THE SUPREM
SOURCEBOOK

ASPEN COURSEBOOK SERIES

THE SUPREME COURT SOURCEBOOK

Richard Seamon
Professor of Law
University of Idaho College of Law

Andrew Siegel
Associate Professor of Law
Seattle University School of Law

Joseph Thai
Presidential Professor of Law
University of Oklahoma College of Law

Kathryn Watts
Garvey Schubert Barer Professor of Law
University of Washington School of Law

Wolters Kluwer
Law & Business

To contact Customer Service, e-mail customer.service@wolterskluwer.com, call 1-800-234-1660, fax 1-800-901-9075, or mail correspondence to:

Wolters Kluwer Law & Business
Attn: Order Department
PO Box 990
Frederick, MD 21705

Printed in the United States of America.

1 2 3 4 5 6 7 8 9 0

ISBN 978-1-4548-0609-7

Library of Congress Cataloging-in-Publication Data

Seamon, Richard H., 1959-
The Supreme Court sourcebook / Richard Seamon, professor of law, University of Idaho College of Law; Andrew Siegel, associate professor of law, Seattle University School of Law; Joseph Thai, presidential professor of law, University of Oklahoma College of Law; Kathryn Watts, Garvey Schubert Barer Professor of Law, University of Washington School of Law.
    pages cm. — (Aspen coursebook series)
Includes index.
ISBN 978-1-4548-0609-7
    1. United States. Supreme Court. 2. Courts of last resort—United States. I. Siegel, Andrew (Law teacher) II. Thai, Joseph. III. Watts, Kathryn A., 1976- IV. Title.
KF8742.S425 2013
347.7326—dc23

                                                                        2013010720

About Wolters Kluwer Law & Business

Wolters Kluwer Law & Business is a leading global provider of intelligent information and digital solutions for legal and business professionals in key specialty areas, and respected educational resources for professors and law students. Wolters Kluwer Law & Business connects legal and business professionals as well as those in the education market with timely, specialized authoritative content and information-enabled solutions to support success through productivity, accuracy and mobility.

Serving customers worldwide, Wolters Kluwer Law & Business products include those under the Aspen Publishers, CCH, Kluwer Law International, Loislaw, Best Case, ftwilliam.com and MediRegs family of products.

CCH products have been a trusted resource since 1913, and are highly regarded resources for legal, securities, antitrust and trade regulation, government contracting, banking, pension, payroll, employment and labor, and healthcare reimbursement and compliance professionals.

Aspen Publishers products provide essential information to attorneys, business professionals and law students. Written by preeminent authorities, the product line offers analytical and practical information in a range of specialty practice areas from securities law and intellectual property to mergers and acquisitions and pension/benefits. Aspen's trusted legal education resources provide professors and students with high-quality, up-to-date and effective resources for successful instruction and study in all areas of the law.

Kluwer Law International products provide the global business community with reliable international legal information in English. Legal practitioners, corporate counsel and business executives around the world rely on Kluwer Law journals, looseleafs, books, and electronic products for comprehensive information in many areas of international legal practice.

Loislaw is a comprehensive online legal research product providing legal content to law firm practitioners of various specializations. Loislaw provides attorneys with the ability to quickly and efficiently find the necessary legal information they need, when and where they need it, by facilitating access to primary law as well as state-specific law, records, forms and treatises.

Best Case Solutions is the leading bankruptcy software product to the bankruptcy industry. It provides software and workflow tools to flawlessly streamline petition preparation and the electronic filing process, while timely incorporating ever-changing court requirements.

ftwilliam.com offers employee benefits professionals the highest quality plan documents (retirement, welfare and non-qualified) and government forms (5500/PBGC, 1099 and IRS) software at highly competitive prices.

MediRegs products provide integrated health care compliance content and software solutions for professionals in healthcare, higher education and life sciences, including professionals in accounting, law and consulting.

Wolters Kluwer Law & Business, a division of Wolters Kluwer, is headquartered in New York. Wolters Kluwer is a market-leading global information services company focused on professionals.

Summary of Contents

Contents

Chapter 4
Certiorari

Chapter 6
Oral Argument   **397**

Preface

We thank you for opening this book. In this preface we describe how the book came about and what we hope it and its companion website offer the reader.

Each of us has had the joy and privilege of teaching a law school course on the Supreme Court of the United States. Each of us has always created our own set of materials for the course. None of us believes in reinventing the wheel: We created our own course material because we could not find anything in the market suited to our approach. We found, instead, many excellent works that take a primarily theoretical approach to the Court and others that take a primarily historical approach. We believe it is important to expose students to theoretical and historical materials, as well as to comparative materials, but we have chosen to do so as part of an approach that also emphasizes a practice-oriented, experiential study of the Court.

We conceived this book project because we realized that we were not alone in our desire to provide students with materials that emphasize practice as well as history, theory and comparative perspectives. When some of us began teaching our courses on the Court in the early 2000s, there were no more than perhaps 15 to 20 such courses being taught at U.S. law schools. Since then, the number has more than quadrupled, and this does not include what we understand to be a burgeoning numbers of courses on the Court taught in other graduate programs and at the undergraduate level. Indeed, outside of academia, too, it seems that interest in the Court has grown exponentially since *Bush v. Gore.*

As we investigated other law school courses on the Court and spoke with professors who taught the course in other graduate and undergraduate settings, we were impressed (and humbled) by their variety. We therefore decided to (1) organize the book into self-contained modules in an attempt to maximize flexibility and (2) create a true sourcebook by offering a wide variety of material, including not only academic literature and Court decisions but also historical material, articles and litigation documents written by experienced Supreme Court practitioners, and internal documents such as draft opinions, memoranda, and cert pool memos. We have aimed, in short, for versatility and variety.

Whereas the book provides evergreen material, its companion website provides teachable examples of materials on cases currently before the Court. By creating the website, we intend to spare teachers the highly time- and labor-intensive chore of culling pedagogically useful current material from the thousands of cert petitions filed in, and the dozens of cases decided by, the Court on the merits each Term. We fold in the current material partly to give students a vibrant sense of the operations and concerns of the Court in "real time." More instrumentally, we use the current material for simulations and exercises in which students take on the roles of the Justices—by, for example, conferencing on a pending petition for certiorari or drafting an opinion in a pending case; their law clerks—by, for example, writing a pool memo on a pending petition for certiorari; or advocates before the Court—by, for example, presenting oral argument in a current case. We believe this hands-on use of material on pending cases deepens students' understanding of the Court and equips them with valuable practice skills. By selecting and packaging current material based on its value for teaching courses on the Court, our website will serve a function distinct from that of other websites on the Court, several of which are quite excellent but which are not designed to support classroom activities.

We have benefited greatly from the suggestions and advice of colleagues who teach courses on the Court, including anonymous reviewers of drafts of our book, and from our students. We have also benefited greatly from our experiences clerking on and practicing before the Court, which offered us privileged views of its workings from both sides of the bench. Needless to say, none of us have disclosed any confidential information within these pages. We invite readers of the finished product and users of our website to share ideas for future improvement with us.

R.S.
A.S.
J.T.
K.W.

May 2013

Acknowledgments

We gratefully acknowledge the following authors and publishers who granted us permission to reprint copyrighted material:

Alfred A. Knopf, a division of Random House, Inc., for excerpts from The Supreme Court by William H. Rehnquist, copyright © 1987, 2001 by William H. Rehnquist. Used by permission of Alfred A. Knopf, a division of Random House, Inc. Any third party use of this material, outside of this publication, is prohibited. Interested parties must apply directly to Random House, Inc., for permission.

ALM Media, Inc., for Jonathan Groner, *How University Got Support of Military Leaders: Diversity Brief by Ex-Officials Came Together Over Four Years*, Legal Times, June 30, 2003, at 1; copyright © 2004; and for Tony Mauro, *Bush Got a Conservative High Court, with Caveats*, The Nat'l L. J., Nov. 3, 2008, copyright © 2008. Reproduced with permission of ALM Media, Inc.; permission conveyed through Copyright Clearance Center, Inc.

American Bar Association, for excerpts from Andrew L. Frey & Roy T. Engelert, Jr., *How to Write a Good Appellate Brief*, Litigation, Winter 1994, at 6; copyright © 1994 by the American Bar Association; and for excerpts from Paul M. Smith, *The Sometimes Troubled Relationship Between Courts and Their "Friends,"* Litigation, Summer 1998, at 24; copyright © 1998 by the American Bar Association. Reprinted with permission. This information or any portion thereof may not be copied or disseminated in any form or by any means or stored in an electronic database or retrieval system without the express written consent of the American Bar Association.

Amanda Tyler and the George Washington Law Review, for excerpts from Amanda Tyler, *Setting the Supreme Court's Agenda: Is There a Place for Certification?*, 78 Geo. Wash. L. Rev. 1310 (2010), copyright © 2010. Reproduced with permission of Amanda Tyler and the George Washington Law Review.

Barbara A. Perry and ABC-Clio Inc., for excerpts from Barbara A. Perry, A "Representative" Supreme Court?: The Impact of Race, Religion, and Gender on Appointments (1991), copyright © 1991 Barbara A. Perry. Reproduced with permission of Barbara A. Perry and ABC-Clio Inc.; permission from ABC-Clio Inc. conveyed through Copyright Clearance Center, Inc.

Berkeley La Raza Law Journal, for Sonia Sotomayor, *A Latina Judge's Voice*, 13 Berkeley La Raza L.J. 87 (2002), copyright © 2002. Reproduced with permission of Berkeley La Raza Law Journal; permission conveyed through Copyright Clearance Center, Inc.

Blackwell Publishing, Inc., for excerpts from Thomas G. Walker, Lee Epstein & William Dixon, *On the Mysterious Demise of Consensual Norms in the United States Supreme Court*, 50 J. Pol. 361 (1988), copyright © 1988. Reproduced with permission of Blackwell Publishing, Inc.; permission conveyed through Copyright Clearance Center, Inc.

Bryan A. Garner and Scribes—The American Society of Legal Writers, for
    excerpts from Bryan A. Garner, *Interviews with United States Supreme Court
    Justices*, 13 The Scribes Journal of Legal Writing 1 (2010), copyright ©
    2010. Reproduced with permission of Bryan A. Garner and Scribes.
Catholic University Law Review, for excerpts from Stephen M. Shapiro, *Oral
    Argument in the Supreme Court of the United States*, 33 Cath. U.L. Rev. 529
    (1984), copyright © 1984; and for excerpts from James vanR. Springer,
    *Some Suggestions on Preparing Briefs on the Merits in the Supreme Court of the
    United States*, 33 Cath. U.L. Rev. 593 (1984), copyright © 1984.
    Reproduced with permission of The Catholic University of America
    Press, Inc.
Columbia Law Review, for excerpts from Peter Linzer, *The Meaning of Certiorari
    Denials*, 79 Colum. L. Rev. 1227 (1979), copyright © 1979. Reproduced
    with permission of the Columbia Law Review Association, Inc.; permission
    conveyed through the Copyright Clearance Center, Inc.
Columbia Law Review, for excerpts from Rebecca L. Brown, *Accountability,
    Liberty, and the Constitution*, 98 Colum. L. Rev. 531 (1998), copyright ©
    1998. Reproduced with permission of the Columbia Law Review
    Association, Inc.; permission conveyed through the Copyright Clearance
    Center, Inc.
Cornell Law Review, for excerpts from Paul D. Carrington & Roger C.
    Cramton, *Judicial Independence in Excess: Reviving the Judicial Duty of the
    Supreme Court*, 94 Cornell L. Rev. 587 (2009), copyright © 2009.
    Reproduced with permission of Cornell University Law School; permis-
    sion conveyed through the Copyright Clearance Center, Inc.
Constitutional Commentary, for excerpts from Barbara Palmer, *The "Bermuda
    Triangle?" The Cert Pool and Its Influence over the Supreme Court's Agenda*, 18
    Const. Comment. 105 (2001), copyright © 2001. Reproduced with
    permission of Constitutional Commentary.
David Margolick, for excerpts from David Margolick, Evgenia Peretz & Michael
    Shnayerson, *The Path to Florida: What Really Happened in the 2000 Election
    and What's Going Down Right Now!*, Vanity Fair, Oct. 2004, at 310, copyright
    © 2004. Reproduced with permission of David Margolick.
David M. O'Brien, for excerpts from *Join-3 Votes, the Rule of Four, the* Cert. *Pool,
    and the Supreme Court's Shrinking Plenary Docket*, 13 J.L. & Pol. 779 (1997),
    copyright © 1997. Reproduced with permission of David M. O'Brien.
Denver Bar Association, for excerpts from Wiley Rutledge, *The Appellate Brief*, 19
    Dicta 109 (1942); copyright © 1942. Reproduced with permission of the
    Denver Bar Association.
Edward Lazarus, for excerpts from Edward Lazarus, *The Supreme Court Must Bear
    Scrutiny*, Washington Post, July 6, 1998, at A19, copyright © 1998.
    Reprinted with permission from Edward Lazarus.
Edward Lazarus and FindLaw.com, for excerpts from *The Supreme Court's
    Excessive Secrecy: Why It Isn't Merited*, FindLaw.com, Sept. 30, 2004,
    copyright © 2004. Reproduced with permission of Edward Lazarus and
    FindLaw.com.
Harvard Law Review, for excerpts from Aharon Barak, *Foreword: A Judge on
    Judging: The Role of a Supreme Court in a Democracy*, 116 Harv. L. Rev. 16

(2002), copyright © 2002. Reproduced with permission of the Harvard Law Review Association; permission conveyed through the Copyright Clearance Center, Inc.

Jeffrey Bleich, Kelly Klaus & Lise Earle Beske, for excerpts from Jeff Bleich, Kelly Klaus & Lise Earle Beske, *Closed Chambers: Has the Integrity of the Supreme Court Been Breached?*, Oregon State Bar Bulletin, July 1998, at 15, copyright © 1998. Reproduced with permission of Jeffrey Bleich, Kelly Klaus & Lise Earle Beske.

John P. Kelsh and the Washington University Law Review, for excerpts from John P. Kelsh, *The Opinion Delivery Practices of the United States Supreme Court 1790-1945*, 77 Wash. U. L.Q. 137 (1999), copyright © 1999. Reproduced with permission of John P. Kelsh and the Washington University Law Review.

John Paul Stevens, for excerpts from John Paul Stevens, Five Chiefs: A Supreme Court Memoir (2011), copyright © 2011. Reproduced with permission of John Paul Stevens.

John Paul Stevens, for excerpts from John Paul Stevens, *The Life Span of a Judge-Made Rule*, 58 N.Y.U. L. Rev. 1 (1983), copyright © 1983. Reproduced with permission of John Paul Stevens.

John Wiley & Sons, Inc., for excerpts from Antonin Scalia, *The Dissenting Opinion*, J. Sup. Ct. Hist. 33 (1994), copyright © 1994. Reproduced with permission of John Wiley & Sons, Inc.

Journal of Appellate Practice and Process, for excerpts from Robert L. Brown, *Just a Matter of Time? Video Cameras at the United States Supreme Court and the State Supreme Courts*, 9 J. App. Prac. & Process 1, 7-14 (2007), copyright © 2007. Reproduced with permission from the Journal of Appellate Practice and Process.

Kathryn A. Watts, for excerpts from *Constraining Certiorari Using Administrative Law Principles*, 160 U. Penn. L. Rev. 1 (2011), copyright © 2011 Kathryn A. Watts. Reproduced with permission of Kathryn A. Watts.

Kelly J. McFadden, for excerpts from Kelly J. Lynch, *Best Friends? Supreme Court Law Clerks on Effective* Amicus Curiae *Briefs*, 20 J. L. & Pol. 33 (2004), copyright © 2004 Kelly J. Lynch. Reproduced with permission of Kelly J. McFadden.

Law and Society Review, for excerpts from Gregory Caldeira & John R. Wright, *The Discuss List: Agenda Building in the Supreme Court*, 24 Law & Soc'y Rev. 807, 809-815 (1990), copyright © 1990. Reproduced with permission of John Wiley & Sons Ltd.

Louis Michael Seidman and the Federalist Society for Law and Public Policy Studies, for excerpts from Louis Michael Seidman, *The Federalist Society Online Debate Series, The Sotomayor Nomination, Part II*, July 13, 2009, http://www.fed-soc.org/debates/dbtid.30/default.asp; copyright © 2009. Reprinted with permission of Louis Michael Seidman and the Federalist Society for Law and Public Policy Studies.

Lee Epstein, Andrew Martin, Kevin Quinn and Jeffrey Segal, for excerpts from Lee Epstein, Andrew D. Martin, Kevin Quinn and Jeffrey Segal, *Circuit Effects: How the Norm of Federal Judicial Experience Biases the Supreme Court*, 157 U. Pa. L. Rev. 833 (2009), copyright © 2009. Reproduced with permission from Lee Epstein, Andrew Martin, Kevin Quinn and Jeffrey Segal.

Lee Epstein, Jack Knight, and CQ Press, for excerpts from Lee Epstein & Jack Knight, The Choices Justices Make (1998), copyright © 1998. Reproduced with permission of Lee Epstein, Jack Knight, and CQ Press.

Linda Sandstrom Simard, for excerpts from *An Empirical Analysis of Amici Curiae in Federal Court: A Fine Balance of Access, Efficiency, and Adversarialism*, 27 Rev. Litig. 669 (2008); copyright © 2008. Reproduced with permission of Linda Sandstrom Simard.

Margaret Meriwether Cordray, Richard Cordray and the Washington and Lee Law Review, for excerpts from Margaret Meriwether Cordray & Richard Cordray, *The Supreme Court's Plenary Docket*, 58 Wash. Lee L. Rev. 737 (2001), copyright © 2001. Reprinted with permission from Margaret and Richard Cordray and the Washington and Lee Law Review.

Margaret Meriwether Cordray, Richard Cordray and the Washington University Law Review, for excerpts from Margaret Meriwether Cordray & Richard Cordray, *The Philosophy of Certiorari: Jurisprudential Considerations in Supreme Court Case Selection*, 82 Wash. U. L. Q. 389 (2004), copyright © 2004. Reproduced with permission from Margaret and Richard Cordray and the Washington University Law Review.

Margaret Meriwether Cordray, Richard Cordray & the Kansas Law Review, for excerpts from Margaret Meriwether Cordray & Richard Cordray, *Setting the Social Agenda: Deciding to Review High-Profile Cases at the Supreme Court*, 57 U. Kan. L. Rev. 313 (2009), copyright © 2009. Reprinted with permission from Margaret and Richard Cordray and the Kansas Law Review.

Michigan Law Review and Bruce D. Collins, for excerpts from Bruce D. Collins, *C-SPAN's Long and Winding Road to a Still Un-Televised Supreme Court*, 106 Mich. L. Rev. First Impressions 12 (2007), copyright © 2007. Reproduced with permission from the Michigan Law Review and Bruce D. Collins.

National School Boards Association, for excerpts from John G. Roberts, Jr., *Thoughts on Presenting an Effective Oral Argument*, in School Law in Review 1997, copyright © 1997. Reproduced with permission of the National School Boards Association.

New Republic, for Andrew M. Siegel, *Nice Disguise: Alito's Frightening Geniality*, The New Republic, Nov. 14, 2005, at 20, copyright © 2005. Reproduced with permission of The New Republic.

New York University Press, for excerpts from Bernard Schwartz, Super Chief: Earl Warren and His Supreme Court—A Judicial Biography (1983), copyright © 1983. Reproduced with permission of New York University Press.

Ohio Northern University Law Review, for excerpts from Theresa M. Beiner, *Diversity on the Bench and the Quest for Justice for All*, 33 Ohio N.U. L. Rev. 481 (2007), copyright © 2007. Reproduced with permission of the Ohio Northern University Law Review.

Oxford University Press, for excerpts from The Supreme Court in Conference (1940-1985) (Del Dickson ed., 2001), copyright © 2001. Reproduced with permission of Oxford University Press.

Richard J. Lazarus and the Georgetown Law Journal, for excerpts from Richard J. Lazarus, *Advocacy Matters Before and Within the Supreme Court: Transforming the Court by Transforming the Bar*, 96 Geo. L.J. 1487 (2008), copyright © 2008. Reproduced with permission of Richard J. Lazarus and the Georgetown Law Journal.

Ross Guberman, for excerpts from Ross Guberman, *Five Ways to Write Like Paul Clement*, http://www.legalwritingpro.com/briefs/clement.pdf, copyright © 2012. Reproduced with permission of Ross Guberman.

San Francisco Attorney, for excerpts from Jeff Bleich & Kelly Klaus, *White Marble Walls and Marble White Males*, San Francisco Attorney at 17 (April-May 1999), copyright © 1999. Reproduced with permission from the San Francisco Attorney, the magazine of The Bar Association of San Francisco.

South Carolina Law Review, for excerpts from Richard H. Seamon, *Preparing for Oral Argument in the United States Supreme Court*, 50 S.C. L. Rev. 603 (1999), copyright © 1999. Reproduced with permission of the South Carolina Law Review.

Southwestern University Law Review, for excerpts from Ruth Bader Ginsburg, *The Supreme Court: A Place for Women*, 32 Southwestern Univ. L. Rev. 189 (2003), copyright © 2003. Reproduced with permission of the Southwestern University Law Review.

Stanford University Press, for excerpts from Todd C. Peppers, Courtiers of the Marble Palace: The Rise and Influence of the Supreme Court Law Clerk, copyright © 2006 by the Board of Trustees of the Leland Stanford Jr. University. All rights reserved. Used with the permission of Stanford University Press, www.sup.org.

Supreme Court of the United States, for the following photographs, all from the Collection of the Supreme Court of the United States: portraits of Chief Justice Roberts and Justices Thomas, Ginsburg, Breyer, Alito, Sotomayor, and Kagan, and photograph of the conference room, all by Steve Pettaway; portrait of Justice Scalia, by Mollie Isaacs; portrait of Justice Kennedy, by Robin Reid; and photographs of the exterior of the building and of the courtroom, by Franz Jantzen. Reproduced with permission of the Curator's Office of the Supreme Court of the United States.

Thomson Reuters, for excerpts from Dave Frederick, Supreme Court and Appellate Advocacy (2003), copyright © 2003. Reproduced with permission of Thomson Reuters.

Timothy R. Johnson, James F. Spriggs II, Paul Wahlbeck, and the Washington University Law Review, for excerpts from Timothy R. Johnson, James F. Spriggs II & Paul Wahlbeck, *Oral Advocacy Before the United States Supreme Court: Does It Affect the Justices' Decisions?*, 85 Wash. U. L. Rev. 457 (2007), copyright © 2007. Reproduced with permission of Timothy R. Johnson, James F. Spriggs II, Paul Wahlbeck, and Washington University.

Timothy S. Bishop, Jeffrey Sarles & Stephen Kane and The Circuit Rider, for excerpts from Timothy S. Bishop, Jeffrey Sarles & Stephen Kane, *Tips on Petitioning for Certiorari in the United States Supreme Court*, The Circuit Rider 28 (May 2007), copyright © 2007. Republished with permission of The Circuit Rider and Timothy S. Bishop, Jeffrey Sarles & Stephen Kane.

Timothy S. Bishop, Jeffrey W. Sarles & Stephen Kane, for excerpts from Timothy S. Bishop, Jeffrey W. Sarles & Stephen Kane, *Tips on Petitioning*

and Opposing Certiorari in the U.S. Supreme Court, 34 Litigation 26, at pp.
30-31 (2008), copyright © 2008. Reproduced with permission of Timothy
S. Bishop, Jeffrey Sarles and Stephen Kane.

The University of California-Davis Law Review, for excerpts from John C.
Eastman, *The Limited Nature of the Senate's Advice and Consent Role*, 33 U.Cal.
Davis. L. Rev. 633 (2003), copyright © 2003. Reproduced with permission
of the University of California Davis Law Review; permission conveyed
through Copyright Clearance Center, Inc.

University of Chicago, for excerpts from Doris Marie Provine, Case Selection in
the United States (1980), copyright © 1980 The University of Chicago. All
rights reserved. Reproduced with permission of the University of Chicago
Press.

University of Chicago, for excerpts from David Alistair Yalof, Pursuit of Justices:
Presidential Politics and the Selection of Supreme Court Nominees
(1999), copyright © 1999 The University of Chicago. All rights reserved.
Reproduced with permission of the University of Chicago Press and David
Alistair Yalof.

University of Pennsylvania Law Review, for excerpts from Joseph D. Kearney &
Thomas W. Merrill, *The Influence of* Amicus Curiae *Briefs in the Supreme
Court*, 148 U. Pa. L. Rev. 743 (2000), copyright © 2000. Republished with
permission of the University of Pennsylvania Law Review; permission
conveyed through Copyright Clearance Center, Inc.

Vanderbilt Law Review, for excerpts from William E. Nelson, Harvey Rishikof,
I. Scott Messinger & Michael Jo, *The Liberal Tradition of the Supreme Court
Clerkship: Its Rise, Fall, and Reincarnation?*, 62 Vand. L. Rev. 1749 (2009),
copyright © 2009. Reproduced with permission of the Vanderbilt Law
Review.

Virginia Law Review, for excerpts from Amanda Frost, *Overvaluing Uniformity*,
94 Va. L. Rev. 1567 (2008), copyright © 2008. Republished with
permission of the Virginia Law Review; permission conveyed through
Copyright Clearance Center, Inc.

W. W. Norton & Company, Inc., for excerpts from David M. O'Brien, Storm
Center: The Supreme Court in American Politics (8th ed. 2008),
copyright © 2008. Reproduced with permission of W. W. Norton &
Company, Inc.

Yale Law Journal, for Richard J. Lazarus, *Docket Capture at the High Court*, 119
Yale L.J. Online 89 (2010), copyright © 2010; for excerpts from Alex
Kozinski, *Conduct Unbecoming*, 108 Yale L.J. 835 (1999), copyright © 1999;
and for excerpts from David A. Strauss & Cass R. Sunstein, *The Senate, the
Constitution, and the Confirmation Process*, 101 Yale L.J. 1491 (1992),
copyright © 1992. Reproduced with permission of the Yale Law Journal
Company, Inc.; permission conveyed through the Copyright Clearance
Center, Inc.

Yale University Press, for excerpts from Alexander M. Bickel, The Least
Dangerous Branch: The Supreme Court at the Bar of Politics (2d ed.
1986), copyright © 1986, originally published in 1962 by The Bobbs-
Merrill Company, Inc. Republished with permission of Yale University
Press.

1

A Supreme Court

What should be the role of a supreme court in a democracy? As the highest court in a judicial system, a supreme court obviously shoulders responsibility for ensuring the uniform interpretation and application of national law. But beyond ensuring uniformity, should a supreme court in a free society play any other roles?

Subsequent chapters of this book will examine the actual functions of our own Supreme Court in the United States today. To prepare you to critically assess what our Court does, first consider on a clean slate what a high court in a democracy ideally should—and should not—do. In considering this predicate question, reflect as well on whether the roles you would assign a supreme court depend on, and in turn affect, the nature of the democracy it serves.

A. EXTERNAL PERSPECTIVE

The normative question posed by this chapter is not of unique interest to the United States. It is one that scholars and jurists in other democracies have examined as well. An external perspective from another modern democracy with a vigorous judicial system may challenge our existing conceptions and assumptions about the proper place for a supreme court in a free society. Accordingly, consider the views of Aharon Barak, who served on the Supreme Court of Israel from 1978 to 2006 as a Justice and then as its President, and who "dominated his court as completely as John Marshall dominated our Supreme Court." Richard A. Posner, *Enlightened Despot*, The New Republic, Apr. 23, 2007, http://www.tnr.com/article/enlightened-despot.

Aharon Barak, *Foreword: A Judge on Judging: The Role of a Supreme Court in a Democracy*

116 Harv. L. Rev. 16, 19, 27-29, 34-36, 38-40, 48-50 (2002)

I am not a philosopher. I am not a political scientist. I am a judge—a judge in the highest court of my country's legal system. So I ask myself a question that many supreme court judges—and, in fact, all judges on all courts in modern democracies—ask themselves: what is my role as a judge? Certainly it is my role— and the role of every judge—to decide the dispute before me. Certainly it is my role, as a member of my nation's highest court, to determine the law by which the dispute before me should be decided. Certainly it is my role to decide cases according to the law of my legal system. But is that all that can be said about my role? . . .

The primary concern of the supreme court in a democracy is not to correct individual mistakes in lower court judgments. That is the job of courts of appeal. The supreme court's primary concern is broader, systemwide corrective action. This corrective action should focus on two main issues: bridging the gap between law and society, and protecting democracy. The judge is charged with both jobs simultaneously, and in most cases, they are complementary. . . .

A. BRIDGING THE GAP BETWEEN LAW AND SOCIETY

The law regulates relationships between people. It prescribes patterns of behavior. It reflects the values of society. The role of the judge is to understand the purpose of law in society and to help the law achieve its purpose. But the law of a society is a living organism. It is based on a given factual and social reality that is constantly changing. Sometimes the change is drastic, sudden, and easily identifiable. Sometimes the change is minor and gradual, and cannot be noticed without the proper distance and perspective. Law's connection to this fluid reality implies that it too is always changing. Sometimes change in law precedes societal change and is even intended to stimulate it. In most cases, however, a change in law is the result of a change in social reality. Indeed, when social reality changes, the law must change too. Just as change in social reality is the law of life, responsiveness to change in social reality is the life of the law. It can be said that the history of law is the history of adapting the law to society's changing needs. A thousand years of common law are a thousand years of changes in the law in order to adapt it to the needs of a changing reality. The judge is the primary actor in effecting this change. He is the senior partner in making common law. The legislature is the junior partner. Its role is to correct mistakes in case law or in the margins of case law, and not to try to replace the judge in his primary role as developer of the common law. Similarly, the history of legislation is the history of adapting law to society's changing needs. Here the main role lies, of course, with the legislature. It is the senior partner. . . .

. . . [The legislature's] democratic nature (in the sense of its being chosen by the people), the tools at its disposal, and the ways in which it receives information about different policies and different alternatives all make the legislature chiefly responsible for bridging the gap between law and society.

. . . But the statute itself cannot be implemented without being interpreted. The task of interpreting belongs to the judge. Through his or her interpretation, a judge must give effect to the purpose of the law and ensure that the law in fact bridges the gap between law and society. The judge is a partner in the legislature's creation and implementation of statutes, even if this partnership is a limited one.

. . . From this perspective, the judge's role in creating common law (as a senior partner) is similar to the judge's role in interpreting legislation (as a junior partner). In both cases, the judge works in the interstices of legislation. Of course, he or she has a different degree of freedom in each situation, but his or her role is primarily the same: to bridge the gap between law and society. . . . This approach directly impacts the formation of a proper system of interpretation. It should be a system that bridges law and society's needs. It should be a system that ensures dynamic interpretation, giving a statute a meaning compatible with social life in the present and, as far as can be anticipated, in the future, too.

B. PROTECTING THE CONSTITUTION AND DEMOCRACY

. . . The second role of the judge in a democracy is to protect the constitution and democracy itself. Legal systems with formal constitutions impose this task on judges, but judges also play this role in legal systems with no formal constitution. Israeli judges have regarded it as their role to protect Israeli democracy since the founding of the state, even before the adoption of a formal constitution. In England, notwithstanding the absence of a written constitution, judges have protected democratic ideals for many years. . . .

. . . Everyone agrees that a democracy requires the rule of the people, which is often effectuated through representatives in a legislative body. Therefore, frequent elections are necessary to keep these representatives accountable to their constituents. However, real or substantive democracy, as opposed to formal democracy, is not satisfied merely by these conditions. Democracy has its own internal morality, based on the dignity and equality of all human beings. Thus, in addition to formal requirements, there are also substantive requirements. These are reflected in the supremacy of such underlying democratic values and principles as human dignity, equality, and tolerance. There is no (real) democracy without recognition of basic values and principles such as morality and justice. Above all, democracy cannot exist without the protection of individual human rights—rights so essential that they must be insulated from the power of the majority. As Justice Iacobucci of the Canadian Supreme Court observed, "[t]he concept of democracy is broader than the notion of majority rule, fundamental as that may be." Real democracy is not just the law of rules and legislative supremacy; it is a multidimensional concept. It requires recognition of both the power of the majority and the limitations on that power. It is based on legislative supremacy and on the supremacy of values, principles, and human rights. When there is internal conflict, the formal and substantive elements of democracy must be balanced to protect the essence of each of these aspects. In this balance, the system must place limits on both legislative supremacy and on the supremacy of human rights.

To maintain real democracy—and to ensure a delicate balance between its elements—a formal constitution is preferable. To operate effectively, a constitution should enjoy normative supremacy, should not be as easily amendable as a normal statute, and should give judges the power to review the constitutionality of legislation. Without a formal constitution, there is no legal limitation on legislative supremacy, and the supremacy of human rights can exist only by the grace of the majority's self-restraint. A constitution, however, imposes legal limitations on the legislature and guarantees that human rights are protected not only by the self-restraint of the majority, but also by constitutional control over the majority. Hence the need for a formal constitution.

The need for judicial review is less intense when one can rely on the self-restraint of the majority. This is apparently the situation in the United Kingdom. The Human Rights Act—an ordinary statute—allows judges to hold legislation incompatible with it, without authorizing them to void the incompatible legislation. I hope that this arrangement will work well in the United Kingdom and that it will guarantee the proper combination of parliamentary supremacy and human rights. Personally, however, I am skeptical. In hard situations, like terrorist attacks or other emergencies, this self-restraint is unlikely to suffice. . . . Therefore, while a written constitution and judicial review are not necessary conditions for the existence of democracy, they are important conditions that should be preferred. . . .

. . . Critics of my theory argue that the non-accountability of judges should deprive them of the power to void statutes. Such power must only be given to the representatives of the people, who are accountable to them. This is the counter-majoritarian argument made again and again. In my opinion, this argument is extremely problematic. First, some constitutions contain express provisions for judicial review of the constitutionality of statutes. In such circumstances, the legitimacy of judicial review should not be in doubt. . . . Second, if the countermajoritarian argument is correct, then states ought to refrain from making a constitution. After all, a constitution is not a democratic document, since it negates, in certain circumstances, the power of the current majority. Therefore, if a constitution is desirable, we cannot attribute much weight to countermajoritarian considerations. But if a constitution is democratic, then its implementation by courts is democratic; if democracy is not merely the rule of the majority, but also the protection of human rights, then judicial review for constitutionality that implements substantive democracy—thereby giving expression to the role of the judge—is not antidemocratic. I discussed this in one case, where I said:

> Democracy is a delicate balance between majority rule and the fundamental values of society that rule the majority. . . . [W]hen the majority deprives the minority of human rights, this harms democracy. . . . [W]hen judges interpret provisions of the Constitution and void harmful laws, they give expression to the fundamental values of society, as they have evolved throughout the history of that society. Thus they protect constitutional democracy and uphold the delicate balance on which it is based. Take majority rule out of constitutional democracy, and you have harmed its essence. Take the rule of fundamental values out of constitutional democracy, and you have harmed its very existence. Judicial review of the constitutionality of statutes allows society to be honest with itself and to respect its fundamental tenets. This is the basis for the substantive legitimacy of judicial review. . . . [T]hrough judicial review we are faithful to the fundamental values that we imposed on ourselves in the past, that reflect our essence in the present, and that will guide us in our national development as a society in the future.

Notes and Questions

1. Justice Barak contends that a basic responsibility of judges in a democracy, and ultimately supreme court judges, is to "bridge the gap between law and society." What does he mean by that phrase? Do you agree with him or with critics who charge that his view of judicial responsibility "opens up a vast realm for discretionary judgment" to "rewrite" laws in accord with judges' social preferences, as Judge Richard Posner of the Court of Appeals for the Seventh Circuit contends? Richard A. Posner, *Enlightened Despot*, The New Republic, Apr. 23, 2007, http://www.tnr.com/article/enlightened-despot.

2. Justice Barak also argues that "the main role" of a supreme court in a democracy is "to maintain and protect the constitution and democracy." Is it consistent with protecting democracy for a supreme court whose members are *not* elected to strike down laws passed by elected representatives—that is, to exercise the power of judicial review? Does the answer depend on how one defines "democracy"? This question may be worth revisiting after considering modern debates over the "countermajoritarian difficulty" of judicial review in Section C, *infra*.

3. Justice Barak conceives of democracy not only as "formal" but moreover as "substantive." What do those terms mean to him? Do you agree with Justice Barak's conception of democracy? If one agrees, is it also necessary to agree that a supreme court should be the ultimate guardian of "substantive democracy"?

4. Like Justice Barak, Learned Hand, one of the longest serving and most respected judges in American history, saw the necessity in a constitutional democracy of having "some arbiter" keep the state within its prescribed powers. Learned Hand, *The Bill of Rights* 15, 29 (1958). Like Justice Barak, Judge Hand also concluded that courts were the best repository for such power, "since by the independence of their tenure they [are] least likely to be influenced by diverting pressure." *Id.* at 29. However, unlike Justice Barak, he was never completely comfortable with assigning courts such power. He wrote:

> Each one of us must in the end choose for himself how far he would like to leave our collective fate to the wayward vagaries of popular assemblies. No one can fail to recognize the perils to which the last forty years have exposed such governments. We are not indeed forced to choose between absolutism and the kind of democracy that so often prevailed in Greek cities during the sixth to fourth centuries before our era. The Founding Fathers were acutely, perhaps overacutely, aware of the dangers that had followed that sort of rule, though . . . they differed widely as to what curbs to impose. For myself it would be most irksome to be ruled by a bevy of Platonic Guardians, even if I knew how to choose them, which I assuredly do not. If they were in charge, I should miss the stimulus of living in a society where I have, at least theoretically, some part in the direction of public affairs. Of course I know how illusory would be the belief that my vote determined anything; but nevertheless when I go to the polls I have a satisfaction in the sense that we are all engaged in a common venture. If you retort that a sheep in the flock may feel something like it; I reply, following Saint Francis, "My brother, the Sheep."

Id. at 73-74.

Is Justice Barak's ideal supreme court—one that protects democracy from itself by invalidating laws that stray from society's fundamental values—the kind of "Platonic Guardians" whose rule Judge Hand would reject? Would you feel more comfortable leaving democratic rule, instead, to "the wayward vagaries of popular assemblies"?

5. Would giving elected officials power to select judges mitigate any unease over courts deciding constitutional disputes in a democracy? Consider the work of political scientists such as Robert Dahl, who argued that the Supreme Court of the United States is not merely a legal institution but "also a political institution" that often must choose among competing policy alternatives when neither cases, statutes, nor the Constitution gives a definitive answer. Robert A. Dahl, *Decision-Making in a Democracy: The Supreme Court as a National Policy-Maker*, 6 J. Pub. L. 279, 281 (1957). From an empirical study of the Court's cases, Professor Dahl concluded that the Court's policy views "are never for long out of line with the policy views dominant among the lawmaking majorities of the United States." *Id.* at 285. To Professor Dahl, that conclusion was hardly surprising, given that members of the Court are nominated by Presidents who "are not famous for appointing justices hostile to their own views on public policy," and confirmed by "the dominant majority in the Senate." *Id.* at 284; *see also* Robert G. McCloskey, *The American Supreme Court* 209 (Sanford Levinson ed., 2d ed. 1994) (arguing that "the Court seldom strayed very far from the mainstreams of American life" because "the Court learned to be a political institution and to behave accordingly"). Does Professor Dahl's work suggest that Judge Hand's concern about unaccountable judicial rule is unfounded, or does it suggest that Justice Barak's idealism about judicial protection of "fundamental values" from majority rule is unrealistic, or both?

6. What criteria do you think Justice Barak would use to select members of his ideal supreme court? What criteria would you use? For materials on the process and considerations for selecting Justices for the Supreme Court, *see infra* Chapter 2, Section B. In addition, for a discussion of whether the Justices on the Court should reflect and represent America's diverse population along racial, gender, religious, and other lines, *see infra* Chapter 8, Section A.

7. Even if Justice Barak is right that "real" democracy is not just formal majority rule but also recognition of fundamental substantive rights, is a supreme court even necessary to safeguard the latter? Consider the example of the United Kingdom, to which Justice Barak alludes. Despite a lengthy constitutional history dating back to the Magna Carta—a tradition from which we draw many of our rights—the United Kingdom did not have a supreme court until 2005, and none of its courts ever has enjoyed the power to void acts of Parliament as unconstitutional. The judiciary can develop common law, interpret statutory law, and declare legislation incompatible with the Human Rights Act, which the United Kingdom passed in 1998 to give domestic effect to the European Convention on Human Rights. Human Rights Act, 1998, c. 42 (U.K.). However, laws declared incompatible remain valid and retain their full effect.

Moreover, prior to the creation of the Supreme Court of the United Kingdom, the final judicial authority in the system was not even an independent court but the Appellate Committee of the House of Lords—that is, a committee of the upper house of Parliament. When the government of the United Kingdom proposed the creation of a supreme court in 2003, the impetus was to "put the relationship between the executive, the legislature and the judiciary on a modern footing, which takes account of people's expectations about the independence and transparency of the judicial system." Department for Constitutional Affairs, *Constitutional Reform: A Supreme Court for the United Kingdom*, 2003, at 10 (U.K.). But the modernization of the judicial system in the United Kingdom did not endow the new supreme court with the power to protect "substantive" democracy by invalidating legislation on higher grounds. The government explained:

> In our democracy, Parliament is supreme. There is no separate body of constitutional law which takes precedence over all other law. The constitution is made up of the whole body of the laws and settled practice and convention, all of which can be amended or repealed by Parliament. . . . Such amendment or repeal would certainly be very difficult in practice and Parliament and the executive regard themselves as bound by the obligations they have taken on through that legislation, but the principle remains intact.

Id. at 21.

Few would question that the United Kingdom is a robust democracy. Yet the legislature is the judge of its own powers in its system of parliamentary supremacy. What does the example of the United Kingdom say about the necessity of having a supreme court serve as an institutional guardian of rights in *a* democracy? In *our* democracy?

B. EARLY DISAGREEMENT

Debates about the proper place for a supreme court in a democracy—and the Supreme Court in our democracy—are not new. As the readings below highlight, prominent figures from the Founding generation who drafted, promoted, interpreted, and applied the Constitution disagreed fundamentally over the role of the judiciary in our system of government. Consider whether their disagreements should impact our modern understanding of the Supreme Court's role in our constitutional system.

The Federalist No. 78

490-494 (Alexander Hamilton) (Benjamin Wright ed., 1961)

. . . Whoever attentively considers the different departments of power must perceive, that in a government in which they are separated from each other, the judiciary, from the nature of its functions, will always be the least dangerous to the political rights of the Constitution; because it will be least in a capacity to annoy or injure them. The Executive not only dispenses the honors, but holds the sword of the community. The legislature not only commands the purse, but prescribes the rules by which the duties and rights of every citizen are to be regulated. The judiciary, on the contrary, has no influence over either the sword or the purse; no direction either of the strength or of the wealth of the society; and can take no active resolution whatever. It may truly be said to have neither FORCE nor WILL, but merely judgment; and must ultimately depend upon the aid of the executive arm even for the efficacy of its judgments. . . .

The complete independence of the courts of justice is peculiarly essential in a limited Constitution. By a limited Constitution I understand one which contains certain specified exceptions to the legislative authority; such, for instance, as that it shall pass no bills of attainder, no *ex post facto* laws, and the like. Limitations of this kind can be preserved in practice no other way than through the medium of courts of justice, whose duty it must be to declare all acts contrary to the manifest tenor of the Constitution void. Without this, all the reservations of particular rights or privileges would amount to nothing.

Some perplexity respecting the right of the courts to pronounce legislative acts void, because contrary to the Constitution, has arisen from an imagination that the doctrine would imply a superiority of the judiciary to the legislative power. It is urged that the authority which can declare the acts of another void, must necessarily be superior to the one whose acts may be declared void. As this doctrine is of great importance in all the American constitutions, a brief discussion of the grounds on which it rests cannot be unacceptable.

There is no position which depends on clearer principles, than that every act of a delegated authority, contrary to the tenor of the commission under which it is exercised, is void. No legislative act, therefore, contrary to the Constitution, can be valid. To deny this, would be to affirm, that the deputy is greater than his principal; that the servant is above his master; that the representatives of the people are superior to the people themselves; that men acting by virtue of powers, may do not only what their powers do not authorise, but what they forbid.

If it be said that the legislative body are themselves the constitutional judges of their own powers, and that the construction they put upon them is conclusive upon the other departments, it may be answered, that this cannot be the natural presumption, where it is not to be collected from any particular provisions in the Constitution. It is not otherwise to be supposed that the Constitution could intend to enable the representatives of the people to substitute their *will* to that of their constituents. It is far more rational to suppose, that the courts were designed to be an intermediate body between the people and the legislature, in order, among other things, to keep the latter within the limits assigned to their authority. The interpretation of the laws is the proper and peculiar province of the courts. A constitution is, in fact, and must be regarded by the judges, as a fundamental law. It therefore belongs to them to ascertain its meaning, as well as the meaning of any particular act proceeding from the legislative body. If there should happen to be an irreconcilable variance between the two, that which has the superior obligation and validity ought, of course, to be preferred; or, in other words, the Constitution ought to be preferred to the statute, the intention of the people to the intention of their agents.

Nor does this conclusion by any means suppose a superiority of the judicial to the legislative power. It only supposes that the power of the people is superior to both; and that where the will of the legislature declared in its statutes, stands in opposition to that of the people, declared in the Constitution, the judges ought to be governed by the latter rather than the former. They ought to regulate their decisions by the fundamental laws, rather than by those which are not fundamental. . . .

It can be of no weight to say that the courts, on the pretence of a repugnancy, may substitute their own pleasure to the constitutional intentions of the legislature. This might as well happen in the case of two contradictory statutes; or it might as well happen in every adjudication upon any single statute. The courts must declare the sense of the law; and if they should be disposed to exercise WILL instead of JUDGMENT, the consequence would equally be the substitution of their pleasure to that of the legislative body. The observation, if it prove any thing, would prove that there ought to be no judges distinct from that body.

If, then, the courts of justice are to be considered as the bulwarks of a limited Constitution against legislative encroachments, this consideration will afford a strong argument for the permanent tenure of judicial offices, since nothing will contribute so much as this to that independent spirit in the judges which must be essential to the faithful performance of so arduous a duty.

James Madison, Address to U.S. House of Representatives: Amendments to the Constitution (June 8, 1789)

5 *The Writings of James Madison* 385 (Gaillard Hunt ed., 1904)

. . . It has been said that it is unnecessary to load the constitution with [a proposed bill of rights], because it was not found effectual in the constitution of the particular states. It is true, there are a few particular States in which some of the most valuable articles have not, at one time or other, been violated; but does it not follow but they may have, to a certain degree, a salutary effect against the abuse of power. If they are incorporated into the Constitution, independent tribunals of justice will consider themselves in a peculiar manner the guardians of those rights; they will be an impenetrable bulwark against every assumption of power in the Legislative or Executive; they will be naturally led to resist every encroachment upon rights expressly stipulated for in the Constitution by the declaration of rights.

Marbury v. Madison

5 U.S. (1 Cranch) 137, 177-180 (1803)

Opinion of the court.

. . . Certainly all those who have framed written constitutions contemplate them as forming the fundamental and paramount law of the nation, and consequently the theory of every such government must be, that an act of the legislature, repugnant to the constitution, is void. . . .

If an act of the legislature, repugnant to the constitution, is void, does it, notwithstanding its invalidity, bind the courts, and oblige them to give it effect? Or, in other words, though it be not law, does it constitute a rule as operative as if it was a law? This would be to overthrow in fact what was established in theory; and would seem, at first view, an absurdity too gross to be insisted on. . . .

It is emphatically the province and duty of the judicial department to say what the law is. Those who apply the rule to particular cases, must of necessity expound and interpret that rule. If two laws conflict with each other, the courts must decide on the operation of each.

So if a law be in opposition to the constitution; if both the law and the constitution apply to a particular case, so that the court must either decide that case conformably to the law, disregarding the constitution; or conformably to the constitution, disregarding the law; the court must determine which of these conflicting rules governs the case. This is of the very essence of judicial duty.

If then the courts are to regard the constitution; and the constitution is superior to any ordinary act of the legislature; the constitution, and not such ordinary act, must govern the case to which they both apply.

Those then who controvert the principle that the constitution is to be considered, in court, as a paramount law, are reduced to the necessity of maintaining that courts must close their eyes on the constitution, and see only the law.

This doctrine would subvert the very foundation of all written constitutions. It would declare that an act, which, according to the principles and theory of our government, is entirely void; is yet, in practice, completely obligatory. It would declare, that if the legislature shall do what is expressly forbidden, such act, notwithstanding the express prohibition, is in reality effectual. It would be giving to the legislature a practical and real omnipotence, with the same breath which professes to restrict their powers within narrow limits. It is prescribing limits, and declaring that those limits may be passed as pleasure. . . .

The judicial power of the United States is extended to all cases arising under the constitution.

Could it be the intention of those who gave this power, to say that, in using it, the constitution should not be looked into? That a case arising under the constitution should be decided without examining the instrument under which it arises?

This is too extravagant to be maintained. . . .

It is also not entirely unworthy of observation, that in declaring what shall be the *supreme* law of the land, the *constitution* itself is first mentioned; and not the laws of the United States generally, but those only which shall be made in *pursuance* of the constitution, have that rank.

Thus, the particular phraseology of the constitution of the United States confirms and strengthens the principle, supposed to be essential to all written constitutions, that a law repugnant to the constitution is void; and that *courts*, as well as other departments, are bound by that instrument.

Letter from Thomas Jefferson to Spencer Roane (Sept. 6, 1819)

10 *The Writings of Thomas Jefferson* 140-141 (Paul Leicester Ford ed., 1899)

In denying the right [that the courts] usurp of exclusively explaining the constitution, I go further than you do. . . . If this opinion be sound, then indeed is our constitution a complete *felo de se*. For intending to establish three departments, co-ordinate and independent, that they might check and balance one another, it has given, according to this opinion, to one of them alone, the right to prescribe rules for the government of the others, and to that one too, which is unelected by, and independent of the nation. For experience has already shown that the impeachment it has provided is not even a scare-crow. . . . The constitution, on this hypothesis, is a mere thing of wax in the hands of the judiciary, which they may twist and shape into any form they please. It should be remembered, as an axiom of eternal truth in politics, that whatever power in any government is independent, is absolute also; in theory only, at first, while the spirit of the people is up, but in practice, as fast as that relaxes. Independence can be trusted nowhere but with the people in mass. They are inherently independent of all but moral law. My construction of the constitution is very different from that you quote. It is that each department is truly independent of the others, and has an equal right to decide for itself what is the meaning of the constitution in the cases submitted to its action; and especially, where it is to act ultimately and without appeal.

Andrew Jackson, Veto Message Regarding the Bank of the United States (July 10, 1832)

The Statesmanship of Andrew Jackson 154, 163-164 (Francis Newton Thorpe ed., 1909)

. . . It is maintained by the advocates of the bank that its constitutionality in all its features ought to be considered as settled by precedent and by the decision of the Supreme Court. To this conclusion I can not assent. Mere precedent is a dangerous source of authority, and should not be regarded as deciding questions of constitutional power except where the acquiescence of the people and the States can be considered as well settled. . . .

If the opinion of the Supreme Court covered the whole ground of this act, it ought not to control the coordinate authorities of this Government. The Congress, the Executive, and the Court must each for itself be guided by its own opinion of the Constitution. Each public officer who takes an oath to support the Constitution swears that he will support it as he understands it, and not as it is understood by others. It is as much the duty of the House of Representatives, of the Senate, and of the President to decide upon the constitutionality of any bill or resolution which may be presented to them for passage or approval as it is of the supreme judges when it may be brought before them for judicial decision. The opinion of the judges has no more authority over Congress than the opinion of Congress has over the judges, and on that point the President is independent of both. The authority of the Supreme Court must not, therefore, be permitted to control the Congress or the

Executive when acting in their legislative capacities, but to have only such influence as the force of their reasoning may deserve.

Notes and Questions

1. Alexander Hamilton was one of the drafters and chief supporters of the proposed Constitution. His *Federalist No. 78* remains one of the most vigorous and famous defenses of the constitutional role of the federal judiciary. What role *(p. 8)* did Hamilton believe the Constitution conferred on the courts? *Court as intermed*

2. Hamilton responds to concerns that the new judiciary would be supreme and unaccountable by asserting that it would, to the contrary, be "the least dangerous" branch. Why? Are you persuaded, or would you regard the label in quotations with irony, as one influential modern scholar has? *See infra* Section C.

3. On what grounds does Hamilton reject the view that the legislature should *p. 7* be "the constitutional judges of their own powers"? Why does he believe that judging the constitutionality of laws is "the proper and peculiar province of the courts"?

4. If the Constitution lodges the power of judicial review—"to pronounce legislative acts void, because contrary to the Constitution"—in the courts, what assurance does Hamilton give that judges would interpret it more faithfully than the legislature?

5. In 1982, Canada adopted a constitutional bill of rights called the Canadian Charter of Rights and Freedoms, and secured those rights with a constitutional provision that declared: "The Constitution of Canada is the supreme law of Canada, and any law that is inconsistent with the provisions of the Constitution is, to the extent of the inconsistency, of no force or effect." Canadian Charter of Rights and Freedoms, §52(1), Part 1 of the Constitution Act, 1982, *being* Schedule B to the Canada Act, 1982, c. 11 (U.K.). Does this provision authorize judicial review? Is it necessary considering the "proper and peculiar province of the courts"?

If explicit authorization for judicial review is desirable, apart from whether it is necessary, consider whether Section 52(1) is an improvement on the Supremacy Clause of the U.S. Constitution. That provision states: "This Constitution, and the Laws of the United States which shall be made in Pursuance thereof; and all Treaties made, or which shall be made, under the Authority of the United States, shall be the supreme Law of the Land; and the Judges in every State shall be bound thereby, any Thing in the Constitution or Laws of any State to the Contrary notwithstanding." U.S. Const. art. VI, cl. 2.

6. James Madison, the primary author of the U.S. Constitution, drafted and introduced the Bill of Rights to the First Congress of the United States in 1789. The excerpt above comes from his statement to the House of Representatives in support of those amendments. Does Madison's conception of "independent tribunals of justice," serving as "guardian" of the proposed rights against encroachments by the legislative and executive branches, assume the existence of judicial review? Is his conception akin to Justice Barak's notion of the judiciary as protectors of "substantive" democracy?

7. *Marbury v. Madison* is widely credited with establishing the judiciary's supremacy in interpreting the Constitution. Chief Justice John Marshall's famous proclamation—that "[i]t is emphatically the province and duty of the judicial department to say what the law is"—has served as authority for courts to have the last word on the meaning of the Constitution and consequently for the Supreme

Court to be the final arbiter of constitutional disputes in the United States. In *Cooper v. Aaron*, the Court lectured state officials resisting desegregation under the authority of *Brown v. Board of Education*, 347 U.S. 483 (1954), reminding states that *Marbury* "declared the basic principle that the federal judiciary is supreme in the exposition of the law of the Constitution," and that the principle "has ever since been respected by this Court and the Country as a permanent and indispensable feature of our constitutional system." 358 U.S. 1, 18 (1958). But do Chief Justice Marshall's famous words actually advance that view? Or are they a more modest assertion of authority for the judiciary to decide for itself what the Constitution means in the limited context of adjudicating cases? *See* Larry D. Kramer, *The Supreme Court 2000 Term—Foreword: We the Court*, 115 Harv. L. Rev. 4, 88-90 (2001) ("[I]t does not say, 'it is the job of courts, more so than others, to say what the Constitution means.' What it says is, 'courts, too, can say what the Constitution means.'"). Put another way, can *Marbury v. Madison* be read to reflect, not a Hamiltonian understanding of the role of the courts in our constitutional system, but a view closer to those expressed by Thomas Jefferson and Andrew Jackson?

8. Jefferson asserts that giving courts—and hence the Supreme Court—the last word on the meaning of the Constitution amounts to a "*felo de se*," that is, a suicide. But if he believes that "whatever power in any government is independent, is absolute also," why does he favor letting the legislative and executive branches independently judge for themselves the constitutionality of their own conduct?

9. In President Jackson's message explaining his veto of legislation to recharter the Bank of the United States (drafted with the help of then-Attorney General Roger Taney), he gives reasons for not accepting as binding the Supreme Court's precedent upholding the constitutionality of the bank, *McCulloch v. Maryland*, 17 U.S. 316 (1819). Are Jackson and Jefferson kindred spirits in their view of the limited domain of the Supreme Court in our constitutional system?

10. Consider the response Byron White gave, after his Supreme Court confirmation hearings over a century later, to a reporter asking him to define the constitutional role of the Court. He replied curtly, "To decide cases." Dennis J. Hutchinson, *The Man Who Once Was Whizzer White: A Portrait of Justice Byron R. White* 331 (1998). Are Jackson and Jefferson's views any more (or less) than White's answer?

11. Is it problematic for a sitting President to declare that the Supreme Court's interpretation of the Constitution does not bind the executive or legislative branch? Consider whether our democratic society would be better off if the President and Congress chose to ignore judicial interpretations of the Constitution with which they disagree, such as *Dred Scott v. Sandford*, 60 U.S. 393 (1856), *Brown v. Board of Education*, 347 U.S. 483 (1954), or *Roe v. Wade*, 410 U.S. 113 (1973)? Or if "the people" asserted ultimate authority for interpreting and enforcing the Constitution—ignoring, disobeying, or even rebelling against contrary constitutional decisions of the courts as well as the political branches.

A leading advocate of the second scenario, dubbed "popular constitutionalism," is former Dean Larry Kramer of Stanford Law School. He argues that "we the people" should "insist[] that the Supreme Court is our servant and not our master: a servant whose seriousness and knowledge deserves much deference, but who is ultimately supposed to yield to our judgments about what the Constitution means and not the reverse." Larry D. Kramer, *The People Themselves: Popular Constitutionalism and Judicial Review* 248 (2004). In the end, would you prefer judicial supremacy over what critics of Kramer's theory describe as "constitutional interpretation by [the] mob"? Larry Alexander & Lawrence B. Solum, *Popular? Constitutionalism?*, 118 Harv. L. Rev. 1594, 1640 (2005) (book review).

C. A MODERN DIFFICULTY

Contemporary disputes over the proper role of the Supreme Court echo those of the Founding generation. Modern debates have centered, time and again, on the legitimacy of judicial review. In the words of one scholar: "Before, the central obsession was the inconsistency between judicial review and democracy. Now, it is the inconsistency between judicial review and democracy." Barry Friedman, *The Birth of an Academic Obsession: The History of the Countermajoritarian Difficulty, Part 5*, 112 Yale L.J. 153, 155 (2002). The modern terms of the debate were framed by Professor Alexander Bickel in his 1962 book, *The Least Dangerous Branch: The Supreme Court at the Bar of Politics*, the title of which refers ironically to Hamilton's disarming description of the third branch of government. Professor Bickel's criticism of judicial review as "counter-majoritarian" bedeviled a generation of scholars attempting to justify its place in a democracy. Professor Rebecca Brown's response offers a creative way out of this difficulty.

Alexander M. Bickel, *The Least Dangerous Branch: The Supreme Court at the Bar of Politics*

1, 16-18 (1962)

[handwritten: Judicial review as counter majoritarian]

The least dangerous branch of the American government is the most extraordinarily powerful court of law the world has ever known. The power which distinguishes the Supreme Court of the United States is that of constitutional review of actions of the other branches of government, federal and state. Curiously enough, this power of judicial review, as it is called, does not derive from any explicit constitutional command. The authority to determine the meaning and application of a written constitution is nowhere defined or even mentioned in the document itself. . . .

The root difficulty is that judicial review is a counter-majoritarian force in our system. There are various ways of sliding over this ineluctable reality. Marshall did so when he spoke of enforcing, in behalf of "the people," the limits that they have ordained for the institutions of a limited government. . . . Marshall himself followed Hamilton, who in the 78th Federalist denied that judicial review implied a superiority of the judicial over the legislative power—denied, in other words, that judicial review constituted control by an unrepresentative minority of an elected majority. "It only supposes," Hamilton went on, "that the power of the people is superior to both; and that where the will of the legislature, declared in its statutes, stands in opposition to that of the people, declared in the Constitution, the judges ought to be governed by the latter rather than the former." But the word "people" so used is an abstraction. Not necessarily a meaningless or pernicious one by any means; always charged with emotion, but nonrepresentational—an abstraction obscuring the reality that when the Supreme Court declares unconstitutional a legislative act or the action of an elected executive, it thwarts the will of representatives of the actual people of the here and now; it exercises control, not in behalf of the prevailing majority, but against it. That, without mystic overtones, is what actually happens. It is an altogether different kettle of fish, and it is the reason the charge can be made that judicial review is undemocratic.

Most assuredly, no democracy operates by taking continuous nose counts on the broad range of daily governmental activities. Representative democracies—that is to say, all working democracies—function by electing certain men for certain periods of time, then passing judgment periodically on their conduct of public office. It is a matter of a laying on of hands, followed in time by a process of holding to account—all through the exercise of the franchise. The elected officials, however, are expected to delegate some of their tasks to men of their own appointment, who are not directly accountable at the polls. The whole operates under public scrutiny and criticism—but not at all times or in all parts. What we mean by democracy, therefore, is much more sophisticated and complex than the making of decisions in town meeting by a show of hands. It is true also that even decisions that have been submitted to the electoral process in some fashion are not continually resubmitted, and they are certainly not continually unmade. Once run through the process, once rendered by "the people" (using the term now in its mystic sense, because the reference is to the people in the past), myriad decisions remain to govern the present and the future despite what may well be fluctuating majorities against them at any given time. A high value is put on stability, and that is also a counter-majoritarian factor. Nevertheless, although democracy does not mean constant reconsideration of decisions once made, it does mean that a representative majority has the power to accomplish a reversal. This power is of the essence, and no less so because it is often merely held in reserve.

. . . [N]othing in these complexities can alter the essential reality that judicial review is a deviant institution in the American democracy.

Rebecca L. Brown, *Accountability, Liberty, and the Constitution*

98 Colum. L. Rev. 531, 531-536, 574 (1998)

Honk if you are tired of constitutional theory. More than ever before thought, the blame lies with Alexander Bickel. At his instigation, contender after contender has stepped forward to try a hand at pulling the sword of judicial review from the stone of illegitimacy. Each suggests a different way to ease the discomfort of unaccountable decisionmaking in a democracy. . . . The curious thing about these defenses of judicial review, however, is that they suggest not that unaccountable decisionmaking is legitimate, but only that it is not really unaccountable. The arguments take the form of a confession and avoidance, rather than a rebuttal, of Bickel's charge.

The vast majority of theorists have failed to challenge Bickel's basic assumption, that political accountability is the *sine qua non* of legitimacy in government action. As a consequence, that assumption for decades framed the debate in constitutional law. Even the most sympathetic theorists tended to assume the role of apologist for judicial review, while the unsympathetic made concerted efforts to exploit that widespread assumption in order to engender profound skepticism about judging itself. Judgment was no longer the proper and revered sphere of judges, but was recast as the unforgivable "value imposition." These attacks on the legitimacy of judgment in a democracy have left their mark not only on the academy, but also on the public understanding of the judicial role and on the Supreme Court's understanding of its own role. These effects, in turn, have had palpable implications for the recognition and enforcement of individual rights.

I do not emulate Arthur. It seems to me that too much effort has been expended in the quest to solve Bickel's difficulty, especially since efforts to "solve" the difficulty serve rather to entrench the insidious assumption underlying it. Instead, I seek to contribute to the budding effort to resist the siren song of popular sovereignty as the foundation of constitutional thought. I do so by examining the character of accountability itself.

My claim is that political accountability—broadly, the requirement that public officials stand periodically for election—has been misunderstood. Almost universally, it has erroneously been cast as the servant of the constitutional value of majoritarianism. Readers of the Constitution routinely look to the various textual provisions establishing different types of accountability as compelling evidence of an overarching constitutional commitment to a telos of majority rule. This understanding contains two important errors: First, it wrongly identifies majoritarianism as the primary constitutional value, and second, it misconceives the purpose of political accountability. . . .

[A]ccountability is best understood, not as a utilitarian means to achieve maximum satisfaction of popular preferences, but as a structural feature of the constitutional architecture, the goal of which is to protect liberty. In this respect it is much like the other structural constitutional features such as separation of powers, checks and balances, and federalism—all of which are more comfortably accepted as devices for protecting individual rights. It may seem counterintuitive to consider that a system of electorally accountable government might also be designed to serve the end of individual liberty. We have been trained to view popular will as antithetical to the protection of rights. But it is counterintuitive only because we have not properly honed our intuitions about the Constitution that we have.

The resolution of this conundrum asks the reader to abandon the deeply entrenched prejudices that haunt a generation weaned on the countermajoritarian difficulty. It asks the reader to turn Bickel's difficulty on its head and wonder instead how one might justify a system of majority rule in a government whose final cause is the protection of individual rights. The resolution lies in the almost instinctive realization that unless a government is politically accountable, an independent judiciary that vigorously protects rights from government encroachment could not survive.

Imagine how one would proceed to design a government if one were committed to the principle that the primary goal of government is to protect the liberty of the people from government invasion. Accept with me for the purpose of argument that this was the Framers' commitment, and consider what kinds of structures would plausibly advance the newly formed polity toward that goal. One might well start by designing an institutional body whose job it is to ensure that the laws of the polity—however they may come to be created—are applied to individual cases in a way that preserves basic individual rights. The obvious question then is how to ensure that such a rights-protecting body could itself be sufficiently protected in its independent status to allow it to do that job effectively without being overcome by the very organs of government that the rights-protecting body is designed to cabin. It turns out that a very good answer to that question is the establishment and maintenance of a politically accountable government. Indeed, it may be that a politically accountable government is the only effective means of governing a polity while still enabling an independent judiciary to survive.

Thus, the structural feature of accountability for political actors can be under-stood, not as a means to maximize the preferences of the majority of the people on matters of routine governance, as it has been widely understood, which is a purpose always in tension with a commitment to individual rights, but rather as a means primarily to minimize the risk of tyranny in government, which is not. Accountability serves this goal in two ways: by allowing the people to check abuse of power at the polls if they detect a threat and wish to eradicate it (a traditionally majoritarian check on tyranny) and, more importantly, by involving the polity in standing behind a political structure which includes a judicial branch empowered to step in if the majority is itself carried away by an impulse to tyrannize (a countermajoritarian check). . . .

. . . Thus, if the executive refused to enforce the orders of the court, or if the legislature tried to impeach the members of the court without warrant, the people would still stand outside of those actions and could pass judgment on them through their retained political powers by holding elected officials accountable for any such breach of trust. Thus, the encroachment into the independence of the judiciary that seemed inevitable under any form of autocratic government is subject to an extrinsic check by the people under their own Constitution. And this role for the people gives meaning to the Constitution's commitment to accountability, without making it necessary to jettison its equally clear commitment to liberty.

There lies the hard answer to the question why, in a system whose final cause is liberty, the powers of government should be housed in an accountable body, elected by the people: to support the existence of the judiciary and thus to allow for the continual protection of liberty.

Notes and Questions

1. It would not be an overstatement to say that Professor Bickel's identification of the "root difficulty" of judicial review as "counter-majoritarian" is one of the most influential and debated ideas in modern constitutional law. *See, e.g.,* Alexander Bickel Symposium, SCOTUSblog (Aug. 2012), http://www.scotusblog.com/category/special-features/alexander-bickel-symposium. Yet his criticism of judicial review as unaccountable and undemocratic is not new, but reaches back to Jefferson and Jackson and through many critics in between. Nor, for that matter, are the responses new. How, for instance, did Hamilton counter this line of criticism? How might Madison or Marshall respond? More recently, what answer does Barak give from abroad?

2. Does Professor Bickel's argument lead to the conclusion that there is no role for an unelected judiciary, much less a supreme court, in a democratic system? What about other government institutions whose members are not directly elected or directly accountable to the electorate, such as the Federal Reserve, whose monetary policy arguably affects people more on a day-to-day basis than the constitutional decisions of the Supreme Court, or the Senate, whose members prior to the adoption of the Seventeenth Amendment were selected by state legislatures rather than by popular vote of "the people"?

3. Is it necessarily incompatible with or undesirable in a democracy to have politically insulated institutions such as an unelected supreme court? Does your answer, as Justice Barak argues, depend on how you define "democracy"? If so, what is Professor Bickel's definition?

Consider, by contrast, the suggestion by Professors Daniel Farber and Suzanna Sherry that the legitimacy of a democracy be assessed not institution by institution but "as a whole": *interesting*

> One reason for applying the concept of legitimacy at the systemic level is that our conception of democracy is actually quite complex. Our constitutional scheme elaborately divides power among different organs of government, some (such as the Senate) being democratic in only a qualified sense [because it is not proportionately representational]. In their actual operations, the decisions of these institutions are shaped by extraconstitutional features such as political parties, government bureaucracies, and legislative committees—none of them directly representative of a majority of the public. The system as a whole operates reasonably democratically, but this does not mean that every individual component is majoritarian, or that we would want a wholly majoritarian form of government.

Daniel A. Farber & Suzanna Sherry, *Desperately Seeking Certainty: The Misguided Quest for Constitutional Foundations* 149-150 (2004).

4. Professor Rebecca Brown turns the "countermajoritarian difficulty" on its head by arguing that electoral accountability is not the measure of legitimacy in our constitutional system, but rather a means for the people to protect their liberty by checking the political branches from undermining the judiciary's protection of individual rights. Put in Hamiltonian terms, Professor Brown's argument is essentially that the people (through elections) act as "an intermediate body" between the courts and the legislature so that the courts (through judicial review) can act as "an intermediate body" between the people and the legislature. There is no "countermajoritarian difficulty" because majoritarianism and countermajoritarianism work symbiotically to keep elected officials within constitutional limits and thereby protect individual liberties. Is this description of the ends and means of our constitutional system accurate?

5. Even if Professor Brown aptly describes how our constitutional system should operate in theory, does it fall short in practice? For instance, would "the people" more likely side with politicians who supported popular legislation or with judges who strike it down? Does history provide any guide? Can you think of examples one way or the other?

D. THE SUPREME COURT OF THE UNITED STATES

In many respects, the actual role played by the Supreme Court of the United States over the course of its existence has been more mundane than suggested by the above debates or by the tendency of law schools and the media to focus on "sexy" constitutional law cases. The reality on the ground can be fairly run-of-the-mill and has been subject to revision as the nation itself has grown and evolved.

In the Court's first century of existence, its primary role was one of error correction. The Judiciary Act of 1789 assigned the Court mandatory jurisdiction over appeals from federal trial courts, including diversity cases raising pure questions of state law, and appeals from state courts in broad categories of cases involving federal law. As a result, litigants on the losing side in the lower courts often could oblige the Court to reexamine their case regardless of whether the issues were of consequence to the nation or only to the parties.

The Court's assigned role as final arbiter in cases great and small did not present a problem in its early years. Its caseload was light—less than fifty total during its first decade, and climbing gradually to around 70 a year by 1850. For every great case of constitutional law that the Court decided, it adjudicated dozens more "dull and unimportant cases." William H. Rehnquist, *The Changing Role of the Supreme Court,* 14 Fl. St. U. L. Rev. 1, 3 (1986). In fact, the Court only sat for a few months at most, and the more time-consuming and arduous task of its members was to "ride circuit," fanning out by horse, stagecoach, and riverboat across different multistate judicial regions created by Congress to act as federal trial judges. One such road and river warrior was Justice John McKinley, who reported to the Senate in 1838 that he had traveled "10,000 miles" through his circuit states of Alabama, Louisiana, Mississippi, and Arkansas, though he had failed to visit the judicial seat of Little Rock, because "it could not be conveniently approached in the spring of the year, except by water, and by that route the distance would be greatly increased." *Id.* at 4 (quoting Sen. Doc. No. 50, 25th Cong., 3d Sess. 39 (1838)).

As detailed in Chapter 4, the second century of the Court's existence witnessed an inversion of its original role, driven by a docket explosion in the decades following the Civil War as the country—and the Court—confronted Reconstruction, expansion, industrialization, and the burgeoning regulation necessary to govern an increasingly complex society. The Court had over 250 cases docketed for argument in 1860, over 600 in 1870, over 1,200 in 1880, and over 1,800 in 1890. Many of these cases lacked national importance but not legal difficulty, causing an overextended Court to take more than three years to decide a typical case.

With the creation of the federal courts of appeals in 1891 to relieve some of the Court's obligatory caseload, Congress began a century-long transformation of the Court's docket from one consisting mainly of mandatory appeals to one filled primarily by the Court's own selection of cases. The pivotal moment came in 1925 with the passage of the "Judges' Bill" drafted by the Justices themselves, which sharply reduced the types of appeals the Court had to take and correspondingly widened its discretion to shape most of its docket via the writ of certiorari. In 1988, Congress completed its turnaround work by purging almost all of the remains of the Court's mandatory jurisdiction. Rather than having its role defined by losing litigants, the Court for the past century has largely set its own agenda. *See infra* Chapter 4, Section A.

If a court's role is shaped by what it decides, then the Supreme Court's self-defined role may be gleaned from criteria that it has used since 1925 to characterize its case selection. Foremost, the Court ensures uniformity of federal law by resolving conflicting decisions of lower courts—particularly federal courts of appeals, which each cover extensive regions of the country—over "important" federal questions. Sup. Ct. R. 10(a) & 10(b). It bears mention that the great majority of conflicting decisions reviewed by the Court do not involve "hot-button" social or political issues that the general public may consider "important," but rather raise prosaic legal questions that may affect the nation, the states, or the people in considerable ways. To take just one example, a workaday case decided during the Court's 2004-2005 term—out of the 76 that it granted review from a pool of more than 7,000 petitions for certiorari—involved a conflict between two federal courts of appeals over whether workers in meat and poultry processing plants are entitled to compensation under the Fair Labor Standards Act for the time it takes them to put on protective gear and walk to their production area. *See IBP, Inc. v. Alvarez,* 546 U.S. 21 (2005).

Since passage of the Judges' Bill, the Court has taken cases of broad public importance even in the absence of conflicting lower court decisions. Generally speaking, these cases tend to make less frequent appearances on the Court's docket but more frequent appearances on the front pages. The kinds of questions the Court has considered appropriate for its position as the highest court in the land has evolved over time, influenced partly by shifting social forces and partly by competing views inside the Court over its role in our democracy. For instance, New Deal legislation adopted in response to the Great Depression led the Court to confront questions over the constitutional limits of the federal government's economic regulatory power. World War II prompted decisions over civil liberties at home and abroad in wartime. The Civil Rights Movement, the Vietnam War, and the Great Society shaped, and were shaped by, expansive decisions under Chief Justice Earl Warren on substantive and procedural rights. And ever since, an increasingly divided Court has struggled over its proper role in the lives of individuals and the life of the nation.

In short, beyond ensuring the uniformity of federal law across the country, the Supreme Court's role in our democratic society is one that is continually under construction. Yet despite the Court's evolving role, its business—whether mandated by Congress or self-selected by the Court—has generally mirrored the business of the nation, from its early years under John Marshall to its recent years under John Roberts. That is to say, the more things change, the more they stay the same.

2

The Justices

The Constitution announces that "the judicial power of the United States shall be vested in one Supreme Court," lays out the basic contours of federal jurisdiction, and establishes the principle that federal judges possess life tenure. U.S. Const. art. III, §§1-2. Beyond those simple provisions, the document leaves the size and shape of the federal judiciary to the discretion of later generations. Much of that power resides with Congress, which is responsible for setting the size of the Supreme Court, determining whether there will be lower federal courts and in what form, establishing the precise jurisdiction of each court, and making numerous logistical decisions about the funding, calendar, and structure of the federal courts. During its first year, Congress passed the Judiciary Act of 1789, fulfilling these responsibilities, and it has continued to manage the structure of the courts through a series of judiciary acts and amendments.

While Congress has been responsible for creating the structure of the federal courts, including the Supreme Court, it has been the judges and Justices themselves who have given the courts their character. The culture of the federal courts, indeed the very nature of American judicial power, has been forged at crucial moments by the abilities, values, and personalities of the men and women who happened to be wearing judicial robes. The Supreme Court that exists today is a tradition-bound institution whose habits and procedures reflect the influence of each of its 112 Justices. To take only the most obvious examples, John Marshall played a crucial role in establishing both the Court's confidence in exercising the power of judicial review and its habit of wherever possible handing down a single majority opinion, while Earl Warren's influence is felt every time the modern Court embraces a central role in resolving a politically-charged constitutional dispute. To take a lesser example of keen interest to contemporary Supreme Court advocates, Antonin Scalia owns the lion's share of responsibility for creating the current courtroom culture in which lawyers face a challenging and well-prepared bench and often find it impossible to string more than two or three sentences together before being hit with the next barrage of judicial questions.

The material in this chapter provides an introduction to the Justices. Part A offers a collective biography of the Court's 112 Justices, providing information about their demographics, backgrounds, and careers. Part B focuses on the Supreme Court selection process, looking first at the process by which Presidents decide whom to nominate for the Court and then at the process through which the

Senate determines whether or not to confirm the nominee. Finally, Part C offers profiles of each of the current Justices.

A. THE JUSTICES THROUGHOUT HISTORY:
A GROUP PORTRAIT[1]

The size of the Supreme Court varied widely for the first 80 years of the Court's existence but has remained stable at nine since 1869. The Judiciary Act of 1789 created a six-member Supreme Court, two Justices for each of the three judicial circuits created by the Act. The Judiciary Act of 1801 eliminated the requirement that Justices ride circuit to hear intermediate appeals and reduced the number of Justices to five; the Act was repealed in 1802, restoring a six-member Court. Between 1807 and 1863, Congress added Justices several times as the nation expanded across the continent, gradually increasing the Court's size to ten members. An 1866 statute, motivated in large measure by a desire to prevent the unpopular Andrew Johnson from appointing any Justices, prospectively reduced the Court's number to seven through attrition. In 1869, after Johnson left office, a new Judiciary Act fixed the Court's membership at nine, one more than was then serving. Since 1869, there have been periodic proposals to change the size of the Court, most notably Franklin Delano Roosevelt's 1937 proposal to significantly increase the Court's size in order to "pack" it with Justices supportive of the New Deal, but none have succeeded.

One hundred and twelve men and women have served on the Supreme Court (two of whom left the Court and were later reappointed for a second term). As discussed in more detail in Chapter 8, of the 112 Justices, 108 have been men and 4—Justice Sandra Day O'Connor (who served from 1981-2006), and current Justices Ruth Bader Ginsburg, Sonia Sotomayor, and Elena Kagan—women. Justices Thurgood Marshall (1967-1991) and current Justice Clarence Thomas are African American; Sonia Sotomayor is of Puerto Rican descent; and all the remaining Justices have been white.[2] Historically, the Court has been heavily Protestant; there have been 12 Roman Catholic Justices, 8 Jewish Justices, and 92 Protestant Justices. Since 2010, however, the Court has lacked a Protestant member; currently 6 of the Justices are Catholics and 3 are Jewish.

For most of the Court's history, the professional and educational backgrounds of the Justices varied considerably. Approximately 65 percent of the Justices had judicial experience before joining the Court. Less than half were sitting judges at the time of their appointment and a significant percentage of those with experience had served for only a short time, often on a minor court. Roughly the same percentage of Justices have had prior experience serving in executive roles in federal, state, or local government, including 19 cabinet members, 7 governors, and 1 President (William Howard Taft). Slightly less than half of all Justices also had prior experience as elected legislators. At the time of their appointment, 30 Justices were federal court judges, 21 were state court judges, 13 were serving

1. The biographical data reported in this section is largely drawn from Lee Epstein et al., *The Supreme Court Compendium* (5th ed. 2012).
2. When Justice Sotomayor was nominated, there was a modest debate about whether she was in fact that Court's first "Latino/a" Justice, as Benjamin Cardozo was of Spanish Jewish ancestry, a background that fits some, though not most, modern understandings of what it means to be "Latino."

in the Cabinet, 9 were serving in other executive branch positions, 8 were members of the Senate or United States House of Representatives, 3 were governors, 2 were serving in state legislatures, 24 were in private practice, and 2 were full-time law professors.

Sixty-nine of the Court's members received at least some degree of formal school-based legal education at 29 different institutions, though many of those studied in an era before law degrees were offered. By contrast, 43 Justices read the law outside of a school setting, including at least 9 who were completely self-taught. The last member of the Court without a law degree was Justice Stanley Reed, who served from 1938-1957.

In recent decades, the résumés of the Justices have become both more elite and less varied. Nine of the last 10 appointees, 13 out of the last 16, and 16 out of the last 23 have been federal appeals court judges at the time of their nomination. From 2006 to 2010, for the first time in the Court's history, all nine Justices had served previously on the federal appellate bench.[3] All nine members of the current court attended either Harvard or Yale Law School (though Justice Ginsburg graduated from Columbia). Three of the current Justices (along with three of their immediate predecessors) began their legal careers as Supreme Court law clerks.[4]

President George Washington, who had the privilege of appointing the initial Supreme Court, appointed the most Justices, ten. Despite a slow start, Franklin Roosevelt nominated eight new Justices, while Abraham Lincoln and Andrew Jackson each appointed six and William Howard Taft appointed five. Every President has appointed at least one Justice except William Henry Harrison and Zachary Taylor, who died early in their terms; Andrew Johnson, whose ability to make nominations was blocked by a hostile Congress; and Jimmy Carter, who seems to have drawn the historical short straw.

Well more than half of the Justices were in their fifties when they joined the Court, approximately a quarter were in their forties, a little more than 15 percent were in their sixties, and four Justices were in their thirties. The youngest Justice to join the Court was Joseph Story, who was 32; the oldest was Horace Lurton, who was 65, unless you count Charles Evans Hughes, who returned to the Court for his second tour of duty at age 67. Whether you count by median or mean, the average Justice has served approximately 15 years on the Court, though that number has been exceeded by every Justice to leave the Court since 1970. Fourteen Justices served at least 30 years and 29 more (including three current Justices) have served at least 20. The longest serving Justice is William Douglas, who served for 36 years and 6 months; the shortest service belongs to Thomas Johnson, who was in office for only 5 months. Oliver Wendell Holmes and John Paul Stevens, both of whom retired at age 90, are the only two Justices to serve into their nineties.

There have been 17 Chief Justices of the United States (the official name for the Court's leader). George Washington appointed the first three; since then, no

---

3. For a pair of interesting articles on the development of an expectation that Justices have prior experience on the federal court of appeals and its consequences for the Court, see Lee Epstein et al., *Circuit Effects: How the Norm of Federal Judicial Experience Biases the Supreme Court,* 157 U. Pa. L. Rev. 833 (2009) (which is excerpted in Chapter 8) and Lee Epstein et al., *The Norm of Prior Judicial Experience and Its Consequences for Career Diversity on the U.S. Supreme Court,* 91 Cal. L. Rev. 903 (2003). The consequences of this new norm are discussed and analyzed in Chapter 8.

4. The former law clerks are: Byron White (clerk for Chief Justice Vinson); William Rehnquist (clerk for Justice Jackson); John Paul Stevens (clerk for Justice Wiley Rutledge); Stephen Breyer (clerk for Justice Goldberg); John Roberts (clerk for then-Justice Rehnquist); and Elena Kagan (clerk for Justice Thurgood Marshall).

President has appointed more than one. Three of these men were serving as Associate Justices at the time of their appointments (Edward Douglas White, Harlan Fiske Stone, and William Rehnquist); two more were former Associate Justices (John Rutledge and Charles Evans Hughes); and the rest were new to the Court. The 12 new to the Court ran the gamut from major national political figures (John Marshall, William Howard Taft, Salmon Chase, and Earl Warren) to relatively obscure lawyers (Morrison Waite and Melvin Fuller). Two of the last three Chief Justices, Warren Burger and John Roberts, were appointed directly from the United States Court of Appeals for the District of Columbia Circuit; they are the only sitting lower federal court judges to be appointed Chief Justice.

B. SELECTING THE JUSTICES

The Constitution lays out the basic blueprint for the selection of Supreme Court Justices. Article II states that "[t]he President . . . shall nominate, and by and with the Advice and Consent of the Senate, shall appoint . . . Judges of the supreme Court. . . ." U.S. Const. art. II, §2. At a basic level, the Constitution's design is clear: the President has the initial responsibility for selecting candidates for the high court but a nominee must be acceptable to both the President and Senate to ascend to the bench. On a deeper level, however, the Constitution provides little guidance, leaving unanswered crucial questions about the details of the process, the relative power of the two elected branches, and the proper standards for evaluating potential or pending nominees.

Like most aspects of our constitutional culture, the nomination process has evolved over time, as different generations have experimented with different mechanisms for fulfilling the Constitution's open-ended commands. This section begins with a brief sketch of how the process has evolved over time, then turns to a deeper discussion of how both the presidential selection and Senate confirmation processes have operated over the last few decades.

1. An Evolving Process: A Short History of Supreme Court Nominations

When President George Washington set out to appoint the original Justices of the Supreme Court, the hoopla of the modern confirmation process was still centuries in the future. Washington sent to the Senate the names of six relatively well-known lawyers and judges, each from a different state and each generally loyal to Washington's political and judicial views. Two days later, the Senate confirmed all six nominees by voice vote. In a move that would be repeated several times over the next few decades, one of the newly confirmed Justices (Robert Harrison of Maryland) declined his seat on the Court and was replaced by a like-minded candidate from a seventh state. Washington ran into some trouble with two of his later nominees, having to briefly delay the nomination of William Patterson in 1793, because he had been a member of the then-sitting Congress which had voted to increase the salary of the Justices, making him temporarily ineligible for the Court, and then watching the Senate reject the nomination of former Justice John Rutledge for Chief Justice, based largely on his opposition to the recently negotiated Jay Treaty. (Rutledge had also received a recess appointment to the Court and was already serving as Chief

Justice when his nomination was rejected. He is the only nominee in history to take up service and not ultimately win confirmation to that seat.)

The nominations of the next four Presidents followed a similar pattern. When vacancies occurred, Presidents quickly settled on nominees, usually selecting from their most legally accomplished friends and political allies and often sending their names up without first consulting with them. Congress then acted quickly, confirming most nominees by voice vote within a matter of days. At that point, the nominated candidate either accepted the seat and joined the Court or declined the position (something done four times before 1811, including by the future President John Quincy Adams).[5] During that time, only one nomination was rejected by the Senate: Alexander Wolcott, a leading Connecticut Jeffersonian who combined limited legal credentials with a politically unpopular career as a customs inspector during the embargoes that preceded the War of 1812 and was rejected by an overwhelming 24-9 vote in 1811.

Between the election of 1824 and the coming of the Civil War, national politics was intensely riven by partisan and sectional differences and the presidency changed hands with great frequency. During this period, Congress, responding both to the sharp divisions in the body politic and the weakness of many Presidents, began to more closely scrutinize Supreme Court nominees. Of the 30 nominations made during this period, the Senate confirmed only 16 Justices, barely more than 50 percent. Whereas up until that point all of the confirmed nominees save one had been confirmed by voice vote, during this period only seven nominees were so confirmed. Seven of the eight Presidents during this period saw at least one nominee go down to defeat, led by John Tyler, an accidental President without home in either political party, who nominated five candidates a total of nine times and saw only one of his picks confirmed. Early in this period, Andrew Jackson renominated a defeated Associate Justice nominee, Roger Taney, for Chief Justice after an intervening election returned a more hospitable Senate. Taney was confirmed as Chief Justice, making him the only nominee ever to join the Court after initially being rejected by the Senate.

Abraham Lincoln won easy support for each of his five nominees, four of whom were approved on voice votes. The Senate was so hostile to the prospect of the unpopular Andrew Johnson appointing Justices that they prospectively reduced the size of the Court to deprive him of any nominations. The next seven Presidents achieved mixed results; between 1866 and 1894, the vast majority of nominees were confirmed, but five nominees were defeated or forced to withdraw, several others survived close votes, one declined his seat, and Edwin Stanton had the misfortune to die before ever taking the oath of office. Twice during this period, presidential searches to fill seats bogged down amidst a new level of press interest and increasing intra-party competition for seats on the Court. In 1874, President Ulysses Grant withdrew two nominees for Chief Justice under intense pressure and publicly floated several other candidates before settling on Morrison Waite, a compromise choice who was unanimously confirmed. In 1893 and 1894, President Grover Cleveland, a New York native, twice nominated citizens of his own state for a seat

5. Most historians attribute the relative frequency with which confirmed nominees declined Supreme Court seats during the early republic to the comparatively low prestige of the Court, the modest pay, and the rigors of riding circuit. Presumably, the fact that Presidents often sent nominations to the Senate without consulting with the potential Justice also had something to do with the frequency with which seats were declined; after all, some highly qualified modern candidates decline to be considered when approached by the President.

traditionally held by a New Yorker, but both nominees were rejected, largely as a result of intra-party squabbles back in the Empire State. Annoyed with his fellow New Yorkers, Cleveland then nominated Louisiana Senator Edward Douglas White, who—owing in large measure to the Senate's traditional courtesy to its own members—was confirmed by voice vote on the same day.

Starting in the late 1890s, a new series of norms began to take hold. As the presidency became stronger as an institution, and as Presidents began to take a more active role as the leaders of their parties, the Senate became much more likely to approve presidential nominations for the high court. In fact, between 1895 and 1968, the Senate rejected only one nominee, Judge John Parker, who was nominated by President Herbert Hoover in 1930 but rejected by a 41-39 vote after a series of contentious hearings focusing on the nominee's record with regard to labor and civil rights issues.

At the same time as it was becoming more likely to approve nominees, the Senate was also becoming more thorough in its process for vetting them. When President Woodrow Wilson nominated noted attorney Louis Brandeis to be the Court's first Jewish member in 1916, many establishment figures balked at the selection of the supposedly "radical" Boston attorney. The Senate responded by holding a series of public hearings on Brandeis's suitability and taking testimony from many leading figures, though not from the nominee himself. After a still-record four-month delay, the Senate confirmed Brandeis 47-22. In 1925, Harlan Fiske Stone became the first nominee to personally testify at a Senate hearing, appearing to dispel corruption allegations. Just five years later, a coalition of progressive interest groups targeted two of President Hoover's nominees, Charles Evans Hughes and, as mentioned above, John Parker, forcing substantial hearings and ultimately defeating Judge Parker.

Having seen much of his first-term legislative agenda struck down by a hostile Supreme Court, President Franklin Delano Roosevelt paid particular attention to the political and judicial views of his eight nominees, selecting staunch defenders of the New Deal and leading advocates of judicial deference to legislative judgments, whether they be found in his own administration, in the Senate, in academia, or on the bench. Only two of his nominees provoked significant controversy, Hugo Black—whose rumored membership in the Ku Klux Klan caused 16 of his fellow Senators to vote against him and whose seat seemed briefly in jeopardy as post-confirmation news reports confirmed those rumors—and Felix Frankfurter—whose (Jewish) religion, foreign birth, and academic career briefly evoked speculation that he was a Communist, forcing him to offer memorable live testimony refuting that speculation.

The next four Presidents pursued varied nomination strategies but all saw their nominees confirmed with little fuss. Harry Truman favored Washington insiders with broad government experience, preferably ones with whom he had played poker. Dwight Eisenhower used two of his appointments to serve political ends (paying off a debt to California Governor Earl Warren who had provided crucial support on the Republican convention floor and pursuing the votes of northern Catholics by appointing William Brennan) and used his other three picks to attempt to establish a norm that nominees ought to have experience on the federal appellate bench. John Kennedy largely delegated his search to others in his administration before selecting two candidates from their list already serving in his administration, Deputy Attorney General Byron White and Labor Secretary Arthur Goldberg. Lyndon Johnson identified two individuals he wanted on the Court and then took the perhaps unprecedented step of maneuvering two Justices into resigning in order to create vacancies.[6] Though the Senate largely rubber-stamped these nominees, they also continued to formalize the process for considering them, expanding their hearings and establishing a norm (unbroken since 1957) that all nominees would testify in person.

The presidency's long run of success in gaining Senate approval for its nominees ran into some speed bumps in the late 1960s and early 1970s. First, in 1968, the Senate successfully filibustered President Johnson's nomination of his longtime advisor, Associate Justice Abe Fortas, as Chief Justice. The next year, the Senate rejected two of President Richard Nixon's nominees, Southern federal judges Clement Haynsworth and G. Harrold Carswell, for a complicated mix of reasons that included concern from civil rights groups about the consequences of appointing a Southern judge at such a crucial moment in civil rights history, a desire to strike a blow against a polarizing President, minor ethical concerns about Haynsworth, and serious concerns about Carswell's abilities. Two years later, President Nixon floundered for several months in his efforts to fill two vacant seats, floating a series of mostly implausible names that met with opposition from the press, key congressional leaders, and the American Bar Association, before finally settling on Assistant Attorney General William Rehnquist—who had initially been considered too young—and former American Bar Association president Lewis Powell of Virginia—who had originally been considered too old.

The next 15 years went by quietly as President Gerald Ford purposefully searched for an experienced centrist to fill his one vacancy, Jimmy Carter's presidency passed without a vacancy, and Ronald Reagan filled his first vacancy with the Court's first female Justice, the unanimously confirmed Sandra Day O'Connor. In the aftermath of President Reagan's overwhelming reelection in 1984, however, officials in his administration concerned with the direction of the Court over the previous several decades committed to appointing to the Court the intellectual leaders of their conservative insurgency, Antonin Scalia and Robert Bork. The first part of their strategy worked swimmingly, with Scalia charming the Senate Judiciary Committee and winning unanimous confirmation. By the next year, however, the Democratic Party had won control of the Senate and, sensing the importance of the contested seat, set out to defeat Judge Bork. In events chronicled in more detail below, Democratic Senators joined forces with left-wing interest groups to make a very public—and often very shrill—case against Judge Bork, a task made easier by the untelegenic nominee's poorly received performance before the Judiciary Committee. After Judge Bork was defeated by a fairly large margin and another prospective nominee was forced to withdraw in minor scandal, the administration settled on the relatively moderate Californian Anthony Kennedy to fill the seat.

By this point in time, the Senate side of the selection process had largely coalesced in its modern form. After the President makes a nomination, the Senate asks the nominee to fill out a long written questionnaire, independently investigates the candidate, and schedules a hearing before the Judiciary Committee. At that hearing, panels of supporters and opponents testify, the candidate gives an opening

---

6. Justice Arthur Goldberg was pressured into resigning from the Court in order to become Ambassador to the United Nations and Justice Tom Clark was manipulated into resigning by the appointment of his son as Attorney General, a move that raised the prospect of too many recusals by the Justice.

statement, and the members of the committee take turns questioning the nominee.[7] The Judiciary Committee then votes on whether or not to approve the candidate, but, regardless of the vote, the nomination is forwarded to the full Senate, where it is voted upon by the body's members. The efficacy of this process is a subject of sharp debate, as is the standard which Senators are supposed to use in assessing and voting on nominees. Those issues are explored more thoroughly below.

While the Senate had largely fixed on a process for performing its duties, the White House had not yet done the same. Though Presidents George H.W. Bush and Bill Clinton ultimately settled on four sitting federal appeals court judges to fill the next four vacancies on the Court, inside accounts of the White House decision-making process (some of which are referenced below) reveal chaos, confusion, and a series of false starts. Perhaps in response to the perceived flaws of their recent predecessors, the last two Presidents (George W. Bush and Barack Obama) have used relatively formal and relatively public procedures in filling three of the last four vacancies. In each of those cases, the President has had advisors come up with a relatively long list of potential candidates, then winnowed the list to four or five names, personally interviewed those finalists, revealed the fact of those interviews to the press, and selected one of the interviewed candidates within days of the interviews. The likelihood that future Presidents will use a similar procedure was certainly enhanced by the results of the one search that varied from this path, in which President George W. Bush nominated his White House Counsel Harriet Miers to the Court, only to withdraw the nomination in the face of intense bipartisan criticism.

Though expectations about the level of deference Senators ought to give to Supreme Court nominees have ebbed and flowed over the last 220 years, events over the last decade suggest that we may have reached (temporary?) equilibrium. Each of the last four nominees faced a variety of partisan criticisms and careful scrutiny of every aspect of their pasts by those opposed to their perceived judicial ideology. At the end of that process, Senators of the President's party lined up almost uniformly behind their nominees, while members of the opposing party engaged in a complicated calculus, weighing various principled, political, and pragmatic considerations before deciding how to cast their votes. In each of the four cases, a substantial but far-from-unanimous number of the opposing-party Senators voted against the nominees, resulting in their confirmations by comfortable but not overwhelming margins (votes of 78-22, 58-42, 68-31, and 63-37, respectively).

2. Presidential Selection

As indicated above, Presidents throughout American history have used different criteria and procedures for identifying and selecting potential Supreme Court Justices. Nevertheless, there are some common themes. For the most part, Presidents

7. The extraordinary confirmation hearing of Justice Clarence Thomas required a variation on this procedure, as late allegations of sexual harassment by a former employee required a second round of hearings, a second appearance by the candidate, and a delayed vote by the judiciary committee. Those anomalous and still wildly controversial hearings are chronicled most fully in Jane Mayer & Jill Abramson, *Strange Justice: The Selling of Clarence Thomas* (1994). For those interested in these events, then-Judge Thomas's angry statement to the committee is also required reading. *See Nomination of Judge Clarence Thomas to Be Associate Justice of the Supreme Court of the U.S.: Hearings Before the Senate Judiciary Committee,* 102d Cong., 1st Sess. 605-617 (1991).

have considered the following categories of criteria, though each has employed them differently and given them different relative weight:

- **General political and legal affinity:** From the very beginning, Presidents have been much more likely to nominate members of their own political party and, to the extent that they have had legal and constitutional views, to nominate candidates who share them.

- **Demographic considerations:** Presidents have consistently taken demographic factors into account, though the nature of those factors has shifted over time. Initially, state of residence and regional representation were crucial factors. For awhile, ensuring some, but not too much, religious diversity seemed to play a significant role. In recent years, concerns about racial and gender diversity have figured prominently in some nomination decisions.

- **Legal acumen:** In selecting among candidates who meet their other criteria, many Presidents have given the strength of a potential candidate's reputation as a lawyer and/or judge considerable weight. In a handful of situations (most notably the selection of Justice Benjamin Cardozo), Presidents have decided to appoint candidates based primarily on the perception that they were uniquely or especially qualified for the high court.

- **Confirmability:** In eras (such as the present one) where the Senate has more actively scrutinized nominees, Presidents have had to take into account both the likelihood that particular candidates might eventually win confirmation and the amount of political capital they might have to spend to ensure confirmation. This factor has been particularly important for Presidents who have faced hostile Senates or who have already sent up unsuccessful nominees.

- **Prior personal relationships and political promises:** Throughout history, a significant minority of Supreme Court nominees have been friends or close personal and political allies of the President or his leading advisors. In addition, a few Justices (most famously Earl Warren) have owed their seats to express or implied political deals made by the President or on his behalf.

- **Personal rapport:** In recent years, Presidents (and, at times, their senior staff) have made it a habit to interview potential nominees before making a final selection. Anecdotal evidence (particularly from the administrations of Gerald Ford, Bill Clinton, and George W. Bush) suggests that the Presidents who have gone to the trouble of interviewing potential nominees have relied heavily on the degree of rapport achieved in these conversations in making their selections.

The excerpts below try to provide an insider perspective on how Presidents go about selecting nominees. First, political scientist David Yalof identifies three different models Presidents have used to manage the selection process. Then, a leading legal journalist offers a detailed account of how President George W. Bush went about making his choices. In reading these excerpts and the notes that follow, it is worth thinking about whether the process the President utilizes is likely to have a significant influence on the candidate he or she ultimately selects and, if so, whether the particular mechanisms and procedures utilized by the last few administrations have been well designed to produce the optimal nominees.

David Alistair Yalof, Pursuit of Justices: Presidential Politics and the Selection of Supreme Court Nominees

1-8 (1999)

On June 27, 1992, the Supreme Court inserted itself once again into the national debate over abortion with its surprising decision in *Planned Parenthood v. Casey*. Specifically, five of the nine justices refused to cast aside *Roe v. Wade*, the Court's controversial 1973 opinion establishing a constitutional right to abortion. Included among *Roe*'s saviors that day were Sandra Day O'Connor and Anthony Kennedy, both appointees of former President Ronald Reagan. As a candidate for the presidency in 1980 and 1984, Reagan had supported a constitutional amendment to overturn *Roe*, a ruling considered to be among the most vilified of public targets for social conservatives in his party. As president, Reagan had publicly promised to appoint justices to the Supreme Court willing to reverse *Roe v. Wade*. Yet just the opposite occurred in *Casey*: a majority of the Court reaffirmed the core right to privacy first discovered in *Roe*. And in a touch of irony, two of President Reagan's own nominees had played significant roles in safeguarding the decision from the Court's conservatives.

Obviously the selection of Supreme Court nominees is among the president's most significant duties. Yet as the outcome in *Casey* demonstrates, it is a task beset with difficulties and potential frustrations. On one hand, a president ordinarily tries to choose a nominee whose influence will reach beyond the current political environment. As a beneficiary of life tenure, a justice may well extend that president's legacy on judicial matters long into the future. Yet in selecting a nominee the president must also successfully maneuver through that immediate environment, lest he suffer politically or (as in some cases) see his nominee rejected by the Senate outright. In recent years internal strife and factionalism within the executive branch have only further complicated what was already a delicate undertaking.

Beyond merely overcoming the constitutional requirement of Senate approval, Ronald Reagan confronted numerous obstacles in selecting his nominees for the Supreme Court. During the 1980s a disjunction eventually arose within his administration between the ardently conservative "Reagan revolutionaries" in the Justice Department, who were campaigning to transform the constitutional landscape at all costs, and the pragmatic White House officials concerned with protecting the president's more immediate political interests. Certainly the U.S. Senate deserves some of the credit for *Roe*'s last-minute resuscitation. President Reagan's first choice for the Court in 1987 had been Court of Appeals Judge Robert Bork, an admitted opponent of *Roe;* the Senate's defeat of Bork by a 58-42 vote set the stage for Anthony Kennedy's ultimate appointment to the Court in January 1988. Still, all of the president's nominees (including Kennedy) first had to survive political struggles within the administration itself. High-level advisors to the president waged these civil wars long before the Senate had its say in the appointment process.

Prior to the respective nominations of O'Connor and Kennedy, various officials in the Reagan administration became aware that each had evidenced some ambiguity on the critical issue of abortion rights. Despite such clear warnings, a select group of high-level officials mustered enough support in each case to ensure that its favored candidate remained high on the administration's "short-lists." A combination of assets in O'Connor's case, including youth (she was just fifty-one years old) and a conservative record on law enforcement issues, convinced Attorney General

William French Smith to look past troubling ambiguities about her abortion position. Similarly, Anthony Kennedy's youth (he was also just fifty), his stature in the legal community, and his eminent confirmability made him a top candidate for a Supreme Court vacancy as early as 1986. After witnessing two consecutive nominations to the Supreme Court go awry (Robert Bork and Douglas Ginsburg), Chief of Staff Howard Baker and White House Counsel Arthur B. Culvahouse were able to seize the upper hand from Reagan's other chief advisor, Attorney General Edwin Meese III, in November 1987. Kennedy's star thus rose despite Justice Department officials' qualms over his judicial record on privacy rights. Few of these same officials could have been surprised five years later when Kennedy joined the controlling opinion in *Casey.*

A central question remains: why were these particular candidates chosen over others possessing similar—and in some cases superior—qualifications? The classic "textbook" portrayal of the Supreme Court nomination process depicts presidents as choosing Supreme Court justices more for their judicial politics than for their judicial talents. By this version of events, presidents, by nominating justices whose political views appear compatible with their own, try to gain increased influence over the Supreme Court. Once on the Court, a justice may then satisfy or disappoint the appointing president by his decisions. Such an oversimplified view of nomination politics usually ignores the more complex political environment in which modern presidents must act, including the various intricacies and nuances of executive branch politics.

. . . I contend that modern presidents are often forced to arbitrate among factions within their own administrations, each pursuing its own interests and agendas in the selection process. At first glance, presidential reliance on numerous high-level officials equipped with a variety of perspectives might seem a logical response to the often hostile and unpredictable political environment that surrounds modern appointments to the Court. Yet conflicts within the administration itself may have a debilitating effect on that president's overall interests. High-level advisors may be sincerely pursuing their own conceptions of what makes up the administration's best interests; but to achieve their own maximum preferred outcomes, they may feel compelled to skew the presentation of critical information, if not leave it out altogether. In recent administrations the final choice of a nominee has usually reflected one advisor's hard-won victory over his rivals, without necessarily accounting for the president's other political interests. Analysis of these intra-executive branch conflicts, and the role such conflicts play in the Supreme Court selection process as a whole, constitutes the central aspect of this work.

EVALUATING THE POLITICAL LANDSCAPE THAT SHAPES NOMINEE SELECTIONS

In studying the various pathways that lead to a Supreme Court nomination, my assumption throughout is that presidents enjoy considerable discretion in considering and selecting candidates for the Supreme Court. No candidate ever forces himself or herself upon a president of the United States. Even if a Supreme Court seat is offered in fulfillment of a promise, political or otherwise, it remains the case that the president originally exercised his discretion when issuing that promise in the first place. Certainly he could have showed his appreciation by some means other than a Supreme Court bid. One must nevertheless distinguish between the discretion a president technically enjoys as a matter of constitutional prerogative from that which he can realistically wield without causing undue political hardship to his presidency.

As to the latter, a president's personal prestige and ability to influence other public matters suffer when the selection of a Supreme Court nominee fails to adequately account for the hostile forces at work in the immediate political context.

The *timing* of a vacancy usually plays a critical role in the selection of a nominee. When a vacancy arises just before a pending presidential election, the president may be forced to nominate a noncontroversial moderate as a means of achieving the requisite support in the Senate. The nominations of Benjamin Cardozo by President Hoover in 1932 and John Paul Stevens by President Ford in late 1975 were each heavily influenced by such political reality. A Supreme Court vacancy may also occur when public attention to issues surrounding the Supreme Court is relatively high. In those cases, a president must take careful account of public perceptions. Having tried to sell his 1937 "court-packing" plan as a means of reducing the workload for older justices, Franklin D. Roosevelt was understandably reluctant to nominate an older justice to the Court in subsequent years; the seventy-one-year-old Learned Hand thus stood little chance of landing a Supreme Court nomination in 1943 despite enjoying considerable support in some legal circles. After the abortion issue rocketed into the national spotlight during the late 1970s, the Reagan administration was forced to consider abortion politics in its evaluation of Supreme Court nominees throughout the following decade.

The *composition of the Senate* will constrain presidential discretion in this context. The Democrats' comfortable twelve-seat advantage in the Senate made it easier for President Truman to name two close personal associates to the bench in 1949. Truman suffered some harsh criticism initially for his nominations of Tom Clark and Sherman Minton, but each candidate was confirmed handily. More than anyone, Ronald Reagan saw first-hand what a difference a year makes. The Republicans' 53-47 edge in the Senate during the summer of 1986 eased the confirmation paths for two ardently conservative Supreme Court nominees, Antonin Scalia and William Rehnquist. In fact, Rehnquist was confirmed as chief justice by a thirty-two-vote margin despite some harsh allegations by Democrats. By contrast, a year later, after the Republicans had lost their Senate majority, the nomination of Robert Bork ran into more serious resistance from newly empowered Senate Democrats.

Public approval of the president similarly shapes the setting for each Supreme Court nomination. A president who enjoys high public support may comfortably submit almost any nominee of his choosing. By contrast, an unpopular president stands little chance of seeing any nominee confirmed easily, if at all. One scholar doubts "the Senate would have approved God himself" had he been nominated by the highly unpopular Andrew Johnson after the Civil War. (Even Johnson's cautious selection of Attorney General Henry Stanbury, a well-respected Ohio Republican and Unionist, stood little real chance of success in 1865.) Sophisticated new polling techniques today give presidents yet another tool in deciding whether to choose a controversial nominee. Rising poll ratings in early 1970 actually may have spurred President Nixon to respond to the defeat of his second nominee to the Court, Court of Appeals Judge Clement Haynsworth, with an even more controversial candidate for the Court, G. Harrold Carswell.

Attributes of the outgoing justice, including his or her status in the legal community and perceived position on the Court's ideological spectrum, may also influence expectations for a prospective replacement. In seeking a nominee for the seat vacated by the legendary Justice Oliver Wendell Holmes in 1932, President Hoover fully realized that the highly esteemed Court of Appeals judge from New York, Benjamin Cardozo, was one of few candidates in the country capable of filling such lofty shoes. Perhaps Robert Bork's strong opinions on abortion, affirmative action, and other social issues would have resonated less with senators and the public had he been selected to replace a fellow conservative on the Court instead of the critical "swing" justice, Lewis F. Powell Jr.

In all cases *the realistic pool of candidates* available to the president necessarily restricts his selection of Supreme Court nominees. This field has been winnowed in advance by traditional norms of political and professional advancement. Richard Watson and Rondal Downing have employed a "progressive winnowing theory" to explain the phenomenon of judicial recruitment in general. At one end of the process lies the "particular subculture" from which judges are drawn, especially the legal community of persons admitted to the bar. Additional stages eliminate more and more candidates on the basis of acceptability to interest groups, personal desire, and other factors. Finally, at the other end a chosen few emerge as the final products of the entire process: the pool of those eligible for nomination.

Although the Constitution does not specify qualifications for a justice of the Supreme Court, even the most daring president would find it difficult to ignore de facto norms of advancement that define the pool of candidates available to him. Historically, every justice has been a lawyer. Since 1943, every justice has formally graduated from an accredited law school. Some limited participation in politics, however broadly defined, colors the background of nearly all Supreme Court justices. Many carry past partisanship as a badge of honor, having risen through the ranks of a political party before catching the attention of a senator, governor, presidential advisor, or even the president himself. Others were themselves governors, members of Congress, or high-level executives before appointment to the Supreme Court. Still others were active in local bar association politics or interest groups such as the AFL-CIO, the ACLU, and the NAACP. As J. Woodford Howard Jr. remarked, even the final stages of judicial recruitment involve "an intricate web of vocational and political contacts developed long before the denouement."

How do modern presidents go about the complicated task of selecting Supreme Court nominees? Presidents since 1945 have tended to utilize one of three decisional frameworks in considering candidates: (1) an "*open*" selection framework, in which all critical decisions about the next Supreme Court nominee are rendered *after* a particular vacancy arises; (2) *a single-candidate focused* framework, in which the identity of the next justice has been decided in advance of a vacancy (usually based on previous political promises, commitments, or other such circumstances); and (3) a *criteria-driven* framework for selection in which—prior to any actual vacancy arising—the president and his advisors set forth specific criteria to be met by prospective nominees (without settling on any specific candidate). Under the more flexible "open" framework, the president (with or without the assistance of advisors) may respond quickly and effectively to changes in the immediate political environment and adjust his goals accordingly. On the other hand, the president's long-term goals for the Court (to the extent he has any) may be obscured in his efforts to achieve more immediate gains. That risk is reduced whenever a criteria-driven framework for selection is utilized.

Key decisionmakers and the roles they play in executing these frameworks must also be identified. Modern presidents may utilize any of a number of approaches to structuring their administration's selection processes. On one end of a continuum lies a strictly personal approach to selection, in which the president primarily keeps his own counsel in considering and selecting nominees. On the other end lies a more bureaucratic approach, in which presidential advisors and subordinates make many critical selection decisions about Supreme Court nominations on behalf of the president. Some presidents hope to draw on positive aspects of both approaches: the final product may thus emerge from a dialogue between the president and the decisionmaking bureaucracy beneath him.

Regardless of the precise balance struck, during the past thirty years some form of delegation to bureaucratic structures has become a defining characteristic of the selection process. Both the Nixon and Reagan administrations—together responsible for filling eight of nine vacancies that arose on the Court between 1969 and 1987—established more bureaucratic, subordinate-driven mechanisms for vetting Supreme Court candidates. These systems featured (1) the promulgation of political and/or legal criteria for nominees that administration officials could interpret and apply, and (2) the participation of multiple officials and/or agencies in the process of choosing nominees. Both presidents hoped such a system would identify a broader pool of candidates. In fact, these innovations often failed to serve the president's overall interests. Officials forced to compete for influence within the administration often assume alternate roles as advocates of their *own* political agendas or causes in the selection process. And those concerns do not always represent those of their boss.

Tony Mauro, Bush Got a Conservative High Court, with Caveats

The National Law Journal, Nov. 3, 2008

If cameras were allowed in the Supreme Court, it would have been a Kodak moment. As it was, few spectators were on hand for the first oral argument on the morning of April 14, 2008.

The question before the justices: Do tribal courts have jurisdiction over a dispute between a nontribal bank and an Indian-owned corporation? Halfway into the hearing, Chief Justice John Roberts Jr. leaned forward to say he was trying to understand the concept of an "Indian corporation." With a faint smile he nodded toward his colleagues on the bench. "If Justices Scalia and Alito form a corporation," he asked, "is that an Italian corporation?"

Antonin Scalia and Samuel Alito Jr. laughed heartily, even though Scalia makes a point of telling people he is Italian-American, not Italian. "Do we get personal loan guarantees?" asked Scalia, going along with the joke.

It was a brief interlude, but it displayed the easy, confident style of the new chief justice and the comfortable camaraderie of the Court's reconstituted conservative wing. Conservative Justice Clarence Thomas was smiling, too. Two months later, those four and Justice Anthony Kennedy ruled 5-4 against the tribe and for the bank.

Most Court commentators believe conservatives are finally riding high in the saddle at the Supreme Court—and enjoying it. Increasingly, their ascendancy is being viewed, as author Jeffrey Toobin puts it, as President George W. Bush's "most enduring triumph." In *The New York Times*, Linda Greenhouse, now retired from the beat, wrote that it is "the Supreme Court that conservatives had long yearned for and that liberals feared." NPR's Nina Totenberg chimed in that conservatives "seem to have reached the promised land."

Without being churlish, it is fair to wonder whether even this part of the Bush legacy is the shining success it is cracked up to be. Has the Court yet gotten all the way to conservative nirvana? A new law review study of the Roberts Court's decisions

Sauter as "mystery" candidate?

concludes, in a play on Greenhouse's 2007 assessment, that "conservatives should continue to yearn, and liberals should not fear." . . .

"A VERY TRICKY BUSINESS"

Few dispute that Bush's campaign to move the Court to the right was a deliberate journey, launched by Federalist Society Republicans who had been awaiting their moment for decades. But serendipity and lucky moments of history helped enormously to create the Roberts Court. If key events had broken differently, the Supreme Court might have been added to the list of unconsummated Bush administration projects, right next to Social Security reform and energy independence.

As one top former Justice Department official put it, "Roberts and Alito were inspired picks, but I don't think anyone should ever forget who his second choice was." Even the proudest architects of the Bush Supreme Court legacy wince at the memory of Harriet Miers.

The administration's obsession with Supreme Court appointments began even before George W. Bush was elected in 2000. In 1999, Bush invited conservative lawyers—among them, Reagan Attorney General Edwin Meese III—to Austin, Texas, to discuss judicial selection, says conservative lawyer Leonard Leo, an informal adviser on the subject from that point on. "There was a sensitivity that judicial selection was a very tricky business," Leo recalls, and a desire to get started early. As a son of the first President Bush, George W. Bush had seen and felt the disappointment (Souter), the agony (Clarence Thomas), and the success (again, Thomas) that the power to appoint justices could bring.

Then came the 2000 election itself, producing a baptism by fire called *Bush v. Gore.* The ordeal left an unavoidable, black-robed birthmark on the Bush administration, a profound reminder that the Supreme Court matters. "It was impossible to have had that supercharged judicial experience and not walk away with a deep sense of the awesome power of the judiciary," says Leo.

When Bush was inaugurated, "we prepared from day one," according to one top staffer. The goal was to prevent a mystery candidate like Souter from sneaking to the front of the line. While some administrations task the Justice Department with judicial selection, Leo says, "it was flipped in this Bush administration" to the White House counsel's office, headed by Alberto Gonzales. "That's where the president had his closest friends," Leo adds.

The list of potential Supreme Court nominees that emerged from the counsel's office was heavy with Texans and a fair sprinkling of Hispanics. Roberts, then in private practice, was not on the list, and neither was Miers. But Alito, a solid conservative on the U.S. Court of Appeals for the 3rd Circuit, was.

The important thing was that there was a list to work from. Mistakes come when the staff is caught unprepared, officials believed, leaving a vacuum for mystery candidates—like Souter—to fill. "Heaven help you aren't ready when the time comes," says Timothy Flanigan, then-deputy White House counsel and now a partner at McGuireWoods in Richmond, Va. "Everybody hopes for and dreads a vacancy at the same time."

As the years went by without vacancies, according to another former senior official who requested anonymity, Alito and Judge J. Michael Luttig of the U.S. Court of Appeals for the 4th Circuit emerged as front-runners. Alito's early prominence comes as something of a surprise; he rarely appeared near the top of media short lists. "I've never seen much of a correlation between the real list and the one that is spoken of publicly," shrugs Flanigan.

The passage of time also helped Roberts. He'd been nominated to the U.S. Court of Appeals for the D.C. Circuit, and began serving in June 2003. By 2005 he had enough judicial heft that his biggest fan, deputy White House counsel David Leitch (now vice president and general counsel of Ford Motor Co.), could push him for the Supreme Court. Any earlier and it would have been a tough sell.

Hitting Home Runs

What the administration was seeking, according to conversations with participants, was a mix of ideology and excellence. The goal was to find impeccable Supreme Court nominees whose talents and intellect were so unimpeachable that their strongly conservative stripes would not defeat them.

"The conversation isn't, 'he'll vote right on abortion,'" says Leo, "because conservatives have learned you can play that game all you want and you'll still have a 50 percent chance of being wrong." Instead, the "cafeteria talk," Leo continues, was, "do you hit a home run or trade up?" Leo defines "trading up" disdainfully as appointing someone who is only a notch more conservative than his or her predecessor instead [of] going for full ideological purity. In 2005, Leo took a leave of absence from his job as executive vice president of the Federalist Society to serve as one of the president's key advisers on high court nominations. By then, Leo says, the debate over what kind of nominees should be sought was over. "It was all about hitting home runs," he says, rather than appointing "85-percenters."

Leo was one of the "four horsemen," as they were called, who consulted daily with the White House on high court nominations. The others were Meese, Christian-right attorney Jay Sekulow, and C. Boyden Gray, White House counsel under the first President Bush.

So the stage was set when the events of the summer of 2005 began. Just before the term ended in June, Justice Sandra Day O'Connor went to chat with her ailing, longtime friend Chief Justice William Rehnquist about the future. A strong institutional impulse at the Court compels justices not to burden the nation with more than one vacancy at a time, so she wanted to see what Rehnquist's plans were. O'Connor's husband, whose Alzheimer's disease was worsening, needed her, but if Rehnquist was about to announce his retirement, she'd defer to him and stay on. Rehnquist, suffering from a virulent form of thyroid cancer, said he would not resign. "Well, okay, I'll retire then," was O'Connor's reply, according to Jan Crawford Greenburg in her authoritative 2007 book *Supreme Conflict.*

On July 1, after the term had ended, O'Connor stunned Washington by announcing she would retire when her successor was confirmed.

The White House was ready for a vacancy—though staffers had expected they would be looking for a replacement for Rehnquist. Conservative activists were ready, too, and they quickly snuffed out Gonzales' chances to be named. "Gonzales is Spanish for Souter" was one fatal slogan.

Though Leitch pushed hard for Roberts, doubts remained about his conservative credentials, partly because he had not written many decisions on the appeals court in his brief time there. Leo recalls a White House meeting where Miers, then White House counsel, bluntly said of Roberts' conservatism, "Prove it. I'm not sure I see it." The case was made, and Bush nominated Roberts to replace O'Connor.

Then Rehnquist died, just before Roberts' confirmation hearings were to begin. Roberts would not get to serve on the Court next to his mentor and the man who had hired him as a law clerk more than two decades before.

Faced suddenly with task of replacing Rehnquist, Bush no longer felt he had to start from scratch; he had his man right in front of him. Roberts had benefited from the summer of scrutiny, and with Hurricane Katrina devastating the Gulf Coast at the same time, Bush wanted to move fast. Naming Roberts to the Court's center chair two days after Rehnquist's death, Bush said that after getting to know Roberts, Americans "like what they see."

The discipline broke down when Bush then had to find someone else to replace O'Connor. He was under pressure to nominate a woman, but for whatever reason, insiders say the vetted list contained few "home run" candidates who were female. So Bush looked elsewhere—not very far, it turns out—and went with Miers, his White House counsel. "I know the president felt she was a quality candidate," Leo says. "In his own heart, he was not compromising."

But in little over three weeks, she was gone—a victim of conservative outrage that she would be a moderate mistake worse than Souter, and with fewer credentials than Souter. Miers did not help her own cause. During a courtesy call, when Sen. Patrick Leahy (D-Vt.) asked her to name her favorite justice, she said "Warren." Surprised, Leahy sought clarification; did she mean Earl Warren or Warren Burger? She gave the correct conservative answer—Warren Burger—but the exchange left Leahy doubting that she had any more than a passing knowledge of the institution she was seeking to join.

A COURT TRANSFORMED?

Even before Miers withdrew, it appears, Bush had settled on her replacement: Sam Alito. During earlier interviews, Bush had liked Alito more than Luttig, says Toobin in his book *The Nine*. And the line on Alito among White House lawyers was that in his 15 years on the 3rd Circuit—he'd been appointed by Bush's father—Alito had never written a wrong opinion.

The dramatic chronology was crucial to the almost accidental success of Bush's Supreme Court nominations. If the cards had been dealt in a different order, Roberts might not be chief justice at all. If Rehnquist had retired before 2005, as many expected, either of the more experienced 4th Circuit judges—J. Michael Luttig or J. Harvie Wilkinson III—probably would have been picked to replace him. And if Rehnquist had retired in 2005, as was widely expected, or passed away earlier, O'Connor would have stayed on at least one more term, to avoid a double vacancy. By then her husband John's Alzheimer's disease, the reason she wanted to leave, had deteriorated to the point where he could not be cared for at home; O'Connor might never have stepped down at all.

In short, Bush might have given life to a Luttig Court that included Justice O'Connor. Conservatives would have a lot less legacy to boast about. . . .

Notes and Questions

1. In making his two nominations to the high court, President Barack Obama has utilized a selection process quite similar to that employed by his immediate predecessor: soliciting and reviewing reports prepared by his staff on approximately ten candidates, selecting four candidates from among the larger group to interview, then rapidly settling on a nominee at the end of the interview process. Presumably because of his experience as a lawyer and law school lecturer, President Obama played a somewhat more active role in the selection than President Bush, for example, requesting that his advisors prepare reports on particular candidates and reviewing many of their judicial opinions. For a summary of the White House decision making process in 2009, leading to the selection of Justice Sonia Sotomayor, see Peter Baker and Adam Nagourney, *Sotomayor Pick a Product of Lessons from Past Battles*, N.Y. Times, May 27, 2009, at A1. For a summary of the process in 2010, leading to the selection of Justice Elena Kagan, *see Obama Picks Kagan as Justice Nominee*, N.Y. Times, May 10, 2010, at A1.

2. The orderly selection processes employed by the last two Presidents are in sharp contrast with the approaches of the two prior White Houses, both of which were more haphazard in their search process. According to many reports, President Bill Clinton was initially committed to appointing a nonjudge to the Supreme Court. When a vacancy occurred, he initially offered the seat to New York Governor Mario Cuomo, who vacillated before turning it down; then settled on Interior Secretary Bruce Babbitt, only to eliminate him for seemingly minor reasons; nearly pulled the trigger on Arkansas Federal Judge Richard Arnold; settled on Judge Stephen Breyer, only to reject him after a poor interview; and finally turned to Judge Ruth Bader Ginsburg. For two slightly different versions of these events, see Jan Crawford Greenburg, *Supreme Conflict: The Inside Story of the Struggle for Control of the United States Supreme Court* 166-170 (2007) and Jeffrey Toobin, *The Nine: Inside the Secret World of the Supreme Court* 60-73 (2007). According to the leading chronicler of Republican judicial nominations, Jan Crawford Greenburg, President George H.W. Bush went through a similar process of indecision when he first had a vacancy to fill. The problem in his case came about as the result of overconfidence and underpreparedness on the part of some of his senior advisors, who assumed that a Supreme Court vacancy would go to Solicitor General and former appellate judge Kenneth Starr or, in the alternative, to Judge Laurence Silberman. When the two candidates were quickly eliminated from consideration, due in the first case to unexpected opposition within the administration and in the second to questions about judicial temperament, the administration had no further list of candidates to turn to and was highly susceptible to Chief of Staff John Sununu's advocacy for his former colleague, the relatively unknown David Souter. For the full story, see Crawford Greenburg, *Supreme Conflict* at 87-107.

3. The processes utilized by the last two Presidents have certainly been more organized and disciplined than those catalogued in the note above, but they have been far from perfect. President Bush went off script for his second nominee, Harriet Miers, and was ultimately forced to withdraw her nomination. President Obama's vetting team failed to understand the degree to which Judge Sotomayor's controversial speeches (one of which is excerpted below) provided ammunition for her opponents and, by many accounts, did not sufficiently prepare her for her hearings.

4. What lessons, if any, should we draw from the failed nomination of Harriet Miers? Is it a story about cronyism? The dangers of affirmative action? The necessity of prior judicial experience (or perhaps equivalent experience in constitutional litigation) for service on the modern court? The rising power of judicial and cultural conservatives within the Republican coalition? The risks a President takes when he deviates from his process when making crucial decisions? The failure of White House political officials to shore up their base before launching an important initiative?

5. If you were in charge of organizing the process through which the President arrived at a Supreme Court nominee, how would you organize the process? What modifications, if any, would you make to the processes used by the last two Presidents? To what degree and in what way would you include the President him or herself in the process?

6. What do you think about the greater transparency involved in recent selections? Notice that it is a strange sort of transparency—the White House is releasing the names and dates of all Supreme Court interviews but only after the nomination has been made; beforehand, they continue to take extraordinary steps to maintain confidentiality. Is this a substantial step in the direction of open government or merely an attempt to satisfy different constituencies that their preferred candidates have been considered? Should the White House move toward greater transparency by publicly revealing whom the President will be interviewing before the President settles on a nominee?

7. News accounts suggests that President Obama extensively consulted with members of the Judiciary Committee before making his selection of Justice Sotomayor. See, for example, Baker and Nagourney, *supra* note 1, at A1. Though Obama probably made more calls to legislators before making a nomination than any previous President, conversations with legislative leaders are not uncommon. For example, Utah Senator Orrin Hatch reportedly recommended Justices Stephen Breyer and Ruth Bader Ginsburg to President Clinton before their nominations. Given the language of the Constitution (the President shall act "with the advice and consent" of the Senate), do you think the President should more actively involve Senators in his prenomination deliberations, or do you think such a step dangerously muddies the roles of the various branches of government?

8. There exists a very rich literature on the dynamics of Supreme Court nominations. In addition to Yalof's book, those interested in the subject might also consult Henry Abraham, *Justices, Presidents, and Senators* (1999); Stephen Carter, *The Confirmation Mess* (1994); Chrisopher L. Eisgruber, *The Next Justice: Repairing the Supreme Court Appointments Process* (2009); John Anthony Maltese, *The Selling of Supreme Court Nominees* (1999); Benjamin Wittes, *Confirmation Wars: Preserving Independent Courts in Angry Times* (2006); Paul A. Freund, *Appointment of Justices: Some Historical Perspectives*, 101 Harv. L. Rev. 1146 (1988); and Michael Gerhardt, *Toward a Comprehensive Understanding of the Federal Appointments Process*, 21 Harv. J.L. & Pub. Pol'y 467 (1997).

3. Senate Confirmation

Once a President selects a Supreme Court nominee, the battle shifts to the Senate, which must "consent" to the nomination by majority vote.[8] As discussed above, the Senate confirmation process has become a stylized affair, with coordinated panels of advocates testifying on both sides, carefully choreographed opening statements, and predictable banter between posturing committee members and nominees

---

8. Senate rules allow for the filibustering of nominees who cannot muster the 60 votes necessary to invoke cloture and cut off debate. This is a nontrivial concern for Presidents, as Senators have successfully filibustered more than a few lower court appointees in recent years, have threatened (and in one recent instance briefly attempted) to filibuster Supreme Court nominees, and did in fact successfully filibuster the nomination of Abe Fortas for Chief Justice 40 years ago. That having been said, the political dynamics of a modern Supreme Court nomination make it difficult—though not impossible—to keep a nominee who enjoys majority support in the Senate off the Court.

unwilling to get bogged down in substantive conversation. This section breaks the Senate confirmation process down into a series of stages and offers an eclectic set of materials illustrating the dynamics of each stage.

a. The Campaign for the Hearts and Minds of the Public

As soon as a nominee is selected (and often before), supporters and opponents of the candidate work to shape the public's perception of the candidate and control the nomination's narrative. The readings below offer materials from recent confirmation battles. First is a famous speech given by Senator Edward Kennedy within minutes of the nomination of Judge Robert Bork. Second is an article from a news magazine in which one of this book's authors (writing in a very different context) unsuccessfully opposed the confirmation of Justice Samuel Alito. Finally, we include a controversial speech given by then-Judge Sonia Sotomayor that proved to be a primary focus for critics of her nomination.

Senator Edward Kennedy, "Robert Bork's America"

133 Cong. Rec. S9188 (daily ed. July 1, 1987)
(statement of Sen. Kennedy)

[Senate floor speech made in response to the announcement of Bork's nomination; June 23, 1987:]

Mr. President, I oppose the nomination of Robert Bork to the Supreme Court, and I urge the Senate to reject it.

In the Watergate scandal of 1973, two distinguished Republicans—Attorney General Elliot Richardson and Deputy Attorney General William Ruckelshaus—put integrity and the Constitution ahead of loyalty to a corrupt President. They refused to do Richard Nixon's dirty work, and they refused to obey his order to fire Special Prosecutor Archibald Cox. The deed devolved on Solicitor General Robert Bork, who executed the unconscionable assignment that has become one of the darkest chapters for the rule of law in American history.

That act—later ruled illegal by a Federal court—is sufficient, by itself, to disqualify Mr. Bork from this new position to which he has been nominated. The man who fired Archibald Cox does not deserve to sit on the Supreme Court of the United States.

Mr. Bork should also be rejected by the Senate because he stands for an extremist view of the Constitution and the role of the Supreme Court that would have placed him outside the mainstream of American constitutional jurisprudence in the 1960s, let alone the 1980s. He opposed the Public Accommodations Civil Rights Act of 1964. He opposed the one-man one-vote decision of the Supreme Court the same year. He has said that the First Amendment applies only to political speech, not literature or works of art or scientific expression.

Under the twin pressures of academic rejection and the prospect of Senate rejection, Mr. Bork subsequently retracted the most neanderthal of these views on civil rights and the first amendment. But his mind-set is no less ominous today.

Robert Bork's America is a land in which women would be forced into back-alley abortions, blacks would sit at segregated lunch counters, rogue police could break down citizens' doors in midnight raids, schoolchildren could not be taught about evolution, writers and artists would be censored at the whim of government, and the doors of the federal courts would be shut on the fingers of millions of citizens for whom the judiciary is often the only protector of the individual rights that are the heart of our democracy.

America is a better and freer nation than Robert Bork thinks. Yet in the current delicate balance of the Supreme Court, his rigid ideology will tip the scales of justice against the kind of country America is and ought to be.

The damage that President Reagan will do through this nomination, if it is not rejected by the Senate, could live on far beyond the end of his presidential term. President Reagan is still our President. But he should not be able to reach out from the muck of Irangate, reach into the muck of Watergate, and impose his reactionary vision of the Constitution on the Supreme Court and on the next generation of Americans. No justice would be better than this injustice. . . .

Andrew M. Siegel, Nice Disguise: Alito's Frightening Geniality

The New Republic, Nov. 14, 2005, at 20

The nomination this week of Judge Samuel A. Alito Jr. to succeed Justice Sandra Day O'Connor set off a predictable scurry to divine what kind of justice he might make and, in particular, to decipher whether the judge commonly tagged "Scalito" would live up to that moniker. The verdict on the latter question was swift. After skimming his opinions and interviewing his friends and associates, nearly every source concluded that Alito and Justice Antonin Scalia share little beyond Italian-American heritage, Catholicism, and a conservative voting record.

In particular, those familiar with Alito stressed that his even-keeled temperament, collegiality, and lawyerly writing style distinguished his professional demeanor from that of the volatile, sarcastic, and often hectoring Scalia. The nearly universal conclusion was that Alito was less of a Scalia clone than some of the other federal judges considered for the post, most notably the rumored runner-up, Judge J. Michael Luttig.

The implication of this conclusion was that liberals should breathe a sigh of relief, since Alito is no Scalia 2.0. The reality, however, is much more complicated. While Scalia's bellicose tone and general lack of civility have long been fodder for his left-wing critics, they have also served to hold back his judicial agenda, both by alienating potential allies within the Court and by marking his ideas as extreme in the court of public opinion.

But Alito, who marries Scalia's conservative jurisprudence with tact, politeness, and a deferential writing style, is infinitely more dangerous to liberals. In Alito, they may have met their worst nightmare. In 15 years on the bench, Alito has had opportunities to weigh in on almost all of the controversial constitutional issues facing the Supreme Court today—from abortion and the death penalty to the scope of federal power and the role of religion in the public square. The opinions that he has written in these cases share two essential characteristics. First, each is calm, rational, and well-written. Second, on virtually every significant issue where his conclusion is not mandated by direct Supreme Court precedent, the result is conservative.

These traits are notable in Alito's first major constitutional opinion, his partial dissent in *Planned Parenthood v. Casey*. In that 1991 case, Alito was one of three judges responsible for evaluating the constitutionality of a number of new abortion restrictions adopted by Pennsylvania, including a controversial spousal notification provision. Alito was the only judge who argued that the spousal notification provision passed constitutional muster (a conclusion ultimately rejected by the Supreme Court). But, in reaching that conclusion, Alito moved cautiously toward his bold result, carefully mustering quotations from O'Connor's various abortion opinions (ultimately using nearly two dozen different quotations from her abortion writings), debating countervailing evidence, and repeatedly downplaying the scope of his disagreement with his colleagues (at one point all but admitting that the case turns on how one interprets a single cryptic sentence in an O'Connor concurring opinion). Read in isolation, Alito's opinion gives the impression of a conscientious jurist doing his best to tame and apply difficult legal texts. The author's will is largely absent from the text of the opinion.

In a 1996 case challenging Congress's power to ban the possession of machine guns, Alito again faced a hot-button constitutional issue on which the Supreme Court's decisions were cryptic and in flux. The other two judges on the panel joined all of the other federal courts of appeals in rejecting the gun owner's challenge, but Alito dissented. Again, he parsed the relevant Supreme Court opinions in painstaking detail; again, he openly acknowledged and engaged countervailing evidence (for example, noting, with regard to the majority's central argument, that "I take this theory very seriously"); again, he played down the scope of his disagreement with his colleagues (by commenting that the majority "quite properly focuses its analysis" on a particular doctrinal point). And, again, he reached a boldly conservative result.

In recent years, Alito has honed his ability to write lucid, polite opinions reaching invariably conservative positions on a string of issues that have divided the current Court—from the scope of a capital defendant's right to the effective assistance of counsel during the penalty phase of his trial, to the breadth of governmental officials' immunity from liability when they inadvertently violate the constitutional rights of citizens, to the proper interpretation of the Establishment Clause.

For example, in the 1999 case *American Civil Liberties Union of New Jersey v. Schundler,* Alito wrote an opinion for a divided panel evaluating the constitutionality of a Jersey City holiday display containing, among other things, a menorah, a creche, a Christmas tree, and large plastic figures of Santa Claus and Frosty the Snowman. The heart of his opinion is an almost comically detailed dissection of the Supreme Court's relevant writings and their implications for this case. He notes, for example, that the display in one of the Supreme Court cases "included fewer religious symbols" than the one in Jersey City—a "menorah only" versus "both a menorah on the left side of City Hall and a creche on the right." Along the way, Alito, as usual, finds time to acknowledge the aspects of the Supreme Court precedents that potentially cut against his argument before reaching the predictable conclusion that Jersey City's display does not violate the Establishment Clause. Whatever one thinks of the opinion's conclusion, it is hard to come away from it with anything other than affection for its careful and patient author.

Two lessons can be drawn from the substance and tone of Alito's appellate opinions. First, contrary to what many commentators want you to believe, the individual predilections and judgments of jurists have a substantial effect on the direction of U.S. constitutional law. While many legal questions can be resolved through a relatively straightforward application of reason to the relevant legal texts, most of the controversial constitutional questions that reach the Court are not susceptible to such simple resolution. When confronting such cases, judges are forced back—almost inexorably—to their own, often inchoate, ideas about human behavior, social policy, and the judicial role. For most Supreme Court nominees, we need to guess how these "priors" will shape their jurisprudence, but, for Alito, we have a long and consistent answer: He will tack hard to the right.

The second lesson is really a caveat about the first. With the opinions of most justices—particularly the savvy—it's hard for a reader to separate the application of legal sources and precedents from individual will. The norms of the legal profession push judges to ground their opinions directly in the legal sources, whatever the wellspring of their decisions. Those who are accomplished at this task have the ability to make even the most controversial result sound inevitable. In a substantial percentage of their cases, Scalia and Luttig eschew these professional conventions and lay bare their motivation. Alito never does. In many ways, the scrupulous fidelity of Alito's opinions makes him a more powerful advocate for his conclusions and a bigger danger to those who sport opposing legal or constitutional visions.

If Alito were to join the Supreme Court, his opinions would instantly gain a larger audience and a more central role in U.S. jurisprudence. Moreover, freed from the shackles of operating with a higher court looking over his shoulder, he would almost certainly expand his horizons. If one follows the little clues dropped (modestly) into his appellate opinions, Alito is brimming with ideas for pushing the boundaries of existing doctrine to the right in a number of crucial, albeit low-profile, areas, such as federal employment discrimination law, search and seizure law, and the rules governing the susceptibility of public officials to lawsuits.

In the end, however, if Judge Alito becomes Justice Alito, his greatest influence might stem not from his vote or his pen but from his collegiality. For more than three decades, efforts to assemble a consistent right-wing majority on the Supreme Court have foundered, at least in part because of personality conflicts among the conservative justices. To take the highest- profile example, as the history of the Rehnquist Court gradually comes to light, it becomes increasingly clear that Scalia's unwillingness to credit the intelligence and good faith of those who disagree with him took a particular toll on his relationship with O'Connor, potentially costing him a decisive vote to overturn *Roe v. Wade* and almost certainly costing him majorities in a slew of lower-profile cases.

Unless Alito undergoes a personality transplant if he enters the Beltway, it is literally impossible to imagine him demeaning the qualifications of a colleague, exasperating his fellow justices by hogging the spotlight at oral argument, or running his mouth off in a speech or a dissenting opinion to blow off steam. In his years on the Third Circuit, Alito's decency and civility have earned him respect across ideological lines. Recently, former colleague Timothy Lewis endorsed his Supreme Court candidacy and said that another colleague, the late Chief Judge A. Leon Higginbotham Jr., a notoriously hostile critic of Scalia and Justice Clarence Thomas, had also praised Alito.

If you are a fan of the justices who fought throughout the Rehnquist years to pull the Supreme Court to the right, Alito is a home run—a strong and consistent conservative with the skill to craft opinions that make radical results appear inevitable and the ability to build trusting professional relationships across ideological lines. If, on the other hand, you are a committed opponent of the Scalia-Thomas-Rehnquist agenda who has been carefully evaluating O'Connor's potential replacements with concern for the Court's future direction, Alito might be the most dangerous possible nominee.

Sonia Sotomayor, A Latina Judge's Voice

13 Berkeley La Raza L.J. 87 (2002)

Judge Reynoso, thank you for that lovely introduction. I am humbled to be speaking behind a man who has contributed so much to the Hispanic community. I am also grateful to have such kind words said about me.

I am delighted to be here. It is nice to escape my hometown for just a little bit. It is also nice to say hello to old friends who are in the audience, to rekindle contact with old acquaintances and to make new friends among those of you in the audience. It is particularly heart warming to me to be attending a conference to which I was invited by a Latina law school friend, Rachel Moran, who is now an accomplished and widely respected legal scholar. I warn Latinos in this room: Latinas are making a lot of progress in the old-boy network.

I am also deeply honored to have been asked to deliver the annual Judge Mario G. Olmos lecture. I am joining a remarkable group of prior speakers who have given this lecture. I hope what I speak about today continues to promote the legacy of that man whose commitment to public service and abiding dedication to promoting equality and justice for all people inspired this memorial lecture and the conference that will follow. I thank Judge Olmos' widow Mary Louise's family, her son and the judge's many friends for hosting me. And for the privilege you have bestowed on me in honoring the memory of a very special person. If I and the many people of this conference can accomplish a fraction of what Judge Olmos did in his short but extraordinary life we and our respective communities will be infinitely better.

I intend tonight to touch upon the themes that this conference will be discussing this weekend and to talk to you about my Latina identity, where it came from, and the influence I perceive it has on my presence on the bench.

Who am I? I am a "Newyorkrican." For those of you on the West Coast who do not know what that term means: I am a born and bred New Yorker of Puerto Rican-born parents who came to the states during World War II.

Like many other immigrants to this great land, my parents came because of poverty and to attempt to find and secure a better life for themselves and the family that they hoped to have. They largely succeeded. For that, my brother and I are very grateful. The story of that success is what made me and what makes me the Latina that I am. The Latina side of my identity was forged and closely nurtured by my family through our shared experiences and traditions. For me, a very special part of my being Latina is the *mucho platos de arroz, gandules y perniel*—rice, beans and pork— that I have eaten at countless family holidays and special events. My Latina identity also includes, because of my particularly adventurous taste buds, *morcilla*, pig intestines[;] *patitas de cerdo con garbanzo*[,] pigs' feet with beans[;] and *la lengua y orejas de cuchifrito*, pigs' tongue and ears. I bet the Mexican-Americans in this room are thinking that Puerto Ricans have unusual food tastes. Some of us, like me, do. Part of my Latina identity is the sound of *merengue* at all our family parties and the heart wrenching Spanish love songs that we enjoy. It is the memory of Saturday afternoon at the movies with my aunt and cousins watching Cantinflas, who is not Puerto Rican, but who was an icon Spanish comedian on par with Abbot and Costello of my generation. My Latina soul was nourished as I visited and played at my grandmother's house with my cousins and extended family. They were my friends as I grew up. Being a Latina child was watching the adults playing dominos on Saturday night and us kids playing *lotería*, bingo, with my grandmother calling out the numbers which we marked on our cards with chick peas.

Now, does any one of these things make me a Latina? Obviously not because each of our Caribbean and Latin American communities has their own unique food and different traditions at the holidays. I only learned about tacos in college from my Mexican-American roommate. Being a Latina in America also does not mean speaking Spanish. I happen to speak it fairly well. But my brother, only three years younger, like too many of us educated here, barely speaks it. Most of us born and bred here, speak it very poorly.

If I had pursued my career in my undergraduate history major, I would likely provide you with a very academic description of what being a Latino or Latina means. For example, I could define Latinos as those peoples and cultures populated or colonized by Spain who maintained or adopted Spanish or Spanish Creole as their language of communication. You can tell that I have been very well educated. That antiseptic description however, does not really explain the appeal of *morcilla*—pig's intestine—to an American-born child. It does not provide an adequate explanation of why individuals like us, many of whom are born in this completely different American culture, still identify so strongly with those communities in which our parents were born and raised.

America has a deeply confused image of itself that is in perpetual tension. We are a nation that takes pride in our ethnic diversity, recognizing its importance in shaping our society and in adding richness to its existence. Yet, we simultaneously insist that we can and must function and live in a race and color-blind way that ignore these very differences that in other contexts we laud. That tension between "the melting pot and the salad bowl"—a recently popular metaphor used to described New York's diversity—is being hotly debated today in national discussions about affirmative action. Many of us struggle with this tension and attempt to maintain and promote our cultural and ethnic identities in a society that is often ambivalent about how to deal with its differences. In this time of great debate we must remember that it is not political struggles that create a Latino or Latina identity. I became a Latina by the way I love and the way I live my life. My family showed me by their example how wonderful and vibrant life is and how wonderful and magical it is to have a Latina soul. They taught me to love being a Puerto Riqueña and to love America and value its lesson that great things could be achieved if one works hard for it. But achieving success here is no easy accomplishment for Latinos or Latinas, and although that struggle did not and does not create a Latina identity, it does inspire how I live my life.

I was born in the year 1954. That year was the fateful year in which *Brown v. Board of Education* was decided. When I was eight, in 1961, the first Latino, the wonderful Judge Reynaldo Garza, was appointed to the federal bench, an event we are celebrating at this conference. When I finished law school in 1979, there were no women judges on the Supreme Court or on the highest court of my home state, New York. There was then only one Afro-American Supreme Court Justice and then and now no Latino or Latina justices on our highest court. Now in the last twenty plus years of my professional life, I have seen a quantum leap in the representation of women and Latinos in the legal profession and particularly in the judiciary. In addition to the appointment of the first female United States Attorney General, Janet Reno, we have seen the appointment of two female justices to the Supreme Court and two female justices to the New York Court of Appeals, the highest court of my home state. One of those judges is the Chief Judge and the other is a Puerto Riqueña, like I am. As of

today, women sit on the highest courts of almost all of the states and of the terri-
tories, including Puerto Rico. One Supreme Court, that of Minnesota, had a
majority of women justices for a period of time.

As of September 1, 2001, the federal judiciary consisting of Supreme, Circuit
and District Court Judges was about 22% women. In 1992, nearly ten years ago, when
I was first appointed a District Court Judge, the percentage of women in the total
federal judiciary was only 13%. Now, the growth of Latino representation is
somewhat less favorable. As of today we have, as I noted earlier, no Supreme
Court justices, and we have only 10 out of 147 active Circuit Court judges and 30
out of 587 active district court judges. Those numbers are grossly below our
proportion of the population. As recently as 1965, however, the federal bench
had only three women serving and only one Latino judge. So changes are happening, although in some areas, very slowly. These figures and appointments are heart-
warming. Nevertheless, much still remains to happen.

Let us not forget that between the appointments of Justice Sandra Day O'Connor in 1981 and Justice Ginsburg in 1992, eleven years passed. Similarly, between
Justice Kaye's initial appointment as an Associate Judge to the New York Court of
Appeals in 1983, and Justice Ciparick's appointment in 1993, ten years elapsed.
Almost nine years later, we are waiting for a third appointment of a woman to
both the Supreme Court and the New York Court of Appeals and of a second
minority, male or female, preferably Hispanic, to the Supreme Court. In 1992
when I joined the bench, there were still two out of 13 circuit courts and about
53 out of 92 district courts in which no women sat. At the beginning of September of
2001, there are women sitting in all 13 circuit courts. The First, Fifth, Eighth and
Federal Circuits each have only one female judge, however, out of a combined total
number of 48 judges. There are still nearly 37 district courts with no women judges
at all. For women of color the statistics are more sobering. As of September 20, 1998,
of the then 195 circuit court judges only two were African-American women and two
Hispanic women. Of the 641 district court judges only twelve were African-American
women and eleven Hispanic women. African-American women comprise only
1.56% of the federal judiciary and Hispanic-American women comprise only 1%.
No African-American, male or female, sits today on the Fourth or Federal circuits.
And no Hispanics, male or female, sit on the Fourth, Sixth, Seventh, Eighth, District
of Columbia or Federal Circuits.

Sort of shocking, isn't it? This is the year 2002. We have a long way to go.
Unfortunately, there are some very deep storm warnings we must keep in mind.
In at least the last five years the majority of nominated judges the Senate delayed
more than one year before confirming or never confirming were women or
minorities. I need not remind this audience that Judge Paez of your home
Circuit, the Ninth Circuit, has had the dubious distinction of having had his
confirmation delayed the longest in Senate history. These figures demonstrate
that there is a real and continuing need for Latino and Latina organizations and
community groups throughout the country to exist and to continue their efforts
of promoting women and men of all colors in their pursuit for equality in the
judicial system.

This weekend's conference, illustrated by its name ["Raising the Bar: Latino
and Latina Presence in the Judiciary and the Struggle for Representation"], is
bound to examine issues that I hope will identify the efforts and solutions that
will assist our communities. The focus of my speech tonight, however, is not
about the struggle to get us where we are and where we need to go but instead to

discuss with you what it all will mean to have more women and people of color on the bench. The statistics I have been talking about provide a base from which to discuss a question which one of my former colleagues on the Southern District bench, Judge Miriam Cederbaum, raised when speaking about women on the federal bench. Her question was: What do the history and statistics mean? In her speech, Judge Cederbaum expressed her belief that the number of women and by direct inference people of color on the bench, was still statistically insignificant and that therefore we could not draw valid scientific conclusions from the acts of so few people over such a short period of time. Yet, we do have women and people of color in more significant numbers on the bench and no one can or should ignore pondering what that will mean or not mean in the development of the law. Now, I cannot and do not claim this issue as personally my own. In recent years there has been an explosion of research and writing in this area. On one of the panels tomorrow, you will hear the Latino perspective in this debate.

For those of you interested in the gender perspective on this issue, I commend to you a wonderful compilation of articles published on the subject in Vol. 77 of the *Judicature, the Journal of the American Judicature Society* of November-December 1993. It is on Westlaw/Lexis and I assume the students and academics in this room can find it.

Now Judge Cedarbaum expresses concern with any analysis of women and presumably again people of color on the bench, which begins and presumably ends with the conclusion that women or minorities are different from men generally. She sees danger in presuming that judging should be gender or anything else based. She rightly points out that the perception of the differences between men and women is what led to many paternalistic laws and to the denial to women of the right to vote because we were described then "as not capable of reasoning or thinking logically" but instead of "acting intuitively." I am quoting adjectives that were bandied around famously during the suffragettes' movement.

While recognizing the potential effect of individual experiences on perception, Judge Cedarbaum nevertheless believes that judges must transcend their personal sympathies and prejudices and aspire to achieve a greater degree of fairness and integrity based on the reason of law. Although I agree with and attempt to work toward Judge Cedarbaum's aspiration, I wonder whether achieving that goal is possible in all or even in most cases. And I wonder whether by ignoring our differences as women or men of color we do a disservice both to the law and society. Whatever the reasons why we may have different perspectives, either as some theorists suggest because of our cultural experiences or as others postulate because we have basic differences in logic and reasoning, are in many respects a small part of a larger practical question we as women and minority judges in society in general must address. I accept the thesis of a law school classmate, Professor Steven Carter of Yale Law School, in his affirmative action book that in any group of human beings there is a diversity of opinion because there is both a diversity of experiences and of thought. Thus, as noted by another Yale Law School Professor—I did graduate from there and I am not really biased except that they seem to be doing a lot of writing in that area—Professor Judith Resnik says that there is not a single voice of feminism, not a feminist approach but many who are exploring the possible ways of being that are distinct from those structured in a world dominated by the power and words of men. Thus, feminist theories of judging are in the midst of creation and are not and perhaps will never aspire to be as solidified as the established legal doctrines of judging can sometimes appear to be.

That same point can be made with respect to people of color. No one person, judge or nominee will speak in a female or people of color voice. I need not remind you that Justice Clarence Thomas represents a part but not the whole of African-American thought on many subjects. Yet, because I accept the proposition that, as Judge [sic] Resnik describes it, "to judge is an exercise of power" and because as, another former law school classmate, Professor Martha Minnow of Harvard Law School, states "there is no objective stance but only a series of perspectives—no neutrality, no escape from choice in judging," I further accept that our experiences as women and people of color affect our decisions. The aspiration to impartiality is just that—it's an aspiration because it denies the fact that we are by our experiences making different choices than others. Not all women or people of color, in all or some circumstances or indeed in any particular case or circumstance but enough people of color in enough cases, will make a difference in the process of judging. The Minnesota Supreme Court has given an example of this. As reported by Judge Patricia Wald formerly of the D.C. Circuit Court, three women on the Minnesota Court with two men dissenting agreed to grant a protective order against a father's visitation rights when the father abused his child. The Judicature Journal has at least two excellent studies on how women on the courts of appeal and state supreme courts have tended to vote more often than their male counterpart to uphold women's claims in sex discrimination cases and criminal defendants' claims in search and seizure cases. As recognized by legal scholars, whatever the reason, not one woman or person of color in any one position but as a group we will have an effect on the development of the law and on judging.

In our private conversations, Judge Cedarbaum has pointed out to me that seminal decisions in race and sex discrimination cases have come from Supreme Courts composed exclusively of white males. I agree that this is significant but I also choose to emphasize that the people who argued those cases before the Supreme Court which changed the legal landscape ultimately were largely people of color and women. I recall that Justice Thurgood Marshall, Judge Connie Baker Motley, the first black woman appointed to the federal bench, and others of the NAACP argued *Brown v. Board of Education.* Similarly, Justice Ginsburg, with other women attorneys, was instrumental in advocating and convincing the Court that equality of work required equality in terms and conditions of employment.

Whether born from experience or inherent physiological or cultural differences, a possibility I abhor less or discount less than my colleague Judge Cedarbaum, our gender and national origins may and will make a difference in our judging. Justice O'Connor has often been cited as saying that a wise old man and wise old woman will reach the same conclusion in deciding cases. I am not so sure Justice O'Connor is the author of that line since Professor Resnik attributes that line to Supreme Court Justice Coyle. I am also not so sure that I agree with the statement. First, as Professor Martha Minnow has noted, there can never be a universal definition of wise. Second, I would hope that a wise Latina woman with the richness of her experiences would more often than not reach a better conclusion than a white male who hasn't lived that life.

Let us not forget that wise men like Oliver Wendell Holmes and Justice Cardozo voted on cases which upheld both sex and race discrimination in our society. Until 1972, no Supreme Court case ever upheld the claim of a woman in a gender discrimination case. I, like Professor Carter, believe that we should not be so myopic as to believe that others of different experiences or backgrounds are incapable of understanding the values and needs of people from a different group. Many are so capable. As Judge Cedarbaum pointed out to me, nine white men on the Supreme Court in the past have done so on many occasions and on many issues including *Brown*.

However, to understand takes time and effort, something that not all people are willing to give. For others, their experiences limit their ability to understand the experiences of others. Other[s] simply do not care. Hence, one must accept the proposition that a difference there will be by the presence of women and people of color on the bench. Personal experiences affect the facts that judges choose to see. My hope is that I will take the good from my experiences and extrapolate them further into areas with which I am unfamiliar. I simply do not know exactly what that difference will be in my judging. But I accept there will be some based on my gender and my Latina heritage.

I also hope that by raising the question today of what difference having more Latinos and Latinas on the bench will make will start your own evaluation. For people of color and women lawyers, what does and should being an ethnic minority mean in your lawyering? For men lawyers, what areas in your experiences and attitudes do you need to work on to make you capable of reaching those great moments of enlightenment which other men in different circumstances have been able to reach? For all of us, how do change the facts that in every task force study of gender and race bias in the courts, women and people of color, lawyers and judges alike, report in significantly higher percentages than white men that their gender and race has shaped their careers, from hiring, retention to promotion and that a statistically significant number of women and minority lawyers and judges, both alike, have experienced bias in the courtroom?

Each day on the bench I learn something new about the judicial process and about being a professional Latina woman in a world that sometimes looks at me with suspicion. I am reminded each day that I render decisions that affect people concretely and that I owe them constant and complete vigilance in checking my assumptions, presumptions and perspectives and ensuring that to the extent that my limited abilities and capabilities permit me, that I reevaluate them and change as circumstances and cases before me requires. I can and do aspire to be greater than the sum total of my experiences but I accept my limitations. I willingly accept that we who judge must not deny the differences resulting from experience and heritage but attempt, as the Supreme Court suggests, continuously to judge when those opinions, sympathies and prejudices are appropriate.

There is always a danger embedded in relative morality, but since judging is a series of choices that we must make, that I am forced to make, I hope that I can make them by informing myself on the questions I must not avoid asking and continuously pondering. We, I mean all of us in this room, must continue individually and in voices united in organizations that have supported this conference, to think about these questions and to figure out how we go about creating the opportunity for there to be more women and people of color on the bench so we can finally have statistically significant numbers to measure the differences we will and are making.

I am delighted to have been here tonight and extend once again my deepest gratitude to all of you for listening and letting me share my reflections on being a Latina voice on the bench. Thank you.

Notes and Questions

1. The vision of "Robert Bork's America" that Senator Kennedy invoked draws upon Judge Bork's academic and popular press writings, extrapolating the potential consequences of some of his legal and jurisprudential positions. It is a political document that paints everything Judge Bork had written in the worst possible light, holds him responsible for things written decades before, and does not pay heed to the possibility that a judge might oppose particular practices politically but not believe that they are prohibited by the Constitution. Given the significant role that the modern Supreme Court plays in resolving crucial questions of constitutional politics, is such a speech fair game, or did Senator Kennedy—in treating Judge Bork as a political enemy who needed to be defeated—step over some sort of line?

2. Judge Bork's nomination was ultimately rejected by a 58-42 vote. His opponents' coordinated campaign to shape the narrative about the nomination and turn the public against him became such a cultural touchstone that it gave rise to the verb "to bork," which is now commonly used to refer to a campaign to defeat a nominee for public office by publicly besmirching his or her character, background, or views.

3. For Judge Bork's response to these events, see Robert H. Bork, *The Tempting of America: The Political Seduction of the Law* (1990), especially pages 268-269 (claiming that "[n]ot one line of [Senator Kennedy's] tirade was true").

4. The Siegel article is a fairly standard example of the kinds of articles and speeches that academics have been writing in favor of or in opposition to recent Supreme Court nominees. In what ways is it similar to Senator Kennedy's speech? In what ways is it different?

5. Judge Sotomayor's speech became the fulcrum of opposition to her nomination. In particular, critics bristled at her statement "I would hope that a wise Latina woman with the richness of her experiences would more often than not reach a better conclusion than a white male who hasn't lived that life." That statement was used—often in conjunction with President Obama's assertion that he wanted to pick Justices who had "empathy"—to suggest that Judge Sotomayor would not simply follow the law but would instead favor racial minorities or other sympathetic categories of litigants. In the full context of the speech, is that a fair critique? Even if not, does this quotation or any other part of the speech raise concerns for you about Justice Sotomayor's world view or jurisprudential philosophy?

b. Nominees Present Themselves: Statements Before the Senate Judiciary Committee

As the modern confirmation process has developed, the first and most important opportunity nominees have to introduce themselves to the nation are their opening statements during their hearings before the Senate Judiciary Committee. Depending on the candidate's prior stature, the political dynamics between the President and the Senate, and the initial public reception of the nomination, each recent nominee has faced a series of slightly different tasks when preparing his or her statement. The opening statements of four of the current Justices (or substantial excerpts from them) are reproduced below.

Opening Statement of John G. Roberts, Before the Senate Judiciary Committee

Confirmation Hearing on the Nomination of John G. Roberts, Jr. to be Chief Justice of the United States: Hearing Before the S. Comm. on the Judiciary, 109th Cong. 55 (2005)

. . . I know that I would not be here today were it not for the sacrifices and help over the years of my family, who you met earlier today, friends, mentors, teachers and colleagues—many of whom are here today.

Last week one of those mentors and friends, Chief Justice William Rehnquist, was laid to rest. I talked last week with the nurses who helped care for him over the past year, and I was glad to hear from them that he was not a particularly good patient. He chafed at the limitations they tried to impose.

His dedication to duty over the past year was an inspiration to me and, I know, to many others.

I will miss him.

My personal appreciation that I owe a great debt to others reinforces my view that a certain humility should characterize the judicial role.

Judges and justices are servants of the law, not the other way around. Judges are like umpires. Umpires don't make the rules; they apply them.

The role of an umpire and a judge is critical. They make sure everybody plays by the rules.

But it is a limited role. Nobody ever went to a ball game to see the umpire.

Judges have to have the humility to recognize that they operate within a system of precedent, shaped by other judges equally striving to live up to the judicial oath.

And judges have to have the modesty to be open in the decisional process to the considered views of their colleagues on the bench.

Mr. Chairman, when I worked in the Department of Justice, in the office of the solicitor general, it was my job to argue cases for the United States before the Supreme Court.

I always found it very moving to stand before the justices and say, "I speak for my country."

But it was after I left the department and began arguing cases against the United States that I fully appreciated the importance of the Supreme Court and our constitutional system.

Here was the United States, the most powerful entity in the world, aligned against my client. And yet, all I had to do was convince the court that I was right on the law and the government was wrong and all that power and might would recede in deference to the rule of law.

That is a remarkable thing.

It is what we mean when we say that we are a government of laws and not of men. It is that rule of law that protects the rights and liberties of all Americans. It is the envy of the world. Because without the rule of law, any rights are meaningless.

President Ronald Reagan used to speak of the Soviet constitution, and he noted that it purported to grant wonderful rights of all sorts to people. But those rights were empty promises, because that system did not have an independent judiciary to uphold the rule of law and enforce those rights. We do, because of the wisdom of our founders and the sacrifices of our heroes over the generations to make their vision a reality.

Mr. Chairman, I come before the committee with no agenda. I have no platform. Judges are not politicians who can promise to do certain things in exchange for votes.

I have no agenda, but I do have a commitment. If I am confirmed, I will confront every case with an open mind. I will fully and fairly analyze the legal arguments that are presented. I will be open to the considered views of my colleagues on the bench. And I will decide every case based on the record, according to the rule of law, without fear or favor, to the best of my ability. And I will remember that it's my job to call balls and strikes and not to pitch or bat.

Senators Lugar and Bayh talked of my boyhood back home in Indiana. I think all of us retain, from the days of our youth, certain enduring images. For me those images are of the endless fields of Indiana, stretching to the horizon, punctuated only by an isolated silo or a barn. And as I grew older, those endless fields came to represent for me the limitless possibilities of our great land.

Growing up, I never imagined that I would be here, in this historic room, nominated to be the chief justice. But now that I am here, I recall those endless fields with their promise of infinite possibilities, and that memory inspires in me a very profound commitment.

If I am confirmed, I will be vigilant to protect the independence and integrity of the Supreme Court, and I will work to ensure that it upholds the rule of law and safeguards those liberties that make this land one of endless possibilities for all Americans.

Thank you, Mr. Chairman.

Thank you, members of the committee.

I look forward to your questions.

Opening Statement of Clarence Thomas, Before the Senate Judiciary Committee

S. Hrg. 102-1084, Part 1, Sept. 10, 1991

. . . Much has been written about my family and me over the past 10 weeks. Through all that has happened throughout our lives and through all adversity, we have grown closer and our love for each other has grown stronger and deeper. I hope these hearings will help to show more clearly who this person Clarence Thomas is and what really makes me tick.

My earliest memories, as alluded to earlier, are those of Pin Point, Georgia, a life far removed in space and time from this room, this day and this moment. As kids, we caught minnows in the creeks, fiddler crabs in the marshes, we played with pluffers, and skipped shells across the water. It was a world so vastly different from all this.

In 1955, my brother and I went to live with my mother in Savannah. We lived in one room in a tenement. We shared a kitchen with other tenants and we had a common bathroom in the backyard which was unworkable and unusable. It was hard, but it was all we had and all there was.

Our mother only earned $20 every two weeks as a maid, not enough to take care of us. So she arranged for us to live with our grandparents later, in 1955. Imagine, if you will, two little boys with all their belongings in two grocery bags.

Our grandparents were two great and wonderful people who loved us dearly. I wish they were sitting here today. Sitting here so they could see that all their efforts, their hard work were not in vain, and so that they could see that hard work and strong values can make for a better life.

I am grateful that my mother and my sister could be here. Unfortunately, my brother could not be.

I attended segregated parochial schools and later attended a seminary near Savannah. The nuns gave us hope and belief in ourselves when society didn't. They reinforced the importance of religious beliefs in our personal lives. Sister Mary Virgilius, my eighth grade teacher, and the other nuns were unyielding in their expectations that we use all of our talents no matter what the rest of the world said or did.

After high school, I left Savannah and attended Immaculate Conception Seminary, then Holy Cross College. I attended Yale Law School. Yale had opened its doors, its heart, its conscience to recruit and admit minority students. I benefitted from this effort.

My career is as [has] been delineated today. I was an Assistant Attorney General in the State of Missouri. I was an attorney in the corporate law department of Monsanto Company. I joined Senator Danforth's staff here in the Senate, was an Assistant Secretary in the Department of Education, Chairman of EEOC, and since 1990 a judge on the U.S. Court of Appeals for the District of Columbia Circuit.

But for the efforts of so many others who have gone before me, I would not be here today. It would be unimaginable. Only by standing on their shoulders could I be here. At each turn in my life, each obstacle confronted, each fork in the road someone came along to help.

I remember, for example, in 1974 after I completed law school I had no money, no place to live. Mrs. Margaret Bush Wilson, who would later become chairperson of the NAACP, allowed me to live at her house. She provided me not only with room and board, but advice, counsel and guidance.

As I left her house that summer, I asked her, "How much do I owe you?" Her response was, "Just along the way help someone who is in your position." I have tried to live by my promise to her to do just that, to help others.

So many others gave their lives, their blood, their talents. But for them I would not be here. Justice Marshall, whose seat I have been nominated to fill, is one of those who had the courage and the intellect. He is one of the great architects of the legal battles to open doors that seemed so hopelessly and permanently sealed and to knock down barriers that seemed so insurmountable to those of us in the Pin Point, Georgias of the world.

The civil rights movement, Reverend Martin Luther King and the SCLC, Roy Wilkins and the NAACP, Whitney Young and the Urban League, Fannie Lou Haemer, Rosa Parks and Dorothy Hite, they changed society and made it reach out and affirmatively help. I have benefited greatly from their efforts. But for them there would have been no road to travel.

My grandparents always said there would be more opportunities for us. I can still hear my grandfather, "Y'all goin' have mo' of a chance then me," and he was right. He felt that if others sacrificed and created opportunities for us we had an obligation to work hard, to be decent citizens, to be fair and good people, and he was right.

You see, Mr. Chairman, my grandparents grew up and lived their lives in an era of blatant segregation and overt discrimination. Their sense of fairness was molded in a crucible of unfairness. I watched as my grandfather was called "boy." I watched as my grandmother suffered the indignity of being denied the use of a bathroom. But through it all they remained fair, decent, good people. Fair in spite of the terrible contradictions in our country.

They were hardworking, productive people who always gave back to others. They gave produce from the farm, fuel oil from the fuel oil truck. They bought groceries for those who were without, and they never lost sight of the promise of a better tomorrow. I follow in their footsteps and I have always tried to give back.

Over the years I have grown and matured. I have learned to listen carefully, carefully to other points of views and to others, to think through problems recognizing that there are no easy answers to difficult problems, to think deeply about those who will be affected by the decisions that I make and the decisions made by others. But I have always carried in my heart the world, the life, the people, the values of my youth, the values of my grandparents and my neighbors, the values of people who believed so very deeply in this country in spite of all the contradictions.

It is my hope that when these hearings are completed that this committee will conclude that I am an honest, decent, fair person. I believe that the obligations and responsibilities of a judge, in essence, involve just such basic values. A judge must be fair and impartial. A judge must not bring to his job, to the court, the baggage of preconceived notions, of ideology, and certainly not an agenda, and the judge must get the decision right. Because when all is said and done, the little guy, the average person, the people of Pin Point, the real people of America will be affected not only by what we as judges do, but by the way we do our jobs.

If confirmed by the Senate I pledge that I will preserve and protect our Constitution and carry with me the values of my heritage: fairness, integrity, open-mindedness, honesty, and hard work.

Thank you, Mr. Chairman.

Opening Statement of Ruth Bader Ginsburg, Before the Senate Judiciary Committee

S. Hrg. 103-482, July 20, 1993, at 53

. . . I am, as you know from my responses to your questionnaire, a Brooklynite, born and bred—a first-generation American on my father's side, barely second-generation on my mother's. Neither of my parents had the means to attend college, but both taught me to love learning, to care about people, and to work hard for whatever I wanted or believed in. Their parents had the foresight to leave the old country, when Jewish ancestry and faith meant exposure to pogroms and denigration of one's human worth. What has become of me could only happen in America. Like so many others, I owe so much to the entry this Nation afforded to people yearning to breathe free. . . .

Indeed, in my lifetime, I expect to see three, four, perhaps even more women on the High Court Bench, women not shaped from the same mold, but of different complexions. Yes, there are miles in front, but what a distance we have traveled from the day President Thomas Jefferson told his Secretary of State: "The appointment of women to [public] office is an innovation for which the public is not prepared. Nor," Jefferson added, "am I."

The increasingly full use of the talent of all this nation's people holds large promise for the future, but we could not have come to this point—and I surely would not be in this room today—without the determined efforts of men and women who kept dreams of equal citizenship alive in days when few would listen. People like

Susan B. Anthony, Elizabeth Cady Stanton, and Harriet Tubman come to mind. I stand on the shoulders of those brave people.

Supreme Court Justices are guardians of the great charter that has served as our nation's fundamental instrument of government for over 200 years, the oldest written constitution still in force in the world. But the Justices do not guard constitutional rights alone. Courts share that profound responsibility with the Congress, the President, the States, and the People. Constant realization of a more perfect union, the Constitution's aspiration, requires the widest, broadest, deepest participation on matters of government and government policy. . . .

Some of you asked me, during recent visits, why I want to be on the Supreme Court. It is an opportunity, beyond any other, for one of my training to serve society. The controversies that come to the Supreme Court, as the last judicial resort, touch and concern the health and well-being of our nation and its people; they affect the preservation of liberty to ourselves and our posterity. Serving on this Court is the highest honor, the most awesome trust that can be placed in a judge. It means working at my craft—working with and for the law—as a way to keep our society both ordered and free.

Let me try to state in a nutshell how I view the work of judging. My approach, I believe, is neither "liberal" nor "conservative." Rather, it is rooted in the place of the judiciary of judges—in our democratic society. The Constitution's preamble speaks first of We, the People, and then of their elected representatives. The Judiciary is third in line, and it is placed apart from the political fray so that its members can judge fairly, impartially, in accordance with the law and without fear about the animosity of any pressure group.

In Alexander Hamilton's words: the mission of judges is "to secure a steady, upright, and impartial administration of the laws." I would add that the judge should carry out that function without fanfare, but with due care: she should decide the case before her without reaching out to cover cases not yet seen. She should be ever mindful, as Judge and then Justice Benjamin Nathan Cardozo said: "Justice is not to be taken by storm. She is to be wooed by slow advances." . . .

Federal judges may long outlast the President who appoints them. They may serve as long as they can do the job, as the Constitution says, they may remain in office "during good Behavior." Supreme Court Justices, particularly, participate in shaping a lasting body of constitutional decisions; they continuously confront matters on which the Framers left many things unsaid, unsettled, or uncertain. For that reason, when the Senate considers a Supreme Court nomination, the Senators are properly concerned about the nominee's capacity to serve the nation, not just for the here and now, but over the long term.

You have been supplied, in the five weeks since the President announced my nomination, with hundreds of pages about me, and thousands of pages I have penned—my writings as a law teacher, mainly about procedure; ten years of briefs filed when I was a courtroom advocate of the equal stature of men and women before the law; numerous speeches and articles on that same theme; thirteen years of opinions—well over 700 of the decisions I made as a member of the U.S. Court of Appeals for the District of Columbia Circuit; several comments on the roles of judges and lawyers in our legal system. That body of material . . . is the most tangible, reliable indicator of my attitude, outlook, approach, and style. I hope you will judge my qualifications principally on that written record spanning thirty-four years. . . .

You are well aware that I came to this proceeding to be judged as a judge, not as an advocate. Because I am and hope to continue to be a judge, it would be wrong for me to say or preview in this legislative chamber how I would cast my vote on questions the Supreme Court may be called upon to decide. Were I to rehearse here what I would say and how I would reason on such questions, I would act injudiciously.

A judge sworn to decide impartially can offer no forecasts, no hints, for that would show not only disregard for the specifics of the particular case, it would display disdain for the entire judicial process. . . .

It is fitting, as I conclude this opening statement, to express my deep respect for, and abiding appreciation to Justice Byron R. White for his thirty-one years and more of fine service on the Supreme Court . . . He expressed a hope shared by all lower court judges; he hoped "the [Supreme] Court's mandates will be clear [and] crisp . . . leav[ing] as little room as possible for disagreement about their meaning." If confirmed, I will take the counsel to heart and strive to write opinions that both "get it right" and "keep it tight."

Opening Statement of Sonia Sotomayor, Before the Senate Judiciary Committee

S. Hrg. 111-503, July 13, 2009, at 58

. . . The progression of my life has been uniquely American. My parents left Puerto Rico during World War II. I grew up in modest circumstances in a Bronx housing project. My father, a factory worker with a third grade education, passed away when I was nine years old.

On her own, my mother raised my brother and me. She taught us that the key to success in America is a good education. And she set the example, studying alongside my brother and me at our kitchen table so that she could become a registered nurse. We worked hard. I poured myself into my studies at Cardinal Spellman High School, earning scholarships to Princeton University and then Yale Law School, while my brother went to medical school. Our achievements are due to the values that we learned as children, and they have continued to guide my life's endeavors. I try to pass on this legacy by serving as a mentor and friend to my many godchildren and students of all backgrounds.

Over the past three decades, I have seen our judicial system from a number of different perspectives—as a big-city prosecutor, a corporate litigator, a trial judge and an appellate judge. My first job after law school was as an assistant District Attorney in New York. There, I saw children exploited and abused. I felt the suffering of victims' families torn apart by a loved one's needless death. And I learned the tough job law enforcement has protecting the public safety. In my next legal job, I focused on commercial, instead of criminal, matters. I litigated issues on behalf of national and international businesses and advised them on matters ranging from contracts to trademarks.

My career as an advocate ended—and my career as a judge began—when I was appointed by President George H.W. Bush to the United States District Court for the Southern District of New York. As a trial judge, I decided over four hundred and fifty cases, and presided over dozens of trials, with perhaps my best known case involving the Major League Baseball strike in 1995.

After six extraordinary years on the district court, I was appointed by President William Jefferson Clinton to the United States Court of Appeals for the Second Circuit. On that Court, I have enjoyed the benefit of sharing ideas and perspectives with wonderful colleagues as we have worked together to resolve the issues before us. I have now served as an appellate judge for over a decade, deciding a wide range of Constitutional, statutory, and other legal questions.

Throughout my seventeen years on the bench, I have witnessed the human consequences of my decisions. Those decisions have been made not to serve the interests of any one litigant, but always to serve the larger interest of impartial justice.

In the past month, many Senators have asked me about my judicial philosophy. It is simple: fidelity to the law. The task of a judge is not to make the law—it is to apply the law. And it is clear, I believe, that my record in two courts reflects my rigorous commitment to interpreting the Constitution according to its terms; interpreting statutes according to their terms and Congress's intent; and hewing faithfully to precedents established by the Supreme Court and my Circuit Court. In each case I have heard, I have applied the law to the facts at hand.

The process of judging is enhanced when the arguments and concerns of the parties to the litigation are understood and acknowledged. That is why I generally structure my opinions by setting out what the law requires and then by explaining why a contrary position, sympathetic or not, is accepted or rejected. That is how I seek to strengthen both the rule of law and faith in the impartiality of our justice system. My personal and professional experiences help me listen and understand, with the law always commanding the result in every case.

Since President Obama announced my nomination in May, I have received letters from people all over this country. Many tell a unique story of hope in spite of struggles. Each letter has deeply touched me. Each reflects a belief in the dream that led my parents to come to New York all those years ago. It is our Constitution that makes that Dream possible, and I now seek the honor of upholding the Constitution as a Justice on the Supreme Court.

I look forward in the next few days to answering your questions, to having the American people learn more about me, and to being part of a process that reflects the greatness of our Constitution and of our nation. Thank you.

Notes and Questions

1. What were John Roberts's primary objectives in his statement? Did he achieve them? What did you think of his analogy between the roles of a judge and an umpire? Is it persuasive? Is it accurate? You might be interested to know that this analogy has probably provoked more commentary than any other single statement ever made in a confirmation hearing. *See, e.g.*, Michael P. Allen, *A Limited Defense of (at Least Some of) the Umpire Analogy*, 32 Seattle U. L. Rev. 525 (2009); Theodore A. McKee, *Judges as Umpires*, 35 Hofstra L. Rev. 1709 (2007); Neil S. Siegel, *Umpires at Bat: On Integration and Legitimation*, 24 Const. Comment. 701, 702 & n.5 (2007); Aaron Zelinsky, *The Justice as Commissioner: Benching the Judge-Umpire Analogy*, 119 Yale L.J. Online 113 (Mar. 4, 2010); Jon O. Newman, *Judging's a Lot More Than Balls and Strikes*, Hartford Courant, Sept. 8, 2009, at A11.

2. What were Clarence Thomas's primary objectives in his statement? Did he achieve them? Remember that Thomas was appointed to succeed Thurgood

Marshall, the civil rights lion who had become the first (and to that point only) African-American Justice. In a press conference the day after submitting his resignation, Justice Marshall warned President Bush against nominating Thomas (albeit without naming him), commenting that race should not be used as an "excuse . . . - for picking the wrong Negro" and noting that "[t]here's no difference between a white snake and black snake. They'll both bite." Toobin, *The Nine*, at 25. How do the dynamics created by Marshall's comments play into the narrative choices Thomas made?

3. What were Ruth Ginsburg's primary objectives in her statement? Did she achieve them? Note that her statement is more detailed in some ways than those offered by other nominees and more reticent in others. Relatedly, her statement seems more self-conscious about defining the terms of a constitutionally appropriate encounter with the Judiciary Committee, and with the Senate more broadly. What do you think are the terms of an appropriate hearing as she understands them? Do you agree with her vision?

4. What were Sonia Sotomayor's primary objectives in her statement? Did she achieve them? Remember the controversy raised by some of her speeches, including the "Wise Latina" speech included above. How do you think that controversy shaped her statement?

c. Questioning Before the Judiciary Committee

The vast majority of a modern Judiciary Committee hearing involves the nominee orally and immediately answering questions posed sequentially by the members of the committee. The dynamics of the questioning can make for intriguing theater as skeptical Senators and cagey nominees engage each other in a game of intellectual and political cat-and-mouse. At moments, they can also be revealing—demonstrating, for example, the intellectual gifts of John Roberts and Elena Kagan; the relative moderation of David Souter; and the staggering anger that appears to motivate Clarence Thomas.

However, a wide range of judges, politicians, and commentators have expressed profound skepticism as to whether, on balance, the questioning as currently structured produces much insight. They make a series of related criticisms. First, some are concerned that the whole process is too stylized, that it has become a kind of "kabuki dance" in which Senators ask predictable questions and nominees produce predictable anodyne answers that reveal little about their true judicial philosophies. *See, e.g.*, Richard Brust, *No More Kabuki Confirmations*, 95 A.B.A. J. 39, 39 (2009) (discussing phenomena and citing then-Senator Joe Biden as the originator of the "kabuki" reference). Second, some believe that many Senators behave inappropriately, using their questions as an opportunity to recite political talking points and score points against political opponents, neither caring about, nor even really listening to, the nominees' answers. *See, e.g.*, Geoffrey R. Stone, *Understanding Supreme Court Confirmations*, 2010 S. Ct. Rev. 381, 466 (offering reforms designed to stop Senators from "grandstanding"). Finally, many believe that the nominees themselves share part of the blame, exaggerating legitimate concerns about maintaining judicial impartiality in order to invoke a general immunity from answering questions properly designed to test their judicial philosophies. *See, e.g.*, Robert Post & Reva Siegel, *Questioning Justice: Law and Politics in Judicial Confirmation Hearings*, 115 Yale L.J. Pocket Part 38, 44-51 (2006) (criticizing recent nominees for claiming too broad an immunity from questioning and proposing a new norm that nominees can be questioned in detail about already-decided Supreme Court cases).

The excerpt that follows includes several crucial exchanges between Sonia Sotomayor and Senators skeptical about her nomination. In reading through the transcript, consider the degree to which the excerpts support or contradict the criticisms laid out above.

Excerpt from the Sotomayor Hearings

S. Hrg. 111-503, July 14, 2009, at 66-70, 120-125

[Senator Jeff] **SESSIONS:** Welcome. It's good to have you back, Judge, and your family and friends and supporters. And I hope we'll have a good day today, look forward to dialogue with you. I got to say that I liked your statement on the fidelity of the law yesterday and some of your comments this morning.

And I also have to say had you been saying that with clarity over the last decade or 15 years, we'd have a lot fewer problems today because you have evidenced, I think it's quite clear, a philosophy of the law that suggests that the judge's background and experiences can and should—even should and naturally will impact their decision what I think goes against the American ideal and oath that a judge takes to be fair to every party. And every day when they put on that robe, that is a symbol that they're to put aside their personal biases and prejudices.

So I'd like to ask you a few things about it. I would just note that it's not just one sentence, as my chairman suggested, that causes us difficulty. It's a body of thought over a period of years that causes us difficulties.

And I would suggest that the quotation he gave was not exactly right of the wise Latina comment that you made. You've said, I think six different times, quote, "I would hope that a wise Latina woman, with the richness of her experiences, would more often than not reach a better conclusion." So that's a matter that I think we'll talk about as we go forward.

Let me recall that yesterday you said it's simple fidelity to the law. The task of a judge is not to make law; it's to apply law. I heartily agree with that. However, you previously have said the court of appeals is where policy is made. And you said on another occasion the law that lawyers practice and judge declare is not a definitive—capital L—Law that many would like to think exists, close quote.

So I guess I'm asking today what do you really believe on those subjects. That there is no real law and that judges do not make law? Or that there is no real law and the court of appeals is where policy is made? Discuss that with us, please.

SOTOMAYOR: I believe my record of 17 years demonstrates fully that I do believe that law—that judges must apply the law and not make the law. Whether I've agreed with a party or not, found them sympathetic or not, in every case I have decided, I have done what the law requires.

With respect to judges making policy, I assume, Senator, that you were referring to a remark that I made in a Duke Law student dialogue. That remark, in context, made very clear that I wasn't talking about the policy reflected in the law that Congress makes. That's the job of Congress to decide what the policy should be for society.

In that conversation with the students, I was focusing on what district court judges do and what circuit court judges do. And I know noted that district court judges find the facts, and they apply the facts to the individual case. And when they do that, their holding, their finding doesn't bind anybody else.

Appellate judges, however, establish precedent. They decide what the law says in a particular situation. That precedent has policy ramifications because it binds not just the litigants in that case, it binds all litigants in similar cases, in cases that may be influenced by that precedent.

I think if my speech is heard outside of the minute and a half that YouTube presents and its full context examined, that it is very clear that I was talking about the policy ramifications of precedent and never talking about appellate judges or courts making the policy that Congress makes.

SESSIONS: Judge, I would just say, I don't think it's that clear. I looked at that on tape several times, and I think a person could reasonably believe it meant more than that.

But yesterday you spoke about your approach to rendering opinions and said, quote, "I seek to strengthen both the rule of law and faith in the impartiality of the justice system," and I would agree. But you have previously said this: "I am willing to accept that we who judge must not deny differences resulting from experiences and heritage, but attempt, as the Supreme Court suggests, continuously to judge when those opinions, sympathies and prejudices are appropriate."

So first, I'd like to know, do you think there's any circumstance in which a judge should allow their prejudices to impact their decision making?

SOTOMAYOR: Never their prejudices. I was talking about the very important goal of the justice system is to ensure that the personal biases and prejudices of a judge do not influence the outcome of a case.

What I was talking about was the obligation of judges to examine what they're feeling as they're adjudicating a case and to ensure that that's not influencing the outcome. Life experiences have to influence you. We're not robots to listen to evidence and don't have feelings. We have to recognize those feelings and put them aside. That's what my speech was saying . . .

SESSIONS: Well, Judge . . .

SOTOMAYOR: . . . because that's our job.

SESSIONS: But the statement was, "I willingly accept that we who judge must not deny the differences resulting from experience and heritage, but continuously to judge when those opinions, sympathies and prejudices are appropriate." That's exactly opposite of what you're saying, is it not?

SOTOMAYOR: I don't believe so, Senator, because all I was saying is, because we have feelings and different experiences, we can be led to believe that our experiences are appropriate. We have to be open-minded to accept that they may not be, and that we have to judge always that we're not letting those things determine the outcome. But there are situations in which some experiences are important in the process of judging, because the law asks us to use those experiences.

SESSIONS: Well, I understand that, but let me just follow up that you say in your statement that you want to do what you can to increase the faith and the impartiality of our system, but isn't it true this statement suggests that you accept that there may be sympathies, prejudices and opinions that legitimately can influence a judge's decision? And how can that further faith in the impartiality of the system?

SOTOMAYOR: I think the system is strengthened when judges don't assume they're impartial, but when judges test themselves to identify when their emotions are driving a result, or their experience are driving a result and the law is not.

SESSIONS: I agree with that.

SESSIONS: I know one judge that says that if he has a feeling about a case, he tells his law clerks to, "Watch me. I do not want my biases, sympathies or prejudices to influence this decision, which I've taken an oath to make sure is impartial." I just am very concerned that what you're saying today is quite inconsistent with your statement that you willingly accept that your sympathies, opinions and prejudices may influence your decision-making.

SOTOMAYOR: Well, as I have tried to explain, what I try to do is to ensure that they're not. If I ignore them and believe that I'm acting without them, without looking at them and testing that I'm not, then I could, unconsciously or otherwise, be led to be doing the exact thing I don't want to do, which is to let something but the law command the result.

SESSIONS: Well, yesterday, you also said that your decisions have always been made to serve the larger interest of impartial justice, a good—good aspiration, I agree. But in the past, you've repeatedly said this: "I wonder whether achieving the goal of impartiality is possible at all in even most cases and I wonder whether by ignoring our differences as women, men or people of color we do a disservice to both the law and society." Aren't you saying there that you expect your background and—and heritage to influence your decision-making?

SOTOMAYOR: What I was speaking about in that speech was—harkened back to what we were just talking about a few minutes ago, which is life experiences to influence us, in good ways. That's why we seek the enrichment of our legal system from life experiences.

That can affect what we see or how we feel, but that's not what drives a result. The impartiality is an understanding that the law is what commands the result.

And so, to the extent that we are asking the questions, as most of my speech was an academic discussion about, what should we be thinking about, what should we be considering in this process, and accepting that life experiences could make a difference. But I wasn't encouraging the belief or attempting to encourage the belief that I thought that that should drive the result.

SESSIONS: Judge, I—I think it's consistent in the comments I've quoted to you and your previous statements that you do believe that your backgrounds will accept—affect the result in cases, and that's troubling me. So that is not impartiality. Don't you think that is not consistent with your statement, that you believe your role as a judge is to serve the larger interest of impartial justice?

SOTOMAYOR: No, sir. As I've indicated, my record shows that at no point or time have I ever permitted my personal views or sympathies to influence an outcome of a case. In every case where I have identified a sympathy, I have articulated it and explained to the litigant why the law requires a different result.

SESSIONS: Judge. . .

SOTOMAYOR: I do not permit my sympathies, personal views, or prejudices to influence the outcome of my cases.

SESSIONS: Well, you—you—you said something similar to that yesterday, that in each case I applied the law to the facts at hand, but you've repeatedly made this statement: Quote, I "accept the proposition"—I "accept the proposition that a difference there will be by the presence of women and people of color on the bench, and that my experiences affect the facts I choose to see as a judge."

First, that's troubling to me as a lawyer. When I present evidence, I expect the judge to hear and see all the evidence that gets presented. How is it appropriate for a judge ever to say that they will choose to see some facts and not others?

SOTOMAYOR: It's not a question of choosing to see some facts or another, Senator. I didn't intend to suggest that. And in the wider context, what I believe I was—the point I was making was that our life experiences do permit us to see some facts and understand them more easily than others.

But in the end, you're absolutely right. That's why we have appellate judges that are more than one judge because each of us, from our life experiences, will more easily see different perspectives argued by parties.

But judges do consider all of the arguments of litigants. I have. Most of my opinions, if not all of them, explain to parties [why] the law requires what it does.

SESSIONS: Do you stand by your statement that my experiences affect the facts I choose to see?

SOTOMAYOR: No, sir. I don't stand by the understanding of that statement that I will ignore other facts or other experiences because I haven't had them. I do believe that life experiences are important to the process of judging. They help you to understand and listen but that the law requires a result. And it would command you to the facts that are relevant to the disposition of the case.

SESSIONS: Well, I will just note you made that statement in individual speeches about seven times over a number of years span. And it's concerning to me. So I would just say to you I believe in Judge Cederbaum's formulation. She said—and you disagreed. And this was really the context of your speech. And you used her—her statement as sort of a beginning of your discussion.

And you said she believes that a judge, no matter what their gender or background, should strive to reach the same conclusion. And she believes that's possible. You then argued that you don't think it's possible in all, maybe even most, cases. You deal with the famous quote of Justice O'Connor in which she says a wise old man should reach the same decision as a wise old woman. And you pushed backed from that. You say you don't think that's necessarily accurate. And you doubt the ability to be objective in your analysis.

So how can you reconcile your speeches which repeatedly assert that impartiality is a near aspiration which may not be possible in all or even most cases with your oath that you've taken twice which requires impartiality?

SOTOMAYOR: My friend, Judge Cederbaum is here this afternoon, and we are good friends. And I believe that we both approach judging in the same way which is looking at the facts of each individual case and applying the law to those facts.

I also, as I explained, was using a rhetorical flourish that fell flat. I knew that Justice O'Connor couldn't have meant that if judges reached different conclusions—legal conclusions—that one of them wasn't wise.

That couldn't have been her meaning, because reasonable judges disagree on legal conclusions in some cases. So I was trying to play on her words. My play was—fell flat.

It was bad, because it left an impression that I believed that life experiences commanded a result in a case, but that's clearly not what I do as a judge. It's clearly not what I intended in the context of my broader speech, which was attempting to inspire young Hispanic, Latino students and lawyers to believe that their life experiences added value to the process.

SESSIONS: Well, I can see that, perhaps as a—a layperson's approach to it. But as a judge who's taken this oath, I'm very troubled that you had repeatedly, over a decade or more, made statements that consistently—any fair reading of these speeches—consistently argues that this ideal and commitment I believe every judge is committed, must be, to put aside their personal experiences and biases and make sure that that person before them gets a fair day in court.

Judge, on the—so philosophy can impact your judging. I think it's much more likely to reach full flower if you sit on the Supreme Court, and then you will—than it will on a lower court where you're subject to review by your colleagues in the higher court. . . .

* * *

[Senator John] KYL: . . . Let me ask you about what the president said—and I talked about it in my opening statement—whether you agree with him. He used two different analogies. He talked once about the 25 miles—the first 25 miles of a 26-mile marathon.

And then he also said, in 95% of the cases, the law will give you the answer, and the last 5 percent legal process will not lead you to the rule of decision. The critical ingredient in those cases is supplied by what is in the judge's heart. Do you agree with him that the law only takes you the first 25 miles of the marathon and that that last mile has to be decided by what's in the judge's heart?

SOTOMAYOR: No, sir. That's—I don't—I wouldn't approach the issue of judging in the way the president does. He has to explain what he meant by judging. I can only explain what I think judges should do, which is judges can't rely on what's in their heart. They don't determine the law. Congress makes the laws. The job of a judge is to apply the law. And so it's not the heart that compels conclusions in cases. It's the law. The judge applies the law to the facts before that judge.

KYL: Appreciate that. And has it been your experience that every case, no matter how tenuous it's been and every lawyer, no matter how good their quality of advocacy, that in every case, every lawyer has had a legal argument of some quality it make? Some precedent that he's cited? It might not be the Supreme Court. It might not be the court of appeals. It might be a trial court somewhere. It might not even be a court precedent. It may be a law review article or something. But have you ever been in a situation where a lawyer said I don't have any legal argument to me, Judge, please go with your heart on this or your gut?

SOTOMAYOR: Well, I've actually had lawyers say something very similar to that. (LAUGHTER) I've had lawyers where questions have been raised about the legal basis of their argument. I thought one lawyer who put up his hands and said, but it's just not right. (LAUGHTER) But it's just not right is not what judges consider. What judges consider is what the law says.

KYL: You've always been able to find a legal basis for every decision that you've rendered as a judge?

SOTOMAYOR: Well, to the extent that every legal decision has—it's what I do in approaching legal questions is, I look at the law that's being cited. I look at how precedent informs it. I try to determine what those principles are of precedent to apply to the facts in the case before me and then do that. And so one—that is a process. You use. . .

KYL: Right. And—and all I'm asking—this is not a trick question.

SOTOMAYOR: No, I wasn't. . . .

KYL: I can't imagine that the answer would be otherwise than, yes, you've always found some legal basis for ruling one way or the other, some precedent, some reading of a statute, the Constitution or whatever it might be. You haven't ever had to throw up your arms and say, "I can't find any legal basis for this opinion, so I'm going to base it on some other factor"?

SOTOMAYOR: It's—when you say—use the words "some legal basis," it suggests that a judge is coming to the process by saying, "I think the result should be here, and so I'm going to use something to get there."

KYL: No, I'm not trying to infer that any of your decisions have been incorrect or that you've used an inappropriate basis. I'm simply confirming what you first said in response to my question about the president, that, in every case, the judge is able to find a basis in law for deciding the case. Sometimes there aren't cases directly on point. That's true. Sometimes it may not be a case from your circuit. Sometimes it may be somewhat tenuous and you may have to rely upon authority, like scholarly opinions and law reviews or whatever.

But my question is really very simple to you: Have you always been able to have a legal basis for the decisions that you have rendered and not have to rely upon some extra-legal concept, such as empathy or some other concept other than a legal interpretation or precedent?

SOTOMAYOR: Exactly, sir. We apply law to facts. We don't apply feelings to facts.

KYL: Right. Now, thank you for that. Let me go back to the beginning. I raised this issue about the president's interpretation, because he clearly is going to seek nominees to this court and other courts that he's comfortable with and that would imply who have some commonality with his view of the law in judging. It's a concept that I also disagree with.

But in this respect, it is—the speeches that you have given and some of the writings that you've engaged in have raised questions, because they appear to fit into what the president has described as this group of cases in which the legal process or the law simply doesn't give you the answer.

And it's in that context that people have read these speeches and have concluded that you believe that gender and ethnicity are an appropriate way for judges to make decisions in cases. Now, that's—that's my characterization.

I want to go back through the—I've read your speeches, and I've read all of them several times. The one I happened to mark up here is the Seton Hall speech, but it was virtually identical to the one at Berkeley.

You said this morning that your—the point of those speeches was to inspire young people. And I think there is some in your speeches that certainly is inspiring, and, in fact, it's more than that. I commend you on several of the things that you talked about, including your own background, as a way of inspiring young people, whether they're minority or not, and regardless of their gender. You said some very inspirational things to them.

And I take it that, therefore, in some sense, your speech was inspirational to them. But, in reading these speeches, it is inescapable that your purpose was to discuss a different issue, that it was to discuss—in fact, let me put it in your words. You said, "I intend to talk to you about my—I—my Latina identity, where it came from, and the influence I perceive gender, race, and national original representation will have on the development of the law."

And then, after some preliminary and sometimes inspirational comments, you got back to the theme and said, "The focus of my speech tonight, however, is not about the struggle to get us where we are and where we need to go, but instead to discuss what it will mean to have more women and people of color on the bench."

You said, "No one can or should ignore asking and pondering what it will mean, or not mean, in the development of the law." You talked to—you cited some people who had a different point of view than yours, and then you came back to it and said, "Because I accept the proposition that, as Professor Resnik explains, to judge is an exercise of power, and because as Professor Martha Minow of Harvard Law School explains, there is no objective stance, but only a series of perspectives. No neutrality, no escape from choice in judging. . . . I further accept that our experiences as women and people of color will in some way affect our decisions."

Now, you're deep into the argument here. You've agreed with Resnik that there is no objective stance, only a series of perspectives, no neutrality—which just as an aside, it seems to me, is relativism run amok.

But then you say, "What Professor Minow's quote means to me is not all women are people of color or all in some circumstances, or me in any particular case or circumstance, but enough women and people of color in enough cases will make a difference in the process of judging." You're talking here about different outcomes in cases, and you go on to substantiate your case by, first of all, citing a Minnesota case in which three women judges ruled differently than two male judges in a father's visitation case.

You cited two excellent studies, which tended to demonstrate differences between women and men in making decisions in cases. You said, "As recognized by legal scholars, whatever the cause is, not one woman or person of color in any one position, but as a group, we will have an effect on the development of law and on judging."

So, you develop the theme. You substantiated it with some evidence to substantiate your point of view. Up to that point, you had simply made the case, I think, that judging could certainly reach—or judges could certainly reach different results and make a difference in judging depending upon their gender or ethnicity. You hadn't rendered a judgment about whether that—they would be better judgments or not.

But then, you did. You quoted Justice O'Connor to say that, a wise old woman, wise old man, would reach the same decisions, and then you said: "I'm also not sure I agree with that statement." And that's when you made the statement that's now relatively famous. "I would hope that a wise Latina woman with the richness of her experiences would more often than not reach a better conclusion."

So here, you're reaching a judgment that, not only will it make a difference, but that it should make a difference. And you went on. And—and this is the last thing that I'll quote here. You said: In short, I—well, I think this is important.

You note that some of the old white guys made some pretty good decisions eventually—Oliver Wendell Holmes, Cardozo and others. And—and you acknowledge that they made a big difference in discrimination cases. But it took a long time to understand. It takes time and effort, something not all people are willing to give, and so on.

And then you concluded this: "In short, I accept the proposition that difference will be made by the presence of women and people of color on the bench, and that my experiences will affect the facts that I choose to see."

You said: "I don't know exactly what the difference will be in my judging. But I accept that there will be some based on gender and my Latina heritage."

You don't, as—as you said in your response to Senator Sessions, you said that you weren't encouraging that. And you—you talked about how we need to set that aside. But you didn't, in your speech, say that this is not good. We need to set this aside. Instead, you seem to be celebrating it. The clear inference is, it's a good thing that this is happening.

So, that's why some of us are concerned, first with the president's elucidation of his point of view here about judging, and then these speeches, several of them, including speeches that were included in Law Review articles that you edited, that all say the same thing.

And it would certainly lead one to a conclusion that, a, you understand it will make a difference; and b, not only are you not saying anything negative about that, but you seem to embrace the difference in—in concluding that you'll make better decisions. That's the basis of concern that a lot of people have. Please take the time you need to respond to my question.

SOTOMAYOR: Thank you. I have a record for 17 years. Decision after decision, decision after decision. It is very clear that I don't base my judgments on my personal experiences or—or my feelings or my biases. All of my decisions show my respect for the rule of law, the fact that regardless about if I identify a feeling about a case, which was part of what that speech did talk about, there are situations where one has reactions to speeches—to activities.

It's not surprising that, in some cases, the loss of a victim is very tragic. A judge feels with those situations in acknowledging that there is a hardship to someone doesn't mean that the law commands the result. I have any number of cases where I have acknowledged the particular difficulty to a party or disapproval of a party's actions and said, "No, but the law requires this."

So, my views, I think, are demonstrated by what I do as a judge. I'm grateful that you took notice that much of my speech, if not all of it, was intended to inspire. And my whole message to those students, and that's the very end of what I said to them, was: I hope I see you in the courtroom somebody. I don't know if I said it in that speech, but I often end my speeches with saying, "And I hope someday you're sitting on the bench with me."

And so, the intent of the speech, it's structure, was to inspire them to believe, as I do, as I think everyone does, that life experiences enrich the legal system.

I used the words "process of judging." That experience that you look for in choosing a judge, whether it's the ABA rule that says the judge has to be a lawyer for X number of years or it's the experience that your committee looks for in terms of what's the background of the judge, have they undertaken serious consideration of constitutional questions. All those experiences are valued because our system is enriched by a variety of experiences.

And I don't think that anybody quarrels with the fact that diversity on the bench is good for America. It's good for America because we are the land of opportunity. And to the extent that we're pursuing and showing that all groups can be lawyers and judges, that's just reflecting the values of our society.

KYL: And if I could just interrupt you right now, to me, that's the key. It's good because it shows these young people that you're talking to that, with a little hard work, it doesn't matter where you came from. You can make it. And that's why you hope to see them on the bench. I totally appreciate that.

The question though is whether you leave them with the impression that it's good to make different decisions because of their ethnicity or gender. And it strikes me to you could have easily said in here now, of course, blind lady justice doesn't permit us to base decisions in cases on our ethnicity or gender. We should strive very hard to set those aside when we can.

I found only one rather oblique reference in your speech that could be read to say that you warned against that. All of the other statements seemed to embrace it or, certainly, to recognize it and almost seem as if you're powerless to do anything about it. I accept that this will happen, you said. So while I appreciate what you're saying, it still doesn't answer to me the question of whether you think that these—that ethnicity or gender should be making a difference.

SOTOMAYOR: I—there are two different, I believe, issues to address and to look at because various statements are being looked at and being tied together. But the speech, as it's structured, didn't intend to do that and didn't do that.

Much of the speech about what differences there will be in judging was in the context of my saying or addressing an academic question. All the studies that you reference I cited in my—in my speech were just that, studies. They were suggesting that there could be a difference. They were raising reasons why. I was inviting the students to think about that question.

Most of the quotes that you had and reference say that. We have to ask this question. Does it make a difference? And if it does, how? And the study about differences in outcomes was in that context.

That was a case in which three women judges went one way and two men went the other, but I didn't suggest that that was driven by their gender. You can't make that judgment until you see what the law actually said.

And I wasn't talking about what law they were interpreting in that case. I was just talking about the academic question that one should ask.

KYL: If I could just interrupt, I think you just contradicted your speech because you said in the line before that, "enough women and people of color in enough cases will make a difference in the process of judging."

Next comment, the Minnesota Supreme Court has given us an example of that. So you did cite that as an example of gender making a difference in judging.

Now, look, I'm not—I—I don't want to be misunderstood here as disagreeing with a general look into question—into the question of whether people's gender, ethnicity or background in some way affects their—their judging. I suspect you can make a very good case that that is true in some cases. You cite a case here for that proposition.

Neither you nor I probably know whether for sure that was the reason, but one could infer it from the decision that was rendered. And then you cite two other studies.

I am not questioning whether the studies are not valuable. In fact, I would agree with you that it's important for us to be able to know these things so that we are on guard to set aside prejudices that we may not even know that we have.

Because when you do judge a case—I mean, let me just go back in time. I tried a lot of cases, and it always depended on the luck of the draw, what judge you got; 99 times out of 100 it didn't matter. So what we got? Judge Jones, fine. We got Judge Smith, fine. It didn't matter, because you knew they would all apply the law.

In federal district court in Arizona, there was one judge you didn't want to get. All—all of the lawyers knew that, because they knew he had predilections that was really difficult for him to set aside. It's a reality. And I suspect you've seen that on some courts, too.

So it is a good thing to examine whether or not those biases and prejudices exist in order to be on guard and to set them aside. The fault I have with your speech is that you not only don't let these students know that you need to set it aside; you don't say that that's what you need this information for. But you're almost celebrating. You think—you say, if there are enough of us, we will make a difference, inferring that it is a good thing if we begin deciding cases differently.

Let me just ask you one last question here. I mean, can you—have you ever seen a case where, to use your example, the wise Latina made a better decisions than the non-Latina judges?

SOTOMAYOR: No. What I've seen. . . . (CROSSTALK)

KYL: I mean, I know you like all of your decisions, but. . . .

(UNKNOWN): (OFF-MIKE)

KYL: I was just saying that I know that she appreciates her own decisions, and I'm—I don't mean to denigrate her decisions, Mr. Chairman (inaudible)

SOTOMAYOR: I was using a rhetorical riff that hearkened back to Justice O'Connor, because her literal words and mine have a meaning that neither of us, if you were looking at it, in their exact words make any sense.

Justice O'Connor was a part of a court in which she greatly respected her colleagues. And yet those wise men—I'm not going to use the other word—and wise women did reach different conclusions in deciding cases. I never understood her to be attempting to say that that meant those people who disagreed with her were unwise or unfair judges.

As you know, my speech was intending to inspire the students to understand the richness that their backgrounds could bring to the judicial process in the same way that everybody else's background does the same.

I think that's what Justice Alito was referring to when he was asked questions by this committee and he said, you know, when I decide a case, I think about my Italian ancestors and their experiences coming to this country. I don't think anybody thought that he was saying that that commanded the result in the case.

These were students and lawyers who I don't think would have been misled, either by Justice O'Connor's statement, or mine, in thinking that we actually intended to say that we could really make wiser and fairer decisions.

I think what they could think, and would think, is that I was talking about the value that life experiences have, in the words I used, to the process of judging. And that is the context in which I understood the speech to be doing.

The words I chose, taking the rhetorical flourish, it was a bad idea. I do understand that there are some who have read this differently, and I understand why they might have concern.

But I have repeated—more than once—and I will repeat throughout, if you look at my history on the bench, you will know that I do not believe that any ethnic, gender or race group has an advantage in sound judging. You noted that my speech actually said that. And I also believe that every person, regardless of their background and life experiences, can be good and wise judges. . . .

Notes and Questions

1. What were Senators Sessions and Kyl trying to accomplish with their questioning? How successful were they in achieving their objectives? Was one more successful than the other?

2. At several points during their questioning, the Senators became frustrated with Judge Sotomayor, because they felt that, while her answers were excellent, they were also in conflict with her prior writings. This dynamic—in which nominees attempt to distance themselves from their most provocative (and often most interesting) prior statements, leaving Senators at a loss how to proceed—is a common staple of confirmation hearings. During the Robert Bork hearings, the nominee's Democratic opponents described his similar attempts to distance himself from his prior writings as a "confirmation conversion" and refused to accept that it was genuine. *See, e.g.*, Linda Greenhouse, *The Bork Hearings: Senators Question the Sincerity of Bork's New Views*, N.Y. Times, Sept. 18, 1987, at A22.

3. It was not only right-wing critics who were concerned by some of the anodyne statements about the role of judges that Justice Sotomayor made in her opening statement and in her answers to questions. Left-wing Georgetown Law Professor Louis Michael Seidman received national attention for this scathing critique, originally offered as part of an online symposium on the Sotomayor hearings:

> Speaking only for myself (I guess that's obvious), I was completely disgusted by Judge Sotomayor's testimony today. If she was not perjuring herself, she is intellectually unqualified to be on the Supreme Court. If she was perjuring herself, she is morally unqualified. How could someone who has been on the bench for seventeen years possibly believe that judging in hard cases involves no more than applying the law to the facts? First year law students understand within a month that many areas of the law are open textured and indeterminate—that the legal material frequently (actually, I would say always) must be supplemented by contestable presuppositions, empirical assumptions, and moral judgments. To claim otherwise—to claim that fidelity to uncontested legal principles dictates results—is to claim that whenever Justices disagree among themselves, someone is either a fool or acting in bad faith. What does it say about our legal system that in order to get confirmed Judge Sotomayor must tell the lies that she told today? That judges and justices must live these lies throughout their professional careers?
>
> Perhaps Justice Sotomayor should be excused because our official ideology about judging is so degraded that she would sacrifice a position on the Supreme Court if she told the truth. Legal academics who defend what she did today have no such excuse. They should be ashamed of themselves.

The Federalist Society Online Debate Series, The Sotomayor Nomination, Part II, July 13, 2009, http://www.fed-soc.org/debates/dbtid.30/default.asp.

4. As noted above, in recent decades, nominees have become increasingly unwilling to talk about their views on particular cases and issues that might come before the Court. As a result, advocates of different constitutional visions and different conceptions of the role of the courts have been forced to address their support for or concerns about nominees more obliquely. To what extent are the colloquies above actually subtle debates about the content of Justice Sotomayor's future jurisprudence? To the extent that they are, what specifically are Senators Sessions and Kyl worried about?

5. Certainly, many nominees for the Court have enhanced or diminished their reputations by the overall impression left by their hearing testimony. Rarely, however, has a candidate's answer to a particular question been especially newsworthy or especially influential in the course of his or her confirmation. One arguable exception occurred during the Bork hearings, when Judge Bork was thrown a softball question by a Republican Senator and wiffed badly, offering a stilted answer that reinforced the image his detractors were trying to establish:

[Republican of Wyoming] ALAN K. SIMPSON: And now I have one final question. Why do you want to be an Associate Justice of the United States Supreme Court?

BORK: Senator, I guess the answer to that is that I have spent my life in the intellectual pursuits in the law. And since I've been a judge, I particularly like the courtroom. I like the courtroom as an advocate and I like the courtroom as a judge. And I enjoy the give-and-take and the intellectual effort involved. It is just a life and that's of course the Court that has the most interesting cases and issues and I think it would be an intellectual feast just to be there and to read the briefs and discuss things with counsel and discuss things with my colleagues. That's the first answer.

The second answer is, I would like to leave a reputation as a judge who understood constitutional governance and contributed his bit to maintaining it in the ways I have described before this committee. Our constitutional structure is the most important thing this nation has and I would like to help maintain it and to be remembered for that.

S. Hrg. 100-1011, Part 1, at 854 (Sept. 10, 1991).

d. The Confirmation Vote

Once the committee hearings are over, each of the 100 Senators must determine how to vote on the nomination. The judiciary committee members are the first to reveal their intentions, either in the days leading up to the committee's vote on the nominee or, in rarer cases, at the hearing in which the vote is cast. Once the nomination moves on to the full Senate, each Senator is given an opportunity to make a speech explaining his or her vote and many take advantage of this opportunity. Others announce their positions in a variety of venues, including in press releases, televised interviews, and posts to their Web sites. Depending on the level of controversy generated by the nomination, a small number of Senators may simply cast their votes without further public comment.

In deciding whether to support a particular nominee, Senators take into account the same sorts of factors that Presidents weigh in making nominations—including the nominee's objective qualifications, the potential political ramifications of a vote to confirm or deny, and, in most cases, the extent to which the nominee's views seem compatible with the Senator's own, at least in comparison with other possible nominees. However, there is—and always has been—substantial disagreement as to which standard Senators ought to use in casting a confirmation vote. Many argue that the Constitution gives the President the primary responsibility for selecting judges and that Senators ought to defer to a President's judicial nominations, unless a candidate is unqualified or corrupt. Others believe that Senators have the right—and perhaps even the responsibility—to independently evaluate judicial nominees to determine whether they will make the kind of judge that the Senator could support. As one recent article astutely observes, those who advocate the second position come in two varieties: (1) Those who argue that there is a clear separation between law and politics and that Senators need to participate aggressively in the confirmation process in order to ferret out judges who will not respect that line, and (2) those who argue that law and politics are so inextricably bound together that it is incoherent or dangerous or both to assess judicial nominees without at least broadly considering their views. *See* Wm. Grayson Lambert, *The Real Debate over the Senate's Role in the Confirmation Process*, 61 Duke L.J. 1283 (2012). In the excerpts that follow, law professors, advocates, and Senators offer their various takes on this important issue.

David A. Strauss & Cass R. Sunstein, The Senate, the Constitution, and the Confirmation Process

more deference

101 Yale L.J. 1491, 1492 (1992)

One possible response to divided government, and to the troubled Supreme Court confirmation process it has produced, is for the Senate to be more deferential to the Administration's preferences. The Senate might confine itself to a role similar to that traditionally played by the American Bar Association and other advisory groups: to inquire into whether the nominee meets certain standards of character and professional distinction. Under this approach, the Senate could not appropriately consider a nominee's basic commitments or views on controversial issues, unless those views were so extreme as to call into question the nominee's character or competence.

Confining the Senate to this deferential role would certainly eliminate some of the current complaints about the antagonistic nature of the confirmation process, and to this extent it would be an advance. But there is not much else to commend it. From the constitutional standpoint, this recommendation seems perverse. The Constitution requires that the Senate give its "Advice and Consent" to nominations; this language contemplates a more active role than simple acquiescence whenever a nominee is not deeply objectionable. Beyond that, nothing in the structure of the Constitution or the nature of Supreme Court appointments suggests that the Senate should be so deferential. The Senate, no less than the President, is elected by the people. Supreme Court Justices, unlike executive branch appointees, are not the President's subordinates. Often the Court must mediate conflicts between the President and the Congress; one party to a conflict should not have the dominant role in choosing the mediator.

In our view there are other ways, more consistent with the constitutional plan, to deal with the defects of the current confirmation process. The first step is essentially the opposite of the proposal for Senate deference. We suggest that the Senate should assert its constitutional prerogatives more forcefully, unabashedly claiming an independent role. Specifically, the Senate should insist that it has both the authority to "advise" the President and the power to withhold its "consent" because it disagrees with the nominee's basic commitments on the kinds of issues that are likely to come before the Court.

When Congress considers the President's legislative initiatives, it is not deferential. No one would suggest that Congress should pass every bill the President proposes unless the bill fails some minimal test, analogous to a minimal test of character and competence. Congress is free to reject proposed legislation for political reasons. This is a most familiar part of the system of checks and balances. There is no reason for nominations to the Supreme Court to command greater deference.

John C. Eastman, The Limited Nature of the Senate's Advice and Consent Role

33 U.C. Davis L. Rev. 633, 652 (2003)

Despite the original understanding of the Senate's limited role in the confirmation process, and despite the lessons learned from these early historical flirtations with the use of political ideology as a criteria for judicial confirmation, the Senate today appears bent on using its limited confirmation power to impose ideological litmus tests on presidential nominees. In this way, the Senate seems to be arrogating to itself the nomination as well as the confirmation power.

The Senate's expanded use of its confirmation power should perhaps come as no surprise. As a result of the growing role of the judiciary, the Senate's part in the nomination process has become a powerful political tool. And, like any powerful political tool, it is the subject of a strenuous competition among interest groups every time the President seeks to fill a judicial vacancy. Nevertheless, it is a tool that poses grave dangers to our constitutional system of government. In its current manifestation, the Senate's ideological use of the confirmation power threatens the separation of powers in three ways. First, it undermines the responsibility for appointments given to the President. Second, it demands of judicial nominees a commitment to a role not appropriate to the courts. Third, and, perhaps most importantly, the Senate's ideological use of the confirmation power threatens the separation of powers by threatening the independence of the judiciary itself.

Marcia Greenberger, Hearing Before the Senate Committee on the Judiciary Subcommittee on Administrative Oversight and the Courts on "Should Ideology Matter?: Judicial Nominations 2001"

Hearings Before Subcomm. on Administration Oversight and the Courts, Sen. Comm. on the Judiciary, 107th Cong. (June 26, 2001)

The "advice and consent" language of the Constitution itself, and the history of the Framers' adoption of this formulation, make it clear that the Constitution creates an independent role and set of responsibilities for the Senate in the confirmation process. And, as in so many other ways, the Framers of the Constitution were right. The judiciary, after all, is independent from the Executive and Legislative Branches, and indeed is sometimes called upon to resolve disputes between the two. If the President were given a superior role in judicial appointments, it would upset the neutrality of the judiciary and the system of checks and balances of which it is a part. Unlike cabinet members or other appointments to the Executive Branch, judges do not work for the President or serve at the pleasure of the President only while he, or someday, she, is in office. So while it may be appropriate for Senators to give deference to a President's choices of the personnel who will work for him and implement his policies in the departments and agencies of the federal government—and even then, deference is not a blank check—it would be entirely inappropriate to give deference to the President's selection of judicial candidates.

The late Charles L. Black, Jr., said it well in an article in the Yale Law Journal in 1970. After arguing that a Senator should let the President have wide latitude in filling Executive Branch posts, "These are his people; they are to work with him,"

Professor Black continues: "Just the reverse, just exactly the reverse, is true of the judiciary. The judges are not the President's people. God forbid! They are not to work with him or for him. They are to be as independent of him as they are of the Senate, neither more nor less."

At bottom, no judicial nominee enjoys a presumption in favor of confirmation. Rather, as numerous legal scholars have shown, it is the nominee who carries the burden of convincing the Senate that he or she should be confirmed, and any doubts should be resolved against confirmation. Articulating this shared view, Professor Chemerinsky has written:

> Under the Constitution there is no reason why a President's nominees for Supreme Court are entitled to any presumption of confirmation. The Constitution simply says that the President shall appoint federal court judges with the advice and consent of the Senate. The Senate is fully entitled to begin with a presumption against the nominee and confirm only if persuaded that the individual is worthy of a lifelong seat on the Supreme Court.

No person has an entitlement to a lifetime seat on the federal bench, and if a nominee cannot clearly satisfy the Senate that he or she meets all of the criteria for confirmation, the American people should not be asked to bear the risk of entrusting that individual with the reigns of judicial power.

Senator Barack Obama, Statement on the Floor of the United States Senate Announcing Vote Not to Confirm Judge John Roberts, Sept. 28, 2005

. . . [T]he decision with respect to Judge Roberts' nomination has not been an easy one for me to make. As some of you know, I have not only argued cases before appellate courts but for 10 years was a member of the University of Chicago Law School faculty and taught courses in constitutional law. Part of the culture of the University of Chicago Law School faculty is to maintain a sense of collegiality between those people who hold different views. What engenders respect is not the particular outcome that a legal scholar arrives at but, rather, the intellectual rigor and honesty with which he or she arrives at a decision.

Given that background, I am sorely tempted to vote for Judge Roberts based on my study of his resume, his conduct during the hearings, and a conversation I had with him yesterday afternoon.

There is absolutely no doubt in my mind Judge Roberts is qualified to sit on the highest court in the land. Moreover, he seems to have the comportment and the temperament that makes for a good judge. He is humble, he is personally decent, and he appears to be respectful of different points of view. It is absolutely clear to me that Judge Roberts truly loves the law. He couldn't have achieved his excellent record as an advocate before the Supreme Court without that passion for the law, and it became apparent to me in our conversation that he does, in fact, deeply respect the basic precepts that go into deciding 95 percent of the cases that come before the Federal court—adherence to precedence, a certain modesty in reading statutes and constitutional text, a respect for procedural regularity, and an impartiality in presiding over the adversarial system. All of these characteristics make me want to vote for Judge Roberts.

The problem I face—a problem that has been voiced by some of my other colleagues, both those who are voting for Mr. Roberts and those who are voting against Mr. Roberts—is that while adherence to legal precedent and rules of statutory or constitutional construction will dispose of 95 percent of the cases that come before a court, so that both a Scalia and a Ginsburg will arrive at the same place most of the time on those 95 percent of the cases—what matters on the Supreme Court is those 5 percent of cases that are truly difficult. In those cases, adherence to precedent and rules of construction and interpretation will only get you through the 25th mile of the marathon. That last mile can only be determined on the basis of one's deepest values, one's core concerns, one's broader perspectives on how the world works, and the depth and breadth of one's empathy.

In those 5 percent of hard cases, the constitutional text will not be directly on point. The language of the statute will not be perfectly clear. Legal process alone will not lead you to a rule of decision. In those circumstances, your decisions about whether affirmative action is an appropriate response to the history of discrimination in this country or whether a general right of privacy encompasses a more specific right of women to control their reproductive decisions or whether the commerce clause empowers Congress to speak on those issues of broad national concern that may be only tangentially related to what is easily defined as interstate commerce, whether a person who is disabled has the right to be accommodated so they can work alongside those who are nondisabled— in those difficult cases, the critical ingredient is supplied by what is in the judge's heart.

I talked to Judge Roberts about this. Judge Roberts confessed that, unlike maybe professional politicians, it is not easy for him to talk about his values and his deeper feelings. That is not how he is trained. He did say he doesn't like bullies and has always viewed the law as a way of evening out the playing field between the strong and the weak.

I was impressed with that statement because I view the law in much the same way. The problem I had is that when I examined Judge Roberts' record and history of public service, it is my personal estimation that he has far more often used his formidable skills on behalf of the strong in opposition to the weak. In his work in the White House and the Solicitor General's Office, he seemed to have consistently sided with those who were dismissive of efforts to eradicate the remnants of racial discrimination in our political process. In these same positions, he seemed dismissive of the concerns that it is harder to make it in this world and in this economy when you are a woman rather than a man.

I want to take Judge Roberts at his word that he doesn't like bullies and he sees the law and the Court as a means of evening the playing field between the strong and the weak. But given the gravity of the position to which he will undoubtedly ascend and the gravity of the decisions in which he will undoubtedly participate during his tenure on the Court, I ultimately have to give more weight to his deeds and the overarching political philosophy that he appears to have shared with those in power than to the assuring words that he provided me in our meeting.

The bottom line is this: I will be voting against John Roberts' nomination. I do so with considerable reticence. I hope that I am wrong. I hope that this reticence on my part proves unjustified and that Judge Roberts will show himself to not only be an outstanding legal thinker but also someone who upholds the Court's historic role as a check on the majoritarian impulses of the executive branch and the legislative branch. I hope that he will recognize who the weak are and who the strong are in our society. I hope that his jurisprudence is one that stands up to the bullies of all ideological stripes. . . .

Senator Barack Obama, Statement on the Floor of the United States Senate Announcing Vote Not to Confirm Judge Samuel Alito, Jan. 26, 2006

As we all know, there's been a lot of discussion in the country about how the Senate should approach this confirmation process. There are some who believe that the President, having won the election, should have the complete authority to appoint his nominee, and the Senate should only examine whether or not the Justice is intellectually capable and an all-around nice guy. That once you get beyond intellect and personal character, there should be no further question whether the judge should be confirmed.

I disagree with this view. I believe firmly that the Constitution calls for the Senate to advise and consent. I believe that it calls for meaningful advice and consent that includes an examination of a judge's philosophy, ideology, and record. And when I examine the philosophy, ideology, and record of Samuel Alito, I'm deeply troubled.

I have no doubt that Judge Alito has the training and qualifications necessary to serve. He's an intelligent man and an accomplished jurist. And there's no indication he's not a man of great character.

But when you look at his record—when it comes to his understanding of the Constitution, I have found that in almost every case, he consistently sides on behalf of the powerful against the powerless; on behalf of a strong government or corporation against upholding American's individual rights.

If there is a case involving an employer and an employee and the Supreme Court has not given clear direction, he'll rule in favor of the employer. If there's a claim between prosecutors and defendants, if the Supreme Court has not provided a clear rule of decision, then he'll rule in favor of the state. He's rejected countless claims of employer discrimination, even refusing to give some plaintiffs a hearing for their case. He's refused to hold corporations accountable numerous times for dumping toxic chemicals into water supplies, even against the decisions of the EPA. He's overturned a jury verdict that found a company liable for being a monopoly when it had over 90% of the market share at the time.

It's not just his decisions in these individual cases that give me pause—it's that decisions like these are the rule for Samuel Alito, not the exception.

When it comes to how checks and balances in our system are supposed to operate—the balance of power between the Executive Branch, Congress, and the Judiciary, Judge Alito consistently sides with the notion that a President should not be constrained by either Congressional acts or the check of the Judiciary. He believes in the overarching power of the President to engage in whatever the President deems to be appropriate policy. As a consequence of this, I'm extraordinarily worried about how Judge Alito might approach issues like wiretapping, monitoring of emails, or other privacy concerns that we've seen surface over the last several months.

In sum, I've seen an extraordinarily consistent attitude on the part of Judge Alito that does not uphold the traditional role of the Supreme Court as a bastion of equality and justice for United States citizens.

Should he be confirmed, I hope that he proves me wrong. I hope that he shows the independence that I think is absolutely necessary in order for us to preserve our liberties and protect our citizens.

Senator Lindsey Graham, Statement on the Floor of the United States Senate Announcing Vote to Confirm Judge Sonia Sotomayor, July 22, 2009

Madam President, I take to the floor to inform the Senate and my colleagues about how I intend to vote on the pending nomination of Supreme Court nominee Judge Sotomayor. I understand the path of least resistance for me personally would be to vote no. That is probably true anytime you are in the minority party and you lose an election. But I feel compelled to vote yes, and I feel this is the right vote for me and, quite frankly, for the country in this case.

Why do I say that? Well, elections have consequences. I told Judge Sotomayor in the hearing that if I had won the election, even though I wasn't running, or Senator McCain had, she would probably not have been chosen by a Republican. We would have chosen someone with a more conservative background—someone similar to a Chief Justice Roberts or Miguel Estrada. She is definitely more liberal than a Republican would have chosen, but I do believe elections have consequences.

It is not as though we hid from the American people during the campaign that the Supreme Court selections were at stake. Both sides openly campaigned on the idea that the next President would be able to pick some justices for the Supreme Court. That was known to the American people and the American people spoke.

In that regard, having been one of the chief supporters of Senator McCain and one of the chief opponents of then-Senator Obama, I feel he deserves some deference on my part when it comes to his first selection to the Supreme Court. I say that understanding, under our Constitution, I or no other Senator would be bound by the pick of a President. But when you look at the history of this country, generally speaking, great deference has been given to that selection by the Senate.

While I am not bound to vote for Judge Sotomayor—voting no would be the path of least political resistance for me—I choose to vote for Judge Sotomayor because I believe she is well qualified.

We are talking about one of the most qualified nominees to be selected for the Supreme Court in decades. She has 17 years of judicial experience. Twelve of those years she was on the Second Circuit Court of Appeals. I have looked at her record closely. I believe she follows precedent; that she has not been an activist judge in the sense that would make her disqualified, in my view. She has demonstrated left-of-center reasoning but within the mainstream. She has an outstanding background as a lawyer. She was a prosecutor for 4 years in New York. Her record of academic achievement is extraordinary—coming up from very tough circumstances, being raised by a single mother, going to Princeton, being picked as the top student there, and doing an extraordinary job in law school. She has a strong work ethic. That all mattered to me. It is not just my view that her legal reasoning was within the mainstream. She received the highest rating by the ABA—the American Bar Association—as "well qualified."

The reason I mention that is not because I feel bound by their rating, but during the Alito and Roberts confirmation hearings for the Supreme Court under President Bush, I used that as a positive for both those nominees. I feel, as a

Republican, I can't use it one time and ignore it the other. So the fact that she received the highest rating from the American Bar Association made a difference to me.

Her life story, as I indicated before, is something every American should be proud of. If her selection to the Supreme Court will inspire young women, particularly Latina women, to seek a career in the law, that is a good thing, and I hope it will. . . .

I am not voting for her believing I know how she will decide a case. I am voting for her because I find her to be well qualified, because elections matter, and because the people who have served along her side for many years find an extraordinary woman in Judge Sotomayor, and I confirm their findings.

What standard did I use? Every Senator in this body, at the end of the day, has to decide how to give their advice and consent. One of the things I chose not to do was to use Senator Obama's standard when it came to casting my vote for Judge Sotomayor. If those who follow the Senate will recall, Senator Obama voted against both Justice Alito and Justice Roberts, and he used the rationale that they were well qualified; that they were extraordinarily intellectually gifted; but the last mile in the confirmation process, when it came to Judge Roberts, was the heart. Because 5 percent of controversial cases may change society, one has to look and see what is in a judge's heart.

I totally reject that.

If the Senate tries to have a confirmation process where we explore another person's heart, I think we are going to chill out people wanting to become members of the judiciary. Who would want to come before the Senate and have us try to figure out what is in their heart? Can you imagine the questions we would be allowed to ask? I think it would have a tremendous chilling effect on the future recruitment of qualified candidates to be judges. Let me say this: Judge Sotomayor agreed with me and Senator Kyl that trying to find out what is in a judge's heart is probably not a good idea.

Senator Obama also indicated that judicial philosophy and ideology were outcome determinative when it came to Judge Alito. If I used his standard, knowing that her philosophy is different than mine, her ideology is different than mine, she would have no hope of getting my vote. I daresay not one Republican, using the Obama standard, would provide her with a confirmation vote. So I decided to reject that because I believe it is not in the long-term interest of the Senate or the judiciary.

I went back to a standard I think has stood the test of time—the qualifications standard. Is this person qualified to sit on the Court? Are they a person of good character? Do they present an extraordinary circumstance—having something about their life that would make them extraordinary to the point they would be unqualified?

There was a time in this country where a Justice, such as Justice Ginsburg, who is clearly left of center, received 90-something votes in this body. There was a time in this country, not long ago, where a conservative judge, such as Justice Scalia, received over 95 votes from this body. Every Democrat who voted for Justice Scalia could not have been fooled as to what they were getting. They were getting an extremely qualified, talented, intellectual man who was qualified for the job but had a different philosophy from most Democrats. Someone on our side of the aisle who voted for Justice Ginsburg had to know what they were getting. They were getting someone who was very talented, extremely well qualified, incredibly smart, and who was general counsel for the ACLU. You had to know what you were getting, but you understood that President Clinton, in that case, had the right to make that decision.

What happened to those days? I would say to my Democratic colleagues—and I am sure Republicans have made our fair share of mistakes when it comes to judges—that this effort, not too far in the past, of filibustering judges, declaring war on the Judiciary, has hurt this body. In my opinion, the politicization of our Judiciary has to stop for the good of this country, for the good of the Senate, and for the good of the rule of law in America.

What am I trying to do today? I am trying to start over. The political "golden rule" is: Do unto others as they did unto you. The actual Golden Rule is: Do unto others as you would have them do unto you. I hope we can get back to the more traditional sense of what the Senate has been all about. . . .

I do not know what is ahead for this country when it comes to picking Supreme Court Justices. I don't know what openings may occur and when they will occur. I know this. Elections have to matter. I don't want to invalidate elections by disagreeing with someone against whom I ran or I opposed politically because when the election is over, everything has to change to some extent. I am not bound to agree with every pick of President Obama, but when it comes to trying to show some deference, I will. I will try to do better for him than he was able to do for President Bush.

I don't want to turn over the confirmation of judges to special interest groups on the left or the right, and that is where we are headed if we don't watch it. Special interest groups are important, they have their say, they have every right to have their say, but we can't make every Supreme Court vacancy a battle over our culture.

I am trying to start over. I have only been here one term plus a few months. But since I have been here, I have been worried about where this country is going when it comes to judges. I happen to be here at a time when we are about to change the rules of the Senate in a way it had never been done in 200 years. I was new to the body, but I was understanding of the law and how our system works well enough to know that I did not want to be part of that. I had not been here long, but I understood what would happen to this country if we changed the rules of the Senate, even though people felt frustrated and justified to do so.

As a member of the minority, I promised President Obama that I would look hard at his nominees. I will try to help him where I can, but I will not abandon the right to say no and to stop, in an extraordinary circumstance, a nominee who I think would be bad for the country and would dramatically change the power of a branch of the government, the Supreme Court, that is very important to every American.

As to my colleagues who find a different decision on the Republican side, I can understand and appreciate why they did not feel comfortable giving their confirmation votes to Judge Sotomayor. But I am trying to look beyond this moment, look to the future and come up with a reason to support her that will create a different way of doing business, that will help the judiciary, the Senate, and the country as a whole. . . .

I choose to vote for Judge Sotomayor looking at her from the most optimistic perspective, understanding I could be wrong but proud of the fact that my country is moving in the right direction when anybody and everybody can hit it out of the park. I would not have chosen her if I had to make this choice as President, but I understand why President Obama did choose her and I am happy to vote for her.

C. THE CURRENT JUSTICES

The remainder of this chapter offers sketches of each of the current Justices of the Supreme Court, providing necessary or intriguing information about their backgrounds, their personalities, and their jurisprudence. Each sketch draws heavily on the voluminous literature about the Justices (much of which is cited below), but the observations and conclusions contained in the profiles are ultimately our own.

1. Chief Justice John G. Roberts

 Chief Justice Roberts was born in Buffalo, New York, on January 27, 1955, and raised in a well-to-do family in small-town Indiana. He was something of a golden boy from day one, shining in school, sports, and other activities. He received his bachelor's degree from Harvard College in 1976 and his law degree from Harvard Law School in 1979, both with high honors. After graduation, he served as a law clerk for legendary Judge Henry J. Friendly of the United States Court of Appeals for the Second Circuit and for then-Associate Justice William H. Rehnquist.

After his clerkships, he moved directly into the Reagan administration, serving first as a Special Assistant to the Attorney General, then as an Associate Counsel in the White House Counsel's Office. During his years in the Reagan administration he was perhaps the brightest star in a group of young conservative lawyers committed to remaking the federal judiciary and rolling back the liberal jurisprudence of the previous decades. He wrote many memos on controversial issues during these years, expressing positions that caused mild problems for him during his confirmation hearings.

After leaving the White House, Roberts joined the law firm Hogan & Hartson, where he practiced for three years, before becoming the Principal Deputy Solicitor General of the United States in 1989. He served with distinction in that role, arguing more than a dozen cases before the United States Supreme Court. Toward the end of his tenure as Deputy Solicitor General, the 38-year old Roberts was nominated by President George H.W. Bush for a seat on the United States Court of Appeals for the District of Columbia Circuit, but the Senate failed to act on his nomination. When President Bush left office, Roberts returned to Hogan & Hartson, where he worked for another decade, arguing more than 20 further cases before the Supreme Court and building a reputation as perhaps the finest appellate litigator of his generation.

When President George W. Bush took office, he promptly renominated Roberts for the D.C. Circuit. His confirmation was delayed for almost exactly two years as a result of the partisan wrangling surrounding President Bush's initial judicial appointments. Roberts was finally confirmed and took his seat in 2003. When Associate Justice Sandra Day O'Connor announced her retirement during the summer of 2005, President Bush nominated Judge Roberts for her seat, after a series of interviews in which Roberts's intellectual abilities and personal humility vaulted him over several higher profile candidates. When Chief Justice Rehnquist died later in the summer, the President withdrew that nomination and nominated Judge Roberts to replace his former boss as Chief Justice of the United States.

During his confirmation hearings, Roberts impressed everyone with his intellect and charm. Republican Senators almost uniformly championed his candidacy, while Democratic Senators were divided. In large measure, the Democrats struggled with the question of whether Judge Roberts was still the young firebrand with bracing conservative views who had served in the Reagan White House or whether the intervening years, and particularly his decade in private practice, had turned him into a "lawyer's lawyer," who—while still quite conservative—now placed greater emphasis on civility, consensus, and the expression of diverse viewpoints. Roberts was ultimately confirmed 78-22, winning the votes of slightly more than half of the Democrats, and he joined the Court on September 29, 2005.

To some extent, the jury is still out on the question that divided Democratic Senators at his confirmation. With one obvious exception discussed below, Roberts has done little to disappoint the Bush administration, establishing an almost uniformly conservative voting record and leading the Court to the right on a variety of issues, ranging from campaign finance to abortion to gun rights. Though he has thus far been less likely than prior Chief Justices to assign himself the majority opinions in major cases, he has, by all reports, worked hard to shape the Court's decision in these cases and to hold together tentative conservative majorities.[9] In one of his most famous opinions, *Parents Involved in Community Schools v. Seattle School District No. 1*, 551 U.S. 701, 748 (2007), Chief Justice Roberts categorically rejected the assignment of students to schools on the basis of race even when done in order to achieve greater integration, insisting that "[t]he way to stop discriminating on the basis of race is to stop discriminating on the basis of race" (albeit in a plurality opinion whose scope was limited by Justice Kennedy's concurring opinion). Over the full run of cases, his voting record is largely indistinguishable from the other strongly conservative members of the Court; in each of his terms on the Court, he has voted with each of them at least 79 percent of the time.[10]

That having been said, there are some signals that Chief Justice Roberts puts a higher premium on consensus than do some of his conservative colleagues. In every year that he has been on the Court, he has dissented in fewer cases than any Justice except Justice Kennedy. In a small but significant number of cases, particularly early in his tenure, he has led the Court to narrow rulings that eschewed opportunities to push the law substantially to the right on high profile issues. *See, e.g., Northwest Austin Municipal Utility District No. 1 v. Holder*, 557 U.S. 193 (2009) (constitutionality of Voting Rights Act); *Ayotte v. Planned Parenthood of Northern New England*, 546 U.S. 320 (2006) (abortion). He has at times provided the sixth or seventh vote in cases where Justice Kennedy has joined the Court's more liberal members to create a majority. *See, e.g., Graham v. Florida*, 130 S. Ct. 2011 (2010) (constitutionality of life without parole sentences for juveniles). In fact, the percentage of cases in which he has agreed with the allegedly moderate Justice Kennedy does not deviate significantly from the percentage of cases in which he has agreed with his more conservative colleagues. One statistical study ranks him as the Court's fourth most conservative

9. Journalist Jeffrey Toobin has repeatedly made this point. *See, e.g.,* Jeffrey Toobin, *Money Unlimited: How John Roberts Orchestrated the* Citizens United *Decision*, The New Yorker, May 21, 2012, at 36; Jeffrey Toobin, *No More Mr. Nice Guy: The Supreme Court's Stealth Hardliner*, The New Yorker, May 25, 2009, at 42.

10. All statistics about the voting records of the Justices are taken or calculated from the wonderful statistical reports that the staff of "SCOTUSblog" compiles at the end of each Supreme Court term. Their reports for recent years can be accessed at http://www.scotusblog.com/reference/stat-pack.

member, albeit placing him closer on the ideological spectrum to the most conservative member than he is to Justice Kennedy, the median Justice.[11]

In June 2012, Chief Justice Roberts delivered the Court's opinion in the consolidated cases challenging the constitutionality of the Patient Protection and Affordable Care Act, the controversial health care reform legislation at the heart of President Obama's first-term agenda. To the surprise of many, his opinion in that case gave continued grist to both readings of the Chief Justice. On the one hand, the opinion accepted the aggressive arguments of the Act's challengers that (1) the Act's requirement that most Americans purchase health insurance or pay a penalty (the so-called individual mandate) is not valid legislation under Congress's Commerce Clause powers and (2) that the Act's provisions requiring states to substantially expand Medicaid coverage or decline *all* federal Medicaid funds is unconstitutionally coercive. On the other hand, his opinion (1) provided the crucial vote to uphold the individual mandate, on the grounds that it is valid legislation under the taxing power, and (2) allowed the expansion of the Medicaid program to go forward as long as states that declined to participate in the expanded program were allowed to keep their existing Medicaid funding. *See generally Nat'l Fed'n of Indep. Business v. Sebelius*, 132 S. Ct. 2566 (2012).

2. Justice Antonin Scalia

Justice Scalia was born in Trenton, New Jersey, on March 11, 1936, the only child of a Professor of Romance Languages and a schoolteacher, his father and his maternal grandparents having emigrated from Italy. He grew up in Queens, New York, attending and excelling in Jesuit schools. He received his undergraduate degree from Georgetown University in 1957 and his law degree from Harvard Law School in 1960, both with high honors.

After graduating from law school, he spent seven years practicing with a large law firm in Cleveland, Ohio, before entering academia. Justice Scalia taught at the University of Virginia School of Law from 1967-1971 and the University of Chicago School of Law from 1977-1982. In the interim, he held a series of increasingly important positions in the Nixon and Ford administrations: as General Counsel of the Office of Telecommunications Policy from 1971-1972, as Chairman of the Administrative Conference of the United States from 1972-1974, and as Assistant Attorney General for the Office of Legal Counsel from 1974-1977.

During his years in government and academia, Justice Scalia developed a strong reputation in conservative legal and political circles as an intellectual heavyweight who tenaciously advocated for his views. President Reagan appointed him to the United States Court of Appeals for the District of Columbia Circuit early in his first term and nominated him for the Supreme Court early in his second term. The nominee charmed the nation and the Senate, reveling in his Italian roots, displaying characteristic humor and charm, and demonstrating the power of his intellect; he was unanimously confirmed 98-0 and joined the Court on September 26, 1986.

---

11. *See* Nate Silver, *Supreme Court May Be the Most Conservative in History,* FiveThirtyEight, http://fivethirtyeight.blogs.nytimes.com/2012/03/29/supreme-court-may-be-most-conservative-in-modern-history, Mar. 29, 2012, 8:06 P.M.

Since joining the Court, Scalia has been the Court's most outspoken conservative, with heavy emphasis on both of those words. Substantively, he is a strong advocate of the position that statutes should be interpreted exclusively with regards to their text, going so far as to refuse to join any portion of a Court opinion that cites to legislative history.[12] In constitutional cases, he is a self-described "faint-hearted originalist," who believes that the Constitution is a fixed document whose content is set by the original popular meaning of its words but who admittedly shies away from the implications of this theory in a handful of areas where following it might disturb centuries of precedent or have other particularly unpalatable consequences. *See* Antonin Scalia, *Originalism: The Lesser Evil*, 57 U. Cinn. L. Rev. 849, 864 (1989). In structural matters involving issues of federalism and separation of powers, he has been a firm, though not absolute, vote in favor of imposing judicially enforced limits upon the federal legislative branch.

Justice Scalia has consistently taken strong rhetorical positions against expansive visions of the judicial role both in high-profile constitutional cases and in more technical cases involving questions of procedure and remedy. (Whether this rhetorical embrace of judicial restraint is matched by his actions is a question that divides commentators, largely along ideological lines.) An expert in administrative and regulatory law, Justice Scalia has developed his own jurisprudence in this area, offering an iconoclastic reading of the all-important *Chevron* doctrine, *see, e.g., United States v. Mead Corp.*, 533 U.S. 218, 239 (2001) (Scalia, J., dissenting), and sharply critiquing many aspects of the modern administrative state, albeit without significantly scaling back its constitutional license.

While broadly, and in many cases sharply, conservative, Justice Scalia's jurisprudence does not uniformly map onto the political platform of any modern party. He has, for example, been an occasional ally of criminal defendants, leading a left/right coalition (sometimes called the Court's "formalist" wing) that has reinvigorated the Sixth Amendment's Confrontation and Jury Trial Clauses[13] and offering occasional support for broader Fourth Amendment protections against illegal searches and seizures. He has also been a less reliable vote to strike down regulatory measures anathema to big business than some of his more pragmatic conservative colleagues, rejecting, for example, the notion that the Fifth Amendment's Due Process Clause bars "excessive" punitive damage awards. In one high-profile case challenging Congress's power to regulate homegrown marijuana under the Commerce Clause, *Gonzalez v. Raich*, 545 U.S. 1 (2005), Justice Scalia voted to uphold the law, breaking with the majority of his conservative colleagues and authoring a separate opinion, which suggests his vision of Congress's powers may be moderately broader than theirs (though his signing of—and likely authorship of—a strident joint dissent in the recent health care cases has obviously complicated this calculus).

Justice Scalia is probably as famous for his personality as for his views. He is by far the most voluble Justice at oral argument—interrupting advocates with whom he disagrees with acerbic questions, filling in missing arguments for advocates with whom he agrees, and cracking jokes at everyone's expense. He is equally strident

---

12. For the fullest explanation of his views on statutory and constitutional interpretation, see Antonin Scalia, *A Matter of Interpretation: Federal Courts and the Law* (1997).

13. On the Confrontation Clause, the key opinion is *Crawford v. Washington*, 541 U.S. 36 (2004). In the jury trial context, the crucial cases are *Apprendi v. New Jersey*, 530 U.S. 466 (2000); *Blakeley v. Washington*, 542 U.S. 296 (2004); and *United States v. Booker*, 543 U.S. 220 (2005).

in his opinions, mocking the views and occasionally the abilities of Justices with whom he disagrees. When on the losing side in a high-profile case, his dissents can become quite caustic.[14] While Justice Scalia has maintained some close relationships across the aisle while on the Court (he and Justice Ginsburg have long been close personal friends), his relentless public and private criticism has, according to many commentators, taken a toll on other crucial relationships (most notably with former Justice Sandra Day O'Connor), limiting his ability to build coalitions on the Court. Indeed, several court-watchers have gone so far as to suggest that Justice Scalia's intense criticism of Justice O'Connor is largely responsible for the Court's failure to overrule *Roe v. Wade*.[15]

3. Justice Anthony Kennedy

 Justice Kennedy was born in Sacramento, California, on July 23, 1936, the son of one of the California capital's leading lawyers and lobbyists. He received his undergraduate degree from Stanford University in 1958 and his law degree from Harvard Law School in 1961. Returning to California, he practiced briefly in San Francisco and then returned to Sacramento to take over his father's practice upon the elder Kennedy's sudden death. He practiced in Sacramento from 1963-1975; during almost all of that time, he also taught Constitutional Law at the University of the Pacific's McGeorge School of Law. During the mid-1970s, Kennedy assisted then-governor Ronald Reagan on a series of legal matters, impressing the governor and his staff, who in turn recommended him to President Gerald Ford, who promptly nominated him for a seat on the United States Court of Appeals for the Ninth Circuit. He took his seat in 1976 at the age of 39 and served for 12 years.

In 1987, after two prior nominees were defeated or forced to withdraw, President Reagan nominated Justice Kennedy for the high court. He was unanimously confirmed 97-0 and took office in February 1988. Justice Kennedy had developed a reputation on the Ninth Circuit as a moderately conservative jurist, and on the Supreme Court he has largely lived up to that reputation. In many significant areas of the law—including federalism, affirmative action, criminal procedure, and the Takings Clause—he has provided a crucial vote for the Court's conservative wing, helping to push the law to the right, albeit not always as far or as fast as some of his colleagues might have liked. He is widely reported to have been the primary author of the Court's per curiam opinion in *Bush v. Gore*, the much-discussed case that resolved the disputed 2000 Presidential election. *See, e.g.*, Jeffrey Toobin, *Too Close to Call* 264-65 (2011) (explaining that "the wording [of the opinion] was mostly Kennedy's"). Over the run of cases, he votes substantially more often with the Court's more conservative members; in recent terms, he has voted with Chief Justice Roberts more frequently than he has with any other member of the Court.

---

14. Identifying the sharpest, funniest, or most over-the-top Scalia dissent is a matter of personal taste. For a collection of candidates, already out-of-date, see Kevin A. Wing, *Scalia Dissents: Writings of the Supreme Court's Wittiest, Most Outspoken Justice* (2005).

15. For one scholar's assessment of these events and their implications, see Jeffrey Rosen, *The Supreme Court: The Personalities and Rivalries That Divided America* (2007).

Justice Kennedy's conservatism is occasionally reinforced, but more often undercut, by his other defining jurisprudential trait: a deep-seated commitment to protecting individual liberty, even when doing so requires expansive constitutional interpretation.[16] He is the member of the Court who votes most frequently in favor of claims that a government action violates the First Amendment's Free Speech Clause and the author of the Court's extremely controversial opinion in *Citizens United v. Fed. Election Commn.*, 558 U.S. 50 (2010), striking down restrictions on corporate campaign speech as violative of that provision. He is also the author of the Court's two significant gay and lesbian rights decisions, *Lawrence v. Texas*, 539 U.S. 558 (2003) and *Romer v. Evans*, 517 U.S. 620 (1996). On abortion, he has proven to be a crucial swing vote—overcoming initial skepticism to coauthor the Court's opinion in *Planned Parenthood v. Casey*, 505 U.S. 833 (1992) (upholding *Roe v. Wade*'s "core holding" while allowing for greater government regulation), only to later advocate for a particularly narrow reading of the right protected by the *Casey* opinion. He articulated his constitutional vision in a famous passage originally crafted for the *Casey* opinion, which has been both widely critiqued and widely applauded: "At the heart of liberty is the right to define one's own concept of existence, of meaning, of the universe, and of the mystery of human life. Belief about these matters could not define the attributes of personhood if they were formed under compulsion of the State." *Id.* at 851.

Since Justice Sandra Day O'Connor left the Court in 2006, Justice Kennedy has been the Court's unequivocal swing Justice, the fulcrum of power in most closely contested cases. In each of the full terms since Justice O'Connor left the Court, Justice Kennedy has been in the majority between 87 and 97 percent of the time, leading the Court each time but one in that category. In cases decided by a 5-4 vote, no Justice has been with the majority more often than Justice Kennedy in any term during this period. During October Term 2006, he was in the majority in a full 100 percent of the cases decided by a 5-4 vote.

Early in his career, Justice Kennedy developed a reputation as a judge who vacillated in his opinions and had a hard time making up his mind, an impression that he himself helped cultivate during a famous interview he gave the morning that the *Casey* decision came down. In recent years, as he has developed a distinctive voice in liberty cases, that criticism has died down, only to be replaced in some circles by suggestions that he enjoys the judicial role a bit too much.[17] Though that criticism may be unfair—and is any case too subjective to analyze—Justice Kennedy has certainly been an eager participant in off-the-court activities, addressing numerous professional associations and actively representing the American judiciary at a wide variety of international conferences and events.

---

16. Libertarians disagree among themselves as to whether to count Justice Kennedy among their members. *Compare* Randy Barnett, *Kennedy's Libertarian Revolution*, National Review, July 10, 2003, at 17 *with* Ilya Shapiro, *Book Review: A Faint-Hearted Libertarian at Best: The Sweet Mystery of Justice Anthony Kennedy*, 33 Harv. J.L. & Pub. Pol'y 333 (Winter 2010).

17. For a fascinating article that both documents in detail the criticisms of Justice Kennedy and submits them to critical analysis, see Douglas M. Parker, *Justice Kennedy: The Swing Voter & His Critics*, 11 Green Bag 2d 317 (2008).

4. Justice Clarence Thomas

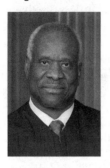

Justice Thomas was born in Pin Point, Georgia, near Savannah, on June 23, 1948. He was raised primarily by a strict and religious grandfather. He attended Immaculate Conception Seminary for a year, largely at his grandfather's insistence, before transferring to Holy Cross College, from which he received his undergraduate degree in 1971. He received his J.D. from Yale Law School in 1974 and then became an Assistant Attorney General for the State of Missouri from 1974-1977, working under future Senator John Danforth. He worked as an attorney for the Monsanto Company from 1977-1979, before returning to work for then-Senator Danforth as a Legislative Assistant from 1979-1981.

Thomas joined the Reagan administration in 1981, serving first as Assistant Secretary for Civil Rights at the U.S. Department of Education, and then for eight years as Chairman of the U.S. Equal Employment Opportunity Commission (EEOC). President George H.W. Bush appointed him to the United States Court of Appeals for the District of Columbia Circuit in 1990 and briefly considered him for a seat on the Supreme Court that same year. When Justice Thurgood Marshall, the Court's only African-American Justice retired the next year, President Bush surprised no one by nominating Thomas—the highest-ranking conservative African-American judge in the country—to fill the vacancy.

Thomas's appointment was controversial from the onset as critics raised concerns about his experience and his views. Thomas nonetheless seemed poised to win a close confirmation vote until allegations of sexual harassment of a former employee caused the Senate Judiciary Committee to schedule further proceedings. These contentious hearings concluded with a powerful statement by Justice Thomas proclaiming his innocence and expressing anger at the course of events. Without ever really resolving the truth of the allegations, the Senate voted to confirm Thomas 52-48, and he joined the Court in October 1991.

Since joining the Court, Justice Thomas has been a staunch member of the Court's conservative wing, consistently joining opinions enhancing federalism, accommodating religion, and rejecting constitutional claims brought by death row prisoners and other criminal defendants. He has strenuously advocated for the overturning of *Roe v. Wade* and dissented from the Court's decisions expanding the constitutional rights of gays and lesbians. In affirmative action cases, racial districting cases, and other cases involving the allegedly benign use of racial classifications by government bodies, Thomas has been a strong advocate for a color-blind Constitution, often focusing on the pernicious consequences even allegedly benign racial classification can have for racial minorities.

Justice Thomas has voted with Justice Scalia more often than with any other Justice, but he has deviated from his conservative counterpart in a number of ways, most significantly by rejecting Justice Scalia's "faint-hearted" originalism in favor of a more potent originalism committed to following the Constitution's original public meaning even if doing so requires the overruling of venerated precedents.[18] He has joined Justice Scalia in the great majority of decisions that have divided the Court

18. In recent years, many commentators on both the left and the right have begun to favorably compare Justice Thomas's abilities and principled jurisprudence to those of Justice Scalia. For one prominent example, see Mark Tushnet, *A Court Divided: The Rehnquist Court and the Future of Constitutional Law* 71-103 (2005).

along formalist vs. pragmatist lines, providing, for example, the crucial fifth vote in *Apprendi v. New Jersey*, 530 U.S. 466 (2000). Justice Thomas is significantly more likely than his conservative colleagues to vote to uphold state regulations challenged on preemption grounds (see, for example, *Wyeth v. Levine*, 555 U.S. 555 (2009)) and, perhaps influenced by his years at the EEOC, slightly more likely to vote in favor of a claim made by an employee against an employer (see, for example, *CSX Transport v. McBride*, 131 S. Ct. 2630 (2011)).

In recent years, Justice Thomas has received increasing attention for his unwillingness to speak in oral argument. In sharp contrast with his verbose colleagues who participate in almost every argument, Justice Thomas spoke rarely during his early years on the Court and has largely stopped speaking at all; as of May 2013, he has gone more than seven years since asking a question at oral argument (though he did interject a comment in January 2013). Over the years, he has offered different explanations for his silence, attributing it at various times to a childhood stutter that inculcated an appreciation for sitting quietly and listening, his own willingness to shun the spotlight combined with the skill of his colleagues in asking questions, and the belief that it is a waste of time to engage in banter with the litigants if a Justice has already developed an understanding of the legal principles necessary to resolve a dispute.

5. Justice Ruth Bader Ginsburg

Justice Ginsburg was born in Brooklyn, New York, on March 15, 1933. She received her B.A. from Cornell University in 1954, and then attended Harvard Law School for two years, where she excelled. When her husband graduated and accepted a job in New York, she transferred to Columbia Law School, from which she received her law degree in 1959, graduating first in her class. She had so impressed her professors at Harvard that they recommend her for a clerkship with Justice Felix Frankfurter. Though Frankfurter normally accepted their recommendations, he declined to hire Ginsburg, perhaps because he was not yet ready to work that closely with a woman.

Justice Ginsburg instead served as a law clerk for Judge Edmund Palmieri on the United States District Court for the Southern District of New York. After completing her clerkship, she joined academia, researching international civil procedure for two years as part of a Columbia University project, then serving as a Professor of Law at Rutgers University School of Law (1963-1972) and Columbia (1972-1980).

As a law professor, her academic specialty was civil procedure, but Justice Ginsburg gained greater notoriety as the first director of the American Civil Liberties Union's Women's Rights Project. In that role, she was instrumental in developing the legal strategy that resulted in the dismantling of a system of gender-based classifications that had limited women's civic participation for most of the nation's history. She personally argued six key cases before the Supreme Court, winning five.

President Jimmy Carter appointed her to the United States Court of Appeals for the District of Columbia Circuit in 1980. In her 13 years on that Court, Justice Ginsburg developed a reputation for moderation and close personal relationships with many of the judges on the court, including Antonin Scalia. In 1993, after a series of false starts, President Clinton nominated the 60-year-old Ginsburg to the high court. After confirmation hearings where she acquitted herself well but also exasperated some Senators with her insistence that many seemingly innocuous questions were off-limits, she was overwhelmingly confirmed 96-3, becoming the second woman to serve on the Court.

Since joining the Court, Justice Ginsburg has been a reliable member of the Court's more liberal wing, joining the Court's opinions expanding protection for gays and lesbians, maintaining the constitutionality of affirmative action, and curtailing the executive branch's authority to act unilaterally in fighting the so-called war on terror, while regularly dissenting in federalism, church and state, and criminal procedure cases. She has been a particular defender of women's rights and abortion rights, authoring, for example, the Court's 1996 opinion in *United States v. Virginia*, 518 U.S. 515 (1995), which came close to adopting strict scrutiny for gender classifications, and a stinging dissent from the Court's decision in *Gonzalez v. Carhart*, 550 U.S. 124 (2007), upholding a federal law barring certain late-term abortion procedures despite a five-year old precedent striking down a nearly identical state law.[19]

On issues like the Confrontation Clause and the Sixth Amendment right to a jury trial, Justice Ginsburg has been part of the "formalist" coalition of left- and right-wing Justices who have voted to expand constitutional protections. Though she is a reliable vote for the left in constitutional cases, she is—as one might expect—something of a stickler for procedure, and occasionally votes with the Court's more conservative members to strictly enforce time limits or other rules or to literally construe a statute. As the mother of an intellectual property professor and the long-time wife of one of the nation's elite tax lawyers, Justice Ginsburg has become, largely by default, one of the Court's leading voices in those areas.

With the retirement of Justice Stevens in 2010, Justice Ginsburg became the Court's oldest member. She has also survived two recent bouts with cancer and the loss in 2010 of her husband of 56 years. While those facts have combined to stir regular rumors of her retirement from the Court, Justice Ginsburg has asserted her inclination to remain in the job for at least a few more years and has, in many ways, seemed re-energized by the recent appointment to the Court of two like-minded female Justices.

6. Justice Stephen Breyer

Justice Breyer was born in San Francisco, California, on August 15, 1938, the son of a lawyer; he was raised in an affluent, politically active household. He received his undergraduate degree from Stanford University in 1959, was a Marshall Scholar at Oxford University from 1959-1961, and received his law degree from Harvard Law School in 1964. After graduating from law school, he served as a law clerk to Justice Arthur Goldberg and as a Special Assistant to the Assistant U.S. Attorney General for Antitrust from 1965-1967, before returning to Harvard as an assistant professor in 1967. Specializing in antitrust law, administrative law, and other regulatory fields, Breyer continued to teach at Harvard—first

---

19. For commentaries that emphasize the continuity between Justice Ginsburg's career as an advocate and her time as a Justice, see Tushnet, *A Court Divided*, 104-129; and Judith Baer, "Advocate on the Court: Ruth Bader Ginsburg and the Limits of Formal Equality," in *Rehnquist Justice: Understanding the Court Dynamic* 216-240 (Earl M. Maltz, ed., 2003).

as a full-time faculty member and then, after he joined the bench, as a lecturer—until 1994.

During his time on the Harvard faculty, Breyer took several leaves from teaching to work in government, serving as an assistant to the Watergate Special Prosecutor in 1973, as special counsel to a Senate Judiciary Committee subcommittee from 1974-1975, and as Chief Counsel to the full Judiciary Committee in 1979-1980. President Jimmy Carter nominated him to the United States Court of Appeals for the First Circuit in November 1980 during the last months of his term, and the Judiciary Committee rewarded him for his service by making him the last of President Carter's judicial nominees to win confirmation. He served on the First Circuit from 1980 until 1994, the last four years as Chief Justice. From 1985 to 1989, he was also a member of the United States Sentencing Commission; in that position, he played a leading role in developing and administering the new federal sentencing guidelines. After considering and rejecting him the prior year, President Clinton nominated Breyer to the Supreme Court in 1994. His nomination met with broad bipartisan approval, and he was confirmed by an 87-9 vote.

Since joining the Court, Justice Breyer has cultivated two somewhat contradictory images. On the one hand, he has been a fairly reliable member of the Court's left-of-center block, voting with the Court's other liberals on nearly every significant noncriminal constitutional issue, writing an important (though since limited) opinion in *Stenberg v. Carhart*, 530 U.S. 914 (2000) broadly construing *Casey*'s protection of a right to abortion, and dissenting sharply from the bench in the *Seattle Schools* case. He has also attempted to claim intellectual leadership of the Court's left wing, writing several books meant to offer an alternative to Justice Scalia's theories of statutory and constitutional interpretation.[20] His extrajudicial writing focuses on the idea that the Constitution is designed to protect "active liberty"—the ability of citizens to come together to collectively solve problems and pursue the public welfare—and ought to be interpreted so as to facilitate that project.

On the other hand, Justice Breyer can also be a cautious, technocratic judge, writing moderate opinions that reflect his prior scholarship and forming coalitions with Justices across the proverbial aisle. He is the leader of the Court's so-called pragmatic wing, offering spirited opposition to the Court's expansion of criminal defendants' rights under the Sixth Amendment and taking particular umbrage at the Court's decisions declaring substantial portions of federal and state sentencing guidelines unconstitutional. In general, he is less sympathetic to the rights of criminal defendants than his usual liberal allies, adopting narrower views of the available protections in the Fourth Amendment context as well. He is also somewhat less sympathetic to free speech claims than many of his colleagues, voting in some cases to uphold well-intentioned regulatory schemes that arguably limit constitutionally protected expression. *See, e.g., Brown v. Entertainment Merchants Association*, 131 S. Ct. 2729 (2011) (dissenting from opinion striking down California's ban on sales of violent video games to minors).

During oral arguments, Justice Breyer is the absentminded professor of the Court, asking long, complicated, hypothetical questions that at times cut to the heart of the case and at other times serve only to confuse the advocates. His writing style is also distinctive, in that he eschews footnotes almost entirely, instead relying

---

20. *See* Stephen Breyer, *Making Our Democracy Work: A Judge's View* (2010); Stephen Breyer, *Active Liberty: Interpreting Our Democratic Constitution* (2005).

heavily on long appendixes overflowing with legislative testimony and social science data. Despite his scholarly bent, Justice Breyer is one of the Court's most sociable Justices, a trait that has helped him nurture relationships with the Court's swing Justices, particularly now-retired Justice Sandra Day O'Connor.

7. Justice Samuel Alito

Justice Alito was born in Trenton, New Jersey, on April 1, 1950, the son of a longtime state government official and a school-teacher. He graduated from Princeton University and Yale Law School before embarking on a distinguished legal career entirely in federal governmental service. After graduating from law school, he returned to New Jersey and served as a law clerk for Judge Leonard Garth of the United States Court of Appeals for the Third Circuit from 1976-1977 and in the United States Attorney's Office for the District of New Jersey from 1977-1981.

After the election of Ronald Reagan, he moved to Washington and worked as an Assistant to the Solicitor General and as a Deputy Assistant Attorney General. Having impressed his superiors with both his skills and his conservatism, Alito was sent back to New Jersey six years later to lead the United States Attorney's office for which he had once worked and, in 1990, was appointed a judge on the court for which he had once clerked. Judge Alito served on the Third Circuit for 16 years, developing a reputation as an excellent judge, a friendly person, and a rock-solid conservative vote. When a vacancy on the Supreme Court opened in 2006, Judge Alito impressed President George W. Bush in his interview but lost out to fellow Reagan Administration alum John Roberts. However, the death of Chief Justice William Rehnquist soon created a second vacancy, which President Bush eventually turned to Judge Alito to fill after an ill-fated attempt to nominate White House Counsel Harriet Miers. Judge Alito's nomination drew some sharp objection from Democratic Senators and liberal commentators who were worried about the effect his appointment would have on the balance of power within the Court. Buoyed on the margins by the genuine affection he elicited from some of his more liberal colleagues and former clerks, Judge Alito was confirmed 58-42.

Since joining the Court, Justice Alito has been the reliable conservative vote that his record suggested. During his first full term on the Court, Justice Alito provided the decisive fifth vote in *Gonzalez v. Carhart*, 550 U.S. 124 (2007), to effectively overturn a recent precedent striking down a ban on particular late-term abortion procedures. Since then, he has cast crucial votes to overturn campaign finance laws, to limit the use of racial preferences in school assignments, and to recognize a potent individual right under the Second Amendment. He has also become probably the Court's most consistent vote against claims that police and prosecutors violated the rights of criminal defendants. Indeed, his deference to governmental action transcends the criminal law. Like Justice Breyer, he appears to have a basic trust in government that manifests itself in a variety of contexts, most notably in the First Amendment area, where he has cast several lone votes to uphold regulatory schemes targeting particularly unpleasant categories of speech. *See, e.g., Snyder v. Phelps*, 131 S. Ct. 1207 (2011) (dissenting alone from decision protecting funeral protestors from state tort liability); *United States v. Stevens*, 130 S. Ct. 1577 (2010) (dissenting alone from decision striking down federal law prohibiting videos that depict animal cruelty).

By all reports, Justice Alito lived up to his reputation in his first few years on the Court, making friends across the political spectrum and projecting an image of moderation. Over the last few terms, however, Justice Alito's relationship with the Court's left wing appears to have become a little more tense, as the strains of consistent high-stakes disagreements have begun to take their toll. In 2010, Justice Alito also garnered substantial press attention when he mouthed "not true" during the State of the Union address in response to President Obama's criticism of the Court's controversial decision in *Citizens United v. Fed. Election Commn.*, 558 U.S. 50 (2010).

8. Justice Sonia Sotomayor

Justice Sotomayor was born in the Bronx, New York, on June 25, 1954 and raised in a working-class Latino family. Her father died when she was nine, leaving the family under constant financial stress. She excelled in Catholic school, earning scholarships to Princeton University (from which she earned her undergraduate degree summa cum laude in 1976) and Yale Law School (from which she earned her law degree in 1979). After graduation, she served as an Assistant District Attorney in the New York County District Attorney's Office from 1979-1984 and as a commercial litigator at a small New York firm from 1984-1992. In 1991, President George H.W. Bush nominated her to the United States District Court for the Southern District of New York, where she served for six years, adjudicating a wide variety of criminal and civil matters including the case that ended the 1995 Major League Baseball work stoppage. President Clinton appointed her to the United States Court of Appeals for the Second Circuit in 1998, and she was confirmed a year later, after a delay precipitated by concerns that she was being groomed for a seat on the Supreme Court. She served on the Court of Appeals for slightly more than a decade, developing a reputation as an excellent judge but making no particular jurisprudential mark.

When Justice David Souter announced his retirement in 2009, Justice Sotomayor was widely considered the favorite for the seat. Both her nomination and her confirmation stirred up a moderate amount of controversy, as intra-party rivals and political opponents took to the press with a variety of concerns, on matters ranging from her temperament to her ideology. After some relatively contentious hearings, Judge Sotomayor was confirmed by a comfortable but not overwhelming 68-31 vote and took her seat in August 2009.

Since joining the Court, Justice Sotomayor—like most of her recent predecessors—has largely lived up to the expectations of her supporters and opponents. She has been a reliable member of the Court's left-leaning bloc, voting with each of Justices Stevens, Ginsburg, Breyer, and Kagan at least 80 percent of the time in each term and often much more frequently. Though occasionally breaking from some or all of them in a low-profile case, she has not yet done so in any of the Court's more hotly contested cases. Contrary to some preappointment speculation, the former prosecutor has not shown any special solicitude for the state in criminal cases; indeed, her highest profile majority opinion to date, *J.D.B. v. North Carolina*, 131 S. Ct. 2394 (2011), was a 5-4 decision requiring courts to take into account the youth of suspects when determining whether they voluntarily consented to police interrogation.

By all reports, Justice Sotomayor has hit the ground running as a Justice. She has been one of the more active Justices in oral argument, trailing only Justice Scalia and occasionally Justice Breyer in this department.[21] Her experience as the only former District Judge on the Court has served her well, providing useful real-world knowledge about trial-level litigation and procedure. She is yet to author an especially high-profile majority opinion but has been the author of several powerful dissents on significant issues. *See, e.g., Berghuis v. Thompkins,* 130 S. Ct. 2250 (2010) (contesting what dissenters considered to be a substantial rollback of the protections afforded under *Miranda*).

9. Justice Elena Kagan

Justice Kagan was born in New York, New York, on April 28, 1960, the child of a lawyer and a teacher. Like most of her colleagues, she was an academic superstar, earning her bachelor's degree summa cum laude from Princeton University in 1981, her master's of philosophy from Oxford University in 1983, and her law degree magna cum laude from Harvard Law School in 1986. After law school, she clerked for Judge Abner Mikva of the United States Court of Appeals for the District of Columbia Circuit and Justice Thurgood Marshall. She then worked briefly in private practice before joining the faculty of University of Chicago Law School in 1991, where she specialized in constitutional and administrative law. From 1995-1999, she served in the Clinton administration in both law and policy positions. In 1999, President Clinton nominated the 39-year old Kagan to a vacant seat on the D.C. Circuit but, as with John Roberts, the Senate never acted on the nomination.

She joined Harvard Law School as a visiting professor in 1999 and became a professor of law in 2001. Two years later, she was appointed the school's Dean. During her time as Dean at Harvard, Justice Kagan won widespread praise for working well with colleagues of all political stripes, for breaking a hiring logjam and recruiting dozens of new faculty members, and for making the law school more responsive to students' needs.

Despite her lack of judicial experience, Dean Kagan was frequently mentioned as a possible Supreme Court candidate during the run-up to the 2008 presidential election. After the election, President Obama nominated her to serve as Solicitor General of the United States, the nation's top appellate advocate. After she had served a year in that role, President Obama nominated her to the Supreme Court in 2010. Like Justice Sotomayor, her hearings were moderately contentious, as political opponents raised questions about her lack of political philosophy, her lack of judicial experience, and the large number of cases she would initially have to recuse herself from because of her service as Solicitor General. She was confirmed on a largely 63-37 party-line vote and joined the Court in August 2010.

In her first two terms on the Court, Justice Kagan has proven to be a reliable ally for Justices Ginsburg, Breyer, and Sotomayor, voting with each well over 80 percent of the time and with Justice Sotomayor approximately 90 percent of the time. She has also proven herself to be a deft writer, authoring several pointed dissenting opinions that earned substantial attention during the last days of the 2010-2011 term, including public praise from Justice Ginsburg, who called them "powerful"

---

21. As of 2010, data on oral argument participation is now part of the SCOTUSblog "Statpack," available at http://www.scotusblog.com/reference/stat-pack.

and "forceful." During the closing days of the 2012 term, she issued her first significant majority opinion in *Miller v. Alabama*, 132 S. Ct. 2455 (2012), concluding that the Eighth Amendment prohibits a sentencing scheme that imposes mandatory sentences of life in prison without parole on juveniles convicted of homicide. Those opinions and the leading role that she has played during oral arguments in some of the Court's most politically charged cases have fueled speculation—admittedly premature—that she is poised to become the intellectual leader of the Court's more liberal wing.[22]

22. The notable dissents from her first term are *Arizona Christian School Tuition Organization v. Winn*, 131 S. Ct. 1436, 1450 (2011) (Kagan, J., dissenting) and *Arizona Free Enterprise Institute v. Bennett*, 131 S. Ct. 2806, 2829 (2011) (Kagan, J., dissenting). Justice Ginsburg offered her comments in praise of Justice Kagan's first term in several public speeches, including a speech entitled "A Survey of the 2010 Term for presentation to the Otsego County Bar Association Cooperstown Country Club, July 22, 2011," available at http://www.supremecourt.gov/publicinfo/speeches/viewspeeches.aspx?Filename=sp_07-22-11.html. *See also* Joan Biskupic, *Analysis, Justice Kagan—Giving Liberals a Rhetorical Lift*, Reuters, Apr. 26, 2012.

3

Jurisdiction

Although the United States Supreme Court sits atop the U.S. court system, the Court is in one way just like any other federal court: It is a court of limited jurisdiction. An understanding of the Court's jurisdiction is helpful to understanding the Court and practicing before it.

This chapter explores the Court's jurisdiction in three steps. Section A briefly reviews how Article III distributes the Court's jurisdiction between original and appellate jurisdictions. Section B explores the Court's original jurisdiction with the primary aim of illuminating its purpose and continued significance. Section C explores the Court's appellate jurisdiction, in which role the Court indeed serves as the capstone of the U.S. judicial system.

A. ARTICLE III'S DISTRIBUTION OF ORIGINAL AND APPELLATE JURISDICTION TO THE COURT *original & appellate jurisdiction*

Article III of the United States Constitution defines the extent of federal judicial power and distributes that power between the Court's original jurisdiction and its appellate jurisdiction. An understanding of Article III's distribution scheme is helpful even if your study of the Court focuses on its appellate jurisdiction. This section briefly examines that distribution scheme.

Section 1 of Article III vests the "judicial Power of the United States" in "one supreme Court, and in such inferior Courts as the Congress may from time to time ordain and establish." Section 2 of Article III, in the first clause, extends the judicial power of the United States to nine types of cases and controversies, which are called the nine "heads" of federal jurisdiction. The first clause states:

Section 2. [Clause 1:] The judicial Power shall extend to all Cases, in Law and Equity, arising under this Constitution, the Laws of the United States, and Treaties made, or which shall be made, under their Authority;—to all Cases affecting Ambassadors, other public Ministers and Consuls;—to all Cases of admiralty and maritime Jurisdiction;—to Controversies to which the United States shall be a Party;—to Controversies between two or more States;—between a State and Citizens of another State;—between Citizens of different States;—between Citizens of the same State claiming Lands under Grants of different States, and between a State, or the Citizens thereof, and foreign States, Citizens or Subjects.

9 HEADS OF FED JURISDICTION

93

The second clause of Section 2 divides cases between the United States Supreme Court's original jurisdiction and its appellate jurisdiction:

[handwritten: ORIGINAL V. APPELLATE JURISDICTION]

> Section 2. . . . [Clause 2:] In all Cases affecting Ambassadors, other public Ministers and Consuls, and those in which a State shall be Party, the supreme Court shall have original Jurisdiction. In all the other Cases before mentioned, the supreme Court shall have appellate Jurisdiction, both as to Law and Fact, with such Exceptions, and under such Regulations as the Congress shall make.

The judicial power granted in the first clause of Section 2 is restricted by the Eleventh Amendment, which provides:

> AMENDMENT XI.
>   The Judicial power of the United States shall not be construed to extend to any suit in law or equity, commenced or prosecuted against one of the United States by Citizens of another State, or by Citizens or Subjects of any Foreign State.

These constitutional provisions have been implemented by statute, and both the constitutional provisions and the implementing statutes have been construed by the Court. The resulting law governing the Court's jurisdiction is explored in the next sections, which respectively examine the Court's original and appellate jurisdiction.

B. ORIGINAL JURISDICTION

The material in this section illuminates the scope, purpose, and modern significance of the Court's original jurisdiction. The section begins by discussing the statute and Court Rule governing the Court's original jurisdiction. Then it excerpts the most famous case in which the Court has held that it lacked original jurisdiction: *Marbury v. Madison*. Thereafter, the material is organized by the party alignment of cases in which the Court has discussed the scope of its original jurisdiction:

[handwritten: → only category of exclusive OG jurisdiction]

1. Controversies between two or more states.
2. Actions by the United States against a state.
3. Actions by a foreign state against a state.
4. Actions by a Native American tribe against a state.
5. Actions by a state against a citizen of another state.

Of these five categories of cases, the most important category is the first: Controversies between two or more states. Interstate disputes are the only category in which the Court's original jurisdiction is exclusive, and they account for the vast majority of cases over which the Court exercises original jurisdiction today.

1. Statute and Court Rule

a. Statute

28 U.S.C. §1251. Original jurisdiction

(a) The Supreme Court shall have original and exclusive jurisdiction of all controversies between two or more States.

(b) The Supreme Court shall have original but not exclusive jurisdiction of:

(1) All actions or proceedings to which ambassadors, other public ministers, consuls, or vice consuls of foreign states are parties;

(2) All controversies between the United States and a State;

(3) All actions or proceedings by a State against the citizens of another State or against aliens.

Notes and Questions

1. Article III's grant of original jurisdiction to the Court is self-executing. *See, e.g., Kentucky v. Dennison*, 65 U.S. (24 How.) 66, 74 (1860). This means that the Court could have exercised its original jurisdiction even if Congress had not enacted implementing legislation. In any event, Congress enacted legislation implementing the Court's original jurisdiction in the first Judiciary Act. *See* Act of Sept. 24, 1789, §13, ch. 20, 1 Stat. 73, 80-81. What do you think would have happened if Congress had not enacted implementing legislation?

2. The statutes implementing the Court's original jurisdiction have always provided that some of its original jurisdiction is not exclusive. The Court has upheld Congress's power to make portions of the Court's original jurisdiction nonexclusive. *Ames v. Kansas*, 111 U.S. 449 (1884); *Bors v. Preston*, 111 U.S. 252 (1884). As you study the material in this chapter, consider why the current statute gives the Court exclusive jurisdiction over controversies between two or more states but only concurrent jurisdiction over other cases within its original jurisdiction.

3. The Court discussed the purpose of the Court's original jurisdiction in *Ames v. Kansas*:

> The evident purpose was to open and keep open the highest court of the nation for the determination, in the first instance, of suits involving a state or a diplomatic or commercial representative of a foreign government. So much was due to the rank and dignity of those for whom the provision was made.

111 U.S. at 464; *see also The Federalist No. 81*, at 487 (Alexander Hamilton) (Clinton Rossiter ed. 1961) (Court's original jurisdiction over cases to which states were parties reflected that "it would ill suit [a state's] dignity to be turned over to an inferior [federal] tribunal"; Court's original jurisdiction over cases affecting foreign envoys reflected that those cases were often connected with "public peace" and that envoys were entitled to "respect").

The Court has heard many original jurisdiction cases to which a state was a party. In contrast, the Court has not exercised original jurisdiction over actions affecting foreign envoys since its early days, and then only in two cases. *See* Vincent L. McKusick, *Discretionary Gatekeeping: The Supreme Court's Management of Its Original Jurisdiction Docket since 1961*, 45 Maine L. Rev. 185, 187 (1993). The paucity of foreign envoy cases partly reflects that diplomatic immunity bars many actions against foreign envoys. *See* 22 U.S.C. §254d. Moreover, the Court's original jurisdiction over actions involving foreign envoys is concurrent with that of the federal district courts. 28 U.S.C. §§1251(b)(1) & 1351.

4. You may have noticed that 28 U.S.C. §1251 defines the Court's original jurisdiction solely by reference to the parties to the suit, and without reference to the subject matter of the suit. Indeed, the Court has not construed its original jurisdiction as extending to any case based solely on its subject matter. For example, it appears that the Court would not construe its original jurisdiction to extend to a suit by a state against one of its own citizens, even if the suit arose under federal law and even though Article III, §2, clause 2 gives the Court original jurisdiction over cases to which a state is a party. Does the exclusion of such a case from the Court's original jurisdiction accord with your reading of the relevant portions of Article III?

5. Today the Court's original docket is small, with no more than three or four original jurisdiction cases pending on the docket at any one time. *See, e.g., The Supreme Court—The Statistics*, 125 Harv. L. Rev. 362, 369 Table II.A (2011) (reporting that during the October 2010 Term, two original jurisdiction cases were disposed of, and two remained on the docket).

b. Court Rule

The Court's Rule 17 governs the procedures in original cases. At this point please read Rule 17, which you will find in Appendix B.

Notes and Questions

1. Rule 17.3 requires the party seeking to file an original action first to move for leave to file the action. Rule 17.3 thus reflects the Court's view that its original jurisdiction is discretionary, a view most famously associated with a decision excerpted later in this chapter: *Ohio v. Wyandotte Chemicals Corp.*, 401 U.S. 493 (1971). Although Rule 17 does not address the Court's internal process for deciding whether to grant a motion for leave to file an original action, the leading authority on practice before the Court states that "[t]he vote of a majority of the participating Justices is required" to grant the motion for leave to file. Eugene Gressman et al., *Supreme Court Practice: For Practice in the Supreme Court of the United States* 634 (9th ed. 2007).

2. If the Court grants leave to file, the Court usually appoints a special master to the case. The Court typically authorizes the special master to take evidence on factual matters; make recommendations on motions; and, ultimately, to recommend findings of fact, conclusions of law, and final decrees. The special master reports on these matters to the Court. The parties may file exceptions and objections to the special master's reports; the parties may also file briefs and present oral argument to the Court. The Court is thus ordinarily in the position of reviewing the special master's work, though the Court retains complete authority to decide all issues and render the final decree. *See* Gressman et al., *supra* note 1, at 642-645. The Court's practice of appointing special masters dates back to the early twentieth century (before which time the Court employed commissions or commissioners for similar duties). *See* Anne-Marie C. Carstens, *Lurking in the Shadows of Judicial Process: Special Masters in the Supreme Court's Original Jurisdiction Cases*, 86 Minn. L. Rev. 625, 644 (2001). One notable characteristic of special masters is that, with apparently only one exception, all have been men. *See id.* at 628 n.13.[1] Why do you suppose that is? We further explore the issue of diversity on the Court in Chapter 8.

---

1. A Westlaw search using a phrase that seems to appear in all Court orders appointing special masters—that is, "appointed special master"—discloses only one order appointing a special master who (1) had a name traditionally given more often to women than men and (2) upon research turned out indeed to be a woman. *See South Carolina v. North Carolina*, 552 U.S. 1160 (2008).

2. *Marbury v. Madison*

We included an excerpt of *Marbury v. Madison*, 5 U.S. (1 Cranch) 137 (1803), in material in Chapter 1 on the role of a supreme court. Now we reproduce the portion of *Marbury* addressing whether the Court had original jurisdiction over Marbury's suit. This portion of the opinion has significance because of its discussion of (1) the scope of the Court's original jurisdiction; (2) Congress's lack of power to add to the Court's original jurisdiction; and (3) the meaning of "appellate jurisdiction."

Marbury v. Madison

5 U.S. (1 Cranch) 137 (1803)

Opinion of the Court.

At the last term on the affidavits then read and filed with the clerk, a rule was granted in this case, requiring the Secretary of State to shew cause why a mandamus should not issue, directing him to deliver to William Marbury his commission as a justice of the peace for the county of Washington, in the district of Columbia.

No cause has been shewn, and the present motion is for a mandamus. . . .

This . . . is a plain case for a mandamus, either to deliver the commission, or a copy of it from the record; and it only remains to be inquired,

Whether it can issue from this court.

The act to establish the judicial courts of the United States authorizes the Supreme Court "to issue writs of mandamus, in cases warranted by the principles and usages of law, to any courts appointed, or persons holding office, under the authority of the United States." [Quoting Judiciary Act of 1789, ch. 20, §13, 1 Stat. 81.]

The Secretary of State, being a person holding an office under the authority of the United States, is precisely within the letter of the description; and if this court is not authorized to issue a writ of mandamus to such an officer, it must be because the law is unconstitutional, and therefore absolutely incapable of conferring the authority, and assigning the duties which its words purport to confer and assign.

The [C]onstitution vests the whole judicial power of the United States in one Supreme Court, and such inferior courts as [C]ongress shall, from time to time, ordain and establish. This power is expressly extended to all cases arising under the laws of the United States; and consequently, in some form, may be exercised over the present case; because the right claimed is given by a law of the United States.

In the distribution of this power it is declared that "the Supreme Court shall have original jurisdiction in all cases affecting ambassadors, other public ministers and consuls, and those in which a state shall be a party. In all other cases, the Supreme Court shall have appellate jurisdiction."

It has been insisted, at the bar, that as the original grant of jurisdiction, to the supreme and inferior courts, is general, and the clause, assigning original jurisdiction to the Supreme Court, contains no negative or restrictive words; the power remains to the legislature, to assign original jurisdiction to that court in other cases than those specified in the article which has been recited; provided those cases belong to the judicial power of the United States.

If it had been intended to leave it in the discretion of the legislature to apportion the judicial power between the supreme and inferior courts according to the will of that body, it would certainly have been useless to have proceeded further than to have defined the judicial power, and the tribunals in which it should be vested. The subsequent part of the section is mere surplusage, is entirely without meaning, if such is to be the construction. If [C]ongress remains at liberty to give this court appellate jurisdiction, where the constitution has declared their jurisdiction shall be original; and original jurisdiction where the [C]onstitution has declared it shall be appellate; the distribution of jurisdiction, made in the constitution, is form without substance.

Affirmative words are often, in their operation, negative of other objects than those affirmed; and in this case, a negative or exclusive sense must be given to them or they have no operation at all.

It cannot be presumed that any clause in the constitution is intended to be without effect; and therefore such a construction is inadmissible, unless the words require it.

If the solicitude of the convention, respecting our peace with foreign powers, induced a provision that the supreme court should take original jurisdiction in cases which might be supposed to affect them; yet the clause would have proceeded no further than to provide for such cases, if no further restriction on the powers of [C]ongress had been intended. That they should have appellate jurisdiction in all other cases, with such exceptions as [C]ongress might make, is no restriction; unless the words be deemed exclusive of original jurisdiction.

When an instrument organizing fundamentally a judicial system, divides it into one supreme, and so many inferior courts as the legislature may ordain and establish; then enumerates its powers, and proceeds so far to distribute them, as to define the jurisdiction of the supreme court by declaring the cases in which it shall take original jurisdiction, and that in others it shall take appellate jurisdiction; the plain import of the words seems to be, that in one class of cases its jurisdiction is original, and not appellate; in the other it is appellate, and not original. If any other construction would render the clause inoperative, that is an additional reason for rejecting such other construction, and for adhering to their obvious meaning.

To enable this court then to issue a mandamus, it must be shewn to be an exercise of appellate jurisdiction, or to be necessary to enable them to exercise appellate jurisdiction.

It has been stated at the bar that the appellate jurisdiction may be exercised in a variety of forms, and that if it be the will of the legislature that a mandamus should be used for that purpose, that will must be obeyed. This is true, yet the jurisdiction must be appellate, not original.

It is the essential criterion of appellate jurisdiction, that it revises and corrects the proceedings in a cause already instituted, and does not create that cause. Although, therefore, a mandamus may be directed to courts, yet to issue such a writ to an officer for the delivery of a paper, is in effect the same as to sustain an original action for that paper, and therefore seems not to belong to appellate, but to original jurisdiction. Neither is it necessary in such a case as this, to enable the court to exercise its appellate jurisdiction.

The authority, therefore, given to the Supreme Court, by the act establishing the judicial courts of the United States, to issue writs of mandamus to public officers, appears not to be warranted by the [C]onstitution. . . .

. . . [A] law repugnant to the [C]onstitution is void; and . . . courts, as well as other departments, are bound by that instrument.

The rule must be discharged.

Notes and Questions

1. Modern readers of Article III may wonder whether Marbury or Madison qualified as "public Ministers" under the language in Article III, §2, clause 2, giving the Court original jurisdiction over "all Cases affecting Ambassadors, other public Ministers and Consuls." The answer is no: The Court in a later case held that the quoted phrase encompasses only representatives of foreign countries, not U.S. officials. *See* Ex parte *Gruber*, 269 U.S. 302, 303 (1925).

2. The Court held in *Marbury* that Congress cannot add to the Court's original jurisdiction. Does the Court's reasoning imply that Congress also cannot *restrict* the Court's original jurisdiction?

Whatever *Marbury* may imply, the Court in later cases has suggested that Congress cannot restrict the Court's original jurisdiction. For example, in *California v. Arizona*, 440 U.S. 59 (1979), the Court interpreted a federal statute to avoid "a grave constitutional question" that would arise if the statute were interpreted to restrict the Court's original jurisdiction. *Id.* at 65; *see also id.* at 66 (calling it "extremely doubtful" that Congress could restrict the Court's original jurisdiction to prevent it from hearing California's action). The text of Article III probably provides the strongest basis for doubting Congress's power to restrict the Court's original jurisdiction: Article III allows Congress to regulate and create exceptions to the Court's *appellate* jurisdiction but has no similar provision applicable to the Court's *original* jurisdiction.

3. Like the writ of mandamus sought in *Marbury*, a writ of habeas corpus is directed to a nonjudicial officer—namely, to the custodian of the person who is challenging his or her custody by seeking the writ. Even so, the Court has held that an application to the Court for an original writ of habeas corpus invokes the Court's appellate jurisdiction when it seeks review of a lower court's decision putting the challenger in custody. *See* Ex parte *Bollman*, 8 U.S. (4 Cranch) 75, 101 (1807). The Court's continuing authority to issue an original writ of habeas corpus is reflected in current statutes. *See* 28 U.S.C. §§2241(a) & 2254(a). The Court's rules, however, emphasize that an original writ of habeas corpus is "rarely granted." U.S. Supreme Court Rule 20.4(a); *see also Felker v. Turpin*, 518 U.S. 651 (1996) (holding that Antiterrorism and Effective Death Penalty Act of 1996 did not preclude Court's consideration of application for original writ of habeas but does affect standards governing granting of such relief to state prisoners).

3. Controversies Between Two or More States

Both historically and today, controversies between two or more states constitute the largest and most important category of original jurisdiction cases. The material below explores the history and scope of the Court's original jurisdiction over these interstate controversies and the discretion the Court exercises in determining when it will exercise its original jurisdiction over them.

Charles Warren, The Supreme Court and Sovereign States

31-33 (Princeton ed. 1924)

The Virginia delegation to the Federal Convention had traits of the diplomats of Great Britain; they arrived on the field first, and they brought with them a fully developed plan for a Constitution. Hence, naturally, it was their plan (probably drafted by James Madison and presented by Governor Edmund Randolph) which became the basis of the final draft of the Constitution. From the clause, which it contained, providing for a Supreme Court with jurisdiction to determine questions "which may involve the national peace and harmony," there was developed Article III of the Constitution as finally adopted, setting forth more specifically the various controversies over which the Court should have jurisdiction—and thus there appeared, for the first time in history, the provision for a permanent Supreme Court with compulsory jurisdiction over "controversies between two or more States."

"And now is accomplished," said James Wilson in the Pennsylvania Convention, "what the great mind of Henry IV had in contemplation—a system of government for large and respectable dominions, united and bound together in peace, under a superintending head by which all their differences may be accommodated without the destruction of the human race."

. . . Never before in history had there existed a Court with the powers which this new tribunal was to exercise. For the first time, there now came into existence a permanent Court, which should have the power to summon before it sovereign States in dispute and to determine their respective rights by a judgment which should be enforceable against them.

Such a Court . . . is the cement which has fixed firm the whole Federal structure. Or, to change the metaphor and to use Jefferson's quaint words: "They are setting up a kite to keep the henyard in order."

Undoubtedly, the idea of such a Court is traceable somewhat to the familiarity of the Colonists with the various political and judicial committees of the British Privy Council, which had in the past given advisory opinions to the King in settlement of boundary and territorial disputes between the Colonies. . . .

Though the homely prophesy made by Francis Hopkinson that, "no sooner will the chicken be hatched but everyone will be for plucking a feather," was fulfilled by the immediate and widespread assault which was made upon every other part of the Constitution, it is to be especially noted that the clause which gave jurisdiction to the Supreme Court over controversies between the States of the new Union received not a breath of opposition. The reason for this was the realization by the States of the danger that lay in any less vigorous expedient. As to this part of the Constitution certainly, the words of John Quincy Adams may be truly applied, that it was "wrung from a reluctant people by grinding necessity." . . .

Rhode Island v. Massachusetts

37 U.S. 657 (1838)

Mr. Justice BALDWIN delivered the Opinion of the Court:

. . . [Rhode Island filed an original action asking the Court to resolve a boundary dispute with Massachusetts.] [T]he case is now before us for consideration, on a motion by the defendant, to dismiss the bill for want of jurisdiction in the cause. . . .

That it is a controversy between two states, cannot be denied; and though the Constitution does not, in terms, extend the judicial power to all controversies between two or more states, yet it in terms excludes none, whatever may be their nature or subject. It is, therefore, a question of construction, whether the controversy in the present case is within the grant of judicial power. . . .

. . . It is a part of the public history of the United States, of which we cannot be judicially ignorant, that at the adoption of the Constitution, there were existing controversies between eleven states respecting their boundaries, which arose under their respective charters, and had continued from the first settlement of the colonies. . . . With the full knowledge that there were at its adoption, not only existing controversies between two states singly, but between one state and two others, we find the words of the Constitution applicable to this state of things, "controversies between two or more states." It is not known that there were any such controversies then existing, other than those which relate to boundary; and it would be a most forced construction to hold that these were excluded from judicial cognizance, and that it was to be confined to controversies to arise prospectively on other subjects. This becomes the more apparent, when we consider the context and those parts of the Constitution which bear directly on the boundaries of states; by which it is evident, that there remained no power in the contending states to settle a controverted boundary between themselves, as states competent to act by their own authority on the subject matter, or in any department of the government, if it was not in this.

By the first clause of the tenth section of the first article of the Constitution, there was a positive prohibition against any state entering into "any treaty, alliance, or confederation[";] no power under the government could make such an act valid, or dispense with the constitutional prohibition. In the next clause is a prohibition against any state entering "into any agreement or compact with another state, or with a foreign power, without the consent of Congress; or engaging in war, unless actually invaded, or in imminent danger, admitting of no delay." By this surrender of the power, which before the adoption of the Constitution was vested in every state, of settling these contested boundaries, as in the plenitude of their sovereignty they might; they could settle them neither by war, or in peace, by treaty, compact or agreement, without the permission of the new legislative power which the states brought into existence by their respective and several grants in conventions of the people. . . .

In looking to the practical construction of this clause of the Constitution, . . . it is most manifest . . . the words "agreement" and "compact," are construed to include those which relate to boundary. . . .

Every reason which has led to this construction, applies with equal force to the clause granting to the judicial power jurisdiction over controversies between states, as to that clause which relates to compacts and agreements. . . . Bound hand and foot by the prohibitions of the Constitution, a complaining state can neither treat, agree, or fight with its adversary, without the consent of congress: a resort to the judicial power is the only means left for legally adjusting, or persuading a state which has possession of disputed territory, to enter into an agreement or compact, relating to a controverted boundary. Few, if any, will be made, when it is left to the pleasure of the state in possession; but when it is known that some tribunal can decide on the right, it is most probable that controversies will be settled by compact.

There can be but two tribunals under the Constitution who can act on the boundaries of states, the legislative or the judicial power; the former is limited in express terms to assent or dissent, where a compact or agreement is referred to them by the states; and as the latter can be exercised only by this Court, when a state is a party, the power is here, or it cannot exist. For these reasons we cannot be persuaded that it could have been intended to provide only for the settlement of boundaries, when states could agree; and to altogether withhold the power to decide controversies on which the states could not agree, and presented the most imperious call for speedy settlement. . . .

There is but one power in this Union paramount to that by which, in our opinion, this jurisdiction has been granted, and must be brought into action if it can. That power has been exerted in the 11th Amendment: but while it took from this Court all jurisdiction, past, present, and future of all controversies between states and individuals; it left its exercise over those between states as free as it had been before. . . .

The motion of the defendants is, therefore, overruled.

[The dissenting opinion of Chief Justice Taney and the concurring opinion of Justice Barbour are omitted.]

Mr. Justice Story did not sit in this case. . . .

Notes and Questions

1. The Court says that the Compact Clause provided one way to resolve boundary disputes when the disputing states could not reach agreement. Indeed, Felix Frankfurter and James M. Landis reported in 1925: "Boundary disputes . . . have been the most continuous occasions for invoking the Compact Clause." *The Compact Clause of the Constitution: A Study in Interstate Adjustments*, 34 Yale L.J. 685, 696 (1925). Given the Compact Clause's use for this purpose, why was it necessary to give the Court original jurisdiction over boundary disputes between states?

2. Boundary disputes between states account for many of the cases in which the Court has exercised original jurisdiction and issued published opinions. Vincent L. McKusick, *Discretionary Gatekeeping: The Supreme Court's Management of Its Original Jurisdiction Docket Since 1961*, 45 Maine L. Rev. 185, 188, 198 (1993) ("Historically, interstate boundary disputes are the paradigm subject matter for original jurisdiction cases.").

3. One might think that the number of boundary disputes between states would diminish over time. However that may be, boundary disputes continue to arise because natural and man-made events produce changes in land and water courses. One of the more prominent boundary disputes in recent memory arose between New York and New Jersey over a portion of Ellis Island. The portion in dispute comprised some 24.5 acres that the federal government added to expand the size of the island to accommodate the processing of immigrants. *New Jersey v. New York*, 523 U.S. 767, 775-777 (1998).

Missouri v. Illinois

180 U.S. 208 (1901)

Mr. Justice SHIRAS . . . delivered the opinion of the Court.

[Missouri sued Illinois and the Sanitary District of Chicago, alleging that the Sanitary District, acting under Illinois state law, was dumping tons of sewage into the water and that the sewage-tainted water flowed into Missouri via the Mississippi River. The defendants by demurrer challenged Missouri's capacity to bring the suit.]

... [The Court's original jurisdiction cases] show that such jurisdiction has been exercised in cases involving boundaries and jurisdiction over lands and their inhabitants, and in cases directly affecting the property rights and interests of a State. But such cases manifestly do not cover the entire field in which such controversies may arise, and for which the Constitution has provided a remedy; and it would be objectionable, and, indeed, impossible, for the court to anticipate by definition what controversies can and what cannot be brought within the original jurisdiction of this court.

An inspection of the bill discloses that the nature of the injury complained of is such that an adequate remedy can only be found in this court at the suit of the State of Missouri. It is true that no question of boundary is involved, nor of direct property rights belonging to the complainant State. But it must surely be conceded that, if the health and comfort of the inhabitants of a State are threatened, the State is the proper party to represent and defend them. If Missouri were an independent and sovereign State all must admit that she could seek a remedy by negotiation, and, that failing, by force. Diplomatic powers and the right to make war having been surrendered to the general government, it was to be expected that upon the latter would be devolved the duty of providing a remedy and that remedy, we think, is found in the constitutional provisions we are considering.

The allegations of the bill plainly present such a case. The health and comfort of the large communities inhabiting those parts of the State situated on the Mississippi River are not alone concerned, but contagious and typhoidal diseases introduced in the river communities may spread themselves throughout the territory of the State. Moreover, substantial impairment of the health and prosperity of the towns and cities of the State situated on the Mississippi River, including its commercial metropolis, would injuriously affect the entire State. ...

The demurrers are overruled, and leave is given to the defendants to file answers to the bill.

[The dissenting opinion of Chief Justice Fuller, in which Justices Harlan and White joined, is omitted.]

Notes and Questions

1. Missouri brought this action on behalf of its residents, alleging that their health and safety were threatened by the defendants' conduct. When a state sues on behalf of its residents to address some sort of widespread harm to them, the state is said to be suing as *parens patriae* ("parent of his or her country"). The ability of a state to sue as *parens patriae* can get complicated, but for our purposes it is not necessary to plumb the complexity. *See* Note, *The Original Jurisdiction of the United States Supreme Court,* 11 Stan. L. Rev. 665, 672 (1959). *See generally* Richard H. Fallon et al., *Hart and Wechsler's the Federal Courts and the Federal System* 259, 261-266 (6th ed. 2009). We introduce the concept here because states have sued as *parens patriae* in some important original jurisdiction cases, including the two cases excerpted below: *Ohio v. Wyandotte Chemicals Corp.,* 401 U.S. 493 (1971), and *Maryland v. Louisiana,* 451 U.S. 725 (1981).

2. Although Missouri successfully invoked the Court's original jurisdiction to sue Illinois and the Sanitary District of Chicago, Missouri lost on the merits. *See Missouri v. Illinois,* 200 U.S. 496 (1906). In denying relief, the Court (per Justice Holmes) assumed that, without applicable federal legislation, the Court itself would have to devise principles governing the rights of one state to be free from pollution produced by another state. *See id.* at 520. The Court emphasized the difficulties of framing such principles. *See id.* Those difficulties warranted "great and serious caution" in deciding "whether a case is proved." *Id.* The Court cited these same difficulties as a reason for declining to exercise original jurisdiction in *Ohio v. Wyandotte Chemicals Corp.*, 401 U.S. 493 (1971).

3. *Ohio v. Wyandotte Chemicals Corp.* is excerpted next. It is not a controversy between two or more states. We reproduce it now because it provides essential background for the case that follows it, *Maryland v. Louisiana*, 451 U.S. 725 (1981), in which the Court discussed the discretionary nature of its original jurisdiction in a controversy between two or more states. The Court's decision to decline original jurisdiction in a controversy between two or more states has particular significance because its original jurisdiction over those controversies is exclusive; there is no other forum in which these interstate controversies may be brought, though, as the Court emphasizes in this context, there may be other forums in which the underlying issues can be litigated.

Ohio v. Wyandotte Chemicals Corp.

401 U.S. 493 (1971)

Mr. Justice HARLAN delivered the opinion of the Court.

By motion for leave to file a bill of complaint, Ohio seeks to invoke this Court's original jurisdiction. . . . For reasons that follow we deny the motion for leave to file.

The action, for abatement of a nuisance, is brought on behalf of the State and its citizens, and names as defendants Wyandotte Chemicals Corp. (Wyandotte), Dow Chemical Co. (Dow America), and Dow Chemical Company of Canada, Ltd. (Dow Canada). Wyandotte is incorporated in Michigan and maintains its principal office and place of business there. Dow America is incorporated in Delaware, has its principal office and place of business in Michigan, and owns all the stock of Dow Canada. Dow Canada is incorporated, and does business, in Ontario. A majority of Dow Canada's directors are residents of the United States.

The complaint alleges that Dow Canada and Wyandotte have each dumped mercury into streams whose courses ultimately reach Lake Erie, thus contaminating and polluting that lake's waters, vegetation, fish, and wildlife, and that Dow America is jointly responsible for the acts of its foreign subsidiary. . . . Ohio seeks a decree: (1) declaring the introduction of mercury into Lake Erie's tributaries a public nuisance; (2) perpetually enjoining these defendants from introducing mercury into Lake Erie or its tributaries; (3) requiring defendants either to remove the mercury from Lake Erie or to pay the costs of its removal into a fund to be administered by Ohio and used only for that purpose; (4) directing defendants to pay Ohio monetary damages for the harm done to Lake Erie, its fish, wildlife, and vegetation, and the citizens and inhabitants of Ohio. . . .

While we consider that Ohio's complaint does state a cause of action that falls within the compass of our original jurisdiction, we have concluded that this Court should nevertheless decline to exercise that jurisdiction.

I

That we have jurisdiction seems clear enough. . . . [T]his Court has often adjudicated controversies between States and between a State and citizens of another

State seeking to abate a nuisance that exists in one State yet produces noxious consequences in another. See *Missouri v. Illinois*, 180 U.S. 208 (1901) (complaint filed), 200 U.S. 496 (1906) (final judgment). . . .[2]

Ordinarily, the foregoing would suffice to settle the issue presently under consideration: whether Ohio should be granted leave to file its complaint. For it is a time-honored maxim of the Anglo-American common-law tradition that a court possessed of jurisdiction generally must exercise it. *Cohens v. Virginia*, 6 Wheat. 264, 404 (1821). Nevertheless, although it may initially have been contemplated that this Court would always exercise its original jurisdiction when properly called upon to do so, it seems evident to us that changes in the American legal system and the development of American society have rendered untenable, as a practical matter, the view that this Court must stand willing to adjudicate all or most legal disputes that may arise between one State and a citizen or citizens of another, even though the dispute may be one over which this Court does have original jurisdiction.

As our social system has grown more complex, the States have increasingly become enmeshed in a multitude of disputes with persons living outside their borders. Consider, for example, the frequency with which States and nonresidents clash over the application of state laws concerning taxes, motor vehicles, decedents' estates, business torts, government contracts, and so forth. It would, indeed, be anomalous were this Court to be held out as a potential principal forum for settling such controversies. . . . And the evolution of this Court's responsibilities in the American legal system has brought matters to a point where much would be sacrificed, and little gained, by our exercising original jurisdiction over issues bottomed on local law. This Court's paramount responsibilities to the national system lie almost without exception in the domain of federal law. . . . We have no claim to special competence in dealing with the numerous conflicts between States and nonresident individuals that raise no serious issues of federal law.

This Court is, moreover, structured to perform as an appellate tribunal, ill-equipped for the task of factfinding and so forced, in original cases, awkwardly to play the role of factfinder without actually presiding over the introduction of evidence. . . . [T]he problem . . . is compounded by the fact that for every case in which we might be called upon to determine the facts and apply unfamiliar legal norms we would unavoidably be reducing the attention we could give to those matters of federal law and national import as to which we are the primary overseers.

Thus, we think it apparent that we must recognize "the need [for] the exercise of a sound discretion in order to protect this Court from an abuse of the opportunity to resort to its original jurisdiction in the enforcement by States of claims against citizens of other States." *Massachusetts v. Missouri*, 308 U.S. 1, 19 (1939), opinion of Chief Justice Hughes. . . .[3] We believe, however, that the focus of concern

2. While we possess jurisdiction over Dow America and Wyandotte simply on the basis of their citizenship, the problem with respect to Dow Canada is quite different with regard to two major issues: whether that foreign corporation has "contacts" of the proper sort sufficient to bring it personally before us, and whether service of process can lawfully be made upon Dow Canada. Were we to decide to entertain this complaint, however, it seems reasonably clear that the better course would be to reserve this aspect of the jurisdictional issue pending ascertainment of additional facts, rather than to resolve it now. Thus, for purposes of ruling on Ohio's motion for leave to file its complaint, we treat the question of jurisdiction over all three defendants as a unitary one.

3. In our view the federal statute, 28 U.S.C. §1251(b)(3), providing that our original jurisdiction in cases such as these is merely concurrent with that of the federal district courts, reflects this same judgment. However, this particular case cannot be disposed of by transferring it to an appropriate federal district court since this statute by itself does not actually confer jurisdiction on those courts and no other

embodied in the above-quoted statement of Chief Justice Hughes should be somewhat refined. In our opinion, we may properly exercise such discretion, not simply to shield this Court from noisome, vexatious, or unfamiliar tasks, but also, and we believe principally, as a technique for promoting and furthering the assumptions and value choices that underlie the current role of this Court in the federal system. Protecting this Court *per se* is at best a secondary consideration. What gives rise to the necessity for recognizing such discretion is pre-eminently the diminished societal concern in our function as a court of original jurisdiction and the enhanced importance of our role as the final federal appellate court. A broader view of the scope and purposes of our discretion would inadequately take account of the general duty of courts to exercise that jurisdiction they possess.

Thus, at this stage we go no further than to hold that, as a general matter, we may decline to entertain a complaint brought by a State against the citizens of another State or country only where we can say with assurance that (1) declination of jurisdiction would not disserve any of the principal policies underlying the Article III jurisdictional grant and (2) the reasons of practical wisdom that persuade us that this Court is an inappropriate forum are consistent with the proposition that our discretion is legitimated by its use to keep this aspect of the Court's functions attuned to its other responsibilities.

II

In applying this analysis to the facts here presented, we believe that the wiser course is to deny Ohio's motion for leave to file its complaint.

A

Two principles seem primarily to have underlain conferring upon this Court original jurisdiction over cases and controversies between a State and citizens of another State or country. The first was the belief that no State should be compelled to resort to the tribunals of other States for redress, since parochial factors might often lead to the appearance, if not the reality, of partiality to one's own. The second was that a State, needing an alternative forum, of necessity had to resort to this Court in order to obtain a tribunal competent to exercise jurisdiction over the acts of nonresidents of the aggrieved State.

Neither of these policies is, we think, implicated in this lawsuit. The courts of Ohio, under modern principles of the scope of subject matter and *in personam* jurisdiction, have a claim as compelling as any that can be made out for this Court to exercise jurisdiction to adjudicate the instant controversy, and they would decide it under the same common law of nuisance upon which our determination would have to rest. . . . While this Court, and doubtless Canadian courts, if called upon to assess the validity of any decree rendered against either Dow Canada or Wyandotte, would be alert to ascertain whether the judgment rested upon an even-handed application of justice, it is unlikely that we would totally deny Ohio's competence to act if the allegations made here are proved true. . . . And while we

---

statutory jurisdictional basis exists. The fact that there is diversity of citizenship among the parties would not support district court jurisdiction under 28 U.S.C. §1332 because that statute does not deal with cases in which a State is a party. Nor would federal question jurisdiction exist under 28 U.S.C. §1331. So far as it appears from the present record, an action such as this, if otherwise cognizable in federal district court, would have to be adjudicated under state law. *Erie R. Co. v. Tompkins*, 304 U.S. 64 (1938).

cannot speak for Canadian courts, we have been given no reason to believe they would be less receptive to enforcing a decree rendered by Ohio courts than one issued by this Court. . . .

B

Our reasons for thinking that, as a practical matter, it would be inappropriate for this Court to attempt to adjudicate the issues Ohio seeks to present are several. History reveals that the course of this Court's prior efforts to settle disputes regarding interstate air and water pollution has been anything but smooth. In *Missouri v. Illinois*, 200 U.S. 496, 520-522 (1906), Justice Holmes was at pains to underscore the great difficulty that the Court faced in attempting to pronounce a suitable general rule of law to govern such controversies. . . .

The nature of the case Ohio brings here is equally disconcerting. It can fairly be said that what is in dispute is not so much the law as the facts. And the factfinding process we are asked to undertake is, to say the least, formidable. We already know, just from what has been placed before us on this motion, that Lake Erie suffers from several sources of pollution other than mercury; that the scientific conclusion that mercury is a serious water pollutant is a novel one; that whether and to what extent the existence of mercury in natural waters can safely or reasonably be tolerated is a question for which there is presently no firm answer; and that virtually no published research is available describing how one might extract mercury that is in fact contaminating water. . . . The notion that appellate judges, even with the assistance of a most competent Special Master, might appropriately undertake at this time to unravel these complexities is, to say the least, unrealistic. . . .

Finally, in what has been said it is vitally important to stress that we are not called upon by this lawsuit to resolve difficult or important problems of federal law. . . .

Ohio's motion for leave to file its complaint is denied without prejudice to its right to commence other appropriate judicial proceedings. . . .

[The dissenting opinion of Justice Douglas is omitted.]

Notes and Questions

1. *Wyandotte Chemicals* is most significant for the Court's determination that it has discretion to decline original jurisdiction despite the "time-honored maxim of the Anglo-American common-law tradition that a court possessed of jurisdiction generally must exercise it." 401 U.S. at 496-497. As *Wyandotte Chemicals* illustrates, that time-honored maxim is sometimes found to be better honored in the breach than the observance. Of particular importance is a school of thought that argues that the Court should decline to decide some cases within its jurisdiction to mitigate the "counter-majoritarian difficulty." Alexander Bickel, *The Least Dangerous Branch* 16 (1962). The "counter-majoritarian difficulty" refers to the idea that a federal court is thwarting the will of the majority when it strikes down, as unconstitutional, a statute or other law produced through the political process by either officials accountable to the people or the people themselves (for example, through the initiative process). To mitigate that difficulty, Professor Alexander Bickel argued that the United States Supreme Court should exercise the "passive virtues" of sometimes declining, through various "devices" such as justiciability doctrines, to

exercise jurisdiction over cases presenting such constitutional challenges. *Id.* at 111, 112. Whether or not one agrees with Bickel's argument, it demonstrates that the Court's decision *not* to decide a case—including on jurisdictional grounds—can be as important as its decision to decide a case. Its importance, and Bickel's argument about the counter-majoritarian difficulty, are explored elsewhere in this book—specifically, in Chapters 1 and 4.

2. The Court in *Wyandotte Chemicals* cited *Massachusetts v. Missouri*, 308 U.S. 1 (1939), as precedent for its discretion to decline original jurisdiction. The Court in *Wyandotte Chemicals* believed, however, that "the focus of concern embodied in" some language in the *Massachusetts v. Missouri* opinion needed to be "somewhat refined." *Wyandotte Chemicals*, 401 U.S. at 499. Why did the Court believe refinement was necessary? How did the Court refine the "focus of concern"? As refined, what does the focus imply about the purpose of the Court's original jurisdiction and its importance compared to that of the Court's appellate jurisdiction?

3. In footnote 3 the Court in *Wyandotte Chemicals* said that, "[s]o far as it appears from the present record," Ohio's public nuisance claim would "have to be adjudicated under state law." By contrast, in the later case of *Illinois v. City of Milwaukee*, the Court held that federal common law governed Illinois' claim that Milwaukee and other units of local government had created a public nuisance by polluting an interstate waterway. 406 U.S. 91, 99-103 (1972); *id.* at 102 n.3 (noting that *Wyandotte Chemicals* assumed applicability of state law "based on the preoccupation of that litigation with public nuisance under Ohio law"). Indeed, the Court declined original jurisdiction in *Illinois v. City of Milwaukee* partly because the case could be brought in the federal district courts under those courts' federal question jurisdiction. *Id.* at 99-103. Since 1972, when *Illinois v. City of Milwaukee* was decided, the increase in federal legislation governing interstate pollution has to some extent displaced federal common law. *See Am. Elec. Power v. Connecticut*, _____ U.S. _____, 131 S. Ct. 2527 (2011). What effect, if any, would you predict the increasing predominance of federal legislation will have on the Court's exercise of original jurisdiction over interstate pollution cases?

Maryland v. Louisiana

451 U.S. 725 (1981)

Justice WHITE delivered the opinion of the Court.

In this original action, several States, joined by the United States and a number of pipeline companies, challenge the constitutionality of Louisiana's "First-Use Tax" imposed on certain uses of natural gas brought into Louisiana, principally from the Outer Continental Shelf (OCS), as violative of the Supremacy Clause and the Commerce Clause of the United States Constitution.

I

The lands beneath the Gulf of Mexico have large reserves of oil and natural gas. . . .

The ownership and control of these large reserves of natural gas have been much disputed. . . . In 1953, Congress passed the Submerged Lands Act, 43 U.S.C. §§1301-1315, ceding any federal interest in the lands within three miles of the coast, while confirming the Federal Government's interest in the area seaward of the 3-mile limit. In the same year, Congress passed the Outer Continental Shelf

Lands Act, 43 U.S.C. §§1331–1343 (OCS Act), which declared that the "subsoil and seabed of the outer Continental Shelf appertain to the United States and are subject to its jurisdiction, control, and power of disposition. . . ." §1332. The OCS Act also established procedures for federal leasing of OCS land to develop mineral resources. . . .

In 1978, the Louisiana Legislature enacted a tax of seven cents per thousand cubic feet of natural gas on the "first use" of any gas imported into Louisiana which was not previously subjected to taxation by another State or the United States. . . . Since most States impose their own severance tax, it is acknowledged that the primary effect of the First-Use Tax will be on gas produced in the federal OCS area and then piped to processing plants located within Louisiana. It has been estimated that Louisiana would receive at least $150 million in annual receipts from the First-Use Tax. . . .

. . . [In 1979,] eight States filed a motion for leave to file a complaint under this Court's original jurisdiction pursuant to Art. III, §2, of the Constitution. The complaint sought a declaratory judgment that the First-Use Tax was unconstitutional. . . . We granted plaintiffs' motion for leave to file. . . . Subsequently, as is usual, we appointed a Special Master to facilitate handling of the suit. . . . [T]he Special Master recommended that the Court approve the motions of New Jersey, the United States, the Federal Energy Regulatory Commission (FERC), and 17 pipeline companies to intervene as plaintiffs. The Master's second report . . . recommended that we deny Louisiana's motion to dismiss and reject the submissions that the plaintiff States had no standing to bring the action and that the case was not an appropriate one for the exercise of our original jurisdiction. . . . We heard oral argument on the exceptions filed to the reports.

II . . .

Louisiana [first] asserts that this case should be dismissed for want of standing because the Tax is imposed on the pipeline companies and not directly on the ultimate consumers. . . .

Jurisdiction is . . . supported by the States' interest as *parens patriae*. A State is not permitted to enter a controversy as a nominal party in order to forward the claims of individual citizens. But it may act as the representative of its citizens in original actions where the injury alleged affects the general population of a State in a substantial way. See, *e.g., Missouri v. Illinois*, 180 U.S. 208 (1901). . . .

. . . Plaintiff States have alleged substantial and serious injury to their proprietary interests as consumers of natural gas as a direct result of the allegedly unconstitutional actions of Louisiana. This direct injury is also supported by the States' interest in protecting its citizens from substantial economic injury presented by imposition of the First-Use Tax. Nor does the incidence of the Tax fall on a small group of citizens who are likely to challenge the Tax directly. Rather, a great many citizens in each of the plaintiff States are themselves consumers of natural gas and are faced with increased costs aggregating millions of dollars per year. . . .

With respect to Louisiana's second argument, it is true that we have construed the congressional grant of exclusive jurisdiction under §1251(a) as requiring resort to our obligatory jurisdiction only in "appropriate cases." *Illinois v. City of Milwaukee*, 406 U.S. 91, 93 (1972). . . . In *City of Milwaukee*, we noted that what is "appropriate" involves not only "the seriousness and dignity of the claim," but also "the availability of another forum where there is jurisdiction over the named parties, where the issues tendered may be litigated, and where appropriate relief may be had." Louisiana urges that presently pending state lawsuits raising the identical constitutional issues presented here constitute sufficient reason to forgo the exercise of our original jurisdiction.

There have been filed in various lower courts several suits challenging the constitutionality of the First-Use Tax. The first suit was brought by Louisiana in state court seeking a declaratory judgment that the First-Use Tax is constitutional. . . . Other lawsuits were filed in state court seeking a refund of taxes paid under protest. . . . Neither the plaintiff States, the United States, nor the FERC is a named party in any of the state actions nor have they filed leave to intervene, although Louisiana represented at oral argument that such a motion would not be opposed.[17] The final suit was commenced by the FERC [in federal district court] against various state officials, seeking to enjoin enforcement of the First-Use Tax on constitutional grounds. That action is presently stayed.

In *City of Milwaukee*, on which Louisiana relies, the proposed suit by Illinois against four municipalities did not fall within our exclusive grant of original jurisdiction because political subdivisions of the State could not be considered as a State for purposes of 28 U.S.C. §1251(a) (1976 ed., Supp. III). Similarly, the decision in *Wyandotte Chemicals* did not involve §1251(a), since it was a suit between a State and citizens of another State and so did not fall under our exclusive jurisdiction. Louisiana also relies, however, on *Arizona v. New Mexico* for an example of a case where we determined not to exercise our exclusive jurisdiction in a case between States because the matter was "inappropriate" for determination.

In that case, we denied Arizona's motion for leave to file a complaint against New Mexico. Arizona was suing to challenge New Mexico's electrical energy tax which imposed a net kilowatt hour tax on any electric utility generating electricity in New Mexico. Arizona sought a declaratory judgment that the tax constituted, *inter alia*, an unconstitutional discrimination against interstate commerce. Arizona brought the suit in its proprietary capacity as a consumer of electricity generated in New Mexico and as *parens patriae* for its citizens. Arizona further alleged that it had no other forum in which to vindicate its interests. New Mexico asserted that the three Arizona utilities affected by the statute had chosen not to pay the tax and instead had jointly filed suit in state court seeking a declaratory judgment that the tax was unconstitutional. This Court held that "[i]n the circumstances of this case, we are persuaded that the pending state-court action provides an appropriate forum in which the issues tendered here may be litigated." . . . Despite the facial similarity with *Arizona v. New Mexico*, there are significant differences from the present case that compel an opposite result. . . . [O]ne of the three electric companies involved in the state-court action in New Mexico was a political subdivision of the State of Arizona. Arizona's interests were thus actually being represented by one of the named parties to the suit. In this case, none of the plaintiff States is directly represented in the tax refund case.[19] . . .

The tax at issue in the Arizona case did not sufficiently implicate the unique concerns of federalism forming the basis of our original jurisdiction. . . . Given the

---

17. See Tr. of Oral Arg. 55-58. It is acknowledged that but for the "invitation" there exists no procedural mechanism in Louisiana for the plaintiff States or the United States to be made parties to the state refund suit.

19. Despite the fact that these parties have been invited to intervene, the Louisiana refund action is an imperfect forum, primarily because no injunctive relief prior to the determination on the merits is possible under Louisiana law.

underlying claim that Louisiana is attempting, in effect, to levy the Tax as a substitute for a severance tax on gas extracted from areas that belong to the people at large to the relative detriment of the other States in the Union, it is clear that the First-Use Tax implicates serious and important concerns of federalism fully in accord with the purposes and reach of our original jurisdiction.

The exercise of our original jurisdiction is also supported by the fact that the First-Use Tax affects the United States' interests in the administration of the OCS—a factor totally absent in *Arizona v. New Mexico.* While we do not have exclusive jurisdiction in suits brought by the United States against a State, we may entertain such suits as original actions in appropriate circumstances. . . . [I]t is clear that a district court action brought by the United States, which necessarily would not include the plaintiff States, would be an inadequate forum in light of the present posture of this case. In addition, because of the interest of the United States in protecting its rights in the OCS area, with ramifications for all coastal States, as well as its interests under the regulatory mechanism that supervises the production and development of natural gas resources, we believe that this case is an appropriate one for the exercise of our original jurisdiction under §1251(b)(2). . . .

JUSTICE POWELL took no part in the consideration or decision of the case.

[The concurring opinion of Chief Justice Burger is omitted.]

Justice REHNQUIST, dissenting. . . .

. . . Because of the nature of the interests which the plaintiff States seek to vindicate in this original action, and because of the existence of alternative forums in which these interests can be vindicated, I do not consider this an "appropriate case" for the exercise of original jurisdiction. . . .

If all that is required to invoke our original jurisdiction is an injury to the State as consumer caused by the regulatory activity of another State, the list of cases which could be pressed as original-jurisdiction cases must be endless. . . .

I would require that the State's claim involve some tangible relation to the State's sovereign interests. Our original jurisdiction should not be trivialized and open to run-of-the-mill claims simply because they are brought by a State, but rather should be limited to complaints by States *qua* States. This would include the prototypical original action, boundary disputes, and the familiar cases involving disputes over water rights. In such cases, the State seeks to vindicate its rights as a State, a political entity. Since nothing about the complaint in this case involves sovereign interests, I would hold that there is no jurisdiction on the basis of the States' own purchases of natural gas.[4]

Nor is this an appropriate case for the plaintiff States to invoke original jurisdiction as *parens patriae.* . . .

---

4. It is true that the Court has exercised original jurisdiction in cases where the right asserted by a complaining State cannot truly be considered a right affecting sovereign interests. I do not doubt the Court's *power* to exercise original jurisdiction in such cases, nor do I in this case. The decision that a particular type of case was an "appropriate" one for original jurisdiction a century ago, however, does not mean that the same sort of case is an appropriate one today. Justice Harlan explicitly recognized in *Ohio v. Wyandotte Chemicals Corp.*, 401 U.S. 493, 497-499 (1971), that societal changes and "the evolution of this Court's responsibilities in the American legal system" affected the determination of what was an appropriate case in which to exercise original jurisdiction. The increase in state regulatory efforts on the one hand and the role of States as consumers on the other suggests that new considerations need to be brought to bear on the present question.

Here the plaintiff States are not suing to advance a sovereign or quasi-sovereign interest. Rather they are suing to promote the economic interests of those of their citizens who purchase and use natural gas. Advancing the economic interests of a limited group of citizens, however, is not sufficient to support *parens patriae* original jurisdiction. . . .

The exercise of original jurisdiction in this case is particularly inappropriate since the issues the plaintiff States would have us decide not only can be, but in fact are being, litigated in other forums. . . .

. . . I consider *Arizona v. New Mexico* controlling. . . . Although the Court in this case stresses that the plaintiff States are not parties in the Louisiana state-court proceedings, in *Arizona v. New Mexico* we specifically emphasized that the relevant question was whether the *issues* could be litigated elsewhere. . . .

. . . The absence of limiting principles in the Court's opinion, I fear, "could well pave the way for putting this Court into a quandary whereby we must opt either to pick and choose arbitrarily among similarly situated litigants or to devote truly enormous portions of our energies to such matters." *Ohio v. Wyandotte Chemicals Corp.*, 401 U.S., at 504. The problem is accentuated in this case because it falls within our original and exclusive jurisdiction, which means that similar cases not only can be but must be brought here. . . .

Notes and Questions

1. As discussed in the majority and dissenting opinions in *Maryland v. Louisiana*, the Court has declined original jurisdiction even in cases between two or more states, which fall within the Court's exclusive jurisdiction, when the Court believes the issues presented can be resolved in another forum. Dissenting from the Court's decision to decline original jurisdiction in one such case, Justice White objected that "this is no way to treat a sovereign State that wants its dispute with another State settled in this Court." *Louisiana v. Mississippi*, 488 U.S. 990 (1988) (White, J., dissenting, joined by Stevens and Scalia, JJ.). Do you side with the Court's approach or Justice White's view? Why?

2. Sometimes an apparent alternative forum to resolve disputes between states turns out to be unavailable. One such case involved the estate of billionaire eccentric Howard Hughes. California sought leave to bring an original action against Texas to settle a dispute over which state could tax Hughes's estate. The Court declined jurisdiction in 1978, partly because at least four Justices thought the dispute might be adjudicated by the administrator of the estate in federal district court under the Federal Interpleader Act. See *California v. Texas*, 437 U.S. 601 (1978) (Brennan, J., concurring); *id.* at 608 n.10 (Stewart, J., concurring, joined by Powell and Stevens, JJ.); *id.* at 615 (Powell, J. concurring). The Court later held, however, that the administrator's interpleader action was barred by the Eleventh Amendment. *Cory v. White*, 457 U.S. 85 (1982). On the same day that the Court issued its Eleventh Amendment ruling barring the interpleader action in federal district court, it granted California's new motion for leave to file an original action against Texas to resolve which state could tax Howard Hughes's estate. *California v. Texas*, 457 U.S. 164 (1982). The case later settled. See George Gleason Bogert et al., *Bogert's Trusts and Trustees* §287, at 220 n.41 (2d rev. ed. 1992).

Do situations like this one cast doubt on the wisdom (or legitimacy) of the Court's declining original jurisdiction in cases over which it has exclusive jurisdiction, as long as it appears that "the *issues*" may be resolved in an alternative forum? *Arizona v. New Mexico*, 425 U.S. 794, 797 (1976) (emphasis in original). *See* Richard H. Fallon et al., *Hart and Wechsler's the Federal Courts and the Federal System* 256 (6th ed. 2009) (asking whether declining original, exclusive jurisdiction when "issues" can be litigated elsewhere "deprive[s] the state of the opportunity to litigate those issues itself—an opportunity that Congress apparently afforded in §1251(a)"); *see also* David L. Shapiro, *Jurisdiction and Discretion*, 60 N.Y.U. L. Rev. 543 (1985) (describing as "unanswerable" opinion of Justice Stevens dissenting from Court's refusal to exercise its original, exclusive jurisdiction in *California v. West Virginia*, 454 U.S. 1027 (Stevens, J., dissenting)).

3. The Court in *Maryland v. Louisiana* distinguished *Arizona v. New Mexico*, in which the Court declined original jurisdiction, because that earlier case "did not sufficiently implicate the unique concerns of federalism forming the basis of our original jurisdiction." 451 U.S. at 743. How would you characterize the "unique" federalism concerns that led the Court to exercise original jurisdiction in *Maryland v. Louisiana* but not in *Arizona v. New Mexico*?

4. Interstate pollution cases such as *Ohio v. Wyandotte Chemicals* and *Illinois v. City of Milwaukee* implicate federalism concerns. Does the Court's decision to decline original jurisdiction in those two cases suggest that the federalism concerns in those cases were not "unique"? What other factors might lead the Court to decline jurisdiction in interstate pollution cases? Before you conclude that their complexity contributes to the Court's reluctance, consider that boundary disputes and water-rights disputes can be highly complex, yet "the Court takes those cases almost without exception." Vincent L. McKusick, *Discretionary Gatekeeping: The Supreme Court's Management of Its Original Jurisdiction Docket Since 1961*, 45 Maine L. Rev. 185, 198 (1993).

5. In his dissent in *Maryland v. Louisiana*, then-Justice Rehnquist reiterated his previously expressed concerns that, in exercising original jurisdiction, the Court is "not suited to functioning as a *nisi prius* [that is, a fact-finding] tribunal" and that "expending its time and resources on original-jurisdiction cases detracts from its primary responsibility as an appellate tribunal." 451 U.S. at 761-762 (Rehnquist, J., dissenting). Justice Rehnquist added that that those concerns are not "adequately answered by the expedient of employing a Special Master to conduct hearings, receive evidence, and submit recommendations for our review":

> It is no reflection on the quality of the work by the Special Master in this case or any other master in any other original-jurisdiction case to find it unsatisfactory to delegate the proper functions of this Court. Of course this Court cannot sit to receive evidence or conduct trials—but that fact should counsel reluctance to accept cases where the situation might arise, not resolution of the problem by empowering an individual to act in our stead. I for one think justice is far better served by trials in the lower courts, with appropriate review, than by trials before a Special Master whose rulings this Court simply cannot consider with the care and attention it should. It is one thing to review findings of a district court or state court, empowered to make findings in its own right, and quite another to accept (or reject) recommendations when this Court is in theory the primary factfinder.

Id. at 762-763 (Rehnquist, J. dissenting). Is the Court's substantial reliance on special masters consistent with the "rank and dignity" rationale for original jurisdiction that the Court has articulated? *See supra* this chapter, Note 3 following 28 U.S.C. §1251.

6. You may wonder how the Court's use of special masters squares with any jury trial right available in original actions. The Seventh Amendment "preserve[s]" the "right of trial by jury" in "Suits at common law" where the amount in controversy exceeds $20. U.S. Const. amend. VII. In addition, 28 U.S.C. §1872 states, "In all original actions at law in the Supreme Court against citizens of the United States, issues of fact shall be tried by a jury." The Court apparently has not had jury trials in its original jurisdiction cases since its early days. *See* Richard H. Fallon et al., *Hart and Wechsler's the Federal Courts and the Federal System* 253 & n.1 (6th ed. 2009); Eugene Gressman et al., *Supreme Court Practice: For Practice in the Supreme Court of the United States* 645-646 & n.45 (9th ed. 2007). The Court held in *United States v. Louisiana*, 339 U.S. 699, 706 (1950), that §1872 and the Seventh Amendment, "assuming they extend to cases under our original jurisdiction, are applicable only to actions at law." They therefore did not apply to the case before it, which was "an equity action for an injunction and accounting." *Id.*

In deciding whether to exercise original jurisdiction over a particular case, may the Court legitimately consider a party's demand for a jury trial as a factor weighing against the exercise of original jurisdiction?

4. Actions by the United States Against a State

United States v. Texas

143 U.S. 621 (1892)

Mr. Justice HARLAN delivered the opinion of the Court.

This suit was brought by original bill in this court pursuant to the act of May 2, 1890, providing a temporary government for the Territory of Oklahoma. The 25th section [of the 1890 legislation] recites the existence of a controversy between the United States and the State of Texas as to the ownership of what is designated on the map of Texas as Greer County, and provides that the act shall not be construed to apply to that county until the title to the same has been adjudicated and determined to be in the United States. In order that there might be a speedy and final judicial determination of this controversy the Attorney General of the United States was authorized and directed to commence and prosecute on behalf of the United States a proper suit in equity in this court against the state of Texas. . . .

The state of Texas appeared and filed a demurrer. . . . The case is now before the court only upon the demurrer, the principal grounds of which are [among other grounds] . . . that it is not competent for the general government to bring suit against a State of the Union in one of its own courts. . . .

It is apparent upon the face of these clauses [that is, Article III, §2, clauses 1 and 2,] that in one class of cases the jurisdiction of the courts of the Union depends "on the character of the cause, whoever may be the parties," and, in the other, on the character of the parties, whatever may be the subject of controversy. *Cohens v. Virginia*, 6 Wheat. 264, 378, 393. The present suit falls in each class, for it is, plainly, one arising under the Constitution, laws and treaties of the United States, and, also, one in which the United States is a party. It is, therefore, one to which, by the express words of the Constitution, the judicial power of the United States extends. That a Circuit Court of the United States has not jurisdiction, under existing statutes, of a suit by the United States against a State, is clear; for by the Revised Statutes it is declared—as was done by the Judiciary Act of 1789—that "the Supreme Court shall have exclusive jurisdiction of all controversies of a civil nature where a State is a party, except between a State and its citizens, or between a State and citizens of other States or aliens, in which latter cases it shall have original, but not exclusive, jurisdiction." Such exclusive jurisdiction was given to this court, because it best comported with the dignity of a State, that a case in which it was a party should be determined in the highest, rather than in a subordinate judicial tribunal of the nation. Why then may not this court take original cognizance of the present suit, involving a question of boundary between a territory of the United States and a State?

The words, in the Constitution, "in all cases . . . in which a State shall be party, the Supreme Court shall have original jurisdiction," necessarily refer to all cases mentioned in the preceding clause in which a State may be made, of right, a party defendant, or in which a State may, of right, be a party plaintiff. It is admitted that these words do not refer to suits brought against a State by its own citizens or by citizens of other States, or by citizens or subjects of foreign States, even where such suits arise under the Constitution, laws and treaties of the United States, because the judicial power of the United States does not extend to suits of *individuals* against States. *Hans v. Louisiana*, 134 U.S. 1. It is, however, said that the words last quoted refer only to suits in which a State is a party, and in which, also, the opposite party is another State of the Union or a foreign State. This cannot be correct, for it must be conceded that a State can bring an original suit in this court against a citizen of another State. Besides, unless a State is exempt altogether from suit by the United States, we do not perceive upon what sound rule of construction suits brought by the United States in this court—especially if they be suits, the correct decision of which depends upon the Constitution, laws or treaties of the United States—are to be excluded from its original jurisdiction as defined in the Constitution. . . . We cannot assume that the framers of the Constitution, while extending the judicial power of the United States to controversies between two or more States of the Union, and between a State of the Union and foreign States, intended to exempt a State altogether from suit by the General Government. They could not have overlooked the possibility that controversies, capable of judicial solution, might arise between the United States and some of the States, and that the permanence of the Union might be endangered if to some tribunal was not entrusted the power to determine them according to the recognized principles of law. And to what tribunal could a trust so momentous be more appropriately committed than to that which the people of the United States . . . have constituted with authority to speak for all the people and all the States, upon questions before it to which the judicial power of the nation extends? It would be difficult to suggest any reason why this court should have jurisdiction to determine questions of boundary between two or more States, but not jurisdiction of controversies of like character between the United States and a State.

. . . *Hans v. Louisiana*, 134 U.S. 1, . . . and others in this court relating to the suability of States, proceeded upon the broad ground that "it is inherent in the nature of sovereignty not to be amenable to the suit of an *individual* without its consent."

The question as to the suability of one government by another government rests upon wholly different grounds. Texas is not called to the bar of this court at the suit of an individual, but at the suit of the government established for the common and equal benefit of the people of all the States. The submission to judicial solution of controversies arising between these two governments, "each sovereign, with respect to the objects committed to it, and neither sovereign with respect to the objects committed to the other," *McCulloch v. State of Maryland,* but both subject to the supreme law of the land, does no violence to the inherent nature of sovereignty. The States of the Union have agreed, in the Constitution, that the judicial power of the United States shall extend to *all* cases arising under the Constitution, laws and treaties of the United States, without regard to the character of the parties, (excluding, of course, suits against a State by its own citizens or by citizens of other States, or by citizens or subjects of foreign States,) and equally to controversies to which the United States shall be a party, without regard to the subject of such controversies, and that this court may exercise original jurisdiction in all such cases, "in which a State shall be party," without excluding those in which the United States may be the opposite party. The exercise, therefore, by this court, of such original jurisdiction in a suit brought by one state against another to determine the boundary line between them, or in a suit brought by the United States against a State to determine the boundary between a Territory of the United States and that State, so far from infringing, in either case, upon the sovereignty, is with the consent of the State sued. Such consent was given by Texas when admitted into the Union upon an equal footing in all respects with the other States.

We are of opinion that this court has jurisdiction to determine the disputed question of boundary between the United States and Texas. . . .

Demurrer overruled.

[The dissenting opinion of Chief Justice Fuller, in which Justice Lamar joined, is omitted.]

Notes and Questions

1. The Court bases its original jurisdiction upon the presence of a federal question and the presence of a state as a party. In later cases, however, the Court has *not* construed Article III as giving it original jurisdiction of state-party cases based on the presence of a federal question. For example, the Court would not have original jurisdiction over a suit by a state against its own citizen, even though the suit arose under federal law. *See California v. S. Pac. Co.,* 157 U.S. 229, 261 (1895) (determining that Court would not have original jurisdiction over action by state against its own citizen and a citizen of another state, even if a federal question were involved, "since the original jurisdiction of this court in cases between a state and citizen of another state rests upon the character of the parties, and not at all upon the nature of the case"); *see also Texas v. Interstate Commerce Commn.,* 258 U.S. 158, 164 (1922) (holding that Court would lack original jurisdiction over Texas's challenge to the constitutionality of a federal statute if citizens of Texas whose interests were directly involved in the challenge were joined (apparently as defendants)); Eugene Gressman et al., *Supreme Court Practice: For Practice in the Supreme Court of the United States* 612 (9th ed. 2007).

Does it seem odd that the Court cannot exercise original jurisdiction in state-party cases that arise under federal law? Professor James Pfander has argued that Article III *did* give the Court original jurisdiction over federal claims brought by and against states. Indeed, he argues that this was necessary and intended by the Framers to ensure that the only federal court created by the Constitution itself—that is, the "supreme Court" established in Article III, §1—could ensure state compliance with federal law. Consistent with this argument, Professor Pfander disputes the Court's "rank and dignity" rationale for the Court's original jurisdiction of state-party cases. James E. Pfander, *Rethinking the Supreme Court's Original Jurisdiction in State-Party Cases*, 82 Cal. L. Rev. 555 (1994); *see also supra* this chapter, Note 3 following 28 U.S.C. §1251 (describing "rank and dignity" rationale).

   2. Section 1251 of Title 28 provides for the Court to have "original but not exclusive jurisdiction of [a]ll controversies between the United States and a State." 28 U.S.C. §1251(b)(2). That is why federal district courts may exercise original jurisdiction over some actions by the United States against states. For example, the district court can hear actions by the United States against a state that present a federal question. *See* 28 U.S.C. §1331. Indeed, the United States has often invoked federal question jurisdiction to sue states in district courts to invalidate state actions that violate the Constitution or federal statutes, or that are preempted by federal law. *See, e.g., Arizona v. United States,* _____ U.S. _____, 132 S. Ct. 2492 (2012) (United States sued Arizona and other defendants in federal district court, arguing that federal law preempted Arizona law regulating immigration-related matters); *United States v. Virginia,* 518 U.S. 515 (1996) (United States sued Virginia and other defendants in federal district court, challenging, on equal protection grounds, male-only admission policy of a state college, Virginia Military Institute). As the Court held in *United States v. Texas,* states lack sovereign immunity from federal court lawsuits brought by the United States.

   3. Dicta in *United States v. Texas* could be read to suggest that the Eleventh Amendment would not bar a foreign state from bringing an original action against a state. Can you find that dicta in the excerpt above? In any event, the Court in the next case held that the Eleventh Amendment bars a suit against a state by a foreign state.

5. Actions by a Foreign State Against a State

Principality of Monaco v. Mississippi

292 U.S. 313 (1934)

Mr. Chief Justice HUGHES delivered the opinion of the Court.

   The Principality of Monaco asks leave to bring suit in this Court against the State of Mississippi upon bonds issued by the State and alleged to be the absolute property of the Principality. . . .

   . . . [The Principality alleged] that the bonds were transferred and delivered to the Principality . . . as an absolute gift. [The Principality submitted] a letter of the donors, dated September 26, 1933, stating . . . that the donors had been advised that there was no basis upon which they could maintain a suit against Mississippi on the bonds, but that "such a suit could only be maintained by a foreign government or one of the United States"; and that in these circumstances the donors were making an unconditional gift of the bonds to the Principality to be applied "to the causes of any of its charities, to the furtherance of its internal development or to the benefit of its citizens in such manner as it may select."

   We find it necessary to deal with but one [issue], that is, the question whether this Court has jurisdiction to entertain a suit brought by a foreign State against a State without her consent. That question, not hitherto determined, is now definitely presented.

The Principality relies upon the provisions of §2 of Article III of the Constitution of the United States that the judicial power shall extend to controversies "between a State, or the Citizens thereof, and foreign States, Citizens or Subjects" (Clause one), and that in cases "in which a State shall be Party" this Court shall have original jurisdiction (Clause two). The absence of qualification requiring the consent of the State in the case of a suit by a foreign State is asserted to be controlling. And the point is stressed that the Eleventh Amendment of the Constitution, providing that the judicial power shall not be construed to extend to any suit against one of the United States "by Citizens of another State, or by Citizens or Subjects of any Foreign State," contains no reference to a suit brought by a foreign State.

The argument drawn from the lack of an express requirement of consent to be sued is inconclusive. Thus there is no express provision that the United States may not be sued in the absence of consent. Clause one of §2 of Article III extends the judicial power "to Controversies to which the United States shall be a Party." . . . But by reason of the established doctrine of the immunity of the sovereign from suit except upon consent, the provision of Clause one of §2 of Article III does not authorize the maintenance of suits against the United States. . . .

Similarly, neither the literal sweep of the words of Clause one of §2 of Article III, nor the absence of restriction in the letter of the Eleventh Amendment, permits the conclusion that in all controversies of the sort described in Clause one, and omitted from the words of the Eleventh Amendment, a State may be sued without her consent. . . . [A]lthough a case may arise under the Constitution and laws of the United States, the judicial power does not extend to it if the suit is sought to be prosecuted against a State, without her consent, by one of her own citizens. *Hans v. Louisiana,* 134 U.S. 1. . . . Again, the Eleventh Amendment mentions only suits "in law or equity"; it does not refer to suits in admiralty. But this Court has held that the Amendment does not "leave open a suit against a State in the admiralty jurisdiction by individuals, whether its own citizens or not." *Ex parte State of New York, No. 1,* 256 U.S. 490, 498.

Manifestly, we cannot rest with a mere literal application of the words of §2 of Article III, or assume that the letter of the Eleventh Amendment exhausts the restrictions upon suits against non-consenting States. Behind the words of the constitutional provisions are postulates which limit and control. . . . There is . . . the postulate that States of the Union, still possessing attributes of sovereignty, shall be immune from suits, without their consent, save where there has been "a surrender of this immunity in the plan of the convention." The Federalist, No. 81. The question is whether the plan of the Constitution involves the surrender of immunity when the suit is brought against a State, without her consent, by a foreign State.

The debates in the Constitutional Convention do not disclose a discussion of this question. But Madison, in the Virginia Convention, answering objections to the ratification of the Constitution, clearly stated his view as to the purpose and effect of the provision conferring jurisdiction over controversies between States of the Union and foreign States. That purpose was suitably to provide for adjudication in such cases if consent should be given but not otherwise. Madison said: "The next case provides for disputes between a foreign state and one of our states, should such a case ever arise; and between a citizen and a foreign citizen or subject. I do not conceive that any controversy can ever be decided, in these courts, between an American state and a foreign state, without the consent of the parties. If they consent, provision is here made." 3 Elliot's Debates, 533. . . .

. . . We think that Madison correctly interpreted Clause one of §2 of Article III of the Constitution as making provision for jurisdiction of a suit against a State by a foreign State in the event of the State's consent but not otherwise. In such a case, the grounds of coercive jurisdiction which are present in suits to determine controversies between States of the Union, or in suits brought by the United States against a State, are not present. The foreign State lies outside the structure of the Union. The waiver or consent, on the part of a State, which inheres in the acceptance of the constitutional plan, runs to the other States who have likewise accepted that plan, and to the United States as the sovereign which the Constitution creates. We perceive no ground upon which it can be said that any waiver or consent by a State of the Union has run in favor of a foreign State. As to suits brought by a foreign State, we think that the States of the Union retain the same immunity that they enjoy with respect to suits by individuals whether citizens of the United States or citizens or subjects of a foreign State. The foreign State enjoys a similar sovereign immunity and without her consent may not be sued by a State of the Union.

The question of the right of suit by a foreign State against a State of the Union is not limited to cases of alleged debts or of obligations issued by a State and claimed to have been acquired by transfer. Controversies between a State and a foreign State may involve international questions in relation to which the United States has a sovereign prerogative. One of the most frequent occasions for the exercise of the jurisdiction granted by the Constitution over controversies between States of the Union has been found in disputes over territorial boundaries. See *Rhode Island v. Massachusetts*. Questions have also arisen with respect to the obstruction of navigation, the pollution of streams, and the diversion of navigable waters. But in the case of such a controversy with a foreign power, a State has no prerogative of adjustment. No State can enter "into and Treaty, Alliance, or Confederation" or, without the consent of Congress, "into any Agreement or Compact with a foreign Power." Const. Art. I, §10. The National Government, by virtue of its control of our foreign relations is entitled to employ the resources of diplomatic negotiations and to effect such an international settlement as may be found to be appropriate, through treaty, agreement of arbitration, or otherwise. It cannot be supposed that it was the intention that a controversy growing out of the action of a State, which involves a matter of national concern and which is said to affect injuriously the interests of a foreign State, or a dispute arising from conflicting claims of a State of the Union and a foreign State as to territorial boundaries, should be taken out of the sphere of international negotiations and adjustment through a resort by the foreign State to a suit under the provisions of §2 of Article III. In such a case, the State has immunity from suit without her consent and the National Government is protected by the provision prohibiting agreements between States and foreign powers in the absence of the consent of the Congress. While, in this instance, the proposed suit does not raise a question of national concern, the constitutional provision which is said to confer jurisdiction should be construed in the light of all its applications. . . .

Rule discharged, and leave [to bring suit] denied.

Notes and Questions

1. *Principality of Monaco* is one of many cases in which the Court has held that states have sovereign immunity broader than that indicated by the text of the

Eleventh Amendment. (Despite the Court's nonliteral approach, we use the term "Eleventh Amendment immunity" hereafter to refer to state sovereign immunity from federal court actions.) *Principality of Monaco* shows that Eleventh Amendment immunity restricts the original jurisdiction of the United States Supreme Court, as well as the original and removal jurisdiction of the lower federal courts. It makes sense for Eleventh Amendment immunity to restrict the Court's original jurisdiction inasmuch as the Eleventh Amendment was meant to overrule *Chisholm v. Georgia*, 2 U.S. (2 Dall.) 419 (1793), in which the Court held that it had original jurisdiction over a suit brought against a state by a citizen of another state.

2. Do you think the Court's decision in *Principality of Monaco* was influenced by the way that Monaco came to own the bonds—namely, because the Eleventh Amendment would have barred a federal court action by the bonds' original owners? *See* Thomas H. Lee, *The Supreme Court of the United States as Quasi-International Tribunal: Reclaiming the Court's Original and Exclusive Jurisdiction over Treaty-Based Suits by Foreign States Against States*, 104 Colum. L. Rev. 1765, 1810-1811 (2004) (arguing that this fact would have justified discretionary decision by the Court not to exercise original jurisdiction in *Principality of Monaco*, but that Court did have original jurisdiction over Monaco's action).

6. Actions by a Native American Tribe Against a State

Cherokee Nation v. Georgia

30 (5 Pet.) U.S. 1 (1831)

Mr[.] Chief Justice MARSHALL delivered the opinion of the Court.

This bill is brought by the Cherokee nation, praying an injunction to restrain the state of Georgia from the execution of certain laws of that state, which, as is alleged, go directly to annihilate the Cherokees as a political society, and to seize, for the use of Georgia, the lands of the nation which have been assured to them by the United States in solemn treaties repeatedly made and still in force.

If courts were permitted to indulge their sympathies, a case better calculated to excite them can scarcely be imagined. A people once numerous, powerful, and truly independent, found by our ancestors in the quiet and uncontrolled possession of an ample domain, gradually sinking beneath our superior policy, our arts and our arms, have yielded their lands by successive treaties, each of which contains a solemn guarantee of the residue, until they retain no more of their formerly extensive territory than is deemed necessary to their comfortable subsistence. To preserve this remnant, the present application is made.

Before we can look into the merits of the case, a preliminary inquiry presents itself. Has this court jurisdiction of the cause?

The third article of the constitution describes the extent of the judicial power. The second section closes an enumeration of the cases to which it is extended, with "controversies" "between a state or the citizens thereof, and foreign states, citizens, or subjects." A subsequent clause of the same section gives the supreme court original jurisdiction in all cases in which a state shall be a party. The party defendant may then unquestionably be sued in this court. May the plaintiff sue in it? Is the Cherokee nation a foreign state in the sense in which that term is used in the constitution? . . .

The counsel have shown conclusively that they are not a state of the union, and have insisted that individually they are aliens, not owing allegiance to the United

States. An aggregate of aliens composing a state must, they say, be a foreign state. Each individual being foreign, the whole must be foreign. . . .

Though the Indians are acknowledged to have an unquestionable, and, heretofore, unquestioned right to the lands they occupy, until that right shall be extinguished by a voluntary cession to our government; yet it may well be doubted whether those tribes which reside within the acknowledged boundaries of the United States can, with strict accuracy, be denominated foreign nations. They may, more correctly, perhaps, be denominated domestic dependent nations. They occupy a territory to which we assert a title independent of their will, which must take effect in point of possession when their right of possession ceases. Meanwhile they are in a state of pupilage. Their relation to the United States resembles that of a ward to his guardian. . . .

. . . [T]he peculiar relations between the United States and the Indians occupying our territory are such, that we should feel much difficulty in considering them as designated by the term *foreign state*, were there no other part of the constitution which might shed light on the meaning of these words. But we think that in construing them, considerable aid is furnished by that clause in the eighth section of the third article; which empowers congress to "regulate commerce with foreign nations, and among the several states, and with the Indian tribes."

In this clause they are as clearly contradistinguished by a name appropriate to themselves, from foreign nations, as from the several states composing the union. . . . We cannot assume that the distinction was lost in framing a subsequent article, unless there be something in its language to authorize the assumption.

. . . We find nothing in the context, and nothing in the subject of the article, which leads to it.

The court has bestowed its best attention on this question, and, after mature deliberation, the majority is of opinion that an Indian tribe or nation within the United States is not a foreign state in the sense of the constitution, and cannot maintain an action in the courts of the United States. . . .

The motion for an injunction is denied.

[The opinions of Justices Johnson and Baldwin concurring in the result, and the dissenting opinion of Justice Thompson, in which Justice Story joined, are omitted.]

Notes and Questions

1. The Court held in *Cherokee Nation* that Native American tribes are not "foreign States" within the meaning of the language in Article III, §2, clause 1, that extends federal judicial power to controversies "between a State . . . and foreign States." But in *Blatchford v. Native Village of Noatak*, 501 U.S. 775 (1991), the Court analogized Native American tribes to foreign states in holding that Eleventh Amendment immunity barred a tribe from asserting a federal claim against a state in federal district court under 28 U.S.C. §1362. The Court in *Blatchford* reasoned: "Just as in *Monaco* with regard to foreign sovereign, so also here with regard to Indian tribes, there is no compelling evidence that the Founders thought . . . a surrender [by the States of their sovereign immunity] inherent in the constitutional compact." *Id.* at 781. Are the Court's decisions in *Cherokee Nation* and *Blatchford* consistent except insofar as they both deny relief to a tribe suing a state?

2. In *Cherokee Nation*, counsel for the Cherokee Nation argued that its members were aliens. In the Indian Citizenship Act of 1924, Congress explicitly provided that a tribal member born in the United States is a U.S. citizen at birth. *See* Act of June 2, 1924, 43 Stat. 253 (current statute at 8 U.S.C. §1401(b)).

7. Actions by a State Against a Citizen of Another State

South Carolina v. Katzenbach

383 U.S. 301 (1966)

Mr. Chief Justice WARREN delivered the opinion of the Court.

By leave of the Court, South Carolina has filed a bill of complaint, seeking a declaration that selected provisions of the Voting Rights Act of 1965 violate the Federal Constitution, and asking for an injunction against enforcement of these provisions by the Attorney General. Original jurisdiction is founded on the presence of a controversy between a State and a citizen of another State under Art. III, §2, of the Constitution.[2] Because no issues of fact were raised in the complaint, and because of South Carolina's desire to obtain a ruling prior to its primary elections in June 1966, we dispensed with appointment of a special master and expedited our hearing of the case.

Recognizing that the questions presented were of urgent concern to the entire country, we invited all of the States to participate in this proceeding as friends of the Court. A majority responded by submitting or joining in briefs on the merits, some supporting South Carolina and others the Attorney General. Seven of these States also requested and received permission to argue the case orally at our hearing. . . .

The Voting Rights Act was designed by Congress to banish the blight of racial discrimination in voting, which has infected the electoral process in parts of our country for nearly a century. The Act creates stringent new remedies for voting discrimination where it persists on a pervasive scale, and in addition the statute strengthens existing remedies for pockets of voting discrimination elsewhere in the country. Congress assumed the power to prescribe these remedies from §2 of the Fifteenth Amendment, which authorizes the National Legislature to effectuate by "appropriate" measures the constitutional prohibition against racial discrimination in voting. We hold that the sections of the Act which are properly before us are an appropriate means for carrying out Congress' constitutional responsibilities and are consonant with all other provisions of the Constitution. We therefore deny South Carolina's request that enforcement of these sections of the Act be enjoined. . . .

The bill of complaint is . . . dismissed. . . .

[The opinion of Justice Black, "concurring and dissenting," is omitted.]

Notes and Questions

1. *Oregon v. Mitchell*, 400 U.S. 112 (1970) is another well-known original action by a state against a diverse U.S. Attorney General challenging the constitutionality of voting rights legislation. *See id.* at 117 n.1 (noting that Oregon's original action

---

2. Attorney General Katzenbach was a citizen of New Jersey. Richard H. Fallon et al., Hart and Wechsler's the Federal Courts and the Federal System 251 n.4 (6th ed. 2009).

against Attorney General Mitchell was consolidated with original actions by Texas against Mitchell and by the United States against Arizona and Idaho). In *Oregon v. Mitchell*, the Court held that Congress exceeded its power in enacting federal legislation giving people 18 years old and older the right to vote in state and local elections. That holding was "overruled" by the 26th Amendment.

2. The Court has original, but not exclusive, jurisdiction over actions by a state against a citizen of another state. *See* 28 U.S.C. §1251(b)(3). The federal district courts' diversity jurisdiction does not extend to actions by a state against citizens of another state. *See* 28 U.S.C. §1332(a). As a result, a state can sue a citizen of another state in federal district court only if the suit arises under federal law, in which case the diversity of the parties is irrelevant. Thus, for example, the district courts can entertain actions by a state against federal officials challenging the constitutionality of federal legislation. *See* 28 U.S.C. §1331; *see, e.g., Natl. Fedn. of Indep. Business v. Sebelius,* _____ U.S. _____, 132 S. Ct. 2566 (2012) (action by 26 states and other plaintiffs challenging constitutionality of Patient Protection and Affordable Care Act of 2010, as amended by the Health Care and Education Reconciliation Act of 2010).

C. APPELLATE JURISDICTION

1. Review of Federal Court Decisions

a. Overview

The United States Supreme Court has appellate jurisdiction over cases from four types of federal courts:

1. *Cases from the U.S. Courts of Appeals.* The vast majority of the federal court cases reviewed by the Court come from 13 federal courts of appeals, which include 12 regional courts of appeals and the United States Court of Appeals for the Federal Circuit. The Court's appellate jurisdiction over cases from these courts rests on 28 U.S.C. §1254, which is reproduced below.

2. *Cases from federal district courts.* A very small number of federal court cases reviewed by the Court can come from any of 94 district courts, including district courts in the U.S. Virgin Islands, Guam, and the Northern Mariana Islands. In some cases—now rare—Congress authorizes the Court to hear appeals from three-judge panels of the district courts. *See* 28 U.S.C. §§1253 & 2284; *see, e.g., Citizens United v. Fed. Election Commn.,* 558 U.S. 310 (2010) (reviewing decision of three-judge district court panel in case challenging constitutionality of provisions in Bipartisan Campaign Reform Act). Still rarer are certain antitrust cases in which Congress has authorized appeals to the Court from decisions of the district courts. *See* 15 U.S.C. §29(b); *see also Microsoft Corp. v. United States,* 530 U.S. 1301 (2000) (denying direct appeal from district court judgment sought under 15 U.S.C. §29(b), and remanding the case to the court of appeals); *Microsoft Corp. v. United States,* 534 U.S. 952 (2001) (denying petition for certiorari to review decision of court of appeals on remand).

3. *Cases from the Court of Appeals for the Armed Forces.* The Court has authority to review certain decisions of the United States Court of Appeals for the Armed Forces (CAAF). The CAAF, unlike the other federal courts of appeals, is an

"Article I court"—as distinguished from an "Article III court"—because its judges do not enjoy the protections that Article III gives the judges of Article III courts: namely, lifetime tenure during good behavior and irreducible salaries. The Court may review decisions of the CAAF under 28 U.S.C. §1259. *See, e.g., Edmond v. United States,* 520 U.S. 651 (1997) (reviewing CAAF decision presenting Appointments Clause challenge to appointment of judges on Coast Guard Court of Criminal Appeals); *Davis v. United States,* 512 U.S. 452 (1994) (reviewing CAAF decision presenting issue of the effectiveness of ambiguous invocation of right to counsel during custodial interrogation).

4. *Cases from the Foreign Intelligence Surveillance Court of Review.* The Court has authority to review decisions of the Foreign Intelligence Surveillance Court of Review, which was created in 2001 to review the decisions of federal judges on applications for surveillance under the Foreign Intelligence Surveillance Act. The Court of Review's decisions are subject to United States Supreme Court review under 50 U.S.C. §1803(b), but the Court has not yet granted plenary review of any decisions of that court. *Cf. American Civil Liberties Union v. United States,* 538 U.S. 920 (2003) (denying ACLU motion to intervene for purposes of petitioning for certiorari to review *In re Sealed Case,* 310 F.3d 725 (Foreign Intell. Surveillance Ct. Rev. 2002)).

Because the vast majority of federal court cases reviewed by the Court fall into the first category—that is, cases in the federal courts of appeals—the material in this section focuses on the Court's review of those cases.

b. Statutes

The Court reviews cases from the federal courts of appeals under 28 U.S.C. §1254.

28 U.S.C. §1254. Court of appeals; certiorari; certified questions

Cases in the courts of appeals may be reviewed by the Supreme Court by the following methods:

(1) By writ of certiorari granted upon the petition of any party to any civil or criminal case, before or after rendition of judgment or decree;

(2) By certification at any time by a court of appeals of any question of law in any civil or criminal case as to which instructions are desired, and upon such certification the Supreme Court may give binding instructions or require the entire record to be sent up for decision of the entire matter in controversy.

The Court rarely reviews cases by certification under §1254(2), though it has been argued that the Court should make greater use of the certification procedure. *See* Amanda L. Tyler, *Setting the Supreme Court's Agenda: Is There a Place for Certification?,* 78 Geo. Wash. L. Rev. 1310 (2010) (excerpt reproduced in Chapter 4, *infra*). Because of the infrequency of review by certification under §1254(2), the material in this section focuses instead on the Court's review of cases in the federal courts by writ of certiorari under §1254(1).

In addition to §1254(1), another statute, 28 U.S.C. §2101, addresses the timing rules for petitions for writ of certiorari, including petitions for certiorari under §1254(1). Section 2101(e) also authorizes petitions for writ of certiorari under §1254(1) to be filed before a judgment has been rendered in the federal court of appeals. Section 2101 provides in relevant part:

28 U.S.C. §2101. Supreme Court; time for appeal or certiorari; docketing; stay . . .

[handwritten: 90 days if appeal from judgment in civil action]

(c) . . . [A]ny writ of certiorari intended to bring any judgment or decree in a civil action, suit or proceeding before the Supreme Court for review shall be taken or applied for within ninety days after the entry of such judgment or decree. A justice of the Supreme Court, for good cause shown, may extend the time for applying for a writ of certiorari for a period not exceeding sixty days.

(d) The time for appeal or application for a writ of certiorari to review the judgment of a State court in a criminal case shall be as prescribed by rules of the Supreme Court. *[handwritten: Criminal cases the court decides how long to file cert]*

(e) An application to the Supreme Court for a writ of certiorari to review a case before judgment has been rendered in the court of appeals may be made at any time before judgment. . . . *[handwritten: if unrelated to judgment, file @ any time.]*

The organization of §2101 can be confusing until you work your way through each subsection. Section 2101(c) prescribes a 90-day time limit for all cert petitions in civil actions, whether those actions are in federal or state court. Section 2101(d) refers you to the Court's rules for the timing of cert petitions in criminal cases in state court. In fact, though, the Court's Rule 13.1 provides that "[u]nless otherwise provided by law," the time for filing *all* cert petitions is 90 days, whether the petition concerns a civil or criminal case, and whether the case is in federal or state court. Thus, 90 days after entry of judgment is the outer limit for all cert petitions (unless the Court grants an extension of time). In addition, §2101(e) authorizes the filing of a cert petition *before* judgment has been entered in a case in a federal court of appeals. This last option, available only in cases in the federal courts of appeals, is known as "seeking cert before judgment."

[handwritten: In reality crim & civil both 90 days after judgment]

c. Summary of Five Restrictions on Court's Review of Cases from the Federal Courts of Appeals

We provide material concerning five limits on the Court's review of federal-court decisions by certiorari under §1254:

First, §1254 requires that a "[c]as[e]" be "in" a federal court of appeals to be subject to review by the Court. For a case to be "in" a court of appeals, the court of appeals must have before it an appealable decision (for example, a decision by a federal district court or a federal agency) that has been properly appealed to it. *[handwritten: ① be in fed ct. app.]*

Second, although the Court can review a case in the court of appeals before the court of appeals has rendered any judgment, the Court ordinarily reviews cases in the court of appeals only after the court of appeals has rendered a final judgment—that is, a judgment that "ends the litigation on the merits and leaves nothing for the court to do but execute the judgment." *Catlin v. United States*, 324 U.S. 229, 233 (1945). *[handwritten: ② usually S. ct. waits til judgment @ lower court]*

Third, although §1254(1) allows "any party" to petition for certiorari, the Court generally does not grant petitions filed by the party who prevailed in the court of appeals. *[handwritten: ③ usually losing party]*

Fourth, although §1254(1) does not limit the Court to reviewing only court of appeals decisions that are based on *federal* law, the Court seldom grants certiorari to review a federal court of appeals' determination of *state* law. *[handwritten: ④ rarely state law]*

Fifth, in addition to its usual insistence on the presence of a federal issue, the Court usually requires the federal issue to have been pressed or passed upon in the lower courts. *[handwritten: ⑤ fed issue handled @ lower court]*

Before we delve into these limits, we note that these are not the only limits on the Court's jurisdiction. For example, like other federal courts, the U.S. Supreme

Court's appellate jurisdiction, like its original jurisdiction, is limited by Article III's justiciability doctrines of, for example, standing, ripeness, and mootness.

d. The Requirement of a Case "in" a Court of Appeals

United States v. Nixon

418 U.S. 683 (1974)

Mr. Chief Justice BURGER delivered the opinion of the Court.

This litigation presents for review the denial of a motion, filed in the District Court on behalf of the President of the United States, in the case of *United States v. Mitchell* to quash a third-party subpoena *duces tecum* issued by the United States District Court for the District of Columbia, pursuant to Fed. Rule Crim. Proc. 17(c). The subpoena directed the President to produce certain tape recordings and documents relating to his conversations with aides and advisers. The court rejected the President's claims of absolute executive privilege, of lack of jurisdiction, and of failure to satisfy the requirements of Rule 17(c). The President appealed to the Court of Appeals. We granted both the United States' petition for certiorari before judgment (No. 73-1766), and also the President's cross-petition for certiorari before judgment (No. 73-1834),[2] because of the public importance of the issues presented and the need for their prompt resolution.

On March 1, 1974, a grand jury of the United States District Court for the District of Columbia returned an indictment charging seven named individuals[3] with various offenses, including conspiracy to defraud the United States and to obstruct justice. Although he was not designated as such in the indictment, the grand jury named the President, among others, as an unindicted coconspirator. On April 18, 1974, upon motion of the Special Prosecutor, . . . a subpoena *duces tecum* was issued . . . to the President by the United States District Court and made returnable on May 2, 1974. This subpoena required the production, in advance of the September 9 trial date, of certain tapes, memoranda, papers, transcripts, or other writings relating to certain precisely identified meetings between the President and others. The Special Prosecutor was able to fix the time, place, and persons present at these discussions because the White House daily logs and appointment records had been delivered to him. On April 30, the President publicly released edited transcripts of 43 conversations; portions of 20 conversations subject to subpoena in the present case were included. On May 1, 1974, the President's counsel filed a "special appearance" and a motion to quash the subpoena. . . . This motion was accompanied by a formal claim of privilege. . . .

On May 20, 1974, the District Court denied the motion to quash. . . .

. . . [T]he President filed a timely notice of appeal from the District Court order, and the certified record from the District Court was docketed in the United States Court of Appeals for the District of Columbia Circuit. . . .

---

2. The cross-petition in No. 73-1834 raised the issue whether the grand jury acted within its authority in naming the President as an unindicted coconspirator. Since we find resolution of this issue unnecessary to resolution of the question whether the claim of privilege is to prevail, the cross-petition for certiorari is dismissed as improvidently granted and the remainder of this opinion is concerned with the issues raised in No. 73-1766. . . .

3. The seven defendants were John N. Mitchell, H. R. Haldeman, John D. Ehrlichman, Charles W. Colson, Robert C. Mardian, Kenneth W. Parkinson, and Gordon Strachan. Each had occupied either a position of responsibility on the White House staff or a position with the Committee for the Re-election of the President. Colson entered a guilty plea on another charge and is no longer a defendant.

. . . [T]he Special Prosecutor . . . filed, in this Court, a petition for a writ of certiorari before judgment. . . . [T]he petition was granted. . . . [T]he President filed, under seal, a cross-petition for writ of certiorari before judgment. This cross-petition was granted. . . .

I. JURISDICTION

The threshold question presented is whether the May 20, 1974, order of the District Court was an appealable order and whether this case was properly "in" the Court of Appeals when the petition for certiorari was filed in this Court. 28 U.S.C. §1254. The Court of Appeals' jurisdiction under 28 U.S.C. §1291 encompasses only "final decisions of the district courts." Since the appeal was timely filed and all other procedural requirements were met, the petition is properly before this Court for consideration if the District Court order was final. 28 U.S.C. §§1254(1), 2101(e).

The finality requirement of 28 U.S.C. §1291 embodies a strong congressional policy against piecemeal reviews, and against obstructing or impeding an ongoing judicial proceeding by interlocutory appeals. This requirement ordinarily promotes judicial efficiency and hastens the ultimate termination of litigation. In applying this principle to an order denying a motion to quash and requiring the production of evidence pursuant to a subpoena *duces tecum,* it has been repeatedly held that the order is not final and hence not appealable. This Court has ~~For production of evidence~~

"consistently held that the necessity for expedition in the administration of the criminal law justifies putting one who seeks to resist the production of desired information to a choice between compliance with a trial court's order to produce prior to any review of that order, and resistance to that order with the concomitant possibility of an adjudication of contempt if his claims are rejected on appeal." *United States v. Ryan,* 402 U.S., at 533.

The requirement of submitting to contempt, however, is not without exception and in some instances the purposes underlying the finality rule require a different result. For example, in *Perlman v. United States,* 247 U.S. 7 (1918), a subpoena had been directed to a third party requesting certain exhibits; the appellant, who owned the exhibits, sought to raise a claim of privilege. The Court held an order compelling production was appealable because it was unlikely that the third party would risk a contempt citation in order to allow immediate review of the appellant's claim of privilege. That case fell within the "limited class of cases where denial of immediate review would render impossible any review whatsoever of an individual's claims." *United States v. Ryan,* 402 U.S., at 533.

Here too, the traditional contempt avenue to immediate appeal is peculiarly inappropriate due to the unique setting in which the question arises. To require a President of the United States to place himself in the posture of disobeying an order of a court merely to trigger the procedural mechanism for review of the ruling would be unseemly, and would present an unnecessary occasion for constitutional confrontation between two branches of the Government. Similarly, a federal judge should not be placed in the posture of issuing a citation to a President simply in order to invoke review. The issue whether a President can be cited for contempt could itself engender protracted litigation, and would further delay both review on the merits of his claim of privilege and the ultimate termination of the underlying criminal action for which his evidence is sought. These considerations lead us to conclude that the order of the District Court was an appealable order. The appeal from that order was therefore properly "in" the Court of Appeals, and the case is now properly before this Court on the writ of certiorari before judgment. . . .

Mr. Justice REHNQUIST took no part in the consideration or decision of these cases.

Notes and Questions

1. *Nixon* illustrates that, for a case to be "in" a federal court of appeals for purposes of 28 U.S.C. §1254(1), the federal court of appeals must have jurisdiction over the case. That is why the Court's jurisdiction under §1254(1) depends on the court of appeals' jurisdiction. In *Nixon*, the court of appeals' jurisdiction rested on 28 U.S.C. §1291, which generally gives the courts of appeals jurisdiction over "appeals from all *final* decisions of the district courts." 28 U.S.C. §1291 (emphasis added). Thus, the Court had to determine whether the court of appeals had before it a "final" decision of the district court. What decision by the district court did the Court in *Nixon* find "final"? On what rationale? Does the rationale extend to cases beyond those involving a sitting President? If not, is it appropriate to have special rules of jurisdiction for the President?

2. The "collateral order" doctrine treats some interlocutory decisions by federal district courts as final, and therefore appealable to a federal court of appeals, under §1291. *See, e.g., Cohen v. Beneficial Indus. Loan Corp.*, 337 U.S. 541, 546 (1949). The Court relied on the collateral order doctrine in *Nixon v. Fitzgerald*, 457 U.S. 731 (1982). Fitzgerald sued by-then former President Nixon for money damages in federal court, claiming that Nixon was part of a conspiracy that forced Fitzgerald out of his government job. Nixon claimed absolute immunity from the suit. The district court rejected Nixon's immunity defense. Nixon took an interlocutory appeal of the district court's immunity ruling to the federal court of appeals, which dismissed his appeal for lack of jurisdiction. Petition for a Writ of Certiorari at 54, *Nixon v. Fitzgerald*, 457 U.S. 731 (No. 79-1738). The Court relied on the collateral order doctrine to hold that that the district court's immunity ruling was appealable as a final order under §1291; the "case" was thus "in" the court of appeals within the meaning of §1254(1) and thus reviewable by the Court on Nixon's petition for certiorari. *Nixon v. Fitzgerald*, 457 U.S. at 742-743.

3. In addition to having appellate jurisdiction over final decisions of the district courts under §1291, the federal courts of appeals have jurisdiction over appeals from certain interlocutory decisions of district courts, such as orders granting or denying preliminary injunctions, under 28 U.S.C. §1292(a). For example, a properly appealed district court order denying a preliminary injunction can be "in" a federal court of appeals, and the Court can review the court of appeals' decision on that appeal under 28 U.S.C. §1254(1). *See, e.g., City of Indianapolis v. Edmond*, 531 U.S. 32 (2000) (reviewing court of appeals' decision reversing district court's denial of preliminary injunction against drug interdiction checkpoint). As discussed later in this chapter, however, the Court ordinarily does not review federal court of appeals decisions on review of interlocutory orders by district courts, preferring instead to review only final judgments of the federal courts of appeals.

4. Section 1254(1) of Title 28 authorizes the Court to grant certiorari "before or after rendition of [a] judgment or decree" by the court of appeals. *See also* 28 U.S.C. §2101(e). The Court in *Nixon* granted certiorari before the federal court of

appeals made any judgment in *Nixon* "because of the public importance of the issues presented and the need for their prompt resolution." 418 U.S. at 687. The Court's Rule 11 provides that the Court will grant certiorari before judgment "only upon a showing that the case is of such imperative public importance as to justify deviation from normal appellate practice and to require immediate determination in this Court." *See generally* Eugene Gressman et al., *Supreme Court Practice: For Practice in the Supreme Court of the United States* 285 (9th ed. 2007).

In the years after *Nixon*, the Court has arguably shown greater willingness than before to grant certiorari before judgment in order to decide cases on the merits. *See, e.g., United States v. Booker*, 543 U.S. 220, 229 (2005) (opinion deciding two cases in which Court granted certiorari before judgment to consider constitutionality of U.S. Sentencing Guidelines); *Gratz v. Bollinger*, 539 U.S. 244, 259-260 (2003) (granting certiorari before judgment to consider constitutionality of affirmative action plan for admission to undergraduate program at University of Michigan at the same time as Court considered affirmative action plan for admission to the university's law school); *Mistretta v. United States*, 488 U.S. 361 (1989) (constitutional challenges to U.S. Sentencing Guidelines); *Dames & Moore v. Regan*, 453 U.S. 654, 668 (1981) (constitutional challenge to executive settlement ending Iranian hostage crisis).

Nonetheless, the Court still denies certiorari before judgment in cases that raise issues important enough to warrant a later grant of certiorari after a judgment in the court of appeals. For example, the State of Virginia sought certiorari before judgment in a lawsuit challenging the constitutionality of a provision in the Patient Protection and Affordable Care Act of 2010 that was called the "individual mandate" and that requires people to have health insurance. The Court denied certiorari before judgment but later granted certiorari after judgment in two other cases to review the constitutionality of the individual mandate. *See Natl. Fedn. of Indep. Business v. Sebelius*, _____ U.S. _____, 132 S. Ct. 2566 (2012) (decision on the merits). Well-known cases before *Nixon* in which the Court granted certiorari before judgment include: *Youngstown Sheet & Tube Co. v. Sawyer*, 343 U.S. 937 (1952) (Memorandum of Burton J., joined by Frankfurter, J.) (expressing disagreement with Court's decision to grant certiorari before judgment), *decision on the merits*, 343 U.S. 579 (1952) (constitutional challenge to President's executive order directing government takeover of the nation's steel mills); *Ex parte Quirin*, 317 U.S. 1 (1942) (constitutional challenge to trial by military commission of Nazi saboteurs); *Carter v. Carter Coal Co.*, 298 U.S. 238 (1936) (constitutional challenge to Bituminous Coal Conservation Act). Why do you suppose that, in general, the Court rarely grants certiorari before judgment?

5. In *Nixon*, the Court granted certiorari before judgment to both the United States *and* Richard Nixon, but later dismissed Nixon's cross-petition as improvidently granted. The Court thus decided the case on the United States' cert petition. Recall, however, that the United States prevailed in the district court (and had not yet gotten any decision, favorable or unfavorable, from the court of appeals). Thus, the Court in *Nixon* reviewed the case on petition of the party who prevailed below. The governing statute, 28 U.S.C. §1254(1), authorizes review "upon the petition of *any* party." (Emphasis added.) As the Court recently reaffirmed, "[t]hat language covers petitions brought by litigants who have prevailed, as well as those who have lost, in the court below." *Camreta v. Greene*, _____ U.S. _____, 131 S. Ct. 2020, 2028 (2011). The Court in several cases before *Nixon* had granted certiorari before judgment on a petition filed by the party who had prevailed in the district court.

See *Mistretta*, 488 U.S. at 371; *Youngstown Sheet & Tube*, 343 U.S. at 937; *United States v. United Mine Workers of America*, 330 U.S. 258, 269 (1947).

e. The Rule Disfavoring Review of Nonfinal Judgments of the Courts of Appeals

As discussed above, 28 U.S.C. §1254 authorizes the Court to review a "[c]as[e] in the court of appeals" even before the court of appeals renders a judgment in the case. The Court exercised that authority, for example, in *United States v. Nixon*, 418 U.S. 683 (1974). Nonetheless, the Court rarely grants certiorari before a judgment has been entered in the court of appeals. More than that: As a matter of prudence, the Court generally will not review a case until the court of appeals has rendered a final judgment, as distinguished from a nonfinal judgment. The material below illustrates the Court's prudential rule disfavoring review of nonfinal judgments by the federal courts of appeals.

United States v. Virginia

976 F.2d 890 (4th Cir. 1992)

[Virginia Military Institute (VMI) is a state college in Virginia. Before this litigation, VMI had a policy of admitting only men. The United States brought this civil action to challenge VMI's men-only admission policy as a violation of the Equal Protection Clause of the Fourteenth Amendment. The action named as defendants the State of Virginia, VMI, and various officials (referred to collectively hereafter as "Virginia").

Virginia defended the men-only policy as necessary to VMI's mission of producing "citizen-soldiers" through a unique, "adversative" educational model. The adversative method entailed, among other things, absence of privacy and communal living. VMI contended that forcing it to become coeducational would destroy this model of education.

On the case's first trip to the United States Court of Appeals for the Fourth Circuit, the Fourth Circuit held that Virginia violated the Equal Protection Clause by offering women no public education program of higher education comparable to that offered by VMI to men. See *United States v. Virginia*, 976 F.2d 890 (4th Cir. 1992). The closing paragraphs of the Fourth Circuit's opinion follow:]

Before PHILLIPS and NIEMEYER, Circuit Judges, and WARD, Senior District Judge for the Middle District of North Carolina, sitting by designation. . . .

NIEMEYER, Circuit Judge: . . .

We are thus left with three conclusions: (1) single-gender education, and VMI's program in particular, is justified by a legitimate and relevant institutional mission which favors neither sex; (2) the introduction of women at VMI will materially alter the very program in which women seek to partake; and (3) the Commonwealth of Virginia, despite its announced policy of diversity, has failed to articulate an important policy that substantially supports offering the unique benefits of a VMI-type of education to men and not to women.

Although neither the goal of producing citizen soldiers nor VMI's implementing methodology is inherently unsuitable to women, the Commonwealth has elected, through delegation or inaction, to maintain a system of education which offers the program only to men. In the proceedings below, Virginia had the opportunity to meet its burden of demonstrating that it had made an important and meaningful distinction in perpetuating this condition. As the record stands, however, evidence of a legitimate and substantial state purpose is lacking.

In light of our conclusions and the generally recognized benefit that VMI provides, we do not order that women be admitted to VMI if alternatives are available. But VMI's continued status as a state institution is conditioned on the Commonwealth's satisfactorily addressing the findings we affirm and bringing the circumstances into conformity with the Equal Protection Clause of the Fourteenth Amendment. By commenting on the potential benefits of single-gender education while discussing the alleged governmental interest in support of VMI's admissions policies, we do not mean to suggest the specific remedial course that the Commonwealth should or must follow hereafter. Rather, we remand the case to the district court to give to the Commonwealth the responsibility to select a course it chooses, so long as the guarantees of the Fourteenth Amendment are satisfied. Consistent therewith, the Commonwealth might properly decide to admit women to VMI and adjust the program to implement that choice, or it might establish parallel institutions or parallel programs, or it might abandon state support of VMI, leaving VMI the option to pursue its own policies as a private institution. While it is not ours to determine, there might be other more creative options or combinations.

Accordingly, we vacate the judgment and remand the case to the district court: (1) to require the defendants to formulate, adopt, and implement a plan that conforms with the Equal Protection Clause of the Fourteenth Amendment, (2) to establish appropriate timetables, and (3) to oversee the implementation of the plan. . . .

Virginia Military Institute v. United States

No. 92-1213
C.A. 4th Cir. *cert. denied*

Justice THOMAS took no part in the consideration or decision of this petition. Reported below: 976 F.2d 890. [508 U.S. 946 (1993)]

Opinion of Justice SCALIA, respecting the denial of the petition for writ of certiorari.

Whether it is constitutional for a State to have a men-only military school is an issue that should receive the attention of this Court before, rather than after, a national institution as venerable as the Virginia Military Institute [(VMI)] is compelled to transform itself. This present petition, however, seeks our intervention before the litigation below has come to final judgment. The Court of Appeals vacated the judgment that had been entered in favor of petitioners, and remanded the case to the District Court for determination of an appropriate remedy. It expressly declined to rule on the "specific remedial course that the Commonwealth should or must follow hereafter," and suggested permissible remedies other than compelling the Virginia Military Institute to abandon its current admissions policy.

We generally await final judgment in the lower courts before exercising our certiorari jurisdiction. *See, e.g., American Constr. Co. v. Jacksonville, T. & K.W.R. Co.,* 148 U.S. 372, 384 (1893); *Locomotive Firemen v. Bangor & Aroostook R. Co.,* 389 U.S. 327, 328 (1967) (*per curiam*); see generally R. Stern, E. Gressman, & S. Shapiro, Supreme Court Practice §4.18, pp. 224-226 (6th ed. 1986). I think it prudent to take that course here. Our action does not, of course, preclude VMI from raising the same issues in a later petition, after final judgment has been rendered. See, *e.g.*, *Hamilton-Brown Shoe Co. v. Wolf Brothers & Co.*, 240 U.S. 251, 257-259 (1916); *Hughes Tool Co. v. Trans World Airlines, Inc.*, 409 U.S. 363, 365-366, n.1 (1973); Stern, Gressman, & Shapiro, supra, §4.18, at 226; 17 C. Wright, A. Miller, & E. Cooper, Federal Practice and Procedure §4036, p. 32 (2d ed. 1988).

Notes and Questions

1. The Court's practice of "generally await[ing] final judgment in the lower courts before exercising [its] certiorari jurisdiction" is not compelled by §1254(1), for that statute authorizes review "before or after rendition of judgment." Thus, "there is no absolute bar to review of nonfinal judgments of the lower federal courts." *Mazurek v. Armstrong*, 520 U.S. 968, 975 (1997); *see also Randolph Cent. Sch. Dist. v. Aldrich*, 506 U.S. 965 (1992) (White, J., dissenting from denial of certiorari) ("Respondent does not, and cannot, question this Court's jurisdiction to review a nonfinal judgment of a court of appeals under 28 U.S.C. §1254(1)."). In contrast, as discussed *infra*, 28 U.S.C. §1257(a) limits the Court to reviewing only "[*f*]*inal* judgments or decrees" from the state court systems. (Emphasis added.)

2. If the Court had granted certiorari to review the Fourth Circuit's decision, could the Court have reviewed the constitutionality of Virginia's offering a VMI-type program of public education only to men? If so, why did the Court not do so? What, do you suppose, are the reasons for the Court's general practice of awaiting a final judgment by a court of appeals before exercising its certiorari power under §1254(1)?

3. As you may know, the Court eventually granted review in the *VMI* case after the Fourth Circuit entered a final judgment, and held that Virginia had violated the Equal Protection Clause by offering a VMI-type program of public higher education only to men. *See United States v. Virginia*, 518 U.S. 515 (1996).

4. Despite the Court's general practice of reviewing only final judgments of the court of appeals, the Court often departs from that practice, usually without explanation. For example, the Court reviewed the nonfinal judgment of a federal court of appeals in *Bowers v. Hardwick*, 478 U.S. 186 (1986), *overruled by Lawrence v. Texas*, 539 U.S. 558 (2003). Hardwick sued Georgia Attorney General Bowers in federal court, challenging the constitutionality of the Georgia statute criminalizing sodomy. The federal district court dismissed the suit. The U.S. Court of Appeals for the Eleventh Circuit, however, reversed and remanded. The Eleventh Circuit held that the Georgia statute violated Hardwick's fundamental rights, and the court remanded the case for a trial at which, to win, Georgia would have to prove that its statute served a compelling interest and was the most narrowly tailored way to achieve that interest. *See id.* at 189. The Court granted certiorari without addressing the nonfinal nature of the Eleventh Circuit's judgment. The Court did observe, however, "[O]ther Courts of Appeals have arrived at judgments contrary to that of the Eleventh Circuit in this case." *Id.*

If you were representing Georgia, what arguments might you have made about why the Court should not grant review of the case in this nonfinal posture? If you were representing Hardwick, what arguments would you make in favor of reviewing the nonfinal judgment?

f. The Rule Disfavoring Grant of Petition by Party Prevailing in the Court of Appeals

Section 1254(1) of Title 28 authorizes the Court to review a case in the court of appeals upon the petition for certiorari "of any party." The Court has construed this "any party" language to allow the Court to grant certiorari before judgment on the petition of a party who won in the district court, once there has been a timely, proper appeal to the federal court of appeals. For example, the Court in *United States v. Nixon* granted certiorari before judgment on petition of the United States, which had prevailed in the district court against Nixon's challenge to a subpoena. *See* 418 U.S. at 686. When the Court grants certiorari in that situation, the Court reviews the case in lieu of the court of appeals. *See* Eugene Gressman et al., *Supreme Court Practice: For Practice in the Supreme Court of the United States* 86 (9th ed. 2007).

The next case appears to be the first time in which the Court has granted certiorari on petition of the party who prevailed—not in the district court—but, instead, in the court of appeals. *See Kalka v. Hawk*, 215 F.3d 90, 96 n.9 (D.C. Cir. 2000) ("The Court has apparently never granted the certiorari petition of a party who prevailed in the appellate court.") (citing Robert L. Stern et al., *Supreme Court Practice* 45 (7th ed. 1993)). As you read the case, consider why it matters whether the party petitioning for certiorari prevailed in the district court or, instead, in the court of appeals.

Camreta v. Greene

563 U.S. _____, 131 S. Ct. 2020 (2011)

[The plaintiff, Sarah Greene, sued two Oregon officials in federal court on behalf of her daughter, "S.G." Greene claimed that the officials violated S.G.'s Fourth Amendment rights and were therefore liable to S.G. in damages under 42 U.S.C. §1983. According to Greene, the officials violated the Fourth Amendment when, without a warrant, they interviewed S.G. at school about alleged sexual abuse by her father.

On appeal from the district court, the United States Court of Appeals for the Ninth Circuit agreed with Greene that the officials violated the Fourth Amendment. The Ninth Circuit further held, however, that the officials had qualified immunity—which shielded them from a judgment awarding damages under §1983—because the unconstitutionality of their conduct had not been clearly established when they acted. Based on this immunity ruling, the Ninth Circuit entered a judgment in favor of the officials by affirming the district court's order granting summary judgment in their favor.

The officials each petitioned for certiorari, seeking review of the Ninth Circuit's holding that their conduct violated the Fourth Amendment. One of the officials, Bob Camreta, also presented the question: "Is the Ninth Circuit's constitutional ruling reviewable, notwithstanding that it ruled in petitioner's favor on qualified immunity grounds?" Petition for Certiorari at i, *Camreta v. Greene*, 131 S. Ct. 2020 (No. 09-1454). The Court granted the officials' petitions. 131 S. Ct. 456, 457 (2010). In the following excerpt, the Court explained its decision to grant petitions filed by parties who prevailed in the court of appeals.]

Justice KAGAN delivered the opinion of the Court. . . .

II

We first consider our ability to act on a petition brought by government officials who have won final judgment on grounds of qualified immunity, but who object to an appellate court's ruling that they violated the plaintiff's constitutional rights. Camreta and Alford are, without doubt, prevailing parties. The Ninth Circuit's decision shielded them from monetary liability, and S.G. chose not to contest that ruling. So whatever else follows, they will not have to pay S.G. the damages she sought. The question we confront is whether we may nonetheless review the Court of Appeals' holding that the officials violated the Constitution.

The statute governing this Court's jurisdiction authorizes us to adjudicate a case in this posture, and S.G. does not contend otherwise. The relevant provision confers unqualified power on this Court to grant certiorari "upon the petition of *any* party." 28 U.S.C. §1254(1) (emphasis added). That language covers petitions brought by litigants who have prevailed, as well as those who have lost, in the court below. See E. Gressman, K. Geller, S. Shapiro, T. Bishop, & E. Hartnett, Supreme Court Practice 87 (9th ed. 2007) (hereinafter Stern & Gressman).

S.G., however, alleges two impediments to our exercise of statutory authority here, one constitutional and the other prudential. First, she claims that Article III bars review because petitions submitted by immunized officials present no case or controversy. Second, she argues that our settled practice of declining to hear appeals by prevailing parties should apply with full force when officials have obtained immunity. We disagree on both counts.

A

Article III of the Constitution grants this Court authority to adjudicate legal disputes only in the context of "Cases" or "Controversies." To enforce this limitation, we demand that litigants demonstrate a "personal stake" in the suit. . . .

We have previously recognized that an appeal brought by a prevailing party may satisfy Article III's case-or-controversy requirement. See *Deposit Guaranty Nat. Bank v. Roper*, 445 U.S. 326, 332-336 (1980). Indeed, we have twice before allowed a party for whom judgment was entered to challenge an unfavorable lower court ruling. See *ibid.*; *Electrical Fittings Corp. v. Thomas & Betts Co.*, 307 U.S. 241 (1939). . . .

This Article III standard often will be met when immunized officials seek to challenge a ruling that their conduct violated the Constitution. That is not because a court has made a retrospective judgment about the lawfulness of the officials' behavior, for that judgment is unaccompanied by any personal liability. Rather, it is because the judgment may have prospective effect on the parties. The court in such a case says: "Although this official is immune from damages today, what he did violates the Constitution and he or anyone else who does that thing again will be personally liable." If the official regularly engages in that conduct as part of his job (as Camreta does), he suffers injury caused by the adverse constitutional ruling. So long as it continues in effect, he must either change the way he performs his duties or risk a meritorious damages action. . . . Only by overturning the ruling on appeal can the official gain clearance to engage in the conduct in the future. . . .

B

Article III aside, an important question of judicial policy remains. As a matter of practice and prudence, we have generally declined to consider cases at the request of a prevailing party, even when the Constitution allowed us to do so. Our resources are not well spent superintending each word a lower court utters en route to a final judgment in the petitioning party's favor. See *California v. Rooney*, 483 U.S. 307, 311 (1987) (*per curiam*). . . . We therefore have adhered with some rigor to the principle that "[t]his Court reviews judgments, not statements in opinions." *Ibid.* (internal quotation marks omitted). On the few occasions when we have departed from that principle, we have pointed to a "policy reaso[n] . . . of sufficient importance to allow an appeal" by the winner below. *Deposit Guaranty*, 445 U.S., at 336, n.7.

We think just such a reason places qualified immunity cases in a special category when it comes to this Court's review of appeals brought by winners. The constitutional determinations that prevailing parties ask us to consider in these cases are not mere dicta or "statements in opinions." *Rooney*, 483 U.S., at 311. . . . They are rulings that have a significant future effect on the conduct of public officials—both the prevailing parties and their co-workers—and the policies of the government units to which they belong. And more: they are rulings self-consciously designed to produce this effect, by establishing controlling law and preventing invocations of immunity in later cases. And still more: they are rulings designed this way with this Court's permission, to promote clarity—and observance—of constitutional rules. We describe in more detail below these features of the qualified immunity world and why they came to be. We hold that taken together, they support bending our usual rule to permit consideration of immunized officials' petitions.

To begin, then, with the nature of these suits: Under §1983 (invoked in this case) and *Bivens v. Six Unknown Fed. Narcotics Agents*, 403 U.S. 388 (1971), a plaintiff may seek money damages from government officials who have violated her constitutional or statutory rights. But to ensure that fear of liability will not "unduly inhibit officials in the discharge of their duties," *Anderson v. Creighton*, 483 U.S. 635, 638 (1987), the officials may claim qualified immunity; so long as they have not violated a "clearly established" right, they are shielded from personal liability, *Harlow v. Fitzgerald*, 457 U.S. 800, 818 (1982). That means a court can often avoid ruling on the plaintiff's claim that a particular right exists. If prior case law has not clearly settled the right, and so given officials fair notice of it, the court can simply dismiss the claim for money damages. The court need never decide whether the plaintiff's claim, even though novel or otherwise unsettled, in fact has merit.

And indeed, our usual adjudicatory rules suggest that a court *should* forbear resolving this issue. After all, a "longstanding principle of judicial restraint requires that courts avoid reaching constitutional questions in advance of the necessity of deciding them." *Lyng v. Northwest Indian Cemetery Protective Assn.*, 485 U.S. 439, 445 (1988); see also *Ashwander v. TVA*, 297 U.S. 288, 346-347 (1936) (Brandeis, J., concurring). In this category of qualified immunity cases, a court can enter judgment without ever ruling on the (perhaps difficult) constitutional claim the plaintiff has raised. Small wonder, then, that a court might leave that issue for another day.

But we have long recognized that this day may never come—that our regular policy of avoidance sometimes does not fit the qualified immunity situation because it threatens to leave standards of official conduct permanently in limbo. . . . Qualified immunity thus may frustrate "the development of constitutional precedent" and the promotion of law-abiding behavior. *Pearson v. Callahan*, 555 U.S. 223, 237 (2009).

For this reason, we have permitted lower courts to avoid avoidance—that is, to determine whether a right exists before examining whether it was clearly established. . . . In general, courts should think hard, and then think hard again, before turning small cases into large ones. But it remains true that following the two-step sequence—defining constitutional rights and only then conferring immunity—is sometimes beneficial to clarify the legal standards governing public officials.

Here, the Court of Appeals followed exactly this two-step process. . . . [T]he court adopted constitutional standards to govern all in-school interviews of suspected child abuse victims. . . . With the law thus clearly established, officials who conduct this kind of interview will not receive immunity in the Ninth Circuit. . . .

Given its purpose and effect, such a decision is reviewable in this Court at the behest of an immunized official. No mere dictum, a constitutional ruling preparatory to a grant of immunity creates law that governs the official's behavior. If our usual rule pertaining to prevailing parties applied, the official would "fac[e] an unenviable choice": He must either acquiesce in a ruling he had no opportunity to contest in this Court, or "defy the views of the lower court, adhere to practices that have been declared illegal, and thus invite new suits and potential punitive damages." *Pearson*, 555 U.S., at 240-241. . . . And if our usual bar on review applied, it would undermine the very purpose served by the two-step process, "which is to clarify constitutional rights without undue delay." *Bunting* [*v. Mellen*], 541 U.S. [1019, 1024 (2004)] (SCALIA, J., dissenting from denial of certiorari). This Court, needless to say, also plays a role in clarifying rights. Just as that purpose may justify an appellate court in reaching beyond an immunity defense to decide a constitutional issue, so too that purpose may support this Court in reviewing the correctness of the lower court's decision.

We emphasize, however, two limits of today's holding. First, it addresses only our own authority to review cases in this procedural posture. The Ninth Circuit had no occasion to consider whether it could hear an appeal from an immunized official: In that court, after all, S.G. appealed the judgment in the officials' favor. We therefore need not and do not decide if an appellate court, too, can entertain an appeal from a party who has prevailed on immunity grounds. Second, our holding concerns only what this Court *may* review; what we actually will choose to review is a different matter. That choice will be governed by the ordinary principles informing our decision whether to grant certiorari—a "power [we] . . . sparingly exercis[e]." *Forsyth v. Hammond*, 166 U.S. 506, 514 (1897). Our decision today does no more than exempt one special category of cases from our usual rule against considering prevailing parties' petitions. Going forward, we will consider these petitions one by one in accord with our usual standards.

III

Although we reject S.G.'s arguments for dismissing this case at the threshold, we find that a separate jurisdictional problem requires that result: This case, we conclude, is moot. . . .

. . . S.G. can no longer claim the plaintiff's usual stake in preserving the court's holding because she is no longer in need of any protection from the challenged practice. After we granted certiorari, we discovered that S.G. has "moved to Florida, and ha[s] no intention of relocating back to Oregon." What is more, S.G. is now only months away from her 18th birthday—and, presumably, from her high school graduation. S.G. therefore cannot be affected by the Court of Appeals' ruling; she faces not the slightest possibility of being seized in a school in the Ninth Circuit's jurisdiction as part of a child abuse investigation. . . .

We thus must decide how to dispose of this case. When a civil suit becomes moot pending appeal, we have the authority to "direct the entry of such appropriate judgment, decree, or order, or require such further proceedings to be had as may be just under the circumstances." 28 U.S.C. §2106. Our "established" (though not exceptionless) practice in this situation is to vacate the judgment below. "A party who seeks review of the merits of an adverse ruling, but is frustrated by the vagaries of circumstance," we have emphasized, "ought not in fairness be forced to acquiesce in" that ruling. *U.S. Bancorp Mortgage Co. v. Bonner Mall Partnership*, 513 U.S. 18, 25 (1994). The equitable remedy of vacatur ensures that "those who have been prevented from obtaining the review to which they are entitled [are] not . . . treated as if there had been a review." [*United States v.*] *Munsingwear*, 340 U.S. [36, 39 (1950)].

In this case, the happenstance of S.G.'s moving across country and becoming an adult has deprived Camreta of his appeal rights. Mootness has frustrated his ability to challenge the Court of Appeals' ruling that he must obtain a warrant before interviewing a suspected child abuse victim at school. We therefore vacate the part of the Ninth Circuit's opinion that addressed that issue, and remand for further proceedings consistent with this opinion.[11]

Justice SCALIA, concurring.

I join the Court's opinion, which reasonably applies our precedents, strange though they may be. The alternative solution, as Justice Kennedy suggests, is to end the extraordinary practice of ruling upon constitutional questions unnecessarily when the defendant possesses qualified immunity. See *Saucier v. Katz*, 533 U.S. 194 (2001). The parties have not asked us to adopt that approach, but I would be willing to consider it in an appropriate case.

Justice SOTOMAYOR, with whom Justice BREYER joins, concurring in the judgment.

I agree with the Court's conclusion that this case is moot and that vacatur is the appropriate disposition; unlike the majority, however, I would go no further. . . .

Justice KENNEDY, with whom Justice THOMAS joins, dissenting.

Today's decision results from what is emerging as a rather troubling consequence from the reasoning of our recent qualified immunity cases. . . . It does seem that clarification is required. In my view, however, the correct solution is not to override jurisdictional rules that are basic to the functioning of the Court and to the necessity of avoiding advisory opinions. . . .

I

. . . A party that has already obtained the judgment it requested may not seek review to challenge the reasoning of a judicial decision. As we have said on many occasions, "This Court reviews judgments, not statements in opinions." . . .

---

11. Our disposition of this case differs slightly from the normal *Munsingwear* order vacating the lower court's judgment and remanding the case with instructions to dismiss the relevant claim. We leave untouched the Court of Appeals' ruling on qualified immunity and its corresponding dismissal of S.G.'s claim because S.G. chose not to challenge that ruling. We vacate the Ninth Circuit's ruling addressing the merits of the Fourth Amendment issue because, as we have explained, that is the part of the decision that mootness prevents us from reviewing but that has prospective effects on Camreta. But we emphasize that this unique disposition follows from the unique posture of this case and signals no endorsement of deviations from the usual *Munsingwear* order in other situations.

The rule against hearing appeals or accepting petitions for certiorari by pre-vailing parties is related to the Article III prohibition against issuing advisory opin-ions. This principle underlies, for example, the settled rule against hearing cases involving a disputed judgment based on grounds of state law. As Justice Jackson explained for the Court: "[O]ur power is to correct wrong judgments, not to revise opinions. We are not permitted to render an advisory opinion, and if the same judgment would be rendered by the state court after we corrected its views of federal laws, our review could amount to nothing more than an advisory opinion." *Herb v. Pitcairn*, 324 U.S. 117, 125-126 (1945).

The Court defends its holding with citations to just two of our cases. Neither provides support for the Court's result.

The first case is *Electrical Fittings Corp. v. Thomas & Betts Co.*, 307 U.S. 241 (1939). There, a plaintiff alleged the infringement of two patent claims. The District Court found the plaintiff's first claim valid but not infringed and the second claim invalid. Rather than issuing a judgment "dismissing the bill without more," the District Court instead "entered a decree adjudging claim 1 valid" and "dismissing the bill for failure to prove infringement." *Id.*, at 241-242. The District Court thus issued a formal judgment regarding the validity of the first claim. The defendant appealed to dispute that claim's validity. This Court noted, without qualification, that a party "may not appeal from a judgment or decree in his favor, for the purpose of obtain-ing a review of findings he deems erroneous which are not necessary to support the decree." *Id.*, at 242. "But," this Court went on to explain, "here the decree itself purports to adjudge the validity of claim 1, and though the adjudication was imma-terial to the disposition of the cause, it stands as an adjudication of one of the issues litigated." *Ibid.* In other words, the District Court had entered an unnecessary legal conclusion into the terms of the judgment itself, making it possible, for example, that the decree would have estoppel effect as to an issue whose resolution was unnecessary to the proper judgment of dismissal. *Electrical Fittings* therefore con-cluded that "the petitioners were entitled to have this portion of the decree elim-inated." *Ibid.* The sole relief provided was an order for the "reformation of the decree." *Ibid.* That result accords with, indeed flows from, the settled rule that this Court reviews only judgments, not statements in opinions.

The second case is *Deposit Guaranty Nat. Bank v. Roper*, 445 U.S. 326 (1980). In that case plaintiffs attempted to bring a class action against a bank. After the District Court denied class certification, the defendant tendered to the plaintiffs the maximum value that they could recover as individuals. Of course, that offer did not amount to "all that ha[d] been requested in the complaint"—namely, "relief for the class." *Id.*, at 341 (Rehnquist, J., concurring). It is therefore no surprise that the plaintiffs responded with "a counteroffer of judgment in which they attempted to reserve the right to appeal the adverse class certification ruling." *Id.*, at 329 (opinion of the Court). But that proposal was denied. "Based on the bank's offer, the District Court entered judgment in respondents' favor, over their objec-tion." *Id.*, at 330. The District Court thus issued a judgment other than the one the plaintiffs had sought. The would-be class plaintiffs appealed, and this Court later granted certiorari. The Court held that appeal was not barred by the prevailing-party rule: "We view the denial of class certification as an example of a procedural ruling, collateral to the merits of a litigation, that is appealable after the entry of final judgment." *Id.*, at 336. . . . Because the purported prevailing parties were injured by their failure to obtain the class-based judgment they had sought, the Court held there was "jurisdiction to entertain the appeal only to review the asserted procedural error, not for the purpose of passing on the merits." *Ibid.* The Court was clear that the District Court's denial of class certification had a direct effect on the judgment: "As in *Electrical Fittings*," the purported prevailing parties "were entitled to have [a] portion of the District Court's judgment reviewed." *Ibid.*

. . . [*Electrical Fittings* and *Deposit Guaranty*] held that, in the unusual circumstances presented, particular parties who at first appeared to have prevailed below had in fact failed to obtain the judgments they had sought. This Court therefore had jurisdiction, including of course jurisdiction under Article III, to provide relief for the harm caused by the adverse judgments entered below. . . . In contrast the Court appears to assume that the petitioners in the present case are true prevailing parties. They have obtained from the Court of Appeals the only formal judgment they requested: denial of respondent's claim for damages. . . .

III

It is most doubtful that Article III permits appeals by any officer to whom the reasoning of a judicial decision might be applied in a later suit. Yet that appears to be the implication of the Court's holding. The favorable judgment of the Court of Appeals did not in itself cause petitioner Camreta to suffer an Article III injury entitling him to appeal. On the contrary, Camreta has been injured by the decision below to no greater extent than have hundreds of other government officers who might argue that they too have been affected by the unnecessary statements made by the Court of Appeals. . . . [E]ven if Congress were to give explicit permission for certiorari petitions to be filed by "any person" instead of by "any party," 28 U.S.C. §1254(1), the constitutional definition of a case or controversy would still constrain this Court's jurisdiction. . . .

Notes and Questions

Does *Camreta* support review in cases beyond those involving constitutional rulings otherwise "cloaked by" immunity rulings? Suppose, for example, the government prevails in the federal court of appeals on a recurring issue of federal tax law the resolution of which has divided the courts of appeals. *See* Eugene Gressman et al., *Supreme Court Practice: For Practice in the Supreme Court of the United States* 87 (9th ed. 2007) (posing similar hypothetical situation). Does *Camreta* support granting the government's petition for certiorari? Why or why not?

g. The Rule Disfavoring Review of Determinations of State Law by Courts of Appeals

Leavitt v. Jane L.

518 U.S. 137 (1996)

PER CURIAM.

The State of Utah seeks review of a ruling by the Court of Appeals for the Tenth Circuit which declared invalid a provision of Utah law regulating abortions "[a]fter 20 weeks gestational age." Utah Code Ann. §76-7-302(3) (1995). The court made that declaration, not on the ground that the provision violates federal law, but rather on the ground that the provision was not severable from another provision of the same statute, purporting to regulate abortions up to 20 weeks' gestational age, which had been struck down as unconstitutional. The court's severability ruling was based on its view that the Utah Legislature would not have wanted to regulate the later-term abortions unless it could regulate the earlier-term abortions as well. Whatever the validity of such speculation as a general matter, in the present case it is flatly contradicted by a provision in the very part of the Utah Code at issue, explicitly stating that each statutory provision was to be regarded as having been enacted independently of the others. Because we regard the Court of Appeals' determination as to the Utah Legislature's intent to be irreconcilable with that body's own statement on the subject, we grant the petition for certiorari as to this aspect of the judgment of the Court of Appeals, and summarily reverse. . . .

We have summarily set aside unsupportable judgments in cases involving only individual claims. Much more is that appropriate when what is at issue is the total invalidation of a state-wide law. To be sure, we do not normally grant petitions for certiorari solely to review what purports to be an application of state law; but we have done so, see *Steele v. General Mills, Inc.*, 329 U.S. 433, 438, 440-441 (1947); *Wichita Royalty Co. v. City Nat. Bank of Wichita Falls*, 306 U.S. 103, 107 (1939), and undoubtedly should do so where the alternative is allowing blatant federal-court nullification of state law. The dissent argues that "[t]he doctrine of judicial restraint" weighs against review, but it is an odd notion of judicial restraint that would compel us to cast a blind eye on overreaching by lower federal courts. The fact observed by the dissent, that the "underlying substantive issue in this case" is a controversial one, generating "a kind of 'hydraulic pressure' that motivates ad hoc decisionmakin[g]," provides a greater, not a lesser, justification for reversing state-law determinations that seem plainly wrong. In our view, these considerations combine to make this an "extraordinary cas[e]" worth our effort of summary review.

. . . [T]he dissent's appeal to the supposed greater expertise of courts of appeals regarding state law is particularly weak (if not indeed counterindicative) where a Court of Appeals panel consisting of judges from Oklahoma, Colorado, and Kansas has reversed the District Court of Utah on a point of Utah law. If, as we have said, the courts of appeals owe no deference to district court adjudications of state law, see *Salve Regina College v. Russell*, 499 U.S. 225, 239-240 (1991), surely there is no basis for regarding panels of circuit judges as "better qualified" than we to pass on such questions. Our general presumption that courts of appeals correctly decide questions of state law reflects a judgment as to the utility of reviewing them in most cases, not a belief that the courts of appeals have some natural advantage in this domain.

. . . The opinion of the Tenth Circuit in this case is not sustainable. Accordingly, we grant the petition as to the severability question, summarily reverse the judgment, and remand the case to the Court of Appeals for further proceedings. . . .

Justice STEVENS, with whom Justice SOUTER, Justice GINSBURG, and Justice BREYER join, dissenting.

The severability issue discussed in the Court's *per curiam* opinion is purely a question of Utah law. It is contrary to our settled practice to grant a petition for certiorari for the sole purpose of deciding a state-law question ruled upon by a federal court of appeals. The justifications for that practice are well established: The courts of appeals are more familiar with and thus better qualified than we to interpret the laws of the States within their Circuits; the decision of a federal court (even this Court) on a question of state law is not binding on state tribunals; and a decision of a state-law issue by a court of appeals, whether right or wrong, does not have the kind of national significance that is the typical predicate for the exercise of our certiorari jurisdiction.

The underlying substantive issue in this case generates what Justice Holmes once described as a kind of "hydraulic pressure" that motivates ad hoc decision-making. *Northern Securities Co. v. United States*, 193 U.S. 197, 401 (1904) (dissenting opinion). Even if the court of appeals has rendered an incorrect decision, that is no reason for us to jettison the traditional guides to our practice of certiorari review. The doctrine of judicial restraint counsels the opposite course.

. . . [I]n 1980 we codified our already longstanding practice by eliminating as a consideration for deciding whether to review a case the fact that "a court of appeals has . . . decided an important state or territorial question in a way in conflict with applicable state or territorial law." Compare this Court's Rule 19(1)(b) (1970) with this Court's Rule 17.1 (1980). That deletion—the *only* deletion of an entire category of cases—was intended to communicate our view that errors in the application of state law are not a sound reason for granting certiorari, except in the most extraordinary cases. . . .

Notes and Questions

1. Section 1254(1) of Title 28 permits the Court to review cases in the federal courts of appeals regardless whether the court of appeals' decision rests on federal law or some other body of law, including state law. May the Court review a federal court of appeals' decision in a diversity-of-citizenship case? *See Wichita Royalty Co. v. City Natl. Bank of Wichita Falls*, 306 U.S. 103 (1939). If so, under what circumstances should the Court do so, under the Court's decision in *Leavitt*?

2. Would the Tenth Circuit's interpretation of Utah law (unless reversed by the Court) have bound the Utah federal courts or the Utah state courts? Is the United States Supreme Court's interpretation of Utah state law binding on lower federal courts or on the Utah state courts?

h. The Rule Disfavoring Review of Issues Not Pressed or Passed Upon Below

United States v. Williams

504 U.S. 36 (1992)

Justice SCALIA delivered the opinion of the Court.

The question presented in this case is whether a district court may dismiss an otherwise valid indictment because the Government failed to disclose to the grand jury "substantial exculpatory evidence" in its possession.

I

On May 4, 1988, respondent John H. Williams, Jr., . . . was indicted by a federal grand jury on seven counts of "knowingly mak[ing] [a] false statement or report . . . for the purpose of influencing . . . the action [of a federally insured financial institution]," in violation of 18 U.S.C. §1014 (1988 ed., Supp. II). According to the indictment, between September 1984 and November 1985 Williams supplied four Oklahoma banks with "materially false" statements that variously overstated the value of his current assets and interest income in order to influence the banks' actions on his loan requests. . . .

Shortly after arraignment, the District Court granted Williams' motion for disclosure of all exculpatory portions of the grand jury transcripts. See *Brady v. Maryland*, 373 U.S. 83 (1963). Upon reviewing this material, Williams demanded that the District Court dismiss the indictment, alleging that the Government had failed to fulfill its obligation under the Tenth Circuit's prior decision in *United States v. Page*, 808 F.2d 723, 728 (1987), to present "substantial exculpatory evidence" to the grand jury (emphasis omitted). . . .

The District Court [held] . . . that the withheld evidence . . . "render[ed] the grand jury's decision to indict gravely suspect[.]" . . . Upon the Government's appeal, the Court of Appeals affirmed the District Court's order, following its earlier decision in *Page*. . . .

II

Before proceeding to the merits of this matter, it is necessary to discuss the propriety of reaching them. Certiorari was sought and granted in this case on the following question: "Whether an indictment may be dismissed because the government failed to present exculpatory evidence to the grand jury." The first point discussed in respondent's brief opposing the petition was captioned "The 'Question Presented' in the Petition Was Never Raised Below." Brief in Opposition 3. In granting certiorari, we necessarily considered and rejected that contention as a basis for denying review. . . .

Our traditional rule, as the dissent correctly notes, precludes a grant of certiorari only when "the question presented was not pressed or passed upon below." That this rule operates (as it is phrased) in the disjunctive, permitting review of an issue not pressed so long as it has been passed upon, is illustrated by some of our more recent dispositions. . . .

There is no doubt in the present case that the Tenth Circuit decided the crucial issue of the prosecutor's duty to present exculpatory evidence.[4] Moreover, this is not, as the dissent paints it, a case in which, "[a]fter losing in the Court of Appeals, the Government reversed its position[.]" The dissent describes the Government as having "expressly acknowledged [in the Court of Appeals] *the responsibilities described in Page*[.]" It did no such thing. Rather, the Government acknowledged "*that it has certain responsibilities under . . . Page.*" Brief for United States in Response to

---

4. Relying upon, and to some extent repeating, the reasoning of its earlier holding in *United States v. Page*, 808 F.2d 723 (1981), the Court of Appeals said the following:

"We have previously held that a prosecutor has the duty to present substantial exculpatory evidence to the grand jury. Although we do not require the prosecutor to 'ferret out and present every bit of potentially exculpatory evidence,' we do require that substantial exculpatory evidence discovered during the course of an investigation be revealed to the grand jury. Other courts have also recognized that such a duty exists. This requirement promotes judicial economy because 'if a fully informed grand jury cannot find probable cause to indict, there is little chance the prosecution could have proved guilt beyond a reasonable doubt to a fully informed petit jury.'" 899 F.2d 898, 900 (1990) (citations omitted).

This excerpt from the opinion below should make abundantly clear that, contrary to the dissent's mystifying assertion, we premise our grant of certiorari not upon the Tenth Circuit's having "passed on" the issue in its prior *Page* decision, but rather upon its having done so in this case. We discuss *Page* only to point out that, had the Government *not* disputed the creation of the binding Tenth Circuit precedent in that case, a different exercise of discretion might be appropriate.

Appellee's Brief in Nos. 88-2827, 88-2843 (CA10), p. 9 (emphasis added). It conceded, in other words, not that the responsibilities *Page* had imposed were proper, but merely that *Page* had imposed them—over the protests of the Government, but in a judgment that was nonetheless binding precedent for the panel below. The dissent would apparently impose, as an absolute condition to our granting certiorari upon an issue decided by a lower court, that a party demand overruling of a squarely applicable, recent circuit precedent, even though that precedent was established in a case to which the party itself was privy and over the party's vigorous objection, see *Page*, 808 F.2d, at 727 ("The government counters that a prosecutor has no duty to disclose exculpatory evidence [to a grand jury]"), and even though no "intervening developments in the la[w]" had occurred. That seems to us unreasonable.

In short, having reconsidered the precise question we resolved when this petition for review was granted, we again answer it the same way. It is a permissible exercise of our discretion to undertake review of an important issue expressly decided by a federal court[5] where, although the petitioner did not contest the issue in the case immediately at hand, it did so as a party to the recent proceeding upon which the lower courts relied for their resolution of the issue, and did not concede in the current case the correctness of that precedent. Undoubtedly the United States benefits from this rule more often than other parties; but that is inevitably true of most desirable rules of procedure or jurisdiction that we announce, the United States being the most frequent litigant in our courts. Since we announce the rule to be applicable to all parties; since we have recently applied a similar rule (indeed, a rule even more broadly cast) to the *disadvantage* of the United States, see *Stevens v. Department of Treasury*, 500 U.S. 1 (1991); and since the dissenters themselves have approved the application of this rule (or a broader one) in circumstances rationally indistinguishable from those before us, the dissent's suggestion that in deciding this case "the Court appears to favor the Government over the ordinary litigant[t]" and compromises its "obligation to administer justice impartiall[y]" needs no response. . . .

Justice Stevens, with whom Justice Blackmun and Justice O'Connor join, and with whom Justice Thomas joins as to Parts II and III, dissenting. . . .

I . . .

In this case the Government expressly acknowledged the responsibilities described in *Page*, but argued that the withheld evidence was not exculpatory or significant. Instead of questioning the controlling rule of law, it distinguished the facts of this case from those of an earlier case in which an indictment had been dismissed because the prosecutor had withheld testimony that made it factually impossible for the corporate defendant to have been guilty. The Government concluded its principal brief with a request that the court apply the test set forth in *Bank of Nova Scotia v. United States*, 487 U.S. 250 (1988), "follow the holding of *Page*," and

---

5. Where certiorari is sought to a state court, "due regard for the appropriate relationship of this Court to state courts," *McGoldrick v. Compagnie Generale Transatlantique*, 309 U.S. 430, 434-435 (1940), may suggest greater restraint in applying our "pressed or passed upon" rule. In that context, the absence of challenge to a seemingly settled federal rule deprives the state court of an opportunity to rest its decision on an adequate and independent state ground. See *Illinois v. Gates*, 462 U.S. 213, 222 (1983). . . . But cf. *Cohen v. Cowles Media Co.*, 501 U.S. 663, 667 (1991) ("It is irrelevant to this Court's jurisdiction whether a party raised below and argued a federal-law issue that the state supreme court actually considered and decided").

hold that dismissal was not warranted in this case because the withheld evidence was not substantial exculpatory evidence and respondent "was not prejudiced in any way."

After losing in the Court of Appeals, the Government reversed its position and asked this Court to grant certiorari and to hold that the prosecutor has no judicially enforceable duty to present exculpatory evidence to the grand jury. In his brief in opposition to the petition, respondent . . . appropriately called our attention to many of the cases in which we have stated, repeated, and reiterated the general rule that precludes a grant of certiorari when the question presented was "not pressed or passed upon below." Apart from the fact that the United States is the petitioner, I see no reason for not following that salutary practice in this case. . . .

The Court explains that the settled rule does not apply to the Government's certiorari petition in this case because the Government raised the same question three years earlier in the *Page* case and the Court of Appeals passed on the issue in that case. This is a novel, and unwise, change in the rule. We have never suggested that the fact that a court has repeated a settled proposition of law and applied it, without objection, in the case at hand provides a sufficient basis for our review. . . .

This Court has a special obligation to administer justice impartially and to set an example of impartiality for other courts to emulate. When the Court appears to favor the Government over the ordinary litigant, it seriously compromises its ability to discharge that important duty. For that reason alone, I would dismiss the writ of certiorari as improvidently granted. . . .

Notes and Questions

1. What is the purpose of the "pressed or passed upon" rule?

2. According to the majority, how did the court of appeals in this case "pass upon" the issue of the government's duty to present to the grand jury substantially exculpatory evidence in its possession? Does the majority's application of the "pressed or passed upon rule" accord with the purpose of the rule?

3. How does the majority's application of the "pressed or passed upon" rule in this case favor the government? Why is this pro-government application a basis for criticism, according to the dissent?

4. Under the dissent's view, how could the government have satisfied the "pressed or passed upon" rule in this case?

Citizens United v. Federal Election Commission

558 U.S. 310 (2010)

[This case concerned the constitutionality of provisions in the Bipartisan Campaign Reform Act of 2002 (BCRA). Section 203 of the BCRA prohibited corporations and unions from using their general treasury funds to make independent expenditures for speech designed as an "electioneering communication" or for speech expressly advocating the election or defeat of a candidate. 2 U.S.C. §441b (2006). Other provisions in the BCRA that were challenged in this case imposed disclaimer and disclosure requirements in connection with certain election-related communications.

The provisions were challenged on First Amendment grounds by the organization Citizens United. Citizens United had made a documentary about then-Senator Hillary Clinton, who was a candidate in the Democratic Party's 2008 presidential primary elections. Citizens United wanted to advertise the documentary and show it on cable television. Citizens United feared that doing so, however, would expose it to civil and criminal sanctions under the BCRA. To address that risk, Citizens United sued the Federal Election Commission, which administers the BCRA, in federal court.

Citizens United initially argued that the potentially applicable BCRA provisions, both on their face and as applied to the documentary and the advertising for it, violated the First Amendment. Citizens United later stipulated to a dismissal of its facial challenge, however, and pursued only its as-applied challenge. A three-judge district court panel granted summary judgment for the Commission.

On Citizens United's appeal, the Court granted review. The case was reargued after the Court asked the parties to file supplemental briefs addressing whether the Court should overrule *Austin v. Michigan Chamber of Commerce*, 494 U.S. 652 (1990), and the part of *McConnell v. Federal Election Commission*, 540 U.S. 93 (2003), that addressed the facial validity of 2 U.S.C. §441b.

In the portion of the opinion presented below, the Court and dissent discussed the appropriateness of addressing whether *Austin* and *McConnell* should be overruled.]

Justice KENNEDY delivered the opinion of the Court.

. . . The Government argues that Citizens United waived its challenge to *Austin* by dismissing . . . [the count in its complaint asserting a facial challenge to §441b]. We disagree.

First, even if a party could somehow waive a facial challenge while preserving an as-applied challenge, that would not prevent the Court from reconsidering *Austin* or addressing the facial validity of §441b in this case. "Our practice 'permit[s] review of an issue not pressed [below] so long as it has been passed upon. . . .'" *Lebron* [*v. Natl. R. Passenger Corp.*], 513 U.S. [374, 379 (1995)] (quoting *United States v. Williams*, 504 U.S. 36, 41 (1992)). . . . And here, the District Court addressed Citizens United's facial challenge. See 530 F. Supp. 2d, at 278 ("Citizens wants us to enjoin the operation of BCRA §203 as a facially unconstitutional burden on the First Amendment right to freedom of speech"). In rejecting the claim, it noted that it "would have to overrule *McConnell*" for Citizens United to prevail on its facial challenge and that "[o]nly the Supreme Court may overrule its decisions." The District Court did not provide much analysis regarding the facial challenge because it could not ignore the controlling Supreme Court decisions in *Austin* or *McConnell*. Even so, the District Court did "'pas[s] upon'" the issue. Furthermore, the District Court's later opinion, which granted the FEC summary judgment, was "[b]ased on the reasoning of [its] prior opinion," which included the discussion of the facial challenge. After the District Court addressed the facial validity of the statute, Citizens United raised its challenge to *Austin* in this Court. In these circumstances, it is necessary to consider Citizens United's challenge to *Austin* and the facial validity of §441b's expenditure ban. . . .

Justice STEVENS, with whom Justice GINSBURG, Justice BREYER, and Justice SOTOMAYOR join, concurring in part and dissenting in part. . . .

. . . Before turning to the question whether to overrule *Austin* and part of *McConnell*, it is important to explain why the Court should not be deciding that question. . . .

The first reason is that the question was not properly brought before us. In declaring §203 of BCRA facially unconstitutional on the ground that corporations' electoral expenditures may not be regulated any more stringently than those of individuals, the majority decides this case on a basis relinquished below, not included in the questions presented to us by the litigants, and argued here only in response to the Court's invitation. This procedure is unusual and inadvisable for a court. . . .

In the District Court, Citizens United initially raised a facial challenge to the constitutionality of §203. In its motion for summary judgment, however, Citizens United expressly abandoned its facial challenge and the parties stipulated to the dismissal of that claim. The District Court therefore resolved the case on alternative grounds,[3] and in its jurisdictional statement to this Court, Citizens United properly advised us that it was raising only "an as-applied challenge to the constitutionality of . . . BCRA §203." Juris. Statement 5. The jurisdictional statement never so much as cited *Austin*, the key case the majority today overrules. And not one of the questions presented suggested that Citizens United was surreptitiously raising the facial challenge to §203 that it previously agreed to dismiss. . . . [E]ven in its merits briefing, when Citizens United injected its request to overrule *Austin*, it never sought a declaration that §203 was facially unconstitutional as to all corporations and unions; instead it argued only that the statute could not be applied to it because it was "funded overwhelmingly by individuals." "'It is only in exceptional cases coming here from the federal courts that questions not pressed or passed upon below are reviewed,'" *Youakim v. Miller*, 425 U.S. 231, 234 (1976) (*per curiam*) (quoting *Duignan v. United States*, 274 U.S. 195, 200 (1927)), and it is "only in the most exceptional cases" that we will consider issues outside the questions presented, *Stone v. Powell*, 428 U.S. 465, 481, n.15 (1976). The appellant in this case did not so much as assert an exceptional circumstance, and one searches the majority opinion in vain for the mention of any. That is unsurprising, for none exists.

Setting the case for reargument was a constructive step, but it did not cure this fundamental problem. Essentially, five Justices were unhappy with the limited nature of the case before us, so they changed the case to give themselves an opportunity to change the law. . . .

Notes and Questions

1. How did the district court "pass upon" the issue of *Austin* and *McConnell*'s validity? Considering a lower court's duty to follow Supreme Court precedent, could the district court have done more by way of addressing their validity?

2. Perhaps the most famous instance of the Court's addressing an issue that was not pressed or passed upon below—but that was first raised by the Court on its own initiative—is *Erie Railroad Co. v. Tompkins*, 304 U.S. 64 (1938). The Court began its

---

3. The majority states that, in denying Citizens United's motion for a preliminary injunction, the District Court "addressed" the facial validity of BCRA §203. That is true, in the narrow sense that the court observed the issue was foreclosed by *McConnell v. FEC*, 540 U.S. 93 (2003). See 530 F. Supp. 2d 274, 278 (D.D.C. 2008) (*per curiam*). Yet as explained above, Citizens United subsequently dismissed its facial challenge, so that by the time the District Court granted the Federal Election Commission's (FEC) motion for summary judgment, any question about statutory validity had dropped out of the case. That latter ruling by the District Court was the "final decision" from which Citizens United appealed to this Court. . . . As regards the lower court decision that has come before us, the claim that §203 is facially unconstitutional was neither pressed nor passed upon in any form.

opinion in *Erie*: "The question for decision is whether the oft-challenged doctrine of *Swift v. Tyson*, [41 U.S. (16 Pet.) 1 (1842),] shall now be disapproved." 304 U.S. at 69 (footnote omitted). As Justice Butler objected in dissent, however, the constitutionality of *Swift v. Tyson* was not challenged in the lower federal courts or in the petition for certiorari, "[a]nd as a general rule, this Court will not consider any question not raised below and presented by the petition." *Id.* at 82 (Butler, J., dissenting). Although petitioner Erie Railroad prevailed in Tompkins' lawsuit against it because of *Swift v. Tyson*'s overruling, the lawyer for Erie Railroad disclaimed an intention to challenge *Swift* in his brief and oral argument to the Court. *See* Edward Purcell, Jr., Brandeis and the Progressive Constitution: *Erie*, the Judicial Power, and the Politics of the Federal Courts in Twentieth-Century America 97-100 (2000). Edward Purcell argued that Erie Railroad's lawyer did not challenge *Swift* because the lawyer believed that, in the long term, *Swift*'s regime of federal common law "was more valuable in litigating and settling claims brought against [Erie Railroad] than was a victory in Tompkins's individual suit." *Id.* at 100. Why would a continuation of the *Swift* regime favor the railroad, compared to the approach adopted in *Erie*? Should the Court in *Erie* have set the case for reargument and requested supplemental briefing on the validity of *Swift*, as it did in *Citizens United* with respect to *Austin* and *McConnell*?

3. Could the Court in *Citizens United* have, on its own, raised and decided the issue of the validity of *Austin* and the relevant part of *McConnell*, even if the issue had not been pressed or passed upon below?

2. Review of State Court Decisions

The materials in this section concern the Court's power to review state court decisions. The materials are organized to address (a) the current statutory provisions governing the Court's review; (b) the requirement that the issues to be decided by the Court have been "pressed or passed upon" by the state courts; (c) the doctrine that prevents the Court from reviewing a state court judgment or decree that rests on an "adequate and independent state ground"; and (d) the statutory requirement that limits the Court to reviewing only the "final" judgment or decree of a state court.

a. Statutes

28 U.S.C. §1257. State courts; certiorari

(a) Final judgments or decrees rendered by the highest court of a State in which a decision could be had, may be reviewed by the Supreme Court by writ of certiorari where the validity of a treaty or statute of the United States is drawn in question or where the validity of a statute of any State is drawn in question on the ground of its being repugnant to the Constitution, treaties, or laws of the United States, or where any title, right, privilege, or immunity is specially set up or claimed under the Constitution or the treaties or statutes of, or any commission held or authority exercised under, the United States.

(b) For the purposes of this section, the term "highest court of a State" includes the District of Columbia Court of Appeals.

28 U.S.C. §2101. Supreme Court; time for appeal or certiorari; docketing; stay ...

(c) Any ... writ of certiorari intended to bring any judgment or decree in a civil action, suit or proceeding before the Supreme Court for review shall be taken or applied for within ninety days after the entry of such judgment or decree. A justice of the Supreme Court, for good cause shown, may extend the time for applying for a writ of certiorari for a period not exceeding sixty days.

(d) The time for appeal or application for a writ of certiorari to review the judgment of a State court in a criminal case shall be as prescribed by rules of the Supreme Court. . . .

Notes and Questions

1. Section 1257 is the modern counterpart to §25 of the Judiciary Act of 1789, which authorized the Court to review certain cases from the state courts by writ of error. The Court upheld the constitutionality of §25 in *Martin v. Hunter's Lessee*, 14 U.S. (1 Wheat.) 304 (1816). The Court in *Martin* rejected the view that its "appellate" jurisdiction under Article III, §2, clause 2, permitted it to review only cases from the lower federal courts. In another important case interpreting §25, *Cohens v. Virginia*, the Court held that its jurisdiction to review a state court decision was not defeated by the presence of the State as a party. *See Cohens v. Virginia*, 19 U.S. (6 Wheat.) 264 (1821). In particular, the Court in *Cohens* rejected the argument that the Eleventh Amendment barred its appellate jurisdiction. Although *Cohens* was a state court action brought *by* the State, the Court in a later case relied on *Cohens* to hold that the Court can exercise appellate jurisdiction to review state court judgments entered in actions brought *against* a State, at least when the state court itself entertains the action without regard to the State's sovereign immunity from suits in its own courts. *See McKesson Corp. v. Div. of Alcoholic Beverages & Tobacco*, 496 U.S. 18, 26-29 (1990); *see also* Richard H. Fallon et al., Hart and Wechsler's the Federal Courts and the Federal System 720-721 (6th ed. 2009).

2. Section 1257 restricts the Court to reviewing final judgments or decrees "by the highest court of a State in which a decision could be had." This restriction dates back to §25 of the Judiciary Act of 1789, the earliest provision authorizing the Court to review cases from the state courts. The highest-state-court restriction requires the petitioner seeking certiorari under §1257 first to "exhaust" the "possibilities of review by all state courts." *Gorman v. Washington Univ.*, 316 U.S. 98, 100 (1942).

The Court can review a case from a state court below the state's highest court when all courts above the lower state court lack appellate jurisdiction or have exercised discretion to decline review of the case. For example, the Court in *Cohens v. Virginia* reviewed the case on a writ of error to the Quarterly Session Court of Hustings for the borough of Norfolk, Virginia. Because the Virginia Supreme Court of Appeals refused an appeal from the Hustings Court, "there was no higher State tribunal which could take cognizance of the case." *Cohens*, 19 U.S. at 376 n.31. To cite another example, the Court reviewed the decision of a municipal "police court" in *Thompson v. City of Louisville*, 362 U.S. 199 (1960). That court had convicted Thompson and fined him $10 on each of two charges—one for loitering, the other for disorderly conduct. *Id.* at 200. Police court decisions imposing such small fines were "not appealable or otherwise reviewable in any other Kentucky Court," as shown by Thompson's unsuccessful attempts to get further review in the state court system. *Id.* at 202.

3. Please review §1257. In which three situations does it authorize the Court to review a final judgment or decree by the highest state court in which a decision could be had? Does §1257 authorize the Court to review cases from the state court system based on the diverse citizenship of the parties? If not, why not? Now, please review

§1254. Does it authorize the Court to review cases in the federal courts of appeals that fall within federal jurisdiction because of diversity of citizenship? If so, why so? Could Congress amend §1257 to allow the Court to review state court decisions in cases between citizens of diverse citizenship? *See* John Harrison, *Federal Appellate Jurisdiction Over Questions of State Law in State Courts,* 7 Green Bag 2d 353 (2004).

b. The "Pressed or Passed Upon" Rule

As discussed earlier in this chapter, when the Court reviews cases from the federal courts of appeals, it generally refuses to consider issues that have not been "pressed or passed upon" in the lower federal courts. The "pressed or passed upon" rule is apparently prudential when the Court reviews cases from the federal courts of appeals; the rule does not appear in that context to be required by the Constitution or the governing statute, 28 U.S.C. §1254(1).

As the material in this section shows, the Court also applies the "pressed or passed upon" rule when reviewing decisions from state courts. (In the next case, though, the Court calls it the "*not* pressed or passed upon" rule.) Please examine the governing statute, 28 U.S.C. §1257, to see if any language in that provision provides a textual hook for a "pressed or passed upon" rule in this context. Then consider the following material. As you do, identify what justifications for the rule exist—apart from its arguably being required by the text of §1257.

Illinois v. Gates

462 U.S. 213 (1983)

Justice REHNQUIST delivered the opinion of the Court.

Respondents Lance and Susan Gates were indicted for violation of state drug laws after police officers, executing a search warrant, discovered marihuana and other contraband in their automobile and home. Prior to trial the Gateses moved to suppress evidence seized during this search. The Illinois Supreme Court affirmed the decisions of lower state courts granting the motion. It held that the affidavit submitted in support of the State's application for a warrant to search the Gateses' property was inadequate under this Court's decisions in *Aguilar v. Texas,* 378 U.S. 108 (1964) and *Spinelli v. United States,* 393 U.S. 410 (1969).

We granted certiorari to consider the application of the Fourth Amendment to a magistrate's issuance of a search warrant on the basis of a partially corroborated anonymous informant's tip. After receiving briefs and hearing oral argument on this question, however, we requested the parties to address an additional question:

> "[W]hether the rule requiring the exclusion at a criminal trial of evidence obtained in violation of the Fourth Amendment, *Mapp v. Ohio,* 367 U.S. 643 (1961); *Weeks v. United States,* 232 U.S. 383 (1914), should to any extent be modified, so as, for example, not to require the exclusion of evidence obtained in the reasonable belief that the search and seizure at issue was consistent with the Fourth Amendment."

We decide today, with apologies to all, that the issue we framed for the parties was not presented to the Illinois courts and, accordingly, do not address it. Rather, we consider the question originally presented in the petition for certiorari. . . . Initially, however, we set forth our reasons for not addressing the question regarding modification of the exclusionary rule framed in our order of November 29, 1982.

I

Our certiorari jurisdiction over decisions from state courts derives from 28 U.S.C. §1257, which provides that "[f]inal judgments or decrees rendered by the highest court of a State in which a decision could be had, may be reviewed by the Supreme Court as follows: . . . (3) By writ of certiorari, . . . where any title, right, privilege or immunity is specially set up or claimed under the Constitution, treaties or statutes of . . . the United States." The provision derives, albeit with important alterations, from the Judiciary Act of 1789, §25, 1 Stat. 85.

Although we have spoken frequently on the meaning of §1257 and its predecessors, our decisions are in some respects not entirely clear. We held early on that §25 of the Judiciary Act of 1789 furnished us with no jurisdiction unless a federal question had been both raised and decided in the state court below. . . .

Notwithstanding these decisions, however, several of our more recent cases have treated the so-called "not pressed or passed upon below" rule as merely a prudential restriction. . . .

In addition to this lack of clarity as to the character of the "not pressed or passed upon below" rule, we have recognized that it often may be unclear whether the particular federal question presented in this Court was raised or passed upon below. In *Dewey v. Des Moines*, 173 U.S. 193, 197-198 (1899), the fullest treatment of the subject, the Court said that "[i]f the question were only an enlargement of the one mentioned in the assignment of errors, or if it were so connected with it in substance as to form but another ground or reason for alleging the invalidity of the [lower court's] judgment, we should have no hesitation in holding the assignment sufficient to permit the question to be now raised and argued. Parties are not confined here to the same arguments which were advanced in the courts below upon a Federal question there discussed." We have not attempted, and likely would not have been able, to draw a clear-cut line between cases involving only an "enlargement" of questions presented below and those involving entirely new questions.

The application of these principles in the instant case is not entirely straightforward. It is clear in this case that respondents expressly raised, at every level of the Illinois judicial system, the claim that the Fourth Amendment had been violated by the actions of the Illinois police and that the evidence seized by the officers should be excluded from their trial. It also is clear that the State challenged, at every level of the Illinois court system, respondents' claim that the substantive requirements of the Fourth Amendment had been violated. The State never, however, raised or addressed the question whether the federal exclusionary rule should be modified in any respect, and none of the opinions of the Illinois courts give any indication that the question was considered.

The case, of course, is before us on the State's petition for a writ of certiorari. Since the Act of Dec. 23, 1914, jurisdiction has been vested in this Court to review state court decisions even when a claimed federal right has been upheld. Our prior decisions interpreting the "not pressed or passed on below" rule have not, however, involved a State's failure to raise a defense to a federal right or remedy asserted below. As explained below, however, we can see no reason to treat the State's failure to have challenged an asserted federal claim differently from the failure of the proponent of a federal claim to have raised that claim.

We have identified several purposes underlying the "not pressed or passed upon" rule: for the most part, these are as applicable to the State's failure to have opposed the assertion of a particular federal right, as to a party's failure to have asserted the claim. First, "[q]uestions not raised below are those on which the record is very likely to be inadequate since it certainly was not compiled with those questions in mind." *Cardinale v. Louisiana*, 394 U.S. 437, 439 (1969). Exactly the same difficulty exists when the State urges modification of an existing constitutional right or accompanying remedy. Here, for example, the record contains little, if anything, regarding the subjective good faith of the police officers that searched the Gateses' property—which might well be an important consideration in determining whether to fashion a good-faith exception to the exclusionary rule. Our consideration of whether to modify the exclusionary rule plainly would benefit from a record containing such facts.

Likewise, "due regard for the appropriate relationship of this Court to state courts," *McGoldrick v. Compagnie Generale Transatlantique*, 309 U.S. [430, 435-436 (1940)], demands that those courts be given an opportunity to consider the constitutionality of the actions of state officials, and, equally important, proposed changes in existing remedies for unconstitutional actions. Finally, by requiring that the State first argue to the state courts that the federal exclusionary rule should be modified, we permit a state court, even if it agrees with the State as a matter of federal law, to rest its decision on an adequate and independent state ground. Illinois, for example, adopted an exclusionary rule as early as 1923 and might adhere to its view even if it thought we would conclude that the federal rule should be modified. In short, the reasons supporting our refusal to hear federal claims not raised in state court apply with equal force to the State's failure to challenge the availability of a well-settled federal remedy. Whether the "not pressed or passed upon below" rule is jurisdictional, as our earlier decisions indicate, or prudential, as several of our later decisions assume, or whether its character might be different in cases like this from its character elsewhere, we need not decide. Whatever the character of the rule may be, consideration of the question presented in our order of November 29, 1982, would be contrary to the sound justifications for the "not pressed or passed upon below" rule, and we thus decide not to pass on the issue.

The fact that the Illinois courts affirmatively applied the federal exclusionary rule—suppressing evidence against respondents—does not affect our conclusion. . . . [I]n the present case, although the Illinois courts applied the federal exclusionary rule, there was never "any real contest" upon the point. The application of the exclusionary rule was merely a routine act, once a violation of the Fourth Amendment had been found, and not the considered judgment of the Illinois courts on the question whether application of a modified rule would be warranted on the facts of this case. In such circumstances, absent the adversarial dispute necessary to apprise the state court of the arguments for not applying the exclusionary rule, we will not consider the question whether the exclusionary rule should be modified.

Likewise, we do not believe that the State's repeated opposition to respondents' substantive Fourth Amendment claims suffices to have raised the question whether the exclusionary rule should be modified. . . . The question whether the exclusionary rule's remedy is appropriate in a particular context has long been regarded as an issue separate from the question whether the Fourth Amendment rights of the party seeking to invoke the rule were violated by police conduct. . . .

Finally, weighty prudential considerations militate against our considering the question presented in our order of November 29, 1982. The extent of the continued vitality of the rules that have developed from our decisions in *Weeks v. United States*,

232 U.S. 383 (1914), and *Mapp v. Ohio*, 367 U.S. 643 (1961), is an issue of unusual significance. . . . Where difficult issues of great public importance are involved, there are strong reasons to adhere scrupulously to the customary limitations on our discretion. By doing so we "promote respect . . . for the Court's adjudicatory process [and] the stability of [our] decisions." *Mapp v. Ohio*, 367 U.S., at 677 (dissenting opinion). Moreover, fidelity to the rule guarantees that a factual record will be available to us, thereby discouraging the framing of broad rules, seemingly sensible on one set of facts, which may prove ill-considered in other circumstances. In Justice Harlan's words, adherence to the rule lessens the threat of "untoward practical ramifications," *id.*, at 676 (Harlan, J., dissenting), not foreseen at the time of decision. The public importance of our decisions in *Weeks* and *Mapp* and the emotions engendered by the debate surrounding these decisions counsel that we meticulously observe our customary procedural rules. By following this course, we promote respect for the procedures by which our decisions are rendered, as well as confidence in the stability of prior decisions. A wise exercise of the powers confided in this Court dictates that we reserve for another day the question whether the exclusionary rule should be modified. . . .

Justice WHITE, concurring in the judgment.

In my view, the question regarding modification of the exclusionary rule framed in our order of November 29, 1982, is properly before us and should be addressed. . . .

We have never suggested that the jurisdictional stipulations of §1257 require that all arguments on behalf of, let alone in opposition to, a federal claim be raised and decided below. . . .

As a jurisdictional requirement, I have no doubt that the exclusionary rule question is before us as an indivisible element of the claim that the Constitution requires exclusion of certain evidence seized in violation of the Fourth Amendment. As a prudential matter, I am unmoved by the Court's lengthy discourse as to why it must avoid the question. First, the Court turns on its head the axiom that "'due regard for the appropriate relationship of this Court to state courts,' *McGoldrick v. Compagnie Generale Transatlantique*, 309 U.S. [430, 434-435 (1940)], demands that those courts be given an opportunity to consider the constitutionality of the actions of state officials[.]" This statement, written to explain why a state statute should not be struck down on federal grounds not raised in the state courts, hardly applies when the question is whether a rule of federal law articulated by this Court should now be narrowed to reduce the scope of federal intrusion into the State's administration of criminal justice. Insofar as modifications of the federal exclusionary rule are concerned, the Illinois courts are bound by this Court's pronouncements. I see little point in requiring a litigant to request a state court to overrule or modify one of this Court's precedents. Far from encouraging the stability of our precedents, the Court's proposed practice could well undercut *stare decisis*. Either the presentation of such issues to the lower courts will be a completely futile gesture or the lower courts are now invited to depart from this Court's decisions whenever they conclude such a modification is in order. . . .

[The dissenting opinion of Justice Brennan, in which Justice Marshall joined, and the dissenting opinion of Justice Stevens, in which Justice Brennan joined, are omitted.]

Notes and Questions

1. The Court indicates in *Illinois v. Gates* that it has appellate jurisdiction under the portion of §1257 authorizing review "where any title, right, privilege or immunity is specially set up or claimed under the Constitution, treaties or statutes of . . . the United States." What "title, right, privilege or immunity" is being "specially set up or claimed" in *Illinois v. Gates*? What is the relationship between that "title, right, privilege or immunity" and the question that the Court ultimately declines to decide because it was "not pressed or passed upon" in the state courts?

2. Does the Court in *Illinois v. Gates* treat the "not pressed or passed upon" rule as prudential or jurisdictional?

3. In some cases, the Court has traced the "not pressed or passed upon" rule to the language in §1257(a) requiring the federal constitutional right to be "specially set up or claimed." For example, the Court said in *Howell v. Mississippi*, 543 U.S. 440, 443 (2005) (*per curiam*):

> Congress has given this Court the power to review "[f]inal judgments or decrees rendered by the highest court of a State in which a decision could be had . . . where any . . . right . . . is *specially set up or claimed* under the Constitution or the treaties or statutes of . . . the United States." 28 U.S.C. §1257(a) (emphasis added). Under that statute and its predecessors, this Court has almost unfailingly refused to consider any federal-law challenge to a state-court decision unless the federal claim "was either addressed by or properly presented to the state court that rendered the decision we have been asked to review."

In *Illinois v. Gates*, the federal right "specially set up or claimed" was the Fourth Amendment right to be free from unreasonable searches, a right claimed by the Gateses. There was no dispute that the Gateses had properly raised their Fourth Amendment claim in the state courts. The issue instead was whether the Court should consider modifying the exclusionary rule when the State of Illinois had not argued for such a modification in the state courts. The Court's determination that this modification should have been pressed or passed upon below, before the Court decided it, cannot be readily tied to any language in §1257. Perhaps the "not pressed or passed upon" rule is jurisdictional when it is rooted in the text of §1257, as in *Howell*, but prudential when it has no such textual basis, as in *Illinois v. Gates*.

4. Somewhat like §1257(a)'s requirement that a federal right be "specially set up or claimed," §1257(a) provides for review when the validity of a treaty or a federal statute "is drawn in question," and when the validity of a state statute "is drawn in question on the ground of its being repugnant" to federal law. Section 1257 does not identify *who* must "specially set up" the federal right or "draw in question" the validity of a federal statute, a treaty, or a state statute. Section 1257 thus appears to permit review if the *state* court raises and decides the federal issue without prior prompting from any of the parties. *See, e.g., Orr v. Orr*, 440 U.S. 268, 274-275 (1979) (citing the "elementary rule that it is irrelevant to inquire . . . when a Federal question was raised in a court below when it appears that such question was actually considered and decided.") (quoting *Manhattan Life Ins. Co. v. Cohen*, 234 U.S. 123, 134 (1914)).

5. In the *Williams* case reproduced earlier in this chapter, the Court said:

> Where certiorari is sought to a state court, "due regard for the appropriate relationship of this Court to state courts," *McGoldrick v. Compagnie Generale Transatlantique*, 309 U.S. 430, 434-435 (1940), may suggest greater restraint in applying our "pressed or passed upon" rule. In that context, the absence of challenge to a seemingly settled federal rule

deprives the state court of an opportunity to rest its decision on an adequate and independent state ground.

504 U.S. at 44 n.5. Is this "greater restraint" illustrated by comparing (1) the Court's refusal in *Illinois v. Gates* to consider modifying the exclusionary rule, even though the state court below applied that rule, albeit unquestioningly, to suppress evidence with (2) the Court's willingness in *Citizens United* (reproduced earlier in this chapter) to consider the validity of precedent (namely *Austin* and *McConnell*) that the lower federal court considered itself bound to apply?

6. The Court's comparatively rigorous adherence to the "pressed or passed upon" rule when reviewing state-court cases is reflected in the Court's Rule 14.1(g)(1), which requires petitions for certiorari to include:

> (g) A concise statement of the case setting out the facts material to consideration of the questions presented, and also containing the following:
>
> (i) If review of a *state-court* judgment is sought, specification of the stage in the proceedings, both in the court of first instance and in the appellate courts, when the federal questions sought to be reviewed were raised; the method or manner of raising them and the way in which they were passed on by those courts; and pertinent quotations of specific portions of the record or summary thereof, with specific reference to the places in the record where the matter appears (*e.g.*, court opinion, ruling on exception, portion of court's charge and exception thereto, assignment of error), so as to show that the federal question was timely and properly raised and that this Court has jurisdiction to review the judgment on a writ of certiorari. When the portions of the record relied on under this subparagraph are voluminous, they shall be included in the appendix referred to in subparagraph 1(i).
>
> (ii) If review of a judgment of a *United States court of appeals* is sought, the basis for federal jurisdiction in the court of first instance.

(Emphasis added.) This rule does not require a petition for review of the judgment of a federal court of appeals to explain how, and where in the record, the issues on which certiorari is sought were pressed and passed upon. Even so, it is wise to include this information, in light of the "pressed or passed upon" rule applied in this context by the Court in *Williams* and other cases.

c. The Adequate and Independent State Ground Doctrine

The United States Supreme Court will not review a state court's decision of a federal issue if the state court's judgment rests on an adequate and independent state ground. The material below elaborates on the adequate and independent state ground doctrine. The first case, *Herb v. Pitcairn*, states the doctrine and expresses the Court's modern view that the doctrine is jurisdictional. 324 U.S. 117 (1945). The second major case, *Michigan v. Long*, adopts the Court's current approach to situations where it is unclear whether a state-court judgment rests on an adequate and independent state ground. 463 U.S. 1032 (1983).

Herb v. Pitcairn

324 U.S. 117 (1945)

Mr. Justice JACKSON delivered the opinion of the Court. . . .

Herb alleged injury while employed as a switchman on the Wabash Railroad at or near the City of Decatur, Mason County, Illinois. . . . He filed complaint under the Federal [Employers' Liability] Act in the City Court of Granite City, Madison County, Illinois. . . . A verdict of $30,000 was returned, which the trial court set aside. Further proceedings in the Appellate Court and the Supreme Court resulted in remand to the City Court. On March 16, 1942, in other cases, the Supreme Court of Illinois decided that, under the Illinois Constitution, a city court is without jurisdiction in any case where the cause of action arose outside the city where the court is located. When these decisions were rendered, plaintiff [Herb] moved in the City Court for a change of venue, under the Illinois Venue Statute, to the Circuit Court of Madison County, a court of general jurisdiction. Meanwhile the two-year period within which an action could be instituted under the Employers' Liability Act had long expired. The motion for change of venue was granted and the papers certified and transferred accordingly. The defendant . . . moved, in the Circuit Court, to dismiss on the grounds that the City Court had no jurisdiction either to entertain or to transfer the case; that, since all proceedings theretofore were utterly void, no action was pending or properly commenced by the City Court process, nor by the transfer; that, since no action had been commenced in a court of competent jurisdiction, any right under the Federal Act had expired by its limitation, which provided that "No action shall be maintained under this Act unless commenced within two years from the day the cause of action accrued." The Circuit Court granted the motion to dismiss and the Supreme Court of Illinois affirmed. Its affirmance is here claimed to involve a federal question, erroneously decided.

First. Whether any case is pending in the Illinois courts is a question to be determined by Illinois law, as interpreted by the Illinois Supreme Court. . . .

. . . The [Illinois] Supreme Court used language which can mean that no valid proceeding was pending in either court as a matter of state law. We think that the Supreme Court probably has decided that as matter of Illinois law no action is pending against these defendants in any court and that all of the proceedings have been of no effect whatever. . . .

The freedom of the state courts so to decide is, of course, subject to the qualification that the cause of action must not be discriminated against because it is a federal one. But we cannot say that the court below, in so far as it did hold the city courts without power, construed the state jurisdiction and venue laws in a discriminatory fashion. . . .

Second. The case went to the Supreme Court of Illinois with a certification by the Circuit Court that a federal question was involved. The federal question, whether the action was barred by the federal statute of limitations, was raised by respondents in their motion to dismiss in the Circuit Court. In the course of its opinion the Illinois Supreme Court used language from which it seems reasonably clear that the question was decided, either necessarily, because the Court had not disposed of the case on state law grounds, or hypothetically. For purposes of passing on this question the Court seems to have assumed that an action is pending under state law; for only if one is pending is there occasion to consider whether the cause of action is barred.

Petitioners contend therefore that the judgment below does not rest upon a state ground but upon an erroneously decided federal ground—namely, that even though the City Court had power to transfer the case, the action is barred because not "commenced" until it arrived in Circuit Court.

Third. This Court from the time of its foundation has adhered to the principle that it will not review judgments of state courts that rest on adequate and independent state grounds. The reason is so obvious that it has rarely been thought to warrant statement. It is found in the partitioning of power between the state and federal judicial systems and in the limitations of our own jurisdiction. Our only power over state judgments is to correct them to the extent that they incorrectly adjudge federal rights. And our power is to correct wrong judgments, not to revise opinions. We are not permitted to render an advisory opinion, and if the same judgment would be rendered by the state court after we corrected its views of federal laws, our review could amount to nothing more than an advisory opinion. If the Illinois court means to hold that the city courts could not adjudge, transfer, or begin these cases and that no case is pending in its courts at the present time, it is manifest that no view we might express of the federal Act would require its courts to proceed to the trial of these actions.

But what to do with cases in which the record is ambiguous but presents reasonable grounds to believe that the judgment may rest on decision of a federal question has long vexed the Court. In many cases the answer has been a strict adherence to the rule that it must affirmatively appear that the federal question was decided and that its decision was essential to disposition of the case; and that where it is not clear whether the judgment rests on a federal ground or an adequate state one, this Court will not review.

. . . [I]n *State of Minnesota v. National Tea Co.*, 309 U.S. 551, uncertainty as to the grounds of the decision below led the Court to vacate and remand for further consideration. . . .

. . . [I]n cases where the answer is not clear to us, it seems consistent with the respect due the highest courts of states of the Union that they be asked rather than told what they have intended. If this imposes an unwelcome burden it should be mitigated by the knowledge that it is to protect their jurisdiction from unwitting interference as well as to protect our own from unwitting renunciation.

. . . We think the simplest procedure to do so, where the record is deficient, is to hold the case pending application to the state court for clarification or amendment. . . .

These causes are continued for such period as will enable counsel for petitioners with all convenient speed to apply to the Supreme Court of Illinois for amendment, or certificate, which will show whether it intended to rest the judgments herein on an adequate and independent state ground or whether decision of the federal question was necessary to the judgment rendered.

[The dissenting opinion of Justice Black, in which Justices Douglas and Murphy joined, and the dissenting opinion of Justice Rutledge are omitted.]

Notes and Questions

1. The adequate and independent state ground doctrine prevents review by the Court when the state ground is both adequate and independent. The Court indicated in *Herb* that Illinois law would not have been an "adequate" ground if the law discriminated against a federal cause of action. More generally, the state-law ground for a state court's judgment is not "adequate" if it violates federal law.

The well-known case of *Bush v. Gore*, 531 U.S. 98 (2000), provides an example of a state-law ground that violated federal law. The Florida Supreme Court relied on Florida law to order a partial, manual recount of votes cast in the State's general election in 2000 for president and vice president. On review under §1257, the United States Supreme Court held that the Florida Supreme Court's state-law decision violated the Equal Protection Clause of the Fourteenth Amendment. *See Bush v. Gore*, 531 U.S. at 103. On this view, the state-law ground for the Florida Supreme Court's decision violated the U.S. Constitution.

In a concurring opinion in *Bush v. Gore*, Chief Justice Rehnquist, joined by Justices Scalia and Thomas, concluded that the Florida Supreme Court's decision also violated Article II, §1, clause 2, which provides for electors for president and vice president to be appointed "in such Manner as the Legislature [of the State] may direct." In the concurrence's view, the Florida Supreme Court interpreted Florida election statutes "so as to wholly change" the legislative scheme and thereby to violate Article II's requirement that state legislation control the "appointment" (*i.e.*, election) process. *Bush v. Gore*, 531 U.S. at 114.

Whether the Florida Supreme Court's interpretation of state law violated the Equal Protection Clause or Article II (or both), the state-law basis for the decision was not an "adequate" state ground so as to preclude review by the United States Supreme Court.

2. Sometimes a state court refuses to consider an issue of federal law because the issue was not presented as required by a state rule of procedure. For instance, a state rule of procedure may prevent a party from raising an issue in the state appellate court if the issue was not first raised in the state trial court. Such a state rule of procedure generally provides an adequate ground for disposing of a federal issue if the rule is "firmly established and regularly followed" by the state courts. *E.g.*, *Walker v. Martin*, _____ U.S. _____, 131 S. Ct. 1120, 1127 (2011). On the other hand, a state rule of procedure is inadequate if it is "without any fair or substantial support" in state law. *NAACP v. Alabama*, 357 U.S. 449, 455 (1958) (internal quotation marks omitted). In *NAACP v. Alabama*, the Alabama Supreme Court rejected the NAACP's constitutional claim supposedly because the NAACP had used the wrong appellate procedure to present that claim. The United States Supreme Court found no support in Alabama case law to support that procedural ruling. *Id.* at 454-458.

The Court has said that, even when a state rule of procedure is "firmly established and regularly followed," there is a "limited category" of "exceptional cases in which exorbitant application of a generally sound [procedural] rule renders the state ground inadequate to stop consideration of a federal question." *Walker*, 131 S. Ct. at 1128 n.4. An example of such an exceptional case is *Lee v. Kemna*, 534 U.S. 362 (2002). In that case, defendant Remon Lee moved for a continuance of his state-court criminal trial when, for reasons unknown to Lee, his alibi witnesses left the courthouse on the day they were supposed to testify. The trial judge denied Lee's motion for a continuance because the judge had a family obligation the next day and another trial scheduled for the day after that. Lee's trial resumed without his alibi witnesses; Lee was convicted of first-degree murder and sentenced to life in prison without parole. The state appellate court upheld the denial of a continuance on the ground that Lee's lawyer failed to follow state procedural rules for motions for a continuance.

The United States Supreme Court held that those state procedural rules did not provide an adequate ground for the state court's rejection of Lee's federal claim, which was that the denial of the continuance violated due process. For one thing, the state procedural rules were designed for the benefit of the trial judge's consideration of continuance motions, but the trial judge in this case did not even raise the issue of Lee's noncompliance with those rules and apparently would have denied Lee's motion even if Lee had complied with them. Second, no published state court opinion required "flawless compliance" with the state procedural rules under the unusual circumstances presented in Lee's case, in which the alibi witnesses unexpectedly disappeared after showing up to testify in compliance with subpoenas. Finally, the purposes of the procedural rules were fulfilled by the submissions that Lee's counsel made in support of a continuance. These "special circumstances" made the application of otherwise sound state procedural rules an inadequate ground for disposing of the federal claim. *Id.* at 365-385.

From exceptional cases such as *Lee*, and from the Court's inquiry in the run of cases—which asks whether a state procedural rule is "firmly established" or is instead "without substantial support"—it is obvious that the Court treats state court procedural rulings differently from state court rulings on matters of substantive state law. There are various theories for why state procedural rules are treated differently from state substantive law under the adequate and independent state ground doctrine. *See* Richard H. Fallon et al., Hart and Wechsler's *The Federal Courts and the Federal System* 515-518 (6th ed. 2009).

3. In *Herb*, the Court put the case on hold pending a request to the Illinois Supreme Court for "clarification or amendment" of its decision. In the next case the Court rejected that approach (and others that it had taken in similar cases) in favor of the one that prevails today.

Michigan v. Long

463 U.S. 1032 (1983)

[Michigan police watched Long drive his car into a ditch. When the police approached Long's car, they saw a hunting knife inside the car in plain view. They then searched Long's car for other weapons, and found marijuana. The marijuana was admitted in the state court trial at which Long was convicted of a drug offense. The Michigan Court of Appeals affirmed Long's conviction, holding that the search of Long's car was valid under *Terry v. Ohio*, 392 U.S. 1 (1968). The Michigan Supreme Court reversed.]

Justice O'CONNOR delivered the opinion of the Court. . . .

We granted certiorari in this case to consider the important question of the authority of a police officer to protect himself by conducting a *Terry*-type search of the passenger compartment of a motor vehicle during the lawful investigatory stop of the occupant of the vehicle. . . .

Before reaching the merits, we must consider Long's argument that we are without jurisdiction to decide this case because the decision below rests on an adequate and independent state ground. The court below [*i.e.*, the Michigan Supreme Court] referred twice to the State Constitution in its opinion, but otherwise relied exclusively on federal law. Long argues that the Michigan courts have provided greater protection from searches and seizures under the State Constitution than is afforded under the Fourth Amendment, and the references to the State Constitution therefore establish an adequate and independent ground for the decision below.

It is, of course, "incumbent upon this Court . . . to ascertain for itself . . . whether the asserted non-federal ground independently and adequately supports the judgment." . . . [W]e openly admit that we have thus far not developed a satisfying and consistent approach for resolving this vexing issue. . . .

This ad hoc method of dealing with cases that involve possible adequate and independent state grounds is antithetical to the doctrinal consistency that is required when sensitive issues of federal-state relations are involved. Moreover, none of the various methods of disposition that we have employed thus far recommends itself as the preferred method that we should apply to the exclusion of others, and we therefore determine that it is appropriate to reexamine our treatment of this jurisdictional issue in order to achieve the consistency that is necessary.

The process of examining state law is unsatisfactory because it requires us to interpret state laws with which we are generally unfamiliar, and which often, as in this case, have not been discussed at length by the parties. Vacation and continuance for clarification have also been unsatisfactory both because of the delay and decrease in efficiency of judicial administration, and, more important, because these methods of disposition place significant burdens on state courts to demonstrate the presence or absence of our jurisdiction. Finally, outright dismissal of cases is clearly not a panacea because it cannot be doubted that there is an important need for uniformity in federal law, and that this need goes unsatisfied when we fail to review an opinion that rests primarily upon federal grounds and where the *independence* of an alleged state ground is not apparent from the four corners of the opinion. . . .

Respect for the independence of state courts, as well as avoidance of rendering advisory opinions, have been the cornerstones of this Court's refusal to decide cases where there is an adequate and independent state ground. It is precisely because of this respect for state courts, and this desire to avoid advisory opinions, that we do not wish to continue to decide issues of state law that go beyond the opinion that we review, or to require state courts to reconsider cases to clarify the grounds of their decisions. Accordingly, when, as in this case, a state court decision fairly appears to rest primarily on federal law, or to be interwoven with the federal law, and when the adequacy and independence of any possible state law ground is not clear from the face of the opinion, we will accept as the most reasonable explanation that the state court decided the case the way it did because it believed that federal law required it to do so. If a state court chooses merely to rely on federal precedents as it would on the precedents of all other jurisdictions, then it need only make clear by a plain statement in its judgment or opinion that the federal cases are being used only for the purpose of guidance, and do not themselves compel the result that the court has reached. In this way, both justice and judicial administration will be greatly improved. If the state court decision indicates clearly and expressly that it is alternatively based on bona fide separate, adequate, and independent grounds, we, of course, will not undertake to review the decision.

. . . We believe that such an approach will provide state judges with a clearer opportunity to develop state jurisprudence unimpeded by federal interference, and yet will preserve the integrity of federal law. . . .

The principle that we will not review judgments of state courts that rest on adequate and independent state grounds is based, in part, on "the limitations of our own jurisdiction." *Herb v. Pitcairn*, 324 U.S. 117, 125 (1945).[7] The jurisdictional concern is that we not "render an advisory opinion." *Id.*, at 126. Our requirement of

7. In *Herb v. Pitcairn*, the Court also wrote that it was desirable that state courts "be asked rather than told what they have intended." It is clear that we have already departed from that view in those cases in which we have examined state law to determine whether a particular result was guided or compelled by federal law. Our decision today departs further from *Herb* insofar as we disfavor further requests to state courts for clarification, and we require a clear and express statement that a decision rests on adequate and

a "plain statement" that a decision rests upon adequate and independent state grounds does not in any way authorize the rendering of advisory opinions. Rather, in determining, as we must, whether we have jurisdiction to review a case that is alleged to rest on adequate and independent state grounds, we merely assume that there are no such grounds when it is not clear from the opinion itself that the state court relied upon an adequate and independent state ground and when it fairly appears that the state court rested its decision primarily on federal law.[8]

Our review of the decision below under this framework leaves us unconvinced that it rests upon an independent state ground. Apart from its two citations to the State Constitution, the court below relied *exclusively* on its understanding of *Terry* and other federal cases. Not a single state case was cited to support the state court's holding that the search of the passenger compartment was unconstitutional. Indeed, the court declared that the search in this case was unconstitutional because "[t]he Court of Appeals erroneously applied the principles of *Terry v. Ohio* . . . to the search of the interior of the vehicle in this case." 413 Mich., at 471. The references to the State Constitution in no way indicate that the decision below rested on grounds in any way *independent* from the state court's interpretation of federal law. Even if we accept that the Michigan Constitution has been interpreted to provide independent protection for certain rights also secured under the Fourth Amendment, it fairly appears in this case that the Michigan Supreme Court rested its decision primarily on federal law.

. . . [W]e find that we have jurisdiction in the absence of a plain statement that the decision below rested on an adequate and independent state ground. It appears to us that the state court "felt compelled by what it understood to be federal constitutional considerations to construe . . . its own law in the manner it did." . . .

Justice BLACKMUN, concurring in part and concurring in the judgment.
. . . While I am satisfied that the Court has jurisdiction in this particular case, I do not join the Court . . . in fashioning a new presumption of jurisdiction over cases coming here from state courts. Although I agree with the Court that uniformity in federal criminal law is desirable, I see little efficiency and an increased danger of advisory opinions in the Court's new approach.

[The dissenting opinion of Justice Brennan, in which Justice Marshall joined, is omitted.]

---

independent state grounds. However, the "plain statement" rule protects the integrity of state courts for the reasons discussed above. The preference for clarification expressed in *Herb* has failed to be a completely satisfactory means of protecting the state and federal interests that are involved.

8. . . . In dissent, Justice Stevens proposes the novel view that this Court should never review a state court decision unless the Court wishes to vindicate a federal right that has been endangered. The rationale of the dissent is not restricted to cases where the decision is arguably supported by adequate and independent state grounds. Rather, JUSTICE STEVENS appears to believe that even if the decision below rests exclusively on federal grounds, this Court should not review the decision as long as there is no federal right that is endangered.

The state courts handle the vast bulk of all criminal litigation in this country. . . . The state courts are required to apply federal constitutional standards, and they necessarily create a considerable body of "federal law" in the process. It is not surprising that this Court has become more interested in the application and development of federal law by state courts in the light of the recent significant expansion of federally created standards that we have imposed on the States.

Justice STEVENS, dissenting.

The jurisprudential questions presented in this case are far more important than the question whether the Michigan police officer's search of respondent's car violated the Fourth Amendment. The case raises profoundly significant questions concerning the relationship between two sovereigns—the State of Michigan and the United States of America.

The Supreme Court of the State of Michigan expressly held "that the deputies' search of the vehicle was proscribed by the Fourth Amendment to the United States Constitution and *art. 1, §11 of the Michigan Constitution.*" 413 Mich. 461, 472-473, 320 N.W. 2d 866, 870 (1982) (emphasis added). The state law ground is clearly adequate to support the judgment, but the question whether it is independent of the Michigan Supreme Court's understanding of federal law is more difficult. Four possible ways of resolving that question present themselves: (1) asking the Michigan Supreme Court directly, (2) attempting to infer from all possible sources of state law what the Michigan Supreme Court meant, (3) presuming that adequate state grounds are independent unless it clearly appears otherwise, or (4) presuming that adequate state grounds are *not* independent unless it clearly appears otherwise. This Court has, on different occasions, employed each of the first three approaches; never until today has it even hinted at the fourth. . . . I cannot accept the Court's decision to choose the fourth approach over the third—to presume that adequate state grounds are intended to be dependent on federal law unless the record plainly shows otherwise. . . .

Even if I agreed with the Court that we are free to consider as a fresh proposition whether we may take presumptive jurisdiction over the decisions of sovereign States, I could not agree that an expansive attitude makes good sense. It appears to be common ground that any rule we adopt should show "respect for state courts, and [a] desire to avoid advisory opinions." . . .

. . . These are not cases in which an American citizen has been deprived of a right secured by the United States Constitution or a federal statute. Rather, they are cases in which a state court has upheld a citizen's assertion of a right, finding the citizen to be protected under both federal and state law. . . .

Such cases should not be of inherent concern to this Court. . . .

In this case the State of Michigan has arrested one of its citizens and the Michigan Supreme Court has decided to turn him loose. The respondent is a United States citizen as well as a Michigan citizen, but since there is no claim that he has been mistreated by the State of Michigan, the final outcome of the state processes offended no federal interest whatever. Michigan simply provided greater protection to one of its citizens than some other State might provide or, indeed, than this Court might require throughout the country.

I believe that in reviewing the decisions of state courts, the primary role of this Court is to make sure that persons who seek to *vindicate* federal rights have been fairly heard. . . .

Notes and Questions

1. Which approach do you think is better when it is not clear whether a state court's judgment or decree rests on adequate and independent state grounds: the approach taken in *Herb* or that taken in *Michigan v. Long*? Why? Does your answer depend on whether you consider the question from the perspective of a United States Supreme Court Justice, a State Supreme Court Justice, or a lawyer seeking (or opposing) United States Supreme Court review?

2. It may be hard under *Michigan v. Long* for a state court to establish that its decision rests independently on a state constitutional provision when the State's highest court has interpreted that state constitutional provision to be coextensive with the cognate provision in the U.S. Constitution and upholds a claim based on the state constitutional provision. *See, e.g., Florida v. Powell*, _____ U.S. _____, 130 S. Ct. 1195, 1202 (2010) (applying *Michigan v. Long* to review a state court decision when "the Florida Supreme Court treated state and federal law as interchangeable and interwoven . . . [and] at no point expressly asserted that state-law source gave Powell rights distinct from, or broader than, those delineated in *Miranda*"). Can the state court in this situation decide the case in a way that precludes United States Supreme Court review?

3. The United States Supreme Court has independently reviewed state court determinations of state law when those determinations are logically antecedent to—rather than independent of—the resolution of an issue of federal law. *Martin v. Hunter's Lessee* provides an example. 14 U.S. (1 Wheat.) 304 (1816). The *Martin* case arose from a dispute over land in Virginia. Hunter claimed that he got title to the land from the State of Virginia after Virginia validly confiscated the land from Martin (a British subject). Martin argued that the land was protected from confiscation by treaties of 1783 and 1794. Hunter responded that Virginia law effectively divested Martin and his predecessors of title to the land before the treaties took effect. To resolve these arguments, the Court first had to address whether Virginia law had divested Martin of his property rights before the treaties took effect. If Virginia law did cause a prior divestiture, then the later treaties had nothing to protect; Martin's treaty claims would fail. If, on the other hand, Virginia law did not cause a divestiture before the treaties took effect, the Court would have to determine whether the treaties protected Martin's rights to the land. In either case, the divestiture issue (the issue of state law) was logically antecedent to the treaty issue (the issue of federal law). The Court's jurisdiction to review the federal (treaty) issue authorized the Court to review the antecedent state law (divestiture) issue. *See* Richard H. Fallon et al., Hart and Wechsler's the Federal Courts and the Federal System 434-438, 458 (6th ed. 2009); Charles F. Hobson, *John Marshall and the Fairfax Litigation: The Background of* Martin v. Hunter's Lessee, J. Sup. Ct. History 1996, vol. 21 no. 2, at 36; Herbert Wechsler, *The Appellate Jurisdiction of the Supreme Court: Reflections on the Law and the Logistics of Direct Review*, 34 Wash. & Lee L. Rev. 1043, 1051 (1977).

4. The Court in *Herb v. Pitcairn* treated the adequate and independent state ground doctrine as a constitutional restriction on the Court's jurisdiction to review state court decisions under 28 U.S.C. §1257 and its predecessor statutes. The Court has not always treated the doctrine as constitutional, however; in early cases, the Court seemed to treat the doctrine as prudential. Richard H. Fallon et al., Hart and Wechsler's the Federal Courts and the Federal System 461 (6th ed. 2009). How does the Court treat the doctrine in *Michigan v. Long*?

5. The Court applies the adequate and independent state ground doctrine when it reviews state prisoners' petitions for habeas corpus under 28 U.S.C. §2254, which are ordinarily filed after state court litigation for collateral review has ended and which challenge the state courts' adjudication of federal law. The doctrine "is not technically jurisdictional" in the habeas context, however, "since . . . [the Court] is not formally reviewing a [state court] judgment, but is determining whether the prisoner is 'in custody in violation of the Constitution or laws or treaties of the United States.'" *Lambrix v. Singletary*, 520 U.S. 518, 523 (1997) (quoting 28 U.S.C. §2254). Despite the different nature of the doctrine in the habeas context, the Court in habeas cases applies non-habeas precedent on the doctrine. *See, e.g., Beard v. Kindler,* 558 U.S. 53, ____, 130 S. Ct. 612, 617-618 (2009).

d. The Finality Requirement

As discussed above, the Court generally awaits a final judgment by a federal court of appeals before reviewing a case from that court. *See Virginia Military Inst. v. United States,* 508 U.S. 946 (1993) (opinion of Scalia, J., respecting denial of certiorari). The final judgment rule as applied to review of cases from the federal courts of appeals is prudential. It is not required by the governing statute, 28 U.S.C. §1254(1), which authorizes review "before or after rendition of judgment or decree." The Court also applies a final judgment rule to its review of decisions from the state courts. In that context, the rule is required by the relevant statute, 28 U.S.C. §1257, as discussed in the next case.

Cox Broadcasting Corp. v. Cohn

420 U.S. 469 (1975)

Mr. Justice WHITE delivered the opinion of the Court.

[A Georgia statute, §26-9901, made it a misdemeanor to publish or broadcast the name of a rape victim. A television station owned by appellant Cox Broadcasting aired news reports identifying appellee Cohn's daughter as a rape victim. A reporter for the station learned her identity from public records. Cohn sued Cox Broadcasting and the reporter in state court for money damages. Cohn claimed that his right to privacy had been invaded by the broadcasts' naming his by-then-deceased daughter as a rape victim, in violation of the state statute.]

. . . Appellants admitted the broadcasts but claimed that they were privileged under both state law and the First and Fourteenth Amendments. The trial court, rejecting appellants' constitutional claims and holding that the Georgia statute gave a civil remedy to those injured by its violation, granted summary judgment to appellee as to liability, with the determination of damages to await trial by jury. . . .

The Georgia Supreme Court held that §26-9901 did not create a civil cause of action in favor of Cohn; Cohn's complaint did, however, state a common law cause of action. In its initial decision the Georgia Supreme Court found it unnecessary to rule on the constitutionality of §26-9901.

Upon motion for rehearing the Georgia [Supreme] [C]ourt countered the argument that the victim's name was a matter of public interest and could be published with impunity by relying on §26-9901 as an authoritative declaration of state policy that the name of a rape victim was not a matter of public concern. This time the court felt compelled to determine the constitutionality of the statute and sustained it as a "legitimate limitation on the right of freedom of expression contained in the First Amendment." . . .

We postponed decision as to our jurisdiction over this appeal to the hearing on the merits. We conclude that the Court has jurisdiction, and reverse the judgment of the Georgia Supreme Court. . . .

Since 1789, Congress has granted this Court appellate jurisdiction with respect to state litigation only after the highest state court in which judgment could be had has rendered a "[f]inal judgment or decree." The Court has noted that "[c]onsiderations of English usage as well as those of judicial policy" would justify an interpretation of the final-judgment rule to preclude review "where anything further remains to be determined by a State court, no matter how dissociated from the only federal issue that has finally been adjudicated by the highest court of the State." *Radio Station WOW, Inc. v. Johnson,* 326 U.S. 120, 124 (1945). But the Court there observed that the rule had not been administered in such a mechanical fashion and that there were circumstances in which there has been "a departure from this requirement of finality for federal appellate jurisdiction." *Ibid.*

These circumstances were said to be "very few," *ibid.*; but as the cases have unfolded, the Court has recurringly encountered situations in which the highest court of a State has finally determined the federal issue present in a particular case, but in which there are further proceedings in the lower state courts to come. There are now at least four categories of such cases. . . . In most, if not all, of the cases in these categories, these additional proceedings would not require the decision of other federal questions that might also require review by the Court at a later date,[6] and immediate rather than delayed review would be the best way to avoid "the mischief of economic waste and of delayed justice," as well as precipitate interference with state litigation.[7] In the cases in the first two categories considered below, the federal issue would not be mooted or otherwise affected by the proceedings yet to be had because those proceedings have little substance, their outcome is certain, or they are wholly unrelated to the federal question. In the other two categories, however, the federal issue would be mooted if the petitioner or appellant seeking to bring the action here prevailed on the merits in the later state-court proceedings, but there is nevertheless sufficient justification for immediate review of the federal question finally determined in the state courts.

In the first category are those cases in which there are further proceedings—even entire trials—yet to occur in the state courts but where for one reason or another the federal issue is conclusive or the outcome of further proceedings preordained. In these circumstances, because the case is for all practical purposes concluded, the judgment of the state court on the federal issue is deemed final. In *Mills v. Alabama,* 384 U.S. 214 (1966), for example, a demurrer to a criminal complaint was sustained on federal constitutional grounds by a state trial court. The State Supreme Court reversed, remanding for jury trial. This Court took jurisdiction on the reasoning that the appellant had no defense other than his federal claim and could not prevail at trial on the facts or any nonfederal ground. To dismiss the appeal "would not only be an inexcusable delay of the benefits Congress intended

---

6. Eminent domain proceedings are of the type that may involve an interlocutory decision as to a federal question with another federal question to be decided later. "For in those cases the federal constitutional question embraces not only a taking, but a taking on payment of just compensation. A state judgment is not final unless it covers both aspects of that integral problem." *North Dakota State Board of Pharmacy v. Snyder's Drug Stores, Inc.,* 414 U.S. 156, 163 (1973).

7. *Gillespie v. United States Steel Corp.,* 379 U.S. 148 (1964), arose in the federal courts and involved the requirement of 28 U.S.C. §1291 that judgments of district courts be final if they are to be appealed to the courts of appeals. In the course of deciding that the judgment of the District Court in the case had been final, the Court indicated its approach to finality requirements:

"And our cases long have recognized that whether a ruling is 'final' within the meaning of §1291 is frequently so close a question that decision of that issue either way can be supported with equally forceful arguments, and that it is impossible to devise a formula to resolve all marginal cases coming within what might well be called the 'twilight zone' of finality. Because of this difficulty this Court has held that the requirement of finality is to be given a 'practical rather than a technical construction.' *Cohen v. Beneficial Industrial Loan Corp.* [337 U.S. 541, 546.] *Dickinson v. Petroleum Conversion Corp.,* 338 U.S. 507, 511, pointed out that in deciding the question of finality the most important competing considerations are 'the inconvenience and costs of piecemeal review on the one hand and the danger of denying justice by delay on the other.'" 379 U.S., at 152-153.

to grant by providing for appeal to this Court, but it would also result in a completely unnecessary waste of time and energy in judicial systems already troubled by delays due to congested dockets." *Id.*, at 217-218 (footnote omitted).

② Second, there are cases such as *Radio Station WOW, supra,* and *Brady v. Maryland,* 373 U.S. 83 (1963), in which the federal issue, finally decided by the highest court in the State, will survive and require decision regardless of the outcome of future state-court proceedings. In *Radio Station WOW,* the Nebraska Supreme Court directed the transfer of the properties of a federally licensed radio station and ordered an accounting, rejecting the claim that the transfer order would interfere with the federal license. The federal issue was held reviewable here despite the pending accounting on the "presupposition . . . that the federal questions that could come here have been adjudicated by the State court, and that the accounting which remains to be taken could not remotely give rise to a federal question . . . that may later come here. . . ." 326 U.S., at 127. . . . Nothing that could happen in the course of the accounting, short of settlement of the case, would foreclose or make unnecessary decision on the federal question. . . .[9]

③ In the third category are those situations where the federal claim has been finally decided, with further proceedings on the merits in the state courts to come, but in which later review of the federal issue cannot be had, whatever the ultimate outcome of the case. Thus, in these cases, if the party seeking interim review ultimately prevails on the merits, the federal issue will be mooted; if he were to lose on the merits, however, the governing state law would not permit him again to present his federal claims for review. . . . *California v. Stewart,* 384 U.S. 436 (1966) (decided with *Miranda v. Arizona*), epitomizes this category. There the state court reversed a conviction on federal constitutional grounds and remanded for a new trial. Although the State might have prevailed at trial, we granted its petition for certiorari and affirmed, explaining that the state judgment was "final" since an acquittal of the defendant at trial would preclude, under state law, an appeal by the State. . . .

④ Lastly, there are those situations where the federal issue has been finally decided in the state courts with further proceedings pending in which the party seeking review here might prevail on the merits on nonfederal grounds, thus rendering unnecessary review of the federal issue by this Court, and where reversal of the state court on the federal issue would be preclusive of any further litigation on the relevant cause of action rather than merely controlling the nature and character of, or determining the admissibility of evidence in, the state proceedings still to come. In these circumstances, if a refusal immediately to review the state court decision might seriously erode federal policy, the Court has entertained and decided the federal issue, which itself has been finally determined by the state courts for purposes of the state litigation.

In *Construction Laborers v. Curry,* 371 U.S. 542 (1963), the state courts temporarily enjoined labor union picketing over claims that the National Labor Relations Board had exclusive jurisdiction of the controversy. The Court took jurisdiction for two independent reasons. First, the power of the state court to proceed in the face of the preemption claim was deemed an issue separable from the merits and ripe for

---

9. In *Brady v. Maryland,* 373 U.S. 83 (1963), the Maryland courts had ordered a new trial in a criminal case but on punishment only, and the petitioner asserted here that he was entitled to a new trial on guilt as well. We entertained the case, saying that the federal issue was separable and would not be mooted by the new trial on punishment ordered in the state courts.

review in this Court, particularly "when postponing review would seriously erode the national labor policy requiring the subject matter of respondents' cause to be heard by the . . . Board, not by the state courts." *Id.*, at 550. Second, the Court was convinced that in any event the union had no defense to the entry of a permanent injunction other than the preemption claim that had already been ruled on in the state courts. Hence the case was for all practical purposes concluded in the state tribunals.

In *Mercantile National Bank v. Langdeau,* 371 U.S. 555 (1963), two national banks were sued, along with others, in the courts of Travis County, Tex. The claim asserted was conspiracy to defraud an insurance company. The banks as a preliminary matter asserted that a special federal venue statute immunized them from suit in Travis County and that they could properly be sued only in another county. Although trial was still to be had and the banks might well prevail on the merits, the Court, relying on *Curry*, entertained the issue as a "separate and independent matter, anterior to the merits and not enmeshed in the factual and legal issues comprising the plaintiff's cause of action." *Id.*, at 558. Moreover, it would serve the policy of the federal statute "to determine now in which state court appellants may be tried rather than to subject them . . . to long and complex litigation which may all be for naught if consideration of the preliminary question of venue is postponed until the conclusion of the proceedings." *Ibid.*

Miami Herald Publishing Co. v. Tornillo, 418 U.S. 241 (1974), is the latest case in this category. There a candidate for public office sued a newspaper for refusing, allegedly contrary to a state statute, to carry his reply to the paper's editorial critical of his qualifications. The trial court held the act unconstitutional, denying both injunctive relief and damages. The State Supreme Court reversed, sustaining the statute against the challenge based upon the First and Fourteenth Amendments and remanding the case for a trial and appropriate relief, including damages. The newspaper brought the case here. We sustained our jurisdiction . . . observing:

> "Whichever way we were to decide on the merits, it would be intolerable to leave unanswered, under these circumstances, an important question of freedom of the press under the First Amendment; an uneasy and unsettled constitutional posture of [the state statute] could only further harm the operation of a free press."

In light of the prior cases, we conclude that we have jurisdiction to review the judgment of the Georgia Supreme Court rejecting the challenge under the First and Fourteenth Amendments to the state law authorizing damage suits against the press for publishing the name of a rape victim whose identity is revealed in the course of a public prosecution. The Georgia Supreme Court's judgment is plainly final on the federal issue and is not subject to further review in the state courts. Appellants will be liable for damages if the elements of the state cause of action are proved. They may prevail at trial on nonfederal grounds, it is true, but if the Georgia court erroneously upheld the statute, there should be no trial at all. Moreover, even if appellants prevailed at trial and made unnecessary further consideration of the constitutional question, there would remain in effect the unreviewed decision of the State Supreme Court that a civil action for publishing the name of a rape victim disclosed in a public judicial proceeding may go forward despite the First and Fourteenth Amendments. Delaying final decision of the First Amendment claim until after trial will "leave unanswered . . . an important question of freedom of the press under the First Amendment," "an uneasy and unsettled constitutional posture [that] could only further harm the operation of a free press." *Tornillo, supra,* at 247 n.6. On the other hand, if we now hold that the First and Fourteenth Amendments bar civil liability for broadcasting the victim's name, this litigation ends. Given these factors—that the litigation could be terminated by our decision on the merits and that a failure to decide the question now will leave the press in Georgia operating in the shadow of the civil and criminal sanctions of a rule of law and a statute the constitutionality of which is in serious doubt—we find that reaching the merits is consistent with the pragmatic approach that we have followed in the past in determining finality. See *Gillespie v. United States Steel Corp.,* 379 U.S. 148 (1964). . . .

[The separate opinions of Chief Justice Burger and Justice Douglas (each concurring in the judgment) and of Justice Powell (concurring), are omitted.]

Mr. Justice Rehnquist, dissenting.

Because I am of the opinion that the decision which is the subject of this appeal is not a "final" judgment or decree, as that term is used in 28 U.S.C. §1257, I would dismiss this appeal for want of jurisdiction. . . .

The Court has taken what it terms a "pragmatic" approach to the finality problem presented in this case. In so doing, it has relied heavily on *Gillespie v. United States Steel Corp.,* 379 U.S. 148 (1964). . . . *Gillespie* involved 28 U.S.C. §1291, which restricts the appellate jurisdiction of the federal courts of appeals to "final decisions of the district courts." . . . I believe that the underlying concerns are different, and that the difference counsels a more restrictive approach when §1257 finality is at issue.

According to *Gillespie,* the finality requirement is imposed as a matter of minimizing "the inconvenience and costs of piecemeal review." This proposition is undoubtedly sound so long as one is considering the administration of the federal court system. . . . The case before us, however, is an appeal from a state court, and this fact introduces additional interests which must be accommodated in fashioning any exception to the literal application of the finality requirement. I consider §1257 finality to be but one of a number of congressional provisions reflecting concern that uncontrolled federal judicial interference with state administrative and judicial functions would have untoward consequences for our federal system.[4] . . .

. . . [T]he greatest difficulty with the test enunciated today is that it totally abandons the principle that constitutional issues are too important to be decided save when absolutely necessary, and are to be avoided if there are grounds for decision of lesser dimension. The long line of cases which established this rule makes clear that it is a principle primarily designed, not to benefit the lower courts, or state-federal relations, but rather to safeguard this Court's own process of constitutional adjudication. . . .

In this case there has yet to be an adjudication of liability against appellants, and unlike the appellant in *Mills v. Alabama,* they do not concede that they have no nonfederal defenses. Nonetheless, the Court rules on their constitutional defense. Far from eschewing a constitutional holding in advance of the necessity for one, the

---

4. See, *e.g.,* 28 U.S.C. §1341 (limitation on power of district courts to enjoin state taxing systems); 28 U.S.C. §1739 (requiring that state judicial proceedings be accorded full faith and credit in federal courts); 28 U.S.C. §§2253-2254 (prescribing various restrictions on federal habeas corpus for state prisoners); . . . 28 U.S.C. §2283 (restricting power of federal courts to enjoin state-court proceedings).

Court construes §1257 so that it may virtually rush out and meet the prospective constitutional litigant as he approaches our doors. . . .

Notes and Questions

1. Into which of the four categories does the Court in *Cox* find that case falls?

2. What are the purposes of the "finality" requirement in §1257? What are the justifications for the four categories identified in *Cox*?

3. Is the Court's conclusion that it has jurisdiction influenced by its view of the correctness of the state court's decision on the federal issue? Should the Court be influenced by this factor?

4. Which of the categories are in tension with the doctrine of constitutional avoidance discussed in the dissent? Does any such tension support a narrow understanding of the exception?

5. The *Cox* categories can be difficult to apply, especially the fourth category. A case illustrating the difficulty is *Flynt v. Ohio*, 451 U.S. 619 (1981), which is excerpted next. Notice that the Court in *Flynt* refers to the *Cox* "categories" as "exceptions" to the (formal) finality requirement.

Flynt v. Ohio

451 U.S. 619 (1981)

[Ohio prosecuted the Flynts for obscenity based on two issues of *Hustler* magazine. The Flynts persuaded the state trial court to dismiss the prosecution on the ground that the Flynts had been subjected to selective and discriminatory prosecution, in violation of the Equal Protection Clause. The state trial court based its finding of selective, discriminatory prosecution on evidence, including a public statement by the prosecutor, that the prosecution had been prompted by public complaints about a political cartoon in one of the allegedly obscene issues of *Hustler*. The cartoon, as petitioners described it, depicted "President Ford, Henry Kissinger, and Nelson Rockefeller attempting to do rude things to the Statue of Liberty, obviously without her consent." Petitioners' Brief on the Merits 3 n.**, *Flynt v. Ohio*, 451 U.S. 619 (No. 80-420).

The Ohio court of appeals reversed the dismissal of the prosecution and remanded the case for trial, and the Ohio Supreme Court affirmed. The United States Supreme Court initially granted the Flynts' petition for certiorari but in this opinion dismissed the writ "for want of jurisdiction."]

PER CURIAM.

Consistent with the relevant jurisdictional statute, 28 U.S.C. §1257, the Court's jurisdiction to review a state-court decision is generally limited to a final judgment rendered by the highest court of the State in which decision may be had. *Cox Broadcasting Corp. v. Cohn*, 420 U.S. 469, 476-477 (1975). In general, the final-judgment rule has been interpreted "to preclude reviewability . . . where anything further remains to be determined by a State court, no matter how dissociated from the only federal issue that has finally been adjudicated by the highest court of the State." *Radio Station WOW, Inc. v. Johnson*, 326 U.S. 120, 124 (1945). Applied in the context of a criminal prosecution, finality is normally defined by the imposition of the sentence. Here there has been no finding of guilt and no sentence imposed.

The Court has, however, in certain circumstances, treated state-court judgments as final for jurisdictional purposes although there were further proceedings to take place in the state court. Cases of this kind were divided into four categories in *Cox Broadcasting Corp. v. Cohn*, and each category was described. We do not think that the decision of the Ohio Supreme Court is a final judgment within any of the four exceptions identified in *Cox*.

In the first place, we observed in *Cox* that in most, if not all, of the cases falling within the four exceptions, not only was there a final judgment on the federal issue for purposes of state-court proceedings, but also there were no other federal issues to be resolved. There was thus no probability of piecemeal review with respect to federal issues. Here, it appears that other federal issues will be involved in the trial court, such as whether or not the publication at issue is obscene.

Second, it is not even arguable that the judgment involved here falls within any of the first three categories identified in the *Cox* opinion, and the argument that it is within the fourth category, although not frivolous, is unsound. The cases falling within the fourth exception were described as those situations:

> "[w]here the federal issue has been finally decided in the state courts with further proceedings pending in which the party seeking review here might prevail on the merits on nonfederal grounds, thus rendering unnecessary review of the federal issue by this Court, and where reversal of the state court on the federal issue would be preclusive of any further litigation on the relevant cause of action rather than merely controlling the nature and character of, or determining the admissibility of evidence in, the state proceedings still to come. In these circumstances, if a refusal immediately to review the state-court decision might seriously erode federal policy, the Court has entertained and decided the federal issue, which itself has been finally determined by the state courts for purposes of the state litigation." 420 U.S., at 482-483.

Here, it is apparent that if we reversed the judgment of the Ohio Supreme Court on the federal defense of selective enforcement, there would be no further proceedings in the state courts in this case. But the question remains whether delaying review until petitioners are convicted, if they are, would seriously erode federal policy within the meaning of our prior cases. We are quite sure that this would not be the case and that we do not have a final judgment before us.

The cases which the *Cox* opinion listed as falling in the fourth category involved identifiable federal statutory or constitutional policies which would have been undermined by the continuation of the litigation in the state courts. *Miami Herald Publishing Co. v. Tornillo*, 418 U.S. 241 (1974); *Mercantile National Bank v. Langdeau*, 371 U.S. 555 (1963); *Construction Laborers v. Curry*, 371 U.S. 542 (1963). Here there is no identifiable federal policy that will suffer if the state criminal proceeding goes forward. The question presented for review is whether on this record the decision to prosecute petitioners was selective or discriminatory in violation of the Equal Protection Clause. The resolution of this question can await final judgment without any adverse effect upon important federal interests. A contrary conclusion would permit the fourth exception to swallow the rule. Any federal issue finally decided on an interlocutory appeal in the state courts would qualify for immediate review. That this case involves an obscenity prosecution does not alter the conclusion. Obscene material, properly defined, is beyond the protection of the First Amendment. *Miller v. California*, 413 U.S. 15, 23-24 (1973). As this case comes to us, we are confronted only with a state effort to prosecute an unprotected activity, the dissemination of obscenity. The obscenity issue has not yet been decided in the state courts, and no federal policy bars a trial on that question. There is no reason to treat this selective prosecution claim differently than we would treat any other claim of selective prosecution.

Accordingly, the writ is dismissed for want of jurisdiction.

Justice STEWART, with whom Justice BRENNAN and Justice MARSHALL join, dissenting.

I believe that a criminal trial of the petitioners under this Ohio obscenity law will violate the Constitution of the United States. It is clear to me, therefore, that "identifiable . . . constitutional polic[y]" will be "undermined by the continuation of the litigation in the state courts."

Accordingly, I think that under the very criteria discussed in the opinion of the Court, the judgment before us is "final for jurisdictional purposes." . . .

Justice STEVENS, dissenting.

. . . In my opinion, the interest in protecting magazine publishers from being prosecuted criminally because state officials or their constituents are offended by the content of an admittedly nonobscene political cartoon is not merely "an identifiable federal policy"; it is the kind of interest that motivated the adoption of the First Amendment to the United States Constitution. . . .

Notes and Questions

1. The state court decision on which the Court initially granted certiorari concerned only the selective prosecution issue; there had been no trial yet on the obscenity charges. Considering there had not yet been a trial on the obscenity charges and that the Flynts had presented evidence that the prosecution was based on "an admittedly nonobscene political cartoon" (as Justice Stevens described it), is the majority begging the question when it says, "As this case comes to us, we are confronted only with a state effort to prosecute an unprotected activity, the dissemination of obscenity"?

2. The Court in *Flynt* suggests that the fourth *Cox* exception has the potential, if broadly interpreted, to "swallow" the final judgment rule. Why does the fourth exception have that potential?

3. Another case illustrating the difficulty of determining finality under *Cox* is *Florida v. Thomas*, 532 U.S. 774 (2001). In that case, a state trial court granted Thomas's pretrial motion to suppress evidence (drugs). The trial court ruled that the drugs were found during a police search of Thomas's car that violated the Fourth Amendment. The state immediately appealed the trial court order suppressing the evidence. The state court of appeals reversed the suppression order, holding that the search was permissible under *New York v. Belton*, 453 U.S. 454 (1981), which had held that the police can search the passenger compartment of a car incident to the arrest of its occupant. The Florida Supreme Court reversed the state court of appeals' decision. The Florida Supreme Court held that the search was not valid under *Belton*, because Thomas was not an occupant of his car when the police first approached Thomas; instead, Thomas had already gotten out of his car and was walking away. But, the Florida Supreme Court determined, the search of Thomas's car might have been permissible as a search incident to arrest under the principles of *Chimel v. California,* 395 U.S. 752 (1969). The Florida Supreme Court remanded the case for further fact-finding on whether the search of Thomas's car was valid under *Chimel.*

The Florida Supreme Court's decision was not final under the formal conception of finality, because that court remanded the case for further proceedings, which could include a trial on the drug charges against Thomas. Even so, the United States Supreme Court granted Florida's petition for certiorari to decide whether the "*Belton* rule" applies when the police initiate contact with a person only after the person has gotten out of the car. None of the parties raised a finality problem in their briefs to the Court on the merits. Indeed, the posture of the case seemed similar to prior cases, such as *New York v. Quarles,* 467 U.S. 649 (1984). In *Quarles,* the Court had reviewed a decision by the New York Court of Appeals (the state's highest court) affirming the suppression of statements obtained from an arrestee without *Miranda* warnings. The Court in *Quarles* had found the New York state court's decision final under the third *Cox* category, as a situation in which "the federal claim has been finally decided . . . but in which later review of the federal issue cannot be had, whatever the ultimate outcome of the case." *Id.* at 651 n.1 (internal quotation marks omitted). *Florida v. Thomas* differed from *Quarles,* however, because the Florida courts had *not* finally decided the federal issue—that is, the constitutionality of the police's search of Thomas's car—and because, if the trial court on remand in *Florida v. Thomas* had again suppressed the evidence on federal constitutional grounds, the state could again take an interlocutory appeal. *See Florida v. Thomas,* 532 U.S. at 779-780.

The Court in *Florida v. Thomas* dismissed certiorari after the case had been briefed and argued on the merits, holding that the case did not fall within any of the *Cox* categories. *See* 532 U.S. at 777-780. The nonfinality of the state court's judgment became evident only after oral argument. The complexity of finality analysis under *Cox* raises two normative questions. First, does the very complexity of the doctrine count against it, considering the policy, often enunciated by the Court itself, that threshold issues of jurisdiction should not be overly complicated? *E.g. Hertz Corp. v. Friend,* _____ U.S. _____, 130 S. Ct. 1181, 1193 (2010). Second, is the complexity of the doctrine justified by the relative flexibility it gives the Court to review cases that would not be considered final under a stricter, more formal approach?

4

Certiorari

Many litigants seek certiorari from the United States Supreme Court but very few litigants succeed in convincing the Court to take their cases. Hence, securing a prized slot on the Supreme Court's docket via a petition for a writ of certiorari is a bit like winning the lottery from the advocate's perspective. In recent years, the Court has routinely received approximately 8,000 petitions for certiorari per Term. *See* Eugene Gressman et al., *Supreme Court Practice: For Practice in the Supreme Court of the United States* 312 (9th ed. 2007). Yet when both *in forma pauperis* petitions—petitions filed by parties who cannot afford to pay litigation costs—and paid petitions are considered, the Court grants certiorari in only about 1 percent of all petitions filed each year. If only paid petitions are considered, then the grant rate increases slightly, but the odds of the Court granting certiorari still are very low. In the 2010 Term, for example, the Court granted just 4.7 percent of paid petitions and only 0.2 percent of all *in forma pauperis* petitions. *See The Supreme Court, The Statistics,* 125 Harv. L. Rev. 362, 369 (2011).

Given the long odds of successfully persuading the Court to grant certiorari in any given case, it is not surprising that the Court's certiorari decisions have been called "crucial" and "second to none in importance." Margaret Meriwether Cordray & Richard Cordray, *The Philosophy of Certiorari: Jurisprudential Considerations in Supreme Court Case Selection,* 82 Wash. U. L.Q. 389, 397 (2001); *see also* William J. Brennan, *The National Court of Appeals: Another Dissent,* 40 U. Chi. L. Rev. 473, 482 (1973). Through its case-selection decisions at the cert stage, the Court not only sets its own priorities and agenda but also sends signals about what role the Court will play in our society. In addition, the Court's certiorari decisions help "shape political discourse in our society," and they help to determine the degree to which the Court "will become involved in confrontations among the various branches and levels of government," including the "relationship of the Court to the other branches of the national government and to the state and local governments." Doris Marie Provine, *Case Selection in the United States Supreme Court* 2 (1980).

The materials in this chapter explore certiorari and are divided into five sections. Section A describes the historical origins, development, and size of the Court's certiorari docket, explaining how the Court morphed from a court of obligatory jurisdiction to a court of discretionary jurisdiction as a result of various congressional enactments, including the Evarts Act of 1891, the Judiciary Act of 1925, and the Supreme Court Case Selections Act of 1988. Section B analyzes what makes a petition certworthy, looking at various rule-based, ideological, jurisprudential,

[handwritten margin note: court evolves from court of obligatory jurisdiction to a court of discretionary jurisdiction]

173

and strategic factors that might influence the Justices' certiorari decisions. Section C discusses the process used to determine which petitions will be granted and which will be denied, walking through the process from the briefing stage through voting by the Justices at conference. Section D focuses on the meaning of a certiorari denial and discusses the practice of dissents from denial of certiorari. Finally, Section E sets forth various proposals for certiorari reform, including a 1972 proposal to create a National Court of Appeals and a more recent proposal to create a Certiorari Division to help the Justices with the certiorari screening process.

A. HISTORICAL DEVELOPMENT OF THE COURT'S CERTIORARI DOCKET

Today we are well-accustomed to the notion that the Supreme Court enjoys broad discretion to set its docket via the writ of certiorari. The Court, however, has not always enjoyed this discretion. Rather than beginning as a court of discretionary jurisdiction, the Court initially stood as a court of obligatory jurisdiction.[1] Indeed, as Chief Justice John Marshall put it in 1821 in *Cohens v. Virginia*, the Court felt it had "no more right to decline the exercise of jurisdiction which is given than to usurp that which is not given." 19 U.S. (6 Wheat.) 264, 404 (1821). Then beginning in 1891, Congress began to invest the Court with some discretion to control its docket. Over time, Congress gave the Court more and more docket control, eventually transforming the Court from a court of obligatory jurisdiction to one of almost entirely discretionary jurisdiction.[2]

1. The Introduction of Certiorari via the Evarts Act of 1891

When Congress enacted the Judiciary Act of 1789, it created two types of inferior federal courts: thirteen district courts, as well as three multidistrict circuit courts consisting of two Supreme Court Justices and a district judge from within the circuit. Both the district and the circuit courts generally operated as trial courts, with the circuit courts enjoying only a very limited appellate jurisdiction and the Supreme Court operating as a court of obligatory jurisdiction. However, as the country grew in scale and complexity in the wake of the Civil War, the number of cases on the Court's docket rose sharply from 253 cases pending in 1850 to 1,816 at the beginning of the 1890 October Term. Not surprisingly, as this happened, the obligatory nature of the Court's docket proved overwhelming and unworkable. By 1890, for example, the Court's docket was so congested that it took more than three years from the time a case was docketed to the time it was argued.

As the Supreme Court's docket soared in the late 1800s, Congress chose to restructure the federal judicial system in 1891 by creating nine intermediate federal appellate courts, called the circuit courts of appeals, via the Evarts Act. Circuit Court of Appeals Act, ch. 517, 26 Stat. 826 (1891). As the Supreme Court has explained, "The essential purpose of the Evarts Act was to enable the Supreme Court to

---

1. Portions of this section on the history of certiorari are adapted from Kathryn A. Watts, *Constraining Certiorari Using Administrative Law Principles*, 160 U. Pa. L. Rev. 1 (2011).

2. For an extremely detailed and thorough history of the Court's transformation from a court of obligatory jurisdiction to one of discretionary jurisdiction, *see generally* Edward A. Hartnett, *Questioning Certiorari: Some Reflections Seventy-Five Years After the Judges' Bill*, 100 Colum. L. Rev. 1643 (2000).

discharge its indispensable functions in our federal system by relieving it of the duty of adjudication in cases that are important only to the litigants." *Dick v. New York Life Insur. Co.*, 359 U.S. 437, 448 (1959) (Frankfurter, J., dissenting).

In the Evarts Act, Congress generally continued the longstanding practice of making the Court's jurisdiction obligatory. For example, cases from the district courts or existing circuit courts that involved the construction or application of the U.S. Constitution were still appealable as of right directly to the United States Supreme Court, as were cases involving the conviction of a capital or otherwise infamous crime. Congress, however, also vested the new circuit courts of appeals with power to review—and generally to render final decisions—in certain limited classes of cases, including in diversity cases and suits under the revenue and patent laws. Congress enabled Supreme Court review of these limited classes of final court of appeals decisions only if: (1) the court of appeals certified questions from the case to the Court; or (2) the Supreme Court granted a "writ of certiorari" to bring the judgment before it for review. The thinking was that these limited classes of cases were "rarely of moment except to the parties" and thus generally should not burden the Supreme Court's docket. *Dick*, 359 U.S. at 448 (Frankfurter, J., dissenting).

Congress did not invent the writ of certiorari via the Evarts Act. Rather, certiorari—which means "to be more fully informed" in Latin—has its roots as an English prerogative writ that allowed the record of a subordinate tribunal to be called up. *See* Harold Weintraub, *English Origins of Judicial Review by Prerogative Writ: Certiorari and Mandamus*, 9 N.Y. L. Forum 478, 504 (1963); Frank J. Goodnow, *The Writ of Certiorari*, 6 Poli. Sci. Q. 493 (1891). Indeed, as early as 1789, Congress authorized certiorari in its common law sense as an "auxiliary process" to "supply imperfections in the record of a case already before" the Court. *American Construction Co. v. Jacksonville, T. & K.W. Ry. Co.*, 148 U.S. 372, 380 (1893). The Evarts Act, however, did break new ground by using the writ of certiorari as a means of achieving docket control, thereby planting the seeds for what was later to morph into our contemporary practice of a discretionary docket largely selected via the certiorari process.

The following materials describe the impetus for the enactment of the Evarts Act in 1891, as well as the circumscribed role that certiorari was initially intended to play.

Forsyth v. City of Hammond

166 U.S. 506, 511-13 (1897)

Mr. Justice BREWER . . . delivered the opinion of the Court.

Up to the time of the passage of the act of 1891, creating the circuit courts of appeal, the theory of federal jurisprudence had been a single appellate court, to wit, the supreme court of the United States, by which a final review of all cases of which the lower federal courts had jurisdiction was to be made. It is true there existed certain limitations upon the right of appeal and review, based on the amount in controversy and other considerations; but such limitations did not recognize or provide for the existence of another appellate court, and did not conflict with the thought that this court was to be the single tribunal for reviewing all cases and questions of a federal nature. The rapid growth of the country and the enormous amount of litigation involving questions of a federal character so added to the number of cases brought here for review that it was impossible for this court to keep even pace with the growing docket. The situation had become one of great peril, and many plans for relief were suggested and discussed.

The outcome was the act of March 3, 1891, the thought of which was the creation in []each of the nine circuits of an appellate tribunal composed of three judges, whose decision in certain classes of cases appealable thereto should be final. While this division of appellate power was the means adopted to reduce the accumulation of business in this court, it was foreseen that injurious results might follow if an absolute finality of determination was given to the courts of appeal. Nine separate appellate tribunals might by their differences of opinion, unless held in check by the reviewing power of this court, create an unfortunate confusion in respect to the rules of federal decision. As the courts of appeal would often be constituted of two circuit judges and one district judge, a division of opinion between the former might result in a final judgment where the opinions of two judges of equal rank were on each side of the questions involved. Cases of a class in which finality of decision was given to the circuit courts of appeal might involve questions of such public and national importance as to require that a consideration and determination thereof should be made by the supreme tribunal of the nation. It was obvious that all contingencies in which a decision by this tribunal was of importance could not be foreseen, and so there was placed in the act creating the courts of appeal, in addition to other provisions for review by this court, this enactment:

> "And excepting also that in any such case as is hereinbefore made final in the circuit court of appeals it shall be competent for the supreme court to require, by certiorari or otherwise, any such case to be certified to the supreme court for its review and determination with the same power and authority in the case as if it had been carried by appeal or writ of error to the supreme court."

The general language of this clause is noticeable. It applies to every case in which but for it the decision of the circuit court of appeals would be absolutely final, and authorizes this court to bring before it for review and determination the case so pending in the circuit court of appeals, and to exercise all the power and authority over it which this court would have in any case brought to it by appeal or writ of error. Unquestionably the generality of this provision was not a mere matter of accident. It expressed the thought of congress distinctly and clearly, and was intended to vest in this court a comprehensive and unlimited power. . . . Obviously, a power so broad and comprehensive, if carelessly exercised, might defeat the very thought and purpose of the act creating the courts of appeal. So exercised it might burden the docket of this court with cases which it was the intent of congress to terminate in the courts of appeal, and which, brought here, would simply prevent that promptness of decision which in all judicial actions is one of the elements of justice.

So it has been that this court, while not doubting its power, has been chary of action in respect to certiorari.

Peter Linzer, The Meaning of Certiorari Denials

79 Colum. L. Rev. 1227, 1234-1236 (1979)

From where did certiorari emerge? Today, a distinction is commonly made between "statutory" certiorari—the Supreme Court's discretionary power to review judgments of other courts—and "common law" certiorari—the writ used by many courts to review administrative agencies such as tax assessors and zoning boards. But the language . . . [in the 1891 Act] indicates rather clearly that no such distinction was in Congress's mind in 1891. Rather, after making some judgments of the circuit courts of appeals "final," it was avoiding complete finality by giving the Supreme Court the power to use certiorari in the classic common law manner: to order certified up a record from an inferior jurisdiction where circumstances did not permit normal appellate procedure to be used. It is obviously very different from the device that today controls most of the Supreme Court's docket.

There are very few references to certiorari in the legislative history of the 1891 Act. The House version, H.R. 9014, had no provision for certiorari. It did permit the judges of the circuit courts (which would have had an exclusive appellate function under H.R. 9014) to certify questions to the Supreme Court, and, in fact, required them to do so if there was a conflict among the circuits. The House passed H.R. 9014, but the Senate Judiciary Committee substituted for it a bill based on one prepared by a committee of the American Bar Association. This bill, which, largely unchanged, became the 1891 Act, already contained the language . . . relating to certiorari. Virtually the only reference to this provision occurred during remarks of its proponent, Senator William M. Evarts, a famous New York lawyer and former Secretary of State, by then chairman of the Senate Judiciary Committee. Evarts was discussing the possibility of conflict between circuits. After citing the option of the circuit courts of appeals to certify questions to the Supreme Court, he continued:

> Mr. President, another guard against the occurring diversity of judgments or of there being a careless or inadvertent disposition of important litigation by these courts; I should deprecate any opinion in advance that these courts would not fully meet the interest and confidence that should be invited for them, but still there should be something besides a mere judgment within these courts as to what ought to be reviewed in the interest of jurisprudence and uniformity of decision, and that is that the Supreme Court shall have a right in any of these cases that are thus made final, by certiorari to take up to itself for final determination this or that case, and in that way the scheme of the committee does firmly and peremptorily make a finality on such subjects as we think in their nature admit of finality, and at the same time leaves flexibility, elasticity, and openness for supervision by the Supreme Court.

One of certiorari's key features was that it was a discretionary writ. Evart[s'] remarks make clear that the draftsmen of the 1891 Act intended the specific reference to certiorari not to create a totally new statutory form of discretionary appeal but simply to serve as a safety valve to permit the Supreme Court, by use of common law certiorari, occasionally to take up important cases, primarily involving conflicts between circuits, in areas of law as to which the circuit courts of appeals had "final" jurisdiction.

---

2. The Expansion of Certiorari Leading to the Judges' Bill of 1925

After the Evarts Act of 1891, the Court's docket continued to grow, and Congress proceeded to include certiorari in additional jurisdictional acts. For example, in 1914, Congress responded to concerns about the state courts invalidating progressive-era state legislation on the grounds that it violated federal constitutional rights. The 1914 legislation enabled the Court to use the discretionary writ of certiorari to review state court judgments upholding federal rights. Act of Dec. 23, 1914, ch. 2, 38 Stat. 790. Prior to this Act, only state court judgments that denied (rather than upheld) a claim of federal right were reviewable via a writ of error. In expanding the Court's jurisdiction to also reach cases upholding a federal right in 1914, Congress chose to use the discretionary writ of certiorari rather than a mandatory writ to "protect the already over-loaded Court from further obligatory jurisdiction." Felix Frankfurter & James M. Landis, *The Business of the Supreme Court* 196 (Transaction Publishers 2007) (1928).

Following this enactment, Congress quickly passed another law, the Webb Act of 1916, which further empowered the Court to use certiorari. Act of Sept. 6, 1916, ch. 448, §2, Pub. L. No. 258, 39 Stat. 726. The Webb Act narrowed the Court's mandatory jurisdiction by allowing discretionary review of various lower court decisions, including cases involving state court judgments denying a federal claim or defense, that had been part of the Court's obligatory jurisdiction since 1789.

Next came the most significant congressional expansion of certiorari: the passage of the Judges' Bill of 1925. Judiciary Act of 1925, Pub. L. No. 68-415, ch. 229, 43 Stat. 936. The bill—called the Judges' Bill because the Justices themselves drafted the legislation and Chief Justice William Howard Taft tirelessly lobbied for the bill—withdrew all but a few categories of cases from the Court's mandatory docket and gave the Court broad control over its docket. *See generally* Edward A. Hartnett, *Questioning Certiorari: Some Reflections Seventy-Five Years After the Judges' Bill,* 100 Colum. L. Rev. 1643 (2000) (detailing Taft's persistent lobbying in helping to draft the bill and pushing the bill through Congress). While lobbying Congress for the bill, various Justices including Chief Justice Taft, made representations to Congress about the necessity of increasing the Court's discretion and about how the Court would handle petitions for certiorari and decide which types of petitions the Court would grant. *See id.* For example, Justice Van Devanter "reiterated that discretionary jurisdiction 'does not mean that the court is authorized merely to exercise a will in the matter but rather that the petition is to be granted or denied according to a sound judicial discretion,'" which means that the Court takes into account whether the "'questions presented are of public importance or of wide general interest," or whether the Court should consider the case "in the interest of uniformity.'" *Id.* at 1685. Justice Van Devanter also assured Congress that the Court would grant cases presenting conflicts among the lower courts. *Id.* at 1677.

Consider this description of the history and purposes behind the Judges' Bill written by Justice Felix Frankfurter in 1959, a few decades after the passage of the Judges' Bill.

Dick v. New York Life Insurance Co.

359 U.S. 437, 451-454 (1959)

Mr. Justice FRANKFURTER, whom Mr. Justice WHITTAKER, joins, dissenting.

In 1925 Congress enacted the "Judges' Bill," called such because it was drafted by a committee of this Court composed of Van Devanter, McReynolds, and Sutherland, JJ. At the hearings on the bill these Justices and Mr. Chief Justice Taft explained the bill and also the Court's past practice in respecting the limitations of its certiorari jurisdiction. These authoritative expositions and assurances to Congress, on the basis of which Congress sharply restricted the Court's obligatory jurisdiction, admit of no doubt, contain no ambiguity. Mr. Chief Justice Taft said:

"No litigant is entitled to more than two chances, namely, to the original trial and to a review, and the intermediate courts of review are provided for that purpose. When a case goes beyond that, it is not primarily to preserve the rights of the litigants. The Supreme Court's function is for the purpose of expounding and stabilizing principles of law for the benefit of the people of the country, passing upon constitutional questions and other important questions of law for the public benefit. It is to preserve uniformity of decision among the intermediate courts of appeal."

The House Report, in recommending to the House of Representatives passage of the bill, stated the matter succinctly:

"The problem is whether the time and attention and energy of the court shall be devoted to matters of large public concern, or whether they shall be consumed by matters of less concern, without especial general interest, and only because the litigant wants to have the court of last resort pass upon his right."

Though various objections to certain jurisdictional changes worked by the bill were voiced on the floor of the Senate, even critical Senators recognized the great difference between the Supreme Court and other appellate tribunals. Thus Senator Copeland:

"The United States Supreme Court is one of the three great coordinate branches of the Government, and its time and labor should, generally speaking, be devoted to matters of general interest and importance and not to deciding private controversies between citizens involving no questions of general public importance."

In correspondence between Senator Copeland and Mr. Chief Justice Taft, the latter wrote: "The appeal to us should not be based on the right of a litigant to have a second appeal."

This understanding of the role of the Supreme Court and the way in which it is to be maintained in observing the scope of certiorari jurisdiction, are clearly set forth in a contemporary exposition by Mr. Chief Justice Taft of the purposes of the Judiciary Act of 1925:

"The sound theory of that Act (Act of 1891) and of the new Act is that litigants have their rights sufficiently protected by a hearing or trial in the courts of first instance, and by one review in an intermediate appellate Federal court. The function of the Supreme Court is conceived to be, not the remedying of a particular litigant's wrong, but the consideration of cases whose decision involves principles, the application of which are of wide public or governmental interest, and which should be authoritatively declared by the final court."

Notes and Questions

1. Is it problematic that the Judges' Bill—which proved instrumental in transforming the Court from a court of obligatory jurisdiction to a court of discretionary jurisdiction—came about as a result of tireless lobbying by the Justices themselves? Why or why not?

2. Should assurances and representations made by the Justices in lobbying for the Judges' Bill bind the Court today? For example, should Justice Van Devanter's representation that the Court would grant cases presenting a conflict bind the Court today? What about representations made by the Justices that every Justice personally examined the certiorari papers and that each petition was discussed and voted upon, with four, and sometimes only three, votes being necessary to grant the petition? Should these representations bind the Court today? *See generally* John Paul Stevens, *The Life Span of a Judge-Made Rule*, 58 N.Y.U. L. Rev. 1, 11-14 (1983) (noting that most of the certiorari practices the Justices described in lobbying for the Judges' Bill have been discarded or discontinued, with the exception of the so-called Rule of Four, which requires four votes to grant certiorari).

3. The Supreme Court Case Selections Act of 1988

Even the dramatic expansion of certiorari brought about by the Judges' Bill did not ultimately prove to be enough to deal with the Court's workload issues. The Court's docket continued to grow. For example, "approximately three times as many cases were filed in the 1971 Term as in the 1951 Term." Federal Judicial Center, Report of the Study Group on the Caseload of the Supreme Court, 57 F.R.D. 573, 578 (1972). This growth in the Court's docket was fueled by the growing economy, the rise of the administrative state, and the Court's recognition of new constitutional rights, as well as an explosion in cases filed *in forma pauperis* by litigants unable to pay litigation costs.

Ultimately, in 1988, Congress responded to the Court's continuing workload problems by passing legislation that eliminated nearly all the Court's obligatory jurisdiction. *See* Supreme Court Case Selections Act of 1988, Pub. L. No. 100-352, 102 Stat. 662. As a result of the 1988 Act, today only a very small number of cases fall within the Court's mandatory appellate jurisdiction. These mandatory jurisdiction cases arise out of statutes in which Congress has called for mandatory review of the decisions of three-judge district courts, such as decisions in voting rights cases and other cases in which Congress determines expedited review is warranted.[3] *See, e.g.,* 42 U.S.C. §1973c(a); *see also* 28 U.S.C. §1253; 28 U.S.C. §2284(a). For example, the Court's decision in *Bowsher v. Synar*, 478 U.S. 714 (1986), arose from the Balanced Budget and Emergency Deficit Control Act of 1985, Pub. L. No. 99-177, 99 Stat. 1037, in which Congress provided for direct appeal to the Court. Similarly, *Turner Broadcasting System v. FCC*, 512 U.S. 622 (1994), arose out of the Cable Television Consumer Protection and Competition Act of 1992, 47 U.S.C. §555(c)(1), which provided for direct appeal to the Court. However, other than these sorts of narrow situations in which Congress has expressly provided for direct appeal to the Court, the Court today enjoys nearly unfettered discretion to set its own docket.

4. The Court's Shrinking Docket

Shortly after the 1988 legislative changes gave the Court nearly complete discretion over its docket, the Court's problem suddenly became not one of too many cases but rather one of too few cases. Although the number of petitions for certiorari continued to climb, the Court started placing fewer and fewer cases on its "plenary" docket—meaning its docket consisting of all those cases that receive briefing and oral argument. Whereas the Court issued 145 plenary decisions in the 1988 Term, by the 1989 Term, "the number fell to 132; and in the 1990 Term, it fell to 116."

---

3. There is also a very narrow category of antitrust cases that are eligible for a direct appeal to the Supreme Court from a one-judge district court ruling—although the Supreme Court has some discretion as to whether to entertain these direct appeals. *See* 15 U.S.C. §29(b) (giving the Court "discretion" to "deny the appeal and remand the case to the courts of appeals").

Margaret Meriwether Cordray & Richard Cordray, *The Supreme Court's Plenary Docket*, 58 Wash. Lee L. Rev. 737, 747 (2001). "It dropped slightly to 110 in the 1991 Term, held steady at 111 during the 1992 Term, then plunged to 90 in the 1993 Term." *Id.* In recent years, this trend has continued. In the 2007 Term, for example, the Court's plenary docket hit just 76 opinions. *See The Statistics,* 122 Harv. L. Rev. 516, 524 (2008). Similarly, in the 2010 Term, there were just 80 cases reviewed via the writ of certiorari that were disposed of via a full opinion. *See The Supreme Court, The Statistics,* 125 Harv. L. Rev. 362, 370 (2011).

What caused this dramatic decline in the Court's docket has not gone undetected. Rather, it has been splashed across national headlines and debated in leading law journals. *See, e.g.,* Adam Liptak, *The Case of the Plummeting Supreme Court Docket,* N.Y. Times, Sept. 28, 2009, at A18; Philip Allen Lacovara, *The Incredible Shrinking Court,* 25 Am. Law. 53 (2003); Charles Lane, *Caseload Reflects Court's Altered Role,* Wash. Post, Feb. 2, 2004, at A15; Margaret Cordray & Richard Cordray, *Numbers That Don't Befit the Court,* Wash. Post, July 11, 2006, at A17; Kenneth Starr, *The Supreme Court and Its Shrinking Docket: The Ghost of William Howard Taft,* 90 Minn. L. Rev. 1363, 1366 (2006).

What caused this dramatic decline in the Court's plenary docket? Was it Congress's decision to eliminate most of the Court's mandatory jurisdiction in 1988? Consider the following views on these questions written by two prolific scholars who study the Court—one a law professor and the other a former Supreme Court law clerk who began serving as the Director of the United States Consumer Financial Protection Bureau in 2012.

Margaret Meriwether Cordray & Richard Cordray, The Supreme Court's Plenary Docket

58 Wash. Lee L. Rev. 737, 743-744, 750-753 (2001)

Beginning in the 1989 Term, the Court's docket—which had remained fairly constant at about 150 plenary decisions for the past decade—suddenly began to decline. . . .

This unexpected development surprised and puzzled both participants and observers. At his confirmation hearings in 1986, then-Justice Rehnquist said, "I think the 150 cases that we have turned out quite regularly over a period of 10 or 15 years is just about where we should be at." Indeed, in response to questioning about whether the size of that caseload might be too great for effective administration, he stated more pointedly, "[m]y own feeling is that all the courts are so much busier today than they have been in the past, that there would be something almost unseemly about the Supreme Court saying, you know, everybody else is deciding twice as many cases as they ever have before, but we are going to go back to two-thirds as many as we did before." Justice Souter, who arrived at the Court in the midst of this dramatic decline, said he has been "amazed" at the trend, which he suggests has "just happened" without any conscious decision on the Justices' part.

Commentators also recognized and were perplexed by the marked decline. Although some offered possible explanations for the decline, most of that discussion was tentative and came too soon to benefit from the kind of detailed investigation of additional data that is necessary to test the various hypotheses adequately. Some commentators on the decline expressed frustration that the Court's already precious resources were not being fully utilized, whereas others dispensed praise or blame, according to their views about the proper role of the Supreme Court in national life. . . .

Lawyers, commentators, and even the Justices themselves have hypothesized a variety of causes for the drop in the Supreme Court's plenary docket over the past decade. For the most part, however, these theories have remained mostly speculative and have not been satisfactorily evaluated in light of numerical data that would allow them to be either verified or falsified. This problem occurs because the close secrecy of the Court's internal deliberations makes it difficult to quantify the Justices' voting behavior in conference. . . .

In seeking explanations for the recent decline in the Court's plenary docket, one obvious (but ultimately unpersuasive) candidate is the almost wholesale repeal of the Court's mandatory jurisdiction. Prior to 1988, the Supreme Court enjoyed discretion to determine whether to review most of the cases coming before it, but several important statutes gave litigants a right of appeal to the Supreme Court. In 1988, at the Court's urging, Congress eliminated virtually all of these mandatory appeal provisions, substituting instead discretionary review on certiorari.

The 1988 legislation made three major changes: First, it repealed 28 U.S.C. §1252, which allowed any party in a civil action to appeal directly to the Supreme Court from any decision of any federal court declaring a federal statute to be unconstitutional, if the United States was a party to the lawsuit. Second, the Act repealed 28 U.S.C. §1254(2), which allowed a party to appeal to the Supreme Court from a decision of a federal court of appeals striking down a state statute as violative of the federal Constitution, treaties, or laws. Third, the legislation repealed 28 U.S.C. §§1257(1) and (2), which allowed a party to appeal to the Supreme Court from a judgment of a state court of last resort holding either that a federal statute or treaty was invalid, or that a state statute was valid despite a challenge based on the federal Constitution, treaties, or laws. . . .

There were at least three reasons to believe that this virtual elimination of the Court's mandatory jurisdiction might have been a significant factor contributing to the decline in the docket. First, . . . Congress's 1925 modifications of the Supreme Court's jurisdictional statutes led to an immediate and dramatic drop in the Court's caseload. Although the amount of mandatory jurisdiction remaining in 1988 was much diminished, it would be sensible to expect some further decline to flow from additional legislative changes made in the same direction. Second, the timing is right, as the enactment of the 1988 legislation occurred around the beginning of the decline. Third, the Justices themselves seemed convinced that this change would relieve some of the pressure on their docket, at a minimum by freeing up precious time for cases of greater import. . . .

Notes and Questions

1. Despite the various reasons that Cordray and Cordray set forth for why the 1988 legislation may have significantly contributed to the decline in the Court's docket, Cordray and Cordray ultimately conclude that the 1988 legislative changes actually had little or no effect on the Court's plenary docket. If they are right, then what does account for the drop in the Court's plenary docket?

Cordray and Cordray posit that a number of factors may be at play, including a decrease in *cert* filings by the Solicitor General of the United States and changes in Supreme Court personnel:

> Changes in the Court's personnel . . . have played a substantial role in shrinking the docket. To begin with, the substitution of Justice Scalia for Chief Justice Burger and Justice Kennedy for Justice Powell, along with Justice Rehnquist's promotion to Chief Justice, provided a considerable impetus to reduce the docket. This was followed in short order by the retirements of Justices Brennan and Marshall, which had less impact than might have been expected. . . . The final substantial shift occurred with the retirements, soon afterwards, of Justices White and Blackmun. By their votes at conference, as well as by Justice White's frequent prodding both in public and private statements, these two Justices had strongly supported the Court granting review on the merits in more cases. When Justices who appear to have more moderate viewpoints on this issue replaced Justices White and Blackmun, the docket immediately plunged. Not since 1949—the year in which Justices Clark and Minton replaced Justices Murphy and Rutledge—had such a massacre of certiorari votes occurred on the Court.
>
> In addition, an important influence that has independently contributed to the decline is the changing pattern of federal civil litigation involving government parties. Over the same period, the federal government was winning more of its fewer civil cases in the lower courts and thus was seeking plenary review less frequently. Similar factors were also at work in civil litigation involving the state and local governments and in criminal cases (though the numbers here were partially offset by a rising tide of federal criminal prosecutions), as for a generation the Supreme Court had asserted its control over the direction of the lower courts and presided over some version of a judicial realignment. Our analysis indicates that these factors—even apart from any changes in the Court's personnel—may have been responsible for as much as half of the overall reduction in the plenary docket.
>
> Given these explanations for the declining docket, it is likely that the current situation will endure for some time to come, unless or until significant changes occur from new appointments to the Court. The consequences of the changes in personnel to date have been so great that it would take a real and sustained shift in the Court's direction to reverse them. Barring the appointment of a jurist whose approach to certiorari is cast in the highly unusual mold of a Justice White or a Justice Douglas, it will take several new members with a definite inclination to grant more cases to effect a substantial increase in the Court's caseload. At the same time, the confirmed pattern of government attorneys bringing fewer cases to the Court is likely to persist, for though they can anticipate paddling into rougher waters again at some point in the future, there is no apparent reason to believe that this will happen any time soon. For the time being, therefore, the Supreme Court's plenary docket has stabilized at levels that are unprecedented in the modern era.

Margaret Meriwether Cordray & Richard Cordray, *The Supreme Court's Plenary Docket*, 58 Wash. Lee. L. Rev. 737, 794 (2001). Likewise, David Stras found evidence to suggest that "changes in the Court's membership have contributed to the decline in the Supreme Court's plenary docket." David R. Stras, *The Supreme Court's Declining Plenary Docket: A Membership-Based Explanation*, 27 Const. Comment. 151, 152, 161 (2010) ("every Justice appointed between 1986 and 1993 voted to grant plenary review less often than his or her predecessor").

There are, however, many other possible explanations. One prominent view is that the Court's conception of its proper role has become "Olympian," which makes the Court shy about taking more ordinary cases. Carolyn Shapiro, *The Limits of the Olympian Court: Common Law Judging versus Error Correction in the Supreme Court*, 63

Wash. Lee L. Rev. 271 (2006). Another view is that the "cert pool," which is explored *infra* at page 227, is to blame because law clerks writing pool memos are reluctant to recommend granting petitions that may turn out not to be certworthy.

3. Is the Court's declining docket necessarily a bad thing? Does your answer to this question depend on what you view as the proper judicial role and function of the United States Supreme Court, which was explored initially in Chapter 1?

B. SUBSTANTIVE CONSIDERATIONS IMPACTING CERTIORARI DECISIONS: WHAT MAKES A CASE CERTWORTHY?

Given that the Court today grants certiorari in only a small number of cases each year, it is important to understand what makes a case "certworthy." What makes the Court exercise its discretion to take a certain case but to deny certiorari in a different case? As the materials below illustrate, the Justices may consider many different factors. High on the list of usual considerations are whether a "conflict" exists on the question and the "importance" of the issues presented. However, various strategic, ideological, and jurisprudential considerations may also come into play.

1. Rule-Based Considerations

Supreme Court Rule 10, which sets forth considerations governing review on certiorari, makes clear that "[r]eview on a writ of certiorari is not a matter of right, but of judicial discretion." Please read the text of Rule 10, which is provided below. In doing so, note how the Court makes clear that a "petition for a writ of certiorari will be granted only for compelling reasons."

Rule 10. Considerations Governing Review on Certiorari

Review on a writ of certiorari is not a matter of right, but of judicial discretion. A petition for a writ of certiorari will be granted only for compelling reasons. The following, although neither controlling nor fully measuring the Court's discretion, indicate the character of the reasons the Court considers:

(a) a United States court of appeals has entered a decision in conflict with the decision of another United States court of appeals on the same important matter; has decided an important federal question in a way that conflicts with a decision by a state court of last resort; or has so far departed from the accepted and usual course of judicial proceedings, or sanctioned such a departure by a lower court, as to call for an exercise of this Court's supervisory power;

(b) a state court of last resort has decided an important federal question in a way that conflicts with the decision of another state court of last resort or of a United States court of appeals;

(c) a state court or a United States court of appeals has decided an important question of federal law that has not been, but should be, settled by this Court, or has decided an important federal question in a way that conflicts with relevant decisions of this Court.

A petition for a writ of certiorari is rarely granted when the asserted error consists of erroneous factual findings or the misapplication of a properly stated rule of law.

---

a. Conflict and Importance

In defining what considerations the Court might—in its discretion—take into account in exercising its discretion to grant certiorari, Rule 10 provides that the Court may consider various factors, including the "importance" of the questions presented and the presence of a "conflict." *See, e.g., New Process Steel, L.P. v. NLRB,* 130 S. Ct. 2635, 2639 (2010) (justifying the Court's decision to grant certiorari in order to resolve a "conflict"); *Wyeth v. Levine,* 555 U.S. 555, 563 (2009) (granting certiorari to decide preemption case, in part, because of the importance of the issue at stake); *Gonzales v. Raich,* 545 U.S. 1, 9 (2005) ("The obvious importance of the case prompted our grant of certiorari."). While assessing the importance of the issues presented in a case is a somewhat subjective exercise, assessing the presence of a conflict is much more objective. This is because a conflict can be said to exist when one can say with certainty, based on published decisions, that the case conflicts with a Supreme Court precedent or that it would have come out differently in another circuit or highest state court.

It is uniformly agreed that these two factors expressly mentioned in Rule 10— the presence of a conflict and the importance of the issues presented—are the two most important factors in determining whether the Court will grant certiorari. However, the Court does not appear to treat these two factors equally. Rather, as the excerpt below discusses, the presence of a conflict appears to be the most important criteria in the Court's case selection process, and the importance of the legal question—although still quite significant—is secondary.

[handwritten marginalia: most impart. factors = • presence of a conflict • importance of the issues]

[handwritten: - presence of a conflict is most important]

Amanda Frost, Overvaluing Uniformity

94 Va. L. Rev. 1567, 1631-1636 (2008)

Supreme Court Rule 10, which lists the reasons the Court might choose to grant certiorari, states that a relevant factor is whether a state court of last resort or federal court of appeals "has entered a decision in conflict with the decision" of another such court on a federal question. In 1995, Rule 10 was amended to provide that the Supreme Court's review should be limited to conflicts on an "important federal question." Nonetheless, the presence of a conflict remains by far the most important criteria in the Court's case selection; the "importance" of the question is decidedly secondary. The Stern and Gressman treatise on Supreme Court practice notes that "the Court continues to grant certiorari in many cases that do not appear to be 'certworthy' for any reason other than the existence of a conflict, real or alleged."[191]

The Court's focus on resolving lower court conflicts is obvious from the high percentage of certiorari grants involving questions over which the lower courts have differed. Professor David Stras reviewed petitions for certiorari, lower court opinions, and Supreme Court opinions for all the cases decided in the 2004, 2005,

---

191. Robert L. Stern et al., Supreme Court Practice §4.4, at 228 (8th ed. 2002).

Standardization of federal law 70% of the cases were resolving lower court disputes

and 2006 terms and discovered that approximately seventy percent of the cases resolved by the Court during those years involved a split among the lower courts.[192] Professor Hellman conducted similar research for the 1983-1985 terms and the 1993-1995 terms, but limited his study to conflicts between federal courts of appeals.[193] From 1983-1985, forty-five percent of the Court's cases concerned a conflict, and from 1993-1995, that percentage increased to sixty-nine percent. Professor Stras reviewed cases from the 2003-2005 terms using criteria identical to Professor Hellman's and found that approximately sixty percent of the cases involved a conflict between the courts of appeals.

Of course, the high percentage of conflict cases, standing alone, does not prove that the Court has prioritized standardization of federal law over other values. Perhaps the presence of a circuit split is a relatively minor factor and serves only to move an issue higher up the Supreme Court's queue. The Justices may have a short list of areas of law they think important to clarify, and they will first take up those issues that have continually produced a difference of opinion among the circuits and state supreme courts. Thus, the presence of a split may simply be a reason to prioritize the resolution of an issue the Court would have eventually chosen to address in any case. Another possibility is that divisions among the lower courts are just a proxy for other factors that make a case certworthy. For example, a complicated statute affecting large numbers of people is likely to produce more divergent judicial opinions than a straightforward statute that generates little litigation.

The evidence does not support these alternative explanations, however. In his [1991] book *Deciding to Decide: Agenda-Setting in the United States Supreme Court*, political scientist H.W. Perry investigated the factors involved in the current Court's case selection. His data came primarily from interviews with five Supreme Court Justices and sixty-four former Supreme Court law clerks about the certiorari process. Time and again, these individuals emphasized the importance of lower court conflicts in determining whether a case was "certworthy." When Professor Perry asked one Justice "[w]hat would make a case an obvious grant?" the Justice replied, "Conflict among the circuits might." At least one Justice believed that "virtually every conflict should be taken as long as the issue is not completely trivial." While other Justices were more circumspect, all viewed conflicts as "very important." As Perry put it, "[a] circuit split is not simply a formal criterion for cert.; it is probably the single most important criterion."

The Justices and former law clerks interviewed by Perry described a split as a primary, not secondary, factor affecting the certiorari determination. Perry reported that "informants almost invariably would say that first they looked to see if there were a circuit conflict, and then they looked to see if the conflict involved an important issue." One law clerk told Perry, "I really do believe that a conflict is the reason that most cases are taken. In some ways it is the driving force." Another explained, "[conflicts] really dominated and were clearly the most important reason for taking cert." Although Perry acknowledged that a conflict was neither a necessary nor sufficient factor in determining whether to grant certiorari, he wrote that the "overwhelming majority of my informants, indeed almost all, listed this as the first and most important thing they looked for in a petition." In short, conflicts

192. David R. Stras, *The Supreme Court's Gatekeepers: The Role of Law Clerks in the Certiorari Process*, 85 Tex. L. Rev. 947, 981 (2007).

193. [Arthur D. Hellman, *The Shrunken Docket of the Rehnquist Court*, 1996 Sup. Ct. Rev. 403, 414-417 (1997).]

seem to drive the Court's interest in a case, rather than serving merely as a method of triaging the issues the Court wished to address.

Furthermore, some of the Supreme Court's recent cases involve trivial legal questions that would never have come before the Court absent lower court disagreement. Admittedly, no one could accuse the Roberts or Rehnquist Courts of dodging the hard cases, as well illustrated by their decisions upholding the partial birth abortion ban, striking down anti-sodomy laws, rejecting military commissions, and resolving disputes over presidential elections. Yet sprinkled among these blockbuster cases are a host of issues so minor as to be laughable. . . .

Murphy Brothers, Inc. v. Michetti Pipe Stringing, Inc. provides a good example. In that case, the Court addressed whether a defendant's "receipt" of a complaint transmitted by facsimile, rather than delivered by mail, triggered the 30-day time limit for removal from state to federal court under 28 U.S.C. Section 1446(b). The Court explained that it had granted certiorari "[b]ecause lower courts have divided on th[at] question." Likewise, in *Becker v. Montgomery,* the Court tackled the question whether a typewritten name on a notice of appeal could satisfy the signature requirement in the Federal Rules of Civil Procedure, and, if not, whether that defect deprived a federal court of jurisdiction—a question over which the circuits disagreed.

It would appear that the only reason these cases merited review was that they involved a question over which the lower courts were divided. Yet there was no special need for uniformity in these areas of the law. The issues in these two cases primarily affected lawyers who practice in the federal courts—a group that has a professional responsibility to keep abreast of the rules governing the practice of law in their jurisdictions. Moreover, the conflicts were not debilitating. If the lower courts had remained divided on these questions, lawyers would either have had to keep track of which jurisdictions followed which rules, or they could have played it safe and made sure to remove every case within thirty days of receipt of the complaint, whether by fax or regular service of process, and to handwrite rather than type any signature—hardly a great inconvenience. Although *Murphy Brothers* and *Becker* are the most vivid examples, dozens of other certiorari grants over the last few years are more notable for the depth of the splits involved than for their legal significance. Cases such as these illustrate more vividly than statistics the Court's focus on resolving lower court conflict.

Notes and Questions

1. Do you find it troubling that the Court may elevate conflicts over the importance of legal issues? If you were a Justice on the Court today, would you place a greater premium on the presence of a conflict or the importance of the issues presented? What might be some of the potential costs and benefits of valuing one consideration over the other?

2. Given the importance of the presence of a conflict, some petitioners may allege "the existence of a conflict in the hope of increasing the probability that the Court will grant their petition." Kevin H. Smith, *Certiorari and the Supreme Court Agenda: An Empirical Analysis,* 54 Okla. L. Rev. 727, 748 (2001). The Justices and their law clerks, however, recognize this strategy and will objectively verify whether a conflict actually exists. For example, "[a]n allegation of a conflict by a more impartial observer, [such as] by a dissenting judge in the court below, . . . may carry more

This is how you show a conflict

weight than an allegation of conflict in the petition." *Id.* (noting that "[t]he Supreme Court was more likely to grant certiorari if a judge in a dissenting opinion in the court immediately below the Supreme Court alleged a conflict with Supreme Court precedent than if such an allegation was absent.").

3. The presence or absence of a conflict involves a largely objective assessment. In contrast, assessing the "importance" of legal issues is much more subjective. How might one go about assessing the "importance" of the legal issues presented in a petition for certiorari? Rule 10 neither defines importance nor provides a standard for assessing the importance of the issues presented in a petition for certiorari. Hence, the Court enjoys significant flexibility in assessing the importance of the issues presented, and many factors might be considered by the Justices. For example, as Kevin Smith has described, a Justice might take into account whether the case involves great social issues of the day or whether the case involves essential governmental functions. *See id.* at 751-752. In addition, Smith has described how a Justice might consider the views of others concerning the importance of the questions presented by, for example, looking at whether a brief in opposition, a reply brief, or any *amicus* briefs were filed, whether a dissenting opinion was filed in the court below, whether the lower court opinion was published or unpublished, and whether the petitioner proceeded pro se or with retained counsel. *Id.* at 752-758.

In assessing the importance of a case, why do you think that Justices might take into account the *pro se* status of a petitioner? Do you think it is because of discrimination against the poor or because *pro se* petitions tend to contain frivolous (and hence unimportant) legal claims? *See id.* at 767 (concluding that "as compared to non-*pro se* petitions, *pro se* petitions are much more likely to contain frivolous issues and are much less likely to contain attributes (such as the allegation of a conflict with Supreme Court precedent) that are associated with the granting of certiorari").

Likewise, in assessing the importance of a case, why might the Justices take into account whether any *amicus curiae* briefs—meaning "friend of the Court" briefs—have been filed? Note that various studies have found that there is a relationship between the filing of an *amicus curiae* brief and the likelihood that the Court will grant certiorari. *See, e.g.,* Gregory Caldeira & John Wright, *Organized Interests and Agenda Setting in the U.S. Supreme Court,* 82 Am. Pol. Sci. Rev. 1109, 1119-1122 (1988) (finding that the filing of an *amicus* brief in support of a petition increases the likelihood that the Court will grant certiorari by 40 to 50 percent); *see also* Tony Mauro & Marcia Coyle, *To Get on the Argument Docket, It Helps to Have Friends,* Natl. L.J., July 28, 2010 (noting the rising trend of *amicus* briefs filed at the certiorari stage); Kelly J. Lynch, *Best Friends? Supreme Court Law Clerks on Effective Amicus Briefs,* 20 J.L. & Pol. 33 (2004) (exploring former Supreme Court clerks' views on what makes *amicus* briefs effective). For more on *amicus* briefs, see Chapter 5, at pages 356-395.

4. If you were a Justice on the Court, what proxies do you think you would look to in assessing the importance of the issues presented in petitions for certiorari?

b. Legal Rather Than Factual Issues

In addition to highlighting the emphasis that will be given to the presence of a conflict and the importance of the issues, Rule 10 also expressly states that "[a] petition for a writ of certiorari is rarely granted when the asserted error consists of erroneous factual findings or the misapplication of a properly stated rule of law." Hence, to be certworthy, a case generally must raise not just important issues but important *legal* issues. The dissenting opinion that follows explores this point, highlighting how the Court is not inclined to resolve factual disputes but rather prefers to decide important legal questions.

Dick v. New York Life Insurance Co.

359 U.S. 437, 454-460 (1959)

Mr. Justice FRANKFURTER, whom Mr. Justice WHITTAKER, joins, dissenting.

Questions of fact have traditionally been deemed to be the kind of questions which ought not to be recanvassed here unless they are entangled in the proper determination of constitutional or other important legal issues. In *Newell v. Norton,* 3 Wall. 257, Mr. Justice Grier stated the considerations weighing against Supreme Court review of factual determinations: "It would be a very tedious as well as a very unprofitable task to again examine and compare the conflicting statements of the witnesses in this volume of depositions. And, even if we could make our opinion intelligible, the case could never be a precedent for any other case, or worth the trouble of understanding." 3 Wall. at page 267. And he issued this caveat: "Parties ought not to expect this court to revise their decrees merely on a doubt raised in our minds as to the correctness of their judgment, on the credibility of witnesses, or the weight of conflicting testimony." 3 Wall. at page 268. In *Houston Oil Co. of Texas v. Goodrich,* 245 U.S. 440, certiorari was dismissed as improvidently granted after it became apparent that the only question in the case was the "propriety of submitting" certain questions to the jury and this "depended essentially upon an appreciation of the evidence." 245 U.S. at page 441. Testifying before the Senate Judiciary Committee in hearings concerning the Judges' Bill, Mr. Justice Van Devanter related a similar incident. The proper use of the discretionary certiorari jurisdiction was on a later occasion thus expounded by Mr. Chief Justice Hughes:

> "Records are replete with testimony and evidence of facts. But the questions on certiorari are questions of law. So many cases turn on the facts, principles of law not being in controversy. It is only when the facts are interwoven with the questions of law which we should review that the evidence must be examined and then only to the extent that it is necessary to decide the questions of law.
>
> This at once disposes of a vast number of factual controversies where the parties have been fully heard in the courts below and have no right to burden the Supreme Court with the dispute which interests no one but themselves."

What are the questions which petitioner here presses upon us? The petition for certiorari sets forth as the questions presented: (1) was petitioner deprived of her constitutional right to a jury trial guaranteed by the Seventh Amendment? (2) did the Court of Appeals refuse to follow North Dakota law as it was required to do under *Erie R. Co. v. Tompkins,* 304 U.S. 64? If this case raises a question under the Seventh Amendment, so does every granted motion for dismissal of a complaint calling for trial by jury, every direction of verdict, every judgment notwithstanding the verdict. Fabulous inflation cannot turn these conventional motions turning on appreciation of evidence into constitutional issues, nor can the many diversity cases sought to be brought here on contested questions of evidentiary weight be similarly transformed by insisting before this Court that the Constitution has been violated. This verbal smoke screen cannot obscure the truth that all that is involved is an appraisal of the fair inferences to be drawn from the evidence. . . .

Alike in Congress and here it has been repeatedly insisted that a question like that raised by petitioner—was there sufficient evidence for submission to a jury—is not proper for review in this Court. The circumstances in the type of situation before us are infinite in their variety. Judicial judgments upon such circumstances are bound to vary with the particularities of the individual situation. The decision in each case is a strictly particular adjudication—a unique case since it turns on unique facts—and cannot have precedential value. Of course it is of interest, perhaps of great importance to the parties, but only as such and not independently of any general public interest.

The considerations that demand strict adherence by the Court to the rules it has laid down for the bar in applying for the exercise of the Court's "sound judicial discretion" in granting a writ of certiorari are not technical, in the invidious sense of the term. They go to the very heart of the effective discharge of this Court's functions. To bring a case here when there is no "special and important" reason for doing so, when there is no reason other than the interest of a particular litigant, especially when the decision turns solely on a view of conflicting evidence or the application of a particular local doctrine decided one way rather than another by a Court of Appeals better versed in the field of such local law than we can possibly be, works inroads on the time available for due study and reflection of those classes of cases for the adjudication of which this Court exists. . . .

. . . In 1925 the Congress, by withdrawing all but a few categories of cases which can come to the Court as a matter of right, gave to the Court power to control its docket, to control, that is, the volume of its business. Congress conferred this discretionary power on the Court's own urging that this was necessary if the proper discharge of the Court's indispensable functions were to be rendered feasible. The process of screening those cases which alone justify adjudication by the Supreme Court is in itself a very demanding aspect of the Court's work. The litigious tendency of our people and the unwillingness of litigants to rest content with adverse decisions after their cause has been litigated in two and often in three courts, lead to attempts to get a final review by the Supreme Court in literally thousands of cases which should never reach the highest Court of the land. The examination of the papers in these cases, to sift out the few that properly belong in this Court from the very many that have no business here, is a laborious process in a Court in which every member is charged and properly charged with making an independent examination of the right of access to the Court.

Every time the Court grants certiorari in disregard of its own professed criteria, it invites disregard of the responsibility of lawyers enjoined upon the bar by the Court's own formal rules and pronouncements. It is idle to preach obedience to the justifying considerations for filing petitions for certiorari, which Mr. Chief Justice Taft and his successors and other members of the Court have impressively addressed to the bar year after year if the Court itself disregards the code of conduct by which it seeks to bind the profession. Lawyers not unnaturally hope to draw a prize in the lottery and even conscientious lawyers who feel it their duty, as officers of the Court, to obey the paper requirements of a petition for certiorari, may feel obligated to their clients not to abstain where others have succeeded. No doubt the most rigorous adherence to the criteria for granting certiorari will not prevent too many hopeless petitions for certiorari from being filed. But laxity by the Court in respecting its own rules is bound to stimulate petitions for certiorari with which the Court should never be burdened. . . .

Notes and Questions

1. Why do you think Rule 10 provides that certiorari "is rarely granted when the asserted error consists of erroneous factual findings or the misapplication of a properly stated rule of law"? Should this rule apply in all cases? Or should some cases, like death penalty cases involving allegations of erroneous factual findings, be treated differently? Why or why not? For a general discussion of the Court's prominent role in capital punishment cases, *see generally* Franklin E. Zimring, *Inheriting the Wind: The Supreme Court and Capital Punishment in the 1990s,* 20 Fla. St. U. L. Rev. 7 (1992).

2. By asserting that the Court granted certiorari in *Dick* in disregard of its own criteria, Justice Frankfurter seems to suggest that the Court's own certiorari criteria do in fact provide rules and constraining criteria. Is Justice Frankfurter correct? Do you think that Rule 10 provides constraining factors to guide the Court's discretion? Does Rule 10's emphasis on the importance of the legal questions and whether a conflict exists provide sufficiently constraining factors to guide the Court's discretion?

3. If you were tasked with proposing suggested changes to Rule 10's language, what changes, if any, would you suggest? How would your proposed changes alter how the Court approaches its certiorari decisions?

2. Other Considerations: Ideological, Strategic, and Jurisprudential Factors

In addition to the two primary rule-based factors (conflict and importance), the Justices may also take a variety of ideological, strategic, and jurisprudential factors into account when deciding whether or not to grant certiorari in a given case. For example, the Justices might consider the merits of the case and might be inclined to vote to grant certiorari when they are ideologically uncomfortable with the result reached below. Or a Justice might make a strategic decision to vote to deny certiorari in a case—despite the Justice's own preference for deciding the case—to try to defensively avoid an undesirable result on the merits. The following two excerpts explore some of these various strategic, ideological, and jurisprudential factors that might motivate the Justices' certiorari decisions.

Margaret Meriwether Cordray & Richard Cordray, The Philosophy of Certiorari: Jurisprudential Considerations in Supreme Court Case Selection

82 Wash. U. L.Q. 389, 390, 395-396, 406-412, 414-435, 441 (2004)

The importance of [the Court's self-made agenda] is all the more striking in view of the unusual manner in which it is performed. In sharp contrast to traditional judicial decisionmaking, the Justices typically make decisions about whether to grant certiorari according to vague guidelines that afford them maximum discretion, based on very little collegial deliberation, with virtually no public disclosure or explanation of their actions and subject to no precedential constraints. . . .

The connection between the Court's agenda-setting function and its more prominent responsibility to decide cases is reflected in the consequences that each decision to grant or deny review has for the Court's agenda. At stake in the aggregate is the overall size of the Court's docket and thus its capacity to decide cases well while processing its caseload in a timely and effective manner. Also at stake are the contours of the Court's agenda—what kinds of issues will be addressed while others go unheard. The shape of the Court's agenda in turn produces a broad range of effects.

At a more concrete level, the choice of a particular case, with its peculiar set of facts, among the many that are generally available to resolve an issue can influence the scope and content of the Court's opinion on the merits—and possibly the outcome. Indeed, even delaying adjudication of an issue may affect its ultimate disposition, perhaps by putting it off to a later Court with different personnel or by causing the issue to be considered within a changed political climate or an evolved legal landscape.

At a more general level, the decisions that the Justices make about which cases to hear (and not to hear) play a part in determining the magnitude of the Court's profile in American life. . . .

II. RULE-BASED AND STRATEGIC FACTORS AFFECTING CERTIORARI DECISIONS

There have been a number of useful attempts to identify and prioritize the key determinants in the Court's case selection process. Scholars and researchers, primarily from the social sciences, have used various modes of analysis to illuminate the extent to which the Justices' case selection decisions may be motivated by two distinct concerns: (1) fidelity to the explicit rule-based criteria set out in Rule 10 and sensible proxies for those criteria; and (2) ideological or strategic concern about the result on the merits in each case. This second category includes concerns about whether the case was rightly or wrongly decided by the court below and whether it is likely to be rightly or wrongly decided by the Supreme Court if plenary review were to be granted. . . .

A. Rule-Based Determinants in the Certiorari Process

The key criteria set out in Rule 10, which lists the reasons that the Court considers in deciding whether to grant or deny a petition for certiorari, are whether the lower court decision creates a conflict and whether the case presents an important federal question. Researchers have studied both criteria in an effort to gauge their significance in the decisionmaking process.

Not surprisingly, researchers have found that the existence of an actual conflict between the lower courts or between the lower court and a Supreme Court precedent is a potent determinant. There is strong evidence that the presence of genuine conflict between the circuit courts of appeals, between state supreme courts, between federal courts and state courts, or between the lower court and Supreme Court precedent dramatically increases the probability that the Court will grant a case. Indeed, even allegations of a conflict between lower court decisions, where actual conflict is absent, increase the likelihood that the Court will grant certiorari.

In determining whether the case presents an important federal question, the second key criterion in Rule 10, the Court looks to a variety of indicators. Among these, a consistent standout is the presence of the United States as a petitioner in the case. When the Solicitor General seeks review on behalf of the United States, the Court is far more likely to grant certiorari. Indeed, the Court consistently grants over fifty percent of the Solicitor General's petitions for certiorari, whereas it grants only about three percent of paid petitions filed by other parties. The Solicitor General's success is attributable in part to the rigorous screening that he performs to cull out cases appropriate for review, as well as the general expertise and quality of the lawyers in his office. But perhaps most significantly, the key "importance" criterion for review is almost necessarily met when the federal government seeks review asserting that the government is directly and substantially affected by a lower court decision or that decisional conflicts are requiring it to operate differently in various parts of the country. . . .

Researchers have also suggested that a case is more likely to be granted if the court immediately below reversed the lower court, or if a judge dissented from the decision. There has also been some attempt to correlate the likelihood of a grant with substantive areas—for example, it has been suggested that the Court is more inclined to grant cases involving civil liberties than economic issues—but recent analysis raises questions about the extent to which the Court may favor certain issue areas over others. In any event, these factors appear[] to exert far less influence on the Court's decision to grant certiorari than the three major determinants of genuine conflict, the United States as petitioner, and the presence of amicus briefs.

① genuine conflict ② US as petitioner ③ amicus briefs

B. Ideological and Strategic Considerations on Certiorari

Researchers have also identified other, more political, influences on the Court's decisionmaking at the certiorari stage. In considering the extent and impact of these influences, it is useful to distinguish between the various ways in which a Justice could give play to ideological preferences in his or her certiorari votes. *national importance/ ideology*

First, Justices might vote to grant or deny certiorari not merely because of the national importance of the issue or the existence of conflicting decisions in the lower courts, but also based on their own ideological predilections. Thus, a Justice *personally* would be more likely to vote to grant a case where he or she was uncomfortable with the ideological result below and would be inclined to vote to reverse on the merits. *view on the likely outcome* Second, Justices might vote to grant or deny certiorari in a somewhat more sophisticated manner that takes into account the likely positions of their colleagues, with a view to the ultimate outcome on the merits. Engaging in this kind of strategic voting, a Justice might vote to deny certiorari even if he or she disagreed with the result below if the Justice believed that the unappealing result would likely be affirmed in any decision on the merits. And third, in pursuing these objectives, it is also possible *build coalitions on the bench* that the Justices might not act as independent decisionmakers guided exclusively by their own ideological inclinations or predictions, but could consciously form explicit coalitions that would work as power blocs in setting the Court's plenary agenda.

Numerous scholars have contended that the Justices' agenda-setting decisions are motivated, at least in part, by their own ideological inclinations; in other words, a Justice is more likely to vote to grant a case when the result reached by the court below is out of step with his or her own ideological preferences. . . . The extent to which the Justices' decisionmaking is driven by ideology is unclear, however. Studies have demonstrated a statistically significant relationship between a Justice's vote to grant a case and his or her vote to reverse on the merits. But there is not a clear delineation in the political science literature between cases in which a Justice's inclination for error correction is rooted in ideology and those in which this inclination is based on non-ideological legal considerations.

Further, a growing body of scholarship indicates that the Justices do engage in strategic voting at the certiorari stage. One form of strategic, or sophisticated, voting occurs when a voter does not vote for his or her preferred alternative at an early stage of a voting process in hopes of bringing about a more desirable outcome at a later stage. The Supreme Court's two-stage voting process (deciding to grant certiorari and then deciding the case on the merits) is ripe for strategic manipulation since the decisionmaking at the first (certiorari) stage occurs in the secrecy of the Justices' private conference, with no justification provided publicly, and the Justices have sufficient familiarity with the preferences of their colleagues to predict with some confidence how they will cast their votes at the later (merits) stage. Yet the conditions for manipulation are not ideal because the Justices' concerns for the rule of law and for compliance with established norms of proper judicial behavior may constrain their willingness to exploit the potential for power-based voting at the case selection stage. . . .

The weight of the evidence, however, now favors the view that the Justices do act strategically in their decisionmaking at the certiorari stage. In a recent study, Gregory Caldeira, John Wright, and Christopher Zorn provided strong empirical evidence that strategic voting not only occurs but is routine and has a substantial impact on the content of the Court's plenary docket.[119] Using data from the 1982 Term, they had two key findings: (1) there was a substantial correlation between a Justice's own ideological position and his or her vote on certiorari; and (2) there was strong evidence that the Justices consider the likely result on the merits in deciding how to vote. Further, they estimated that the strategic use of "defensive denials"— that is, a vote to deny certiorari to fend off an undesirable result on the merits, despite the Justice's own preference to grant the case—accounted for at least eighteen omissions from the Court's plenary docket in the 1982 Term. . . .

In the end, the question seems to be less whether the Justices engage in strategic voting than how extensively they do so. . . .

III. THE INFLUENCE OF THE INDIVIDUAL JUSTICES' VIEWS ON THE PROPER ROLE OF THE SUPREME COURT

The set of rule-based and strategic factors discussed above does much to explain the Court's agenda-setting decisions. But given how much is at stake for the Court in building its docket—the size of its caseload, the Court's profile and image in American society, selection of a case mix that will enable it to supervise and guide the lower courts most effectively, and setting the Court's priorities—one would expect the Justices to take an even broader array of considerations into account in their decisionmaking.

Moreover, the rule-based and strategic factors fail to account for important phenomena. Although the Justices consider the very same materials, and apply the same guidelines articulated in Rule 10, they reach dramatically different conclusions about which cases merit plenary review. In the 1982 Term, for example, Justices White and Rehnquist examined the thousands of applications and each voted to grant review in over 230 cases. Yet in the same term, based on the same sample of cases, Justice Powell and Chief Justice Burger each voted to grant review in more than 100 fewer cases. In the 1990 Term, to take another example, Justice

---

119. [Gregory A. Caldeira et al., *Sophisticated Voting and Gate-Keeping in the Supreme Court*, 15 J.L. Econ. & Org. 549, 553-71 (1999).]

White again voted to grant review in more than 200 cases, whereas Justices Scalia, Kennedy, and Stevens voted to grant review only half as often. Earlier studies of the Vinson Court show that the same kinds of disparities have persisted for decades, even with different personnel and different universes of legal issues.

Equally paradoxical is the fact that even though some Justices routinely win on the merits, they vote infrequently to grant review. Justice Kennedy, for example, dissented in only fourteen cases during the 1990 Term. Yet he voted to grant only 101 cases that Term, the second fewest on the Court, and considerably fewer than Justice O'Connor, who was the only Justice to dissent less often on the merits. By contrast, Justice Blackmun was one of the more frequent dissenters during the 1990 Term and yet he voted to grant 142 cases that Term, more than anyone except Justice White. Similarly paradoxical examples from an earlier period include Justice Jackson, who voted infrequently to grant review on the Vinson Court and yet regularly was part of the controlling swing bloc that made up the prevailing side on the merits, and Justices Douglas and Black, who voted the most frequently to grant review on the Vinson Court yet were not part of its controlling swing bloc and instead were frequent dissenters on the merits.

To understand these various phenomena, analysis of the agenda-setting function requires greater emphasis on each Justice's distinctive views and voting record, as opposed to focusing on the Court's aggregate decisionmaking. Further, analysis should include factors that go beyond the rule-based and strategic considerations discussed above. As the Justices apply the key criterion of Rule 10—that the case present an "important question" that is either unsettled or is the source of a conflict in the lower courts—each Justice's sense of what is "important" is shaped by his or her philosophy about the Court's proper role in the judicial system and in society. . . .

A. The Complex and Uniquely Impressionistic Nature of Decisionmaking on Certiorari

Because decisionmaking at the certiorari stage is completely unfettered, the voting behavior of each Justice is constrained only by his or her own individual sense of what kinds of cases merit the Court's attention. Over the years, Justices across the ideological spectrum have acknowledged the uniquely impressionistic nature of the task. Chief Justice Rehnquist, for example, commented that "[w]hether or not to vote to grant certiorari strikes me as a rather subjective decision, made up in part of intuition and in part of legal judgment." . . .

Interestingly, this "feel" for which cases are most appropriate for plenary review seems to remain fairly stable for each Justice over time. Studies of the conference votes from both the Vinson and the Warren Courts have demonstrated that the Justices "tend to be consistent in the strength of their propensity to grant review" and so the "rank order of the justices thus remained fairly constant over the entire period," especially in periods of a "natural" Court that was not subject to personnel changes. . . . [T]here are exceptions to this pattern in more recent terms, but general consistency in voting behavior remains the norm. This consistency is likely attributable to the lack of collegial deliberation at the certiorari stage, as the isolated nature of the decisionmaking process prevents the kind of peer influence that might cause an individual Justice's approach to case selection to evolve. The consistency also suggests that each Justice has an innate formula, which apparently remains remarkably steady in the face of the varying procession of legal issues that arise from one year to the next.

But more fundamentally, what elements combine to create this "feel"? As we have seen, this "feel" is significantly influenced by rule-based and strategic considerations. These considerations, however, do not appear to account fully for the voting patterns of the individual Justices in the case selection process. Indeed, even as the Justices strive to implement the guidelines of Rule 10, their central notions of what constitutes an "important question" or a "conflict" worthy of resolution are inevitably colored by their own views on a complex web of other factors. In other words, the "feel" or sense that each Justice develops is molded by subtle elements in his or her outlook on a variety of matters. . . .

. . . Because decisions about case selection are so subjective, a Justice's "feel" for when an issue is sufficiently "important" to merit plenary review is necessarily informed by his or her conception of the essential nature of the Supreme Court's responsibility to supervise and guide the lower courts and to shape the law. Recognizing the potency of these ingredients, Justice Frankfurter observed: "'As is true of so many matters that come before us, one's view of the appropriate treatment of these cases derives from one's attitude toward the true functions of the Court and the best way to discharge them.'" . . .

B. The Significance of Jurisprudential Approach for Decisionmaking on Certiorari

1. Views on How Precedent Guides and Superintends the Lower Courts

There is extensive discussion in the legal literature about the different approaches that the Justices take in resolving cases on the merits. The discussion centers on the competing claims of a "rule-articulating" approach, a "standard-setting" approach, and an "incrementalist" approach.

Under a rule-articulating approach, the Court sets out broad and clear rules that not only control the outcome in the particular case on its specific set of facts, but are also consciously intended to govern many other situations where the facts are somewhat different but the same principles are nonetheless operative. Advocates of this approach contend, in essence, that the Court should generate opinions that cast a substantial precedential shadow covering a meaningful amount of legal terrain. The chief virtues of this approach are that rules enhance fairness by requiring decisionmakers to act consistently, and they increase the predictability of results.

Under a standard-setting approach, the Court applies the background principle or policy to the fact situation, taking into account all relevant factors. This approach is epitomized by reliance on the "balancing test," through which the Court identifies multiple factors as the relevant criteria for decisionmaking in a particular area, and then instructs the lower courts to apply a prescribed formula that leaves them with discretion to weigh those factors in deciding future cases. The primary advantages of a standard-setting approach are that standards promote fairness by enabling decisionmakers to consider all factors relevant to the individual case, and standards are sufficiently flexible to permit decisionmakers to adapt to changing circumstances.

Under an incrementalist approach, the Court seeks only to resolve the dispute before it, allowing the law to develop "not through the pronouncement of general principles, but case-by-case, deliberately, incrementally, one-step-at-a-time." The core of this approach is the notion that judges do not pronounce the law in their role as authors (either by articulating broader rules or by formulating balancing tests), but rather they shape the law by resolving disputes and ultimately creating a pattern of judgments through deciding a sufficient number of discrete cases in an area. This approach is the antipode to the rule-articulating approach but is akin to the standard-setting approach in that both focus closely on the facts of the particular case before the Court. The incrementalist approach, however, differs from a standard-setting approach in one key aspect: a Justice employing a standard-setting approach seeks to lay down a formula that identifies the most relevant factors to guide further judicial decisionmaking in the area, whereas a Justice employing an incrementalist approach consciously seeks to decide cases as narrowly as possible, without providing much of a road map for deciding future cases. To return to the earlier illustration, incrementalist opinions cast pinpoint shadows; they are intended, individually, to cover very little of the legal terrain. The main benefits of an incrementalist approach are that it reduces the risk and cost of errors in judicial decisionmaking and leaves maximum room for further deliberation and action by the other political branches.

. . . These approaches, and the Justices' preferences for them, fall along a continuum, and none of the Justices is perfectly consistent in his or her approach. But particularly at the poles, each Justice's sense of how the Supreme Court most effectively creates precedent to guide and supervise the lower courts can provide important context for his or her decisions about which cases merit plenary review.

Justice Scalia, for example, has championed the rule-articulating approach. He has argued strongly that, wherever it is possible to do so, opinions should be written expansively to explain the rules of general application that control the result in the particular case because "the establishment of broadly applicable general principles is an essential component of the judicial process." Justice Scalia has justified this view, in part, based on a functional understanding of how the Supreme Court should fulfill its supervisory role at the apex of the judicial system. He has noted, in particular, that a "common-law, discretion-conferring approach is ill suited . . . to a legal system in which the supreme court can review only an insignificant proportion of the decided cases." It is difficult to be "gradually closing in on a fully articulated rule of law by deciding one discrete fact situation after another" when the Court "will revisit the area in question with great infrequency."

We focus here on the effect that these views would tend to have on Justice Scalia's approach to the case selection process. All other things being equal, it would seem that he would be disinclined, on average, to vote to grant certiorari as often as a Justice with a narrower view of precedent. Justice Scalia has candidly stated that little is to be gained from granting certain kinds of cases, or cases in certain areas of the law, where the Court has already developed the governing rules to the maximum degree of productiveness, and he cites as examples of such unhelpful cases those raising issues under the Commerce Clause and disputes about whether a given search or seizure was reasonable. In these and other cases where the Court either decides outcomes based explicitly on the unique circumstances or employs balancing tests involving an evaluation of multiple factors to arrive at results, Justice Scalia contends that it unproductively "begins to resemble a finder of fact more than a determiner of law."

Moreover, Justice Scalia has also expressed his disagreement with the notion that the Court should continue to revisit a particular issue as a means of "gradually closing in on a fully articulated rule of law by deciding one discrete fact situation after another until (by process of elimination, as it were) the truly operative facts become apparent." At bottom, the main consequences of his jurisprudential approach on the merits appear to be twofold: altering the mix of cases to favor areas that are more susceptible to articulation of clear legal rules, and necessitating fewer total precedents since the Court can effectively guide the lower courts with a more selective group of opinions that provide general rules with broad applicability.

And, in fact, the information available about Justice Scalia's voting record is consistent with this expectation. In his first four full terms after joining the Court, he voted to grant review in fewer cases than any other Justice—averaging almost ten fewer grant votes per term than Justice Stevens, who was next in rank. One would not predict this stingy record based on Justice Scalia's votes on the merits during those same terms, since he was regularly winning at that stage; indeed, only Justices White and Kennedy dissented from the majority's ultimate disposition in substantially fewer cases than Justice Scalia, who dissented in relatively few cases, with about the same frequency as Justice O'Connor and Chief Justice Rehnquist. Therefore, it was not that Justice Scalia was voting "strategically" based on a calculation that he would not prevail on the merits. Instead, his different approach to the case selection process seems to derive from his distinct conception of the appropriate mode of decisionmaking and hence his views on how many precedents are required to fulfill the Court's central responsibilities.

Sanford Levinson has suggested that Justice Scalia's voting behavior on certiorari is out of step with his "unrelenting [advocacy] for the notion of the judge as positivistic enforcer of formalistic rules."[185] Noting that Justice Scalia did not vote to grant many of the cases presenting conflicts among the circuits that Justice White and others felt strongly about, Levinson questions how Justice Scalia can "fit his own behavior within the commitment to rules that he has so insistently proclaimed." Viewed through a merits prism, Justice Scalia's willingness to bypass many cases involving conflicts—which Rule 10 states is one of the principal bases for granting certiorari—does appear paradoxical.

But Justice Scalia undoubtedly sees case selection through a different prism, where the job at the certiorari stage is simply to identify those cases most appropriate for plenary review. Given that Rule 10 itself is so emphatically discretion-conferring, it seems consistent, and even natural, for Justice Scalia to use that discretion to promote the selection of those cases through which he judges that his merits-stage approach can be advanced. In other words, it seems that Justice Scalia sees the task of case selection as distinct from the task of deciding cases on the merits because the goals at each stage are so fundamentally different. Whereas equal treatment and predictability are essential values at the merits stage, the key focus at the certiorari stage is to build a docket that will best enable the Court to carry out its crucial supervisory responsibilities at the head of the judicial system. This leads Justice Scalia to be willing to "tolerate a fair degree of diversity" in lower court decisions in order to reserve space on the Court's docket for cases in which it can best accomplish the more compelling work of crafting and issuing opinions that lay down clear rules of broad applicability. . . .

---

185. [Sanford Levinson, *Strategy, Jurisprudence, and Certiorari*, 79 Va. Rev. 717, 738 (1993).]

At the opposite pole from the rule-articulating approach, Justice White epitomized the incrementalist approach. "The function of a judge, as White often reiterated, is to decide cases, not to write essays or to expound theories." In implementing this view, he "remained an incrementalist, deciding issues a case at a time, and he perfected an opinion style that was intentionally opaque and self-effacing." Although Justice White was respectful of the principle of stare decisis, he tended to regard the decision reached in each case as the specific judgment rendered on a particular set of facts. When the constellation of facts differed in a later case, he was not reluctant to conclude that statements and observations made in the opinion from the earlier case would not control the Court's judgment, exemplifying Justice Cardozo's observation that "[j]udges differ greatly in their reverence for the illustrations and comments and side-remarks of their predecessors, to make no mention of their own." "For White, the focus on the discrete case imposed a discipline that deterred loose or expansive exercise of the judicial power."

Another general adherent of the incrementalist approach, though less uniformly, is Chief Justice Rehnquist, who narrowly interprets precedents and places primary emphasis on their specific holdings rather than the broader language contained in the Court's opinions. This preference for narrow decisionmaking is reflected in his readiness to dispatch contrary precedents with little elaboration when he sees them as not controlling the circumstances of the case at hand. It also shows up in his apparent embrace of "a premise more associated with the civil law than the common law tradition, to wit that only a consistent line of cases . . . rather than a single case, has any strong precedential force."

This less sweeping approach to judging also has ramifications for case selection. All other things being equal, it would seem that these Justices would be inclined, on average, to vote to grant certiorari in a different mix of cases and more frequently than those with a more robust view of precedent. In order for the incrementalist approach to be effective, the Court must take a sufficient number of cases in each distinct area to be able to create the body of judgments that are necessary to guide the lower courts. The Court might thus need several decisions to supply the guidance that Justice Scalia would prefer to provide through declaration of a broad, general rule in a single case. But under the incrementalist approach, the Court does not need to formulate a rule that will produce acceptable results in a broad run of cases; rather the Court focuses on resolving only the dispute at hand, which eases the burdens of deciding each case. The main consequence of this jurisprudential approach on the merits is thus to require more precedents in each area but with each precedent expected to carry a lighter load in terms of illuminating the law.

Justice White's voting record on certiorari is consistent with this hypothesis. On both the Burger and the Rehnquist Courts, he invariably cast the most votes each term to grant review on the merits. Moreover, in cases that were granted on a bare four votes during that period, Justice White provided the essential fourth vote for review more often than any other Justice. As an Associate Justice, Justice Rehnquist was comparable to Justice White in his frequency of voting to grant review, and both were far more active in this respect than their colleagues. After his elevation to Chief Justice in 1986, Justice Rehnquist's voting behavior on certiorari changed markedly, an exception to the general rule of consistency which we discuss further below. But his voting pattern as an Associate Justice is in line with what might be expected from a Justice who favors a narrow view of Supreme Court precedents: voting to grant large numbers of cases in order to produce enough of a pattern of judgments to provide satisfactory guidance to the lower courts.

The Justices who incline more generally to a "standard-setting" or "balancing" approach present yet another perspective on case selection. One would expect that adherents to this view of precedent, all else being equal, would not tend to be extreme in their decisions on certiorari—neither seeking to confine the Court to a smaller number of opinions written with an eye to settling broad principles nor demanding a large number of judgments to create the pattern necessary to set a direction for the lower courts. In recent decades, Justice Powell has been the most devoted proponent of a balancing approach in many areas of the law and, to a lesser extent, Justice O'Connor has as well. . . .

In the end, we do not wish to suggest that the jurisprudential hypotheses we have posited in this section are determinative of Justices' voting behavior on certiorari. As discussed further below, the blend of influences that affect each Justice's decisionmaking is far more complex than these artificially-tidy pigeonholes might indicate. Yet among the considerations constituting the subjective "feel" for the importance of an issue that each Justice brings to bear on case selection is undoubtedly his or her own understanding of what the Court is trying to accomplish when it decides cases on the merits. Indeed, it seems likely that the Justices formulate their differing perspectives on the proper mode of judicial decisionmaking prior to their arrival at the Court, and this factor thus tends to be one of the more invariable components of their overall approach to case selection.

2. Views on the Importance of Ensuring Uniformity by Resolving Conflicts

Another consideration for each Justice is the degree to which he or she is willing to tolerate disagreements among the lower courts. . . . If, for example, a Justice believes that every conflict presents an "important federal question," then regardless of his or her views about how precedents should be fashioned this priority will motivate that Justice to vote to grant cases more aggressively than a Justice less concerned about national uniformity.

All of the Justices no doubt agree, on some level, that resolving conflicts among the lower courts is an essential task of the Supreme Court, and Rule 10 expressly recognizes that certiorari may be granted where a circuit court or a state court of last resort "has entered a decision in conflict with" another such court on "an important federal question." But there appears to be a surprisingly large variance in the importance that individual Justices attach to achieving uniformity in the application of federal law. . . .

3. Special Interest in Certain Legal Issues and in Effectuating Social Change

Another element in the "feel" that individual Justices have for which cases are sufficiently important to deserve plenary review is their special concern for, or particular interest in, certain areas of the law. These particular interests range from constitutional matters, such as capital cases and abortion, to statutory matters, such as water rights and securities law. It is, of course, not surprising that the Justices would have their own personal interests both from their experiences prior to joining the Court and from their service on it. But the Justices themselves have acknowledged that these idiosyncratic interests affect their behavior on certiorari. Justice Brennan, for example, observed that an essential feature of the certiorari process is that it "provides a forum in which the particular interests or sensitivities of individual justices may be expressed." . . .

Margaret Meriwether Cordray & Richard Cordray, Setting the Social Agenda: Deciding to Review High-Profile Cases at the Supreme Court

57 U. Kan. L. Rev. 313, 324-329 (2009)

Each individual Justice has a complex and highly individualized process for culling out those special cases that warrant plenary review. Our question is whether, consciously or subconsciously, they treat high-profile cases differently from the other cases in the select group of nonfrivolous certiorari petitions. Although the Justices are relatively isolated from the daily concerns and struggles of most Americans, it seems certain that they not only are aware of which issues lie at the heart of the country's social and political agenda, but have their own deeply held views about those issues. What we seek to assess, as far as the Justices' voting records permit, is how the Justices approach the cases that present these issues.

One possibility is that the Justices behave even more strategically than usual in such cases to achieve the results that they desire. Individual passions run high when issues such as abortion, religious freedom, gay rights, and affirmative action are involved. With regard to such issues, each Justice generally has clearly formed views and a keen interest in seeing those views reflected in legal doctrine. Moreover, each Justice usually is able to develop a strong sense of the other Justices' positions, and how the Court will likely resolve the case on the merits. There would thus seem to be strong temptation to vote based on the expected outcome, given the ideological stakes and the ease of casting a forward-looking vote at the threshold stage.

Based on his extensive interviews of five Justices and sixty-two former law clerks, Professor H. W. Perry concluded that the Justices do act differently and more strategically in ideologically laden, socially important cases. Perry found that in most cases the Justices follow a "jurisprudential mode" of decisionmaking, where in essence they take each nonfrivolous petition through a series of gates, considering whether there is a conflict in the circuits, how important the issue is, how urgent resolution of the issue is, and whether the particular case is a good vehicle substantively and procedurally.[51]

However, Perry contended that in those cases where a Justice cares deeply about a particular issue—as is almost invariably true in the high-profile cases—he or she tends to employ a far more outcome-oriented decisional calculus: "When entering the outcome decision mode, the first thing that the [J]ustice does is try to make an assessment of whether or not he will win on the merits. If he thinks he will not, he will vote to deny the case." If, on the other hand, "the [J]ustice thinks he will win on the merits, and if [the case] allows him to move doctrine in the way he wishes," then the Justice will vote to grant. A second possibility, however, is that the Justices act with a greater institutional sense of the Supreme Court's role in the high-profile cases. This possibility is almost diametrically opposed to the first: rather than voting strategically with a view to advancing their own social and political agendas, the core factor in the Justices' decisionmaking is the importance of the case to the Supreme Court's institutional standing and integrity. Each individual Justice's particular conception of the Supreme Court's essential role and responsibilities is no doubt somewhat distinct and influenced by many factors. But the Justices nevertheless must recognize the disproportional importance of these cases to the Court's

---

51. [H.W. Perry, Jr., *Deciding to Decide: Agenda Setting in the United States Supreme Court* 277-79 (1991).]

image with the American public and its authority within our tripartite system of government.

To the extent these considerations carry weight, they would tend to lead the Justices to vote non-strategically in the high-profile cases. Rather than asking whether he or she will win on the merits, the Justice instead would ask whether it is necessary and expected that the United States Supreme Court should decide this case or this issue at this time. Although the internal dynamics of the Justices' conference are largely unknown, it is quite plausible that the importance of these high-profile cases to the Court as an institution may cause the Justices to spend more time in conference deliberating as a body over whether to grant or deny them. This additional collective consideration as a Court, rather than the usual tallying of predetermined votes that were reached in relative isolation, might also lead to greater consensus about the need for Supreme Court review.

Professor Doris Marie Provine has championed the view that the Justices' sense of judicial responsibility leads them to act non-strategically in case-selection decisions. Noting that the certiorari process allows the Justices virtually limitless discretion, she nonetheless argued that "members of the Supreme Court share a conception of their role which prevents them from using their votes simply to achieve policy preferences."[59] Based on her examination of Justice Burton's papers, Provine found that the Justices' voting records on certiorari indicated "that the [J]ustices selected cases with something more than the result they desired on the merits in mind. More particularly, these voting patterns seem to reflect judicial sensitivity to the role of the Supreme Court on the merits." While Provine's analysis was not focused on high-profile cases, and while she recognized the possibility that "some [J]ustices calculate outcomes in cases that are particularly important to them," she strongly advocated that "the [J]ustices' perceptions of a judge's role and of the Supreme Court's role in our judicial system" are central to their case selection decisions. Professor Walter F. Murphy, in his classic study of judicial strategy, likewise observed:

> It would be . . . difficult to deny that much of the force of self-restraint can be traced to individual Justices' concepts of their proper role in American government, to a realization that they are equipped by training, availability of information, and choice of legal remedies to offer only partial solutions to many problems and no solution at all to many others.[63]

Yet a third possibility is that the Justices treat case selection in high-profile cases in the same manner that they treat all other cases. The Justices' sense of the judicial role, as opposed to the institutional role of the Supreme Court, might lead them to apply the same standards through the same selection process in every case, whether the issue involves patent law, the tax code, abortion, or affirmative action. In other words, the Justices may use the same blend of strategic and institutional factors in high-profile cases as they do in more ordinary cases, rather than giving greater emphasis to strategic (or institutional) considerations. At a minimum, the Justices may feel an obligation to try to follow their usual procedures in these cases, which may affect their case selection decisions.

To gain a better sense of how the Justices approach the cases that present high-profile issues, we collected information on the Justices' certiorari votes from the

59. [Doris Marie Provine, *Case Selection in the United States Supreme Court* 174 (1980).]
63. [Walter F. Murphy, *Elements of Judicial Strategy* 29 (1964).]

private papers of Justices Blackmun, Brennan, and Marshall for the 1983 Term through the 1993 Term. We used this information to make four types of comparisons between the Justices' behavior in high-profile cases and their behavior in low-profile cases. First, we compared the frequency with which each Justice voted to grant high-profile cases as opposed to low-profile cases. Second, we compared the degree of unanimity (and divisiveness) with which the Court granted high-profile cases as opposed to low-profile cases. Third, we looked at whether Justices who are ideologically aligned on the merits tend to vote together more frequently on certiorari in high-profile cases as opposed to the full set of cases granted (and, conversely, whether Justices who are ideologically opposed on the merits tend to vote together less frequently on certiorari in high-profile cases as opposed to the full set of cases granted). Fourth, for five of the Terms in our dataset, we tracked how each Justice voted on certiorari and then on the merits, to assess whether the Justices behave more strategically in high-profile versus low-profile cases. . . . [W]e did so by considering whether each Justice tended to "win" more frequently in high-profile cases, and also whether each Justice tended to vote to reverse more frequently in such cases.

In comparing the frequency with which each Justice voted to grant cases, the degree of unanimity in voting on certiorari, and the Justices' voting alignments, we saw strong evidence that the Justices' tendency to vote with an eye to the merits is even more pronounced in high-profile cases, but the results also suggested that the Justices are voting at least in some cases based on a sense of the Court's institutional responsibility. In the five Terms for which we tracked the Justices' voting behavior from certiorari through the merits, we found that in the cases the Justices voted to grant, they tended to vote to reverse with the same frequency in high-profile versus low-profile cases. But the Justices tended to win less often in high-profile cases that they voted to grant than they did in low-profile cases that they voted to grant. Although the reasons for this voting behavior are not entirely clear, we think it provides some further evidence that the Justices' sense of the Court's institutional responsibilities has an effect on their decisionmaking in high-profile cases.

Notes and Questions

1. In his famous book *The Least Dangerous Branch*, which was originally published in 1962, Alexander M. Bickel argued in favor of the "passive virtues" of the Court—meaning the Court's refusal to decide certain matters. In extolling the virtues of the Court's passive virtues, he pointed to certiorari as a tool through which the Court could avoid deciding certain political matters that might harm the Court's institutional credibility and stature. In describing certiorari as a tool of avoidance, Bickel noted that certiorari cannot "be principled in the sense in which we have a right to expect adjudications on the merits to be principled." Alexander M. Bickel, *The Least Dangerous Branch: The Supreme Court at the Bar of Politics* 132 (1986). Rather, in Bickel's view, certiorari decisions mark "where the Court is the most political animal." *Id.* Is Bickel right that certiorari cannot be truly "principled"?

2. Should the names of the attorneys who have drafted a petition for certiorari impact the likelihood that the Court will grant certiorari? Whether or not the experience level of the attorneys *should* impact the likelihood of certiorari being granted, it appears that there is some relationship. *See* Richard J. Lazarus, *Docket*

Capture at the High Court, 119 Yale L.J. 89 (2010). According to Lazarus, expert Supreme Court advocates—meaning those who have presented at least five oral arguments before the Court or are affiliated with a practice whose current members have argued at least ten cases—were responsible for only 5.8 percent (6 of 102 cases) of the petitions granted plenary review during October Term 1980. *Id.* at 90. In contrast, by October Term 2000, "that same percentage had increased to 25% (seventeen of sixty-eight cases) and has steadily increased since—36% in October Term 2005 and 44% in October Term 2006—to boast more than 50% of the Court's docket during both the October Terms 2007 (53.8%) and 2008 (55.5%)." *Id.* Lazarus's study is explored in more detail at page 276. But for now, consider why certain attorneys might enjoy greater success before the Court. Is it because more experienced appellate attorneys have a better sense of what the Justices are looking for? Or is it because they craft better petitions? Or do they have the luxury of attracting clients with more certworthy cases?

3. If you were a Justice on the Court today, which considerations would you give the most weight to in assessing petitions for certiorari? The presence of a conflict? The importance of the legal issues? Whether you think the lower court reached an erroneous decision? Whether you think the Court would reach a desirable result on the merits? The quality of the lawyering in the petition? Would you gravitate toward a rule-articulating approach, a standard-setting approach, or an incrementalist approach? Why?

C. PROCEDURAL CONSIDERATIONS: THE PROCESS OF DECIDING TO DECIDE

Separate from the issue of which substantive considerations individual Justices might take into account when deciding whether to vote to grant cert, there is the question of process. Specifically, what process does the Court follow when considering and ruling upon cert petitions?

This section will walk through the process governing certiorari decisions, detailing its four main stages: (1) preparing and filing of cert-stage papers by the litigants; (2) in-chambers review of the cert papers, generally through what is known as the "cert pool" whereby one law clerk reviews and writes a memorandum on each petition for the benefit of those Justices who participate in the cert pool; (3) creating and internally circulating the "discuss list," which lists those petitions that the Justices have selected for conference discussion and voting; and (4) voting at the conference guided by the so-called Rule of Four, which requires the votes of four Justices before certiorari can be granted.

1. Preparation and Filing of Certiorari Briefs by the Litigants

The first step in the certiorari process comes when a losing party in the lower courts decides to seek Supreme Court review and files a petition for a writ of certiorari. When a litigant chooses to file a petition for a writ of certiorari, that litigant bears the burden of convincing at least four Justices that the case warrants the Court's attention and deserves a prized slot on the Court's docket.

The materials that follow detail the required contents and organizational structure of petitions for certiorari, as well as "briefs in opposition," which a respondent opposing certiorari may file, and "reply" briefs, which a petitioner may file to respond to points raised in a brief in opposition. In addition, the materials provide various Supreme Court experts' tips on how to craft successful cert-stage papers, as well as illustrative examples of cert-stage papers.

a. Drafting Petitions for Certiorari

As a federal appellate judge and former Supreme Court practitioner has put it, "[t]o be effective at the certiorari stage," the petitioners "must recognize that their opposition is no longer merely the prevailing party in the lower court, but the other certiorari petitions vying for the Court's attention during the term." A. Raymond Randolph, *Certiorari Petitions in the Supreme Court*, ABA Litigation Manual: Special Problems and Appeals 363 (1999). In other words, "the certiorari practice in the Supreme Court is a contest of cases." *Id.* Crafting a petition for certiorari so that it stands out and separates itself from the thousands of denied petitions takes significant skill as well as knowledge of what the Court is looking for in petitions for certiorari.

In exploring how to craft petitions for certiorari, Supreme Court Rules 13 and 14 stand as good places to begin. Please read both rules. (See Appendix B, pages 644-649.) As you will see, Rule 13 governs the time for petitioning, and Rule 14 governs the contents of petitions for certiorari. As Rule 14 makes clear, a petition for certiorari generally contains a variety of things, including the questions presented for review, a list of all parties, a table of contents, a table of cited authorities, a concise statement of the basis for jurisdiction, a concise statement of the case that sets out the material facts, and a direct and concise argument amplifying the reasons relied on for allowance of the writ. The excerpt that follows explores the art of crafting effective petitions for certiorari and highlights the special importance of carefully crafting the question or questions presented, the statement of the case, and the reasons for granting certiorari.

Timothy S. Bishop, Jeffrey W. Sarles & Stephen J. Kane, Tips on Petitioning for Certiorari in the U.S. Supreme Court

The Circuit Rider, May 2007, at 28

For many lawyers, representing a client in a case that is a candidate for review by the United States Supreme Court is a once in a lifetime experience. Yet the art of seeking certiorari in the Supreme Court—with its focus on conflicts among lower courts and the importance of the case to non-parties—is decidedly foreign to many litigators, who spend their days engaged in the underlying merits of a dispute. This article seeks to make certiorari practice a little less foreign by providing some tips on the factors the Supreme Court considers in deciding whether to review a case. . . .

The first question that any prospective Supreme Court petitioner should consider is whether to file a petition at all. While the number of petitions filed in the Supreme Court has increased from roughly 4,000 in the mid-1970s to 7,496 in the 2004 Term, the number of annual grants has decreased from about 150 to only 80 during that same period. Whatever the cause of the Court's shrinking docket—the theories include repeal of much of the Court's mandatory jurisdiction, changes in the composition of the Court, increased reliance on clerks, and homogeneity in the lower courts—the stark reality for petitioners is that the chances of a grant are slim at best. In fact, the approximately 4 percent rate at which the Court grants certiorari in paid cases (as opposed to petitions filed in *forma pauperis*, which are granted at an even lower rate) is misleadingly high because petitions filed by governmental entities stand a far better chance of success than do petitions filed by private litigants. The Office of the Solicitor General—the entity that represents the federal government in the Supreme Court—has a particularly impressive track record, with the Court granting about 44 percent of the petitions filed by the SG in the ten terms between 1995 and 2004. What's more, much of the Court's docket is taken up by criminal and habeas cases, leaving few openings if your case involves a business issue. The Justices have frequently commented on the ease with which they are able to dispatch many petitions. Justice Brennan observed that 60 percent of paid petitions are "utterly without merit," while Chief Justice Rehnquist remarked that "several thousand" of the petitions filed each year are so implausible that "no one of the nine [Justices] would have the least interest in granting them." Brennan, *The National Court of Appeals, Another Dissent*, 40 U. Chi. L. Rev. 473, 476-78 (1973); Rehnquist, *The Supreme Court* 233 (2d ed. 2001). One of the principal reasons why so many petitions are poor candidates for review is that they reflect a fundamental misconception about the role of the Supreme Court. As Chief Justice Vinson noted over fifty years ago, "[t]he Supreme Court is not, and never has been, primarily concerned with the correction of errors in lower court decisions." Vinson, *Work of the Federal Courts*, Address Before the ABA (Sept. 7, 1949). Today's Supreme Court Rule 10 confirms that a petition "is rarely granted when the asserted error consists of factual findings or the misapplication of a properly stated rule of law." Yet litigants continue to flood the Court with petitions arguing that review is warranted in large part because the lower court erred. To be sure, the merits are not irrelevant at the certiorari stage. The Court affirmed in less than 28 percent of the cases it reviewed on a writ of certiorari and decided with a full opinion during the 2004 Term, suggesting that the Court is more likely to issue a grant when it believes that the lower court got it wrong. But the fact that the court below erred is generally not nearly enough to merit a spot on the Supreme Court's docket. . . .

If you decide to face the long odds and file a petition for certiorari in the Supreme Court, there are three initial steps you should take. First, if you are not already a member of the Supreme Court Bar, you should apply for admission. The requirements are not onerous. Sup. Ct. R. 5, 9. Second, you should determine the due date for your petition. A petition must be filed within 90 days after entry of the judgment below or the denial of rehearing. Sup. Ct. R. 13. The petition is timely if you file it with the Clerk within 90 days; send it to the Clerk on the 90th day via U.S. mail with a postmark (not a commercial postage meter label); or deliver it on the 90th day "to a third-party commercial carrier for delivery to the Clerk within 3 calendar days." Sup. Ct. R. 29.2. Although requests for an extension of time are "not favored," you may obtain an extension of up to 60 days "[f]or good cause" by filing an application with the Clerk at least 10 days before the date the petition is due. Sup. Ct. R. 13.5. Regardless of whether you obtain an extension, make sure that you calculate your due date correctly because the Clerk will not file an untimely petition. Sup. Ct. R. 13. Third, you should identify and contact potential amici. Although amici need not file their briefs until after the petition is due—generally 30 days after the petition is docketed—you should begin the critical process of obtaining amici early in the game. Sup. Ct. R. 37.2(a).

. . . Rule 14 sets forth the petition's required content, which we need not detail here. There are three critical components to any petition. The Question Presented—which appears on the first page—may well be the most important part of the petition. Justice Brennan frequently decided that a case was not "certworthy" simply by looking at the Question Presented. To avoid that type of reaction, your question should briefly describe the essential features of the case while conveying the necessity of Supreme Court intervention. A short introductory paragraph is sometimes helpful to place the question in context. To determine whether your question is effective, try inserting the words "We hold that" before the question to make it an affirmative statement. If that statement reflects a clear and important ruling in your favor that would have an impact beyond your case, then you are well on your way. See Shapiro, *Certiorari Practice: The Supreme Court's Shrinking Docket*, 24 Litigation 25 (Spring 1998). Finally, a cautionary note about the number of questions presented: try to limit yourself to one or two questions. There are few cases that present a single question that merits the Court's review; it is unlikely that your case presents three or more, and you may lose credibility suggesting otherwise.

The second key component is the Statement, which provides a brief recitation of the factual background and a description of the decisions below. A punchy introductory paragraph that orients the reader about what is to follow is often useful. Make sure to keep the description of the facts to a minimum. A lengthy factual summary, loaded with references to the types of background controversies that are the focus of trial counsel, may only serve to show that your case is convoluted and fact-dependent—defects that usually result in a denial. If your case revolves around the interpretation of a statute or regulatory scheme, it may be helpful to write a brief section detailing that framework. Finally, in your description of the decisions below, be sure to emphasize any dissent or votes in favor of rehearing en banc and to note the identity of any judge(s) who saw things your way, particularly if they are well-respected.

for my case, specifically!

REASONS TO GRANT CERT

The "Reasons for Granting the Petition" forms the heart of the petition. An introductory paragraph or two often helps to highlight the reasons why your case is certworthy. Like any brief, subheadings are useful to direct the reader to your key points and provide a roadmap of the argument. If your case presents conflicts among the lower courts, you might begin with a section captioned "The First Circuit Joined the Second Circuit in Expressly Rejecting Decisions from the Third and Fourth Circuits." In this section, prove that the lower courts are deeply divided on an issue of federal law by quoting from the leading cases. If you are lucky enough that the lower courts have acknowledged the split, emphasize that fact.

• lower court split

Regardless of whether there are conflicts, the petition must show that the issue presented is of great importance beyond the narrow interests of the litigants and that Supreme Court intervention is therefore imperative. This section might argue, for example, that the lower court's decision threatens to open the floodgates to a dramatic increase in litigation or makes it impossible for litigants to comply with discrepant rulings from across the country. Finally, the petitioner should almost always include a short section at the end arguing that the court below erred, both because the merits play a minor role in the certiorari decision and because the Court on rare occasions simultaneously grants certiorari and summarily affirms.

In writing this section, focus on the Supreme Court's own precedents, as well as any relevant constitutional or statutory language. Reliance on respected scholars in the field and public policy arguments may bolster your position. Above all else, keep this section short; there will be plenty of time to argue the merits if the Court grants your petition.

---

b. Drafting Briefs in Opposition and Reply Briefs

Once a petition for a writ of certiorari has been filed, then the respondent has a strategic choice to make: the respondent may either file a brief in opposition ("BIO") opposing certiorari, or the respondent may waive the opportunity to file a BIO. *See* S. Ct. R. 15. Given the allure of briefing a case before the United States Supreme Court, why would a respondent ever choose to waive the opportunity to file a BIO? There are many possible reasons for doing so. For example, the petition for a writ of certiorari might be frivolous and might not warrant the time and resources necessary to prepare a response, or the respondent might determine that filing a response would call unwanted attention to the petition and might actually increase the odds of certiorari being granted. Or alternatively, the respondent might decide to waive the right to file a BIO knowing that if the Court is truly interested in a particular certiorari petition, the Court generally will issue an order calling for a response (known as a "CFR") before granting cert. *See generally* David C. Thompson & Melanie F. Wachtell, *An Empirical Analysis of Supreme Court Certiorari Petition Procedures: The Call for Response and the Call for the Views of the Solicitor General,* 16 Geo. Mason L. Rev. 237, 247-249 (2009) (describing how any one Justice has the power to call for a response and noting that the Supreme Court calls for responses "relatively frequently").

If the respondent files a BIO, then the petitioner has the right to file a reply brief. According to Supreme Court Rule 15, a reply brief should be "addressed to new points raised in the brief in opposition." S. Ct. Rule 15.

Please read Supreme Court Rule 15 found in Appendix B (page 646), and then consider the following excerpt, which provides some tips for opposing certiorari.

Timothy S. Bishop, Jeffrey W. Sarles & Stephen J. Kane, Tips on Petitioning and Opposing Certiorari in the U.S. Supreme Court

34 Litigation 26 (2008)

If you are the respondent, congratulations are in order. The court below gave you a well-deserved victory, and the odds overwhelmingly suggest that your victory will not be disturbed. The first question you should consider is whether to file a brief in opposition at all. You may waive your right to file a brief, and that may be the appropriate course if your opponent has filed a frivolous petition. In fact, some commentators suggest that respondents should waive a response in all cases because the clerk will "call for a response" if one of the justices votes to include the petition on the discuss list. That could be a mistake. If a clerk bases the pool memo solely on the petition, the justices could form an opinion about the certiorari decision without the benefit of your views. In any event, consider consulting an experienced Supreme Court practitioner before deciding to waive.

If you decide to file a brief in opposition, do not feel compelled to use the 9,000 words allotted to you. A short brief that points out the two or three principal reasons why certiorari is unwarranted often suffices. Be sure to deter would-be amici from filing briefs in support of your position. Studies have shown that amicus briefs filed in support of the respondent actually increase the likelihood of a grant, probably because such briefs highlight the importance of the issue to parties not before the Court. [Gregory A.] Caldeira & [John R.] Wright, "The Discuss List: Agenda Building in the Supreme Court," 24 *Law & Soc. Rev.* 807, 828 (1990).

The question presented is generally less important in a brief in opposition than it is in a petition for certiorari. In fact, simply adopting the petitioner's question presented may be to your benefit if the question is so confused as to make it unclear what issue the petitioner wants the Court to review. More commonly, however, you will want to reformulate the question to make it clear that the case is not certworthy. For example, your question may indicate that the case is highly fact-bound or that the lower court's decision is no more than a routine application of settled law.

In rare cases, you may find it beneficial to adopt the petitioner's statement or to direct the Court to a comprehensive statement of the facts in an opinion below. That is usually a mistake. Perhaps your case is rife with messy factual disputes that the Court would have to resolve to address the question presented. Perhaps the court below based its decision on the unique facts presented by your case. A good statement can bring these points to light and cause a clerk drafting the pool memo to conclude that your case is a poor vehicle to resolve the question presented. In any event, be careful to correct any misstatement in the petitioner's statement. If you fail to do so, the Court may decide that you have waived the point. Rule 15.2 ("Counsel are admonished that they have an obligation to the Court to point out in the brief in opposition, and not later, any perceived misstatement made in the petition.").

The heart of the brief in opposition is the argument section, Reasons for Denying the Petition. The good news is that the clerk who drafts the pool memo will be eager to seize upon any infirmity in the petition. Clerks tend to be risk-averse. They know that a truly important issue will resurface, while a grant recommendation could lead to embarrassment should an overlooked defect in the case lead the Court to dismiss a case as improvidently granted ("DIG" in Court parlance). Your job is to play upon the pool clerk's "just-say-no" predisposition by providing reasons to doubt that the petition presents a certworthy issue. In this task, there is a lengthy catalog of potential arguments from which you may choose.

If you are lucky, you will be able to knock out the petition before even addressing any conflicts that allegedly exist in the lower courts. *See generally* [Andrew L.] Frey, [Kenneth S.] Geller & [Daniel] Harris, "Opposing Review: The Art of Finding 'Uncertworthiness,'" I *Inside Litigation* 27 (Mar. 1987). Consider the following questions:

- Was the petition timely filed? In civil cases, the Supreme Court lacks jurisdiction to review an untimely petition. Rule 13.2.
- Does the petition present an issue of state law? The Supreme Court does not sit to review questions of state law. Indeed, you should raise any plausible argument that the court below relied on state law. A risk-adverse clerk is unlikely to recommend a grant in a case that requires the Court to expend resources resolving a close question concerning the applicable law before deciding whether it even can reach the issue presented.
- If the petition presents an issue of federal law, did the court below include an adequate and independent state law ground to support the judgment? Such decisions are generally immune from Supreme Court review. *E.g., Michigan v. Long*, 463 U.S. 1032 (1983).

- Did the court below provide an alternative federal law basis for its judgment that is clearly not certworthy? The Court is sensitive to the need to avoid advisory opinions and is thus unlikely to grant certiorari in a case where a decision in favor of the petitioner would have no effect on the judgment below.
- Did the petitioner preserve the issue presented in the lower courts? The Court usually will deny review where the lower courts had no opportunity to pass on the issue presented.
- Is the decision below interlocutory? The Court does not have jurisdiction to review interlocutory decisions issued by state courts. 28 U.S.C. §1257. Although the Court may review interlocutory decisions issued by federal courts, you should nevertheless highlight the interlocutory nature of a federal court decision. Absent a compelling reason why immediate intervention is necessary, the Court will likely deny review of an interlocutory decision because the petitioner may well ultimately win the case on another ground, thereby obviating the need for review. If the respondent ultimately prevails, the petitioner may seek certiorari again upon entry of a final judgment.
- Is there a problem with ripeness, mootness, or standing? The Court has been increasingly strict about the case-or-controversy requirement in recent years and is unlikely to grant review where there is a plausible argument that the issue is moot or the petitioner lacks standing.

Even if none of the factors described above applies to your case and the petition alleges a conflict among the lower courts, the petition may be unworthy of Supreme Court review. For example, the conflicting decisions cited by the petitioner may have been issued by the wrong type of court. As we noted, intra-circuit conflicts and conflicts among district courts or lower state courts are generally insufficient to merit certiorari. Moreover, the conflict alleged by the petitioner may not be "real." . . . Perhaps the language that the petitioner cites as creating the conflict is mere dicta not essential to the lower court's decision. Or perhaps the allegedly conflicting cases are distinguishable on their facts. If possible, the respondent should try to reconcile the conflicting decisions and argue that the conflicts alleged by the petitioner do not prove that the lower courts would reach different decisions if faced with the same or very similar facts. Justice Breyer has explained that "attorneys often present cases that involve not actual divides among the lower courts, but merely different verbal formulations of the same underlying legal rule. And we are not particularly interested in ironing out minor linguistic discrepancies among the lower courts because those discrepancies are not outcome determinative." [Stephen G.] Breyer, "Reflections on the Role of Appellate Courts: A View from the Supreme Court," 8 *J. App. Prac. & Process* 91, 96 (2006).

To the extent the petition presents a square conflict among the federal courts of appeal or state courts of last resort, there remain a number of reasons why the Court may decline review. For instance, the conflict may be tolerable because the issue arises infrequently or involves a question on which national uniformity is not essential. You may want to cite past denials of certiorari on the same issue to remind the Court that it previously found the issue to be unworthy of review. The conflict cited by the petitioner may be of recent vintage, requiring further percolation among the lower courts to assist the Court when it ultimately resolves the issue. As Justice Stevens has noted, "experience with conflicting interpretations of federal rules may help to illuminate an issue before it is finally resolved and thus may play a constructive role in the lawmaking process." [Justice John Paul] Stevens, "Some Thoughts on Judicial Restraint," 66 *Judicature* 177, 183 (1982). Conversely, the conflict may be based on a decades-old decision that has been discredited due to an intervening Supreme Court decision. The Court is unlikely to grant review if there is reason to believe that the lower court would no longer adhere to an old decision of dubious continuing vitality. Along the same lines, the conflict may be too narrow—i.e., every circuit but one has adopted the same rule, holding open the possibility that the dissenting circuit will ultimately fall in line.

Even a petition that presents a deep conflict among the lower courts on an important issue of federal law may not warrant review if the case is a poor vehicle to resolve the issue. The Court shies away from cases involving messy or convoluted facts that may prevent the Court from reaching the issue presented. You should inform the Court if there is another case in the pipeline that presents the same issue without the knotty factual problems that predominate in your case. Perhaps Congress or an administrative agency has amended or is considering amendments to the statute or regulation at issue in your case. If so, the Court may allow the conflict to persist in the hope that legislative changes will enable the lower courts to harmonize their decisions.

Like the petition, a brief in opposition should conclude with a short section addressing the merits of the dispute. In this section, you should show that the lower court's decision is consistent with both the Supreme Court's precedents in the area and common sense. If, however, the lower court's reasoning is indefensible, you should try to identify an alternative basis to support the judgment. A justification that is at least plausible will likely stave off a simultaneous grant and summary reversal.

Respondents should also be aware of the possibility of a "hold" and subsequent "GVR" (grant, vacate, and remand). If the justices believe that the Court's resolution of a case awaiting argument or decision may affect the issues raised in a petition, the Court often will hold the petition until the pending case is decided. Once the pending case is decided, the Court may dispose of the petition through a GVR and order the lower court to reconsider the case in light of the Supreme Court's intervening decision. Although a GVR does not spell automatic defeat for the respondent in the court below, respondents should be alert for cases on the Court's docket that could affect the petition and should try to distinguish those cases (if at all possible) in the brief in opposition.

---

c. Sample Cert Filings from *Bowers v. Hardwick*

Now that you have a sense of what a petition for a writ of certiorari, a brief in opposition and a reply brief should contain and what they should emphasize, it is time to review some illustrative examples of real cert-stage papers filed with the Court. Accordingly, the materials that follow provide the petition for a writ of certiorari, the brief in opposition, and the reply brief filed in *Bowers v. Hardwick*, 478 U.S. 186 (1986), a case involving the constitutionality of a Georgia anti-sodomy statute.

In reading the *Bowers* certiorari papers, pay particular attention to how the petitioner seeking certiorari tries to play up the existence of a circuit split, the importance of the issues presented, the errors in the decision below, and the broad impact the lower court's opinion would have if left standing. In turn, note how the respondents opposing certiorari try to downplay the importance of the legal issues, to undercut the petitioner's claims that a circuit split exists, and to emphasize the correctness of the opinion below. As you will see, much of the disagreement between the parties at the certiorari stage concerns what might be seen as procedural technicalities, such as whether the Supreme Court's summary affirmance in *Doe v. Commonwealth's Attorney*, 425 U.S. 901 (1976), *summ. aff'g* 403 F. Supp. 1199 (E.D. Va. 1975), constituted binding precedent that should have been followed by the lower court in *Bowers*. Summary affirmances result when the Court finds that the decision below was correct and that no substantial question was raised, leading the Court to summarily affirm the decision below.

i. The Petition for a Writ of Certiorari

MICHAEL J. BOWERS,
ATTORNEY GENERAL OF GEORGIA,
Petitioner,
v.
MICHAEL HARDWICK, AND
JOHN AND MARY DOE,
Respondents.

PETITION FOR A WRIT OF CERTIORARI TO THE UNITED STATES COURT OF APPEALS FOR THE ELEVENTH CIRCUIT

MICHAEL J. BOWERS
Attorney General
MARION O. GORDON
First Assistant, Attorney General
DARYL A. ROBINSON
Senior Assistant, Attorney General
MICHAEL E. HOBBS
Senior Assistant, Attorney General . . .

QUESTIONS PRESENTED

1. Whether the Court of Appeals erred in concluding that *Doe v. Commonwealth's Attorney for the City of Richmond*, 425 U.S. 901 (1976), *aff'g*. 403 F. Supp. 1199 (E.D. Va. 1975), which upheld the constitutionality of Virginia's sodomy statute, does not constitute precedent binding upon lower federal courts.
2. Whether the Court of Appeals erred in concluding that Georgia's sodomy statute infringes upon the fundamental rights of homosexuals and in requiring the State of Georgia to demonstrate a compelling state interest in order to support the constitutionality of the statute.

LIST OF PARTIES

Michael Hardwick and John and Mary Doe were the Plaintiffs in the United States District Court for the Northern District of Georgia. Michael J. Bowers, Attorney General of the State of Georgia, Lewis Slaton, District Attorney, for Fulton County, Georgia and George Napper, Commissioner of Public Safety for the City of Atlanta were named as Defendants in this action. . . .

The Petitioner, Michael J. Bowers, Attorney General of the State of Georgia, respectfully prays that a writ of certiorari issue to review the judgment and opinion of the United States Court of Appeals for the Eleventh Circuit entered in this proceeding on May 21, 1985.

OPINION BELOW

The opinion of the Court of Appeals appears at 760 F.2d 1202 (11th Cir. 1985). The opinion of the United States District Court for the Northern District of Georgia was not reported. . . .

JURISDICTION

The judgment of the Court of Appeals for the Eleventh Circuit was entered on May 21, 1985. A timely suggestion for rehearing en banc was filed on May 30, 1985, and denied on June 13, 1985. This petition for certiorari is filed within 90 days of the denial of rehearing. This Court's jurisdiction is invoked under 28 U.S.C. §1254(1) (1982).

STATUTORY PROVISION INVOLVED

Official Code of Georgia Annotated, Section 16-6-2(a) (1984).

"A person commits the offense of sodomy when he performs or submits to any sexual act involving the sex organs of one person and the mouth or anus of another."

STATEMENT OF THE CASE

Respondents, Michael Hardwick and John and Mary Doe, filed their complaint in this case on February 14, 1983. Hardwick alleged that he was a practicing homosexual who regularly engages in private homosexual acts, and that he will do so in the future. The Does alleged that they were lawfully married and had the ambition to engage in activities proscribed by the Georgia sodomy statute, O.C.G.A. §16-6-2 (1984). The Respondents alleged that the statute was unconstitutional in that it violated their right of privacy under the First, Third, Fourth, Fifth, Ninth and Fourteenth Amendments to the United States Constitution and that it violated due process of law, was unconstitutionally overbroad, and violated their freedom of expression and association. Respondents sought declaratory judgment to this effect.

Each Defendant, including Petitioner Bowers, filed separate motions to dismiss. The District Court, in an order entered by the Honorable Robert H. Hall, dismissed the complaint as to the Does on the basis of their lack of standing. As to Hardwick, the complaint was dismissed on the ground that all of his constitutional claims had been rejected by this Court in *Doe v. Commonwealth's Attorney for the City of Richmond*, 403 F. Supp. 1199 (E.D. Va. 1975), *aff'd* 425 U.S. 90 (1976).

Respondents appealed Judge Hall's decision to the United States Court of Appeals for the Eleventh Circuit and on May 21, 1985, in an opinion authored by the Honorable Frank M. Johnson, Circuit Judge, a majority of the panel found (1) that Hardwick possessed sufficient standing to pursue this action, while the Does lacked standing; (2) that this Court's summary affirmance in *Doe v. Commonwealth's Attorney, supra,* is not binding precedent; and (3) that Georgia's sodomy statute infringes upon Hardwick's fundamental constitutional right of privacy and that the State of Georgia would be required, upon the trial of the case, to establish the existence of a compelling state interest in proscribing consensual homosexual sodomy.

The Honorable Phyllis A. Kravitch, Circuit Judge, filed a separate opinion concurring in part with the majority panel decision, but dissenting from the majority
holding that *Doe v. Commonwealth's Attorney* is not binding on the lower federal
courts.

On May 30, 1985, a suggestion for rehearing *en banc* was filed on behalf of
Petitioner Bowers, and was denied on June 13, 1985.

REASONS FOR GRANTING THE WRIT

I. THE DECISION BELOW CONFLICTS DIRECTLY WITH THE DECISION OF THE COURT OF APPEALS FOR THE DISTRICT OF COLUMBIA IN *DRONENBURG V. ZECH*, 741 F. 2D 388, *REH. DENIED*, 746 F.2D 1579 (D.C.CIR. 1984) BY ERRONEOUSLY CONCLUDING THAT *DOE V. COMMONWEALTH'S ATTORNEY*, 425 U.S. 901 (1976), *SUM. AFF'G* 403 F.SUPP. 1199 (E.D. VA. 1975), DOES NOT CONSTITUTE BINDING PRECEDENT.

In *Doe v. Commonwealth's Attorney for the City of Richmond*, 407 F. Supp. 1199 (E.D.
Va. 1975) a three-judge district court upheld the constitutionality of Virginia's sodomy statute against allegations that the statute violated due process, freedom of
expression, and the right of privacy as it related to homosexual conduct.

On appeal, the district court's decision was summarily affirmed by this Court.
425 U.S. 901 (1976). This summary affirmance formed the basis for Petitioner's
motion to dismiss Respondent Hardwick's claims, which was granted by the district
court.

The Court of Appeals for the Eleventh Circuit disagreed with the district court's
decision and concluded that *Doe* is not binding precedent. While the Court of
Appeals recognized that a summary affirmance by the Supreme Court has binding
precedential effect, *Hicks v. Miranda*, 422 U.S. 332, 344-45 (1975), it decided that *Doe*
was not binding since this Court ". . . could have approved the result reached by the
district court without addressing the constitutional issues because the Plaintiffs in
Doe plainly lacked standing to sue." *Hardwick v. Bowers,* 760 F.2d 1202, 1207 (11th
Cir. 1985).

Additionally, the Court of Appeals determined that even if *Doe*'s summary affirmance could have been considered a decision on the merits at one time, subsequent
doctrinal developments have occurred which would release lower courts from the
bonds of *Doe*.

The Court of Appeals concluded that two footnotes in this Court's decision in
Carey v. Population Services International, 431 U.S. 678 n.5, n.17 (1977), and this
Court's dismissal of the writ of certiorari in *New York v. Uplinger,* __ U.S. __, 104
S. Ct. 2332 (1984) were indications that this court now considers the issue of privacy
in the context of homosexual sodomy to be an open question, and fair game for
lower court interpretations.

It is urged that the court of appeals has made unwarranted assumptions in its
efforts to evade *Doe v. Commonwealth's Attorney*. These assumptions have resulted in a
direct conflict with the Court of Appeals for the District of Columbia's decision in
Dronenburg v. Zech, 741 F.2d 1388, 1392, *reh. denied,* 746 F.2d 1579 (1984). In a
unanimous panel opinion authored by Circuit Judge Bork, that court found that
the summary affirmance in *Doe v. Commonwealth's Attorney* was binding on the lower
courts as a decision on the merits of the issues expressly ruled on by the district
court.

As in the case *sub judice* it was urged in *Dronenburg* that *Doe* should be viewed not as an affirmance based upon the constitutionality of Virginia's sodomy statute, but rather upon the plaintiff's alleged lack of standing in the case. The *Dronenburg* court noted, however, that the three-judge district court made its decision on the merits of the constitutional claims, and not on standing, and further noted that the summary affirmance gave no indication that this Court "proceeded upon any other rationale." *Dronenburg,* 741 F.2d 1388, 1392. The court stated:

> Under these circumstances, we doubt that a court of appeals ought to distinguish a Supreme Court precedent on the speculation that the Court might possibly have had something else in mind.

Id. at 1392.

In addition, the *Dronenburg* opinion examined this Court's previous privacy decisions, ranging from *Griswold v. Connecticut,* 381 U.S. 479 (1965) to *Carey v. Population Services International,* 431 U.S. 678 (1977), and concluded as follows:

> . . . We do not find any principle articulated even approaching in breadth that which appellant seeks to have us adopt. The [Supreme] Court has listed as illustrative of the right of privacy such matters as activities relating to marriage, procreation, contraception, family relationships, and child rearing and education. It need hardly be said that none of these covers a right to homosexual conduct.

Id. at pp. 1395-96.

Thus, the District of Columbia Circuit Court was unable to discern doctrinal developments or any indications from this Court that the right of privacy may extend as far as is urged by the Respondents herein or as found by the Eleventh Circuit panel.

As Circuit Judge Kravitch indicated in her dissent from the decision below, this Court has made it clear that summary affirmances are decisions on the merits of a case and the lower courts are bound to follow summary decisions "until such time as the Court informs [them] that [they] are not" *Hicks v. Miranda,* 422 U.S. at 345-346, 95 S. Ct. at 2289 (quoting *Doe v. Hodgson,* 478 F.2d 537, 539 (2d Cir.) *cert. denied,* 414 U.S. 1096, 96 S. Ct. 732, 38 L. Ed. 2d 555 (1973))." *Hardwick, supra* at 1214. (Kravitch, J., dissenting).

Moreover, Judge Kravitch correctly concluded that even if the perceived "doctrinal developments" of *Carey* and *Uplinger* might indicate a willingness on the part of this Court to reconsider the wisdom of *Doe,* the Court of Appeals is not free to ignore it as binding precedent.

As the Eleventh Circuit stated in *Jaffre v. Wallace,* 705 F.2d 1526 (11th Cir. 1983) *aff'd,* U.S., 105 S. Ct. 2479 (1985):

> Federal district courts and circuit courts are bound to adhere to the controlling decisions of the Supreme Court. *Hutto v. Davis,* 454 U.S. 370, 375, 102 S. Ct. 703, 706, 70 L. Ed. 2d 556 (1982). . . . Justice Rehnquist emphasized the importance of precedent when he observed that "unless we wish anarchy to prevail within the federal judicial system, a precedent of this Court must be followed by the lower courts no matter how misguided the judges of those courts may think it to be." *Davis,* 45 U.S. at 375, 102 S. Ct. at 706. *See also, Thurston Motor Lines, Inc. v. Jordan K. Rand, Ltd.,* [460] U.S. [533, 535] 103 S. Ct. 1343, 1344, 75 L. Ed. 2d 260 1983). (The Supreme Court in a per curiam decision recently stated: "Needless to say, only this Court may overrule one of its precedents.")

Id. at 1532.

Petitioner maintains that the court below has failed to adhere to its own admonition in this case. In doing so it has created a direct conflict with another Circuit's ruling on the effect of *Doe v. Commonwealth's Attorney* on the present controversy. Its opinion is contrary to the weight of authority, since most federal courts which have had occasion to consider *Doe* have recognized it as binding and as limiting the constitutional right of privacy to heterosexual conduct. *See Beller v. Middendorf,* 632 F.2d 788, 809 (9th Cir. 1980). It is urged that this conflict, and the importance of the issues involved in this matter, warrant review by this Court.

II. THE COURT BELOW ERRED IN CONCLUDING THAT GEORGIA'S SODOMY STATUTE INFRINGES UPON FUNDAMENTAL CONSTITUTIONAL RIGHTS OF HOMOSEXUALS AND BY REQUIRING THE STATE TO SHOW A COMPELLING INTEREST TO SUPPORT ITS CONSTITUTIONALITY, THUS RAISING SIGNIFICANT AND RECURRING QUESTIONS AS TO THE ABILITY OF THE STATES TO REGULATE PRIVATE CONDUCT.

In *Paris Adult Theatre I v. Slaton,* 413 U.S. 49 (1973) this Court stated:

Our prior decisions recognizing a right to privacy guaranteed by the Fourteenth Amendment included "only personal rights that can be deemed 'fundamental' or 'implicit in the concept of ordered liberty.'" [Citations omitted.] This privacy right encompasses and protects the personal intimacies of the home, the family, marriage, motherhood, procreation and child rearing. [Citations omitted.]

Id. at 65.

It is urged that these traditional zones of protected privacy have not been enlarged in any subsequent decisions of this court. Even *Carey v. Population Services International, supra,* dealt with the individual's right to make decisions to prevent contraception. 431 U.S. at 688.

After recounting these zones of privacy, the lower court in the case *sub judice* perceived an analogy between the zone of marital intimacy and homosexual sodomy stating that "[f]or some, the sexual activity in question here serves the same purpose as the intimacy of marriage." *Hardwick* at 122. The panel also concluded that the same privacy interests identified in *Stanley v. Georgia,* 394 U.S. 557 (1969) (the right to be free from governmental interference with the private possession of obscene material) are implicated in private consensual sodomy.

As noted by Judge Gabrielli in his dissenting opinion in *People v. Onofre,* 51 N.Y.2d 476, 415 N.E.2d 936, *cert. denied* 451 U.S. 987 (1980), decisions relating purely to sexual gratification have been subject to government regulation and proscription throughout the history of western civilization.

Scholars from Aquinas to Blackstone considered even consensual sodomy to be as heinous as the crime of rape (43 Aquinas, *Summa Theologiae,* pp. 246-249 [Gilby ed.], 4 *Blackstone's Commentaries,* 215; see, generally, Richards, Unnatural Acts and the Constitutional Right to Privacy: A Moral Theory, 45 Fordham L. Rev. 1281, 1292-98). Indeed, as early as 1553 during the reign of Henry VIII, England enacted statutes prohibiting sodomy which became part of the American common law at the time of the American Revolution and were later embodied in the penal codes of the various states. . . . [I]t simply cannot be said that such freedom is an integral part of our concept of ordered liberty as embodied in the due process clauses of the Fifth and Fourteenth Amendments.

Id. at 503-504, 4215 N.E.2d at 949 (Gabrielli, J., dissenting). In contrast, this Court in *Roe v. Wade,* 410 U.S. 113 (1973) [,] in finding a limited right of privacy with respect to abortion decisions, conducted a historical review of ancient attitudes, and the common law and statutory laws of England and America, and concluded that at the time of the adoption of our Constitution, and through a major portion of the 19th Century, ". . . a woman enjoyed a substantially broader right to terminate pregnancy than she does in most states today." 410 U.S. at 140, 93 S. Ct. at 720. No similar right to engage in sodomy existed at the time of the adoption of our Constitution. It is therefore urged that sodomy of any kind, including that which perchance takes place in private, cannot be considered a fundamental right or implicit in the concept of ordered liberty. Such a right is not contemplated by the Constitution. *See generally, Paris Adult Theatre I, supra.*

Members of this Court have indicated that they would not go so far as the lower court has in this case. In *Carey, supra,* Justice White, in his concurring opinion, stated, "I do not regard the opinion, however, as declaring unconstitutional any state law forbidding extra-marital relations." 431 U.S. at 702. Justice Powell, in his concurrence, rejected any view which would subject all state regulation affecting adult sexual relations to the strictest standard of review. "Neither our precedents nor sound principles of constitutional analysis require state legislation to meet the exacting 'compelling state interest' standard wherever it implicates sexual freedom." 431 U.S. at 705. Justice Rehnquist, in a footnote to his dissent, referred to the fact that the facial constitutionality of sodomy statutes has "definitively" been established, citing *Doe v. Commonwealth's Attorney, supra,* 431 U.S. at 718, n.2. (Rehnquist, J. dissenting).

Indeed the majority opinion in *Carey,* in footnote 5, expressly denied that it was holding that state laws must meet the compelling state interest test whenever sexual freedom is implicated, but only when they infringe upon an individual's decision to prevent conception or terminate pregnancy. 431 U.S. at 688, n.5.

Justice Blackmun, in writing for the Court in *Roe v. Wade, supra,* recognized that the right of privacy is not absolute:

> In fact, it is not clear to us that the claim asserted by some *amici* that one has an unlimited right to do with one's body as one pleases bears a close relationship to the right of privacy previously articulated in the Court's decisions. The Court has refused to recognize an unlimited right of this kind in the past. *Jacobson v. Massachusetts,* 197 U.S. 11 (1905). [Other citation omitted.]

This Court in *Paris Adult Theatre I, supra,* made it clear that the states do have the right to make unprovable assumptions lacking in scientifically certain criteria, in order to protect a social interest in order and morality. "As Chief Justice Warren stated, there is a 'right of the nation and of the states to maintain a decent society. . . .'" *Paris Adult Theatre I v. Slaton,* 413 U.S. at 59-60, quoting *Jacobellis v. Ohio,* 378 U.S. 184, 199 (1964) (Warren, C.J., dissenting). Thus it was held that even though there might be no conclusive proof of a connection between antisocial behavior and obscene material, it was within the power of the General Assembly of Georgia to make that determination. The State of Georgia has made a similar conclusion with respect to sodomy.

Finally, the Court in *Dronenburg v. Zech,* 741 F.2d 1388, *reh. denied,* 746 F.2d 1579 (D.C. Cir. 1984) [,] was unable to find any principle which would apply a right of privacy to homosexual conduct. 741 F.2d at 1395-96.

It is urged that the Eleventh Circuit's opinion purports to create a right of privacy where none has previously existed. It will substantially impede the ability of Georgia and her sister states to legislate in any area which touches upon moral issues. The decision below calls into question numerous statutes proscribing personal, private consensual conduct such as suicide, prostitution, polygamy, adultery, and fornication, *Paris Adult Theatre I v. Sloton, supra,* 413 U.S. at 69, 93 S. Ct. at 2641, n.15, and those laws prohibiting the private possession and use of illegal drugs, such as marijuana. The decision raises significant questions relating to the relationships of government, the Constitution, state laws and individual actions which substantially impact on the traditional mores of this nation.

CONCLUSION

Petitioner shows that the decision below is erroneous and constitutes a precedent-setting error of exceptional importance. The Court of Appeals for the Eleventh Circuit has failed to follow binding precedent of this Court and has rendered an opinion in direct conflict with that of the Court of Appeals for the District of Columbia. *Dronenburg v. Zech,* 741 F.2d 388, *reh. denied,* 748 F.2d 1579 (D.C. Cir. 1984).

The lower court's opinion purports to create a new right under the federal Constitution which has never been recognized by this Court. In doing so, the lower court's opinion has substantially diminished the ability of the state to enact legislation having as its object the preservation of a decent and moral society. The effects of the opinion, if left to stand, will reach well beyond the issues presented herein. For these reasons, a writ of certiorari should issue to review the judgment and opinion of the Eleventh Circuit.

---

ii. The Brief in Opposition

MICHAEL J. BOWERS,
ATTORNEY GENERAL OF GEORGIA,
Petitioner,
v.
MICHAEL HARDWICK, AND
JOHN AND MARY DOE,
Respondents.

BRIEF OF RESPONDENTS IN OPPOSITION TO PETITION FOR A WRIT OF CERTIORARI TO THE UNITED STATES COURT OF APPEALS FOR THE ELEVENTH CIRCUIT

KATHLEEN L. WILDE
Attorney for Respondents
Cooperating Attorney, ACLU of Georgia . . .

STATEMENT OF THE CASE

On August 3, 1982, Respondent Michael Hardwick, a 29-year-old gay man, was arrested and charged by the Atlanta Police Department with committing sodomy with another consenting adult in the bedroom of his home. The offense of sodomy, punishable by one to twenty years in prison, criminalizes "any sexual act involving the sex organs of one person and the mouth or anus of another." Official Code of Georgia Annotated (O.C.G.A.) §16-6-2 (1984). The statute applies to all persons, whether single or married, heterosexual or homosexual.

Hardwick's case was heard by the Atlanta Municipal Court, and bound over to the Superior Court of Fulton County. However, the District Attorney's office has not presented the case to the grand jury, and has formally stated that, unless further evidence develops, the case will not be presented. Hence, there is no prosecution pending; but neither is there any criminal state court forum in which Hardwick can raise his constitutional claims. And, as Hardwick regularly engages in private homosexual acts, and will do so in the future, he, like all other homosexuals in Georgia, is in imminent danger of arrest, prosecution, and potential imprisonment.

On February 14, 1983, Hardwick, together with John and Mary Doe, a married couple who feared prosecution under the same statute, filed their complaint in Federal Court, seeking a declaratory judgment that O.C.G.A. §16-6-2 (1984), as applied to private sexual conduct between consenting adults, is unconstitutional.

SUMMARY OF ARGUMENT

The Eleventh Circuit correctly concluded that this Court's summary affirmance in *Doe v. Commonwealth's Attorney* was not binding precedent which required the dismissal of Hardwick's constitutional claims. That conclusion was based on well-established rules as to the limited precedential value of summary affirmances. Petitioner's contention that a summary affirmance without opinion was intended to resolve the complex constitutional question of privacy protection for homosexuals is rebutted by decisions of this Court issued subsequent to *Doe,* and by substantial authority from both state and federal courts that have considered the issue.

In its present procedural posture, the *Hardwick* case neither presents a ripe conflict with any other circuit nor frames an issue sufficiently concrete to merit this Court's attention. The Eleventh Circuit did not hold the challenged statute unconstitutional, but merely stated the appropriate constitutional standard in the abstract and remanded the case for trial. The instant case thus does not yet present a ripe conflict with the recent Fifth Circuit decision in *Baker v. Wade,* nor does it conflict with the D.C. Circuit decision in *Dronenburg v. Zech,* a military case not involving a challenge to the military sodomy law.

The Eleventh Circuit correctly found that the Georgia sodomy statute, to the extent that it sought to criminalize private sexual conduct between consenting homosexual adults, infringes upon the fundamental constitutional right to personal autonomy and privacy. The statute implicates important associational interests which cannot be impeded without a compelling state interest. In reaching its conclusion, the Eleventh Circuit properly applied precedent regarding the right of privacy in intimate personal relationships to the specific factual situation presented by Hardwick.

The Eleventh Circuit decision in this case involves no unwarranted extensions of existing law, and in no way jeopardized Georgia's ability to legislate in legitimate spheres of state regulation. The narrow constitutional right at issue here protects only private, consensual, sexual conduct between adults.

REASONS FOR DENYING THE WRIT

I. THE ELEVENTH CIRCUIT CORRECTLY CONCLUDED THAT *DOE V. COMMONWEALTH'S ATTORNEY* DOES NOT CONSTITUTE BINDING PRECEDENT.

After careful review, the Eleventh Circuit concluded that this Court's summary affirmance of *Doe v. Commonwealth's Attorney for the City of Richmond,* 425 U.S. 901 (1976), *aff'g mem,* 403 F. Supp. 1199 (E.D. Va. 1975), *reh'g denied,* 425 U.S. 985 (1976) was not binding precedent which required the dismissal of Hardwick's constitutional claims. In doing so, the Court applied well-established rules on the limited precedential value of such affirmances. That it reached the proper conclusion is supported by this Court's earlier decisions in *Carey v. Population Services,* 431 U.S. 678 (1977) and *New York v. Uplinger,* 58 N.Y.2d 936 (1983), *writ dismissed as improvidently granted,* __ U.S. __, 104 S. Ct. 2332 (1984).

Defendants below had contended, and the District Court had agreed, that the summary affirmance in *Doe* precluded consideration of Plaintiff Hardwick's constitutional claims. The threshold issue on appeal thus became the meaning of *Doe.* While clearly acknowledging that a summary affirmance by the Supreme Court has binding precedential effect, *Hicks v. Miranda,* 422 U.S. 332, 344 (1975), the Eleventh Circuit undertook the difficult task of identifying the precise limits of the summary affirmance in *Doe v. Commonwealth's Attorney.* The panel diligently applied the principles established in *Mandel v. Bradley,* 432 U.S. 173 (1977), *Illinois State Board of Elections v. Socialist Workers Party,* 440 U.S. 173, 181-83 (1979) and *Metromedia, Inc. v. City of San Diego,* 453 U.S. 490, 499 (1981), carefully examining both the jurisdictional statement and the facts in *Doe.* It concluded that the "most narrow plausible rationale for [this Court's] summary decision" in *Doe* was plaintiffs' lack of standing. Accordingly, the Court held that the summary affirmance of *Doe* was not based upon, nor did it foreclose consideration of, the constitutional issues raised by Hardwick in the instant case.

Petitioner's contention that a summary affirmance without opinion was intended to resolve the complex constitutional question of privacy protection for homosexuals is rebutted by this Court's decisions in *Carey* and *Uplinger,* issued subsequent to *Doe.* Those cases demonstrate that the Eleventh Circuit analysis of the meaning of *Doe* was not based on mere "speculation" or "unwarranted assumptions," as the Petitioner contends, Petition for *Certiorari, Bowers v. Hardwick,* No. 85-140, at 5, and that the Eleventh Circuit properly performed its difficult task in defining the limits of *Doe.*

Footnotes 5 and 7 in *Carey* and the opinion dismissing *certiorari* in *Uplinger* clearly established that *Doe* is not binding precedent on the specific issues raised by Hardwick, and that sexual privacy between homosexuals is among the "important constitutional issues", *New York v. Uplinger,* 104 S. Ct. at 2334, which the Court has yet to definitively address. Indeed, as the panel correctly noted, those decisions constitute "doctrinal developments" sufficient in and of themselves to relieve lower Courts from any obligation to adhere to the reasoning of the three judge district court's decision in *Doe. Hardwick v. Bowers,* 760 F.2d 1202, 1209-1210 (11th Cir. 1985).

Other state and federal courts, when presented with this question, have taken the same view as the Eleventh Circuit on the meaning of *Doe v. Commonwealth's Attorney.* In a decision in which this Court denied *certiorari,* the New York Court of Appeals held that *Doe* was not an obstacle to declaring that homosexuals are covered under the constitutional right to privacy. *People v. Onofre,* 51 N.Y.2d 476

(N.Y. 1980), *cert. denied,* 451 U.S. 987 (1981). *See also State v. Saunders,* 75 N.J. 200, 381 A.2d 333, 341 (N.J. 1977); *Neville v. State,* 430 A.2d 570, 574 (Md. 1981). Similarly, the Tenth Circuit recently concluded that "whether some private consensual homosexual activity is constitutionally protected appears to be an unsettled question." *Rich v. Secretary of the Army,* 735 F.2d 1220, 1228 n.8 (10th Cir. 1984). *See also Beller v. Middendorf,* 632 F.2d 788 (9th Cir. 1980). The Eastern District of Wisconsin also has noted that "the law remains unsettled" on whether private homosexual acts are protected by the right of privacy. *Ben Shalom v. Secretary of Army,* 489 F. Supp. 964, 976 (E.D. Wis. 1980).

Thus, the conclusion reached by the Eleventh Circuit, that *Doe v. Commonwealth's Attorney* does not constitute binding precedent on the question of Hardwick's right to privacy, was eminently correct, and need not be examined by this Court.

II. THE ELEVENTH CIRCUIT HOLDING, WHICH LEAVES THE GEORGIA STATUTE IN PLACE PENDING DETERMINATION OF WHETHER IT IS JUSTIFIED BY A COMPELLING STATE INTEREST, NEITHER PRESENTS A RIPE CONFLICT WITH ANY OTHER CIRCUIT NOR FRAMES AN ISSUE SUFFICIENTLY CONCRETE TO MERIT THIS COURT'S ATTENTION.

In its present procedural posture, the *Hardwick* case neither presents a ripe conflict with any other circuit nor frames an issue sufficiently concrete to merit this Court's attention. After thorough analysis and discussion, the Eleventh Circuit properly concluded that *Doe v. Commonwealth's Attorney* was not binding on the merits, and that it was free to examine the substantial constitutional issues raised by *Hardwick.* The court did not hold the statute unconstitutional. It merely stated the appropriate constitutional test in the abstract, and remanded the case for trial. The Eleventh Circuit held that in order to prevail at trial, Georgia must prove "a compelling interest in regulating this behavior and that this statute is the most narrowly drawn means of safeguarding that interest," *Hardwick v. Bowers,* 760 F.2d at 1213. Accordingly, review by this Court would be premature.

Petitioner's contention that the Eleventh Circuit decision creates a "conflict in the circuits", Petition for *Certiorari* at 8, with *Dronenburg v. Zech,* 741 F.2d 388, *reh'g denied,* 746 F.2d 1579 (D.C. Cir. 1984), is incorrect. *Dronenburg* was a military case, and the panel discussion of the precedential value of *Doe* was *dicta.* Furthermore, the military regulation criminalizing private consensual sodomy was not even directly challenged in the case.

Nor is there yet a ripe conflict between the instant case and the recent Fifth Circuit decision in *Baker v. Wade,* F.2[d] *(en banc),* No. 82-1590 (5th Cir. Aug. 26, 1985). *Baker,* like the present case, involved a declaratory judgment challenge to the constitutionality of a state sodomy law. Unlike *Hardwick,* however, a full trial on the merits was held in *Baker,* after which a federal district court found the Texas sodomy law to be unconstitutional. *Baker v. Wade,* 553 F. Supp. 1121 (N.D. Tex. 1982), *appeal dismissed,* 743 F.2d 236 (5th Cir. 1984). In *Hardwick,* the Eleventh Circuit has not struck down the challenged statute, but has instead remanded the case for trial with instructions as to the appropriate constitutional standards to apply. Therefore, the issues presented by *Hardwick* are not yet framed concretely, and there is no ripe conflict with *Baker.*

III. THE FUNDAMENTAL CONSTITUTIONAL RIGHTS AT ISSUE IN *HARDWICK V. BOWERS* ARE WELL-ROOTED IN PRIOR CONSTITUTIONAL PRECEDENTS ON THE RIGHT OF PRIVACY AND DO NOT REQUIRE THIS COURT'S REVIEW.

The Eleventh Circuit found that Georgia sodomy statute, insofar as it sought to criminalize private sexual conduct between consenting homosexual adults, infringed upon Hardwick's fundamental constitutional right to personal autonomy and privacy. The statute, it held, implicated important intimate associational interests, which could not be impeded without a compelling state interest.

In reaching that conclusion, the Eleventh Circuit properly applied precedent regarding the right of privacy in intimate personal relationships to the factual situation presented by Hardwick. Its holding that the associational interests at issue fall within the protection of the Due Process clause of the Fourteenth Amendment construed in light of the Ninth Amendment was grounded firmly in this Court's recent decisions on privacy, including *Griswold v. Connecticut,* 381 U.S. 479 (1965), *Carey v. Population Services,* 431 U.S. 678, *Eisenstadt v. Baird,* 405 U.S. 438 (1972), and *Zablocki v. Redhail,* 434 U.S. 374 (1978). The opinion does not represent a departure from existing constitutional principles, as Petitioner contends, Petition for *Certiorari* at 8-12, but is, rather, the logical result of their application.

The full scope of the privacy right is as yet undefined. Its "outer limits" have not been established. *Carey v. Population Services, Inc.,* 431 U.S. at 684. However, this Court's decisions in *Carey* and *Eisenstadt* make it clear that the right of sexual privacy is the right of the individual to be free from unwarranted government intrusion into matters fundamentally affecting intimate personal decisions. Given the fact, as the Eleventh Circuit found in *Hardwick,* that "for some the sexual activity in question here serves the same purpose as the intimacy of marriage," 760 F.2d at 1212, there is no basis for excluding acts of sodomy carried out between consenting adults in private from the scope of constitutional protection.

Indeed, given the underlying purposes of the "associational" aspect of the privacy right, as explained by this Court in *Roberts v. United States Jaycees,* ____ U.S. ____, 104 S. Ct. 3244 (1984), the conduct sought to be protected in *Hardwick* falls squarely within the ambit of the First Amendment:

> []choices to enter into and maintain certain intimate human relationships must be secured against undue intrusion by the State because of the role of such relationships in safeguarding the individual freedom that is central to our constitutional scheme. In this respect, freedom of association receives protection as a fundamental element of personal liberty. . . .
>
> [T]he constitutional shelter afforded such relationships reflects the realization that individuals draw much of their emotional enrichment from close ties with others. Protecting these relationships from unwarranted state interference therefore safeguards the ability independently to define one's identity that is central to any concept of liberty. See, e.g., *Quilloin v. Walcott,* 434 U.S. 246, 255 (1978); *Smith v. Organization of Foster Services Int'l,* 431 U.S. 678, 684-6 (1977); *Cleveland Board of Education v. LaFleur,* 414 U.S. 632, 639-640 (1974); *Stanley v. Illinois,* 405 U.S. 645, 651-2 (1972); *Stanley v. Georgia,* 394 U.S. 557, 564 (1969); *Olmstead v. United States,* 277 U.S. 438, 478 (1928) (Brandeis, J. dissenting).

104 S. Ct. at 3249-50.

Moreover, the privacy rights previously recognized by this Court are not limited to marriage and family. As this Court stated in *Paris Adult Theatre I v. Slaton*, 413 U.S. 49, 65 (1973):

> Our prior decisions recognizing a right to privacy guaranteed by the Fourteenth Amendment included "only personal rights that can be deemed 'fundamental' or 'implicit' in the concept of ordered liberty." *Palko v. Connecticut*, 302 U.S. 319, 325 (1937); *Roe v. Wade*, 410 U.S. 113, 152 (1973). *This privacy right encompasses and protects the personal intimacies of the home*, the family, marriage, motherhood, procreation, and child rearing . . . [citing] *Stanley v. Georgia*. . . . (emphasis supplied).

It is significant that Hardwick was arrested for conduct which occurred in the privacy of his own bedroom. That arrest therefore implicated the heightened protections which come into play when a state attempts to regulate consensual intimate activities in the home, a "castle" historically protected from state interference. In light of this Court's decisions in *Payton v. New York*, 445 U.S. 573, 589-90 (1980), and *Stanley v. Georgia*, 394 U.S. 557 (1969), the Eleventh Circuit was compelled to conclude that the privacy interests articulated by Hardwick were of constitutional dimension. Whatever the State's power to regulate certain activities in public, the acts which underlie this case occurred in the home, and require a compelling governmental interest to justify intrusion upon them by the State.

Georgia's contention that the *Hardwick* decision, unless reviewed and reversed by this Court, will somehow wreak havoc in the courts and streets of Georgia and its sister states is simply unfounded. *Hardwick* involves no unwarranted extensions of existing law, and does not present the issue of Georgia's capacity to legislate in such spheres of regulation as suicide, drug abuse, prostitution or bigamy. As this Court noted in *Paris Adult Theatre I v. Slaton*, it is not for the courts "to resolve empirical uncertainties underlying state legislation, save in the exceptional case where that legislation plainly impinges upon rights protected by the Constitution itself." 413 U.S. at 60. The "rights protected by the Constitution" in this case are narrow. The only activity which the Eleventh Circuit has said is not a proper area for state regulation, absent a compelling state interest, is private, consensual sexual activity between adults.

The decision of the Eleventh Circuit was thus well-grounded in established constitutional principles, and contrary to Petitioner's assertion, does not involve the creation of any new rights. Accordingly, there is no basis for this Court's review.

CONCLUSION

The decision of the Eleventh Circuit as to both the meaning of this Court's summary affirmance in *Doe v. Commonwealth's Attorney* and the constitutional standard by which Georgia's sodomy statute must be reviewed is eminently correct, and requires no review by this Court. Accordingly, the petition for *certiorari* should be denied.

———————————————

iii. The Reply Brief

MICHAEL J. BOWERS,
ATTORNEY GENERAL OF GEORGIA,
Petitioner,

v.

MICHAEL HARDWICK, AND
JOHN AND MARY DOE,
Respondents.

BRIEF OF PETITIONER IN REPLY TO RESPONDENT'S BRIEF IN OPPOSITION TO THE PETITION FOR CERTIORARI

> MICHAEL J. BOWERS
> Attorney General
> MARION O. GORDON
> First Assistant, Attorney General
> DARYL A. ROBINSON
> Senior Assistant, Attorney General
> MICHAEL E. HOBBS
> Senior Assistant, Attorney General . . .

STATEMENT OF THE CASE

Petitioner hereby adopts and incorporates herein by reference the statement of the case contained in the petition for a writ of certiorari, and will not restate the statement of the case herein.

SUMMARY OF ARGUMENT

Contrary to Respondents' assertion, the recent decision of the Fifth Circuit Court of Appeals in *Baker v. Wade,* 769 F.2d 289 (5th Cir. 1985) (en banc) does present a ripe conflict with the Eleventh Circuit's decision in the case *sub judice.* The en banc decision in *Baker,* which upheld the constitutionality of Texas' sodomy statute, was founded squarely upon this Court's summary affirmance in *Doe v. Commonwealth's Attorney for the City of Richmond,* 425 U.S. 901 (1976), *aff'g* 403 F. Supp. 1199 (E.D. Va. 1975, *reh'g denied,* 425 U.S. 985 (1976). The *Baker* decision held that *Doe*'s summary affirmance is binding precedent, and that it should be followed until this Court determines otherwise. This presents a clear conflict with the decision below. *See also Dronenburg v. Zech,* 741 F.2d 388, *reh'g denied* 746 F.2d 1579 (D.C. Cir. 1984).

In addition, homosexual sodomy, like polygamy, is not protected by any "associational interest" embodied in a constitutional right of privacy. See *Potter v. Murray City,* 760 F.2d 1065 (10th Cir. 1985).

REASONS FOR GRANTING WRIT

I. THE DECISION BELOW CONFLICTS DIRECTLY WITH THE DECISION OF THE COURT OF APPEALS FOR THE FIFTH CIRCUIT IN *BAKER V. WADE* BY ERRONEOUSLY CONCLUDING THAT *DOE V. COMMONWEALTH'S ATTORNEY* DOES NOT CONSTITUTE BINDING PRECEDENT.

In the petition for certiorari, Attorney General Bowers demonstrated that the decision below was contrary to *Dronenburg v. Zech,* 741 F.2d 1388, 1392, *reh'g denied,*

746 F.2d 1579 (D.C. Cir. 1984). Since the filing of the petition for certiorari, the Fifth Circuit Court of Appeals, in an en banc decision, upheld the constitutionality of Texas' sodomy statute. *Baker v. Wade,* 769 F.2d 289 (5th Cir. 1985) (en banc). The decision in that case was specifically founded upon the continuing efficacy of *Doe v. Commonwealth's Attorney,* 425 U.S. 901 (1976). The *Baker* court stated as follows:

> We consider the decision of the Court in *Doe* to be binding upon us for the reasons stated by the District of Columbia circuit in *Dronenburg v. Zech,* 741 F.2d 1388, 1391-92 (D.C. Cir. 1984), and by Judge Kravitch in her dissent to the Eleventh Circuit opinion in *Hardwick v. Bowers,* 760 F.2d 1202, 1213-16 (11th Cir. 1985). There can be no question but that the decision of the Supreme Court in *Doe* was on the merits of the case, not on the standing of the plaintiffs to bring the suit. We should follow that controlling authority until the Supreme Court itself has issued an unequivocal statement that *Doe* no longer controls.

Id., at 292.

    Respondents claim that the issues presented by the *Hardwick* opinion are not yet framed concretely, and that there is no ripe conflict between *Hardwick* and *Baker.* To the contrary, Petitioner shows that the issues are certainly framed with exacting clarity: Is *Doe* binding precedent? Is there a fundamental right of privacy protecting homosexual conduct? If there is such a fundamental right, must Georgia's sodomy statute withstand the strict scrutiny required in the demonstration of a "compelling state interest?"

    The decision below found that *Doe* is not binding and that there is a fundamental right to engage in homosexual sodomy. The Eleventh Circuit has mandated that the statute be tested under the compelling state interest criteria. On the other hand, both *Baker* and *Dronenburg* conclude that *Doe* is binding precedent. Both *Baker* and *Dronenburg* conclude that there is no right of privacy to engage in consensual sodomy. Both *Baker* and *Dronenburg* conclude that the standard of review is whether the statute is rationally related to a legitimate state purpose.

    In *Baker,* albeit in the context of equal protection, the Fifth Circuit stated:

> In view of the strong objection to homosexual conduct, which has prevailed in western culture for the past seven centuries, we cannot say that §21.06 is 'totally unrelated to the pursuit of' *Id.,* at 809, 89 S. Ct. at 1408, 22 L. Ed. 2d at 745, implementing morality, a permissible goal, *Burman v. Parker,* 348 U.S. 26, 32, 75 S. Ct. 98, 102, 99 L. Ed. 27 (1954); *Dronenburg v. Zech,* 741 F.2d 1388, 1398 (D.C. Cir. 1984).

Id., at 292.

    It is thus urged that there is a remarkable conflict between the Eleventh Circuit and the Fifth and District of Columbia Circuits. It is also urged that this conflict is ripe for reconciliation by this Court.

II. THE ASSOCIATIONAL ASPECTS OF THE RIGHT OF PRIVACY DO NOT EXTEND TO HOMOSEXUAL ACTS OF SODOMY.

    The opinion below held that while homosexual sodomy is not procreative, "it does involve important associational interests." *Hardwick v. Bowers,* 760 F.2d 1202, 1211 (11th Cir. 1985). The Court then proceeded to equate sodomy with the intimacy of marriage. Respondents urge that the Eleventh Circuit's conclusion that sodomy serves the same purpose, for at least some homosexuals, as marital intimacy, demands the conclusion that sodomy is an activity protected as a fundamental right of privacy, because of its "associational" aspects.

However, Petitioner maintains that if this were the law, then statutes prohibiting polygamy must also fall. The polygamous marriage, it can certainly be argued, serves the same purpose for some as the monogamous marriage. Associational aspects are certainly present. Yet, in *Potter v. Murray City,* 760 F.2d 1065 (10th Cir. 1985), the Court of Appeals for the Tenth Circuit found no authority for extending the right of privacy to polygamous marriages. *Cf. Paris Adult Theater I v. Slaton,* 413 U.S. 49, 68 at n.15 (1973). Likewise, it is asserted that the decision below is unsupported by authority and represents an extension of constitutional protections well beyond what has been recognized by this Court.

CONCLUSION

For the foregoing reasons, and those set forth in the original petition for a writ of certiorari, it is urged that the writ should be issued to review the judgment and opinion below.

Notes and Questions

1. As noted above, much of the disagreement between the parties in the *Bowers* certiorari papers involved the precedential authority of a summary affirmance issued by the Supreme Court. Summary affirmances arise when the Court finds that the decision below was correct and that no substantial question was raised, leading the Court to decline plenary consideration and summarily affirm the decision below. The Court has declared that summary affirmances are decisions on the merits entitled to precedential effect. *See, e.g., Meek v. Pittenger,* 421 U.S. 349, 367 n.16 (1975); *Richardson v. Ramirez,* 418 U.S. 24, 53 (1974). Nevertheless, other statements by the Court have created questions and confusion surrounding the precedential authority of summary affirmances. *See, e.g., Edelman v. Jordan,* 415 U.S. 651, 670-671 (1974) ("summary affirmances obviously are of precedential value" but "[e]qually important obviously they are not of the same precedential value as would be an opinion of this Court treating the question on the merits").

2. Consistent with Supreme Court Rule 10, the parties focused largely on the presence or absence of a circuit split and the importance of the issues presented in their cert papers. What other factors do the parties highlight in their certiorari papers?

3. What is the strongest argument made by petitioner in favor of granting certiorari? What was the strongest argument made by respondent in favor of denying certiorari? If you had been counsel for either the petitioner or the respondent, what, if anything, would you have done differently in your cert-stage papers?

4. If you were a Justice on the Court in the 1985 Term reviewing the certiorari petition filed in *Bowers,* would you have voted to grant or deny certiorari? Why or why not?

2. In-Chambers Review of Cert Papers and the Role of the Cert Pool

Once a petition for a writ of certiorari is filed and distributed within the Court, in-chambers review of the certiorari petition (and any accompanying brief in opposition, reply brief, and amicus briefs that have been filed) begins. It is at this stage that the Justices—with the help of their law clerks—must determine which petitions for certiorari should be granted and thereby win a spot on the Court's prized docket. All but one of the current Justices (Justice Samuel Alito) manage this time-consuming process of separating the wheat from the chaff by relying upon the "cert pool." The cert pool involves the Justices pooling their law clerks and assigning one law clerk from the pool to each certiorari petition. The assignments are made randomly through an administrative process rather than based on the subject matter of the petitions or the law clerk's individual preferences. Once a law clerk is assigned to a particular petition, the law clerk must analyze and write up a pool memorandum on the petition for the benefit of all of the Justices who participate in the pool. Law clerks who have participated in the pool "have estimated that they spend from 15 minutes to (in rare cases) one day preparing pool memos, which typically run from 2-5 pages in length." Timothy S. Bishop, Jeffrey Sarles & Stephen Kane, *Tips on Petitioning for Certiorari in the United States Supreme Court,* The Circuit Rider 28 (May 2007). Clerks in the other chambers then "annotate the pool memo or draft a supplemental memo" for their individual Justices to highlight any issues that might interest their own Justices or to note how their views differ from the pool writer. *Id.*

In contrast, in Justice Alito's chambers, Justice Alito's law clerks, rather than a pool clerk, help Justice Alito review and analyze all cert petitions. Similarly, when Justice Stevens was on the Court, he opted not to participate in the cert pool. Instead, Justice Stevens asked his law clerks to divide the certiorari petitions among themselves and to write short memos only for petitions that the clerks felt warranted the Justice's attention.

a. An Introduction to the Cert Pool

William H. Rehnquist, The Supreme Court

232-234 (2001)

During the first term in which I served on the Court, there was no "cert pool," and each chambers did all of its own certiorari work as well as its other work. I could not help but notice that my clerks were frequently pressed for time, scrambling between having memos describing the certiorari petitions ready when they should be, and drafts or revisions of Court opinions or dissents ready when they should have been. Lewis Powell, who had come on the Court at the same time I had, was also bothered by this phenomenon, and suggested that all the law clerks be pooled for purposes of writing memos describing the facts and contentions in each petition for certiorari. As it turned out, only five members of the Court as it then stood decided to join the pool, but when Sandra O'Connor was appointed in 1981 she became the sixth member of the pool. . . .

Each of the thirty-odd law clerks in the pool divide among themselves the task of writing memos outlining the facts and contentions of each of the . . . petitions for certiorari that are filed each term, and these memos are then circulated to the chambers whose clerks comprise the pool. When the memos come into my chambers, I ask my clerks to divide them up three ways, and that each law clerk read the memo and, if necessary, go back to the petition and response in order to make a recommendation to me as to whether the petition should be granted or denied. . . .

When I get the annotated certiorari memos from my law clerks, I review the memos and indicate on them the way I intend to vote at conference. I don't necessarily always vote the way I had planned to vote, however; something said at conference may persuade me either to shift from a "deny" to a "grant" or vice versa.

... As soon as I am confident that my new law clerks are reliable, I take their word and that of the pool memo writer as to the underlying facts and contentions of the parties in the various petitions, and with a large majority of the petitions, it is not necessary to go any further than the pool memo. In cases that seem from the memo perhaps to warrant a vote to grant certiorari, I may ask my clerk to further check out one of the issues, and may review the lower court opinion, the petition, and the response myself. ...

... I have been asked whether or not the use of the law clerks in a cert pool didn't represent the abandonment of the justices' responsibilities to a sort of internal bureaucracy. I certainly do not think so. The individual justices are quite free to disregard whatever recommendation the writer of the pool memo may have made, as well as the recommendation of his own law clerks, but this is not a complete answer to the criticism. It is one thing to do the work yourself, and it is another thing to simply approve the recommendation of another person who has done the work. But the decision whether to grant certiorari is a much more "channeled" decision than the decision as to how a case should be decided on the merits; there are really only two or three factors involved in the certiorari decision—conflict with other courts, general importance, and perception that the decision is wrong in light of Supreme Court precedent. Each of these factors is one that a well-trained law clerk is capable of evaluating, and the justices, of course, having been in the certiorari-granting business term after term, are quite familiar with many of the issues that come up. I would feel entirely different about a system that assigned preparation of "bench memos"—memoranda that summarize the contention of the parties and recommend a particular result in an argued case—to one law clerk in a large pool of clerks.

Barbara Palmer, The "Bermuda Triangle?" The Cert Pool and Its Influence over the Supreme Court's Agenda

18 Const. Comment. 105-116, 118-120 (2001)

It has been called a "monopoly," a "swamp," a "Leviathan," and even "the Bermuda Triangle." The culprit: the Supreme Court's cert pool, the system of randomly assigning petitions for review to a single clerk for a recommendation regarding acceptance or denial of a case. Former Supreme Court clerk and solicitor general, Kenneth Starr, recently lamented that Supreme Court justices have abdicated their responsibility in screening cases for review and have ceded too much power to their clerks; cases worthy of the justices['] attention go into the cert pool, but they never come out. According to Starr, the cert pool "is at war with Justice Louis Brandeis' proud proclamation that the justices, unlike high government officials from the other branches, do their own work." Moreover, the cert pool "squander[s] a precious national resource—the time and energy of the justices themselves." Others agree that the cert pool is a "very dangerous proposition." In 1998, *USA Today* conducted a five-month study on the "effect and growing influence of law clerks," with several stories devoted to the influence of the cert pool. In addition, at least one

Justice has been publicly critical of this practice, Justice Stevens. All of this has created a perception of the justices shirking their duties and clerks determining access to the nation's highest bench.

We actually know, however, very little about the role of the cert pool and the potential influence of clerks. Until now, there have been no systematic assessments of the role of the cert pool in determining the Court's agenda. With data from the 1971-1974 and 1984-1985 Terms, this analysis focuses on two criticisms of the cert pool: (1) the cert pool largely determines case selection; and (2) the cert pool fosters the creation of a "cert-pool voting bloc" among the Justices in the pool. . . .

I. THE CREATION OF THE CERT POOL

The cert pool was implemented in October of 1972, but there is very little historical record of its creation. Justice Powell is usually credited with the idea of streamlining the process of case selection, but Chief Justice Warren Burger also claimed that the cert pool was his idea. Unfortunately, archival documentation sheds little light on the development of the cert pool. In fact, if Powell was the primary force behind the cert pool, his personal papers are decidedly lacking in any kind of written records or memoranda regarding its creation.

Although the genesis of the cert pool is unclear, the logic behind its creation is clear: to save time and increase efficiency. During the 1960's, the Court's docket had grown rapidly, reaching over 4000 cases by the early 1970s, and the process of disposing of cases was unique to each Justice's chamber. With the cert pool, rather than each chamber reviewing every petition that came to the Court, petitions would be randomly assigned in equal numbers to each chamber that participated in the pool. A clerk would then evaluate the petition and write a "cert-pool memo," ranging from two to twenty pages long. The memo had a standard format, beginning with a statement of the issues raised, followed by summaries of the facts of the case, the lower court opinion, and the contentions and arguments presented by the parties. At the end of the memo, the clerk would discuss reasons why the cert petition should or should not be granted. This memo would be circulated to all the chambers in the pool. Upon receiving the pool memo, another clerk would "mark up" the memo for his or her specific justice, providing further analysis or disagreeing with the pool memo's assessment.

Unlike decisions on the merits and the circulation of opinion drafts, the Justices rarely debate the decision to grant review to a case. The time pressures created by the docket simply prohibit meaningful discussion of all but a few noteworthy cases. Given this, clerks in the cert pool could conceivably have a great deal of influence over the Court's agenda. With Justices spending so little time reviewing each petition, those in the pool would almost have to rely on cert-pool recommendations. The Justices in the pool share an important source of information that the non-cert pool justices lack, the cert-pool memo. As a result, the Justices in the pool would probably tend to vote together, creating a "cert pool voting bloc." Thus, it does seem logical to expect that the clerks in the cert-pool would largely determine which cases were selected. . . .

II. LOOKING AT CERT POOL MEMOS

Empirically assessing the influence of the cert pool poses some significant challenges. Agreement between Justices' votes and clerk recommendations "does not prove that the justice[s] [are] being influenced; the law clerks might be merely following the guidelines established" by the Court; in other words, they might be using the same criteria that the Justices are using. The Justices have specified particular criteria for screening cases, conflict among the circuits being one of the most important, and clerks in the cert pool obviously look for cases with these characteristics. On the other hand, some correlation between Justices' votes and pool-memo recommendations must be shown as a precondition of any inferences regarding influence. If there is little to no association between pool-memo recommendations, the Justices' choices, and the Court's docket, the cert pool is not influencing case selection.

The most substantial problem posed by any kind of study of the cert pool is the availability of data. Currently, Justice Lewis Powell's papers are the only public source of cert-pool memos. While Justice Powell did keep pool memos from cases the Court decided during his tenure, unfortunately he destroyed all his records on cases that were denied review. Consequently, it is impossible to assess how many times the Court voted to deny review when the cert-pool memo recommended that a case should be granted. It is also impossible to assess how many times the Court agreed when the cert-pool memo recommended that a case should be denied review. On the other hand, the vast majority of cases that come to the Court are "frivolous," particularly those filed in forma pauperis [i.f.p.] by prisoners. It stands to reason that, in i.f.p. cases in particular, the clerks and the justices would be in agreement regarding the denial of review, not because the clerks are exerting "influence" over the Justices in the cert pool, but because these are indeed cases that are not worthy of the Court's time. At any rate, while the lack of data from cases denied review results in an incomplete picture of the influence of the cert pool, until we have better data, it is the best we can do.

With these caveats, this analysis uses data from the cert-pool memos in the papers of Justice Lewis Powell from cases decided during the 1972-1974 Terms and the 1984-1985 Terms. This allows us to assess possible changes that may have developed over time. It is conceivable that the influence of the cert pool was relatively limited during the first years of its operation given its novelty, but grew over time as the practice became institutionalized. During the 1972-1974 terms, the members of the cert pool were Justices White, Blackmun, Powell, Rehnquist and Chief Justice Burger. Justices Douglas, Brennan, Stewart and Marshall were not members. During the 1984-1985 terms, the members of the cert pool were Justices White, Blackmun, Powell, Rehnquist, Chief Justice Burger, joined by Justice O'Connor. Justices Stevens, Marshall and Brennan were not members.

Data on justices' cert votes were collected from the papers of Justice William Brennan from the 1971-1974 terms and the 1984-1985 terms. With cert votes from before and after the implementation of the cert pool in 1972, not only can we assess the impact of the cert pool on the Court's agenda, but we can also explore whether there were any changes in the voting behavior of individual Justices.

When cases arrive at the Court, justices and their clerks have several options at their disposal in deciding what to do with a particular case. The most obvious are granting or denying review to petitions for certiorari, or noting probable jurisdiction or dismissing appeals. The Justices may also withhold a decision on review until more information has been gathered. They may "call for a response" (CFR), which allows the respondent (the winning party below) to file a brief in opposition to certiorari, or "call for the views of the solicitor general" (CVSG), in which the Court invites the solicitor general to file an amicus brief, typically in cases that will potentially effect the federal government. Cases can also be "held," pending a decision in another case, or treated summarily and vacated and remanded without full plenary review. . . .

How often did the Court actually do what the pool memo recommended? . . . In the early years of the cert pool, the decision to grant review was largely left open by the clerks. During the 1972-1974 period, the clerks specifically recommended that the Court grant review to the cert petition or appeal in only 24% of the cases that were granted review. . . .

III. The Cert Pool's Influence over the Court's Agenda

In other words, the cert-pool memo suggested that the Court grant review in only one-fourth of the cases that made it onto the Court's agenda.

In another 9% of cases, the cert-pool memo did not specifically state that the case should be granted review; but the recommendation was implied. These were cases in which the pool memo indicated that the criteria for granting review were present in a particular case, but did not specifically state that a case should be granted review.

In 15 cases, or 5%, the pool memo recommended that the case be denied, but the Court granted review; and in another 3%, the pool memo implied that there were no reasons to grant the case, but the Court did anyway. Thus, 8% of the time, the Court did the opposite of what the cert pool recommended.

During the first three years of the pool, by far the most common recommendation made by a cert-pool memo was no recommendation at all. In 47% of the cases that were granted review during the 1972-1974 terms, the clerk writing the memo did not take a specific position regarding whether the Court should grant review. In fact, it was quite common for the clerk to give reasons why the case should be granted, but also reasons why it should not be granted. In almost half of all cases, the clerk discussed pros and cons regarding whether the case should be granted, specifically leaving the judgment up to the Justices. . . .

In fact, it was not until the 1981 Term, almost ten years after the pool's creation, that clerks began consistently recommending a specific course of action in the "discussion" section at the end of the memo. In the beginning of the 1983 term, a change occurred in the format of pool memos, with the addition of a final section entitled "Recommendation." This section was typically only one to three sentences and provided a specific statement regarding what the Justices should do with the case. . . .

With cert-pool memos now making specific recommendations in every case, we would expect that the cert pool would have substantially more influence over the Court's agenda. It seems logical to expect that if the Justices now required the clerk writing the cert-pool memo to make a specific recommendation, they would follow it, at least most of the time. The addition of a short "Recommendation" section to the end of the pool memo suggests that, along with summary information, the Justices wanted to know what the cert-pool clerk thought should be done with the case.

. . . The Court took the pool memo's suggestion to grant cases about twice as often as it did in the early years of its operation, but this is at least partly due to the increased number of recommendations in the cert-pool memos. On the other hand, it is quite remarkable that during the 1984-1985 Terms, the pool memo recommended that a case be granted review in only half of the cases that were actually granted review. Even more strikingly, the cert pool had recommended that the

Court deny review in 24% of the cases granted. Thus, in almost one-fourth of the cases that were granted review, the Court ignored the recommendation of the cert-pool memo. This is also a substantial increase over the earlier period.

With the Court accepting half of the cases that the cert-pool memo recommended, the cert pool may have played a much larger role in the development of the Court's agenda by the 1984-85 terms. On the other hand, the high number of cases in which the Court rejected the cert-pool recommendation indicates that even when clerks suggested a specific course of action, the Justices still made their own independent judgments regarding case selection. Even in this later period, it appears that cert-pool memos were still serving primarily as summaries and not a screening-method. . . .

IV. The Cert Pool's Influence over the Cert-Pool Justices

If the Court did what the cert-pool memo recommended about half the time, was it, in fact, the Justices in the cert pool who voted to accept these cases, or was it some combination of Justices in and out of the pool? If the Justices in the pool were voting together in these cases, this would suggest that the pool fostered a voting bloc that was able to determine half of the Court's docket. The influence of the cert pool on the Court's agenda would be more indirect, but still important. . . .

Prior to the creation of the cert pool, during the 1971-1972 terms, Justices White, Blackmun, Powell, Rehnquist and Chief Justice Burger, the five Justices who eventually made up the cert pool, voted together as a bloc of five 32% of the time. Once the cert pool was implemented, they voted as a bloc of five 41% of the time, an increase of 9%. This does suggest that the cert pool contributed to the development of a cert-pool voting bloc. Further analysis, however, suggests a much murkier picture. Only four Justices' votes are needed to grant review, so a more accurate picture of the influence of the cert pool on the Court's agenda is drawn by considering whether the cert pool fostered a bloc of four Justices among the five in the cert pool. In other words, how often did at least four of the five justices in the cert pool vote together and ensure that a case was granted? . . . [T]here was virtually no difference between the 1971-1972 and the 1972-1974 periods in the number of cases that at least four cert-pool justices voted together. If anything, there was a slight decline, from 74% to 71%.

What is quite clear, however, is that by the 1984-1985 period, ten years later, vote cohesion among pool justices had substantially declined. Admittedly, the addition of one more Justice, O'Connor, increasing the pool to six, simply makes it harder for them to vote as a bloc. On the other hand, the other five Justices who were in the pool from 1972-1974 were still there in 1984-1985. They voted as a bloc of six in only 15% of the cases granted review. They voted as a bloc of four or more only 64% of the time, a measurable decrease from the earlier periods, particularly the pre-cert pool years. It should also be noted that by the 1984-85 period, in 5% of the cases granted review, no more than two Justices could agree on a chosen course of action; there were at least three different voting blocs among the Justices in the cert pool.

Although vote cohesion among the Justices in the cert pool declined over time, were these Justices still more cohesive than the Justices who were not in the pool? Given that the number of non-cert-pool Justices has always been smaller than the number of cert-pool Justices, comparisons between the two groups are not precise, but the data are noteworthy. . . . [V]ote cohesion among the four Justices who were not in the pool, Justices Douglas, Brennan, Stewart and Marshall, declined from 48% to 40% during the 1971-1972 to 1972-1974 periods. They did vote as a bloc of three, however, well over 80% of the time during both periods. Without a cert pool, these Justices' votes were still relatively cohesive. During the 1984-1985 period, the three remaining non-cert pool Justices voted together as a bloc only half the time, in 48% of the cases granted review, suggesting that the decline in vote cohesion over this ten-year period was a Court-wide phenomenon.

In the years immediately after the implementation of the cert pool, there was virtually no change in the vote cohesion of the Justices who joined the pool. Moreover, by the mid 1980s, when cert-pool memos were making explicit recommendations regarding which cases should be granted review, vote cohesion among the Justices in the pool declined. The Justices who were not in the cert pool also showed a relatively high level of vote cohesion that declined over time. All of this suggests that factors other than the cert pool were influencing the Justices' votes regarding certiorari. . . .

During the 1972-1974 period, in 41% of the cases in which the pool memo made a recommendation, all five Justices in the pool voted accordingly. In an additional 17%, four of the cert-pool Justices voted as the cert pool recommended. If these two categories are added, at least four of the Justices in the cert pool agreed with the cert pool recommendation 58% of the time. But it is important to keep in mind that during this early period, the data include only half of the cases granted review, given the high number of cases in which the cert-pool memo made no recommendation. Thus, during the early years of the cert pool, the cert-pool Justices voted cohesively as the cert-pool memo recommended in only one-fourth of the cases that made it onto the Court's docket. What is even more surprising is that 22% of the time, or about just as often, the Justices in the cert pool unanimously rejected the cert-pool recommendation.

During the 1984-1985 period, the Justices in the pool voted as a bloc of four or more in support of the cert-pool recommendation 55% of the time, essentially the same rate as the earlier period. Thus, even when the pool memo was more likely to make a recommendation, the Justices were not any more likely to follow it. The Justices were much less likely, however, to unanimously reject the cert-pool recommendation; they voted as a bloc of six against the cert-pool memo only 10% of the time.

None of this, however, accounts for the votes of the non-cert pool Justices. If the non-cert pool Justices are voting with the pool Justices in these cases, then something other than the pool-memo is catching the justices' attention. Unanimous cases are a prime example. During the 1972-1974 period, 22% of the time (17 cases) the Court unanimously agreed with the pool memo recommendation to grant review. During the 1984-1985 period, 8% of the time (16 cases) the Court unanimously agreed with the pool memo to grant review. These are cases that more than likely would have been granted review even without a cert-pool recommendation. Once these are accounted for, the potential influence of the cert pool declines even more.

In addition, the cert-pool Justices rarely voted as a bloc against the non-cert-pool Justices. During the 1972-1974 period, there was only one case in which the cert-pool memo recommended a grant, the cert-pool Justices agreed and voted as a bloc of four to grant, and the non-cert-pool justices voted as a unanimous bloc to deny. There were no cases in which all five cert-pool Justices voted against all four non-cert-pool Justices. During the 1984-1985 period, there were 29 cases in which the cert-pool memo recommended a grant, the cert-pool justices agreed and voted as a bloc of four or more to grant, and the non-cert-pool justices voted as a unanimous bloc to deny. This is a substantial increase from the earlier period, but is still only 19% of the cases in which the cert-pool memo recommended a grant. As a proportion of all cases ultimately granted review by the Court, this is a mere 10%. Thus, only in a few cases did a cert-pool voting bloc thwart the wishes of the non-cert pool Justices. In the vast majority of cases, Justices in the cert pool and out of the cert pool were voting together to determine which cases were selected. Once again, this suggests that the influence of the cert pool over the Court's agenda is mitigated by the independent judgments of the Justices themselves. Whatever influence the cert pool may have over the Court's agenda is more than likely attributable to the fact that the Justices and the clerks are using the same criteria to evaluate cases. . . .

. . . Thus, it appears that the cert pool serves primarily as a time-saver and not an initial case-screener; it merely provides the Justices with summarized versions of case records. To a surprisingly large extent, the cert pool does not determine which cases the Court ultimately decides. The decision to grant review is still based on the independent judgments of the Justices.

b. Sample Certiorari Memos

The following materials provide three illustrative examples of certiorari memoranda written by law clerks. The first memo, which is entitled a "preliminary memorandum," is the pool memo written in *Bowers v. Hardwick*, No. 85-140, which the Court ultimately granted and decided on the merits. 478 U.S. 186 (1986). The second memorandum, which is headed "TO: Justice Powell," is a short memo written by Justice Powell's law clerk "Bill" in *Bowers* explaining how his views on the cert petition in *Bowers* differed from the views of the author of the pool memo. The third memorandum is not from *Bowers* but rather is the pool memo written in the 1993 Term on whether to grant certiorari in a much more routine case, *Perreault v. Fishman*, No. 93-838, which the Court ultimately denied. 510 U.S. 1047 (1994). At the time these memoranda were written, they were internal Court documents, which were not available to the public or to the parties. As Chapter 8 discusses in more detail, it is only through the passage of time—as Justices retire or die and then choose to make their papers public—that these sorts of memoranda written by law clerks often surface for public viewing and scrutiny. The first two memoranda were pulled from the papers of Justice Lewis F. Powell, Jr., which are housed at Washington and Lee University School of Law. The third memorandum was taken from Justice Harry A. Blackmun's papers, which are now housed in the Library of Congress.

In reviewing the three memoranda, pay close attention to the different components of the memoranda and to how the law clerks characterize the parties' contentions. Also, be sure to contrast the level of attention given to the *Bowers* petition with that given to the *Perreault* petition, and consider whether you think giving law clerks significant power to decide how to characterize and frame the issues presented in certiorari papers gives law clerks too much power in the Court's docket-setting process.

i. The Cert Pool Memo in Bowers

Ginny - Flag for me.
Also attach
Bill's news

CA11 (2-1) ~~court and ability of~~ invalidated Ga's ~~sodomy~~ statute that makes sodomy a crime. & Decision based on "privacy" right.
In Doe v Commonwealth's atty, 425 U.S. 901 ('76) we summarily affirmed a three judge court decision that such a statute is valid. We wrote no opinion, & since have declined to take one of these case.
In this case, CA11 majority ~~s~~ held Doe was not controlling because it ~~t~~was based on standing concerns. J. Kravitch correctly argued that CA11 misread Doe.
CA5 has recognized ~~Doe~~ as controlling & follows it.

PRELIMINARY MEMORANDUM

We can again avoid this highly controversial issue by holding that CA11 misread Doe — i.e. reiterate binding effect of affirming a 3J/ct summarily.

October 11, 1985 Conference
List 1, Sheet 2

Or we simply could Deny despite conflict

No. 85-140-CFX

Bowers (Ga. Atty. Gen.)

v.

Hardwick et al.   OK
  (engaged in illegal,
  consensual sex acts)

Cert to CA11 (<u>Johnson</u>, Tuttle
  [Sr.CJ]; Kravitch, conc/diss)

Federal/Civil   Timely

1. <u>SUMMARY</u>: Petrs challenge CA11's conclusion that Ga.'s
sodomy statute implicates a fundamental right of a homosexual to
engage in private sexual activity with another consenting adult,
and CA11's holding that <u>Doe</u> v. <u>Commonwealth's Attorney for the</u>

GRANT only if the Court wishes to decide the case on the procedural issue (effect of summary affirmances). Otherwise, DENY. -
Bill (See my memo attached.)

- 2 -

City of Richmond, 425 U.S. 901 (1976), summarily aff'g, 403
F.Supp. 1199 (E.D. Va. 1975) did not prevent CAll from reaching
the merits.

2. FACTS AND PROCEEDINGS BELOW: A Ga. sodomy statute makes
it illegal to engage in oral or anal sex, and carries a penalty
of from one to 20 years in prison. O.C.G.A. §16-6-2. Resp Hardwick, a 29-year-old homosexual, was arrested for committing this
crime with a consenting male adult in the bedroom of Hardwick's
home. Charges were filed against Hardwick and after a hearing in
Municipal Court, he was bound over to the Superior Court. The
DA's office then declined to present the case to a grand jury
unless additional evidence developed.

Hardwick and a married couple, John and Mary Doe, (all three
are resps here) filed a declaratory judgment action in DC seeking
to have the statute declared unconstitutional. Hardwick alleged
in the complaint that he regularly engages in homosexual acts and
will continue to do so. The Does alleged that they wanted to
engage in sexual activity proscribed by the statute, but had been
chilled and deterred by the statute and Hardwick's arrest. The
defendants, who include petr, filed a motion to dismiss for failure to state a claim. The DC (ND Ga. Hall, J.) dismissed the
case on the authority of Doe v. Commonwealth's Attorney for the
City of Richmond, 425 U.S. 901 (1976), summarily aff'g, 403
F.Supp. 1199 (E.D. Va. 1975), in which the Court affirmed a
three-judge DC decision upholding the constitutionality of a
Virginia statute that prohibited consensual homosexual intercourse between adults in private.

- 3 -

CA11 reversed. Standing: Hardwick had standing because
there was a real and immediate threat of prosecution. Steffel v.
Thompson, 415 U.S. 452, 459 (1974). The State's past enforcement
of the statute against him raises a strong inference that the
state intends to prosecute him in the future. Hardwick contends
that his homosexual lifestyle will lead him to violate the statute regardless of its legality. And Hardwick is well suited to
challenge the law. Therefore, even if the State is not threatening to enforce the law, the existence of the statute provides a
sufficient basis on which to confer standing. See Babbitt v.
United Farm Workers National Union, 442 U.S. 289, 302-03 (1979).

The Does did not have standing. In the DC, the Does relied
on the existence of the statute, its literal application to their
situation, and the State's refusal to promise not to prosecute.
Before the appeal to CA11 they did not request discovery or an
evidentiary hearing to determine whether there was a threat of
future prosecution. Younger v. Harris, 401 U.S. 37, 40-42
(1971).

Judge Kravitch concurred on the standing issue.

Summary affirmance: The summary affirmance in Doe does not
control this case. A summary affirmance has binding precedential
effect, but represents approval of the judgment below and not the
reasoning. Mandel v. Bradley, 432 U.S. 173 (1975). The scope of
a summary affirmance is determined by examining the issues necessarily decided in reaching the result and the issues mentioned in
the jurisdictional statement. Illinois State Board of Elections
v. Socialist Workers Party, 440 U.S. 173, 181-83 (1979). In Doe,

- 4 -

the two indicia conflict. The jurisdictional statement asked whether Virginia's sodomy statute violated constitutional rights to privacy, due process and equal protection under the First, Fourth, Fifth, Ninth, and Fourteenth Amendments. But a narrower ground was available: the plaintiffs in Doe clearly lacked standing because they had neither been arrested nor presented any evidence of threatened or past prosecutions under the statute. A lower court should presume that the case was decided on the narrower ground. Otherwise, litigants would have too much control over the scope of summary dispositions.

The fact that the Court in Doe affirmed the dismissal on the merits does not demonstrate that the Court reached the merits of the case. Although an appellate court that finds a lack of standing normally vacates the judgment with instructions to dismiss for lack of subject matter jurisdiction, the Court has not uniformly followed that course. See Rizzo v. Goode, 423 U.S. 362 (1976); O'Shea v. Littleton, 414 U.S. 488 (1974). There is less reason to vacate with instructions to dismiss for lack of subject matter jurisdiction if the case presents prudential standing problems—as Doe appeared to—which do not bear on the power of a court to hear the case.

Similarly, the Court was not required to dismiss for lack of appellate jurisdiction over a three-judge court. Appellate jurisdiction is conferred only when the three-judge court is properly convened. 28 U.S.C. §1253. When a three-judge court dismisses a case due to a plaintiff's lack of constitutional standing, the Court will often dismiss an appeal and vacate the judg-

- 5 -

ment below. <u>Gonzalez</u> v. <u>Automatic Employees Credit Union</u>, 419 U.S. 90 (1974). But the Court has not held that it lacks jurisdiction over an appeal from a dismissal by a three-judge court where the plaintiff lacks standing. A three-judge court may be properly convened when it could decide the case on nonconstitutional grounds. <u>Alexander</u> v. <u>Fioto</u>, 430 U.S. 634 (1977). Therefore, if there was a prudential standing problem, the Court could affirm a dismissal by a three-judge court.

Judge Kravitch dissented, finding that <u>Doe</u> governed this case. A summary affirmance is a decision on the merits of a case. <u>Hicks</u> v. <u>Miranda</u>, 442 U.S. 332, 344 (1975). The jurisdictional statement, which limits the range of permissible lower court interpretations of a summary disposition, mentioned the substantive contitutional issues in the case but did not mention the issue of standing. Most important, if the plaintiffs in <u>Doe</u> lacked standing, the Court would not have had jurisdiction to decide the case. The Court would have had to dismiss the appeal instead of summarily affirming the lower court, which had decided the case on the merits. This would have been the case whether the lack of standing was on constitutional or prudential grounds. See <u>Poe</u> v. <u>Ullman</u>, 367 U.S. 497, 509 (1961).

Judge Kravitch conceded that the Court does not always vacate the judgment and remand for dismissal when it finds that the plaintiffs lacked standing. But the crucial issue is whether the Court could have summarily affirmed the lower court in <u>Doe</u> on the basis of lack of standing, or whether dismissal of the appeal would have been required. In <u>Rizzo</u> and <u>O'Shea</u>, the cases cited

- 6 -

by the majority, the Court <u>reversed</u> a lower court decision rendered on the merits in favor of the <u>plaintiffs.</u> The Court cites
no case in which the Court has <u>affirmed</u>, on the basis of lack of
standing, a lower court decision rendered on the merits in favor
of the <u>defendants</u>.

The majority said that even if <u>Doe</u> had resolved the merits,
later cases indicate that the Court views the constitutional
question as open. In <u>Carey</u> v. <u>Population Services</u>, 431 U.S. 678,
688 n. 5 (1977), the Court stated that it was not reaching the
question of whether and to what extent the Constitution prohibits
state statutes from regulating private consensual sexual behavior
among adults. A dissent criticized that language as conflicting
with <u>Doe</u>. The Court also indicated that the constitutionality of
a state law prohibiting consensual sodomy had been raised in <u>New
York</u> v. <u>Uplinger</u>, cert. granted, 104 S.Ct. 64 (1983), dismissed
as improvidently granted, 104 S.Ct. 2332 (1984).

Judge Kravitch did not think the question was open. <u>Carey</u>
simply acknowledges that the Court has not yet passed on the
validity of many kinds of state statutes regulating sexual conduct. It does not purport to overrule cases such as <u>Doe</u>. The
majority also infers too much from the dismissal of the writ of
cert in <u>Uplinger</u>.

<u>Merits:</u> The Court's right of privacy cases prohibit state
interference with certain decisions critical to personal autonomy. The Court has indicated that the intimate associations protected by the Constitution are not limited to those with a procreative purpose. See <u>Griswold</u> v. <u>Connecticut</u>, 381 U.S. 479

- 7 -

(1965) (striking down state law prohibiting the use of contraceptives because it interfered with sanctity of marriage relationship); Zablocki v. Redhail, 434 U.S. 374, 385-86 (1978) (listing
"associational interests" and procreation as separate interests
protected by the right to marry). The intimate associations
protected against state interference extend beyond the marriage
relationship. See Eisenstadt v. Baird, 405 U.S. 438 (1972) (prohibiting distribution of contraceptives to unmarried persons
unconstitutional because treats married and unmarried persons
differently). "For some, the sexual activity in question here
serves the same purpose as the intimacy of marriage," CA11 said.

In addition, having privacy in one's home covers some activities that would not normally merit constitutional protection.
See Payton v. New York, 445 U.S. 573, 589-90 (1980); Stanley v.
Georgia, 394 U.S. 557 (1969) (unconstitutional to criminalize the
possession of obscene films in one's home). Hardwick presents an
interest at least as substantial to that in Stanley, and one that
presents no public ramifications.

CA11 found that the statute implicated a fundamental right
protected by the Ninth Amendment and by substantive due process.
Accordingly, CA11 remanded the case for trial, at which time the
State must prove a compelling interest in regulating this behavior and a narrowly drawn statute.

3. CONTENTIONS: Petr contends that CA11's decision conflicts with the CADC's opinion in Dronenburg v. Zech, 741 F.2d
1388, 1392, reh'g denied, 746 F.2d 1579 (CADC 1984), which found
that Doe was binding on the lower courts as a decision on the

- 8 -

merits. Dronenberg also held that the Court's privacy cases do not cover a right to engage in homosexual conduct. Id., at 1395-96.

Decisions related purely to sexual gratification have been regulated by government throughout the history of Western civilization. By contrast, the Court said in Roe v. Wade, 410 U.S. 113, 140 (1973), that at the time the Constitution was adopted, a woman had a substantially broader right to terminate a pregnancy than she did in 1973. But no similar right to engage in sodomy existed or was contemplated when the Constitution was adopted. Therefore, sodomy of any kind, including that which takes place in private, cannot be considered a fundamental right or implicit in the concept of ordered liberty.

The Court in Paris Adult Theatre I v. Slaton, 413 U.S. 49 (1973) permitted States to make unprovable assumptions lacking in scientifically certain criteria in order to protect a social interest in order and morality. CA11's opinion will impede the States' ability to legislate in any area touching upon moral issues, and calls into question statutes proscribing such personal conduct as suicide, prostitution, polygamy, adultery, fornication, and the private possession and use of illegal drugs.

Resps largely adopt CA11's arguments in contending that Doe does not constitute binding precedent. This Court employed similar reasoning in Akron v. Akron Center for Reproductive Health, 462 U.S. 416 (1983) in discussing the precedential effects of a summary affirmance. Other circuits have interpreted Doe similarly, see Rich v. Sec'y of the Army, 735 F.2d 1220, 1228 n. 8 (CA10

- 9 -

1984); <u>Beller</u> v. <u>Middendorf</u>, 632 F.2d 788, 809 (CA9 1980); as
have the highest courts of New York, New Jersey, and Maryland.
In addition, <u>Doe</u> did not address any claim of a First Amendment
right of association, which is involved here.

The Court should not grant cert. CA11 did not hold the
statute unconstitutional. Rather, it stated an appropriate constitutional test in the abstract and remanded the case for trial.
Accordingly, review by this Court is premature. The State virtually concedes the case is premature by filing a petn for cert
rather than an appeal pursuant to 28 U.S.C. §1254(2) from a decision holding a state statute unconstitutional.

The prematurity of the case precludes it from conflicting
with any other Circuit. Moreover, <u>Dronenburg</u> was a military
case, and its discussion of <u>Doe</u> was dicta. At issue there was
the constitutionality of a naval discharge regulation, and not
the military sodomy law. The case indicated that the standard by
which military regulations must be judged is much lower than in a
civilian context. <u>Dronenburg</u> v. <u>Zech</u>, <u>supra</u>, at 1392. In addition, there is no ripe conflict between this case and CA5's decision in <u>Baker</u> v. <u>Wade</u>, slip op. No. 82-1590 (CA5 August 26, 1985)
(en banc). <u>Baker</u>, like this case, involved a declaratory judgment challenge to the constitutionality of a state sodomy law,
and CA5 reversed the DC's holding that the law was unconstitutional. <u>Baker</u> v. <u>Wade</u>, 553 F.Supp. 1121 (N.D. Tex. 1982). Since
the issues here are not framed concretely yet, there is no conflict with <u>Baker</u>.

- 10 -

On the merits, resps' argument is similar to CA11's opinion.
Affirming CA11 will not wreak havoc on the States. Twenty-two
States have decriminalized private homosexual acts, and the
courts in two other States have struck down sodomy statutes.
States will still be able to prohibit suicide, drug abuse, pros-
titution, and bigamy.

4. <u>DISCUSSION</u>: There is no bar to granting cert in a case
where a CA has disposed of an appeal from a final judgment in a
way that requires further action in the DC. See, e.g., <u>Estelle</u>
v. <u>Gamble</u>, 429 U.S. 97, 98 (1976) (CA reversed DC's dismissal of
§1983 complaint and remanded with instructions to reinstate complaint; Court granted cert over dissent stating that Court's
normal practice is to deny interlocutory review, <u>id.</u>, at 114);
<u>Butz</u> v. <u>Economou</u>, 438 U.S. 478, 480-481 (1978) (DC dismissed
action on ground of absolute immunity; CA reversed, finding officials entitled to qualified immunity). Although the Court has at
times suggested that such a CA ruling must be "fundamental to the
further conduct of the case," that standard is arguably met by
any CA reversal of a final judgment that requires further proceedings, See 17 Wright, Miller and Cooper, Federal Practice and
Procedure §4036, at 23-24 (1978), and is met in this case. On
the other hand, the Court has also denied cert on the grounds
that the case is not ripe for review. See e.g., <u>Brotherhood of</u>
<u>Locomotive Firemen & Enginemen</u> v. <u>Bangor & A.R. Co.</u>, 389 U.S.
327, 328 (1967) ("because the Court of Appeals remanded the case,
it is not yet ripe for review by this Court"); <u>Hamilton-Brown</u>
<u>Shoe Co.</u> v. <u>Wolf Bros. & Co.</u>, 240 U.S. 251, 258 (1916) (lack of

- 11 -

finality "funished sufficient ground for the denial"). These
cases thus could support a decision either way.

Hardwick appears to have standing, so that would be no bar
to taking the case either, even though the Does will probably
drop out for lack of standing.

The debate between the CA11 majority and dissent about the
summary affirmance standards does not control this Court's decision on whether to reconsider the issue in Doe. Summary decisions carry less authority in this Court than do opinions rendered after plenary consideration, and the Court needs less justification for reconsidering them. Metromedia, Inc. v. City of
San Diego, 453 U.S. 490, 500 (1981) (plurality) (citing cases).
"It is not at all unusual for the Court to find it appropriate to
give full consideration to a question that has been the subject
of previous summary action." Id. (quoting Washington v. Yakima
Indian Nation, 439 U.S. 463, 477 n. 20 (1979)).

It is clear that the issue here is important enough to merit
the Court's attention. The Court is procedurally able to decide
the case if it wants to. CA11's decision is in confict with
CA5's in Baker, and Dronenburg adds to the debate. The statute
in Baker forbid engaging in oral or anal sex in a homosexual
encounter. CA5 held that Doe controlled and that engaging in
homosexual conduct was therefore not a protected liberty interest. CA5 also rejected the plaintiff's equal protection claim,
finding that homosexuals were not a suspect class, and that the
"strong objection to homosexual conduct, which has prevailed in
Western culture for the past seven centuries" provided a rational

- 12 -

basis for upholding the statute. <u>Baker</u> v. <u>Wade</u>, <u>supra</u>, slip op.,
at 6448. There is also a case pending before CA4 in which the DC
held that Virginia's fornication and cohabitation statutes violated the privacy rights of unmarried, heterosexual adults who
engage in sexual activity in private. <u>Doe</u> v. <u>Duling</u>, 603 F.Supp.
960 (E.D. Va. 1985), appeal pending. Last term, this Court affirmed by an equally divided Court a CA10 case that upheld an
Okla. statute providing that teachers could be fired for "public
homosexual activity," but struck down a restriction on their
"public homosexual conduct," which included advocacy. <u>Bd. of Ed.</u>
<u>of the City of Oklahoma City</u> v. <u>National Gay Task Force</u>, 105
S.Ct. 1858 (1985), aff'd by an equally divided court, 729 F.2d
1270 (CA10 1984).

The Court could put off the confrontation by allowing this
case to go to trial for development of the facts and presentation
of the state interest. It is possible that CA11 next time will
hear the case en banc and come out the other way. Also, the
Court may want to delay in the hope that it will receive a case
raising the issue in the context of heterosexuals, in which it
might be less controversial and a smaller step to find a right of
sexual privacy.

On the other hand, it does not seem essential to have a
trial before deciding the constitutional issue. The Court does
not need additional facts to decide the case, and the State can
present its interests in its brief to this Court. Also, CA11 is
unlikely to go en banc on the appeal from the trial. If CA11
wanted to address en banc the essential issue in this case, it

- 13 -

would have done so with this opinion. While a case involving
heterosexuals will likely filter up from CA4 or a similar case
might arise, heterosexuals may run into greater standing problems
than does resp here. In the CA4 case, the unmarried, heterosexual adult plaintiffs had engaged in sex and cohabited with other
unmarrieds, and desire to do so in the future although they have
abstained since the filing of the suit, partly because they fear
prosecution. The defendants said there was a low probability of
prosecution, but admitted that the statutes would be enforced if
complaints were received and they had manpower available. Doe v.
Duling, 603 F.Supp., supra, at 964. Further, although it would
be a smaller step to find a right of sexual privacy among heterosexuals, it might be difficult to preclude homosexuals from its
coverage. And perhaps homosexuals need the protection more. If
the Court finds no right to sexual privacy, it might be more
desirable to render such a decision in case involving homosexuals. The Court might also want to grant cert to discuss what
standards it wishes CAs to apply in connection with summary affirmances.

    5. RECOMMENDATION: I recommend grant.

       There is a response.

September 25, 1985   Morrison   Opn in petn *ii. Memo to Justice Powell from His Law Clerk in* Bowers

Helpful

TO: Justice Powell

FROM: Bill

DATE: September 28, 1985

RE: <u>Bowers</u> v. <u>Hardwick, et al.</u>, No. 85-140
       Cert petition

This petn raises the question whether a state statute criminalizing sodomy is constitutional under the line of cases beginning with <u>Griswold</u> v. <u>Connecticut</u>, 381 U.S. 479 (1965). The Court summarily affirmed a three-judge DC decision that such a statute is constitutional in <u>Doe</u> v. <u>Commonwealth's Attorney</u>, 425 U.S. 901 (1976). Since <u>Doe</u>, the Court has declined to discuss the issue. See <u>Carey</u> v. <u>Population Services</u>, 431 U.S. 678, 688 n. 5 (1977).

In this case, the CA11 found that (1) <u>Doe</u> was not controlling, since the Court's summary affirmance might have been based on standing concerns and not a decision on the merits, and (2) under the right-to-privacy cases, the Georgia sodomy statute is unconstitutional. Judge

2.

Kravitch authored a persuasive dissent, arguing that Doe is controlling. Judge Kravitch contended that if the Court's decision had been based on standing, the Court would have dismissed the appeal rather than summarily affirming.

Since the CA11's decision was rendered in this case, CA5 (en banc, Reavley writing for the court) decided in a similar case that Doe controls and that the Texas sodomy statute is not unconstitutional. Baker v. Wade, 769 F.2d 289 (CA5 1985).

There is an argument that the Court should deny, and wait for the DC to try the case on remand. (CA11 remanded for trial on the question whether the statute is a narrowly tailored means of advancing a compelling state interest.) Unlike the memo writer, I think this argument is strong. The decision in this case is an important one that may have implications for other forms of regulated private conduct (e.g., some kinds of recreational drug use). The Court should therefore decide it on a proper record. (It's possible the state will be able to make a record for the proposition that this statute is related to state efforts to control various diseases; that kind of

3.

interest would be hard for the state to discuss adequately in an appellate brief.)

On the other hand, this case gives the Court an opportunity to decide the issue without discussing it (if that's what the Court wishes to do). That is what Doe appeared to accomplish, and the CA11 misunderstood the binding effect of the summary affirmance in Doe. The Court could take this case and write a brief opinion on the proper application of summary affirmances. That would (1) reverse the CA11's decision in this case, and (2) put other federal courts on notice that Doe decided this issue.

Consequently, I recommend DENY unless the Court wishes to decide the merits issue simply by discussing the procedural issue -- the effect of summary affirmances.

----

iii. Cert Pool Memo in Perreault v. Fishman

PRELIMINARY MEMORANDUM

January 7, 1994 Conference
List 1, Sheet 4 (Page 4)

No. 93-838-CFX

Richard Perreault (deadbeat dad)   Cert to CA1 (Breyer (cj), Selya, Boudin)
                                              (unpub pc)
v.

Harriet Fishman (Marital Master)   Federal/Civil   Timely

1. *Summary:* Pro se petr seeks review of dct dismissal of his action challenging NH's order that he pay education expenses for his children by former marriage.

2. *Facts and Decisions Below:* Petr was divorced in 1979. In 1992, former wife sought ct order requiring petr to contribute to college education of the children of their marriage. St ct issued such an order. NH Sup Ct dismissed petr's appeal. Petr sued in fed dct, which dismissed the complaint b/c of res judicata. Petr appealed.

   CA1 affirmed: Having had an opportunity to challenge the child support award in st ct, petr may not raise in fed ct either the same challenges or new ones which could have been presented to the st ct. *Migra v. Warren City Sch. Dist.*, 465 U.S. 75 (1984). There's no merit to petr's claim that NH Sup Ct denied him DP by summarily rejecting his appeal, since petr has no constl right to appeal. *Lindsey v. Normet,* 405 U.S. 56 (1972).

3. *Contentions:* My constl rights have been violated. The lower cts say I'm trying to appeal or relitigate. But my complaint is an original action, not an appeal. §1983 entitles me to sue in fed ct for violation of constl rights.

4. *Discussion:* Petr never comes to grips w/ CA1's (& d ct's) res judicata argument. Factbound, splitless, meritless, unpub.

5. *Recommendation: DENY.*

Response waived.

December 11, 1993   Feldman   Opin. In Petn

Notes and Questions

1. The pool memos in the *Bowers* and *Perreault* cases contained five main sections: (1) a summary; (2) facts and proceedings/decisions below; (3) contentions of the parties; (4) discussion; and (5) a recommendation. In contrast, the memo written to Justice Powell by his law clerk "Bill" was much shorter and more casual. Why would Justice Powell want his law clerk Bill to write a separate memo reacting to the pool memo in *Bowers?* Why wouldn't Justice Powell simply rely upon the pool memo?

2. In the 1985 Term, Justice Powell had four law clerks: C. Cabell Chinnis, who is now a partner at Mayer Brown, where he specializes in tax law; Anne Coughlin, who is currently a law professor at the University of Virginia; Michael Mosman, who is now a federal district court judge; and William J. Stuntz, an influential legal scholar who is now deceased. The "Bill" who wrote the memo to Justice Powell was presumably William Stuntz.

3. Note how the "discussion" section of the *Bowers* pool memo focuses first on various vehicle issues that might prevent the Court from granting certiorari or deciding the merits of the case, such as Article III standing issues and whether the Court can grant certiorari in a case where the court of appeals disposed of the appeal from a judgment in a way that required further action from the district court. Only after addressing these various procedural issues did the pool writer assess whether the issue presented was "important enough to merit the Court's attention" and whether a "conflict" in the lower courts existed. This is a reminder of how the Court looks not only for cases that present important legal questions dividing the lower courts, but also how it also looks for clean vehicles that are free of various procedural defects that might prevent the Court from getting to the heart of the issues presented. For more on vehicle defects, *see supra* at page 263.

4. Note that in the "recommendation" section of the pool memo in *Perreault,* the pool writer highlights that the petition is, among other things, "[f]actbound" and "splitless." The pool writer's emphasis on the factbound nature of the petition helps to highlight Rule 10's admonition that the Court will rarely grant certiorari to decide erroneous factual findings, *see* S. Ct. Rule 10, and it also highlights the importance of the presence of a conflict or a split on the issues presented. The pool writer's reference to "unpub"—meaning that the lower-court opinion in the case was unpublished—suggests a preference for reviewing published opinions, and the pool writer's reference to the petitioner's claims being "meritless" highlights how the Court may consider the merits of a case in deciding whether to grant certiorari.

5. The *Perreault* cert pool memo identifies the author only as "Feldman." However, in the Blackmun chambers, someone annotated the cert-pool memo in pencil and handwrote beneath "Feldman" the following: "AS/Wallace/Penn." This notation indicates that the clerk named Feldman was a law clerk for Justice Antonin Scalia ("AS"), that the clerk formerly clerked for Judge Wallace ("Wallace"), and that the clerk was a graduate of the University of Pennsylvania ("Penn"). Why would the Blackmun chambers take note of this biographical information about the pool writer?

6. Pool memos from the 1986 to 1993 Term can be found online via a digital archive of the Harry A. Blackmun Papers. *See* Lee Epstein, Jeffrey A. Segal, & Harold J. Spaeth, The Digital Archive of the Papers of Justice Harry A. Blackmun (2007), available at: http://epstein.usc.edu/research/BlackmunArchive.html. For example, the *Perreault* pool memo—along with the handwritten annotations written on Justice Blackmun's copy of the pool memo—can be viewed in the digital archive at http://epstein.usc.edu/research/blackmunMemos/1993/Denied-pdf/93-838.pdf.

7. Can the rise of the cert pool be blamed for the Court's shrinking docket? *See generally* David Stras, *The Supreme Court's Gatekeepers: The Role of Law Clerks in the Certiorari Process,* 85 Tex. L. Rev. 947, 997 (2007) (reporting results of pilot study that suggest that "the impact of the cert pool on the Court's declining plenary docket" has been too quickly dismissed). If you were a law clerk at the Court faced with analyzing the certworthiness of a case, do you think you would err on the side of recommending that the Court grant or deny certiorari? What are the possible risks of recommending that the Court grant certiorari in a particular case? And what are the risks of recommending that the Court deny certiorari in a particular case?

3. The Discuss List

The third step in the cert process involves what is called the "discuss list." After the pool memo is circulated within the Court, the Justices who participate in the cert pool review the memo, and sometimes the cert papers too, before deciding whether a particular cert petition should be placed on the Court's "discuss list." The discuss list serves as an internal court document—not circulated to the public or to the parties—that lists those cert petitions that have been selected for discussion at conference by at least one Justice. Any one Justice has the power to place a cert petition on the discuss list simply by asking that it be placed on the list. Cert petitions not placed on the list are automatically denied without conference discussion, whereas those cert petitions that are placed on the discuss list are discussed and voted on. Justice Ginsburg estimated in 2003 that approximately 85 percent of all petitions fail to make the discuss list and hence are automatically denied with no discussion. *See* Ruth Bader Ginsburg, *Thomas Jefferson Lecture: Workways of the Supreme Court,* 25 Thomas Jefferson L. Rev. 517, 519-520 (2003).

Although the discuss list is well entrenched today, it has not always played a role in the certiorari process. Consider the following article, which describes the origins, history, and purposes of the discuss list.

Gregory Caldeira & John R. Wright, The Discuss List: Agenda Building in the Supreme Court

24 Law & Soc'y Rev. 807, 809-815 (1990)

During the hearings on the Judges' Bill, the justices made a special point of the rational and comprehensive manner in which the Court screened cases and arrived at the plenary docket: the Clerk distributed the record and briefs for each case to all the justices, each of the brethren prepared a memorandum, the members of the Conference discussed each of the petitions, and the Court bound the matter over for decision on the merits if four or more justices thought it worthy. The justices promised to give full consideration to all candidates for plenary review.

Until the 1930s, so far as we can tell, the justices prepared for and the Conference discussed, however briefly, each case on the docket. Sometime during the 1930s—the precise year is not clear—the Supreme Court began to work with two lists of cases—a practice apparently established at the behest of Chief Justice Charles Evans Hughes. There was then and continues to be widespread agreement among the justices that most cases, more than half, coming up on a writ of certiorari have little or no merit. The first list, a "dead list," received no attention during the Conference. Chief Justice Hughes would circulate among the justices a second list he regarded as sufficiently meritorious for discussion in the Conference. Prior to the next Conference, any one of the justices could remove a case from what eventually became known as the "dead list" and require discussion among the justices. This summary treatment of many cases fit neatly with Chief Justice Hughes's well-known reputation for efficiency and austerity. It is not clear whether the cases on the docket during Hughes's tenure were any less meritorious than those in Taft's time, or whether Hughes had simply decided to focus the energies of the Court more than had his predecessors.

The process of retrenchment has continued. Mr. Justice Stevens has commented: "In the 1975 Term, when I joined the Court, I found that other procedural changes had occurred. The 'dead list' had been replaced by a 'discuss list'; now the chief justice circulates a list of cases he deems worthy of discussion and each of the other members of the Court may add cases to it". In a sense, nothing has changed since the tenure of Chief Justice Hughes. But, as Justice Stevens remarks, "there is a symbolic difference. In 1925, every case was discussed unless it was on the dead list; today, no case is discussed unless it is placed on a special list". . . .

These days, the chief justice circulates two lists to the chambers of the justices prior to "noon on the Wednesday before the Friday conference". Initially, the office of the chief justice, but actually the Conference Secretary, sends around to each chamber a "Conference List"; it includes all of the matters, including petitions for certiorari, jurisdictional statements, motions, and cases submitted, awaiting a disposition from the Court. The second list—the "Discuss List"—includes jurisdictional statements and petitions for certiorari that the chief justice or at least one associate justice thinks worthy of discussion. After an initial list for discussion from the office of the chief justice goes out to the members of the Court, each justice, including the chief justice, adds cases. Normally, the justices discuss between forty and fifty cases in each Conference. The third list—the "dead list"—contains the cases no one regards as important enough or appropriate for discussion in the Conference. It is simply the residual, and it never actually circulates among the justices. By law, the Court must decide appeals on the merits, so all jurisdictional statements go on to the discuss list for at least a brief discussion. Each term, approximately 70 percent of the "paid" cases filed[] go directly on to the Supreme Court's dead list and never reach the Conference.

What purpose does the discuss list serve on the Supreme Court? Members of the Court describe it as a neutral, administrative measure, a result of the widespread agreement on the frivolousness of 60 to 70 percent of the caseload. None of the justices—not even that apostle of access, William O. Douglas—has argued that more than 30 percent of the cases filed deserves serious attention. With the frivolous cases out of the path, the Conference can concentrate on the important legal issues in the remaining subset. The discuss list simplifies the Court's work. It might also function as a device to keep a persistent minority relatively satisfied with the Court's operation. Theoretically, of course, a single justice may shift any case from the dead to the discuss list. Although a justice in the minority normally cannot hope to win on the merits, he or she may nonetheless prevail on the Conference to justify a decision not to consider the matter. Others see the members of the Court as making the same sorts of judgments about which cases to discuss as they do on which to grant or deny certiorari. Does it contain a conflict? Does the case raise an important issue? Discussion of cases in Conference, then, represents a repetition of the initial phase but with a smaller group of cases from which to choose.

We see a substantial element of truth in all these views of the roles of the discuss list in the Court. Undoubtedly, the discuss list, in varying degrees, serves administrative goals, releases tensions among the justices, and represents at least some of the same political/legal judgments as the decision to grant or deny. Yet, our theoretical framework leads us to an emphasis somewhat different from previous research. . . .

. . . [T]he strategic situation in the initial winnowing permits—indeed, invites—wide sway for the policy orientations of the justices. If, as we assume . . . , the justices pursue policy goals, then they should do so here as well. . . .

In our view, the formation of the discuss list is, first and foremost, a political process, driven by the ideological stakes so often at issue in the great matters brought before the justices. It is the initial skirmish in the battle for public policy; and the content of the discuss list holds enormous implications for the eventual shape of decisions on the merits.

4. Voting at Conference and the Rule of Four

If a petition is placed on the discuss list, then the Justices will discuss and vote upon the petition at a conference. The conferences are generally held weekly while the Court is in session. Only the Justices attend conference; no law clerks, secretaries, or aides are allowed into the room. As each certiorari petition on the discuss list is considered during conference, the Chief Justice begins by stating his

recommendation for disposition, and then the other Justices state their recommended disposition in order of seniority. The key at conference is that it takes
the votes of four Justices for certiorari to be granted. This rule is referred to as
the "Rule of Four." The first excerpt below describes and considers the impact
of the Rule of Four, and the second excerpt discusses so-called "Join-3" votes—
meaning votes to provide a fourth vote if three others vote to grant review.

John Paul Stevens, The Life Span of a Judge-Made Rule

58 N.Y.U. L. Rev. 1, 10-21 (1983)

Whenever four justices of the United States Supreme Court vote to grant a petition
for a writ of certiorari, the petition is granted even though a majority of the Court
votes to deny.... [T]he origins of this so-called Rule of Four are somewhat
obscure.... It was first publicly described by the justices who testified in support
of the Judges' Bill that became the Judiciary Act of 1925. . . .

In their testimony in support of the Judges' Bill, members of the Court
explained that they had exercised discretionary jurisdiction in a limited number
of federal cases since 1891 when the Circuit Courts of Appeals were created, and also
in a limited number of cases arising in the state courts since 1914. They described in
some detail the procedures they had followed in processing their discretionary
docket and made it clear that they intended to continue to follow those practices
in managing the enlarged certiorari jurisdiction that would be created by the enactment of the Judges' Bill.

Several features of the Court's practice were emphasized in order to demonstrate that the discretionary docket was being processed in a responsible, nonarbi-
trary way. These four are particularly worthy of note: (1) copies of the printed
record, as well as the briefs, were distributed to every justice; (2) every justice personally examined the papers and prepared a memorandum or note indicating his
view of what should be done; (3) each petition was discussed by each justice at
conference; and (4) a vote was taken, and if four, or sometimes just three, justices
thought the case should be heard on its merits, the petition was granted. In his
testimony, Justice Van Devanter pointed out that in the 1922 and 1923 Terms the
Court had acted on 398 and 370 petitions respectively. Since these figures indicate
that the Court was processing only a handful of certiorari petitions each week, it is
fair to infer that the practice of making an individual review and having a full
conference discussion of every petition was not particularly burdensome. Indeed,
at that time the number was so small that the Court was then contemplating the
possibility of granting an oral hearing on every petition for certiorari. Times have
changed and so have the Court's practices.

In the 1947 Term, when I served as a law clerk to Justice Rutledge, the practice of
discussing every certiorari petition at conference had been discontinued. It was then
the practice for the Chief Justice to circulate a so-called 'dead list' identifying the
cases deemed unworthy of conference discussion. Any member of the Court could
remove a case from the dead list, but unless such action was taken, the petition
would be denied without even being mentioned at conference.

In the 1975 Term, when I joined the Court, I found that other significant
procedural changes had occurred. The 'dead list' had been replaced by a 'discuss

list'; now the Chief Justice circulates a list of cases that he deems worthy of discussion and each of the other members of the Court may add cases to that list. In a sense, the discuss list practice is the functional equivalent of the dead list practice, but there is a symbolic difference. In 1925, every case was discussed; in 1947 every case was discussed unless it was on the dead list; today, no case is discussed unless it is placed on a special list. . . .

The rule that four affirmative votes are sufficient to grant certiorari has, however, survived without change. Indeed, its wisdom has seldom, if ever, been questioned. Perhaps it is time to do so. . . .

. . . I am neither persuaded myself nor prepared to shoulder the burden of persuading my colleagues, that the Rule of Four should be abandoned—either temporarily or permanently. I am, however, prepared to demonstrate that it would be entirely legitimate to reexamine the rule, that some of the arguments for preserving the rule are unsound, and that there are valid reasons for making a careful study before more drastic solutions to the Court's workload problems are adopted.

First, I would put to one side any suggestion that the representations made to Congress when the 1925 Judges' Bill was enacted created some sort of estoppel that would make it dishonorable for the Court to change the Rule of Four. The Justices' testimony in 1924 contained a complete and candid explanation of the practices then being followed and a plain expression of an intent to continue to follow essentially the same practices in the future. The purposes of the testimony were to demonstrate that the selection of cases for review would be based on neutral and relevant considerations, rather than the arbitrary choice of particular justices, and that the Court would continue to hear an adequate number of cases. The testimony, however, contained no representation or even suggestion that the Court might not make various procedural changes in response to changes in the condition of its docket. I have found nothing in the legislative history of the 1925 Act that limits the Court's power to modify its internal rules governing the processing of its certiorari docket.

But even if I have misread that history, ample precedent—and therefore the doctrine of *stare decisis*—supports the proposition that the Court has the authority to modify the certiorari procedures that were being followed in the 1920's. The Court has already eliminated the record filing requirement; it has abandoned the practice of individual discussion of every petition at conference; there have been substantial changes in the way each individual justice evaluates each certiorari petition. In my judgment, each of those procedural modifications was an entirely legitimate response to a dramatic change in the character of the docket. They are precedents that establish the legitimacy of making such other internal procedural changes—specifically including a possible modification of the Rule of Four—as may be appropriate to cope with a problem whose present dimensions were not foreseen in 1925.

During most of the period in which the Rule of Four was developed, the Court had more capacity than it needed to dispose of its argument docket. The existence of the rule in 1924 provided a persuasive response to the concern—expressed before the Judges' Bill was enacted—that the Court might not accept enough cases for review if its discretionary docket were enlarged. In my judgment, it is the opposite concern that is now dominant. For I think it is clear that the Court now takes far too many cases. Indeed, I am persuaded that since the enactment of the Judges' Bill in 1925, any mismanagement of the Court's docket has been in the direction of taking too many, rather than too few, cases.

In his talk on *stare decisis* in 1944, Justice Jackson noted that the substitution of discretionary for mandatory jurisdiction had failed to cure the problem of overloading because judges found it so difficult to resist the temptation to correct perceived error or to take on an interesting question despite its lack of general importance. In a letter written to Senator Wheeler in 1937 describing the workload of the Supreme Court, Chief Justice Hughes, after noting that less than twenty percent of the certiorari petitions raised substantial questions, stated: 'I think that it is the view of the members of the Court that if any error is made in dealing with these applications it is on the side of liberality.' In a recent letter Paul Freund, who served as Justice Brandeis' law clerk in 1932, advised me that the Justice 'believed the Court was granting review in too many cases—not only because of their relative unimportance for the development or clarification of the law but because they deprived the Court of time to pursue the really significant cases with adequate reflection and in sufficient depth.'

It can be demonstrated that the Rule of Four has had a significant impact on the number of cases that the Court has reviewed on their merits. A study of Justice Burton's docket book for the 1946 and 1947 Terms reveals that, in each of those Terms, the decision to grant certiorari was supported by no more than four votes in over twenty-five percent of the granted cases. It is, of course, possible that in some of those cases a justice who voted to deny might have voted otherwise under a Rule of Five, but it does seem fair to infer that the Rule of Four had a significant impact on the aggregate number of cases granted.

A review of my own docket sheets for the 1979, 1980, and 1981 Terms confirms this conclusion. No more than four affirmative votes resulted in granting over twenty-three percent of the petitions granted in the 1979 Term, over thirty percent of those granted in the 1980 Term, and about twenty-nine percent of those granted in the 1981 Term. In my judgment, these are significant percentages. If all—or even most—of those petitions had been denied, the number of cases scheduled for argument on the merits this Term would be well within the range that all justices consider acceptable.

Mere numbers, however, provide an inadequate measure of the significance of the cases that were heard because of the rule. For I am sure that some Court opinions in cases that were granted by only four votes have made a valuable contribution to the development of our jurisprudence. My experience has persuaded me, however, that such cases are exceptionally rare. I am convinced that a careful study of all of the cases that have been granted on the basis of only four votes would indicate that in a surprisingly large number the law would have fared just as well if the decision of the court of appeals or the state court had been allowed to stand. To enable interested scholars to consider the validity of this judgment, I have prepared footnotes listing twenty-five cases granted certiorari by a mere four votes in the 1946 Term and thirty-six such cases granted certiorari in the 1979 Term.

The Rule of Four is sometimes justified by the suggestion that if four justices of the Supreme Court consider a case important enough to warrant full briefing and argument on the merits, that should be sufficient evidence of the significance of the question presented. But a countervailing argument has at least equal force. Every case that is granted on the basis of four votes is a case that five members of the Court thought should not be granted. For the most significant work of the Court, it is assumed that the collective judgment of its majority is more reliable than the views of the minority. Arguably, therefore, deference to the minority's desire to add additional cases to the argument docket may rest on an assumption that whether the Court hears a few more or a few less cases in any term is not a matter of first importance.

History and logic both support the conclusion that the Rule of Four must inevitably enlarge the size of the Court's argument docket and cause it to hear a substantial number of cases that a majority of the Court deems unworthy of review. What light does this conclusion shed on the current debate over possible solutions to the problems created by the Court's crowded docket? I shall mention just two points. First, this conclusion refutes one of the arguments that is made to support the creation of a new National Court of Appeals to enlarge the federal judiciary's lawmaking powers by deciding cases referred to it by the Supreme Court. It has been argued that because the Court now grants a smaller percentage of certiorari petitions than it did in the past, it is not granting enough. But that argument rests on the untenable assumption that the correct standard was set at some unspecified time in the past—an assumption that simply ignores the impact of the Rule of Four.

Second, reflection about the impact of the Rule of Four on the size of the docket demonstrates that the Court has a greater capacity to solve its own problems than is often assumed. We might, for example, simply abandon the Rule of Four, or perhaps refuse to follow it whenever our backlog reaches a predetermined point. But there are reasons to beware of such a procedural change. For even if the Rule of Four had nothing more than a distinguished parentage, an unblemished reputation, and a venerable age to commend itself to posterity, it would be entitled to the presumptive protection provided by the rule of *stare decisis*. Moreover, the Rule of Four has additional redeeming virtues. It gives each member of the Court a stronger voice in determining the makeup of the Court's docket. It increases the likelihood that an unpopular litigant, or an unpopular issue, will be heard in the country's court of last resort. Like the danger of awakening a sleeping dog, the costs of change are not entirely predictable. Surely those costs should not be incurred if less drastic solutions to the Court's problems are available.

At least two such solutions are quite obvious. If Congress were concerned about our plight, it could provide us with significant help by promptly removing the remainder of our mandatory jurisdiction. Second, as I suggested last summer, in the processing of our certiorari docket we are often guilty of ignoring the teachings of the doctrine of judicial restraint; if we simply acted with greater restraint during the case selection process, we might be able to manage the docket effectively under the Rule of Four. But if neither of these remedies materializes or is effective, we may find it necessary to acknowledge that the Rule of Four is a luxury we can no longer afford. I hope we can retain the rule, but I would much prefer temporary, or possibly even permanent abandonment of the Rule of Four to certain kinds of major surgery that have been suggested.

In conclusion, I will merely note that my primary objective has been neither to praise nor to bury the Rule of Four, but rather to suggest that one may legitimately ask questions about its future life span.

David M. O'Brien, Join-3 Votes, the Rule of Four, the *Cert.* Pool, and the Supreme Court's Shrinking Plenary Docket

13 J.L. & Pol. 779, 784-789, 795 (1997)

In the early 1970s Chief Justice Burger and some other justices began casting "Join-3" votes, rather than simply voting to grant or deny petitions for certiorari. Because earlier in this century the Court adopted the so-called informal "Rule of Four"—namely, that at least four justices must agree that a case merits review—a Join-3 vote is a vote to provide a fourth vote if others vote to grant review, but is otherwise considered as voting to deny. The introduction of Join-3 votes, arguably, contributed to the Court's taking more cases by lowering the threshold for granting review established by the Rule of Four. . . .

. . . In [1983], Justice John Paul Stevens concluded that between 20 to 30 percent of the plenary docket was typically granted on only four votes and that those "are significant percentages." He did so after reviewing Justice Harold Burton's docket books and determining that during 1946-1947 about 25 percent of the cases granted had the support of no more than four justices. . . .

Justice Stevens thus proposed abandoning the Rule of Four and adopting a "Rule of Five." . . . By abandoning the Rule of Four, Justice Stevens pointed out, as much as a quarter of the cases then granted review might be eliminated. . . .

When proposing a Rule of Five, Justice Stevens did not mention that other justices cast Join-3 votes. Still, he had clearly identified the main cause of the Court's workload problem: the Rule of Four no longer imposed the kind of self-restraint it previously had. The introduction of and propensity of some justices to cast Join-3 votes lowered the threshold imposed by the Rule of Four for granting cases, thereby inflating plenary docket. Accordingly, returning to a firm Rule of Four or adopting a Rule of Five would have raised the threshold for granting review and moved the Court toward resolving its workload problem.

Although the origin of Join-3 votes remains unclear, such votes were not recorded prior to Burger's chief justiceship. . . . Justice Harry A. Blackmun, who came aboard in 1970, recalls neither who began the practice nor any "definite discussion about the use of the vote." Asked about the Join-3 votes, Chief Justice Rehnquist responded:

> It is hard to remember back nearly twenty-five years, which is the length of time I have been a member of the Court; but I do not remember the "join-three" vote striking me as a novelty after I was here. I therefore think it must have been used, albeit rarely, from the time I came on the Court. It may be that this vote has various meanings, depending on who casts it. But my sense has always been that it is a more tentative vote than a "grant," and that if there are three to join, the person who casts the vote may nonetheless reconsider it.

Whatever their origin, Join-3 votes were established by the time Justice Stevens joined the Court in 1975. One possible explanation is that in leading conferences, Chief Justice Burger began voting to join three and other justices did the same. Within a few years, Join-3 votes became almost routine, though still relatively infrequent. . . .

Regardless of the exact origin of Join-3 votes, the practice of casting such votes was accepted in the 1970s and 1980s. Furthermore, some justices cast an extraordinary share of such votes, whereas others rarely do, if ever. Justice Blackmun led in Join-3 votes. By comparison, Justice Stevens never casts such votes. On and off the

·h, he repeatedly warned colleagues not to take cases pointlessly. His view of voting to grant was undoubtedly influenced by clerking for Justice Wiley Rutledge in 1947-1948, at a time when the Rule of Four was respected.

Notes and Questions

1. Justice Stevens wrote about the Rule of Four in 1983 when the Court heard approximately 150 cases per Term in contrast to the 70 to 80 cases per Term it hears today. In other words, Justice Stevens wrote about the Rule of Four when the Court's docket suffered from too many cases, *not* too few. In light of the Court's significantly lighter docket today, should the Rule of Four be reduced to a Rule of Three to facilitate the granting of *more* petitions for certiorari? Or should Join-3 votes be used with greater regularity to increase the number of cases that the Court hears? Why or why not?

2. Imagine that five Justices vote to deny certiorari in a particular case and that four vote to grant certiorari, so certiorari is granted. Also imagine that when the Justices are reviewing the merits briefs in the case, five Justices become convinced that the Court improvidently granted certiorari because, for example, the Court failed to spot the presence of a jurisdictional flaw or some other defect in the case. Can the five Justices vote to dismiss the case as improvidently granted (also known as a vote to "DIG" the case)? *See generally* Michael Solimine & Rafael Gely, *The Supreme Court and the Sophisticated Use of DIGs*, 18 Sup. Ct. Econ. Rev. 155, 158 (2010) ("[I]t appears that the Court will usually only DIG a case when at least six Justices vote to do so, otherwise known as the Rule of Six. The difference is justified on the basis that if a supermajority vote to DIG a case were not required, then in theory the Rule of Four could be regularly subverted by five Justices who did not vote to hear the case."); Michael E. Solimine & Rafael Gely, *The Supreme Court and the DIG: An Empirical and Institutional Analysis,* 2005 Wis. L. Rev. 1421 (2005) (noting that the Court generally adheres to a Rule of Six when deciding to DIG a case, but finding that the Court has sometimes voted to DIG a case based on just five votes).

3. Voting to grant or deny are not the only options available to a Justice at conference. For example, the Justices might vote to "hold" a case pending resolution of another case already on the Court's docket and then vote to grant, vacate, and remand (GVR) once the other case on the Court's docket is decided. Or a Justice might vote to grant certiorari limited to a certain question presented but not others, thereby granting only a limited question. In addition, instead of voting to grant or deny outright, a Justice might instead vote to Call for the Views of the Solicitor General (also known as a "CVSG"). When the Court CVSGs, it issues an order "requesting" that the Solicitor General of the United States file an amicus brief weighing in on whether certiorari should be granted. The Court has not publicly clarified how many Justices must vote to CVSG. *See generally* David C. Thompson & Melanie F. Wachtell, *An Empirical Analysis of Supreme Court Certiorari Petition Procedures: The Call for Response and the Call for the Views of the Solicitor General,* 16 Geo. Mason L. Rev. 237, 272 (2009) (noting that various former Supreme Court clerks, a former Chief Deputy Clerk of the Court, and Justice Breyer have stated that four votes are required to CVSG whereas Chief Justice Rehnquist reportedly stated in a letter that only three votes are required).

D. CERTIORARI DENIALS

Given that the Court denies approximately 99 percent of all petitions for certiorari, it is important to ask what a denial of certiorari signifies. The following materials explore certiorari denials, examining the significance and meaning of certiorari denials as well as dissents from a denial of certiorari, which occur when a Justice decides to note his or her dissent to a denial of certiorari.

1. The (In?)significance of Cert Denials

Can a denial of certiorari be read to provide an opinion on the merits of a case? Or does a denial of certiorari inherently say nothing about the merits of a given case, signaling no more than that the Court refused to decide the merits of the case? The following materials explore these questions.

Maryland v. Baltimore Radio Show

338 U.S. 912, 917-919 (1950)

Opinion of Mr. Justice FRANKFURTER respecting the denial of the petition for writ of certiorari.

The sole significance of such denial of a petition for writ of certiorari need not be elucidated to those versed in the Court's procedures. It simply means that fewer than four members of the Court deemed it desirable to review a decision of the lower court. . . . A variety of considerations underlie denials of the writ, and as to the same petition different reasons may lead different Justices to the same result. This is especially true of petitions for review on writ of certiorari to a State court. Narrowly technical reasons may lead to denials. Review may be sought too late; the judgment of the lower court may not be final; it may not be the judgment of a State court of last resort; the decision may be supportable as a matter of State law, not subject to review by this Court, even though the State court also passed on issues of federal law. A decision may satisfy all these technical requirements and yet may commend itself for review to fewer than four members of the Court. Pertinent considerations of judicial policy here come into play. A case may raise an important question but the record may be cloudy. It may be desirable to have different aspects of an issue further illumined by the lower courts. Wise adjudication has its own time for ripening.

Since there are these conflicting and, to the uninformed, even confusing reasons for denying petitions for certiorari, it has been suggested from time to time that the Court indicate its reasons for denial. Practical considerations preclude. In order that the Court may be enabled to discharge its indispensable duties, Congress has placed the control of the Court's business, in effect, within the Court's discretion. . . . If the Court is to do its work it would not be feasible to give reasons, however brief, for refusing to take [] cases. The time that would be required is prohibitive, apart from the fact as already indicated that different reasons not infrequently move different members of the Court in concluding that a particular case at a particular time makes review undesirable. . . .

Inasmuch, therefore, as all that a denial of a petition for a writ of certiorari means is that fewer than four members of the Court thought it should be granted, this Court has rigorously insisted that such a denial carries with it no implication whatever regarding the Court's views on the merits of a case which it has declined to review. The Court has said this again and again; again and again the admonition has to be repeated.

Doris Marie Provine, Case Selection in the United States Supreme Court

54-56 (1980), University of Chicago

Denial of review is an attractive means of avoiding consideration on the merits because the vote is secret and the Court never issues its reasons for denial. Even when one or more justices dissent from the denial, the views of the rest of the Court remain unknown. The [Court's] criteria [for granting certiorari] . . . are sufficiently vague and various to prevent even likely guesses about reasons for denial. In addition, the Court has repeatedly warned that the reasons for denial may be totally unrelated to the merits of the dispute. . . .

The comparative attractiveness of using denial of review to avoid volatile disputes led Alexander Bickel, an advocate of the "passive virtues" of nondecision, to recommend that the Court use denials for this purpose. In Bickel's analysis, such outcome-oriented denials could release the Court from the danger of overinvolvement in the political process without sacrificing the Court's capacity to resolve disputes when it did intervene:

> Some do and some do not care to recognize a need for keeping the Court's constitutional interventions within bounds that are imposed, though not clearly defined, by the theory and practice of political democracy. Those who do recognize this need have the choice of either limiting the occasions of the Court's interventions, so that the times will be relatively few when the Court interjects itself decisively into the political process, or of restricting the category of principles that the Court may evolve and enforce. [Alexander M. Bickel, *The Least Dangerous Branch: The Supreme Court at the Bar of Politics* (1962).]

Bickel's recommendation that the Court limit the occasions of review rather than the principles of decision, carries with it certain difficulties of implementation. . . .

[One] . . . consideration tending to limit the Court's use of case selection to avoid resolving volatile disputes is external to the Court: the Court must take account of the public's interpretation of such denials. Regardless of the technical wording of [the Court's rule governing certiorari], commentators and litigants tend to interpret denials of review in practical and political terms. . . . Newspaper reports are even more likely to consider the denial of review as a decision against the validity of the petitioner's claim. A long-range pattern of denials tends to be interpreted among observers as indicating negative Supreme Court policy making on the avoided issue. . . .

A more general problem with dispute avoidance as a means of preserving Supreme Court prestige is that denials in such circumstances can actually damage the standing of the Court. Denials can damage the Court's credibility because the Court is popularly perceived as a guardian of constitutional rights. Thus even if one accepts Bickel's warning against the Court's overextending itself, the costs of denial must also be recognized. . . .

Notes and Questions

1. Think back to Chapter 1's discussion of the role of a supreme court in a democracy. Given the Court's countermajoritarian role in our democracy, do you agree with Bickel's suggestion that the Court should avoid deciding political cases that could damage the Court's credibility as an institution? Or do you agree with Provine that there are potentially significant costs to the denial of certiorari in cases presenting important federal questions?

2. Is it true that the denial of certiorari should *never* be read as a reflection on the merits of a case? In considering this question, think back to the pool memo written for the *Perreault* case, which can be found at page 250. Remember that the pool writer justified a denial by noting, among other things, that the petitioner's claims were "meritless."

3. Occasionally the Court will repeatedly deny certiorari in cases presenting the same issue of federal law before eventually granting certiorari to decide the issue that the Court repeatedly declined to decide previously. Why might this be? Many different factors could be at play. One possible explanation might be the existence of what are called "vehicle" problems in the initial petitions for certiorari. The term "vehicle" problems refers to how some certiorari petitions—although they raise important legal issues in need of the Court's resolution—contain jurisdictional issues or other procedural defects, such as problems with Article III standing or mootness, that could prevent the Court from deciding the heart of the important legal questions that the Court wants to decide in the case. Hence, the Court might decline to grant certain petitions for certiorari because it wants to wait for a cleaner case that is free of vehicle defects.

Another potential explanation is that the Court might have wanted to let the important legal issue presented "percolate" in the lower courts before stepping in to resolve the issue. What do you think the benefits and costs of percolation might be? *See generally* Comment, Todd J. Tiberi, *Supreme Court Denials of Certiorari in Conflicts Cases: Percolation or Procrastination?*, 54 U. Pitt. L. Rev. 861, 891 (1993) (studying percolation and suggesting that "percolation does not lead to demonstrably better statutory decisions from the Supreme Court"). If you were a Justice faced with deciding whether to grant certiorari in a case presenting an important question of federal law that two circuits had previously addressed and decided differently, do you think the benefits of percolation would outweigh the costs of waiting for a definitive answer from the Supreme Court? Why or why not?

2. Dissents from Denials of Certiorari

Most petitions for certiorari are denied without any dissenting votes being noted. However, occasionally a Justice will choose to note or to explain his dissent from the denial of a petition for certiorari. The following excerpt from *Singleton v. Commissioner of Internal Revenue* provides an example of a dissent from a denial of certiorari in which Justice Blackmun questions the Court's denial of certiorari in a tax case and also provides Justice Stevens's views on the meaning of dissents from denials of certiorari.

Singleton v. Commissioner of Internal Revenue

439 U.S. 940, 940-942, 944-946 (1978)

On petition for writ of certiorari to the United States Court of Appeals for the Fifth Circuit.

The petition for a writ of certiorari is denied.

Mr. Justice BLACKMUN, with whom Mr. Justice MARSHALL and Mr. Justice POWELL join, dissenting.

The issue in this federal income tax case is whether a cash distribution that petitioner husband (hereafter petitioner) received in 1965 with respect to his shares in Capital Southwest Corporation (CSW) was taxable to him as a dividend, as the United States Court of Appeals for the Fifth Circuit held, or whether that distribution was a return of capital and therefore not taxable, as the Tax Court held. I regard the issue as of sufficient importance in the administration of the income tax laws to justify review here, and I dissent from the Court's failure to grant certiorari.

CSW was the parent of a group of affiliated corporations. Consolidated returns were filed for CSW and the group for the fiscal years ended March 31, 1964 and 1965. This was advantageous taxwise, for it enabled income of Capital Wire & Cable Corporation (CW), one of the subsidiaries, to be offset against losses sustained by CSW. CW's board formally recognized a saving in tax of about $863,000 through the filing of consolidated returns for the two fiscal years. That board then distributed $1 million in March 1965, not solely to CSW, its principal shareholder, but ratably to all its shareholders. As primary shareholder, CSW received $803,750 of that distribution.

The Internal Revenue Service subsequently determined that the consolidated returns for fiscal 1964 and 1965 did not accurately reflect the earnings of the group. Asserted deficiencies were settled in 1972 for approximately $900,000. Of this amount, about $755,000 was allocated to CW.

Petitioner takes the position that CW's allocable share of the 1965 tax must be accrued to that fiscal year; that CW's 1965 payment to CSW was thus not a dividend entering into the determination of CSW's earnings and profits at all, but was a constructive payment of CW's share of the tax bill; that this left CSW with no earnings and profits for 1965; and that, as a consequence, CSW's 1965 distribution to petitioner could only be a nontaxable return of capital and could not be a taxable dividend. The Tax Court, in a reviewed decision, with six judges dissenting, accepted this view. 64 T.C. 320 (1975). The Fifth Circuit reversed. 569 F.2d 863 (1978). . . .

For me, the answer to this tax question is by no means immediately apparent. Each side advances a forceful argument. The deep division among the judges of the Tax Court is indicative and significant. I cannot regard the issue as one that is too fact-specific or incapable of precedential effect. On the contrary, it features important aspects of tax accounting and tax law. CSW and CW, after all, were accrual-basis taxpayers. Normally, when a deficiency in tax of an accrual-basis taxpayer is ultimately determined, it is to be accrued as of the tax year of the deficiency and it affects earnings and profits accordingly. A consideration opposing this accepted proposition is the fact that the portion of CW's 1965 distribution paid to minority shareholders obviously qualified and apparently was reported as taxable dividends;

it would be at least somewhat anomalous to have the portion paid to CSW constitute, in contrast, a return of capital.

I hope that the Court's decision to pass this case by is not due to a natural reluctance to take on another complicated tax case that is devoid of glamour and emotion. . . .

Opinion of Mr. Justice STEVENS respecting the denial of the petition for writ of certiorari.

One characteristic of all opinions dissenting from the denial of certiorari is manifest. They are totally unnecessary. They are examples of the purest form of dicta, since they have even less legal significance than the orders of the entire Court which . . . have no precedential significance at all.

Another attribute of these opinions is that they are potentially misleading. Since the Court provides no explanation of the reasons for denying certiorari, the dissenter's arguments in favor of a grant are not answered and therefore typically appear to be more persuasive than most other opinions. Moreover, since they often omit any reference to valid reasons for denying certiorari, they tend to imply that the Court has been unfaithful to its responsibilities or has implicitly reached a decision on the merits when, in fact, there is no basis for such an inference.

In this case, for example, the dissenting opinion suggests that the Court may have refused to grant certiorari because the case is "devoid of glamour and emotion." I am puzzled by this suggestion because I have never witnessed any indication that any of my colleagues has ever considered "glamour and emotion" as a relevant consideration in the exercise of his discretion or in his analysis of the law. With respect to the Court's action in this case, the absence of any conflict among the Circuits is plainly a sufficient reason for denying certiorari. Moreover, in allocating the Court's scarce resources, I consider it entirely appropriate to disfavor complicated cases which turn largely on unique facts. A series of decisions by the courts of appeals may well provide more meaningful guidance to the bar than an isolated or premature opinion of this Court. . . .

Admittedly these dissenting opinions may have some beneficial effects. Occasionally a written statement of reasons for granting certiorari is more persuasive than the Justice's oral contribution to the Conference. For that reason the written document sometimes persuades other Justices to change their votes and a case is granted that would otherwise have been denied. That effect, however, merely justifies the writing and circulating of these memoranda within the Court; it does not explain why a dissent which has not accomplished its primary mission should be published.

It can be argued that publishing these dissents enhances the public's understanding of the work of the Court. But because they are so seldom answered, these opinions may also give rise to misunderstanding or incorrect impressions about how the Court actually works. Moreover, the selected bits of information which they reveal tend to compromise the otherwise secret deliberations in our Conferences. There are those who believe that these Conferences should be conducted entirely in public or, at the very least, that the votes on all Conference matters should be publicly recorded. The traditional view, which I happen to share, is that confidentiality makes a valuable contribution to the full and frank exchange of views during the decisional process; such confidentiality is especially valuable in the exercise of the kind of discretion that must be employed in processing the thousands of certiorari petitions that are reviewed each year. In my judgment, the importance of preserving the tradition of confidentiality outweighs the minimal educational value of these opinions.

In all events, these are the reasons why I have thus far resisted the temptation to publish opinions dissenting from denials of certiorari.

Notes and Questions

1. Dissents from denial of certiorari were more common at the time of *Singleton* than they are today. According to the leading Supreme Court treatise, "the tide of dissenting votes" appears "to be ebbing; the number of publicly recorded dissenting votes has dropped off sharply in recent years." Eugene Gressman et al., *Supreme Court Practice* 332 (9th ed. 2007). For example, in the 1991 Term, 167 dissenting votes from the denial of certiorari were noted in nearly 6,000 petitions, whereas by the 1998 Term, only 14 dissents were noted out of more than 7,500 petitions. Hence, although Justice Stevens's colleagues chose to ignore him at the time he wrote *Singleton,* more Justices seem to be following his advice today. Do you think this general decrease in denials from certiorari is a beneficial development? Why or why not? What might be some of the advantages of denials of certiorari?

2. Is there a tension between Justice Frankfurter's pronouncements in *Baltimore Radio Show* to the effect that denials of certiorari have no legal significance beyond ending the review process in the particular case and the Justices' desire to publish a written dissent from certiorari in certain cases? On this, *see generally* Peter Linzer, *The Meaning of Certiorari Denials,* 79 Colum. L. Rev. 1227, 1260 (1979) ("Except for [a] few, including . . . [Justice] Stevens, who attack the use of dissents from certiorari denials, Justices rarely explore the paradox of dissents from an act said to have no legal significance besides ending the review process in a particular case.").

E. PROPOSALS FOR CERTIORARI REFORM

Complaints about certiorari are commonplace today. Many critics have focused on the Court's shrinking docket, arguing that the Court should be hearing many more cases than it does. Other critics have focused on the types of cases the Court frequently hears, arguing that the Court is taking the wrong kinds of cases. In addition, some critics have articulated concerns with the process the Court uses to make its cert decisions. It is here that the cert pool and the role of law clerks have come under attack. Kenneth Starr, for example, has argued that the cert pool has become "too powerful," giving clerks "an unjustifiable influence over which cases the Supreme Court reviews." Kenneth Starr, *The Supreme Court and Its Shrinking Docket: The Ghost of William Howard Taft,* 90 Minn. L. Rev. 1363, 1366, 1376 (2006); *see also* Carolyn Shapiro, *The Limits of the Olympian Court: Common Law Judging Versus Error Correction in the Supreme Court,* 63 Wash. & Lee L. Rev. 271, 285-86 (2006) (arguing that the Court's reliance on the cert pool "increases the likelihood that chaotic areas of the law may be given short shrift, due to the law clerks' and Justices' unfamiliarity with more mundane areas of the law"); David R. Stras, *The Supreme Court's Gatekeepers: The Role of Law Clerks in the Certiorari Process,* 85 Tex. L. Rev. 947, 997 (2007) (reporting that empirical evidence from a pilot study suggests that "many scholars have too quickly dismissed the impact of the cert pool on the Court's declining plenary docket").

In order to address some of these concerns surrounding certiorari, numerous proposals for cert reform have been floated over the years. The materials that follow include a few of the many proposals, including: (1) a well-known study published in 1972—when the Court's docket was overly congested—known as the "Freund Report," named after Paul Freund of Harvard Law School, who served as the chair of the group that conducted the study; and (2) examples of more recent scholarly cries for cert reform made during the past few years against the backdrop of perceptions that the Court's problem now—unlike in the 1970s—is too few cases, not too many.

1. The Freund Report's Attempt to Deal with an Overloaded Docket

In 1971, the Chief Justice of the United States appointed a group to study the Court's docket, which was considered too heavy and unmanageable at the time. The study group was made up of lawyers, professors, and former law clerks. Ultimately, the study group published the Freund Report in 1972. In the report, the study group concluded that the "Court is now at the saturation point, if not actually overwhelmed," and it proceeded to assess various means of taking some pressure off the Court and its docket. As the following excerpt from the Freund Report illustrates, the mechanism for reform that the study group ultimately found the most appealing was the creation of a National Court of Appeals, which would screen all petitions for review then filed in the Supreme Court, and hear and decide on the merits many cases of conflicts between circuits.

Federal Judicial Center, Report of the Study Group on the Caseload of the Supreme Court

57 F.R.D. 573, 590-595 (1972)

Our own recommendation builds on the Judiciary Act of 1925. Its aim is twofold. It deals first with that part of the solution embodied in the Act of 1925 which has since itself become a problem, namely the screening of a mass of petitions for review; and, second, with the pressure exerted on the Supreme Court by cases of conflict between circuits that ought to be resolved but that are otherwise not of such importance as to merit adjudication in the Supreme Court.

We recommend creation of a National Court of Appeals which would screen all petitions for review now filed in the Supreme Court, and hear and decide on the merits many cases of conflicts between circuits. Petitions for review would be filed initially in the National Court of Appeals. The great majority, it is to be expected, would be finally denied by that court. Several hundred would be certified annually to the Supreme Court for further screening and choice of cases to be heard and adjudicated there. Petitions found to establish a true conflict between circuits would be granted by the National Court of Appeals and the cases heard and finally disposed of there, except as to those petitions deemed important enough for certification to the Supreme Court.

The composition of the National Court of Appeals could be determined in a number of ways. The method of selection outlined here draws on the membership

of the existing courts of appeals, vesting the judges of those courts with new functions in relation to the new Court. The National Court of Appeals, under this plan,
would consist of seven United States circuit judges in active service. Assignment to
this Court should be for limited, staggered terms. Thus the opportunity to serve on
the National Court of Appeals would be made available to many circuit judges, the
Court would draw on a wide range of talents and varied experience while not losing
its identity and continuity as a court, and the burden of any personal inconvenience
would not fall too heavily on any small group of judges. Appointments should be
made by a method that will ensure the rapid filling of vacancies, and itself tend to
provide the court with the widest diversity of experience, outlook and age, in order
to help secure for it the confidence of the profession, of the Supreme Court, and of
the country.

Assignment of circuit judges to the National Court of Appeals could be made for
three-year staggered terms by a system of automatic rotation, as follows. A list of all
United States circuit judges in active service would be made up in order of seniority.
All judges serving as chief judges, or who would have succeeded to a chief judgeship
during their term of service on the National Court of Appeals had they been
selected, and all judges with less than five years' service as United States circuit
judges would be struck from the list. Appointments to the National Court of Appeals
would be made from the resulting list by alternating the judge most senior in service
and the most junior, except that each judge would have the privilege of declining
appointment for good cause; no two judges from the same circuit could serve at the
same time on the National Court of Appeals, and no judge who had served once
would be selected again until all other eligible judges had served. It is to be noted
that some additional circuit judgeships would have to be created. . . .

The threshold jurisdiction of the National Court of Appeals would be co-exten-
sive with the present appellate jurisdiction of the Supreme Court. We assume, as we
shall urge, that access to that jurisdiction will be entirely by certiorari. . . .

The National Court of Appeals would have discretion to deny review, governed
by the considerations . . . of the Rules of the Supreme Court, or in such further
Rules of the Supreme Court as may be made, or in Rules of the National Court of
Appeals made subject to the supervening rule-making power of the Supreme Court.
Denial of review by the National Court of Appeals would be final, and there would
then be no access to the Supreme Court.

The National Court of Appeals would also have discretion, similarly governed,
to certify a case to the Supreme Court for disposition. Possibly the concurrence of
three judges (one less than a majority) of the National Court of Appeals might
suffice for a decision to certify a case to the Supreme Court. In cases where a
court of appeals has rendered a decision in conflict with a decision of another
court of appeals, the National Court of Appeals would certify the case to the
Supreme Court for disposition if it finds the conflict to be real and if the issue
on which the conflict arises, or another issue in the case, is otherwise of adequate
importance. In all other cases of real conflict between circuits, the National Court of
Appeals would set the case down for argument, and proceed to adjudication on the
merits of the whole case. Its decision would be final, and would not be reviewable in
the Supreme Court.

It should be plain on the face of the proposal, and if found necessary could be
made plain by statement, that where there is serious doubt, the National Court of
Appeals should certify a petition rather than denying review. The expectation would
be that the National Court of Appeals would certify several times as many cases as the

Supreme Court could be expected to hear and decide-perhaps something of the order of 400 cases a year. These cases would constitute the appellate docket of the Supreme Court, except that the Court would retain its power to grant certiorari before judgment in a Court of Appeals, before denial of review in the National Court of Appeals, or before judgment in a case set down for hearing or heard there. The expectation would be that exercises of this power would be exceptional.

Once a case had been certified to it, the Supreme Court would, as now, have full discretion to grant or deny review or limited review, to reverse or affirm without argument, or to hear the case. In cases of conflict among circuits, the Supreme Court would, in addition, be able to grant review and remand to the National Court of Appeals with an order that the case be heard and adjudicated. This would be the disposition indicated in a case in which the Supreme Court agreed that the conflict was a true one, but did not view the issue involved as being of sufficient comparative importance to warrant a hearing in that Court. . . .

We are aware of objections that can be raised against this recommendation. But relief is imperative, and among possible remedies, none of which is perfect, this appears to us to be the least problematic.

Undoubtedly some room is opened up for the play of the subjectivity of the judges of the National Court of Appeals in the exercise of discretionary judgments to deny review. But someone's subjectivity is unavoidable. We believe our recommendation minimizes the chances of an erratic subjectivity. There are safeguards in the method of designation of the judges; and if the vote of three of the seven judges were to suffice for certification to the Supreme Court the concurrence of five of the seven would be required to deny the certification. We believe that a National Court of Appeals such as we propose would succeed in gaining the confidence of the country, the Supreme Court and the profession.

Again, some measure of loss of control by the Supreme Court itself is inevitable if the Court's burden is to be lessened. We believe this recommendation involves the least possible loss of control. The Supreme Court would select cases for decision on the merits from a docket of several times the number it would be expected thus to decide. Certiorari before final action in the court below, though not a procedure to be encouraged, remains available. Finally, the Supreme Court's readiness to reopen what had seemed to be settled issues, its impatience with, or its interest in, one or another category of cases—all this, we think, would communicate itself to the National Court of Appeals, and would be acted upon. We suggest, however, that the Supreme Court would be well-advised to return to the early practice of writing an occasional opinion to accompany a denial or dismissal of certiorari, and to offer a sentence or two in opinions on the merits by way of explanation of the grant.

We know of no way to quantify the relief that this recommendation would provide for the Supreme Court. Obviously, the chaff on the docket is less time-consuming than the marginal cases that hover between a grant and a denial, and of the latter the Court would still see some few hundred. But when the chaff is counted in the thousands, the burden is bound to be considerable. We are confident that a substantial amount of Justices' and law clerks' time would be conserved, and more imponderably, that there would be an appreciable lessening of pressure. We think that the costs of the proposal recommend—not merely the material ones, and not merely to litigants, but in terms of the values of the legal order and of the judicial process—are minimal. Balancing these costs against probable benefits, we are entirely persuaded that the proposal is worth adopting. An incidental advantage is that it would allow for experimentation for a period of years without a commitment to a permanent new tier of judicial review and a permanent new judicial body. It may turn out merely to palliate, or it may serve as a cure for at least as long as the reforms of 1891 and 1925 did in their time. Only experience will tell. We believe it should be allowed to tell. . . .

Notes and Questions

1. The Freund Report's suggestion that a National Court of Appeals be created stirred debate and controversy. *See, e.g., Retired Chief Justice Warren Attacks, Chief Justice Burger Defends Freund Study Group's Composition and Proposal,* 59 A.B.A. J. 721, 730 (1973). Why do you think it was controversial?

2. The Freund Report's recommendation in favor of a National Court of Appeals was never adopted. Instead, to deal with the Court's overcrowded docket, Congress passed legislation in 1988, described *supra* at page 180, that eliminated nearly all of the Court's mandatory jurisdiction.

2. Current Calls for Cert Reform in an Era of a Shrunken Docket

Unlike when the Freund Report was written, the Court's docket today is not overcrowded. Nonetheless, cries for cert reform have continued. The materials that follow include four representative examples of recent calls for certiorari reform written decades after the Freund Report at a time when the Court's docket is widely perceived as being too light, not too heavy. The first proposal provided below calls for the creation of a new "Certiorari Division." The second argues that new life should be breathed into the practice of "certification," whereby the lower federal courts can identify cases that warrant the Court's attention and "certify" them to the Court for decision. The third argues that the Court should be wary of docket capture whereby the Supreme Court's docket is being "captured" by the more powerful economic interests that know best how to influence the decision making of the Justices at the jurisdictional stage. Finally, the fourth analogizes to administrative law principles and argues that the Court's certiorari discretion—which was delegated to the Court by Congress—should be subject to greater transparency, accountability, and monitoring through vote disclosure and through greater public participation in the certiorari process. In reading the four proposals set forth below, think about which—if any—you find to be persuasive.

Paul D. Carrington & Roger C. Cramton, Judicial Independence in Excess: Reviving the Judicial Duty of the Supreme Court

94 Cornell L. Rev. 587, 632-636 (2009)

We would replace the "cert pool" of law clerks with a panel of experienced federal judges. These judges would be empowered to hear all petitions for certiorari and evaluate the petitions on the basis of standards supplied by Congress. They would place a specified and substantial number of cases on the docket of the Court, and the Court would be obligated to decide these cases on their merits. We tentatively designate the group as the Certiorari Division of the Supreme Court. Specifically, we suggest that a group of thirteen Article III judges be assigned the task of selecting perhaps as many as 120 cases a term that the Court would be obliged to decide in the manner of *Marbury v. Madison.* One member of the group might be drawn from each of the regional circuits to preclude suspicion of geographical bias. They might be selected automatically by a principle enacted by Congress. This service could, for example, be performed for limited part-time terms by circuit judges with at least ten years of federal judicial experience. All members of this Certiorari Division would still have ample time to bear a substantial share of the regular duties of circuit judges. Senior Justices who have retired from regular duty on the Court might also be asked to sit in the Division.

We envision that five members of the Division would be summoned in regularly scheduled sessions by the Clerk of the Supreme Court to meet and rule on pending certiorari petitions. It would be the duty of the Clerk to transmit petitions as they are received to the members of the next incoming panel. Their duty roster would be designed, perhaps by the Judicial Conference of the United States, to rotate the duty so that membership of the panels would not be constant. A circuit judge summoned to certiorari duty in three annual terms might thereafter be returned to full duty in the circuit and replaced by a colleague.

It would be the duty of the members of the Certiorari Division at each session to grant an appropriate number of pending certiorari petitions in accord with standards expressed by Congress. Given that the Court's present practice purporting to set standards for the exercise of this power is "hopelessly indeterminate and uni-lluminating," Congress or the Judicial Conference should be able to improve the law governing those decisions. It might prudently, as Justice White so long urged, give priority to the resolution of conflicts in the interpretation of federal law by the courts of appeals and to substantial issues of federal constitutional law presented by the decisions of the highest state courts.

We do not propose to prevent the Supreme Court from overruling a denial of certiorari by the Certiorari Division. Given the Court's workload and the dynamics of the situation, this would seem likely to be an infrequent event, but history indicates that the Justices could pick another hundred cases if they were highly motivated to do so. They would also retain the power to grant a petition for certiorari in order to vacate a judgment and remand the case to the lower court to revise its judgment in light of recent developments. Perhaps the Certioriari Division might on some occasions recommend that course to the Court.

The Certiorari Division would not write or publish an opinion to explain why a petition was granted, but an individual member of the ruling panel would be allowed to opine or dissent. A dissenting opinion might attract the interest of the Justices, who might then grant a petition that was not granted by the Division. The personal law clerks of the Justices might independently identify a case that their Justice might seek to bring before the Court. . . .

Richard Arnold observed that "the courts, like the rest of the government, depend on the consent of the governed," and they need often to be reminded of that dependence. Our present proposal is a response to his wise advice. It promises at least five important benefits. First, and most important in our view, the restructuring of the certiorari process would restore the Supreme Court to the more judicial and less legislative role that it generally performed prior to 1925. The Justices, like real judges, would have to decide many cases placed on their docket. This would partially restore the validity of Chief Justice Marshall's justification of the Court's power to review legislation, that it is obliged under Article III to decide cases and can only decide them in compliance with the text of the overriding Constitution. We would hope that thus restored to the role of a law court, the Supreme Court might rediscover the virtues of humility and acquiescence that Jefferson Powell has identified as the moral dimensions of the Justices' work. Perhaps it might also serve to scale down the excessively elevated expectations of the legal profession observed by Robert Nagel.

Second, relieving the Justices of the certiorari task they currently perform would provide them with increased time to decide a larger number of cases that raise important issues of national law. The Court so structured could be expected to leave fewer conflicts in the interpretation of federal law of the sort that have increasingly plagued the system. There would be a reduced need for courts of appeals to sit en banc. This in turn would ease the problems associated with the appointment of additional circuit judges needed to give proper and transparent attention to all the appeals filed in their courts.

Third, the new arrangement would vest the power to select a large part of the Court's cases in judges who are in the best position to know what issues of national law are most in need of authoritative attention: the veteran circuit judges who are the object of the Court's oversight and who have experience sitting on three-judge panels.

Fourth, we hope that our proposal will be perceived as an elevation of the status and authority of circuit judges, many of whom might expect to serve a three-year term on a division of the Supreme Court responsible for identifying the issues of national law needing authoritative resolution.

Finally, this reform would provide a modest measure of transparency to the Court's decisions to select cases for review and would reduce the influence on the selection process of instrumental considerations of the sort to which the public choice theory adverts. One might indeed view the proposed device as a source of judicial independence; those selecting the cases for the Court to decide would seldom if ever have the professional stake in their decisions that the Justices inevitably have. Judges sitting on a Certiorari Division panel would also be tempted to be instrumental in their choices of cases, but these temptations would not be constant or persistent. The increased transparency in case selection might also encourage a restoration of transparency in the proceedings in the lower courts. More oral arguments in the courts of appeals, at least in electronic form, might be provided.

Notwithstanding these benefits, we anticipate that the Justices will not join in urging Congress to adopt our proposal. Justice White to the contrary notwithstanding, we have been told that "the Justices are unanimous in their praise for the virtues of the discretionary court." On that issue, we can respond with confidence that none of the Justices bring judicial independence to the question of whether others should have a say in defining their workload. They are disqualified to opine on the subject.

Notes and Questions

1. Do you agree with Carrington and Cramton that creating a "Certiorari Division" would be desirable? Why or why not?

2. Why should the "certiorari court" proposed by Carrington and Cramton be composed only of experienced appellate judges? Professor Sanford Levinson has suggested that the idea of a "certiorari court" composed only of "'experienced appellate judges' is doubtful . . . unless one believes, entirely contrary to the main developments of constitutional theory in the twentieth century, the decisions as to which cases to take are entirely 'technical' and devoid of politics." Sanford Levinson, *Assessing the Supreme Court's Current Caseload: A Question of Law or Politics?*, 119 Yale L.J. 99, 111 (2010). Professor Levinson suggests that "if one wants to go the route of the Carrington-Cramton proposal, . . . its members should include not only a variety of judges drawn from all levels of the federal and *state* judiciary, but also (and just as importantly) some 'public representatives' who would be happily devoid of any legal training whatsoever." *Id.* According to Professor Levinson, "[i]f there really is a point to the Supreme Court's doing anything beyond providing uniform 'solutions' to conflicts below, then ordinary citizens should be able to offer their own valuable perspectives as to when intervention is needed (and when it is just fine to leave well enough alone)." *Id.* In light of Article III's text, do you think Professor Levinson's proposal would pass constitutional muster?

Amanda Tyler, Setting the Supreme Court's Agenda: Is There a Place for Certification?

78 Geo. Wash. L. Rev. 1310, 1311-1312, 1319-1327 (2010)

Professors Carrington and Cramton have added an important new chapter to the debate over the role of the Supreme Court in our judicial system. Specifically, they have offered a provocative suggestion as to how we might rethink the manner in which the Court's cases are chosen. Nonetheless, there are formidable problems with the proposal, not least of which is its questionable political viability. Notwithstanding these problems, a major attribute of the Carrington-Cramton proposal is that it seeks to involve in the case selection process the very judges who increasingly have called for greater guidance from the Court on questions that divide them. I agree with Professors Carrington and Cramton that these judges "are in the best position to know what issues of national law are most in need of authoritative attention." Significantly, there is already a procedural tool in place by which lower federal court judges may participate formally in composing the Court's docket: certification. . . .

. . . Certification is "essentially a simple appellate procedure." It allows one court to put questions of law to another court, the resolution of which will assist the certifying court in reaching a judgment in a case pending before it. When used as a means of putting questions from the courts of appeals to the Supreme Court, certification accomplishes the very same thing that Professors Carrington and Cramton highlight as a benefit of their proposal: namely, it involves those "judges who are in the best position to know what issues of national law are most in need of authoritative attention" in the dialogue on how the Supreme Court focuses its attention. . . .

My point of departure is the recent case of *United States v. Seale.*[58] This is a case in which the en banc Fifth Circuit divided 9-9 over an important statute of limitations issue that has come up in a host of decades-old Klan-violence cases currently being prosecuted by the federal government. When the judges could not agree on how to

---

58. *United States v. Seale* (*Seale II*), 570 F.3d 650 (5th Cir. 2009) (per curiam opinion by an equally divided en banc court), *vacating United States v. Seale* (*Seale I*), 542 F.3d 1033 (5th Cir. 2008) (panel opinion).

resolve the very complicated statute of limitations question that governed whether the government could even bring these prosecutions, a majority of the en banc Fifth Circuit certified the question to the Supreme Court. Ultimately, the Court declined the Fifth Circuit's invitation to resolve the issue. This was in keeping with the Court's modern practice of treating certification as discretionary, notwithstanding the fact that—technically speaking—the certification statute is one of few remnants of the mandatory appellate jurisdiction scheme of old.

Justices Stevens, joined by Justice Scalia, dissented from dismissal of the certification, lamenting that the Court has, in effect, abandoned this important means by which lower court judges can prod the Court to take up issues of great importance to the lower courts. Speaking to this particular case, the dissenters observed that there was "no benefit and significant cost to postponing the question's resolution." They continued: "A prompt answer from this Court will expedite the termination of this litigation and determine whether other similar cases may be prosecuted." The two Justices were, for whatever reason, unable to find two more of their colleagues who shared their views.

This is unfortunate. Indeed, the *Seale* case presented a strong candidate for certification. There was nothing to be gained by waiting for the case to return later on certiorari, for the factual record would shed absolutely no light on the purely legal statute of limitations question that the Fifth Circuit certified to the Court. In brief, depending on how one interprets the intersection of various statutes and the Court's precedents on point, either there is or is not a limitations period that curtails the government's ability to prosecute Seale and others like him on kidnapping charges arising out of their alleged actions in the 1960s. By denying certification in Seale's case, the result is a continuation of appellate proceedings, when it may well be the case, legally speaking, that the charges against him never should have been brought.

But whatever the merits of *Seale* as a candidate for certification, it is the larger complaint registered in Justice Stevens's opinion in that case that warrants special attention. As he noted, the Court has not taken up a certified question from one of the circuits for almost three decades. As Justice Stevens also observed:

> The certification process has all but disappeared in recent decades. The Court has accepted only a handful of certified cases since the 1940s and none since 1981; it is a newsworthy event these days when a lower court even tries for certification. [The certification rules] remain part of our law because the certification process serves a valuable, if limited, function. We ought to avail ourselves of it in an appropriate case.

This view echoes a similar dissent once registered by Justice Holmes, who viewed certification in cases involving "questions of pure law" as eminently appropriate. In his words: "[S]uch questions are to be encouraged as a mode of disposing of cases in the least cumbersome and most expeditious way."

Some history is illuminating. Congress enacted the first certification statute in 1802, providing in it that the Supreme Court "shall . . . finally decide[ ]" questions put to it by circuit court judges unable to reach agreement on the matter. In the Evarts Act of 1891, Congress modified the statute to account for the creation of the courts of appeals, giving the Supreme Court the option of either resolving only the certified question or calling for the record in order to decide the "whole matter in controversy." Importantly, Senator Evarts saw certification as playing a key role in ensuring that matters that divided the newly created courts of appeals (what today we often refer to as "circuit splits") would be resolved by the Supreme Court. Thus, he viewed certification as a means by which the courts of appeals could "guard against diversity of judgment in these different courts" by "send[ing] up" those questions of law that had divided them.

Certification also played a significant role in the passage of the Judges' Bill. As Professor Hartnett's work on that legislation summarizes: "In the hearings on the Judges' Bill, it was repeatedly noted that the Supreme Court would not alone control its jurisdiction, but that the courts of appeals, by use of certification, would share in that control." So, for example, Chief Justice Taft told Congress that certification would serve as a means pursuant to which the courts of appeals could exercise their own "discretion" to "place" particular legal issues before the Supreme Court. And Justice Van Devanter, in the final testimony on the bill prior to its passage, highlighted that the bill allowed the circuit courts "[w]henever they are so disposed" to certify "important questions of law" to the Supreme Court. The understanding that emerged in the wake of the Judges' Bill, reflected in Frankfurter and Landis's 1930 Harvard Law Review foreword, was that "[p]etitions for certiorari the Court can deny, but questions certified must be answered."

It did not take long, however, for that understanding to fall by the wayside. In the decade following the passage of the Judges' Bill in 1925, the circuits issued on average approximately seven certification[s] per Supreme Court Term. In the next decade, however, the average dropped to two per Term, and it has steadily declined ever since, such that today, "certification is practically a dead letter." . . .

Ironically, the demise of certification as a means of formal communication between the courts of appeals and the Supreme Court has taken place as the Supreme Court itself has increased its own practice of certifying questions to the highest courts of the states. The Court also now takes the position that certification to the state courts is the preferred course of action for lower federal courts faced with resolving important and unsettled questions of state law. . . .

This trend highlights the fact that both federal and state courts have grown to develop a certain comfort level with certification as a means of communicating— except in this particular context, which, ironically, is the form of certification with the richest historical pedigree. It also bears noting that the principal criticism of new forms of certification—namely, that they occasion delays in the final resolution of cases—does not apply in the context of certification by courts of appeals to the Supreme Court. On the contrary, the latter form of certification often results in more efficient resolution of cases. Consider again, in this regard, the *Seale* case.

In addition, comparable provisions that Congress enacted in 1958 to provide for interlocutory review in the courts of appeals when the district and circuit courts agree that such review is appropriate "have worked fairly well." There is no reason to think that reinvigorating the practice as a means of communication between the courts of appeals and the Supreme Court could not work equally well. As the Federal Practice and Procedure treatise notes, moreover, "certification, if wisely used, would have several advantages," including that "[i]t would sharply distinguish a small handful of cases from the flood of frequently worthless certiorari petitions that engulf the Court." Another possible advantage is that certification allows the Court to ignore "[i]ncidental issues" that otherwise "might encumber a petition [for certiorari]." But my focus on the practice sees a more immediate benefit: certification allows lower court judges themselves to inform the Court—directly and formally—that an issue is important, recurring, and in need of its resolution. . . .

Skeptics will suggest that the Supreme Court is unlikely to alter its practices without new legislation compelling it to do so. Thus, one could imagine calls to make certification truly mandatory or at least mandatory where an issue has been certified by more than one court of appeals. For now, I hesitate to go this far, in part from an appreciation for the benefits that discretion brings to the exercise of jurisdiction, and in part because I suspect that the Supreme Court is likely to be more receptive to a practice promoted within its own ranks in contrast to one imposed on it by Congress. With that said, if Congress were to revisit the certification rules, it should consider adding a means by which the highest courts of the states could certify questions to the Supreme Court, given that they too are in a position to gauge which unsettled issues of federal law are of great concern to the lower courts.

Notes and Questions

1. Do you think that the Supreme Court would be receptive to reinvigorating the practice of certification? Or do you think that if greater certification is to be achieved, Congress must revisit the certification rules and mandate greater use of certification?

2. Which proposal for cert reform—Tyler's call for a reemergence of certification or Carrington and Cramton's call for a Certiorari Division—do you find more appealing? Which do you think has the greater likelihood of being successfully implemented?

3. Might part of the reason why the Court has let certification fall by the wayside be because the Court has become increasingly willing to grant certiorari before judgment? *See* Chapter 3 *supra* at pages 128-129 (discussing the Court's practice of granting certiorari before judgment).

Richard J. Lazarus, Docket Capture at the High Court

119 Yale L.J. Online 89 (2010)

The declining number of cases on the Supreme Court's plenary docket may or may not be a problem. After all, there are many good reasons that such a decline could be happening, including the obvious possibility that the Court was previously hearing too many cases that did not warrant plenary review and is now doing a better, not worse, job of picking cases. But while having fewer cases is not necessarily problematic, what is worrisome is the very real possibility that the Court's plenary docket is increasingly captured by an elite group of expert Supreme Court advocates, dominated by those in the private bar. The same way that powerful economic interests can capture an agency or any other entity that purports to exercise authority over those interests, so too may the Supreme Court's docket be "captured" by the more powerful economic interests that know best how to influence the decision-making of the Justices at the jurisdictional stage. It is, accordingly, not the number of cases on the plenary docket but rather their content that is the real problem.

I. THE RISING INFLUENCE OF THE SUPREME COURT BAR AT THE JURISDICTIONAL STAGE

The statistics are striking. While the number of merits cases has roughly declined by one half during the past three decades, the influence of the expert Supreme Court bar over the plenary docket during this same time period has increased approximately tenfold; expert practitioners now represent the successful petitioner at the jurisdictional stage in more than fifty percent of the cases. What is the basis of this measurement? I examined the petitions granted plenary review in several Supreme Court Terms, ranging back to October Term 1980 and extending to the most recently completed October Term 2008. I deliberately eliminated from consideration cases in which the Solicitor General was the petitioner or one of the petitioners because her influence is well established. And, I chose a fairly tough measure of what it means to be an "expert Supreme Court advocate": an attorney either has to have presented at least five oral arguments before the Court or be affiliated with a practice whose current members have argued at least ten cases. Based on this measure, expert Supreme Court advocates were responsible for 5.8% (6 of 102 cases) of the petitions granted plenary review during October Term 1980. By October Term 2000, that same percentage had increased to 25% (seventeen of sixty-eight cases) and has steadily increased since—36% in October Term 2005 and 44% in October Term 2006—to boast more than 50% of the Court's docket during both the most recently completed October Terms 2007 (53.8%) and 2008 (55.5%). I do not doubt that there is some inexactitude at the margins in counting cases and oral arguments and comparing Supreme Court Terms, but these trends are beyond marginal. They reflect a shift of an order of magnitude.

Why should we worry? Good advocacy is not a bad thing, of course, and it should not be especially surprising to discover that those who are more experienced advocates before the Court are especially successful in persuading the Court to grant their certiorari petitions. What is worrisome is the potential for an undesirable skewing in the content of the Court's docket. The public should expect that the Court will devote its limited resources to address the legal issues that are truly the most important for the nation rather than those legal issues important to those who can secure representation of their interests by the Supreme Court bar.

II. The Environmental Law Cases of October Term 2008

It is not numbers alone that strongly suggest that the private Supreme Court bar is increasingly capturing the Court's docket. A look at the cases themselves reinforces that suggestion. As described further below, the Court regularly grants cases at the urging of leading members of the private sector Supreme Court bar that are marginally certiorari worthy at best, at a time when the rates of granting certiorari are otherwise rapidly declining. No one may be more skilled in this respect right now than Sidley Austin's Supreme Court practice, as underscored by the extraordinary number of cases arising under the Federal Employer Liability Act in which the firm has obtained High Court review on behalf of railroad clients.

Especially illustrative are the environmental cases from October Term 2008. For the first time, a series of industry clients last Term turned repeatedly to the expert Supreme Court bar for assistance in a host of cases arising under federal pollution control laws. The result was palpable and formed the basis of the best Term that industry has ever enjoyed before the Court in environmental cases.

The Court granted review in four cases that, absent the involvement of expert practitioners, would not have seemed to have had a remote chance of review. Two were Clean Water Act cases (*Entergy Corp. v. Riverkeeper, Inc.* and *Coeur Alaska, Inc. v. Southeast Alaska Conservation Council*) in which industry parties were merely intervenors in the lower courts and the federal agency that had lost the case declined to petition on its own and opposed Supreme Court review. Such federal opposition is almost always the death knell of a petition. If the Solicitor General is advising the

Court that the federal agency that lost below is not seeking review that tends to end the matter. In one of those cases (*Entergy*), not only was there no circuit court conflict, but the lower court ruling was the first court of appeals ever to construe statutory language that has been on the books for more than thirty-six years. The third and fourth cases, *Burlington Northern & San Francisco Railroad v. United States* and *Shell Oil v. United States*, both arose under the federal Superfund law and raised legal issues of diminishing practical significance the Court declined to hear for decades. Not only is Superfund a retrospective liability law that has naturally dissipated in its application over time, but Congress has declined since 1995 to reauthorize the federal tax that funds the Act, so resources for the law's administration have been running out ever since.

In all four cases, a high-profile member of the private Supreme Court bar served as lead counsel for industry petitioners: Maureen Mahoney in *Entergy* and *Burlington Northern,* Ted Olson in *Coeur Alaska, Inc.,* and Kathleen Sullivan in *Shell Oil.* The bar's *coup de grâce* last Term, however, was the Court's denial of the Solicitor General's petition in yet another Clean Water Act case, *McWane, Inc. v. United States. McWane* presented all the traditional criteria of a case warranting review—an express, deep, and wide conflict in the circuits regarding a legal issue of national importance; yet, the Court denied review after Ted Olson's partner at Gibson Dunn, Miguel Estrada, filed an especially skillful brief in opposition to the government's petition. There is hardly anything in Supreme Court advocacy as difficult as obtaining plenary review, but defeating a Solicitor General's petition runs a close second. The Court grants the Solicitor General's petitions for writ of certiorari about seventy percent of the time compared to between three and four percent for others.

III. The Susceptibility to Capture of the Court's Jurisdictional Decisionmaking

Some might respond that even if the Court's plenary docket has been captured, this is not the result of a hostile takeover. Any such development, it could be contended, results from the predilections of business-friendly members of the Court rather than the heightened skills of the advocates. Such an assessment, however, would both overestimate the role Justices play at the jurisdictional stage and underestimate the influence of the advocates. To be sure, the Justices—and not the advocates—are the ones with the votes necessary to grant certiorari. But the Justices are far more dependent on the skills of the advocates than is routinely appreciated.

Even with the introduction of the "cert" pool, neither the Justices nor their clerks can in fact spend significant time evaluating the certiorari worthiness of the literally thousands of petitions that must be reviewed. Once one subtracts the significant time necessary to decide increasingly complex merits cases and the other activities of a Justice these days, the clerks can spend on average only minutes for each cert pool memo, or at most a few hours for a handful. The Justices have, in theory, at most only a few minutes to review a petition and may in fact never read the petitions themselves. The Justices instead delegate the task to their law clerks—inexperienced recent law school graduates who lack both the requisite background and time necessary to consider the competing legal arguments on the merits, and to evaluate in a truly informed and independent manner the petitioner's claims of circuit conflict and practical importance.

The upshot is a huge tactical advantage for those attorneys who know best how to pitch their cases to the law clerks. The expert attorneys know the trends in the Court's recent precedent and the predilections of each individual Justice as evidenced in recent oral argument transcripts, speeches, and writings. Having once served as Supreme Court clerks themselves, the experts are also well versed in the generic limitations, susceptibilities, and tendencies of the clerks.

Their expertise extends to the securing of multiple amicus briefs at the jurisdictional stage in support of their request for the Court's plenary review. They appreciate how amicus support substantiates their assertions regarding the importance of the legal issues proffered for review. And they have the professional connections with other members of the Supreme Court bar and the economic clout to generate the necessary amicus submissions. If news article and op-ed columns contemporaneous to the Court's jurisdictional determination might be helpful, they can and will obtain them.

The expert advocates also invariably enjoy an advantage by dint of their sheer celebrity, at least within the confines of One First Street, N.E. The clerks know of the outstanding reputation of these expert advocates for working on important Supreme Court cases. Many of the clerks hope to and do in fact work for these experts' law firms immediately or soon after their clerkships. And, for no reason more than the appearance of the name of the advocate on the cover of the brief, their petitions will receive more attention and respect. This is not an incidental advantage. In the barrage of petitions under review, visibility alone can make all the difference at the jurisdictional stage, especially when buttressed by multiple amicus briefs supporting plenary review.

The effect is twofold. Not only are the expert Supreme Court counsel able to make their petitions seem more compelling, but they are simultaneously able to make petitions filed by others less expert seem relatively weaker by comparison. The experts have, in practical effect, raised the bar for Supreme Court review through their outstanding presentations and significant amicus support.

IV. Reforming the Court's Decisionmaking Process at the Jurisdictional Stage

The question is what, if anything, to do about the disproportionate influence the high Court bar increasingly has on the Court's plenary docket. A full answer to that question, however, lies far beyond the purpose of this Essay, which seeks to initiate, and not end, the conversation. Nonetheless, I offer a few preliminary thoughts. First, part of the answer could, of course, be to improve the Supreme Court advocacy available to a wide range of interests beyond those who can afford to pay its market value. Mitigation already occurs to an extent as reflected in the private bar's willingness to offer pro bono services, the development of expert solicitors general in many states, and the recent emergence of Supreme Court clinics in several of the nation's leading law schools.

But, such mitigating efforts fall far short of filling the gap between those who have access to the resources of the expert Supreme Court bar and those who do not. Much of the private law firm pro bono effort occurs at the merits stage rather than at the certiorari stage and there are many subject matters (e.g., environmental, employment discrimination) that the private bar, because of conflicts with paying clients, will not take up, including when they oversee the law school Supreme Court clinics. It is undeniably a positive development to have the states represented more effectively than in the past, but they too are limited in their perspective and, for instance, may deepen rather than reduce the advocacy gap existing in criminal cases. Finally, the Supreme Court clinics offer some promise, but law students even at schools like Harvard, Northwestern, Stanford, Texas, Virginia, and Yale are still just that: students.

The disproportionate influence that the expert Supreme Court bar exerts on the content of the Court's plenary docket is the problem, not solved by which cases the bar takes—business or public interest—but by the Court itself asserting more control. For this reason, I expect the fuller solution to the docket capture problem will be found, by analogy, to the kinds of structural reforms that have been made in administrative agencies to reduce the risk of agency capture.

As applied to the Court, such reforms would require changes in the Court's internal decisionmaking process at the cert stage. The place to start is questioning the existing cert pool as the primary basis for evaluating which cases warrant plenary review. As currently structured, the law clerks lack the time, experience, and resources at the jurisdictional stage to evaluate in a meaningful way the claims made by expert counsel or to make up for the deficits of below-par counsel.

. . . One modest recommendation would be to replace the existing single cert pool with two competing cert pools, thereby increasing the number of clerks who provide a petition with a close review. Another would be the introduction of a two-step process to jurisdictional review in which the clerks would first identify potentially cert-worthy cases and then next examine that smaller subset of petitions more closely prior to recommending in favor of certiorari.

A more ambitious reform would be for the Justices to be more willing at the jurisdictional stage to seek input from those outside the Court who are knowledgeable about the issues raised by a pending petition. The Court currently seeks such input several times a year on pending petitions, but exclusively from the Solicitor General by way of formal orders inviting the Solicitor General to express the views of the United States on a pending petition. The Court could make similar requests from other knowledgeable organizations as a method of ensuring the wisdom of the Court's jurisdictional determinations.

An even more dramatic structural reform would be the addition to the Court of an office of seasoned, career lawyers akin in skills to assistants to the Solicitor General; the attorneys in such an office would assist the Court at the jurisdictional stage in assessing the worthiness of cases for judicial review, by both questioning the exaggerated claims of some advocates and making up for the deficiencies of other advocates. Whatever the best approach, it is increasingly likely that the current potential for capture of the Court's docket is a significant problem that warrants the Court's attention.

Notes and Questions

1. Do Lazarus's findings—which suggest that expert Supreme Court advocates were responsible for 53.8 percent of the petitions granted plenary review during the October 2007 Term compared with only 5.8 percent of plenary grants in the 1980 Term—trouble you? What implications do his findings have for access to justice?

2. Which of the structural reforms proposed by Lazarus to help minimize docket capture at the Court do you think would be most viable? Most effective?

3. Besides those listed by Lazarus, can you think of other possible ways of helping to minimize or avoid capture of the Court's docket? In thinking about this question, perhaps the next excerpt will give you some ideas to consider.

Kathryn A. Watts, Constraining Certiorari Using Administrative Law Principles

160 U. Pa. Law Rev. 1, 43-50, 52-62 (2011)

A. LEGISLATING MORE SPECIFIC STANDARDS

The most obvious way to provide a check on the Court's certiorari discretion would be for Congress to pass legislation that more specifically delineates the standards to be used in certiorari decisions. . . .

. . . In the past, some have argued that Congress should try to more carefully delineate the kinds of cases that warrant certiorari review. Herbert Wechsler, for example, argued in 1961 that "much would be gained if the governing statutes could be revised to play a larger part in the delineation of the causes that make rightful call upon the time and energy of the Supreme Court."[225] The fact that Congress has not done so—despite mounting criticism of the certiorari process—seems to highlight a fairly widely held assumption: certiorari decisions are driven by a variety of factors, including the importance of the questions, the presence of a conflict in the lower courts, the need for further percolation of the issues, and the need for clarification of the law. Hence, some level of flexibility seems desirable in certiorari decisions. . . .

Consistent with this notion that flexibility is valuable in the agenda-setting process, most states have chosen to leave their highest courts with docket-setting discretion. In Kansas, for example, a statute lists various non-binding factors that the court should consider, such as the "general importance of the question presented" and the "existence of a conflict." Similarly, in Minnesota, a statute delineates factors that its court "should" take into account when deciding whether to grant a petition for further review, including the importance of the question and whether a statute has been held unconstitutional, but these factors are merely "intended to be instructive" and are "neither mandatory nor exclusive." . . . This highlights the need to look to other more indirect forms of constraint in the certiorari context. . . .

B. MANDATING DISCLOSURE TO ENABLE GREATER TRANSPARENCY AND MONITORING

An alternative means of reining in the Court's discretion and enabling greater oversight and transparency would be for Congress to mandate—or for the Court to voluntarily impose upon itself—some kind of disclosure requirements. Two possible disclosure requirements are considered here: (1) requiring the Court to explain the reasons behind certiorari decisions; and (2) requiring disclosure of the Justices' certiorari votes. . . .

1. Imposing a Reason-Giving Requirement

. . . [A] few scholars—including one writing shortly after the passage of the Judges' Bill—have considered the possibility of requiring the Court to explain its certiorari decisions. This kind of reform, however, would likely face numerous legal and practical hurdles.

First, it might not be feasible for the Court to explain all of its certiorari decisions. Various Justices have indicated that it would be plainly impractical for the Court to do so. For example, in 1950 when the Court acted on approximately 1500

---

225. Herbert Wechsler, Principles, Politics, and Fundamental Law 15 (1961).

certiorari petitions per term, Justice Frankfurter explained that "it would not be feasible to give reasons, however brief, for refusing to take" cases because the "time that would be required" would be "prohibitive." Similarly, writing in 1977 when the Court heard about 150 out of 4000 cases per term, then-Justice Rehnquist suggested that "there simply is not the time available to formulate statements of reasons why review is denied." Today, concerns about the time-intensive nature of explaining certiorari decisions would likely be even more acute given that the Court now receives approximately 8000 or 9000 petitions per term.

While it might seem that issuing a brief order stating that a certain certiorari petition was denied because it is "splitless and factbound" or because it alleges the "misapplication of a properly stated rule of law" would not take that much time, this may not be true. For the most part, the Justices act on their own—without the benefit of collegial discussion—when deciding which cases merit discussion as a group, and even those certiorari petitions that are deemed worthy of group discussion receive fairly perfunctory discussion at conference. Given that certiorari decisions tend to be made individually, it seems likely that different Justices might have different reasons for granting or denying certain petitions. Accordingly, it might be quite difficult for the Court to quickly formulate any kind of unified certiorari explanations.

Second, it might be argued that reason-giving requirements are most applicable to decisions that are driven by legal or technocratic factors and less applicable to highly discretionary decisions driven by strategic or political concerns. . . .

Finally, if a reason-giving requirement were to be imposed, there is still the question of who would impose it. It seems highly unlikely that the Justices would agree to voluntarily adopt such a requirement, especially in light of statements made by various Justices, such as Chief Justice Rehnquist and Justice Frankfurter, suggesting that the Justices believe that the Court simply does not have the time to explain its certiorari decisions.

So any reason-giving requirement would likely have to come from Congress. Yet congressional attempts to impose a reason-giving requirement on the Court would almost certainly elicit constitutional objections on separation of powers grounds. . . .

In any event, this constitutional question might well be mere academic sport because of a serious practical hurdle that would likely get in the way of any congressionally imposed reason-giving requirement: the Court might choose to thumb its nose at Congress by providing only very vague and general explanations in response to any such statute. The nub of the problem is *quis custodiet ipsos custodes*: who would guard the guardians? The experiences of two states—Michigan and Maryland—corroborate this concern.

A provision of the Michigan constitution mandates that the state's supreme court provide "reasons for each denial of leave to appeal." . . .

. . . [This requirement, however, has] failed to yield meaningful explanations. In fact, in Michigan, "[a]ll that is filed in the clerk's office and sent to the litigants is a standard form order filled in with the title and docket number of the case" and accompanied by boilerplate language stating that the court is "'not persuaded that the question(s) presented should be reviewed.' "[274] . . .

---

274. Maurice Kelman, *Case Selection by the Michigan Supreme Court: The Numerology of Choice,* 1992 Detroit C.L. Rev. 1, 12.

Maryland's experience with a reason-giving requirement is quite similar. A Maryland state statute provides that its highest court (the Maryland Court of Appeals), which can grant review when the court determines it is "desirable and in the public interest," shall provide the "reasons for the denial of the writ . . . in writing." As in Michigan, the requirement has not resulted in illuminating explanations of certiorari denials. Rather, the Court of Appeals will generally issue nothing more than formulaic language to the effect that the petition is "denied as there has been no showing that review by certiorari is desirable and in the public interest." . . .

In short, with no means of enforcing a reason-giving requirement against the Court, the success of any such requirement would likely depend on the receptiveness of the Court. Given that it seems quite unlikely that the Court would look kindly upon a congressional mandate or would voluntarily impose such a requirement on itself, other mechanisms for constraining the Court's certiorari jurisdiction warrant consideration.

2. Requiring Disclosure of Certiorari Votes

. . . [O]ne less intrusive and much more promising means of forcing an alternative kind of disclosure might simply be to require publication of the Court's votes on certiorari petitions. This could be a backdoor way of obtaining reasons for some of the Court's certiorari decisions since the Justices—knowing that their certiorari votes would be made public and fearing that their votes could be misread as a reflection on the merits of the case—might be more inclined to choose on their own initiative to explain their certiorari votes in certain cases. For example, a Justice might opt to write an explanation of a vote to deny a petition by noting that jurisdictional defects in the petition precluded a vote to grant but that the substantive issues raised in the petition warrant review in a future case, thereby signaling to the outside world that the Justice is interested in the merits of the issue raised.

A vote-disclosure requirement also might be a way of encouraging the Justices to rely less on their law clerks for petition screening and to pay more careful attention to certiorari petitions. After all, the Justices' own names would be publicly attached to certiorari decisions at the time the decisions are made rather than (as is the case under our current system) years or decades after the fact when a retired colleagues' papers are made public. In addition, publication of the discuss list might help to cut down on frivolous filings. An attorney might be reluctant to recommend that a client spend money on a certiorari petition if the attorney knew that the client would ultimately learn that no Justice on the Court voted to grant certiorari.

Perhaps even more importantly, a vote-disclosure requirement could be used to facilitate public oversight and political monitoring. . . . Specifically, Congress could use vote-disclosure information to consider whether (and how) to revise the Court's jurisdictional statutes. In addition, both the President and the Senate could use the information to put the spotlight on certiorari in the confirmation process and to take nominees' views on certiorari into account when nominating and confirming Justices. . . .

a. Votes on Petitions That Fail to Make the Discuss List

Requiring public disclosure of those certiorari petitions that are automatically denied without discussion would be an easy way to shed some light on the certiorari process and enable greater monitoring. Unlike a reason-giving requirement, such disclosure would not impose a time-consuming burden on the Justices. Since the Court already internally tracks which cases make the discuss list and which do not, it would be quite simple for the Court to release a list of certiorari petitions that were denied without receiving conference discussion. If the Court were to disclose all cases that fail to make the discuss list, it would, by negative inference, also disclose those cases that did make the discuss list.

Certainly, the mere disclosure of those petitions that fail to make the discuss list would not enable the outside world to learn why certain cases did or did not warrant discussion, but such disclosure would reveal—in a minimally intrusive manner— which petitions yielded discussion and which did not, as well as precisely how many petitions fail to yield any conference discussion in a given year. Accordingly, Court watchers and Congress alike would gain valuable information about how the Court is exercising its discretion.

Such a disclosure requirement would not be unheard of in the judicial realm, but rather finds an analog in various federal courts of appeals' en banc procedures. Much like petitions for certiorari filed with the U.S. Supreme Court, petitions for rehearing en banc filed with the courts of appeals are often denied, and rarely even result in a judge requesting a vote on the petition. Notably, three different circuit courts have chosen to adopt rules or internal procedures that provide that orders denying petitions for rehearing en banc shall note when no member of the circuit court requests a poll on the petition. . . .

b. Votes on All Petitions or All Denied Petitions

Alternatively, the Court could be required to disclose the Justices' votes on more than just the subset of petitions that fail to make the discuss list. This could be done by either requiring the Justices to disclose their votes on all denied petitions (not just those petitions that are automatically denied because they fail to make the discuss list), or by requiring the Justices to disclose their votes on all petitions regardless of whether the petition is granted or denied. A major advantage of vote disclosure on all petitions is that it would be easier for those external to the Court, including Congress, to monitor the Court's certiorari decisions and to piece together possible voting patterns. One possible disadvantage, however, of disclosing votes on all petitions might be that if certiorari votes were disclosed at the time certiorari was granted, then litigants in granted cases might try to tailor their merits arguments to certain Justices based on a "tea leaf" reading of the certiorari votes. This problem could be avoided, however, by waiting to disclose certiorari votes on granted petitions until the case is decided on the merits. Alternatively, a vote-disclosure requirement could be limited to denied petitions.

At the en banc level, the Fourth Circuit's local rules provide a useful example of requiring vote disclosure for all denials. In the Fourth Circuit, not only will an order on a petition for rehearing that fails to yield a request for a poll "bear the notation that no member of the Court requested a poll," but also if a poll is requested on a petition and rehearing en banc is denied, then "the order will reflect the vote of each participating judge."

Some other useful examples can be found at the state level. In Arizona, for example, Rule 23(h) of Arizona's Rules of Civil Appellate Procedure provides: "If the Supreme Court denied review, its order shall specify those justices of the Supreme Court, if any, who voted to grant review." . . . Similarly, in California, a court rule also calls for vote disclosure on petitions for review, but unlike the rule in Arizona, it focuses on disclosure of votes in cases where review is granted.

Specifically, this rule provides: "An order granting review must be signed by at least four justices; an order denying review may be signed by the Chief Justice alone." . . .

The fact that some federal and state courts have chosen to promulgate court rules imposing vote-disclosure requirements suggests that it might not be all that unrealistic to believe that the U.S. Supreme Court would be willing to do so as well. . . .

C. ENABLING GREATER PUBLIC PARTICIPATION

One final means of reforming the Court's certiorari discretion would seek to enable greater public participation in the certiorari process by analogizing to public participation mechanisms that exist in the administrative law world. The goal certainly would not be to move the certiorari process to a full-blown notice-and-comment rulemaking model, which is cumbersome and can take years to complete. Rather, the goal would be to increase the opportunity for participation by knowledgeable outsiders through greater invited and uninvited amicus curiae participation and through greater use of "certification," which allows the lower federal courts to certify questions of law to the Court for resolution.

Currently, the primary sources that the Court looks to when making certiorari decisions are the written briefs filed by the petitioner seeking certiorari, any brief in opposition filed by the respondent, and the opinions below. Certiorari decisions are thus based primarily on information presented to the Court in the parties' briefs through a fairly closed judicial process. This highlights how Congress has removed important questions about what kinds of cases the Court should hear from the usual legislative arena where public participation and open deliberation can easily occur. It also highlights how the Court must make certiorari decisions based on limited information regarding the importance of the case. Enabling greater participation by knowledgeable outsiders in the certiorari process could help to open up the process to greater public awareness and deliberation.

Notes and Questions

1. Do you agree that requiring the Justices to provide explanations for their certiorari decisions would be impractical because of the sheer amount of work this would require of the Justices? Would it also be unconstitutional for Congress to impose such a requirement on the Court?

2. Even if the Justices are not required to explain their cert votes, should they nonetheless be required to disclose those votes, as Watts proposes? Why or why not?

3. Whereas Tyler focuses on giving lower federal court and state court judges a greater role in identifying those cases that warrant the Court's attention, Watts suggests that the Court might provide more opportunities for the broader public to weigh in on certiorari petitions. How likely do you think it is that the broader public would have anything worthwhile to offer to the Justices about the certworthiness of cases? And how likely is it that the Justices would listen to the public's views?

4. After reading the different proposals for cert reform set forth above, do you agree that the cert process is broken and needs to be reformed? Or is the status quo preferable? For one federal judge's thoughts on this, *see generally* J. Harvie Wilkinson III, *If It Ain't Broke*, 119 Yale L.J. Online 67 (2010) ("Although critics in recent years have lodged various complaints about the Court's docket, the solutions being urged upon us will neither cure the alleged ills nor avoid significant collateral damage.").

5. As described *supra* at page 174, the Court has not always stood as a Court of discretionary jurisdiction. Would one potential path to certiorari reform involve rethinking the Judges' Bill of 1925 and turning the Court back into a court of predominantly mandatory jurisdiction? For one scholar's views on this question, *see* Edward A. Hartnett, *Questioning Certiorari: Some Reflections Seventy-Five Years After the Judges' Bill*, 100 Colum. L. Rev. 1643, 1738 (2000) (arguing on the 75th anniversary of the Judges' Bill that it was "appropriate to reflect upon and question" the Court's "far-ranging power to set its own agenda and thereby shape the nation's political agenda").

6. If you were tasked with drafting a proposal to reform certiorari, what would you propose? Why? How might your proposed reforms change the Court's approach to certiorari? To its docket?

5

Written Advocacy

If an advocate is skilled or lucky enough to have certiorari granted by the Supreme Court, the counsel's work is just beginning. In a relatively short period of time, counsel must perform four crucial tasks. First, the attorney must, in consultation with opposing counsel, prepare a joint appendix containing key items from the record below including, for example, docket entries, pleadings, opinions, and jury instructions. The details of the time-consuming and often contentious procedure for preparing this crucial document is laid out in Supreme Court Rule 26, which can be found in Appendix B. Second, the attorney must begin preparation for oral argument.[1] Though oral argument preparation is treated in detail in Chapter 6, it is worth mentioning at this earlier stage because, in almost all cases, it proceeds in tandem with merits briefing. As the merits brief is the platform for oral argument, the brief needs to make sure to lay out the points that the oral advocate will want to emphasize before the Court and to frame the issues in terms that lend themselves to effective colloquy with the Justices.

Third, counsel must prepare the required briefs on the merits according to the requirements laid out in Supreme Court Rules 24, 25, 33, and 34. This task imposes somewhat different obligations on petitioners and respondents. In drafting their arguments, petitioners are limited to the issues on which the Court has granted certiorari. As Supreme Court Rule 14.1(a) spells out, "only the questions set out in the petition, or fairly included therein, will be considered by the Court." As discussed in Chapters 3 and 4 above, the Court grants certiorari for the purposes of deciding particular issues, and it therefore usually will not consider issues that are raised by petitioner for the first time in the brief on the merits. The respondent's situation is different. The Court usually allows a respondent to include in his or her brief on the merits any argument that supports the judgment below, as long as (1) the argument was presented below and (2) to the extent the argument calls into question the accuracy or applicability of the question presented, those concerns

---

1. Sometimes the primary author of the merits brief is also the lawyer who will argue the case before the Court, but, for a variety of reasons, that is not always the case. Whenever possible, it is highly desirable to have the lawyer who will be arguing the case involved in reviewing or preparing the brief in some significant capacity. Decisions as to who will be arguing a particular case are usually made either before the petition is filed or quickly after certiorari has been granted, but occasionally drag themselves out as affiliated counsel strategize for their clients and/or compete with each other for the honor. In one recent example, the lawyers representing two government parties in a pending case bickered incessantly, resolved to decide who would argue by coin toss, and then had trouble agreeing on the rules for the coin toss. *See* Katie Mulvaney, *Coin Toss Could Decide Who Takes State Case to High Court*, Provid. J., Oct. 24, 2008.

were raised in the brief in opposition to the petition for certiorari. *See* Supreme Court Rule 15.2 ("Counsel are admonished that they have an obligation to the Court to point out in the brief in opposition, and not later, any perceived misstatement in the petition. Any objection to consideration of a question presented based on what occurred in the proceedings below, if the objection does not go to jurisdiction, may be deemed waived unless called to the Court's attention in the brief in opposition.").

Fourth, counsel must strategize about and, within the limits set by ethical and court rules, coordinate the activity of sympathetic *amicus curiae.* The scope of participation by *amici* in Supreme Court merits litigation has increased dramatically in recent decades. *See* Joseph D. Kearney & Thomas W. Merrill, *The Influence of* Amicus Curiae *Briefs in the Supreme Court,* 148 U. Pa. L. Rev. 743, 749 (2000) (noting an 800 percent increase in amicus briefs between 1965 and 1999). By most, though not all accounts, so too has their influence. *See, e.g., id.,* at 749-750 (finding that *amicus* briefs have a small and uneven but significant influence on the outcome of cases); Paul M. Collins, Jr., *Friends of the Court: Examining the Influence of* Amicus Curiae *Participation in Supreme Court Litigation,* 38 Law & Soc'y Rev. 807, 807 (2004) (reaching similar conclusions). Scholars and advocates have identified a number of ways in which sympathetic *amici* have the ability to influence the Court; they may, for example, raise additional legal arguments, provide relevant historical background or empirical data, illustrate the real-world consequences of potential rulings, or demonstrate the support of particular relevant and persuasive constituencies.

The materials in this chapter explore merits and *amicus* briefing and will be divided into three sections. Section A provides a brief overview of the briefing schedule by which advocates and *amici* must abide. Section B discusses the theory and practice of merits briefing, looking sequentially at the elements of a Supreme Court brief, the literature on how to prepare such a brief (including scattered pearls of wisdom from current and recently retired Justices), and examples of recent briefs. Section C focuses on *amicus* briefs, exploring in turn the proper role of an *amicus,* the requisites of a successful *amicus* brief, and a few particularly influential or noteworthy recent briefs.

A. THE BRIEFING SCHEDULE

Once certiorari has been granted, the briefing schedule is tight. The timetable for filing briefs is primarily governed by Rule 25, which is laid out below. A full briefing cycle (petitioner's brief, respondent's brief, and a reply brief by petitioner) takes 105 days. However, both because the Court's calendar causes scheduling pressure at predictable times in the year and because certworthy cases do not reach the Court at a steady rate, the Rule specifically provides that some cases will be "advanced for hearing" with the time to file briefs "abridged." Sup. Ct. R. 25.5. This provision is used with some regularity, both when the substance of the case requires prompt attention and when necessary to fill the Court's calendar (for example, when there are slots remaining at the end of the Court's argument schedule or when the Court does not grant enough cases before its summer recess to fill its calendar through December). *See generally* Robert Stern et al., *Supreme Court Practice* 700-701, 757-759 (9th ed. 2008). For similar scheduling reasons, petitioners are not guaranteed a full 30 days to file their reply briefs but instead must ensure that they are "received" by the Court a week in advance of oral argument. Sup. Ct. R. 25.3. The Court's Rules state that "[a] case will ordinarily not be called for argument less than two weeks after the brief on the merits of the respondent . . . is due," Sup. Ct. R. 27.1, but even then there are no promises. The Clerk of the Court may grant an extension of time to file a brief on the merits if such a request is "justified" by "specific reasons," Sup. Ct. R. 30.4, but such an application "is not favored," Sup. Ct. R. 25.5. At one point in time, the Court routinely granted extensions for briefs that were due during the Court's long summer recess but were not slated to be argued until later in the term, but that practice appears to have ended.

Amici must abide by a similar, though slightly extended, briefing schedule. Briefs in support of petitioners or respondents are due within seven days of the filing of that party's brief, while briefs labeled as supporting neither party are due within seven days of the expiration of petitioner's time to file. Sup. Ct. R. 37.3(a). All *amici*—other than the Solicitor General, other federal agencies authorized to appear separately at the Court, states, and local government agencies—must obtain either written consent from the parties or permission of the Court in order to file their brief. S. Ct. R. 37.4. In most, but far from all, cases, the parties give blanket consent to the filing of *amicus* briefs rather than reviewing each individually.

Rule 25. Briefs on the Merits: Number of Copies and Time to File

1. The petitioner or appellant shall file 40 copies of the brief on the merits within 45 days of the order granting the writ of certiorari, noting probable jurisdiction, or postponing consideration of jurisdiction. Any respondent or appellee who supports the petitioner or appellant shall meet the petitioner's or appellant's time schedule for filing documents.

2. The respondent or appellee shall file 40 copies of the brief on the merits within 30 days after the brief for the petitioner or appellant is filed.

3. The petitioner or appellant shall file 40 copies of the reply brief, if any, within 30 days after the brief for the respondent or appellee is filed, but any reply brief must actually be received by the Clerk not later than 2 p.m. one week before the date of oral argument. Any respondent or appellee supporting the petitioner or appellant may file a reply brief.

4. If cross-petitions or cross-appeals have been consolidated for argument, the Clerk, upon request of the parties, may designate one of the parties to file an initial brief and reply brief as provided in paragraphs 1 and 3 of this Rule (as if the party were petitioner or appellant), and may designate the other party to file an initial brief as provided in paragraph 2 of this Rule and, to the extent appropriate, a supplemental brief following the submission of the reply brief. In such a case, the Clerk may establish the time for the submission of the briefs and alter the otherwise applicable word limits. Except as approved by the Court or a Justice, the total number of words permitted for the briefs of the parties cumulatively shall not exceed the maximum that would have been allowed in the absence of an order under this paragraph.

5. The time periods stated in paragraphs 1, 2, and 3 of this Rule may be extended as provided in Rule 30. An application to extend the time to file

a brief on the merits is not favored. If a case is advanced for hearing, the time to file briefs on the merits may be abridged as circumstances require pursuant to an order of the Court on its own motion or that of a party.

6. A party wishing to present late authorities, newly enacted legislation, or other intervening matter that was not available in time to be included in a brief may file 40 copies of a supplemental brief, restricted to such new matter and otherwise presented in conformity with these Rules, up to the time the case is called for oral argument or by leave of the Court thereafter.

7. After a case has been argued or submitted, the Clerk will not file any brief, except that of a party filed by leave of the Court.

8. The Clerk will not file any brief that is not accompanied by proof of service as required by Rule 29.

9. An electronic version of every brief on the merits shall be transmitted to the Clerk of Court and to opposing counsel of record at the time the brief is filed in accordance with guidelines established by the Clerk. The electronic transmission requirement is in addition to the requirement that booklet-format briefs be timely filed.

B. MERITS BRIEFS

The stakes are very high in written advocacy before the Supreme Court. The parties' merits briefs represent the only opportunities they will have to lay out their arguments for the Justices without interruption or opposition. An effective merits brief is likely to leave the Justices disposed to ruling in the party's favor and may provide a blueprint for the Court's opinion if the Court ultimately decides in the party's favor. Conversely, a poorly written or inartfully organized brief may well obscure winning arguments or highlight gaps in the party's case.

The benefits of a well-executed brief—and the dangers of a poorly executed one—are magnified by the time pressures the Justices and their clerks face. With very few exceptions, the Court hands down its decisions in all cases argued during a given term by the end of June. In order to adhere to that deadline while allowing time for the drafting of dissenting and concurring opinions, Justices have less than a month to circulate draft majority opinions in the last cases argued each term and less than two months to circulate drafts in all but the most complicated cases argued earlier in the term. Given the other obligations that Justices and their clerks have during this time and the amount of in-chambers back-and-forth that precedes the circulation of a draft opinion, there is little time to waste reinventing the wheel. Thus, powerful arguments from the winning brief often make their way into the pages of the United States Reports with only light editing.

The literature on what makes a good Supreme Court brief is surprisingly thin, relying on either broad generalities about the need for "good writing" and "careful planning" or detailed anecdotes of dubious general applicability. Perhaps outstanding written advocacy is, as many claim, more art than science. *Cf.* Frederick Bernays Wiener, *Briefing and Arguing Federal Appeals* 5-6 (1961 ed.) ("It may be urged—and some friends have suggested—that it would be just as impossible—quite as unhelpful—to attempt to teach advocacy as to write a learned tome on how to paint a picture or how to write a novel."). Or maybe, as others puckishly suggest, the best brief writers are loath to give up their lucrative secrets.

The remainder of this section will attempt to provide a little bit of insight and provoke a lot of questions about what makes a good brief by approaching that question from three different perspectives. First, we will look at the elements of the brief separately, understanding what each is supposed to do. Second, we will review excerpts from some of the most helpful literature. Finally, we will look at the merits briefs in an important case in which the petitioners' briefs have been much applauded and the respondent's brief has been subject to substantial criticism.

1. Elements of the Brief

Rule 24. Briefs on the Merits: In General

1. A brief on the merits for a petitioner or an appellant shall comply in all respects with Rules 33.1 and 34 and shall contain in the order here indicated:
   (a) The questions presented for review under Rule 14.1(a). The questions shall be set out on the first page following the cover, and no other information may appear on that page. The phrasing of the questions presented need not be identical with that in the petition for a writ of certiorari or the jurisdictional statement, but the brief may not raise additional questions or change the substance of the questions already presented in those documents. At its option, however, the Court may consider a plain error not among the questions presented but evident from the record and otherwise within its jurisdiction to decide.
   (b) A list of all parties to the proceeding in the court whose judgment is under review (unless the caption of the case in this Court contains the names of all parties). Any amended corporate disclosure statement as required by Rule 29.6 shall be placed here.
   (c) If the brief exceeds five pages, a table of contents and a table of cited authorities.
   (d) Citations of the official and unofficial reports of the opinions and orders entered in the case by courts and administrative agencies.
   (e) A concise statement of the basis for jurisdiction in this Court, including the statutory provisions and time factors on which jurisdiction rests.
   (f) The constitutional provisions, treaties, statutes, ordinances, and regulations involved in the case, set out verbatim with appropriate citation. If the provisions involved are lengthy, their citation alone suffices at this point, and their pertinent text, if not already set out in the petition for a writ of certiorari, jurisdictional statement, or an appendix to either document, shall be set out in an appendix to the brief.
   (g) A concise statement of the case, setting out the facts material to the consideration of the questions presented, with appropriate references to the joint appendix, e.g., App. 12, or to the record, e.g., Record 12.
   (h) A summary of the argument, suitably paragraphed. The summary should be a clear and concise condensation of the argument made in the body of the brief; mere repetition of the headings under which the argument is arranged is not sufficient.
   (i) The argument, exhibiting clearly the points of fact and of law presented and citing the authorities and statutes relied on.
   (j) A conclusion specifying with particularity the relief the party seeks.

2. A brief on the merits for a respondent or an appellee shall conform to the foregoing requirements, except that items required by subparagraphs 1(a), (b), (d), (e), (f), and (g) of this Rule need not be included unless the respondent or appellee is dissatisfied with their presentation by the opposing party. . . .

Notes and Questions

1. Like in most legal documents, some elements of a Supreme Court brief are mechanistic. The high court's rules are more specific and less flexible than those of some other courts, but it is hardly surprising that the Court wants easy access to the questions presented, the names of all parties, the citations to earlier opinions in the case, and the relevant statutory and constitutional texts. Nor is it surprising that a busy Court demands a table of contents and table of authorities and seeks up-front reassurance as to its jurisdiction. In most instances, these elements are uncontroversial, though jurisdiction is occasionally at issue and, as discussed below, the parties at the merits stage often continue to bicker about the precise wording of the questions presented. Why do you think the Supreme Court insists that these largely factual elements be presented in a particular order and broken out from the main text of the briefs?

2. In looking at the various elements of a merits brief, it is useful to put yourself in the position of an advocate. In drafting the mechanistic portions of a Supreme Court brief (like the list of parties and the table of authorities), are there pitfalls to avoid? What about strategic opportunities to subtly influence the Court?

3. The central strategic importance of the questions presented has already been addressed in Chapter 4, and the jurisdictional consequences of a petitioner's failure to raise potential questions in a cert petition has already been considered in Chapter 3, but both points are worth reiterating in the context of merits briefing. By the time a case reaches the merits stage, parties are more constrained in formulating, raising, and challenging questions presented, but they need to remain vigilant both as to the particular formulations of the questions and as to whether the questions fully encompass all of the issues the parties intend to press in their briefs. Unless the Court has specifically drafted the questions themselves, parties are free to tinker with the language of the questions in their merits briefs, and most avail themselves of the opportunity. For example, during the Supreme Court's March 2012 sitting, the parties in each of the nine argued cases (ranging from the momentous cases challenging the constitutionality of aspects of the Patient Protection and Affordable Care Act to routine cases involving the application of the harmless error doctrine and the meaning of technical provisions of the Social Security Act) offered different variants on the questions presented. *See October Term 2011*, SCOTUSblog, http://www.scotusblog.com/case-files/terms/ot2011/ (linking to the briefs in all the cases).

4. In some cases, the parties choose to include prefatory material before the questions presented, to provide context or predispose the Court to a particular view of the case. How effective are such tactics? Consider one recent example. In *Miller v. Alabama*, 132 S. Ct. 2455 (2012), the petitioners raised a number of issues related to the constitutionality of life without parole sentences for juveniles convicted of murder. The petitioners framed the questions presented as follows:

1. Does imposition of a life-without-parole sentence on a 14-year-old child convicted of homicide violate the Eighth and Fourteenth Amendments' prohibition against cruel and unusual punishments?

2. Does such a punishment violate the Eighth and Fourteenth Amendments when it is imposed on a 14-year-old child as a result of a mandatory sentencing scheme that categorically precludes consideration of the offender's young age or any other mitigating consideration?

Brief for Petitioner, *Miller v. Alabama*, 132 S. Ct. 2455 (No. 10-9646). Here, in contrast, is the respondent's version:

When Evan Miller was 14, he robbed his neighbor, beat him bloody with a baseball bat, set his home on fire, and left him to die in the blaze. The juvenile court transferred him to the criminal system, and a jury convicted him of capital murder. Like most States and the federal government, Alabama requires all persons convicted of certain aggravated murders to be sentenced to, at a minimum, life imprisonment without the possibility of parole. Miller's Eighth Amendment challenge therefore raises the following two questions about governments' ability to punish juveniles who commit these crimes:

I. Does the Eighth Amendment categorically bar governments from imposing life-without-parole sentences on persons who commit aggravated murder when they are 14 years old?

II. If the Eighth Amendment does not categorically bar governments from imposing life-without-parole sentences on these offenders, does it nevertheless require governments to exempt these offenders from statutes that, for the worst forms of murder, make life without parole the minimum sentence?

Brief of Respondent, *Miller v. Alabama*, 132 S. Ct. 2455 (No. 10-9646). Which of these two openings is more likely to garner the Court's attention? Their sympathy? Their trust?

Less controversially, lawyers in highly technical cases and cases involving particularly complicated statutory and regulatory schemes often include explanatory material before their questions in order to clarify the issues for judges or law clerks who might not be sufficiently versed in those matters.

5. Rule 24(1)(g) requires "[a] concise statement of the case, setting out the facts material to the consideration of the questions presented." This, by another name, is the "facts" section familiar to the author of any legal memorandum or brief. In drafting this section, a lawyer must produce a narrative of the relevant events and contexts that is "fair and adequate" but also, to the extent possible, "leaves the impression that right and justice demand a decision in his or her favor." Stern et al., *Supreme Court Practice*, at 713. This is a tall task. Experts in appellate advocacy and legal writing have suggested a number of strategies for threading this particular needle. For example, one of the leading introductory guides to brief writing directs students to (1) "create a favorable context" by inserting the reader into the narrative at a place and time likely to present your client favorably; (2) "tell the story from the client's point of view"; (3) emphasize favorable facts by giving them more "airtime," giving them more "detail," and locating them at the beginning and end of the section, its paragraphs, and its sentences; (4) "choose words carefully" paying special attentions to the nuances of different verbs and adjectives that nominally mean the same thing; and (5) attempt to persuade only at the margins, avoiding misstatements, omissions, and rhetoric that undercut your objectivity. *See* Laurel Currie Oates, Anne Enquist & Connie Krontz, *Just Briefs* 103-116 (2d ed. 2008). In reading through actual Supreme Court briefs, can you identify particular places in which the authors successfully utilized these strategies? Can you identify any other strategies that they used to craft a fair yet persuasive statement of facts?

6. Rule 24(1)(h) requires, "[a] summary of the argument, suitably paragraphed" and goes on to explain, "[t]he summary should be a clear and concise condensation of the argument made in the body of the brief; mere repetition of the headings under which the argument is arranged is not sufficient." In many ways, this is the most difficult element of the brief to draft. It must be sufficiently detailed and persuasive to convince a Justice who does not have the time or inclination to read the entire argument section before oral argument yet sufficiently sleek and transitional to avoid wasting precious words or irritating the majority of Justices who will read the briefs in their entirety. Nor does it help that the Justices appear to be of wildly different views as to the importance of this section. (For two conflicting views on this matter, see the opinions of Justices Scalia and Thomas quoted in subsection B(3) below.) The leading Supreme Court practice guide suggests that the summary should total somewhere between 600 and 1,200 words and should be no more than 10 percent of the length of the argument section. Stern et al., *Supreme Court Practice*, at 714. If you were drafting a Supreme Court brief, which would you write first, the argument section or the summary section, or would you work back and forth between the two?

7. Rule 24(1)(i) simply asks for "[t]he argument, exhibiting clearly the points of fact and of law presented and citing the authorities and statutes relied on." Of course, advocates spend the vast majority of their word limit crafting their arguments, and more cases are won or lost here than in any other part of the brief.[2] Some of the requisites of a successful argument section are discussed below. At this point, however, it is worth noting just how many tasks go into crafting the argument section. Advocates must, at a minimum, identify their central arguments, organize those arguments into both specific contentions and a broader structure, craft and test the particular contours of each claim, identify and highlight supporting authority, identify and mitigate opposing authority, anticipate and preempt the most significant countervailing arguments, and frame the issues in such a way that the Justices come away convinced that the law, if not the world, will be a better place if the advocates' ideas are heeded. Some briefs succeed swimmingly at some of these tasks but flounder at others. In reviewing and evaluating briefs, both in this class and in practice, it is often useful to break these questions out and assess how well the authors performed each task.

8. Rule 24(2) allows respondents to omit from their briefs any or all of the questions presented, the list of parties, the citations to the proceedings below, the statement of jurisdiction, the relevant statutory and constitutional provisions, and/or the statement of the case if they are satisfied with the petitioners' treatment of these elements. Are there some of these elements that lend themselves to such reliance? Are there others that are more likely to require restatement or even refutation?

---

2. How frequently the quality and content of the respective briefs influences the outcome of Supreme Court cases is a question about which many have speculated but few agree. This book does not further address either the competing arguments or the nascent academic literature trying to resolve the question, though Chapter 6 does consider the related question of whether the quality and content of oral argument matters to the disposition of cases. For one of the more interesting recent attempts to measure the impact of briefs, see Chad M. Oldfather, Joseph P. Bockhorst & Brian P. Dimmer, *Triangulating Judicial Responsiveness: Automated Content Analysis, Judicial Opinions, and the Methodology of Legal Scholarship*, 64 Fla. L. Rev. 1189 (2012).

The next two subsections offer advice on how to prepare merits briefs. Subsection (2) provides guidance from leading practitioners, legal writing experts, and a sitting judge (later Justice) about the core tasks and key attributes of a successful Supreme Court brief. Subsection (3) then offers scattered pearls of wisdom from six current Justices, gleaned from a series of wide-ranging interviews each gave to a leading legal writing expert.

2. Preparing an Effective Merits Brief

a. The Advocate's Task

James vanR. Springer, Some Suggestions on Preparing Briefs on the Merits in the Supreme Court of the United States

33 Cath. U. L. Rev. 593 (1984)

Briefs on the merits in the Supreme Court—those filed after the Court has decided to hear a case by granting certiorari or noting probable jurisdiction—are not fundamentally different from briefs filed in any appellate court. The ample general literature on appellate advocacy therefore applies to this subject as well. It should not be necessary to add to this literature, but the day-to-day experience of reading briefs that have been filed and drafts proposed to be filed suggests that perhaps it is. I begin with a few thoughts about the general subject, articulated in the Supreme Court context, and then offer some more specific suggestions on Supreme Court briefs. I do not purport to be exhaustive or to discuss all of the pertinent Supreme Court rules. . . .

The common deficiency of most bad or mediocre briefs is a lack of perspective, which results in a failure to give the audience the information it wants and needs. Since the audience is a panel of nine Justices or three judges, such perspective is obviously best acquired by being one of them or a judicial law clerk. The experience can, however, be simulated—and should be periodically—by simply taking the time to read a few briefs as though one were on the bench. Choose a field in which you have some general knowledge (preferably the field in which you are about to write) and read the briefs and opinions in several recent cases in which you have not been involved. Which briefs do you find most persuasive? Which briefs pave the way followed by the decisions? Which ones leave you troubled by unanswered factual or legal questions suggested by the opposing briefs or by your own reflection? Which briefs are simply difficult to fight your way through? Are there parts that you cannot resist skimming or passing entirely? A modicum of such role-playing will be more instructive than my maxims or those of anyone else.

In your judicial role-playing, and in writing a brief, it is essential to recognize the time constraints under which Supreme Court Justices and other appellate judges must work. In 1959, Professor Hart estimated that on the average each Justice had no more than two hours to devote to reading the briefs in each case heard on the merits before casting his vote at the post-argument conference. With the certiorari workload more than doubled in the intervening years, Professor Hart's estimate must now be regarded as the maximum time available. The role-player should adhere to these same time constraints. And any Supreme Court brief must be written in a manner that allows a Justice to grasp fully, in an hour or less of focused reading, the nature and significance of the issues presented, the essential factual context in which they arise, and the points of the argument. Professor Hart's moral bears repeating:

> [W]ritten arguments filed with the Court are not documents like law review essays which the author is entitled to expect each of his readers to peruse carefully and reflectively from beginning to end. Perhaps the writer of an opinion reads a brief this way. But for other members of the Court these documents necessarily serve a different function than the communication simply of a connected line of thought. They are documents from which busy men have to extract the gist in a hurry. . . . Briefs on the merits need not only tell their story to one who takes the time to read all the way through them, but to be so organized that they can be used, like a book or reference, for quick illumination on any particular point of concern.[3]

From this perspective, it is clear that less is more. Think of the page limitations imposed by the rules not as an arbitrary hindrance but as an essential challenge to the advocate's powers of concise exposition and persuasion.

Bear in mind the functions of the briefs in the deliberative process. Apart from a relatively cursory study some months earlier when certiorari was granted (or probable jurisdiction noted), the briefs are the Justices' introduction to a case and the impressions derived from them are more likely than not to be decisive. The one time when you can be reasonably certain of all nine Justices' undivided attention to the merits of your case—as you choose to present them—is when they first sit down with the briefs in chambers. Oral argument is a much more uncertain thing, with less time available, numerous potential distractions and much less control on your part. First, the brief has to convey what the issues are, in both conceptual and practical terms, and what the relevant facts are. Only then is it time to present your arguments; resist any attempt to convince the Court on the first page that the decision below was outrageous or that the petitioner's arguments are frivolous. Your brief must also anticipate any questions that may linger after the argument, and serve to refresh the Justices' understanding of your position as they review the case before voting at the post-argument conference. In order to fulfill these functions, both the brief for the respondent or appellee and the "topside" brief should be complete in themselves, rather than merely attacking the statements and reasoning in the opponent's brief or the opinion below. The Court should be able to understand the entire case as well as your arguments within the four corners of your brief, and the presentation must be such that the reader can easily refer to particular points whenever the occasion arises.

Think of the proceedings in the Supreme Court (or the court of appeals, for that matter) more as a new case than as an extension of the proceedings below. Keeping this in mind may help avoid the pitfall of viewing the appeal as an exercise in self-vindication—to prove that the trial strategy was correct notwithstanding its failure, that the judge or judges below were stupid or biased, or that opposing counsel misrepresented the facts. Just as the trial lawyer must restrain his client's passions when they interfere with an effective presentation, so also must the appellate lawyer restrain the trial lawyer's passions. The fact that the appellant should have won on a point below does not necessarily mean that it is a strong point on appeal. A misstep below, bad luck, or simply the way the evidence appears in the cold pages of the record may make it necessary to abandon a point or recast it drastically. A fresh look at the whole case is essential. . . .

3. Quoting Henry Hart, *The Supreme Court, 1958 Term, Foreword: The Time Chart of the Justices*, 73 Harv. L. Rev. 84, 94 (1959).

Every brief should have one principal author or editor who is responsible for organization, consistency, and style. Frequently, this should not be the most senior lawyer on the case; it should be one who can devote intensive attention to the task and know the record and the authorities. Good briefs are written by individuals, not committees or assembly lines.

Although the rules prescribe the format of the briefs in broad terms, and include several technical requirements, they leave the writer a great deal of leeway as to both structure and style. There is no single way to write a brief, and the best way to explain what the case is about and show why your position is right will vary from case to case. Brief writing is a creative art rather than merely a mechanical exercise of summarizing the record and recording the results of someone's legal research. The artist must develop and refine an overall concept, must have the daring to take a novel approach, and must have the patience and discipline to rework his material, often throwing away painfully constructed prose that cannot withstand harsh editorial scrutiny.

In format, Supreme Court merits briefs are not significantly different from other appellate briefs. Their contents and tone are obviously affected by the fact that the Court is Supreme. Authority has much less significance, and reasoning has much more, even if it questions the precedents in the lower courts or, sometimes in the Supreme Court itself. With nine Justices and a collection of exceptionally bright law clerks, a Supreme Court brief is subjected to more intense intellectual analysis than most briefs. And while the Court often decides cases on extremely narrow grounds, it is obviously more inclined than lower courts to explore the broader ramifications of the issues before it.

Some suggestions about the major sections of the brief follow: . . .

The Argument.—In any brief, and particularly in the Supreme Court, the Argument section can usefully be viewed as the part of the brief that shows the Court that a compelling opinion can be written in your favor. The purpose is not to display the author's scholarship[,] and straightforward lucidity will be more effective than elaborate or subtle discourse. Your general reading of other Supreme Court briefs and the Court's opinions will have reminded you that the Court starts with a good deal of general learning and—in some areas where it has recently been active—a very detailed knowledge of the law. Your familiarity with your particular field and with the Supreme Court's opinions in it will guide you in deciding the extent to which the argument should (relatively speaking) start in midstream, i.e., when you are joining a legal discussion that was actively going on when you arrived. The Court will be impatient with reiterations of elementary principles or the details of cases with which it is familiar. The result may be a loss of attention to the important parts of your argument. The question here is one of discretion as to how much the Court need be told and the tone in which it should be addressed—something that can only be learned from actual or vicarious experience.

The Argument should ordinarily be broken down into logical and relatively short subsections, each having a brief heading in argumentative language. When all of the headings and subheadings are put together in your table of contents, they alone should show clearly what your points are and how they are interrelated—a kind of summary of the Summary. An Introduction is frequently helpful. This is not a summary but an explanation of the structure of the brief and the interrelationship of the various points. It is essential in any event that the brief of the petitioner or appellant state with particularity, at the outset, exactly what the errors to be corrected are and exactly what relief is sought. In general, if the brief does not state in simple terms what you want and why you should have it, it needs to be reworked.

One advantage the Supreme Court brief-writer has is that of knowing in advance the identity of the 'panel' that will be hearing the case (barring recusals). In an area where a substantial number of the present Justices have written, it may be feasible to strategize about trends and to determine the best way to assemble a majority favoring your position. On the other hand, playing to the presumed biases of individual Justices can be risky if overdone, and rhetoric is of little help. In any event, your points must be intellectually sound and, unless you have made a considered decision to attempt to change the law, must be consistent with the Court's majority decisions.

The nature of the authorities that can be used in support of your arguments is, as previously suggested, extremely broad, but you must keep in mind the Supreme Court's role in the judicial system. Because lower court decisions are pertinent but not decisive, the Court is more influenced by their reasoning than their number and not infrequently reverses positions widely accepted in the lower courts. String citations of cases are almost never convincing, particularly where (as often) their support of a particular point is obscure at best. In most instances, any case that is worth citing to the Supreme Court is worth discussing sufficiently to show why it is particularly on point or sheds analogous light on the question at hand. And be careful with quotations: the excerpts you choose not only must fairly support your point, but must plainly appear to do so without requiring the reader to go to the original source to determine whether you have quoted out of context. Snippets separated by dots or stars are unconvincing; either paraphrase or preferably quote enough so that the language speaks for itself. On the other hand, multipage quotations are seldom helpful.

You will, of course, have fully researched the legislative history of any federal statutes upon which you rely, and will have reviewed the scholarly writings on the legal points at issue. You will also have surveyed other potential sources of relevant historical, scientific or sociological information that are susceptible to the peculiarly generous kind of judicial notice in which the Supreme Court is willing to indulge ("Brandeis brief" materials). The extent to which such materials should be used in the brief and how they should be presented are, of course, matters of judgment under the particular circumstances of each case. The general principle is that, while the brief cannot safely stray far from the record with respect to the facts of the particular case, the Supreme Court will "take judicial cognizance of all matters of general knowledge."

The brief for the petitioner or appellant should present all of the arguments worth making on his side and anticipate and "pull the teeth of" the factual statements and arguments the other side can be expected to make. Do not save anything for the reply brief that you can put in the main brief. Reply briefs should be limited to essential responses to unanticipated points, and you should not hesitate to do without one if there is nothing essential to say. . . .

Notes and Questions

1. The author of this article was a leading appellate attorney in Washington, D.C. for many years until his recent retirement and served as a Deputy Solicitor General from 1968-1971.

2. Mr. vanR. Springer states at the outset that Supreme Court merits briefs "are not fundamentally different from briefs filed in any appellate court," but then goes on to describe a series of salient differences between the Supreme Court and other courts that have an impact on briefing strategy before the high court. Which of those differences did you find most significant? Do they sound like the kind of differences that can be mastered by any experienced appellate advocate, or do they militate in favor of hiring an experienced Supreme Court litigator to handle a matter before that Court?

3. The article matter-of-factly suggests that Justices and their clerks lack sufficient time to read merits briefs with care. While this is conventional wisdom and may in fact be correct, events since the publication of this article arguably have loosened the time pressures under which the Justices work. First, as noted in Chapter 4, the rise of the cert pool has reduced the amount of time each chambers must spend evaluating cert petitions. Second, as also noted in Chapter 4, the number of cases the Supreme Court reviews has dropped substantially since 1984. In recent years, the Supreme Court has decided roughly 80 cases per term by opinion (including argued cases and summary reversals); during the term before the above article was written, the Court decided 168 such cases. *See The Supreme Court, 1983 Term—The Statistics*, 98 Harv. L. Rev. 307, 307 (1984). Finally, the number of clerks hired by many of the Justices has expanded since 1984.

4. Like most experienced Supreme Court advocates, Mr. vanR. Springer urges those briefing and arguing cases before the Supreme Court not to rely too heavily on a long list of cited cases and to emphasize the arguments rather than the authority of the cases they do cite. While he largely limits this advice to lower-court decisions, others have offered similar advice about prior Supreme Court decisions, arguing that few issues on which the Supreme Court grants cert can be resolved by resort to the Court's precedents. *See, e.g.*, Stephen M. Shapiro, *Oral Argument in the Supreme Court of the United States*, 33 Cath. U. L. Rev. 529, 535 (1984) ("Most of the cases that reach the Supreme Court are doubtful, and respectable opinions can be written to justify either affirmance or reversal. In this situation, technical legal reasoning will not suffice."). Does the limited role of precedents in resolving Supreme Court cases (in comparison with, say, an intermediate state court of appeals) surprise or disturb you? *Cf.* Eric J. Segall, *Supreme Myths: Why the Supreme Court Is Not a Court and Its Justices Are Not Judges* (2012) (arguing, as its title suggests, that the Supreme Court's decision-making process is not, in any meaningful sense, a process of legal reasoning). If the close parsing of cases does not resolve most Supreme Court litigation, what mechanisms do the Courts have for ensuring that their decisions remain identifiably "legal"? The following excerpt from a future Supreme Court Justice offers another perspective on these issues.

b. Focus on Principle

[handwritten: Principle?]

Wiley Rutledge, The Appellate Brief

19 Dicta 109, 115-117 (1942)

. . . I turn now to the third function [of the merits brief], the application of the law— in other words, your argument proper. Given the facts, given right and true analysis, two functions remain, argument on principle and argument on authority.

Having been so long a teacher, I suppose I have a predilection for principle, though that does not imply a contempt for authority.

But I find enlightenment in the former respect absent more frequently than in the latter. Perhaps my major criticism of briefs, apart from that relating to analysis, would deal with the lack of discussion on principle. Some cases are so clearly ruled by authority, directly in point and controlling, that discussion of principle is superfluous. But these are not many. I have been surprised to find how many appealed cases present issues not directly or exactly ruled by precedent. That is as it should be. The novel case is the one most appropriate for appeal, and the bar, on the whole, appears to exercise excellent discrimination in selecting such cases for appeal. In a large percentage of the cases, therefore, there is room for discussion and thought as well as for citation. Discussion on principle has direct relation to analysis of facts. If that is clearly and fully made, the former will follow almost automatically. What we want to know is why this case, or line of cases, should apply to these facts rather than that other line on which your opponent relies with equal certitude. . . . Too often the why is left out. The discussion stops with the assertion that this case or line of cases rules the present one. Assertion is not demonstration. And beyond the amount necessary for statement of position and emphasis it may weaken or indicate that you are doubtful of your position. "The lady doth protest too much." The argument which stops at this point gives us the lead you wish us to follow. But it is bobtailed, nevertheless. The lead may be the wrong one, or we may think it such. Your reasons for thinking it the right one may keep us out of error, if perchance we can be saved. In a close case, where the authorities pertinent by analogy are conflicting and especially when they are equally pertinent and numerous on both sides, the discussion of the underlying principles as related to the present application counts heavily to swing the scales. . . .

Finally, I come to the authoritative function. I shall state this as briefly as possible.

1. When available the cases in point—on all fours—are the ones we want. If they are available, your way, and in quantity to settle the law, citation and discussion of others wastes your time and ours.

   There is one exception. That is when the law is settled the wrong way and you think you can play legal Don Quixote successfully. This has become a legal sport more popular in recent than in former years. But it is still a mountain-climbing sport and when one tries to climb perhaps anything goes, principle, law review articles, Brandeis briefs, whatnot. The climb is not recommended for everyday exercise.

2. When the case is not ruled by precedent, then precedent by analogy must take over the functions of persuasion and decision. And this is where much waste occurs. The cases most approximate are the ones we need. But approximation is always a matter of judgment and degree. It is the old question of "when is far too far?" When using cases by analogy (as well as otherwise) and relying heavily upon them, it is always wise to give, in your own words, a brief and accurate statement of the facts. Half or more of the meaning of the case you discuss is lost, unless you do this—or unless your opponent has done it sufficiently for you.

Notes and Questions

1. The author of this piece, Wiley Rutledge (1894-1949), was at the time a Judge of the United States Court of Appeals for the District of Columbia Circuit, arguably the second most prestigious court in the nation. He was the former dean of the law schools at both Washington University in St. Louis and the University of Iowa and an enthusiastic supporter of President Franklin Roosevelt. The year after this article was published, President Roosevelt appointed him to the United States Supreme Court, where he served until his untimely death six years later. The future Justice John Paul Stevens was one of his law clerks.

2. What does it mean to argue "principle"? Is it an alternative to arguing cases, or a mechanism for organizing your arguments about cases? There is language in this excerpt that suggests the former, but such an approach, taken to the extreme, seems in tension with stare decisis and other rule-of-law values. How do you think Justice Rutledge would respond to that concern?

3. Consider an example from earlier in Justice Rutledge's article (remembering, of course, that it is 70 years old and that the underlying law may have changed). Two individuals are arrested for robbery and, unrepresented, "plead guilty" at a preliminary hearing. When they obtain representation, they withdraw their pleas and take their cases to trial. At trial, are their unrepresented "pleas" admissible against them? As Justice Rutledge narrates:

> . . . The prosecution asserted that admissibility was controlled by the law of voluntary or extrajudicial confessions. The defense claimed violation of the right of counsel and of the privilege against self-incrimination. On the prosecution's theory, there was no compulsion sufficient to destroy the probative value of the plea, regarded as a confession of guilt. On the theory of the defense, a serious question arose as to whether the privilege had been violated. There was no controlling authority. But analogies from Supreme Court decisions were close, on both sides, and conflicting. The government relied heavily on cases holding that statements not amounting to a confession or statement of guilt, made under circumstances similar to those existing when the plea was made, were admissible. The defense relied on a decision excluding a plea of guilty made at arraignment. Our case stood exactly between the two lines of Supreme Court decisions. Both analogies were close. In the absence of the other, each probably would have ruled our decision. But there they stood thumbing noses at each other—and with our case in between.
>
> The point in regard to the briefs is this: Each brief was admirable—on its theory. Each cited pertinent authorities, perhaps all of them. Each drew its analogies closely. Each was a lawyer's work of art. But there was one respect in which each failed. Neither discussed on principle why its basic theory of the case, rather than that of the other, should apply. What I wanted to know, and for me it was the controlling issue, was why the rule of evidence rather than the privilege, or vice versa, should be applied in and should control this case. But the arguments largely skipped this question, namely, what considerations dictate that this body of law rather than that one be applied. And because the authorities most controlling were so approximate the pending case on both sides, and so directly contradictory in analogy as to the outcome, this was almost wholly a question of principle, perhaps somewhat of history, as distinguished from one of authority merely. . . .

Id. at 115-116.

4. In a more recent article, two leading Supreme Court advocates offer a similar—albeit more pragmatic—argument for focusing on the principles on which precedents stand rather than on their inherent authority:

> It also is desirable to explain the client's position in a way that makes sense from a policy (or common sense) perspective. Judges are concerned about both the institutional and the real-world consequences of the rules they adopt. Relatively few cases that reach

appellate courts are controlled so squarely by precedent that the judges have no wiggle room. Accordingly, even if favorable precedent is available and you intend to rely heavily on it, write the argument in a way that gives the judges confidence that they should follow that precedent. That is far better than baldly telling them that they must follow it—and daring them to disagree.

Andrew L. Frey & Roy T. Engelert, Jr., *How to Write a Good Appellate Brief*, Litigation, Winter 1994, at 6, 7.

5. Reliance on language in prior Supreme Court cases, even language seemingly essential to the reasoning, can be fatal if the Court, reflecting anew on the area of law, concludes that the language unnecessarily limits the principle that animated the earlier decision. *See, e.g., Board of Education v. Earls*, 536 U.S. 822 (2002) (upholding constitutionality of suspicionless drug testing of students who participated in extracurricular activities despite language in prior case upholding similar testing scheme for student athletes seemingly relying on factors specific to athletics). Similar problems can occur when litigants rely on even an unbroken string of relevant precedents if opposing counsel (or the court below) can identify a coherent animating principle for the prior cases that distinguishes the case under consideration. *See, e.g., City of Indianapolis v. Edmond*, 531 U.S. 32 (2000) (finding Fourth Amendment violation when police stop cars at vehicle checkpoints in order to allow dogs to sniff for drugs despite prior decisions upholding similar checkpoints to investigate other crimes because, under a rationale developed by Judge Richard Posner in the decision under review, the criminal law schemes involved in the other cases could be classified as serving "special needs" and the scheme in this case served only "to detect evidence of ordinary criminal wrongdoing.").

c. Framing the Case

Andrew L. Frey & Roy T. Engelert, Jr., How to Write a Good Appellate Brief

Litigation, Winter 1994, at 6

In theory, every law school graduate should know something about how to write an effective appellate brief. After all, first-year legal writing classes in law school often concentrate on that skill. Moot court competitions do too. Compared to other kinds of legal work, appellate briefs seem tidy and self-contained, with a predictable structure. So they are what law schools teach.

Once in practice, regardless of law school background, trial lawyers sometimes seem to believe that no special talent or training is needed to write a good brief on appeal. The idea appears to be that what works before a jury or is acceptable to a busy trial judge should be more than adequate for an appellate court.

Despite what law students should learn and despite what lawyers think they know, appeal after appeal is lost, or at least made harder to win, because of ineffective briefs. Why? In part, because many lawyers write appellate briefs infrequently. When they do have to brief an appeal, they fail to appreciate that the job is different from much other lawyering. It poses special problems, but presents special opportunities, for advocacy.

The most common mistake made by trial lawyers is to think that they should do the same thing in the appellate court that they did in trial court. They write their jury speech and call it a brief. At best, they address the appellate judges as they would address the trial judge. At worst, they treat the appellate judges like jurors.

Such advocates bog down in irrelevant detail and empty rhetoric. Ninth Circuit Judge Alex Kozinski's comments about oral argument apply even more forcefully to the brief: "When a lawyer resorts to a jury argument on appeal, you can see the judges sit back and give a big sigh of relief. . . . [W]e know, and you know we know, that your case doesn't amount to a hill of beans, so we can go back there in the conference room and flush it with an unpublished disposition."

Even those who understand that a court of appeals is different from a trial court often fail to seize the opportunities for advocacy that an appellate brief offers. They may recall their early law school lessons, but they do not know and do not take (or do not have) the time to study the more sophisticated lessons that actual experience in appellate practice can bring. Their written product is formulaic. It fails to take advantage of the flexibility that an appellate brief writer has in packaging arguments to meet the needs of a particular case.

Packaging Arguments

Here is what we mean by effective packaging: A few years ago, the Supreme Court considered a case that turned on the interpretation of two complex, interrelated statutes. One statute involved regulation by the Food and Drug Administration, and the other involved patent law. Conventional law school wisdom would have called for the brief to begin with a statement of the events giving rise to the controversy, followed by a description of the proceedings below. The winning brief did not do that. Instead, it opened with a four-page description of the statutory scheme. Not one sentence on those four pages was argumentative or even disputable. The passage alerted the Court to the statutory elements that the brief writers knew were most significant and helpful to their side. It gave the Court a framework to understand everything else the brief said—from the statement of facts through the conclusion of the argument.

Ultimately, the Court ruled in favor of the side that had taken the unconventional approach, saying that it found " 'the structure of the [statute] taken as a whole' " to be dispositive. The critical information the Court needed to rule as it did was in those first four pages. Of course, this technique is not right for every appeal (although it probably makes sense more often than not in cases turning solely on statutory construction). But it is one way an advocate can achieve maximum effectiveness while staying within the rules. . . .

Organization Above All

First, never forget the importance of organization. It is vital to organize, not only the writing, but also the theory of the case. Appellate judges know that they are setting precedents. They therefore worry about whether the theory they adopt in one case will or will not apply appropriately to slightly different sets of facts. Appellate lawyers should assist the judges by having—and expressing—clear theories with reasonably clear limits.

Unfortunately, many appellate briefs are organized in ways that do not advance an overall theory. One common but particularly unsatisfactory form of appellate brief (whatever its merit in a trial court) is to quote snippets from one precedent after another without fitting those precedents into an overall pattern. Such filings are long on cut-and-paste, but short on logic or explanation. Likewise, it is tempting (but equally ineffective) to use a brief to take a series of potshots at the opinion below (in an appellant's brief) or the adversary's brief (in an appellee's brief or a reply brief), never bothering to devise an overall theory of the correct approach to the case. And it bears repeating that ad hominem criticisms of adversaries or the decisionmakers below—as opposed to their legal positions— are counterproductive. . . .

Ross Guberman, Five Ways to Write Like Paul Clement

http://www.legalwritingpro.com/briefs/clement.pdf

"Phenomenal," said our new solicitor general, Donald Verrilli, Jr. "I commend it to you as an example of how to write an effective brief," he told the group of lawyers.

Was Mr. Verrilli touting the government's own brief defending the Affordable Care Act's individual mandate?

Not at all. That "phenomenal" model was the brief penned by his dueling partner, Paul Clement. . . .

But what makes Mr. Clement's brief so terrific? Let me share five reasons[4] his brief is as "phenomenal" as the government thinks—or fears.

I. FULL CIRCLE

We lawyers talk a big game about having "a theme of the case," but how many briefs make good on that goal? To succeed, a theme must be at once bite-sized and specific. And it must cascade across the brief from the opening paragraph through the fact section and land on the conclusion.

Mr. Clement pulls no punches here, announcing in the very first sentence that "[t]he individual mandate rests on a claim of federal power that is both unprecedented and unbounded."

"Unprecedented" appears 20 more times in the brief, and "unbounded" another 8 times. The related idea of "limit" or "limiting," also introduced in the brief's opening paragraph, resurfaces no fewer than 40 more times.

Thus this theme is everywhere. Take the facts in the Statement of the Case. Here's the very first sentence:

> The Patient Protection and Affordable Care Act imposes new and substantial obligations on every corner of society, from individuals to insurers to employers to States.

And the theme returns full circle in the argument's parting thought:

> The statute the federal government defends under the tax power is not the statute that Congress enacted. In that statute, the penalty provision is merely the tail and the mandate is the proverbial dog, not vice-versa. And that statute imposes a command that is unprecedented and invokes a power that is both unbounded and not included among the limited and enumerated powers granted to Congress. It is therefore unconstitutional, no matter what power the federal government purports to invoke. . . .

---

4. This excerpt focuses on one of those reasons—his ability to stick to and highlight a theme. The other four tips include: constantly framing the choice between your side and your opponent's in ways that flatter your case; offering creative and memorable examples; keeping your sentences short and your writing "light"; and varying your transition words.

Notes and Questions

1. The two excerpts above, from a pair of experienced Supreme Court advocates and a professional legal writing coach, respectively, strike a common chord: The key to crafting successful Supreme Court briefs is to identify a suitable "theme," "frame," or "theory" and to return to that theme repeatedly throughout the brief. The advocate who builds the cognitive frame through which the Justices view the case has a substantial head start in convincing the Justices of the ultimate wisdom of his or her position.

2. The brief which Mr. Guberman dissects is Brief for State Respondents on the Minimum Coverage Provision, *United States Dep't of Health and Human Services v. Florida*, 132 S. Ct. 2566 (No. 11-398). It is available, along with many of the other briefs in that case, on the *Supreme Court Sourcebook* website. The case, a constitutional challenge to several aspects of President Barack Obama's signature health care law, drew the participation of many of the nation's leading advocates. Mr. Clement, a former Solicitor General and frequent advocate before the high court, drew nearly universal praise for his performance in the case. In the end, of course, Mr. Clement won most of the battles but (arguably) lost the war, as the Court adopted many of his arguments and limited the statute at issue in some crucial ways but upheld the constitutionality of the statute's provisions mandating that most individuals purchase health insurance or pay a penalty, on the grounds that the penalty could be construed as a valid tax. *See generally Natl. Fedn. of Indep. Business v. Sebelius*, 132 S. Ct. 2566 (2012), particularly the controlling opinion of Chief Justice Roberts.

3. Advice from the Justices

Between November 2006 and March 2007, Bryan A. Garner, a nationally recognized expert on legal writing, interviewed eight sitting Supreme Court Justices on their experiences as writers and their views on a variety of issues related to legal writing.[5] The interviews were transcribed and published in *The Scribes Journal of Legal Writing* in 2010. During their interviews, many of the Justices offered intriguing nuggets of advice about brief writing. Some of the highlights appear below.[6]

Bryan A. Garner, Interviews with United States Supreme Court Justices

13 Scribes Journal of Legal Writing 1 (2010)

(A) CHIEF JUSTICE JOHN ROBERTS

Language is the central tool of our trade. You know, when we're looking at a statute, trying to figure out what it means, we're relying on the language. When we're construing the Constitution, we're looking at words. Those are the building blocks of the law. And so if we're not fastidious, as you put it, with language, it dilutes the effectiveness and clarity of the law. And so I think it's vitally important—whether it's a lawyer arguing a case and trying to explain his position, whether it's a legislator

---

5. Video recordings of the interviews are available at http://www.lawprose.org/interviews/supreme-court.php?v=P2yl9x-KPFk.

6. For ease of readability, Professor Garner's questions have been omitted and, where necessary for clarity, replaced by bracketed material in the body of the Justice's comments.

writing a law, whether it's a judge trying to construe it. At every stage, the more careful they are with their language, I think, the better job they're going to do in capturing in those words exactly what they want the law to do; in persuading a judge how to interpret it; and as a judge, in giving a good, clear explanation of what the law is. . . .

The quality of briefs varies greatly. We get some excellent briefs; we get a lot of very, very good briefs. And there are some where the first thing you can tell in many of them is that the lawyer really hasn't spent a lot of time on it, to be honest with you. You can tell that if they'd gone through a couple more drafts, it would be more effective. It would read better. And for whatever reason, they haven't devoted that energy to it. Well, that tells you a lot right there about that lawyer's devotion to his client's cause, and that's very frustrating because we're obviously dealing with very important issues. We depend heavily on the lawyers. Our chances of getting a case right improve to the extent the lawyers do a better job. And when you see something like bad writing, the first thing you think is, "Well, if he didn't have enough time to spend writing it well, how much time did he spend researching it? How much time did he spend thinking out the ramifications of his position?" You don't have a lot of confidence in the substance if the writing is bad. . . .

[A first-rate statement of facts has] got to be a good story. Every lawsuit is a story. I don't care if it's about a dry contract interpretation; you've got two people who want to accomplish something, and they're coming together—that's a story. And you've got to tell a good story. Believe it or not, no matter how dry it is, something's going on that got you to this point, and you want it to be a little bit of a page-turner, to have some sense of drama, some building up to the legal arguments. I also think—again, it varies on your forum—but certainly here at the Supreme Court and in the courts of appeals, you're looking for a couple of hooks in the facts that hopefully are going to be repeated in one form or another later on in the legal argument but also are going to catch somebody's interest. It may not have that much to do with the substantive legal arguments, but you want it to catch their eyes. Certainly here in the Supreme Court, in writing cert petitions, for example, if you're going to be looking at 9,000 of them over the course of a year, you've got to stand out from the crowd a little bit. So you want to put something in there to give them the hooks. And I've seen that with judges when you start talking to them about cases from five or ten years ago. Most of us remember *Marbury v. Madison* and everything else, but otherwise, it's going to be that case about whatever—that case about the coal mine where this happened, or that case about the prescription. But give them some hook, and it kind of helps draw them into the brief and carries them along a little bit. . . .

[Bad writing] sure can [lose a strong case]—because they may not see your strong case. It's not like judges know what the answer is. I mean, we've got to find it out. And so when you say can bad writing lose a strong case, if it's bad writing, we may not see that you've got a strong case. It's not that, oh, this is poorly written, so you're going to lose. It's that it's so poorly written that we don't see how strong the precedents in your favor really are, because you haven't conveyed them in a succinct way. Or we don't see exactly how the statutory language works together to support you, because you haven't adequately explained that. Or even simple things: you haven't put it in there. You're telling us about why it should be read this way when we haven't even seen it yet. . . . [I]f the lawyers don't write clearly enough to convey the arguments, it's going to be very difficult for us to get the case right. . . .

I have been very fortunate as a lawyer to work with some great associates and fellow partners. And I have found that I really have to be on guard when I'm dealing with a good writer because you pick up the draft of a brief, say, or a draft of a memo, and you read it through, and if the writing is good, you put it down, and it sounds right. And sometimes when you go back, it's not right. So it's certainly the case that good writing can cover up some weaknesses. That's for sure.

(b) Justice Antonin Scalia

I see a lot [of briefs that appear hastily written], and it is about the brief-writer, about using ungrammatical words, about sloppy citation, all of this stuff. There's a maxim in evidence law or criminal law or whatever: *falsus in uno, falsus in omnibus.* If you show that a witness lied about one thing, the jury can assume that he lied about everything. False in one, false in all. It's the same thing about sloppiness. If you see somebody who has written a sloppy brief, I'm inclined to think this person is a sloppy thinker. It is rare that a person thinks clearly, precisely, carefully and does not write that way. And contrariwise, it's rare that someone who is careful and precise in his thought is sloppy in his writing. So it hurts you. It really hurts you to have ungrammatical, sloppy briefs. . . .

Judicial readers . . . you know . . . I want to move on to the next brief and the next case, and I just want the kernel of the argument. I want it there in front of me, I want it clear, and I want it fast. And if possible, I want it elegant. But prolixity is probably the worst offense that most unskilled brief-writers are guilty of. . . .

[O]ur form of brief always has a summary section. The first section of the brief is a summary of argument. I usually don't read it because I'm going to read the brief. . . . Why would I read the summary if I'm going to read the brief? Can you tell me why I should read it? Should I feel guilty about not reading it [laughter][7]?

(c) Justice Clarence Thomas

I like the summary of the argument. I think that it gives you a preview. It's like giving you, you know, what's going to be on TV next week. If you watch the television program you know what's going to happen next week. Or it says, "Here's what I'm going to tell you." I remember I got that from Justice Black—he would be very upset when someone left the summary of the argument out. Each of us reads a brief differently. I never read the jurisdiction statement or anything like that. I don't read the facts. I go right to what you have to say. . . .

I don't read [statements of fact]. . . . I can't say ever[], but I don't as a matter of course read them. I read the court-of-appeals opinion, and that has a statement of facts. . . . I think it is because judges are engaged in the exact same job I'm engaged in. They're not advocating a position. They're not trying to push the law in a particular direction. They're judges. They had some parties before them, they had briefs, and they had to decide, and they had to explain their decision. Same thing I have to do. And so I go to them as coparticipants in this process. And that's not to denigrate the lawyers. But if the court-of-appeals judge has already stated the facts, then I take that and I go on.

7. Bracketed aside appears in the original.

(D) JUSTICE RUTH BADER GINSBURG

Of the two components of the presentation of a case, the brief is ever so much more important. It's what we start with; it's what we go back to. The oral argument is fleeting and very concentrated, just a half hour per side. It is a conversation between the Court and counsel. It gives counsel an opportunity to face the decision-makers, to try to answer the questions that trouble the judges. So oral argument is important, but far less important than the brief. . . .

[B]e scrupulously honest because if a brief-writer is going to slant something or miscite an authority, if the judge spots that one time, the brief will be distrusted—the rest of it. And lawyers should remember that most of us do not turn to their briefs as the first thing we read. The first thing we read is the decision we're reviewing. If you read a decision and then find that the lawyer is characterizing it in an unfair way, we will tend to be impatient with that advocate. My other tip is that it isn't necessary to fill all the space allotted. We allow 50 pages for opening briefs. In some cases, complex cases particularly, it may be hard to fit what you have to say into 50 pages. But in single-issue cases, most arguments could be made in 20 to 30 pages. Lawyers somehow can't give up the extra space, so they fill the brief unnecessarily, not realizing that eye-fatigue and even annoyance will be the response they get for writing an overlong brief. . . .

[I]t isn't necessary to get your point across to put down the judge who wrote the decision you are attempting to get overturned. It isn't necessary to say anything nasty about your adversary or to make deriding comments about the opposing brief. Those are just distractions. You should aim to persuade the judge by the power of your reasoning and not by denigrating the opposing side. . . . If the other side is truly bad, the judges are smart enough to understand that themselves; they don't need the lawyer's aid. . . .

If you're on the petitioner's side, to anticipate what is likely to come from the respondent and account for it in your brief [is the most important thing]. Make it part of your main argument. You know the vulnerable points, so deal with them. Don't wait for the reply brief; just incorporate in the main brief as part of your affirmative statement answers to what you think you will most likely find in the responsive brief. And in the responsive brief, I think the principal danger is that it will end up being a series of "not so's": "the petitioner says thus and so," or "the appellant says thus and so." "That's not so." A series of "no's" doesn't really work. In the days when I was writing briefs, I tried to draft a brief for the appellee or for the respondent before I ever got the brief for the appellant or the petitioner because I wanted to avoid that trap. So I told my side affirmatively and then used, for the most part, footnotes to answer points made in the petitioner's brief or the appellant's brief and had not been part of the body of the brief I tried to write even before I got the brief I'm answering.

(E) JUSTICE STEPHEN BREYER

I think in the intermediate court it seemed to me what that attorney was trying to do is to get the judge to see the case in a particular way. Is it a rabbit, or is it a duck? It's like the famous psychological example. You have a figure: it could be seen as a rabbit, or it could be seen as a duck. You're going to win if you get him to see it as a duck, but the other side says, "No, no. This is a rabbit." And the characterization will matter, and that's why I liked oral argument. I wanted to know how the lawyers see this case. I'm trying to think, How do they really see it? And very often—not always, but very often—that helps a lot. In this Court, we're not dealing with the case. It's too late to characterize. We are dealing with a legal issue. And I want to know what the answer to that issue is. . . .

I think[,] in the beginning, I want to see what the question is; and the end, I want to know what the summary is. And I think if I have to emphasize one in a brief in this Court, the description of the argument. I'll go right to the table of contents. I want to know what that argument is, and I want to know the points. I want to know the main points. In part, I want to know if I've already read them in another brief. . . . Questions presented should be fairly presented. . . . Don't try to load the question in your favor; it just won't be read. Say what the question is. . . .

[It is a common failing that briefs are] [t]oo long. Don't try to put in everything. Use a little editing, I would say. If I see something 50 pages, it can be 50 pages, but I'm already going to groan. And I'm going to wonder, Did he really have to write that 50 pages? I would have preferred 30. And if I see 30, I think, Well, he thinks he's really got the law on his side because he only took up 30. Now, I'm not saying that you always do that. But trying to be succinct—absolutely clear—is the main thing. It saves me a lot of time. . . .

(f) Justice Samuel Alito

[Many people seem to write before they know what they want to say.] . . . And I think that's a mistake. I have sometimes seen briefs that I think were written that way. I think you should have a good idea of what you're going to say, and the order in which you're going to say it, before you actually start writing. . . . [On the other hand,] I think no matter how carefully you plan what you're going to write, [some rethinking and reorganizing] will often occur during the writing process. And it goes back to . . . the relationship between language and thought. Judges often say, "It just wouldn't write," and what they mean is that when you have to go through the discipline of actually putting your argument in written form, you see problems with what you had thought out. When you are just thinking about a legal problem, your mind can easily skip over problems. When you have to write it, and if you aim for a tightly reasoned, well-expressed argument, very often that will expose the problems in the kind of argument that you had anticipated you were going to make. . . .

[One of the key skills lawyers need to learn] is to simplify—to leave out the things that are just not important. Of course, you don't want to leave out anything that is important or distort the facts of the case or the law or the argument that you're making. But it takes a real discipline to say, "This really isn't important, and that really isn't important." So often a mediocre brief will have all sorts of extraneous things in it, and it just makes it more complicated for the reader to understand. And I think it can lead to sloppy thinking also on the part of the lawyer. If you really identify what is important and start pushing away all the things that aren't important, what you're left with is what you want to present to the court, and I think it helps you in making your argument if you do that. . . . I will give you just a simple example, a mundane example, that comes up all the time. I used to get, on the court of appeals (a little bit less here), lots of briefs and draft opinions all full of dates. The dates were totally irrelevant. Why did you need to know that something happened on March 2, 2007? Now, of course, if there is a statute-of-limitations issue or something like that, then you have to put the date in, and the one date that you put in will stand out. But on such and such a date, such and such a motion was filed.

Generally, it's of no importance whatsoever, and yet it complicates what you've written. . . .

An old colleague of mine in the Solicitor General's office once said that he spent hours and hours and hours on the summary of the argument in a brief because he thought that was critically important—that would be the first thing he thought that Justices would read, and he wanted to start out with that. I think that's very important in a brief, and a lot of lawyers, particularly in the court of appeals, just sort of blow that off. They've written the whole brief, and now they have to do the summary (it's a requirement of the rules), so they don't devote any attention to it—sometimes it's a few sentences—and I think that's really a missed opportunity. . . . I do in a way [think that it is the most important part of a brief]. I do. I think it should be self-contained. I think that somebody reading the summary of the argument should understand what the case is about and the essence of the argument that is being made and should be persuaded to agree with that argument by what's in the summary. And then in the rest of the brief, you develop the points. . . . I think it's very helpful. It's the first thing I read.

Notes and Questions

1. In addition to the Justices whose remarks are excerpted above, the transcribed interviews include conversations with Justices John Paul Stevens and Anthony Kennedy. Justices Sonia Sotomayor and Elena Kagan had not yet joined the Court, and Justice David Souter (politely) declined the interview request.

2. Among other points, the Justices' comments underscore the degree to which each is a unique consumer of legal briefs. It is noteworthy and somewhat unsettling that Chief Justice Roberts and Justice Alito, respectively, consider the fact section and the summary of the argument of particular importance while Justices Thomas and Scalia each claim not to even read one of those sections.

3. Justice Scalia so enjoyed his colloquy with Professor Garner that they wrote two books together: Antonin Scalia & Bryan A. Garner, *Making Your Case: The Art of Persuading Judges* (2008) and Antonin Scalia & Bryan A. Garner, *Reading Law: The Interpretation of Legal Texts* (2012). The books, as might be expected, are readable and opinionated guides to briefing and arguing cases.

4. Sample Merits Briefs from *Lawrence v. Texas*

The pages that follow contain substantial excerpts from the merits briefs in *Lawrence v. Texas*, 539 U.S. 558 (2003), a landmark Supreme Court case dealing with the constitutionality of laws banning consensual same-sex sexual activity. The petitioners' brief has received a great deal of praise for, among other things, the quality of the writing, the way in which it finessed some difficult strategic decisions, and the degree to which it anticipated the concerns of the swing Justices. The respondent's brief, on the other hand, has been the subject of significant criticism for, among others, the tone of the writing and the decision to focus on tangential issues while ignoring some of the stronger potential arguments in its favor. In reading through the briefs, think about whether you agree with those assessments. In addition, keep an eye on the ways in which each of the advocates utilizes (or fails to utilize) the various elements of the brief and on the degree to which they follow (or ignore) the brief-writing advice offered above.

John Geddes LAWRENCE and Tyron GARNER, Petitioners,
v.
STATE OF TEXAS, Respondent.

No. 02-102. January 16, 2003.

On Writ of Certiorari to the Court of Appeals of Texas Fourteenth District

Brief of Petitioners . . .

QUESTIONS PRESENTED

1. Whether Petitioners' criminal convictions under the Texas "Homosexual Conduct" law—which criminalizes adult, consensual same-sex intimate behavior, but not identical behavior by different-sex couples—violate the Fourteenth Amendment right to equal protection of the laws?
2. Whether Petitioners' criminal convictions for adult consensual sexual intimacy in the home violate their vital interests in liberty and privacy protected by the Due Process Clause of the Fourteenth Amendment?
3. Whether *Bowers v. Hardwick*, 478 U.S. 186 (1986), should be overruled?

TABLE OF CONTENTS

The State of Texas arrested Petitioners Lawrence and Garner, charged them with a crime, and convicted them under the State's "Homosexual Conduct" law for engaging in consensual same-sex intimacy in the privacy of Lawrence's home. The Texas law and Petitioners' convictions are constitutionally indefensible for two reasons. First, the law discriminates without a legitimate and rational State purpose, in violation of the Equal Protection Clause. In 1973, Texas broke with both the even-handed laws of the past and the decisive modern trend toward decriminalization. Instead, the State chose to criminalize consensual, adult sexual behaviors *only* for those whose partners are of the same sex—gay men and lesbians. Texas's decision to classify along that line brands gay men and lesbians as lawbreakers and fuels a whole range of further discrimination, effectively relegating them to a form of second-class citizenship. Second, this criminal law directly implicates fundamental interests in intimate relationships, bodily integrity, and the home. Texas's law and the few other remaining consensual sodomy statutes—both those that discriminate and those that do not—trample on the substantive liberty protections that the Constitution erects in order to preserve a private sphere shielded from government intrusion. Here, where the State authorizes such intrusion into the homes and lives only of same-sex couples, the constitutional injury is especially clear and disturbing. . . .

STATEMENT OF THE CASE

A. Petitioners' Arrests, Convictions, and Appeals

Late in the evening of September 17, 1998, Harris County, Texas, sheriff's officers entered John Lawrence's home and there intruded on Lawrence and Tyron Garner having sex. The officers were responding to a false report of a "weapons disturbance." Pet. App. 129a, 141a.[1] They arrested Petitioners, jailed them, and

---

1. The person who called in the report later admitted his allegations were false and was convicted of filing a false report. *See* R.A. Dyer, *Two Men Charged Under State's Sodomy Law*, Hous. Chron., Nov. 6, 1998, at A1.

did not release them from custody until the next day. Clerk's Record in *State v. Lawrence*, at 3 ("C.R.L."); Clerk's Record in *State v. Garner*, at 3 ("C.R.G.").

The State charged Petitioners with violating the Texas "Homosexual Conduct" statute, Tex. Pen. Code §21.06 (the "Homosexual Conduct Law" or "Section 21.06"), which criminalizes so-called "deviate sexual intercourse" with another person of the same sex, but not identical conduct by different-sex couples, *Id.* The sole facts alleged by the State to make out a violation were that each Petitioner "engage[d] in deviate sexual intercourse, namely anal sex, with a member of the same sex (man)." Pet. App. 127a, 139a. The State did not allege that the conduct was public, non-consensual, with a minor, or in exchange for money. *Id.* The charges rested solely on consensual, adult sexual relations with a partner of the same sex in the privacy of Lawrence's home. *Id.*

After proceedings and initial convictions in the Justice of the Peace Court, Petitioners appealed for a trial *de novo* to the Harris County Criminal Court. C.R.L. 15; C.R.G. 12. They filed motions to quash the charges on the ground that the law violates the Fourteenth Amendment's guarantees of equal protection and privacy, both on its face and as applied to their "consensual, adult, private sexual relations with another person of the same sex." Pet. App. 117a-118a, 121a-122a, 130a-131a, 134a-135a. On December 22, 1998, the court denied the motions to quash. Pet. App. 113a. Lawrence and Garner then pled *nolo contendere*, Pet. App. 114a, preserving, under Texas procedural rules, their right to pursue previously asserted defenses. Tex. Code Crim. P. §44.02. The court imposed on each a fine of $200 and court costs of $141.25. Pet. App. 107a-108a, 109a-110a, 116a.

In consolidated appeals to the Texas Court of Appeals, Lawrence and Garner argued that Section 21.06 impermissibly discriminates between citizens "[u]nder any characterization of the classification." Amended Brief of Appellants at 4, 5, 6-17 (Tex. App. filed Apr. 30, 1999) ("Am. Br."); Additional Brief of Appellants 1 n.1, 14-22 (Tex. App. filed Aug. 11, 2000) ("Add'l Br."); Petition for Discretionary Review at 7-13 (Tex. Crim. App. filed Apr. 13, 2001) ("Pet. Disc. Rev."). Petitioners also argued that the statute invades their right of privacy and preserved their contention that *Bowers v. Hardwick*, 478 U.S. 186 (1986), was wrongly decided. Am. Br. 5, 23-26; Add'l Br. 23 n.20; Pet. Disc. Rev. 16-19.

At oral argument in the Court of Appeals, counsel for the State conceded that "he could not 'even see how he could begin to frame an argument that there was a compelling State interest'" served by Section 21.06. Pet. App. 76a (quoting counsel for Texas). Texas has repeatedly identified its only aim as "enforcement of principles of morality and the promotion of family values." *See, e.g.*, State's Brief in Support of Rehearing En Banc 16 (Tex. App. filed Aug. 23, 2000) ("States' Br. in Supp. of Reh'g En Banc").

On June 8, 2000, a panel of the Court of Appeals reversed Petitioners' convictions under the Texas Equal Rights Amendment, holding that Section 21.06 impermissibly discriminates on the basis of sex. Pet. App. 86a-92a. After rehearing *en banc*, the Court of Appeals reinstated Petitioners' convictions on March 15, 2001. Pet. App. 3a, 4a. Citing *Bowers*, the court rejected Petitioners' substantive due process claim. Pet. App. 24a-31a. As to the federal equal protection claim, the court held that the statute was subject to and survived rational basis review, because it "advances a legitimate state interest, namely, preserving public morals." Pet. App. 13a. The court distinguished *Romer v. Evans*, 517 U.S. 620 (1996), as limited to discrimination in the right to seek legislation. Pet. App. 14a-15a.

Two Justices of the appellate court "strongly" dissented from the rejection of Petitioners' federal equal protection arguments. Pet. App. 42a. The dissent reasoned that:

> where the same conduct, defined as "deviate sexual intercourse[,]" is criminalized for same sex participants but not for heterosexuals[,] [t]he contention that the same conduct is moral for some but not for others merely repeats, rather than legitimizes, the Legislature's unconstitutional edict.

Pet. App. 44a. Petitioners timely sought discretionary review from the Texas Court of Criminal Appeals, which was refused. Pet. App. 1a, 2a.

B. The Homosexual Conduct Law

The Homosexual Conduct Law is of comparatively recent vintage. It was enacted in 1973 when Texas repealed all of its then-existing laws that criminalized private sexual conduct between consenting adults. *See* 1973 Tex. Gen. Laws ch. 399, §§1, 3. Prior to that time, the criminality of consensual sexual conduct in Texas did not depend on whether a couple was same-sex or different-sex. In particular, oral as well as anal sex was a crime for all. 1943 Tex. Gen. Laws ch. 112, §1. *See generally Baker v. Wade*, 553 F. Supp. 1121, 1148-53 (N.D. Tex. 1982) (reviewing history of Texas sodomy laws), *rev'd*, 769 F.2d 289 (5th Cir. 1985) (en banc). Until 1973 Texas also criminalized fornication and adultery. *See* Tex. Pen. Code arts. 499-504 (1952) (repealed by 1973 Tex. Gen. Laws, ch. 399, §3).

The 1973 repeals abolished all those crimes, 1973 Tex. Gen. Laws ch. 399, §3, freeing heterosexual adult couples, married or unmarried, to engage in all forms of consensual, private, noncommercial sexual intimacy without state intrusion. In the same enactment, however, the Legislature adopted Section 21.06, *see id.* §1, which for the first time singled out same-sex couples for criminal sanctions. Section 21.06 applies to "deviate sexual intercourse," which is defined as oral, anal, and certain other sexual conduct without regard to whether the actors are of the same or different sexes. *See* Tex. Pen. Code §21.01(1). But "deviate sexual intercourse" is *not* a crime when engaged in privately by two consenting adults of different sexes. Rather, Section 21.06 criminalizes only "Homosexual Conduct," making it a punishable offense to engage in "deviate sexual intercourse with another individual of the same sex," but not identical conduct by heterosexual couples. Tex. Pen. Code §21.06.

Texas, of course, also has and enforces other laws that criminalize sexual conduct that takes place in public, Tex. Pen. Code §§21.07(a)(2), 21.08, that is violent or without consent, *id.* §22.011(a)(1), that is in exchange for money, *id.* §43.02, or that is committed with a minor, *id.* §§22.011(a)(2), 21.11. All of these prohibitions apply without regard to whether the actors are of the same or different sexes. Section 21.06, in contrast, applies to non-commercial, consensual, private sexual conduct between two adults—but only if they are of the same sex.

Because it singles out same-sex couples, this Texas law is unlike older legal prohibitions of "sodomy," *see infra* Point I.A.3, and differs fundamentally from the facially evenhanded Georgia law considered by the Court in *Bowers, see* 478 U.S. at 188 n.1. The Homosexual Conduct Law was substituted for a facially non-discriminatory law at a time when many States, prompted by changing views about the proper limits of government power that were reflected in the American Law Institute's *Model Penal Code*, were revising their criminal codes and completely abandoning offenses like fornication and sodomy. *See Model Penal Code and Commentaries* §§213.2 cmt. 2, 213.6 note (1980). By 1986, 26 States had invalidated their sodomy laws. *Bowers,* 478 U.S. at 193-94. Today, only nine States retain criminal laws that bar consensual sodomy for all. Between 1969 and 1989, Texas and seven other States legislatively replaced general laws with laws targeting homosexual couples. *See infra* at 21-22 & note 15. Four of those discriminatory laws have already been judicially invalidated, and one has been repealed. *See id.* Now only Texas and two other States criminalize same-sex conduct but not identical different-sex conduct by statute, while one other State has reached the same result through judicial construction of a facially evenhanded law. Similarly, all but a few States have repealed criminal laws prohibiting fornication. *Infra* note 18.

Since its enactment, Section 21.06 has narrowly survived several federal and state constitutional challenges. . . .

SUMMARY OF ARGUMENT

As the experience of Lawrence and Garner vividly illustrates, Section 21.06 puts the State of Texas inside its citizens' homes, policing the details of their most intimate and private physical behavior and dictating with whom they may share a profound part of adulthood. Texas has enacted and enforced a criminal law that takes away—from same-sex couples only—the freedom to make their own decisions, based upon their own values and relationships, about the forms of private, consensual sexual intimacy they will engage in or refrain from. The State defends this law only by saying the majority wants it so. Texas asserts a power of the majority to free itself from state dictates about private, consensual sexual choices, while using the criminal law to condemn and limit the choices of a minority.

This law and its application to Petitioners violate both the guarantee of equal protection *and* fundamental liberties safeguarded by the Fourteenth Amendment. Petitioners explain below why the equality claim and the liberty claim are each well rooted in the Constitution. The Court, however, need not rule on both constitutional violations if it chooses to focus on one infirmity rather than the other. Petitioners discuss the fundamental liberty claim under the Due Process Clause first, because even if the Court were not to reach that issue, a full appreciation of the personal interests affected by Section 21.06 also illuminates and informs the equal protection analysis that follows.

Fundamental liberty and privacy interests in adults' private, consensual sexual choices are essential to the ordered liberty our Constitution protects. The State may not, without overriding need, regiment and limit this personal and important part of its citizens' lives. More so than in 1986, when *Bowers v. Hardwick* was decided, it is clear today that such a fundamental right is supported by our basic constitutional structure, by multiple lines of precedent, and by a decisive historical turn in the vast majority of the States to repudiate this type of government invasion into private life. The well-established fundamental interests in intimate relationships, bodily integrity, and the sanctity of the home all converge in the right asserted here. *See Griswold v. Connecticut,* 381 U.S. 479 (1965); *Eisenstadt v. Baird,* 405 U.S. 438 (1972); *Planned Parenthood of Southeastern Pa. v. Casey,* 505 U.S. 833 (1992). That right belongs to all Americans, including gay men and lesbians, and should be shielded from Section 21.06's unjustified invasion. Much more is needed to outweigh fundamental individual interests than the majority's preferences. Indeed, the Fourteenth Amendment's protection of liberty exists to guard against the very impulse Texas acted on here. Principles of *stare decisis* do not, in these circumstances, justify adherence to *Bowers*.

Texas also has violated the Fourteenth Amendment's guarantee of equal protection of the laws. The Homosexual Conduct Law creates classes of persons, treating the same acts of consensual sexual behavior differently depending on who the participants are. By this law, Texas imposes a discriminatory prohibition on all gay and lesbian couples, requiring them to limit their expressions of affection in ways that heterosexual couples, whether married or unmarried, need not. The law's discriminatory focus sends the message that gay people are second-class citizens and lawbreakers, leading to ripples of discrimination throughout society. Such a discriminatory law cannot satisfy even the minimal requirement that a legislative classification must be rationally related to a legitimate State purpose. *See Romer*, 517 U.S. 620. The bare negative attitudes of the majority, whether viewed as an expression of morality, discomfort, or blatant bias, cannot take away the equality of a smaller group. *See id.; United States Dep't of Agric. v. Moreno*, 413 U.S. 528, 534 (1973); *City of Cleburne v. Cleburne Living Ctr., Inc.*, 473 U.S. 432, 448 (1985).

ARGUMENT

I. Section 21.06 Violates Constitutional Rights to Liberty and Privacy Possessed by All Americans.

"It is a promise of the Constitution that there is a realm of personal liberty which the government may not enter." *Casey*, 505 U.S. at 847. It is well settled that the Due Process Clause of the Fourteenth Amendment guarantees the personal liberty of Americans against encroachment by the States, and that this protection of liberty encompasses substantive fundamental rights and interests that are unenumerated. *See, e.g., Troxel v. Granville*, 530 U.S. 57, 65-66 (2000); *Casey*, 505 U.S. at 846-51; *Cruzan v. Director, Mo. Dep't of Health*, 497 U.S. 261, 278-79 (1990); *Carey v. Population Servs. Int'l*, 431 U.S. 678, 684-85 (1977); *Moore v. City of E. Cleveland*, 431 U.S. 494, 501-03 (1977); *Roe v. Wade*, 410 U.S. 113, 152-53 (1973); *Griswold*, 381 U.S. at 482-85; *Pierce v. Society of the Sisters of the Holy Names of Jesus & Mary*, 268 U.S. 510, 534-35 (1925); *Meyer v. Nebraska*, 262 U.S. 390, 399-400 (1923). Giving substance to "liberty" is necessary to maintain the individual freedoms that are the essence of American democracy, while also allowing government action that is justified by the collective good. *See Casey*, 505 U.S. at 849-51.

Among the liberties protected by the Constitution is the right of an adult to make choices about whether and in what manner to engage in private consensual sexual intimacy with another adult, including one of the same sex. This extremely personal sphere implicates three aspects of liberty that have long been recognized as fundamental: the interests in intimate associations, in bodily integrity, and in the privacy of the home. For the State to limit and dictate the intimate choices of American couples in this realm without any substantial justification is repugnant to ordered liberty. *Stare decisis* does not require continued adherence to the Court's contrary decision in *Bowers*.

A. American Adults Have Fundamental Liberty and Privacy Interests in Making Their Own Choices About Private, Consensual Sexual Relations.

1. Well-Established Protections for Intimate Relationships, Bodily Integrity, and the Privacy of the Home Converge in This Vital Freedom.

Being forced into a life without sexual intimacy would represent an intolerable and fundamental deprivation for the overwhelming majority of individuals. Equally repugnant is any form of external compulsion to engage in sexual relations. There should be no doubt, then, that the Constitution imposes substantive limits on the power of government to compel, forbid, or regulate the intimate details of private sexual relations between two consenting adults.

All adults have the same fundamental liberty interests in their private consensual sexual choices. This fundamental protection is rooted in three well-recognized aspects of personal liberty—in intimate relationships, in bodily integrity, and in the privacy of the home. These aspects of liberty should not be viewed as "a series of isolated points," but are part of a "rational continuum" that constitutes the full scope of liberty of a free people. *Casey,* 505 U.S. at 848 (quotation marks omitted); *see also Board of Regents v. Roth,* 408 U.S. 564, 572 (1972) ("In a Constitution for a free people, there can be no doubt that the meaning of 'liberty' must be broad indeed"). Sexual intimacy marks an intensely personal and vital part of that continuum.

The Court has recognized that "choices to enter into and maintain certain intimate human relationships must be secured against undue intrusion by the State because of the role of such relationships in safeguarding the individual freedom that is central to our constitutional scheme." *Roberts v. United States Jaycees,* 468 U.S. 609, 617-18 (1984). "[T]he constitutional shelter afforded such relationships reflects the realization that individuals draw much of their emotional enrichment from close ties with others. Protecting these relationships from unwarranted state interference therefore safeguards the ability independently to define one's identity that is central to any concept of liberty." *Id.* at 619; *see also Board of Directors of Rotary Int'l v. Rotary Club of Duarte,* 481 U.S. 537, 545-46 (1987).

The adult couple whose shared life includes sexual intimacy is undoubtedly one of the most important and profound forms of intimate association. The Court has rightly recognized that regulation of the private details of sexual relations between two adults sharing an intimate relationship has "a maximum destructive impact upon that relationship." *Griswold,* 381 U.S. at 485. *Griswold* struck down a law that intruded directly into a married couple's private sexual intimacy—and thus their intimate relationship—by criminalizing the use of contraceptives and allowing intercourse only if accompanied by the risk of pregnancy. *Id.* at 485-86. Since *Griswold,* the Court has recognized that all adults, regardless of marital status or other facets of their relationship, have the same interest in making their own intimate choices in this area. *See Eisenstadt,* 405 U.S. at 453 ("If the right of privacy means anything, it is the right of the *individual,* married or single, to be free from unwarranted governmental intrusion into matters so fundamentally affecting a person") (emphasis in original); *Casey,* 505 U.S. at 898 ("The Constitution protects all individuals, male or female, married or unmarried, from the abuse of governmental power"); *id.* at 852 (reaffirming *Eisenstadt* and *Griswold*).

Sexual intimacy is "a sensitive, key relationship of human existence, central to family life, community welfare, and the development of human personality." *Paris Adult Theatre I v. Slaton,* 413 U.S. 49, 63 (1973). One's sexual orientation, the choice of one's partner, and whether and how to connect sexually are profound attributes of personhood where compulsion by the State is anathema to liberty. *Cf. Casey,* 505 U.S. at 851.[8] Thus, the essential associational freedom here is the freedom to structure one's own private sexual intimacy with another adult. Section 21.06 utterly destroys that freedom by forbidding most sexual behavior for all same-sex couples, whether they are in a committed, long-standing relationship, a growing one, or a new one.

State regulation of sexual intimacy also implicates the liberty interest in bodily integrity. "It is settled now . . . that the Constitution places limits on a State's right to interfere with a person's most basic decisions about . . . bodily integrity." *Casey,* 505 U.S. at 849 (citations omitted); *see also id.* at 896 ("state regulation . . . is doubly deserving of scrutiny . . . [where] the State has touched not only upon the private sphere of the family but upon the very bodily integrity of the pregnant woman"). Stated generally, "[e]very human being of adult years and sound mind has a right to determine what shall be done with his own body." [*Washington v.*] *Glucksberg,* 521 U.S. at 777 (Souter, J., concurring) (quotation marks omitted); *see also id.* at 720; *Rochin v. California,* 342 U.S. 165, 166, 173-74 (1952); *Cruzan,* 497 U.S. at 278.

Control over one's own body is fundamentally at stake in sexual relations, involving as they do the most intimate physical interactions conceivable. Like the decision whether to continue or terminate a pregnancy, or the decision whether to permit or decline medical procedures, the physical, bodily dimensions of how two persons express their sexuality in intimate relations are profoundly personal. Indeed, consent is a critically important dividing line in legal and societal views about sexuality for the very reason that individual control over sexual activity is of fundamental importance to every person's autonomy. Texas invades the liberty interest in bodily integrity by dictating that citizens may not share sexual intimacy unless they perform acts approved by the legislature, and by attempting to coerce them to select a sexual partner of the other sex.

The liberty interest at issue here also involves the deeply entrenched interest in the privacy of the home. "In the home, [the Court's] cases show, *all* details are intimate details, because the entire area is held safe from prying government eyes." *Kyllo v. United States,* 533 U.S. 27, 37 (2001) (emphasis in original); *Minnesota v. Olson,* 495 U.S. 91, 98 (1990) (overnight guest receives protection under "everyday expectations of privacy that we all share"). The importance of shielding the home from intrusion goes beyond the Fourth Amendment. In *Frisby v. Schultz,* 487 U.S. 474 (1988), for example, the Court relied on the constitutional status of the home in rejecting a First Amendment challenge to an ordinance against picketing targeted at a home. *Id.* at 484 ("The State's interest in protecting the well-being, tranquility, and privacy of the home is certainly of the highest order in a free and civilized society") (quotation marks omitted). And constitutional protection for the home was an important consideration in *Griswold* itself. *See* 381 U.S. at 485 (rejecting intrusion into "sacred precincts of marital bedrooms"). "[I]f the physical curtilage of the home is protected, it is surely as a result of the solicitude to protect the privacies of the life within." *Poe v. Ullman,* 367 U.S. 497, 551 (1961) (Harlan, J., dissenting); *see also Stanley v. Georgia,* 394 U.S. 557 (1969).

---

8. For many adults in modern society, sexual intimacy is an important aspect of forming or building a committed relationship where one does not already exist. *See Roberts,* 468 U.S. at 618 (Constitution protects "the *formation* and preservation" of "highly personal relationships") (emphasis added); Richard A. Posner, *Sex and Reason* 349 (1992) ("Consensual sex in whatever form is as we know a method of cementing a relationship").

Even without actual physical entry by the police, Section 21.06 directly invades the privacy of the home by criminalizing the private intimate conduct taking place there. *Poe*, 367 U.S. at 549, 551-52 (Harlan, J., dissenting). But this case also graphically illustrates how laws criminalizing consensual adult sexual intimacy permit invasion of the privacy of the home in the starkest sense. Although Petitioners do not challenge the lawfulness of the police entry into Lawrence's home in response to a report of an armed gunman, the officers did not withdraw after discovering the report was false. Instead, under license of Section 21.06, they multiplied their intrusion exponentially by scrutinizing the specific intimate acts in which Petitioners were involved, arresting them, hauling them off to jail, and charging them with a crime for which they were later convicted.

Denying the existence of a liberty interest in private consensual adult sexual activity would give constitutional legitimacy to the grossest forms of intrusion into the homes of individuals and couples. To investigate this "criminal" conduct, the police could use every investigative method appropriate when ordinary criminal activity, such as drug use or distribution, occurs in the home: obtaining warrants to search for physical evidence of sexual activity; interrogating each member of the couple about the intimate details of the relationship; and surveillance, wiretaps, confidential informants, and questioning of neighbors. That these routine police methods are so repugnant and unthinkable in the context of adult consensual sexual relations is a strong indication that the conduct at issue differs in a fundamental way from ordinary criminal conduct that happens to occur in the home. *Cf. Romer*, 517 U.S. at 645 (Scalia, J., dissenting) ("'To obtain evidence [in sodomy cases], police are obliged to resort to behavior which tends to degrade and demean both themselves personally and law enforcement as an institution'") (quoting Kadish, *The Crisis of Overcriminalization*, 374 Annals of Am. Acad. of Pol. & Soc. Sci. 157, 161 (1967)).

The core liberty interests at stake in this case are a bulwark against an overly controlling and intrusive government. The "fundamental theory of liberty upon which all governments in this Union repose excludes any general power of the state to standardize," *Pierce*, 268 U.S. at 535, or "to coerce uniformity," *West Va. State Bd. of Educ. v. Barnette*, 319 U.S. 624, 640 (1943).

> The right of privacy exists because democracy must impose limits on the extent of control and direction that the state exercises over the day-to-day conduct of individual lives. . . . People do not meaningfully govern themselves if their lives are . . . molded into standard, rigid, normalized roles.

Jed Rubenfeld, *The Right of Privacy*, 102 Harv. L. Rev. 783, 804-05 (1989).

2. There Is No Constitutional Exception to Liberty for Gay and Lesbian Citizens.

Gay and lesbian Americans have the same liberty interests as heterosexuals in private consensual sexual intimacy free from unwarranted intrusion by the State. Gay adults, like their heterosexual counterparts, have vital interests in their intimate relationships, their bodily integrity, and the sanctity of their homes. Today, family lives centered on same-sex relationships are apparent in households and communities throughout the country. Likewise, the special interplay between the privacy of the home and individual decisions about sexual expression applies to lesbians and gay men as it does to others.

A gay or lesbian sexual orientation is a normal and natural manifestation of human sexuality. A difference in sexual orientation means a difference only in that one personal characteristic. Mental health professionals have universally rejected the erroneous belief that homosexuality is a disease. For example, in 1973 the American Psychiatric Association concluded that "homosexuality *per se* implies no impairment in judgment, stability, reliability, or general social or vocational capabilities." For gay adults, as for heterosexual ones, sexual expression is integrally linked to forming and nurturing the close personal bonds that give humans the love, attachment, and intimacy they need to thrive. *See, e.g.,* Lawrence A. Kurdeck, *Sexuality in Homosexual and Heterosexual Couples, in Sexuality in Close Relationships* 177-91 (K. McKinney & S. Sprecher eds., 1991); Christopher R. Leslie, *Creating Criminals: The Injuries Inflicted by "Unenforced" Sodomy Laws,* 35 Harv. C.R.-C.L. L. Rev. 103, 119-20 (2000). "[M]ost lesbians and gay men want intimate relationships and are successful in creating them. Homosexual partnerships appear no more vulnerable to problems and dissatisfactions than their heterosexual counterparts." Letitia A. Peplau, *Lesbian and Gay Relationships, in Homosexuality* 177, 195 (J. Gonsiorek & J. Weinrich eds., 1991). Same-sex relationships often last a lifetime, and provide deep sustenance to each member of the couple. *See, e.g.,* A. Steven Bryant & Demian, *Relationship Characteristics of American Gay and Lesbian Couples,* 1 J. Gay & Lesbian Soc. Servs. 101 (1994).

That gay Americans have exactly the same vital interests as all others in their bodily integrity and the privacy of their homes is so plain that it appears never to have been disputed in the law. In contrast, the vital liberty interest that gay adults have in their intimate relationships has not always been recognized. Even a few decades ago, intense societal pressure, including many anti-gay government measures, ensured that the vast majority of gay people hid their sexual orientation— even from their own parents—and thus hid the important intimate relationships that gave meaning to their lives. *See infra* Point II.B.2. Lesbians and gay men, moreover, were falsely seen as sick and dangerous. *See infra* at 46. As recently as 1986, it was still possible not to perceive the existence and dignity of the families formed by gay adults. *See, e.g., Bowers,* 478 U.S. at 191, 195.

Today, the reality of these families is undeniable. The 2000 United States Census identified more than 600,000 households of same-sex partners nationally, including almost 43,000 in Texas. These families live in 99.3% of American counties. Many state and local governments and thousands of private employers have adopted domestic partner benefits or more extensive protections for same-sex couples. Virtually every State permits gay men and lesbians to adopt children individually, jointly and/or through "second-parent adoptions" that are analogous to stepparent adoptions. *See, e.g., Lofton v. Kearney,* 157 F. Supp. 2d 1372, 1374 n.1 (S.D. Fla. 2001) (observing that Florida is currently "the only state" "to statutorily ban adoption by gay or lesbian adults"); American Law Inst., *Principles of the Law of Family Dissolution: Analysis and Recommendations* §2.12 cmt. f, at 312 (2002). These and other legal doctrines have secured parental bonds for many of the estimated millions of children in the United States with gay parents. Ellen C. Perrin, *Technical Report: Coparent or Second-Parent Adoption by Same-Sex Parents,* 109 Pediatrics 341, 341 & n.1 (Feb. 2002) (estimating one to nine million children with at least one lesbian or gay parent); *see also, e.g., T.B. v. L.R.M.,* 786 A.2d 913 (Pa. 2001) (allowing claim for partial custody by lesbian second parent under *in loco parentis* doctrine).

The reality of these families cannot be disregarded just because they do not match the "nuclear" model of a married couple with their biological children. *See, e.g., Troxel,* 530 U.S. at 63 ("The demographic changes of the past century make it difficult to speak of an average American family. The composition of families varies greatly from household to household"); *id.* at 85 (Stevens, J., dissenting); *id.* at

98-101 (Kennedy, J., dissenting); *Michael H. v. Gerald D.,* 491 U.S. 110, 124 n.3 (1989) (plurality opinion) ("The family unit accorded traditional respect in our society . . . includes the household of unmarried parents and their children"). For gay men and lesbians, their family life—their intimate associations and the homes in which they nurture those relationships—is every bit as meaningful and important as family life is to heterosexuals.

Thus, the liberty interest at issue here should not be defined in terms of sexual orientation as the "right of homosexuals to engage in acts of sodomy," *Bowers,* 478 U.S. at 191, or reduced in value on that account. If heterosexual adults have a fundamental interest in consensual sexual intimacy, including the choice to engage in oral or anal sex, then so too must homosexual adults. The Due Process Clause itself does not distinguish among classes of citizens, extending the Constitution's shield to the highly personal associations and choices of some, but not protecting the very same associations and choices for others. These liberties are important to and protected for all Americans.

3. Objective Considerations Support Recognition of Fundamental Interests Here. . . .

B. *Texas Cannot Justify Section 21.06's Criminal Prohibition of Petitioners' and Other Adults' Private Sexual Intimacy.*

Recognition of the fundamental liberty interest at stake here does not end the inquiry, for due regard must also be given to any countervailing interests the State may have and the means used to achieve them. The Court has rejected rigid or mechanical tests in this area. Rather, it has given careful consideration to any weighty governmental interests that stand opposed to a fundamental liberty interest, and has looked closely at the degree and nature of the burden on the liberty interest, before ruling on the ultimate question of constitutionality. *See, e.g., Casey,* 505 U.S. at 849-51 (opinion of Court); *id.* at 871-79 (plurality opinion of O'Connor, Kennedy, and Souter, JJ.); *Troxel,* 530 U.S. at 73 (plurality opinion); *id.* at 101-02 (Kennedy, J., dissenting); *Cruzan,* 497 U.S. at 280-81.

Here, however, there is no countervailing State interest remotely comparable to those weighed by this Court in other recent cases involving fundamental liberties, such as the State's interests in protecting the potentiality of human life, *Casey,* 505 U.S. at 871-79 (opinion of O'Connor, Kennedy, and Souter, JJ.), in protecting the welfare of children, *see Troxel,* 530 U.S. at 73 (plurality opinion), or in protecting and preserving existing human life, *Cruzan,* 497 U.S. at 280-81. *See also Glucksberg,* 521 U.S. at 728-35 (reviewing numerous "important and legitimate" interests furthered by ban on assisted suicide).

In stark contrast to those cases, counsel for Texas has conceded that Section 21.06 furthers no compelling state interest. Pet. App. 76a. The sole justification urged throughout this litigation by the State is the majority's desire to espouse prevailing moral principles and values. *See, e.g.,* State's Br. in Supp. of Reh'g En Banc 16. The State claims no distinct harm or public interest other than a pure statement of moral condemnation. This Court, however, has never allowed fundamental freedoms to be circumscribed simply to enforce majority preferences or moral views concerning deeply personal matters. *See, e.g., Casey,* 505 U.S. at 850-51. Indeed, the discriminatory moral standard employed in the Homosexual Conduct Law is illegitimate under the Equal Protection Clause. *See infra* Point II. . . .

C. Bowers *Should Not Block Recognition and Enforcement of These Fundamental Interests.*

Vindication of Petitioners' constitutionally protected liberty interests should not be blocked by continued adherence to *Bowers*. In light of the fundamental interests at stake and the consistent and profound legal, political, and social developments since *Bowers*, principles of *stare decisis* do not bar the Court's reconsideration of that decision.

Stare decisis is a "principle of policy," not an "inexorable command." *Seminole Tribe of Fla. v. Florida*, 517 U.S. 44, 63 (1996) (quotation marks omitted); *see also, e.g., Agostini v. Felton*, 521 U.S. 203, 235-36 (1997) (same). That is "particularly true in constitutional cases, because in such cases correction through legislative action is practically impossible." *Seminole Tribe*, 517 U.S. at 63 (quotation marks omitted). For these reasons, the Court has not hesitated to overrule earlier constitutional decisions that have been recognized as erroneous. *See, e.g., Payne v. Tennessee*, 501 U.S. 808, 828 & n.1 (1991) (surveying cases); Lewis F. Powell, Jr., *Stare Decisis and Judicial Restraint*, 1991 J. S. Ct. Hist. 13 (same).

Where, as here, a prior decision has erroneously *denied* a fundamental constitutional right of citizens over and against the State and no countervailing rights of other individuals are at stake, there is a compelling need to correct the error. *See, e.g., Barnette*, 319 U.S. at 630-42 (overruling *Minersville Sch. Dist. v. Gobitis*, 310 U.S. 586 (1940)); *see also, e.g., Brown v. Board of Educ.*, 347 U.S. 483, 494-95 (1954) (overruling *Plessy v. Ferguson*, 163 U.S. 537 (1896)). That is especially true here, because laws of the kind upheld by *Bowers*—whether facially evenhanded or discriminatory—are used to legitimize widespread discrimination against gay and lesbian Americans. *See infra* Point II.B.1. Indeed, the holding of *Bowers* itself has been cited as justifying state-sponsored discrimination. *See, e.g., Padula v. Webster*, 822 F.2d 97,103 (D.C. Cir. 1987) ("If the Court [in *Bowers*] was unwilling to object to state laws that criminalize the behavior that defines the class, it is hardly open . . . to conclude that state sponsored discrimination against the class is invidious"); *Romer*, 517 U.S. at 641 (Scalia, J., dissenting) (same).

In this respect *Bowers* is fundamentally different from decisions like *Roe* or *Miranda v. Arizona*, 384 U.S. 436 (1966), which recognized individual rights that then became incorporated into the very fabric of our society. *See Casey*, 505 U.S. at 854; *Dickerson v. United States*, 530 U.S. 428, 443 (2000). Indeed, there are no considerations like those identified in *Casey* or other *stare decisis* cases that might favor continued adherence to *Bowers*.

Unlike the right recognized in *Roe* and its progeny, there is no pattern of individuals who "have relied reasonably on the [*Bowers*] rule's continued application" to their advantage, *Casey*, 505 U.S. at 855; *see also, e.g., Adarand Constructors, Inc. v. Pena*, 515 U.S. 200, 233 (1995). Individuals have only been harmed by the *Bowers* decision. Nor has *Bowers* become "part of our national culture," *Dickerson*, 530 U.S. at 443. Just the opposite is true. Developments in the law and in the facts—or in society's perception of the facts, *see Casey*, 505 U.S. at 863—have steadily eroded any support for *Bowers*. Since *Bowers*, the Nation has continued to reject the extreme intrusion into the realm of personal privacy approved in that case, so that now three-fourths of the States have repealed or invalidated such laws—including the very law upheld by *Bowers*. *See supra* Point I.A.3.

Also since *Bowers*, the Nation has steadily moved toward rejecting second-class-citizen status for gay and lesbian Americans. In *Romer*, this Court held that venerable equal protection principles protect gay and lesbian Americans against invidious discrimination. Thirteen States and the District of Columbia, plus countless municipalities—including at least four in Texas—have now added sexual orientation to laws barring discrimination in housing, employment, public accommodations, and other areas. More than half the States now have enhanced penalties for hate crimes motivated by the victim's sexual orientation. And the reality of gay and lesbian couples and families with children has been increasingly recognized by the law and by society at large. *See supra* at 17-19. This is thus a case in which the Court must respond to basic facts and constitutional principles that the country has "come to understand already, but which the Court of an earlier day . . . had not been able to perceive." *Casey*, 505 U.S. at 863; *see also, e.g., Vasquez v. Hillery*, 474 U.S. 254, 266 (1986) (*stare decisis* must give way when necessary "to bring [the Court's] opinions into agreement with experience and with facts newly ascertained") (quotation marks omitted).

Bowers is an isolated decision that, like the cases overturned in *Payne*, was "decided by the narrowest of margins, over spirited dissents challenging [its] basic underpinnings." *Payne*, 501 U.S. at 828-29. Far from being "an essential feature of our legal tradition," *Mitchell v. United States*, 526 U.S. 314, 330 (1999), *Bowers* stands today as "a doctrinal anachronism discounted by society," *Casey*, 505 U.S. at 855. Many of the bedrock principles of contemporary constitutional law were announced in cases overruling contrary precedent—whether after only a few intervening years, or following decades of legal, political, and social development. *See, e.g., Barnette*, 319 U.S. at 630; *Brown*, 347 U.S. at 494-95; *Gitlow v. New York*, 268 U.S. 652, 666 (1925); *Malloy v. Hogan*, 378 U.S. 1, 4-6 (1964). As in those cases, the Court "cannot turn the clock back." *Brown*, 347 U.S. at 492-93. It accordingly should overturn *Bowers* and protect the fundamental liberty interests of Petitioners.

II. Section 21.06 Discriminates Without Any Legitimate and Rational Basis, Contrary to the Guarantee of Equal Protection.

Texas's Homosexual Conduct Law violates the Fourteenth Amendment for the additional reason that it "singl[es] out a certain class of citizens for disfavored legal status," *Romer*, 517 U.S. at 633, in violation of the most basic requirements of the Equal Protection Clause. The statute directly conflicts with the Constitution's "commitment to the law's neutrality." *Id.* at 623. It fails equal protection scrutiny even under the deferential "rational basis" standard.[24] And this discriminatory classification is "embodied in a criminal statute . . . where the power of the State weighs most heavily," a context in which the Court "must be especially sensitive to the policies of the Equal Protection Clause." *McLaughlin v. Florida*, 379 U.S. 184, 192 (1964).

Of course, if the Court agrees with Petitioners that the challenged law invades a fundamental liberty, analysis of the law's discriminatory classification would be as stringent as the analysis outlined in Point I. *See, e.g., Dunn v. Blumstein*, 405 U.S. 330, 337 (1972). In this Point II, Petitioners urge a distinct constitutional violation that does not depend on the Court finding that a fundamental liberty is at stake.

---

24. Heightened equal protection scrutiny is appropriate for laws like Section 21.06 that use a sexual-orientation-based classification. It is also appropriate where, as here, the law employs a gender-based classification to discriminate against gay people. The classification in this law, however, does not even have a legitimate and rational basis.

By its terms, Section 21.06 treats the *same* consensual sexual behavior differently depending on *who* the participants are. The behaviors labeled "deviate sexual intercourse" by Texas are widely practiced by heterosexual as well as gay adults.[25] But the statute makes this common conduct illegal only for same-sex couples and not for different-sex ones. Tex. Pen. Code §21.06. And the State offers only a tautological, illegitimate, and irrational purported justification for such discrimination.

The group targeted and harmed by the Homosexual Conduct Law is, of course, gay people. Gay people have a same-sex sexual orientation and heterosexuals have a different-sex one. *See, e.g.*, John C. Gonsiorek & James D. Weinrich, *The Definition and Scope of Sexual Orientation, in Homosexuality: Research Implications for Public Policy* 1 (J. Gonsiorek & J. Weinrich eds., 1991) ("sexual orientation is erotic and/or affectional disposition to the same and/or opposite sex"); *cf. Romer*, 517 U.S. at 624, 626-31 (in civil rights laws, "sexual orientation" is defined by an individual's "choice of sexual partners" or "heterosexuality, homosexuality or bisexuality"). The Homosexual Conduct Law overtly uses that defining characteristic to set up its disparate treatment. Section 21.06 "prohibit[s] lesbians and gay men from engaging in the same conduct in which heterosexuals may legally engage." *Morales*, 826 S.W.2d at 204; *see also* [*Commonwealth v.*] *Wasson*, 842 S.W.2d at 502 (where same-sex but not different-sex sodomy is criminalized, "[s]exual preference, and not the act committed, determines criminality, and is being punished").

A straightforward application of the rational basis test shows that this law and Texas's attempted justification for it cannot satisfy the requirement that every classification must at least "bear a rational relationship to an independent and legitimate legislative end." *Romer*, 517 U.S. at 633. When broader realities and history are considered, as this Court appropriately does in any equal protection case, the constitutional violation is only magnified. The Homosexual Conduct Law and its badge of criminality function to make gay people unequal in myriad spheres of everyday life and continue an ignominious history of discrimination based on sexual orientation. Ultimately, the equal protection and liberty concerns in this case reinforce one another, and further underscore that this unequal law and its broad harms are intolerable in this country.

A. Section 21.06's Classification Is Not Rationally Related to Any Legitimate Purpose and Serves Only the Illegitimate Purpose of Disadvantaging One Group.

"[C]onventional and venerable" principles require that legislative discrimination must, at a minimum, "bear a rational relationship to an independent and legitimate legislative end." *Romer*, 517 U.S. at 633, 635; *see also, e.g., Cleburne*, 473 U.S. at 446; *Western & S. Life Ins. Co. v. State Bd. of Equalization*, 451 U.S. 648, 668 (1981). This test is deferential, but meaningful.

> [E]ven in the ordinary equal protection case . . . , [the Court] insist[s] on knowing the relation between the classification adopted and the object to be attained. The search for the link between classification and objective gives substance to the Equal Protection Clause; it provides guidance and discipline for the legislature, which is entitled to know what sort of laws it can pass; and it marks the outer limits of [the judiciary's] own authority.

---

25. *See, e.g.*, Edward O. Laumann *et al.*, *The Social Organization of Sexuality* 98-99 (1994) (comprehensive study by University of Chicago researchers of sexual practices of American adults, finding that approximately 79% of all men and 73% of all women had engaged in oral sex, and 26% of all men and 20% of all women had engaged in anal sex).

Romer, 517 U.S. at 632.

Under the Equal Protection Clause, the *classification*—the different treatment of different people—is what must be justified. *See Board of Trustees of the Univ. of Ala. v. Garrett*, 531 U.S. 356, 366-67 (2001) (rational basis review searches for "distinguishing characteristics" between the two groups that are "relevant to interests the State has the authority to implement") (quotation marks omitted); *Rinaldi v. Yeager*, 384 U.S. 305, 308-09 (1966) (equal protection "imposes a requirement of some rationality in the nature of the class singled out"); *McLaughlin*, 379 U.S. at 191 ("courts must reach and determine the question whether the classifications drawn in a statute are reasonable in light of its purpose . . . whether there is an arbitrary or invidious discrimination between those classes covered . . . and those excluded"). The classification must be rationally connected to an independent and permissible government objective to "ensure that classifications are not drawn for the purpose of disadvantaging the group burdened by the law." *Romer*, 517 U.S. at 633.

Section 21.06 fails that essential test. As the Supreme Court of Kentucky observed in striking down that State's discriminatory consensual sodomy law on state equal protection grounds:

> In the final analysis we can attribute no legislative purpose to this statute except to single out homosexuals for different treatment for indulging their sexual preference by engaging in the same activity heterosexuals are now at liberty to perform. . . . The question is whether a society that no longer criminalizes adultery, fornication, or deviate sexual intercourse between heterosexuals, has a rational basis to single out homosexual acts for different treatment.

Wasson, 842 S.W.2d at 501. That court found no "rational basis for different treatment," and emphasized that "[w]e need not sympathize, agree with, or even understand the sexual preference of homosexuals in order to recognize their right to equal treatment before the bar of criminal justice." *Id.*; *accord Jegley* [*v. Picado*], 80 S.W.3d at 353 ("[w]e echo Kentucky in concluding that 'we can attribute no legislative purpose to this statute except to single out homosexuals'"). That conclusion applies with equal force to the identical classification employed by Texas's law.

When Texas enacted Section 21.06 in the early 1970s, there was no "practical necessity" to draw a classification among its residents with regard to the subject matter of consensual, adult oral and anal sex. *Cf. Romer*, 517 U.S. at 631. For decades, the State had included an evenhanded prohibition on those acts within its criminal code. When the legislature determined that its old law was unduly intrusive, it had the obvious choice of repealing it for *all* its citizens—as three-fourths of the States have done. *See supra* at 23 & n.17. Instead, it decided to single out same-sex couples for intrusive regulation and condemnation, and to free all heterosexual couples to make their own choices about particular forms of intimacy.

Throughout this litigation, the only justification that Texas has offered for this discriminatory classification is the moral judgment of the majority of its electorate. The State asserts that its "electorate evidently continues to believe" that the discriminatory line drawn by the Homosexual Conduct Law is desirable because it expresses the majority's moral views. Pet. Opp. 18.

The Homosexual Conduct Law's classification fails rational basis analysis, for several reasons. *First*, the State's position amounts to no "independent . . . legislative end" at all. *Cf. Romer*, 517 U.S. at 633. This "justification" merely restates that Texas believes in and wants to have this criminal law. The Equal Protection Clause requires that the State's classification serve a distinct legislative end—an objective or purpose—independent of the classification itself. There must be a "link between classification and objective," *id.* at 632, or "some relation between the classification and the purpose it serve[s]," *id.* at 633. The test would be meaningless—a mere rubberstamp for discrimination—unless the purpose is independent of the classification. But the "justification" offered by Texas is circular and not an independent objective served. In the words of the dissenters below, "[t]he contention that the same conduct is moral for some but not for others merely repeats, rather than legitimizes, the Legislature's unconstitutional edict." Pet. App. 44a.

The State's approach gives *carte blanche* to presumed majority sentiment, and leaves those targeted by a discriminatory law without recourse. If majority moral or value judgments were enough to answer an equal protection challenge, the amendment struck down in *Romer* would have survived, because the votes of a majority of Coloradans clearly signaled that including gay people within civil rights protections was antithetical to their values. Instead, this Court recognized that Amendment 2—like Section 21.06 here—was a "classification of persons undertaken for its own sake, something the Equal Protection Clause does not permit." 517 U.S. at 635. Government "may not avoid the strictures of that Clause by deferring to the wishes or objections . . . of the body politic." *Cleburne,* 473 U.S. at 448.

Second, even if Texas's objective could somehow be characterized as independent of the classification, mere negative views about the disfavored group—"moral" or otherwise—are not a legitimate basis for legal discrimination. *Cleburne,* 473 U.S. at 448 ("mere negative attitudes . . . unsubstantiated by factors which are properly cognizable [by government] are not permissible bases" for discriminatory legal rules). This Court has many times repeated the core principle of rejecting bias, however characterized, in law: Legal distinctions may not give effect to the majority's desire to condemn an unpopular group, *see Moreno,* 413 U.S. at 534, the negative reactions of neighbors, *see Cleburne,* 473 U.S. at 448, the fears of people who are different, *see id.,* a reaction of discomfort toward a minority, *see O'Connor v. Donaldson,* 422 U.S. 563, 575 (1975); *Cleburne,* 473 U.S. at 448-49, private prejudice, *Palmore v. Sidoti,* 466 U.S. 429, 433 (1984), or any other manifestation of unfounded animosity toward one group, *Romer,* 517 U.S. at 633-35. History unquestionably teaches that the moral views of a given time, just like fears, dislikes, and blatant prejudices, often reflect prevailing negative attitudes about different groups of people in society. *Cf. Whitney v. California,* 274 U.S. 357, 376 (1927) (Brandeis, J., concurring) ("Men feared witches and burnt women"). Indeed, negative attitudes toward a group can always be recast in terms of a discriminatory moral code. Using a moral lens to describe negative attitudes about a group that are not tied to any distinct, objective and permissible factors cannot cleanse those bare negative attitudes of their illegitimacy in government decisionmaking.

Texas's approach of dictating that same-sex couples are "more 'immoral and unacceptable,'" Pet. Opp. 18, than heterosexual couples under the very same circumstances—if they choose any of the behaviors defined as "deviate sexual intercourse"—must be rejected as impermissible. *Neutral, evenhanded* laws that truly restrict all persons in the same way could, if there were no fundamental interests at stake, be justified by a moral position. Here, however, Texas impermissibly attempts to impose a *discriminatory* moral code. The State's law and its proffered justification embody a bald preference for those with the most common sexual orientation and dislike of a smaller group who are different. Texas simply wants to judge those with a same-sex sexual orientation more harshly for the same behavior.

The Constitution and this Court's precedents forbid that. In *Palmore*, a mother lost custody of her child because her interracial "'life-style'" was "'unaccepta-ble . . . to society.'" 466 U.S. at 431 (quoting investigator's report). But this Court emphatically held that such negative views have no place in the law. *Id.* at 433 ("Private biases may be outside the reach of the law, but the law cannot, directly or indirectly, give them effect"). Likewise, unequal treatment may not be based on archaic and unfounded negative attitudes toward a group, whether grounded in morality, religious conviction, or "nature." In *Mississippi University for Women v. Hogan*, 458 U.S. 718 (1982), for example, the Court stressed the need to set aside archaic ideas about gender, such as that women are "innately inferior" or that unique "'moral and social problems'" would arise if women tended bar or otherwise enjoyed equal opportunities, *Id.* at 725 & n.10.

Similarly, negative attitudes toward those with a particular personal characteristic—even where advanced with the toned down patina of morality—are also not a legitimate justification for discrimination under rational basis scrutiny. In *Romer*, the Court refused to endorse the dissent's position that Amendment 2's anti-gay classification could be sustained as an attempt "to preserve traditional sexual mores," *Romer*, 517 U.S. at 636 (Scalia, J., dissenting). In *Moreno*, faced with a regulation that targeted the morally disfavored group of "hippies," the Court emphasized that "if the constitutional conception of 'equal protection of the laws' means anything, it must at the very least mean that a bare . . . desire to harm a politically unpopular group cannot constitute a *legitimate* governmental interest." *Moreno*, 413 U.S. at 534. Instead, different treatment must be supported by "reference to [some independent] considerations in the public interest." *Id.* (alteration in original). Whether termed a moral judgment, fear, discomfort, or bias, "mere negative attitudes" about one subset of the diverse American population cannot justify distinctions in legal treatment. *See Cleburne*, 473 U.S. at 448.

Third, there is no other legitimate justification that can save this law. The distinction drawn by the Homosexual Conduct Law does not rationally further any permissible goal of the State. There are no valid concerns of the government here that correlate with sexual orientation, which is a deeply rooted personal characteristic that we all have. Variation among heterosexuals, homosexuals, and bisexuals has no "relevan[cy] to interests the State has the authority to implement," *Garrett*, 531 U.S. at 366, or to "factors which are properly cognizable," *Cleburne*, 473 U.S. at 448, in writing the criminal law. Thus, Section 21.06's linedrawing does not turn on or respond to any differences in maturity or age, in intent, or in the specifics of the actors' relationship, other than its same-sex or different-sex nature. It does not incorporate the use of force, a public location, or a commercial context in its elements, to address those types of important concerns. Indeed, Texas has other laws that criminalize sexual conduct that is non-consensual, or public, or commercial, or with a minor. *See supra* at 6. Likewise, the law's discriminatory regulation of "deviate sexual intercourse" is unrelated to any interest in reproduction, for oral and anal sex are obviously not methods of reproduction for any couple.

Where government itself offers a reason that is illegitimate, as Texas has done here, or other factors indicate that the law rests on negative attitudes, the Court has carefully assessed any additional, purportedly rational and legitimate basis for challenged differential treatment. *See Cleburne*, 473 U.S. at 449-50 (careful assessment, and ultimate rejection, of other proffered reasons, where negative attitudes were clearly one basis for legal discrimination); *Moreno*, 413 U.S. at 535-38 (same). In such rational basis cases, the Court has not tried to supply new, "conceivable" reasons to support the classification. *See also Romer,* 517 U.S. at 635. It is, after all, only "*absent some reason to infer antipathy*" that the "Constitution presumes that . . . even improvident decisions will eventually be rectified by the democratic process and that judicial intervention is generally unwarranted." *Vance v. Bradley* 440 U.S. 93, 97 (1979) (emphasis added). Here, Texas offers nothing more than the majority's negative moral judgment to support its discrimination, and that should end the matter with a ruling of unconstitutionality.

This 1970s classification is "divorced from any factual context from which [the Court] could discern a relationship to legitimate state interests." *Romer,* 517 U.S. at 635. It is solely an effort to mark a difference in status, to send a message in the criminal law that one group is condemned by the majority. This impermissible and irrational double standard must be removed from Texas's criminal code.

B. *The Broader Realities Reinforce This Law's Affront to Core Principles of Equal Protection.*

Additional considerations confirm the violation of equal protection here. First, the Homosexual Conduct Law does not just discriminate against gay and lesbian Texans in their private intimate relations, but brands gay persons as second-class citizens and legitimizes discrimination against them in all aspects of life. Second, the discrimination worked by this law reflects and reinforces a century-long history of discrimination against gay Americans. The real-world context and history of discrimination further expose the law's illegitimacy. *See Romer,* 517 U.S. at 623-31 (considering in detail the functioning and historical background of challenged enactment); *Moreno,* 413 U.S. at 537 (considering "practical effect" of classification); *Eisenstadt,* 405 U.S. at 447-52 (considering social and legal backdrop in finding equal protection violation under rational basis standard). Where a law "circumscribe[s] a class of persons characterized by some unpopular trait or affiliation," there is a "special likelihood of bias on the part of the ruling majority." *N.Y. Trans. Auth. v. Beazer,* 440 U.S. 568, 593 (1979). . . .

CONCLUSION

For the foregoing reasons, the judgment of the Texas Court of Appeals upholding Section 21.06 and affirming Petitioners' criminal convictions thereunder should be reversed.

Notes and Questions

1. Though the excerpts from this brief (and the others in this section) contain substantial portions of the briefs, they are not complete. Full copies of these briefs (and many others of interest) are available on the *Supreme Court Sourcebook* Web site.

2. Look at the Table of Contents for this brief. Is it well-organized? Does it effectively preview the argument to come? If you read only the Table of Contents, would you know what the petitioners were arguing?

3. Notice that there is a single unlabeled introductory paragraph before the statement of facts. The relevant rules do not call for (or arguably even allow) such a paragraph, yet most experienced Supreme Court advocates include one. In his interview with Bryan Garner, Chief Justice Roberts indicated that he included such an introduction in almost every appellate brief he filed as a lawyer, even before courts that had shown a propensity for throwing briefs out if they did not exactly conform to the court's rules. Garner, *Interviews with Supreme Court Justices*, at 30. Why do experienced litigators—who are usually sticklers for following the rules—find it so important to push the boundaries in order to include this kind of introductory paragraph?

4. The facts section of the brief begins with the events of the night in question and then pulls out to discuss the history of the relevant statutory provision (including, an omitted discussion of its litigation history). Was this an effective way to frame the case? Does it follow the advice quoted above about how to craft a sympathetic facts section?

5. The facts section begins by asserting, "Late in the evening of September 17, 1998, Harris County, Texas, sheriff's officers entered John Lawrence's home and there intruded on Lawrence and Tyron Garner having sex." Recent scholarship reveals, however, that there is significant uncertainty as to whether that statement is in fact true. According to *Flagrant Conduct: The Story of* Lawrence v. Texas (2011) by law professor Dale Carpenter, only two of the police officers who raided the home claim to have seen the two men engaging in sexual activity and their accounts differ substantially as to the particular acts that they claim to have seen. *Id.* at 61-74. Lawyers for Lawrence and Garner knew from the outset that their clients were very likely innocent of the charges for which they had been indicted, but, with their permission, decided to use the case as a vehicle for this crucial constitutional challenge. In navigating the case through the courts, they never challenged the police account of the night in question but also never volunteered any details about the night in question. Given this general strategy, why do you think the brief begins with that particular sentence? If the sentence is not accurate, was it mistakenly included? If it was intentionally included, was it ethical to do so?

6. At the certiorari stage, the petitioners presented three questions to the Court in the following order: Whether laws like the one in question violate the Fourteenth Amendment's Equal Protection Clause; whether laws like the one in question violate the Fourteenth Amendment's Due Process Clause; and whether a prior Court decision foreclosing that due process argument should be overruled. When it came time to craft their brief, they flipped the order of their arguments, beginning instead with the due process argument and spending slightly more than half of their brief on that argument. Why do you think they decided to switch the order of their points and their emphasis? Can you think of some of the strategic and substantive considerations they might have considered in making that decision?

7. In pushing to make new constitutional law, the brief writers in this case had to make a number of very important and very difficult strategic choices about the structure of their argument and their particular language. Probably one of the most significant was their decision to make a two-step argument for their proposed due process rule, first claiming that prior case law protects private, consensual sexual activity between adults from state interference and then arguing that there is no principled reason to make an "exception" to that rule for gay men. As you will see in Chapter 7, the structure of that argument heavily shaped the majority opinion. Why do you think they framed their due process argument in those terms? Do you think that framing played a decisive role in their victory?

8. Take a look at the sources cited throughout the brief. Do they differ from those normally cited in legal briefs? In what ways? Why do you think they were included? Do you think they are effective?

John Geddes LAWRENCE and Tyron GARNER, Petitioners,
v.
STATE OF TEXAS, Respondent

No. 02-102. February 17, 2003

On Writ of Certiorari to the Texas Court of Appeals for the Fourteenth District

Respondent's Brief . . .

QUESTIONS PRESENTED

1. Whether the petitioners' criminal prosecutions for the offense of engaging in homosexual conduct, as defined by section 21.06 of the Texas Penal Code, violated the Fourteenth Amendment guarantee of equal protection of the law.
2. Whether the petitioners' criminal prosecutions under section 21.06 of the Texas Penal Code violated their constitutional rights to liberty and privacy, as protected by the Due Process Clause of the Fourteenth Amendment.
3. Whether *Bowers v. Hardwick*, 478 U.S. 186 (1986), should be overruled.

TABLE OF CONTENTS

2. Section 21.06 furthers the legitimate governmental interest
   of promotion of morality

III. Summary

CONCLUSION

STATEMENT

A citizen informed Harris County sheriff's deputies that an armed man was "going crazy" in the apartment of petitioner Lawrence. Pet. App. 129a. The investigating officers entered the apartment and observed the petitioners engaged in anal sexual intercourse. *Id.* They were then charged by complaint in a Harris County justice court with the commission of the Class C misdemeanor offense of engaging in homosexual conduct, an offense defined by Tex. Penal Code §21.06(a) (Vernon 1994), as follows: "A person commits an offense if he engages in deviate sexual intercourse with another individual of the same sex." A Class C misdemeanor is punishable only by a fine not to exceed five hundred dollars. Tex. Penal Code §12.23 (Vernon 1994).

After the petitioners were convicted and fined in the justice court, they gave notice of appeal and the proceedings were transferred to Harris County Criminal Court at Law No. 10. The petitioners moved to quash the complaints on various constitutional grounds. Pet. App. 117a, 130a. In support of those motions, the petitioners offered into evidence only the complaints themselves and the supporting "probable cause affidavits" filed by a sheriff's deputy in the justice court. *See* Pet. App. 129a, 141a. . . .

After the county court denied the petitioners' motions to quash the complaints, they entered pleas of *nolo contendere*, and the court found them guilty of engaging in homosexual conduct. The court sentenced each petitioner, pursuant to a plea bargain, to payment of a fine in the amount of two hundred dollars, and the petitioners again gave notice of appeal from their convictions.

A three-judge panel of the Court of Appeals for the Fourteenth District of Texas initially held that the State's prosecution of the petitioners under section 21.06 violated the Equal Rights Amendment of the Texas Constitution, with one justice dissenting. The State's motion for rehearing *en banc* was granted, however, and on March 15, 2001, the *en banc* court of appeals rejected all of the petitioners' constitutional challenges to the enforcement of section 21.06. *See Lawrence v. State,* 41 S.W.3d 349 (Tex. App.-Houston [14th Dist.] 2001, pet. ref'd) (Pet. App. 4a, *et seq.*). The *en banc* opinion of the court of appeals may be briefly summarized as follows:

1. Enforcement of the statute prohibiting homosexual conduct does not violate the Equal Protection Clauses of the Fourteenth Amendment to the United States Constitution and Article I, §3, of the Texas Constitution, because the statute does not implicate fundamental rights or a suspect class, and it has a rational basis in the Texas Legislature's determination that homosexual sodomy is immoral. The fact that heterosexual sodomy is no longer a criminal offense under Texas law is not constitutionally significant, because the Legislature could rationally distinguish between an act performed with a person of the same sex and a similar act performed with a person of different sex. Pet. App. 13a-18a.

2. Enforcement of section 21.06 does not violate the Equal Rights Amendment of the Texas Constitution, because the statute applies equally to both men

and women who engage in the prohibited conduct, and it is not the product of prejudice towards persons of either gender. Pet. App. 20a-24a.

3. The State's prosecution of the petitioners for the offense of engaging in homosexual conduct did not violate any constitutional right to privacy under the State or Federal Constitutions, in light of the long history of the imposition of criminal sanctions for such conduct, because it could not be said that the State of Texas or the United States recognized any "fundamental right" to engage in homosexual activity. Pet. App. 25a-31a.

A petition for discretionary review was denied, without written opinion, by the Texas Court of Criminal Appeals. Pet. App. 1a.

SUMMARY OF ARGUMENT

1. The record is inadequate to serve as a basis for recognition of a limited constitutional right to engage in extramarital sexual conduct, because the absence of information concerning the petitioners and the circumstances of their offense precludes a determination of whether they would actually benefit from the Court's recognition of the limited right which they assert. The record is also inadequate to establish that the petitioners belong to the class for which they seek equal protection relief.

2. The States of the Union have historically prohibited a wide variety of extramarital sexual conduct, a legal tradition which is utterly inconsistent with any recognition, at this point in time, of a constitutionally protected liberty interest in engaging in any form of sexual conduct with whomever one chooses. Nothing in this Court's "substantive due process" jurisprudence supports recognition of a constitutional right to engage in sexual misconduct outside the venerable institution of marriage. This Court should adhere to its previous holding on this issue in *Bowers v. Hardwick,* 478 U.S. 186 (1986), and it should reaffirm that the personal liberties protected by the Due Process Clause of the Fourteenth Amendment from State regulation are limited to those "so rooted in the traditions and conscience of our people as to be ranked as fundamental." *Palko v. Connecticut,* 302 U.S. 319, 325 (1937).

3. Since enforcement of the homosexual conduct statute does not interfere with the exercise of a fundamental right, and the statute is not based upon a suspect classification, it must only be rationally related to a permissible state goal in order to withstand equal protection challenge. This legislative proscription of one form of extramarital sexual misconduct is in keeping with long-standing national tradition, and bears a rational relationship to the worthy governmental goals of implementation of public morality and promotion of family values.

4. The petitioners cannot meet their burden of establishing a discriminatory purpose to the original enactment of a statute which is facially applicable to both persons of exclusively homosexual orientation and persons who regard themselves as bisexual or heterosexual. When the statute is viewed in historical perspective, it can reasonably be inferred that the Texas Legislature acted with non-discriminatory intent in limiting the scope of the predecessor sodomy statute to fit within the commonly understood parameters of this Court's then-emerging privacy jurisprudence.

ARGUMENT

I. Substantive Due Process Under the Fourteenth Amendment

A. The appellate record is inadequate to support the recognition of the limited constitutional right asserted by the petitioners.

The appellate record does not establish that the petitioners would actually benefit from recognition of the particular liberty interest which they assert; therefore, it does not provide this Court with a factual basis for recognizing that interest.

Precise identification of an asserted liberty interest is critical to the determination of whether it falls within the scope of the Due Process Clause of the Fourteenth Amendment. An appellate court's substantive due process analysis "must begin with a careful description of the asserted right," because the "doctrine of judicial self-restraint" requires a court "to exercise the utmost care whenever [it] is asked to break new ground in this field." *Reno v. Flores,* 507 U.S. 292, 302 (1993) (quoting *Collins v. Harker Heights,* 503 U.S. 115, 125 (1992)).

The petitioners initially advocate the recognition of a broadly drawn constitutional right to choose to engage in any "private consensual sexual intimacy with another adult, including one of the same sex." Brief of Petitioners 10. However, the petitioners later clarify that their challenge does not extend to the validity of statutes prohibiting prostitution, incest or adultery, which they describe as implicating additional "state concerns" not present in this case. *Id.* at 22 n.16. In short, the petitioners are asking the Court to recognize a fundamental right of an adult to engage in private, non-commercial, consensual sex with an unrelated, unmarried adult.

The slim record reveals only that the petitioners are adult males and that they engaged in anal intercourse in an apartment that petitioner Lawrence identified as his residence. It does not answer any of the following questions concerning the factual basis of their constitutional claims:

- Whether the petitioners' sexual conduct was non-commercial.
- Whether the petitioners' sexual conduct was mutually consensual.
- Whether the petitioners' conduct was "private."
- Whether the petitioners are related to one another.
- Whether either of the petitioners is married.
- Whether either (or both) of the petitioners is exclusively homosexual.[9]

While the petitioners possess standing to challenge the constitutionality of a statute under which they have actually been prosecuted and convicted, *see Eisenstadt v. Baird,* 405 U.S. 438, 443-444 (1972), they should not be permitted to argue that a protected liberty interest exists under some specified set of circumstances without showing that those circumstances actually exist. This Court will not issue an opinion "advising what the law would be upon a hypothetical state of facts," and it will not "decide questions that cannot affect the rights of litigants in the case before [it]." *North Carolina v. Rice,* 404 U.S. 244, 246 (1971) (citations omitted). For example, in cases not involving expressive activity protected by the First Amendment, litigants have no standing to argue that a statute "would be unconstitutional if applied to

---

9. The sexual orientation of the petitioners appears to be irrelevant to the disposition of their substantive due process argument, because they assert a constitutional right to engage in sodomy with persons of either gender, but it may be significant in determining whether the petitioners are members of any specific class in addressing their arguments premised upon the Equal Protection Clause, *infra.*

third parties in hypothetical situations." *County Court of Ulster County v. Allen,* 442 U.S. 140, 155 (1979).

In recognizing constitutional liberty interests under the Fourteenth Amendment, appellate courts "must use considerable restraint, including careful adherence to the incremental instruction given by the precise facts of particular cases, as they seek to give further and more precise definition to the right." *Troxel v. Granville,* 530 U.S. 57, 95-96 (2000) (Kennedy, J., dissenting).

Simply put, the record in this case provides an insufficient foundation for the meaningful review of the important and complex question of whether there is a constitutional right to engage in private, non-commercial, consensual sex with an unrelated, unmarried adult. At best, the record would support only the recognition of an extremely broad right to engage in sexual conduct with any other adult, regardless of any other circumstance which might attend that conduct—a right so broad that the petitioners themselves disavow any claim to it.

Because the record is inadequate to permit this Court to scrutinize and identify the contours and limitations of any protected liberty interest that might be recognized in this case, the State respectfully suggests that this Court dismiss the petition for writ of certiorari as improvidently granted. In the alternative, the respondent asks that the Court affirm the judgment of the Texas court of appeals on ground that the record is inadequate to support an effort to identify a limited constitutional right to engage in sexual conduct.

B. The Court has adopted an historical approach to the recognition of liberty interests protected under the Due Process Clause.

In addressing claims that a state has interfered with an individual's exercise of a previously unrecognized liberty interest protected by the Fourteenth Amendment, this Court has looked to the nation's history and legal traditions to determine whether the asserted interest is actually so fundamental to our system of ordered liberty as to merit constitutional protection from state regulation. For instance, in *Moore v. City of East Cleveland,* 431 U.S. 494 (1976) (plurality opinion), the Court observed that, "Appropriate limits on substantive due process come not from drawing arbitrary lines but rather from careful 'respect for the teaching of history [and], solid recognition of the basic values that underlie our society'." *Id.* at 503 (quoting *Griswold v. Connecticut,* 381 U.S. 479, 501 (1965) (Harlan, J., concurring)). Thus the "Constitution protects the sanctity of the family precisely because the institution of the family is deeply rooted in this Nation's history and tradition." *Id.*

In *Bowers,* 478 U.S. at 192-194, the Court rejected an asserted fundamental right to engage in homosexual conduct because, in light of pervasive State criminalization of such conduct throughout the nation's history, it could not seriously be asserted that a right to engage in homosexual sodomy was "deeply rooted in this Nation's history and tradition." Three years later, in *Michael H. v. Gerald D.,* 491 U.S. 110 (1989) (plurality opinion), the Court noted that in its attempts to "limit and guide interpretation of the [Due Process] Clause," it has "insisted not merely that the interest denominated as a 'liberty' be 'fundamental' (a concept that in isolation is hard to objectify), but also that it be an interest traditionally protected by our society." *Id.* at 122-123.

Two of the opinions issued in *Planned Parenthood of Southeastern PA. v. Casey,* 505 U.S. 833 (1992), expressed doubt or disagreement that the Due Process Clause protects only those practices, "defined at the most specific level," which were protected by law at the time of ratification of the Fourteenth Amendment. Emphasis upon the nation's legal traditions appeared only in the dissenting opinions. However, less than a year later, the Court's opinion in *Reno v. Flores,* 507 U.S. 292 (1993), unambiguously stated that the "mere novelty" of a claimed constitutional liberty interest was "reason enough to doubt that 'substantive due process' sustains it," because it could not be considered "so rooted in the traditions and conscience of our people as to be ranked as fundamental." *Id.* at 303 (quoting *United States v. Salerno,* 481 U.S. 739, 751 (1987), and *Snyder v. Massachusetts,* 291 U.S. 97, 105 (1934)).

This issue of the importance of national legal tradition in substantive due process jurisprudence was resolved in *Washington v. Glucksberg,* 521 U.S. 702 (1997), in which the Court emphasized the necessity of "examining our Nation's history, legal traditions, and practices" in order to determine whether a claimed liberty interest was, "objectively, 'deeply rooted in this Nation's history and tradition'" and "implicit in the concept of ordered liberty," and, therefore, merited protection under the Fourteenth Amendment:

> Our established method of substantive-due-process analysis has two primary features: First, we have regularly observed that the Due Process Clause specially protects those fundamental rights and liberties which are, objectively, "deeply rooted in this Nation's history and tradition," [*Moore v. City of East Cleveland*], at 503 (plurality opinion); *Snyder v. Massachusetts,* 291 U.S. 97, 105 (1934) ("so rooted in the traditions and conscience of our people as to be ranked as fundamental"), and "implicit in the concept of ordered liberty," such that "neither liberty nor justice would exist if they were sacrificed," *Palko v. Connecticut,* 302 U.S. 319, 325, 326 (1937). Second, we have required in substantive-due-process cases a "careful description" of the asserted fundamental liberty interest. *Flores, supra,* at 302; *Collins* [*v. Harker Heights,* 503 U.S. 115 (1992)] at 125; *Cruzan* [*v. Director, Missouri Department of Health,* 497 U.S. 261 (1990)] at 277-278. Our Nation's history, legal traditions, and practices thus provide the crucial "guideposts for responsible decisionmaking," *Collins, supra,* at 125, that direct and restrain our exposition of the Due Process Clause.

521 U.S. at 720-721.

The Court declined to recognize the constitutional liberty interest proposed in *Glucksberg*—a right to assisted suicide—because its recognition would have required the Court to "reverse centuries of legal doctrine and practice" and to elevate to the status of a protected liberty interest a practice that was traditionally prohibited by state law. *Id.* at 723, 728. . . .

C. *This nation has no deep-rooted tradition of protecting a right to engage in sodomy.*

Turning to the question of whether a right to engage in sodomy is "so rooted in the traditions and conscience of our people as to be ranked as fundamental," the Court's previous resolution of that issue in *Bowers v. Hardwick* is unassailable. As noted in *Bowers,* sodomy was a serious criminal offense at common law; it was forbidden by the laws of the original thirteen states at the time of the ratification of the Bill of Rights; and it was punishable as a crime in all but five of the thirty-seven states in existence at the time of the ratification of the Fourteenth Amendment. *Bowers,* 478 U.S. at 192-193.

As further noted in *Bowers,* sodomy remained punishable as a crime in every state of the Union prior to the year 1961, *id.* at 193, when Illinois became the first state to adopt the American Law Institute's Model Penal Code approach to decriminalization of some sexual offenses. *Id.* at 193 n.7.

Our nation's history has not been rewritten in the seventeen years since *Bowers* was decided, and that history contradicts any assertion that a right to engage in homosexual anal intercourse has been a valued and protected right of American citizens. The fact that the states have traditionally prohibited the act as a crime is utterly inconsistent with any claim that our legal tradition has treated the choice to engage in that act as a "fundamental" right.

It is true that some change has occurred since *Bowers* was decided: three more states and the District of Columbia, in appropriate exercise of the democratic process, have repealed or limited the scope of their statutes prohibiting sodomy in general or homosexual sodomy in particular; and a small number of state appellate courts have found that such statutes violate a state constitutional right to privacy. *See* Brief of Petitioners 23 n.17. The State of Texas is now one of thirteen states in which consensual homosexual sodomy remains a criminal offense. *Id.* at 27 n.21. The fact that several states have ceased treating sodomy as a criminal offense, however, is no evidence of a national tradition of espousing, honoring or safeguarding a right to engage in deviate sexual intercourse.

The petitioners concede that this Court requires "objective guideposts," such as "history and precedent," in the process of identification of liberty interests protected by the Fourteenth Amendment. They point to the gradual trend towards decriminalization of consensual sexual behavior among adults as the necessary objective evidence of a fundamental right firmly rooted in the traditions and conscience of American citizens. *See* Brief of Petitioners 19-25. Four decades of gradual but incomplete decriminalization does not erase a history of one hundred and fifty years of universal reprobation. A recent trend towards uneasy toleration—even a trend involving a majority of the fifty states—cannot establish a tradition "deeply rooted" in our national history and tradition. The petitioners mistake new growth for deep roots. . . .

The petitioners also argue that previously recognized "fundamental interests . . . converge in the right asserted here," Brief of Petitioners 11-16, but considered separately, the recognized liberty interests upon which the petitioners rely do not implicate the conduct in question, and no logical process extends their reach when they are lumped together.

The petitioners first assert a constitutionally protected right to choose to enter into "intimate relationships," citing *Roberts v. United States Jaycees*, 468 U.S. 609, 617-618 (1984), but no court has held that this nebulously defined right extended to the protection of sexual misconduct prohibited by State law. For example, in *Marcum v. McWhorter*, 308 F.3d 635, 641-643 (6th Cir. 2002), the court held that the freedom to choose to enter into personal relationships could not extend to an adulterous relationship, since adultery has been punishable as a crime for centuries. In this case, while the petitioners may have a constitutional right to associate with one another, the right to form an "intimate relationship" does not protect any and all sexual conduct in which they might engage in the context of that relationship.[17]

The petitioners also rely upon the recognized constitutional right to "bodily integrity," but the Court's decisions regarding bodily integrity generally pertain to unwarranted government invasion of an individual's body, and the individual's right to control his own medical treatment, *see Glucksberg*, 521 U.S. at 777-778 (Souter, J., concurring), and those decisions have nothing to do with the manner in which an individual interacts with third parties or invades another person's body.

---

17. Parents might well have a constitutionally protected right to maintain an intimate relationship with their children, but no one would argue that their protected liberty interest would extend to having sexual relations with the children.

The right to privacy in the home has long been recognized under both the First Amendment, *see Stanley v. Georgia*, 394 U.S. 557, 564-565 (1969), and the Fourth Amendment, *see Kyllo v. United States*, 533 U.S. 27, 31 (2001). However, the decision in *Stanley* involved the individual's freedom of thought, rather than conduct, *Stanley*, 394 U.S. at 565-566, and that decision has never been extended to prohibit state regulation of conduct that does not involve expression protected by the First Amendment. The Fourth Amendment protects against unreasonable police entry and search of the home, but it has never been found to protect one from prosecution for otherwise criminal conduct that occurs within that home. . . .

By arguing that their asserted liberty interest under the Fourteenth Amendment may be located at the "convergence" of these previously recognized rights, the petitioners implicitly admit that none of them, standing alone, has ever been construed in a fashion that would protect an individual from state prosecution for sexual misconduct occurring in a private residence. The petitioners' assertion of a patchwork of constitutional rights which do *not* implicate their conduct does not logically prove that the conduct is in fact protected by a previously unrecognized liberty interest.

D. No tradition of protection exists at any level of specificity of designation of an asserted liberty interest.

The petitioners' other quarrel with *Bowers* involves the level of specificity at which the nation's traditions are to be analyzed in assessing the existence of a protected liberty interest under the Fourteenth Amendment, an issue that does not seem to have been definitively resolved at this time. . . . Assuming that issue does remain open at this time, it should not be necessary to resolve it in this case, since the petitioners cannot establish a historical tradition of exalting and protecting the conduct for which they were prosecuted at *any* level of specificity.

At the most specific level, the nation has a long-standing tradition, only recently waning, of criminalizing anal sodomy—the offense once known as "buggery"—as a serious criminal offense. *See Bowers*, 478 U.S. 192-194; William N. Eskridge, Jr., *Gaylaw: Challenging the Apartheid of the Closet* 157-158, 328-337 (App. A) (1999).[20]

But even if the topic is broadened to include other acts of extramarital sexual intercourse, such as fornication, adultery, incest, prostitution, etc., the nation's tradition is still one characterized by prohibition and criminalization. Most of the states have maintained, through most of their history, statutes which made it a criminal offense to engage in fornication and adultery as well as sodomy, and there is no long-standing tradition of protecting the right to engage in any sort of extramarital sexual conduct.

Fornication was a punishable offense in colonial times, and it remained illegal in forty states until the early 1970s. *See* Tracy Shallbettor Stratton, *No More Messing Around: Substantive Due Process Challenges to State Laws Prohibiting Fornication*, 73 Wash. L. Rev. 767, 780 (1998). As of 1998, it was still a crime in thirteen states and the District of Columbia. *See id.* at 767 n.2; *accord*, Richard Green, *Griswold's Legacy: Fornication and Adultery as Crimes*, 16 Ohio N.U. L. Rev. 545, 546 n.8 (1989).

---

20. While acknowledging the widespread and longstanding existence of sodomy statutes, Professor Eskridge is critical of the historical basis for the Court's decision in *Bowers*, on grounds that early sodomy statutes were aimed primarily at the prohibition of buggery and similar forms of unnatural coitus, rather than the oral sex act for which the defendant in *Bowers* was prosecuted. *See* Eskridge at 156-157. That concern is absent in this case, since it is undisputed that the act of anal sodomy was a serious crime—originally a capital offense—from the earliest days of the colonization period.

Adultery was once a capital offense, under some circumstances, in colonial Massachusetts, and it was punished as a crime during the colonial period in almost every jurisdiction. *See Oliverson v. West Valley City*, 875 F. Supp. 1465, 1474 (D. Utah 1995). Adultery was still punishable as a crime "in most states . . . in 1900," *see id.* (quoting Lawrence M. Friedman, *Crime and Punishment in American History* 13 (1993)), and as of 1996, it remained a crime in twenty-five states and the District of Columbia. *City of Sherman v. Henry*, 928 S.W.2d 464, 470 n.3 (Tex. 1996); Green, *supra* at n.7.

Thus, the legislatures of the various states have shown significant concern for the sexual morality of the citizenry, and statutes criminalizing extramarital sexual conduct have been pervasive throughout our national history. The constitutionality of those statutes previously has been thought to be "beyond doubt," *Griswold v. Connecticut*, 381 U.S. 479, 498 (Goldberg, J. concurring), and recent decisions from the lower courts have held that the statutes are, in fact, constitutional. *See, e.g., Henry*, 928 S.W.2d at 471-472; *Marcum*, 308 F.3d at 642-643.

Furthermore, criminal prosecutions aside, the United States had no history whatsoever of *protecting* the right to engage in extramarital sex, at least until a few state appellate courts began in the 1990s to invalidate their sodomy statutes as violative of a state constitutional right to privacy. This Court, in particular, has never recognized any right to engage in extramarital sexual conduct, and it is telling that most of the fundamental liberty interests the Court has recognized under the Fourteenth Amendment are rooted in marriage, procreation and child-rearing. An asserted right to engage in homosexual sodomy is actually inimical to the fundamental rights that this Court has endeavored to protect.

The fact that five state courts have invalidated sodomy statutes in the last eleven years, on state constitutional grounds, is meager evidence of a deeply rooted national tradition of protecting the privacy of the conduct in issue. Too few states have taken such a step, over too brief a period of time, to support any such inference.

The Court catalogued the liberty interests to which it has accorded Fourteenth Amendment protection in *Glucksberg*, 521 U.S. at 720, as follows:

> In a long line of cases, we have held that, in addition to the specific freedoms protected by the Bill of Rights, the "liberty" specially protected by the Due Process Clause includes the rights to marry, *Loving v. Virginia*, 388 U.S. 1 (1967); to have children, *Skinner v. Oklahoma ex rel. Williamson*, 316 U.S. 535 (1942); to direct the education and upbringing of one's children, *Meyer v. Nebraska*, 262 U.S. 390 (1923); *Pierce v. Society of Sisters*, 268 U.S. 510 (1925); to marital privacy, *Griswold v. Connecticut*, 381 U.S. 479 (1965); to use contraception, *ibid.*; *Eisenstadt v. Baird*, 405 U.S. 438 (1972); to bodily integrity, *Rochin v. California*, 342 U.S. 165 (1952), and to abortion, *Casey, supra*. We have also assumed, and strongly suggested, that the Due Process Clause protects the traditional right to refuse unwanted lifesaving medical treatment.

Cruzan, 497 U.S., at 278-279.

The conduct at issue in this case has nothing to do with marriage or conception or parenthood and it is not on a par with those sacred choices. Homosexual sodomy cannot occur within or lead to a marital relationship. It has nothing to do with families or children. The decision to engage in homosexual acts is not like the acts and decisions that this Court previously has found worthy of constitutional protection, and it should not be added to the list of fundamental rights protected by the Fourteenth Amendment.

The difference between protected conduct within the marriage relationship and unprotected sexual conduct outside marriage has been recognized on a number of occasions, most famously in Justice Harlan's dissenting opinion in *Poe v. Ullman*, 367 U.S. 497, 545-546, 552-553 (1961), in which he expressed the view that "any Constitutional doctrine in this area" must be built upon the division between acts occurring within and without the marital relationship. . . .

E. Principles of stare decisis counsel against recognition of a new protected liberty interest.

Stare decisis mandates that the Court adhere to its holdings in *Bowers*. Seventeen years should be considered a very brief period indeed, in the context of the development of fundamental rights under the Fourteenth Amendment, and the principle of stare decisis counsels against rapid change in this area. If a right is truly fundamental, its public acceptance and societal value should not be the subject of vehement and widespread disagreement. Fundamental rights should be rock solid, and vacillation is inconsistent with the level of durability of rights which should be deemed "fundamental" to our society.

"Although adherence to precedent is not rigidly required in constitutional cases, any departure from the doctrine of stare decisis demands special justification." *Arizona v. Rumsey*, 467 U.S. 203, 212 (1984). The petitioners argue that such special justification exists in the steady "erosion" of support for *Bowers* and the concomitant advancement of the gay rights movement, Brief of Petitioners 30-31, but the Court reaffirmed in *Glucksberg* that *Bowers* utilized the correct mode of analysis in the determination of the existence of a new liberty interest under the Fourteenth Amendment. The fact that a few more states have eased criminal sanctions on sodomy or homosexual conduct since 1986 does not logically affect the validity of the conclusion in *Bowers* that no right to engage in homosexual conduct can be found "deeply rooted in this Nation's history and tradition." *Bowers*, 478 U.S. at 192.

"It is one of the happy incidents of the federal system that a single courageous State may, if its citizens choose, serve as a laboratory; and try novel social and economic experiments without risk to the rest of the country." *New State Ice Co. v. Liebmann*, 285 U.S. 262, 311 (1932) (Brandeis, J., dissenting). The principle of federalism that encourages the state to undertake such experiments also operates to permit states to decline to participate in them. All change is not for the better, and the right to be first should be accompanied by a right to be among the last to accept a change of debatable social value. . . .

II. EQUAL PROTECTION UNDER THE FOURTEENTH AMENDMENT

The petitioners also argue that their prosecution for engaging in homosexual conduct violates the Equal Protection Clause of the Fourteenth Amendment. They argue that section 21.06 improperly criminalizes sexual conduct with a person of the same sex that is otherwise legal when done with a person of the opposite sex, and they claim that the State cannot articulate any rational basis for this classification.

This challenge fails on two grounds. First, given the evolution of the Texas sodomy statute towards more liberality with respect to sexual activity, petitioners cannot establish that the Texas Legislature purposefully discriminated against persons engaging in homosexual conduct. Instead, this Court reasonably can infer that the legislature, in good faith, incrementally narrowed the State's neutral proscriptions against sodomy in accordance with contemporaneous developments in due process jurisprudence. As such, instead of being the product of a legislative choice to discriminate against homosexuals, section 21.06 is the vestigial remainder of a predecessor sodomy statute, reduced to its present form as a result of the legislature's 1973 reform of the Texas Penal Code.

Second, this Court can infer a rational basis for the legislature's enactment of section 21.06. The State of Texas has a legitimate state interest in legislatively expressing the long-standing moral traditions of the State against homosexual conduct, and in discouraging its citizens—whether they be homosexual, bisexual or heterosexual—from choosing to engage in what is still perceived to be immoral conduct. Section 21.06 rationally furthers that goal by publishing the State's moral disapproval in a penal code of conduct for its citizens and by creating a disincentive against the conduct. The Legislature reasonably could have concluded that lesser, unenforceable expressions of disapproval would be ineffective to deter that conduct. Moreover, the narrowing of the predecessor sodomy statute to avoid constitutional challenge is in itself a rational basis for the legislative action: viewed in historical context, the Texas Legislature's decision was a reasonable response to the evolving due process jurisprudence of the late 1960s and early 1970s.

This rational-basis analysis is consistent with this Court's analysis in *Bowers v. Hardwick,* 478 U.S. 186 (1986), which addressed the rationality of basing legislation on moral tradition. Although *Bowers* was decided on substantive due process grounds, it stands alone as the only modern case in which this Court has approved moral tradition as a submitted rational basis for legislation. Nothing has changed in the sixteen years since *Bowers* to justify abandonment of its conclusion.

A. The Equal Protection Clause—standard of review.

The Equal Protection Clause of the Fourteenth Amendment creates no substantive rights. *Vacco v. Quill,* 521 U.S. 793, 799 (1997). Instead, it "embodies a general rule that States must treat like cases alike but may treat unlike cases accordingly." *Id.; see also City of Cleburne, Texas v. Cleburne Living Center,* 473 U.S. 432, 439 (1985) (construing Equal Protection Clause as "essentially a direction that all persons similarly situated should be treated alike").

Unless a classification warrants some form of heightened review because it jeopardizes the exercise of a fundamental right or categorizes on the basis of an inherently suspect characteristic, the Equal Protection Clause requires only that the classification rationally further a legitimate state interest. *Nordlinger v. Hahn,* 505 U.S. 1, 10 (1992).

1. Rational-basis review.

Rational-basis review is "the most relaxed and tolerant form of judicial scrutiny under the Equal Protection Clause." *City of Dallas v. Stanglin,* 490 U.S. 19, 26 (1989). "In general, the Equal Protection Clause is satisfied so long as there is a plausible policy reason for the classification, the legislative facts on which the classification is apparently based rationally may have been considered to be true by the governmental decisionmaker, and the relationship of the classification is not so attenuated as to render the distinction arbitrary or irrational." *Nordlinger,* 505 U.S. at 11 (citations omitted); *see also Romer,* 517 U.S. at 632 (1996) ("In the ordinary case, a law will be sustained if it can be said to advance a legitimate government interest, even if the law seems unwise or works to the disadvantage of a particular group, or if the rationale for it seems tenuous.").

The rational-basis standard of review is a paradigm of judicial restraint. *F.C.C. v. Beach Communications, Inc.*, 508 U.S. 307, 314 (1993). Rational-basis review in equal protection analysis is not a license for courts to judge the wisdom, fairness, or logic of legislative choices, nor does it authorize the judiciary to sit as a super-legislature to judge the wisdom or desirability of legislative policy determinations made in areas that neither affect fundamental rights nor proceed along suspect lines. . . .

When social legislation is at issue, the Equal Protection Clause allows the states wide latitude, and the Constitution presumes that even improvident decisions will eventually be rectified by the democratic processes. *Cleburne*, 473 U.S. at 440; *see also Dandridge v. Williams*, 397 U.S. 471, 486 (1970) (holding that the rational basis standard "is true to the principle that the Fourteenth Amendment gives the federal courts no power to impose upon the States their views of what constitutes wise economic or social policy").

2. Heightened review is neither sought nor required.

The petitioners suggest only in a footnote that laws which incorporate a sexual-orientation-based classification, or a gender-based classification to discriminate against homosexuals, should be reviewed pursuant to a heightened scrutiny standard. Brief of Petitioners 32 n.24. This assertion is not implicated by the litigation, briefed by the petitioners, or mandated by law.

The petitioners do not brief their request for heightened review and continue to rely solely on the rational-basis standard of review in their equal protection challenge to the constitutionality of section 21.06. *See Lawrence*, 41 S.W.2d at 378 (Anderson, J., dissenting) (in response to majority's conclusions that there is no fundamental right to engage in sodomy, and homosexuals do not constitute a suspect class, dissent characterizes these conclusions as "irrelevant here because *appellants do not raise these arguments*") (emphasis added). Accordingly, this Court's jurisprudence would be ill-served by consideration of a new standard not actually in controversy between the parties. *See Heller*, 509 U.S. at 319 ("Even if respondents were correct that heightened scrutiny applies, it would be inappropriate for us to apply that standard here. Both parties have been litigating this case for years on the theory of rational-basis review, which . . . does not require the State to place any evidence in the record, let alone the extensive evidentiary showing that would be required for these statutes to survive heightened scrutiny. It would be imprudent and unfair to inject a new standard at this stage in the litigation.").

The appropriateness of applying a rational-basis analysis to classifications based upon sexual orientation is not a matter of controversy in this Court or the federal courts of appeals. In *Romer v. Evans*, 517 U.S. 620 (1996), a case in which the amendment in question specifically classified the affected individuals in terms of sexual orientation, this Court nonetheless utilized the rational-basis test. *Id.* at 631-636. Likewise, in the federal courts of appeals, the profusion of litigation involving the exclusion of homosexuals from military service has provided ample opportunity for consideration of the appropriate standard of review, and it appears that those courts are unanimous in finding that homosexuals do not constitute a suspect class and that there is no fundamental right to engage in homosexual conduct.

Heightened review of section 21.06 as a statute discriminating on the basis of gender is likewise unnecessary. . . .

B. *The petitioners have not established their membership in the class for which equal protection relief is sought.*

Before rational-basis review is necessary, the petitioners must establish that Texas impermissibly discriminated against *them*. From the record and the briefs, however, it is unclear what class the petitioners purport to represent in this challenge.

The classifications challenged in the petitioners' respective motions to quash the complaints against them in the trial court were the criminalization of "consensual sexual acts, including those in private, according to the sex and sexual orientation of those who engage in them," and the "discriminatory classification against gay people." *See* Pet. App. 119a-120a, 131a-132a. However, the record is silent as to the sexual orientation of the petitioners and whether the charged conduct was occurring consensually. *See id.*, Appendices E, F & G, pp. 107a-141a (entirety of trial court record). . . .

In this instance, if the petitioners contend that they were denied equal protection because they belong to the class of individuals who are foreclosed from having deviate sexual intercourse with another person of the same sex, they do not state an equal protection violation. Under the facially neutral conduct prohibitions of section 21.06, everyone in Texas is foreclosed from having deviate sexual intercourse with another person of the same sex. If the petitioners contend, however, that they were denied equal protection because they belong to a class of individuals who have been disproportionately impacted by section 21.06, the record is silent as to whether they in fact belong to such a class.

This Court accords equal protection standing only to "those persons who are personally denied equal treatment." *See id.* at 743-744 (quoting *Allen v. Wright,* 468 U.S. 737, 755 (1984)). While the petitioners clearly have been prosecuted under section 21.06, it is not established in this record that they possess the same-sex orientation that they contend is singled out for discrimination by the statute.

As such, the writ of certiorari should be dismissed as improvidently granted, or standing should be denied to these petitioners for lack of an adequate record to establish an equal protection violation against them personally.

C. *The Texas Legislature did not purposefully discriminate in the passage of section 21.06.*

Although the petitioners assert that the "group targeted and harmed by the Homosexual Conduct Law is, of course, gay people," *see* Brief of Petitioners 33, and much of their briefing is related to the unequal protection of the laws with respect to homosexuals, *see id.* at 40-50, section 21.06 does not expressly classify its offenders on the basis of their sexual orientation. Rather, it criminalizes homosexual conduct without reference to a defendant's sexual orientation. *Lawrence,* 41 S.W.2d at 353; *see also* Editors of the Harvard Law Review, *Sexual Orientation and the Law,* at 16 (Harvard University Press 1990) ("Although litigants and courts have assumed that [same-sex] sodomy statutes classify based on sexual preference, the statutes actually prevent all persons from engaging in same-sex sodomy, regardless of sexual orientation.").

The focus of section 21.06 on conduct, rather than sexual orientation, does not foreclose equal protection review. A statute, though facially neutral, may still be challenged as constitutionally infirm under the Equal Protection Clause if the challenger can prove that the statute was enacted because of a discriminatory purpose. *Personnel Administrator of Massachusetts v. Feeney,* 442 U.S. 256, 279 (1979). This intent component is significant: equal protection jurisprudence focuses on the purposeful marginalization of disfavored groups. *See id.* at 274, 279 (holding that "discriminatory purpose" implies more than intent as volition or intent as awareness of the consequences; it implies that the decisionmaker [in that case a state legislature] selected or reaffirmed a particular course of action at least partly "because of," and not merely "in spite of," its adverse effects upon an identifiable group); *Hernandez v. New York,* 500 U.S. 352, 372-73 (1991) (O'Connor, J., concurring) ("An unwavering line of cases from this Court holds that a violation of the Equal Protection Clause requires state action motivated by discriminatory intent; the disproportionate effects of state action are not sufficient to establish such a violation.").

As such, assuming that petitioners appear as representatives of the class of individuals who are disproportionately affected by section 21.06, it is incumbent upon them to prove the purposeful intent of the Texas Legislature in order to perfect their equal protection claim. *Cf. State v. Baxley,* 656 So. 2d 973, 978 (La. 1995) ("Given the presumption of the constitutionality of legislation which does not classify on its face, it is incumbent upon the challenger of the legislation to prove the discriminatory purpose. In the present case, the record is devoid of any evidence that the crime against nature statute was enacted for the purpose of discriminating against gay men and lesbians. Therefore, the statute is not constitutionally infirm on these grounds.").

The record on appeal—which essentially consists of complaints, "probable cause affidavits," motions to quash, and pleas of guilty—provides no such evidence. Likewise, the petitioners have submitted no evidence of the Legislature's intent to invidiously discriminate.

Although commentators have speculated that section 21.06 was enacted in its present form because of political concerns about the impact of decriminalizing homosexual conduct, an alternative interpretation of the Legislature's intent can be inferred from the historical context within which section 21.06 was passed. . . .

In 1943, the statute was amended to the following form:

ARTICLE 524. SODOMY.
Whoever has carnal copulation with a beast, or in an opening of the body, except sexual parts, with another human being, or whoever shall use his mouth on the sexual parts of another human being for the purpose of having carnal copulation, or who shall voluntarily permit the use of his own sexual parts in a lewd and lascivious manner by any minor, shall be guilty of sodomy, and upon conviction thereof shall be deemed guilty of a felony, and shall be confined in the penitentiary not less than two (2) nor more than fifteen (15) years.

Act of April 5, 1943, 48th Leg., R.S., ch. 112, §1, 1943 Tex. Gen. Laws 194 (hereinafter "article 524").

In 1965, this Court recognized in *Griswold v. Connecticut,* 381 U.S. 479 (1965), a constitutional right of privacy forbidding government regulation of a married couple's access to the use of contraceptives. Decisions followed that further delineated similar rights of privacy, including *Loving v. Virginia,* 388 U.S. 1 (1967), *Eisenstadt v. Baird,* 405 U.S. 438 (1972), and *Roe v. Wade,* 410 U.S. 113 (1973).

As a result of those decisions, article 524 came under attack in federal district court, *see Buchanan v. Batchelor,* 308 F. Supp. 729 (N.D. Tex. 1970), *rev'd on other grounds,* 401 U.S. 989 (1971), and in the Texas Court of Criminal Appeals. *See Pruett v. State,* 463 S.W.2d 191 (Tex. Crim. App. 1971). The *Buchanan* court, a three-judge panel, declared article 524 unconstitutional because it violated the liberty of married couples in their private conduct by subjecting them to felony prosecution for private acts of sodomy, "an intimate relation of husband and wife." *Id.* at 732-33.

The court declined to extend its holding to homosexual conduct, specifically noting the limited applicability of *Griswold* to the marital context. *Id.* at 733. The Court thus held article 524 unconstitutional "insofar as it reaches the private, consensual acts of married couples." *Id.* at 735.

Although *Buchanan* was later reversed by this Court and remanded for consideration as to whether abstention was necessary in light of the Court's decision in *Younger v. Harris,* 401 U.S. 37 (1971), and the Texas Court of Criminal Appeals ultimately declined to find article 524 unconstitutional in *Pruett,* these cases were certainly within the constructive knowledge of the 1973 Texas Legislature as it considered what to do with the sodomy statute.

As such, it is a reasonable inference from this context that the Texas Legislature's enactment of section 21.06 in 1973 was not purposefully discriminatory against homosexuals, but was instead a reform of article 524 in accordance with what then appeared to be the direction in which constitutional privacy law was heading. The reformatory nature of the amendments is indicated as well by the Legislature's reduction of the offense from a felony punishable by confinement in the penitentiary for a minimum two years to a misdemeanor punishable only by a fine of up to two hundred dollars, and the Legislature's formulation of the statute to forbid only certain kinds of homosexual conduct.

The residual differences left over from this kind of benign incremental reform do not amount to purposeful discrimination. *See, e.g., McDonald v. Board of Election Commissioners of Chicago,* 394 U.S. 802, 809 (1969) ("[A] legislature traditionally has been allowed to take reform 'one step at a time, addressing itself to the phase of the problem which seems most acute to the legislative mind,' and a legislature need not run the risk of losing an entire remedial scheme simply because it failed, through inadvertence or otherwise, to cover every evil that might conceivably have been attacked.") (citations omitted); *F.C.C. v. Beach Communications, Inc.,* 508 U.S. 307, 316 (1993) ("[S]cope-of-coverage provisions are unavoidable components of most economic or social legislation. [The necessity of drawing a line of demarcation] renders the precise coordinates of the resulting legislative judgment virtually unreviewable, since the legislature must be allowed leeway to approach a perceived problem incrementally.").

Because there is no evidence establishing that the Texas Legislature acted with discriminatory intent in 1973, the presumption of constitutionality persists. The petitioners have not demonstrated purposeful discrimination against the class they purport to represent.

D. Section 21.06 is rationally related to a legitimate state interest.

If a rational-basis analysis is necessary with regard to the promulgation of section 21.06, the State's legitimate interest in protecting its statute from constitutional challenge was in itself a rational basis for legislative action. In addition, section 21.06 rationally furthers other legitimate state interests, namely, the continued expression of the State's long-standing moral disapproval of homosexual conduct, and the deterrence of such immoral sexual activity, particularly with regard to the contemplated conduct of heterosexuals and bisexuals.

1. Section 21.06 was enacted for the purpose of avoiding litigation and possible invalidation of the predecessor statute.

As noted above, section 21.06 was enacted by a 1973 Texas Legislature which was cognizant of changing judicial attitudes towards the constitutionality of legislation restricting private decisions of married couples. Accordingly, the decision to narrow article 524 was not the irrational product of invidious discrimination against homosexuals, but rather a reasonable retrenchment of the statute to address what may have been perceived to be a constitutional limitation of state authority to regulate marital behavior. No similar concerns existed at that time with respect to the possible constitutional protection of homosexual conduct, thus vitiating the need for immediate legislative reform in that direction.

For the reasons more fully expressed *supra*, this neutral motivation for the amendment of article 524 into the present-day statute—*i.e.*, to avoid a potentially successful challenge to the State's sodomy law by individuals engaging in consensual heterosexual conduct—represents a rational basis for the classification of conduct upon which section 21.06 is based.

2. Section 21.06 furthers the legitimate governmental interest of promotion of morality.

The promotion of morality has long been recognized as a lawful function of government. *See, e.g., Barbier v. Connolly,* 113 U.S. 27, 31 (1884) (holding that the Equal Protection Clause was not intended "to interfere with the power of the state . . . to prescribe regulations to promote the health, peace, morals, education, and good order of the people"); *Louis K. Liggett Co. v. Baldridge,* 278 U.S. 105, 111-12 (1928) ("The police power may be exerted in the form of state legislation . . . only when such legislation bears a real and substantial relation to the public health, safety, morals, or some other phase of the general welfare."); *Berman v. Parker,* 348 U.S. 26, 32 (1954) (identifying "[p]ublic safety, public health, morality, peace and quiet [and] law and order" as appropriate "application[s] of the police power to municipal affairs"); *Barnes v. Glen Theatre, Inc.,* 501 U.S. 560, 569 (1991) (plurality opinion) (holding that police powers of the State extend to "public health, safety and morals").

Similarly, protection of family and morality has motivated many valid governmental actions. *See, e.g., Barnes,* 501 U.S. at 569 (recognizing legislature's right to "protect 'the social interest in order' and morality" in enacting public indecency statutes); *Michael H. v. Gerald D.,* 491 U.S. 110, 131 (1989) (protection of "integrity of the marital union" as legitimate state interest for denying third-party standing to challenge legitimacy of birth); *City of Dallas v. Stanglin,* 490 U.S. 19, 27 (1989) (protection of teenagers from "corrupting influences" as legitimate state interest for limiting access to dancehall); *Ginsberg v. United States,* 390 U.S. 629, 639 (1968) (approving legislature's legislation against distribution of "girlie magazines" to minors because "legislature could properly conclude that parents and others . . . who have this primary responsibility for children's well-being are entitled to the support of laws designed to aid discharge of that responsibility").

This moral component was at the core of the Fifth Circuit's decision affirming the constitutionality of section 21.06 in 1985. Sitting *en banc*, that court found that "in view of the strong objection to homosexual conduct, which has prevailed in Western culture for the past seven centuries," section 21.06 was rationally related to the implementation of "morality, a permissible state goal," and, therefore, did not violate the Equal Protection Clause. *Baker v. Wade,* 769 F.2d 289, 292 (5th Cir. 1985), *cert. denied,* 478 U.S. 1022 (1986). Other courts at that time reached similar conclusions. *See Dronenburg v. Zech,* 741 F.2d 1388, 1397 (D.C. Cir. 1984) (upholding naval regulations excluding homosexuals from service as a permissible implementation of public morality, and noting the unlikelihood that "very many laws exist whose ultimate justification does not rest upon the society's morality"); *State v. Walsh,*

713 S.W.2d 508, 511-12 (Mo. 1986) (holding that "punishing homosexual acts as a Class A misdemeanor . . . is rationally related to the State's constitutionally permissible objective of implementing and promoting the public morality").

Shortly before the courts in *Baker* and *Dronenburg* upheld legislation related to homosexual conduct, the Eleventh Circuit reached an opposite conclusion with respect to Georgia's sodomy statute. *See Hardwick v. Bowers,* 760 F.2d 1202, 1212 (11th Cir. 1985) (holding that the Georgia statute implicated Hardwick's fundamental rights because his homosexual activity was a private and intimate association placed beyond the reach of state regulation by the Ninth Amendment and the "notion of fundamental fairness embodied in the due process clause of the Fourteenth Amendment").

This Court granted the Georgia Attorney General's petition for certiorari, and declined to invalidate Georgia's sodomy statute, finding that there was no fundamental right to engage in homosexual sodomy. *Bowers,* 478 U.S. at 191. In reaching this conclusion, the Court noted the long history of moral disapproval of homosexual conduct, noting that "[p]roscriptions against that conduct have ancient roots," and that, until 1961, sodomy had been illegal in all fifty states. *Id.* at 192; *see also id.* at 196-97 (Burger, C.J., concurring) (detailing historical genesis of sodomy statutes).

This Court dismissed Hardwick's assertion that there was no rational basis for the Georgia sodomy statute, explicitly rejecting the notion that laws may not be based upon perceptions of morality:

> Even if the conduct at issue here is not a fundamental right, respondent asserts that there must be a rational basis for the law and that there is none in this case other than the presumed belief of a majority of the electorate in Georgia that homosexual sodomy is immoral and unacceptable. This is said to be an inadequate rationale to support the law. The law, however, is constantly based on notions of morality, and if all laws representing essentially moral choices are to be invalidated under the Due Process Clause, the courts will be very busy indeed. Even respondent makes no such claim, but insists that majority sentiments about the morality of homosexuality should be declared inadequate. We do not agree, and are unpersuaded that the sodomy laws of some 25 States should be invalidated on this basis.

Id. at 196. This Court shortly thereafter declined to review the constitutionality of section 21.06 of the Texas Penal Code. *See Baker v. Wade,* 478 U.S. 1022 (1986) (denying petition for writ of certiorari).

Nothing in this Court's jurisprudence since *Bowers* justifies revisiting its conclusion that morality constitutes an appropriate basis for legislative action. Petitioners cite *Romer v. Evans,* 517 U.S. 620 (1996) as antithetical to *Bowers,* but a careful review of *Romer* indicates that its application of equal protection principles to an overbroad state constitutional amendment does not implicate the legislature's authority to prohibit what has traditionally been perceived as immoral conduct.

In *Romer,* the citizens of the State of Colorado approved a constitutional amendment that invalidated municipal ordinances banning discrimination on the basis of sexual orientation, and prohibited all legislative, executive or judicial action at any level of state or local government designed to protect homosexuals, lesbians, or bisexuals. *See id.* at 627. The Court summarized the impact of the amendment:

> Homosexuals, by state decree, are put in a solitary class with respect to transactions and relations in both the private and governmental spheres. The amendment withdraws

from homosexuals, but no others, specific legal protection from the injuries caused by discrimination, and it forbids reinstatement of these laws and policies.

Id.

In overturning the amendment on equal protection grounds, the Court found that the statute "has the peculiar property of imposing a broad and undifferentiated disability on a single named group" that is "at once too narrow and too broad," identifying "persons by a single trait and then den[ying] them protection across the board." *Id.* at 632-33. In other words, the Colorado initiative was held unconstitutional because it went beyond punishment of the act of engaging in homosexual conduct and sought to disenfranchise individuals because of the mere tendency or predilection to engage in such conduct.

Section 21.06 does not suffer from that flaw. It is the homosexual conduct that is viewed as immoral, and a statute rendering that conduct illegal is obviously related to the goal of discouraging the conduct and thereby implementing morality. A statute that, say, prohibited all individuals with a homosexual orientation from attending public schools would not be rationally related to that goal and would violate the Equal Protection Clause, but a statute imposing criminal liability only upon persons who actually engage in homosexual conduct is perfectly tailored to implement the communal belief that the conduct is wrong and should be discouraged. . . .

The State does not dispute that invidious intent can be inferred from classifications based on race, gender, economic status, or mental retardation. *See, e.g., Palmore v. Sidoti,* 466 U.S. 429 (1984) (reversing order denying custody based on racial considerations); *Frontiero v. Richardson,* 411 U.S. 677 (1973) (reversing gender-based classification in distribution of military benefits); *United States Department of Agriculture v. Moreno,* 413 U.S. 528 (1973) (striking down grossly overbroad classification discriminating against "individuals who live in households containing one or more members who are unrelated to the rest"); *Cleburne,* 473 U.S. 432 (1985) (striking down zoning restriction against group home for mentally retarded based on negative reactions of neighbors to proximity). In those cases, the Court fairly reduced the asserted bases for discriminatory classifications to unsubstantiated negative views about the affected individuals. *See Romer,* 517 U.S. at 635 (prohibiting "status-based" legislation that is "a classification of persons undertaken for its own sake").

Those classifications do not implicate a moral component, though, as does a classification identifying types of homosexual conduct. As previously noted, the history of prohibitions against homosexual sodomy—in the common law, American law, and Texas law—is ancient, and the legislature's deference to these moral traditions is appropriate and rational.[30]

---

30. *See* Michael McConnell, *The Role of Democratic Politics in Transforming Moral Convictions into Law,* 98 Yale L. Rev. 1501 (1989), arguing that deference to traditions of morality is "natural and inevitable . . . but it is also *sensible*":

> An individual has only his own, necessarily limited, intelligence and experience (personal and vicarious) to draw upon. Tradition, by contrast, is composed of the cumulative thoughts and experiences of thousands of individuals over an expanse of time, each of them making incremental and experimental alterations (often unconsciously), which are then adopted or rejected (again, often unconsciously) on the basis of experience—the experience, that is, of whether they advance the good life.

The prohibition of homosexual conduct in section 21.06 represents the reasoned judgment of the Texas Legislature that such conduct is immoral and should be deterred.[31] Although the application of sodomy statutes is not common because of the nature and circumstances of the offense, the statutes, like many others, express a baseline standard expressing the core moral beliefs of the people of the State. Whether this Court perceives this position to be wise or unwise, long-established principles of federalism dictate that the Court defer to the Texas Legislature's judgment and to the collective good sense of the people of the State of Texas, in their effort to enforce public morality and promote family values through the promulgation of penal statutes such as section 21.06.

III. SUMMARY

Public opinion regarding moral issues may change over time, but what has not changed is the understanding that government may require adherence to certain widely accepted moral standards and sanction deviation from those standards, so long as it does not interfere with constitutionally protected liberties. The legislature exists so that laws can be repealed or modified to match prevailing views regarding what is right and wrong, and so that the citizens' elected representatives can fine-tune the severity of the penalties to be attached to wrongful conduct. Perhaps homosexual conduct is not now universally regarded with the same abhorrence it inspired at the time of the adoption of our Federal Constitution, but any lag in legislative response to a mere change of public opinion—if such a lag actually exists—cannot and must not constitute the basis for a finding that the legislature's original enactment exceeded its constitutional authority.

As stated in *Glucksberg*, 521 U.S. at 735-36, there is "an earnest and profound debate about the morality, legality and practicality" of the statute in question; and the affirmance of the decision of the court of appeals in this case will "permit this debate to continue, as it should in a democratic society."

CONCLUSION

It is respectfully submitted that the petition for writ of certiorari should be dismissed as improvidently granted, or, in the alternative, that the judgment of the Texas Court of Appeals for the Fourteenth District should be in all things affirmed.

Notes and Questions

1. In contrast with the petitioners' brief, the Table of Contents in this brief includes several headings that describe the topic of the section but do not reveal the content of the argument the respondent is making. Does this difference have any impact on the persuasiveness of the brief? Are there other differences in the effectiveness of the Tables of Contents?

---

31. In fact, although the statute is unlikely to deter many individuals with an exclusively homosexual orientation, the Legislature rationally could have concluded that section 21.06 would be effective to some degree in deterring the remaining population (i.e., persons with a heterosexual or bisexual orientation) from detrimentally experimenting in homosexual conduct.

2. The fact section and summary section in this brief are substantially shorter than in the petitioners' brief. Does this reflect the kind of effective, concise writing the Justices begged for above or does it instead reflect incomplete work and lost opportunities?

3. The respondent begins their argument with questions about whether the factual record is sufficient to allow the Court to decide the issues raised by the case and returns to such arguments at some length later in the brief. What exactly are their objections? Is this the proper stage of the proceedings to raise them? Do you find them persuasive on their merits?

4. The respondent in this case has been criticized for failing to raise or down-playing some of their best arguments. What do you think are the best arguments for their side? Do you think they get sufficient airtime in this brief?

5. As noted above, one of the most oft-repeated tips for appellate brief writing is to have a theme that echoes through the brief? Does this brief have such a theme? If, in your mind, it does, how would you describe the theme? If, in your mind, it doesn't, can you suggest a theme that the respondents might have used to structure their argument?

John Geddes LAWRENCE and Tyron GARNER, Petitioners, v.
STATE OF TEXAS, Respondent.

No. 02-102.
March 10, 2003.

On Writ of Certiorari to the Court of Appeals of Texas Fourteenth District

Reply Brief . . .

TABLE OF CONTENTS

The Court should reject Respondent's meritless and untimely arguments for avoiding a decision on the important questions presented and should enforce the core rights of liberty and equal protection that are at stake in this case. Texas has no proper role supplanting the individual decisions of adults with the legislature's or electorate's different judgments concerning the private, intimate relations proscribed by the Homosexual Conduct Law, nor any legitimate basis for singling out same-sex couples for a criminal ban. Through this law, Texas flouts the essential American values of privacy and equal justice for all. Those values, jointly embodied in the Fourteenth Amendment, are critical limits on the power of the State that require vindication here.

I. RESPONDENT'S OBJECTION TO CONSIDERATION OF THE QUESTIONS PRESENTED IS WAIVED AND, IN ANY EVENT, MERITLESS

Texas begins with a belated plea for the Court to dismiss this case. The State now objects to consideration of the questions presented on the ground that the record does not reveal more, beyond the scope of the crime charged, about Petitioners' sexual relations or orientations. That objection is waived because it was not raised in the State's opposition to the petition for certiorari. *See* Sup. Ct. R. 15.2; *City of Canton v. Harris*, 489 U.S. 378, 383-85 (1989). Moreover, it has no merit.

Speculation that Petitioners might have committed some other offense that was neither charged nor proved cannot save the constitutionality of this law or Petitioners' convictions under it. This is a criminal prosecution; therefore, the State must allege and prove the elements necessary for conviction. *In re Winship*, 397 U.S. 358, 364 (1970); *see Apprendi v. New Jersey*, 530 U.S. 466, 477 (2000). Petitioners were charged with and convicted of the crime of "Homosexual Conduct" simply for "engag[ing] in deviate sexual intercourse, namely anal sex, with a member of the same sex (man)." Pet. App. 127a, 129a; *see also id.* 114a-15a (State's evidence offered on Petitioners' pleas of *nolo contendere*). The record also shows that Petitioners are unmarried adults and that the police intruded on and arrested them in Lawrence's home. *Id.* at 129a, 141a. If the State had wanted to premise its actions here on something more, *the State* would have had to allege and prove one or more additional elements. Texas cannot avoid a challenge to this law and Petitioners' convictions by speculating that their conduct might have involved additional facts. *E.g., Eisenstadt v. Baird*, 405 U.S. 438, 464-65 (1972) (White, J., concurring in result). This case cleanly presents the question whether "consensual, adult, private sexual relations," without more, may be punished by the State. Pet. App. 118a, 131a.

Equally meritless is the State's suggestion that Petitioners may not challenge the statute's discriminatory classification because they did not separately prove they are "exclusively homosexual." Resp. Br. 7, 33-34.[2] The State determined that Petitioners fell within the statutory classification and convicted them for conduct that would have been perfectly legal for different-sex intimate partners. They are the direct victims of the discrimination they challenge, discrimination that is explicit in the terms of the statute. It is hard to imagine circumstances that would more strongly support standing and the need to resolve whether Texas employs a permissible classification.

A few *amici*—but not Texas—also contend that Petitioners can assert only a facial challenge and that *United States v. Salerno*, 481 U.S. 739 (1987), governs that challenge. They are incorrect. Section 21.06 was applied to Petitioners in these criminal prosecutions, and they challenge it both as applied and facially. Pet. App. 117a, 130a. Even with respect to the facial challenge, *Salerno* does not apply here. Most importantly, *Salerno* is easily satisfied, because mere proof of a Homosexual Conduct offense is *always* constitutionally defective and discriminatory. The State's potential ability to criminalize sexual conduct under a *different* law that does not use an impermissible classification and that requires proof of additional elements cannot save the facial invalidity of *this* law.

---

2. Texas casts this argument in terms of "standing," Resp. Br. 33-34, yet it concedes that "petitioners possess standing to challenge the constitutionality of a statute under which they have actually been prosecuted and convicted," *id.* at 7. The jurisdictional "case or controversy" requirement is plainly satisfied here. *See, e.g., Eisenstadt*, 405 U.S. at 443-44.

II. THE HOMOSEXUAL CONDUCT LAW UNCONSTITUTIONALLY BURDENS A FUNDAMENTAL RIGHT

The State's defense of the Homosexual Conduct Law against Petitioners' fundamental rights challenge is based almost entirely on history well past, to the exclusion of all other considerations. That single-minded focus is not true to this Court's fundamental rights jurisprudence. It ignores the critical personal interests at stake. And it distorts both the history Texas relies on and the last half-century's decisive rejection of state intrusion in this area.

1. The State's contention that fundamental rights are always circumscribed by legislation in effect in the past cannot be squared with this Court's precedents. How far government may go in reducing its citizens to mere creatures of the State, whose most private lives are policed according to majority sentiment, must be answered through "reasoned judgment" and is "not susceptible of expression as a simple rule." *Planned Parenthood of Southeastern Pa. v. Casey*, 505 U.S. 833, 849 (1992).

   In *Casey*, the Court carefully reviewed its precedents and definitively rejected the position "that the Due Process Clause protects only those practices, defined at the most specific level, that were protected against government interference by other rules of law when the Fourteenth Amendment was ratified," because that contraction of fundamental rights "would be inconsistent with our law." *Id.* at 847; *see also id.* at 848 (citing precedents expanding liberty beyond 19th-century confines). And *Casey* itself struck down a spousal notification law that was "consonant with the common-law status of married women"—and thus with historical legal tradition—but "repugnant to our present understanding of marriage and of the nature of the rights secured by the Constitution." *Id.* at 898.

   Texas relies primarily on the plurality opinion in *Michael H. v. Gerald D.*, 491 U.S. 110 (1989), and on *Washington v. Glucksberg*, 521 U.S. 702 (1997). Yet those cases do not break from the Court's long-standing recognition that traditions and liberties evolve, *see Casey*, 505 U.S. at 850, and do not support a rigid, strictly historical view of fundamental rights. In *Michael H.*, a majority of the Justices expressly *rejected* the plurality's statements on this very point. 491 U.S. at 132 (O'Connor, J., joined by Kennedy, J., concurring in part); *id.* at 137-41 (Brennan, J., joined by White, Marshall, and Blackmun, JJ., dissenting). And *Glucksberg* was a case in which tradition, contemporary legislation, and powerful state interests all coincided to defeat the claim that a fundamental right was at stake. *See* 521 U.S. at 716-19, 728-35. Thus, in *Glucksberg* the Court had no occasion to decide that history alone is decisive, much less to overrule its precedents holding just the opposite. *See also County of Sacramento v. Lewis*, 523 U.S. 833, 857 (1998) (Kennedy, J., concurring). While the Court examines relevant history in all cases, the personal liberty that is protected by the Due Process Clause is not perpetually frozen in the mold set by the laws of 1868 or any other by gone age. Nor is the Court's job merely to mirror all changes around it. The Court must apply its "reasoned judgment" to determine the deeper question of what is required to protect Americans' ordered liberty today.

2. The State here steps over the line and beyond its proper powers to invade an essential American liberty. The fundamental rights question in this case turns on who has the power to make basic decisions about the specifics of

sexual intimacy between two consenting adults behind closed doors. Is the decision about expressions of intimacy and choice of partner for two adults to make through mutual consent, or for the State to control through a criminal law enacted by the legislature?

In this most personal realm of human existence, the Constitution limits government's power to substitute the preferences of the majority for the individual choices of adults. Three previously recognized aspects of liberty point to that conclusion: the liberty interests in intimate relationships, bodily integrity, and the privacy of the home. Texas tries to isolate these liberties as discrete and unrelated legal technicalities, but in truth they are aspects of a single continuum that comprises the fundamental rights of a free people. *See Casey*, 505 U.S. at 848-49.

The virtually unlimited power to regulate sexual intimacy claimed by Texas directly interferes with constitutionally protected intimate associations. The relationship of an adult couple—whether heterosexual or gay—united by sexual intimacy is the very paradigm of an intimate association in which one finds "emotional enrichment" and "independently . . . define[s] one's identity," and it is protected as such from "unwarranted state interference." *Roberts v. United States Jaycees*, 468 U.S. 609, 618-20 (1984) (family and other highly personal relationships protected under rubric of intimate association); *Board of Directors of Rotary Int'l v. Rotary Club of Duarte*, 481 U.S. 537, 545-46 (1987) (same). The State impairs the protected relationship of two adults whose shared life includes sexual intimacy by regulating—or even outright forbidding—the sexual dimension of their relationship. *See, e.g., Griswold v. Connecticut*, 381 U.S. 479, 485 (1965).

In addition, Texas's view of the constitutional status of the home ignores the foundational connection between protection of the home and protection of the private intimacies that are nurtured there. *See, e.g., Poe v. Ullman*, 367 U.S. 497, 551 (1961) (Harlan, J., dissenting). Likewise, the State's dismissive response to Petitioners' fundamental interests in bodily integrity fails to come to grips with the reality that this case concerns the *government's* attempt to *dictate* whom one must take as a sexual partner—a person of the other sex— and the specific state-approved acts that may be performed. That implicates bodily integrity because the State is using the criminal law to impose the majority's own sexual preferences on every individual. Indeed, the State's *amici* would justify the law precisely because it attempts to compel (or "channel" people into) heterosexual relationships. By outlawing most types of sexual intimacy with any partner of the same sex, the State drastically interferes with a core aspect of personal liberty.

3. Gay Americans have the same liberty interests as heterosexuals here. Pet. Br. 16-19; Am. Psych. Assn. Br. 15-23. Texas does not appear to argue otherwise. Instead, although the law at issue does not do so, the State "urges the Court to draw the line at the threshold of the marital bedroom," Resp. Br. 24, thereby permitting government regulation or prohibition of *all* sexual intimacy outside marriage, whether with another adult of the same or different sex. But adult Americans who remain unmarried are not mere wards of the State who have ceded total dominion over the most intimate details of their lives to a majority of their neighbors or legislators. Texas's attempt to limit the fundamental interest at stake in this case to marital unions must be rejected.

Nor is restriction of this fundamental liberty to married persons supported by the Court's decisions. It is true that the Court's earliest privacy decisions, *Griswold* and Justice Harlan's dissent in *Poe*, suggested special solicitude for sexual relations in marriage. Since then, however, the Court has made clear that such rights belong to *individuals*, whether married or unmarried. *Eisenstadt*, 405 U.S. at 453 ("If the right of privacy means anything, it is the right of the *individual*, married or single, to be free from unwarranted governmental intrusion into matters so fundamentally affecting a person as the decision whether to bear or beget a child"); *Carey v. Population Servs. Int'l*, 431 U.S. 678, 687 (1977) (same); *Casey*, 505 U.S. at 898 ("The Constitution protects all individuals . . . , married or unmarried, from the abuse of governmental power . . .").

Of course, the Court's contraception and abortion cases did not directly present the question whether unmarried adults have fundamental liberties regarding *sexual* intimacy, and the Court expressly reserved that question in *Carey*, 431 U.S. at 688 n.5. The logic of those decisions, however, mandates recognition that unmarried as well as married adults have a fundamental liberty interest in their private sexual relations. If the right to decide whether to bear or beget a child is for the *individual*, married or unmarried, the concomitant right to decide whether and with whom to engage in sexual intimacy cannot be for married couples only. Indeed, an unmarried individual could not meaningfully exercise the right to decide to bear or beget a child if the State may ban the sexual relations that lead to procreation. By the same token, the State may not ban sexual relations by unmarried persons that do *not* lead to procreation. The core teaching of the contraception cases is that the State may not force individuals to have only procreative sex. Thus, Texas's far-reaching argument that it may police the sexual choices of all unmarried adults—and may criminalize all same-sex intimacy as one aspect of that unconstrained power—cannot be accepted. Rejecting Texas's argument, and overruling *Bowers v. Hardwick*, 478 US. 186 (1986), will bring coherence to the Constitution's protection of this deeply personal sphere for *all* adult Americans.

4. The history of regulation in this area also supports recognition of the fundamental liberty interests Petitioners assert. Indeed, Americans recognized long ago that government does not belong in the bedrooms of its citizens to mandate or forbid particular expressions of consensual intimacy. Since the Founding, such private policing has not been the norm. There is not a single reported 19th-century case clearly upholding a sodomy conviction for *private* consensual conduct between two adults. *See* Cato Br. 11-12 & App. 2; ACLU Br. 13-15; History Profs. Br. 7-9. Though the facts are not reported in all cases, in many they are, and every one of those involves force, minors, animals, or public places. Cato Br. App. 2.

While the States historically had laws that technically applied to private consensual conduct, the vast majority of the laws proscribed specific conduct whether committed with a person of the same or different sex. Pet. Br. 5 & n.2, 21-22; Cato Br. 9-10 & n.13; History Profs. Br. 7, 10; ACLU Br. 12. Indeed, the laws often applied to married couples. *See Model Penal Code and Commentaries* §213.2, cmt. 1, at 360 (1980). Thus, older laws did not single out "homosexual sodomy," and they applied to conduct that Texas concedes is constitutionally protected today.

Most significantly, over the last half-century the States have rejected altogether laws that criminalize certain forms of private sexual intimacy between two consenting adults. Texas attempts to trivialize this decisive historic turn as a mere "experiment" by a handful of States acting as laboratories. In reality, it reflects a profound judgment about the limits of government control over the intimate and private details of the lives of Americans. . . .

5. Texas and its *amici* expend considerable effort litigating cases that are not before the Court. They conjure up a parade of horribles—invalidation of laws against bestiality, prostitution, incest, adultery, bigamy—that will allegedly follow a ruling for Petitioners. Those are chimeras. Comparison of the intimate relations of two human beings—married or unmarried, same-sex or different-sex—with bestiality is simply offensive. Nor do the other kinds of laws in the parade involve such a wholesale and devastating burden on individual liberty as here—where *all* same-sex partners are prohibited, for a vast range of intimate acts. Moreover, in the other areas conjured up to distract the Court, the State has important interests not present here. *See* Pet. Br. 22 n.16; *infra* at 19.[10]

Petitioners have carefully defined the fundamental liberty interest at stake as freedom from undue State Intrusion Into the particular choices of sexual expression made by two consenting adults in private. A ruling that Section 21.06 violates that liberty interest will affect no laws other than those against sodomy and fornication. Those laws have already been repealed or invalidated in the vast majority of the States and are almost never enforced where they remain on the books. . . .

III. The Homosexual Conduct Law Draws an Explicit Classification That Denies Equal Protection of the Laws

Texas has convicted Petitioners under a criminal law that explicitly targets same-sex couples but not different-sex ones for the same behavior. The State cannot evade equal protection review by attempting to recast this law as a "neutral" conduct regulation, because the law expressly treats identical conduct differently depending on who is engaging in it. There is no permissible justification for that classification, even under the most deferential equal protection review. In this specific context, a judgment that the same conduct is immoral when engaged in by one class of persons, but not when engaged in by the majority, necessarily represents a negative judgment about the targeted class, not the conduct. Equal protection bars laws based on bare negative attitudes toward one group. And any other rationale suggested by Texas or its *amici* also fails, for there is no rational and legitimate basis for this discriminatory criminal law. . . .

Though Texas limits its defense of its law to the two arguments addressed above, various *amici* search for other possible rationales. That search is unavailing. The classification drawn in Section 21.06 bears no rational relation to any conceivable and permissible State purpose.

Many of the *amici* are attempting to defend a law that classifies between married and unmarried couples, but that is not this law. *All* heterosexual couples, whether

---

10. Another chimera concerns the right to marry. Petitioners here assert a shield to be free from government interference, not any right to affirmative state recognition or benefits. *See infra* at 19.

they are in a one-night stand, an adulterous affair, or a committed relationship outside marriage, were freed by the legislature's actions in 1973, while all same-sex couples became the unique targets of the Homosexual Conduct Law. Section 21.06 was adopted as part of a penal code overhaul that abolished criminal penalties not only for all heterosexual "deviate sexual-intercourse," but also for adultery and fornication. Pet. Br. 5. Particularly in the context of the whole code revision that brought it about, this law cannot conceivably be described as promoting or protecting marriage.[17]

Other *amici* contend that the classification here is rationally related to protecting public health, particularly with respect to HIV and AIDS. These arguments seek to tap into the destructive myth that particular persons are responsible for HIV and other diseases to justify a blunt ban that is not a public health tool. As explained in the *amicus* brief of the American Public Health Association *et al.*, the classification in Section 21.06 is wholly unrelated to the prevention of HIV infection. Am. Pub. Health Assn. (APHA) Br. at 10-27.[18] The lack of any fit is not surprising, as the law was enacted well before HIV was even known to exist. The Homosexual Conduct Law bans all oral and anal sex as well as sex with an object for all male-male and female-female couples, but not the same forms of sexual conduct for heterosexual couples. That classification, based solely on the same-sex character of the couple, sweeps vast amounts of very safe sexual intimacy into the prohibition, while leaving much riskier conduct unregulated for a man and a woman. For example, female same-sex couples have exceedingly low rates of HIV and other sexually transmitted diseases—rates that are much lower than those for the heterosexual couples whose sexual conduct is completely unregulated—yet Section 21.06 criminalizes the sexual intimacy of all female same-sex couples. Likewise, it is well known that oral sex (or sex with an object), which is banned for all same-sex couples, is much safer than vaginal or anal intercourse, which are freely permitted for heterosexual couples. In addition, anal intercourse is precisely the same act for any couple that chooses it, yet it is criminalized only for same-sex couples. *See id.* at 10-18. Moreover, the State takes the position that this rarely enforced law does not actually deter any sexual conduct between gay persons. Resp. Br. 48 n.31. It certainly does not even differentiate between safe or protected acts and riskier ones. Far from helping, the Homosexual Conduct Law hampers public health initiatives. APHA Br. 18-27. Like Texas, the Court should reject the *amici*'s "public health" arguments as irrational and unrelated to the challenged classification.

The State's *amici* seek to divert attention from the Homosexual Conduct Law's discriminatory intrusion into private intimacies by asserting that Petitioners' equal protection claim is "tantamount to a challenge to the constitutionality of limiting marriage to a heterosexual couple." Am. Ctr. for Law and Justice (ACLJ) Br. 10. To the contrary, Petitioners seek equality under the criminal law, to keep the State out of their bedrooms, not any affirmative access to marriage or

---

17. Nor does the classification in Section 21.06 serve the purported goal of "funneling sexual activity into the bonds of marriage." Tex. Legislators Br. 23. Section 21.06 and the 1973 changes as a whole actually freed much more non-marital, heterosexual intimacy from criminal regulation and *took away* criminal law pressure on heterosexuals to marry.

18. APHA *et al.* represent the nation's major associations of public health professionals. *See* APHA Br. 1-3. In stark contrast, the State's *amici* who argue for a connection between the discriminatory standard of the Homosexual Conduct Law and HIV prevention do not offer public health expertise. *See* Pro Family Law Ctr. (PFLC) Br. 1-2 (*amici* are advocacy groups "opposing the legitimization of homosexuality"); Tex. Phys. Resource Council Br. 1 (*amici* approach health issues from Christian perspective and "appl[y] principles of faith and morality to modern medical science and practice"). . . .

other legal structures or benefits. This canard was also offered in *Romer* to distract the Court, see Brief of *Amicus Curiae* Concerned Women for America, Inc., 1995 WL 17008430 at *23-24, *Romer v. Evans,* 517 U.S. 620 (1996) (No. 94-1039), and has no more validity here.

Enforcing the guarantee of equal treatment under the law requires not a "sweeping, novel constitutional decision," ACLJ Br. 1, but a decision comporting fully with past precedent and basic fairness. One should not be convicted of a crime, or face stigma and other penalties flowing from a criminal law, for engaging in forms of intimacy that other adults may freely enjoy. . . .

CONCLUSION

The judgment of the Texas Court of Appeals upholding Section 21.06 and affirming Petitioners' criminal convictions thereunder should be reversed.

Notes and Questions

1. The first task of the reply brief is to respond to any unanticipated arguments made in the respondent's merits brief. In this case, the merits brief included several unexpected arguments challenging the petitioners' entitlement to a ruling on the merits. Does this brief effectively handle those arguments?

2. The second task of the reply brief is to reinforce the central themes and arguments of the petitioner's case. Does this brief succeed at that task?

3. This reply brief responds in great detail to arguments raised by the various *amicus* briefs supporting the respondent. Does that surprise you? Do you think it is wise to give that much attention to arguments raised only by *amici?* Is there anything distinctive about this case that may have made petitioners pay extra attention to the arguments raised by *amici?*

4. The reply brief twice starkly rejects the suggestion that a victory by the petitioners would in any way lead towards the recognition of a constitutional right to same-sex marriage. However, in the years since *Lawrence,* the opinion in their favor has been heavily cited by both lawyers advocating for such a right and courts finding in their favor. *See, e.g., In re Marriage Cases,* 43 Cal. 4th 757 (2008) (finding state constitutional right to same-sex marriage); *Goodridge v. Department of Public Health,* 440 Mass. 309 (2003) (same). Did the lawyers in *Lawrence* overstate the difference between their claims and the claims of future litigants seeking constitutional recognition of same-sex marriage and, if they did so, why did they?

C. *AMICUS* BRIEFS

This section explores the function and importance of *amicus* briefs in Supreme Court litigation. The first few excerpts address some of the complicated questions about the role of *amici* and their relationship with the parties in their case. The second set of excerpts take a more pragmatic tack, asking and answering questions about the efficacy of particular *amicus* strategies. This section concludes with excerpts from some notable recent *amicus* briefs.

1. The Role of the *Amicus*

Rule 37. Brief for an *Amicus Curiae*

1. An *amicus curiae* brief that brings to the attention of the Court relevant matter not already brought to its attention by the parties may be of considerable help to the Court. An *amicus curiae* brief that does not serve this purpose burdens the Court, and its filing is not favored. An *amicus curiae* brief may be filed only by an attorney admitted to practice before this Court as provided in Rule 5. . . .

4. No motion for leave to file an *amicus* curiae brief is necessary if the brief is presented on behalf of the United States by the Solicitor General; on behalf of any agency of the United States allowed by law to appear before this Court when submitted by the agency's authorized legal representative; on behalf of a State, Commonwealth, Territory, or Possession when submitted by its Attorney General; or on behalf of a city, county, town, or similar entity when submitted by its authorized law officer. . . .

6. Except for briefs presented on behalf of *amicus curiae* listed in Rule 37.4, a brief filed under this Rule shall indicate whether counsel for a party authored the brief in whole or in part and whether such counsel or a party made a monetary contribution intended to fund the preparation or submission of the brief, and shall identify every person or entity, other than the amicus curiae, its members, or its counsel, who made such a monetary contribution to the preparation or submission of the brief. The disclosure shall be made in the first footnote on the first page of text.

Linda Sandstrom Simard, An Empirical Study of Amici Curiae in Federal Court: A Fine Balance of Access, Efficiency, and Adversarialism

27 Rev. of Litig. 669 (2008)

I. INTRODUCTION

It has long been accepted procedure for courts to allow interested non-parties such as *amici curiae* to influence judicial decisionmaking by offering legal and factual insights that are relevant to the issues in a case but are not found in the trial or appellate record that facilitate the court's decisionmaking process. One of the more famous examples of the U.S. Supreme Court's willingness to accept such data is found in *Muller v. Oregon*, in which the Court upheld the constitutionality of a state law limiting the number of hours that female employees could work. In that case, Louis Brandeis, serving as counsel for the State of Oregon, filed a brief containing social science data regarding the detrimental effects of long work hours on women's health and asserting that the law at issue was necessary to protect women's health and safety. The unanimous Court accepted the brief, notwithstanding the fact that it contained reports and data that were not part of the appellate record, and noted that the information showed "a widespread belief that woman's physical structure, and the functions she performs in consequence thereof, justify special legislation. . . . " *Amicus* briefs have been influential in many other landmark cases declaring social policy, including *Brown v. Board of Education*, in which the Court cited information offered by *amici* that segregation generates a feeling of inferiority among persons of color, and *Roe v. Wade*, in which the Court relied upon information supplied by *amici* describing the risks of abortion and recounting beliefs concerning the beginning of life.

Although non-party participation by *amici curiae* has been acceptable procedure in federal courts for quite some time, there has been a tremendous surge in *amicus* activity over recent decades. In fact, during the last half of the twentieth century, the Supreme Court saw an astonishing 800% increase in the number of *amicus* filings on its docket. This increase manifested as an increase in the number of briefs filed as well as an increase in the number of participants cosigning the *amicus* submissions. Several scholars have studied this tremendous surge in non-party participation and established that the influence of *amicus* briefs on litigation success depends upon many factors, including, for example, the prestige and experience of the entity filing the brief (with the U.S. Solicitor General showing the greatest success), whether the brief supports the respondent or the petitioner (briefs supporting the respondents enjoy higher success rates), and the disparity in number of briefs offered for each side (a small number of briefs for one side with no briefs for the other side sometimes translates into higher success rates, but larger disparities do not).

This surge of *amicus* activity has given rise to concern among some judges. Several circuit courts have criticized the lack of scrutiny that is common in granting leave to file *amicus* briefs and at least one circuit has articulated a policy regarding the limited types of *amicus* filings that it will allow. In March, 2006, a federal circuit court refused to accept *amicus* briefs from three senators, even though none of the parties to the litigation opposed the filing. Notwithstanding these concerns, at least one circuit court has expressed support for an open door model toward granting permission to file *amicus* briefs, expressly rejecting arguments that *amici* must be impartial and not motivated by pecuniary concerns.

In order to evaluate the varying views on *amicus* participation, we must consider the reasons that *amici curiae* are seeking to participate in federal litigation in significantly greater numbers than they did fifty years ago. One important factor appears to be the ripening of the public law model of litigation. In 1976, Professor Abram Chayes identified an emerging model of public law litigation which focused on the vindication of constitutional or statutory policies rather than on private disputes. He predicted that this model would lead to a significant power shift in favor of the judicial branch and would become a formidable tool in the public policy debate. Thirty plus years later, it is fair to say that his prediction has been realized. Public law litigation has responded to the most controversial social and political issues of our day—including racial discrimination, affirmative action, abortion, free speech, church-state relations, and right-to-die cases, just to name a few—and *amici curiae* have been actively involved every step of the way. The continuing relevance of public law litigation in the twenty-first century is evidenced by many recent events, including the Supreme Court's decision in *Hamdan v. Rumsfeld* (declaring constitutional limits of executive power in wartime), the Court's controversial eminent domain decision in *Kelo v. City of New London*, and even by the confirmation hearings for Supreme Court Justices Roberts and Alito, during which many Senators attempted to prognosticate whether a change in the composition of the Court would lead to a new interpretation of the right of privacy under the United States Constitution. These examples, and countless others, illustrate that public law litigation has played, and likely will continue to play, a significant role in driving the public policy debate.

The emergence of the public law model and its maturation over the latter half of the twentieth century created a ripe environment for interested non-parties to weigh in on the development of policy through the courts; the *amicus* brief provided the tool to accomplish this goal. Insights offered by *amici curiae* tend to extend beyond the interests of the parties to the litigation—who are presumably adequately represented by their own lawyers—and are generally aimed at protecting the interests of individuals or organizations who are absent from the proceedings but whose interests are potentially jeopardized by the litigation. Given that public law litigation inherently extends beyond the specific interests of the parties to the litigation and prospectively changes widely applicable public policies, the *amicus* brief has provided a powerful tool for non-party participation in public law litigation affecting the body politic.

If one considers the development of public law litigation as the fuel for the fire which ignited the *amicus curiae* blaze, the Federal Rules of Evidence and the Federal Rules of Civil Procedure played little or no role in controlling the flame. Unlike traditional litigants who are subject to the procedural rules that protect the fundamental values of our adversarial system, *amici* are excused from the requirements of most procedural rules because they are deemed non-parties. Traditional litigants must meet the requirements of justiciability and subject matter jurisdiction, both of which have constitutional underpinnings that define the judicial power and protect the constitutional separation of powers; *amici* need not meet the requirements of justiciability or subject matter jurisdiction. Traditional litigants must satisfy the Federal Rules of Civil Procedure for joinder of parties and claims, rules which protect the fair and efficient administration of the courts and define the scope of the "claim"; *amici* need not satisfy the rules for joinder because they are not "joining" the litigation as a party. Traditional litigants must garner and present evidence which satisfies the Federal Rules of Evidence, rules which are designed to protect the reliability of the evidence. *Amici*, however, are allowed to present some types of factual information without regard to the requirements of the Federal Rules of Evidence. Finally, traditional litigants are limited by the rules of *res judicata* and collateral estoppel from endlessly relitigating the same issues, rules which protect the efficiency and credibility of the system; *amici curiae*, however, are not limited by the rules of res judicata or collateral estoppel. . . .

II. HISTORICAL ANALYSIS: FROM THEN TO NOW

A. The Origins of the *Amicus Curiae*

The role of *amicus curiae*—or "friend of the court"—enjoys a rich pedigree. Dating back to Roman law, the tool allowed an unbiased or neutral outsider to a legal action to provide information to an appellate court in a case in which the *amicus* was not named as a party. Relatively loose procedural restrictions created a flexible doctrine that was capable of responding to a variety of needs. For example, *amici curiae* frequently provided impartial guidance on legal issues ranging from oral shepardizing to referencing the existence of a relevant statute or other source of law.

Over time, *amici curiae* evolved into third party representatives, less concerned with providing unbiased scholarly guidance to the court and more interested in protecting the interests of individuals or entities who were not named parties in a suit. This progression, from neutral informant and servant of the court to defender of third-party rights, marked a significant shift in the role of *amici curiae* and opened the door for *amici curiae* to take sides in a dispute advocating a particular position.

The shift away from neutrality and toward advocacy accelerated under the federal system in the United States. A strict interpretation of federal subject matter jurisdiction and a general hostility to intervention limited the ability of interested entities to formally participate in litigation in federal court and encouraged resort to the *amicus curiae* role. Although the hostility toward intervention eventually softened and courts recognized that it was necessary to allow bystanders to intervene in a suit to protect their interests, *amici curiae* continued to enjoy relatively easy access to federal courts.

The identity of the *amici curiae* also changed. Originally, the role involved a professional relationship between the court and the individual *amicus curiae* (who may or may not have been a lawyer). Organizations could not serve as *amici curiae*. By the early 1900s, however, courts began to identify an *amicus* brief according to the organization who sponsored it rather than according to the individual who drafted it. This shift paved the way for influential groups to weigh in on the merits of a dispute by offering their endorsement to one litigant's position over another.

As a consequence of these doctrinal changes, the *amicus* brief became a formidable tool in the effectuation of social change through litigation. The Department of Justice was one of the first entities to effectively invoke the *amicus* device in pursuit of public policy change and, in the early part of the twentieth century, state attorneys general and minority groups recognized the opportunity to use the tool to shape public policy.

During the latter half of the 1940s and the early 1950s, the use of *amicus* briefs became so prevalent that at least some perceived them to be a "genuine problem" for the Supreme Court. Characterized as "repetitious at best and emotional explosions at worst," the value added by such briefs was far outweighed by the inefficiencies created by them. These attempts at judicial participation created the appearance that the Court was a "political legislative body, amenable and responsive to mass pressures from any source." In an effort to respond to the problem, the Court in November 1949 amended its procedural rules regarding non-governmental *amicus* participation to require either consent of all parties or, if consent was not available, a motion requesting permission to file an *amicus* brief. This rule change resulted in dramatically fewer *amicus* briefs reaching the Court.

During the late 1960s and early 1970s, public law litigation emerged and *amicus curiae* participation once again surged. For example, from 1965 to 1999 the percent of U.S. Supreme Court cases which included *amicus* filings grew from 35% to 95%, and the number of *amicus* filings increased by over 800%. During the late 1970s and 1980s, some courts began to expand the traditional role of *amici curiae* beyond the mere presentation of information through written briefs to allow participation in discovery, introduction of evidence, and presentation of oral arguments. Notwithstanding the occasional use of *amici curiae* in these roles at the trial court, the most common form of *amicus* activity today remains at the appellate level.

B. The Role of *Amici Curiae* in Modern Litigation

At its most basic level, the *amicus curiae* tool allows an entity that is separate from the parties to provide legal or factual information to the court, creating an appearance of neutrality which may or may not be a reality. The information presented can range from a repetition of legal arguments already before the court (in essence, an endorsement backed by the prestige of the entity offering it) to the presentation of new legal arguments or facts that inform the court of potential impacts of the litigation. More subtly, *amici curiae* may play a strategic role by suggesting weak legal arguments that are morally appealing (if the argument is a loser, the party may disassociate itself from the position), an educational role by presenting technical information that creates a fuller context for the court to decide the case, or a census role by providing a barometer of public opinion on an issue, particularly when a large number of entities are involved as cosponsors or separate filers of *amicus* briefs.

In light of the array of uses that *amicus* briefs may serve, it is not surprising that judges have expressed an array of opinions regarding the value of such briefs. For example, Justice Breyer has described the *amicus* brief as a valuable tool in educating judges, particularly on technical matters, but Judge Posner has been critical of the inefficiencies created by *amicus* briefs, noting that "[t]he vast majority of *amicus curiae* briefs are filed by allies of litigants and duplicate the arguments made in the litigants' briefs. . . . " Justice Scalia has suggested that *amici curiae* provide a type of interest group lobbying and has expressed concern that overrepresentation by well-organized interest groups has the potential to impact decisions by the Court. These comments suggest that the value accorded to *amicus* briefs depends upon the function that they are intended to serve.

There are two basic theories on the utility of *amicus* briefs: the affected groups theory and the information theory. The affected groups theory states:

> Insofar as the Justices are assumed to try to resolve cases in accordance with the weight of public opinion, they should look to *amicus* briefs as a barometer of opinion on both sides of the issues. Moreover, the information that *amicus* briefs convey about organized opinion is such that it can largely be assimilated simply by looking at the cover of the brief. The Justices can scan the covers of the briefs to see which organizations care strongly about the issue on either side. The fact that the organization saw fit to file the brief is the important datum, not the legal arguments or the background information set forth between the covers of the brief.

This is an interesting theory, in part because traditional jurisprudence would suggest that the judicial branch is to be insulated from majoritarian pressures, not subject to them. Yet, the judiciary's institutional legitimacy is ultimately dependent upon the influence of its decisions upon society. To the extent that the strength of the judicial system depends upon having decisions followed and not overridden, altered, or ignored, judges have an incentive to fit within the parameters of broadly shared public opinion. Moreover, lacking the purse and the sword, the judicial branch is not equipped to enforce its decisions without the assistance of the other branches of government and the goodwill of the citizenry. Thus, while the judicial branch is theoretically shielded from majoritarian forces, the practical reality suggests that some consideration of public opinion may be prudent.

Alternatively, the information theory suggests that *amicus* briefs are effective not because they provide a barometer of public sentiment, but rather because they supplement the arguments of the parties by providing information not found in the parties' briefs. Such supplemental information might present legal arguments from another perspective, present policy consequences of particular legal interpretations, describe common interpretations of relevant laws, or present factual data such as social science information that is absent from the appellate record. This theory is more in line with the common thought that *amicus* briefs facilitate judicial decisionmaking by educating the decisionmaker. . . .

Paul M. Smith, The Sometimes Troubled Relationship Between Courts and Their "Friends"

Litigation, Summer 1998, at 24

Something is afoot (or amiss) these days with courts' attitudes toward their would-be "friends"—*amici curiae*. As anyone who practices in appellate settings knows from experience, the volume of amicus filings in important appellate cases continues to grow. But the courts seem restive.

Early last year, the Supreme Court issued a Rule 37.6, which requires that every nongovernmental amicus brief filed in that Court "indicate whether counsel for a party authored the brief in whole or in part" and "identify every person or entity, other than the *amicus curiae*, its members, or its counsel, who made a monetary contribution to the preparation or submission of the brief." The Court did not explain its apparent concern about abuse of amicus filings by parties or hidden nonparties.

A few months later, Seventh Circuit Chief Judge Richard Posner issued a remarkable order in *John H. Ryan v. Commodities Futures Trading Comm'n*, 125 F.3d 1062 (7th Cir. 1997), denying the Chicago Board of Trade's motion for leave to file an amicus brief. He explained that the "vast majority of amicus briefs are filed by allies of litigants and duplicate the arguments made in the litigants' briefs, in effect merely extending the length of the litigant's brief. Such amicus briefs should not be allowed." Posner then noted that, while amici curiae once were viewed as neutrals aiding the court, "an adversary role of an amicus curiae has become accepted." But, he added, "there are, or at least should be, limits." He identified only three situations in which an amicus brief "should normally be allowed": (1) when a party is not represented competently or at all, (2) when an amicus has an interest in another case that will be affected, and (3) when the amicus has "unique information or perspective that can help the court beyond the help that the lawyers for the parties are able to provide."

What's going on? Why the concern about undisclosed principals, partisanship, and abuse of amicus filings to extend parties' briefs? And how should these signs of concern affect decisions about whether to file an amicus brief and what kind of brief to file?

One piece of the explanation is that appellate courts in important, high-profile cases are being inundated with amicus briefs. For example, the piles of green briefs on the desk of a Supreme Court Justice preparing for argument in an important civil rights, business, or abortion case often number in the dozens. The judges facing such piles know that few of these briefs are going to have a significant impact on their consideration of the case. So they wonder why organizations persist in filing so many briefs so often. They come to the sometimes-correct conclusion that the real audience for these briefs is not the court, but an organization's friends and members.

But it is a poor answer to duplication concerns to begin applying subjective and after-the-fact judgments about whether a given brief is sufficiently distinctive. After all, an amicus often does not know in advance precisely what arguments and information will be included in the parties' briefs or the briefs of other amici. A partial answer, at least for the federal courts of appeals, is a proposed change to Rule 29 of the Federal Rules of Appellate Procedure allowing amici seven additional days to file after the filing of the brief of the party they support. But even if this change reduces duplication of party briefs, it will not affect duplication among amicus briefs, or eliminate the threat of a court's determination that a given brief does not "add" enough to be accepted. And, if filing an amicus brief becomes a crap shoot, with each filing subjected to the risk of an embarrassing and expensive rejection, courts will soon lose the real benefits provided by some amicus briefs—those that supply needed insights and information, or merely improve on the legal arguments presented by a party.

Certainly, it can hardly be suggested that there is a single "amicus" position to be briefed on each side of every case—a position that can easily be presented in a single consolidated brief. Indeed, any effort to mandate consolidation of amicus briefs would almost certainly be unworkable for the Supreme Court, where the number and diversity of interested groups would often make consolidation into a single (or even a few) briefs logistically impossible. That Court seems to have adopted the position that it will accept nearly all briefs, and give them the attention they appear to deserve.

The increased volume of amicus filings cannot explain the prevailing judicial concern about *party* abuse of amicus briefs, reflected both in the new Supreme Court rule and in Chief Judge Posner's comments. The concern seems to be that parties and their counsel will use amici to present additional arguments they cannot (because of page limitations or for other reasons) fully present in their own briefs— perhaps even "ghostwriting" and/or financing amicus briefs. But that concern cannot logically stem from the courts' daily experience with a high volume of amicus filings. To the contrary, if a party were considering a strategy of transferring most of one argument to the brief of a cooperative amicus, the fact that a large number of other amicus briefs might also be filed would be a powerful deterrent. The party would have no way of knowing that the court would give serious attention to the particular amicus brief in which it was planting additional arguments. The fact of the matter is that a party knows the one brief the court will surely pay attention to is the party's own. A rational party does not omit from that brief an argument that has a substantial chance of winning.

DISCLOSING FINANCIAL ASSISTANCE

Nor is there any other reason to think there is a widespread problem with parties abusing amicus briefs in appellate cases. Certainly, parties do get involved in talking with potential amici and reviewing drafts. But that kind of party involvement is essential if the number of such briefs is going to be *reduced*. The party often is the only one who knows who else is considering filing a brief. At the Supreme Court level, sophisticated parties and counsel often convene meetings of potential amici in an attempt to form coalitions and to influence the nature of the presentations that will be made. Potential amici, in turn, often contact counsel for the party they support, recognizing that such party coordination can be beneficial. But there is little reason to see this common practice as a form of abuse.

So what is lurking behind the suggestion that there is something abusive about many current amicus briefs? Why did Chief Judge Posner look back nostalgically to the day when the few amici curiae who existed were truly neutral advisers? And why did the Supreme Court promulgate a rule requiring disclosure of financial assistance provided by hidden third parties?

It can't be that the courts truly believe there is something wrong with amici "taking sides." Amicus briefs are unsolicited and volunteered. Anyone who files one is very likely to have, and express, a point of view about the proper outcome in the case. Nor can courts operating in an adversarial system truly be worried about their ability to deal with adversarial presentations of legal arguments. Judges decide cases every day based primarily on the legal presentations of interested parties. They are used to seeing through misstatements of the law or faulty legal reasoning by advocates. And if they feel the need for a "neutral" legal analysis, they have their law clerks.

The problem, I submit, arises from two other ways in which amicus briefs can influence courts. First, the nature of the organization or entity submitting the brief can itself be persuasive. When, for example, the leading organizations of mental health providers told the Supreme Court in *Jaffee v. Redmond*, 518 U.S. 1 (1996), that their members rely on and need a psychotherapist-patient privilege in order to treat mental disorders, that empirical assessment was far more persuasive coming from them than it would have been coming from the individual party seeking to prevent disclosure of information disclosed in confidential therapy sessions. The statements by the amici told the Court that this was an issue providers as a whole really cared about because they thought it made a difference in their practice. The Court, in turn, cited some of these briefs as persuasive authority.

The courts, however, want to be sure that the credibility of major organizations like those that filed in *Jaffee* is not being put to use by unnamed persons or entities who are funding the brief because they have particular interests in the case different from those apparent on the face of the brief. It wants to know that the positions stated reflect the actual views of the amicus, and are not designed to satisfy the particular needs of some other party. Hence, the new requirement of disclosure in Supreme Court amicus briefs of any financial assistance provided by unnamed third parties.

Amicus briefs in such cases can also influence courts by presenting empirical evidence about how the world works, in the form of social science research that is described and cited. Such "Brandeis briefs" can be extraordinarily important and helpful to courts. Frequently, a court deciding a legal issue on appeal needs information about how the real world works. Most often, this is information the parties had no occasion to develop through evidence presented in the trial court. Moreover, even where the relevant facts were considered in the trial court, it is doubtful whether the constitutionality of a statute, for example, ought properly to turn on the particular evidence presented by the two parties and the particular findings made by one trial judge.

In many cases, the Supreme Court has relied on social science literature. For example, the Court has turned to nonlegal research to learn whether racially separate schooling is inherently unequal (*Brown v. Board of Education*), whether "death-qualified" jurors unfairly favor the prosecution at the guilt phase of a murder trial (*Lockhart v. McCree*), and how psychotropic medications affect the body (*Riggins v. Nevada*). On many occasions, as in the *Jaffee* case, the Court has simply incorporated by reference the studies that were cited by an amicus.

But the influence exercised by such briefs in the development of the law has also spawned a whole scholarly literature expressing concern about the neutrality and fairness of the presentation of the relevant research. The concern seems to be that when scientific or social science research is presented to appellate courts, without the benefit of prior presentation through expert witnesses subject to cross-examination, courts are not as equipped to see the flaws in the presentation as they would be when dealing with legal arguments and materials. They may not have the cited materials available to them, they may not know where to look for competing studies, and they may not have the training needed to critique research methodologies and statistical arguments. Kenneth Culp Davis, for example, has argued that courts should consider creating bodies of neutral nonlegal experts to sift and analyze research on relevant topics.

That is hardly likely, though. Instead, what courts tend to do is to rely on the fairness of the presentations made by leading professional organizations in each given field. But, say the critics, those presentations take the form of legal briefs, drafted by lawyers, who start from the premise that they want to use the cited research materials in an effort to persuade the court that one side of the case should win. That process, they argue, is inconsistent with a neutral and scholarly presentation of the research, regardless of the name or characteristics of the amicus whose name appears on the cover of the brief.

In my experience representing major national associations filing amicus briefs in the Supreme Court and elsewhere, this concern is overblown. Generally speaking, an amicus organization that is sufficiently eminent and respected to have its description of scientific or social science research taken at face value will appreciate the importance of its own reputation. It will also know that such a brief can be attacked in answering briefs and is highly visible both to its members and to the world at large. It will not deliberately mischaracterize the research in the field it represents just to support a favored outcome. Certainly, the courts are better off with the kind of empirical presentation that can be provided in such an amicus brief than they would be without it. But counsel should be aware of the need to maintain credibility by not describing the state of current research on an issue in a manner that can be revealed to be slanted.

Two Questions

So what does all of this say about what practitioners should do in real cases? That issue breaks into two questions:

1. **Should counsel for a party in an important appeal encourage and work with amici?** The answer is generally a firm "yes." Amicus briefs influence courts to favor your side in lots of different—conscious and unconscious—ways. The mere fact that a given number of entities or groups took the trouble to file tells that court that they consider the outcome important. A good amicus brief augments this effect by describing in detail how the case matters to the broader world, often with examples of other cases. Such a brief can have a substantial impact because a party's predictions about the potential effects of a particular legal rule are always subject to question. Moreover, in many cases, there are factual arguments that amici can make without being confined to a trial record. Done well, such nonlegal argument can be both helpful to the court and effective.

   Counsel for a party in such a case should endeavor to coordinate the amicus briefing process to the extent possible. The goal should be to reduce the number of filings to a manageable number, while improving the quality of what gets submitted. Twenty briefs that just say "rule for appellant" are a lot less helpful than two, with lots of groups joining in, that make cogent, nonduplicative arguments.

2. **What should you do when a client hires you to file an amicus brief?** The key to representing an amicus in an important case is figuring out what kind of brief

will help the favored side to win the case. That depends entirely on the circumstances. The first thing you should do is find out who is representing that party, and make an assessment of the quality of the legal arguments they are likely to present. The most important thing, in any case, is to make sure that someone—the party or an amicus—presents the main legal arguments in a persuasive way.

Depending on your analysis of the case, there are four basic models, which can be combined:

1. *A Brief that Makes the Main Legal Argument.* In some cases, depending on who is representing the party whom the amicus is supporting and on the quality of the legal arguments the party is likely to present, it is essential to devote most of the amicus brief to an improved version of the main legal argument.
2. *A Brief that Makes an Alternative Legal Argument.* Occasionally, it makes more sense for an *amicus* to offer a legal argument that is entirely different from the one presented by the party. Sometimes, counsel for *amici* will conclude that the party is not putting its best legal foot forward. In other cases, differences between the interests of the party and the amicus will prompt the amicus to try to modify the court's legal analysis to favor the distinctive interests of the amicus. Of course, it makes no sense to present an argument when the case is in a procedural posture that would prevent the court from adopting it. But that often is not a problem, especially when an *amicus* is supporting an appellee.
3. *A Brief that Emphasizes the Practical Impact of a Particular Legal Rule.* Often, amicus briefs usefully describe for the court other pending litigation that will be affected by the outcome of the appeal. This can include one case in which the amicus is involved or an entire category of cases pending in many courts. Such descriptions can influence courts by informing them about the breadth of the impact of their decision, as well as possible variations among the cases that may require refinement of the legal analysis.
4. *A Brief that Provides Factual Information Relevant to the Resolution of the Legal Issue.* As noted, many amicus briefs focus on descriptions of research or other factual material that informs the court about the "real world." Almost always, such statements of facts are supported by citations to published nonlegal authorities.

In every case you should tell the court why the amicus is interested in the case, and be careful to adhere to the court's rules about deadlines, consents, and motions for leave to file. Most often, a brief designed to be of use to the court, and presented in compliance with all technical rules, will be well received and given due consideration.

Notes and Questions

1. The author of the previous excerpt, Paul Smith, is a leading appellate lawyer in Washington, D.C., and a former clerk to Justice Lewis Powell. He is also, coincidentally, the attorney who argued *Lawrence v. Texas* before the Supreme Court.

2. For recent statistics on how frequently the Supreme Court cites *amicus* briefs and some interesting data broken down by Justice, see R. Reeves Anderson & Anthony J. Franze, *The Supreme Court's Increased Reliance on* Amicus Curiae *in the Past Term*, Nat. L.J., Aug. 24, 2011.

3. Why do you think the volume of *amicus* briefs has grown so dramatically since 1965? Professor Sandstrom Simard identifies one significant cause: The rise of public interest litigation. But surely there are other contributing factors. Can you think of any technological, cultural, professional, political, or jurisprudential changes over the last half century that might have also encouraged or facilitated the growth of *amicus* briefing?

4. Supreme Court Rule 37.6, reproduced above, arose out of concerns about whether *amici* were participating in cases as independent actors or whether they were instead mere pawns of the parties. Beyond adding a new disclosure requirement, its lessons are murky. On the one hand, the Rule might be seen as delineating the line between proper and improper involvement of the parties in preparing *amicus* briefs, countenancing all support short of paying for or actually drafting the brief, and even permitting those actions if appropriately disclosed. On the other hand, the Rule might reflect a more general judicial expectation that *amici* appear as true "friends of the court" rather than as coordinated allies of the parties. Which do you think is a better reading of the Rule? Would it surprise you to find out that the Supreme Court bar has uniformly adopted the former, narrower view?

5. The kinds of *amicus* briefs courts desire depend a great deal on the functions they expect those briefs to perform. Professor Sandstrom Simard deftly summarizes the major theories regarding the role of *amicus* briefs in modern litigation. If you were a judge, would you only want to hear from parties with special information to impart, or would you welcome a broader set of briefs to give you a concise overview of community and interest group sentiments about the issues in question?

6. Even groups that have no expectation of influencing the substance of the Supreme Court's deliberation in a pending case may have reasons to file an *amicus* brief. Elected officials may see political upside in stating their support for a particular position or party. Leaders of advocacy organizations may need to demonstrate their commitment to their membership or may see an opportunity to enhance their publicity or fundraising. Ad hoc coalitions on one side of an issue or another may find the preparation of a brief to be an important site for organization, community-building, or symbolic civic participation. For one famous recent example, see Brief of *Amici Curiae* 13,922 Current Law Students at Accredited American Law Schools, *Grutter v. Bollinger*, 539 U.S. 306 (2002) (No. 02-241). Professor Robert Chang, an advocate for the liberal use of *amicus* briefing to build community among civil rights groups has argued that such briefs are an appropriate response to the stark reality that

> [t]he courts are a quintessentially undemocratic institution. Courts make decisions in cases and establish precedents that affect many people beyond the litigants in a particular case. Non-litigants whose rights are at stake in the case typically have no voice. If the case involves justice claims based on race, gender, sexual orientation, and disability, the undemocratic nature of the courts is especially problematic because the groups affected are those that are historically and currently less powerful politically. The undemocratic nature of the institution is amplified with regard to individuals or groups that are less politically powerful or have fewer resources.

Robert S. Chang, *The Fred T. Korematsu Center for Law and Equality and Its Vision for Social Change*, 7 Stan. J. C.R. & C.L. 197, 200 (2011); *see also* Omari Scott Simmons, *Picking Friends from the Crowd:* Amicus *Participation as Political Symbolism*, 42 Conn. L. Rev. 185 (2009).

7. A small fraction of *amicus* briefs filed at the Supreme Court are actually solicited by the Justices. In argued cases in which all the parties (1) agree that the judgment below should be reversed; (2) take very similar positions on the questions presented; or (3) fail to support a plausible position about which a majority of the Justices would like to hear more, the Court occasionally appoints a lawyer to provide the missing argument as an *amicus*. A lawyer appointed in this manner is expected to file a brief and, in most circumstances, to participate in oral argument. For some recent examples of briefs filed by lawyers in such a role, see Brief for Court-Appointed *Amicus Curiae* Supporting Complete Severability, Natl. Fedn. of Indep. Business v. Sebelius, 132 S. Ct. 2566 (2012) (No. 11-393); Brief of the Court-Appointed *Amicus Curiae* in Support of the Judgment Below, *Dorsey v. United States*, 132 S. Ct. 2321 (No. 11-5683).

8. In the fall of 2011, a draft article by Harvard Law Professor Richard Fallon, Jr., caused a controversy in legal academia. Professor Fallon politely but firmly challenged the widespread practice of law professors signing on to *amicus* briefs in pending Supreme Court cases without first reading, understanding, and endorsing the validity of the arguments made in the briefs. He argued that law professors damage their credibility and misuse their professional credentials when they apply a lower standard for signing on to briefs than they would for putting their names on law review articles. *See* Richard H. Fallon, Jr., *Scholars' Briefs and the Vocation of a Law Professor*, 4 J. Leg. Analysis 223 (2012).

C. Effective *Amicus* Briefing

In recent years, both advocates and scholars have become more interested in and more sophisticated about the comparative utility of different strategies for recruiting *amici* and drafting *amicus* briefs. Scholars have produced a rich empirical literature that seems to suggest that, over the run of cases, *amicus* support has a small but significant correlation with a party's prospects in a given case. Scholars have also been able to identify a hierarchy of *amici*—identifying groups whose briefs are more likely to be read and whose advice is more likely to be heeded. Finally, advocates, scholars, and other commentators have spent a substantial amount of time and energy microanalyzing the handful of *amicus* briefs that appear to have been most effective, trying to identify the characteristics of a case-changing brief. The following excerpts offer windows into each of those avenues of exploration.

Joseph D. Kearney & Thomas W. Merrill, The Influence of *Amicus Curiae* Briefs in the Supreme Court

148 U. Pa. L. Rev. 743 (2000)

III. Previous Studies of the Influence of *Amicus* Briefs on Supreme Court Outcomes

By far the most important question about *amicus* briefs is not whether they are easy to file, or whether, if filed, they are likely to be cited or quoted. Rather, it is whether such briefs have any influence on the decisions reached by the Court.

If *amicus* briefs have a demonstrable impact on the supported party's chances of prevailing in the Court, or on the Court's rationale for its judgment, then this would readily explain the high rate of *amicus* filings we have seen in recent decades. On the other hand, if *amicus* briefs have no impact on the Court's decision-making process, then the tidal wave of *amicus* briefs becomes harder to explain. There have been a number of studies by legal scholars and political scientists over the last thirty years that shed light on the phenomenon of the *amicus curiae* brief. Most of these studies describe the role of *amicus* briefs in particular cases or in the resolution of particular issues. For example, they examine the strategic considerations underlying the filing of *amicus* briefs in the Court's decisions invalidating racial covenants, expanding the constitutional rights of women, addressing the constitutionality of affirmative action, and in numerous other areas. These studies are valuable, and suggest that groups seeking social change through litigation assume that *amicus* support can in some circumstances influence the Court's adoption of a particular position on a critical issue or can at least frame the debate. . . .

Though illuminating, only rarely do these case studies address the question of whether *amicus* briefs have an impact on the Court, even in specific areas. Furthermore, even in these areas, the exact role of the *amici* is often open to interpretation. Clearly, more extensive empirical data about the relationship between *amicus curiae* filings and Supreme Court outcomes are needed. Unfortunately, only a handful of studies have attempted to use quantitative data to assess the relationship between the filing of *amicus curiae* briefs and the outcomes reached by the Court. Moreover, the studies that do exist reach strikingly inconsistent conclusions about whether such briefs have an effect on the Court.

The first empirical survey of the influence of *amicus* briefs on Supreme Court decision making was undertaken in a doctoral dissertation by Steven Puro completed in 1971. Puro's study contains much valuable information. His data set consisted of all *amicus* briefs filed in reported decisions of the Supreme Court from the 1920 Term to the 1966 Term. In order to provide some basis for comparing the role of *amicus* briefs over time and across different filing entities, Puro computed what he called the "success rate" of various *amicus* filers. This was a kind of *amicus curiae* batting average—the number of cases in which an entity files an *amicus* brief supporting the prevailing party divided by the total number of *amicus* filings by that entity.

Overall, Puro found that *amicus* filers had a success rate of .550—that is, they filed briefs supporting the winning side 55% of the time. Moreover, he found that the success rate of *amicus* filers increased over time: the success rate was only 44.4% in the period 1920-1936; it increased to 54.9% in 1937-1952; and it rose to 60.3% in 1953-1966. . . .

Standing alone, Puro's findings regarding success rates might suggest that *amicus* filings have some modest but positive influence on outcomes, and that this influence was increasing during the period of his study. However, Puro did not claim to have uncovered any causal connection between *amicus* filings and Supreme Court outcomes. He noted that the Court tended to favor liberal positions during the period of his investigation, and that "underdog" groups were at that time more likely to file *amicus* briefs than were business groups or other conservative organizations. Thus, to the extent he suggested any explanation for his findings, it was that the Court was ideologically inclined to reach liberal outcomes, and that groups advocating liberal results were more likely to file *amicus* briefs, and hence more likely to be on the winning side.

Puro was well advised to exercise caution in drawing any strong causal conclusions from his success rates, if only because his aggregate data did not control for the impact of institutional litigants. Specifically, Puro's overall success rate of 55% was based on a sample of *amicus* filings which included such institutional litigants as the Solicitor General (who filed in over 17% of the *amicus* cases during the period), the ACLU (12.3% of the cases), and the AFL-CIO (5.7% of the cases). These institutional litigants enjoyed unusually high success rates during the period of his study. Moreover, the high success rates of such players in turn might be at least partly a function of their legal strategies. For example, they might seek to build up their credibility with the Court by filing frequently on the side they would predict to be more likely to win. Or as Puro himself suggested, interest groups might file *amicus* briefs out of a desire to "look good" with their members, which might also cause them to file in cases in which they are most likely to win. To the extent interest groups pursue such a strategy, they will presumably lift their success rates, and hence to a degree the overall success rate for all *amicus* filers. But this would not signify any causal connection between *amicus* filings and outcomes.

More recently, Donald Songer and Reginald Sheehan attempted to measure the efficacy of *amicus* briefs by using a different investigative strategy. They sought to identify "matched pairs" of cases in which, in one case, only one party was supported by one or more *amicus curiae* briefs filed by an interest group and, in the other case, neither party had *amicus* support. The matched pairs had to be decided in the same Term, had to involve parties of the same status (viz., private individual, business, union, state or local government, or the federal government), and had to involve the "same issue" (i.e., both cases had to fall into one of thirteen general subject matter categories). Using data from ten Terms over a twenty-year period (1967 to 1987), Songer and Sheehan identified 132 such matched pairs of cases.

Analyzing their case pairs, Songer and Sheehan found no evidence of *amicus* group influence. The success rate of parties supported by interest group *amicus* briefs was virtually identical to that of parties without such support. Restricting the comparison to cases in which one side had at least two or three *amicus* supporters, they again found "no support for the thesis that interest groups have a substantial impact on Court outcomes through their use of *amicus curiae* briefs." They also found no variation in success rates among different categories of litigants, and no evidence of change in the pattern of influence over the twenty-year period under examination.

In contrast, recent studies applying multivariate regression analysis to limited subsets of Supreme Court decisions have detected signs of a positive impact of *amicus* briefs on outcomes. Kevin McGuire has published two such studies, one seeking to identify the factors that affect the outcome of obscenity cases in the Supreme Court, the other focusing on the relationship between the use of experienced lawyers and the probability of success in the Supreme Court. Both studies found that the probability of success was significantly related to the level of *amicus curiae* support for a party. But the more directly relevant of these studies—the one seeking to determine the factors influencing the outcome of obscenity cases—is vulnerable to the same criticism noted above in connection with Puro's study: it does not control for the influence of institutional litigants such as the Solicitor General.

Finally, a number of studies have sought to determine the degree of influence that particular institutional litigants, most prominently the Solicitor General, have achieved through their *amicus* filings. Jeffrey Segal has conducted a number of studies of the Solicitor General's *amicus curiae* activities. Looking at all cases decided between the 1952 and 1982 Terms, Segal found that the Solicitor General's *amicus* filings supported the winning side approximately 75% of the time overall. This high rate of success applied across all categories of issues, all changes in the Court's membership, and regardless of whether the Solicitor General was urging a liberal or a conservative result. Segal's other studies show that *amicus* support by the Solicitor General is highly influential in determining the outcome of sex discrimination cases, after a number of other variables are controlled for, and that the Solicitor General's success is not related to the number of Justices appointed by Presidents of the same party as the Solicitor General. Rebecca Mae Salokar, reviewing all *amicus* cases decided by a full Court between 1959 and 1986, obtained similar results: the Solicitor General supported the winning side in 72% of the cases in which he filed an *amicus* brief, with no significant variations from one administration to the next.

Studies of other institutional litigants have found less reason to believe that these litigants have a major impact on the Court. A paper by Thomas Morris suggested that state attorneys general are less successful than the Solicitor General in influencing the Supreme Court through *amicus* filings. A study undertaken by Gregg Ivers and Karen O'Connor found that the ACLU and Americans for Effective Law Enforcement achieved some success as *amici curiae*, but only when the Court was ideologically predisposed to reach the outcomes they favored.

In sum, the existing empirical literature on the relationship between *amicus* briefs and Supreme Court outcomes provides confusing and contradictory results. Some studies, including those of Puro and the issue-specific multivariate regression analyses, suggest that *amicus* support is associated with enhanced chances of success. Other studies, such as Songer and Sheehan's matched pair study and the studies of institutional litigants other than the Solicitor General, show no relationship between *amicus* support and outcomes. The only finding that has been consistently replicated is that the Solicitor General enjoys a unique degree of success as an *amicus* filer. . . .

Conclusion

Amicus curiae briefs have become an increasingly important phenomenon in Supreme Court litigation. Once a rarity, such briefs are currently filed in the Supreme Court at the rate of about 500 per year. If nothing else, these briefs consume significant amounts of legal resources—and a significant portion of the shelf space devoted to the Court's records and proceedings. As the number of *amicus* submissions has soared, so have the citations and quotations of amicus briefs found in the Justices' opinions.

The obvious question is whether, or to what extent, these submissions influence the decisions rendered by the Court. Although political scientists and, to a lesser degree, law professors have turned increasingly to empirical analysis in recent years, no one has undertaken to try to answer this question by analyzing the patterns of *amicus* participation and associated outcomes in a large number of cases decided over a significant span of time. One reason such a study has not been done is that the political scientists who study the Supreme Court overwhelmingly start from the attitudinal model, which explains outcomes in terms of the preexisting political beliefs of the Justices. Such a model suggests that *amicus* briefs should have little or no impact on outcomes. Perhaps not surprisingly, therefore, the database political scientists use to study the Court (which was developed by attitudinal scholars) does not include information on the number of amicus briefs filed in each case in support of each side or by key institutional litigants. The lack of readily accessible data has undoubtedly discouraged empirical research.

In this Article, we report our efforts to fill this gap in our knowledge by developing and analyzing a database consisting of over 6000 Supreme Court decisions over fifty years. Some of our results confirm the findings of previous, more limited studies. Most prominently, our survey shows that the Solicitor General enjoys a unique degree of success as an *amicus* filer. We also show that other institutional litigants—the ACLU, the AFL-CIO, and the States—enjoy above-average success, although their success rates fluctuate depending on whether they support petitioners or respondents and never reach the same level achieved by the Solicitor General.

In two respects, however, our study generates results wholly unanticipated by the prior literature. First, we show that *amicus* filers supporting respondents consistently enjoy more success than do amicus filers supporting petitioners. For example, *amicus* filers who support respondents are in general 7% more successful than those who support petitioners, and the Solicitor General is 9% more successful when supporting respondents than when supporting petitioners.

Second, we find that although small disparities of *amicus* support (one or two briefs to none) may be associated with increased success for the supported party, larger disparities (three briefs or more to none) show little sign of increased success and may possibly even be counterproductive. Undoubtedly one reason we find little support for higher success rates with larger disparities of filings is that there are very few cases that have such disparities. In most cases the *amicus* briefs are symmetrically distributed between the parties; patterns like that encountered in *Jaffee v. Redmond*, where fourteen briefs supported respondent and none supported petitioner, are extremely rare.

Regarding the implications our results have in terms of identifying the factors that motivate Supreme Court Justices, we must speak much more tentatively. The attitudinal model, at least in its undiluted form, seems to find the least support in our findings. *Amicus* briefs clearly do matter in many contexts, and this means that the Court is almost certainly influenced by additional information supplementing that provided by the parties to the case. The strategic actor variation on the attitudinal model fares better, since the Court appears to be more attentive to information supplied by the Solicitor General (representing the executive branch) and, to a lesser degree, to information coming from the States than it is to the information supplied by amicus filers in general. The interest group model, which predicts that the Justices will respond to signals suggesting that organized interest groups disproportionately favor one side over the other, finds only equivocal support. Small disparities of support for one side may matter, although only weakly. Large disparities, however, perhaps because they occur so rarely, cannot be shown to have any impact; indeed, they appear often to work against the interests of the supported party.

We think the explanatory model that fares the best overall is the traditional legal model reflected in the rules and procedures of the Court. *Amicus* briefs matter insofar as they provide legally relevant information not supplied by the parties to the case—information that assists the Court in reaching the correct decision as defined by the complex norms of our legal culture. This explanation can account for the fact that respondents benefit from *amicus* support more than petitioners, since it is likely that respondents on the whole are less likely to be represented by experienced counsel. It can also account for the apparent pattern that small disparities of support for one side over the other are associated with greater success on the part of the supported party, since the low-profile nature of these cases may make the Court more attentive to legal arguments. Finally, of course, it is consistent with the remarkable success of the Solicitor General and the significant if less dramatic success of other institutional litigants that employ skilled and experienced Supreme Court advocates. This does not mean that the legal model explains all the Court's decisions. Nevertheless, we think our findings support the conclusion that legal doctrine matters in at least a significant portion of the Court's business.

Kelly J. Lynch, Best Friends? Supreme Court Law Clerks on Effective *Amicus Curiae* Briefs

20 J.L. & Pol. 33 (2004)

Precisely what influences the justices of the United States Supreme Court? Numerous scholars have pondered this question, addressing it from many different perspectives: the influence of law clerks, the preferences of Congress, and the role of public opinion. To date, however, none have examined the influence of *amicus curiae* briefs ("*amicus* briefs") from the perspective of former Supreme Court law clerks. This article draws upon a new data set featuring seventy interviews with former Supreme Court law clerks who served from 1966-2001. Their personal insights clarify the role of these unsolicited briefs—a judicial lobbying tool that organizations and individuals aspiring to influence the Court's decision-making process increasingly employ. . . .

The clerk sample included one clerk from 1966, eight clerks from the 1970s, sixteen clerks from the 1980s, thirty clerks from the 1990s, and fifteen clerks from the 2000 and 2001 terms. Interviewees included at least three former clerks from the chambers of each of the current justices, as well as clerks from the Brennan, Stewart, White, Marshall, Burger, Blackmun and Powell chambers. Given the unavailability of any central listing of former clerks, it was not possible to use a random sample. Instead, I constructed a database of clerk contacts obtained by personal referrals and by conducting searches of law firms, law school faculties, the *National Law Journal* and *The Legal Times*. All interviews were conducted between November 2002 and January 2003. . . .

III. CLERKS' PROCESS FOR REVIEWING *AMICUS* BRIEFS

A. When Are *Amicus* Briefs Most Useful to the Court?

The survey began with an inquiry into whether there were particular areas of law or specific kinds of cases where clerks found *amicus* briefs to be especially helpful. The majority of clerks (56%) explained that *amicus* briefs were most helpful in cases involving highly technical and specialized areas of law, as well as complex statutory and regulatory cases. Some of the most frequently mentioned types of cases were those involving tax, patent, and trademark law, as well as cases relating to the Employment Retirement Income Security Act ("ERISA"). Other noteworthy areas of law included: railroad preemption, water rights, marine labor, immigration and Native American law. One clerk explained that, generally speaking, there existed a positive correlation between legal obscurity of subject matter and helpfulness of *amicus* briefs. . . .

Clerks citing the serviceability of *amicus* briefs in technical, statutory, regulatory and medical cases alike frequently noted that it was largely the non-legal information presented in these briefs that made them useful. Seventeen percent of the clerks volunteered that this type of information was most helpful.

Conforming to the views of legal scholars and Court observers, twenty-three percent of clerks offered that *amicus* briefs were extremely valuable in cases lacking quality legal representation. Generally, the clerks relied heavily on the merits briefs when they prepared for cases or wrote bench memoranda. In cases where the merits briefs were deficient, however, clerks would resort to the typically subordinate *amicus* briefs for assistance. According to one clerk, *amicus* briefs were most helpful in "cases where a side happened to be represented by a poor lawyer, such as a local trial lawyer who should have given the case to someone else [after certiorari was granted]." . . .

IV. DOES THE IDENTITY OF AN *AMICUS* FILER MATTER?

A. Are the Briefs of Any Particular Groups Considered More Carefully?

The clerks reported that *amicus* briefs from the Office of the Solicitor General were given a higher level of consideration than those of any other advocate. Approximately 70% of the seventy clerks interviewed emphatically cited the solicitor general as the most important filer. According to one particular clerk, "*Amicus* briefs from the solicitor several are always read closely." (C21). Multiple similar responses from clerks in all chambers and across all decades were offered with regards to the solicitor general, including phrases such as "always considered" and "most important without a doubt." (E.g. C14, C18, C38, C39, C62). Clerks repeatedly noted that the solicitor general was the only regular *amicus* filer always given special consideration. (C32). One clerk reported, "*Amicus* briefs from the solicitor general are 'head and shoulders' above the rest, and are often considered more carefully than party briefs." (C39). Since merits briefs generally receive more attention than *amicus* briefs, the solicitor general's *amicus* briefs are thus highly significant.

Clerks offered several explanations for why the solicitor general receives extraordinary attention. First and foremost, the Office of the Solicitor General has a well-deserved reputation for excellent written and oral advocacy. As one clerk commented, "The solicitor general has instant credibility and a reputation for good legal work with respect to case holdings and case logic." (C65). Another explained, "You may not agree with the solicitor general's argument, but the *amicus* brief will always be well researched." (C60).

The solicitor general's impartial analyses further distinguish his filings. According to one clerk, "*Amicus* briefs from the solicitor general are of excellent quality; they provide an extremely reliable, objective assessment." (C26). Thus, if the *amicus* briefs from the solicitor general are as outstanding as the interviewees suggest, it is not surprising that clerks appear to develop a quick appreciation for the consistent standard of excellence characterizing his briefs.

A final explanation offered for why the solicitor general's *amicus* briefs are read more carefully than any other filing entity is the Court's general concern for the interests of the United States as an institution. According to one clerk, "The solicitor general is always considered very carefully. He often gets argument time, like a party. If a normal *amicus* brief raises a new argument, the Court is not obligated to respond. But the Court is compelled to address the United States." (C44). While the Supreme Court Rules say nothing about the Court's obligation to respond to arguments raised by the United States, the Court's concern for the interest of the United States is evidenced by its rule that the government need not seek the permission of the litigants in order to file an *amicus* brief.

Following the solicitor general, *amicus* briefs filed by states were the next most frequently cited government entity as being important enough to always warrant close consideration. While a number of clerks claimed that *amicus* briefs from states were always carefully considered (21%), most clerks cited briefs from the solicitor general first, followed by briefs from states. Unlike *amicus* briefs from the solicitor general, briefs from states or coalitions of states were not generally regarded for their outstanding legal expertise. Rather, it is the Court's concern for the states as an integral component of the American system of government that seems to account for the consideration it confers to states' *amicus* briefs. . . .

After government entities, public interest groups comprised the most popular category of responses. First and foremost among those cited was the ACLU, noted by thirty-three percent of clerks. Clerks gave the ACLU's *amicus* briefs more consideration principally on account of their consistent superiority. As one clerk put it, certain groups that are habitually better filers—such as the ACLU—always make the "first cut" of *amicus* review. (C50). Another clerk commented, "The ACLU has quality people, and experience writing briefs; you know that they will raise good arguments." (C4). While a few clerks noted an ideological preference for ACLU briefs, most clerks' comments related to the excellence of the staff attorneys and their ability to raise the most salient legal arguments.

Clerks' plaudits of ACLU *amicus* briefs were remarkably similar across all chambers. Certainly for the category of public interest group *amici*, one might expect that chambers would have favored filers, and that such preferences would be linked to common perceptions of chamber ideology. When it came to the *amicus* briefs of the ACLU, however, this was not the case. Interestingly, even some clerks do not realize the extent to which ACLU *amicus* briefs are uniformly respected by the justices. For example, a clerk for Justice Ginsburg explained that she "always reads the briefs from the ACLU, because she wants to know what arguments they have raised." The clerk continued on to note that, "this is probably different in the Scalia or Thomas chambers." (C3). However, multiple clerks from both Justice Scalia's and Justice Thomas's chambers listed the ACLU as an organization that always receives closer attention. One possible explanation is that the clerks have significant discretion in choosing which *amicus* briefs they read, and that the briefs that interest the clerks may not necessarily correspond to the briefs that interest their justices. It is more likely, however, that clerks and justices use *amicus* briefs to prepare for cases by seeking out the best arguments presented by the opposing side, and that the ACLU is uniformly perceived to be outstanding. According to one of Justice Scalia's clerks, "Justice Scalia does respect the views of the ACLU; he views himself as being intellectually honest, and likes to consider other viewpoints." (C45). The suggestion that one would be challenged by ACLU viewpoints necessarily implies that they are generally thoughtful and of high quality.

Consistent with the theory that the justices will often rely upon the best briefs—regardless of ideological preference—another clerk reported that he considered most carefully the *amicus* briefs from those organizations he most respected, including the ACLU, the NAACP Legal Defense Fund, Inc., and the Brennan Center for Justice. However, he added that he also "considered carefully some conservative counterparts thought to be standard bearers for arguments of that side, since they would raise the most difficult arguments." (C70).

In addition to the ACLU, clerks consistently cited other public interest groups whose *amicus* briefs always receive closer attention, including the NAACP Legal Defense Fund (11%), the AFL-CIO (7%), and the Chamber of Commerce (7%). With the exception of the Chamber of Commerce, the liberal orientation of these groups is noteworthy. According to one clerk who served in the early 1980s, "The conservative equivalents [that are active Supreme Court amicus litigators and filers today] were just getting started then." (C15). The increasing tendency for conservative interest groups to file *amicus* briefs is a recent phenomenon and the delayed emergence of these organizations as *amici* likely accounts for the ideological imbalance reflected in the research.

As discussed previously, professional associations comprised another oft-cited but separate category of organizations whose *amicus* briefs receive extra consideration. Sixteen percent of clerks specifically cited the briefs of the American Medical Association, the American Psychological Association, and American Bar Association as consistently trustworthy. According to one clerk, "Professional groups are considered to be more reliable than ideological groups." (C58). . . .

B. Does the Author of an *Amicus* Brief Make a Difference? . . .

The overwhelming majority of clerks (88%) indicated that they would be inclined to give an *amicus* brief filed by an academic closer attention—at least initially. Several clerks reported that they always took an interest in *amicus* briefs filed by academics. According to one, "It is good to get a diversity of academic briefs. It is interesting to get different perspectives, even if some of the academic filers are not as famous." (C27). In most cases, however, clerks' affirmations of academic *amicus* filers were usually qualified in some way; many claimed only to give extra attention to well-known academics or professors they happened to know personally. (C38). Clerks repeatedly asserted that name recognition alone would not necessarily warrant closer consideration of an *amicus* brief. For example, two clerks specifically noted that an *amicus* brief authored by Harvard Law Professor Laurence Tribe would be given more deference than a brief authored by Harvard Law Professor Alan Dershowitz. (C9, C51). Other clerks recounted a wariness of *amicus* briefs filed by large groups of law professors. According to one, "Many law professors are just causing trouble, and just file *amicus* briefs as a vanity project." (C36). Another ventured, "*Amicus* briefs from large groups of professors can have an impact, but those are generally overdone." (C63). . . .

Coincidentally, the percentage of clerks claiming to lend additional consideration to an *amicus* brief authored by a reputed attorney was exactly equivalent to the percentage claiming to note a brief authored by an academic (88%). According to one such clerk, "If a famous lawyer filed, you would pay attention and take a closer look." (C45). Most specified that only established members of the "Supreme Court Bar"—the "inner circle," as McGuire described it—would always receive closer consideration. One clerk suggested, "Depending on whom you ask, there will be 10-25 lawyers in this category read more carefully." (C19). . . .

Jonathan Groner, How University Got Support of Military Leaders: Diversity Brief by Ex-Officials Came Together over Four Years

Legal Times, June 30, 2003, at 1

It began four years ago in a private conversation between James Cannon, a retired journalist and political operative, and former President Gerald Ford, whom Cannon served as a domestic affairs assistant.

Cannon was Ford's biographer and remains his friend. He is also a former chairman of the board of visitors of the U.S. Naval Academy in Annapolis.

That chat between two political old-timers in the summer of 1999, over dinner in Ann Arbor, Mich., proved to be the catalyst for what may be remembered as one of the most important amicus curiae briefs ever submitted to the Supreme Court.

The pair of cases testing undergraduate and law school affirmative action at the University of Michigan drew an avalanche of amicus briefs, on both sides of the issue. But after the Supreme Court's landmark June 23 ruling, a brief filed by 29 high-ranking former leaders of the U.S. military stands out for having had a direct impact.

"It was a very unusual amicus brief," says Marvin Krislov, the university's vice president and general counsel, who played a major role in coordinating the brief-writing process. "It evidently made a difference to the Court."

When Cannon and Ford met in Ann Arbor, trial courts had not yet even ruled. To many, the university's legal position seemed precarious.

"I talked with President Ford about the suits that had been filed," says Cannon, now 85. At the time, Ford, a 1935 graduate of the University of Michigan, had just written an op-ed article supporting the affirmative action programs at his alma mater which was published in *The New York Times* in August 1999.

Cannon says the two men agreed at the dinner that a court-ordered end to minority preference programs at Michigan could be a "real handicap" for the university, and that they should try to take steps to shore up the school's position.

Former President Ford confirms this account.

"I got involved very early in supporting the university," Ford says.

Soon thereafter, Cannon met with Lee Bollinger, then the president of the university, and raised the issue with him.

Cannon says his own "instant reaction" upon discussing the cases with Bollinger was that a ruling against Michigan would not only hurt the university but would also be "devastating to the continued efforts by the service academies to recruit and train minorities."

"I tried to think of a way to file a separate brief," says Cannon, who is not a lawyer, but is well-versed on military concerns from his stint on the board of the Naval Academy. "Bollinger liked my idea, and I continued to keep him informed."

Krislov, the general counsel, recalls, "Jim Cannon had serious concerns about the cohesiveness of the military [if affirmative action were curtailed]. There was serious concern in military circles that the military would not be able to do their jobs. It all started from this discussion."

The military brief, filed in February 2003, strongly asserted that maintaining racial diversity programs in higher education is crucial to the needs of all branches of the service and thus to national security.

This turned out to be a central point in Justice Sandra Day O'Connor's 5-4 majority opinion last week that upheld the law school's affirmative action plan in *Grutter v. Bollinger.*

Signers of the brief, in addition to Cannon, included such heavy hitters as retired Gen. Norman Schwartzkopf, former Defense Secretary William Cohen, and Sen. Carl Levin (D-Mich.), a former chairman of the Senate Armed Services Committee.

The final lineup of former Defense Department and military officials wasn't exactly what Cannon originally had in mind.

In October 2002, after the lower courts had ruled on the Michigan cases but before the Supreme Court had agreed to hear them, Cannon stepped into action.

"I went to the Pentagon and spoke with the assistant secretary for manpower," Cannon says. "I said, 'You ought to initiate an amicus brief.'"

At the time, however, the Bush administration had not yet formulated its position on the Michigan cases. The Defense Department rejected Cannon's proposal. "[I] told them I would go ahead and do it anyway," Cannon says.

Cannon had remained in touch with university GC Krislov. Cannon suggested that if current Pentagon officials couldn't sign a brief, former leaders of the U.S. military, both uniformed and civilian, certainly could.

On Dec. 2, 2002, the Supreme Court agreed to hear the case, and things started moving quickly.

Krislov, 42, a former associate White House counsel under President Bill Clinton, reached out to Joe Reeder, a former undersecretary of the Army whom he knew from his days in government. He asked Reeder, the managing partner of the D.C. office of Greenberg Traurig, to help put an amicus brief together and to find the best possible retired military leaders to sign on.

"I worked very hard to bring in people who were household names and whose reputations were unimpeachable. They included Republicans, Democrats, apolitical people—a wide range, so that no one could possibly say this is a partisan effort," Reeder says.

At the same time, the Michigan lawyers decided they also needed a leading Supreme Court advocate to be part of the effort to write an amicus brief.

The university had already enlisted two teams from elite firms to argue its own case—a group from Wilmer, Cutler & Pickering, led by John Payton, and one from Latham & Watkins, led by Maureen Mahoney.

For the amicus brief, Mahoney recommended Sidley Austin Brown & Wood, where Carter Phillips leads the appellate practice. Mahoney spoke with Phillips and with his partner Virginia Seitz, and they agreed to participate on a pro bono basis.

Seitz took the lead in writing the brief, while Reeder and Cannon used their extensive contacts in the military to bring new signers in.

"Joe Reeder is the man who moved this from my modest idea to a dynamic case," says Cannon, a former correspondent for *Time* and *Newsweek.* "I began to realize that there was a force behind this movement."

Krislov kept the process moving smoothly, and some of the former generals themselves contributed suggestions to the brief. Cannon wrote a two-page memorandum to Seitz with his own ideas.

"We had two large research tasks," Seitz says. "We had to figure out exactly what the affirmative action policies were in each branch of the military, and we had to review the history of the desegregation of the military to understand the relevance of these policies."

Payton says that at one meeting, the generals told the lawyers that half the nation's officer corps comes from the ROTC.

"I stopped the meeting at that point," Payton recalls. "I told them, 'I see that you're depending on student bodies like that of Michigan to develop your officers.'"

Parts of the brief were rewritten to emphasize the need for diversity in ROTC programs, as well as in the service academies.

At oral argument on April 1, the justices showed that they had read the military brief closely.

As soon as he began his argument, Solicitor General Theodore Olson was peppered with questions from several justices about the amicus brief.

Justice Ruth Bader Ginsburg asked Olson if he recognized that "all of the military academies do have race preference programs in admissions."

He replied, "The Coast Guard does not. . . . I do acknowledge, Justice Ginsburg, that the other academies are doing so."

The O'Connor decision handed down June 23 reflected the military leaders' arguments.

"High-ranking retired officers and civilian leaders of the United States military assert that . . . a highly qualified, racially diverse officer corps is essential to the military's ability to fulfill its principal mission to provide national security," O'Connor noted.

Reeder and the others who put the brief together could not have asked for a better result.

"It's kind of hard to ignore 29 people who are four-star generals or on a similar level," says Reeder. "Nor should anyone ignore what they have to say."

Notes and Questions

1. The Kearney and Merrill article excerpted above is over a decade old. More recent studies on the influence of *amicus* briefs have added more nuance to an already complicated story, but have, on balance, only reinforced their general conclusion: *Amicus* briefs have a small but noticeable impact on the results of Supreme Court cases, but that impact is uneven, varying significantly based on the nature of the case, the identity of the *amici*, the kind of information offered by the *amici*, and the side of the litigation supported by the *amici*. *See, e.g.*, Paul M. Collins, Jr., *Friends of the Court: Examining the Influence of* Amicus Curiae *Participation in Supreme Court Litigation*, 38 Law & Soc'y Rev. 807 (2004).

2. One of the more surprising findings of the Kearney and Merrill study was that a small advantage in the number of *amicus* filings on its behalf made a party more likely to win a Supreme Court case, but a large advantage had virtually no effect. The authors hint at their favored explanation for this seemingly anomalous result in their conclusion, but explain it more clearly earlier in their article: It is possible that the pool of cases with only a few *amicus* briefs and the pool of cases with a large number "reflect different sorts of controversies" with the former consisting largely of "low profile" cases involving technical statutory and procedural question in which a few well-executed *amicus* briefs might be helpful and the latter consisting largely of "high profile" cases in which the Justices are already ideologically disposed and are unlikely to be persuaded by *amicus* briefs. Kearney & Merrill, at 818.

3. Ms. Lynch's article suggests that the overrepresentation of left-wing groups in the clerks' account of the most respected *amicus* organizations may be an artifact of an earlier era in which liberal groups were more committed to litigation in general and to *amicus* briefs in particular and posits that it may be disappearing as conservative groups put more efforts into their *amicus* briefing. Events since the publication of her article seem to support her thesis, as conservative groups have increased the quality and quantity of their Supreme Court filings and met with positive press for doing so. *See, e.g.*, Tony Mauro, *Rachel Brand Headed to U.S. Chamber Litigation Center to Fight Regulation*, BLT: Blog of the Legal Times, http://legaltimes.typepad.com/blt/2011/05/rachel-brand-heading-to-us-chamber-litigation-center-to-fight-regulation.html (May 25, 2011 3:22 P.M.) (announcing that United States Chamber of Commerce was hiring two high-profile former Supreme Court clerks to lead litigation efforts in part because of high volume of cases in which they are participating as *amici* at the Supreme Court).

4. The *amicus* brief for the military officials in *Grutter v. Bollinger* is the Consolidated Brief of Lt. Gen. Julius W. Becton, Jr., et al. as *Amici Curiae* in Support of Respondents in *Grutter v. Bollinger*, 539 U.S. 306 (2002) (No. 02-241). It is excerpted below and appears in its entirety on the *Supreme Court Sourcebook*'s Web site.

5. As you follow pending Supreme Court cases or read decisions in older cases, it is intriguing and valuable to ask yourself: If I were counsel for each of the parties, what types of *amicus* briefs would I solicit? What types of arguments and information might be helpful to the Justices in deciding the case (in your favor)? What kinds of supporters might draw the Justices' attention?

3. Sample *Amicus* Briefs

The remaining pages of this chapter offer excerpts from three of the most widely discussed *amicus* briefs of this century. You have already been introduced to one of the briefs: the retired generals' brief in *Grutter v. Bollinger*, 539 U.S. 306 (2003). The second, a brief by leading historians of gender and sexuality offered in support of the plaintiffs' arguments in *Lawrence v. Texas*, 539 U.S. 558 (2003), reinforces many of the arguments made in the petitioners' brief in that case, which is excerpted above. The third is a provocative and controversial brief filed by the Alabama Solicitor General's office on behalf of six states in *Roper v. Simmons*, 543 U.S. 551 (2005), a case in which the Court was asked to overturn a prior decision and conclude that the Eighth Amendment's Cruel and Unusual Punishment Clause prohibits the execution of individuals for crimes committed while they were juveniles. Taking a page from the left-wing playbook, Solicitor General Kevin Newsom, a former law clerk for Justice Souter, attempted to humanize the case by providing detailed descriptions of several grisly murders committed by juveniles in Alabama.

In looking through these *amicus* briefs, consider why the particular *amici* chose to participate in the case, why they chose to emphasize the kinds of facts and arguments that appear below, and to whom were there arguments directed. In addition, try and evaluate the efficacy of these briefs, considering both how well each brief was conceptualized and how well those concepts were executed.

United States Supreme Court Amicus Brief.
Barbara A. GRUTTER, Petitioner,
v.
Lee BOLLINGER, et al., Respondents.
Jennifer GRATZ and Patrick HAMACHER, Petitioners,
v.
Lee BOLLINGER, et al., Respondents.

Nos. 02-241, 02-516.
February 21, 2003.

On Writs of Certiorari to the United States Court of Appeals for the Sixth Circuit

Consolidated Brief of Lt. Gen. Julius W. Becton, Jr., Adm. Dennis Blair, Maj. Gen. Charles Bolden, Hon. James M. Cannon, Lt. Gen. Daniel W. Christman, Gen. Wesley K. Clark, Sen. Max Cleland, Adm. Archie Clemins, Hon. William Cohen, Adm. William J. Crowe, Gen. Ronald R. Fogleman, Lt. Gen. Howard D. Graves, Gen. Joseph P. Hoar, Sen. Robert J. Kerrey et al. as Amici Curiae in Support of Respondents . . .

TABLE OF CONTENTS

INTEREST OF *AMICI*

Amici are former high-ranking officers and civilian leaders of the Army, Navy, Air Force, and Marine Corps, including former military-academy superintendents, Secretaries of Defense, and present and former members of the U.S. Senate. They are deeply interested in this case, because its outcome could affect the diversity of our nation's officer corps and, in turn, the military's ability to fulfill its missions. *Amici*'s judgment is based on decades of experience and accomplishment at the very highest positions in our nation's military leadership. The responsibilities highlighted below do not begin to describe the full scope of their service. . . .

SUMMARY OF ARGUMENT

Based on decades of experience, amici have concluded that a highly qualified, racially diverse officer corps educated and trained to command our nation's racially diverse enlisted ranks is essential to the military's ability to fulfill its principal mission to provide national security. The primary sources for the nation's officer corps are the service academies and the Reserve Officers Training Corps, the latter comprised of students already admitted to participating colleges and universities. At present, the military cannot achieve an officer corps that is both highly qualified and racially diverse unless the service academies and the ROTC use limited race-conscious recruiting and admissions policies. Accordingly, these institutions rely on such policies, developed to comport with this Court's instruction in *Regents of the University of California v. Bakke*, 438 U.S. 265 (1978).

The military has made substantial progress towards its goal of a fully integrated, highly qualified officer corps. It cannot maintain the diversity it has achieved or make further progress unless it retains its ability to recruit and educate a diverse officer corps. This Court and others have recognized that in certain contexts, the government may take race-conscious action not only to remedy past discrimination, but to further other compelling government interests. *See Bakke*; *Wittmer v. Peters*, 87 F.3d 916 (7th Cir. 1996) (penological benefits justify consideration of race in selecting correctional officers; collecting similar cases). The rules should not be changed. The military must be permitted to train and educate a diverse officer corps to further our compelling government interest in an effective military.

More than 50 years ago, President Truman issued an executive order ending segregation in the United States armed services. That decision, and the resulting integration of the military, resulted not only from a principled recognition that segregation is unjust and incompatible with American values, but also from a practical recognition that the military's need for manpower and its efficient, effective deployment required integration. Since that time, men and women of all races have trained and fought together in our armed services, from Korea to Vietnam to Afghanistan. Today, almost 40% of servicemen and women are minorities; 61.7% are white, and the remaining almost 40% are minorities, including 21.7% African-American, 9.6% Hispanic, 4% Asian-American and 1.2% Native American. Dep't of Def. ("DoD"), Statistical Series Pamphlet No. 02-5, *Semiannual Race/Ethnic/Gender Profile By Service/Rank of the Department of Defense & Coast Guard* 4 (Mar. 2002) ("DoD Report").

In the 1960s and 1970s, however, while integration increased the percentage of African-Americans in the enlisted ranks, the percentage of minority officers remained extremely low, and perceptions of discrimination were pervasive. This deficiency in the officer corps and the discrimination perceived to be its cause led to low morale and heightened racial tension. The danger this created was not theoretical, as the Vietnam era demonstrates. As that war continued, the armed forces suffered increased racial polarization, pervasive disciplinary problems, and racially motivated incidents in Vietnam and on posts around the world. "In Vietnam, racial tensions reached a point where there was an inability to fight." D. Maraniss, *United States Military Struggles to Make Equality Work*, Wash. Post, Mar. 6, 1990, at A01 (quoting Lt. Gen. Frank Petersen, Jr.). By the early 1970s, racial strife in the ranks was entirely commonplace. B. Nalty, *Strength for the Fight: A History of Black Americans in the Military* 308-10 (1986). The lack of minority officers substantially exacerbated the problems throughout the armed services. LTC E.J. Mason, U.S. Army War Coll. Strategy Research Project, *Diversity: 2015 and the Afro-American Army Officer* 2-3 (1998). The military's leadership "recognized that its racial problem was so critical that it was on the verge of self-destruction. That realization set in motion the policies and initiatives that have led to today's relatively positive state of affairs." *Id.* at 3.

"It is obvious and unarguable that no governmental interest is more compelling than the security of the Nation." *Haig v. Agee*, 453 U.S. 280, 307 (1981) (internal quotations omitted). The absence of minority officers seriously threatened the military's ability to function effectively and fulfill its mission to defend the nation. To eliminate that threat, the armed services moved aggressively to increase the number of minority officers and to train officers in diverse educational environments. In full accord with *Bakke* and with the DoD Affirmative Action Program, the service academies and the ROTC have set goals for minority officer candidates and worked hard to achieve those goals. They use financial and tutorial assistance, as well as recruiting programs, to expand the pool of highly-qualified minority candidates in a variety of explicitly race-conscious ways. They also employ race as a factor in recruiting and admissions policies and decisions.

These efforts have substantially increased the percentage of minority officers. Moreover, increasing numbers of officer candidates are trained and educated in racially diverse educational settings, which provides them with invaluable experience for their future command of our nation's highly diverse enlisted ranks. Today, among active duty officers, 81% are white, and the remaining 19% are minority, including 8.8% African-American, 4% Hispanic, 3.2% Asian American, and .6% Native American. *DoD Report* at 4. A substantial difference between the percentage of African-American enlisted personnel (21.7%) and African-American officers (8.8%) remains. The officer corps must continue to be diverse or the cohesiveness essential to the military mission will be critically undermined. *See infra* at 17.

In specific contexts, the courts have approved race-conscious action to achieve compelling, but non-remedial government interests. For example, the government's interest in "the promotion of racial diversity has been found sufficiently 'compelling,' at least in the context of higher education, to support the use of racial considerations in furthering that interest." *Wygant v. Jackson Bd. of Educ.*, 476 U.S. 267, 286 (1986) (O'Connor, J., concurring in part); *Metro Broad., Inc. v. FCC*, 497 U.S. 547, 568 (1990) (same) (citing *Bakke*). *Amici* submit that the government's compelling interest in promoting racial diversity in higher education is buttressed by its compelling national security interest in a cohesive military. That requires both a diverse officer corps and substantial numbers of officers educated and trained in diverse educational settings, including the military academies and ROTC programs. *See Haig*, 453 U.S. at 307; *Sweatt v. Painter*, 339 U.S. 629, 634 (1950) (students in racially-homogenous classrooms are ill-prepared for productive lives in our diverse society). President George Washington eloquently underscored the vital importance of direct association among diverse individuals in education and in the profession of arms:

> [T]he Juvenal period of life, when friendships are formed, & habits established that will stick by one; the Youth, or young men from different parts of the United States would be assembled to-gether, & would by degrees discover that there was not that cause for those jealousies & prejudices which one part of the Union had imbibed against another part. . . . What, but the mixing of people from different parts of the United States during the War rubbed off these impressions? A century in the ordinary intercourse, would not have accomplished what the Seven years association in Arms did. [Letter from Pres. George Washington, to Alexander Hamilton (Sept. 1, 1796), *reproduced* in J. Ellis, *Founding Brothers: The Revolutionary Generation* 960-61 (2001).]

The crisis that mandated aggressive integration of the officer corps in the service academies and in ROTC programs is a microcosm of what exists in our society at large, albeit with potentially more severe consequences to our nation's welfare.

Broad access to the education that leads to leadership roles is essential to public confidence in the fairness and integrity of public institutions, and their ability to perform their vital functions and missions.

At present no alternative exists to limited, race-conscious programs to increase the pool of high quality minority officer candidates and to establish diverse educational settings for officers. The armed services must have racially diverse officer candidates who satisfy the rigorous academic, physical, and personal prerequisites for officer training and future leadership. It is no answer to tell selective institutions such as the service academies or the ROTC automatically to admit students with a specified class rank, even if such a system were administratively workable and would result in a diverse student body. This one-dimensional criterion forces the admission of students with neither the academic nor physical capabilities nor the leadership qualities demanded by these institutions, damaging the corps and the military mission in the process. The military must both maintain selectivity in admissions and train and educate a racially diverse officer corps to command racially diverse troops. The device of admitting a top percentage will not simultaneously produce high quality and diversity.

Like numerous selective educational institutions, the military already engages in aggressive minority recruiting programs and utilizes the service preparatory academies and other programs to increase the pool of qualified minority candidates. These important steps are vital to the continuing integration of the officer corps. The fact remains: Today, there is no race-neutral alternative that will fulfill the military's, and thus the nation's, compelling national security need for a cohesive military led by a diverse officer corps of the highest quality to serve and protect the country. . . .

John Geddes LAWRENCE and Tyron GARNER, Petitioners,
v.
STATE OF TEXAS, Respondent.

No. 02-102.
January 16, 2003.

On Writ of Certiorari to the Court of Appeals of Texas, Fourteenth District

Brief of Professors of History George Chauncey, Nancy F. Cott, John D'Emilio, Estelle B. Freedman, Thomas C. Holt, John Howard, Lynn Hunt, Mark D. Jordan, Elizabeth Lapovsky Kennedy, and Linda P. Kerber as Amici Curiae in Support of Petitioners . . .

TABLE OF CONTENTS

III. Tolerance Toward Homosexuals Has Increased, Resulting in Acceptance
by Many, But Not All, Mainstream Institutions

CONCLUSION

APPENDIX (qualifications and affiliations of *amici*)

INTRODUCTION AND SUMMARY OF ARGUMENT

Amici, as historians, do not propose to offer the Court legal doctrine to justify a
holding that the Texas Homosexual Conduct Law violates the U.S. Constitution.
Rather, *amici* believe they can best serve the Court by elaborating on two *historical*
propositions important to the legal analysis: (1) no consistent historical practice
singles out same-sex behavior as "sodomy" subject to proscription, and (2) the
governmental policy of classifying and discriminating against certain citizens on
the basis of their homosexual status is an unprecedented project of the twentieth
century, which is already being dismantled. The Texas law at issue is an example of
such irrational discrimination.

In colonial America, regulation of non-procreative sexual practices—regulation
that carried harsh penalties but was rarely enforced—stemmed from Christian
religious teachings and reflected the need for procreative sex to increase the population. Colonial sexual regulation included such non-procreative acts as masturbation, and sodomy laws applied equally to male-male, male-female, and human-
animal sexual activity. "Sodomy" was not the equivalent of "homosexual conduct."
It was understood as a particular, discrete, act, not as an indication of a person's
sexuality or sexual orientation.

Not until the end of the nineteenth century did lawmakers and medical writing
recognize sexual "inversion" or what we would today call homosexuality. The
phrase "homosexual sodomy" would have been literally incomprehensible to the
Framers of the Constitution, for the very concept of homosexuality as a discrete
psychological condition and source of personal identity was not available until the
late 1800s. The Court in *Bowers v. Hardwick* misapprehended this history.

Proscriptive laws designed to suppress all forms of non-procreative and non-
marital sexual conduct existed through much of the last millennium. Widespread
discrimination against a class of people on the basis of their homosexual status
developed only in the twentieth century, however, and peaked from the 1930s to
the 1960s. Gay men and women were labeled "deviants," "degenerates," and "sex
criminals" by the medical profession, government officials, and the mass media.
The federal government banned the employment of homosexuals and insisted that
its private contractors ferret out and dismiss their gay employees, many state governments prohibited gay people from being served in bars and restaurants, Hollywood
prohibited the discussion of gay issues or the appearance of gay or lesbian characters
in its films, and many municipalities launched police campaigns to suppress gay life.
The authorities worked together to create or reinforce the belief that gay people
were an inferior class to be shunned by other Americans. Sodomy laws that exclusively targeted same-sex couples, such as the statute enacted in 1973 in Texas (1973
Tex. Gen. Laws ch. 399, §§1, 3), were a development of the last third of the twentieth
century and reflect this historically unprecedented concern to classify and penalize
homosexuals as a subordinate class of citizens.

Since the 1960s, however, and especially since the *Bowers* decision in 1986,
official and popular attitudes toward homosexuals have changed, though vestiges
of old attitudes—such as the law at issue here—remain. Among other changes, the

medical profession no longer stigmatizes homosexuality as a disease, prohibitions on employment of homosexuals have given way to antidiscrimination protections, gay characters have become common in movies and on television, 86 percent of Americans support gay rights legislation, and family law has come to recognize gays and lesbians as part of non-traditional families worthy of recognition. These changes have not gone uncontested, but a large majority of Americans have come to oppose discrimination against lesbians and gay men.

In this case, the Court should construe the Equal Protection Clause and the Due Process Clause with a thorough and nuanced history of the subject in mind.

ARGUMENT

I. *Bowers v. Hardwick* Rests on a Fundamental Misapprehension of the History of Sodomy Laws

In *Bowers v. Hardwick,* this Court concluded, by a 5-4 vote, that the Constitution does not confer a fundamental right to engage in "homosexual sodomy." The majority's conclusion was based, in large measure, on the "ancient roots" of laws prohibiting homosexuals from engaging in acts of consensual sodomy. 478 U.S. 186, 192 (1986). The Court stated that in 1791 "sodomy" "was forbidden by the laws of the original thirteen States," that in 1868 "all but 5 of the 37 States in the Union had criminal sodomy laws," and that, "until 1961, all 50 States outlawed sodomy." *Id.* at 192-193. Accordingly, the Court reasoned, the right of homosexuals to engage consensually in the acts that have been labeled "sodomy" is not "deeply rooted in this Nation's history and tradition." *Id.* at 192-194. In a concurring opinion, Chief Justice Burger relied on a similar historical interpretation. In his view, "[d]ecisions of individuals relating to homosexual conduct have been subject to state intervention throughout the history of Western civilization." *Id.* at 196. To consider the right to engage in homosexual sodomy a fundamental right, Chief Justice Burger wrote, "would be to cast aside millennia of moral teaching." *Id.* at 197.

Recent historical scholarship demonstrates the flaws in the historical accounts endorsed by the Court and Chief Justice Burger. We concur with the accounts given of the history of sodomy laws and of their enforcement in colonial America and the United States by the American Civil Liberties Union and the Cato Institute in their amicus briefs. We will not endeavor to replicate their historical accounts here, but we do wish to stress two points about this history.

First, contrary to the Court's assumption in *Bowers,* sodomy prohibitions have varied enormously in the last millennium (and even since our own colonial era) in their definition of the offense and in their rationalization of its prohibition. The specification of "homosexual sodomy" as a criminal offense does not carry the pedigree of the ages but is almost exclusively an invention of the recent past.

Prohibitions against sodomy are rooted in the teachings of Western Christianity, but those teachings have always been strikingly inconsistent in their definition of the acts encompassed by the term. When the term "sodomy" was first emphasized by medieval Christian theologians in the eleventh century, they applied it inconsistently to a diverse group of non-procreative sexual practices. In subsequent Latin theology, canon law, and confessional practice, the term was notoriously confused with "unnatural acts," which had a very different origin and ranged even more widely (to include, for example, procreative sexual acts in the wrong position or with contraceptive intent). "Unnatural acts" is the older category, because it comes directly from Paul in *Romans* 1, but Paul does not associate such acts with (or even mention) the story of Sodom (*Genesis* 19) and appears not to have considered that story to be concerned with same-sex activity. (Cf. *Ezekiel* 16:49-50, where the sin of Sodom is the arrogant and inhospitable refusal to share wealth and leisure.)

Later Christian authors did combine *Romans* 1 with *Genesis* 19, but they could not agree on what sexual practices were meant by either "unnatural acts" or "sodomy." For example, in Peter Damian, who around 1050 championed the term "sodomy" as an analogy to "blasphemy," the "sins of the Sodomites" include solitary masturbation. In Thomas Aquinas, about two centuries later, "unnatural acts" cover every genital contact intended to produce orgasm except penile-vaginal intercourse in an approved position. See Mark D. Jordan, The Invention of Sodomy in Christian Theology 46, 144-145 (1997). Many later Christian writers denied that women could commit sodomy at all; others believed that the defining characteristic of unnatural or sodomitic sex was that it could not result in procreation, regardless of the genders involved. See Mark D. Jordan, The Silence of Sodom 62-71 (2000). In none of these authors does the term "sodomy" refer systematically and exclusively to same-sex conduct. Certainly it was not used consistently through the centuries to condemn that conduct. The restrictive use of the term in the Texas law at issue must itself be regarded as a historically recent innovation.

The English Reformation Parliament of 1533 turned the religious injunction against sodomy into the secular crime of buggery when it made "the detestable and abominable vice of buggery committed with mankind or beast" punishable by death. The English courts interpreted this to apply to sexual intercourse between a human and animal and anal intercourse between a man and woman as well as anal intercourse between two men. See William Eskridge, Jr., *Law and the Construction of the Closet: American Regulation of Same-Sex Intimacy, 1880-1946*, 82 Iowa L. Rev. 1007, 1012 (1997); Ed Cohen, *Legislating the Norm: From Sodomy to Gross Indecency*, 88 S. Atlantic Q. 181, 185 (1989).

Colonial American statutes variously drew on the religious and secular traditions and shared their imprecision in the definition of the offense. Variously defining the crime as (the religious) sodomy or (the secular) buggery, they generally proscribed anal sex between men and men, men and women, and humans and animals, but their details and their rationale varied, and the New England colonies penalized a wider range of "carnall knowledge," including (but by no means limited to) "men lying with men." Puritan leaders in the New England colonies were especially vigorous in their denunciation of sodomitical sins as contrary to God's will, but their condemnation was also motivated by the pressing need to increase the population and to secure the stability of the family. Thus John Winthrop mused that the main offense of one man hanged in New Haven in 1646 for having engaged in masturbation with numerous youths—not, in other words, for "sodomy" as it is usually understood today—was his "frustratinge of the Ordinance of marriage & the hindringe the generation of mankinde." See John Murrin, *"Things Fearful to Name": Bestiality in Early America, in* American Sexual Histories 17 (Elizabeth Reis ed., 2001); see also Robert F. Oaks, *"Things Fearful to Name": Sodomy and Buggery in Seventeenth-century New England*, 12 J. Soc. Hist. 268 (1978); Jonathan Ned Katz, *The Age of Sodomitical Sin, 1607-1740, in* Gay/Lesbian Almanac 23 (1983).

Another indication that the sodomy statutes were not the equivalent of a statute against "homosexual conduct" is that with one brief exception they applied exclusively to acts performed by men, whether with women, girls, men, boys, or animals, and not to acts committed by two women. Only the New Haven colony penalized "women lying with women," and this for only ten years. For the entire colonial period we have reports of only two cases involving two women engaged in acts with one another. As one historian notes, both cases "were treated as lewd and lascivious behavior, not as potential crimes against nature." See Murrin at 15; Katz, Gay/Lesbian Almanac, at 29-30.

Statutes enacted in the early decades after independence followed the English authorities, but by the mid-nineteenth century most statutes defined the offense as a crime against nature rather than as a crime against God. Such statutes were still not the equivalent of a statute proscribing "homosexual conduct." In 1868, no statute criminalized oral sex, whether between two men, two women, or a man and woman. See William Eskridge, Jr., Hardwick *and Historiography*, 1999 U. Ill. L. Rev. 631, 656.

It was only beginning in the 1970s that a handful of States, including Texas, passed legislation specifying homosexual sodomy while decriminalizing heterosexual sodomy. This legislation had no historical precedent, but resulted from a uniquely twentieth-century form of animus directed at homosexuals, which will be detailed in the next section of this brief.

Second, throughout American history, the authorities have rarely enforced statutes prohibiting sodomy, however defined. Even in periods when enforcement increased, it was rare for people to be prosecuted for consensual sexual relations conducted in private, even when the parties were of the same sex. Indeed, records of only about twenty prosecutions and four or five executions have surfaced for the entire colonial period. Even in the New England colonies, whose leaders denounced "sodomy" with far greater regularity and severity than did other colonial leaders and where the offense carried severe sanctions, it was rarely prosecuted. The trial of Nicholas Sension, a married man living in Westhersfield, Connecticut, in 1677, revealed that he had been widely known for soliciting sexual contacts with the town's men and youth for almost forty years but remained widely liked. Likewise, a Baptist minister in New London, Connecticut, was temporarily suspended from the pulpit in 1757 because of his repeatedly soliciting sex with men, but the congregation voted to restore him to the ministry after he publicly repented. They understood his sexual transgressions to be a form of sinful behavior in which anyone could engage and from which anyone could repent, not as a sin worthy of death or the condition of a particular class of people. See Richard Godbeer, *"The Cry of Sodom": Discourse, Intercourse, and Desire in Colonial New England*, 3.52 Wm. & Mary Q. 259, 259-260, 275-278 (1995); Eskridge, 1999 U. Ill. L. Rev. at 645; John D'Emilio & Estelle B. Freedman, Intimate Matters: A History of Sexuality in America 30 (2d ed. 1997).

The relative indifference of the public and the authorities to the crime of sodomy continued in the first century of independence. For instance, only twenty-two men were indicted for sodomy in New York City in the nearly eight decades from 1796 to 1873. D'Emilio & Freedman, Intimate Matters 123. The number of sodomy prosecutions increased sharply in the last two decades of the nineteenth century and in the twentieth century. This was made possible by the decision of many States to criminalize oral intercourse for the first time. But it resulted in large measure from the pressure applied on district attorneys by privately organized and usually religiously inspired anti-vice societies, whose leaders feared that the growing size and complexity of cities had loosened the constraints on sexual conduct and increased the vulnerability of youth and the disadvantaged. The increase in sodomy prosecutions was only one aspect of a general escalation in the policing of sexual activity, which also included stepped-up campaigns against prostitution, venereal disease, and contraception use. Although in this context a growing number of sodomy prosecutions involved adult males who had engaged in consensual relations, most such relations had taken place in semi-public spaces rather than in the privacy of the home, and the great majority of cases continued to involve coercion and/or minor boys or girls. See D'Emilio & Freedman, Intimate Matters 150-156, 202-215; George Chauncey, Gay New York: Gender, Urban Culture, and the Making of the Gay Male World 137-141 (1994); Paul Boyer, Urban Masses and Moral Order in America, 1820-1920 (1978); Eskridge, 1999 U. Ill. L. Rev. at 655-659.

Thus, the majority in *Bowers* misinterpreted the historical record. Laws singling out sexual (or "sodomitical") conduct between partners of the same sex for proscription are an invention of our time, not the legacy of "millennia of moral teaching." And in practice, regulating sodomy has never been a major concern of the state or the public.

When reexamining a prior holding, this Court ordinarily considers "whether facts have so changed, or come to be seen so differently, as to have robbed the old rule of significant application or justification." *Planned Parenthood v. Casey,* 505 U.S. 833, 855 (1992). See also *Church of Lukumi Babalu Aye v. City of Hialeah,* 508 U.S. 520, 574-575 (1993) (Souter, J., concurring in part) (arguing that recent historical scholarship correcting incomplete historical assessments by the Court justifies reexamination of constitutional precedent). Because, in this case, historical scholarship demonstrates that the use of sodomy laws to regulate exclusively same-sex behavior and to restrict homosexuals is a recent invention, this Court should reconsider its earlier opinion in *Bowers,* which rested on an inaccurate historical assessment. And, at the very least, it should recognize that Texas's singling out of same-sex sodomy for prohibition lacks a significant historical pedigree.

Furthermore, in its analysis of the Equal Protection Clause issue in this case, the Court should recognize what the foregoing history shows: sodomy laws have not only varied in content over time, but have also depended on the kinds of status-based distinctions and shifting justifications that are typical of irrational discrimination. Neither millennia of moral teachings nor the American experience teach *any* consistent message about which sexual practices between consenting adults should be condemned and why. Rather, the unprecedented enactment in recent decades of sodomy laws that exclusively penalize homosexual conduct is one indication of the growth of a uniquely twentieth-century form of discrimination. . . .

Supreme Court of the United States.
Donald P. ROPER, Superintendent, Potosi Correctional
Center Petitioner,
v.
Christopher SIMMONS, Respondent.

No. 03-633.
April 20, 2004.

On Writ of Certiorari to the Supreme Court of Missouri

Brief of the States of Alabama, Delaware, Oklahoma, Texas, Utah, and Virginia as Amici Curiae in Support of Petitioner ...

TABLE OF CONTENTS

SUMMARY OF ARGUMENT

Amici's experience strongly indicates that a bright-line rule categorically exempting 16- and 17-year-olds from the death penalty—no matter how elaborate the plot, how sinister the killing, or how sophisticated the cover-up—would be arbitrary at best, and downright perverse at worst. Using abbreviated descriptions of a handful of murders committed by "juvenile" offenders currently on Alabama's death-row, this brief will show that, despite their chronological age, *at least some* 16- and 17-year-old killers most assuredly are able to distinguish right from wrong and to appreciate fully the consequences of their murderous actions. Because a prophylactic constitutional rule taking capital punishment off the table for *all* such offenders would have no footing in the real world, it should be rejected.

Although this brief uses examples drawn from Alabama to make its point, the other amici hasten to note that their experiences have been no different. There simply is no basis to conclude that 16- and 17-year-olds are categorically incapable of committing heinous (and meticulously planned) murders, and there is no justification for categorically exempting them from the death penalty.[1]

ARGUMENT

Once again, this Court is asked to "'draw a line' that would prohibit the execution of any person who was under the age of 18 at the time" he or she committed capital murder. *Thompson v. Oklahoma*, 487 U.S. 815, 838 (1988); *see also Stanford v. Kentucky*, 492 U.S. 361 (1989). As it has done twice before, this Court should decline to impose that sort of constitutional prophylaxis.

The States' purpose in filing this brief is a limited one. It is simply to show—using the facts of real-world cases—that there is no principled basis for concluding that 16- and 17-year-old murderers, as a class, are categorically incapable of acting with a degree of moral culpability deserving of society's severest punishment.

---

1. Virginia notes its own experience with Lee Boyd Malvo—one of the snipers who plagued Virginia and Maryland in 2002. This experience illustrates both the heinousness of the crimes of which juveniles are capable as well as the ability of jurors to take a juvenile's age into account along with other factors in determining whether to impose the death penalty. *See Commonwealth v. Malvo*, Sentencing Order, Criminal No. K102888 (Fairfax Co. Cir. Ct., March 10, 2004) available at http://www.fairfaxcounty. gov/courts/cases/malvo_orders.htm (reciting conviction of capital murder, but ordering life without parole, on jury's recommendation). The fate of such criminals should be decided on a case-by-case basis rather than by the categorical rule sought by respondent.

Adolescents are fundamentally distinguishable from the mentally retarded in that respect. This Court's decision in *Atkins v. Virginia*, 536 U.S. 304 (2002), exempting mentally retarded murderers from the death penalty rests, at bottom, on a judgment that retarded offenders are, by virtue of their limited cognitive abilities, less blame-worthy than non-retarded offenders. That sort of clinical assessment simply does not hold for adolescents. Some juvenile offenders, to be sure, are not capable of the sort of cold-blooded calculation to which the death penalty is properly addressed. But others most assuredly are. And that is the point: a juvenile offender's moral culpa-bility, if it is to have any mooring in reality, must be assessed on an individualized basis.

As this Court held in *Stanford*, "[i]n the realm of capital punishment in particular, 'individualized consideration [is] a constitutional requirement.'" 492 U.S. at 375 (quoting *Lockett v. Ohio*, 438 U.S. 586, 605 (1978)). Indeed, "one of the individualized mitigating factors that sentencers must be permitted to consider is the defendant's age." *Id.* (citing *Eddings v. Oklahoma*, 455 U.S. 104, 115-16 (1982)). There simply is no warrant, either in law or in fact, for abandoning the touchstone of individualized sentencing, which sensibly has characterized this Court's death-penalty jurisprudence for nearly a quarter century, in favor of a prophylactic rule that bears no necessary relationship to an adolescent offender's actual moral cul-pability. Where an individual offender—whether adolescent or adult—truly cannot appreciate the wrongfulness of his actions, he should by all means be spared the death penalty. But where an individual—again, adolescent or adult—*can* make informed moral choices, he should be held fully responsible for the human con-sequences of those choices.

The following summaries, abbreviated descriptions of murders committed by current Alabama death-row inmates when they were 16 or 17 years old, leave little room for doubt that *at least some* adolescent killers most assuredly have the mental and emotional wherewithal to plot, kill, and cover up in cold blood. They should not evade full responsibility for their actions by the serendipity of chronological age.

1. Mark Anthony Duke—Age 16

Angry at being refused permission to borrow the family truck, Mark Duke (16 at the time) enlisted the aid of three co-conspirators—Brandon Samra (19), Michael Ellison (16), and David Collums (17)—to help him kill his father, Randy Duke. Aware that he would need to conceal his crime, Duke insisted that "they could not leave any witnesses." *Duke v. State*, 2002 WL 1145829, at *1 (Ala. Crim. App. May 31, 2002). Accordingly, Duke also plotted the murders of his father's girlfriend, Dedra Hunt, and her two young children, Chelisa (6 years old) and Chelsea (7 years old). *Id.* at *1-3.

Even the bare-bones facts of the crime show vividly the careful calculation with which Duke planned, executed, and tried to cover up the murders. On the evening of March 22, 1997, Duke and the three co-conspirators went to the Duke residence to ask permission to use the family truck. When his father refused, Duke became angry; he told his friends that he was tired of his father being so bossy and not letting him do what he wanted to do. Duke said that he wanted to kill his father. *Id.* at *1.

When the group returned to Ellison's house, Duke reiterated—in all seriousness—that he wanted to kill his father. Accordingly, Duke wiped the fingerprints from a .45 caliber pistol, the gun's clip, and bullets; Ellison cleaned the prints off of a .32 caliber pistol. When he had finished his preparations, Duke again said that he wanted to go to his house and kill his father—so they went. *Id.* at *1.

When the four arrived at Duke's house, Duke said—again—that he was going to kill his father (R. 1810) and, further, that he would have to kill the two little girls and their mother so as to eliminate witnesses. *Duke*, 2002 WL 1145829, at *1; R. 1812. Duke, who still had the .45, asked Samra (now carrying the .32) to go in with him. R. 1812-13. After instructing Collums and Ellison to meet them in the neighborhood behind the house, Duke led Samra inside his father's house. R. 1813. According to Duke's plan, Samra was to kill Dedra Hunt; Duke would take care of his father and the little girls. R. 1814.

Dedra Hunt and her girls were on the couch by the fireplace, watching television. R. 1813. After initially waiting for Duke's father in the master bedroom, Duke and Samra went into the kitchen as Randy Duke came up from the basement and sat on the fireplace. R. 1814. Pursuant to Duke's instruction, Samra went after Dedra while Duke approached his father and shot him at close range. R. 1815. Samra shot Dedra in the face, knocking out teeth but not killing her. Dedra (now bleeding profusely) and the girls fled upstairs, with Samra in pursuit. *Duke*, 2002 WL 1145829, at *2. Meanwhile, Randy Duke begged his son to spare his life; in response, the younger Duke said that he was tired of his father not letting him do what he wanted. R. 1816. Duke raised his gun to fire another shot at his father, but the gun jammed. R. 1817. After clearing the chamber, stabbing his father numerous times, and hitting him with his fist (R. 2257-59), Duke said that he would see his father in hell and shot him between the eyes. *Duke*, 2002 WL 1145829, at *2.

Dedra Hunt had also begged for mercy. R. 1817. As she and her little girls ran upstairs, Samra chased after her, shooting at her again. Dedra managed to lock herself and one of her daughters, Chelisa, in the master bathroom. When Samra was unable to pry the door open, Duke arrived from downstairs and kicked a hole in the door, reached through, and unlocked it. Duke shot Dedra Hunt in the forehead, killing her instantly. Duke then found 6-year-old Chelisa cowering in the shower; telling her that it would only hurt for a minute, Duke slit the child's throat. *Duke*, 2002 WL 1145829, at *2.

Duke then told Samra that they had to find the other little girl, 7-year-old Chelsea. They found her hiding under a bed in one of the upstairs bedrooms. R. 1821-22. As Duke pulled Chelsea from underneath the bed, she pleaded for her life. R. 1822-23. Duke tried to slit Chelsea's throat as he had her sister's, but she struggled, in the process sustaining 15 lacerations to her face and hands. R. 1823. Samra refused to help finish the little girl off until Duke yelled at him. *Id.* Duke then held Chelsea down while Samra slit her throat. *Id.*

The gruesome murders complete, the elaborate cover-up began. Duke stole his father's wallet, fled the house, and ditched the knives in a nearby storm drain. *Duke*, 2002 WL 1145829, at *2. Afterwards, Duke and Samra met back up with Collums and Ellison—just as Duke had instructed—in the neighborhood behind the Duke home. R. 1825. Duke and Samra washed up and stashed the guns. While fleeing the scene in Ellison's truck, Duke warned his co-conspirators that he would kill them if they told anyone about the murders. R. 1826.

In an attempt to establish an alibi, the group went to see the movie "Scream" and kept the ticket stubs. *Duke*, 2002 WL 1145829, at *2. They stayed at the movie only a short time, however, before deciding to get something to eat and to play pool. R. 1829-30. During the night, they threw their bloody clothes and Randy Duke's wallet into a trash dumpster near Ellison's house. R. 1830.

The following day, at Duke's instruction, all four co-conspirators returned to the Duke home to ransack it so that police would think that a robbery had occurred. R. 1831-34. Duke then planned to telephone the police to tell them that his family had been murdered. R. 1836. Before placing the call, the four rehearsed the alibi they would give the police if questioned. R. 1838. Duke called the police and, when questioned later, gave a statement consistent with the agreed-upon alibi.

According to the state medical examiner, Randy Duke died as a result of the gunshot between his eyes inflicted by his son. R. 2254. Another shot delivered by the younger Duke traveled downward from Randy Duke's cheek and into his shoulder. R. 2255-56. Examination of the father also revealed numerous stab wounds to the head, face, neck, and chest, as well as many contusions and bruises. R. 2257-59. Dedra Hunt suffered three gunshot wounds. R. 2263. The fatal wound was a shot to the head—again delivered by Duke. R. 2264.

Chelisa suffered two 5 1/4 inch lacerations—at Duke's hands—across her throat. R. 2268. She aspirated her own blood for several minutes, and then died. R. 2268-70. Chelsea sustained deep cuts on her face and neck, as well as the fatal cut across her throat. R. 2272-73. She also suffered 15 defensive wounds to her right hand and several more to her left. R. 2275-77. Like her younger sister, Chelsea aspirated her own blood for a few minutes before she died. R. 2274.

Both Duke and Samra were sentenced to death for their roles in the quadruple murders of Randy Duke and Dedra, Chelisa, and Chelsea Hunt. Under the bright-line rule advanced by respondent, Duke—who was by all accounts the mastermind and ring-leader of the attack, and was in any event the trigger-man (or knife-wielder, as the case may be) in three of the four murders—would escape capital punishment, while his minion, Samra, would not. That, at least as a principle of constitutional law, is nonsensical. . . .

4. William Thomas Knotts—Age 17

In October of 1989, William Thomas Knotts (17) and another teenager escaped from a juvenile detention facility and spent some 24 hours wandering around Montgomery County, Alabama. Angered by what he perceived to be an insult directed at him by Helen Rhodes—namely, splashing water on him with her car—Knotts located Rhodes' house so that he could "get back at her" later. *Knotts v. State*, 686 So. 2d 431, 442 (Ala. Crim. App. 1995).

After being returned to the juvenile facility, Knotts escaped again some two weeks later. Knotts headed straight for Helen Rhodes' home, stopping on the way to burglarize two other houses to steal guns, ammunition, cash, food, and clothing. *Id.* at 442.

Knotts broke into Helen Rhodes' home, placed his wet clothes and shoes in her dryer, and waited for her to return. Knotts waited there, he said, "approximately an hour and a half . . . for her to come home so he could shoot her for splashing water on him." *Id.* at 443. While he waited, Knotts watched television and wrote a note to be left at the scene—intended to mislead police to believe that the murder he planned to commit was gang-related. When Helen arrived home with her two-year-old son, Knotts shot her in the arm. As her young son screamed, Knotts shot Helen a second time in the back. She died almost immediately. *Id.* at 442.

Fearing that someone might have heard the shots, Knotts gathered his loot from the earlier burglaries along with Helen's purse and her husband's shoes and travel kit, and then left town in her car. Helen's husband returned four to five hours later to discover "his wife's body and his son, whose clothing was soaked with his mother's blood, sitting beside her body, crying." *Id.* at 443. . . .

CONCLUSION

If the cases detailed in this brief show anything, it is that there is no magic in the age 18. Just as there are adults who, for whatever reason, cannot fully comprehend the wrongfulness of their actions, there are adolescents—16 and 17 year-olds, to be sure—who *can*. A teenager who plots like an adult, kills like an adult, and covers up like an adult should be held responsible for his choices like an adult.

Because 18 is not "the age before which *no one* can reasonably be held fully responsible" for the murder of another human being, *Stanford,* 492 U.S. at 376 (plurality opinion), the judgment of the Supreme Court of Missouri—which rests on an arbitrary and ultimately unsupportable prophylactic line—should be reversed.

Notes and Questions

1. These *amicus* briefs are available in their entirety on the *Supreme Court Sourcebook* Web site along with other examples of successful or intriguing *amicus* briefs.

2. Why was the Generals' Brief in *Grutter* so successful? Do you think the Court was impressed with the legal argument that affirmative action programs are necessary to protect national security and therefore meets strict scrutiny? Alternatively, do you think that the strong support for affirmative action by a bipartisan coalition of military leaders signaled to the Court that mainstream Americans or American elites or some combination of the two favored continued experimentation with affirmative action programs? With regard to the second possible explanation, note that the Court also received a large number of *amicus* briefs from major corporations, almost all of which supported the continued use of affirmative action. *See, e.g.,* Brief of Exxon Mobil Corp. as *Amicus Curiae* Supporting Neither Party at 4, *Grutter,* 539 U.S. 306 (No. 02-241); Brief for 65 Leading American Businesses as *Amicus Curiae* in Support of Respondents at 2, *Grutter,* 539 U.S. 306 (No. 02-241); Brief of General Motors Corp. as *Amicus Curiae* in Support of Respondents at 12, *Grutter,* 539 U.S. 306 (No. 02-241); Brief of Massachusetts Institute of Technology, Leland Stanford Junior University, E.I. Du Pont De Nemours and Company, International Business Machines Corp., National Academy of Sciences, National Academy of Engineering, National Action Council for Minorities in Engineering, Inc., as *Amicus Curiae* Supporting Respondents at 9, *Grutter,* 539 U.S. 306 (No. 02-241).

3. How persuasive do you find the historians' brief in *Lawrence*? How objective do you find the brief? Does your answer to the first question depend on your answer to the second question?

4. Notice that most of the historians' brief in *Lawrence* addresses a question that, from a purely doctrinal perspective, is peripheral. Under prevailing substantive due process precedent, the central *historical* question before the Court is whether there is a longstanding historical tradition of treating a particular species of conduct as outside the power of government to regulate. The historians are not suggesting that there is any such tradition but instead are challenging the Court's assumption in *Bowers* that the conduct in question has always been regulated by statutes similar to those at issue in this case. Though winning on this latter question is neither necessary nor sufficient for prevailing on a substantive due process claim, the plaintiffs and the *amici* historians speculated that replacing the historical account offered in *Bowers* with a more nuanced picture would substantially increase their chance of victory. Justice Kennedy's opinion in the case, which draws heavily on the historians' brief, suggests that they were correct. *See Lawrence v. Texas,* 539 U.S. 558, 568-571 (2003) (adopting plaintiffs' and historians' understanding of history).

5. What do you think of Alabama's brief in *Roper*? Is it a reasonable attempt to force the Court to face the consequences of a potential ruling in Simmons' favor or an inappropriate attempt to play on base emotions of fear and vengeance? Is it effective? On the last point, note that the defenders of the juvenile death penalty were able to win the vote of one of the two swing Justices whose support they needed to prevail and that both the majority and one of the two dissents cited the Alabama brief. *See Roper v. Simmons,* 543 U.S. 551, 572 (2005); *id.* at 608, 618-619 (Scalia, J., dissenting).

6

Oral Argument

After the briefs on the merits have been filed in a case before the Court, the Court hears oral argument in the case. The oral argument is an important stage of the decision-making process strategically and symbolically.

The oral argument has strategic importance for three reasons. For one thing, oral argument is the first time all the Justices gather to discuss the case. For another thing, oral argument enables the Justices to question the attorneys and the attorneys to respond. Third, oral argument occurs shortly before the conference at which the Justices cast preliminary votes on the case and at which opinion-writing assignments are made. In short, the oral argument has distinctive features and occurs at an important stage of the decision-making process.

Oral argument also has symbolic importance, largely because it is the only part of the decision-making process open to the public. This public part of the process can be dramatic, as the Justices come face to face with counsel for the parties whose case the Court will decide. In addition, oral argument lets the public see what arguments are made to influence the Justices and how the Justices respond to them. Oral argument thus provides a window into a dynamic and rather improvisational part of the decision-making process.

The Justices recognize the symbolic importance of oral argument. As a result, we can infer from oral argument the image of the Court and of themselves that the Justices want to cultivate among the public.

This chapter explores oral argument in five sections. Section A sets the stage by describing the physical setting in which oral argument occurs. Section B addresses the Court's Rules on oral argument. Section C's material discusses what *should* happen before and during oral argument, and Section D's material gives you a sense of what *does* happen during oral argument. Finally, material in Section E assesses the impact of oral argument on the Court's decisions.

A. SETTING THE STAGE

As discussed in Chapter 8.B, the Court does not televise oral arguments. Thus, if you want to see and hear an oral argument, you must go to Washington, D.C. where the Court hears oral arguments starting each year on the first Monday in October and ending, typically, the following April. The physical setting for oral argument warrants a brief description because it influences public perception of the Court and helps you visualize the process.

1. The Supreme Court Building

Jeffrey Toobin, The Nine: Inside the Secret World of the Supreme Court

1 (2008)

The architect Cass Gilbert had grand ambitions for his design of a new home for the Supreme Court—what he called "the greatest tribunal in the world, one of the three great elements of our national government." Gilbert knew that the approach to the Court, as much as the structure itself, would define the experience of the building, but the site presented a challenge. . . . [I]n 1928 Congress had designated for the Court a cramped and asymmetrical plot of land, wedged tightly between the Capitol and the Library of Congress. How could Gilbert convey to visitors the magnitude and importance of the judicial process taking place within the Court's walls?

The answer, he decided, was steps. Gilbert pushed back the wings of the building, so that the public face of the building would be a portico with a massive and imposing stairway. Visitors would not have to walk a long distance to enter, but few would forget the experience of mounting those forty-four steps to the double row of eight massive columns supporting the roof. The walk up the stairs would be the central symbolic experience of the Supreme Court, a physical manifestation of the American march to justice. The stairs separated the Court from the everyday world—and especially from the earthly concerns of the politicians in the Capitol—and announced that the justices would operate, literally, on a higher plane. . . .

Notes and Questions

1. Toobin follows this description with the remark that, despite Cass Gilbert's intention to depict the Court as operating "on a higher plane" than the political branches, "The truth about the Court has always been more complicated." Do you believe the Court is generally above the political fray? In any event, would it be better for the Court to be housed in a building that is less apparently elevated? Why or why not?

2. Gilbert's aim in designing the front entrance has arguably been affected by current building entry and entrance procedures, under which the doors at the top of the front steps can no longer be used to enter the building. Today, the public enters by a side entrance. Do you think it's a problem that the public can no longer use the front door? *See* Memorandum of Justice Breyer, with whom Justice Ginsburg joins, U.S. Supreme Court Journal, October Term 2009, at 831 (May 3, 2010) (statement opposing closing of front entrance).

3. One well-known feature of the Supreme Court building is the phrase engraved above the front entrance: "Equal Justice Under Law." Despite this egalitarian motto, the imposing design and scale of the building have earned it the nickname "the Marble Palace." *See, e.g.*, John Frank, *The Marble Palace: The Supreme Court in American Life* (1958). Chief Justice Harlan Stone is said to have remarked when the Justices first moved into the building in 1935 that "he felt like a beetle entering the temple of Karnak." William H. Rehnquist, *The Supreme Court* 12-13 (revised and updated ed. 2001). Is the conflict between the egalitarian motto and the grandeur of the building emblematic of actual tension between the ideal and the reality of access to justice? Do you think most members of the public believe that the Court is dedicated to "equal justice under law"?

2. The Supreme Court Courtroom

You will find the courtroom on the first floor of the Supreme Court building at the east end of the Great Hall. The courtroom is distinctive for its 44-foot-high ceiling; its wall friezes depicting "great lawgivers of history"; and the red velvet curtains behind the judges' bench, from which the Justices emerge to take their seats on argument days.

Argument days begin promptly at 10 A.M, according to the large clock that sits high on the wall behind the Justices. At that time, the Marshal pounds the gavel, commands that "all rise," and intones the traditional cry:

> The Honorable, the Chief Justice and the Associate Justices of the Supreme Court of the United States. Oyez! Oyez! Oyez! All persons having business before the Honorable, the Supreme Court of the United States, are admonished to draw near and give their attention, for the Court is now sitting. God save the United States and this Honorable Court!

The Justices emerge from behind the red velvet curtains and stand by their respective seats until the Marshal pounds the gavel again, at which point the Justices and everyone else sit down.

The bench is "wing shaped," rather than straight, so the Justices who sit at each end of the bench can see each other better than would be possible on a straight bench. Seating is by seniority. The Chief Justice, deemed most senior by virtue of his office, sits in the center. The next most senior Justice sits to the immediate left of the Chief Justice (as viewers see the bench); the Justice third in seniority sits to the Chief's immediate right; and so on. The current seating arrangement is as follows:

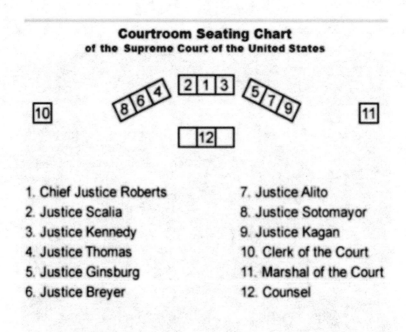

Courtroom Seating Chart
of the Supreme Court of the United States

1. Chief Justice Roberts
2. Justice Scalia
3. Justice Kennedy
4. Justice Thomas
5. Justice Ginsburg
6. Justice Breyer
7. Justice Alito
8. Justice Sotomayor
9. Justice Kagan
10. Clerk of the Court
11. Marshal of the Court
12. Counsel

The Court usually allows one hour for oral argument of each case; each side has 30 minutes.[1] The counsel for petitioner argues first; respondent argues second; petitioner may then offer rebuttal. When counsel have finished their arguments, the Chief Justice announces, "The case is submitted." Thus ends the public part of the Court's decision-making process.

B. COURT RULES

Oral argument is addressed in the Court's Rules 27 and 28. Please read Rule 27 in Appendix B. It addresses the calendaring of oral argument and the consolidation of cases for oral argument. Rule 28 addresses additional aspects of oral argument. It is reproduced below.

Rule 28. Oral Argument

1. Oral argument should emphasize and clarify the written arguments in the briefs on the merits. Counsel should assume that all Justices have read the briefs before oral argument. Oral argument read from a prepared text is not favored.

2. The petitioner or appellant shall open and may conclude the argument. A cross-writ of certiorari or cross-appeal will be argued with the initial writ of certiorari or appeal as one case in the time allowed for that one case, and the Court will advise the parties who shall open and close.

3. Unless the Court directs otherwise, each side is allowed one-half hour for argument. Counsel is not required to use all the allotted time. Any request for additional time to argue shall be presented by motion under Rule 21 in time to be considered at a scheduled Conference prior to the date of oral argument and no later than 7 days after the respondent's or appellee's brief on the merits is filed, and shall set out specifically and concisely why the case cannot be presented within the half-hour limitation. Additional time is rarely accorded.

4. Only one attorney will be heard for each side, except by leave of the Court on motion filed in time to be considered at a scheduled Conference prior to the date of oral argument and no later than 7 days after the respondent's or appellee's brief on the merits is filed. Any request for divided argument shall be presented by motion under Rule 21 and shall set out specifically and concisely why more than one attorney should be allowed to argue. Divided argument is not favored.

5. Regardless of the number of counsel participating in oral argument, counsel making the opening argument shall present the case fairly and completely and not reserve points of substance for rebuttal.

---

1. The Court made a notable, recent exception to the customary, one-hour allotment of time for oral argument in a set of cases challenging the constitutionality of the Patient Protection and Affordable Care Act, legislation popularly known as the "Obamacare Act." In those cases, the Court allocated a total of six hours, spread over three days, to oral arguments. *See Nat'l Fed'n of Indep. Bus. v. Sebelius*, ___ U.S. ___, 132 S. Ct. 1618 (2012).

6. Oral argument will not be allowed on behalf of any party for whom a brief has not been filed.

7. By leave of the Court, and subject to paragraph 4 of this Rule, counsel for an *amicus curiae* whose brief has been filed as provided in Rule 37 may argue orally on the side of a party, with the consent of that party. In the absence of consent, counsel for an *amicus curiae* may seek leave of the Court to argue orally by a motion setting out specifically and concisely why oral argument would provide assistance to the Court not otherwise available. Such a motion will be granted only in the most extraordinary circumstances.

Notes and Questions

1. Rule 28 refers to "petitioners" and "respondents," which are, of course, the designations used for the parties in cases within the Court's certiorari jurisdiction. Rule 28 also refers to "appellants" and "appellees," which are the designations used for the parties in cases that come before the Court on appeal, rather than by certiorari. As discussed in Chapter 3, presently, appeals account for an extremely small portion of the Court's docket.

2. Rule 28.7 allows counsel for *amicus curiae* to argue by leave of the Court. In practice, the Court seldom allows counsel for an *amicus* to argue except when the *amicus* is the United States or a state. States seldom seek time to argue as *amici*. In contrast, the United States regularly seeks and is granted leave to present oral argument as an *amicus*. For example, the United States will ordinarily seek argument time as an *amicus* in criminal cases that come to the Court from a state court system and present issues under the Fourth, Fifth, or Sixth Amendment (since the Court's resolution of those issues will generally apply equally to federal criminal cases). In that example, the United States would typically seek and be granted leave to take ten minutes of the state's oral argument time to present oral argument as *amicus* supporting the state's position. The oral argument for the United States would ordinarily be presented by a lawyer in the Solicitor General's Office. Although the state's argument time would be reduced from the usual 30 minutes to 20 minutes (to accommodate the Solicitor General's argument time), states usually believe it is valuable to have the federal government's support at oral argument, even at the cost of their own argument time.

C. WHAT SHOULD HAPPEN BEFORE AND AT ORAL ARGUMENT

The material in this section describes what lawyers should do when preparing for and presenting oral argument to the Court. The material includes guidance from the Court itself, the Justices, and experienced Supreme Court advocates.

1. The Court's Guide for Counsel

The Clerk of the Court publishes a guide for counsel with cases before the Court. The guide is especially useful for lawyers who have not previously argued before the Court. Below is the portion of the guide that addresses oral argument.

U.S. Supreme Court, Guide for Counsel in Cases to Be Argued Before the Supreme Court of the United States

(October Term 2011)

II. ORAL ARGUMENT

A. Scheduling and Preparation

Oral arguments are normally conducted from October through April. A two-week session is held each month with arguments scheduled on Monday through Wednesday of each week.... The Court generally hears argument in two cases (hours) each day beginning at 10 a.m. and adjourns after the argument in the second case ends, usually around noon. If more than two cases are to be argued in one day, the Court will reconvene at 1 p.m. to hear the additional arguments....

B. Day of Argument

... Arguing counsel and co-counsel should enter the building through the southwest door. It is located on the ground level, to your right as you face the front of the building. Do not walk up the front steps.... Arguing counsel and co-counsel who will be seated at the counsel tables for cases to be argued in the morning must report to the Lawyers' Lounge on the first floor of the Court between 9:00 and 9:15 a.m. on the day of argument. The Clerk will brief counsel at this time on Courtroom protocol, answer any last minute questions they may have, and issue counsel and co-counsel identification cards. Arguing counsel and co-counsel whose cases are scheduled for the afternoon session need not be present in the morning for the Clerk's briefing or the oral arguments. They must report to the Lawyers' Lounge between 12:15 and 12:30 p.m. for a briefing by the Clerk. . . .

Appropriate attire for counsel is conservative business dress in traditional dark colors (*e.g.,* navy blue or charcoal gray). . . .

The Court has a large, residential corps of journalists who follow its docket closely. No interviews or news cameras are permitted in the Court building; however, they are allowed on the front plaza on argument days, where reporters frequently wait . . . to talk to counsel after argument has concluded. . . .

C. Seating for Counsel . . .

The quill pens at counsel table are gifts to you—a souvenir of your having argued before the highest Court in the land. Take them with you. They are hand-crafted and usable as writing quills.

It is appropriate for co-counsel to occupy the arguing counsel's chair when the latter is presenting argument. Except in extraordinary circumstances, co-counsel do not pass notes to arguing counsel during argument. . . .

D. In the Courtroom—Order of Business

. . . The Marshal of the Court cries the Court in at 10 a.m. The Chief Justice makes routine announcements (*e.g.,* orders are released). Opinions, if any, are then released. The authoring Justice will read a summary of the opinion; this takes about five minutes for each opinion. Motions for admission to the Bar occur next. The Chief Justice will then announce that the Court will hear argument in the first case for argument that day. If you are counsel for the petitioner, you should proceed promptly to the lectern—do not wait for the Chief Justice to issue an invitation. Remain standing at the lectern and say nothing until the Chief Justice recognizes you by name. Once he has done so, you may acknowledge the Court by the usual: "Mr. Chief Justice and may it please the Court. . . ." Do not introduce yourself or co-counsel. Under the present practice, "Mr." is only used in addressing the Chief Justice. Others are referred to as "Justice Scalia," "Justice Ginsburg," or "Your Honor." Do not use the title "Judge." If you are in doubt about the name of a Justice who is addressing you, it is better to use "Your Honor" rather than mistakenly address the Justice by another Justice's name.

E. Your Argument

1. Preparation . . .

Remember that briefs are different from oral argument. . . . Oral arguments are not designed to summarize briefs, but to present the opportunity to stress the main issues of the case that might persuade the Court in your favor.

It has been said that preparing for oral argument at the Supreme Court is like packing your clothes for an ocean cruise. You should lay out all the clothes you think you will need, and then return half of them to the closet. When preparing for oral argument, eliminate half of what you initially planned to cover. Your allotted time passes quickly, especially when numerous questions come from the Court. Be prepared to skip over much of your planned argument and stress your strongest points.

Some counsel find it useful to have a section in their notes entitled "cut to the chase." They refer to that section in the event that most of their time has been consumed by answering questions posed by the Justices. . . .

If your argument focuses on a statute, regulation, or ordinance, be sure that the law is printed in full in one of your pleadings so that you can refer the Justices to it and they can be looking at it during your argument.

Do not bring numerous volumes to the lectern. One notebook will suffice. Please note that a legal-sized pad does not fit on the lectern properly. Turning pages in a notebook appears more professional than flipping pages of a legal pad. . . .

Know the record, especially the procedural history of the case. Be prepared to answer a question like: "Why didn't you make a motion for summary judgment?" You have the opportunity to inform the Justices about facts of which they are not aware. Justices frequently ask: "Is that in the record?" Be prepared to answer. It is impressive when you can respond with the volume and page where the information is located. It is also quite effective to quote from the joint appendix. Do not make assertions about issues or facts not in the record.

Know your client's business. One counsel representing a large beer brewing corporation was asked the following by a Justice during argument: "What is the difference between beer and ale?" The question had little to do with the issues, but the case involved the beer brewing business. Counsel gave a brief, simple, and clear answer that was understood by everyone in the Courtroom. He knew the business of his client, and it showed. The Justice who posed the question thanked counsel in a warm and gracious manner. . . .

The following are excellent sources of information for arguing counsel: *Making Your Case, the Art of Persuading Judges,* by Justice Antonin Scalia and Bryan Garner; Chapter 14, Oral Argument, *Supreme Court Practice* (9th ed.), by Eugene Gressman, Kenneth Geller, Stephen Shapiro, Timothy Bishop, and Edward Hartnett; and *Supreme Court Appellate Advocacy: Mastering Oral Argument,* by David Frederick.

2. Time

Your argument time is normally limited to 30 minutes. You need not use all your time. . . .

Unless you make other arrangements with the Marshal, the white light on the lectern will be activated when five minutes of your allotted time remains. The red light will be activated when your time has expired. Upon request prior to argument, the Marshal will flash the white light at a time requested by counsel.

When the Marshal activates the white light you should be prepared to stop your argument in five minutes. When the red light comes on, terminate your argument immediately and sit down. If you are answering a question from a Justice, you may continue your answer and respond to any additional questions from that Justice or any other Justice. In this situation you need not worry that the red light is on. Do not, however, continue your argument after the red light comes on.

In a divided argument, it is effective for counsel to inform the Court of their argument plan. For example, petitioner's counsel might say: "I will cover the Fourth Amendment aspects of this case and counsel for the *amicus* will argue the Fifth Amendment issues."

Regardless of how many attorneys argue in a case, only one is permitted to present rebuttal argument. If two counsel argue for the petitioner, the one who argued first should be the one to present rebuttal. A petitioner's counsel who wants to reserve time for rebuttal should, about five minutes before the allotted time is to expire (white light), say, "If there are no further questions, I would like to reserve the remainder of my time for rebuttal." Petitioner's counsel then sits down and the Chief Justice calls on the respondent's counsel for argument. Respondent's counsel proceeds to the lectern, waits for acknowledgment by the Chief Justice, and then opens with: "Mr. Chief Justice and may it please the Court." When respondent's counsel has finished and gathered all items from the lectern, petitioner's counsel should return to the lectern and wait for acknowledgment by the Chief Justice at which time he will say, *e.g.*, "You have five minutes remaining." You may begin your rebuttal at this time without having to repeat, "Mr. Chief Justice and may it please the Court."

Promptly and quietly vacate the front argument table after the Chief Justice announces that "The case is submitted." . . .

3. Protocol

The Supreme Court is not a jury. A trial lawyer tries to persuade a jury with facts and emotion. At this Court, counsel should try to persuade the Court by arguing points of law.

Your argument should focus only on the question or questions presented in the petition that was granted. Do not deviate from it.

Ordinarily, the Justices will know whether you are making your first argument before the Court. Be assured that some first-time arguments have been far superior to presentations from counsel who have argued several times.

As noted, if your argument focuses on a statute, regulation, or ordinance, be sure that the law is printed in full in one of your pleadings so that you can refer the Justices to it and they can be looking at it during your argument.

Counsel for the petitioner need not recite the facts of the case before beginning argument. The facts are set out in the briefs, which have been read by the Justices.

You should speak in a clear, distinct manner, and try to avoid a monotone delivery. Speak into the microphone so that your voice will be audible to the Justices and to ensure a clear recording. Avoid having notes or books touch the microphones, since this interferes with the recording process. Under no circumstances should you read your argument from a prepared script.

You should not attempt to enhance your argument time by a rapid fire, staccato delivery.

Exhibits can be useful in appropriate cases, but be very careful to ensure that any exhibit you use is appealing, accurate, and capable of being read from a distance of about 25 feet. Be sure to explain to the Court precisely what the exhibit is. Counsel must advise the Clerk of the intent to use an exhibit as soon as possible. For a good example of an exhibit used at oral argument in this Court, see *Shaw v. Reno*, 509 U. S. 630, 658 (1993).

You should be knowledgeable about what is and is not in the record in your case. Justices frequently ask counsel if particular matters are in the record. If you are asked a question that will require you to refer to matters not in the record, your answer should so state; then proceed to respond to the question unless advised otherwise by the Justice.

Never interrupt a Justice who is addressing you. Give your full time and attention to that Justice—do not look down at your notes, and do not look at your watch or at the clock located high on the wall behind the Justices. If you are speaking and a Justice interrupts you, cease talking immediately and listen.

When a Justice makes a point that is adverse to you, do not "stonewall." Either concede the point, as appropriate, or explain why the point is not dispositive of your case and proceed with your argument.

Do not "correct" a Justice unless the matter is essential. In one case a Justice asked a question and mentioned "waiver." Counsel responded by stating that a "forfeiture" rather than a "waiver" was involved. The distinction was irrelevant, but the comment generated more questions and wasted valuable time.

Be careful to use precise language. In one case, counsel stated, "The Supremacy Clause does not apply in this case." A Justice responded: "The Supremacy Clause applies in every case. Perhaps counsel meant that the statute in question does not conflict with the Supremacy Clause."

Be careful not to use the "lingo" of a business or activity. The Court may not be familiar with such terms, even if widely understood within that business or activity. For example, you should not say "double-link connector" or "section 2b claims" unless you have explained what those terms mean. Similarly, do not use the familiar name of your client during argument. For instance, say "Mr. Clark denied the request" rather than "Buddy denied the request."

Strunk and White warned us to "avoid fancy words" when writing. The same is true for oral argument. Counsel used the word "orthogonal" in a recent case. This caused a minor disruption that detracted from the argument. Counsel could just as easily have said "right angle."

Do not refer to an opinion of the Court by saying: "In Justice Ginsburg's opinion." You should say: "In the Court's opinion, written by Justice Ginsburg."

If you quote a document verbatim (*e.g.*, a statute or ordinance), tell the Court where to find the document (*e.g.*, page 4, appendix B to the petition).

Attempts at humor usually fall flat. The same is true of attempts at familiarity. For example, do not say something like: "This is similar to a case argued when I clerked here." Do not denigrate opposing counsel. It is far more appropriate and effective to be courteous to your opponent.

Avoid emotional oration and loud, impassioned pleas. A well-reasoned and logical presentation without resort to histrionics is easier for listeners to comprehend. Do not argue facts. Argue to the question or questions of law presented in the petition for a writ of certiorari that was granted.

Counsel for respondents are often effective when they preface their argument by answering questions that petitioner's counsel could not answer or answered incorrectly or ineffectively. This can often get you off to a positive start.

If your opponent is persuasive on a certain theme during argument, especially one that was not anticipated, you should address that issue at the outset of argument or rebuttal argument rather than adhere to a previously planned presentation. You take a great risk if you ignore a persuasive point made by your opponent.

Rebuttal can be very effective. But you can be even more effective if you thoughtfully waive it when your opponent has not been impressive. If you have any rebuttal, make it and stop. There is no requirement that you use all your allotted time.

4. Answering Questions

You should assume that all of the Justices have read the briefs filed in your case, including *amicus curiae* briefs. Expect questions from the Court, and make every effort to answer the questions directly. If at all possible, say "yes" or "no," and then expand upon your answer if you wish. If you do not know the answer, it is suggested you so state. On one occasion, instead of responding to a question from a Justice, an attorney posed a question to the Justice, only to have another Justice chastise him for doing so.

Anticipate what questions the Justices will ask and be prepared to answer those questions. If a case with issues similar to yours was previously argued in this Court, consider obtaining a transcript of the oral argument in that case to review. That might help you anticipate questions that those Justices who heard the previous case might ask in your case.

If a counsel stumbles on a question from the Court or does not fully answer it, it is a good tactic for an *amicus curiae* counsel supporting that counsel's side to begin argument by repeating the question and answering it correctly and completely. The *amicus* counsel will have had time to reflect on the initial question and perhaps develop a better answer.

A Justice will often ask counsel seeking to establish a new precedent: "Do any cases from this Court support your position?" Be ready for the question, but be careful to cite only those cases that truly support your position. Do not distort the meaning of a precedent. The author of the opinion is likely to be a member of the Court and to have a remarkable memory of exactly what the opinion says. If you are relying on a case that was announced by a "plurality opinion," be sure to mention that there was no "opinion for the Court" in the case.

In appropriate cases, suggest to the Court that bright-line rules should be adopted and suggest what they should be.

If a question seems hostile to you, do not answer with a short and abrupt response. It is far more effective to be polite and accurate.

If a Justice poses a hypothetical question, you should respond to that question on the facts given therein. In the past, several attorneys have responded: "But those aren't the facts in this case!" The Justice posing the question is aware that there are different facts in your case, but wants and expects your answer to the hypothetical question. Answer, and thereafter, if you feel it is necessary, say something such as: "However, the facts in this case are different," or "The facts in the hypothetical question are not the facts in this case." A "yes" or "no" answer might be suitable for a narrow question. Nevertheless, your answer should be carefully tailored to fit the question. A simple "yes" or "no" in response to a broad question might unintentionally concede a point and prompt a follow-on question or statement which ultimately may be damaging to your position.

When other Justices ask questions before you complete your answer to the first Justice, you should take a commonsense approach in determining which of the questions to answer first. You might consider responding to the last question, indicating, if you believe it to be the proper thing to do, that you will answer that question first before completing your answer to the prior question. Alternatively, you may indicate to the last questioner that it would assist you in making your response if you could first conclude your answer to the first Justice's question, at which time you would complete your response to the first Justice. There is no definite rule of protocol. However, ordinarily if two Justices start to speak at once, the junior Justice will withdraw in deference to the senior. Perhaps by analogy you could respond to the senior Justice's question first, and then address questions from junior Justices. . . .

Notes and Questions

1. Are you surprised by how directive the guide is in discussing oral argument? Why do you think it is so directive?

2. What pointers does the guide mention more than once? More generally, what are the main takeaways from the guide?

2. Advice from Experts

The material in this section comes from experienced practitioners and the Justices. They discuss the purposes of oral argument and how to prepare and present oral argument to achieve those purposes. In evaluating the perspectives of the practitioners and the Justices, you may benefit from considering the view of John W. Davis, a former Solicitor General who argued 140 cases before the Court. In a famous article on oral argument, Davis likened oral argument to archery and fishing:

> . . . [A] discourse on the argument of an appeal would come with superior force from a judge who is in his judicial person the target and the trier of the argument than from a random archer like myself. Or, supposing fishes had the gift of speech, who would listen to a fisherman's weary discourse on flycasting, the shape and color of the fly, the size of the tackle, the length of the line, the merit of different rod makers and all the other tiresome stuff that fisherman talk about, if the fish himself could be induced to give his views on the most effective methods of approach. For after all it is the fish that the angler is after and all his recondite learning is but the hopeful means to that end. . . .

John W. Davis, *The Argument of an Appeal*, 26 A.B.A. J. 895, 895 (1940); *see also* William Henry Harbaugh, *Lawyer's Lawyer: the Life of John W. Davis* 531 (1973) (listing Davis's 140 arguments).

a. The Purposes of Oral Argument

Stephen M. Shapiro, Oral Argument in the Supreme Court of the United States

33 Cath. U. L. Rev. 529, 529-532 (1984)

. . . [I]t is useful for the attorney, facing his or her first argument in the Supreme Court, to try to envision what it is that the Justices expect to accomplish through oral argument, and likewise to bear in mind what experienced advocates seek to accomplish. . . .

. . . [T]he Justices utilize the oral argument process to achieve the following objectives:

a) *Clarification of the record.* In nearly every argument, the Justices attempt to bring into better focus important record facts, including details of relevant pleadings, findings at the trial or administrative level, holdings of the lower courts, steps taken to preserve points in the trial court and on appeal, and the adequacy of the specification of questions presented in the petition for certiorari or jurisdictional statement.

b) *Clarification of the substance of claims.* Despite the best efforts of the brief writer, it is common for the Justices to insist upon a further explanation concerning the precise nature of the claims presented to the Court. What exactly is counsel contending in the Supreme Court?

c) *Clarification of the scope of claims.* More so than most lower courts, the Supreme Court is interested in the scope of arguments and principles relied on by the parties. How far does the principle go that counsel invokes? This, of course, is the domain of the hypothetical question, which the Justices propound with frequency during oral argument.

d) *Examination of the logic of claims.* The Justices commonly require attorneys to explain apparent inconsistencies between oral statements and positions articulated in the briefs, or discrepancies between findings made by the lower courts and positions taken in the Supreme Court. Still more frequently, the Justices require counsel to explain how his or her position can be reconciled with past relevant decisions of the Supreme Court, or the plain language, structure, or history of controlling statutes.

e) *Examination of the practical impact of claims.* Since the Justices are responsible for rendering decisions that embody wise policy consistent with the intent of Congress and the framers of the Constitution, they persistently inquire into the practical impact of the positions advocated by counsel. Will a particular position impose excessive burdens on law enforcement officers, interfere unreasonably with the freedoms of private citizens, or hamper the legitimate activities of honest businessmen?

f) *Lobbying for or against particular positions.* Several of the Justices use oral argument as an early opportunity to make known their tentative views to the other Justices, and to express, at least indirectly, their agreement or disagreement with the submission of counsel. Thus, to some extent, the argument serves as an early conference, where the views of both lawyers and judges can be expressed and debated. . . .

It also is useful to consider the objectives of oral argument from the point of view of experienced Supreme Court advocates. . . .

a) *Motivating the Justices to view the case sympathetically.* Every advocate is, in an important sense, a salesperson, and the object of advocacy is persuasion of other human beings. Oral argument is the lawyer's only opportunity to meet the decision-makers eye to eye, without "screening" from law clerks. . . . Oral argument gives the advocate the opportunity to personally motivate the Justices to rule in his or her favor by conveying the impression that fairness, common sense, and the general public interest strongly support his position.

b) *Simplifying information needed to decide the case in counsel's favor.* Oral argument offers the opportunity to separate out the truly important, pivotal considerations in a case, and to give the Justices the few specific "implements of decision" which are needed to resolve the case in a correct manner. Counsel must bear in mind that the Justices cast their votes in conference only a few days after hearing oral argument. . . . It is essential, therefore, to give the Justices the few specific points that are needed to resolve the case correctly, and which rem[ain] stuck in the Justices' minds until conference.

c) *Laying to rest concerns or difficulties that the Justices express.* In nearly every oral argument, the Justices express their misgivings, concerns, and doubts about counsel's submission. Some of them may tell counsel precisely what their pivotal uncertainty is and invite him to dispel that uncertainty. This, of course, is an opportunity to lay to rest not only their concerns, but also those of other Justices who share the same point of view. Although the observation is hardly original, it is important to reiterate that oral argument is counsel's only opportunity to effectively "participate in the conference" and come to grips with the real questions that trouble the Court.

d) *Making a positive and memorable personal impression.* Cases in the Supreme Court frequently are close, and the Justices look to counsel for guidance and leadership. If the Court has confidence in counsel, this will smooth the way to acceptance of counsel's arguments. By contrast, an attorney who makes a poor personal impression necessarily raises obstacles to acceptance of his or her contentions. The personal impression that one must convey is that of respectfulness, utmost candor, reliability, complete knowledge of the record, and sincere conviction. . . .

e) *Demonstrating that the argument hangs together under fire.* Oral argument is the anvil on which a solid position is hammered out and confirmed—or shattered entirely by repeated blows. Effective advocates use oral argument to dramatically demonstrate that his position is sound. Thus, despite difficult questions and criticisms, there always is a logical response and the argument hangs together in a coherent way. There are, in short, no hidden defects, gaps in reasoning, or unanticipated consequences. Some arguments fall apart entirely under the pressure of argument. Other arguments, which have been carefully honed in advance, are strengthened and confirmed by the process of debate. . . .

William H. Rehnquist, The Supreme Court

244-245 (revised and updated ed. 2001)

There is more to oral argument than meets the eye—or the ear. Nominally, it is the hour allotted to opposing counsel to argue their respective positions to the judges who are to decide the case. Even if it were in fact largely a formality, I think it would still have the value that many public ceremonies have: It forces the judges who are going to decide the case and the lawyers who represent the clients whose fates will be affected by the outcome of the decision to look at one another for an hour, and talk back and forth about how the case should be decided. . . .

. . . [A] second important function of oral argument can be gleaned from the fact that it is the only time before conference discussion of the case later in the week when all of the judges are expected to sit on the bench and concentrate on one particular case. The judges' questions, although nominally directed to the attorney arguing the case, may in fact be for the benefit of their colleagues. A good advocate will recognize this fact and make use of it during his presentation. Questions may reveal that a particular judge has a misunderstanding about an important fact in the case, or perhaps reads a given precedent differently from the way in which the attorney thinks it should be read. . . . Each attorney arguing a case ought to be much, much more familiar with the facts and the law governing it than the judges who are to decide it. Each of the nine members of our Court must prepare for argument in at least two cases a day, on three successive days of each week. One can do his level best to digest from the briefs and other reading what he believes necessary to decide the case, and still find himself falling short in one aspect or another of either the law or the facts. Oral argument can cure these shortcomings. . . .

Notes and Questions

1. Chief Justice Rehnquist wrote that oral argument can help a Justice decide the case by providing information that the Justice has not otherwise been able to garner. Other Justices have similarly emphasized the value of oral argument in helping them do their job of deciding cases. Justice Byron White explained:

[Oral argument] . . . is [when] all of the Justices are working on the case together, having read the briefs and anticipating that they will have to vote very soon, and attempting to clarify their own thinking and perhaps that of their colleagues.

Consequently, <u>we treat lawyers as a resource rather than as orators</u> who should be heard out according to their own desires.

Byron White, *The Work of the Supreme Court: A Nuts and Bolts Description*, N.Y. State Bar J. 346, 383 (Oct. 1982); *see also* John M. Harlan, *What Part Does the Oral Argument Play in the Conduct of an Appeal?*, 41 Cornell L.Q. 6, 7 (1955) ("[T]he job of courts . . . is to search out the truth . . . and that is ultimately the job of lawyers, too. And in that joint effort, the oral argument gives an opportunity for interchange between court and counsel which the briefs do not give."). This suggested role of the advocate as an aid to the Justices' decision making implies that oral argument can affect the outcome of the case, an issue examined separately later in Section E of this chapter.

   2. Chief Justice Rehnquist wrote that Justices sometimes use oral argument to influence each other. More recently, Justice Sotomayor described one of the purposes of oral argument as providing an opportunity for the Justices to hear each other's concerns about a case. Adam Liptak, *Sotomayor Reflects on First Years on Court*, N.Y. Times, Jan. 31, 2011, at A17. Stephen Shapiro likewise notes in the excerpt above that one of the Justices' objectives at oral argument is "[l]obbying for or against particular positions." *See also* David C. Frederick, *Supreme Court and Appellate Advocacy: Mastering Oral Argument* 6 (2003); E. Barrett Prettyman, Jr., *The Supreme Court's Use of Hypothetical Questions at Oral Argument*, 33 Cath. U. L. Rev. 555, 556 (1984). Is this an appropriate use of oral argument? Why or why not?

b. Preparing for Oral Argument

Richard H. Seamon, Preparing for Oral Argument in the United States Supreme Court

50 S.C. L. Rev. 603-614 (1999)

Because it is rare to encounter a cold Court these days, . . . [t]he advocate should . . . spend his time anticipating the Justices' questions and preparing answers to them. In doing so, the advocate must identify the small handful of key points that have to be made during oral argument. . . .

   Under the system that I developed, I kept my brief on the merits (including any reply brief) in front of me on the desk. I initially spent most of my time reviewing every single line of that brief with the objective of thinking up questions that each line might prompt the Justices to ask. . . .

   The review process should begin with the cover of the brief. The caption may prompt questions about, for example, who the parties are (including their domicile, their occupation, and their history); how they are related to one another (for example, by familial or corporate ties); why they brought this suit or were named as defendants; when they entered the lawsuit; why certain parties dropped out of the case; why entities or individuals whom one might have expected to be named in the case were not named; and whether the alignment of the parties reflected in the caption accurately reflects the various interests. The questions that Justices ask about the personnel of the lawsuit may be the same questions that occurred to the advocate upon entering the case.

   The first page of the brief, which sets forth the question or questions presented, can be another fruitful source of questions. Is there a dispute about what questions are properly before the Court? Were the questions properly raised below? Where in the record is it indicated that the questions were presented? How did the courts below rule on the questions presented? Where does the record reflect those rulings? Have the respondents restated the question presented? If so, what is the significance, if any, of that restatement? Have any amici curiae attempted to inject additional issues into the case? If so, what is counsel's position about whether and how those issues should be addressed? Are there any factual wrinkles that might prevent the Court from squarely addressing the questions presented? Are there potential legal barriers, such as the existence of an adequate and independent state ground for the judgment below? If the case presents more than one question, how are the questions related? Is it necessary for the Court to decide all of the issues? How might its ruling on one issue affect its ruling on another?

The next major section of the brief, the statement of jurisdiction, also can generate questions. The advocate should anticipate questions about the statutes and the procedural rules (including the timing rules) that governed the jurisdiction of each court below. Particular care is warranted for cases from a state-court system. Each such system has distinct features that may be second-nature to the advocate but strike a Justice as peculiar or, at least, sufficiently unfamiliar to prompt a question.

In reviewing the statement of facts, an advocate should do at least five things for each factual assertion. First, review the parts of the record that support the assertion. Second, recall whether the evidence supporting the assertion is weak or disputed. Third, identify what, if anything, the opponent (or its amici) says about that factual assertion. Fourth, determine how the assertion is relevant to the case. Fifth, consider how the legal analysis might change if the fact asserted were changed or omitted. Going through these steps will spark additional questions that should be written down.

The steps just described entail preparation of a defensive nature. The advocate must also scrutinize the statement of facts to devise an affirmative strategy. In particular, the advocate should decide which factual issues she should downplay and which she should play up. Facts to be downplayed will not be raised at oral argument except in response to questions from the bench, and those responses should be brief. Facts to be played up may well be raised before the Justices pose questions about them; or, if they are raised in response to questions, the advocate will dwell on those facts to the extent necessary to buttress a key point. . . .

The process of reviewing the argument section resembles that for reviewing the statement of facts. For each legal assertion, the advocate should reread the judicial opinion, statutory provision, regulatory provision, or constitutional provision that was cited in support of that assertion. For each source, the advocate should develop a one- or two-sentence description of the source; an explanation of how it supports the advocate's overall position in the case; responses to questions challenging the advocate's reliance on that source; responses to questions about the original reasoning underlying the source (including judicial decisions, which, notwithstanding *stare decisis*, are always open to reexamination); and responses to what the opponent or its amici have to say about the cited source or the assertion for which the advocate has cited it.

In reviewing the argument section, . . . the advocate must . . . begin to identify the weakest and strongest points in her argument. . . . [T]his identification process can be accomplished primarily by determining, respectively, which arguments are most likely to draw the most numerous and difficult questions and which responses will most effectively answer those questions.

Finally, the advocate should not ignore the "conclusion" section of the brief. More than anticipating, the advocate should *hope* to be asked what disposition is appropriate if the Court rules in her favor. The Court usually remands a case for further proceedings of some sort. The advocate should anticipate questions about what issues would remain to be sorted out if the Court decides the case favorably to the advocate; whether there is any dispute about which issues should be left for remand; how the Court's ruling on the issues before it might affect the resolution of issues left for remand; whether (and, if so, why) the Court should include in its opinion any instructions for the courts below on remand; and whether the Court might need, in further proceedings or in a future case, to address any of the issues left for remand.

... [This] process recognizes that the advocate's brief is one of several windows that the Justices use to view the case. The process forces the advocate to think about how to use the oral argument to convince the Justices that her brief provides the clearest, most complete view. ...

If the advocate follows the method described [above] ... she will have imagined dozens of questions. She also will have begun to see a pattern to the questions. The hardest questions cluster around one or a few issues. This is the heart of the case. Only after the advocate has identified these key issues can she prepare effective answers to all of the questions. An effective answer leads the Court to the advocate's statement of her position on the key points. ...

Every answer to a Justice's question may have as many as three parts: (1) a response of three words or fewer; (2) an explanation of item (1); and (3) a transition to a key point. ...

Questions warrant only an answer of one to three words when they are wholly and obviously incidental to the case. ...

Most questions sufficiently relate to the case that they deserve, in addition to an answer of three words or fewer, an explanation. However brief the explanation, it disrupts the argument enough that, after the explanation, some transition back to the affirmative presentation will be needed. The best transitions follow the explanation seamlessly. Making such transitions is most likely when the advocate has, before the argument, anticipated the question and decided on not only the point to which the answer to the question will lead, but also the smoothest, shortest path to get there. ...

In answering a question, the advocate should not always lead the Court back to the point that she was making when the question was asked. When an advocate displays a dogged determination to do so, the argument will feel jagged or inflexible to the Court. Furthermore, a question often gives the advocate a chance to change from one point to another point that has not yet been made or not yet been made adequately. This opportunity will be especially welcome when the advocate has finished, or failed to impress the Court, with the point that she was making when the question arose.

Accordingly, the advocate should plan more than one transition for each anticipated question. This does not require the composition of hundreds of transitions, even if the advocate has anticipated hundreds of questions. A single transition to key point "A" may work for many different questions. ...

Before the argument the advocate should spend as much time as possible talking about the case while on his feet. Well before the advocate feels ready to do so in front of others in a moot court, he should rehearse before an imaginary set of Justices. Indeed, the advocate can use this process not only to refine, but also to compose the substance of his presentation. ...

... The advocate should do the rehearsal in a quiet room where he will not be disturbed for a decent chunk of time. ... The objective ... is to give the advocate time and space to learn the spoken language of his argument. ...

After the rehearsal time ends, the advocate should sit down and analyze the argument. The advocate should write down any additional questions that he anticipated. The advocate should write down the answers that he composed during the rehearsal. Most importantly, the advocate should begin to identify the key points— the small handful of assertions to which the answer to all questions must lead in order for the Court to decide the case in the advocate's favor. The key points emerge with repeated rehearsals. By repeatedly thinking about where the answer to every conceivable question must go, the advocate will discover that only a limited number of destinations exist. These are the key issues—the heart of the case. By deciding how to make the answer to every conceivable question as concise as possible, the advocate will learn that his position on each key issue can be expressed in a single sentence. That sentence is a key point. Each point, of course, can be elaborated. The elaboration should answer the questions that cluster around the key point.

Once the advocate has identified the key points and the appropriate elaboration for each, he should then prepare and rehearse his affirmative presentation— the presentation that he would make if uninterrupted by questions. As a rule, the presentation should last not much longer than half of the time allotted for argument, which usually means fifteen minutes. Although this might seem too short, it is not. If the Court does not consume the additional time with questions, the advocate will win its gratitude by ending early. . . .

Notes and Questions

1. Chief Justice Roberts discussed oral argument preparation in an interview with Bryan A. Garner. *See* Bryan A. Garner, *Chief Justice John Roberts*, 13 Scribes J. Legal Writing 5 (2010). Justice Roberts specifically addressed the needs to identify the key points of the case and to develop transitions from one key point to another in response to questions from the bench:

> I don't care how complicated your case is; it usually reduces to at most four or five major points: here's the key precedent, here's the key language, here's the key regulation, here are the key consequences. You have four or five points. It's called A, B, C, D, and E. And when I'm practicing giving the argument, I'll go through it, and then I'll just shuffle those cards—A, B, C, D, and E—without knowing what they are. Then I'll start again and I'll look down. Okay, my first point is going to be C; and then from point C, I'm going to move to point E; and then from point E to point A. You develop practice on those transitions . . . because . . . [y]ou can't guarantee the first question you're going to get [from the bench is going to concern] . . . your first point. It may be on your third point. And . . . it's very awkward for somebody to say after they answer that third point, "And now I'd like to go back to the point I was making." . . . If you've practiced giving that argument [on your] third point and then [moving] to the first point . . . you can make those transitions, and . . . it makes the argument look fluid no matter what questions you get or in what order the points come out.

Id. at 23-24 (some bracketed text in original source; other bracketed text added).

2. Experienced Supreme Court advocate Carter Phillips recommends that, after the Court grants cert in a case, lawyers for the parties closely scrutinize the lower court opinion, because "[t]he focus of the Supreme Court's attention at the certiorari stage was examining precisely what the appellate court said." Carter G. Phillips, *Advocacy Before the United States Supreme Court*, 15 T.M. Cooley L. Rev. 177,

178 (1998). This recommendation may be particularly true considering that eight of the nine current Justices previously served as judges on the federal courts of appeals.

c. Delivery of Oral Argument

John G. Roberts, Jr., Thoughts on Presenting an Effective Oral Argument

School Law in Review 1997

First, in order to present an effective oral argument, the advocate would do well to ignore all guidance in the abstract and focus instead on the particulars of the case at hand. How a particular case can be effectively argued depends more on the case itself than on any generally applicable set of rules or guidelines. If an adverse decision in your case would truly lead to catastrophic consequences, by all means begin your oral presentation by highlighting those. If you believe the result you seek is compelled by a recent Supreme Court decision, ignore all advice about how to structure the perfect argument; begin and end with that controlling decision. How to play your hand depends largely on the cards you are dealt.

Be particularly skeptical of advice on how to argue an appeal from appellate judges.[2] . . . [M]ost judges give good advice on how to win a winning case. They all say to focus on the language of the statute in a statutory interpretation case, to discuss the facts fairly and objectively, to describe the holdings of any controlling cases. Good advice if the statutory language is helpful, the facts support your position and the precedent leans your way; perhaps not so good advice if the opposite is true. . . .

. . . What follows are procedural suggestions, approaches to handling oral argument that may be helpful no matter how easy, or how desperate, your case on the merits.

The central reality that informs these suggestions is that crowded dockets have severely limited the time available for oral argument. . . .

. . . Given the prevalence of "hot" benches and abbreviated argument times, . . . your preparation should place a premium on making points concisely: you should have at your fingertips 30-second answers to the most likely questions. . . . You will probably never have the chance to deliver an eloquent four-part, five-minute answer to a question, so do not prepare one. Doing so would not only be a waste of time, but trying to deliver such an answer may prevent you from getting out the meat of your reply, which is all the questioner is interested in in any event. Such extended discussion is for the written brief, not the oral argument.

The same concern needs to be kept in mind in deciding what points to attempt to make apart from responding to questions. . . .

. . . [S]ome arguments are more suited to oral presentation than others, and that factor needs to be taken into account in figuring out what you intend to say. Your brief may lead with a rather intricate roadmap through various regulatory provisions, and give second place to an analysis of the purposes of the regulatory program, while the oral argument may lead with the latter point—not because it is stronger than the first, but because it can be more effectively presented orally, while

---

2. John Roberts wrote this article before becoming an appellate judge.

an oral presentation of the first might engender only confusion. The brief and oral argument should work together and complement each other; they do not stand alone. . . .

THE [PETITIONER'S] ARGUMENT

Forget what you may have learned about how to structure an argument: a review of the facts, the holding below, and so on. There simply isn't enough time. Try to have one opening sentence that tees up the issue in an advantageous way, and then proceed immediately to the meat of the argument. Most judges today are well prepared . . . and will move you to the heart of the case with questions if you tarry on background. Much better to get there on your own terms, right away, rather than have even your first point dictated by a question.

THE [RESPONDENT'S] ARGUMENT

It is critically important for those arguing "bottom side" . . . to act, when they stand up, as if they have been listening to what was going on during their opponent's presentation. You are entering the unfolding drama midstream, and if you do not pick up the flow (redirecting it, if necessary), you will lose any chance to be effective. When arguing bottom side, prepare several different openings, and use the one that corresponds most closely to the court's interest, as revealed by the judges' questions to your adversary. If the court has just spent one-half hour peppering the other side with questions on issue B, you look silly and as if you have something to hide if you rise and announce that you would like to talk about issue A. By all means get to issue A if you need to, but deal with what the court is interested in first.

TIME

. . . [T]ry not to use all your time. Having the red light end your argument conveys the impression that you did not do what you set out to do, that you were derailed somewhere along the line, that you were still in the process of persuading rather than having accomplished that result. . . .

REBUTTAL

Always leave time for rebuttal, if only a minute. Even if you do not use it, it will help keep your opponent honest. If you are arguing at the Supreme Court and have not saved any rebuttal time, you're out of luck. . . .

If you are . . . [a respondent] and your opponent has saved time for rebuttal, you can often effectively turn that time to your advantage. If it fits in with the flow of your argument, you can end with an indirect challenge to the [petitioner] . . . , along the lines of "We argued in our brief that . . . [petitioner] had no answer to X, and we did not hear one in . . . [petitioner's] opening argument. Perhaps we will hear it in his remaining time." This can completely disarm your adversary, who has no doubt been preparing an effective rebuttal. He either has to respond to your challenge (and presumably, since you get to select the challenge, the response is weak), or he has effectively to concede your point, if he fails to respond and adheres to his (presumably stronger) planned rebuttal. Even then, in many instances the judges will say "Wait a minute. What is your answer to your opponent's last point?" As . . . [a respondent] you do not have the last word, but you may be able to select the last subject.

QUESTIONS

Perhaps the most important skill for today's appellate oralist is handling questions. . . . As noted earlier, you should have prepared very concise answers to every question you can reasonably anticipate. But be sure and listen carefully to the question before delivering one of your prepared replies: don't assume the judge is asking a question you're ready for, just because that makes the answering easier. And don't assume that the question is hostile—don't fire on the lifeboats coming to save you.

In fact, many lawyers react too defensively to questioning in general, as if the judge is trying to trip them up. These lawyers try to get in an answer that does no perceptible harm to their position and get back to what they were saying as soon as possible. That approach is wrong. Oral argument is not some quiz show, in which you win so long as you avoid any pitfalls the judges may try to spring on you. Try to react to what you can learn from the questions, and adjust your approach accordingly: If you had planned on making points A, B, and C, in that order, but the judges jump in with questions on point C, by all means deal with that first—and not just to the extent necessary to answer the questions. Such flexibility will give a more natural flow to your argument, and facilitate a meaningful dialogue with the bench. Indeed, in rehearsing, you should present your argument in every conceivable order—ABC, BCA, CAB BAC, ACB, CBA—precisely so that you can readily adjust it in response to the order of the questioning.

REFERENCES TO EXHIBITS, APPENDICES, AND THE LIKE

By all means *cite* to the record, if it helps you: "Petitioner contends that we failed to object to this evidence. Of course we objected, Joint Appendix page 32." But generally do *not* invite the court to *look* at the record, briefs, or anything else. You may think that would be more effective, but for some reason it almost never works out well. First, it takes an enormous amount of time. . . . Second, you automatically lose eye contact with [the judges]. . . . Third, you may never get that contact back. . . . If you give the correct reference, any judge who's interested can check it out later.

───────────────────

In this era of abbreviated argument times and prepared, active judges, the advocate must be flexible . . . The only way to develop the necessary flexibility is relentless preparation—at the end of the day, that remains the one overriding key to presenting an effective oral argument.

Notes and Questions

1. Then-attorney Roberts stresses the importance of the opening of your argument and explains that the crafting of the opening depends on the nature of the case. The opening seconds of the oral argument may be the only time when the advocate will have a chance to string a few sentences together without being interrupted by questions from the bench. Below are five openings. Which are effective? Which are not? What distinguishes the effective ones from the ineffective ones?

a. In *National Federation of Independent Business v. Sebelius*, 132 S. Ct. 2566 (2012), the Court upheld a federal statute—the so-called individual mandate—requiring people to buy health insurance. Paul Clement argued on behalf of those challenging the individual mandate on the ground, among others, that it exceeded Congress's power under the Commerce Clause. Clement opened his argument as follows:

> **MR. CLEMENT:**   Mr. Chief Justice and may it please the Court. The mandate represents an unprecedented effort by Congress to compel individuals to enter commerce in order to better regulate commerce.
>
> The Commerce Clause gives Congress the power to regulate existing commerce. It does not give Congress the far greater power to compel people to enter commerce to create commerce essentially in the first place.
>
> Now, Congress when it passed the statute did make findings about why it thought it could regulate the commerce here, and it justified the mandate as a regulation of the economic decision to forego the purchase of health insurance. That is a theory without any limiting principle.

b. In *Citizens United v. Federal Election Commission*, 558 U.S. 310 (2009), the Court held that the First Amendment's Free Speech Clause invalidated a federal statute that restricted corporations and unions from spending money for certain electioneering communications. On reargument, then-Solicitor General Elena Kagan opened the government's argument in support of the statute as follows:

> **GENERAL KAGAN:**   Mr. Chief Justice and may it please the Court:
>
> I have three very quick points to make about the government position. The first is that this issue has a long history. For over 100 years Congress has made a judgment that corporations must be subject to special rules when they participate in elections and this Court has never questioned that judgment.
>
> Number two—
>
> **JUSTICE SCALIA:**   Wait, wait, wait, wait. We never questioned it, but we never approved it, either. And we gave some really weird interpretations to the Taft-Hartley Act in order to avoid confronting the question.
>
> **GENERAL KAGAN:**   I will repeat what I said, Justice Scalia: For 100 years this Court, faced with many opportunities to do so, left standing the legislation that is at issue in this case—first the contribution limits, then the expenditure limits that came in by way of Taft-Hartley—and then of course in *Austin* [*v. Michigan Chamber of Commerce*] specifically approved those limits.
>
> **JUSTICE SCALIA:**   I don't understand what you are saying. I mean, we are not a self, self-starting institution here. We only disapprove of something when somebody asks us to. And if there was no occasion for us to approve or disapprove, it proves nothing whatever that we didn't disapprove it.

c. In *Arthur Andersen v. United States*, 544 U.S. 696 (2005), the Court reversed the conviction of the Arthur Andersen accounting firm. The conviction had been based on Arthur Andersen officials instructing employees of the Enron Corporation to destroy documents that were later sought by the Securities and Exchange Commission. The conviction rested on the federal witness tampering statute, which makes it a crime for someone to "knowingly ... corruptly persuade" another person to withhold or alter documents for use in an official proceeding. In reversing the conviction, the Court held that the trial court's jury instructions did not adequately convey the requirement that Arthur Andersen had acted with "the requisite consciousness of wrongdoing." *Id.* at 706. Maureen Mahoney, the attorney for Arthur Andersen, opened her argument on behalf of Arthur Andersen as follows:

MS. MAHONEY: Mr. Chief Justice, and may it please the Court:

The Government concedes that the destruction of documents in anticipation of a proceeding was not a crime in the fall of 2001 based upon a statutory rule that Congress had preserved for over a century. The central question in this case is whether Congress, nevertheless, intended to make a polite request to engage in that lawful conduct, a form of witness tampering punishable by ten years in prison. We ask this Court to reject that interpretation of the statute and to hold that Arthur Andersen did not commit a crime.

I'd like to turn first to the term "corruptly persuade" as it's used in Section 1512 and explain why Arthur Andersen's interpretation represents not only a reasonable reading, but the best reading of the language in the statute.

The first thing that we see when we look at the statutory context is that Congress did not prohibit—did not prohibit—all persuasion to destroy documents for the specific purpose of making them unavailable for use in an official proceeding. It did not, because it did not simply say, "Anyone who persuades a witness to do this has violated the statute." It added a very important limitation, and that is the word "corruptly"—"corruptly persuades."

So what kinds of requests are excluded from the definition? When is it that it's okay to persuade someone to destroy a document for use in an official proceeding? And the answer, we think, based on the traditional meaning of the term "corruptly," is that "corruptly" means that you have persuaded someone in a fashion that uses improper means, such as bribery, or you've asked the witness to violate duties imposed by other law, whether that's the duties imposed by contempt or the duties imposed by a whole range of statutes that govern the obligations of people in our society.

d. In *Kelo v. City of New London*, 545 U.S. 469 (2005), the Court held that the City of New London, Connecticut, took private property for a "public use," within the meaning of the Just Compensation Clause of the Fifth Amendment, when the City took property for the purpose of selling it to private developers. The City justified the taking on the ground that the developers would use the land to generate tax revenues for the economically depressed city. Scott G. Bullock was the attorney for Kelo and other property owner who challenged the taking on the ground that it was not for a "public use." Bullock began his argument as follows:

MR. BULLOCK: Justice O'Connor, and may it please the Court:

This case is about whether there are any limits on government's eminent domain power under the public use requirement of the Fifth Amendment. Every home, church or corner store would produce more tax revenue and jobs if it were a Costco, a shopping mall or a private office building. But if that's the justification for the use of eminent domain, then any city can take property anywhere within its borders for any private use that might make more money than what is there now.

e. In *Drye v. United States*, 528 U.S. 49 (1999), the Court held that the Internal Revenue Service could seize Rohn Drye's beneficial interest in a trust, despite Drye's exercise of a right under state law to disclaim an interest in the assets that formed the corpus of the trust. Counsel for Drye, Daniel Traylor, opened his argument by holding up a Bible and an apple, and stating as follows:

> **MR. TRAYLOR:**   Mr. Chief Justice, members of the Court, may it please the Court:
>   For our Socratic dialogue I am armed with a borrowed Gideon and the fruit. This is—these aids go right to the jugular of this case, and the genesis of the case, which is Chapter 3 of Genesis.
>   What we have here is, when the serpent extended the fruit to the offeree, free will said that the offeree had a right to accept or reject the gift. Assuming that that offeree was a tax delinquent, the Government's position is that their 6321 Federal tax lien attached at the moment that the serpent extended the fruit. That is not—
> **QUESTION:**   Well, of course, the IRS was not in Paradise.
> (Laughter.)

2. Roberts advises advocates to get quickly to the "meat" of the argument. In later remarks as Chief Justice, he suggested that this may entail tackling, head on, the strongest argument against the advocate's position. *See* Robert Barnes, *Chief Justice Counsels Humility*, Wash. Post, Feb. 6, 2007, at A15. Many other experts on oral advocacy before the Court similarly emphasize getting to the main point of your argument as soon as possible and sticking to it. Former Solicitor General Seth Waxman referred to it as "the kernel of the case—the one, two, or at the very most, three points that you must impress upon the court before you sit down." Seth P. Waxman, *In the Shadow of Daniel Webster: Arguing Appeals in the Twenty-First Century*, 3 J. App. Prac. & Process 521, 530 (2001); *see also* John W. Davis, *The Argument of an Appeal*, 26 A.B.A. J. 895, 897 (1940) ("More often than not there is in every case a cardinal point around which lesser points revolve like planets around the sun . . . a central fortress which if strongly held will make the loss of all the outworks immaterial."); John M. Harlan, *What Part Does the Oral Argument Play in the Conduct of an Appeal?*, 41 Cornell L.Q. 6, 8 (1955) ("Most cases have one or only a few master issues. In planning his oral argument the wise lawyer will ferret out and limit himself to the issues which are really controlling.").

3. Roberts, like many experts on oral appellate advocacy, says that effectively responding to questions from the bench is one of the most important skills. *See, e.g.,* Stephen M. Shapiro, *Oral Argument in the Supreme Court of the United States*, 33 Cath. U. L. Rev. 529, 542 (1984); *see also* Neil D. McFeeley & Richard J. Ault, *Supreme Court Oral Argument: An Exploratory Analysis*, 20 Jurimetrics J. 52 (1979) (empirical analysis of content of Justices' questions at oral argument). "From the standpoint of the bench," Chief Justice Charles Evans Hughes explained, "the desirability of questions is quite obvious as the judges are not there to listen to speeches but to decide the case. They have an irrepressible desire for immediate knowledge as to the points to be determined." Charles Evans Hughes, *The Supreme Court of the United States* 62 (1928). Stephen Shapiro offers this typology of questions and advice on how to handle them:

> a) *Questions that go to the heart of the case.* . . . [S]ome Justices ask questions which go to the central issue in the case. The answer to such a question may well determine the vote of the Justice asking the question and also may affect the judgment of other Justices who share the same point of view. . . . These critical questions . . . can be used as a springboard for development of related substantive points that counsel intends to cover during the argument.
> b) *Background questions.* Many questions during argument simply require a clarification of some record fact. Other questions manifest curiosity about matters such as

relevant geography, the identity of the judges below, or the votes cast by the judges below. Counsel should give a quick and accurate answer to such questions and move on without delay.

c) *Fencing or debating questions.* The Justices sometimes engage in extended debates with counsel, which may or may not relate to central matters in the case. Of course, counsel cannot cut off such debates, despite his belief that the matter is tangential. Nonetheless, one must avoid getting bogged down too long on a peripheral point. It is essential in this instance to give the best possible answer, and find a tactful way to get back to the main points.

d) *Humorous questions or observations.* Counsel should enjoy the remark and then get back to business. . . .

e) *Irrelevant questions.* It is not uncommon for counsel to hear questions which he believes are related only remotely to the dispositive issues in the case. In fact, however, the matter of relevance is personal and relative, and one should never display irritation over questions that appea[r] to be beside the point. Counsel should . . . give a brief response and then explain why the present case raises a "somewhat different issue."

f) *Hostile questions.* Counsel should assume from the very beginning that some of the Justices will present hostile or unfriendly questions, manifesting their disagreement with his position. This is no occasion to be unnerved or disappointed. Hostility frequently is a sign of frustration that the questioner is in the minority. Counsel should remember that, while one or more Justices may seem dissatisfied with his positions or answers, a majority of the Court may well be on his side. In dealing with hostile questions, counsel should give a polite but firm response and get back to his main contentions.

Shapiro, *supra*, at 542-543. Other commentators have agreed that one way *not* to handle questions from the Justices is by displaying resentment of the questions as interruptions. Justice Robert Jackson, who argued many cases before the Court as a Solicitor General prior to serving on it, recognized the difficulty of advocates resenting interruptions and remarked that lawyers who betrayed impatience with interruptions would no doubt wish

> to respond as did a British barrister in an incident related to me by Arthur Goodhart, K.E.B., K.C: The Judge said: "I have been listening to you now for four hours and I am bound to say I am none the wiser." The barrister replied: "Oh, I know that, my Lord, but I had hoped you would be better informed."

Robert H. Jackson, *Advocacy Before the United States Supreme Court*, 37 Cornell L.Q. 1, 11 (1951).

4. It can be hard to gauge the effectiveness of an oral argument from the transcript. It is better to listen to the argument. Fortunately, you can listen to the oral arguments in many of the Court's cases on the Web site Oyez, which is produced by the Chicago-Kent College of Law of the Illinois Institute of Technology, http://www.oyez.org.

5. One of the most well-known types of question asked at oral argument are hypothetical questions. The next excerpt offers advice on how to handle them.

David C. Frederick, Supreme Court and Appellate Advocacy

102-105 (2003)

Supreme Court arguments are notable for the frequent, and creative use of hypothetical questions posed by the justices. . . .

An advocate should keep at least three points in mind when preparing for hypothetical questions. First, the hypothetical can be most soundly answered in almost all cases by having a well-considered theory of the case. The theory of the case will provide an ordering frame of reference that gives a coherent explanation of what happened factually and how those facts relate to the applicable legal principle being advanced. It also provides the reference point through which many difficult hypotheticals may be answered.

Second, if possible, the advocate should try to answer a hypothetical question with a "yes" or "no" and then explain the answer. In court, an observer can see the way members of the court lean forward in anticipation of getting the answer to a hypothetical and then lean back when the advocate answers, "Yes, because ___." Alternatively, when an advocate begins with the explanation rather than the simple answer, members of the court tend to become frustrated. They lean forward even more and become more prone to interrupt.

Third, if the advocate plans to distinguish the hypothetical [from] . . . the case under submission, she should give that distinction *after* directly answering the question. A question may well seek a concession about the limits of the advocate's theory of the case. The advocate should recognize that motivation, give the concession against interest, articulate the necessary distinction, and transition back to an affirmative point.

[One hypothetical that was much commented on at the time was posed at oral argument in *California v. Deep Sea Research, Inc.*, 523 U.S. 491 (1998). That case involved a historic shipwreck off the coast of California that was alleged to contain $2 million in gold and other valuables. One of the issues before the Court was whether the shipwreck had been abandoned, in which event, under a federal statute, the treasure would be owned by its finder, a treasure salvor company; otherwise, the treasure would belong to California.]

. . . [As *amicus curiae* supporting California in part,] [t]he United States had put forward a standard for inferring abandonment under traditional principles of maritime law that took into account the passage of time and the owner's efforts to salvage the wreck. . . . The . . . [government lawyer's] objective . . . was to support that theory of the case when Justice Scalia asked the following hypothetical:

> Suppose I drop a silver dollar down a grate, and I try to bring it up with a piece of gum on a stick, and I can't do it, and I shrug my shoulders and walk off because I have not gotten it, and then somebody comes up and lifts up the grate and gets my silver dollar. Is that his silver dollar? Have I abandoned it just because I could not get it? I still think it's my silver dollar. I haven't said, you know, I don't want it anymore.

. . . [T]he government lawyer treated the question on its own terms and answered by invoking the government's theory of the case: "Justice Scalia, if you waited 130 years without attempting . . . to get your silver dollar, it might be appropriate to infer that you have abandoned it." . . .

Notes and Questions

1. Not all hypotheticals are as whimsical as Justice Scalia's silver dollar hypothetical. In the next section we reproduce the transcript of the oral argument in *Lawrence v. Texas*, 539 U.S. 558 (2003). You will see in that oral argument that some "hypothetical" questions require the lawyers to apply the legal positions for which they contend to *actual* situations that are likely to become the subject of future litigation and thus are "hypothetical" only in the sense that they differ from the situation then before the Court.

2. Frederick writes that a hypothetical question "may well seek a concession about the limits of the advocate's theory of the case." An example can be found in *Rasul v. Bush*, 542 U.S. 466 (2004). In *Rasul*, the Court held that federal district courts had jurisdiction under the federal habeas corpus statute, 28 U.S.C. §2241, over actions by aliens challenging their detention at the U.S. Naval Base at Guantánamo Bay, Cuba. In rejecting the government's argument against jurisdiction, the Court relied in part on the government's concession at oral argument that the district court *would* have jurisdiction over similar actions brought by U.S. citizens:

> Respondents themselves concede that the habeas statute would create federal-court jurisdiction over the claims of an American citizen held at the base. Tr. of Oral Arg. 27. Considering that the statute draws no distinction between Americans and aliens held in federal custody, there is little reason to think that Congress intended the geographical coverage of the statute to vary depending on the detainee's citizenship.

Id. at 481. In another case, the Court cited an attorney's failure to provide a hypothetical situation illustrating the limits of his legal position as a reason to reject that position. The case is *United States v. Lopez*, 514 U.S. 549 (1995). In *Lopez*, the Court held that a federal statute criminalizing possession of a gun within 1,000 feet of a school exceeded Congress's power under the Commerce Clause. The Court observed: "When asked at oral argument if there were *any* limits to the Commerce Clause, the Government was at a loss for words. Tr. of Oral Arg. 5." The cited passage in the oral argument transcript reads in relevant part as follows:

> **CHIEF JUSTICE REHNQUIST:** Well, . . . if this case is . . . [one] Congress can reach under the interstate commerce power, what would be an example of a case which you couldn't reach?
> **DREW S. DAYS, III:** Well, Your Honor, I'm not prepared to speculate generally. . . .

Do you think Drew Days, the attorney for the United States, anticipated this question? Do you think his answer was effective? Would you have answered differently? If so, how? In considering these questions, you may find it useful to read the Court's discussion of the government's unsuccessful attempts to establish a limiting principle for Congress's assertion of powers in a more recent case, which involved federal health care legislation. *See Natl. Fedn. of Indep. Bus. v. Sebelius*, ____ U.S. ____, 132 S. Ct. 2566, 2591 (2012) (opinion of Roberts, J.); *id.* at 2647, 2650 (Scalia, J., dissenting).

D. WHAT DOES HAPPEN AT ORAL ARGUMENT

Below is the edited transcript of the oral argument in *Lawrence v. Texas*, 539 U.S. 558 (2003), in which the Court held unconstitutional a Texas statute making homosexual sodomy a crime. The *Lawrence* Court overruled its decision in *Bowers v. Hardwick*, 478 U.S. 186 (1986), which had upheld a Georgia anti-sodomy law against constitutional challenge.

As you read the *Lawrence* oral argument transcript (or listen to it on Oyez.org), notice ways in which the attorneys follow or depart from the current Guide for Counsel and the expert advice reproduced in Section C of this chapter. Please pay particular attention to: (1) how each counsel begins his argument, (2) the questions that the Justices ask (and the apparent purposes of those questions), and (3) counsel's responses to the questions.[3]

Supreme Court of the United States

John Geddes LAWRENCE and Tyron Garner, Petitioners
v.
TEXAS

No. 02-102. Washington, D.C.
Wednesday, March 26, 2003

The above-entitled matter came on for oral argument before the Supreme Court of the United States at 11:09 a.m.

APPEARANCES

PAUL M. SMITH, ESQ., Washington, DC; on behalf of the Petitioners.
CHARLES A. ROSENTHAL, ESQ., District Attorney, Harris County Houston, Tex.; on behalf of Texas. . . .

CHIEF JUSTICE REHNQUIST: We'll hear argument next in No. 02-102, John Geddes Lawrence and Tyron Garner v. Texas.
Mr. Smith.

ORAL ARGUMENT OF PAUL M. SMITH
ON BEHALF OF THE PETITIONERS

MR. SMITH: Mr. Chief Justice, and may it please the Court.
The State of Texas in this case claims the right to criminally punish any unmarried adult couple for engaging in any form of consensual sexual intimacy that the State happens to disapprove of.

It further claims that there's no constitutional problem raised by a criminal statute that is directed not just at conduct, but at a particular group of people, a law that criminalizes forms of sexual intimacy only for same-sex couples and not for anyone else in the State who has—has the right to make a free choice to engage in the identical conduct.

Petitioners are two adults who were arrested in a private home and criminally convicted simply because they engaged in one of the forms of sexual intimacy that is on the banned list in the State of Texas for same-sex couples.

---

3. In the edited version of the transcript below, we have italicized case names, though they are not italicized in the original transcript, to enhance readability. We have also identified the Justices who ask questions and make other statements during the argument, though that information is not included in the original transcript. In identifying the Justices, we rely on the version of the transcript found on the Oyez Web site maintained by the Illinois Institute of Technology Chicago-Kent College of Law, http://www.oyez.org/cases/2000-2009/2002/2002_02_102 (last visited Sept. 29, 2012).

They bring two constitutional claims to the Court today. First, among the fundamental rights that are implicit in our concept of order of liberty, must be the right of all adult couples, whether same-sex or not, to be free from unwarranted State intrusion into their personal decisions about their preferred forms of sexual expression. Second, there's no legitimate and rational justification under the Equal Protection Clause for a law that regulates forms of sexual intimacy that are permitted in the State only for same-sex couples, thereby creating a kind of a second class citizenship to that group of people.

CHIEF JUSTICE REHNQUIST: On your substantive due process submission, Mr. Smith, certainly, the kind of conduct we're talking about here has been banned for a long time.

Now you point to a trend in the other direction, which would be fine if you're talking about the Eighth Amendment, but I think our case is like *Glucksberg*, say, if you're talking about a right that is going to be sustained, it has to have been recognized for a long time. And that simply isn't so.

MR. SMITH: The Court's cases, Mr. Chief Justice, say that history is a starting point, not the end point of the analysis. And I think that it's important to look at history as a whole and one of the errors that I think that the Court made in *Bowers v. Hardwick* was only looking at the issue in terms of homosexual sodomy and not looking at the issue in general terms, which is the right of everyone to decide for themselves about consensual private sexual intimacy. If you look at the history as a whole, you find a much more complicated picture. First of all, you find that sodomy was regulated going back to the founding for everyone and indeed the laws in the 19th century didn't focus on same-sex couples, they focused on particular—

JUSTICE SCALIA: Well, you're getting to your equal protection argument now. Let's—let's separate the two. The first is, your—your—your fundamental right argument, which has nothing to do with equal protection?

MR. SMITH: Well, Your Honor—

JUSTICE SCALIA: So the same-sex/other-sex aspect doesn't come into it—

MR. SMITH: I think it does come into it, because if you're going to suggest that the state of the law in the books in the 19th century is the touchstone you have to take into account that in the 19th century at least on the face of the law married couples were regulated in terms of their forms of sexual intimacy that were created for them.

JUSTICE SCALIA: It may well be, but so were same-sex couples.

MR. SMITH: Indeed, they all were, Your Honor.

JUSTICE SCALIA: So all same-sex couples could not—could not perform this act lawfully. What more do you need than that? It was prohibited. When you go beyond that and say, oh, but it was also prohibited for—for other sex couples, you're getting into an equal protection argument, it seems to me, not a fundamental right argument

MR. SMITH: I guess I'm suggesting Mr.—Justice Scalia, that it's been conceded here by this State, it was conceded by the State of Georgia 17 years ago, that married couples can't be regulated as a matter of substantive due process in their personal sexual expression in the home.

That means that the state of the law on the books in the 19th century can't be the deciding factor.

JUSTICE SCALIA: They conceded it. I haven't conceded it.

MR. SMITH: Your Honor. That may well be true. I was—I was working with the assumption that there may be Justices who—of the view that married couples do have such a right and I am suggesting that the real issue here is whether that fundamental right extends outside the marital context into other unmarried couples who form bonds and have—and—for whom sexual intimacy plays an equally important role in their lives.

JUSTICE GINSBURG: Were you talking specifically about this *Eisenstadt against Baird* where there was an unmarried couple—while there was an unmarried person and the conduct in question would have been perhaps in the 19th century, early 19th century, criminal? Are you talking about fornication?

MR. SMITH: Yes, Justice Ginsburg. I think the Court in—has moved from *Griswold* to *Eisenstadt*—has moved in the contraception area outside of the marital context to the unmarried context, certainly the right—the qualified right to abortion applies to unmarried people, as well as married people. And I think that the Court in—in looking at this issue of the scope of the fundamental right to make choices about sexual intimacy ought to take into account not just the state of law on the books in the 19th century but a couple of other factors, one the change in enforcement in the last 50 years because the Court's fundamental rights cases all do look at current laws, as well as 19th century law and also even in the 19th century, the fact that there's no record of active enforcement of these laws against conduct—of adults consensual occurring in the private setting and that's true for married couples, it's true for different-sex couples who weren't married, it's true for same-sex couples. The enforcement of the sodomy laws of this country going back to the founding involves coercion, it involves children. It involves public activity. It doesn't involve the kind of conduct that's at issue here.

So you really have a tradition of respect for the privacy of couples in their—in their home, going back to the founding and I think then what began to happen in 1960 was a recognition that we should take that tradition and—and turn it into positive law on the books.

And so you now had three quarters of the States who no longer regulate this conduct for anyone based on a recognition that it's not consistent with our basic American values about the relationship between the individual and the State.

JUSTICE SCALIA: Well, it depends on what you mean by our basic American values, to revert to what the Chief Justice was suggesting earlier. Really what's at issue in this case is whether we're going to adhere to—in the first part of the case, not the equal protection aspect. It's whether we're going to adhere to what—what we said in—in *Glucksberg*, mainly that before we find a substantive due process right, a fundamental liberty, we have to assure ourselves that that liberty was objectively deeply rooted in this Nation's history and tradition.

That's what we said in *Glucksberg* and we've said it in other cases. Or are we going to depart from that and go to the approach that we've adopted with regard to the Eighth Amendment, which is it evolves and changes in—in social values will justify a new perception of what is called unusual punishment.

Now, why should we—why should we slip into the second mode? I'm—I mean, suppose all the States had laws against flagpole sitting at one time, you know, there was a time when it was a popular thing and probably annoyed a lot of communities, and then almost all of them repealed those laws.

Does that make flagpole sitting a fundamental right?

MR. SMITH: No, Your Honor, but the Court's decisions don't look just at history, they look at the—at the function that a particular claimed freedom plays in the lives of real people. That's why contraception became an issue. That's why abortion became an issue.

JUSTICE SCALIA: I don't know what you mean by the function it plays in the lives of real people.

MR. SMITH: The Court has said that—

JUSTICE SCALIA: Any law stops people from doing what they really want to do.

MR. SMITH: The Court has said that it's going to use reasoned judgment to identify a realm of personal liberty that involves matters of central and core [importance] to how a person defines their own lives, and relates to key other people.

It's about moral upbringing of children in the home. It's about procreation or nonprocreation in your sexual relations with your mate. It's about basic questions of what kind of a family you're going to live with and other intimate associations.

CHIEF JUSTICE REHNQUIST: Well, you say it's about procreation or nonprocreation, but none of the cases that you have talked about involved nonprocreation, did they?

MR. SMITH: They certainly involved the right to decide to engage in sexual relations with—while preventing procreation, that's what—that's what *Griswold* and *Eisenstadt* and *Carey* all say you have a right to do. That there's a right to decide whether to bear and beget children and then that right resides with unmarried people as much as it resides with married people.

And I submit to you that it's illogical, fundamentally illogical to say that an unmarried couple has a right free of State intrusion to decide whether or not to have procreative sex or nonprocreative sex, but doesn't have the right to be free from State intrusion—free from a law that says you can't have any sexual intimacy at all. There's a—there's a jagged piece missing from the edifice of this Court's substantive fundamental rights jurisprudence.

JUSTICE SCALIA: It doesn't say you can't have—you can't have any sexual intimacy. It says you cannot have sexual intimacy with a person of the same sex.

MR. SMITH: This particular law does that, yes, Your Honor, but certainly our—our submission is that fornication laws and—and laws involving sodomy regulation more broadly would be equally unconstitutional, because they involve—

JUSTICE SOUTER: But your position, as I understand it, is even if you take the narrowest view of *Glucksberg* and even if you say there's got to be a positive historical sanction, that in fact there is no historical—no substantial historical evidence to the contrary because, A, the—the sodomy laws were not enforced against consensual activity historically and B, they were not aimed at homosexual as opposed to sodomy in general?

MR. SMITH: Right.

JUSTICE SOUTER: Is that—your historical point, you say even if I accept your argument, I should win?

MR. SMITH: Yes, Your Honor. I think first of all that the positive law, the law on the books proves too much because it intruded right into the marital bedroom and that the record of enforcement which may be more informative actually supports us rather than supporting the notion that this is something that can be regulated.

JUSTICE SCALIA: What do you mean by the record of enforcement, that there were—that what happened in this case was an accidental intrusion of the police?

They didn't come into the bedroom looking for people conducting illicit sexual relations? They were there for another reason and happened to discover these—these men in that conduct.

What do you mean by lack of enforcement? The police have not gone around knocking on bedroom doors to see if anyone—I mean—this is not the kind of a crime that the police go around looking for, but do you have any evidence to show that when they—when they found it being committed, they turned a blind eye to it and did not prosecute it?

MR. SMITH: The evidence we have is the—is the absence of reported cases discussing arrests for that kind of conduct.

JUSTICE SCALIA: Well, that's because it's—it's an act committed in private, and—and the police respect the privacy of—of one's home, of one's bedroom, and so they don't investigate and find it.

But it seems to me what you would need is evidence that when the police discovered this matter, they said, oh, well, these are not laws that we enforce. I don't see any evidence of that sort.

MR. SMITH: Certainly it seems to us there's a significance to the fact that it has never been treated as, for example, drug use in the home has been treated. And people do—the police obviously do actively seek to infiltrate homes to find that kind of activity, it's been treated in a categorically different way. But perhaps—

JUSTICE BREYER: To what extent can you characterize it? . . . What is the real record?

MR. SMITH: The argument about 19th century enforcement is that they didn't prosecute anyone for private and consensual crimes involving adults, that they worried about children, they worried about public activity, they worried about coercion, but that they didn't worry about same-sex or different-sex sodomy. Now as to the equal protection point which I think I should get to in my remaining time. This is a statute which in addition to intruding into that area of important fundamental protections, limits its focus just to one small minority of the people of the State of Texas. It says that these specified forms of sexual intimacy called deviate sexual intercourse are illegal only for same-sex couples and not for anyone else in the State of Texas.

JUSTICE O'CONNOR: Well, what about a statute that covered both?

MR. SMITH: Well, I think that would be unconstitutional under my first point, Your Honor.

JUSTICE O'CONNOR: Right.

MR. SMITH: I think there is a multiple—multiply unconstitutional statute, because it does the second thing as well, it says that—

JUSTICE KENNEDY: Well, if the statute covered both, would there be an equal protection argument?

MR. SMITH: If there was a record of enforcement almost exclusively as to same-sex couples, I think there would be potential constitutional problems there, but the statutory language itself would not involve an equal protection problem of the same sort that we're dealing with here. . . .

MR. SMITH: Well, the one thing that I submit, the Court, the State should not be able to come in to say is we are going to permit ourselves the majority of people in our society full—full and free rein to make these decisions for ourselves but there's one minority of people don't get that decision and the only reason we're going to give you is we want it that way. We want them to be unequal in their choices and their freedoms, because we think we should have the right to commit adultery, to commit fornication, to commit sodomy and the State should have no basis for intruding into our lives but we don't want those people over there to have the same right.

JUSTICE SCALIA: I mean you . . . can put it that way, but society always—in a lot of its lives makes these moral judgments, you can make it sound very puritanical, the—you know, the laws—the laws against bigamy, I mean, who are you to tell me that I can't have more than one wife? You blue-nose bigot. Sure. You can make it sound that way, but these are laws dealing with public morality. They've always been on the book, nobody has ever told them they're unconstitutional simply because there are moral perceptions behind them. Why is this different from bigamy?

MR. SMITH: First of all, the first law that's appeared on the books in the States of this country that singles out only same sex sodomy appeared in the '60s and the '70s and it did not—and it does not go way back, this kind of discrimination. Now, bigamy involves protection of an institution that the State creates for its own purposes and there are all sorts of potential justifications about the need to protect the institution of marriage that are different in kind from the justifications that could be offered here involving merely a criminal statute that says we're going to regulate these [people's] . . . behaviors, we include a criminal law which is where the most heightened form of—of people protection analysis ought to apply. This case is very much like *McLaughlin*, Your Honor, where you have a statute that said we're going to give an specially heightened penalty to cohabitation, but only when it involves a white person with a black person. That interracial cohabitation is different, and the State there made the argument we're merely regulating a particular form of conduct, and that's a different form of conduct than—than . . . [interracial] cohabitation. And this Court very clearly said no. You're classifying people. And that classification has to be justified.

And this Court at many times said a mere disapproval of one group of people, whether it be the hippie communes in *Moreno* or the mentally retarded in *Cleburne*, or indeed gay people.

CHIEF JUSTICE REHNQUIST: But all—almost all laws are based on disapproval of either some people or some sort of conduct. That's why people legislate.

MR. SMITH: And what this Court does under the equal protection clause . . . [stands as a bulwark] against arbitrary government when the—when there is no rational justification for the line that is drawn.

JUSTICE O'CONNOR: Well, do you—do you—understood in order to win under an equal protection argument, do you have to apply some sort of heightened scrutiny?

MR. SMITH: We certainly do not think we do, Your Honor. We think this fails rational basis scrutiny, just as the law did in *Romer*, in *Cleburne*, in *Moreno*, in *Eisenstadt*, all of those laws were thrown out under rational basis scrutiny, because the State basically didn't come up with anything other than we want it that way. We want these people to be excluded. We'd had distaste for them. We disapprove of them. It's mere disapproval, or hostility, however historically based, is not sufficient. And certainly even applying the rational basis—

JUSTICE SCALIA: We said the opposite in [*B*]*owers*, didn't we? Overrule [*Bowers*] . . . essentially on that point?

MR. SMITH: Well, certainly [*B*]*owers* is not an equal protection case and it didn't involve this kind of discrimination.

JUSTICE SCALIA: The equal protection and on to the—

MR. SMITH: No I was still talking about the level of scrutiny under equal protection, Your Honor. . . .

. . . [T]he Court in applying even the rational basis standard has not been insensitive to the reality of what the world is like, and to the fact that some groups of—some classifications tend to be involving minorities that have had histories of discrimination against them and that the overall effect of some line-drawing can be very harmful. In *Romer* itself, the Court looked at the actual effects of the—of the amendment in the Constitution and all of the many ways in which it caused harm. Here you have a statute that while it—while it purports . . . just to regulate sexual behavior, has all sorts of collateral effects on people. People in the States who still regulate sodomy everyday they're denied visitation to their own children, they're denied custody of children, they're denied public employment. They're denied private employment, because they're labeled as criminals merely because they've been identified as homosexuals. And that we submit—

CHIEF JUSTICE REHNQUIST: If you prevail, Mr. Smith, and this law is struck down, do you think that would also mean that a State could not prefer heterosexuals to homosexuals to teach kindergarten?

MR. SMITH: I think the issue of—of preference in the educational context would involve very different criteria, Your Honor, very different considerations, the State would have to come in with some sort of a justification.

JUSTICE SCALIA: A justification is the same that's alluded to here, disapproval of homosexuality.

MR. SMITH: Well, I think it would be highly—highly problematic, such a—such a justification.

JUSTICE SCALIA: Yes, it would?

MR. SMITH: If that were the only justification that could be offered, there was not some showing that there would be any more concrete harm to the children in the school.

JUSTICE SCALIA: Only that the children might—might be induced to—to follow the path of homosexuality. And that would not be—that would . . . not be enough?

MR. SMITH: Well, I—I think the State has to have a greater justification for its discrimination than we prefer pushing people towards heterosexuality. That amounts to the same thing as disapproval of people's choices in this area and there has to be a more—more reasons and justifiable distinction than simply we prefer this group of people, the majority, instead of this group of people, the minority.

Justice Jackson in the [R]*ailway* [E]*xpress* case said very eloquently that the equal protection clause is an important bulwark against arbitrary government because it's there to make sure that legislators don't avoid political retribution by imposing onerous burdens only on one minority, but that in fact the majority will live by the same rules as purpor[t] to impose on everybody else.

JUSTICE GINSBURG: Mr. Smith before you continue down to the equal protection line. Your first argument was the right of personal privacy in one's most intimate sexual relations, you were asked and you didn't get a chance to answer because you went back on your equal protection track, you are asking the Court to overrule [B]*owers against Hardwick.* I thought that was very—

MR. SMITH: Yes, Your Honor.

We're asking you to overrule it and we think that the right of—of the fundamental right of unmarried people to make these choices about private adult consensual intimacy applies to different sex couples as well as same sex couples and that *Bowers* was wrong for essentially three reasons, first it posed the question too narrowly by focusing just on homosexual sodomy, which is just one of the moral choices that couples ought to have—that people ought to have available to them.

And second in its analysis of history, which I think I explained already and third, and perhaps most importantly, in the assumptions that the Court made in 1986 about the realities of gay lives and gay relationships, the Court simply asserted in the *Bowers* case that there's no showing that has been demonstrated between the opportunity to engage in this conduct and family.

And certainly while it may not have been shown in that case or even apparent to the Court in 1986, I submit it has to be apparent to the Court now that there are gay families that family relationships are established, that there are hundreds of thousands of people registered in the Census in the 2000 [C]ensus who have formed gay families, gay partnerships, many of them raising children and that for those people, the opportunity to engage in sexual expression as they will in the privacy of their own homes performs much the same function that it does in the marital context, that you can't protect one without the other, that it doesn't make sense to draw a line there and that you should protect it for everyone.

That this is a fundamental matter of American values.

So those are the three reasons we ask you to overrule *Bowers v. Hardwick* as to the fundamental rights aspect of the case and that we think that that is an area where the Court should go—should go back and reconsider itself.

The Court has now left open for nearly 30 years the question of whether anybody outside has a right—has a privacy right to engage in consensual sexual intimacy in the privacy of their home.

And I submit to you, you know, while the Court has left that unanswered, the American people have moved on to the point where that right is taken for granted for everyone.

Most Americans would be shocked to find out that their decision to engage in sexual intimacy with another person in their own home might lead to a knock on the door as occurred here and a criminal prosecution.

And that—that reality is something that the Court needs to take into account and certainly in so doing, it shouldn't—in constructing its fundamental rights edifice draw distinctions between gay couples and other couples.

JUSTICE SCALIA: You probably say the same about adultery, you think adultery laws are unconstitutional?

MR. SMITH: I think that the [S]tate has—

JUSTICE SCALIA: I . . . think people probably feel the same way about that, you know.

It may not be a nice thing to do, but I certainly don't expect a knock on the door and go to jail for it.

MR. SMITH: Your Honor, adultery is a very different case. It involves the State interests in protecting the marital contract which people voluntarily take on. And—and so in assessing.

JUSTICE SCALIA: Why is the marital contract important to the State? Because it's the source of—of the next generation, right?

MR. SMITH: Sure, the State is—

JUSTICE SCALIA: And you think that there's not some of the same thinking behind the conscious choice of the State to favor heterosexual and marital sex over homosexual sex?

MR. SMITH: Well, I can understand a law which says we're going to attempt to channel heterosexuals towards marriage by making them—making it illegal for them to have sex without marriage. I can't understand that law under—under that kind of rational[e] which only regulates same sex couples and says you can't have sex but everyone else has a right to do that.

As for adultery and all of the other parade of horribles which people have raised in their briefs, it seems to me you've got to look at the individual interests and the State interests and . . . [they're] dramatically different in all of those cases incest, prostitution, all of these—bestiality, all of these things either there's very little individual interests or there's very heightened State interest or both, in all of those cases . . .

If I could reserve the balance of my time, Your Honor.

CHIEF JUSTICE REHNQUIST: Very well, Mr. Smith.

Mr. Rosenthal, we'll hear from you.

ORAL ARGUMENT OF CHARLES A. ROSENTHAL, JR.
ON BEHALF OF TEXAS

MR. ROSENTHAL: Give me just a moment. Mr. Chief Justice, and may it please the Court.

The State humbly submits that enforcement of Texas Penal Code Statute 21.06 does not violate the 14th Amendment of the Constitution because this Court has never recognized a fundamental right to engage in extramarital sexual conduct and because there is a rational basis for the statute sufficient to withstand equal protection scrutiny.

I'd like to begin with a brief discussion of substantive due process. From a practitioner's standpoint, it appears that the jurisprudence of this Court appears to resolve the means by which the Court entertains a claim of novel protected liberty interests.

Since the Constitution does not expressly address the issue of privacy or of sexual conduct, we look to the Court's precedents and to the history of our people.

If a historical, traditional analysis applies, it then serves as objective guideposts to guide this Court, as long as those ideals and laws do not infringe on fundamental rights.

The Court has maintained that designation of a liberty interest is done— not done with impunity. But only those interests that appear to be carefully identified asserted rights should be drawn and should be considered as liberty interests. The record in this case does not particularly show which rights the petitioners are asking to uphold.

JUSTICE SCALIA: I—I don't understand what you mean by that. Aren't we clear what right they're seeking to uphold?

MR. ROSENTHAL: No, sir, they're—they're asking for the right of homosexuals to engage in homosexual conduct.

JUSTICE SCALIA: Right.

MR. ROSENTHAL: But there's nothing in the record to indicate that these people are homosexuals. They're not homosexuals by definition if they commit one act. It's our position that a heterosexual person can also violate this code if they commit an act of deviate sexual intercourse with another of the same sex.

JUSTICE SCALIA: Why aren't—why aren't they seeking to vindicate the right of either homosexuals or heterosexuals to commit homosexual act[s]? What difference does that make?

MR. ROSENTHAL: The difference it makes is as the—as the record is set out, it does not really define the issues such that the Court can actually give the petitioners a—a specific form of relief.

JUSTICE GINSBURG: But the—the—the statute, Texas has already decided that for us. It has called this homosexual conduct, so whether it's a heterosexual person or a homosexual person, the crime is engaging in homosexual conduct.

MR. ROSENTHAL: That's correct.

JUSTICE SOUTER: You don't even have to get to the—as I understand it, you don't even have to get to the characterization of homosexual. The statute clearly defines certain acts committed by or together with individuals of the same sex and that's your class, isn't it?

MR. ROSENTHAL: Yes, it is.

JUSTICE SOUTER: What more do we need?

MR. ROSENTHAL: We're—the class actually is people who violate the act, not classes of individuals based upon sexual orientation.

JUSTICE KENNEDY: Well, I—I can see that your point may have some relevance on the equal protection side of the equation, some relevance, I don't think it may be controlling.

It—it doesn't seem to meet the arguments that's made under the substantive liberty part of the argument with reference to *Bowers*. . . .

MR. ROSENTHAL: Well, of course we—we believe that *Bowers versus Hardwick* is—is good law. It's substantial law and that this Court should not overrule *Bowers*—

JUSTICE KENNEDY: But that question is certainly clearly before us. I mean this is your statute.

You convicted the people for these acts and you have to be—you have to defend it.

MR. ROSENTHAL: Yes, sir. And it's our position that *Bowers versus Hardwick* is still good law, that there's nothing that's changed about the fundamental liberties or the—or the history or traditions of our country that should make the analysis in *Bowers* incorrect any longer.

The petitioner also claims that the mores of our nation have changed to the point where physical homosexual intimacy is now part of the fabric of American values. And it's our position this cannot be correct.

Even if you infer that various States acting through their legislative process have repealed sodomy laws, there is no protected right to engage in extrasexual—extramarital sexual relations, again, that can trace their roots to history or the traditions of this nation.

JUSTICE BREYER: Their basic argument, I think—

JUSTICE SCALIA: I—I'm sorry.

I didn't get that argument. I thought you were going to say—you were responding to the argument that the morals haven't changed, or that the morals have changed so that homosexuality is now approved. And you respond to that by saying that there's no tradition? I mean, that's—that's a totally different argument from tradition. I mean, the—the argument is tradition doesn't matter.

MR. ROSENTHAL: Well, history—tradition does not matter in terms of whether or not it—it can be a protected liberty interest.

JUSTICE SCALIA: Why—why do you think that the public perception of—of homosexual acts has—has not changed? Do you think it hasn't?

MR. ROSENTHAL: The public perception of it?

JUSTICE SCALIA: Yes, yes. Do you think there's public approval of it?

MR. ROSENTHAL: Of homosexuals, but not of homosexuality activity.

JUSTICE SCALIA: What do you base that on?

MR. ROSENTHAL: I beg your pardon?

JUSTICE SCALIA: What do you base that on?

MR. ROSENTHAL: Well, even—

JUSTICE SCALIA: I mean I think there ought to be some evidence which—which you can bring forward?

MR. ROSENTHAL: Sure.

JUSTICE SCALIA: Like perhaps the failure of the Federal Congress to add the sexual preference to the list of protected statuses against which private individuals are not permitted to discriminate, that addition has been sought several times and it's been rejected by the Federal Congress, hasn't it?

MR. ROSENTHAL: Yes, sir, and—and in addition, what I was trying to say by the fact that various States have changed their position on sodomy, they've done it through the legislative process. And that's where we believe this belongs, is in the State House of Texas, not this Court.

JUSTICE SCALIA: Yes, but I thought you were responding to the argument that the public perception hasn't changed. That there still is—is a public disapproval of homosexual acts.

And you can't establish that by saying that the States have repealed their homosexual laws.

MR. ROSENTHAL: Well, I think it goes back to whether the—where—whether people in Texas and people in the other States that had this law on their books actually accepted through their representative government. I think it comes down to the—the actual people who—who determine the consensus and mores of the State or the—or the elected legislators.

JUSTICE SCALIA: Might there be a difference between the people's willingness to prosecute something criminally and the people's embracing of that as a fundamental right?

MR. ROSENTHAL: Well, certainly. And just because someone has decriminalized sodomy doesn't mean that they embraced that practice as something that ought to be taught in the schools as was mentioned before.

JUSTICE BREYER: But the argument of—of *Bowers*, to overrule *Bowers* is not directly related to sodomy. It's related, but not directly. It's that people in their own bedrooms, which have their right to do basically what they want, it's not hurting other people. And they—the other side—says *Bowers* understated the importance of that. It got the history wrong. It didn't understand the relationship of the sodomy to families and in addition, *Bowers* has proved to be harmful to thousands and thousands and thousands of people, if not because they're going to be prosecuted, because they fear it—they might be, which makes it a possible instrument of repression in the hands of the prosecutors. Now, that's the kind of argument that they're making. Harmful in consequence, wrong in theory, understating the constitutional value.

MR. ROSENTHAL: All right—

JUSTICE BREYER: All right, now how do you respond to that?

MR. ROSENTHAL: Okay. First of all, let me—let me correct something that—that's very minor at this point, but the allegation was made in petitioners' argument that people can—convicted of homosexual conduct are banned from jobs and housing and all—and all that kind of thing. In Texas, homosexual conduct is a class C misdemeanor. That is, it is the lowest misdemeanor—or the lowest prohibition that Texas has.

JUSTICE BREYER: That I didn't bring in in my question.

MR. ROSENTHAL: Yes, sir.

JUSTICE BREYER: My question was, getting those sort of three or four basic points, I would like to hear your—your straight answer to those points—
    [Laughter]

JUSTICE BREYER: —because on their face, they're—I mean, I'm not—not a criticism, I mean, directly responding, directly responding to the—to the—to the question.

MR. ROSENTHAL: Well, it's our position that the line should be drawn at the marital bedroom, through which we can—through the law enforcement or anyone else cannot pass unless something illegal happens inside that bedroom.

JUSTICE BREYER: Well, if this is drawing the line at the bedroom door, this case is inside the bedroom, not outside. That's the statute makes criminal, to my understanding, . . . what takes place within the bedroom through consent. Am I right about that?

MR. ROSENTHAL: You're right about that, but—

JUSTICE BREYER: And why isn't that something that the State has no business getting involved in—

MR. ROSENTHAL: First of all, let me say—

JUSTICE BREYER: —as long as it doesn't hurt anybody?

MR. ROSENTHAL: First of all, let me say that consent may be alleged in this case, but consent is not proven in the record in this case. . . . [T]his Court having determined that there are certain kinds of conduct that it will accept and certain kinds of conduct it will not accept may draw the line at the bedroom door of the heterosexual married couple because of the interest that this Court has that this Nation has and certainly that the State of Texas has for the preservation of marriage, families and the procreation of children.

JUSTICE GINSBURG: Does Texas permit same-sex adoptions—two women or two men to adopt a child or to be foster parents?

MR. ROSENTHAL: I don't know the answer to that, Justice.

JUSTICE GINSBURG: Well, in portraying what Texas sees as a family and distinguishing both married and unmarried heterosexual people from homosexual people, those things wouldn't go together if the State at the same time said same sex couples are qualified to raise a family. You can adopt children, you can be foster parents.
    You don't know what—what the Texas law is on that?

MR. ROSENTHAL: I do not know what that Texas law—what the Texas law says in that regard.

JUSTICE GINSBURG: I think it would be relevant to your argument that they're making—that Texas is making the distinction between kinds of people who have family relationships and can be proper guardians of children and those who can't.

MR. ROSENTHAL: Well, again, Your Honor, we're not saying that they can't be proper guardians and we can't say that they can't raise children. . . . [W]e're also not—not penalizing their—their status. We're penalizing only the particular activity that those unmarried couples may have with respect to whether they have sexual intimacies.

JUSTICE STEVENS: Does Texas prohibit sexual intercourse between unmarried heterosexuals?

MR. ROSENTHAL: Well, it used to. It does not do that now, unless the sexual intimacy is in public or where someone might view—

JUSTICE STEVENS: No, say in a—a private situation like this, it would not—it would not be prohibited?

MR. ROSENTHAL: It does not criminalize it, it does not condone it.

JUSTICE SCALIA: What about adultery?

MR. ROSENTHAL: I beg your pardon?

JUSTICE SCALIA: What about adultery?

MR. ROSENTHAL: Again, adultery is not penalized in Texas, but it is certainly not condoned in Texas.

[Laughter]

JUSTICE BREYER: All right, so you said—you said procreation, marriage and children, those are your three justifications. Now from what you recently said, I don't see what it has to do with marriage, since, in fact, marriage has nothing to do with the conduct that either this or other statutes do or don't forbid. I don't see what it has to do with children, since, in fact, the gay people can certainly adopt children and they do. And I don't see what it has to do with procreation, because that's the same as the children.

All right. So—so what is the justification for this statute, other than, you know, it's not what they say on the other side, is this is simply, I do not like thee, Doctor Fell, the reason why I cannot tell.

[Laughter]

JUSTICE BREYER: Now, what is aside—aside from that?

MR. ROSENTHAL: I think what—what I'm saying is—and I had not gotten into the equal protection aspect of the—of the argument yet, but under the equal protection argument, Texas has the right to set moral standards and can set bright line moral standards for its people. And in the setting of those moral standards, I believe that they can say that certain kinds of activity can exist and certain kinds of activity cannot exist. . . .

JUSTICE BREYER: Could they say, for example, it is against the law at the dinner table to tell really serious lies to your family?

MR. ROSENTHAL: Yes, they can make that a law, but there would be no rational basis for the law.

JUSTICE BREYER: Oh, really. It's very immoral. I mean, I know there's certainly—it's certainly immoral to tell very serious harmful lies to your own family under certain circumstances and around the dinner table, some of the worst things can happen.

[Laughter]

JUSTICE BREYER: But the—the—so Texas could go right in there and any kind of morality that they think is just immoral or bad, cheating, perhaps. What about rudeness, serious rudeness, et cetera?

MR. ROSENTHAL: Well, again, if—if Texas did pass the law, it would have to—have to show through some rational basis test that it's rationally related to some State interest.

JUSTICE SCALIA: Mr. Rosenthal, don't you think that what laws a State may constitutionally pass has a lot to do with what laws it has always been thought that a State can constitutionally pass, so that if you have a 200-year tradition of a certain type of law—and I don't know of a 200-year tradition of laws against lying at the dinner table—the presumption is that the State can within the bounds of—of the Constitution to pass that law in—as declaring what it has proscribed as *contra bonos mores*, a term that's been in the common law from the beginning as against good morals, bigamy, adultery, all sorts of things like that, and isn't that determined pretty much on the basis of what kind of laws the State has traditionally been allowed to pass?

MR. ROSENTHAL: Certainly. And it goes—it goes to things as diverse as—

JUSTICE STEVENS: I don't suppose you're going to argue that *Loving against Virginia* was incorrectly decided, are you?

MR. ROSENTHAL: Oh, certainly not.

JUSTICE STEVENS: And that was certainly a long tradition that supported that—

MR. ROSENTHAL: But it also violated a fundamental right.

JUSTICE STEVENS: And that's the issue here.

[Laughter]

MR. ROSENTHAL: Yes, sir. And the fundamental right that was asserted there is—is a long-established fundamental right that we don't—we don't treat races differently because we think that one's inferior or we stereotype someone—

JUSTICE SCALIA: There was a constitutional text there, wasn't there, with *Loving versus Virginia.* I thought there was something about a Civil War and no discrimination on the basis of race. . . .

JUSTICE SOUTER: When—when did Texas select homosexual sodomy as—as a subject of specific criminal prohibition? . . .

MR. ROSENTHAL: In 1973, in the passage of the 1974 Penal Code.

JUSTICE SOUTER: So the issue here doesn't have much of a longstanding tradition specific to this statute, does it?

MR. ROSENTHAL: Well, not specific to—not specific to that statute, but it has a longstanding tradition in Texas as being something that should be proscribed and something that is regarded as immoral and unwholesome.

JUSTICE SCALIA: Well, homosexual sodomy was unlawful in Texas from when? There was not a statute addressed just to that. It was addressed to sodomy in general, but homosexual—but homosexual sodomy included, and that law goes back how long? To 1803?

MR. ROSENTHAL: To the—to the time that Texas was a republic. . . .

JUSTICE BREYER: But what about the statute which this Court I think had to grapple with, people felt during World War I that it was immoral to teach German in the public schools. So then would you say that the State has every right to do that, parents want their children to learn German, but the schools forbid it? See, the hard question here is can the State, in fact, pass anything that it wants at all, because they believe it's immoral. If you were going to draw the line somewhere, I guess you might begin to draw it when the [person] . . . is involved inside his own bedroom and not hurting anybody else. Now that—that now—so you say it's morality. I—I agree many people do believe that that's a question of morality. Many do not, but nonetheless, what can you add to what you're saying, other than simply asserting its morality? Because I don't think you think that the State could pass anything in the name of morality?

MR. ROSENTHAL: Certainly not. But it would have—any law that would pass would have to have some rational basis to the State interest.

JUSTICE BREYER: You've not given a rational basis except to repeat the word morality.

JUSTICE SCALIA: Is the rational basis . . . that the State thinks it immoral just as the State thinks adultery immoral or bigamy immoral[?]

JUSTICE BREYER: Or teaching German.

JUSTICE SCALIA: Well, that—

[Laughter]

CHIEF JUSTICE REHNQUIST: Maybe we should go through counsel, yes.

JUSTICE SOUTER: Isn't the—Mr. Rosenthal, isn't the thrust of Justice Breyer's question that when—when the State criminalizes behavior as immoral, customarily what it points to is not simply an isolated moral judgment or the moral judgment alone, but it points to a moral judgment which is backed up by some demonstration of harm to other people.

We—we've heard questions for example about harm to a—a marital institution. It makes sense to say whether you think the law is enforceable or not. It makes sense to say that adultery threatens the—the durability of a particular instance of marriage.

What kind of harm to others can you point to in this case to take it out of the category of simple moral disapproval, per se?

MR. ROSENTHAL: Well, part of the—part of the rationale for the law is to discourage similar conduct, that is, to discourage people who may be in jail together or want to experiment from doing the same kind of thing and I think—and I think that the State can do that. People can harm themselves and still be—and still have it be against the law. But they can take drugs and do that.

JUSTICE SOUTER: Well, do you point to a kind of harm here to an individual or to the individual's partner, which is comparable to the harm that results from the—the harm to the deterioration of the body and the mind from drug-taking? I mean, I don't see the parallel between the two situations.

MR. ROSENTHAL: Well, not—not only do we say that morality is a basis for this, but of course the antecedents have raised that there may also be health considerations. I don't know whether there are or not.

JUSTICE SOUTER: That is not the State's claim in any case?

MR. ROSENTHAL: That's not the State's claim, but I can't say that it's not true. . . .

MR. ROSENTHAL: . . . I did want to briefly distinguish this case from your decision in *Romer v. Evans.* And obviously the distinction there was—was that the Colorado amendment sought to classify people based on their orientation and not their conduct. And by so doing, they excluded a certain class of people from the political debate. Now, on the contrary, Texas welcomes all into the political debate and—in the last Texas legislature, fortunately our legislature meets only every other year, but in the last Texas legislature, there was a hate crime statute passed which made it a more heinous crime to make someone a victim of crime based upon their sexual orientation and it included all sexual orientations. It included homosexuals, bisexuals and heterosexuals, all, so I don't think we can say across the board that there's some sort of Texas policy that we're trying to overall discriminate against—against homosexuals as a group.

JUSTICE GINSBURG: Somebody wants to participate in the political process, run for political office who is homosexual and the charge is made on the other side don't—don't vote for this person, this person is a law breaker, there is a closer connection to *Romer* in that regard, isn't there?

MR. ROSENTHAL: Well, that would be true, if it weren't that the historical fact that that's not in fact true. That there have been people who have campaigned in Texas and have admitted their homosexuality and have been elected to office.

JUSTICE GINSBURG: But the charge—they could be charged as law-breakers.

MR. ROSENTHAL: No, ma'am, they can't be charged as law-breakers for having that orientation. They can only be charged as law-breakers if they commit that particular act. And then, again, the State does not allow any disabilities to come from class C misdemeanor acts.

I'm sure it's obvious to this Court that the issues of homosexual rights are highly emotional for the petitioner in these quarters but equally anxious in this Court's—for this Court's decision are those who are, number one, concerned with the rights of States to determine their own destiny, and, two, and possibly more important, those persons who are concerned that the invalidation of this little Texas statute would make—would make marriage law subject to constitutional challenge.

Then again, how far behind that can there be other acts of sexual gratification brought for constitutional challenge also[?] There's already movements to lower the age limit of consent for children engaged in sexual practices. And there are secondary effects, particularly in Texas law, where we are a common law state and the common law is based upon community property shared by both spouses. The State of Texas is asking this Court to be mindful of the far-reaching aspects of your decision in this case, so as not to disenfranchise 23 million Texans who ought to have the right to participate in questions having to do with moral issues. We ask you to affirm the Texas Court of Appeals.

CHIEF JUSTICE REHNQUIST: Thank you, Mr. Rosenthal.

Mr. Smith, you have 4 minutes remaining.

REBUTTAL ARGUMENT OF PAUL M. SMITH
ON BEHALF OF THE PETITIONERS

MR. SMITH: Thank you, Mr. Chief Justice. I just have a couple of points to make. I thought I might address this question of what it was that we proved in the record below and whether or not we have, as a result, adequately teed up the issues before the Court without having put into evidence directly that this was a non-coercive act or a noncommercial act or a nonpublic act or things of that kind.

Our position is that this is a criminal statute that has only two elements, it has a list of particular kinds of sexual intimacy that you're not allowed to engage in and . . . they have to prove as well that the two people involved were of the same sex.

There was a complaint that was filed that listed those two elements. My clients pleaded no contest to those two elements but said that there is an insufficient basis for imposing criminal liability on them, because, first of all, they invade fundamental rights and second of all, because the law is discriminatory, while it's supposedly got a moral basis, it's a discriminatory morality, a morality imposed only on one category of couples in a State which does not penalize in any way adultery, fornication or sodomy for people of—of couples that are different sex.

Those are the arguments that were made and—so our position is that . . . the statute is unconstitutional both facially and as applied here, because the State purports to impose liability based on those two elements alone and that they are constitutionally insufficient bases both for fundamental rights reasons and because it's a discriminatory state.

The other point I thought I might just address for the moment is the public health rationale which didn't come up before. Essentially, what the facts are—and I think this comes out to a large extent, it's undisputed in the amicus briefing—the issue is not briefed in here because the Texas brief doesn't even attempt to make this argument, but it is—the facts are that if this was the line between safe and unsafe forms of sexual intimacy it's as if the law cuts right across it. Regulating some of the most safe forms of sexual activity possible, including, for example, lots of safe sex—same-sex activity involving women and leaving completely unregulated all sorts of forms of unsafe sexual activity involving different sex couples.

So if there was ever a case of a law where the fit is egregiously improper and insufficient to justify the law under the rational basis test, this would be such a case.

Unless the Court has further questions, thank you very much.

CHIEF JUSTICE REHNQUIST: Thank you Mr. Smith. The case is submitted.

Notes and Questions

1. Which argument do you think was more effective: petitioners' or respondent's? Why?

2. What were the central points—what Seth Waxman would call "the kernel"—of each counsel's argument? How effectively did they make those points?

3. Were any of the Justices' questions to the advocates designed to influence the other Justices' view of the case? Which ones? Notice in particular that some of the questions that Justice Scalia asked the advocate for Texas were designed to help the advocate by suggesting supportive arguments for the advocate to adopt as his own.

4. What hypothetical questions did the Court ask each side? What was the purpose of those hypothetical questions? Did the counsel respond effectively?

5. Chapter 5 includes material from the briefs in *Lawrence* (see pages 310-356). If you have studied that material, consider how the arguments in the briefs were presented at oral argument. Also consider how you might have presented the oral arguments for each side differently, based on your study of the briefs. Do you think the oral argument in this case affected the outcome?

6. Chapter 7 examines the resulting opinions in *Lawrence v. Texas* (see pages 536-564). You will see that the opinion for the Court adopts many of the points made at oral argument by the attorney for the petitioners. You will also find in Justice Scalia's dissenting opinion many of the points that Justice Scalia himself made at oral argument.

7. Paul M. Smith, who argued for the petitioners Lawrence and Geddes, was a Supreme Court clerk for Justice Lewis Powell in 1980-1981. Smith later became a highly regarded appellate practitioner in Washington, D.C. who is openly gay and regularly appears before the Court. Professor John Brigham argues that Smith's elevation to a position as part of the elite institutional life of the Court reflected and contributed to a shift in the Court's attitude toward homosexuality between the time of *Bowers v. Hardwick* and *Lawrence v. Texas.* In the process, the Court had come to recognize and show sensitivity to homosexuality "as part of its institutional life," and this sensitivity contributed to its decision protecting homosexual acts. *See* John Brigham, "Some Thoughts on Institutional Life and 'The Rest of the Closet,'" in *The Future of Gay Rights in America,* at 105 (H.N. Hirsch ed., 2005). Do you agree? Why or why not? We return in Chapter 8 to the issue of how the diversity or lack of diversity among advocates before the Court may affect its decision making.

E. THE IMPORTANCE OF ORAL ARGUMENT

Many wonder whether oral argument really affects the outcome of cases. The issue arises partly because during its history, the Court has steadily reduced the time for oral argument while increasing reliance on written briefs. This section briefly discusses the evolution of oral argument. Then it shows what some Justices and political scientists have said about the impact of oral argument. As you will see, there is dispute about what, if any, impact oral argument has on the Court's decisions, and the Justices themselves appear to disagree about its utility.

1. Evolution of Oral Argument

David C. Frederick, Supreme Court and Appellate Advocacy

15-49 (2003)

In the first year and a half of the Supreme Court's existence, the rules of practice led to much uncertainty among practitioners. On August 8, 1791, the court issued an order . . . advis[ing] that "this court consider[s] the practice of the courts of king's bench, and of chancery, in England, as affording outlines for the practice of this court. . . ."

By long-standing tradition, advocates at the King's Bench presented their material orally to the court. For arguments to the House of Lords, the highest tribunal in Britain, advocates would even go so far as to state orally the decision of the court from which the appeal was being taken, and then proceed with a long presentation of the facts and precedents. . . . [T]he rationale for that practice in England has been that the entire judicial process is completely open to public scrutiny: everything the judge learns about the case is presented in open court, which thus diminishes the possibility of out-of-court influence.

. . . [In early oral arguments before the U.S. Supreme Court,] [s]ome advocates resorted to such sources as scripture, history, and Roman law in arguing their cases. . . . Hence, in 1795, a change in the rules advised that "[t]he Court . . . hereafter . . . will expect to be furnished with a statement of the material points of the case." . . . [This rule change was] treated . . . as a requirement by counsel to fill their oral presentations with citations and long excerpts of learned treatises in support of the argument.

As befitting other changes in the Supreme Court under the leadership of Chief Justice John Marshall, oral advocacy practice also evolved in the decades between

1803 and 1835. In 1812, the court issued a rule limiting oral argument to only two counsel per side. That rule contributed to a growing trend of Supreme Court specialists who came to dominate advocacy before the court. In the 1814 Term, for example, . . . William Pinckney . . . argued more than half of the cases decided by the court that term. A contemporary of Pinckney's, Luther Martin, was known for his "iron memory" and the "fullness of his legal knowledge" notwithstanding the fact that he "often appeared in [the Supreme] Court evidently intoxicated." . . . Martin was one of the losing advocates in the celebrated case of *McCulloch v. Maryland*, a case whose importance was acknowledged at the time by the court itself, in waiving its rule limiting argument to two counsel per side. . . .

The court made no effort at this time . . . to limit the length of attorney presentations. Oral argument could and did consume numerous days in important cases. In *McCulloch*, for example, the argument began on February 22 and did not end until February 27, a Saturday afternoon. . . .

In 1833, the Supreme Court . . . ordered that, "in all cases brought here on appeal, writ of error, or otherwise, the court will receive printed arguments, if the Counsel on either or both sides shall choose so to submit the same." Thus began the practice of submitting written briefs to the court, but the hortatory nature of the "order" meant that change was to proceed at the pace promoted by the bar. . . .

. . . [A] number of competing pressures combined to culminate in the issuance of a rule [in 1849] limiting the time for argument of a case to two hours. One such pressure was occasioned by the Supreme Court's workload, which increased from 98 cases in 1810 to 253 cases in 1850. . . .

A second dynamic was the susceptibility of the justices to illness, which could cause interruptions in a justice's ability to hear the entire argument and which meant that evenly divided cases had to be reargued. . . .

Finally, oral argument was perceived by some of the justices as overly long and not particularly helpful to the court's decision-making process. . . .

. . . [The 1849 rule generally limiting oral argument to two hours] also stated that no counsel would be permitted to speak in a case unless having first filed a printed abstract of points and authorities. . . .

. . . By 1911, the rules of the court provided that each side would have one-and-a-half hours for oral argument. . . . In certain cases, such as those certified from the circuit courts of appeals that had been created under the Evarts Act of 1891, the Supreme Court limited argument to 45 minutes per side. The theory behind that limitation was the expectation that the recently created circuit courts of appeals would help to filter the issues that the Supreme Court needed to resolve. In both instances, the court had the discretion to provide leave for an expansion of time. The court retained the rule limiting arguing counsel to two advocates per side. In the 1920s, the court divided its docket between the "regular" docket and the "summary" docket. Cases on the "regular" docket were allotted one hour per side, and no more than two counsel per side were permitted to argue. In cases on the "summary" docket, only one-half hour per side was apportioned, and the court permitted no more than one counsel per side, except by special leave of court. . . .

The change in the rules limiting the time for oral argument affected advocacy in the Supreme Court, particularly during the New Deal era. Although the court occasionally heard extended arguments in important cases, increasingly the court used the limited time for argument to put questions to counsel. By the 1930s, the transformation of oral argument from oration to question-and-answer was not quite complete, but the signs of that trend were well in evidence in some . . . cases. . . .

[In the New Deal period,] . . . the Supreme Court was much more willing than at any previous time in its history to use the time at oral argument to put questions to counsel. Part of that dynamic resulted from the increasing pressures on time placed on the advocates; part of it was the disposition of the justices themselves. Justice Pierce Butler, for instance, was incessant in his questioning, particularly of government counsel during Franklin Roosevelt's Administration. And when he served on the court, Justice Felix Frankfurter could dominate oral arguments with his questions, leading Justice Douglas to recall that "[s]ome of us would often squirm at Frankfurter's seemingly endless questions that took the advocate round and round and round." . . .

By 1970, arguments of 30 minutes per side had long become the norm in more than 80 percent of the cases argued in the Supreme Court. The court achieved that control over its docket by designating cases deemed to be of lesser importance for the "summary calendar." . . . In 1970, the court changed the rules to conform to that practical reality. Under those new rules, each case would be allotted 30 minutes per side for argument, although in exceptional cases a party could request additional time. That schedule has persisted to the present day.

The compression of time in Supreme Court argument has invariably heightened the pressure on counsel to make their points succinctly and precisely. Since the 1970s, the trend increasingly has been for arguments to be marked by the quick thrust and parry of question-and-answer that so fundamentally has changed the nature of advocacy in the Supreme Court. . . .

. . . Unlike the set-piece orations of the nineteenth century, in which advocates droned on for days about their case, oral argument in the twenty-first century very much mirrors the society: argument often seems as though it is a series of sound [bites] . . . , strung together amid frequent interruptions from the bench. . . .

Notes and Questions

1. Frederick identifies "[t]he two most important dynamics" in the evolution of oral argument as the Court's increasing reliance on written briefs and its gradual decrease of the amount of time allotted for oral argument. He also cites two other dynamics that he believes "have contributed to substantial changes in how oral argument is conducted in the Supreme Court." One is the establishment and development of the Office of the Solicitor General as the unit in the U.S. Department of Justice that represents the United States in cases before the Court. This, he says, has raised the standards for appellate advocacy. The other dynamic is the composition of the Court, which in Frederick's view has come to include more and more inquisitive justices. If you were a Justice, which approach would you favor: the oral tradition of the English or the written tradition that the United States Supreme Court and other appellate courts in the United States have adopted? Why? Would your answers change if you considered them from the perspective of an advocate?

2. In 1981, Justice Sandra Day O'Connor circulated a proposal to address the Court's heavy caseload by changing its rules to give it the option of deciding cases without oral arguments. *See* Joan Biskupic, *Sandra Day O'Connor* 119-121 (2005). Most of the other Justices then on the Court were at least open to discussing the proposal. Justice Lewis Powell worried, however: "[W]e might abuse this privilege." *Id.* at 120. Powell continued:

> I believe in the utility of oral argument, and also in the symbolism it portrays for the public. Accordingly, if the rule is changed as suggested, I would hope that we would use this option sparingly.

Id. Justice Stevens wanted to postpone a decision on O'Connor's suggested change for consideration together with other changes in the Court's procedure. *See id.* Justice William Brennan was flatly opposed to O'Connor's proposed change. Brennan agreed with Powell about the importance of oral argument for the quality of decision making and its symbolic value. On the latter point, Brennan wrote in an internal memo:

> Lewis [Powell] rightly says that one of the values of oral argument is the "symbolism it portrays for the public." For me, that is a very cherished value because it enhances the public image of our complete impartiality.

Id. at 120-121. Brennan's opposition ended the discussion of O'Connor's suggested change. *See id.* at 121.

Do you agree that oral argument enhances public perception of the Court's impartiality? Would this alone justify retaining oral argument? Why or why not?

3. One of the most famous and highly regarded oral advocates before the Court was Daniel Webster. One of Webster's most famous arguments may be the one he gave in *Trustees of Dartmouth College v. Woodward*, 17 U.S. (4 Wheat.) 518 (1819). That case involved a New Hampshire law that purported to amend the charter of the College, which had been made by the British Crown before the American Revolution. The amendments would in effect have converted Dartmouth from a private college to a public one, governed by trustees appointed by the governor of New Hampshire. The majority of the trustees who ran the college before the New Hampshire law was enacted brought suit to challenge the law on the ground that it impaired the obligation of a contract (the charter), in violation of the U.S. Constitution, Art. I, §10, cl. 1. Webster, an alumnus of Dartmouth, successfully argued the case for the trustees.

The account of Webster's 1818 argument in the next excerpt comes from a speech delivered at Dartmouth in 1853 by another Dartmouth graduate and famous orator, Rufus Choate. In his speech, Choate quoted a description of the argument by Dr. Chauncy A. Goodrich.

Rufus Choate, A Discourse Commemorative of Daniel Webster: Delivered Before the Faculty, Students, and Alumni of Dartmouth College, July 27, 1853

in 1 Samuel Gilman Brown, The Works of Rufus Choate with a Memoir of His Life 514-517 (1862)

". . . The Supreme Court of the United States held its session, that winter [of 1818-1819], in a mean apartment of moderate size—the Capitol not having been built after its destruction in 1814 [by the British during the War of 1812]. The audience, when the case came on, was therefore small, consisting chiefly of legal men, the *élite* of the profession throughout the country. Mr. Webster entered upon his argument in the calm tone of easy and dignified conversation. His matter was so completely at his command that he scarcely looked at his brief, but went on for more than four hours with a statement so luminous, and a chain of reasoning so easy to be understood, and yet approaching so nearly to absolute demonstration, that he seemed to carry with him every man of his audience without the slightest effort or weariness on either side. It was hardly *eloquence*, in the strict sense of the term; it was pure reason. Now and then, for a sentence or two, his eye flashed and his voice swelled into a bolder note, as he uttered some emphatic thought; but he instantly fell back into the tone of earnest conversation, which ran throughout the great body of his speech. A single circumstance will show you the clearness and absorbing power of his argument.

"I observed that Judge Story, at the opening of the case, had prepared himself, pen in hand, as if to take copious minutes. Hour after hour I saw him fixed in the same attitude, but, so far as I could perceive, with not a note on his paper. The argument closed, and *I could not discover that he had taken a single note*. Others around me remarked the same thing; and it was among the *on dits* of Washington, that a friend spoke to him of the fact with surprise, when the Judge remarked, 'Every thing was so clear, and so easy to remember, that not a note seemed necessary, and, in fact, I thought little or nothing about my notes.'

"The argument ended. Mr. Webster stood for some moments silent before the Court, while every eye was fixed intently upon him. At length, addressing the Chief Justice, Marshall, he proceeded thus:—

"'*This, Sir, is my case!* It is the case, not merely of that humble institution, it is the case of every College in our land. It is more. It is the case of every Eleemosynary Institution throughout our county,—of all those great charities founded by the piety of our ancestors to alleviate human misery, and scatter blessings along the pathway of life. It is more! It is, in some sense, the case of every man among us who has property of which he may be stripped; for the question is simply this: Shall our State Legislatures be allowed to take that which is not their own, to turn it from its original use, and apply it to such ends or purposes as they, in their discretion, shall see fit!

"'Sir, you may destroy this little Institution; it is weak; it is in your hands! I know it is one of the lesser lights in the literary horizon of our country. You may put it out. But if you do so, you must carry through your work! You must extinguish, one after another, all those great lights of science which, for more than a century, have thrown their radiance over our land!

"It is, Sir, as I have said, a small College. And yet, *there are those who love it—*

"Here the feeling which he had thus far succeeded in keeping down, broke forth. . . . I will not attempt to give you the few broken words of tenderness in which he went on to speak of his attachment to the College. . . . Every one saw that it was wholly unpremeditated, a pressure on his heart, which sought relief in words and tears.

"The courtroom during these two or three minutes presented an extraordinary spectacle. Chief Justice Marshall, with his tall and gaunt figure bent over as if to catch the slightest whisper, the deep furrows of his check expanded with emotion, and eyes suffused with tears. . . .

"Mr. Webster had now recovered his composure, and fixing his keen eye on the Chief Justice, said, in that deep tone with which he sometimes thrilled the heart of an audience,—

"'Sir, I know not how others may feel,' (glancing at the opponents of the College before him,) 'but, for myself, when I see my Alma Mater surrounded, like

Caesar in the senate-house, by those who are reiterating stab upon stab, I would not, for this right hand, have her turn to me, and say, *Et tu quoque mi fili! And thou too, my son!'*

"He sat down. There was a deathlike stillness throughout the room for some moments; every one seemed to be slowly recovering himself, and coming gradually back to his ordinary range of thought and feeling." . . .

Notes and Questions

1. Do you think an oral advocate today could captivate an audience as effectively as Webster apparently did in the *Dartmouth* case? Why or why not?

2. Do you think an advocate today could effectively use oratorical devices—for example, classical allusions—like the ones Webster used? Why or why not?

3. Though Webster used high-flown oratory that might not fly today, Webster also articulated a "chain of reasoning so easy to be understood" and remembered that Justice Story thought it unnecessary to take a single note. In writing about Webster's argument later, Justice Story himself referred to the "lucid order and elegant arrangement" of Webster's argument, "by which each progressive position sustained and illustrated every other." Everett Pepperell, *Daniel Webster: Expounder of the Constitution* 29 (1905) (reprinting Story's account of the argument). Webster's ability to articulate an easy-to-follow chain of reasoning would certainly stand him in good stead as an oral advocate today. *See* Seth P. Waxman, *In the Shadow of Daniel Webster: Arguing Appeals in the Twenty-First Century*, 3 L. App. Prac. & Process 522 (2001).

4. Webster was also highly esteemed for his oral argument in *Gibbons v. Ogden*, 22 U.S. (9 Wheat.) 1 (1824). *See* William H. Rehnquist, *The Supreme Court* 242-243 (revised and updated ed. 2001) (describing the argument). Webster gave a well-known account of the effect on Chief Justice John Marshall of Webster's argument in *Gibbons*:

> I can see the Chief Justice as he looked at that moment. Chief Justice Marshall always wrote with a quill. He never adopted the barbarous invention of steel pens. That abomination had not been introduced. And always, before counsel began to argue, the Chief Justice would nib his pen; and then, when everything was ready, pulling up the sleeves of his gown, he would nod to the counsel who was to address him, as much as to say, "I am ready; now you may go on." I think I never experienced more intellectual pleasure than in arguing that novel question to a great man who could appreciate it, and take it in; and he did take it in, as a baby takes in its mother's milk.

1 Charles Warren, *The Supreme Court in United States History* 603 (rev. ed. 1926) (quoting Webster's description). Though Webster may be exaggerating the effect of his argument, Justice Story also praised Webster's argument in *Gibbons* effusively. *Id.* at 603-604.

2. Impact of Oral Argument

Does oral argument matter? This section examines what current and recent Justices and some political scientists have said about that question.

a. Views of the Justices

William H. Rehnquist, The Supreme Court

243-244 (revised and updated ed. 2001)

Lawyers often ask me whether oral argument "really makes a difference." Often the question is asked with an undertone of skepticism, if not cynicism, intimating that the judges have really made up their minds before they ever come on the bench and oral argument is pretty much of a formality. Speaking for myself, I think it does make a difference: In a significant minority of the cases in which I have heard oral argument, I have left the bench feeling differently about a case than I did when I came on the bench. The change is seldom a one-hundred-and-eighty-degree swing, and I find that it is most likely to occur in cases involving areas of law with which I am least familiar. . . .

Notes and Questions

1. Current Chief Justice John Roberts explained his view of oral argument in an interview with Bryan A. Garner:

> **BRYAN A. GARNER:** When you approach an oral argument as a judge, to what extent do you have a tentative vote in mind? Is there a kind of rebuttable presumption?
> **CHIEF JUSTICE ROBERTS:** It really varies on the case. Some cases seem clear. You look at the briefs, and you're just not persuaded by one side, and you are by another, so you do go in with kind of . . . I'm kind of leaning this way. Usually, you've got concerns. I'm leaning this way, but I need a better answer to this problem. Or I'm leaning this way, but I'm worried about this case. Does it really seem to cut the other way? I'm leaning this way, but is it really going to cause this issue? So even when you're tentatively leaning, you have issues that you want to raise that give the other side a chance to sway you. Some cases, you go in and you don't have a clue. And you're really looking forward to the argument because you want a little greater degree of certainty. . . . Other cases, you go in and there are competing certainties. The language sure seems pretty clear this way. It really leads to some bad results. What are you going to do? Or, yes, this precedent does seem to control, but I think this consequence is too troubling, or the Congress seemed to have a different idea in mind here, and then you've got to work that out. That's a much more typical situation going into argument. . . .

Chief Justice John Roberts, 13 Scribes J. Legal Writing 5, 31-32 (2010).

2. Justice Scalia said the following about oral argument in his interview with Bryan A. Garner:

> [Y]ou should know that oral advocacy is important, that judges don't often have their minds changed by oral advocacy, but very often have their minds made up. I often go into a case right on the knife's edge, and persuasive counsel can persuade me that I ought to flip to this side rather than the other side.

Justice Antonin Scalia, 13 Scribes J. Legal Writing 51, 68 (2010).

3. Justice Clarence Thomas appears to consider oral argument less important than some of the other current Justices. Thomas said the following in an interview with Garner:

> **BRYAN A. GARNER:** How often does your mind change during an oral argument?

JUSTICE THOMAS: Almost never. You can go whole terms without it ever changing. That's my point. And I'm almost certain that my colleagues' minds don't change in maybe max 10 percent, 5 percent of the cases. Or it does change in 5 or 10 percent of the cases, maybe, and I'm being generous there. . . .

Justice Clarence Thomas, 13 Scribes J. Legal Writing 99, 105 (2010). Just as Justice Thomas goes "whole terms" without changing his mind during oral argument, he also goes whole terms without asking questions at oral argument. Thomas has said he does not want to add to what he considers the "unnecessarily intense" questioning by Justices that currently characterizes most oral arguments before the Court. *Id.* at 104.

b. Views of Political Scientists

Timothy R. Johnson, James F. Spriggs II & Paul Wahlbeck, Oral Advocacy Before the United States Supreme Court: Does It Affect the Justices' Decisions?

85 Wash. U. L. Rev. 457 (2007)

A rarely challenged assertion among appellate court judges, lawyers who engage in appellate work, and scholars who teach and study appellate practice is the following: oral argument is an important, if not key, element in the process of successfully appealing a case. . . .

This received wisdom among lawyers and judges, however, is generally not shared by political scientists who study appellate courts. . . . Segal and Spaeth articulate the textbook political science view, noting that there is no systematic empirical evidence that "oral argument regularly, or even infrequently, determines who wins and who loses."[10]

This divergence between the conventional wisdom in the legal academy and the almost dismissive viewpoint of the political science literature raises the empirical question at the heart of our study: do oral arguments actually matter at the U.S. Supreme Court? . . .

To plumb the extent to which arguments put forth by counsel during oral arguments can affect the Justices' decisions, we analyze . . . Justice Harry Blackmun's contemporaneous evaluations of the arguments presented by attorneys who participated in these proceedings. Appointed by President Richard M. Nixon in 1970, Justice Blackmun served on the Court until his retirement in 1994. During this time, Justice Blackmun took extensive notes while he sat on the bench for oral arguments. . . . [The notes are now] at the Library of Congress. . . .

. . . Justice Blackmun's . . . notes include substantive comments about each attorney's positions and a grade for oral argument. . . . For example, in *Florida Department of State v. Treasure Salvors*, Blackmun wrote ten substantive comments about the argument made by the respondent's attorney, Paul Horan, and then noted that "[h]e makes t[he] most o[f] a thin, tough case." The attorney then earned a 6 on Blackmun's 8-point grading scale. . . . Blackmun also offered harsher evaluations at times. He commented on the Nebraska Assistant Attorney General's

---

10. [Jeffrey A. Segal & Harold J. Spaeth, *The Supreme Court and the Attitudinal Model Revisited* (2002),] at 280. *See* Thomas G. Walker & Lee Epstein, *The Supreme Court of the United States: An Introduction* 106 (1993) (suggesting that, while orals are relevant, "[p]robably few [of the Justices'] minds are significantly changed").

argument in *Murphy v. Hunt* by noting, "very confusing talk about Nebraska's bail statutes;" the attorney received a grade of 4. . . .

The first step in our analysis is an examination of the factors . . . associated with Justice Blackmun's evaluations of an attorney's oral arguments. . . . [T]his analysis will help to establish the underlying validity of these data as a measure of the quality of oral argumentation. . . . We contend, and show empirically, that Blackmun's evaluations of attorneys' arguments can plausibly be seen as a measure of their quality. . . .

We posit that attorneys with more litigating experience, better legal education and training, and greater reputational resources will receive higher evaluations because such attorneys will offer the Court more credible and compelling arguments than will less experienced or less resourceful attorneys. The results [of our analysis] . . . provide support for this expectation. Specifically, they show that any single measure of attorney credibility has a modest effect on their oral argument grades, but when one examines a set of these attorney characteristics, we observe considerable variation across the model's predictions of the attorneys' grades. . . .

The results [of our analysis] . . . show that the Justices do indeed respond to the quality of oral argumentation. . . . Even when controlling for the most compelling alternative explanation—a Justice's ideology—and accounting for other factors affecting Court outcomes, the oral argument grades correlate highly with the Justices' final votes on the merits. This relationship is illustrated with the substantive results of this model. When all the independent variables are held at their mean values (or modal value for a categorical variable), there is a 59.2% chance that a Justice will vote to reverse. If we set the value of *Oral Argument Grade* at one standard deviation above its mean, indicating that the appellant's attorney offered a higher quality argument, then this probability increases to 65.0%. The difference is seen more clearly as the quality of competing counsel diverges; when the appellant's attorney is manifestly better than the appellee's attorney, there is an 81.4% chance that a Justice will vote for the petitioner, while this likelihood decreases to 32.9% when the appellee's attorney is clearly better.[4] This statistical result confirms our argument that the relative quality of the competing attorneys' oral arguments influences the Justices' votes on the merits. . . .

One might wonder whether this finding is an artifact of Justices being more responsive to arguments provided by lawyers who advocate positions consistent with their policy preferences. We can definitively state that this is not the case. Our data show that the effect of the difference between the petitioner's and respondent's oral argument quality varies with the Justice's ideological support of the lawyer's position. Nevertheless, even though the impact of oral arguments is statistically different depending on the Justice's ideological predilections, the effect of *Oral Argument Grade* is positive and statistically significant through nearly the entire range of *Ideological Compatibility*. Thus, even Justices who are ideologically opposed to the position advocated by a lawyer have an increased probability of voting for that side of the case if the lawyer provides a higher quality oral argument than the opposing counsel. The magnitude of this effect is sizeable, as [the illustration below] indicates.[133] It demonstrates that nearly all Justices are influenced

---

4. [Editors' note: The authors of this excerpt treat "appellant" and "petitioner" as synonymous terms, and likewise treat "appellee" and "respondent" as synonymous.]

133. *Quality of Oral Argumentation* represents the difference between the quality of oral advocacy by the appellant's and appellee's attorneys, with larger scores indicating that the appellant presented better arguments. . . .

by the quality of oral arguments, but those Justices who are ideologically closer to a lawyer's position have an enhanced tendency to support that lawyer if he or she presents better oral advocacy than does the opposing counsel. In short, oral advocacy has a generally large and robust effect on the way in which Supreme Court Justices vote.

3. The Effect of Oral Advocacy Conditional on Justice Ideology

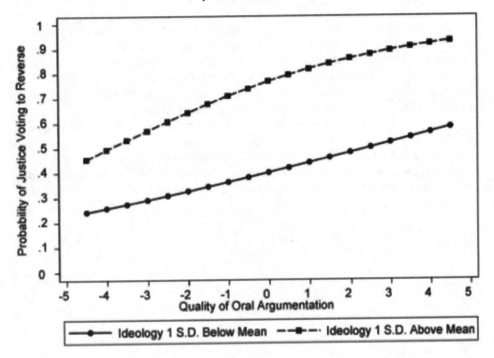

For instance, consider a Justice who is ideologically opposed to the petitioner (specifically, a Justice who is one standard deviation below the mean on *Ideological Compatibility with Appellant*). This Justice has a 35.6% chance of supporting the petitioner when the respondent presents oral advocacy that is considerably better than the petitioner's. By contrast, the likelihood of voting for the petitioner's position increases to 43.8% when this Justice encounters a petitioner who outmatches the respondent's attorney at oral arguments. As seen in Figure 3, the magnitude of the effect of oral advocacy is even more pronounced for Justices who are ideologically supportive of the attorney with the stronger oral argument. When the Justice favors the appellant ideologically but the appellee offers more credible arguments, the Justice has a 70.0% chance of voting for the appellant; when the appellant provides better oral arguments, then this percentage increases to 81.6%. . . .

As we predicted, the effect of ideological distance is also conditioned by the relative quality of the attorneys' oral advocacy. For instance, consider a Justice who is supportive of the petitioner's position. . . . [W]hen the petitioner's attorney is better than the respondent's (one standard deviation above the mean value of *Oral Argument Grade*), a Justice has an 83.6% chance of voting for the petitioner. When the respondent's attorney is better (one standard deviation above the mean value of *Oral Argument Grade*), this number drops to 72.3%. . . .

In summary, our data analyses show convincingly that Supreme Court Justices' final votes on the merits of a case are heavily influenced by oral advocacy. The litigant whose attorney provides the stronger oral argument is substantially more likely to win the case, even after we control statistically for other factors likely to influence Justices' votes. . . .

Notes and Questions

1. As discussed in Chapter 8 (see page 598), the last 25 years have witnessed the emergence of a "Supreme Court bar" comprising a relatively small number of lawyers who appear regularly before the Court. Does this article support the wisdom of choosing one of them to represent you if you have a case before the Court? Does this article have implications for the Court's aspiration to provide "equal justice under law" whether or not a party can afford one of these lawyers?

2. For other published works by political scientists on the role of oral argument, see Lawrence S. Wrightsman, *Oral Arguments Before the Supreme Court: An Empirical Approach* (2008); Neil D. McFeeley & Richard J. Ault, *Supreme Court Oral Argument: An Exploratory Analysis*, 20 Jurimetrics J. 52 (1979); Stephen Wasby, Anthony A. D'Amato & Rosemary Metrailer, *The Functions of Oral Argument in the U.S. Supreme Court*, 62 Q. J. Speech 410 (1976).

7

Deciding Cases

At the close of oral argument, the Chief Justice bangs his gavel and declares, "The case is submitted." The Justices then rise from the bench and, in order of seniority, file through the red velvet curtain that separates the public courtroom from their private chambers. Out of the public eye, they deliberate, vote, and draft opinions justifying—or attacking—the outcome of the case.

Months later, after striking the gavel to call the Court into session, the Chief Justice announces without any forewarning that the case is decided. The author of the main opinion summarizes it to those in the courtroom. Sometimes, in a contentious case, a colleague follows with an oral dissent. The case is then published, and becomes precedent.

What happened behind the curtain between the two bangs of the gavel? This chapter examines what occurred. Section A gives a behind-the-scenes view of the Court's decision-making process from the time a case is submitted to the time it is decided, and offers historical, scholarly, and judicial perspectives on that process. Section B examines the structure, style, and strategy of majority, concurring, and dissenting opinions by contemporary Justices with distinctive and differing approaches to deciding cases.

A. PROCESS

1. The Conference

How does the Supreme Court decide a case? The formal process begins within days of oral argument, when the Justices confront a decision point. They must each cast a vote at a private meeting in the Chief Justice's conference room, pictured below. Former Chief Justice William Rehnquist gives an insider's account of the conference.

William H. Rehnquist, The Supreme Court

252-259 (2001)

... When one thinks of the important ramifications that some of the constitutional decisions of the Supreme Court have, it seems that one could never know as much as he ought to know about how to cast his vote in a case. But true as this is, each member must cast votes in each case decided on the merits each year, and there must come a time when pondering one's own views must cease, and deliberation with one's colleagues and voting must begin.

That time is each Wednesday afternoon after we get off the bench for those cases argued on Monday, and Friday for those cases argued on Tuesday and Wednesday. .... A buzzer sounds—or, to put it more accurately, is supposed to sound—in each of the nine chambers five minutes before the time for conference, and the nine members of the Court then congregate in the conference room next to the chambers of the Chief Justice. We all shake hands with one another when we come in, and our vote sheets and whatever other material we want are at our places at the long, rectangle conference table. Seating is strictly by seniority: the Chief Justice sits at one end and the senior Associate Justice at the other end. Unlike those ranged along the sides of the table, we have unrestricted elbow room. But even along the sides the seating is by seniority: The three associate justices next in seniority sit on one side, and the four associates having the least seniority are on the opposite side.

To anyone familiar with the decision-making process in other governmental institutions, the most striking thing about our Court's conference is that only the nine justices are present. There are no law clerks, no secretaries, no staff assistants, no outside personnel of any kind. If a messenger from the Marshal's Office—the agency responsible for guarding the door of the conference—knocks on the door to indicate that there is a message for one of the justices, the junior Justice opens the door and delivers it. The junior Justice is also responsible for dictating to the staff of the clerk's office at the close of conference the text of the orders that will appear on the Court's order list issued on the Monday following the conference.

I think that the tradition of having only the justices themselves present at the Court's conference is salutary for more than one reason. Its principal effect is to implement the observation of Justice Brandeis . . . that the Supreme Court is respected because "we do our own work." If a justice is to participate meaningfully in the conference, the justice must himself know the issues to be discussed and the arguments he wishes to make. Some cases may be sufficiently complicated as to require written notes to remind one of various points, but any extended reading of one's position to a group of only eight colleagues is bound to lessen the effect of what one says. . . .

In discussions of cases that have been argued, the Chief Justice reviews the facts and the decision of the lower court, outlining his understanding of the applicable case law, and indicating either that he votes to affirm the decision of the lower court or to reverse it. The discussion then proceeds to senior Associate on down to the most junior. For many years there has circulated a tale that although the discussion in conference proceeds in order from the Chief Justice to the junior Justice, the voting actually begins with the junior Justice and proceeds back to the Chief Justice in order of seniority. But, at least during my thirty years on the Court, this tale is very much of a myth; I don't believe I have ever seen it happen at any of the conferences that I have attended.

The time taken in discussion of a particular case by each justice will naturally vary with the complexity of the case and the nature of the discussion that has preceded his. The Chief Justice, going first, takes more time than any one Associate in a typical case, because he feels called upon to go into greater detail as to the facts and the lower-court holding than do those who come after him. The truth is that there simply are not nine different points of view in even the most complex and difficult case, and all of us feel impelled to a greater or lesser degree to try to reach some consensus that can be embodied in a written opinion that will command the support of at least a majority of the members of the Court. The lack of anything that is both previously unsaid, relevant, and sensible is apt to be frustrating to those far down the line of discussion, but this is one of the prices exacted by the seniority system. With rare exceptions, each justice begins and ends his part of the discussion without interruption from his colleagues, and in the great majority of cases, by the time the most junior justice is finished with his discussion it will be evident that a majority of the Court has agreed upon a basis for either affirming or reversing the decision of the lower court in the case under discussion.

When I first went on the Court, I was both surprised and disappointed at how little interplay there was between the various justices during the process of conferring on a case. Each would state his views, and a junior justice could express agreement or disagreement with views expressed by a justice senior to him earlier in the discussion, but the converse did not apply; a junior justice's views were seldom commented upon, because votes had been already cast up the line. Probably the most junior justices before me felt as I did, that they had some very significant contributions to make, and were disappointed that they hardly ever seemed to influence anyone because people didn't change their votes in response to their, the junior justices', contrary views. I felt then it would be desirable to have more of a round-table discussion of the matter after each of us had expressed our ideas. Having now sat in conferences for nearly three decades, and having risen from ninth to first in seniority, I realize—with newfound clarity—that my idea as a junior justice, while fine in the abstract, probably would not have contributed much in practice, and at any rate was doomed by the seniority system to which the senior justices naturally adhere.

Each member of the Court has done such work as he deems necessary to arrive at his own views before coming into conference; it is not a bull session in which off-the-cuff reactions are traded, but instead a discussion in which considered views are stated. We are all working with the same materials, dealing with the same briefs, the same cases, and have heard the same oral argument; unlikely as it may seem to the brand-new justice, the point that he seizes upon probably has been considered by some of the others and they have not found it persuasive. It is not as if we were trying to find a formula for squaring the circle, and all of those preceding the junior justice have bumblingly admitted their inability to find the formula; then suddenly the latter solves the riddle, and the others cry "Eureka! He has found it." The law is at best an inexact science, and the cases our Court takes to decide are frequently ones upon which able judges in lower courts have disagreed. There simply is no demonstrably "right" answer to the question involved in many of our difficult cases.

I have heard both Felix Frankfurter and William O. Douglas describe the conferences presided over by Chief Justice Charles Evans Hughes in which they sat, and I have heard Douglas describe the conferences presided over by Chief Justice Harlan F. Stone. Their styles were apparently very different. Hughes has rightly been described as Jovian in appearance, and, according to Frankfurter, he "radiated authority." He was totally prepared in each case, lucidly expressed his views, and said no more than was necessary. In the words of Frankfurter, you did not speak up in that conference unless you were very certain that you knew what you were talking about. Discipline and restraint were the order of the day.

Understandably, some of the justices appointed by President Roosevelt in the last part of Hughes's tenure resented his tight rein—imposed albeit only by example. Stone was one of those who had disliked the taut atmosphere of the Hughes conference, and when he became Chief Justice, he opened up the floor to more discussion. But, according to Douglas, Stone was unable to shake his former role as a law-school professor, and as a result he would lead off the discussion with a full statement of his own views, then turn the floor over to the senior Associate Justice; but at the conclusion of the latter's presentation Stone would take the floor once more to critique the analysis of the senior Associate. The conference totally lost the tautness it had under Hughes, and on some occasions went on interminably.

The conferences under Warren Burger were somewhere in between those presided over by Hughes and those by Stone. Since I have become Chief Justice, I have tried to make my opening presentation of a case somewhat shorter than Burger made his. I do not believe that conference discussion changes many votes, and I do not think that the impact of the Chief Justice's presentation is necessarily proportional to its length. I don't mean to give the impression that the discussion in every case is stated in terms of nine inflexible positions; on occasion, one or more of those who have stated their views toward the beginning of the discussion, upon seeing that those views as stated are not in agreement with those of the majority, may indicate a willingness to alter those views along the lines of the thinking of the majority. But there is virtually no institutional pressure to do this, and one only need read the opinions of the Court to see that it is practiced by all of us.

I quite strongly prefer the Hughes style over the Stone style insofar as interruptions of conference discussion are concerned. I think it is very desirable that all members of the Court have an opportunity to state their views before there is any cross-questioning or interruption, and I try to convey this sentiment to my colleagues. But the chief justices are not like the speaker of the House of Representatives; it is unheard of to declare anyone out of order, and the chief justice is pretty much limited to leading by example. On rare occasions, questioning of a justice who is speaking by one who has already spoken may throw added light on a particular issue, but this practice carries with it the potential for disrupting the orderly participation of each member of the Court in the discussion. At the end of the discussion, I announce how I am recording the vote in the case, so that others may have the opportunity to disagree with my count if they believe I am mistaken.

The upshot of the conference discussion of a case will, of course, vary in its precision and detail. If a case is a relatively simple one, with only one real legal issue in it, it will generally be very clear where each member of the Court stands on that issue. But many of the cases that we decide are complex ones, with several interrelated issues, and it is simply not possible in the format of the conference to have nine people answering either yes or no to a series of difficult questions about constitutional law. One justice may quite logically believe that a negative answer to the very first of several questions makes it unnecessary to decide the subsequent ones, and having answered the first in the negative will say no more. But if a majority answers the first question in the affirmative, then the Court's opinion will have to go on and discuss the other questions. Whether or not the first justice agrees with the majority on these other issues may not be clear from the conference discussion. The comment is frequently heard during the course of a discussion that "some things will have to be worked out in the writing," and this is very true in a number of cases. Oral discussion of a complex case will usually give the broad outlines of each justice's position, but it is simply not adequate to fine-tune the various positions in the way that the written opinion for the majority of the Court, and the dissenting opinions, eventually will. The broad outlines emerge from the conference discussion, but often not the refinements.

So long as we rely entirely on oral discussion for the exposition of views at conference, I do not see how it could do more than it now does in refining the various views on particular issues. I understand that judges of other courts rely on written presentations circulated by each judge to his colleagues before the conference discussion; this practice may well flesh out more views on the details of a case, but the need to reconcile the differences in the views expressed still remains. There is also a very human tendency to become more firmly committed to a view that is put in writing than one that is simply expressed orally, and therefore the possibility of adjustment and adaptation might be lessened by this approach. At any rate, we do not use it, and I know of no one currently on the Court who believes we should try it.

Our conference is a relatively fragile instrument which works well for the purposes to which we put it, but which also has significant limitations. As I have said, probably every new justice, and very likely some justices who have been there for a while, wish that on occasion the floor could be opened up to a free-swinging exchange of views rather than a structured statement of nine positions. I don't doubt that courts traditionally consisting of three judges, such as the federal courts of appeals, can be much more relaxed and informal in their discussion of a case they have heard argued. But the fact that we are nine, and not three, or five, or seven, sets limits on our procedure. We meet with one another week after week, year after year, to discuss and deliberate over some of the most important legal questions in the United States. Each of us soon comes to know the general outlook of each of his eight colleagues, and on occasion I am sure that each of us feels, listening to the eight others, that he has "heard it all before." If there were a real prospect that extended discussion would bring about crucial changes in position on the part of one or more members of the Court, that would be a strong argument for having that sort of discussion even with its attendant consumption of time. But my years on the Court have convinced me that the true purpose of the conference discussion of argued cases is not to persuade one's colleagues through impassioned advocacy to alter their views, but instead, by hearing each justice express his own views, to determine therefrom the view of the majority of the Court. This is not to say that minds are never changed in conference; they certainly are. But it is very much the exception and not the rule, and if one gives some thought to the matter, this should come as no surprise.

The justices sitting in conference are not, after all, like a group of decision-makers who are hearing arguments pro and con about the matter for the first time. They have presumably read the briefs, they have heard the oral arguments of the lawyers who generally know far more about the particular case than the justices do, and they have had an opportunity to discuss the case with one or more of their law clerks. The party who wishes to have the decision of the lower court reversed has attempted to show the Court, by citation of relevant case law and statutes, how and why this should be done; the party who wishes to sustain the judgment of the lower court has made a similar effort on behalf of his point of view. The conference of our Court is the penultimate stage in our decision-making process, and we have all been dealing with much the same arguments on both sides of the case since we first began considering it. The fact that one or more justices feels very strongly about his view of the case is no indication that other justices who may be less hortatory in their discussion feel less strongly about their views. All in all, I think our conference does about all that it can be expected to do in moving the Court to a final decision of a case by means of a written opinion.

During a given two-week session of oral argument, we will usually hear twelve cases. By Friday of the second week we will have conferred about all of them. . . .

Notes and Questions

1. Chiseled above the front entrance of the Supreme Court are the words, "Equal Justice Under Law." Yet for an institution tasked with upholding the Constitution's command of equal protection, the Court can be a curiously hierarchical place. As noted, the Justices enter and exit the courtroom in order of seniority. When a chambers becomes available, selection proceeds by seniority, with prime real estate closer to the courtroom (and hence a shorter walking distance) generally preferred by the more senior Justices. At lunch, the members of the Court sit around their dining table in order of seniority, and abide by their seating assignment regardless of the number in attendance. Similarly, as Chief Justice Rehnquist relates, seniority determines the place of each Justice around the conference table, which in turn determines the order by which the members of the Court express their views and cast their votes. Consequently, in a conference without much back-and-forth discussion, the more junior the Justice, the less likely his or her views will even be heard, much less considered, before a case has already been decided by majority vote. Does this strike you as an unfair or undesirable method for the highest court in the land to decide cases?

2. Might there be a better way to order the voicing of views and votes at the Justices' conference? Consider, for example, a conference in which discussion proceeds in order of seniority, and then voting occurs in reverse order. Chief Justice Rehnquist avers that the conference never operated that way during his time on the Court. But apparently, that was how conferences generally proceeded until Chief Justice Warren Burger. *See* John Paul Stevens, *Five Chiefs* 154-155 (2011). What advantages or disadvantages might flow from the prior procedure? In practice, would it give junior Justices any more sway over colleagues who have already announced their views, if not their votes? Why do you think it was abandoned in favor of the process Chief Justice Rehnquist describes?

In contemplating these questions, consider two common justifications for reverse-order voting. Justice Felix Frankfurter explains that it was done "[i]n order that the junior [justices] shouldn't be influenced" or "coerce[d]" by more senior colleagues. Felix Frankfurter, *Chief Justices I Have Known*, 39 Va. L. Rev. 883, 903 (1953). On the other hand, a more cynical observer has noted that "[b]y speaking first and voting last, the Chief Justice could see how the vote was going and cast his lot with the majority in order to control the opinion." *The Supreme Court in Conference* (1940-1985) 12 (Del Dickson ed., 2001). That said, according to some social science research into small-group dynamics, "separating discussion from voting encourages flexibility and accommodation on the part of group members," as positions tend not to harden until formal votes are taken. *Id.* at 10.

3. The Chief Justice of the Supreme Court has been described as the "first among equals" because his vote carries no more weight than that of his colleagues. However, as Chief Justice Rehnquist observes, the Chief Justice can, by example if not by command, exert considerable influence over how much—or how little—discussion occurs at conference. In Chief Justice Rehnquist's case, by his own admission, it was very little. Each Justice said enough to explain his or her vote, but not much more. Indeed, as his colleague Justice Antonin Scalia once remarked, "[T]o call our discussion of a case a conference is really something of a misnomer. It's much more a statement of the views of each of the nine justices." David M. O'Brien, *Storm Center: The Supreme Court in American Politics* 207 (8th ed. 2008). Why did Chief Justice Rehnquist not allow the conference to turn into a "bull session" in which views could be developed fully and debated vigorously? Do you find his reasons persuasive? If not, how much latitude would you allow for discussion and debate? Do you believe that longer exchanges could change minds or produce better decisions?

4. There are no rules or manuals on how conferences should be run; historically, they have varied greatly in both form and substance. In fact, in the first years of the Court, the Justices did not even meet for conference because they decided cases in the traditional English seriatim style—that is, by the individual opinions of each justice rather than a collective judgment of the Court. Then, for a good part of Chief Justice John Marshall's tenure, the Justices lived together in a boardinghouse during the few months when the Court was in session. Chief Justice Marshall engineered this close living arrangement with the goal of promoting unity. Argument back then had no time limits and could last days. Afterward, at the boardinghouse, Justice Joseph Story recounted that "[w]e moot every question as we proceed, and my familiar conferences at our lodgings often come to a very quick, and, I trust, a very accurate opinion, in a few hours." Letter from Joseph Story to Samuel Fay

(Feb. 24, 1812), reprinted in 1 *Life and Letters of Joseph Story* 215-216 (William W. Story ed. 1851). In fact, Justice Story reported, living "very harmoniously and familiarly" in close quarters, the Justices "derive no inconsiderable advantage from the pleasant and animated interchange of legal acumen." Letter from Joseph Story to Nathaniel Williams (Feb. 16, 1812), reprinted in 1 *Life and Letters of Joseph Story* at 214; *see also* G. Edward White, *The Working Life of the Marshall Court, 1815-1835*, 70 Va. L. Rev. 1, 39 (1984) ("The boardinghouse provided not only an informal forum in which the justices could discuss issues until they were resolved but also a fraternal setting in which one justice might not want to disagree openly with another justice"). Considering the Marshall Court's experience, do you think the Court today would be less—or more—divided if its members lived and worked together?

5. During the rest of the nineteenth century, conferences varied in length and formality. For example, contemporaneous accounts by various Justices suggest that, under Marshall's successor, Roger B. Taney, discussion could last days and was "free and open among the Justices till all were satisfied," while under his successors, conferences became briefer but often more contentious as Justices grew increasingly willing to "lock horns and fight." *The Supreme Court in Conference (1940-1985)* 46, 60 (Del Dickson ed., 2001) (quotations of Justice John Archibald Campbell and Justice David Brewer, respectively).

6. In the first half of the twentieth century, conferences acquired their modern efficiency and formality and saw a return to civility. In particular, under the diplomatic but strong leadership of Chief Justice (and former President) William Howard Taft, disagreements no longer devolved into "a cockfight," and the meetings went "as smoothly as possible," according to Justice Oliver Wendell Holmes. Bernard Schwartz, *A History of the Supreme Court* 213-214 (1993). Under Chief Justice Taft's successor, Chief Justice Charles Evans Hughes, whose style Chief Justice Rehnquist "strongly prefer[red]," conferences became even more economical. Justice Felix Frankfurter gives the following account:

> . . . Hughes was dynamic and efficient. That's a bad word to apply to Hughes, because it implies regimentation. It implies something disagreeable, at least to me. I don't like to have a man who is too efficient. He's likely to be not human enough. That wasn't true of Hughes. He simply was effective—not efficient, but effective. Stone was much more easy-going. The conference was more leisurely. The atmosphere was less taut, both in the courtroom and the conference room. It has been said that there wasn't free and easy talk in Hughes's day in the conference room. Nothing could be further from the truth. There was less wasteful talk. There was less repetitious talk. There was less foolish talk. You just didn't like to talk unless you were dead sure of your ground, because that gimlet mind of his was there ahead of you.

Frankfurter, *supra*, at 902-903.

7. To say that conferences under Chief Justice Hughes's successor, Chief Justice Harlan Fiske Stone, were "more leisurely" may be a bit of an understatement. Some conferences lasted not hours, but days. As Justice Frankfurter noted in his diary, Chief Justice Stone had

> a habit . . . of not allowing a Justice to state his views uninterruptedly when contrary to those of the C[hief]) J[ustice] but to argue almost every word that is uttered, thereby breaking up the discussion and making of it a needless contention, and, of course, causing a frightful waste of time. Several of the Brethren, especially Roberts and Black, have talked to me complainingly of this. When, last year, Lauson Stone, the Chief's oldest son, asked me confidentially how his Dad was carrying on as C.J., I told him that I

had only one qualification to make, and that is precisely the practice of which today's performance was an egregious example, namely, his failure to observe what seems to me to be an indispensably wise order of procedure—for the C.J. to have his say, and then in order of seniority, for every other member of the Court to have his say without any interruption.

Excerpt from Felix Frankfurter's diary (Jan. 16, 1943), in *From the Diaries of Felix Frankfurter* 160 (Joseph P. Lash ed., 1975).

Yet Justice Frankfurter himself was not free from blame. A former Harvard Law School professor, he was not above condescending to instruct and correct his colleagues in memos, at oral argument, and during conference. Chief Justice Hughes may have held Justice Frankfurter in check with his "gimlet mind," but Chief Justice Stone did not restrain Justice Frankfurter's "never-let-go" personality. John M. Ferren, *Salt of the Earth, Conscience of the Court: The Story of Justice Wiley Rutledge* 277 (2004). Consequently, according to Justice Potter Stewart, Justice Frankfurter frequently "would speak for fifty minutes, no more or less, because that was the length of the lecture at the Harvard Law School." Melvin I. Urofsky, *William O. Douglas and Felix Frankfurter: Ideology and Personality on the Supreme Court*, in 24 The History Teacher 7, 9 (1990). During these lectures, Justice William O. Douglas had no qualms about getting up and going away until Justice Frankfurter was finished.

8. In the second half of the twentieth century, the feel and format of conferences continued to change under the contrasting leadership of three Chief Justices. First was Chief Justice Earl Warren, of whom Justice William Brennan remarked, "To many of his colleagues, certainly to me, he was the Super-Chief." William J. Brennan, Jr., *In Memoriam: Earl Warren*, 88 Harv. L. Rev. 1, 4-5 (1974). One of Chief Justice Warren's "super" powers was his skill at leading conferences and forging consensus in landmark cases such as *Brown v. Board of Education*. His colleague, Justice Abe Fortas, for example, observed that "[i]t was Warren's great gift that, in presenting the case and discussing the case, he proceeded immediately and very calmly and graciously to the ultimate values involved—the ultimate constitutional values, the ultimate human values," and that "opposition based on hemstitching and embroidery of the law appeared petty" by contrast. Bernard Schwartz, *Decision: How the Supreme Court Decides Cases* 89 (1996).

9. Of the conferences of Earl Warren's successor, Warren Burger, Chief Justice Rehnquist simply states that they were "somewhere in between those presided over by Hughes and those by Stone." Rehnquist, *supra*, at 256. Other colleagues have been willing to say more publicly. Justice Lewis Powell recalled that Chief Justice Burger would allow other Justices to "speak as long as you wanted, and [to] interrupt another justice if you wanted." O'Brien, *supra*, at 204. Justice John Paul Stevens adds that Chief Justice Burger himself "would interrupt the discussion to add a point he had omitted or even to repeat a point that had already been made." Stevens, *supra*, at 154. Inside the Court, then-Associate Justice Rehnquist privately wrote to Chief Justice Burger after a protracted conference that he "had the feeling that . . . we may have fitted Matthew Arnold's closing lines in 'Dover Beach' wherein he refers to those 'Swept with confused alarms of Struggle and flight Where ignorant armies clash by night.'" O'Brien, *supra*, at 205. As a student of history and sufferer under Chief Justice Burger, it is hardly surprising that when Rehnquist took over as Chief Justice, he pulled back sharply on discussion and frowned on interruptions. Besides failing to change minds, Rehnquist came to conclude that "[a]nother disadvantage of endless conference discussions is the very visible tension which prolonged dispute, even of the most friendly kind, engenders among nine justices deciding cases of great significance both to themselves and to the country." William H. Rehnquist, *Chief Justices I Never Knew*, 3 Hastings Const. L.Q. 637, 647 (1976).

10. If you were appointed Chief Justice, would you model conferences after any of the above predecessors? If, instead, you were appointed associate Justice, would your preference differ? If none of these models seems satisfactory, consider the way the current Chief Justice, John Roberts, runs conferences. He maintains the seniority system for expressing views and casting votes, but according to Stevens, he also "welcome[s] more discussion of the merits of the argued cases than his predecessor—including expansions of the reasoning behind his own votes," while "maintain[ing] the appropriate impartiality in giving each of us an opportunity to speak." Stevens, *supra*, at 210.

2. Case Study: Conference in *Miranda v. Arizona*

Would you like to be a fly on the wall inside the conference room listening to the Justices decide cases? Although the Justices do not allow anyone else, or any recording devices, into the room during conference, they do take notes for themselves and their clerks. A number of Justices in modern times have given their papers, including their conference notes, to institutions such as the Library of Congress for release after their death. *See infra* Chapter 8.B.2. Below is a reconstruction, based on the conference notes of Justices William Douglas and William Brennan, of the Justices' deliberations in the landmark case of *Miranda v. Arizona*, 384 U.S. 436 (1966), and its companion cases.

Along with *Brown v. Board of Education*, 347 U.S. 483 (1954), and *Reynolds v. Sims*, 377 U.S. 533 (1964), Chief Justice Earl Warren's opinion for the Court in *Miranda v. Arizona* ranks as one of his most enduring legacies. For decades prior to *Miranda*, the Court struggled to regulate police interrogations and to root out confessions obtained through physical or psychological coercion. Initially relying on the Due Process Clause, the Court invalidated confessions that were involuntary due to a suspect's will being "overborne" by police tactics. *See, e.g., Spano v. New York*, 360 U.S. 315 (1959). But that case-by-case approach, with its vague metaphysical standard, proved too infrequent and unpredictable to be effective except in extreme situations. In 1964, the Court turned to the Sixth Amendment right to counsel as another tool for regulating interrogations, excluding confessions that police "deliberately elicited" in the absence of counsel after the initiation of adversarial proceedings. *See Massiah v. United States*, 377 U.S. 201, 204 (1964). However, because interrogations mostly occur before formal charges have been filed, and often before the police have even "focused" on a suspect, *see Escobedo v. Illinois*, 378 U.S. 478 (1964) (extending the Sixth Amendment right to counsel under narrow circumstances to targets of police investigation), the Sixth Amendment proved inadequate in reach. Accordingly, under Warren's leadership, the Court in *Miranda* settled on the Fifth Amendment privilege against self-incrimination as the basis for concrete rules to remedy the "inherently compelling pressures" of custodial interrogations. *Miranda*, 384 U.S. at 467. The decision required police to give suspects in custodial interrogation the now-famous set of *Miranda* warnings: That they have a right to remain silent, that anything they say can be used against them, that they have a right to an attorney before and during interrogation, and that an attorney will be provided if they cannot afford one. *Miranda*'s mandate provoked a firestorm of criticism by police and politicians on the day of its release, and the status, scope, and desirability of the *Miranda* warnings continue to be debated to this day by policy makers, scholars, and the Justices themselves. *See, e.g., United States v. Dickerson*, 530 U.S. 428 (2000); Commentary Symposium, Miranda *at Forty*, 5 Ohio St. J. Crim. L. 161 (2007).

Like most other decisions great and small, *Miranda* started to take shape with the views and votes set forth by the Justices at conference.

Del Dickson, The Supreme Court in Conference (1940-1985)

515-557 (2001)

Eleven days after an eighteen-year-old Phoenix woman was kidnapped and raped, police found her 1953 Packard parked in front of Ernesto A. Miranda's house. The victim picked Miranda out of a lineup, and following a routine two-hour interrogation Miranda confessed. Miranda's lawyer acknowledged that there had been no physical coercion during the interrogation but argued that Miranda had not been informed of his rights and had waived them without knowing the consequences of his decision.

By the time the case reached the Supreme Court, it included similar interrogation cases from California, Missouri, New Jersey, and New York. In each case the suspects had been questioned without being warned of their constitutional rights, and in each case the suspects made incriminating statements used against them at trial.

CONFERENCE OF MARCH 18, 1966

WARREN: [Douglas: The Chief reads a printed statement he had prepared.] I do not accept New York's approach that this is a legislative problem only. I do not accept the Solicitor General's view that "totality" governs. Basically, the issue is under the Fifth Amendment and "being a witness against himself." It also might be under the Sixth Amendment, in case there was a lawyer being sought. The right against interrogation involves the Fifth Amendment. Talking to the police is different from being interrogated by the police. The right to counsel commences at least when a man is taken into custody, or when police undertake to put him there. Our system is accusatory; there is no right to arrest for investigation, only on probable cause or with a warrant. His right to counsel commences at that moment—the case commences then. This does not mean that a lawyer must be appointed then, but later—interrogation is such a "later" time. He must be advised (1) of his right to remain silent; (2) that what he says may be used against him; (3) that in time the court may appoint a lawyer; (4) he must be given an opportunity to get a lawyer before he is interrogated, unless he waives that right; (5) the burden is on the government to show a waiver; and (6) no distinction should be made between one who has a lawyer and one who does not, or between one who can hire one and one who cannot. *Gideon* controls this case. The routine of "booking" is not a violation of the Fifth Amendment. I would follow *Linkletter* and not make it retroactive.

The solicitor general's letter on FBI practice states my views down to the point where the man does not have a lawyer. The FBI leaves it to the discretion of the agent whether there has been a "waiver," but I do not agree with that. I reverse in *Miranda*. There was no warning by police. I also reverse in *Vignera* on the same ground, plus the fact that the state barred the petitioner from proving at trial that no warnings were given. In *Westover*, I reverse because he was not advised of his right to counsel. In *Johnson*, I affirm. The rule is not retroactive, and also there was no involuntariness issue, as it was waived at trial. In *California v. Stewart*, I affirm on the failure to give adequate warnings.

BLACK: I agree with a large part of what the Chief says. But I think that the focus is on the privilege against being a witness against one's self. Look at the Magna Carta. The right to counsel comes in as to a confession as having a bearing on whether the confession was taken in defiance of this privilege. A man is entitled to all of the benefits of a defendant when the government moves against him. I said in *Ashcraft v. Tennessee* that this act was "inherently coercive," and that thereafter you can't make him be a witness against himself. He has a constitutional right not to be witness against himself. There is no right of questioning while he is in custody. When a man is in custody, he is a witness against himself. I am not sure at that stage whether he can be put into a lineup or fingerprinted. When arrested, he cannot be asked questions—you can't get him a lawyer then. I think that it is coercion. I give no credence to "warning the accused." I would reverse all of these cases, except *California v. Stewart*. I will probably go along in affirming *Johnson*, though at least for now I will vote to reverse.

DOUGLAS: I agree largely with the Chief, but I think that this is a critical stage and is largely, therefore, a right to counsel case.

CLARK: I am pretty close to the Chief. When does government "move" against a suspect? When you put it under the Fifth Amendment, you must put it under "interrogation." We do not have to pass on investigation, fingerprinting, lineup, or photography issues here. Once the police are thinking of interrogation, they must warn him on (1) his right to silence; (2) anything he says can be used against him; (3) he can have a lawyer; (4) he is entitled to court-appointed counsel if he can't afford one. But statements not elicited by interrogation should not be barred. In *Stewart*, the record is silent. The burden is on the state to show a waiver.

HARLAN: What the Chief Justice, Hugo, and Bill Douglas have said repudiate all of our precedents and history and the American Bar Association proposals. I would leave law reforms to others who have more information and ability. Our conference room is in an abstract medium—I can't see why we should reverse the course of history and make these radical changes. All of the studies that are going on will become abortive. I am not prepared to slam the door on more deliberation and more empirical data being assembled. What we do, if the Chief's views obtain a majority, should be done by constitutional amendment. I would modify *Linkletter* to make this new rule applicable only to cases that start after these decisions.

BRENNAN: I agree substantially with the Chief. I would make the new rule applicable to all pending cases, not just to these five alone. As for the timing of the warning, if you wait until "interrogation," rather than arrest, you will get into difficulties. "Focus" on him is not enough. When he is arrested is the better test. As to retroactivity, we might make them apply back to the date of *Malloy*. In *Tehan*, we made it retroactive from the date of *Griffin*. Perhaps it should be made retroactive to *Escobedo*.

STEWART: I disagree with the Chief. The privilege against self-incrimination is only a testimonial privilege. "Compulsion" is not present here within the framework of our coerced confession cases. "Compelling" means only coerced statements. I would stick to the totality of facts on coercion. I more or less agree with John Harlan.

WHITE: I also disagree with the Chief Justice, and agree with John and Potter.

FORTAS: In general, I agree with the Chief.

Notes and Questions

1. What was the vote count for the *Miranda* case? Was there a clear majority to affirm or reverse? If so, was there a clear majority for a *rationale* supporting that result?

2. Who should have assigned the opinion? If you had been the senior Justice in the majority, to whom would you have assigned the opinion? Why?

3. Are you surprised at the seemingly calm tone of discussion? Of course, the conference notes of the Justices record votes and views, not tone of voice, so the prose on the page may not reflect the emotion in the room. But Justice John Paul Stevens attests that, in his 35 years on the Court, he has "no memory of any member of the Court raising his or her voice during any conference . . . or showing any disrespect for a colleague during our discussions." Stevens, *supra*, at 244. Given the many contentious issues that come before the Court—and are decided in conference—are you surprised? Or do you suspect that the positive portrayals of the conference discussions by Justice Stevens and Chief Justice Rehnquist above may perhaps reflect a desire to protect the institutional reputation of their Court?

4. Notice that the views expressed by the Justices seem to get more abbreviated as the discussion proceeds from the Chief Justice to the junior Justice. Assuming that the length of the notes for each Justice actually approximates the length of time spoken, does this reconstruction lend credence to the view that the order of speaking at conference favors more senior Justices in general and the Chief Justice in particular? For example, in what ways did Chief Justice Warren's initial exposition shape the subsequent discussion? On the other end, by the time the discussion reached Justice Abe Fortas, did it matter what he said or how he voted?

5. Justice William Douglas's conference notes state that Chief Justice Warren read from a printed statement. The former Chief Justice's papers at the Library of Congress contain what appears to be typed-out conference notes as well as five pages of handwritten notes on which they were based. From the latter, a page of which is reproduced below, do you recognize the *Miranda* warnings that, in the words of Chief Justice William Rehnquist four decades later, "have become part of our national culture"? *United States v. Dickerson*, 530 U.S. 428, 443 (2000).

do is to interrogate him unless he
is adequately advised of his rights and
legally waives them.

He must be advised fully of right to remain
silent etc and of his right to counsel, that
if he is indigent the court will appoint
a lawyer for him. He must be offered
an opportunity to communicate with
a lawyer or friend if he has either
and if neither is available to him
at that time there must be no
interrogation until he does have
one unless he intelligently waives
his rights and manifests a willingness
to be interrogated. He cannot be
either threatened, or cajoled into such
a waiver. If this is done the waiver is not effective.

No distinction should be made between
a deft who already has a lawyer as
did Escobedo and one who has none
at the time; nor between one who can
retain a lawyer at the time and one who for any reason cannot.
Nor should any distinction be made
between those who have the means
to hire a lawyer and those who do not.
(Gideon has wiped out that distinction)

The above principles do not and should not
retard the police from making any investigation
of the deft while he is in custody —
that it would be lawful for them to make otherwise

3. The Assignment

The votes at conference decide the outcome of a case. And each case is ultimately decided, not necessarily based on the better view of the law, but based on the outcome that gets at least five votes and, therefore, a majority on a court of nine justices. The importance of this "rule of five" is illustrated by Justice William Brennan's practice of catechizing new law clerks. He would ask them to identify the most important rule in constitutional law. Predictably, they would nominate one of the great protections of the Constitution, such as the First Amendment's guarantee of free speech. Justice Brennan would smile wryly, savoring the moment, before unfurling the fingers of one raised hand. "Five," he would respond, meaning that "[w]ith five votes, a justice could do anything." Adam Winkler, *The Real Void Stevens Leaves*, The Daily Beast (Apr. 10, 2010), http://www.thedailybeast.com/articles/2010/04/10/the-void-left-by-stevens.html.

The most senior member in the majority assigns the case to a Justice for opinion writing. The most senior Justice in the minority assigns the main dissenting opinion. Notably, as "the first among equals," the Chief Justice is the most senior in any majority or minority to which he or she belongs. After the majority and dissenting opinions are circulated among the Justices, others can and often do write separate concurring and dissenting opinions.

Below, William Rehnquist gives us a Chief Justice's perspective on the assignment process. Justice John Paul Stevens then adds his reflections on assigning opinions as "the second among equals."

William H. Rehnquist, The Supreme Court

259-260 (2001)

In every case in which the chief justice votes with the majority, he assigns the case; where he has been in the minority, the senior associate justice in the majority is the assigner. Although one would not know it from reading the press coverage of the Court's work, the Court is unanimous in a good number of its opinions, and these of course are assigned by the chief justice. Since the odds of his being in a minority of one or two are mathematically small, he assigns the great majority of cases in which there is disagreement within the Court but which are not decided by a close vote. When the conference vote produces three or even four dissents from the majority view, the odds of course increase that the chief justice will be one of the dissenters. During my tenure as an associate justice I received assignments not only from the chief justice but from Justices Douglas, Brennan, White, and Marshall. Sometimes the assignments come around during the weekend after the second week of oral argument, but they can also be delayed until early the following week. Since there are nine candidates to write twelve opinions, the law of averages again suggests that most chambers will ordinarily receive only one assignment.

I know from the time during which I was an associate justice how important the assignment of the cases is to each member of the Court. The signed opinions are to a very large extent the only visible record of a justice's work on the Court, and the office offers no greater reward than the opportunity to author an opinion on an important point of constitutional law. As an Associate Justice I eagerly awaited the assignments, and I think that my law clerks awaited them more than I did. Clerks serve for only a year, and if I was assigned seventeen or eighteen opinions during the course of the year, each of the clerks would have an opportunity to work on five or six opinions. My clerks were always in high hopes that one of the cases on which they had worked or in which they were really interested and regarded as very important would be assigned to me. Unfortunately, they were frequently disappointed in this respect, because not every case argued during a two-week term is both interesting and important.

As Chief Justice, of course, I have the responsibility for assigning the writing of opinions for the Court in cases where I have voted with the majority. This is an important responsibility, and it is desirable that it be discharged carefully and fairly. The chief justice is expected to retain for himself some opinions that he regards as of great significance, but he is also expected to pass around to his colleagues some of this kind of opinion. I think it also pleases the other members of the Court if the chief justice occasionally takes for himself a rather routine and uninteresting case, just as they are expected to do as a result of the assignment process. At the start of each October term, I try to be as evenhanded as possible as far as numbers of cases assigned to each justice, but as the term goes on I take into consideration the extent to which the various justices are current in writing and circulating opinions that have previously been assigned.

John Paul Stevens, Five Chiefs

231, 235-237 (2011)

The most senior associate Supreme Court justice might reasonably be called the "second among equals." I began to occupy that status when Harry Blackmun retired, in 1994. The duties associated with the position are identical to those performed by every other associate justice, with two exceptions: he or she must sometimes substitute for the chief when the chief is unavailable and also must often assign the preparation of Court opinions when the chief is in dissent.

The unavailability of the chief may result from his disqualification in particular cases, from illness that prevents his participation while he is unable to come to Court, or, of course, from his death. For all of those reasons, I presided over a significant number of oral arguments and conferences during the final year of Bill Rehnquist's tenure as chief. . . .

My most significant memory about making assignments of majority opinions when the chief was in dissent is one of satisfaction with a result that I believed to be just. A dissenting judge is never happy, because it is obvious that either the majority has come to the wrong conclusion or his own reasoning is flawed. . . .

On the relatively few occasions when I had majority opinions to assign, Bill Rehnquist and John Roberts would follow the practice of allowing me to make my assignments before they assigned the other majorities. That practice was courteous to me and it also made it easier for them to make an equitable disposition of the other assignments. I seldom, if ever, made an assignment without asking my first choice about his or her willingness to take on the task. And there were few, if any, occasions when my preferred author voiced any objection.

The task of assigning majority opinions is much less burdensome for the "second among equals" than for the chief justice because he or she has relatively few opinions to assign and is not confronted with the need to distribute the work equitably among all nine justices. My principal guideline in making assignments was my judgment about which eligible author would produce the best draft. There were occasions when I kept assignments for myself either because I felt that I had learned some things about a case that I wanted to emphasize in an opinion or because keeping a case or two for myself avoided the risk of receiving a less desirable assignment from the chief. My memory of certain earlier assignments may also have influenced my choice in a few instances.

For example, cases raising First Amendment issues are typically the subject of extensive coverage in the press. I had the impression that Warren Burger would assign the opinions in such cases to himself when the First Amendment claim was vindicated but to Byron White when the opinion would receive a hostile reception on the editorial pages. That practice contributed to Byron's reputation in the press as an enemy of the First Amendment. Because of that history, I tried to avoid assignments that might be interpreted as associating a particular justice with a particular issue.

In cases in which the Court was almost evenly divided, Warren Burger would often assign the opinion to the justice who had the most doubts about the outcome. His reasoning, I believe, was that even if the author changed his mind while drafting the opinion, he would presumably still be able to speak for the Court because the original dissenters would be likely to join his opinion.

I thought that practice wise for quite a different reason. As a practicing lawyer I often began my representation of a client with uncertainty about the validity of his or her position but found that my efforts to justify that position convinced me that it was absolutely right. As a justice there were a few occasions when I changed my mind about the outcome while I was working on the draft of an opinion, but that much more frequently I became even more certain that I was right as the drafting process progressed.

Notes and Questions

1. The Chief Justice is "among equals" because, like every other member of the Court, he or she has only one vote in each case. But because the Chief Justice is first in seniority, he or she also typically ends up assigning more opinions than any other colleague. For example, during the 2007, 2008, 2009, 2010, and 2011 terms, Chief Justice John Roberts was in the majority 90 percent, 81 percent, 91 percent, 91 percent, and 92 percent of the time, respectively, which meant that he determined who drafted the Court's opinion that set forth the law of the land in most cases decided during those years. Do you think it matters who assigns—and hence who writes—majority opinions? Why or why not? Consider this question again after you have had a chance either to review the opinion-drafting materials below or to draft your own majority opinion.

2. By all accounts, as Chief Justice, William Rehnquist discharged his assignment power fairly. He aimed to give each of his colleagues an equal share of majority opinions, took his share of the "dogs," and punished a Justice with fewer assignments only if he or she lagged in completing their current ones. He never played favorites. *See* David J. Garrow, *The Rehnquist Reins*, N.Y. Times, Oct. 6, 1996, http://www.nytimes.com/1996/10/06/magazine/the-rehnquist-reins.html?scp=1&sq=rehnquist%20reins&st=cse.

3. According to *The Brethren*, a controversial behind-the-scenes account of the Court by two *Washington Post* reporters, Chief Justice Warren Burger "carefully made sure that important cases in criminal law, racial discrimination and free speech were kept away from Douglas, Brennan and Marshall, his ideological 'enemies,' as he called them." Bob Woodward & Scott Armstrong, *The Brethren: Inside the Supreme Court* 65 (1979). Chief Justice Burger also had a "willingness to change his position in conference," and an "unwillingness to commit himself before he had figured out which side had a majority," so that he could join the winning side to control the assignment. *Id.* at 174. Furthermore, either through bad note taking or bad strategy, Chief Justice Burger occasionally assigned a majority opinion to someone in the minority, including himself. Finally, he sometimes insisted that the vote count was not clear—though it may have seemed so to others—and took it upon himself to assign the opinion as the senior Justice among undecided colleagues. That was apparently the case in *Roe v. Wade*, 410 U.S. 113 (1973). The vote sheets from conference reveal a majority of which Chief Justice Burger was not part. Nevertheless, he assigned the case to his childhood friend and (at the time) ideological ally, Justice Harry Blackmun. The actual senior Justice in the majority, William Douglas, sent a bristling "Dear Chief" letter objecting to the assignment as a potential waste of "future time and trouble," but the Chief Justice responded that there were so many positions at conference that he "marked down no votes," and asserted that "this was a case that would have to stand or fall on the writing." Bernard Schwartz, *The Unpublished Opinions of the Burger Court* 86 (1988). If the descriptions of Chief Justice Burger's assignment practices are accurate, do you think they reflect appropriate principles for assigning opinions? What other principles would you regard as either appropriate or inappropriate?

4. Opinion Writing and Negotiation

After a case is assigned, work begins in earnest on drafting the opinion that justifies its outcome. For most of the public, the opinion-writing process is invisible. The text that is eventually published may seem inevitable, like writings discovered on tablets rather than words debated by people. Indeed, even Chief Justice William Rehnquist marveled that the Court's typeset opinions appear "vastly improved over the final draft, even though not a word in the draft has been changed." Rehnquist, *supra,* at 264. Yet every published opinion begins as a blank page, filled one word at a time by a single Justice or, increasingly, a lone law clerk in chambers or at home. It can be a solitary process as well as a private one until the Justice authoring the opinion decides that it is ready for circulation to the other members of the conference. Then the wait begins.

Other Justices may circulate the three simplest, and most gratifying, words to an opinion's author: "Please join me." They may suggest or demand changes before joining. They may decide to write a separate concurring opinion. Or they may await or try their hand at writing a dissent.

Below, Court scholar David O'Brien provides an overview of the opinion-writing and negotiation process, Chief Justice Rehnquist again gives us an insider account of the sausage making, and political scientists Lee Epstein and Jack Knight explore the strategic choices that opinion authors make to anticipate, and respond to, their colleagues's views and votes.

David M. O'Brien, Storm Center: The Supreme Court in American Politics

265-266, 275-277, 281-284, 288-290, 292, 295, 299-300, 304-305
(8th ed. 2008)

OPINION-WRITING PROCESS

Opinions justify or explain votes at conference. The opinion for the Court is the most important and most difficult to write because it represents a collective judgment. Writing the Court's opinion, as Holmes put it, requires that a "judge can dance the sword dance; that is, he can justify an obvious result without stepping on either blade of opposing fallacies." Holmes in his good-natured way often complained about the compromises he had to make when writing an opinion for the Court. "I am sorry that my moderation," he wrote Chief Justice Edward White, "did not soften your inexorable heart—But I stand like St. Sebastian ready for your arrows."

Justice Blackmun agreed that opinions must often be revised "because other justices say, if you put in this kind of a paragraph or say this, I'll join your opinion. So you put it in. And many times the final result is a compromise. I think the public doesn't always appreciate this but many times the final result is not what the author would originally have liked to have. But five votes are the answer and that's what the coached judgment is. So you swallow your pride and go along with it if you can."

Since conference votes are tentative, the assignment, drafting, and circulation of opinions are crucial to the Court's rulings. At each stage, justices compete for influence in determining the Court's final decision and opinion. . . .

WRITING AND CIRCULATING OPINIONS

. . . Justices differ in their styles and approaches to opinion writing. They now delegate responsibility to their clerks for assistance in the preparation of opinions. . . . Justice Stevens still regularly does the first draft of his opinions; he does them, as he says, "for self-discipline." For opinions in cases that they deem important, Justice[s] Scalia and Souter also tend to undertake their own first drafts; the latter does so in a hand-written draft since he is the only justice who does not use a computer in his chambers. The first drafts of all the other justices' opinions are usually prepared by their clerks. Still, only after a justice is satisfied with an initial draft does the opinion go to the other justices for their reactions.

The circulation of opinions among the chambers added to the Court's workload and changed the process of opinion writing. The practice of circulating draft opinions began around the turn of the twentieth century and soon became pivotal in the Court's decision-making process. The circulation of opinions provides more opportunities for the shifting of votes and further coalition building or fragmentation within the Court. Chief Justice Marshall, with his insistence on unanimity and nightly conferences after dinner, achieved unsurpassed unanimity. Unanimity, however, was based on the reading of opinions at conferences. No drafts circulated for other justices' scrutiny. Throughout much of the nineteenth century, when the Court's sessions were shorter and the justices had no law clerks, opinions were drafted in about two weeks and then read at conference. If at least a majority agreed with the main points, the opinion was approved.

In the twentieth century, the practice became that of circulating draft opinions, initially carbon copies, later two photocopies, and now electronically for each justice's examination and comments. Because they and their law clerks gave more attention to each opinion, the justices found more to debate. The importance of circulating drafts and negotiating language in an opinion was underscored when Jackson announced from the bench, "I myself have changed my opinion after reading the opinions of the members of the Court. And I am as stubborn as most. But I sometimes wind up not voting the way I voted in conference because the reasons of the majority didn't satisfy me." Similarly, Brennan noted, "I converted more than one proposed majority into a dissent before the final decision was announced. I have also, however, had the more satisfying experience of rewriting a dissent as a majority opinion for the Court." In one case, Brennan added, he "circulated 10 printed drafts before one was approved as the Court's opinion."

As the amount of time spent on the considering of proposed opinions grew, so did the workload. More law clerks were needed, and they were also given a greater role in opinion writing. Though clerks are now largely responsible for drafting and commenting on opinions, they remain subordinates when it comes to negotiating opinions for the Court. . . . But even with clerks assuming more responsibility for working on opinions, the justices ultimately must account for what is circulated. . . .

Justices may suggest minor editorial or major substantive changes. Before joining one of Arthur Goldberg's opinions, Harlan requested that the word "desegregation" be substituted for "integration" throughout the opinion. As he explained, "'Integration' brings blood to Southerners' eyes for they think that 'desegregation' means just that—'integration.' I do not think that we ought to use the word in our opinions." Likewise, Stewart strongly objected to some of the language in Abe Fortas's proposed opinion in *Tinker v. Des Moines School District* (1969), which upheld the right of students to wear black armbands in protest of the government's involvement in Vietnam. "At the risk of appearing eccentric," Stewart wrote, "I shall not join any opinion that speaks of what is going on in Vietnam as a 'war' [since Congress never formally declared a war in Vietnam]."

Justice O'Connor's circulated draft in *Shaw v. Reno* (1993), the leading decision in a series of rulings striking down the creation of "minority-majority" congressional districts, drew similar criticism from two justices in her bare majority. Chief Justice Rehnquist agreed to join her opinion for the Court if she dealt "with two nonsubstantive concerns" that in fact challenged her characterization of the history and role of the Fourteenth Amendment. As the chief justice explained:

> First, on page 7 you say that the Civil War was fought in part to secure the elective franchise to black Americans. One can certainly say that the Civil War was fought to end slavery, but I don't think it is an accurate statement to say that it was fought to secure the elective franchise for blacks. This view gained majority support only during the period of Reconstruction after the Civil War was over.
>
> Second, on page 23, you say that the Fourteenth Amendment embodies "the goal of a fully integrated society." The Fourteenth Amendment prohibits discrimination; it does not require integration, and I think it is a mistake to intimate that it does even as a "goal."

. . . Occasionally, proposed changes lead to a recasting of the entire opinion. Douglas was assigned the Court's opinion in *Griswold v. Connecticut* (1965), in which he announced the creation of a constitutional right of privacy based on the "penumbras" of various guarantees of the Bill of Rights. His initial draft, however, did not develop this theory. Rather, Douglas sought to justify the decision on the basis of earlier cases recognizing a First Amendment right of associational privacy. The analogy and precedents, he admitted, "do not decide this case." "Marriage does not fit precisely any of the categories of First Amendment rights. But it is a form of association as vital in the life of a man or a woman as any other, and perhaps more so." Both Black and Brennan strongly objected to Douglas's extravagant reliance on First Amendment precedents. In a three-page letter, Brennan detailed an alternative approach, as the following excerpt indicates:

> I have read your draft opinion in *Griswold v. Connecticut*, and while I agree with a great deal of it, I should like to suggest a substantial change in emphasis for your consideration. It goes without saying, of course, that your rejection of any approach based on *Lochner v. New York* is absolutely right. . . . And I agree that the association of husband and wife is not mentioned in the Bill of Rights, and that that is the obstacle we must hurdle to effect a reversal in this case.
>
> But I hesitate to bring the husband-wife relationship within the right to association we have constructed in the First Amendment context. . . . In the First Amendment context, in situations like *NAACP v. Alabama* [1964], privacy is necessary to protect the capacity of an association for fruitful advocacy. In the present context, it seems to me that we are really interested in the privacy of married couples quite apart from any interest in advocacy. . . . Instead of expanding the First Amendment right of association to include marriage, why not say that what has been done for the First Amendment can also be done for some of the other fundamental guarantees of the Bill of Rights? In other words, where fundamentals are concerned, the Bill of Rights guarantees are but expressions or examples of those rights, and do not preclude applications or extensions of those rights to situations unanticipated by the Framers.

The restriction on the dissemination and use of contraceptives, Brennan explained,

> [w]ould, on this reasoning, run afoul of a right to privacy created out of the Fourth Amendment and the self-incrimination clause of the Fifth, together with the Third, in much the same way as the right of association has been created out of the First. Taken together, those amendments indicate a fundamental concern with the sanctity of the home and the right of the individual to be alone.

"With this change of emphasis," Brennan concluded, the opinion "would be most attractive to me because it would require less departure from the specific guarantees and because I think there is a better chance it will command a Court." Douglas subsequently revised his opinion and based the right of privacy on the penumbras of the First, Third, Fourth, Fifth, and Ninth Amendments. . . .

William H. Rehnquist, The Supreme Court

260-266 (2001)

When I assign a case to myself, I sit down with the clerk who is responsible for the case and go over my conference notes with him. These notes are unfortunately not as good as they should be, because my handwriting, always poor, has with advancing age become almost indecipherable to anyone but me. But the combination of the notes and my recollection of what was said at conference generally proves an adequate basis for discussion between me and the clerk of the views expressed by the majority at the conference, and of the way in which an opinion supporting the result reached by the majority can be drafted. After this discussion, I ask the clerk to prepare a first draft of a Court opinion and to have it for me in ten days or two weeks.

I know this sort of deadline may seem onerous to the new crop of law clerks when, after the October oral argument session, they undertake the first drafting of an opinion for me. I am sure that every clerk coming to work for a justice of the Supreme Court fancies that the opinion he is about to draft will make an important contribution to jurisprudence, and in the rare case he may be right. But with this goal in mind the clerk is all too apt to first ponder endlessly, and then write and rewrite, and then polish to a fare-the-well. This might be entirely appropriate if his draft were a paper to be presented in an academic seminar, or an entry in a poetry contest. But it is neither of these things; it is a rough draft of an opinion embodying the views of a majority of the Court expressed at conference, a draft that I may very well substantially rewrite. It is far more useful to me to get something in fairly rough form in two weeks than to receive after four or five weeks a highly polished draft that I feel obligated nonetheless to substantially revise. It is easy in October, when the work of the Court is just starting up for the term, to imagine that there is an infinite amount of time in which to explore every nuance of a question and to perfect the style of every paragraph of the opinion. But, as I learned long ago, and as the clerks soon find out, there is not an infinite amount of time. By the last week in October, we are already busy preparing for the November oral-argument session, at the end of which we will be assigned more cases in which to prepare opinions for the Court. I feel strongly that I want to keep as current as I possibly can with my work on the Court, in order not to build up that sort of backlog of unfinished work that hangs over one like an incubus throughout the remainder of the term.

When I receive a rough draft of a Court opinion from a law clerk, I read it over, and to the extent necessary go back and again read the opinion from the lower court and selected parts of the parties' briefs. The drafts I get during the first part of the term from the clerks require more revision and editing than the ones later in the term, after the clerks are more accustomed to my views and my approach to writing. I go through the draft with a view to shortening it, simplifying it, and clarifying it. A good law clerk will include in the draft things that he might feel could be left out, simply to give me the option of making that decision. Clerks also have been exposed to so much "legal writing" on law reviews and elsewhere that their prose tends to stress accuracy at the expense of brevity and clarity. Frank Wozencraft, who was my predecessor as assistant attorney general for the Office of Legal Counsel in the Justice Department, imparted to me a rule of thumb that he used in drafting opinions, which I have used since: If a sentence takes up more than six lines of type on an ordinary page, it is probably too long. This rule is truly stark in its simplicity, but every draft I review is subjected to it. Occasionally, but not often, a draft submitted by a law clerk will seem to me to have simply missed a major point I think necessary to support the conclusion reached by the majority at conference; I will of course rewrite the draft to include that point.

The practice of assigning the task of preparing first drafts of Court opinions to clerks who are usually just one or two years out of law school may undoubtedly and with some reason cause raised eyebrows in the legal profession and outside of it. Here is the Supreme Court of the United States, picking and choosing with great care less than one hundred of the most significant cases out of the seven thousand presented to it each year, and the opinion in each case is drafted by a law clerk! I think the practice is entirely proper; the justice must retain for himself control not merely of the outcome of the case but of the explanation for the outcome, and I do not believe this practice sacrifices either.

I hope it is clear from my explanation of the way that opinions are drafted in my chambers that the law clerk is not simply turned loose on an important legal question to draft an opinion embodying the reasoning and result favored by the clerk. Quite the contrary is the case. The clerk is given, as best I can, a summary of the conference discussion, a description of the result reached by the majority in that discussion, and my views as to how a written opinion can best be prepared embodying that reasoning. The clerk is not off on a frolic of his own, but is instead engaged in a highly structured task that has been largely mapped out for him by the conference discussion and my suggestions to him.

This is not to say that the clerk who prepares a first draft does not have a considerable responsibility in the matter. The discussion in conference has been entirely oral and, as I have previously indicated, nine statements of position suffice to convey the broad outlines of the views of the justices; but these statements do not invariably settle exactly how the opinion will be reasoned through. Something that sounded very sensible to a majority of the Court at conference may, when an effort is made to justify it in writing, not seem so sensible, and it is the law clerk who undertakes the draft of the opinion who will first discover this difficulty. The clerk confronting such a situation generally comes back to me and explains the problem, and we discuss possible ways of solving it. It may turn out that I do not share the clerk's dissatisfaction with the reasoning of the conference, and I simply tell him to go ahead. If I agree with the objection or difficulty he sees, we then undertake an exploration for alternative means of writing the same passage in the draft. Similarly, the conference discussion may have passed over a subsidiary point without even treating it; it is not until the attempt is made to draft a written opinion that the necessity of deciding the subsidiary question becomes apparent. Here again, we do the best we can, recognizing that the proof of the pudding will be the reaction of those who voted with the majority at conference when they see the draft Court opinion.

After I have finished my revisions of the draft opinion, I return it to the law clerk, who then refines and on occasion may suggest additional revisions. We then print the finished product. . . .

. . . [W]e wait anxiously to see what the reaction of the other justices will be, especially those who voted with the majority at conference. If a justice agrees with the draft and has no criticisms or suggestions, he will simply send a letter saying something like[,] "Please join me in your opinion in this case." If a justice agrees with the general import of the draft but wishes changes to be made in it before joining, a letter to that effect will be sent, and the writer of the opinion will, if possible, accommodate the suggestions. The willingness to accommodate on the part of the author of the opinion is often directly proportional to the number of votes supporting the majority result at conference; if there were only five justices voting to affirm the decision of the lower court, and one of those five wishes significant changes to be made in the draft, the opinion writer is under considerable pressure to work out something that will satisfy the critic, in order to obtain five votes for the opinion. Chief Justice Hughes once said that he tried to write his opinions clearly and logically, but if he needed the fifth vote of a colleague who insisted on putting in a paragraph that did not "belong," in it went, and he let the law reviews figure out what it meant.

But if the result at conference is reached by a unanimous or a lopsided vote, a critic who wishes substantial changes in the opinion has less leverage. I willingly accept relatively minor suggestions for change in emphasis or deletion of language that I do not regard as critical, but resist where possible substantial changes with which I don't agree. Often much effort is expended in negotiating these changes, and it is usually effort well spent in a desire to agree upon a single opinion that will command the assent of a majority of the justices.

The senior justice among those who disagreed with the result reached by the majority at conference usually undertakes to assign the preparation of the dissenting opinion in the case, if there is to be one. In the past it was common practice for justices who disagreed with the opinion of the Court simply to note their dissent without more ado, but this practice is rare today. The justice who will write the dissent notifies the author of the opinion and the other justices of his intention, and will circulate that opinion in due course. Perhaps it would be a more rational system if, in a case where a dissent is being prepared, all of those, except the opinion writer, who voted with the majority at conference, as well as those who dissented, would await the circulation of the dissent, but in most cases this practice is not followed. One reason for the current practice is probably that dissents are usually sent around weeks, and often months, after the majority opinion is circulated. A justice who is doubtful as to his vote at conference, or who has reservations about the draft of the Court opinion, may tell the author that he intends to await the dissent before deciding which opinion to join. But this is the exception, not the rule; ordinarily those justices who voted with the majority at conference, if they are satisfied with the proposed Court opinion, will join it without waiting for the circulation of the dissent.

At our Friday conferences the first order of business is to decide what opinions are ready to be handed down. The chief justice goes in order, beginning with the junior justice, and will ask if any of his opinions are ready to be handed down. If all of the votes have been received in a case where he authored the draft of the Court's opinion, he will so advise the conference, and unless there is some objection his opinion will be handed down at one of the sittings the following week. On that day at 10:00 a.m. the Clerk's Office will have available copies of his opinion in that particular case for anyone who wishes it. Meanwhile, the first order of business after the Court goes on the bench will be the announcement by that justice of his opinion from the bench. He will describe the case, summarize the reasoning of the Court, announce the result, and announce whatever separate or dissenting opinions have been filed. The decision-making process has now run full circle: A case in which certiorari was granted somewhere from six months to a year ago has been briefed, orally argued, and now finally decided by the Supreme Court of the United States.

Lee Epstein & Jack Knight, The Choices Justices Make

95-106 (1998)

In *Keyes v. Denver School District*, involving a school desegregation plan, Brennan circulated a majority opinion that distinguished between de jure segregation, which occurs as a result of law or government action, and de facto or actual segregation. But, in an uncirculated memo, perhaps meant for his clerks, Brennan wrote:

> At our original conference discussion of this case, Lewis [Powell] first expressed his view that the de jure/de facto distinction should be discarded. I told him then that I too was deeply troubled by the distinction. Nevertheless, it appeared that a majority of the Court was committed to the view that the distinction should be maintained, and I

therefore drafted *Keyes* within the framework established in our earlier cases. . . . I would be happy to recast the opinion and jettison the distinction if a majority of the Court was prepared to do so.

In light of this memo, Brennan's first draft in *Keyes* provides an example of another form of strategic behavior: sophisticated opinion writing. Brennan sincerely wanted to write an opinion that would have eradicated the distinction between de facto and de jure segregation, but did not believe he could marshal a Court for that position. *Craig* [*v. Boren*] provides another. There Brennan wrote in sophisticated fashion to attain the best possible outcome (heightened scrutiny) and to avoid his least favored alternative (rational basis).

That Brennan engaged in sophisticated writing in these cases is not a surprise. Given the requirement of a majority for the establishment of precedent and the fact that it would be difficult to imagine any case in which the opinion writer fully agreed with the majority on every point, all opinions of the Court are, to greater and lesser degrees, the product of strategic calculations.

Indeed, Powell made this point explicit in a private memo he sent to Chief Justice Burger after conference on *Nixon v. Fitzgerald,* a case asking whether the president had absolute immunity from civil damage suits for official actions taken during his term. The justices met twice to discuss this case, but remained divided on how to dispose of it. Powell nicely summed up the situation in a memo to the chief justice: "Bill Brennan and Harry [Blackmun] would DIG [dismiss as improvidently granted] the *Nixon* case. Byron [White] and Thurgood [Marshall] would dispose of it narrowly as a case in which no private cause of action could be implied, limiting the analysis to the special relationship of government employment." Burger, Rehnquist, and O'Connor wanted to hold that the president has absolute immunity from damage suit liability. Stevens and Powell agreed with Burger, Rehnquist, and O'Connor, but also wanted to address the cause of action question. As Powell put it, "It is evident that a Court opinion is not assured if each of us remains with our first preference votes." He went on to say, "As I view the *Nixon* case as uniquely requiring a Court opinion, I am now prepared to defer to the wishes of you, Bill Rehnquist, and Sandra [O'Connor] and prepare a draft opinion holding that the President has absolute immunity from damage suit liability." Powell, then, was willing to give up his sincere preference for the sake of obtaining an opinion of the Court—an outcome he viewed as essential, but one that would have been difficult to obtain given the various divisions of opinion.

When there is a conference consensus and opinion writers attempt to diverge substantially from it by attempting to write their sincere preferences into law, however, rebuff can be swift—as Burger found out in *Palmore v. Sidoti.* Among the questions this case presented was whether trial court judges can take race into account when deciding on child custody arrangements. The Court could have offered the following responses: (1) it is permissible to take race into account; (2) it is permissible to take race into account so long as race is not the dispositive factor; or (3) it is never permissible to take race into account. Stressing during conference that the "racial factor was [the] dominant if not exclusive" grounds on which the trial judge had rested his order, Chief Justice Burger seemed to favor the second approach. The majority, however, was closer to the third. Nonetheless, Burger circulated an opinion reflecting his sincere preferences—to which Brennan quickly responded:

My recollection of the consensus reached at Conference differs slightly from that reflected in your draft opinion. As I understood the discussion, it was agreed that race would be an improper consideration in the child custody context, irrespective of whether it was the "dispositive" factor in the Court's decision.

To this end, I hope you can make some minor revisions so that I could join your opinion.

Burger conceded the point, thereby preserving the unanimity that had prevailed at conference.

Palmore, Keyes, Craig, and many other cases illustrate the extent to which opinion writers will put aside their most preferred position to generate a definitive ruling of the Court—and one that represents the best they feel they can do under the circumstances.

More systematic data also shore up the frequency of strategic writing during the circulation process: opinion writers produce 3.2 drafts in the average case and nearly 4 in disputes that lead to landmark rulings. These figures suggest that justices are willing to recast their opinions in ways that do not necessarily reflect the preferences revealed in the initial draft of their writing, but they do not tell us whether sophisticated opinion writing has any importance for the policy that the Court produces. Do many opinions undergo significant change in their rationale or in the policy they generate? Or are *Palmore, Keyes,* and *Craig* exceptions?

To answer these important questions—after all, the most fundamental and significant manifestations of strategic interaction are the major alterations in the policy the Court produces or in the rationale the majority uses to decide a case—we compared the policy and rationale adopted in the opinion writer's first circulation with that contained in the published opinion. The samples are those we used throughout this chapter: cases decided during the 1983 term and those that led to landmark rulings during the Burger Court era. . . . [I]n more than 50 percent of the cases a significant change—from the first draft through the published version—occurred in the language of the opinion. Changes were more likely to occur in landmark cases than in less important cases (65 percent versus 45 percent). This finding is especially interesting because it suggests that precedents set in a fair share of the Burger Court's most important cases would have been quite different in the absence of sophisticated opinion writing.

Policy Changes in Select Landmark Cases

Case	Policy in First Draft	Reaction to First Draft	Policy in Published Opinion
Argersinger v. Hamlin, 407 U.S. 25 (1972)	Douglas's first draft held that individuals accused of a crime that carries with it the possibility of imprisonment are entitled to an attorney, even if imprisonment is	The first draft garnered almost no immediate support from the members of the conference majority. Burger said he could not join it. Stewart wrote a memo to Douglas setting out	The published opinion enumerated the actual imprisonment standard: no person can be imprisoned "for any offense . . . unless he was

continues

Case	Policy in First Draft	Reaction to First Draft	Policy in Published Opinion
	virtually never imposed for the crime.	a few "difficulties," including the standard Douglas adopted. Stewart wanted to adopt an "actual imprisonment" approach.	represented by counsel at his trial."
Ballew v. Georgia, 435 U.S. 223 (1978)	Blackmun's original draft included a long section on why the Court's decision—holding unconstitutional five-person juries—would not be applied retroactively.	Three members of the eight-person conference majority took issue with the retroactive holding. Blackmun wrote to Stewart: "Bill Brennan and John [Stevens] have now indicated a preference to say nothing about retroactivity. You are inclined to feel that we should decide in *Ballew* that the decision is retroactive. This is enough of an indication for me to drop [that portion] of the opinion."	The final opinion deleted the section on retroactivity, meaning that the Court chose not to address the issue.
Garcia v. SAMTA, 469 U.S. 528 (1985)	The conference split 4-4; Burger eventually cast his vote to affirm and assigned the opinion to Blackmun. Blackmun produced a first draft that reversed but did not overturn *National League of Cities v. Usery*, 426 U.S. 833	After Blackmun circulated his draft, Burger wrote a memo to Blackmun and to conference saying that he thought the case should be reargued. This generated a long response from Stevens, who had voted to reverse: "Your motion to	After the case was reargued, Blackmun wrote a new draft that overturned *National League of Cities*.

continues

Case	Policy in First Draft	Reaction to First Draft	Policy in Published Opinion
	(1976), in which the Court struck down an amendment to the Fair Labor Standards Act.	reargue this case prompts me to suggest that perhaps it would be useful to have a conference discussion of the standard that should be applied to such motions." He gave "four alternative grounds for reargument," none of which covered *Garcia.* But Stevens did not prevail, and the case was reargued.	
H.L. v. Matheson, 451 U.S. 398 (1981)	In his draft majority opinion, Marshall struck down a Utah law requiring doctors to "notify if possible" a minor's parents prior to performing an abortion. He asserted that a pregnant minor always has the right to decide for herself whether to obtain an abortion free from any parental notification.	When Stewart and Powell (two of the five who had voted with the majority in conference) wrote that they would be unable to join Marshall's opinion, Burger circulated a draft of a proposed opinion for the Court, which upheld the Utah law.	Burger's draft became the majority opinion.
Michelin Tire Corporation v. Wages, 423 U.S. 276 (1976)	Brennan's first draft discussed the question of whether a nondiscriminatory ad valorem property tax was prohibited by the Import and Export	After a majority of the justices expressed interest in Brennan's notion of overruling *Low,* Brennan circulated a "completely rewritten" opinion,	The final opinion overruled *Low v. Austin.*

continues

Case	Policy in First Draft	Reaction to First Draft	Policy in Published Opinion
	Clause. Allowing the tax would require a reexamination of *Low v. Austin*, 13 Wall. 29 (1872), which held that it was prohibited. Brennan thought that overruling *Low* would "have far-reaching consequences," although he was prepared to do so.	taking that step.	
Roe v. Wade, 410 U.S. 113 (1973)	Blackmun's first draft struck the Texas abortion ordinance on the narrowest possible grounds, vagueness, asserting that the law's "sole criterion for exemption as 'saving the life of the mother' is insufficiently informative to the physician." The draft avoided the core constitutional questions of individual liberty and "freedom from bodily restraint" that the conference majority had framed.	Upon reading Blackmun's first draft, Brennan and Douglas asked him to recast it. But Burger reinitiated efforts to have the case (along with *Doe v. Bolton*, 410 U.S. 179) reargued. After considerable debate, the Court went along with Burger's suggestion. In the meantime, Blackmun continued to revise his initial circulation.	The final opinion struck the Texas law as an infringement of the Fourteenth Amendment's concept of personal liberty, which "is broad enough to encompass a woman's decision whether or not to terminate a pregnancy."
Swann v. Charlotte-Mecklenburg Board of Education, 402 U.S. 1 (1971)	Despite the fact that only Justices Black and Blackmun fully agreed with his position—that a	A memorandum Douglas wrote for his own records says: "When [Burger's] opinion at last came around	The published opinion fully repudiated Burger's original approach and disposition and

continues

Case	Policy in First Draft	Reaction to First Draft	Policy in Published Opinion
	lower court had gone too far in attempting to remedy a segregated school system—Burger assigned the majority opinion to himself. His first draft reflected his conference position and remanded the case.	reversing the District Court, the six [of us] were astounded. I wrote a separate opinion. Brennan did; Marshall did; and finally Stewart did. Brennan and I saw Stewart and made several changes, indicating that if he made them he'd have a court opinion. So he made the changes. Instead of circulating, he went to the Chief Justice saying he thought he had a court for the opposed view. That started a slow turn-around that eventually ended in the unanimous opinion of April 20, 1971." Brennan's case files substantiate Douglas's account. The one major exception is that Burger's first draft remanded rather than reversed the cases.	provided judges with a great deal of remedial power to dismantle segregated school districts.
Tennessee v. Garner, 471 U.S. 1 (1985)	White's original draft held that police may shoot a fleeing suspect if the suspect is "armed with a lethal weapon or if there is probable cause to believe the	Shortly after the draft was circulated, Brennan asked White to modify the holding. At the time Brennan requested the change, only three	The final opinion for the Court adopted a modified version of Brennan's suggestion and held that reason to believe that the suspect is armed is

continues

Case	Policy in First Draft	Reaction to First Draft	Policy in Published Opinion
	suspect has committed a violent crime."	justices had joined White's opinion; a dissent was circulating; and Burger, who had voted with the majority at conference, informed White that he was, for the moment, deferring a decision to join.	not in itself sufficient grounds to use deadly force to prevent escape.
United States v. Nixon, 418 U.S. 683 (1974)	During conference discussion, the justices agreed that some form of an executive privilege exists, but that it is neither absolute nor unreviewable by courts. Yet Burger's first draft was closer to the interests of the executive than the conference had desired: it suggested that presidents might win their claims of executive privilege if "core functions" are shown to be at stake.	The other justices would not go along with the "core functions" notion because they believed it could be used to support Nixon's executive privilege claim. Stewart redrafted this portion of Burger's decision; other justices worked on the balance of the Burger draft, which they also viewed as weak.	The published version—largely Stewart's draft—dropped the "core functions" notion.
Wallace v. Jaffree, 472 U.S. 38 (1985)	Stevens's initial drafts for the majority in this case, involving the constitutionality of a moment of silence in public schools, held that "the First Amendment requires that a	When a member of the five-person conference majority— O'Connor— circulated an opinion concurring in judgment, Stevens was worried about losing his opinion of the	The final opinion for the Court modified the language the way Powell wanted: "For even though a statute that is motivated in part by a religious purpose may satisfy the first criterion

continues

Case	Policy in First Draft	Reaction to First Draft	Policy in Published Opinion
	statute must be invalidated if it is entirely motivated by a purpose to advance religion."	Court; without O'Connor's support, his opinion would amount to a mere judgment or even a dissent if O'Connor joined with the opposing camp. So when Powell, who had been in the conference minority, suggested a change in the Stevens circulation, Stevens jumped at the chance of converting his vote. He wrote in a memo to those who had already joined his opinion: "Although there is nothing definite at this point, I think there is a strong possibility that this change would enable Lewis to change his vote and to join our opinion."	[that the statute have a secular legislative purpose], the First Amendment requires that a statute must be invalidated if it is entirely motivated by a purpose to advance religion."

Data Sources: Case files of Justices William J. Brennan Jr., William O. Douglas, and Thurgood Marshall, Library of Congress; and Justice Lewis F. Powell Jr., Washington and Lee University School of Law; and Bernard Schwartz, *The Ascent of Pragmatism* (Reading, Mass.: Addison-Wesley, 1990). [Formatting modified.]

[The table above] drives home the point by detailing policy changes that occurred in landmark cases. Some of the alterations are not as dramatic as others, and the kinds of changes differ from case to case, as do the reasons for the shifts. Nevertheless, virtually all reflect strategic calculations by opinion writers about the preferences of their colleagues and the actions they expected them to take and, occasionally, about the preferences of other relevant actors and their expected actions. *Swann v. Charlotte-Mecklenburg Board of Education* (1971) is a good example. From the beginning of this case, which concerned a school desegregation plan,

Burger had imparted to his colleagues the need for unanimity, as a memo accompanying his first opinion draft makes clear:

> I am sure it is not necessary to emphasize the importance of our attempting to reach an accommodation and a common position, and I would urge that we consult or exchange views by memoranda or both. Separate opinions, expressing divergent views or conclusion [sic] will, I hope, be deferred until we have exhausted all other efforts to reach a common view. I am sure we must all agree that the problems of remedy are at least as difficult and important as the great Constitutional principle in *Brown*.

In fact, it was not "necessary to emphasize" the point: Burger's colleagues understood that a unanimous opinion in such a major case would have a greater chance of remaining undisturbed by external political actors than a divided opinion. The value of unanimity was one of the lessons of *Brown v. Board of Education*; and it is also the moral of scholarly research on the Court, suggesting that rulings on which the entire Court agrees are less susceptible to overturning and more likely to be followed. Nonetheless, the reaction to Burger's first draft did not bode well for a unanimous outcome. As Douglas later put it, most of the justices were "astounded" by Burger's rationale, which reflected the position that Burger and only two other justices, Blackmun and Black, had expressed at conference, and four others (Douglas, Stewart, Marshall, and Brennan) began to draft separate opinions. Finally, after Stewart went to Burger to inform him that he had more support for his view than did the chief, Burger circulated new drafts designed to avoid division—including, as he put it, adopting "points that [are] in conflict with my own position."

Seen in this way, *Swann* provides a quintessential example of sophisticated opinion writing. It is difficult, we think, to . . . fail to reach the conclusion that this form of strategic behavior exists, as do the others we have considered. Simply put, the data we have presented and the cases we have recounted throughout this chapter show that the justices are, in fact, strategic actors—they bargain and accommodate, they think prospectively, and they alter their opinions—and that these behaviors have a nontrivial effect on the policy the Court ultimately produces.

Notes and Questions

1. As Professor O'Brien notes, Justices in the nineteenth century read their drafts at conference for approval rather than circulating them beforehand for scrutiny. As the twentieth century progressed, with the practice of circulation and the assistance of law clerks, draft opinions became subject to an increasing level of comment, criticism, and negotiation. However, more scrutiny and wrangling over draft language has not produced more consensus. Rather, as detailed in the next section, modern decisions have become more fragmented. Is the modern approach nonetheless preferable to the nineteenth-century one? Is your view affected by Justice Douglas's switch in *Griswold v. Connecticut* (1965), as recounted in the O'Brien excerpt, or by the changes to landmark decisions during the Burger Court era, as summarized by the table in the Epstein and Knight book?

2. Professors Epstein and Knight demonstrate that Justices indeed may draft—and redraft—their opinions strategically to attract the support of colleagues, even at the expense of their own views. The two further find that this kind of "sophisticated opinion writing" occurs more frequently in landmark cases, where the Justices may feel a greater political need for consensus. Is it desirable for the Justices to attempt to find common ground rather than stand (or fall) on their own individual views? Section A.6 below will explore this question further.

3. Chief Justice Rehnquist relates that most Justices who voted in the majority at conference end up joining the draft majority opinion before the dissent has even circulated, partly because they are not willing to wait for a response that may be weeks or months in coming. He acknowledges that "a more rational system" would have the Justices withhold their joins until the circulation of the dissent. But neither Chief Justice Rehnquist nor any other Chief Justice has imposed such an embargo. Why do you think they have not? As Chief Justice, would you?

4. Justice Louis Brandeis famously opined that the public respects the members of the Supreme Court in no small part because "they are almost the only people in Washington who do their own work." Charles E. Wyzanski, Jr., *Whereas—A Judge's Premises: Essays in Judgment, Ethics, and the Law* 61 (1965). When Brandeis served on the Court in the early half of the twentieth century, the Justices did largely do their own work. They sifted through certiorari petitions to select cases for review, and they drafted judicial opinions that decided selected cases. With respect to opinion writing, Chief Justice Charles Evans Hughes recalled keeping his clerks "busy with dictation, hating to write in longhand," and a clerk for Justice Brandeis recollected that his boss "wrote the opinion; I wrote the footnotes." Bernard Schwartz, *Decision: How the Supreme Court Decides Cases* 49 (1996). But over the course of the century, the Justices delegated more and more of their workload to law clerks. As Chapter 4 discusses, by the end of the century, all but one of the Justices had combined their law clerks into a "cert pool" for screening certiorari petitions. Furthermore, in the final decades of the twentieth century, Justice John Paul Stevens became the last Justice to regularly write the first drafts of his opinions. Since his retirement in 2010, law clerks have had primary responsibility for drafting opinions in each of the nine chambers. Put another way, the modern Court's definitive interpretations of the Constitution and federal laws have been written mainly by young lawyers just a few years out of law school.

Is this troubling? One scholar, Philip Kurland, believes that "Brandeis would be aghast." *Id.* at 50. As Justice Stevens has explained, personally drafting an opinion is "terribly important" because "you often don't understand a case until you've tried to write it out." Jeffrey Rosen, *The Dissenter*, N.Y. Times Magazine at 50, 72 (Sept. 23, 2007). In accord, Judge Richard Posner of the Court of Appeals for the Seventh Circuit criticizes delegation of opinion writing to law clerks as "a mistake on a number of grounds: The more you write, the faster you write; only the effort to articulate a decision exposes the weak joints in the analysis; and the judge-written opinion provides greater insight into the judge's values and reasoning process and so provides greater information—not least to the judge." Richard Posner, *Diary: Entry 1*, SLATE (Jan. 14, 2002), http://www.slate.com/articles/arts_and_life/diary/features/2002/_34/entry_1.html; *see also* William Domnarski, *Judges Should Write Their Own Opinions*, N.Y. Times (May 31, 2012), http://www.nytimes.com/2012/06/01/opinion/judges-should-write-their-own-opinions.html?_r=1 (criticizing widespread reliance by federal circuit judges on law clerks for opinion drafting). On the other hand, Chief Justice William Rehnquist defends the practice of delegating opinion drafting to law clerks as "entirely proper," because a Justice ultimately retains control of both the outcome of the case and the explanation for it. Which view do you find more persuasive?

5. Opinions drafted personally by Justices in the nineteenth century tended to be shorter, simpler, and less academic than opinions today. With law clerks assuming increasing responsibility in the twentieth century for researching and writing opinions, the opinions have grown in length and complexity, resulting in "the ascendency of the law-review type of opinion." O'Brien, *supra*, at 305. For example, compare one of the most important opinions in the history of the Court, *Marbury v. Madison* (1803), which announced the principle of judicial review and clocked in at 9,350 words and no footnotes, with Justice Antonin Scalia's landmark opinion in *District of Columbia v. Heller* (2008), which interpreted the Second Amendment and clocked in at more than 17,500 words and 29 footnotes. Is the trend toward more exhaustively detailed, documented, and developed opinions desirable? Why or why not?

5. Case Study: Opinion Writing and Negotiation in *Miranda v. Arizona*

The excerpt below from Professor Bernard Schwartz's *Super Chief* and internal documents from Chief Justice Warren's *Miranda* files highlight some of the substantive, strategic, and stylistic choices that helped shape the landmark opinion that has been vaunted and vilified ever since. For additional background on *Miranda, see supra* Section A.2 in this chapter. As you study the sausage making in *Miranda*, keep in mind the high stakes of the case, decided against a backdrop of intense national debate over public safety versus civil and criminal rights, and won by a single-vote margin. Not surprisingly, Chief Justice Warren's draft language underwent close scrutiny and successive revisions to satisfy not only the opinion's author but also his allies in the majority, as well as to address (albeit indirectly) concerns raised by the dissenters. By contrast, in cases of lesser moment, colleagues on the same side of a case often—but not always—give a fair amount of deference to the opinion writer's general approach and choice of words as the author's prerogative, so long as they are satisfied with the formulation of the holding and the basic reasons supporting it.

After reviewing the internal *Miranda* materials, consider whether your peek into the production of this landmark opinion lowers or raises your estimation of the completed product.

a. Background

Bernard Schwartz, Super Chief: Earl Warren and His Supreme Court—A Judicial Biography

589-593 (1983)

According to former Justice Fortas, the *Miranda* decision "was entirely his"—i.e., Warren's. At the March 4, 1966, conference, Warren left no doubt where he stood. As at the argument, the Chief stressed that no warning had been given by the police. In such a case, the police must warn someone like Miranda of his right to silence, that anything he said could be used against him, that he could have a lawyer, and that he could have counsel appointed if he could not afford one. Warren said that such warnings had been given by his staff when he was district attorney. He placed particular emphasis upon the practice followed by the Federal Bureau of Investigation and explained how it worked. The "standard" F.B.I. warning covered the essential requirements Warren had posited. The F.B.I.'s record of effective law enforcement showed that requiring similar warnings in all police interrogations would not impose too great a burden. Another Justice who was present says, "the statement that the F.B.I. did it . . . was a swing factor. I believe that was a tremendously important factor, perhaps the critical factor in the *Miranda* vote."

Harlan led the presentation the other way. To him, Warren's approach meant an unwarranted extension of the Fifth Amendment. Harlan said that the privilege under it "is only a testimonial privilege. 'Compelling' means only coerced statements."

The conference was closely divided. Black, Douglas, Brennan, and Fortas supported Warren, though they were not united on the grounds for reversal. Thus, Douglas felt that the reversal should be based on the [Sixth Amendment] right to counsel and the interrogation by the police "without providing one." Black, on the other hand, said, "I think the focus is on the [Fifth Amendment] privilege against being a witness against himself. From the time government begins to move against a man, when they take him into custody, his rights attach. This . . . was inherently coercive and [they] can't make him be a witness against himself."

Brennan also urged that the decision should turn on the Fifth, rather than the Sixth, Amendment. His view, as he summarized it in a May 11 memorandum, was "that the extension of the privilege against the states by *Malloy v. Hogan* . . . inevitably required that we consider whether police interrogation should be hedged about with procedural safeguards effective to secure the privilege as we defined it in *Malloy*, namely, 'The right of a person to remain silent unless he chooses to speak in the unfettered exercise of his own will.'"

Warren assigned *Miranda* to himself. He had a draft ready early in May. He sent Brennan a copy on May 9, writing, "This is not in circulation but I would appreciate your views." Brennan feared that the opinion was too rigid because it failed to leave room for legislatures to devise alternative procedures for safeguarding the Fifth Amendment privilege.

Brennan explained his concern in a May 11 "Dear Chief" memorandum: "We cannot prescribe rigid rules . . . we are justified in policing interrogation practices only to the extent required to prevent denial of the right against compelled self-incrimination as we defined that right in *Malloy*. I therefore do not think, as your draft seems to suggest, that there is only a single constitutionally required solution to the problems of testimonial compulsion inherent in custodial interrogation. I agree that, largely for the reasons you have stated, all four cases must be reversed for lack of any safeguards against denial of the right. I also agree that warnings and the help of counsel are appropriate. But should we not leave Congress and the States latitude to devise other means (if they can) which might also create an interrogation climate which has the similar effect of preventing the fettering of a person's own will?"

In response, Warren inserted in his opinion the second paragraph of Part III, which indicates that Congress and the states may devise alternative procedures to protect the Fifth Amendment privilege. Another important change was also made at Brennan's suggestion. As explained in his May 11 memo, "It goes to the basic thrust of the approach to be taken. In your very first sentence you state that the root problem is 'the *role* society must *assume*, consistent with the federal Constitution, in prosecuting individuals for crime.' I would suggest that the root issue is 'the *restraints* society must *observe*, consistent with the federal Constitution, in prosecuting individuals for crime.'"

In addition, other minor alterations were made in Warren's draft. The first paragraph was extended to make it plain that the case was concerned with procedures to assure that the individual was accorded his Fifth Amendment privilege. The paragraph at the end of the introductory material summarizing the holding was changed to define "custodial interrogation," to meet the suggestion in the Brennan memo, "Isn't it necessary to give a precise definition and show how it differs from the 'focus' concept of *Massiah* and *Escobedo* . . . ?" The original paragraph concluded with the following sentence (omitted from the final opinion): "We are not here concerned with the right of a person to talk to the police, but with the circumstances under which the police may interrogate him when he is in their custody."

In the draft, after Warren referred to studies showing interrogation abuses, such as the third degree, he wrote, "In a series of cases decided by this Court long after these studies, Negro defendants were subjected to physical brutality—beatings, hanging, whipping—employed to extort confessions. In 1947, the President's Committee on Civil Rights probed further into police violence upon minority groups. The files of the Justice Department, in the words of the Committee, abounded 'with evidence of illegal official action in southern states.'"

Brennan's memo questioned this passage. "I wonder if it is appropriate in this context to turn police brutality into a racial problem. If anything characterizes the group this opinion concerns it is poverty more than race." The reference to blacks and the South was omitted.

Warren also deleted a statement that the Fifth Amendment "privilege is neither an historical relic nor a legal eunuch," as well as language stressing the indispensability of counsel to protect the privilege: "The presence of counsel at the interrogation may serve several significant subsidiary functions as well. He will prove a substantial restraint on the coercive police practices demonstrated in numerous cases. . . . Further, his presence as a third party to the proceedings can provide corroboration for the defendant as to precisely what transpired at the questioning and thus avoid the inevitable conflict of testimony between police and defendant which has plagued courts in cases involving the issue of voluntariness."

At a later point, the draft read, "Incommunicado interrogation, by contrast, does not necessarily afford the innocent an opportunity to clear themselves." The first two words were changed to "Custodial interrogation."

In the draft, the last full paragraph began, "We affirm. We will not presume that there have been warnings of the right to remain silent and the right to counsel at interrogation on a record that does not show that a person was advised of these rights." This was changed to stress the privilege against self-incrimination during custodial interrogation and the failure to give warnings or show "any effective alternative."

Apart from these changes, the opinion of the Court that the Chief Justice delivered in *Miranda* was essentially the same as the draft he had shown Brennan. After he had made the changes noted (particularly those suggested by Brennan), Warren circulated his opinion. It was speedily agreed to by Black, Douglas, Brennan, and Fortas and delivered as the opinion of the Court on June 13, 1966. But

Clark, Harlan (joined by Stewart and White), and White (joined by Harlan and Stewart) delivered dissents. The dissents were notable for their sharp tone as they charged that the "Court's *per se* approach" would "have a corrosive effect on the criminal laws as an effective device to prevent crime."

When he had read Harlan's dissent, Brennan prepared a short concurrence that began, "I join the Court's opinion in these cases and write merely to emphasize that the Court has not, as the dissents suggest, allowed no room for other systems that might as effectively safeguard against denial of the privilege." The draft concurrence then quoted the passage that Warren had inserted in his opinion at Brennan's suggestion, pointing out the power of Congress and the states to devise alternative procedures to protect the person being interrogated.

"It is certainly true," Brennan's concurrence went on, "as my Brother Harlan observes, that the rules we have found necessary in lieu of such creative action are not airtight safeguards against the possibility of prevarication by the police, as to whether warnings have been given or not, or whether waivers have been received. Through Federal Rule of Criminal Procedure 5(a) and the exercise of our supervisory authority over federal courts, the Court has found it possible to fashion a prophylactic rule designed to escape the 'evil potentialities' of a contest over such issues in federal criminal prosecutions. See *Mallory v. United States,* 354 U.S. 449, 456, 457. That avenue is not open to this Court in its review of convictions in state courts. But nothing we hold today prevents the States from devising and applying similar prophylactic means for avoiding the dangers of interrogation which at the same time eliminate the possibility of such contests of veracity between the police and the accused."

Brennan showed his draft concurrence to Warren. The Chief expressed concern at the prospect of a separate opinion by a member of the majority. He was also troubled by Brennan's implication that the required warnings need not be given if alternative safeguards were created. Though Brennan explained that the proposition was already embodied in the Court opinion and that the concurrence was being written solely for emphasis, Warren was not mollified. Brennan finally agreed neither to circulate nor issue the concurrence.

---

b. Internal Documents

i. *Chief Justice Warren's Conference Notes*

Chief Justice Earl Warren spent ten weeks working on his draft *Miranda* opinion before sharing it privately with Justice William Brennan, who was his closest ally and his theoretical architect on the Court. One biography of the Chief Justice recounts that he drafted an outline that the clerks expanded into a draft opinion, which he in turn "edited and reedited." Ed Cray, *Chief Justice: A Biography of Earl Warren* 459 (1997). However, from a review of Chief Justice Warren's files in the Library of Congress, it appears that he did not produce a post-conference opinion outline for his clerks, and that the clerks more likely relied on his five-page typewritten conference notes. Those notes are reproduced in full below.

I cannot accept the New York approach to the effect that the <u>Escobedo</u> cases raise problems which the Legislature and the Executive are to solve, and that they do not raise constitutional questions.

I cannot accept the position of the Federal Government that although the Constitution may be involved that the issues should be decided according to the totality of the circumstances.

I do believe that the cases do raise constitutional issues and that they must be decided here.

Basically the issue is under the Fifth Amendment - the prohibition against compelling a person to be a witness against himself.

They might also in some instances raise the question of the Sixth Amendment - the right to counsel - as in <u>Escobedo</u> where the lawyer was in the building and he was not permitted to see his client even though both he and the defendant were demanding an opportunity to talk together.

But, in the last analysis, where the question is one of the right to interrogate the defendant, we must always go back to the Fifth Amendment.

The fundamental question is not whether a defendant can <u>talk</u> to the police without the benefit of counsel if he is in custody, but whether he can be <u>interrogated</u>.

- 2 -

Exclamatory, or spontaneous, or remorseful admissions, or where
a person seeks out the police for the purpose of confessing are not barred by
the Fifth Amendment.

Defendant's right to counsel, unless he knowingly and intelligently
waives it, commences at least when he is taken into custody. I can envision
some circumstances where it would commence even before that.

Our system of criminal justice is an accusatory one as distinguished
from the civil law investigatory system. Our police, under the Constitution,
have no right to arrest a person merely for investigation. They are limited
to arrest for probable cause or under a warrant issued by a magistrate which
is based upon his belief of probable cause. However, whatever reason is
assigned for depriving the defendant of his liberty, his right to counsel commences at that moment. There is no more right to interrogate petitioner
at the scene of the crime if he is there deprived of his freedom or in his home
if he is arrested there, or in the automobile on the way to the station than
there is when he is actually in the station or the jail. Under the Constitution -
the accusatory system - the case against the defendant commences then.

This does not mean that a lawyer must be appointed for him at that
moment. The Government or the State may provide a system for appointing
a lawyer for him at a later time if he cannot, because of indigency, employ one
himself. And this appointment need not be made until some further meaningful action is taken against him.

- 3 -

One of the meaningful things the police cannot do is to interrogate

him unless he is adequately advised of his rights and knowingly and intel-

ligently waives them.

(1) He must be advised fully of his right to remain silent;

(2) Of the fact that anything he says can and will be used against him;

(3) Of his right to counsel, and that if he is an indigent the Court at

an appropriate time will appoint a lawyer to represent him.

(4) He must be offered an opportunity to communicate with a lawyer

or friend for that purpose, and if neither is available to him at that time there

must be no interrogation until he does have one unless he intelligently waives

his rights and manifests a willingness to be interrogated, *and the burden is on
the govt. to establish that he waived it*

(5) He cannot be either threatened, cajoled or tricked into such a

waiver. If this is done, the waiver is not effective.

No distinction should be made between a defendant who already has a

lawyer when arrested, as did Escobedo, and one who has none at the time but

desires one before being interrogated, nor between one who can reach a lawyer

at the time and one who for any reason cannot; nor should any distinction be

made between those who have the means to hire a lawyer and those who do not.

(Gideon has wiped out that distinction.)

- 4 -

The above principles do not and should not retard the police from making any investigation of the defendant while he is in custody that would be lawful for them to make otherwise. This can be done under the statutes of many states which authorize the authorities to detain a defendant for a certain number of hours before taking him before a magistrate. But that does not carry with it the constitutional right to interrogate him during that period.

If a defendant is known to have a lawyer, the authorities have no right to interrogate him without affording him an opportunity to consult with his client before so doing.

The routine of booking; that is, photographing, finger printing, searching him, etc., are not of themselves violations of the Fifth Amendment.

I am also of the opinion that in the absence of extraordinary circumstances which would amount to plain error, unless counsel does raise the question involved in these cases at the first possible opportunity the right is waived.

I believe, in keeping with Mapp and Linkletter, that the Escobedo principle should not be applied retroactively.

We should not consider lawyers for defendants to be a menace to law enforcement because they would probably tell a client not to talk to the police until he had an opportunity to investigate the case. In that respect, they are merely doing what they are taught to do in every law school in the country and what they are supposed to do under their oaths as lawyers - to protect to the extent of their ability the constitutional and statutory rights of their clients from the moment of their employment until that employment is terminated.

- 5 -

I do not believe that it is in the public interest for counsel to do as
was done in the New Jersey case (<u>Johnson</u>); namely, to praise the police
for the manner in which they treated the defendant and to vouch for the truth
of the confession before the jury as a trial tactic to gain leniency, and then,
only after the defendant is convicted, repudiate that approach and contend
that the defendant was not advised of his right to remain silent.

These principles, reduced to rules of conduct for the public authorities, would, in my opinion, be consistent with our accusatory or adversary
proceeding, and would not interfere with _civilized_ law enforcement. They would do no
more than to accord to the poor, the illiterate, and the sub-normal defendant
the same kind of treatment which the wealthy and influential always receive
and that organized criminals always demand and receive.

It will not be a protection against all third degree methods or other
impositions on the illiterate or the unwary, but it will afford them much
greater protection of their constitutional rights than they have at the present
time.

ii. First Paragraph of Chief Justice Warren's Majority Opinion

First paragraphs of Court opinions typically serve not only the important substantive function of stating the legal issue, but moreover the key strategic function of framing it. Consider the evolution of the first paragraph of the *Miranda* opinion.

The excerpt below comes from the first draft produced by Chief Justice Warren's clerks. It refers to the consolidated cases as the *"Escobedo* Cases," after *Escobedo v. Illinois*, 378 U.S. 478 (1964). As discussed in Section A.2, *supra*, that case applied the Sixth Amendment right to counsel to police interrogations under limited circumstances. Consistent with Chief Justice Warren's conference notes, the draft opinion instead brings police interrogations under an expansive and robust interpretation of the Fifth Amendment privilege against self-incrimination.

<u>Escobedo Cases</u>

The cases before us raise questions which go to the roots

of our concepts of American criminal jurisprudence: the burden

society must bear, consistent with the federal Constitution, in

prosecuting individuals of crime. More specifically, we deal with

the admissibility of evidence obtained from an individual who is

subjected to incommunicado police interrogation.

During redrafting in chambers, "the burden society must bear" is changed to "the role society must assume." Additionally, "incommunicado police interrogation" is changed to "custodial police interrogation." As a result, the typeset draft that Chief Justice Warren shares privately with Justice Brennan before circulation reads:

5/9/66
Not Circulated

SUPREME COURT OF THE UNITED STATES

Nos. 759, 760, 761 AND 584.—OCTOBER TERM, 1965.

Ernesto A. Miranda, Petitioner, 759 *v.* State of Arizona.	On Writ of Certiorari to the Supreme Court of the State of Arizona.
Michael Vignera, Petitioner, 760 *v.* State of New York.	On Writ of Certiorari to the Court of Appeals of the State of New York.
Carl Calvin Westover, Petitioner, 761 *v.* United States.	On Writ of Certiorari to the United States Court of Appeals for the Ninth Circuit.
State of California, Petitioner, 584 *v.* Roy Allen Stewart.	On Writ of Certiorari to the Supreme Court of the State of California.

[May —, 1966.]

MR. CHIEF JUSTICE WARREN delivered the opinion of the Court.

The cases before us raise questions which go to the roots of our concepts of American criminal jurisprudence: the role society must assume, consistent with the Federal Constitution, in prosecuting individuals for crime. More specifically, we deal with the admissibility of statements obtained from an individual who is subjected to custodial police interrogation.

We dealt with certain phases of this problem recently in *Escobedo* v. *Illinois*, 378 U. S. 478 (1964). There, as in the four cases before us, law enforcement officials took the defendant into custody and interrogated him in a

As Professor Schwartz relates, Justice Brennan's 21-page "Dear Chief" letter two days later suggests one change to this introductory paragraph. The suggestion itself only consists of replacing two words with another two, yet Justice Brennan refers to it as his "major suggestion." Why?

Supreme Court of the United States
Washington 25, D. C.

CHAMBERS OF
JUSTICE WM. J. BRENNAN, JR.   May 11, 1966

RE: Nos. 759, 760, 761 and 584.

Dear Chief:

I am writing out my suggestions addressed to your Miranda opinion with the thought that we might discuss them at your convenience. I feel guilty about the extent of the suggestions but this will be one of the most important opinions of our time and I know that you will want the fullest expression of my views.

I have one major suggestion. It goes to the basic thrust of the approach to be taken. In your very first sentence you state that the root problem is "the role society must assume, consistent with the federal Constitution, in prosecuting individuals for crime." I would suggest that the root issue is "the restraints society must observe, consistent with the federal Constitution, in prosecuting individuals for crime."

Chief Justice Warren accepts the suggestion, as the draft he first circulates to the entire conference shows.

MAY 18 1966

SUPREME COURT OF THE UNITED STATES

Nos. 759, 760, 761 AND 584.—OCTOBER TERM, 1965.

Ernesto A. Miranda, Petitioner, 759 v. State of Arizona.	On Writ of Certiorari to the Supreme Court of the State of Arizona.
Michael Vignera, Petitioner, 760 v. State of New York.	On Writ of Certiorari to the Court of Appeals of the State of New York.
Carl Calvin Westover, Petitioner, 761 v. United States.	On Writ of Certiorari to the United States Court of Appeals for the Ninth Circuit.
State of California, Petitioner, 584 v. Roy Allen Stewart.	On Writ of Certiorari to the Supreme Court of the State of California.

[May —, 1966.]

MR. CHIEF JUSTICE WARREN delivered the opinion of the Court.

The cases before us raise questions which go to the roots of our concepts of American criminal jurisprudence: the restraints society must observe consistent with the Federal Constitution, in prosecuting individuals for crime. More specifically, we deal with the admissibility of statements obtained from an individual who is subjected to custodial police interrogation and the necessity for procedures which assure that the individual is accorded his privilege under the Fifth Amendment to the Constitution not to be compelled to incriminate himself.

The change stuck through publication. Is it an improvement over the first and second versions?

iii. Race Removed

As the Schwartz excerpt described, Justice Brennan was also uncomfortable with how Chief Justice Warren's initial draft cast the problem of custodial interrogation partly in racial terms. The passage in question read:

> An understanding of the nature and setting of this in-custody interrogation is essential to our decisions today. The difficulty in depicting what transpires at such interrogations stems from the fact that in this country they have largely taken place incommunicado. From extensive factual studies undertaken in the early 1930's, including the famous Wickersham Report to Congress by a Presidential Commission, it is clear that police vio-

759, 760, 761 & 584—OPINION

MIRANDA *v.* ARIZONA.   7

> lence and the "third degree" flourished at that time.[4] In a series of cases decided by this Court long after these studies, Negro defendants were subjected to physical brutality—beatings, hanging, whipping—employed to extort confessions.[5] In 1947, the President's Committee on Civil Rights probed further into police violence upon minority groups. The files of the Justice Department, in the words of the Committee, abounded "with evidence of illegal official action in southern states," President's Committee on Civil Rights, To Secure These Rights (1947), 26. The 1961 Commission on Civil Rights found much evidence to indicate that "some policemen still resort to physical force to obtain confessions," 1961 Comm'n on Civil Rights Rep., Justice, pt. 5, 17. Physical brutality is not, however, perpetrated solely on minority groups, nor centralized geographically. Only recently in Kings County, New York, the police brutally beat, kicked and placed lighted cigarette butts on the back of an individual under interrogation for the purpose of se-

8   MIRANDA *v.* ARIZONA.

> curing a statement from him. *People* v. *Portelli*, 15 N. Y. 2d 235, 205 N. E. 2d 857, 257 N. Y. S. 2d 931 (1965).[6]

Justice Brennan felt that highlighting race would hinder public acceptance of the opinion. *See* Seth Stern & Stephen Wermiel, *Justice Brennan: Liberal Champion* 238 (2010). In relevant part, Justice Brennan's letter reads:

> 6. Pages 6 - 8. I have some difficulty with the paragraph that
>
> spans these pages. I wonder if it is appropriate in this context to
>
> - 14 -
>
> turn police brutality into a racial problem. If anything characterizes
>
> the group this opinion concerns it is poverty more than race. I'm

No changes were made in response to this suggestion until after the opinion had circulated to the conference on May 18. Below, in handwriting that does not appear to be Chief Justice Warren's but likely belongs to a law clerk, changes were written onto a circulated draft.

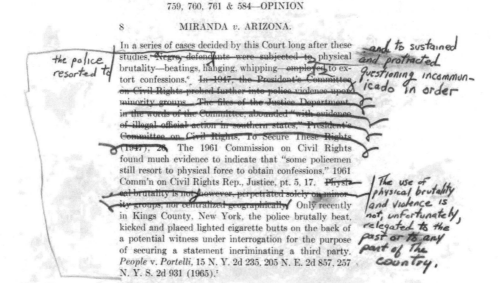

These changes made it to publication. As a result, the sentence which originally read, "In a series of cases decided by this Court long after these studies, Negro defendants were subjected to physical brutality—beatings, hanging, whipping— employed to extort confessions," instead reads, "In a series of cases decided by this Court long after these studies, the police resorted to physical brutality—beating, hanging, whipping—and to sustained and protracted questioning incommunicado in order to extort confessions." *Miranda*, 384 U.S. at 446.

Did Chief Justice Warren make the right call in removing race from the description of "the nature and setting of this in-custody interrogation," an understanding of which the beginning of the paragraph asserts is "essential to our decisions today"? *Id.* at 445.

iv. Rigid Rules?

Justice Brennan's chief concern with Chief Justice Warren's draft opinion was that it appeared too inflexible in insisting on its now famous set of procedures.

> Brennan was uneasy when he read the draft opinion the chief justice circulated privately to him alone on May 9, 1966. He feared that Warren had adopted too rigid a solution and left too little room for state legislatures or Congress to devise alternative procedures. He believed the public would more likely accept the opinion if the Court left legislators greater flexibility in crafting the kind of warning police would be required to give to criminal suspects.

Stern & Wermiel, *supra*, at 238. The first full paragraph of the following passage, among others, gave Justice Brennan pause:

759, 760, 761 & 584—OPINION

46   MIRANDA *v.* ARIZONA.

requirement of the Fifth Amendment of the Constitution, whereas other jurisdictions arrived at their conclusions on the basis of principles of justice not so specifically defined.[54]

It is also urged upon us that we withhold decision on this issue until state legislative bodies and advisory groups have had an opportunity to deal with these problems by rule making.[55] The issues presented are, however, of constitutional dimensions and must be determined by the courts. The admissibility of a statement in the face of a claim that it was obtained in violation of the defendant's constitutional rights is an issue the resolution of which has long since been undertaken by this Court. See *Hopt* v. *Utah,* 110 U. S. 574 (1884). Judicial solutions to problems of constitutional dimension have evolved decade by decade. As courts have been presented with the need to enforce constitutional rights, they have found means of doing so. That was our responsibility when *Escobedo* was before us and it is our responsibility today. Where rights secured by the Constitution are involved, there can be no rule making or legislation which would abrogate them.

In response to this passage, Justice Brennan wrote:

> 16.   Page 46. If I'm right about the basic premise, won't the
> full paragraph on this page have to be substantially revised? It seems
> to suggest that the rules set out in this opinion are constitutionally
> compelled, and the only constitutional solution. Under my approach
> Congress and the States would expressly be left free to devise alter-
> native approaches, restrained only by the requirement, derived from
> Malloy, that any approach, to be sufficient, must effectively assure
> the unfettered exercise of will.

This repeats a similar point he made earlier in the letter that the Court should "leave Congress and the States latitude to devise other means (if they can) which might also create an interrogation climate which has the similar effect of preventing the fettering of a person's own will." William Brennan, Letter to Earl Warren 3 (May 11, 1966). Indeed, appealing to his audience, Justice Brennan went so far as to invoke *Brown v. Board of Education*:

> procedures that will serve the purpose. Yet I think that to allow
> some latitude accomplishes very desirable results: it will make
> it very difficult to criticize our action as outside the scope of
> judicial responsibility and authority, and like Brown v. Board of
> Education, it has an appeal to the conscience of our society, gaining
> on that account social acceptance of its necessity. I repeat that

Chief Justice Warren was not quite as willing as Justice Brennan to allow legislatures latitude to devise "any approach" that "effectively assure[s] the unfettered exercise of will." Perhaps it was just a matter of emphasis, but the revisions which the Chief Justice's clerks worked up, and which he approved, opened the door to alternative procedures while also insisting that the ones set forth in the opinion were the constitutional minimum by which others would be measured.

For example, in a passage summarizing the holding on page 35 of the draft, an insert was added to respond to Justice Brennan's concern:

759, 760, 761 & 584—OPINION

MIRANDA *v.* ARIZONA.   35

privilege while an individual is in custody is not whether he is allowed to talk to the police without the benefit of warnings and counsel, but whether he can be interrogated. There is no requirement that police stop a person who enters a police station and states that he wishes to confess to a crime, or a person who calls the police to offer a confession or any other statement he desires to make. Volunteered statements of any kind are not barred by the Fifth Amendment and their admissibility is not affected by our holding today.

To summarize, we hold that when an individual is taken into custody or otherwise deprived of his freedom by the authorities, he must be warned prior to any questioning that he has the right to remain silent, that anything he says can ~~and will~~ be used against him in a court of law, that he has the right to ~~consult with~~ an attorney, ~~and to have him present at any questioning,~~ and that if he cannot afford an attorney one will be appointed for him prior to any questioning if he so desires. ~~There must be an opportunity afforded to him to exercise these rights.~~ After such warnings have been given, and such opportunity afforded him, the individual may knowingly and intelligently waive these rights and agree to answer questions or make a statement. But unless and until such warnings and waiver are demonstrated by the prosecution at trial, no evidence obtained as a result of interrogation can be used against him.

the presence of

opportunity to exercise these rights must be afforded to him throughout the interrogation.

INSERT 15

ALL ROMAN

and is subjected to questioning, the privilege against self-

is jeopardized

incrimination ~~attaches.~~ Procedural safeguards must be employed

to protect the privilege, and unless other fully effective means are

adopted to notify the person of his right of silence and to assure that

the exercise of the right will be scrupulously honored, the following

measures are required. ~~He must be warned prior to any questioning~~

Similarly, for the language singled out by Justice Brennan on page 46, new language was added:

759, 760, 761 & 584—OPINION

46   MIRANDA *v.* ARIZONA.

requirement of the Fifth Amendment of the Constitution, whereas other jurisdictions arrived at their conclusions on the basis of principles of justice not so specifically defined.[61]

It is also urged upon us that we withhold decision on this issue until state legislative bodies and advisory groups have had an opportunity to deal with these problems by rule making. The issues presented are, however, of constitutional dimensions and must be determined by the courts. The admissibility of a statement in the face of a claim that it was obtained in violation of the defendant's constitutional rights is an issue the resolution of which has long since been undertaken by this Court. See *Hopt* v. *Utah*, 110 U. S. 574 (1884). Judicial solutions to problems of constitutional dimension have evolved decade by decade. As courts have been presented with the need to enforce constitutional rights, they have found means of doing so. That was our responsibility when *Escobedo* was before us and it is our responsibility today. Where rights secured by the Constitution are involved, there can be no rule making or legislation which would abrogate them.

INSERT 1 &

- 5 -

opportunity to deal with this problem by rule-making. We have already pointed out that the Constitution does not require any specific code of procedures for protecting the privilege against self-incrimination during custodial interrogation. Congress and the States are free to develop their own safeguards for the privilege, so long as they are fully as effective as those described above in informing accused persons of their right of silence and in affording a continuous opportunity to exercise it. Beyond this point, however, the issues presented are

In any event

Are the above changes: (1) substantive, altering the holding; (2) strategic, considering internal and external reaction; or (3) stylistic, moderating the tone but not the substance of the opinion? If you had been the author of the draft opinion, would you have approved these changes, made different ones, or kept the passages the way they were?

v. *Justice Brennan's Unpublished Concurrence*

Chief Justice Warren's changes to the privately drafted opinion mollified Justice Brennan for the time being. However, on June 9, Justice John Marshall Harlan circulated a dissent (which Justices Potter Stewart and Byron White quickly joined) that revived Justice Brennan's misgivings by accusing the Court of imposing a "new constitutional code of rules for confessions" on the entire country. In response, as the Schwartz excerpt described, Justice Brennan drafted the following concurring opinion, which quotes another section of the Chief Justice's draft that had been inserted in response to Justice Brennan's May 11 letter:

Nos. 759, 760, 761 & 584 - Miranda, etc.

MR. JUSTICE BRENNAN, concurring.

I join the Court's opinion in these cases and write merely to emphasize that the Court has not, as the dissents suggest, allowed no room for other systems that might as effectively safeguard against denial of the privilege. For the Court expressly states,

> "It is impossible for us to foresee the potential
> alternatives for protecting the privilege which
> might be devised by Congress or the States in
> the exercise of their creative rule-making capacities.
> Therefore, we cannot say that the Constitution nec-
> essarily requires adherence to any particular
> solution for the inherent compulsions of the inter-
> rogation process as it is presently conducted."

Ante at p. 29.

It is certainly true, as my Brother Harlan observes, that the rules we have found necessary in lieu of such creative action are not air-tight safeguards against the possibility of prevarication by the police, as to whether warnings have been given or not, or whether waivers have been received. Through Federal Rule of Criminal Procedure 5(a) and the exercise of our supervisory authority over federal courts, the Court has found it possible to fashion a prophylactic rule designed to escape the "evil potentialities" of a contest over such issues in federal criminal prosecutions. See Mallory v. United States, 354 U.S. 449, 456-457. That avenue is not open to this Court in its review of convictions in State courts. But nothing we hold today prevents the

- 2 -

States from devising and applying ~~similar prophylactic means~~ additional rules
for avoiding the dangers of interrogation ~~which at the same time~~
~~eliminate the possibility of such contests of veracity between the~~
~~police and the accused.~~

Justice Brennan shared the draft with Chief Justice Warren before circulation. The reaction from the Chief Justice's chambers was not positive. In a memo to their boss, the Chief Justice's clerks wrote:

<u>Memorandum</u>

To: The Chief Justice

From: Jim Hale
        Mike Smith
        Ken Ziffren

Re: Justice Brennan's recent suggestion for <u>Miranda</u>,
        <u>et al</u>.

As we all stated yesterday, we think there might be a serious dilution of the power of <u>Miranda</u> if it is decided by a 5-4 vote and one of the five members of the majority appends a concurring opinion that people might construe as not going all the way with the majority.

On the other hand, Justice Brennan is rightly concerned at what amounts to a misreading of the opinion by the dissenters. In order to point up the fact that the majority opinion does not create a system of rules that will cut off all legislative inquiry, two sentences could be added to the existing paragraph (quoted by Justice Brennan in his draft concurrence) which would point up the fallacy of the dissenters' reasoning. There is no need and probably a

- 2 -

disadvantage in referring directly to the dissenting opinions

as such, but their force can be effectively offset by taking

language from their opinions in meeting their argument.

In this light we suggest the sentences appended.

6/10/66

CC

The new sentences referenced in the memo were added to the now-circulated draft opinion to meet Justice Brennan's lingering concerns and the "misreading" by the dissenters. The new language is marked in the margins:

> It is impossible for us to foresee the potential alternatives for protecting the privilege which might be devised by Congress or the States in the exercise of their creative rule-making capacities. Therefore we cannot say that the Constitution necessarily requires adherence to any particular solution for the inherent compulsions of the interrogation process as it is presently conducted. Our decision in no way creates a constitutional straitjacket which will handicap sound efforts at reform, nor is it intended to have this effect. We encourage Congress and the States to continue their laudable search for increasingly effective ways of protecting the rights of the individual while promoting efficient enforcement of our criminal laws. However, unless we are shown other procedures which are at least as effective in apprising accused persons of their right of silence and in assuring a continuous opportunity to exercise it, the following safeguards must be observed.

Did this latest change finally satisfy Justice Brennan? According to his biographers, here is the rest of the story:

> ... After the chief justice made clear his misgivings about a separate concurrence, Brennan agreed not to file it, a decision he was later relieved to have made. The standardized *Miranda* warning became familiar to viewers of every television police show in succeeding decades, in contrast to the confusing medley of fifty different state formulations his concurrence might have encouraged. "Obviously, it would have been just dead wrong," Brennan said. "Thank heavens I woke up."

Stern & Wermiel, *supra,* at 239. Do you agree with Brennan's conclusion?

vi. Brown *and* Miranda

Chief Justice Warren himself wrote the first draft of *Brown v. Board of Education*, and "[t]he opinion delivered was essentially the opinion produced when Warren sat himself down and put pencil to paper." Bernard Schwartz, *The Unpublished Opinions of the Warren Court* 450 (1985). When he turned the draft over to a law clerk for revision, the Chief Justice emphasized:

> [T]he opinion should be as brief as possible, and it was to be written in understandable English, avoiding legalisms. The Chief Justice told [his clerk] he wanted an opinion that could be understood by the layman. This was repeated in Warren's May 7 memorandum transmitting the draft opinion to the Justices. The draft, wrote the Chief Justice, was "prepared on the theory that the opinions should be short, readable by the lay public, non-rhetorical, unemotional and, above all, non-accusatory."

Id. at 448. Chief Justice Warren's first draft was nine handwritten pages on legal paper, without any footnotes. *See id.* at 448-455. The final *Brown* opinion was slightly longer, with 14 footnotes. *See Brown v. Board of Education*, 347 U.S. 483 (1954). Did the Chief Justice's initial five-page outline for *Miranda* live up to the standards he set in *Brown* for being plainspoken, accessible, and unemotional? What about the published *Miranda* opinion, which clocked in at 61 pages and 71 footnotes? *See Miranda v. Arizona, supra; see also* Cray, *supra,* at 459 (characterizing the lengthy opinion as an "interrogation manual"). Is the final opinion an improvement over the Chief Justice's initial outline? Would something more *Brown*-like have been better legally or politically?

6. Separate Opinions

After conference, the author of the majority opinion has the first, but usually not the last, word in a case. In modern times, concurrences and dissents commonly follow, though historically, they were rare. In the first article below, John Kelsh documents the establishment of the Court's "consensual norm" under Chief Justice John Marshall and its subsequent erosion to the present day. Justice Antonin Scalia then gives a vigorous defense of separate opinions.

John P. Kelsh, The Opinion Delivery Practices of the United States Supreme Court 1790-1945

77 Wash. U. L.Q. 137, 139-381 (1999)

A. 1790-1801

. . . In the approximately sixty-three cases that Alexander Dallas reported for the years 1790-1800, the Court used a wide variety of opinion-delivery methods. The most popular was stating that the opinion was being issued "By the Court," without any attribution to a particular Justice. Forty-five of the sixty-three cases (71%) Dallas reported were in this form. These brief opinions usually contained very little legal analysis. . . .

The second most frequently used method was delivering opinions seriatim. This practice was patterned after that of the English common-law courts. In the seriatim style, each Justice prepared and read his own opinion. The individual opinions were frequently followed by a per curiam order stating briefly the Court's disposition of the case. Fifteen of the sixty-three pre-Marshall decisions (24%) were reported in this form. . . .

While the pre-Marshall Court used the per curiam and seriatim styles most frequently, it experimented with other styles as well. Two of its innovations were later adopted by the Court. The first innovative opinion-delivery style was the practice of having the Chief Justice deliver an opinion "for the Court." On at least three occasions, the Reporter identified the opinion of the Court not as being given by the Court itself, but rather as having been delivered by the Chief Justice. . . .

The second innovative opinion-delivery practice is related to the first. This was the practice of having an individual Justice write separately from the Court. In *Sims v. Irvine*, Chief Justice Ellsworth delivered the opinion of the majority of the Court. Justice Iredell, who was unable to attend the reading of the opinion due to "indisposition," later delivered a concurrence which began: "Though I concur with the other Judges of the Court in affirming the Judgment of the Circuit Court, yet as I differ from them in the reasons for affirmance, I think it proper to state my opinion particularly."

This opinion was the first time that an individual Justice had separated himself from an opinion that had been expressed by a single Justice speaking for the Court. This practice became established in the Marshall Court and of course flourishes today. . . .

B. MARSHALL PERIOD

Overview

John Marshall came onto a Supreme Court that had no set procedure for the delivery of opinions. During his tenure three important developments took place. First, nearly all opinions came to be delivered by one Justice speaking for the Court. Second, by the end of his tenure, Justices were free to file concurring and dissenting opinions when they disagreed with the majority. Third, Justices who filed separate opinions felt compelled to explain why they did so. This subsection describes and analyzes these developments.

Chief Justice Marshall, For the Court

The first and perhaps most important development of the Marshall years was that the innovation of having opinions delivered by one Justice speaking for the whole Court was enshrined as normal practice. The contrast with the Court's pre-Marshall years is striking. The early United States Reports include opinions from all of the Justices; the Reports from the early Marshall years are dominated by Marshall himself.

Historians of the period agree that Marshall instituted the practice as a means of strengthening the Court. In an era when the Supreme Court received considerably less attention than the other branches of the federal government, Marshall apparently believed that presenting a unified front would bolster the Court's prestige. Statistics from the Marshall era show how successful Marshall was at establishing his new practice.

In the years between 1801-06, the Court delivered non-per curiam opinions in sixty-seven cases. Marshall delivered the opinion of the Court in sixty of these cases, Justices other than Marshall delivered the opinion in two, and in five cases the Court reverted to the seriatim style. In every one of these five seriatim cases, the Reporter noted that Marshall was either absent or had recused himself. . . .

By 1814, then, after twenty-four years of experimentation, the Court had developed a practice whereby nearly all of its opinions were delivered by an individual Justice speaking for the entire Court. The seriatim opinion had all but disappeared, and the Court had drastically reduced the number of opinions it issued per curiam.

John Marshall had succeeded, but his new practice was soon criticized. The most vocal critic was Thomas Jefferson. Jefferson argued that the practice of having one Justice speak for the entire Court limited the accountability of the individual Justices. In a letter to Justice William Johnson, Jefferson urged a return to the use of seriatim opinions:

> The Judges holding their offices for life are under two responsibilities only. 1. Impeachment. 2. Individual reputation. But this practice compleatly withdraws them from both. For nobody knows what opinion any individual member gave in any case, nor even that he who delivers the opinion, concurred in it himself. Be the opinion therefore ever so impeachable, having been done in the dark it can be proved on no one. As to the 2d guarantee, personal reputation, it is shielded compleatly. The practice is certainly convenient for the lazy, the modest, & the incompetent. It saves them the trouble of developing their opinion methodically and even of making up an opinion at all. That of seriatim argument shews whether every judge has taken the trouble of understanding the case, of investigating it minutely, and of forming an opinion for himself, instead of pinning it on another's sleeve. It would certainly be right to abandon this practice in order to give to our citizens one and all, that confidence in their judges which must be so desirable to the judges themselves, and so important to the cement of the union.

In another letter, Jefferson complained that "an opinion is huddled up in conclave, perhaps by a majority of one, delivered as if unanimous, and with the silent acquiescence of lazy or timid associates, by a crafty chief judge." . . .

Separate Opinions

Dissents and concurrences were relatively rare in the early Marshall years. Justice Chase, who had been one of the most active of the pre-Marshall Justices, was the first to break rank, issuing a one-sentence concurrence in an 1804 insurance case. Justice Washington followed the next year with the Marshall Court's first recorded dissent. This slow pace of separate opinions continued through 1806 and 1807. In each of these years only one separate opinion was filed.

The statistics show, however, that a change took place in 1808. In that year, the Justices began to issue an increased number of separate opinions. This slight increase in dissent activity continued through 1809 and 1810. In 1809 Justice Johnson wrote separately in six cases and Justice Livingston concurred once. In 1810 the separate opinions were more evenly spread. Justices Todd, Johnson, and Livingston each delivered one separate opinion. Even Chief Justice Marshall got into the act, delivering his first dissent in a case that he thought had already been decided.

. . . [T]his initial period when many different Justices found it acceptable to write separately was extremely short-lived. In 1817 the only separate opinion was a dissent from Chief Justice Marshall. In 1818 Justice Johnson delivered four separate opinions. No other Justice delivered any. From 1818 until 1827, Justice Johnson was virtually the only Justice who wrote any separate opinions. In these ten years Justice Johnson wrote a total of seventeen concurrences and dissents. All of the other Justices combined wrote a total of six—and two of these came in *Dartmouth College.*

These statistics suggest that Johnson was alone in fighting to establish the practice of allowing Justices to write separately from the majority of the Court. Writings from the period support this as well. In 1822 Johnson wrote Jefferson in response to Jefferson's urging that he push the Court to return to the use of seriatim opinions. Johnson detailed the difficulty he had encountered in expressing his own opinion:

> Some case soon occurred in which I differed from my brethren, and I thought it a thing of course to deliver my opinion. But, during the rest of the session I heard nothing but lectures on the indecency of judges cutting at each other, and the loss of reputation which the Virginia appellate court had sustained by pursuing such a course. At length I found that I must either submit to circumstances or become such a cypher in our consultations as to effect no good at all.

Marshall himself had made his preference for unanimity public in an 1819 article he published in a Philadelphia newspaper:

> The course of every tribunal must necessarily be, that the opinion which is to be delivered as the opinion of the court, is previously submitted to the consideration of all the judges; and, if any part of the reasoning be disapproved, it must be so modified as to receive the approbation of all, before it can be delivered as the opinion of all.

Marshall was also known to acquiesce silently when his own opinion did not command a majority and even on occasion write opinions with which he did not agree. . . .

Rationales

. . . When dissents began to pick up again in the years between 1827 and 1833, many of the Justices who wrote separately explained their reasons for doing so. The reasons they gave echoed those that Justice Johnson had been giving all along. The Justices spoke of their obligation to make their own opinions known in important cases, in cases presenting constitutional issues, and cases of great public interest. Justice Thompson prefaced an 1827 dissent by writing:

> It is with some reluctance, and very considerable diffidence, that I have brought myself publicly to dissent from the opinion of the Court in this case; and did it not involve an important constitutional question. . . . I should silently acquiesce in the judgment of the Court, although my own opinion might not accord with theirs. . . .

C. The Taney Court

Overview

In the early years of the Taney Court, the opinion-delivery practices of the Marshall Court continued largely unchanged. Opinions were still given by a single Justice speaking for the entire Court and other Justices were allowed to write separately. Nonunanimity rates increased somewhat, but the overwhelming majority of opinions were still presented without recorded dissent. When Justices did dissent, they felt compelled to offer an explanation, and the explanation given most frequently was that the case was important. By the late Taney period, however, there had been a change.

Nonunanimity rates stayed more or less the same, and the form of the opinion did not change, but Justices began to offer different reasons for writing separately. Justices began to say that they were compelled to write separately to maintain personal consistency. The separate opinion was a means by which the individual Justices accomplished the newly-important goal of defending their own judicial records. This new attitude toward dissent was part of a larger shift in the Justices' conception of the Court. Justices for the first time began to think of the Court less as a cohesive whole and more as a collection of individuals.

The Early Taney Court

... When Taney took office for the 1837 Term, the number of dissenting and concurring opinions rose. In 1837 Justices on the Court delivered three concurring opinions and five dissents. In 1838 the Justices delivered a total of seven separate opinions. Both of these totals were higher than all but the most contentious of the Marshall years. As a whole the Taney Court had a higher nonunanimity rate than had the Marshall Court (20% vs. 11%). . . .

Not only were the basic opinion-delivery practices continued, the Justices' attitudes toward dissent also stayed the same. This is evident in two ways. First, Justices in the early Taney period, as had their Marshall Court predecessors, often apologized for dissenting. . . .

... By the end of the Marshall period, nearly all of the Justices had expressed a belief that dissent was acceptable in important cases—importance being defined by the presence of a constitutional issue or the attention of the public. Taney-era Justices apparently shared the belief that dissent was acceptable in these types of cases. . . .

Justice Campbell began his Dred Scott opinion: "I concur in the judgment pronounced by the Chief Justice, but the importance of the cause, the expectation and interest it has awakened, and the responsibility involved in its determination, induce me to file a separate opinion." . . .

Concern with Consistency—A New Reason to Dissent

Up until approximately 1839, Justices who explained why they chose to write separately nearly always placed their emphasis on the issue involved. Beginning in approximately 1841, however, Justices started to express another set of rationales for choosing to write separately. Justices frequently noted that they wrote separately because they did not wish to be individually associated with the majority's opinion. . . .

As the Taney years went on, this rationale began to appear more frequently. . . . In an 1853 case, Justice Catron explained his decision to write separately: "[M]y object here is not to express an opinion in this case further than to guard myself against being committed in any degree to the [following] doctrine. . . . " The next year Justice Daniel dissented briefly in a case involving admiralty jurisdiction. Daniel declined to elaborate on his legal reasons for dissenting—saying that he had made them clear in earlier cases. He closed his dissent by writing: "My purpose is simply to maintain my own consistency in adhering to convictions which are in nowise weakened." . . .

... These explanations for dissent suggest that Taney-era Justices began to conceive of their role more as an individual effort and less as a part of a cohesive unit.

Two other pieces of evidence from the opinion-delivery practices of the Taney Court support this contention. First, the Taney period saw a dramatic increase in the use of dissents and concurrences without opinion. The Marshall Court had used these sparingly, registering a total of forty-one during its thirty-five year run. By contrast, the Taney Court, which ran for thirty-three years, registered 389. The dissent or concurrence without opinion is useful only as a way of separating the individual Justice from the Court. It makes no effort to convince future courts to adopt a different course or to persuade the current majority to tighten its reasoning. It simply preserves for the public and for history that this Justice disagreed. . . .

Second, the late Taney Court saw an increased incidence of hostility in individual opinions. Marshall Court Justices had gone out of their way to express their respect for the opinions of their brethren. During the Taney Court, cordiality was still the norm, but during the Court's later years Justices occasionally began their separate opinions with expressions of scorn or disdain. . . .

D. 1864-1940

Overview

At first glance, it appears the Court's opinion-delivery practices changed little in the period between Chief Justice Taney's death in 1864 and Harlan Fiske Stone's elevation to Chief Justice in 1941. The Court continued to present its opinions in the format it had settled on during the Marshall period. The average nonunanimity rate per term was 18%, very comparable to the Taney Court's 20%. Justices of the period frequently echoed their Taney-era predecessors in expressing their reluctance to dissent.

Despite these superficial similarities, this period saw a significant change in the attitude Justices took toward writing separately. First, the Justices expanded the universe of cases where dissent was appropriate. While the Justices still said that dissent was acceptable in "important" cases, they also said that writing separately was justified when a case had significant practical consequences, or when the majority ignored stare decisis, or when they just plain disagreed. Second, Justices between 1864 and 1940 continued the trend towards viewing the Court more as atomized and less as unified. Citation to the views of individual Justices became more and more frequent and the Court developed distinct ideological blocs. Third, there was an increased sense that dissents were a legitimate and important source of law. Justices began to distinguish between unanimous and nonunanimous cases, citations to dissents for propositions of law became more frequent, and several dissents were written into law. All of these changes laid the groundwork for the post-1941 explosion in nonunanimity rates.

Rationales

1. Case-Specific Rationales

. . . The Justices of the 1864-1940 era inherited most of the case-specific rationales that Justices had expressed during the Taney era. As was the case during that period, the most frequent rationale for writing separately was that the case before the Court was "important." . . .

Justices of this era also followed the Taney Court in explaining that dissent was appropriate in constitutional cases. . . . In 1872 Justice Bradley said, "On a constitutional question involving the powers of the government it is proper that . . . no member of the court should hesitate to express his views." . . .

Post-Taney Justices did not, however, limit themselves to the categories of cases that Taney-era Justices believed warranted dissent. As the years went by, they developed three other rationales for writing separately. . . .

The first new rationale was that the "consequences" of a particular case justified writing separately. Justices frequently opened separate opinions with references to the "far-reaching," "grave," "injurious," "serious," or "alarming" consequences of the Court's opinion. . . .

A second major new rationale that the Justices developed during this period was that it was appropriate to register dissent when the majority departed from principles established by earlier cases. Justices announced in several cases that they had a "duty" to call attention to the Court's disregard of its own precedents. . . .

The third and final new justification for writing separately was the least restrictive of the three. In a number of cases, Justices announced that they were going to state their views separately for no reason other than that they disagreed with the majority of the Court. . . .

One would also expect that this significant broadening of the categories of cases for which dissent was acceptable would lead to a great increase in the nonunanimity rate. To some extent this happened, in that the nonunanimity rate jumped between 1930-40. A far more substantial rise, however, was to occur in the years following 1941, long after these new post-Taney rationales had become established. The explanation for this anomaly is that these new rationales for which types of cases warranted dissent coexisted with the general belief that dissent was to be avoided. The tension between these two ideas kept the nonunanimity rate from rising too high.

2. Justice-Oriented Rationales—"Consistency"

. . . Justices throughout the 1864-1940 period echoed their Taney-era predecessors in stating that dissent was appropriate to explain or protect one's record. Justices frequently stated that they were choosing to write separately to make it clear that they, as individuals, had no part in the majority's opinion. Justice Bradley opened an 1873 concurrence by saying:

> Whilst I concur in the conclusion to which the court has arrived in this case, I think it proper to state briefly and explicitly the grounds on which I distinguish it from the *Slaughter-House Cases*. . . . I prefer to do this in order that there may be no misapprehension of the views which I entertain in regard to the application of the fourteenth amendment to the Constitution.

. . . It was noted above that this pattern of using separate opinions to clarify a Justice's own record was part of a shift during the Taney period toward conceiving of the Court less as a cohesive unit and more as a collection of nine individuals. . . .

[J]ust as individual Justices began to pay more attention to their own records, so too did they begin to pay more attention to the records and analyses of other Justices. Justices began with greater frequency to link propositions of law with the Justice who spoke for the Court, rather than saying simply that the proposition had come from the Court itself. . . .

[Another] piece of evidence from separate opinions that the Court was becoming more atomized was the development of ideological blocs. . . . [F]irst Holmes and Brandeis, later Holmes, Stone, and Brandeis, and later still the Four Horsemen [Justices Willis Van Devanter, James McReynolds, George Sutherland, and Pierce

Butler], seemed to set themselves off from the rest of the Court. These blocs had a particular point to make, and they used separate opinions to repeat that point over and over. Dissents by Holmes very frequently emphasized that the Court was not authorized to act as a superlegislature. The Four Horsemen repeatedly emphasized the limited regulatory powers of state governments. The development of these blocs, which is seen most clearly in the pattern of the separate opinions, made the Court appear less as a unified whole searching for truth and more as a collection of factions, each struggling for votes.

The cumulative effect of all of these developments was to make the Court much more focused on the views of the individual Justice than it had ever been. The Legal Realist perspective, which had come to dominate the academy from which so many of these Justices had been drawn, now dominated the Court as well. Law was no longer considered to be found, rather it was made. Given this shift in conception of law, an increased focus on individual Justices was inevitable. By the end of this period, the Court had moved even further from Marshall's conception of a unified Court and closer to what Justice Holmes purportedly referred to as "nine scorpions trapped in a bottle." . . .

Acceptance of Dissent

There was a final important development in the history of the Court's opinion-delivery practices that took place during this period. To an extent never before seen, during the 1864-1940 period separate opinions became a widely-accepted part of the legal culture. Justices began to view separate opinions as having an important and legitimate role in the process of deciding cases. Four pieces of evidence demonstrate this point.

The first is the frequent reference by Justices to whether or not a relied-upon case had been decided unanimously. Justice McReynolds in *Myers v. United States* attempted to make a point by noting anachronistically that *Marbury v. Madison* had been "concurred in by all." A few years later he used the opposite tactic, noting that "[t]he plan under review in the Legal Tender Cases was declared within the limits of the Constitution, but not without a strong dissent." . . .

The second piece of evidence that separate opinions had come to be regarded as an accepted and legitimate part of the legal culture was the increased frequency with which Justices began citing them. Justices started citing both their own separate opinions and those of other Justices. . . .

The third indication that the separate opinion had become more widely accepted was the relative infrequency with which Justices offered explanations for their decisions to dissent. By the 1930s the familiar judicial language of regret, reluctance, and diffidence had all but disappeared. . . .

The fourth and most compelling sign that separate opinions were now viewed as playing an important role was that during this period, several separate opinions were written into law, either by statute or by subsequent overruling of the opinion for the Court. A number of these elevations of dissent occurred on issues of great public concern. The first and most significant example of this was the passage of the Fourteenth Amendment, which overturned *Dred Scott* and vindicated Justice Curtis' dissent. Other examples abound. . . . Cases such as *Nebbia v. New York* were a sub silentio endorsement of Holmes' dissent in *Lochner v. New York*. Justices seemed to be saving their best efforts for their separate opinions. . . .

E. THE STONE COURT

In 1941 Harlan Fiske Stone assumed leadership of a Court whose opinion-delivery practices had been stable for well over a century. There had been no significant change in the form in which opinions were delivered since the Marshall period. The rate at which these opinions were presented unanimously had also been remarkably constant.

The Stone Court, however, saw the beginnings of a significant change. While the form used to present opinions stayed the same, the rate at which dissent was expressed increased dramatically. Two statistics capture the significance of the Stone Court shift. The first is the nonunanimity rate, which . . . was relatively constant [and generally under 20%] between the beginning of the Marshall Court and the early 1930s. From the early 1930s through 1940 the rate rose slowly but steadily. Beginning in 1941, however, the rate exploded. It peaked at 86% in 1947. It has hovered around 75% ever since.

The second statistic that shows this dramatic change is the ratio of separate opinions to opinions of the Court. . . . As was the case with the nonunanimity rate, this number was remarkably stable between 1800 and 1940. . . . The following table gives the ratio of separate opinions to majority opinions during each of the following Chief Justice's tenure:

John Marshall	.07
Roger B. Taney	.18
Salmon P. Chase	.12
Morrison R. Waite	.08
Melville W. Fuller	.12
Edward D. White	.07
William H. Taft	.10
Charles E. Hughes	.17

As was the case with the nonunanimity rate, however, the 1941 Term was the beginning of a dramatic change. In 1941 the separate opinion to majority opinion ratio jumped from .19 to .34. The ratio continued to climb until 1948, when it topped 1.0 for the first time, meaning that the total number of dissents and concurrences in 1948 was higher than the total number of opinions for the Court. [T]he ratio hovered around 1.0 between 1948 and 1966 and has not dropped below that mark in any subsequent term.

This increase in the frequency of the issuance of separate opinions is a central event in the history of the Court's opinion-delivery practices. Before the shift, unanimity was the norm; afterwards, fragmentation was expected. . . .

At least two groups of scholars . . . have attempted to explain why the rate rose at the time it did. The first scholars to do so were Stephen Halpern and Kenneth Vines. Halpern and Vines argue that the passage of the Judiciary Act of 1925, popularly known as the Judges' Bill, was the primary cause of the Stone-era increase in the nonunanimity rate. The Judges' Bill gave the Justices increased control over their docket. Halpern and Vines note a slight increase in the nonunanimity rate for the years following the passage of the Bill. They tie this increase to the greater freedom the 1925 Bill gave to the Justices, writing: "developing and articulating a coherent judicial philosophy perhaps took on a greater significance for individual Justices after the Act."

The second group of scholars to consider the question, Thomas Walker, Lee Epstein, and William Dixon, conclude that the Judges' Bill is not the primary reason for the Court's increased issuance of separate opinions. This group notes that the rate at which separate opinions were issued did not begin to increase significantly until 1941, fifteen years after the Judges' Bill had taken effect. They reject three other possible explanations as well and argue that it was the leadership of Harlan Fiske Stone that was responsible for the increase in the dissent rate. Not only was Stone ineffective as a leader, he also was the first Chief Justice to believe that "imposed unanimity was no virtue in developing the law." Earlier Chief Justices had created a "no dissent unless absolutely necessary" tradition. Stone rejected this tradition and urged his colleagues to do the same. The Associate Justices, many of whom were new on the bench, readily agreed, and the tradition favoring unanimity was snuffed out forever. . . .

Both of these explanations, however, are limited by a narrow temporal focus. The passage of the Judges' Bill and the elevation of Stone were important, but only as immediate causes. The Stone-era changes can be understood in another way.

Rather than being viewed as the result of specific changes made in 1925 or 1941, the Stone-era rise can also be explained by reference to the historical trends discussed above. By 1941 attitudes toward separate opinions had changed dramatically. Justices no longer needed to justify a decision to write separately. The universe of cases for which dissent was appropriate had expanded dramatically. Much more attention was paid to the thinking of individual Justices, and Justices frequently used separate opinions to explain themselves. Separate opinions were cited for propositions of law and several had ultimately triumphed and become law. . . .

III. Conclusion

As should be apparent, the system the Supreme Court now uses to deliver opinions is a product of the historical choices and changes described above. The basic structure of opinion delivery—whereby opinions are delivered by a single Justice speaking for the Court and other Justices are free to write separately—was first established in the Marshall years. The current attitude that separate opinions play a legitimate role in many different areas of law is an extension of views first developed in the years between 1864-1940. The freedom that Justices today feel to write separately is a product of these views and the Stone-era explosion in individual judicial expression.

It should be equally apparent, however, that the system could have evolved in other ways. Chief Justice Marshall could have continued the early Court's practice of deciding cases by either per curiam or seriatim opinions. Justice Johnson could have decided to follow the lead of his brethren and never write separately. The Justices might never have abandoned the belief that dissent is appropriate only in a narrow category of cases. Had any of this taken place, the Court would undoubtedly today be a very different place.

Antonin Scalia, The Dissenting Opinion

Journal of Supreme Court History 33, 35-42 (1994)

I have chosen to write about the dissenting opinion—a subject, I think, of some interest and importance. First of all, some definitions of terms: In speaking of dissenting opinions, I mean to address opinions that disagree with the Court's reasoning. Some such opinions, when they happen to reach the same disposition as the majority (that is, affirmance or reversal of the judgment below), are technically concurrences rather than dissents. To my mind, there is little difference between the two, insofar as the desirability of a separate opinion is concerned. Legal opinions are important, after all, for the reasons they give, not the results they announce; results can be announced in judgment orders without opinion. An opinion that gets the reasons wrong gets everything wrong, and that is worth a dissent, even if the dissent is called a concurrence.

. . . In assessing the advantages and disadvantages of separate opinions, one must consider their effects both within and without the Court. Let me discuss the latter first: The foremost and undeniable external consequence of a separate dissenting or concurring opinion is to destroy the appearance of unity and solidarity. From the beginning to the present, many great American judges have considered that to be a virtually dispositive argument against separate opinions. So high a value did Chief Justice Marshall place upon a united front that according to his colleague, Justice William Johnson, he not only went along with opinions that were contrary to his own view, but even announced some. Only toward the end of his career—when his effort to suppress separate opinions had plainly failed—did he indulge himself in dissents, a total of only nine dissents in thirty-four years. In more recent times, no less a judicial personage than Judge Learned Hand warned that a dissent "cancels the impact of monolithic solidarity upon which the authority of a bench of judges so largely depends."

I do not think I agree with that. . . . Now it may well be that the people will be more inclined to accept without complaint a unanimous opinion of a court, just as they will be more inclined to accept willingly a painful course decided upon unanimously by their legislature. But to say that the authority of a court depends upon such unanimity in my view overstates the point.

In fact, the argument can be made that artificial unanimity—the suppression of dissents—deprives genuine unanimity of the great force it can have when that force is most needed. United States Supreme Court lore contains the story of Chief Justice Earl Warren's heroic and ultimately successful efforts to obtain a unanimous Court for the epochal decision in *Brown v. Board of Education*, which prohibited racial segregation in all public education. I certainly agree that unanimity was important to achieving greater public acceptance. But would it have had that effect if all the decisions of the Supreme Court, even those decided by 5-4 vote, were announced as unanimous? Surely not.

Perhaps things are different when a newly established court is just starting out. . . . But I have no doubt that for the United States Supreme Court, at its current stage of development and in the current age, announced dissents augment rather than diminish its prestige. . . . Unlike a unanimous institutional opinion, a signed majority opinion, opposed by one or more signed dissents makes it clear that these decisions are the product of independent and thoughtful minds, who try to persuade one another but do not simply "go along" for some supposed "good of the institution."

I think dissents augment rather than diminish the prestige of the Court for yet another reason. When history demonstrates that one of the Court's decisions has been a truly horrendous mistake, it is comforting—and conducive of respect for the Court—to look back and realize that at least some of the justices saw the danger clearly and gave voice, often eloquent voice, to their concern. I think, for example, of the prophetic dissent of Justice John Marshall Harlan (the earlier Justice Harlan) in *Plessy v. Ferguson* (the case essentially overruled by *Brown v. Board of Education* a half century later) which held that, despite the provision of the Constitution requiring equal protection of the laws, the State of Louisiana could require railroads to carry white people and black people in separate cars. Harlan wrote:

> ... [I]n view of the Constitution, in the eye of the law, there is in this country no superior, dominant, ruling class of citizens. There is no caste here. Our Constitution is color-blind. In respect of civil rights, all citizens are equal before the law. The humblest is the peer of the most powerful. The law regards man as man. ...

... At the Supreme Court ... a dissent rarely helps change the law. Even the most successful of our dissenters—Oliver Wendell Holmes, who acquired the sobriquet "The Great Dissenter"—saw somewhat less than 10 percent of his dissenting views ultimately vindicated by later overrulings. Most dissenters are much less successful than that. ...

The dissent most likely to be rewarded with later vindication is, of course, a dissent that is joined by three other justices, so that the decision is merely a 5-4 holding. That sort of a dissent, at least in constitutional cases (in which, under the practice of our Court, the doctrine of stare decisis—i.e., adhering to precedent—is less rigorously observed) emboldens counsel in later cases to try again, and to urge an overruling—which sometimes, although rarely, occurs.

And that observation leads me to another external effect of a dissenting opinion, which is to inform the public in general, and the Bar in particular, about the state of the Court's collective mind. Let me give a concrete example: In 1992 the Court held, in a case called *Lee v. Weisman*, that the Establishment Clause of our Bill of Rights, which prohibits an "Establishment of Religion," forbids public officials from making a nondenominational invocation part of the ceremonies at a public high school graduation. Had the judgment been rendered by an institutional opinion for the Court, that rule of law would have the appearance of being as clear, as unquestionable, and as stable as the rule that denominational prayers cannot be made a mandatory part of the school day. In fact, however, the opinion was 5-4. It is clear to all that the decision was at the very margin of Establishment Clause prohibition; that it would not be extended much further and may even someday be overruled.

Or to take another example, one that involves the provision of our Bill of Rights that forbids laws which prohibit the free exercise of religion. In a case called *Employment Division v. Smith* (1990), the Court held that this did not form the basis for a private exemption from generally applicable laws governing conduct—so that a person could not claim a right to use a proscribed psychotropic drug (peyote) in religious ceremonies. There again, the decision on the point was 5-4, making clear to one and all (and to future litigants, in particular) that this is a highly controverted and thus perhaps changeable portion of our jurisprudence.

I have tried to be impartial in the examples I have chosen; I wrote the dissent in the first case, and the opinion for the Court in the second. In both cases, I think it was desirable and not destructive that the fragility of the Court's holding was apparent. This is not to suggest, by the way, that every 5-4 decision of our Court is a sitting duck for future overruling. In cases involving statutory law, rather than the Constitution, we will almost certainly not revisit the point, no matter how closely it was decided. But even there, disclosure of the closeness of the vote provides useful information to the legal community, suggesting that the logic of the legal principle at issue has been stretched close to its utmost limit and will not readily be extended further.

. . . [O]ne of the undesirable external effects of a system of separate opinions [is that it] produces, or at least facilitates, a sort of vote-counting approach to significant rules of law. Whenever one of the five justices in a 5-4 constitutional decision has been replaced there is a chance, astute counsel must think, of getting that decision overruled. And worse still, when the decision in question is a highly controversial constitutional decision, that thought occurs not merely to astute counsel but to the president who appoints the new justice, to the senators who confirm him, and to the lobbying groups that have the power to influence both. If the decision in question is controversial enough—*Roe v. Wade* is the prime modern example—the appointment of the new justice becomes something of a plebiscite upon the meaning of the Constitution in general and of the Bill of Rights in particular, in effect giving the majority the power to prescribe the meaning of an instrument designed to restrain the majority. That could not happen, or at least it could not happen as readily, if the individual positions of all the justices were not known.

Let me turn to the last, but by no means the least, of the external consequences of our system of separate opinions. By enabling, indeed compelling, the justices of our Court, through their personally signed majority, dissenting, and concurring opinions, to set forth clear and consistent positions on both sides of the major legal issues of the day, this system has kept the Court in the forefront of the intellectual development of the law. In our system, it is not left to the academicians to stimulate and conduct discussion concerning the validity of the Court's latest ruling. The Court itself is not just the central organ of legal judgment; it is center stage for significant legal debate. . . .

I turn now to what I have called the "internal" consequences of separate opinions—their effect within the Court itself. They do not, or at least need not, produce animosity and bitterness among the members of the Court. Dissenting will have that effect, I suppose, if it is an almost unheard-of occurrence, subjecting the writer of the Court's opinion to what may be viewed as a rare indignity. But we come from a tradition in which each judge used to write his own opinion. Dissents are simply the normal course of things. Indeed, if one's opinions were never dissented from, he would begin to suspect that his colleagues considered him insipid, or simply not worthy of contradiction. I doubt whether any two justices have dissented from one another's opinions any more regularly, or any more sharply, than did my former colleague Justice William Brennan and I. I always considered him, however, one of my best friends on the Court, and I think that feeling was reciprocated.

The most important internal effect of a system permitting dissents and concurrences is to improve the majority opinion. It does that in a number of ways. To begin with, the mere prospect of a separate writing renders the writer of the majority opinion more receptive to reasonable suggestions on major points. . . .

The second way in which separate opinions improve the majority opinion is this: Though the fact never comes to public light, the first draft of a dissent often causes the majority to refine its opinion, eliminating the more vulnerable assertions and narrowing the announced legal rule. When I have been assigned the opinion for the Court in a divided case, nothing gives me as much assurance that I have written it well as the fact that I am able to respond satisfactorily (in my judgment) to all the onslaughts of the dissent or separate concurrence. The dissent or concurrence puts my opinion to the test, providing a direct confrontation of the best arguments on both sides of the controverted points. It is a sure cure for laziness, compelling me to make the most of my case. Ironic as it may seem, I think a higher percentage of the worst opinions of my Court—not in result but in reasoning—are unanimous ones.

And finally, the last way in which a separate opinion can improve the majority opinion is by becoming the majority opinion. Not often, but much more than rarely, an effective dissent or concurrence, once it is circulated, changes the outcome of the case, winning over one or more of the justices who formed the original majority. Objections to the proposed majority opinion made at oral conference, or even in an exchange of written memoranda, will never be as fully developed, as thoroughly researched, and as forcefully presented as they are in a full-dress dissenting or concurring opinion prepared for publication.

Besides improving the Court's opinions, I think a system of separate writing improves the Court's judges. It forces them to think systematically and consistently about the law, because in every case their legal views are not submerged within an artificially unanimous opinion, but are plainly disclosed to the world. Even if they do not personally write the majority or the dissent, their name will be subscribed to the one view or the other. . . .

Finally, and to me most important of all, a system of separate opinions renders the profession of a judge—and I think even the profession of a lawyer—more enjoyable. One of the more cantankerous of our justices, William O. Douglas, once wrote that "the right to dissent is the only thing that makes life tolerable for a judge of an appellate court." I am not sure I agree with that, but I surely agree that it makes the practice of one's profession as a judge more satisfying. To be able to write an opinion solely for oneself, without the need to accommodate, to any degree whatever, the more-or-less-differing views of one's colleagues; to address precisely the points of law that one considers important and no others; to express precisely the degree of quibble, or foreboding, or disbelief, or indignation that one believes the majority's disposition should engender—that is indeed an unparalleled pleasure. . . .

Notes and Questions

1. Why do you think Chief Justice John Marshall led his colleagues to abandon the English and initial Court practice of seriatim opinions? Would you agree with one Marshall biographer that having the Court instead speak as one voice was "an act of audacity" and "assumption . . . of power"? 3 Albert J. Beveridge, *The Life of John Marshall* 16 (1919).

2. As the Kelsh article relates, Chief Justice Marshall assiduously cultivated unanimity on the Court, and this consensual norm persisted, more or less, over a century under seven additional chief justices. What caused it to collapse in the 1940s? One influential study, noted by Kelsh, places the blame primarily on Chief Justice Harlan Fiske Stone:

First . . . [i]n a break from the tradition of his predecessors, Stone steadfastly held that justices should be free to assert their individuality—that imposed unanimity was no virtue in developing the law. Second, Stone's attitudes were translated into action. He did not draw back from challenging the majority. He expressed his own views frequently, and by doing so gave a signal to the other members of the Court that it was perfectly permissible to engage in concurring and dissenting opinions. Furthermore, unlike his predecessors, there is no evidence that Stone engaged in any actions to enforce the traditional consensus norms of the Court or to socialize new justices into the no dissent convention. Third, Stone's views appear to have been reinforced by his lack of appreciation for the tightly run conferences of Hughes and what he believed to be the superficial harmony of the Taft years. Stone, in a sense, rebelled against the chiefs under which he had served. . . . Stone thought there was a line beyond which a Chief Justice could not, with propriety, press for compromise.

Thomas G. Walker et al., *On the Mysterious Demise of Consensual Norms in the United States Supreme Court*, 50 J. Pol. 361, 384 (1988). Other factors that "substantially enhanced the impact of [Stone's] leadership style" included the conversion of the Court's docket to a largely discretionary one by the Judiciary Act of 1925, which led the Justices to take an increasing percentage of difficult and controversial cases, *see supra* Chapter 4.A, and associate justices who "had relatively few years of Supreme Court experience," and therefore "had not been deeply immersed in the traditional norms of the institution." *Id.* at 385; *see also* Stephen C. Halpern & Kenneth N. Vines, *Institutional Disunity, The Judges' Bill and the Role of the U.S. Supreme Court*, 30 W. Pol. Q. 471 (1977) (placing blame primarily on the so-called Judges' Bill of 1925).

Perhaps as significantly, once the institutional norm switched from unanimity to individuality, it was difficult to put the genie back in the bottle—though President Truman did try with the appointment of the "affable" Fred Vinson as Stone's replacement.

> Truman's hopes did not materialize. Vinson faced a Court unwilling to return to the old ways. The eight associate justices already in place when the new chief justice opened the October 1946 term represented forty-six years of experience, 74 percent of which had been served under Stone. All of the associates had spent a majority of their Court tenures under the Stone regime. Rutledge, Jackson, and Burton had served only under Stone and had no exposure to pre-Stone consensus norms. Frankfurter, Douglas, and Black, once freed from the expectations of cohesion and consensus, continued to assert their new prerogatives after Vinson's nomination. Significantly, each member of this trio had long years of service after Stone's death: Black and Douglas for more than a quarter-century and Frankfurter for a decade and a half. Vinson was unable to reimpose the norm that individual views should be suppressed in deference to the majority. Instead, the Vinson Court became characterized as "nine scorpions in a bottle". . . . Successive new justices joined and were socialized into a Court with behavioral expectations quite unlike those operative in the pre-Stone years. Consequently, although Stone's term as chief justice was relatively short, his views on individual judicial expression constituted a legacy protected by his surviving associates.

Walker, *supra*, at 385-386.

3. The Kelsh article discusses the explosion of nonunanimous opinions and separate opinions since the 1940s. The number of cases decided by a single vote has also risen dramatically in that time. For example, before the 1940s, no Chief Justice ever saw one-vote majorities exceed 4 percent of decided cases. From the 1940s onward, that percentage jumped under each successive Chief Justice, with the exception of Earl Warren, who had a legendary ability to bring the Court together in critical cases such as *Brown v. Board of Education.* Currently, under Chief Justice John Roberts, a record average 22 percent of cases are decided by a 5-4 vote. The 2006 term alone produced a historic high of 33 percent. *See* David Paul Kuhn, *The Polarization of the Supreme Court*, RealClearPolitics (July 2, 2010), http://www.realclearpolitics.com/articles/2010/07/02/the_polarization_of_the_supreme_court_john_roberts_elena_kagan_106176.html.

4. Whether the soaring rates of nonunanimity, separate opinions, and one-vote majorities are good or bad depend on one's valuation of unanimity and, conversely, of dissent. Are unanimous decisions desirable for the Court? For the country? If your answers differ, why?

5. Even if unanimity is desirable, should it come at the cost of masking internal disagreement on the Court? Consider the views of Chief Justice Charles Evans Hughes:

> When unanimity can be obtained without sacrifice of conviction, it strongly commends the decision to public confidence. But unanimity which is merely formal, which is recorded at the expense of strong, conflicting views, is not desirable in a court of last resort, whatever may be the effect upon public opinion at the time. This is so because what must ultimately sustain the court in public confidence is the character and independence of the judges. They are not there simply to decide cases, but to decide them as they think they should be decided, and while it may be regrettable that they cannot always agree, it is better that their independence should be maintained and recognized than that unanimity should be secured through its sacrifice.

Charles Evans Hughes, *The Supreme Court of the United States* 67-68 (1928).

6. Do you find Justice Scalia's arguments in support of separate opinions persuasive? Do you think his opposition to masking "artificial unanimity" would extend to *Brown v. Board of Education* and the great lengths to which Chief Justice Warren went "to eliminate the danger of dissenting and concurring opinions"? Bernard Schwartz, *The Unpublished Opinions of the Warren Court* 447 (1985). In particular, if Chief Justice Warren had failed to win over southerner Stanley Reed, who reportedly held out until within a month of the decision, *see id.*, do you think Justice Scalia would regard a dissent in *Brown* to have been a benefit to both the Court and the country? Would you?

7. Justice Scalia notes that he did not often see eye to eye with "one of [his] best friends on the Court," Justice William Brennan. Yet they did agree on the subject of dissenting. "Dissents," wrote Justice Brennan, "contribute to the integrity of the process, not only by directing attention to perceived difficulties with the majority's opinion, but . . . also by contributing to the marketplace of competing ideas." William J. Brennan, Jr., *In Defense of Dissents*, 37 Hastings L.J. 427, 435 (1986).

8. Recall Justice Brennan's draft concurrence in *Miranda v. Arizona* (1966), reprinted and discussed in the previous section. Do you think he ultimately decided against publishing it because the draft opinion had already "contribute[d] to the integrity of the process" by prompting Chief Justice Warren to add desirable language? Or do you think Justice Brennan withdrew it strategically to preserve a unified front, as the Chief Justice and his clerks had wished?

9. One study of the impact of concurring opinions concludes that "all concurrences are not the same," and that "expansive concurrences" (that is, those that would go farther than the majority) tend to increase the precedential value of a decision both in the lower courts and at the Court itself, while "doctrinal concurrences" (that is, those that support the result reached by the majority, but not its reasons) tend to decrease a decision's precedential value. Pamela C. Corley, *Concurring Opinion Writing on the U.S. Supreme Court* 97-99 (2010). Assuming the validity of this study, do you think it would be appropriate for a Justice to write (or not write) separately in an attempt to bolster or limit the impact of a majority decision?

10. Between suppressing dissent for the sake of superficial unanimity and writing a full-blown attack on the majority view, would it be a preferable middle ground to simply note a dissenting vote, as was sometimes done early in the Court's history?

Consider Justice Brennan's view that judges have a responsibility to give reasons for their votes:

> I elevate this responsibility to an obligation because in our legal system judges have no power to *declare* law. That is to say, a court may not simply announce, without more, that it has adopted a rule to which all must adhere. That, of course, is the province of the legislature. Courts *derive* legal principles, and have a duty to explain *why* and *how* a given rule has come to be. This requirement serves a function within the judicial process similar to that served by the electoral process with regard to the political branches of government. It restrains judges and keeps them accountable to the law and to the principles that are the source of judicial authority.

Brennan, *supra*, at 435.

11. The Court's increasingly fractured decisions have led other contemporary justices to renew Marshall-like warnings against too much dissension. Justice Ruth Bader Ginsburg has cautioned that "overindulgence in separate opinion writing may undermine both the reputation of the judiciary for judgment and the respect accorded court dispositions." Ruth Bader Ginsburg, *Speaking in a Judicial Voice*, 67 N.Y.U. L. Rev. 1185, 1191 (1992). And early in his tenure as Chief Justice, John Roberts made it a defining priority of his leadership to steer the Court toward unanimity. In an interview just after his first term, Chief Justice Roberts reflected:

> If the Court in Marshall's era had issued decisions in important cases the way this Court has over the past thirty years, we would not have a Supreme Court today of the sort that we have. . . . That suggests that what the Court's been doing over the past thirty years has been eroding, to some extent, the capital that Marshall built up. . . . I think the Court is also ripe for a similar refocus on functioning as an institution, because if it doesn't it's going to lose its credibility and legitimacy as an institution.

Jeffrey Rosen, *Roberts's Rules*, The Atlantic (Jan./Feb. 2007), http://www.theatlantic .com/magazine/archive/2007/01/robertss-rules/305559. Why do you think Chief Justice Roberts has been unable to reverse what he views as the Court's destructive divisiveness?

12. The Roberts Court's 5-4 divisions have typically fallen along ideological lines, so much so that one commentator has observed that the Court is now "just another place where Democrats and Republicans fight." Jeffrey Toobin, *After Stevens*, The New Yorker (March 22, 2010), http://www.newyorker.com/reporting/2010/ 03/22/100322fa_fact_toobin. Furthermore, because retirements and appointments have also made the Court more ideologically conservative in recent decades, another commentator has observed that "[t]he court's deep polarization today is not between the left and the right, but right and middle left." Kuhn, *supra*. Accordingly, even if dissenting opinions may have value in the ways identified by Justice Scalia and Justice Brennan, do they lose their benefits and exacerbate their harms when they reflect ideological voting blocs?

B. MODEL OPINIONS

By this time in your law school career, you will no doubt have read hundreds, if not thousands, of Supreme Court opinions. You likely have read all of them for their substantive content, grappling with their legal issues, analyses, and outcomes. Now try to read the opinions below—or any others that you admire or abhor—from the standpoint, not of a student of the law, but of a critic of opinion writing.

To begin, treat every word, sentence, paragraph, and part of each opinion not as a given, but as a choice made for reasons of structure, strategy, and style as well as substance. Ask why a word was chosen, how it works in a sentence, how the sentence functions in a paragraph, what that paragraph accomplishes, how it fits with those around it, and how the opinion overall is constructed to decide the case. Then ask whether you could have made different—and better—choices along the way.

As you will come to appreciate, the opinions in this section were selected as "models" not necessarily because they are exemplars of opinion writing, but because they are useful subjects for studying the craft. For instance, the majority opinions in the first two cases below, by Chief Justice William Rehnquist and Justice Anthony Kennedy, both decide constitutional questions, but contrast in style, strategy, and scale. The majority opinion in the third case, by Justice Samuel Alito, illustrates how a question of statutory construction may be resolved. After studying these opinions along with the notes and questions that follow them, consider whether you would deem any to be a model majority opinion in the exemplary sense. Do others that you have encountered in law school come to mind as superior models? If so, why? Consider as well the sense in which the selected dissenting and concurring opinions—or others you have come across—are "models" for study.

The paragraphs in the opinions below have been numbered for ease of reference.

1. Bond v. United States

529 U.S. 334, 335-339 (2000): Chief Justice Rehnquist's Majority Opinion

Chief Justice REHNQUIST delivered the opinion of the Court.

[1] This case presents the question whether a law enforcement officer's physical manipulation of a bus passenger's carry-on luggage violated the Fourth Amendment's proscription against unreasonable searches. We hold that it did.

[2] Petitioner Steven Dewayne Bond was a passenger on a Greyhound bus that left California bound for Little Rock, Arkansas. The bus stopped, as it was required to do, at the permanent Border Patrol checkpoint in Sierra Blanca, Texas. Border Patrol Agent Cesar Cantu boarded the bus to check the immigration status of its passengers. After reaching the back of the bus, having satisfied himself that the passengers were lawfully in the United States, Agent Cantu began walking toward the front. Along the way, he squeezed the soft luggage which passengers had placed in the overhead storage space above the seats.

[3] Petitioner was seated four or five rows from the back of the bus. As Agent Cantu inspected the luggage in the compartment above petitioner's seat, he squeezed a green canvas bag and noticed that it contained a "brick-like" object. Petitioner admitted that the bag was his and agreed to allow Agent Cantu to open it.[1]

---

1. The Government has not argued here that petitioner's consent to Agent Cantu's opening the bag is a basis for admitting the evidence.

Upon opening the bag, Agent Cantu discovered a "brick" of methamphetamine. The brick had been wrapped in duct tape until it was oval-shaped and then rolled in a pair of pants.

[4] Petitioner was indicted for conspiracy to possess, and possession with intent to distribute, methamphetamine in violation of 84 Stat. 1260, 21 U.S. C. §841(a)(1). He moved to suppress the drugs, arguing that Agent Cantu conducted an illegal search of his bag. Petitioner's motion was denied, and the District Court found him guilty on both counts and sentenced him to 57 months in prison. On appeal, he conceded that other passengers had access to his bag, but contended that Agent Cantu manipulated the bag in a way that other passengers would not. The Court of Appeals rejected this argument, stating that the fact that Agent Cantu's manipulation of petitioner's bag was calculated to detect contraband is irrelevant for Fourth Amendment purposes. 167 F.3d 225, 227 (CA5 1999) (citing *California v. Ciraolo*, 476 U.S. 207 (1986)). Thus, the Court of Appeals affirmed the denial of the motion to suppress, holding that Agent Cantu's manipulation of the bag was not a search within the meaning of the Fourth Amendment. 167 F.3d, at 227. We granted certiorari, 528 U.S. 927 (1999), and now reverse.

[5] The Fourth Amendment provides that "[t]he right of the people to be secure in their persons, houses, papers, and effects, against unreasonable searches and seizures, shall not be violated. . . . " A traveler's personal luggage is clearly an "effect" protected by the Amendment. See *United States v. Place*, 462 U.S. 696, 707 (1983). Indeed, it is undisputed here that petitioner possessed a privacy interest in his bag.

[6] But the Government asserts that by exposing his bag to the public, petitioner lost a reasonable expectation that his bag would not be physically manipulated. The Government relies on our decisions in *California v. Ciraolo, supra,* and *Florida v. Riley,* 488 U.S. 445 (1989), for the proposition that matters open to public observation are not protected by the Fourth Amendment. In *Ciraolo,* we held that police observation of a backyard from a plane flying at an altitude of 1,000 feet did not violate a reasonable expectation of privacy. Similarly, in *Riley,* we relied on *Ciraolo* to hold that police observation of a greenhouse in a home's curtilage from a helicopter passing at an altitude of 400 feet did not violate the Fourth Amendment. We reasoned that the property was "not necessarily protected from inspection that involves no physical invasion," and determined that because any member of the public could have lawfully observed the defendants' property by flying overhead, the defendants' expectation of privacy was "not reasonable and not one 'that society is prepared to honor.'" See *Riley, supra,* at 449 (explaining and relying on *Ciraolo*'s reasoning).

[7] But *Ciraolo* and *Riley* are different from this case because they involved only visual, as opposed to tactile, observation. Physically invasive inspection is simply more intrusive than purely visual inspection. For example, in *Terry v. Ohio,* 392 U.S. 1, 16-17 (1968), we stated that a "careful [tactile] exploration of the outer surfaces of a person's clothing all over his or her body" is a "serious intrusion upon the sanctity of the person, which may inflict great indignity and arouse strong resentment, and is not to be undertaken lightly." Although Agent Cantu did not "frisk" petitioner's person, he did conduct a probing tactile examination of petitioner's carry-on luggage. Obviously, petitioner's bag was not part of his person. But travelers are particularly concerned about their carry-on luggage; they generally use it to transport personal items that, for whatever reason, they prefer to keep close at hand.

[8] Here, petitioner concedes that, by placing his bag in the overhead compartment, he could expect that it would be exposed to certain kinds of touching and handling. But petitioner argues that Agent Cantu's physical manipulation of his luggage "far exceeded the casual contact [petitioner] could have expected from other passengers." Brief for Petitioner 18-19. The Government counters that it did not.

[9] Our Fourth Amendment analysis embraces two questions. First, we ask whether the individual, by his conduct, has exhibited an actual expectation of privacy; that is, whether he has shown that "he [sought] to preserve [something] as private." *Smith v. Maryland*, 442 U.S. 735, 740 (1979) (internal quotation marks omitted). Here, petitioner sought to preserve privacy by using an opaque bag and placing that bag directly above his seat. Second, we inquire whether the individual's expectation of privacy is "one that society is prepared to recognize as reasonable." *Ibid.* (internal quotation marks omitted).[2] When a bus passenger places a bag in an overhead bin, he expects that other passengers or bus employees may move it for one reason or another. Thus, a bus passenger clearly expects that his bag may be handled. He does not expect that other passengers or bus employees will, as a matter of course, feel the bag in an exploratory manner. But this is exactly what the agent did here. We therefore hold that the agent's physical manipulation of petitioner's bag violated the Fourth Amendment.

[10] The judgment of the Court of Appeals is
Reversed.

Notes and Questions

1. Consider the following paragraph-level outline of Chief Justice William Rehnquist's majority opinion:

¶1	**Introduction** (setting forth question presented)
¶¶2-3	**Facts** (relating relevant facts)
¶4	**Decisions below** (describing results and reasoning of lower courts)
¶5	**Governing law** (setting forth relevant legal provision)
¶¶6-7	**Respondent's precedents** (describing and distinguishing case law relied on by respondent)
¶8	**Petitioner's argument** (setting forth petitioner's main contention)
¶9	**Relevant precedent** (describing and applying relevant case law interpreting governing law)
¶10	**Disposition** (giving outcome of case)

2. The parties properly agree that the subjective intent of the law enforcement officer is irrelevant in determining whether that officer's actions violate the Fourth Amendment. Brief for Petitioner 14; Brief for United States 33-34; see *Whren v. United States*, 517 U.S. 806, 813 (1996) (stating that "we have been unwilling to entertain Fourth Amendment challenges based on the actual motivations of individual officers"); *California v. Ciraolo*, 476 U.S. 207, 212 (1986) (rejecting respondent's challenge to "the authority of government to observe his activity from any vantage point or place if the viewing is motivated by a law enforcement purpose, and not the result of a casual, accidental observation"). This principle applies to the agent's acts in this case as well; the issue is not his state of mind, but the objective effect of his actions.

Does the opinion flow legally or logically, or are there parts that seem unexplained, unnecessary, or out of place? For example, would a reader not knowledgeable in Fourth Amendment case law understand what "privacy" (¶5) and "a reasonable expectation" (¶6) have to do with the text of the just-quoted Fourth Amendment (¶5)? Would the reader only understand after ¶9, which sets out the governing two-part test for determining whether a "search" has occurred within the meaning of the Fourth Amendment ("an actual expectation of privacy" that "society is prepared to recognize as reasonable")?

   2. Consider the following rearrangement of Chief Justice Rehnquist's majority opinion, which is designed to address the problems raised in note 1:

¶1   **Introduction** (setting forth question presented)
¶¶2-3   **Facts** (relating relevant facts)
¶4   **Decisions below** (describing results and reasoning of lower courts)
¶5   **Governing law** (setting forth relevant legal provision)
¶¶8-9   **Relevant precedent/Petitioner's argument** (describing relevant case
                law interpreting governing law and petitioner's argument under it;
                applying relevant case law)
¶¶6-7   **Respondent's precedents** (describing and distinguishing case law
                relied on by respondent)
¶10   **Disposition** (giving outcome of case)

With ¶¶8-9 moved up and combined, and a minimum of other edits (deleted language stricken, added language underlined, new paragraphing preceded by ¶), the revised majority opinion would read as follows:

   Chief Justice REHNQUIST delivered the opinion of the Court.

   [1] This case presents the question whether a law enforcement officer's physical manipulation of a bus passenger's carry-on luggage violated the Fourth Amendment's proscription against unreasonable searches. We hold that it did.

   [2] Petitioner Steven Dewayne Bond was a passenger on a Greyhound bus that left California bound for Little Rock, Arkansas. The bus stopped, as it was required to do, at the permanent Border Patrol checkpoint in Sierra Blanca, Texas. Border Patrol Agent Cesar Cantu boarded the bus to check the immigration status of its passengers. After reaching the back of the bus, having satisfied himself that the passengers were lawfully in the United States, Agent Cantu began walking toward the front. Along the way, he squeezed the soft luggage which passengers had placed in the overhead storage space above the seats.

   [3] Petitioner was seated four or five rows from the back of the bus. As Agent Cantu inspected the luggage in the compartment above petitioner's seat, he squeezed a green canvas bag and noticed that it contained a "brick-like" object. Petitioner admitted that the bag was his and agreed to allow Agent Cantu to open it.[1] Upon opening the bag, Agent Cantu discovered a "brick" of methamphetamine. The brick had been wrapped in duct tape until it was oval-shaped and then rolled in a pair of pants.

   [4] Petitioner was indicted for conspiracy to possess, and possession with intent to distribute, methamphetamine in violation of 84 Stat. 1260, 21 U.S. C. §841(a)(1). He moved to suppress the drugs, arguing that Agent Cantu conducted an illegal search of his bag. Petitioner's motion was denied, and the District Court found him guilty on

---

1. The Government has not argued here that petitioner's consent to Agent Cantu's opening the bag is a basis for admitting the evidence.

both counts and sentenced him to 57 months in prison. On appeal, he conceded that other passengers had access to his bag, but contended that Agent Cantu manipulated the bag in a way that other passengers would not. The Court of Appeals rejected this argument, stating that the fact that Agent Cantu's manipulation of petitioner's bag was calculated to detect contraband is irrelevant for Fourth Amendment purposes. 167 F.3d 225, 227 (CA5 1999) (citing *California v. Ciraolo*, 476 U.S. 207 (1986)). Thus, the Court of Appeals affirmed the denial of the motion to suppress, holding that Agent Cantu's manipulation of the bag was not a search within the meaning of the Fourth Amendment. 167 F.3d, at 227. We granted certiorari, 528 U.S. 927 (1999), and now reverse.

[5] The Fourth Amendment provides that "[t]he right of the people to be secure in their persons, houses, papers, and effects, against unreasonable searches and seizures, shall not be violated. . . . " ~~A traveler's personal luggage is clearly an "effect" protected by the Amendment. See *United States v. Place*, 462 U.S. 696, 707 (1983). Indeed, it is undisputed here that petitioner possessed a privacy interest in his bag.~~ At issue is whether Agent Cantu's physical manipulation of Petitioner's bag constituted a "search" within the meaning of the Fourth Amendment. To determine whether a "search" has occurred, we ask two questions.

[9] ~~Our Fourth Amendment analysis embraces two questions.~~ First, we ask whether the individual, by his conduct, has exhibited an actual expectation of privacy; that is, whether he has shown that "he [sought] to preserve [something] as private." *Smith v. Maryland*, 442 U.S. 735, 740 (1979) (internal quotation marks omitted). Here, petitioner sought to preserve privacy by using an opaque bag and placing that bag directly above his seat.

¶Second, we inquire whether the individual's expectation of privacy is "one that society is prepared to recognize as reasonable." *Ibid.* (internal quotation marks omitted).[2] [8] Here, petitioner concedes that, by placing his bag in the overhead compartment, he could expect that it would be exposed to certain kinds of touching and handling. But petitioner argues that Agent Cantu's physical manipulation of his luggage "far exceeded the casual contact [petitioner] could have expected from other passengers." Brief for Petitioner 18-19. The Government counters that it did not.

¶[9 continued] When a bus passenger places a bag in an overhead bin, he expects that other passengers or bus employees may move it for one reason or another. Thus, a bus passenger clearly expects that his bag may be handled. He does not expect that other passengers or bus employees will, as a matter of course, feel the bag in an exploratory manner. But this is exactly what the agent did here. We therefore hold that the agent's physical manipulation of petitioner's bag ~~violated~~ invaded petitioner's "reasonable expectation of privacy" and thus constituted a "search" under the Fourth Amendment.

[6] But the Government asserts that by exposing his bag to the public, petitioner lost a reasonable expectation that his bag would not be physically manipulated. The Government relies on our decisions in *California v. Ciraolo, supra,* and *Florida v. Riley,* 488

---

2. The parties properly agree that the subjective intent of the law enforcement officer is irrelevant in determining whether that officer's actions violate the Fourth Amendment. Brief for Petitioner 14; Brief for United States 33-34; see *Whren v. United States,* 517 U.S. 806, 813 (1996) (stating that "we have been unwilling to entertain Fourth Amendment challenges based on the actual motivations of individual officers"); *California v. Ciraolo,* 476 U.S. 207, 212 (1986) (rejecting respondent's challenge to "the authority of government to observe his activity from any vantage point or place if the viewing is motivated by a law enforcement purpose, and not the result of a casual, accidental observation"). This principle applies to the agent's acts in this case as well; the issue is not his state of mind, but the objective effect of his actions.

U.S. 445 (1989), for the proposition that matters open to public observation are not protected by the Fourth Amendment. In *Ciraolo*, we held that police observation of a backyard from a plane flying at an altitude of 1,000 feet did not violate a reasonable expectation of privacy. Similarly, in *Riley*, we relied on *Ciraolo* to hold that police observation of a greenhouse in a home's curtilage from a helicopter passing at an altitude of 400 feet did not violate the Fourth Amendment. We reasoned that the property was "not necessarily protected from inspection that involves no physical invasion," and determined that because any member of the public could have lawfully observed the defendants' property by flying overhead, the defendants' expectation of privacy was "not reasonable and not one 'that society is prepared to honor.'" See *Riley, supra*, at 449 (explaining and relying on *Ciraolo*'s reasoning).

[7] But *Ciraolo* and *Riley* are different from this case because they involved only visual, as opposed to tactile, observation. Physically invasive inspection is simply more intrusive than purely visual inspection. For example, in *Terry v. Ohio*, 392 U.S. 1, 16-17 (1968), we stated that a "careful [tactile] exploration of the outer surfaces of a person's clothing all over his or her body" is a "serious intrusion upon the sanctity of the person, which may inflict great indignity and arouse strong resentment, and is not to be undertaken lightly." Although Agent Cantu did not "frisk" petitioner's person, he did conduct a probing tactile examination of petitioner's carry-on luggage. Obviously, petitioner's bag was not part of his person. But travelers are particularly concerned about their carry-on luggage; they generally use it to transport personal items that, for whatever reason, they prefer to keep close at hand.

As a "search," Agent Cantu's physical manipulation of petitioner's bag required either a valid warrant or an applicable warrant exception to be "reasonable." He lacked the former, and the government does not rely on the latter. The search thus violated the Fourth Amendment.

[10] The judgment of the Court of Appeals is
Reversed.

3. Does the revised opinion improve on the original or make it worse? In what ways? Do the revisions work any substantive changes, or merely structural and stylistic ones? If the latter, does any improvement matter?

4. Recall Chief Justice Rehnquist allowed a law clerk only ten days to two weeks to complete a draft opinion, and commented that such a draft need not be polished like "a paper to be presented in an academic seminar or an entry in a poetry contest." William H. Rehnquist, *The Supreme Court* 261 (2001). On the other hand, his longtime colleague, Justice Stevens, has remarked that "the quality of some of [Rehnquist's] opinions may have been adversely affected" by his tight deadline. John Paul Stevens, *Five Chiefs, supra,* 174 (2011). Yet Stevens was also quick to add that "the quality of the writing [is] far less important than the quality of the judgment." *Id.* Do you agree?

5. Consider the majority opinion again in its original form. Review ¶1, which sets out the question presented. Does it frame the issue the Court decides accurately? Objectively? With too little or too much specificity? Can you improve it?

6. Review ¶¶2-3, which set out the facts. Are any facts in these paragraphs relied on later? Are any not? If Chief Justice Rehnquist does not make use of a fact later on, does it nonetheless add something to the opinion? Are there facts mentioned later in the opinion that you would include in these paragraphs?

7. Review ¶4, which describes the decisions below. In a majority opinion, what is the function of such a description? Does this paragraph do the job? Would you prefer a fuller narrative?

8. Review ¶¶5-9, which contain the opinion's legal analysis. Apart from whether the analysis is well structured, is it sufficient or too succinct? What points, if any, could stand further development? In that regard, recall Justice Brennan's view that "a court may not simply announce, without more, that it has adopted a rule to which all must adhere," but instead has "a duty to explain *why* and *how* a given rule has come to be." William J. Brennan, Jr., *In Defense of Dissents*, 37 Hastings L.J. 427, 435 (1986).

9. Review ¶10, which sets forth the outcome. What function does this bottom line serve? To whom does it speak?

2. Bond v. United States

529 U.S. 334, 339-344 (2000): Justice Breyer's Dissenting Opinion

Justice BREYER, with whom Justice SCALIA joins, dissenting.

[1] Does a traveler who places a soft-sided bag in the shared overhead storage compartment of a bus have a "reasonable expectation" that strangers will not push, pull, prod, squeeze, or otherwise manipulate his luggage? Unlike the majority, I believe that he does not.

[2] Petitioner argues—and the majority points out—that, even if bags in overhead bins are subject to general "touching" and "handling," this case is special because "Agent Cantu's physical manipulation of [petitioner's] luggage 'far exceeded the casual contact [he] could have expected from other passengers.'" *Ante*. But the record shows the contrary. Agent Cantu testified that border patrol officers (who routinely enter buses at designated checkpoints to run immigration checks) "conduct an inspection of the overhead luggage by squeezing the bags as we're going out." App. 9. On the occasion at issue here, Agent Cantu "felt a green bag" which had "a brick-like object in it." *Id.*, at 10. He explained that he felt "the edges of the brick in the bag," *id.*, at 12, and that it was a "[b]rick-like object . . . that, when squeezed, you could feel an outline of something of a different mass inside of it," *id.*, at 11. Although the agent acknowledged that his practice was to "squeeze [bags] very hard," he testified that his touch ordinarily was not "[h]ard enough to break something inside that might be fragile." *Id.*, at 15. Petitioner also testified that Agent Cantu "reached for my bag, and he shook it a little, and squeezed it." *Id.*, at 18.

[3] How does the "squeezing" just described differ from the treatment that overhead luggage is likely to receive from strangers in a world of travel that is somewhat less gentle than it used to be? I think not at all. See *United States v. McDonald*, 100 F.3d 1320, 1327 (CA7 1996) ("'[A]ny person who has travelled on a common carrier knows that luggage placed in an overhead compartment is always at the mercy of all people who want to rearrange or move previously placed luggage'"); Eagan, Familiar Anger Takes Flight with Airline Tussles, Boston Herald, Aug. 15, 1999, p. 8 ("It's dog-eat-dog trying to cram half your home into overhead compartments"); Massingill, Airlines Ride on the Wings of High-Flying Economy and Travelers Pay Price in Long Lines, Cramped Airplanes, Kansas City Star, May 9, 1999, p. F4 ("[H]undreds of passengers fill overhead compartments with bulky carry-on bags that they have to cram, recram, and then remove"); Flynn, Confessions of a Once-Only Carry-On Guy, San Francisco Examiner, Sept. 6, 1998, p. T2

(flight attendant "rearranged the contents of three different overhead compartments to free up some room" and then "shoved and pounded until [the] bag squeezed in"). The trial court, which heard the evidence, saw nothing unusual, unforeseeable, or special about this agent's squeeze. It found that Agent Cantu simply "felt the outside of Bond's softside green cloth bag," and it viewed the agent's activity as "minimally intrusive touching." App. 23 (Order Denying Motion to Suppress). The Court of Appeals also noted that, because "passengers often handle and manipulate other passengers' luggage," the substantially similar tactile inspection here was entirely "foreseeable." 167 F.3d 225, 227 (CA5 1999).

[4] The record and these factual findings are sufficient to resolve this case. The law is clear that the Fourth Amendment protects against government intrusion that upsets an "actual (subjective) expectation of privacy" that is objectively "'reasonable.'" *Smith v. Maryland*, 442 U.S. 735, 740 (1979) (quoting *Katz v. United States*, 389 U.S. 347, 361 (1967) (Harlan, J., concurring)). Privacy itself implies the exclusion of uninvited strangers, not just strangers who work for the Government. Hence, an individual cannot reasonably expect privacy in respect to objects or activities that he "knowingly exposes to the public." *Id.*, at 351.

[5] Indeed, the Court has said that it is not *objectively* reasonable to expect privacy if "[a]ny member of the public . . . could have" used his senses to detect "everything that th[e] officers observed." *California v. Ciraolo*, 476 U.S. 207, 213-214 (1986). Thus, it has held that the fact that strangers may look down at fenced-in property from an aircraft or sift through garbage bags on a public street can justify a similar police intrusion. See *ibid.*; *Florida v. Riley*, 488 U.S. 445, 451 (1989) (plurality opinion); *California v. Greenwood*, 486 U.S. 35, 40-41 (1988); cf. *Texas v. Brown*, 460 U.S. 730, 740 (1983) (police not precluded from "'ben[ding] down'" to see since "[t]he general public could peer into the interior of [the car] from any number of angles"). The comparative likelihood that strangers will give bags in an overhead compartment a hard squeeze would seem far greater. See *Riley, supra,* at 453 (O'Connor, J., concurring in judgment) (reasonableness of privacy expectation depends on whether intrusion is a "sufficiently routine part of modern life"). Consider, too, the accepted police practice of using dogs to sniff for drugs hidden inside luggage. See, e.g., *United States v. Place*, 462 U.S. 696, 699 (1983). Surely it is less likely that non-governmental strangers will sniff at other's bags (or, more to the point, permit their dogs to do so) than it is that such actors will touch or squeeze another person's belongings in the process of making room for their own.

[6] Of course, the agent's *purpose* here—searching for drugs—differs dramatically from the intention of a driver or fellow passenger who squeezes a bag in the process of making more room for another parcel. But in determining whether an expectation of privacy is reasonable, it is the *effect*, not the purpose, that matters. See *ante*, at n.2 ("[T]he issue is not [the agent's] state of mind, but the objective effect of his actions"); see also *Whren v. United States*, 517 U.S. 806, 813 (1996); *United States v. Dunn*, 480 U.S. 294, 304-305 (1987). Few individuals with something to hide wish to expose that something to the police, however careless or indifferent they may be in respect to discovery by other members of the public. Hence, a Fourth Amendment rule that turns on purpose could prevent police alone from intruding where other strangers freely tread. And the added privacy protection achieved by such an approach would not justify the harm worked to law enforcement—at least that is what this Court's previous cases suggest. See *Greenwood, supra,* at 41 ("[T]he police

cannot reasonably be expected to avert their eyes from evidence of criminal activity that could have been observed by any member of the public"); *Ciraolo*, supra, at 212-213 (rejecting petitioner's argument that the police should be restricted solely because their actions are "motivated by a law enforcement purpose, and not the result of a casual, accidental observation").

[7] Nor can I accept the majority's effort to distinguish "tactile" from "visual" interventions, even assuming that distinction matters here. Whether tactile manipulation (say, of the exterior of luggage) is more intrusive or less intrusive than visual observation (say, through a lighted window) necessarily depends on the particular circumstances.

[8] If we are to depart from established legal principles, we should not begin here. At best, this decision will lead to a constitutional jurisprudence of "squeezes," thereby complicating further already complex Fourth Amendment law, increasing the difficulty of deciding ordinary criminal matters, and hindering the administrative guidance (with its potential for control of unreasonable police practices) that a less complicated jurisprudence might provide. Cf. *Whren*, *supra*, at 815 (warning against the creation of trivial Fourth Amendment distinctions). At worst, this case will deter law enforcement officers searching for drugs near borders from using even the most nonintrusive touch to help investigate publicly exposed bags. At the same time, the ubiquity of *non*-governmental pushes, prods, and squeezes (delivered by driver, attendant, passenger, or some other stranger) means that this decision cannot do much to protect true privacy. Rather, the traveler who wants to place a bag in a shared overhead bin and yet safeguard its contents from public touch should plan to pack those contents in a suitcase with hard sides, irrespective of the Court's decision today.

[9] For these reasons, I dissent.

Notes and Questions

1. Outline Justice Stephen Breyer's dissent. In what ways does it differ structurally from the majority? What do these differences suggest about the function of a dissent and, by contrast, of a majority opinion? Recall Justice Scalia's observation that a dissent allows a Justice "to write an opinion solely for oneself, without the need to accommodate, to any degree whatever, the more-or-less-differing views of one's colleagues; to address precisely the points of law that one considers important and no others; to express precisely the degree of quibble, or foreboding, or disbelief, or indignation that one believes the majority's disposition should engender." Antonin Scalia, *The Dissenting Opinion*, Journal of Supreme Court History 33, 42 (1994).

2. Review ¶1 of the dissent. How does Justice Breyer's framing of the case differ from the majority's? Is one more accurate than the other? More objective? More effective?

3. Review ¶¶2-8 of the dissent. Is there any obvious organization or order to these paragraphs? Do they "flow" better than the majority opinion? In what ways, if any, would you revise them?

4. Review ¶9 of the dissent. What is the function of this last line? To whom does it speak? Note that in modern times, it is common, but not universal, to insert "respectfully" between "I" and "dissent." Does the omission of "respectfully"

matter? *See* Note, *From Consensus to Collegiality: The Origins of the "Respectful" Dissent,* 124 Harv. L. Rev. 1305 (2011).

5. The dissent lays out its legal argument using plain language that is devoid of emotion or rhetoric. Do you think the dissent would be more or less effective with "zingers" or "firebombs," as some clerks refer to memorable or explosive language? Try your hand at a few and see if they make the dissent more or less persuasive.

6. Notice that the majority opinion does not mention the dissent. Did the majority not grapple with the dissent, or can you point to any text in Chief Justice Rehnquist's opinion that seems responsive to it? Recall that Chief Justice Warren's opinion in *Miranda v. Arizona* (1966) also did not refer directly to the dissenting opinions, but was revised in one respect in response. *See supra,* at A.5.b(5). Why might a majority opinion writer choose not to respond to a dissent? Is such silence desirable?

3. Lawrence v. Texas

539 U.S. 558, 562-580 (2003): Justice Kennedy's Majority Opinion

Justice KENNEDY delivered the opinion of the Court.

[1] Liberty protects the person from unwarranted government intrusions into a dwelling or other private places. In our tradition the State is not omnipresent in the home. And there are other spheres of our lives and existence, outside the home, where the State should not be a dominant presence. Freedom extends beyond spatial bounds. Liberty presumes an autonomy of self that includes freedom of thought, belief, expression, and certain intimate conduct. The instant case involves liberty of the person both in its spatial and in its more transcendent dimensions.

I

[2] The question before the Court is the validity of a Texas statute making it a crime for two persons of the same sex to engage in certain intimate sexual conduct.

[3] In Houston, Texas, officers of the Harris County Police Department were dispatched to a private residence in response to a reported weapons disturbance. They entered an apartment where one of the petitioners, John Geddes Lawrence, resided. The right of the police to enter does not seem to have been questioned. The officers observed Lawrence and another man, Tyron Garner, engaging in a sexual act. The two petitioners were arrested, held in custody overnight, and charged and convicted before a Justice of the Peace.

[4] The complaints described their crime as "deviate sexual intercourse, namely anal sex, with a member of the same sex (man)." The applicable state law is Tex. Penal Code Ann. §21.06(a) (2003). It provides: "A person commits an offense if he engages in deviate sexual intercourse with another individual of the same sex." The statute defines "[d]eviate sexual intercourse" as follows:

"(A) any contact between any part of the genitals of one person and the mouth or anus of another person; or
"(B) the penetration of the genitals or the anus of another person with an object."
§21.01(1).

[5] The petitioners exercised their right to a trial *de novo* in Harris County Criminal Court. They challenged the statute as a violation of the Equal Protection

Clause of the Fourteenth Amendment and of a like provision of the Texas Constitution. Tex. Const., Art. 1, §3a. Those contentions were rejected. The petitioners, having entered a plea of *nolo contendere*, were each fined $200 and assessed court costs of $141.25.

[6] The Court of Appeals for the Texas Fourteenth District considered the petitioners' federal constitutional arguments under both the Equal Protection and Due Process Clauses of the Fourteenth Amendment. After hearing the case en banc the court, in a divided opinion, rejected the constitutional arguments and affirmed the convictions. 41 S.W.3d 349 (2001). The majority opinion indicates that the Court of Appeals considered our decision in *Bowers v. Hardwick*, 478 U.S. 186, to be controlling on the federal due process aspect of the case. *Bowers* then being authoritative, this was proper.

[7] We granted certiorari, 537 U.S. 1044, to consider three questions:

1. Whether petitioners' criminal convictions under the Texas "Homosexual Conduct" law—which criminalizes sexual intimacy by same-sex couples, but not identical behavior by different-sex couples—violate the Fourteenth Amendment guarantee of equal protection of the laws.
2. Whether petitioners' criminal convictions for adult consensual sexual intimacy in the home violate their vital interests in liberty and privacy protected by the Due Process Clause of the Fourteenth Amendment.
3. Whether *Bowers v. Hardwick, supra,* should be overruled.

[8] The petitioners were adults at the time of the alleged offense. Their conduct was in private and consensual.

II

[9] We conclude the case should be resolved by determining whether the petitioners were free as adults to engage in the private conduct in the exercise of their liberty under the Due Process Clause of the Fourteenth Amendment to the Constitution. For this inquiry we deem it necessary to reconsider the Court's holding in *Bowers*.

[10] There are broad statements of the substantive reach of liberty under the Due Process Clause in earlier cases, including *Pierce v. Society of Sisters*, 268 U.S. 510 (1925), and *Meyer v. Nebraska*, 262 U.S. 390 (1923); but the most pertinent beginning point is our decision in *Griswold v. Connecticut*, 381 U.S. 479 (1965).

[11] In *Griswold* the Court invalidated a state law prohibiting the use of drugs or devices of contraception and counseling or aiding and abetting the use of contraceptives. The Court described the protected interest as a right to privacy and placed emphasis on the marriage relation and the protected space of the marital bedroom. *Id.*, at 485.

[12] After *Griswold* it was established that the right to make certain decisions regarding sexual conduct extends beyond the marital relationship. In *Eisenstadt v. Baird*, 405 U.S. 438 (1972), the Court invalidated a law prohibiting the distribution of contraceptives to unmarried persons. The case was decided under the Equal Protection Clause, *id.*, at 454; but with respect to unmarried persons, the Court went on to state the fundamental proposition that the law impaired the exercise of their personal rights, *ibid.* It quoted from the statement of the Court of Appeals finding the law to be in conflict with fundamental human rights, and it followed with this statement of its own:

"It is true that in *Griswold* the right of privacy in question inhered in the marital relationship. . . . If the right of privacy means anything, it is the right of the individual, married or single, to be free from unwarranted governmental intrusion into matters so fundamentally affecting a person as the decision whether to bear or beget a child." *Id.*, at 453.

[13] The opinions in *Griswold* and *Eisenstadt* were part of the background for the decision in *Roe v. Wade*, 410 U.S. 113 (1973). As is well known, the case involved a challenge to the Texas law prohibiting abortions, but the laws of other States were affected as well. Although the Court held the woman's rights were not absolute, her right to elect an abortion did have real and substantial protection as an exercise of her liberty under the Due Process Clause. The Court cited cases that protect spatial freedom and cases that go well beyond it. *Roe* recognized the right of a woman to make certain fundamental decisions affecting her destiny and confirmed once more that the protection of liberty under the Due Process Clause has a substantive dimension of fundamental significance in defining the rights of the person.

[14] In *Carey v. Population Services Int'l*, 431 U.S. 678 (1977), the Court confronted a New York law forbidding sale or distribution of contraceptive devices to persons under 16 years of age. Although there was no single opinion for the Court, the law was invalidated. Both *Eisenstadt* and *Carey*, as well as the holding and rationale in *Roe*, confirmed that the reasoning of *Griswold* could not be confined to the protection of rights of married adults. This was the state of the law with respect to some of the most relevant cases when the Court considered *Bowers v. Hardwick*.

[15] The facts in *Bowers* had some similarities to the instant case. A police officer, whose right to enter seems not to have been in question, observed Hardwick, in his own bedroom, engaging in intimate sexual conduct with another adult male. The conduct was in violation of a Georgia statute making it a criminal offense to engage in sodomy. One difference between the two cases is that the Georgia statute prohibited the conduct whether or not the participants were of the same sex, while the Texas statute, as we have seen, applies only to participants of the same sex. Hardwick was not prosecuted, but he brought an action in federal court to declare the state statute invalid. He alleged he was a practicing homosexual and that the criminal prohibition violated rights guaranteed to him by the Constitution. The Court, in an opinion by Justice White, sustained the Georgia law. Chief Justice Burger and Justice Powell joined the opinion of the Court and filed separate, concurring opinions. Four Justices dissented. 478 U.S., at 199 (opinion of Blackmun, J., joined by Brennan, Marshall, and Stevens, JJ.); *id.*, at 214 (opinion of Stevens, J., joined by Brennan and Marshall, JJ.).

[16] The Court began its substantive discussion in *Bowers* as follows: "The issue presented is whether the Federal Constitution confers a fundamental right upon homosexuals to engage in sodomy and hence invalidates the laws of the many States that still make such conduct illegal and have done so for a very long time." *Id.*, at 190. That statement, we now conclude, discloses the Court's own failure to appreciate the extent of the liberty at stake. To say that the issue in *Bowers* was simply the right to engage in certain sexual conduct demeans the claim the individual put forward, just as it would demean a married couple were it to be said marriage is simply about the right to have sexual intercourse. The laws involved in *Bowers* and here are, to be sure, statutes that purport to do no more than prohibit a particular sexual act. Their penalties and purposes, though, have more far-reaching consequences, touching

upon the most private human conduct, sexual behavior, and in the most private of places, the home. The statutes do seek to control a personal relationship that, whether or not entitled to formal recognition in the law, is within the liberty of persons to choose without being punished as criminals.

[17] This, as a general rule, should counsel against attempts by the State, or a court, to define the meaning of the relationship or to set its boundaries absent injury to a person or abuse of an institution the law protects. It suffices for us to acknowledge that adults may choose to enter upon this relationship in the confines of their homes and their own private lives and still retain their dignity as free persons. When sexuality finds overt expression in intimate conduct with another person, the conduct can be but one element in a personal bond that is more enduring. The liberty protected by the Constitution allows homosexual persons the right to make this choice.

[18] Having misapprehended the claim of liberty there presented to it, and thus stating the claim to be whether there is a fundamental right to engage in consensual sodomy, the *Bowers* Court said: "Proscriptions against that conduct have ancient roots." *Id.*, at 192. In academic writings, and in many of the scholarly *amicus* briefs filed to assist the Court in this case, there are fundamental criticisms of the historical premises relied upon by the majority and concurring opinions in *Bowers*. Brief for Cato Institute as *Amicus Curiae* 16-17; Brief for American Civil Liberties Union et al. as *Amici Curiae* 15-21; Brief for Professors of History et al. as *Amici Curiae* 3-10. We need not enter this debate in the attempt to reach a definitive historical judgment, but the following considerations counsel against adopting the definitive conclusions upon which *Bowers* placed such reliance.

[19] At the outset it should be noted that there is no longstanding history in this country of laws directed at homosexual conduct as a distinct matter. Beginning in colonial times there were prohibitions of sodomy derived from the English criminal laws passed in the first instance by the Reformation Parliament of 1533. The English prohibition was understood to include relations between men and women as well as relations between men and men. See, *e.g.*, *King v. Wiseman*, 92 Eng. Rep. 774, 775 (K.B. 1718) (interpreting "mankind" in Act of 1533 as including women and girls). Nineteenth-century commentators similarly read American sodomy, buggery, and crime-against-nature statutes as criminalizing certain relations between men and women and between men and men. See, *e.g.*, 2 J. Bishop, Criminal Law §1028 (1858); 2 J. Chitty, Criminal Law 47-50 (5th Am. ed. 1847); R. Desty, A Compendium of American Criminal Law 143 (1882); J. May, The Law of Crimes §203 (2d ed. 1893). The absence of legal prohibitions focusing on homosexual conduct may be explained in part by noting that according to some scholars the concept of the homosexual as a distinct category of person did not emerge until the late 19th century. See, *e.g.*, J. Katz, The Invention of Heterosexuality 10 (1995); J. D'Emilio & E. Freedman, Intimate Matters: A History of Sexuality in America 121 (2d ed. 1997) ("The modern terms *homosexuality* and *heterosexuality* do not apply to an era that had not yet articulated these distinctions"). Thus early American sodomy laws were not directed at homosexuals as such but instead sought to prohibit non-procreative sexual activity more generally. This does not suggest approval of homosexual conduct. It does tend to show that this particular form of conduct was not thought of as a separate category from like conduct between heterosexual persons.

[20] Laws prohibiting sodomy do not seem to have been enforced against consenting adults acting in private. A substantial number of sodomy prosecutions and

convictions for which there are surviving records were for predatory acts against those who could not or did not consent, as in the case of a minor or the victim of an assault. As to these, one purpose for the prohibitions was to ensure there would be no lack of coverage if a predator committed a sexual assault that did not constitute rape as defined by the criminal law. Thus the model sodomy indictments presented in a 19th-century treatise, see 2 Chitty, *supra*, at 49, addressed the predatory acts of an adult man against a minor girl or minor boy. Instead of targeting relations between consenting adults in private, 19th-century sodomy prosecutions typically involved relations between men and minor girls or minor boys, relations between adults involving force, relations between adults implicating disparity in status, or relations between men and animals.

[21] To the extent that there were any prosecutions for the acts in question, 19th-century evidence rules imposed a burden that would make a conviction more difficult to obtain even taking into account the problems always inherent in prosecuting consensual acts committed in private. Under then-prevailing standards, a man could not be convicted of sodomy based upon testimony of a consenting partner, because the partner was considered an accomplice. A partner's testimony, however, was admissible if he or she had not consented to the act or was a minor, and therefore incapable of consent. See, *e.g.*, F. Wharton, Criminal Law 443 (2d ed. 1852); 1 F. Wharton, Criminal Law 512 (8th ed. 1880). The rule may explain in part the infrequency of these prosecutions. In all events that infrequency makes it difficult to say that society approved of a rigorous and systematic punishment of the consensual acts committed in private and by adults. The longstanding criminal prohibition of homosexual sodomy upon which the *Bowers* decision placed such reliance is as consistent with a general condemnation of nonprocreative sex as it is with an established tradition of prosecuting acts because of their homosexual character.

[22] The policy of punishing consenting adults for private acts was not much discussed in the early legal literature. We can infer that one reason for this was the very private nature of the conduct. Despite the absence of prosecutions, there may have been periods in which there was public criticism of homosexuals as such and an insistence that the criminal laws be enforced to discourage their practices. But far from possessing "ancient roots," *Bowers*, 478 U.S., at 192, American laws targeting same-sex couples did not develop until the last third of the 20th century. The reported decisions concerning the prosecution of consensual, homosexual sodomy between adults for the years 1880-1995 are not always clear in the details, but a significant number involved conduct in a public place. See Brief for American Civil Liberties Union et al. as *Amici Curiae* 14-15, and n.18.

[23] It was not until the 1970's that any State singled out same-sex relations for criminal prosecution, and only nine States have done so. See 1977 Ark. Gen. Acts no. 828; 1983 Kan. Sess. Laws p. 652; 1974 Ky. Acts p. 847; 1977 Mo. Laws p. 687; 1973 Mont. Laws p. 1339; 1977 Nev. Stats. p. 1632; 1989 Tenn. Pub. Acts ch. 591; 1973 Tex. Gen. Laws ch. 399; see also *Post v. State*, 715 P.2d 1105 (Okla. Crim. App. 1986) (sodomy law invalidated as applied to different-sex couples). Post-*Bowers* even some of these States did not adhere to the policy of suppressing homosexual conduct. Over the course of the last decades, States with same-sex prohibitions have moved toward abolishing them. See, *e.g.*, *Jegley v. Picado*, 80 S.W.3d 332 (Ark. 2002); *Gryczan v. State*, 942 P.2d 112 (Mont. 1997); *Campbell v. Sundquist*, 926 S.W.2d 250 (Tenn. App. 1996); *Commonwealth v. Wasson*, 842 S.W.2d 487 (Ky. 1992); see also 1993 Nev. Stats. p. 518 (repealing Nev. Rev. Stat. §201.193).

[24] In summary, the historical grounds relied upon in *Bowers* are more complex than the majority opinion and the concurring opinion by Chief Justice Burger indicate. Their historical premises are not without doubt and, at the very least, are overstated.

[25] It must be acknowledged, of course, that the Court in *Bowers* was making the broader point that for centuries there have been powerful voices to condemn homosexual conduct as immoral. The condemnation has been shaped by religious beliefs, conceptions of right and acceptable behavior, and respect for the traditional family. For many persons these are not trivial concerns but profound and deep convictions accepted as ethical and moral principles to which they aspire and which thus determine the course of their lives. These considerations do not answer the question before us, however. The issue is whether the majority may use the power of the State to enforce these views on the whole society through operation of the criminal law. "Our obligation is to define the liberty of all, not to mandate our own moral code." *Planned Parenthood of Southeastern Pa. v. Casey*, 505 U.S. 833 (1992).

[26] Chief Justice Burger joined the opinion for the Court in *Bowers* and further explained his views as follows: "Decisions of individuals relating to homosexual conduct have been subject to state intervention throughout the history of Western civilization. Condemnation of those practices is firmly rooted in Judeao-Christian moral and ethical standards." 478 U.S., at 196. As with Justice White's assumptions about history, scholarship casts some doubt on the sweeping nature of the statement by Chief Justice Burger as it pertains to private homosexual conduct between consenting adults. See, *e.g.*, Eskridge, Hardwick and Historiography, 1999 U. Ill. L. Rev. 631, 656. In all events we think that our laws and traditions in the past half century are of most relevance here. These references show an emerging awareness that liberty gives substantial protection to adult persons in deciding how to conduct their private lives in matters pertaining to sex. "[H]istory and tradition are the starting point but not in all cases the ending point of the substantive due process inquiry." *County of Sacramento v. Lewis*, 523 U.S. 833, 857 (1998) (Kennedy, J., concurring).

[27] This emerging recognition should have been apparent when *Bowers* was decided. In 1955 the American Law Institute promulgated the Model Penal Code and made clear that it did not recommend or provide for "criminal penalties for consensual sexual relations conducted in private." ALI, Model Penal Code §213.2, Comment 2, p. 372 (1980). It justified its decision on three grounds: (1) The prohibitions undermined respect for the law by penalizing conduct many people engaged in; (2) the statutes regulated private conduct not harmful to others; and (3) the laws were arbitrarily enforced and thus invited the danger of blackmail. ALI, Model Penal Code, Commentary 277-280 (Tent. Draft No. 4, 1955). In 1961 Illinois changed its laws to conform to the Model Penal Code. Other States soon followed. Brief for Cato Institute as *Amicus Curiae* 15-16.

[28] In *Bowers* the Court referred to the fact that before 1961 all 50 States had outlawed sodomy, and that at the time of the Court's decision 24 States and the District of Columbia had sodomy laws. 478 U.S., at 192-193. Justice Powell pointed out that these prohibitions often were being ignored, however. Georgia, for instance, had not sought to enforce its law for decades. *Id.*, at 197-198, n.2 ("The history of nonenforcement suggests the moribund character today of laws criminalizing this type of private, consensual conduct").

[29] The sweeping references by Chief Justice Burger to the history of Western civilization and to Judeo-Christian moral and ethical standards did not take account

of other authorities pointing in an opposite direction. A committee advising the British Parliament recommended in 1957 repeal of laws punishing homosexual conduct. The Wolfenden Report: Report of the Committee on Homosexual Offenses and Prostitution (1963). Parliament enacted the substance of those recommendations 10 years later. Sexual Offences Act 1967, §1.

[30] Of even more importance, almost five years before *Bowers* was decided the European Court of Human Rights considered a case with parallels to *Bowers* and to today's case. An adult male resident in Northern Ireland alleged he was a practicing homosexual who desired to engage in consensual homosexual conduct. The laws of Northern Ireland forbade him that right. He alleged that he had been questioned, his home had been searched, and he feared criminal prosecution. The court held that the laws proscribing the conduct were invalid under the European Convention on Human Rights. Dudgeon v. United Kingdom, 45 Eur. Ct. H.R. (1981) & ¶52. Authoritative in all countries that are members of the Council of Europe (21 nations then, 45 nations now), the decision is at odds with the premise in *Bowers* that the claim put forward was insubstantial in our Western civilization.

[31] In our own constitutional system the deficiencies in *Bowers* became even more apparent in the years following its announcement. The 25 States with laws prohibiting the relevant conduct referenced in the *Bowers* decision are reduced now to 13, of which 4 enforce their laws only against homosexual conduct. In those States where sodomy is still proscribed, whether for same-sex or heterosexual conduct, there is a pattern of nonenforcement with respect to consenting adults acting in private. The State of Texas admitted in 1994 that as of that date it had not prosecuted anyone under those circumstances. *State v. Morales*, 869 S.W.2d 941, 943.

[32] Two principal cases decided after *Bowers* cast its holding into even more doubt. In *Planned Parenthood of Southeastern Pa. v. Casey*, 505 U.S. 833 (1992), the Court reaffirmed the substantive force of the liberty protected by the Due Process Clause. The Casey decision again confirmed that our laws and tradition afford constitutional protection to personal decisions relating to marriage, procreation, contraception, family relationships, child rearing, and education. *Id.*, at 851. In explaining the respect the Constitution demands for the autonomy of the person in making these choices, we stated as follows:

> "These matters, involving the most intimate and personal choices a person may make in a lifetime, choices central to personal dignity and autonomy, are central to the liberty protected by the Fourteenth Amendment. At the heart of liberty is the right to define one's own concept of existence, of meaning, of the universe, and of the mystery of human life. Beliefs about these matters could not define the attributes of personhood were they formed under compulsion of the State." *Ibid.*

Persons in a homosexual relationship may seek autonomy for these purposes, just as heterosexual persons do. The decision in *Bowers* would deny them this right.

[33] The second post-*Bowers* case of principal relevance is *Romer v. Evans*, 517 U.S. 620 (1996). There the Court struck down class-based legislation directed at homosexuals as a violation of the Equal Protection Clause. *Romer* invalidated an amendment to Colorado's Constitution which named as a solitary class persons who were homosexuals, lesbians, or bisexual either by "orientation, conduct, practices or relationships," *id.*, at 624 (internal quotation marks omitted), and deprived them of protection under state anti-discrimination laws. We concluded that the provision was "born of animosity toward the class of persons affected" and further that it had no rational relation to a legitimate governmental purpose. *Id.*, at 634.

[34] As an alternative argument in this case, counsel for the petitioners and some *amici* contend that *Romer* provides the basis for declaring the Texas statute invalid under the Equal Protection Clause. That is a tenable argument, but we conclude the instant case requires us to address whether *Bowers* itself has continuing validity. Were we to hold the statute invalid under the Equal Protection Clause some might question whether a prohibition would be valid if drawn differently, say, to prohibit the conduct both between same-sex and different-sex participants.

[35] Equality of treatment and the due process right to demand respect for conduct protected by the substantive guarantee of liberty are linked in important respects, and a decision on the latter point advances both interests. If protected conduct is made criminal and the law which does so remains unexamined for its substantive validity, its stigma might remain even if it were not enforceable as drawn for equal protection reasons. When homosexual conduct is made criminal by the law of the State, that declaration in and of itself is an invitation to subject homosexual persons to discrimination both in the public and in the private spheres. The central holding of *Bowers* has been brought in question by this case, and it should be addressed. Its continuance as precedent demeans the lives of homosexual persons.

[36] The stigma this criminal statute imposes, moreover, is not trivial. The offense, to be sure, is but a class C misdemeanor, a minor offense in the Texas legal system. Still, it remains a criminal offense with all that imports for the dignity of the persons charged. The petitioners will bear on their record the history of their criminal convictions. Just this Term we rejected various challenges to state laws requiring the registration of sex offenders. *Smith v. Doe*, 538 U.S. 84 (2003); *Connecticut Dept. of Public Safety v. Doe*, 538 U.S. 1 (2003). We are advised that if Texas convicted an adult for private, consensual homosexual conduct under the statute here in question the convicted person would come within the registration laws of at least four States were he or she to be subject to their jurisdiction. Pet. for Cert. 13, and n. 12 (citing Idaho Code §§18-8301 to 18-8326 (Cum. Supp. 2002); La. Code Crim. Proc. Ann. §§15:540-15:549 S576 (West 2003); Miss. Code Ann. §§45-33-21 to 45-33-57 (Lexis 2003); S.C. Code Ann. §§23-3-400 to 23-3-490 (West 2002)). This underscores the consequential nature of the punishment and the state-sponsored condemnation attendant to the criminal prohibition. Furthermore, the Texas criminal conviction carries with it the other collateral consequences always following a conviction, such as notations on job application forms, to mention but one example.

[37] The foundations of *Bowers* have sustained serious erosion from our recent decisions in *Casey* and *Romer*. When our precedent has been thus weakened, criticism from other sources is of greater significance. In the United States criticism of *Bowers* has been substantial and continuing, disapproving of its reasoning in all respects, not just as to its historical assumptions. See, *e.g.*, C. Fried, Order and Law: Arguing the Reagan Revolution—A Firsthand Account 81-84 (1991); R. Posner, Sex and Reason 341-350 (1992). The courts of five different States have declined to follow it in interpreting provisions in their own state constitutions parallel to the Due Process Clause of the Fourteenth Amendment, see *Jegley v. Picado*, 80 S.W.3d 332 (Ark. 2002); *Powell v. State*, 510 S.E.2d 18, 24 (Ga. 1998); *Gryczan v. State*, 283 Mont. 433, 942 P.2d 112 (Mont. 1997); *Campbell v. Sundquist*, 926 S.W.2d 250 (Tenn. App. 1996); *Commonwealth v. Wasson*, 842 S.W.2d 487 (Ky. 1992).

[38] To the extent *Bowers* relied on values we share with a wider civilization, it should be noted that the reasoning and holding in *Bowers* have been rejected elsewhere. The European Court of Human Rights has followed not *Bowers* but its own decision in *Dudgeon v. United Kingdom.* See *P.G. & J.H. v. United Kingdom,* App. No. 00044787/98, & ¶56 (Eur. Ct. H.R., Sept. 25, 2001); *Modinos v. Cyprus,* 259 Eur. Ct. H.R. (1993); *Norris v. Ireland,* 142 Eur. Ct. H.R. (1988). Other nations, too, have taken action consistent with an affirmation of the protected right of homosexual adults to engage in intimate, consensual conduct. See Brief for Mary Robinson et al. as *Amici Curiae* 11-12. The right the petitioners seek in this case has been accepted as an integral part of human freedom in many other countries. There has been no showing that in this country the governmental interest in circumscribing personal choice is somehow more legitimate or urgent.

[39] The doctrine of *stare decisis* is essential to the respect accorded to the judgments of the Court and to the stability of the law. It is not, however, an inexorable command. *Payne v. Tennessee,* 501 U.S. 808 (1991) ("*Stare decisis* is not an inexorable command; rather, it 'is a principle of policy and not a mechanical formula of adherence to the latest decision'" (quoting *Helvering v. Hallock,* 309 U.S. 106 (1940))). In *Casey* we noted that when a court is asked to overrule a precedent recognizing a constitutional liberty interest, individual or societal reliance on the existence of that liberty cautions with particular strength against reversing course. 505 U.S., at 855-856; see also *id.,* at 844 ("Liberty finds no refuge in a jurisprudence of doubt"). The holding in *Bowers,* however, has not induced detrimental reliance comparable to some instances where recognized individual rights are involved. Indeed, there has been no individual or societal reliance on *Bowers* of the sort that could counsel against overturning its holding once there are compelling reasons to do so. *Bowers* itself causes uncertainty, for the precedents before and after its issuance contradict its central holding.

[40] The rationale of *Bowers* does not withstand careful analysis. In his dissenting opinion in *Bowers* Justice Stevens came to these conclusions:

> "Our prior cases make two propositions abundantly clear. First, the fact that the governing majority in a State has traditionally viewed a particular practice as immoral is not a sufficient reason for upholding a law prohibiting the practice; neither history nor tradition could save a law prohibiting miscegenation from constitutional attack. Second, individual decisions by married persons, concerning the intimacies of their physical relationship, even when not intended to produce offspring, are a form of 'liberty' protected by the Due Process Clause of the Fourteenth Amendment. Moreover, this protection extends to intimate choices by unmarried as well as married persons." 478 U.S., at 216 (footnotes and citations omitted).

Justice Stevens' analysis, in our view, should have been controlling in *Bowers* and should control here.

Bowers was not correct when it was decided, and it is not correct today. It ought not to remain binding precedent. *Bowers v. Hardwick* should be and now is overruled.

[41] The present case does not involve minors. It does not involve persons who might be injured or coerced or who are situated in relationships where consent might not easily be refused. It does not involve public conduct or prostitution. It does not involve whether the government must give formal recognition to any relationship that homosexual persons seek to enter. The case does involve two adults who, with full and mutual consent from each other, engaged in sexual practices common to a homosexual lifestyle. The petitioners are entitled to respect for

their private lives. The State cannot demean their existence or control their destiny by making their private sexual conduct a crime. Their right to liberty under the Due Process Clause gives them the full right to engage in their conduct without intervention of the government. "It is a promise of the Constitution that there is a realm of personal liberty which the government may not enter." Casey, *supra*, at 847. The Texas statute furthers no legitimate state interest which can justify its intrusion into the personal and private life of the individual.

[42] Had those who drew and ratified the Due Process Clauses of the Fifth Amendment or the Fourteenth Amendment known the components of liberty in its manifold possibilities, they might have been more specific. They did not presume to have this insight. They knew times can blind us to certain truths and later generations can see that laws once thought necessary and proper in fact serve only to oppress. As the Constitution endures, persons in every generation can invoke its principles in their own search for greater freedom.

The judgment of the Court of Appeals for the Texas Fourteenth District is reversed, and the case is remanded for further proceedings not inconsistent with this opinion.

It is so ordered.

Notes and Questions

1. Outline Justice Anthony Kennedy's majority opinion. In what ways does the organization of Justice Kennedy's opinion in *Lawrence* differ from that of Chief Justice Rehnquist's opinion in *Bond*? If the Chief Justice were writing the majority opinion in *Lawrence* to reach the same outcome, do you think the structure of the opinion would differ? If so, how?

2. What is the function of ¶1 in the *Lawrence* majority opinion? How does it differ from the function of ¶1 in *Bond*? Do you think the introductory paragraph improves the opinion? Would you revise it, delete it, or leave it as is? In any event, is it clear what Justice Kennedy means in stating that the case "involves liberty of the person both in its spatial and in its more transcendent dimensions"? Why do you think he frames the case in this way?

3. The specific questions presented in *Lawrence* are not listed until ¶7, after a recitation of the facts and lower court decisions (¶¶3-6). What advantages or disadvantages are there to putting the questions presented there rather than at the beginning of the opinion? Regardless, in light of ¶7, is ¶2 necessary or desirable?

4. Does ¶8 seem out of place to you? Why do you think it was included and placed where it was?

5. If, as stated in ¶9, this case requires the Court to reconsider its decision in *Bowers v. Hardwick* (1986), why does the opinion spend the next five paragraphs (¶¶10-14) examining cases decided *before* the Court's decision in *Bowers*?

6. What is the relationship between ¶1 and ¶¶16-17? Is the point of ¶1 clearer in light of these two paragraphs?

7. In ¶16, Justice Kennedy's majority opinion criticizes *Bowers* for framing the issue too narrowly. In what ways is it broadened here? Nevertheless, in ¶17, can you spot specific ways in which the opinion limits the issue in this case? Why do you think the opinion does so?

8. In ¶18, the majority opinion states that it "need not enter" debate over the historical premises on which *Bowers* relied. Nevertheless, it devotes the next six

paragraphs (¶¶19-24) to questioning them before casting them aside as irrelevant (¶¶25-26). Could—or should—those paragraphs have been cut without affecting the meaning or scope of the decision?

9. What is the function of ¶¶26-33? How does it relate to, or differ from, the function of ¶¶18-24? If those preceding paragraphs were cut, could these stand as well on their own?

10. The law at issue was challenged under both the Equal Protection Clause and the Due Process Clause of the Fourteenth Amendment. In ¶9, the majority opinion concludes that the case should be decided under the latter provision. It does not explain why until ¶¶34-35. Does the delay make sense structurally? In any case, does the substantive choice to decide the case on Due Process grounds make strategic sense to you?

11. Conservative critics of *Lawrence* and other recent decisions have lashed out against the Court's use of foreign authority to support its constitutional interpretations, with academic articles against the practice, *see, e.g.*, Steven G. Calabresi, *Lawrence, the Fourteenth Amendment, and the Supreme Court's Reliance on Foreign Constitutional Law: An Originalist Reappraisal*, 65 Ohio State L.J. 1097 (2004), as well as calls for legislative bans or even impeachment, *see* Daniel A. Farber, *The Supreme Court, the Law of Nations, and Citations of Foreign Law: The Lessons of History*, 95 Cal. L. Rev. 1335, 1340-1343 (2007) (summarizing, and responding to, criticisms). At the center of the controversy are ¶¶29, 30, and 38 of Justice Kennedy's majority opinion in *Lawrence*. How are foreign sources of law used in these paragraphs? Are they relied on as dispositive authority or persuasive authority, or are they employed in some other way? Do they make the opinion stronger or weaker? Would you have put them in or taken them out?

12. After devoting two dozen paragraphs (¶¶16-40) to criticizing *Bowers*, the majority opinion overrules it. Did the opinion lay a sufficient foundation for the overruling? Do these paragraphs suggest a template for how to go about overruling a case? Would you alter the majority's method in any material way?

13. Why do you think the majority opinion takes pains (¶41) to say what the case is *not* about? Do you think Justice Kennedy put those points in his original draft opinion, or only inserted them in response to the concern of colleagues or the dissent's slippery slope arguments (¶¶9, 26, 28)? If the latter, why does he not explicitly refer to the dissent here or elsewhere? As in *Bond*, does the lack of direct acknowledgment of the dissenting arguments make sense as a matter of strategy or style?

14. What is the function of ¶42? Is it just a rhetorical finish, or does it do substantive work as well—and if so, what?

15. Compare the first and last paragraphs of Justice Kennedy's majority opinion in *Lawrence* with those of Chief Justice Rehnquist's majority opinion in *Bond*. Do you think the differences in style and scope in these opening and closing paragraphs are more attributable to the different issues involved or to the different authors? Do other opinions by Chief Justice Rehnquist or Justice Kennedy come to mind that either resemble or contrast with *Bond* and *Lawrence*? For example, compare these opinions with Chief Justice Rehnquist's plurality opinion in *Van Orden v. Perry*, 545 U.S. 677 (2005), and Justice Kennedy's majority opinion in *Romer v. Evans*, 517 U.S. 620 (1996).

4. Lawrence v. Texas

539 U.S. 558, 579-585 (2003): Justice O'Connor's Concurring
Opinion

Justice O'Connor, concurring in the judgment.

[1] The Court today overrules *Bowers v. Hardwick*, 478 U.S. 186 (1986). I joined *Bowers,* and do not join the Court in overruling it. Nevertheless, I agree with the Court that Texas' statute banning same-sex sodomy is unconstitutional. See Tex. Penal Code Ann. §21.06 (2003). Rather than relying on the substantive component of the Fourteenth Amendment's Due Process Clause, as the Court does, I base my conclusion on the Fourteenth Amendment's Equal Protection Clause.

[2] The Equal Protection Clause of the Fourteenth Amendment "is essentially a direction that all persons similarly situated should be treated alike." *Cleburne v. Cleburne Living Center, Inc.,* 473 U.S. 432 (1985); see also *Plyler v. Doe,* 457 U.S. 202, 216 (1982). Under our rational basis standard of review, "legislation is presumed to be valid and will be sustained if the classification drawn by the statute is rationally related to a legitimate state interest." *Cleburne v. Cleburne Living Center, supra,* at 440; see also *Department of Agriculture v. Moreno,* 413 U.S. 528 (1973); *Romer v. Evans,* 517 U.S. 620, 632-633 (1996); *Nordlinger v. Hahn,* 505 U.S. 1, 11-12 (1992).

[3] Laws such as economic or tax legislation that are scrutinized under rational basis review normally pass constitutional muster, since "the Constitution presumes that even improvident decisions will eventually be rectified by the democratic processes." *Cleburne v. Cleburne Living Center, supra,* at 440; see also *Fitzgerald v. Racing Assn. of Central Iowa,* 539 U.S. 103 (2003); *Williamson v. Lee Optical of Okla., Inc.,* 348 U.S. 483 (1955). We have consistently held, however, that some objectives, such as "a bare desire to harm a politically unpopular group," are not legitimate state interests. *Department of Agriculture v. Moreno, supra,* at 534. See also *Cleburne v. Cleburne Living Center, supra,* at 446-447; *Romer v. Evans, supra,* at 632. When a law exhibits such a desire to harm a politically unpopular group, we have applied a more searching form of rational basis review to strike down such laws under the Equal Protection Clause.

[4]We have been most likely to apply rational basis review to hold a law unconstitutional under the Equal Protection Clause where, as here, the challenged legislation inhibits personal relationships. In *Department of Agriculture v. Moreno,* for example, we held that a law preventing those households containing an individual unrelated to any other member of the household from receiving food stamps violated equal protection because the purpose of the law was to "'discriminate against hippies.'" 413 U.S., at 534. The asserted governmental interest in preventing food stamp fraud was not deemed sufficient to satisfy rational basis review, at 535-538. In *Eisenstadt v. Baird,* 405 U.S. 438, 447-455 (1972), we refused to sanction a law that discriminated between married and unmarried persons by prohibiting the distribution of contraceptives to single persons. Likewise, in *Cleburne v. Cleburne Living Center, supra,* we held that it was irrational for a State to require a home for the mentally disabled to obtain a special use permit when other residences—like fraternity houses and apartment buildings—did not have to obtain such a permit. And in *Romer v. Evans,* we disallowed a state statute that "impos[ed] a broad and undifferentiated disability on a single named group"—specifically, homosexuals. 517 U.S., at 632.

[5] The statute at issue here makes sodomy a crime only if a person "engages in deviate sexual intercourse with another individual of the same sex." Tex. Penal Code Ann. §21.06(a) (2003). Sodomy between opposite-sex partners, however, is not a crime in Texas. That is, Texas treats the same conduct differently based solely on the participants. Those harmed by this law are people who have a same-sex sexual orientation and thus are more likely to engage in behavior prohibited by §21.06.

[6] The Texas statute makes homosexuals unequal in the eyes of the law by making particular conduct—and only that conduct—subject to criminal sanction. It appears that prosecutions under Texas' sodomy law are rare. See *State v. Morales*, 869 S.W.2d 941, 943 (Tex. 1994) (noting in 1994 that §21.06 "has not been, and in all probability will not be, enforced against private consensual conduct between adults"). This case shows, however, that prosecutions under §21.06 do occur. And while the penalty imposed on petitioners in this case was relatively minor, the consequences of conviction are not. It appears that petitioners' convictions, if upheld, would disqualify them from or restrict their ability to engage in a variety of professions, including medicine, athletic training, and interior design. See, *e.g.*, Tex. Occ. Code Ann. §164.051(a)(2)(B) (2003 Pamphlet) (physician); §451.251(a)(1) (athletic trainer); §1053.252(2) (interior designer). Indeed, were petitioners to move to one of four States, their convictions would require them to register as sex offenders to local law enforcement. See, *e.g.*, Idaho Code §18–8304 (Cum. Supp. 2002); La. Stat. Ann. §15:542 (West Cum. Supp. 2003); Miss. Code Ann. §45-33-25 (West 2003); S.C. Code Ann. §23-3-430 (West Cum. Supp. 2002).

[7] And the effect of Texas' sodomy law is not just limited to the threat of prosecution or consequence of conviction. Texas' sodomy law brands all homosexuals as criminals, thereby making it more difficult for homosexuals to be treated in the same manner as everyone else. Indeed, Texas itself has previously acknowledged the collateral effects of the law, stipulating in a prior challenge to this action that the law "legally sanctions discrimination against [homosexuals] in a variety of ways unrelated to the criminal law," including in the areas of "employment, family issues, and housing." *State v. Morales*, 826 S.W.2d 201, 203 (Tex. App. 1992).

[8] Texas attempts to justify its law, and the effects of the law, by arguing that the statute satisfies rational basis review because it furthers the legitimate governmental interest of the promotion of morality. In *Bowers*, we held that a state law criminalizing sodomy as applied to homosexual couples did not violate substantive due process. We rejected the argument that no rational basis existed to justify the law, pointing to the government's interest in promoting morality. 478 U.S., at 196. The only question in front of the Court in *Bowers* was whether the substantive component of the Due Process Clause protected a right to engage in homosexual sodomy. *Id.*, at 188, n.2. *Bowers* did not hold that moral disapproval of a group is a rational basis under the Equal Protection Clause to criminalize homosexual sodomy when heterosexual sodomy is not punished.

[9] This case raises a different issue than *Bowers*: whether, under the Equal Protection Clause, moral disapproval is a legitimate state interest to justify by itself a statute that bans homosexual sodomy, but not heterosexual sodomy. It is not. Moral disapproval of this group, like a bare desire to harm the group, is an interest that is insufficient to satisfy rational basis review under the Equal Protection Clause. See, *e.g.*, *Department of Agriculture v. Moreno*, 413 U.S., at 534; *Romer v. Evans*, 517 U.S., at 634-635. Indeed, we have never held that moral disapproval, without any other

asserted state interest, is a sufficient rationale under the Equal Protection Clause to justify a law that discriminates among groups of persons.

[10] Moral disapproval of a group cannot be a legitimate governmental interest under the Equal Protection Clause because legal classifications must not be "drawn for the purpose of disadvantaging the group burdened by the law." *Id.*, at 633, 116 S. Ct. 1620. Texas' invocation of moral disapproval as a legitimate state interest proves nothing more than Texas' desire to criminalize homosexual sodomy. But the Equal Protection Clause prevents a State from creating "a classification of persons undertaken for its own sake." *Id.*, at 635. And because Texas so rarely enforces its sodomy law as applied to private, consensual acts, the law serves more as a statement of dislike and disapproval against homosexuals than as a tool to stop criminal behavior. The Texas sodomy law "raise[s] the inevitable inference that the disadvantage imposed is born of animosity toward the class of persons affected." *Id.*, at 634.

[11] Texas argues, however, that the sodomy law does not discriminate against homosexual persons. Instead, the State maintains that the law discriminates only against homosexual conduct. While it is true that the law applies only to conduct, the conduct targeted by this law is conduct that is closely correlated with being homosexual. Under such circumstances, Texas' sodomy law is targeted at more than conduct. It is instead directed toward gay persons as a class. "After all, there can hardly be more palpable discrimination against a class than making the conduct that defines the class criminal." *Id.*, at 641 (Scalia, J., dissenting) (internal quotation marks omitted). When a State makes homosexual conduct criminal, and not "deviate sexual intercourse" committed by persons of different sexes, "that declaration in and of itself is an invitation to subject homosexual persons to discrimination both in the public and in the private spheres." *Ante.*

[12] Indeed, Texas law confirms that the sodomy statute is directed toward homosexuals as a class. In Texas, calling a person a homosexual is slander *per se* because the word "homosexual" "impute[s] the commission of a crime." *Plumley v. Landmark Chevrolet, Inc.*, 122 F.3d 308, 310 (C.A.5 1997) (applying Texas law); see also *Head v. Newton*, 596 S.W.2d 209, 210 (Tex. App. 1980). The State has admitted that because of the sodomy law, *being* homosexual carries the presumption of being a criminal. See *State v. Morales*, 826 S.W.2d, at 202-203 ("[T]he statute brands lesbians and gay men as criminals and thereby legally sanctions discrimination against them in a variety of ways unrelated to the criminal law"). Texas' sodomy law therefore results in discrimination against homosexuals as a class in an array of areas outside the criminal law. See *ibid.* In *Romer v. Evans*, we refused to sanction a law that singled out homosexuals "for disfavored legal status." 517 U.S., at 633. The same is true here. The Equal Protection Clause "'neither knows nor tolerates classes among citizens.'" *Id.*, at 62 (quoting *Plessy v. Ferguson*, 163 U.S. 537, 559 (1896) (Harlan, J., dissenting)).

[13] A State can of course assign certain consequences to a violation of its criminal law. But the State cannot single out one identifiable class of citizens for punishment that does not apply to everyone else, with moral disapproval as the only asserted state interest for the law. The Texas sodomy statute subjects homosexuals to "a lifelong penalty and stigma. A legislative classification that threatens the creation of an underclass . . . cannot be reconciled with" the Equal Protection Clause. *Plyler v. Doe*, 457 U.S., at 239 (Powell, J., concurring).

[14] Whether a sodomy law that is neutral both in effect and application, see *Yick Wo v. Hopkins*, 118 U.S. 356 (1886), would violate the substantive component of the Due Process Clause is an issue that need not be decided today. I am confident,

however, that so long as the Equal Protection Clause requires a sodomy law to apply equally to the private consensual conduct of homosexuals and heterosexuals alike, such a law would not long stand in our democratic society. In the words of Justice Jackson:

> "The framers of the Constitution knew, and we should not forget today, that there is no more effective practical guaranty against arbitrary and unreasonable government than to require that the principles of law which officials would impose upon a minority be imposed generally. Conversely, nothing opens the door to arbitrary action so effectively as to allow those officials to pick and choose only a few to whom they will apply legislation and thus to escape the political retribution that might be visited upon them if larger numbers were affected." *Railway Express Agency, Inc. v. New York*, 336 U.S. 106, 112-113 (1949) (concurring opinion).

[15] That this law as applied to private, consensual conduct is unconstitutional under the Equal Protection Clause does not mean that other laws distinguishing between heterosexuals and homosexuals would similarly fail under rational basis review. Texas cannot assert any legitimate state interest here, such as national security or preserving the traditional institution of marriage. Unlike the moral disapproval of same-sex relations—the asserted state interest in this case—other reasons exist to promote the institution of marriage beyond mere moral disapproval of an excluded group.

[16] A law branding one class of persons as criminal based solely on the State's moral disapproval of that class and the conduct associated with that class runs contrary to the values of the Constitution and the Equal Protection Clause, under any standard of review. I therefore concur in the Court's judgment that Texas' sodomy law banning "deviate sexual intercourse" between consenting adults of the same sex, but not between consenting adults of different sexes, is unconstitutional.

Notes and Questions

1. Outline Justice Sandra Day O'Connor's concurrence. In what ways does it differ structurally from the majority opinion? What do these differences suggest about the function of a concurrence as opposed to a majority opinion?

2. Justice O'Connor concurs in the Court's judgment but not its opinion. She would rather rule that the challenged statute violates the Equal Protection Clause. In your view, does Justice O'Connor have sufficient justification for refusing to join the majority opinion and writing separately? Would Chief Justice Marshall agree? Would Justice Scalia?

3. Compare the first and last paragraphs of Justice O'Connor's concurrence with those of Justice Kennedy's majority opinion. In both opinions, those paragraphs frame the issue in the case. Are there stylistic differences in addition to substantive ones? Whose style do you prefer? Can you divorce the substance of these paragraphs (what they say legally) from their style (how they use language), or are style and substance to some degree inextricable?

4. Like the majority opinion (¶41), the concurrence (¶15) attempts to limit its reach. Why do you think Justice O'Connor does so when she does not need to worry about "getting to five"? Are these limiting paragraphs necessary or desirable? Paradoxically (or perhaps purposefully), do these passages end up suggesting answers to the very matters they purport to avoid? For example, how do you think either the majority or the concurrence would come out on the question of the constitutionality of a ban on same-sex marriage?

5. The majority opinion does not refer specifically to the concurrence. Does it nonetheless answer Justice O'Connor's argument that this case should be decided on equal protection rather than due process grounds? Does Justice O'Connor in turn reply? Compare ¶¶34-35 of the majority opinion with ¶14 of the concurrence. Why do you think the Justices do not respond to each other directly? Does it matter whether or not they do?

5. Lawrence v. Texas

539 U.S. 558, 586-605 (2003): Justice Scalia's Dissenting Opinion

Justice Scalia, with whom The Chief Justice and Justice Thomas join, dissenting.

[1] "Liberty finds no refuge in a jurisprudence of doubt." *Planned Parenthood of Southeastern Pa. v. Casey*, 505 U.S. 833, 844 (1992). That was the Court's sententious response, barely more than a decade ago, to those seeking to overrule *Roe v. Wade*, 410 U.S. 113 (1973). The Court's response today, to those who have engaged in a 17-year crusade to overrule *Bowers v. Hardwick*, 478 U.S. 186 (1986), is very different. The need for stability and certainty presents no barrier.

[2] Most of the rest of today's opinion has no relevance to its actual holding—that the Texas statute "furthers no legitimate state interest which can justify" its application to petitioners under rational-basis review. *Ante* (overruling *Bowers* to the extent it sustained Georgia's antisodomy statute under the rational-basis test). Though there is discussion of "fundamental proposition[s]," and "fundamental decisions," nowhere does the Court's opinion declare that homosexual sodomy is a "fundamental right" under the Due Process Clause; nor does it subject the Texas law to the standard of review that would be appropriate (strict scrutiny) if homosexual sodomy were a "fundamental right." Thus, while overruling the *outcome* of *Bowers*, the Court leaves strangely untouched its central legal conclusion: "[R]espondent would have us announce . . . a fundamental right to engage in homosexual sodomy. This we are quite unwilling to do." 478 U.S., at 191. Instead the Court simply describes petitioners' conduct as "an exercise of their liberty"—which it undoubtedly is—and proceeds to apply an unheard-of form of rational-basis review that will have far-reaching implications beyond this case.

I

[3] I begin with the Court's surprising readiness to reconsider a decision rendered a mere 17 years ago in *Bowers v. Hardwick*. I do not myself believe in rigid adherence to *stare decisis* in constitutional cases; but I do believe that we should be consistent rather than manipulative in invoking the doctrine. Today's opinions in support of reversal do not bother to distinguish—or indeed, even bother to mention—the paean to *stare decisis* coauthored by three Members of today's majority in *Planned Parenthood v. Casey*. There, when *stare decisis* meant preservation of judicially invented abortion rights, the widespread criticism of *Roe* was strong reason to *reaffirm* it:

"Where, in the performance of its judicial duties, the Court decides a case in such a way as to resolve the sort of intensely divisive controversy reflected in Roe [,] . . . its decision has a dimension that the resolution of the normal case does not carry. . . . [T]o over-rule under fire in the absence of the most compelling reason . . . would subvert the Court's legitimacy beyond any serious question." 505 U.S., at 866-867.

[4] Today, however, the widespread opposition to *Bowers*, a decision resolving an issue as "intensely divisive" as the issue in *Roe*, is offered as a reason in favor of *overruling* it. See *ante*. Gone, too, is any "enquiry" (of the sort conducted in *Casey*) into whether the decision sought to be overruled has "proven 'unworkable,'" *Casey, supra*, at 855.

[5] Today's approach to *stare decisis* invites us to overrule an erroneously decided precedent (including an "intensely divisive" decision) *if:* (1) its foundations have been "ero[ded]" by subsequent decisions; (2) it has been subject to "substantial and continuing" criticism; and (3) it has not induced "individual or societal reliance" that counsels against overturning. The problem is that *Roe* itself—which today's majority surely has no disposition to overrule—satisfies these conditions to at least the same degree as *Bowers*.

[6] A preliminary digressive observation with regard to the first factor: The Court's claim that *Planned Parenthood v. Casey, supra*, "casts some doubt" upon the holding in *Bowers* (or any other case, for that matter) does not withstand analysis. As far as its holding is concerned, *Casey* provided a less expansive right to abortion than did *Roe, which was already on the books when* Bowers *was decided*. And if the Court is referring not to the holding of *Casey*, but to the dictum of its famed sweet-mystery-of-life passage, ("'At the heart of liberty is the right to define one's own concept of existence, of meaning, of the universe, and of the mystery of human life'"): That "casts some doubt" upon either the totality of our jurisprudence or else (presumably the right answer) nothing at all. I have never heard of a law that attempted to restrict one's "right to define" certain concepts; and if the passage calls into question the government's power to regulate *actions based on* one's self-defined "concept of existence, etc.," it is the passage that ate the rule of law.

[7] I do not quarrel with the Court's claim that *Romer v. Evans*, 517 U.S. 620 (1996), "eroded" the "foundations" of *Bowers'* rational-basis holding. See *Romer, supra*, at 640-643 (Scalia, J., dissenting). But *Roe* and *Casey* have been equally "eroded" by *Washington v. Glucksberg*, 521 U.S. 702, 721 (1997), which held that only fundamental rights which are "'deeply rooted in this Nation's history and tradition'" qualify for anything other than rational-basis scrutiny under the doctrine of "substantive due process." *Roe* and *Casey*, of course, subjected the restriction of abortion to heightened scrutiny without even attempting to establish that the free-dom to abort *was* rooted in this Nation's tradition.

[8] *Bowers*, the Court says, has been subject to "substantial and continuing [criticism], disapproving of its reasoning in all respects, not just as to its historical assumptions." Exactly what those nonhistorical criticisms are, and whether the Court even agrees with them, are left unsaid, although the Court does cite two books. See *ante* (citing C. Fried, Order and Law: Arguing the Reagan Revolu-tion—A Firsthand Account 81-84 (1991); R. Posner, Sex and Reason 341-350 (1992)). Of course, *Roe* too (and by extension *Casey*) had been (and still is) subject to unrelenting criticism, including criticism from the two commentators cited by the Court today. See Fried, *supra*, at 75 ("*Roe* was a prime example of twisted judging");

Posner, *supra*, at 337 ("[The Court's] opinion in *Roe* . . . fails to measure up to professional expectations regarding judicial opinions"); Posner, *Judicial Opinion Writing*, 62 U. Chi. L. Rev. 1421, 1434 (1995) (describing the opinion in *Roe* as an "embarrassing performanc[e]").

[9] That leaves, to distinguish the rock-solid, unamendable disposition of *Roe* from the readily overrulable *Bowers*, only the third factor. "[T]here has been," the Court says, "no individual or societal reliance on *Bowers* of the sort that could counsel against overturning its holding. . . . " It seems to me that the "societal reliance" on the principles confirmed in *Bowers* and discarded today has been overwhelming. Countless judicial decisions and legislative enactments have relied on the ancient proposition that a governing majority's belief that certain sexual behavior is "immoral and unacceptable" constitutes a rational basis for regulation. See, *e.g.*, *Williams v. Pryor*, 240 F.3d 944, 949 (C.A.11 2001) (citing *Bowers* in upholding Alabama's prohibition on the sale of sex toys on the ground that "[t]he crafting and safeguarding of public morality . . . indisputably is a legitimate government interest under rational basis scrutiny"); *Milner v. Apfel*, 148 F.3d 812, 814 (C.A.7 1998) (citing *Bowers* for the proposition that "[l]egislatures are permitted to legislate with regard to morality . . . rather than confined to preventing demonstrable harms"); *Holmes v. California Army National Guard*, 124 F.3d 1126, 1136 (C.A.9 1997) (relying on *Bowers* in upholding the federal statute and regulations banning from military service those who engage in homosexual conduct); *Owens v. State*, 724 A.2d 43, 53 (Md. App. 1999) (relying on *Bowers* in holding that "a person has no constitutional right to engage in sexual intercourse, at least outside of marriage"); *Sherman v. Henry*, 928 S.W.2d 464, 469-473 (Tex. 1996) (relying on *Bowers* in rejecting a claimed constitutional right to commit adultery). We ourselves relied extensively on *Bowers* when we concluded, in *Barnes v. Glen Theatre, Inc.*, 501 U.S. 560, 569 (1991), that Indiana's public indecency statute furthered "a substantial government interest in protecting order and morality," *ibid.* (plurality opinion); see also *id.*, at 575 (Scalia, J., concurring in judgment). State laws against bigamy, same-sex marriage, adult incest, prostitution, masturbation, adultery, fornication, bestiality, and obscenity are likewise sustainable only in light of *Bowers'* validation of laws based on moral choices. Every single one of these laws is called into question by today's decision; the Court makes no effort to cabin the scope of its decision to exclude them from its holding. See *ante* (noting "an emerging awareness that liberty gives substantial protection to adult persons in deciding how to conduct their private lives *in matters pertaining to sex*" (emphasis added)). The impossibility of distinguishing homosexuality from other traditional "morals" offenses is precisely why *Bowers* rejected the rational-basis challenge. "The law," it said, "is constantly based on notions of morality, and if all laws representing essentially moral choices are to be invalidated under the Due Process Clause, the courts will be very busy indeed." 478 U.S., at 196.

[10] What a massive disruption of the current social order, therefore, the overruling of *Bowers* entails. Not so the overruling of *Roe*, which would simply have restored the regime that existed for centuries before 1973, in which the permissibility of, and restrictions upon, abortion were determined legislatively State by State. *Casey*, however, chose to base its *stare decisis* determination on a different "sort" of reliance. "[P]eople," it said, "have organized intimate relationships and made choices that define their views of themselves and their places in society, in reliance on the availability of abortion in the event that contraception should fail." 505 U.S., at 856. This falsely assumes that the consequence of overruling *Roe* would have been

to make abortion unlawful. It would not; it would merely have *permitted* the States to do so. Many States would unquestionably have declined to prohibit abortion, and others would not have prohibited it within six months (after which the most significant reliance interests would have expired). Even for persons in States other than these, the choice would not have been between abortion and childbirth, but between abortion nearby and abortion in a neighboring State.

[11] To tell the truth, it does not surprise me, and should surprise no one, that the Court has chosen today to revise the standards of *stare decisis* set forth in *Casey*. It has thereby exposed *Casey*'s extraordinary deference to precedent for the result-oriented expedient that it is.

II

[12] Having decided that it need not adhere to *stare decisis*, the Court still must establish that *Bowers* was wrongly decided and that the Texas statute, as applied to petitioners, is unconstitutional.

[13] Texas Penal Code Ann. §21.06(a) (2003) undoubtedly imposes constraints on liberty. So do laws prohibiting prostitution, recreational use of heroin, and, for that matter, working more than 60 hours per week in a bakery. But there is no right to "liberty" under the Due Process Clause, though today's opinion repeatedly makes that claim. *Ante* ("The liberty protected by the Constitution allows homosexual persons the right to make this choice"); ("'These matters . . . are central to the liberty protected by the Fourteenth Amendment'"); ("Their right to liberty under the Due Process Clause gives them the full right to engage in their conduct without intervention of the government"). The Fourteenth Amendment *expressly allows* States to deprive their citizens of "liberty," *so long as "due process of law" is provided*:

> "No state shall . . . deprive any person of life, liberty, or property, *without due process of law.*" Amdt. 14 (emphasis added).

[14] Our opinions applying the doctrine known as "substantive due process" hold that the Due Process Clause prohibits States from infringing *fundamental* liberty interests, unless the infringement is narrowly tailored to serve a compelling state interest. *Washington v. Glucksberg*, 521 U.S., at 721. We have held repeatedly, in cases the Court today does not overrule, that *only* fundamental rights qualify for this so-called "heightened scrutiny" protection—that is, rights which are "'deeply rooted in this Nation's history and tradition,'" *ibid.* See *Reno v. Flores*, 507 U.S. 292, 303 (1993) (fundamental liberty interests must be "so rooted in the traditions and conscience of our people as to be ranked as fundamental" (internal quotation marks and citations omitted)); *United States v. Salerno*, 481 U.S. 739 (1987) (same). See also *Michael H. v. Gerald D.*, 491 U.S. 110, 122 (1989) ("[W]e have insisted not merely that the interest denominated as a 'liberty' be 'fundamental' . . . but also that it be an interest traditionally protected by our society"); *Moore v. East Cleveland*, 431 U.S. 494 (1977) (plurality opinion); *Meyer v. Nebraska*, 262 U.S. 390, 399 (1923) (Fourteenth Amendment protects "those privileges *long recognized at common law as essential* to the orderly pursuit of happiness by free men" (emphasis added)). All other liberty interests may be abridged or abrogated pursuant to a validly enacted state law if that law is rationally related to a legitimate state interest.

[15] *Bowers* held, first, that criminal prohibitions of homosexual sodomy are not subject to heightened scrutiny because they do not implicate a "fundamental right"

under the Due Process Clause, 478 U.S., at 191-194. Noting that "[p]roscriptions against that conduct have ancient roots," *id.*, at 192, that "[s]odomy was a criminal offense at common law and was forbidden by the laws of the original 13 States when they ratified the Bill of Rights," *ibid.*, and that many States had retained their bans on sodomy, *id.*, at 193, *Bowers* concluded that a right to engage in homosexual sodomy was not "'deeply rooted in this Nation's history and tradition,'" *id.*, at 192.

[16] The Court today does not overrule this holding. Not once does it describe homosexual sodomy as a "fundamental right" or a "fundamental liberty interest," nor does it subject the Texas statute to strict scrutiny. Instead, having failed to establish that the right to homosexual sodomy is "'deeply rooted in this Nation's history and tradition,'" the Court concludes that the application of Texas's statute to petitioners' conduct fails the rational-basis test, and overrules *Bowers*' holding to the contrary, see *id.*, at 196. "The Texas statute furthers no legitimate state interest which can justify its intrusion into the personal and private life of the individual." *Ante.*

[17] I shall address that rational-basis holding presently. First, however, I address some aspersions that the Court casts upon *Bowers*' conclusion that homosexual sodomy is not a "fundamental right"—even though, as I have said, the Court does not have the boldness to reverse that conclusion.

III

[18] The Court's description of "the state of the law" at the time of *Bowers* only confirms that *Bowers* was right. The Court points to *Griswold v. Connecticut*, 381 U.S. 479 (1965). But that case *expressly disclaimed* any reliance on the doctrine of "substantive due process," and grounded the so-called "right to privacy" in penumbras of constitutional provisions *other than* the Due Process Clause. *Eisenstadt v. Baird*, 405 U.S. 438 (1972), likewise had nothing to do with "substantive due process"; it invalidated a Massachusetts law prohibiting the distribution of contraceptives to unmarried persons solely on the basis of the Equal Protection Clause. Of course *Eisenstadt* contains well-known dictum relating to the "right to privacy," but this referred to the right recognized in *Griswold*—a right penumbral to the *specific* guarantees in the Bill of Rights, and not a "substantive due process" right.

[19] *Roe v. Wade* recognized that the right to abort an unborn child was a "fundamental right" protected by the Due Process Clause. 410 U.S., at 155. The *Roe* Court, however, made no attempt to establish that this right was "'deeply rooted in this Nation's history and tradition'"; instead, it based its conclusion that "the Fourteenth Amendment's concept of personal liberty . . . is broad enough to encompass a woman's decision whether or not to terminate her pregnancy" on its own normative judgment that antiabortion laws were undesirable. See *id.*, at 153. We have since rejected *Roe*'s holding that regulations of abortion must be narrowly tailored to serve a compelling state interest, see *Planned Parenthood v. Casey*, 505 U.S., at 876 (joint opinion of O'Connor, Kennedy, and Souter, JJ.); *id.*, at 951–953 (Rehnquist, C. J., concurring in judgment in part and dissenting in part)—and thus, by logical implication, *Roe*'s holding that the right to abort an unborn child is a "fundamental right." See 505 U.S., at 843-912 (joint opinion of O'Connor, Kennedy, and Souter, JJ.) (not once describing abortion as a "fundamental right" or a "fundamental liberty interest").

[20] After discussing the history of antisodomy laws, the Court proclaims that, "it should be noted that there is no longstanding history in this country of laws directed at homosexual conduct as a distinct matter." This observation in no way casts into doubt the "definitive [historical] conclusio[n]," *ante* on which *Bowers* relied: that our Nation has a longstanding history of laws prohibiting *sodomy in general*—regardless of whether it was performed by same-sex or opposite-sex couples:

> "It is obvious to us that neither of these formulations would extend a fundamental right to homosexuals to engage in acts of consensual sodomy. Proscriptions against that conduct have ancient roots. *Sodomy* was a criminal offense at common law and was forbidden by the laws of the original 13 States when they ratified the Bill of Rights. In 1868, when the Fourteenth Amendment was ratified, all but 5 of the 37 States in the Union had *criminal sodomy laws*. In fact, until 1961, all 50 States outlawed *sodomy*, and today, 24 States and the District of Columbia continue to provide criminal penalties for *sodomy* performed in private and between consenting adults. Against this background, to claim that a right to engage in such conduct is 'deeply rooted in this Nation's history and tradition' or 'implicit in the concept of ordered liberty' is, at best, facetious." 478 U.S., at 192-194 (citations and footnotes omitted; emphasis added).

[21] It is (as *Bowers* recognized) entirely irrelevant whether the laws in our long national tradition criminalizing homosexual sodomy were "directed at homosexual conduct as a distinct matter." *Ante.* Whether homosexual sodomy was prohibited by a law targeted at same-sex sexual relations or by a more general law prohibiting both homosexual and heterosexual sodomy, the only relevant point is that it *was* criminalized—which suffices to establish that homosexual sodomy is not a right "deeply rooted in our Nation's history and tradition." The Court today agrees that homosexual sodomy was criminalized and thus does not dispute the facts on which *Bowers actually* relied.

[22] Next the Court makes the claim, again unsupported by any citations, that "[l]aws prohibiting sodomy do not seem to have been enforced against consenting adults acting in private." The key qualifier here is "acting in private"—since the Court admits that sodomy laws *were* enforced against consenting adults (although the Court contends that prosecutions were "infrequen[t]"). I do not know what "acting in private" means; surely consensual sodomy, like heterosexual intercourse, is rarely performed on stage. If all the Court means by "acting in private" is "on private premises, with the doors closed and windows covered," it is entirely unsurprising that evidence of enforcement would be hard to come by. (Imagine the circumstances that would enable a search warrant to be obtained for a residence on the ground that there was probable cause to believe that consensual sodomy was then and there occurring.) Surely that lack of evidence would not sustain the proposition that consensual sodomy on private premises with the doors closed and windows covered was regarded as a "fundamental right," even though all other consensual sodomy was criminalized. There are 203 prosecutions for consensual, adult homosexual sodomy reported in the West Reporting system and official state reporters from the years 1880-1995. See W. Eskridge, Gaylaw: Challenging the Apartheid of the Closet 375 (1999) (hereinafter Gaylaw). There are also records of 20 sodomy prosecutions and 4 executions during the colonial period. J. Katz, Gay/Lesbian Almanac 29, 58, 663 (1983). *Bowers'* conclusion that homosexual sodomy is not a fundamental right "deeply rooted in this Nation's history and tradition" is utterly unassailable.

[23] Realizing that fact, the Court instead says: "[W]e think that our laws and traditions in the past half century are of most relevance here. These references show *an emerging awareness* that liberty gives substantial protection to adult persons in deciding how to conduct their private lives *in matters pertaining to sex.*" *Ante* (emphasis added). Apart from the fact that such an "emerging awareness" does not establish a "fundamental right," the statement is factually false. States continue to prosecute all sorts of crimes by adults "in matters pertaining to sex": prostitution, adult incest, adultery, obscenity, and child pornography. Sodomy laws, too, have been enforced "in the past half century," in which there have been 134 reported cases involving prosecutions for consensual, adult, homosexual sodomy. Gaylaw 375. In relying, for evidence of an "emerging recognition," upon the American Law Institute's 1955 recommendation not to criminalize "'consensual sexual relations conducted in private,'" the Court ignores the fact that this recommendation was "a point of resistance in most of the states that considered adopting the Model Penal Code." Gaylaw 159.

[24] In any event, an "emerging awareness" is by definition not "deeply rooted in this Nation's history and tradition[s]," as we have said "fundamental right" status requires. Constitutional entitlements do not spring into existence because some States choose to lessen or eliminate criminal sanctions on certain behavior. Much less do they spring into existence, as the Court seems to believe, because *foreign nations* decriminalize conduct. The *Bowers* majority opinion *never* relied on "values we share with a wider civilization," *ante*, but rather rejected the claimed right to sodomy on the ground that such a right was not "'deeply rooted in *this Nation's* history and tradition,'" 478 U.S., at 193-194 (emphasis added). *Bowers'* rational-basis holding is likewise devoid of any reliance on the views of a "wider civilization," see *id.*, at 196. The Court's discussion of these foreign views (ignoring, of course, the many countries that have retained criminal prohibitions on sodomy) is therefore meaningless dicta. Dangerous dicta, however, since "this Court should not impose foreign moods, fads, or fashions on Americans." *Foster v. Florida*, 537 U.S. 990, (2002) (Thomas, J., concurring in denial of certiorari).

IV

[25] I turn now to the ground on which the Court squarely rests its holding: the contention that there is no rational basis for the law here under attack. This proposition is so out of accord with our jurisprudence—indeed, with the jurisprudence of *any* society we know—that it requires little discussion.

[26] The Texas statute undeniably seeks to further the belief of its citizens that certain forms of sexual behavior are "immoral and unacceptable," *Bowers, supra*, at 196—the same interest furthered by criminal laws against fornication, bigamy, adultery, adult incest, bestiality, and obscenity. *Bowers* held that this was a legitimate state interest. The Court today reaches the opposite conclusion. The Texas statute, it says, "furthers *no legitimate state interest* which can justify its intrusion into the personal and private life of the individual," *ante* (emphasis added). The Court embraces instead Justice Stevens' declaration in his *Bowers* dissent, that "'the fact that the governing majority in a State has traditionally viewed a particular practice as immoral is not a sufficient reason for upholding a law prohibiting the practice,'" *ante*. This effectively decrees the end of all morals legislation. If, as the Court asserts, the promotion of majoritarian sexual morality is not even a *legitimate* state interest, none of the above-mentioned laws can survive rational-basis review.

V

[27] Finally, I turn to petitioners' equal-protection challenge, which no Member of the Court save Justice O'Connor, *ante* (opinion concurring in judgment), embraces: On its face §21.06(a) applies equally to all persons. Men and women, heterosexuals and homosexuals, are all subject to its prohibition of deviate sexual intercourse with someone of the same sex. To be sure, §21.06 does distinguish between the sexes insofar as concerns the partner with whom the sexual acts are performed: men can violate the law only with other men, and women only with other women. But this cannot itself be a denial of equal protection, since it is precisely the same distinction regarding partner that is drawn in state laws prohibiting marriage with someone of the same sex while permitting marriage with someone of the opposite sex.

[28] The objection is made, however, that the antimiscegenation laws invalidated in *Loving v. Virginia*, 388 U.S. 1, 8 (1967), similarly were applicable to whites and blacks alike, and only distinguished between the races insofar as the *partner* was concerned. In *Loving*, however, we correctly applied heightened scrutiny, rather than the usual rational-basis review, because the Virginia statute was "designed to maintain White Supremacy." *Id.*, at 6, 11. A racially discriminatory purpose is always sufficient to subject a law to strict scrutiny, even a facially neutral law that makes no mention of race. See *Washington v. Davis*, 426 U.S. 229, 241-242 (1976). No purpose to discriminate against men or women as a class can be gleaned from the Texas law, so rational-basis review applies. That review is readily satisfied here by the same rational basis that satisfied it in *Bowers*—society's belief that certain forms of sexual behavior are "immoral and unacceptable," 478 U.S., at 196. This is the same justification that supports many other laws regulating sexual behavior that make a distinction based upon the identity of the partner—for example, laws against adultery, fornication, and adult incest, and laws refusing to recognize homosexual marriage.

[29] Justice O'Connor argues that the discrimination in this law which must be justified is not its discrimination with regard to the sex of the partner but its discrimination with regard to the sexual proclivity of the principal actor.

> "While it is true that the law applies only to conduct, the conduct targeted by this law is conduct that is closely correlated with being homosexual. Under such circumstances, Texas' sodomy law is targeted at more than conduct. It is instead directed toward gay persons as a class." *Ante.*

[30] Of course the same could be said of any law. A law against public nudity targets "the conduct that is closely correlated with being a nudist," and hence "is targeted at more than conduct"; it is "directed toward nudists as a class." But be that as it may. Even if the Texas law *does* deny equal protection to "homosexuals as a class," that denial *still* does not need to be justified by anything more than a rational basis, which our cases show is satisfied by the enforcement of traditional notions of sexual morality.

[31] Justice O'Connor simply decrees application of "a more searching form of rational basis review" to the Texas statute. The cases she cites do not recognize such a standard, and reach their conclusions only after finding, as required by conventional rational-basis analysis, that no conceivable legitimate state interest supports the classification at issue. See *Romer v. Evans*, 517 U.S., at 635; *Cleburne v. Cleburne Living Center, Inc.*, 473 U.S. 432, 448-450 (1985); *Department of Agriculture v.*

Moreno, 413 U.S. 528, 534-538 (1973). Nor does Justice O'Connor explain precisely what her "more searching form" of rational-basis review consists of. It must at least mean, however, that laws exhibiting "a desire to harm a politically unpopular group," *ante*, are invalid *even though* there may be a conceivable rational basis to support them.

[**32**] This reasoning leaves on pretty shaky grounds state laws limiting marriage to opposite-sex couples. Justice O'Connor seeks to preserve them by the conclusory statement that "preserving the traditional institution of marriage" is a legitimate state interest. But "preserving the traditional institution of marriage" is just a kinder way of describing the State's *moral disapproval* of same-sex couples. Texas's interest in §21.06 could be recast in similarly euphemistic terms: "preserving the traditional sexual mores of our society." In the jurisprudence Justice O'Connor has seemingly created, judges can validate laws by characterizing them as "preserving the traditions of society" (good); or invalidate them by characterizing them as "expressing moral disapproval" (bad).

[**33**] Today's opinion is the product of a Court, which is the product of a law-profession culture, that has largely signed on to the so-called homosexual agenda, by which I mean the agenda promoted by some homosexual activists directed at eliminating the moral opprobrium that has traditionally attached to homosexual conduct. I noted in an earlier opinion the fact that the American Association of Law Schools (to which any reputable law school *must* seek to belong) excludes from membership any school that refuses to ban from its job-interview facilities a law firm (no matter how small) that does not wish to hire as a prospective partner a person who openly engages in homosexual conduct. See *Romer, supra,* at 653.

[**34**] One of the most revealing statements in today's opinion is the Court's grim warning that the criminalization of homosexual conduct is "an invitation to subject homosexual persons to discrimination both in the public and in the private spheres." It is clear from this that the Court has taken sides in the culture war, departing from its role of assuring, as neutral observer, that the democratic rules of engagement are observed. Many Americans do not want persons who openly engage in homosexual conduct as partners in their business, as scoutmasters for their children, as teachers in their children's schools, or as boarders in their home. They view this as protecting themselves and their families from a lifestyle that they believe to be immoral and destructive. The Court views it as "discrimination" which it is the function of our judgments to deter. So imbued is the Court with the law profession's anti-anti-homosexual culture, that it is seemingly unaware that the attitudes of that culture are not obviously "mainstream"; that in most States what the Court calls "discrimination" against those who engage in homosexual acts is perfectly legal; that proposals to ban such "discrimination" under Title VII have repeatedly been rejected by Congress, see Employment Non-Discrimination Act of 1994, S. 2238, 103d Cong., 2d Sess. (1994); Civil Rights Amendments, H.R. 5452, 94th Cong., 1st Sess. (1975); that in some cases such "discrimination" is *mandated* by federal statute, see 10 U.S.C. §654(b)(1) (mandating discharge from the Armed Forces of any service member who engages in or intends to engage in homosexual acts); and that in some cases such "discrimination" is a constitutional right, see *Boy Scouts of America v. Dale*, 530 U.S. 640 (2000).

[35] Let me be clear that I have nothing against homosexuals, or any other group, promoting their agenda through normal democratic means. Social perceptions of sexual and other morality change over time, and every group has the right to persuade its fellow citizens that its view of such matters is the best. That homosexuals have achieved some success in that enterprise is attested to by the fact that Texas is one of the few remaining States that criminalize private, consensual homosexual acts. But persuading one's fellow citizens is one thing, and imposing one's views in absence of democratic majority will is something else. I would no more *require* a State to criminalize homosexual acts—or, for that matter, display *any* moral disapprobation of them—than I would *forbid* it to do so. What Texas has chosen to do is well within the range of traditional democratic action, and its hand should not be stayed through the invention of a brand-new "constitutional right" by a Court that is impatient of democratic change. It is indeed true that "later generations can see that laws once thought necessary and proper in fact serve only to oppress," *ante*; and when that happens, later generations can repeal those laws. But it is the premise of our system that those judgments are to be made by the people, and not imposed by a governing caste that knows best.

[36] One of the benefits of leaving regulation of this matter to the people rather than to the courts is that the people, unlike judges, need not carry things to their logical conclusion. The people may feel that their disapprobation of homosexual conduct is strong enough to disallow homosexual marriage, but not strong enough to criminalize private homosexual acts—and may legislate accordingly. The Court today pretends that it possesses a similar freedom of action, so that we need not fear judicial imposition of homosexual marriage, as has recently occurred in Canada (in a decision that the Canadian Government has chosen not to appeal). See *Halpern v. Toronto*, 2003 WL 34950 (Ontario Ct. App.); Cohen, Dozens in Canada Follow Gay Couple's Lead, Washington Post, June 12, 2003, p. A25. At the end of its opinion—after having laid waste the foundations of our rational-basis jurisprudence—the Court says that the present case "does not involve whether the government must give formal recognition to any relationship that homosexual persons seek to enter." Do not believe it. More illuminating than this bald, unreasoned disclaimer is the progression of thought displayed by an earlier passage in the Court's opinion, which notes the constitutional protections afforded to "personal decisions relating to *marriage*, procreation, contraception, family relationships, child rearing, and education," and then declares that "[p]ersons in a homosexual relationship may seek autonomy for these purposes, just as heterosexual persons do." *Ante* (emphasis added). Today's opinion dismantles the structure of constitutional law that has permitted a distinction to be made between heterosexual and homosexual unions, insofar as formal recognition in marriage is concerned. If moral disapprobation of homosexual conduct is "no legitimate state interest" for purposes of proscribing that conduct, *ante*; and if, as the Court coos (casting aside all pretense of neutrality), "[w]hen sexuality finds overt expression in intimate conduct with another person, the conduct can be but one element in a personal bond that is more enduring," *ante*; what justification could there possibly be for denying the benefits of marriage to homosexual couples exercising "[t]he liberty protected by the Constitution," *ante*? Surely not the encouragement of procreation, since the sterile and the elderly are allowed to marry. This case "does not involve" the issue of homosexual marriage only if one entertains the belief that principle and logic have nothing to do with the decisions of this Court. Many will hope that, as the Court comfortingly assures us, this is so.

[37] The matters appropriate for this Court's resolution are only three: Texas's prohibition of sodomy neither infringes a "fundamental right" (which the Court does not dispute), nor is unsupported by a rational relation to what the Constitution considers a legitimate state interest, nor denies the equal protection of the laws. I dissent.

Notes and Questions

1. Outline Justice Antonin Scalia's dissent. In what ways does it differ structurally from that of the majority? Does the organization of this dissent have more in common with the structure of the dissent in *Bond* than that of the majority here?

2. Compare the introduction of Justice Scalia's dissent (¶¶1-2) with Justice Breyer's in *Bond* (¶1). Do you detect a difference in style and strategy? Which introduction do you find to be more effective?

3. The dissent (¶2) locates the majority opinion's holding in ¶41, namely, that the law at issue "furthers no legitimate state interest which can justify its intrusion into the personal and private life of the individual." Is Justice Scalia right? If so, do you think the majority opinion makes its holding easy to spot, or would you have made it more prominent? If Justice Scalia is wrong, then what does the majority opinion hold?

4. In addition to locating the majority's holding in ¶41, Justice Scalia asserts (¶2) that "[m]ost of the rest of today's opinion has no relevance to its actual holding." In particular, he contends that the majority opinion's substantive due process discussion is largely beside the point, because the Court does not go on to "declare that homosexual sodomy is a 'fundamental right.'" *Id.*; *see also* ¶16. Do you agree? In any case, what strategic reason might there be for a dissenting opinion to point out not only what the majority does not decide, but also what is irrelevant to its decision?

5. Consider, below, what the majority opinion might look like if cut down to what Justice Scalia might regard as relevant to its holding. In particular, ¶¶1, 10-39, and 42 are deleted. In what ways (besides length) is this extremely truncated version better or worse?

Justice Kennedy delivered the opinion of the Court.

I

[2] The question before the Court is the validity of a Texas statute making it a crime for two persons of the same sex to engage in certain intimate sexual conduct.

[3] In Houston, Texas, officers of the Harris County Police Department were dispatched to a private residence in response to a reported weapons disturbance. They entered an apartment where one of the petitioners, John Geddes Lawrence, resided. The right of the police to enter does not seem to have been questioned. The officers observed Lawrence and another man, Tyron Garner, engaging in a sexual act. The two petitioners were arrested, held in custody overnight, and charged and convicted before a Justice of the Peace.

[4] The complaints described their crime as "deviate sexual intercourse, namely anal sex, with a member of the same sex (man)." The applicable state law is Tex. Penal Code Ann. §21.06(a) (2003). It provides: "A person commits an offense if he engages in

deviate sexual intercourse with another individual of the same sex." The statute defines "[d]eviate sexual intercourse" as follows:

"(A) any contact between any part of the genitals of one person and the mouth or anus of another person; or
"(B) the penetration of the genitals or the anus of another person with an object." §21.01(1).

[5] The petitioners exercised their right to a trial *de novo* in Harris County Criminal Court. They challenged the statute as a violation of the Equal Protection Clause of the Fourteenth Amendment and of a like provision of the Texas Constitution. Tex. Const., Art. 1, §3a. Those contentions were rejected. The petitioners, having entered a plea of nolo contendere, were each fined $200 and assessed court costs of $141.25.

[6] The Court of Appeals for the Texas Fourteenth District considered the petitioners' federal constitutional arguments under both the Equal Protection and Due Process Clauses of the Fourteenth Amendment. After hearing the case en banc the court, in a divided opinion, rejected the constitutional arguments and affirmed the convictions. 41 S.W.3d 349 (2001). The majority opinion indicates that the Court of Appeals considered our decision in *Bowers v. Hardwick*, 478 U.S. 186, to be controlling on the federal due process aspect of the case. *Bowers* then being authoritative, this was proper.

[7] We granted certiorari, 537 U.S. 1044, to consider three questions:

1. Whether petitioners' criminal convictions under the Texas 'Homosexual Conduct' law—which criminalizes sexual intimacy by same-sex couples, but not identical behavior by different-sex couples—violate the Fourteenth Amendment guarantee of equal protection of the laws.
2. Whether petitioners' criminal convictions for adult consensual sexual intimacy in the home violate their vital interests in liberty and privacy protected by the Due Process Clause of the Fourteenth Amendment.
3. Whether *Bowers v. Hardwick, supra,* should be overruled.

[8] The petitioners were adults at the time of the alleged offense. Their conduct was in private and consensual.

II

[9] We conclude the case should be resolved by determining whether the petitioners were free as adults to engage in the private conduct in the exercise of their liberty under the Due Process Clause of the Fourteenth Amendment to the Constitution. For this inquiry we deem it necessary to reconsider the Court's holding in *Bowers*.

[40] The rationale of *Bowers* does not withstand careful analysis. In his dissenting opinion in *Bowers* Justice Stevens came to these conclusions:

"Our prior cases make two propositions abundantly clear. First, the fact that the governing majority in a State has traditionally viewed a particular practice as immoral is not a sufficient reason for upholding a law prohibiting the practice; neither history nor tradition could save a law prohibiting miscegenation from constitutional attack. Second, individual decisions by married persons, concerning the intimacies of their physical relationship, even when not intended to produce offspring, are a form of 'liberty' protected by the Due Process Clause of the Fourteenth Amendment. Moreover, this protection extends to intimate choices by unmarried as well as married persons." 478 U.S., at 216 (footnotes and citations omitted).

Justice Stevens' analysis, in our view, should have been controlling in *Bowers* and should control here.

Bowers was not correct when it was decided, and it is not correct today. It ought not to remain binding precedent. *Bowers v. Hardwick* should be and now is overruled.

[41] The present case does not involve minors. It does not involve persons who might be injured or coerced or who are situated in relationships where consent might not easily be refused. It does not involve public conduct or prostitution. It does not involve whether the government must give formal recognition to any relationship that homosexual persons seek to enter. The case does involve two adults who, with full and mutual consent from each other, engaged in sexual practices common to a homosexual lifestyle. The petitioners are entitled to respect for their private lives. The State cannot demean their existence or control their destiny by making their private sexual conduct a crime. Their right to liberty under the Due Process Clause gives them the full right to engage in their conduct without intervention of the government. "It is a promise of the Constitution that there is a realm of personal liberty which the government may not enter." Casey, *supra*, at 847. The Texas statute furthers no legitimate state interest which can justify its intrusion into the personal and private life of the individual.

The judgment of the Court of Appeals for the Texas Fourteenth District is reversed, and the case is remanded for further proceedings not inconsistent with this opinion.

It is so ordered.

5. If Justice Scalia is correct that the majority's discussion of substantive due process is largely irrelevant, because "the Court does not have the boldness" to overrule *Bowers'* conclusion that "homosexual sodomy" is not a "fundamental right" (¶17), then what is the substantive or strategic point of his devoting an entire section of the dissent (¶¶18-24) to defending *Bowers'* conclusion?

6. In *Lawrence*, the Court was asked to overrule *Bowers*, not *Roe v. Wade* (1973). Yet Justice Scalia devotes pages (¶¶3-11) to contrasting the Court's willingness to overrule the former in this case with its refusal to overrule the latter in *Planned Parenthood of Southeastern Pa. v. Casey* (1992). Does Justice Scalia's focus on *Roe*, and his attack on *Casey*, strengthen or distract from his arguments about this case?

7. Though the majority opinion does not expressly say so, the dissent claims (¶26) that the Court "effectively decrees the end of all morals legislation," including those banning "fornication, bigamy, adultery, adult incest, bestiality, and obscenity." Similarly, though both the majority (¶41) and concurring (¶15) opinions go out of their way to state that they do not reach the question whether states must recognize same-sex marriages, the dissent argues (¶36) that the right to "homosexual marriage" has not been decided "only if one entertains the belief that principle and logic have nothing to do with the decisions of this Court." What benefit is there, from the standpoint of the dissent, in characterizing the majority opinion this broadly and apocalyptically? What risks are there? Relatedly, recall Justice Scalia's view that a dissent "often causes the majority to refine its opinion, eliminating the more vulnerable assertions and narrowing the announced legal rule." Antonin Scalia, *The Dissenting Opinion*, Journal of Supreme Court History 33, 41 (1994). Do the above assertions accomplish this refinement, or do they have the opposite effect?

8. Renowned for the power—and sharpness—of his rhetoric, Justice Scalia includes both "zingers" and "firebombs" in his *Lawrence* dissent. *See, e.g.,* ¶1 ("That was the Court's sententious response . . ."); ¶3 ("I do believe that we should be consistent rather than manipulative"); ¶6 (*Casey's* "sweet-mystery-of-life passage . . . ate the rule of law"); ¶17 ("[T]he Court does not have the boldness to reverse" *Bowers*); ¶33 ("Today's opinion is the product of a Court, which is the product of a law-profession culture, that has largely signed on to the so-called homosexual agenda"); ¶35 ("[I]t is the premise of our system that those judgments are to be made by the people, and not imposed by a governing caste that knows best"); ¶36 (The Court has "laid waste the foundations of our rational-basis juris-prudence"); ¶36 ("[T]he Court coos (casting aside all pretense of neutrality)"). Do you find Justice Scalia's dissenting language and tone more or less effective than Justice Breyer's in *Bond*?

Recall Justice Scalia's observation that dissenting opinions "do not, or at least need not, produce animosity and bitterness among the members of the Court." Scalia, *The Dissenting Opinion, supra*, at 40. If you were the majority opinion writer, would his dissenting rhetoric affect your feelings of collegiality? Should it?

Finally, recall Justice Ginsburg's view that overindulgence in separate opinion writing "may undermine both the reputation of the judiciary for judgment and the respect accorded court dispositions." Ruth Bader Ginsburg, *Speaking in a Judicial Voice*, 67 N.Y.U. L. Rev. 1185, 1191 (1992). No doubt Chief Justice John Marshall would agree. But are they right, or does Justice Scalia have a point that vigorous dissents may "augment rather than diminish the prestige of the Court" by demonstrating beyond doubt that its decisions are "the product of independent and thoughtful minds, who try to persuade one another but do not simply 'go along' for some supposed 'good of the institution'"? Scalia, *The Dissenting Opinion, supra*, at 35.

6. Lawrence v. Texas

539 U.S. 558, 605-606 (2003): Justice Thomas's Dissenting Opinion

Justice Thomas, dissenting.

[1] I join Justice Scalia's dissenting opinion. I write separately to note that the law before the Court today "is . . . uncommonly silly." *Griswold v. Connecticut*, 381 U.S. 479, 527 (1965) (Stewart, J., dissenting). If I were a member of the Texas Legislature, I would vote to repeal it. Punishing someone for expressing his sexual preference through noncommercial consensual conduct with another adult does not appear to be a worthy way to expend valuable law enforcement resources.

[2] Notwithstanding this, I recognize that as a Member of this Court I am not empowered to help petitioners and others similarly situated. My duty, rather, is to "decide cases 'agreeably to the Constitution and laws of the United States.'" *Id.*, at 530. And, just like Justice Stewart, I "can find [neither in the Bill of Rights nor any other part of the Constitution a] general right of privacy," *ibid.*, or as the Court terms it today, the "liberty of the person both in its spatial and more transcendent dimensions," *ante*.

Notes and Questions

1. Outline Justice Clarence Thomas's dissent. In what ways does it differ in function from Justice Scalia's dissent? In what ways is its form and function enabled by his dissent?

2. To whom is Justice Thomas speaking? Is his audience the same as Justice Scalia's?

3. Does the content of Justice Thomas's two paragraphs justify writing sepa-rately? If you were Justice Thomas, would you have written separately or simply joined Scalia's dissent without saying more?

7. Zedner v. United States

547 U.S. 489, 492-509 (2006): Justice Alito's Majority Opinion

Justice ALITO delivered the opinion of the Court.

[1] This case requires us to consider the application of the doctrines of waiver, judicial estoppel, and harmless error to a violation of the Speedy Trial Act of 1974 (Speedy Trial Act or Act), 18 U.S.C. §§3161-3174. The Act generally requires a federal criminal trial to begin within 70 days after a defendant is charged or makes an initial appearance, §3161(c)(1), but the Act contains a detailed scheme under which certain specified periods of delay are not counted. In this case, petitioner's trial did not begin within 70 days of indictment. Indeed, his trial did not commence until more than seven years after the filing of the indictment, but petitioner, at the suggestion of the trial judge, signed a blanket, prospective waiver of his rights under the Act. We address the following questions: whether this waiver was effective; whether petitioner is judicially estopped from challenging the validity of the waiver; and whether the trial judge's failure to make the findings required to exclude a period of delay under a particular provision of the Act, §3161(h)(8), was harmless error.

I

[2] In March 1996, petitioner attempted to open accounts at seven financial institutions using counterfeit $10 million United States bonds. The quality of the counterfeiting was, to put it mildly, not expert. One bond purported to be issued by the "Ministry of Finance of U.S.A." 401 F.3d 36, 39 (C.A.2 2005) (internal quotation marks omitted). Others contained misspelled words such as "Thunted States" and the "Onited States" (United States), "Dhtladelphla" (Philadelphia), "Cgicago" (Chicago), and "forevev" (forever). Id., at 39, n.1 (internal quotation marks omitted). After petitioner presented these bonds, the Secret Service was contacted, and petitioner was arrested. Following arraignment on a criminal complaint, he was released on bond.

[3] On April 4, 1996, a grand jury in the Eastern District of New York indicted petitioner on seven counts of attempting to defraud a financial institution, in violation of 18 U.S.C. §1344, and one count of knowingly possessing counterfeit obligations of the United States, in violation of §472. On June 26, the District Court, citing the complexity of the case, granted what is termed an "ends-of-justice" continuance, see §3161(h)(8)(B)(ii), until September 6. On September 6, the District Court granted another continuance, this time until November 8.

[4] At the November 8 status conference, petitioner requested, without opposition from the Government, a further adjournment to January 1997. Concerned about the difficulty of fitting petitioner's trial into its heavily scheduled calendar and the prospect that petitioner might "only waive [the Act] for so long as it is convenient for [him] to waive," the District Court instructed petitioner as follows: "I think if I'm going to give you that long an adjournment, I will have to take a waiver for all time." App. 71. Petitioner's counsel responded that the defense would "waive for all time. That will not be a problem. That will not be an issue in this case." Id., at 72.

[5] The District Court then addressed petitioner directly and appears to have attempted to explain the operation of a provision of the Act, 18 U.S.C. §3162(a)(2),

under which a defendant whose trial does not begin on time is deemed to have waived the right to move for dismissal of the information or indictment if he or she does not file that motion prior to trial or entry of a guilty plea. The District Court reasoned: "[I]f you can waive [the Act] by inaction, i.e., not raising the motion to dismiss, you can waive affirmatively, knowledgeably, intelligently your right to do so, your right to a speedy trial and your right to make a motion to dismiss for the speedy trial." App. 73. The court told petitioner that it was "prepared to start . . . trial right away," *ibid.*, but that if a continuance was granted, petitioner might have to wait some time for trial because the court had a "fairly big cas[e] . . . which [wa]s set to take eight months for trial." "[I]f that [trial] starts before you start," the court warned, "you may have to wait until that is done." *Id.*, at 74.

[6] The District Court then produced a pre-printed form—apparently of its own devising—captioned "Waiver of Speedy Trial Rights." *Id.*, at 79. The court led petitioner and his counsel through the form, and both signed it. Among other things, the form stated: "I wish to waive my rights to a speedy trial . . . under the Speedy Trial Act of 1974 (18 U.S.C. §3161 et seq.), under the Rules of this Circuit and under the Speedy Trial Plan adopted by this Court." *Ibid.* The form also stated: "I have been advised and fully understand that . . . I also waive any and all rights to make a motion to dismiss the indictment . . . against me for failure of the Court to give me a speedy trial and that I waive all of such rights to a speedy trial and to make such a motion or motions for all time." *Ibid.* After the form was signed, petitioner's counsel requested that a further status conference be scheduled for January 31, 1997, and the court agreed. *Id.*, at 77.

[7] At the January 31 status conference, petitioner sought yet another continuance "to tap . . . the proper channels to authenticate [the] bonds." *Id.*, at 81. Petitioner and the Government emphasized that this request raised no issue under the Act because petitioner had "waived for all time," though the Government suggested that it "would like to try the case sometime in 1997." *Ibid.* After a brief discussion between the court and petitioner's counsel about the need to investigate the authenticity of what seemed such obviously fake bonds, the court offered to set trial for May 5, 1997. *Id.*, at 86. The court admonished petitioner's counsel to "[g]et to work" and noted: "This [case] is a year old. That's enough for a criminal case." *Id.*, at 86, 85. Nevertheless, apparently satisfied with petitioner's waiver "for all time," the District Court made no mention of the Act and did not make any findings to support exclusion of the 91 days between January 31 and petitioner's next court appearance on May 2, 1997 (1997 continuance).

[8] The four years that followed saw a variety of proceedings in petitioner's case, but no trial. See 401 F.3d, at 40-41. Counsel sought to be relieved because petitioner insisted that he argue that the bonds were genuine, and the court ultimately granted counsel's request to withdraw. At the court's suggestion, petitioner was examined by a psychiatrist, who determined that petitioner was competent to stand trial. Petitioner then asked to proceed *pro se* and sought to serve subpoenas on, among others, the President, the Chairman of the Federal Reserve Board, the Attorney General, the Secretary of State, the late Chinese leader Chiang Kai-shek, and "'The Treasury Department of Treasury International Corporation.'" *Id.*, at 40; App. 129. After a year of quashed subpoenas, the District Court set the case for trial, only to conclude on the morning of jury selection that it had to inquire once again into petitioner's competency. The court dismissed the jury panel, found petitioner incompetent, and committed him to the custody of the Attorney General for

hospitalization and treatment. On interlocutory appeal, however, the Court of Appeals vacated that order and remanded for further hearings. In July and August 2000, the District Court held those hearings and received further briefing on the competency issue.

[9] On March 7, 2001, while the competency issue remained under submission, petitioner moved to dismiss the indictment for failure to comply with the Act. The District Court denied the motion on the ground that petitioner had waived his Speedy Trial Act rights "for all time," mentioning in passing that the case was complex. *Id.*, at 128-129. In the same order, the court found petitioner incompetent. *Id.*, at 135. That latter determination was upheld on interlocutory appeal, and petitioner was committed for evaluation. After several months of hospitalization, petitioner was found to be delusional but competent to stand trial, and he was released.

[10] Finally, on April 7, 2003, more than seven years after petitioner was indicted, his trial began. The jury found petitioner guilty on six counts of attempting to defraud a financial institution, and the court sentenced him to 63 months of imprisonment.

[11] The Court of Appeals affirmed the judgment of conviction. Acknowledging that "a defendant's waiver of rights under the Speedy Trial Act may be ineffective" because of the public interest served by compliance with the Act, the Court of Appeals found an exception for situations "'when defendant's conduct causes or contributes to a period of delay.'" 401 F.3d, at 43-44 (quoting *United States v. Gambino*, 59 F.3d 353, 360 (C.A.2 1995)). "[D]oubt[ing] that the public interest in expeditious prosecution would be served by a rule that allows defendants to request a delay and then protest the grant of their request," the Court of Appeals held that petitioner would not be heard to complain of the 91-day delay in early 1997. 401 F.3d, at 45. The Court of Appeals went on to suggest that there "can be no doubt that the district court could have properly excluded this period of time based on the ends of justice" in light of the complexity of the case and defense counsel's request for additional time to prepare. *Ibid.*

[12] We granted certiorari to resolve the disagreement among the Courts of Appeals on the standard for analyzing whether a defendant has made an effective waiver of rights under the Act. 546 U.S. 1085 (2006).

II

[13] As noted above, the Speedy Trial Act generally requires a trial to begin within 70 days of the filing of an information or indictment or the defendant's initial appearance, 18 U.S.C. §3161(c)(1), but the Act recognizes that criminal cases vary widely and that there are valid reasons for greater delay in particular cases. To provide the necessary flexibility, the Act includes a long and detailed list of periods of delay that are excluded in computing the time within which trial must start. See §3161(h). For example, the Act excludes "delay resulting from other proceedings concerning the defendant," §3161(h)(1), "delay resulting from the absence or unavailability of the defendant or an essential witness," §3161(h)(3)(A), "delay resulting from the fact that the defendant is mentally incompetent or physically unable to stand trial," §3161(h)(4), and "[a] reasonable period of delay when the defendant is joined for trial with a codefendant as to whom the time for trial has not run and no motion for severance has been granted," §3161(h)(7).

[14] Much of the Act's flexibility is furnished by §3161(h)(8), which governs ends-of-justice continuances, and which we set out in relevant part in the margin.[3] This provision permits a district court to grant a continuance and to exclude the resulting delay if the court, after considering certain factors, makes on-the-record findings that the ends of justice served by granting the continuance outweigh the public's and defendant's interests in a speedy trial. This provision gives the district court discretion—within limits and subject to specific procedures—to accommodate limited delays for case-specific needs.

[15] To promote compliance with its requirements, the Act contains enforcement and sanctions provisions. If a trial does not begin on time, the defendant may move, before the start of trial or the entry of a guilty plea, to dismiss the charges, and if a meritorious and timely motion to dismiss is filed, the district court must dismiss the charges, though it may choose whether to dismiss with or without prejudice. In making that choice, the court must take into account, among other things, "the seriousness of the offense; the facts and circumstances of the case which led to the dismissal; and the impact of a reprosecution on the administration of [the Act] and on the administration of justice." §3162(a)(2).

[16] This scheme is designed to promote compliance with the Act without needlessly subverting important criminal prosecutions. The more severe sanction (dismissal with prejudice) is available for use where appropriate, and the knowledge that a violation could potentially result in the imposition of this sanction gives the prosecution a powerful incentive to be careful about compliance. The less severe sanction (dismissal without prejudice) lets the court avoid unduly impairing the enforcement of federal criminal laws—though even this sanction imposes some costs on the prosecution and the court, which further encourages compliance. When an indictment is dismissed without prejudice, the prosecutor may of course seek—and in the great majority of cases will be able to obtain—a new indictment, for

---

3. Title 18 U.S.C. §3161(h)(8) provides:

"(A) Any period of delay resulting from a continuance granted by any judge on his own motion or at the request of the defendant or his counsel or at the request of the attorney for the Government, if the judge granted such continuance on the basis of his findings that the ends of justice served by taking such action outweigh the best interest of the public and the defendant in a speedy trial. No such period of delay resulting from a continuance granted by the court in accordance with this paragraph shall be excludable under this subsection unless the court sets forth, in the record of the case, either orally or in writing, its reasons for finding that the ends of justice served by the granting of such continuance outweigh the best interests of the public and the defendant in a speedy trial.

"(B) The factors, among others, which a judge shall consider in determining whether to grant a continuance under subparagraph (A) of this paragraph in any case are as follows:

"(i) Whether the failure to grant such a continuance in the proceeding would be likely to make a continuation of such proceeding impossible, or result in a miscarriage of justice.

"(ii) Whether the case is so unusual or so complex, due to the number of defendants, the nature of the prosecution, or the existence of novel questions of fact or law, that it is unreasonable to expect adequate preparation for pretrial proceedings or for the trial itself within the time limits established by this section.

. . .

"(iv) Whether the failure to grant such a continuance in a case which, taken as a whole, is not so unusual or so complex as to fall within clause (ii), would deny the defendant reasonable time to obtain counsel, would unreasonably deny the defendant or the Government continuity of counsel, or would deny counsel for the defendant or the attorney for the Government the reasonable time necessary for effective preparation, taking into account the exercise of due diligence.

"(C) No continuance under subparagraph (A) of this paragraph shall be granted because of general congestion of the court's calendar, or lack of diligent preparation or failure to obtain available witnesses on the part of the attorney for the Government."

even if "the period prescribed by the applicable statute of limitations has expired, a new indictment may be returned within six calendar months of the date of the dismissal." §3288.

[17] With this background in mind, we turn to the questions presented by the unusual procedures followed in this case.

III

[18] Petitioner contends, and the Government does not seriously dispute, that a defendant may not prospectively waive the application of the Act. We agree.

A

1

[19] As our discussion above suggests, the Speedy Trial Act comprehensively regulates the time within which a trial must begin. Section 3161(h) specifies in detail numerous categories of delay that are not counted in applying the Act's deadlines. Conspicuously, §3161(h) has no provision excluding periods of delay during which a defendant waives the application of the Act, and it is apparent from the terms of the Act that this omission was a considered one. Instead of simply allowing defendants to opt out of the Act, the Act demands that defense continuance requests fit within one of the specific exclusions set out in subsection (h). Subsection (h)(8), which permits ends-of-justice continuances, was plainly meant to cover many of these requests. Among the factors that a district court must consider in deciding whether to grant an ends-of-justice continuance are a defendant's need for "reasonable time to obtain counsel," "continuity of counsel," and "effective preparation" of counsel. §3161(h)(8)(B)(iv). If a defendant could simply waive the application of the Act whenever he or she wanted more time, no defendant would ever need to put such considerations before the court under the rubric of an ends-of-justice exclusion.

[20] The purposes of the Act also cut against exclusion on the grounds of mere consent or waiver. If the Act were designed solely to protect a defendant's right to a speedy trial, it would make sense to allow a defendant to waive the application of the Act. But the Act was designed with the public interest firmly in mind. See, *e.g.*, §3161(h)(8)(A) (to exclude delay resulting from a continuance—even one "granted . . . at the request of the defendant"—the district court must find "that the ends of justice served . . . outweigh the *best interest of the public* and the defendant *in a speedy trial*" (emphasis added)). That public interest cannot be served, the Act recognizes, if defendants may opt out of the Act entirely.

2

[21] This interpretation is entirely in accord with the Act's legislative history. As both the 1974 House and Senate Reports illustrate, the Act was designed not just to benefit defendants but also to serve the public interest by, among other things, reducing defendants' opportunity to commit crimes while on pretrial release and preventing extended pretrial delay from impairing the deterrent effect of punishment. See S. Rep. No. 93-1021, pp. 6-8 (citing "bail problems," offenses committed during pretrial release, and the "seriously undermined . . . deterrent value of the criminal process" as "the debilitating effect[s] of court delay upon our criminal justice system"); H.R. Rep. No. 93-1508, p. 8, U.S. Code Cong. & Admin. News 1974, pp. 7401, 7402 ("The purpose of this bill is

to assist in reducing crime and the danger of recidivism by requiring speedy trials . . ."). The Senate Report accompanying the 1979 amendments to the Act put an even finer point on it: "[T]he Act seeks to protect and promote speedy trial interests that go beyond the rights of the defendant; although the Sixth Amendment recognizes a societal interest in prompt dispositions, it primarily safeguards the defendant's speedy trial right—which may or may not be in accord with society's." S. Rep. No. 96-212, p. 29; see also *id.*, at 6; H.R. Rep. No. 96-390, p. 3 (1979), U.S. Code Cong. & Admin. News 1979, 805, 807. Because defendants may be content to remain on pretrial release, and indeed may welcome delay, it is unsurprising that Congress refrained from empowering defendants to make prospective waivers of the Act's application. See S. Rep. No. 96-212, at 29 ("Because of the Act's emphasis on that societal right, a defendant ought not be permitted to waive rights that are not his or hers alone to relinquish").

B

[21] The District Court reasoned that 18 U.S.C. §3162(a)(2) supports the conclusion that a defendant may prospectively waive the strictures of the Act. This provision states that "[f]ailure of the defendant to move for dismissal prior to trial or entry of a plea of guilty or nolo contendere shall constitute a waiver of the right to dismissal under this section." Because this provision in effect allows a defendant to waive a completed violation of the Act (by declining to move to dismiss before the start of trial or the entry of a guilty plea), it follows, so the District Court's reasoning went, that a defendant should be allowed to make a prospective waiver. We disagree.

[22] It is significant that §3162(a)(2) makes no mention of prospective waivers, and there is no reason to think that Congress wanted to treat prospective and retrospective waivers similarly. Allowing prospective waivers would seriously undermine the Act because there are many cases—like the case at hand—in which the prosecution, the defense, and the court would all be happy to opt out of the Act, to the detriment of the public interest. The sort of retrospective waiver allowed by §3162(a)(2) does not pose a comparable danger because the prosecution and the court cannot know until the trial actually starts or the guilty plea is actually entered whether the defendant will forgo moving to dismiss. As a consequence, the prosecution and the court retain a strong incentive to make sure that the trial begins on time.

[23] Instead of granting broad opt-out rights, §3162(a)(2) serves two unrelated purposes. First, §3162(a)(2) assigns the role of spotting violations of the Act to defendants—for the obvious reason that they have the greatest incentive to perform this task. Second, by requiring that a defendant move before the trial starts or a guilty plea is entered, §3162(a)(2) both limits the effects of a dismissal without prejudice (by ensuring that an expensive and time-consuming trial will not be mooted by a late-filed motion under the Act) and prevents undue defense gamesmanship.

[24] For these reasons, we reject the District Court's reliance on §3162(a)(2) and conclude a defendant may not prospectively waive the application of the Act. It follows that petitioner's waiver "for all time" was ineffective. We therefore turn to the Government's alternative grounds in support of the result below.

IV

A

[25] The Government contends that because "petitioner's express waiver induced the district court to grant a continuance without making an express ends-of-justice finding . . . , basic principles of judicial estoppel preclude petitioner from enjoying the benefit of the continuance, but then challenging the lack of a finding." Brief for United States 10. In this case, however, we see no basis for applying the doctrine of judicial estoppel.

[26] As this Court has explained:

> "'[W]here a party assumes a certain position in a legal proceeding, and succeeds in maintaining that position, he may not thereafter, simply because his interests have changed, assume a contrary position, especially if it be to the prejudice of the party who has acquiesced in the position formerly taken by him.' *Davis v. Wakelee*, 156 U.S. 680, 689 (1895). This rule, known as judicial estoppel, 'generally prevents a party from prevailing in one phase of a case on an argument and then relying on a contradictory argument to prevail in another phase.' *Pegram v. Herdrich*, 530 U.S. 211, 227, n.8 (2000)." *New Hampshire v. Maine*, 532 U.S. 742, 749 (2001).

Although this estoppel doctrine is equitable and thus cannot be reduced to a precise formula or test,

> "several factors typically inform the decision whether to apply the doctrine in a particular case: First, a party's later position must be clearly inconsistent with its earlier position. Second, courts regularly inquire whether the party has succeeded in persuading a court to accept that party's earlier position. . . . A third consideration is whether the party seeking to assert an inconsistent position would derive an unfair advantage or impose an unfair detriment on the opposing party if not estopped." *Id.*, at 750-751 (citations and internal quotation marks omitted).

[27] In applying this doctrine to the present case, we must first identify the "position" of petitioner's that the Government seeks to enforce. There are three possibilities: (1) petitioner's promise not to move for dismissal under §3162(a)(2), (2) petitioner's (implied) position that waivers of the Act are enforceable, and (3) petitioner's claim that counsel needed additional time to research the authenticity of the bonds. None of these gives rise to an estoppel.

[28] First, we are unwilling to recognize an estoppel based on petitioner's promise not to move for dismissal because doing so would entirely swallow the Act's no-waiver policy. We see little difference between granting a defendant's request for a continuance in exchange for a promise not to move for dismissal and permitting a prospective waiver, and as we hold above, prospective waivers are inconsistent with the Act.

[29] Second, petitioner's (mistaken) agreement that Speedy Trial Act waivers are valid also does not provide a ground for estoppel. Petitioner did not "succee[d] in persuading" the District Court to accept the proposition that prospective waivers of Speedy Trial Act rights are valid. On the contrary, it was the District Court that requested the waiver and produced the form for petitioner to sign. And while the other relevant factors (clear inconsistency and unfair advantage or detriment) might in isolation support the Government, we think they do not predominate where, as here, the Government itself accepted the District Court's interpretation without objection.

[30] Finally, petitioner's representation to the District Court at the January 31 status conference that a continuance was needed to gather evidence of the bonds' authenticity does not support the Government's estoppel argument because the position that petitioner took then was not "clearly inconsistent" with the position that he now takes in seeking dismissal of the indictment. This would be a different case if petitioner had succeeded in persuading the District Court at the January 31 status conference that the factual predicate for a statutorily authorized exclusion of delay could be established—for example, if defense counsel had obtained a continuance only by falsely representing that he was in the midst of working with an expert who might authenticate the bonds. In fact, however, the discussion at the January 31 status conference did not focus on the requirements of the Act. Rather, the court and the parties proceeded on the assumption that the court's waiver form was valid and that the Act could simply be disregarded. Nothing in the discussion at the conference suggests that the question presented by the defense continuance request was viewed as anything other than a case-management question that lay entirely within the scope of the District Court's discretion. Under these circumstances, the best understanding of the position taken by petitioner's attorney at the January 31 status conference is that granting the requested continuance would represent a sound exercise of the trial judge's discretion in managing its calendar. This position was not "clearly inconsistent" with petitioner's later position that the continuance was not permissible under the terms of the Act. Accordingly, we hold that petitioner is not estopped from challenging the excludability under the Act of the 1997 continuance.

B

[32] While conceding that the District Court "never made an express finding on the record" about the ends-of-justice balance, Brief for United States 30, the Government argues that such an express finding did not need to be entered contemporaneously—and could be supplied on remand—because, given the circumstances in 1997, the ends-of-justice balance in fact supported the 1997 continuance. We reject this argument. In the first place, the Act requires express findings, and in the second place, it does not permit those findings to be made on remand as the Government proposes.

[33] The Act requires that when a district court grants an ends-of-justice continuance, it must "se[t] forth, in the record of the case, either orally or in writing, its reasons" for finding that the ends of justice are served and they outweigh other interests. 18 U.S.C. §3161(h)(8)(A). Although the Act is clear that the findings must be made, if only in the judge's mind, before granting the continuance (the continuance can only be "granted . . . on the basis of [the court's] findings"), the Act is ambiguous on precisely when those findings must be "se[t] forth, in the record of the case." However this ambiguity is resolved, at the very least the Act implies that those findings must be put on the record by the time a district court rules on a defendant's motion to dismiss under §3162(a)(2). In ruling on a defendant's motion to dismiss, the court must tally the unexcluded days. This, in turn, requires identifying the excluded days. But §3161(h)(8)(A) is explicit that "[n]o . . . period of delay resulting from a continuance granted by the court in accordance with this paragraph shall be excludable . . . unless the court sets forth . . . its reasons for [its] finding[s]." Thus, without on-the-record findings, there can be no exclusion under §3161(h)(8). Here, the District Court set forth no such findings at the January 31 status conference, and §3161(h)(8)(A) is not satisfied by the District Court's passing reference to the case's complexity in its ruling on petitioner's motion to dismiss. Therefore, the 1997 continuance is not excluded from the speedy trial clock.

[34] The Government suggests that this error, stemming as it does from the District Court's technical failure to make an express finding, may be regarded as harmless. Brief for United States 31, n.8. Harmless-error review under Federal Rule of Criminal Procedure 52(a) presumptively applies to "*all* errors where a proper objection is made," *Neder v. United States*, 527 U.S. 1, 7 (1999), and we have required "strong support" to find an implied repeal of Rule 52, *United States v. Vonn*, 535 U.S. 55, 65 (2002). We conclude, however, that the provisions of the Act provide such support here.

[35] The relevant provisions of the Act are unequivocal. If a defendant pleads not guilty, the trial "*shall* commence" within 70 days "from the filing date (and making public) of the information or indictment" or from the defendant's initial appearance, whichever is later. §3161(c)(1) (emphasis added). Delay resulting from an ends-of- justice continuance is excluded from this time period, but "[*n*]*o such period of delay . . . shall be excludable* under this subsection unless the court sets forth, in the record of the case, either orally or in writing, its reasons for finding that the ends of justice served by the granting of such continuance outweigh the best interests of the public and the defendant in a speedy trial." §3161(h)(8)(A) (emphasis added). When a trial is not commenced within the prescribed period of time, "the information or indictment *shall be dismissed* on motion of the defendant." §3162(a)(2) (emphasis added). A straightforward reading of these provisions leads to the conclusion that if a judge fails to make the requisite findings regarding the need for an ends-of-justice continuance, the delay resulting from the continuance must be counted, and if as a result the trial does not begin on time, the indictment or information must be dismissed. The argument that the District Court's failure to make the prescribed findings may be excused as harmless error is hard to square with the Act's categorical terms. See *Alabama v. Bozeman*, 533 U.S. 146, 153-154 (2001) (no "'harmless'" or "'technical'" violations of the Interstate Agreement on Detainers' "antishuttling" provision in light of its "absolute language").

[36] Applying the harmless-error rule would also tend to undermine the detailed requirements of the provisions regulating ends-of-justice continuances. The exclusion of delay resulting from an ends-of-justice continuance is the most open-ended type of exclusion recognized under the Act and, in allowing district courts to grant such continuances, Congress clearly meant to give district judges a measure of flexibility in accommodating unusual, complex, and difficult cases. But it is equally clear that Congress, knowing that the many sound grounds for granting ends-of-justice continuances could not be rigidly structured, saw a danger that such continuances could get out of hand and subvert the Act's detailed scheme. The strategy of §3161(h)(8), then, is to counteract substantive openendedness with procedural strictness. This provision demands on-the-record findings and specifies in some detail certain factors that a judge must consider in making those findings. Excusing the failure to make these findings as harmless error would be inconsistent with the strategy embodied in §3161(h). Such an approach would almost always lead to a finding of harmless error because the simple failure to make a record of this sort is unlikely to affect the defendant's rights. We thus conclude that when a district court makes no findings on the record in support of §3161(h)(8) continuance, harmless-error review is not appropriate.

V

[**37**] We hold that the 91-day continuance granted on January 31 was not excluded from petitioner's speedy trial clock. Because this continuance by itself exceeded the maximum 70-day delay provided in §3161(c)(1), the Act was violated, and we need not address whether any other periods of delay during petitioner's case were not excludable. The sanction for a violation of the Act is dismissal, but we leave it to the District Court to determine in the first instance whether dismissal should be with or without prejudice. See §3162(a)(2). The judgment of the Court of Appeals is therefore reversed, and the case is remanded for further proceedings consistent with this opinion.

It is so ordered.

Notes and Questions

1. Outline Justice Samuel Alito's majority opinion. In what ways does the organization of Justice Alito's opinion differ from that of Chief Justice Rehnquist in *Bond* and Justice Kennedy in *Lawrence?* To what extent are differences attributable to the issue being one of statutory rather than constitutional interpretation? Did you find this opinion easier to follow than the other two?

2. Did the divisions of the opinion into parts help you follow it? Why do you think Chief Justice Rehnquist did not subdivide his opinion in *Bond?*

3. Compare the opening paragraph of this majority opinion with those of *Bond* and *Lawrence.* Would you say that Justice Alito's opinion-writing style is closer to that of Chief Justice Rehnquist or Justice Kennedy? In terms of substance, does Justice Alito give too little, too much, or just enough information to frame the question presented in the case? Which opening paragraph do you prefer—Justice Alito's, Chief Justice Rehnquist's, or Justice Kennedy's?

4. Notice that the recitation of facts (¶¶2-10) proceeds in carefully delineated chronological order. Why do you think it does? Are all the facts necessary to the Court's subsequent legal analysis set forth here? Are any superfluous?

5. In the facts, do you detect mild humor or amusement at the petitioner's expense? If it is there, is it welcome or inappropriate?

6. After reading the introduction and facts, did you develop a sense for which way the Court would go? If so, can you point to ways in which the opinion gave you that sense through its framing of the issue and facts?

7. In ¶12, the majority opinion explains why it granted certiorari. The majority opinions in *Bond* and *Lawrence* did not do so. Why do you think it did here? Do you think it is desirable for the Court generally to state its reasons for taking a case? Might there be difficulties to doing so? *See supra* Chapter 4, Sections B-D.

8. After reading the question presented (¶1), applicable facts (¶¶2-10), and applicable law (¶¶13-17), are you equipped with the necessary information to decide the case on your own? Does Justice Alito do a better job in this case of bringing the reader "up to speed" than Chief Justice Rehnquist in *Bond* or Justice Kennedy in *Lawrence?*

9. What is the function of ¶21? Is it strictly necessary? Regardless, does it strengthen the Court's legal analysis? Why do you think it was segregated into its own section (Part III.A.2)?

10. Note the ordering of the majority opinion's legal analysis. It first gives the affirmative reasons for its decision (¶¶19-21). Next, it addresses the lower court's contrary reasoning (¶¶21-24). Finally, it responds to the losing party's counterarguments (¶¶25-36). Does this ordering work well logically and legally? Would you change it?

11. Both Justice Alito here (¶37) and Chief Justice Rehnquist in *Bond* (¶9) expressly give the Court's holding at the end of their majority opinions. In *Lawrence*, Justice Kennedy does not. Which practice do you prefer? Why do you think a Justice might decide to include—or exclude—an express statement of the Court's holding in the majority opinion?

8. Zedner v. United States

547 U.S. 489, 509-511 (2006): Justice Scalia's Concurring Opinion

Justice SCALIA, concurring in part and concurring in the judgment.

[1] I concur in the opinion of the Court with the exception of its discussion of legislative history in Part III-A-2. For reasons I have expressed elsewhere, I believe that the only language that constitutes "a Law" within the meaning of the Bicameralism and Presentment Clause of Article I, §7, and hence the only language adopted in a fashion that entitles it to our attention, is the text of the enacted statute. See, *e.g.*, *Conroy v. Aniskoff,* 507 U.S. 511, 518-528 (Scalia, J., concurring in judgment). Here, the Court looks to legislative history even though the remainder of its opinion amply establishes that the Speedy Trial Act is unambiguous. The Act's language rejects the possibility of a prospective waiver, and even expresses the very point that the Court relies on legislative history to support—that the Act protects the interests of the public as well as those of the defendant. See *ante* (citing 18 U.S.C. §3161(h)(8)(A)). Use of legislative history in this context thus conflicts not just with my own views but with this Court's repeated statements that when the language of the statute is plain, legislative history is irrelevant. See, *e.g., United States v. Gonzales,* 520 U.S. 1, 6 (1997). "We have stated time and again that courts must presume that a legislature says in a statute what it means and means in a statute what it says there. When the words of a statute are unambiguous, then, this first canon is also the last: judicial inquiry is complete." *Connecticut Nat. Bank v. Germain,* 503 U.S. 249, 253-254 (1992) (citations and internal quotation marks omitted).

[2] It may seem that there is no harm in using committee reports and other such sources when they are merely in accord with the plain meaning of the Act. But this sort of intellectual piling-on has addictive consequences. To begin with, it accustoms us to believing that what is said by a single person in a floor debate or by a committee report represents the view of Congress as a whole—so that we sometimes even will say (when referring to a floor statement and committee report) that "Congress has expressed" thus-and-so. See, *e.g., Conroy, supra,* at 516-517. There is no basis either in law or in reality for this naive belief. Moreover, if legislative history is relevant when it confirms the plain meaning of the statutory text, it should also be relevant when it contradicts the plain meaning, thus rendering what is plain ambiguous. Because the use of legislative history is illegitimate and ill advised in the interpretation of any statute—and especially a statute that is clear on its face—I do not join this portion of the Court's opinion.

Notes and Questions

1. Although the Court lost its tradition of unanimity long before *Zedner*, *see supra* Section A.6, the modern Court nonetheless has a tradition of arranging for a new Justice to issue a unanimous first opinion. *See, e.g., Martin v. Franklin Capital Corp.*, 546 U.S. 132 (2005) (unanimous first opinion of Chief Justice John Roberts). Justice Alito, however, could not keep his first opinion entirely unanimous. In one small paragraph, he refers to legislative history to support the Court's interpretation of the statute at issue. For reasons briefly sketched in his concurrence, and more fully developed elsewhere, *see, e.g.,* Antonin Scalia, *A Matter of Interpretation* 29-37 (1997), legislative history is anathema to Justice Scalia. Everyone who is familiar with Justice Scalia's jurisprudence (certainly including Justice Alito) knows this. Not surprisingly, therefore, Justice Scalia refuses to join that paragraph, and thereby denies Justice Alito a completely unanimous first outing. Why do you think Justice Alito did not simply drop the offending paragraph (¶21)?

2. What do you make of the fact that every other member of the Court joined the paragraph that Justice Scalia objects to, and no one joined Justice Scalia's concurrence? Is it safe to infer that no one on the Court but Justice Scalia believes (¶2) that "the use of legislative history is illegitimate and ill-advised in the interpretation of any statute"? If so, why do you think Justice Alito did not respond to Justice Scalia's attack on his use of legislative history? There is no shortage of developed views from which he could have drawn. *See, e.g.,* Stephen Breyer, *Making Our Democracy Work: A Judge's View* 88-105 (2010); *Zuni Pub. Sch. Dist. No. 89 v. Dept. of Edu.*, 550 U.S. 81, 104 (2007) (Stevens, J., concurring); Abner S. Greene, *The Missing Step of Textualism*, 74 Fordham L. Rev. 1913 (2006). Would you have responded? If so, how?

8

Contemporary Issues Facing
the Court

The Supreme Court stands at the pinnacle of the American legal system, so naturally, controversy, debate, and proposals for reform often swirl around the Court. This final chapter explores two illustrative examples of contemporary debates facing the Court: (a) diversity at the Court; and (b) the public's access to the Court. Both debates serve as good ways of yet again exploring the role of the United States Supreme Court and the function that it should play in our society, which was initially explored in Chapter 1.

A. DIVERSITY AT THE COURT

The Supreme Court does not look like the rest of America. Rather, the Justices, their law clerks, and the advocates who appear before the Court are a fairly homogenous group primarily consisting of white males who attended elite academic institutions. Moreover, the total number of individuals who play a consistent and large role in Supreme Court jurisprudence is extremely small. Is this troubling? Should the Court and the key players operating within and appearing before the Court, look more like the rest of America? What would be the benefits of having a more representative Supreme Court?

The materials in this section will address these and related questions concerning diversity among: (1) the Justices; (2) the Justices' law clerks; and (3) the advocates frequently appearing before the Court.

1. The Justices

Historically, the Court has been dominated by white men. As discussed in Chapter 2, out of the 112 Justices and Chief Justices to have served on the Court to date, four have been women, only two have been African American, and only one has been Hispanic. No Asian Americans or Native Americans have ever served on the Court, and no openly gay or lesbian Justices have sat on the Court. The first African-American Justice (Thurgood Marshall) was not appointed until 1967, and the first woman (Sandra Day O'Connor) was not appointed until 1981. Since then, racial and gender diversity among the Justices has increased a bit. Three women, one African American, and one Hispanic currently sit on the Court. However, the Court is still predominantly white and male.

In terms of religious backgrounds, the Justices started out quite homogeneous but recently have diversified somewhat. During the Court's first 60 years, 30 of the 31 Justices were Protestant Christians. The lone non-Protestant Christian was Chief Justice Roger B. Taney, a Roman Catholic appointed in 1836 by President Andrew Jackson. *See generally* Susan Navarro Smelcer, Congressional Research Service, R40802, Supreme Court Justices: Demographic Characteristics, Professional Experience, and Legal Education, 1789-2010 (April 9, 2010). The next Roman Catholic Justice (Edward Douglass White) was not appointed until 1894. Since that point, the number of Catholic Justices has increased over time. *See generally* Barbara A. Perry, *The Life and Death of the "Catholic Seat" on the United States Supreme Court*, 6 J.L. & Pol. 55, 61 (1989).

Indeed, at present, there are six Catholic Justices (Scalia, Kennedy, Thomas, Roberts, Alito, and Sotomayor) sitting on the Court. The remaining three Justices (Ginsburg, Breyer, and Kagan) are Jewish. The presence of three Jewish Justices on the current Court is quite significant given that the first Jewish Justice (Louis Brandeis) did not join the Court until 1916. *See generally* Thomas Karfunkel & Thomas W. Ryley, *The Jewish Seat* (1978). The Court's current religious composition is also striking because it is the first Court without a sitting Justice that identifies as a Protestant Christian.

Besides gender, racial, and religious diversity, another dimension of diversity among the Justices that has received significant scrutiny recently is the lack of diversity in the professional backgrounds of the Justices. A recent study by several political scientists found that between 1869 (when Congress established separate judgeships for the U.S. circuits) and 1952, just 16 percent of the 62 Supreme Court nominations went to federal circuit court judges. Lee Epstein, Andrew D. Martin, Kevin M. Quinn & Jeffrey A. Segal, *Circuit Effects: How the Norm of Federal Judicial Experience Biases the Supreme Court*, 157 U. Pa. L. Rev. 833, 839 (2009). Yet, since 1953, the figure increased to nearly 66 percent. *Id.*

According to Epstein and her co-authors, increasing "professionalization" of the Justices is troubling because it leads to "circuit effects" whereby the Justices are biased in favor of affirming the decisions of the circuits that they came from. Consider the risks of "professionalization" explored in the following excerpt.

Lee Epstein, Andrew D. Martin, Kevin M. Quinn & Jeffrey A. Segal, Circuit Effects: How the Norm of Federal Judicial Experience Biases the Supreme Court

157 U. Pa. L. Rev. 833, 834-838, 877-880 (2009)

After the appointments of John G. Roberts and Samuel A. Alito, commentators were quick to point to a new source of diversity on the U.S. Supreme Court: religion. For the first time in the Court's history, Protestants do not hold a majority or plurality of seats; Catholics do.

But religion may be the exception. On many other dimensions, the Roberts Court, as it is currently composed, is among the more homogeneous Courts in recent memory. Most noticeably, for the first time in American history all nine Justices came to their positions directly from U.S. courts of appeals.

While this "professionalization" of the Court is without precedent, it has been long in coming. Ever since President Dwight D. Eisenhower made clear that he "would use an appeals court appointment as a stepping stone to the Supreme Court," the vast majority of nominees have come from the federal circuits. Even more to the point, the Senate has not confirmed any Supreme Court nominee lacking circuit court experience since William H. Rehnquist in 1986.[1] Of course, there was President George W. Bush's attempt in 2005 to appoint his White House counsel, Harriet Miers. Ironically enough, this nomination—so roundly criticized on the very ground that Miers had never served on the bench—may have solidified the practice of looking to the circuits for Supreme Court nominees. As one observer noted, "[t]he appointments of Chief Justice Roberts and Justice Alito, and contrastingly the rejection of Harriet Miers, reinforce a trend on the Court that nominees not only have prior judicial experience, but also federal appellate experience."

As new vacancies are likely to arise on the Court in the not-so-distant future, should the next presidential administration and the Senate continue to appoint Justices from the U.S. circuits? Commentators disagree on the best approach. Those who support this so-called "norm" of federal judicial experience point to any number of benefits. Two such benefits appearing on many lists are less contentious confirmation processes and, ultimately, superior products—Justices who reach decisions based on precedent or other neutral sources, and not on their own political preferences. Those opposed to the norm do not necessarily dispute these benefits but instead argue that the costs are substantial. They point to several disadvantages along these lines, perhaps one of the most pernicious being "circuit effects"—the possibility that federal-appellate-judges-turned-Supreme-Court-Justices are predisposed to affirm decisions coming from the circuits they just left.

In what follows, we weigh in on this debate, not by rehashing the existing arguments but rather by exploring them empirically. . . . On balance, we find that the benefits [of the norm of federal appellate judicial experience] are virtually nonexistent—confirmation proceedings are no smoother for candidates coming from the circuits than for other nominees, and former appellate court judges are no more likely to follow precedent or to put aside their policy preferences than are Justices lacking judicial experience. The costs, on the other hand, are considerable. While we do not observe circuit effects in the form of Justices consistently biased towards all the U.S. courts of appeals, the data do reveal a clear predisposition on the part of former federal judges to rule in favor of their home courts. For some Justices the attachment is so strong that they are twice as likely to affirm decisions coming from the circuit on which they served than they are to affirm decisions coming from all other circuits.

Under any circumstances, circuit effects seem problematic; they suggest that when the President and senators follow the norm of federal judicial experience, the Justices they appoint are more likely to give the benefit of the doubt to some circuits than to others. But the problem of bias now transcends individual Justices. Because four of the nine current Justices served on the U.S. Court of Appeals for the District of Columbia, the norm has created a collective presumption in favor of decisions handed down by the D.C. Circuit judges. To provide but one example, while all other federal appellate court judges can expect the U.S. Supreme Court to reverse

---

1. [Editors' note: This article was written prior to the confirmation of Justice Elena Kagan. Like Rehnquist, Justice Kagan came to the Court without any prior judicial experience.]

their decisions in about two out of every three disputes, those sitting on the D.C. Circuit actually enjoy a higher probability of being affirmed than reversed. . . .

. . . An obvious antidote is for the President to look to other pools for potential Court candidates. If confirmation is viewed as an important consideration, one can now feel reasonably certain that sitting federal judges are no less likely to face contentious proceedings than any other candidate; indeed, sitting judges may actually be more difficult to confirm. And if making high-quality appointments is a relevant criterion, the President can now legitimately claim that previous federal judicial experience is no guarantee that the candidate, as a Justice, will be more likely to follow precedent and less likely to follow his or her own political values, or even to go down in the annals as one of the "greats."

A less obvious, though no less plausible, remedy would be for appointers to work toward greater representation of the circuits on the Supreme Court. Arlen Specter implicitly made this point in response to conflict-of-interest concerns that were raised when Justice Alito's colleagues from the Third Circuit testified on his behalf. No one should worry that Alito would be predisposed toward affirming the Third Circuit's rulings, Specter declared, because, "if confirmed, [Alito] would be one of nine people reviewing their cases."

This is true for the Third Circuit: Alito is the first and only Justice elevated from that court. It does not, however, hold for the First Circuit, on which two current Justices served (Souter and Breyer), nor for the D.C. Circuit, now with four representatives on the Supreme Court. In fact, our recommendation of greater diversity in circuit court representation follows from the D.C. Circuit's disproportionate presence on the current Court. Put simply, with its current status as something of a training camp for Supreme Court Justices, the Court of Appeals for the District of Columbia is now at a considerable advantage relative to the other eleven circuits. . . .

If we assume that systematic bias is undesirable in any court, neutralizing it will require appointers to look toward other, unrepresented circuits for the next few appointees. Doing so should not be difficult. For most of the nation's history, geographic diversity was a strong norm—perhaps as strong as the norm of judicial experience is now. If a Supreme Court Justice from the East resigned, the President nominated an easterner; if a southerner departed, the President looked to the South for a replacement. Ensuring greater representation of the circuits should be no more difficult; with little doubt, credible Democratic and Republican candidates reside in each. More to the point, all politicians involved in the appointments process should want to take this approach. With the exception of the northeastern corridor, the home team advantage now so apparent on the nation's high court may well be disadvantaging appellants from all parts of the country. Senators serving in the first Congress would have found this intolerable and it is hard to imagine today's legislators—given their own reelection concerns—finding it any less so.

Notes and Questions

1. This article by Epstein and her co-authors was published in February 2009 prior to Justices Sonia Sotomayor and Elena Kagan joining the bench. Since Justice Sotomayor came to the Court from the Second Circuit, she falls neatly within the professionalization trend identified by Epstein and her co-authors. Justice Kagan bucked this trend, as she came to the Court with no prior judicial experience at

either the federal or the state level. Yet Kagan did fit neatly within other molds. She—like many other recent Justices—came from the Northeastern corridor and Ivy League roots; she not only attended Harvard Law School but also served as Dean of Harvard Law School. Justice Kagan also served as Solicitor General of the United States prior to joining the Court. She also served as a law clerk to Justice Harry Blackmun early in her legal career.

2. If presidents prefer to pick United States Supreme Court nominees from the ranks of federal appellate court judges, could the lack of gender and racial diversity among those lower court judges impede diversity on the United States Supreme Court? In 2006, when Samuel Alito was nominated to replace the country's first female Justice upon her retirement, women occupied less than one-quarter of all U.S. district court and court of appeals seats combined. President George W. Bush's White House lawyers reportedly examined women and minority candidates, but they had trouble finding acceptable candidates. *See* Jan Crawford Greenburg, *Supreme Conflict: The Inside Story of Struggle for Control of the United States Supreme Court* 245, 253 (2007). The overall picture of the federal judiciary, however, might be changing. President Obama is the first President who has nominated more women and minorities than white males for federal judgeships. *See* Jesse J. Holland, *Obama Increases Number of Female, Minority Judges*, Associated Press, Sept. 13, 2011. Indeed, nearly three of every four judges nominated and confirmed to the federal bench under President Obama have been women or minorities. *See id.*

3. In choosing Supreme Court nominees, should presidents take an individual's geographic roots or prior judicial work experience into account in order to create a more "representative" Supreme Court? What about race, gender, or religion? For one take on this, see Barbara A. Perry, *A "Representative" Supreme Court?: The Impact of Race, Religion, and Gender on Appointments* (1991). Perry argues:

> Given the judicial role of the Court and its requirements of expertise, independence, and public confidence, we should enshrine merit as a prime criterion for Supreme Court selection. Nevertheless, other factors can, do, and should enter into the selection process. . . .
>
> Like political and ideological compatibility, "representativeness" is a fact of political life and is destined not only to remain on the judicial appointment scene, but perhaps to complicate matters, as other groups (e.g., Asians and Hispanics) demand a place on the high bench and presidents attempt to meet their demands in return for electoral support. . . .
>
> As a factor in Court appointments, "representativeness" by no means has to entail a diminution of the merit principle. . . . Moreover, a public perception that the high bench is open to all groups in society and is as reflective of American pluralism as the nine seats will allow may be particularly crucial at this time in the nation's development. As the country grows more ethnically and racially heterogeneous, there are increasingly vocal demands to accommodate cultural diversity in all realms of life. Although such demands have aroused ugly controversies, especially in the education field, the application of the diversity principle strikes me as a positive goal—again, as long as merit is at the threshold of any appointment. I reject, however, the "diversity for diversity's sake" argument so prevalent now among extremists in the multiculturalism debate.

Id. at 136-137.

For another take on this topic, see Kevin R. Johnson & Luis Fuentes-Rohwer, *A Principled Approach to the Quest for Racial Diversity on the Judiciary*, 10 Mich. J. Race & L. 5 (2004). Drawing on Critical Race Theory, Johnson and Fuentes-Rohwer argue that diversity on the bench is a "laudable goal" to ensure that judges "bring new and different perspectives to the decision-making process than those offered by a predominantly White judiciary." *Id.* at 10, 52. However, they argue that judgeship candidates should be considered on grounds other than just race, such as ideology, judicial temperament, and life experiences. These considerations ensure that "those appointed do, in fact, have diverse preconceptions about the law and the world." *Id.* at 52-53. As Johnson and Fuentes-Rohwer put it, "[m]any, perhaps most, African Americans . . . would rather have nine William Brennans on the Supreme Court than nine Clarence Thomases." *Id.* at 53.

4. Why strive for a diverse bench? What might be the benefits of a diverse bench? Consider the following possible arguments:

> Political scientists have identified two possible reasons for a diverse bench. First, the purpose behind a diverse bench may be symbolic representation. This means that diversity provides certain groups with the opportunity to have access to positions of influence so that all members of society will believe in the fairness of the system. This adds legitimacy to the judiciary by making it mirror the population. The second reason for diversity is what is known as the functional or substantive representation function. Under this theory, members of under-represented groups will advocate for the interests of the group to which they belong once appointed. This means that judges of differing backgrounds will bring differing perspectives to the bench based on their own life experience, which could potentially lead to different results, or at least the advocating of different results in lawsuits.

Theresa M. Beiner, *Diversity on the Bench and the Quest for Justice for All*, 33 Ohio N.U. L. Rev. 481, 488-489 (2007). Put another way, there are at least two arguments "for diversity on the Supreme Court: diversity as inclusion, and diversity as proxy for values and views." F. Andrew Hessick & Samuel P. Jordan, *Setting the Size of the Supreme Court*, 41 Ariz. St. L.J. 645, 659 (2009).

5. In 2009—just three years after Justice O'Connor retired and left Justice Ginsburg as the only woman on the Court at the time—Justice Ginsburg made clear that the Court needed another woman. *See* Joan Biskupic, *Ginsburg: The Court Needs Another Woman: Panel's Lack of Diversity Wears on Female Justice*, USA Today, May 6, 2009, at 1A. Specifically, a *USA Today* contributor asked Justice Ginsburg about comments her colleagues made the month before in oral argument in a case involving a 13-year old girl who was subjected to a strip search in school based on a tip that she was carrying over-the-counter pain medication in violation of school policy. *Id.* Justice Ginsburg noted that her colleagues, who did not seem to see the seriousness of the strip search, did not understand that 13 is a sensitive age for a girl. She asserted that her colleagues failed to understand this because her colleagues had never been 13-year-old girls. *See id.* Some Court watchers were surprised when the Court subsequently ruled that the search violated the Constitution. *See Safford Unified Sch. Dist. No. 1 v. Redding*, 557 U.S. 364, 368 (2009) ("Because there were no reasons to suspect the drugs presented a danger or were concealed in her underwear, we hold that the search did violate the Constitution, but because there is reason to question the clarity with which the right was established, the official who ordered the unconstitutional search is entitled to qualified immunity from liability."). Indeed, speculation spread that Justice Ginsburg's public comments, made immediately after the *Redding* oral argument, may have influenced the other Justices' votes.

If it is true that Justice Ginsburg's media comments influenced other Justices, does that support the need for more gender diversity on the Court? And what does the anecdote suggest about the propriety of the Justices making public speeches and giving interviews to the media or about the relationship between the Court and the media? On the specific issue of the Justices' extrajudicial speeches and comments, *see generally Judges on Judging: Views from the Bench* 1-12 (David O'Brien ed., 3d ed. 2009); William G. Ross, *Extrajudicial Speech: Charting the Boundaries of Propriety*, 2 Geo. J. Legal Ethics 589 (1989); Alan F. Westin, *Out-of-Court Commentary by United States Supreme Court Justices, 1790-1962: Of Free Speech and Judicial Lockjaw*, 62 Colum. L. Rev. 633 (1962).

6. When President Obama nominated Sonia Sotomayor to the Court in 2009, only one of the nine candidates his administration vetted was an Anglo male, and all four finalists interviewed were women. *See* Peter Baker, *Court Choice Pushes Issue of "Identity Politics" Back to Forefront*, N.Y. Times, May 31, 2009, at A20. President Obama's selection of Justice Sotomayor touched off intense criticism, with some critics calling her a reverse racist because of remarks she had made years earlier at Berkeley, which are excerpted in Chapter 2 (see pages 44–49), referring to how she would hope that "a wise Latina woman with the richness of her experiences would more often than not reach a better conclusion than a white male who hasn't lived that life." Sonia Sotomayor, *A Latina Judge's Voice*, 13 Berkeley La Raza L.J. 87 (2002); *see also* Peter Baker & Neil A. Lewis, *Republicans Press Judge About Bias and Activism*, N.Y. Times, July 15, 2009, at A1 (describing the controversy that Sotomayor's "wise Latina" remarks created during her confirmation proceedings). Responding to the firestorm over her "wise Latina" comment, Sotomayor stressed her objectivity during her confirmation hearing, stating that she does not base her judgments on personal experiences, biases, or feelings. The whole debate raised broad questions about whether personal experiences will necessarily color how a judge views the law, or whether they should. Do you think judges can or should divorce their personal experiences from judging? Why or why not?

7. Should the number of Supreme Court Justices be expanded beyond nine in order to create new seats to increase the representation of various demographic groups on the Court? This has been proposed by at least one scholar. *See* Angela Onwuachi-Willig, *Representative Government, Representative Court? The Supreme Court as a Representative Body*, 90 Minn. L. Rev. 1252, 1258 (2006) (arguing that "the Court should be a demographically representative body" and proposing that the number of Justices be expanded to increase the representativeness of the Court). What objections do you think such a proposal might face?

2. The Law Clerks

Much like the Justices sitting on the Court, the law clerks hired by the Justices historically have been a fairly homogeneous group, largely consisting of white males from Ivy League schools. The following materials explore two different aspects of diversity among the Court's law clerks: (a) gender diversity; and (b) racial diversity. Subsection (c) will explore potential causes of the general lack of diversity among law clerks, as well as some possible means of boosting diversity among the Court's law clerks corps.

a. Gender Diversity Among Law Clerks

The Court's first female law clerk was hired by Justice William O. Douglas for the 1944 Term. Since then, female law clerks have become more and more common at the Court. However, male law clerks still outnumber female law clerks. In the 2002 Term, for example, there were 13 female law clerks out of 35 clerks. In the 2006 Term, the numbers were even more disproportionate: Women accounted for only seven of the 37 clerkships that Term despite the fact that just under 50 percent of new law school graduates in 2005 were women. *See* Linda Greenhouse, *Women Suddenly Scarce Among Justices' Clerks*, N.Y. Times, Aug. 30, 2006, at A1.

During the 2000-2006 Terms, Justice Breyer hired more women as law clerks than did any of the other Justices; of the 28 law clerks he hired during that time period, 15 were women. *Id.* Justice Scalia hired the fewest; out of the 28 law clerks he hired during the same period, just two were women. *Id.*

Consider Justice Ginsburg's description of the history of female law clerks on the Court. As you will see in the excerpt below, Justice Ginsburg was herself passed over for a clerkship by Justice Felix Frankfurter, perhaps because of her gender.

Ruth Bader Ginsburg, The Supreme Court: A Place for Women

32 Sw. U. L. Rev. 189, 193-195 (2003)

The very first woman to clerk at the Court was Lucille Lomen, engaged by Justice William O. Douglas for the 1944 Term. It happened this way. The nation was at war, and the west coast deans who recommended clerks to Douglas found no student worthy of his consideration. Douglas wrote to the Dean at the University of Washington Law School:

> When you say you have 'no available graduates' whom you could recommend for appointment as my clerk, do you include women? It is possible I may decide to take one, if I can find one who is absolutely first-rate.

The Dean recommended, and Douglas hired, Lucille Lomen. Douglas later reported that Lomen was "very able and very conscientious." She served after her clerkship as an assistant Attorney General for the State of Washington, and later became General Electric's counsel for corporate affairs.

Six years after Lucille Lomen's 1944 to 1945 service, Justice Douglas again thought about hiring a woman. He had in mind a "two-for." As he described his thinking:

> It may be that [my] second law clerk [Justices had just two in those days] should be someone who is an accomplished typist, someone who can a half or three-quarters of the time help Mrs. Allen [Douglas's secretary]. In this connection it might be desirable to consider getting a woman [law school graduate], a woman who can qualify as a lawyer and who can assist the regular law clerk for part of the time and help Mrs. Allen part of the time. If that procedure is worked out, the woman selected might stay for more than one year, say two years, perhaps even three.

Now before you put down Justice Douglas for hopelessly chauvinist thinking, consider this. Law clerks provide grand assistance, but their one-year tenure is fleeting. Our secretaries are the people who constantly keep us going. At the Supreme Court, they manage the office and contend with the ceaseless paper flow, mail and e-mail floods, sparing us from countless distractions so we can concentrate on the job of judging.

Justice Douglas never found his double duty person, and it was not until the 1966 Term, over two decades after Lucille Lomen's service, that another woman came to the Court as a clerk. [ ]I have it on reliable authority, however, that the idea was kept alive. In 1960, one of my law school teachers, who selected clerks for Justice Frankfurter, suggested that I might do. The Justice was told of my family situation—I was married and had a 5-year old daughter, also a husband who had just survived successive operations for cancer. For whatever reason, the Justice said "No."

In recent years, I am glad to add, the Justices have seen from the best evidence—law clerks they have engaged—that motherhood need not impede diligent service. In the 1998 Term, for example, a mother of two children, both under the age of 3, commenced a clerkship in my chambers. Despite her heavy work at home, she was always at Court when I needed her aid, and she proved to be a super efficient, most able law clerk. [The] [l]argest facilitator of that young mother's work was her husband, who was determined to make the year successful, and took charge of the children and household much of the time.

For the 1966 Term, Justice Black engaged Margaret Corcoran, daughter of a prominent Democrat, Thomas Corcoran, known around town as Tommy the Cork. Black was not entirely pleased with Margaret's performance. He thought she didn't work hard enough. One time, for example, she told him she couldn't review 35 certiorari petitions (petitions for Supreme Court review) over the weekend, because of plans to attend fundraising dinners with her father. She was, in these extracurricular activities, a dutiful daughter. Corcoran was a widower and sometimes needed a substitute for a spouse at special events.

In 1968, Martha Field, now professor of law at Harvard, clerked for Justice Fortas, and in 1971, Barbara Underwood, once a law professor, later a prosecutor, and last spring Acting Solicitor General, clerked for Justice Marshall. Justice Douglas took the lead again in the 1972 Term, when his selection committee engaged two women. He wrote when told the news:

> The law-clerk-selection committee has informed me that my two clerks for next year are women.
> That's Women's Lib with a vengeance!

That same Term, 1972, Justice White engaged a woman as a law clerk and the following year, then Justice Rehnquist did so too. The 1972 Term, Armstrong and Woodward relate in *The Brethren*, was not a vintage year in Justice Douglas' chambers. Midway through the Term, one of the clerks asked the Justice about a note she had received from him. "Excuse me, Mr. Justice," she said, "I've been looking at this note, I'm afraid I don't understand it." "I'm not running a damn law school," the Justice responded, "read my opinions on the subject." The clerk sent her boss a note:

> I'm very sorry I made a mistake on this case. I'm sure there will be other times this year when I will make other mistakes. However, I've found that civility in professional relationships is most conducive to improved relationships. You can afford to be basically polite to me.

Things went down-hill from there. Eventually, the Justice hired a third law clerk, a young man, with whom he had better rapport.

The other woman engaged by Douglas for the 1972 Term got along well enough with her boss, but had a problem of a different sort. She liked a young man who worked on the Court's staff, a man whose father served as messenger for Chief Justice Burger. The young man had been active in urging improvement in [the] Marshal's office working conditions. Douglas' clerk and the young man first dated, then began living together. He was black, she was white. He continued to press for better working arrangements for staff people. He was fired; she kept her job. The two eventually married.

After the 1973 Term, women law clerks no longer appeared as one-at-a-time curiosities. From 1973 through 1980, the Justices engaged 34 women and 225 men as law clerks. From 1981, Justice Sandra Day O'Connor's first Term on the Court, through 2001, 185 women and 449 men served in Justices' chambers.

Notes

1. One article concluded that the disparity between male and female clerks can be explained, at least in part, by the imbalance between men and women who apply for Supreme Court clerkships. *See* David H. Kaye & Joseph L. Gastwirth, *Where Have All the Women Gone? The Gender Gap in Supreme Court Clerkships,* 49 Jurimetrics J. 411, 432-433 (2009) (concluding that "women at elite law schools do not flow through the pipeline to the initial clerkships in the courts of appeals at the same rate as men" and that there is a pronounced differential in flow into so-called feeder clerkships, meaning clerkships with judges on the lower federal courts who frequently feed their clerks into Supreme Court clerkships).

2. For more views on the gender gap among law clerks, see Mark R. Brown, *Gender Discrimination in the Supreme Court's Clerkship Selection Process,* 75 Or. L. Rev. 359 (1996) (exploring gender preferences in the Court's law clerk selection process over a 35-year period); Lynn K. Rhinehart, Note, *Is There Gender Bias in the Judicial Law Clerk Selection Process?,* 83 Geo. L.J. 575 (1994) (exploring gender bias in the judicial clerkship application and selection process).

b. Racial Diversity Among Law Clerks

Like gender diversity, racial diversity among law clerks has also been quite low. The first African-American Supreme Court law clerk was not hired until the 1948 Term, and the second was not hired until the 1967 Term. Consider the following excerpt, which describes the Justices' record of hiring minority law clerks as well as debate that erupted in the late 1990s after *USA Today* ran two articles detailing the lack of diversity among Supreme Court clerks.

Todd C. Peppers, Courtiers of the Marble Palace: The Rise and Influence of the Supreme Court Law Clerk

22-24 (2006)

While few claim that the selection of Supreme Court law clerks remains riddled with gender bias,[11] the modern Supreme Court has been repeatedly challenged regarding its minority hiring practices. I have been able to collect data on the ethnic backgrounds of 1,507 former Supreme Court law clerks from the years 1882 to 2004. Of those, 1,424 (94 percent) are Caucasian, 42 (2.7 percent) Asian, 27 (1.8 percent) African American, and 10 (.6 percent) Hispanic.

---

11. Mark R. Brown, "Gender Discrimination in the Supreme Court's Clerkship Selection Process," *Oregon Law Review* 75, no. 2 (Summer 1996): 359-88.

William T. Coleman, Jr., was the first African American hired as a Supreme Court law clerk. Coleman graduated summa cum laude from the University of Pennsylvania in 1941 and magna cum laude from Harvard Law School in 1946, where he served as an editor of the *Harvard Law Review*. Selected to clerk for Justice Felix Frankfurter during OT 1948, his hiring was sufficiently noteworthy to merit mention in the *New York Times* and *Washington Post*.[12] It would be almost twenty years before Chief Justice Earl Warren selected the second African American law clerk, Tyrone Brown (OT 1967).[13] The third African American law clerk, and the first female African American clerk, Karen Hastie Williams, clerked for Justice Thurgood Marshall during OT 1974.

I have been unable to determine the precise number of African Americans or other minorities hired in the 1970s and 1980s, but it is clear that racial parity among Supreme Court law clerks proved more elusive than gender parity. In 1998, *USA Today* ran two articles on the Supreme Court by journalist Tony Mauro. He reported that Chief Justice Rehnquist and Associate Justices Scalia, Kennedy, and Souter had never hired an African American law clerk. Collectively, the four justices had hired 218 law clerks while on the Supreme Court. Mauro further reported that Justices O'Connor, Thomas, Ginsburg, and Breyer had each hired only a single African American law clerk since taking the bench.[14] Of all the sitting justices, John Paul Stevens had hired the largest number of African American clerks—three of sixty-one total clerks employed.

The Rehnquist Court's hiring record for other minority groups was slightly better. Mauro reported that Chief Justice Rehnquist and Associate Justice Scalia had never hired an Asian law clerk, while Justices Stevens, Scalia, Thomas, and Ginsburg had never hired a Hispanic clerk. In total, approximately 4 percent of all law clerks hired by the Rehnquist Court were Asian, and 1 percent were Hispanic. None of the sitting justices had ever hired a Native American law clerk. At the time of the reports, approximately 24,000 minority students (roughly 19 percent of all law students) were enrolled in ABA-accredited law schools. Given the historically high number of minorities attending law schools, Court critics were not moved by the justices' claims that qualified minority candidates were difficult to find and hire.

---

12. "Supreme Court Justice to Have a Negro Clerk," *New York Times* (Apr. 27, 1948); "Frankfurter's Negro Clerk to Be First in Court History," *Washington Post* (Apr. 27, 1948). Coleman also applied for a clerkship with Justice Hugo Black. In his application, Coleman writes: "Despite my training due to the fact that I am a negro I have encountered considerable difficulty in getting a suitable position. Your efforts and expressions in your judicial utterances led me to inquire if you would consider me for the position as your legal clerk." Coleman to Black, June 20, 1946, Black Papers. In his reply, Black congratulated Coleman on his "excellent" record but stated that the law clerk for the coming term "was selected some months ago." Black to Coleman, June 24, 1946. After his clerkship, Coleman worked on the NAACP's Legal Defense Fund with Thurgood Marshall and later served as the secretary of transportation in the Ford administration. He was awarded the Presidential Medal of Freedom in 1995.

13. Tyrone Brown did not apply for a Supreme Court clerkship. A Cornell Law School professor submitted his name to Chief Justice Earl Warren, and Brown subsequently interviewed with Warren's selection committee. As for whether race placed a role in his selection, Brown commented: "I would be very surprised if it weren't the case that Chief Justice Warren had said that it would be nice to have a qualified negro law school graduate on the Court," said Brown, "but I don't have any indication that Warren 'put out a net' for qualified black students." Brown downplays the significance of his selection, believing it is more significant that the son of "a common laborer" and graduate of Cornell Law School was selected to clerk on the High Court. (Tyrone Brown, interview with author.) Brown subsequently served as the director of the Black Entertainment Television and as commissioner of the Federal Communications Commission.

14. Tony Mauro, "Only 1 New High Court Clerk Is a Minority," *USA Today* (Sept. 10, 1998). The first article by Mauro on law clerk diversity had appeared six months earlier: Tony Mauro, "Corps of Clerks Lacking in Diversity," *USA Today* (Mar. 13, 1998).

Mauro's articles ignited a controversy over law clerk diversity.[15] Legal scholars now turned their attention to the lack of racial diversity among Supreme Court law clerks.[16] The *USA Today* series sparked NAACP protests on the Supreme Court steps,[17] the grilling of Justices David Souter and Clarence Thomas by congressional subcommittees,[18] the introduction of a Judicial Branch Employment Non-Discrimination Act of 1999 (H.R. 1048) by Congressman Jesse Jackson, Jr., the creation of endless clerkship diversity task forces by various national and state bar associations, and a February 2000 symposium on law clerk diversity at Howard University Law School.

Chief Justice Rehnquist finally entered the debate. In a November 17, 1998, letter in which he declined to meet with congressional and bar association representatives to discuss the law of minority law clerks, the chief justice responded for the High Court. Rehnquist emphasized that none of the justices screened out candidates "because of race, religion, gender, nationality, or any other impermissible reason."

Notes and Questions

1. Do you think that having a more diverse law clerk corps would impact the type of cases the Court hears? What about the Court's substantive rulings on the merits? Why or why not? If you do not think that achieving more diversity among law clerks would lead to substantively different results, then why push for diversity among the law clerks? Might there be other reasons for doing so?

2. What potential benefits might a more diverse law clerk corps confer on the Supreme Court as an institution? For some thoughts on this question, see Christopher R. Benson, Note, *A Renewed Call for Diversity Among Supreme Court Clerks: How a Diverse Body of Clerks Can Aid the High Court as an Institution,* 23 Harv. BlackLetter L.J. 23, 48-49 (2007).

c. Causes of the Lack of Diversity and Potential Solutions

What might be causing the general lack of diversity among law clerks? What possible reforms might help to increase law clerk diversity in the future? Many commentators asked these questions in the late 1990s after *USA Today* published a report showing that African Americans made up fewer than 2 percent of the 394 law clerks hired by

---

15. This was not the first time attention had been focused on the Supreme Court's hiring practices. In a 1979 editorial discussing the number of minority law clerks, the *Washington Post* questioned whether the justices truly comprehended "phrases like employment discrimination and equal opportunity." "Some Deliberate Speed," *Washington Post,* sec. A (June 12, 1979).

16. Examples include: Robert M. Agostisi and Brian P. Corrigan, "Do as We *Say* or Do as We *Do*: How the Supreme Court Law Clerk Controversy Reveals a Lack of Accountability at the High Court," *Hofstra Labor & Employment Law Journal* 18 (Spring 2001): 625-58; Randall Kennedy, "The Clerkship Question and the Court," *American Lawyer* (Apr. 1999): 114-15; Trevor W. Coleman, "Supreme Bias," *Emerge* (July-Aug. 1999): 59-61; Laura Gatland, "A Clerkship for White Males Only," *Student Lawyer* (Oct. 1999): 34-39; William Raspberry, "Clerks and Color," *Washington Post,* sec. C (Dec. 13, 1998).

17. Michael A. Fletcher, "As Term Opens, Lack of Diversity Is Decried," *Washington Post,* sec. A (Oct. 6, 1998).

18. Joan Biskupic, "In Testimony, Justices Defend Court's Hiring Practices," *Washington Post,* sec. A (Mar. 11, 1999); Joan Biskupic, "Two Justices Defend Lack of Minority Court Clerks," *Washington Post,* sec. A (Mar. 6, 2000). At the March 1999 hearing before a House Appropriations subcommittee, Justice Clarence Thomas commented that while the justices wanted to hire more minority clerks, "At this level you just can't take chances." Biskupic, "In Testimony," 1999.

the nine Justices then on the Court during their respective tenures, and that women represented only 25 percent of the total. *See* Tony Mauro, *Corps of Clerks Lacking in Diversity,* USA Today, Mar. 13, 1998, at 12A.

The materials that follow include Justices Souter's and Thomas's views on law clerk diversity, which were expressed during a 1999 congressional subcommittee hearing, as well as the views of two former Supreme Court clerks who wrote an article exploring possible reform.

Hearings Before a Subcomm. of the Comm. on Appropriations H.R., Subcomm. on the Departments of Commerce, Justice, and State, The Judiciary, and Related Agencies, Comm. on Appropriations, 106th Cong.

36-40 (1999)

MR. [JULIAN C.] DIXON [OF CALIFORNIA]:   . . . I certainly join the members of the committee in welcoming you, Mr. Justice Souter and Mr. Justice Thomas. I want to raise an issue that I hope that you are familiar with. It is based on a series of articles that appeared in the *USA Today* and the *Los Angeles Times* and I think several other newspapers. I certainly understand the idea of separation of powers and know that you can only speak about this within limits, but I do feel that . . . there will be discussions about the representation of women and minorities as it relates to the hiring of law clerks. I understand that it is not the Court as a whole that does that, but each Justice is responsible for the selection of their own law clerks.

So my first question is, in the general nature is this codified somewhere? Are there some Court rules that lay out the procedures that are to be followed, or does each Justice have within his own discretion the ability to hire whomever they want?

JUSTICE SOUTER: No, that is an issue that is left strictly to each Justice. There is no Court control. Of course, we are aware of what the others are doing. We are aware of what the pattern is when everybody is finished, but the hiring decision criteria and their application are strictly up to each Justice.

MR. DIXON: So there is no point of reference as it relates to a memorandum of understanding as to how Justices will proceed?

JUSTICE SOUTER: No, there is not.

MR. DIXON: I am wondering if, Justice Souter, you would describe to me the process that you use in this process.

JUSTICE SOUTER: I think in many respects what I do is probably representative of what the others do. In fact, just to say up front, I think the only point on which we probably vary much is some members of the Court will hire two years in advance. Some like me do not hire until the late winter or spring before the term, but with the exception of that, I think the way we go about it is pretty standard.

You really can't probably understand the hiring process without getting into a little bit of the criteria that we all do use. Let me start with the criteria. . . .

The problem that we have in the clerk selection is the fact that the clerks are not—they are not trainees. They have got to come on board and basically be ready immediately. There is no break-in period. And given the work they do and their roles in the research work, you know as well as I, I won't go into it, but the need for the very highest of the high caliber is just unconditional.

We therefore have to go through a winnowing process vicariously. There is no practical way in the world that we could, for example, start at, say, the middle level of law school passage and try to identify people in advance that would be good prospects. What we have to do is basically rely on the law schools and the other courts to make a lot of the cuts for us. Nobody can seriously be considered who has not come to the very top of the law school classes in the most demanding law schools.

Secondly, no one can be considered, I think, for practical purposes today who has not had a Federal clerkship. Some of my colleagues—

MR. DIXON: I am sorry, I didn't hear.

JUSTICE SOUTER: Had a clerkship in one of the other Federal courts, the district court or court of appeals. I know that some of my colleagues have hired out of the State system in the past, and probably there will be occasional exceptions in that respect, but particularly the work on cert petitions in our Court is such that a clerk has got to come with a familiarity with the sort of bread-and-butter Federal statutory work simply in order to be off and running in time.

So there are two levels of distinction. Somebody has got to hit the top in law school, and out of the Federal clerkships somebody has got to hit the top there, too. We, for example, today have in excess of 800 Federal judges in the district and, of course, the courts of appeals. Each of them has several law clerks. The nine of us will end up with slightly less than 36 every year. So we have got to rely on the process of selection within those two levels.

There is also a third level of selection, and it is one of self-selection. I think my experience is probably representative here. I get between—I don't know the exact number, but between 2- and 300 applications a year. Well, again, bear in mind the number of Federal clerks that there are. There is obviously a lot of self-selection going on. It goes on in part because I suppose there is no question that some clerks realize that they are probably not going to be at the top of the eventual heap, and they don't apply. There is, I am sorry to say today, an increasing number of people who do not apply for clerkships because they don't think they can afford to.

MR. DIXON: Afford to?

JUSTICE SOUTER: A clerkship is not going to make you very rich, and these kids are getting out of law school today with debts that are appalling by our standards, and a lot of them feel they can't afford any years clerking. A lot of them, and I know of examples of this from circuits where I have friends, will not apply to the Supreme Court because they figure they can't take 2 years at the salary.

So there is a lot of self-selection that goes on there, but we all end up, I think it is fair to say, just as I do, through that process with about 200 to 300 applications. My first cut is made by my own law clerks. They know what I am looking for. I have got to have somebody with a demonstrated ability to research fast, to write coherently for the drafting work that gets done, and I tell the clerks to go through the resumes and take the grade transcripts, the accomplishment lists and get me the cream from that. They reduce it down depending—I vary from year to year. They usually reduce it down to somewhere between 25 to 50, and then I go through them, and out of the 25 or 50 I will probably select about a dozen to interview and hope that I can get my four out of the dozen. And as I said, with the exception of the timing, which does vary from judge to judge, I think that is probably pretty standard.

MR. DIXON: Mr. Justice Thomas?

JUSTICE THOMAS: Well, I think I differ just a little. I agree with Justice Souter. One of the differences at this level is you simply can't take chances, so we tend to be belt-and-suspenders people on this. I think we all live with the fear that we are going to have a clerk one day who doesn't work out, and at this level and speed at which we work, we simply can't afford a mistake.

I hire four law clerks, as does Justice Souter. There is a vicarious winnowing process, as he so aptly terms it. All of my clerks have clerked on the court of appeals. I think it would be self-defeating to take a clerk who does not have Federal experience when so much of what we do is either codified, or it is certainly Federal Constitution and you have to have a working knowledge. There is no start-up period. Our clerks come on during the summer, and when we come in in September, they have to be up and running. There is no window to learn. There is no learning curve. There are many of us who when we went to law school simply could not that quickly after law school be able to run at that pace that quickly. Well, these are the kids who are able to do it, and these are the ones we select.

We may also differ, and again, it depends on the member of the Court, on which law schools we look at. I tend to look beyond the Ivys on a fairly regular basis. That doesn't always show up in the hiring, but the effort is not to limit it to certain law schools. But there is nothing we can do about the kids who select out of the process for whatever reasons. I certainly was selected out by my performance in law school.

There are individuals with very heavy debt who do not apply, and there are some who just aren't interested. It is a lot of work and perhaps areas in which they are not interested in. And it is 2 years at low income, court of appeals at least, and then the Supreme Court at about $41,000, $42,000.

Beyond that, there is no manual. There is no hiring process. I tend to hire 2 years in advance. . . . I also hire clerks who have been out 4, 5 years, so there is no—some members of the Court hire clerks who have just gotten out of law school. I like to mix mine a bit.

MR. DIXON: I am sorry, Mr. Justice, you hire lawyers that have been out of school 4 or 5 years? Is that what you are saying?

JUSTICE THOMAS: That is right. It depends on the individual. I have one clerk now, for example, who initially applied to me in October term 1992, but could not—I had no room for him, and I asked him whether he could be with me in October term 1998, and he agreed, so here he is. I have clerks who have for whatever reason worked a number of years. That depends on the member of the Court, and it gives you that flexibility. I am more comfortable with clerks who have—some of whom went straight through and are younger and others who are a little bit older and who have other experiences. But they are all uniform in that they are, where there has been class rank, in the single digits in class rank. . . .

MR. DIXON: I recognize and I think several of the *USA Today* articles have pointed out exactly what you are saying—that there are a lot of factors involved here. Some young men and women opt out on their own and may be very good clerks, but they have other goals and desires.

But let me ask you to comment on what I would call the old boy network here. I don't know if these statistics are correct, but the article pointed out that those currently on the Court have had 394 clerks, and half of those have come from four schools. If I were to take your testimony and put it with that statistic, it would suggest to me at least that it is only these schools that can produce young men and women, "up and running."

I know that, Mr. Justice Souter, you are from Harvard, and, Mr. Justice Thomas, you are from Yale. Harvard and Yale have the two highest number[s]. Of the 394, 92 come from Harvard and 64 come from Yale. University of Chicago has 47, and Stanford has 35. That is about half of them. So is the suggestion that only those schools can produce the caliber of person that you are looking for? Because some of the problem, I think, is the school selection part here.

JUSTICE SOUTER: I think to answer your question directly, no, that isn't the assumption. You will find actually a spectrum of belief about that. The Chief Justice, for example, said somewhere—I remember reading it. It had gone into print. His view was that although schools like Harvard, Yale, Stanford and so on are going to be stronger overall simply because of the fact that more people want to go there, so their own selection is going to be more rarified, he nonetheless believes that if you get to the very top of the classes in any major law school, you are going to find people who in quality I think he used the term are pretty fungible. They are going to be about the same.

I think he is right, and I would add one qualification to it, and it is a practical one with me. I have never been over this with other members of the Court. You may get a different view from Justice Thomas, but my qualification to that is this: I not only assume, but I believe that not only in the other large law schools out of the ambit of those that give us the great bulk of our clerks, but in a lot of smaller law schools, too, you will find people who are just as good as the best that I have hired. The rub is in finding them.

MR. DIXON: In training them?

JUSTICE SOUTER: In finding them. I have to work, basically we all do, on a probability judgment. Hiring for all of us, as Justice Thomas said, is meant to be a risk-free business. We cannot afford a mistake. I know that if somebody comes from Harvard Law School, Yale, Stanford, Chicago, the ones where I tend to have experience in the past and from whose faculty members I get a lot of letters, letters that over the years I have assessed, I know who to pay attention to, and I know who to be a little bit wary of. I can make a sounder, less risky judgment than I can make if somebody is coming from a law school that I have not had a lot of experience with and whose references are from people whom I do not know so well.

And I think probably you would get universal agreement in the Court that if any of us was in a situation where we could be absolutely certain of our references from people who knew what we have got to have, that we would probably feel comfortable in going outside the more well-trodden paths, but absent that, I will tell you personally, I am not. I wouldn't dare to. . . .

MR. DIXON: Am I correct in assuming your comments are directed both to minorities and women? The reason I ask that is because it would appear in looking at this, that Justice O'Connor has done very well with hiring women as compared to any of the other Justices. So is it that she is particularly sensitive to looking for women? I mean, of her 68, 29 have been women, but the other Justices don't come close to that.

JUSTICE SOUTER: I don't know what she does. I don't know whether she looks specifically for women on resumes or not. I take them as they come. I almost always have one—last year I had two women law clerks. To the extent that they are looking out for each other, they have got a friend in my chambers, but I do not say I want you to give me, you know, *x* number of women within the 25 or whatever it is that you may end up, or 30 or 40 that you give me.

And the fact is undeniable that you get a lower representation of women in the applicants whom I see than you do in the general law school population, and I have batted this around with women law clerks, and male law clerks for that matter, but the fact is undeniable that it works out that way.

Jeff Bleich & Kelly Klaus, White Marble Walls and Marble White Males

San Francisco Attorney, April-May 1999, 17.

As long as the justices are not discriminating, some commentators have asked, what is the fuss about? They contend that, absent discrimination, there is no reason for any constituency to say who the justices should or shouldn't have to work with. The justices—like the rest of us—are free to hire who they think will do the best job and who they like to work with, as long as they do not discriminate on the basis of race, religion, age, ethnicity, gender or disability.

These commentators dismiss the notion that the courts should make a special effort to have a staff that reflects the racial make-up of law schools or the legal community for a couple of reasons. First, they argue, the tasks performed by law clerks require analytical skills only and race adds nothing to the qualifications of a clerk for the job. Second, to the extent that the idea is to have the Court be more representative, they point out that the courts are not supposed to be so. Rather, the Constitution assigns federal judges and Supreme Court justices awesome, anti-democratic powers and life tenure precisely to allow decisions free from the pressure of being responsive to a cross-section of the population.

On the other hand, critics of the hiring record say that it is not enough that the Court does not intentionally discriminate or that it has no legal duty to be more diverse. The low numbers of minority clerks remain a cause for concern—or, more accurately, several concerns, relating to the Court's legitimacy, decision-making, and role in expanding opportunities for new lawyers.

The first concern goes to issues about the Court's legitimacy. In particular, citizens who are forced to obey the justices' decisions might not perceive the decisions as fair or legitimate if they think the people involved in making them do not reflect the racial mix of society. While this argument may have some weight when the public talks about the justices themselves, it does not make a great deal of sense in the context of justices' clerks. The topic of law-clerk influence on the Court's workings has been much debated . . . but few would seriously argue that clerks are making decisions or that the public thinks this.

It is hard to think of an instance in which the public at large reads about a Court decision with which they disagree—but are bound to obey—and rage about the backgrounds or motives of those clerking for justices in the majority. To the extent that most members of the public think about the justices' staffs at all (which we would hazard to guess is not much), a decision by a particular justice is not more or less palatable based on whether that justice had a minority working in his or her chambers at the time.

The second concern is that—although interpreting law is supposed to have nothing to do with a person's background—there is some relationship between a justice's and a law clerk's backgrounds that can influence the quality of the justice's decision-making process. While almost nobody believes law clerks dictate the outcomes in particular cases, there is virtual unanimity among justices and judges that they value discussing cases with their clerks. Clerks' views do give the decision-maker food for thought and a sounding board against which to test the soundness of the judge's logic. Although on many issues there is no reason to think perspectives will differ depending on a law clerk's particular ethnic background, the Court does deal annually with important cases involving race.

The argument for greater diversity among clerks holds that in cases like these, and probably in other not-so-obvious cases, the experience one has as a member of a minority group might well bring a different, and potentially valuable, perspective to the table. There is no question that this argument has some force. The amount of force, however, depends on how significant one thinks race is in shaping opinions, informing debate and influencing judgments of an individual justice.

Finally, the third concern is that even if hiring a minority will not make a big difference for the Court, it makes a huge difference for the clerk who gets the Supreme Court "credential." While a Supreme Court clerkship does not guarantee success in the legal profession, it is fair to say that it doesn't hurt. A disproportionate share of law professors at major law schools clerked, for example. Former clerks occupy prominent positions in the bar. . . . And then there are the "perks" former clerks enjoy. Signing bonuses paid to clerks at private law firms these days are rapidly eclipsing what the average American family makes in a year (much to the chagrin of those of us from the old, low-bonus days).

Given the benefits of clerking, some have argued that justices should assure that these benefits are spread around more. Justices have the luxury of choosing from a large group of "eligible" people each year, and there is no doubt that there are a lot more than 48 law students qualified to do the job in any given year. Accordingly, as long as the justices are not going to have to compromise getting a qualified clerk, they might as well think about giving a boost to people they think might be good mentors and role models for future lawyers or may help rectify economic disparities among minority and non-minority lawyers.

Again, the strength of this argument depends, in particular, on the importance one attaches to the goals of mentoring and whether one thinks it is fair to have justices make judgments based not solely on what they know a person has done, but also on vague predictions about what that person might do in the future. . . .

Given the different views people have about whether and why justices should try to hire more minority clerks, no one can agree on whether the relative lack of diversity among clerks is an institutional problem or merely a reflection of broader social ills. There is still less consensus about how to deal with the problem, even by people who firmly believe there is a problem.

The truth is that, for whatever reason, the competitive applicant pool over the past few years has not been terribly diverse. As Justice O'Connor explained, the justices "try to get the best" they can. What does "the best" mean in this context? The chief justice explained in his letter to members of Congress that the justices generally "select as clerks those who have very strong academic backgrounds, and have had previously successful law clerk experience, most often in the federal courts."

The fact is that, historically, the pool comprising the top dozen or so graduates from the nation's most elite law schools—Harvard, Yale, Chicago—has not been terribly diverse. Rehnquist, in his letter, expressed optimism that "as the demographic makeup of this pool changes, it seems entirely likely that the underrepresentation of minorities [serving as clerks at the Court] will also change." (Similar to the change in demographic makeup of women, who only a few decades ago were relatively scarce in law schools and had no representation in the clerkship ranks, and today comprise between a third and a half of the students at most top schools and consistently account for a third of clerks.)

Because the top law schools . . . have failed to yield many eligible candidates, much of the current debate has focused on whether the individual justices have drawn from too small a group of schools. In particular, some have urged the justices to expand the pool rather than wait for the current pool to become more diverse. One proposal along these lines, advocated by the president of Michigan's Thomas Cooley Law School would have the deans at each of the nation's 175 accredited law schools nominate one member of their graduating class for a national "dean's list" of available candidates for Supreme Court clerkships. Unfortunately, this sort of proposal does not seem practical or likely to do any real good improving the quality and diversity of the clerkship ranks.

In the first place, delegating "kingmaker" (or "queen-maker") authority to law school deans might, if anything, produce a less-diverse applicant pool. Already it is the case that at many law schools, deans and top professors back their prize candidates for clerkships at the Court, a process that causes much resentment among the "unchosen" and (to date, at least) has not produced a particularly diverse applicant pool.

More fundamentally, though, it is hard to believe any justice (or judge, for that matter) would be willing to allow anyone to limit the available field of applicants. Hiring a confidential assistant to work on sensitive matters is a delicate relationship and justices would no doubt resist being told that they cannot hire someone not approved by a law school dean to perform this task. This resistance would be exacerbated by the tendency of life-tenured judges to play by someone else's arbitrary rules (as evidenced by their annual inability to follow deadlines in the clerkship application process). Most importantly, however, justices and deans will not always value the same qualities in clerkship applicants. Beyond raw academic achievement—that is, high grades—different justices (and judges) may want different talents from their law clerks. Some value speed in turning out written work; others, who enjoy the sword fight of legal argument, might value ideological sparring partners; still others may want clerks with superior research skills.

Finally, expanding the applicant pool is no guarantee. As noted, Rehnquist, who has expressed interest in hiring a diverse group—and has hired clerks from such nontraditional "feeder" schools as the University of Missouri, University of Kentucky, University of Miami, University of Alabama, Boston University, University of Indiana and University of North Carolina—has received relatively few applications from African-Americans and has never had an African-American clerk.

In the end, the problem may be that the issue simply goes beyond the Court's doors. To the extent that our education systems are not preparing or encouraging talented minority students to attend and excel at top law schools, the most competitive ranks of the legal profession will continue to remain predominantly white. This will be true of the Court as much as it is true of law firms and law school faculties.

Notes and Questions

1. What do you think is causing the lack of diversity among law clerks? Chief Justice William Rehnquist once blamed the pool of top law school graduates from which the Court draws its candidates. Specifically, he explained that the Justices pick their clerks from those with the very best academic backgrounds and from those with prior clerkships, and he noted that the underrepresentation of minority clerks at the Supreme Court might change as the pool of top applicants to the Court changes. *See* Tony Mauro, *Rehnquist Blames Grad Pool for Lack of Diversity,* USA Today, Dec. 8, 1998, at 3A. Justice Thomas made a related point, reportedly suggesting that much of the responsibility rests with appeals court judges who send their law clerks to the Supreme Court. *See* Tony Mauro, *Thomas Said to Be Frustrated by Lack of Minority Clerks,* USA Today, Aug. 5, 1998, at 1A. Do you agree with Chief Justice Rehnquist's and Justice Thomas's explanations?

2. In 2009, when questioned by a student at American University Washington College of Law about obtaining Supreme Court clerkships, Justice Scalia said: "By and large, I'm going to be picking from the law schools that basically are the hardest to get into. They admit the best and the brightest, and they may not teach very well, but you can't make a sow's ear out of a silk purse." Anna Persky Stolley, *Shedding Tiers: Look Out, Harvard: Seton Hall Grad Makes It to Clerk Status,* 95 A.B.A. J. 22 (2009). Justice Scalia's professed preference for elite law school graduates seems to be shared by others on the Court. Indeed, from 1986 to 2004, seven elite law schools (Harvard, Yale, Chicago, New York University, Stanford, Michigan, and Virginia) contributed approximately 80 percent of all of the Supreme Court's law clerks. *See* Todd C. Peppers, *Courtiers of the Marble Palace: The Rise and Influence of the Supreme Court Law Clerk* 23-31 (2006).

What might be causing this lack of academic diversity among law clerks? Consider the possibility that the Justices select candidates from elite schools because that is where they have friends (and perhaps former colleagues) on the faculty. If you were a Justice hiring a law clerk, would you give more weight to recommendations from law professors that you knew and trusted? For example, if you were Justice Kagan (the former Dean of Harvard Law School and a graduate of Harvard Law School), would you give more weight to recommendations from Harvard professors? If yes, does this underscore the need for greater diversity in terms of academic backgrounds among the Justices themselves in order to yield greater academic diversity among law clerks?

3. Should Title VII of the Civil Rights Act of 1964, which prohibits employment discrimination, be amended to make it applicable to the judicial branch of the federal government? In 1999, Representative Jesse Jackson, Jr. unsuccessfully sought such an amendment. *See* Judicial Branch Employment Nondiscrimination Act of 1999, H.R. 1048, 106th Cong. (1999); *see also* Robert M. Agostisi & Brian P. Corrigan, Note, *Do As We Say or Do As We Do?: How the Supreme Court Law Clerk Controversy Reveals a Lack of Accountability at the High Court,* 18 Hofstra Lab. & Emp. L.J. 625 (2001) (calling for application of Title VII to the judicial branch).

4. What about creating a system to match law school graduates with the Justices, similar to the system used for matching medical school students with residency programs whereby both medical school students and medical schools submit rank-ordered preferences to a centralized system for matching? Would this type of hiring reform be advisable in an attempt to increase diversity among Supreme Court clerks? *See generally* Patricia M. Wald, *Selecting Law Clerks,* 89 Mich. L. Rev. 152

(1990) (discussing the "match system" in the context of hiring federal judicial law clerks).

5. Is the lack of diversity among law clerks really a problem in need of a solution? Put another way, given that law clerks merely assist the Justices, why has so much attention been given to Supreme Court clerks? Consider this response:

> The institution [of the Supreme Court clerkship] is important for at least two reasons. The first is spelled out in a recent empirical analysis examining "the extent to which both [each] Justice's personal policy preferences and those of his or her law clerks exert an independent influence on the Justice's votes." The analysis found that "clerks' ideological predilections exert an additional, and not insubstantial, influence on the Justices' decisions on the merits" above and beyond the ideological orientation of each Justice.
>
> A second reason to pay attention to Supreme Court clerks is that they exert considerable influence on the legal profession and the law following the conclusion of their clerkships. Upon leaving the Court, former clerks typically find themselves in positions of power in government, private practice, or the academy and use those positions to transmit to others what they learned at the Court. The legal profession and, to a lesser extent, the general public thereby share vicariously in the law clerks' experiences. Above all, law students acquire their formative knowledge of the Court from professors who previously served as clerks or from other professors who have read the scholarship of those clerks. Through processes such as these, the clerks play a key role in communicating how the Supreme Court and, indeed, the judiciary as a whole work.

William E. Nelson, Harvey Rishikof, I. Scott Messinger & Michael Jo, *The Liberal Tradition of the Supreme Court Clerkship: Its Rise, Fall, and Reincarnation?*, 62 Vand. L. Rev. 1749, 1751-52, 1755-1756 (2009) (exploring ideological polarization among law clerks and showing "how clerks who arrive at the Supreme Court already divided among conservative and liberal chambers go on to deeply polarized career tracks in the government, law firms, and law schools.").

6. Justice Lewis Powell provided the fifth vote to uphold Georgia's sodomy law in *Bowers v. Hardwick*, 478 U.S. 186 (1986), and he later regretted his vote. It has been reported that, at the time the Court decided *Bowers*, one of Justice Powell's clerks was gay, but Justice Powell did not know this. Indeed, Justice Powell remarked at least once to one of his clerks and once at a Court conference that he had "never known a homosexual." John C. Jeffries, Jr., *Justice Lewis F. Powell: A Biography* 528 (1994). One commentator has argued that this anecdote demonstrates "limitations on clerk influence, even where it has great potential." Christopher R. Benson, Note, *A Renewed Call for Diversity Among Supreme Court Clerks: How a Diverse Body of Clerks Can Aid the High Court as an Institution*, 23 Harv. BlackLetter L.J. 23, 48 (2007). The anecdote could also lend support to the argument "that, as diversity becomes more commonplace on the High Court, clerks and Justices will feel more comfortable discussing personal experiences and sentiments which may not be accepted by the majority of Americans." *Id.*

3. The Advocates

Much like the Justices who sit on the Court and the law clerks who serve the Justices, the advocates who appear before the Court also represent a fairly homogeneous group primarily consisting of white males. For example, one study concluded that, for the 1993 to 2001 Terms, only 150 (13.91 percent) of the 1,078 attorneys arguing cases orally before the United States Supreme Court were women, even though 2000 statistics put the percent of female members in the national bar at 27 percent. *See* Tammy A. Sarver, Erin B. Kaheny & John J. Szmer, *The Attorney Gender Gap in U.S. Supreme Court Litigation*, 91 Judicature 238, 242 (2008).

Contributing to this general lack of diversity among the advocates is the recent reemergence of an elite Supreme Court bar—a small cadre of experts who dominate Supreme Court litigation. The following article by Professor Richard J. Lazarus, who has himself presented more than a dozen oral arguments before the Court, analyzes this growing trend of elite Supreme Court advocates and highlights the small, clubby nature of Supreme Court advocacy today.

Richard J. Lazarus, Advocacy Matters Before and Within the Supreme Court: Transforming the Court by Transforming the Bar

96 Geo. L.J. 1487, 1488-1492, 1497-1498, 1501-1502, 1521-1522, 1564 (2008)

The fourth Wednesday in April is typically the last regularly scheduled day of oral arguments before the Supreme Court of the United States. For the most recently completed October Term 2006, the date was April 25, 2007, and the Court closed its argument session by hearing two hours of oral argument presented by six advocates in three cases, the first two of which were consolidated for purposes of argument. The Court's rulings on the merits several months later garnered, as to be expected, significant attention from the national news media and will invariably generate a spate of commentary in the nation's law reviews. What is wholly absent, however, from that media scrutiny and scholarly commentary is any recognition of the significance for the Supreme Court and the nation's laws, of the identity of the advocates who argued before the Court on April 25, 2007.

The six advocates before the Court on that final day of argument underscore the emergence of a modern Supreme Court Bar whose expertise in Supreme Court advocacy has quietly transformed the Court's docket and its substantive rulings. In sharp contrast to the typical attorney appearing before the Justices throughout much of the twentieth century, each of the six attorneys was an experienced Supreme Court advocate. The attorney with the least experience had filed briefs in twenty-five cases before the Court and this was his fifth oral argument since 2002. Each of the five other attorneys had all appeared before the Court on multiple occasions that Term and more than twenty other times during their careers. They included the current Solicitor General, who was arguing his eighth case during October Term 2006, an Assistant to the Solicitor General, who has argued thirty-six cases, two former Solicitors General, who have argued before the Court fifty and forty-six times, respectively, and one former Assistant to the Solicitor General, who was not only presenting his twenty-first oral argument, but had argued a little over a week before in another case.

No doubt today's Supreme Court Bar pales in several respects in comparison to the Bar's heyday in the early nineteenth century when a few extraordinary attorneys dominated oral argument before the Court. Arguing as many as three hundred cases, Walter Jones, Daniel Webster, William Wirt, William Pinkney, Thomas Emmett, Littleton Tazewell, Frances Scott Key, and Luther Martin, among a handful of others, presented argument in some of the young nation's most famous cases, including *M'Culloch v. Maryland, Trustees of Dartmouth College v. Woodward, Martin v. Hunter's Lessee,* and *Gibbons v. Ogden.* The Supreme Court Bar today is certainly far less flamboyant—one is unlikely to see a prominent advocate nowadays arguing, like William Pinkney, with "amber-colored doeskin gloves" on, or, like Luther Martin, intoxicated and wearing soiled, old-fashioned clothes. Nor would an advocate today be likely to replicate Daniel Webster's reported feat of "interrupt[ing] oral argument when a bevy of admiring ladies entered the courtroom to listen to him—and beg[inning] again from the beginning for their benefit."

Perhaps because today's Supreme Court advocates lack any comparable color, what has gone wholly unrecognized by all, including legal scholars, is how the re-emergence of a Supreme Court Bar of elite attorneys similar to the early-nineteenth-century Bar in its domination of Supreme Court advocacy is quietly transforming the Court and the nation's laws. The influence of expert advocates is likely greatest at the jurisdictional stage when the Court's resources are stretched the most and the Court most depends on the skills of the advocates in sifting through the thousands of petitions seeking review. But there is good reason to believe that their influence reaches the Court's rulings on the merits as well, just as it did in the early nineteenth century. Indeed, the influence of these new elite lawyers is no longer confined to advocacy *before* the Court. It now extends to advocacy *within* the Court itself as the modern Supreme Court Bar has become a training ground for the Justices themselves, as realized in the President's selection of the newest Chief Justice. . . .

I. The Modern Re-Emergence of a Supreme Court Bar

Strictly speaking, to be a member of the Supreme Court Bar today is not a big deal. Although attorneys routinely tout their membership in the Bar as a meaningful credential of distinction, the Supreme Court Bar is one of the least discerning clubs. The Court itself has characterized an attorney advertisement that emphasizes the fact of membership in its Bar as "at least bad taste."

The qualifications for membership are minimal: three years as a practicing lawyer admitted to any bar of any state, a certificate of good standing from that bar, sponsorship by two current members of the bar, and a $200 check payable to the Court. According to a recent American Bar Association survey, there are currently 1,116,967 licensed lawyers in the United States. The Supreme Court reports that there are 262,684 members of the Supreme Court Bar. Of course, relatively few of the thousands of members of the Supreme Court Bar have ever filed a brief in the Court, let alone represented a party in a case granted review or presented oral argument before the Justices.

Nor, until relatively recently, had those few members of the Bar who do appear before the Court formed the kind of identifiable group of expert Supreme Court practitioners, such as Webster, Jones, and Wirt, that dominated advocacy before the Court during the nineteenth century. The virtual monopoly that a handful of lawyers possessed over Supreme Court advocacy during that early part of the nation's history was largely the result of geography. Washington, D.C., was literally a swampland, and travel from major cities such as New York City or Boston was too difficult for leading members of their respective bars. That is why lawyers from Maryland, Virginia, and Pennsylvania enjoyed such prominence before the High Court. . . . But, for that same reason, as travel became easier, the Supreme Court Bar naturally and gradually lost its cohesiveness by the latter-half of the nineteenth century.

Throughout most of the twentieth century, there were similarly only a few identifiable, highly skilled individuals, such as John W. Davis, Charles Evans Hughes, Charles E. Hughes, Jr., Thomas D. Thacher, Thurgood Marshall, Erwin Griswold, and Archibald Cox, who appeared regularly before the Justices. Most lawyers with Supreme Court cases were newcomers, most likely arguing for the first time. But in no event was there a discrete, coherent group of private lawyers dominating the cases before the Court, capable of boasting a sustained, continuous Supreme Court practice.

The only significant, ongoing concentration of Supreme Court expertise during this time period was in the Office of the Solicitor General, representing the United States before the Court. Not coincidentally, Davis, Thacher, Marshall, Griswold, and Cox each served as Solicitor General. Attorneys in that small office regularly filed briefs and presented oral argument in cases before the Court. . . .

During the first half of the Twentieth Century, several former Solicitor Generals went to New York City law firms where they sought to establish Supreme Court practices: John W. Davis went to Davis Polk where he was the most successful, with 139 career arguments; Charles Evans Hughes, Jr., went to Hughes, Hubbard & Reed where his father practiced before the Court both after resigning his Associate Justice position in 1916 to run for President and before becoming Chief Justice in 1930; and Thomas D. Thacher went to Simpson & Thacher where he had a steady Supreme Court practice. But, by the mid-1980s, there was no coherent private sector Supreme Court Bar able to compete with the Solicitor General's Office. To be sure, there was a smattering of individuals, more likely to be affiliated with an organization like the American Civil Liberties Union or the AFL-CIO than a private law firm who had appeared more than once before the Court, but those non-Solicitor General Office attorneys were the rare exception. Indeed, in commenting on how infrequently he would see a private sector lawyer argue more than once in the same Term, Chief Justice William Rehnquist remarked not long after his appointment in 1986 that "there is no such Supreme Court bar at the present time."

Beginning first slowly in 1985, however, and then quickly accelerating, a private Supreme Court Bar capable of replicating the expertise of the Solicitor General's Office began to develop. . . . [L]eading law firms headquartered at several of the nation's largest cities can now boast of significant Supreme Court practices. . . .

This resurgence of a highly active, successful, specialized Supreme Court Bar has not been confined to the private law firms. In recent years, the states have responded in kind. Several states have created or rejuvenated the position of State Solicitors General modeled after the U.S. Solicitor General. In addition to having primary responsibility for arguing cases before their own state supreme courts, these state solicitors general have increasingly focused their attention on the need to possess expertise in advocacy before the U.S. Supreme Court. Accordingly, Ohio, New York, Illinois, Texas, Alabama, and others recruited to their solicitor general offices highly credentialed attorneys, often former clerks to U.S. Supreme Court Justices, to work within or run those Offices. These state solicitors general now routinely appear before the Court and are quickly developing their own expertise in High Court advocacy. Both the National Association of Attorneys General and the State and Local Legal Center also now commit considerable resources to assisting state and local governmental lawyers with cases before the Court.

Some organizations within the nonprofit sector, such as the ACLU, possess longstanding Supreme Court expertise, but most have little in-house expertise in

Supreme Court practice and, as a result, are highly dependent on the willingness of the private law firms to take on their matters on a pro bono basis. The principal exception is Public Citizen's Supreme Court practice, which has long provided high-quality assistance in the preparation of briefs and presentation of oral argument to public interest advocates with cases before the Court.

More intriguing still has been the recent proliferation in many of the nation's leading law schools of Supreme Court clinics, in which law students—closely supervised by law faculty and many of these same private law firm lawyers—take on pro bono cases on behalf of individuals and organizations. Within just the past five years, Stanford, Harvard, Yale, Virginia, Northwestern, Texas, and New York University have each established such clinics, all based on a similar model. Except for New York University's clinic, which just began in the fall of 2007, each has already had cases before the Court, with Stanford's being the first and the most successful so far. . . .

III. THE SIGNIFICANCE OF THE MODERN SUPREME COURT BAR FOR THE COURT AND THE NATION'S LAWS

The rising dominance of the modern Supreme Court Bar naturally raises the question whether there is any broader significance to that development beyond the implications within the legal profession itself. In the early 19th century, the general consensus was that the extraordinary individuals within the Bar, including Webster, Wirt, and Pinkney, played a major role in influencing no less than the development of the basic legal doctrine upon which the nation, two centuries later, is still based. Can the Bar today make a comparable claim?

Of course, the phenomenon of the re-emerging Supreme Court Bar is still too new for history to evaluate, but the preliminary indications are that the Bar is having a significant, long-term substantive impact. The Bar appears to be having a profound effect on the identity of cases on the Court's plenary docket, shifting that docket to topics more responsive to the concerns of private business. Second, there is good reason to believe that the new Bar is also influencing the Court's rulings on the merits. Better advocates not only win more often, but even more importantly, they influence the content of the opinions themselves, including the words used and the breadth of the ruling or, conversely, the lack thereof. In the longer term, it is the words that the Court uses throughout its opinion, rather than whether the opinion nominally ends with an "affirmed" or "reversed," that tend to have the most significant impact.

There is further reason to speculate that the rise in the professional prestige of the Supreme Court Bar may even be able to change the Court from within. Because of their renewed prominence as leaders of the legal profession, the new, elite Supreme Court advocates have themselves recently become an attractive proving ground for Supreme Court nominees, as demonstrated by the new Chief Justice, John Roberts, whom President Bush plainly picked based on Roberts's record as a leading Supreme Court advocate rather than his judicial record. Not only do their advocacy skills offer the potential of making them effective within the Court, but they can defend whatever positions they have argued as simply those of a lawyer representing a client and do not have the kind of baggage of controversial scholarly writing or judicial opinions that can quickly prove fatal to a judicial nomination.

Finally, precisely because of the potential significance of the modern Supreme Court Bar for the Court's docket, rulings on the merits, and even membership, there is reason for concern that the re-emergence of a Supreme Court Bar may disproportionately favor those monied economic interests more able to afford to pay for such private sector expertise. While better advocacy is generally a good thing, able advocacy on all sides of a case before the Court is the best outcome by far. . . .

. . . [T]he emergence of a modern Supreme Court Bar has the potential for being a positive development for the legal profession and for the Court itself. But it also generates a heightened responsibility within that Bar, as officers of the Court, to strive to ensure that all interests receive a share of such talent, including those not able to pay private market rates for expert Supreme Court advocates. Otherwise, the emergence of a modern Supreme Court Bar risks perversely increasing the advocacy gap in the Court between those who can pay and those who cannot, which would be bad for the legal profession, the Court, and its rulings. Both the Bar and the Court itself should take steps to guard against that result. Sufficient resources are present and need only now to be effectively exploited.

Notes and Questions

1. Who are some of the current members of the elite group of today's Supreme Court experts? As Lazarus describes, many of them are former Supreme Court clerks or former Solicitor Generals, and many graduated from top law schools. For example, on a list of current Supreme Court experts, you might find: Carter Phillips (Northwestern law graduate and former clerk to Chief Justice Warren Burger); Seth Waxman (Yale law graduate and former Solicitor General); Theodore Olson (Berkeley law graduate and former Solicitor General); Paul Smith (Yale law graduate and former clerk to Justice Lewis Powell); and Maureen Mahoney (University of Chicago law graduate and former clerk to then-Associate Justice William Rehnquist).

This is not to say that all members of the elite Supreme Court bar come from the Ivy Leagues, are former Supreme Court clerks, or previously served as Solicitor General. However, the exceptions are few and far between. One such exception is Thomas Goldstein. He arrived as a Supreme Court expert via a much less conventional route. After graduating from American University's Washington College of Law without the benefit of a Supreme Court clerkship, he built a Supreme Court practice for himself by surveying circuit cases for notable certworthy splits, chasing down the cases, and bringing them to the Court. *See* Tony Mauro, *Paper Chaser: How a Young, Self-Employed Lawyer Became the Best Supreme Court Litigator in Washington,* Wash. Monthly, July 1, 2004, at 8. Goldstein has orally argued more than two dozen cases before the Court. He is also the co-founder of SCOTUSblog, the leading blog that follows the Court.

2. Even the popular press has picked up on the clubby nature of the current Supreme Court bar. *See, e.g.,* Joan Biskupic, *Familiar Faces Revolve Through Supreme Court: Elite Lawyers with Ties to Justices Make Multiple Arguments,* USA Today, Dec. 15, 2008, at 9A; *see also* Joan Biskupic, *Lawyers Emerge as Supreme Court Specialists,* USA Today, May 16, 2003, at 6A; Tony Mauro, *At the High Court: The Chosen Few; a Small Group of Advocates Increasingly Dominates Oral Argument,* Legal Times, July 12, 2004, at 1.

3. What caused the recent reemergence of this specialized Supreme Court Bar? According to Lazarus, several factors have played an important role in "promoting and shaping the Supreme Court bar's development in the mid-1980s." Lazarus, at 1503. One factor might have been the entrepreneurial spirit of Rex Lee, an expert appellate advocate who was hired by Sidley Austin, a major national law firm, following his resignation in 1985 as President Reagan's first Solicitor General. Sidley hired Lee to create a Supreme Court and appellate practice, and Lee was "enormously successful" in this endeavor, which quickly prompted other firms to respond to "Lee's success with an unprecedented raid of much of the top talent in the Solicitor General's Office during the spring of 1986" and the creation of Supreme Court practices within the firms. *Id.* at 1498-1499. Lazarus also believes two other factors played significant roles in facilitating the specialized Supreme Court bar's reemergence: The first was industry effort to enlist an expert bar to achieve favorable Supreme Court rulings; the second was "the Rehnquist Court's dramatic shrinking of the Court's docket that, somewhat paradoxically, created opportunities for its domination rather than undermining the Bar by decreasing demand for its expertise." *Id.* at 1503-1504.

4. Besides the reemergence of the traditional Supreme Court Bar, another recent phenomenon is the emergence of law school clinics that litigate cases in the Supreme Court. For a detailed account of Supreme Court clinics and the challenges and opportunities that they face in fulfilling a public service mission, see Jeffrey L. Fisher, *A Supreme Court Clinic's Place in the Supreme Court Bar*, 65 Stan. L. Rev. 137 (2013).

5. Why are women so scarce among Supreme Court advocates despite filling roughly half the classroom seats at law schools across the country and representing one-quarter of all practicing attorneys? Some have suggested that the disparity is largely explained by the fact that women have faced difficulties breaking into certain critical career paths. For example, women at big law firms are still underrepresented as partners as well as in prestigious academic positions. *See* Joan Biskupic, *Women Are Still Not Well-Represented Among Lawyers Facing Supreme Test; Despite Gains for Female Advocates, High Court Is Largely a Man's Venue*, Wash. Post, May 27, 1997, at A03.

6. For another study of the Supreme Court Bar's elite community, see Kevin T. McGuire, *The Supreme Court Bar: Legal Elites in the Washington Community* (1993).

B. THE COURT AND THE PUBLIC EYE

The Court is often described as an institution shrouded in secrecy. Although the Court's argument sessions are open to the public, very few public seats exist in the marble courtroom. Many courtroom seats are reserved for the parties' attorneys, the press, guests of the Justices, and members of the Supreme Court Bar. Those few public seats that do exist are available on a first-come, first-served basis. Before a session begins, two lines form on the plaza in front of the Court: one for those who wish to watch an entire argument session and the other—called the "three-minute" line—for those who wish to watch the Court in session only very briefly. Long lines form outside the Court, with members of the public sometimes camping out overnight (or paying others to camp out for them) to get a good place in line. *See* Adam Liptak, *Tailgating Outside the Supreme Court, Without the Cars*, N.Y. Times, Mar. 3, 2010, at A14.

Furthermore, unlike many state courts that have remotely opened their oral arguments to the public using new audio or video technologies, the Court has been slow to embrace technology as a means of rendering oral arguments more accessible to the public. The Court began audio recording its arguments in 1955. After political scientist Peter Irons ignored Court-imposed restrictions—restrictions that made the recordings available only to researchers and scholars who agreed to use them solely for educational and research purposes—by producing a set of audio cassettes from the audio archives called *May It Please the Court*, the Court decided to lift the use restrictions on archived recordings. However, the Court imposed a delay between the recording of arguments and their distribution, generally not releasing oral argument tapes until the beginning of the following Term. It was not until 2010 that the Court loosened this policy and adopted its current policy, which provides that the audio recordings of all oral arguments heard by the Court will be available free to the public on the Court's Web site at the end of each argument week.

Also contributing to the veil of secrecy surrounding the Court is the fact that the Court's conferences where the Justices cast their votes are closed to everyone but the Justices. As discussed in Chapter 4 (see page 254), not even the Justices' aides or law clerks are allowed to attend these private conferences, which are held in a room at the Court adjoining the Chief Justice's chambers. It is not until a Justice retires or dies and publicly opens up his or her papers that the public can piece together a picture of what went on behind the scenes in various seminal cases by digging through the Justice's papers.

Further contributing to the Court's secrecy is the fact that the Freedom of Information Act and other sunshine in government laws do not reach the Supreme Court. This protects the Court from public scrutiny and disclosure requirements.

In addition, the Court's law clerks are subjected to strict confidentiality rules. The Court has taken various steps to restrict the flow of information from law clerks to the public. For example, the Court created a special, closed-off lunchroom in the otherwise public cafeteria to prevent reporters or members of the public from inadvertently hearing lunchtime conversations among the law clerks about pending cases or Court business. Moreover, all law clerks are subject to a two-year ban on Supreme Court practice after leaving the Court, as well as a permanent ban enjoining them from ever participating in any case that was pending in the Court at the time of the law clerks' employment. Sup. Ct. R. 7.

Together, these factors create a Court that is highly secretive, isolated, and sequestered from the public's view. This veil of secrecy has caused many legal scholars, lawyers, and legislators to debate whether the Court should be more open and transparent, and how such a shift toward transparency, if it is indeed desirable, might be achieved.

In this section, three current debates involving public access to Court information will be explored: (1) recurring proposals to bring cameras into the Court to televise oral proceedings; (2) questions surrounding the appropriate time to publicly release retired Justices' papers; and (3) controversies surrounding law clerks' duties not to publicly divulge confidential Court-related information.

1. Televising the Court

The United States Supreme Court has been steadfast about not allowing cameras in its courtroom. The Court's refusal to let cameras into the Court—despite today's technology-driven culture—has led to many spirited debates among the Justices, legal scholars, and legislators.

On the legislative side, numerous proposals to inject cameras into the Supreme Court have been made. For example, in 2010, Senator Arlen Specter—one of the most relentless voices pushing for cameras in the Court when he was in the Senate—proposed a bill that provided: "The Supreme Court shall permit television coverage of all open sessions of the Court unless the Court decides, by a vote of the majority of justices, that allowing such coverage in a particular case would constitute a violation of the due process rights of 1 or more of the parties before the Court." S. 446, 111th Cong. §678 (2009).

In terms of the Justices' views on the topic, various Justices have spoken on the issue. Some have been positive about introducing cameras. For example, Justice Stevens reportedly stated that cameras in the courtroom would be worth a try. *See* Henry Weinstein, *Televised High Court Hearings Backed: Public Understanding Would Be Enhanced, Stevens Believes*, L.A. Times, July 14, 1989, at I3. In addition, Justice Elena Kagan told the Senate Judiciary Committee during her confirmation proceedings in 2010 that "it would be a terrific thing to have cameras in the courtroom." The Nomination of Elena Kagan to be An Associate Justice of the Supreme Court of the United States: Hearing before S. Comm. on the Judiciary, 111th Cong., S. Hrg. 111-1044, at 83 (2010) (statement of Elena Kagan). Similarly, Justice Ginsburg expressed support for cameras, stating:

> I don't see any problem with having appellate proceedings fully televised. I think it would be good for the public. . . . We have open hearings. If coverage is gavel-to-gavel, I see no problem at all televising proceedings in an appellate court. . . . [T]elevised appellate proceedings can convey at once a picture not easily drawn in words spoken outside the courtroom. One can also view televised proceedings as an extension of the U.S. tradition of open proceedings.

Confirmation Hearing on the Nomination of Ruth Bader Ginsburg to be Associate Justice of the Supreme Court of the United States: Hearing Before the S. Comm. on the Judiciary, 103d Cong. 262, 576 (1993) (statement of Ruth Bader Ginsburg).

In contrast, other Justices have been much more opposed to the notion. Justice David Souter, for example, was reported as stating quite emphatically when he sat on the Court that cameras would have to roll over his "dead body." *See On Cameras in Supreme Court, Souter says, "Over My Dead Body,"* New York Times, Mar. 30, 1996. Justice Scalia has also gone on the record as opposing cameras:

> If I thought that cameras in the Supreme Court would really educate the people, I would be all for it. But I think it would miseducate and misinform. Most of the time the Court is dealing with [the] bankruptcy code, the internal revenue code, [the labor law] ERISA—stuff only a lawyer would love. Nobody's going to be watching that gavel-to-gavel except a few C-SPAN junkies. For every one of them, there will be 100,000 people who will see maybe [2] 15-second take-out on the network news, which I guarantee you will be uncharacteristic of what the Supreme Court does.

S. Rep. 110-448, A Bill to Permit the Televising of Supreme Court Proceedings, 110th Cong. 5 (2008) (quoting statement made by Justice Scalia at Georgetown University in October 2006).

The following materials provide some views from those outside the United States Supreme Court about the issue of bringing cameras to the Court. First, consider an essay written by Bruce D. Collins, Corporate Vice President and General Counsel at C-SPAN. C-SPAN has been at the forefront of pushing for televised coverage of the Court, and Collins's essay details the history of C-SPAN's persistent efforts to seek televised coverage of the United States Supreme Court's proceedings. Second, consider an excerpt from an article written by Robert L. Brown, an Associate Justice on the Arkansas Supreme Court, who contrasts the states' willingness to bring cameras into their own courtrooms with the federal judiciary's reluctance to do so.

Bruce D. Collins, C-SPAN's Long and Winding Road to a Still Un-Televised Supreme Court

106 Mich. L. Rev. First Impressions 12, 12-15 (2007)

In 2005 when Senator Arlen Specter (R-PA) first proposed legislation requiring the Supreme Court of the United States to televise its oral arguments, he resuscitated a twenty-plus-years long effort by several news organizations to achieve the same goal. For at least that long, C-SPAN has been ready to provide the same kind of video coverage of the federal judiciary as it has been providing of the Congress and the president. If cameras are ever permitted in the high Court's chamber, C-SPAN will televise every minute of every oral argument, frequently on a live basis, and will do so in its trademark format of no interruptions or commentary.

This commitment to so-called "gavel-to-gavel" coverage of the Supreme Court is one we make to our audience, and it has an extensive history. Only a few years after C-SPAN began operations, we produced our first Supreme Court oriented program with our full coverage of Sandra Day O'Connor's 1981 Senate confirmation hearings. Four years later, we launched "America & the Courts," a weekly program (Saturday nights at 7 p.m. Eastern Time) focusing on the judiciary with an emphasis on the high court. A few years later, when it seemed to us and others (erroneously, as it turned out) that the Court was open to the possibility of letting the cameras in, we formed an advisory group of former Supreme Court clerks. These nine, mostly younger lawyers had been on the inside of the less-than-transparent Court and were willing to answer our questions about how we should proceed in dealing with it as we urged the Court to become more open to public view. Each of them was careful not to divulge any confidences from their Court service, but as a group they were valuable to us as we decided *which* proposals we might make to the Court and, almost as important, *how* we would make them.

In 1987, the Court accepted an early proposal that allowed C-SPAN to originate live programs from the press room inside the Court building. This was a breakthrough of sorts, albeit a modest one, in terms of the Court's receptiveness to television cameras on its premises. For the first time, the general public was able to see what it looked like inside the Court building as they used our viewer call-in format to talk to the journalists who work in the press room covering the Court, to the lawyers, and even to the parties involved in the pending cases. We were even able to persuade several members of the Court staff to appear on television to describe their jobs and to take questions from viewers. We thought we were slowly but surely easing the Court and its staff into the television age. We believed that by originating television programs from inside the building we were showing them that television coverage could be achieved easily; that it did not disrupt Court operations; that the cables, equipment and power requirements did not stress the building's infrastructure; and that the public was getting an accurate view of the Court.

Early in the following year, 1988, C-SPAN CEO Brian Lamb wrote to then-Chief Justice Rehnquist to make a formal offer. He told the Chief Justice that C-SPAN would televise the entirety of every oral argument if the Court would permit cameras in its chamber. Lamb's offer was made partly in response to our awareness of what a few of the Justices regularly referred to as the "snippet" problem. They did not like the idea of their hour-long arguments being reduced to very brief "snippets" when reported on the evening newscasts. They believed such reporting was inherently distorting and the Court would be better off without it. C-SPAN's offer of gavel-to-gavel coverage was intended to highlight our network's unique format and our ability to televise the whole of each oral argument to an audience that would appreciate such coverage. We realized that the appearance of Court arguments on C-SPAN would not eliminate the Justices' "snippet" concerns, but we hoped our offer would at least mitigate them.

The offer was a long shot, but we hoped its comprehensiveness would appeal to enough of the Justices' concerns that it might overcome their hesitation regarding cameras in their courtroom. For example, we knew some of the Justices recognized courtroom video would generate educational benefits, particularly for law schools. With this in mind, we noted that C-SPAN keeps an archive of all its programming and regularly makes videotapes (now, DVDs) available to educators. We also pointed out that we would not televise the arguments only during the daytime on a live basis, but rather at various times of day when a wider audience would be able to watch.

Chief Justice Rehnquist graciously acknowledged Lamb's offer and said he would refer it to the Conference—meaning the rest of his colleagues. He later responded that the Conference preferred not to change its current practice regarding news media coverage.

Our efforts continued. Toward the end of 1988, C-SPAN joined an informal consortium of other news organizations (including still photographers who wanted the right to take photos of oral arguments—thereby putting the sketch artists out of business). The consortium put on a demonstration inside the Court's chamber to show exactly how televised coverage would work. Our group set up two cameras, one off to the side of the bench and a second facing the lectern from which the attorneys addressed the Court. The director and the switching equipment were set up in a hallway outside the chamber. The production relied on the Court's existing audio system and on available lighting—we did not set up bright lights that would be a distraction. After a 25-minute oral presentation during which three Justices attended (while seated at their usual places on the bench) they watched a playback on tape and asked a few questions. Nothing else came of the demonstration.

C-SPAN's efforts to cover the judicial branch continued. In July 1989 we became the first news organization to televise a federal court argument when the chief judge of the U.S. Court of Military Appeals (now the U.S. Court of Appeals for the Armed Forces) permitted our cameras to tape an argument on drug testing. The next year the same court (which is not subject to the federal courts' rules regarding television coverage) permitted us to provide live coverage of an argument challenging the military death penalty.

Up to this point we had thought the Court, as the iconic Highest Court in the Land, could be persuaded on the merits alone that televised oral arguments would be good for the Court and for the public. We began to think that in light of the Court's deep respect for and reliance on precedent, perhaps it would rather be a follower than a leader in opening the federal judiciary to TV coverage. So, in 1991 C-SPAN and other television news organizations proposed a multiyear experiment during which eight federal trial and appellate courts across the country would be open to televised coverage of civil trials and appellate court oral arguments. The four-year experiment was taken up by the Federal Judicial Center, with the Chief Justice's approval. At the end of the experiment, the official assessment concluded that the television coverage of court proceedings did not adversely affect the administration of justice. We took this as a victory and hoped for a loosening of the rules against televising federal courts including, eventually, the Supreme Court. Although a few of the lower federal courts continued to allow some television coverage after the experiment, its results had no discernible effect on the Supreme Court.

There was little activity in this area from the mid-nineties until the disputed presidential election of 2000. As we watched the Florida Supreme Court's televised proceedings on the vote recount, we realized the election, against all earlier expectations, could be decided in Washington. C-SPAN made an emergency appeal to the Chief Justice to permit televised coverage of the Court's oral arguments in the case that became known as *Bush v. Palm Beach County Canvassing Board.* We pointed out that in this case "the public interest in the Court and its role in our government would likely never be higher" and that "televised coverage of that role would be of immense public service and would help the country understand and accept the outcome of the election." The Court did not agree to televised coverage, but it did break with tradition by offering instead to release audiotapes of the oral arguments immediately upon their conclusion. This led to a media frenzy of coverage as every news channel, including us, put the taped arguments on the air the moment they were available.

A few days later when what turned out to be the dispositive case, *Bush v. Gore*[,] was to be argued, we asked for permission to provide live radio coverage, realizing that televised coverage was unlikely to be approved. Again, the Court consented only to prompt release of the audio, prompting a media frenzy similar to the one experienced days before. . . .

Although we continue to provide extensive coverage of the judiciary and of the Supreme Court in particular, we do so without any real expectation that cameras will be allowed in its chamber any time soon. Still, as recently as October 3, 2005, C-SPAN CEO Brian Lamb renewed the offer originally made to Chief Justice Rehnquist in 1988 in a letter to his successor, Chief Justice John Roberts. The letter described again that if given the chance C-SPAN would televise the entirety of every oral argument. In recognition of the dramatic changes in technology since our first such offer to the Court, we also offered our experience and expertise in creating high-quality and discreet video coverage of arguments should camera coverage ever be permitted. Chief Justice Roberts, like his predecessor, graciously received the offer but ultimately passed on the proposal. . . .

Robert L. Brown, Just a Matter of Time? Video Cameras at the United States Supreme Court and the State Supreme Courts

9 J. App. Prac. & Process 1, 1-2, 7-14 (2007)

The long-running debate over webcasting and broadcasting oral arguments in the Supreme Court of the United States has recently moved to the United States Senate. As the material collected in this article suggests, all indications are that the Supreme Court will continue to drag its heels on the subject. In marked contrast, however, state supreme courts have blazed a significant technological trail, with some twenty-one state supreme courts now offering live video webcasts of their oral arguments, and four additional states planning to do so in the immediate future. . . .

A. THE STATE EXPERIENCE IN GENERAL

So what has been the experience in those state supreme courts that have taken the lead and now provide video of their oral arguments for public consumption? At this writing, twenty-one state supreme courts make video of their oral arguments available, either using in-house production staffs and methods or working in conjunction with third parties, and most archive those recordings for future public access. This development is relatively new, but the trend definitely favors more states doing so, with four states primed and ready to begin in the immediate future. The public's response, according to those state supreme courts that provide these video broadcasts, borders on the exuberant. New Jersey finds webcasting to be "very positive for the court" and to provide "[g]reat exposure to the workings of the court." Florida pronounces the broadcasts "an unqualified success"; Minnesota terms the experience and the feedback "fantastic"; and Chief Justice George of the California Supreme Court says that its videos provide "the best P.R. you can imagine."

The primary motivation for state supreme courts to provide video of their oral arguments is to enhance public education about what appellate courts do. Part and parcel of this goal is the decision to increase public access to our appellate courtrooms, which Justice Ginsb[u]rg noted so appropriately when she discussed "long lines" outside the United States Supreme Court and spoke of "opening" that Court to the public. Rather than a school class of twenty-five children attending oral argument in an appellate courtroom, thousands of children can with a broadcast or webcast see a single argument at the same time. The Director of Communications for the New Jersey Supreme Court makes the point simply and succinctly: The proceedings are "public and important," she says, and because not everyone can be accommodated in the courtroom, "we air for all to see." . . .

B. Specific Examples: Florida, Indiana, Massachusetts, New Hampshire, and Ohio

Florida is a true innovator in this area. In 1997, the Florida Supreme Court made the decision to broadcast its oral arguments. The public television station in Tallahassee agreed then to do the videotaping and archiving, and the Florida legislature appropriated start-up funding of $300,000.00 in the first year. The legislature has continued that funding—to the tune of some $135,000.00 a year—ever since.

Today, the Florida Supreme Court's courtroom has four robotic, broadcast-quality cameras recessed into its architecture. The feed is sent to the Florida State University television channel but also to the Florida Channel, the state's version of C-Span, which reaches three million households. Any television station can downlink the live broadcasts free of charge, and many took advantage of this opportunity during both the Schiavo appeal and the 2000 presidential balloting case. In fact, one estimate was that the court's live broadcast of the arguments in the 2000 election case reached about fifty million Americans and an untold number of foreign viewers.

The Indiana Supreme Court, which first began webcasting oral arguments in 2001, has followed the Florida model with four remotely operated cameras in the courtroom. The initial set-up cost for the project was less than $100,000.00, and today the court is looking forward to upgrading its system and offerings. But Indiana has taken a quantum leap forward in its effort to educate the public about the judiciary. It has developed a "Courts in the Classroom" program, which has been a highly successful offshoot of its webcasts, making the supreme court an active participant in public education through the public schools' internet capability. The Indiana Supreme Court has also partnered with the Indiana Department of Education, Purdue University, Indiana University, and various historical bureaus to aid in the program's production and dissemination. Creative ideas such as focusing on featured cases of interest, dramatic reenactments of famous cases, and lessons on the right to trial by jury and the like have increased public understanding of the role of the appellate courts, while the webcasts also enable the court to provide [Continuing Legal Education] programs for lawyers and judges. Archived oral arguments collected in a database are available to lawyers for legal research and to the public at large as well.

A relative newcomer to broadcasting oral arguments is the Supreme Judicial Court of Massachusetts, which began its live video broadcasts in 2005. Like Florida, Massachusetts also archives its videotapes for future review. A spokesperson for the court says the program has been "a great success," indicating that she frequently receives "positive comments from lawyers, the media, and students in particular." The New Hampshire Supreme Court, using Massachusetts as a model but on a much smaller scale, began televising its oral arguments later in 2005, and now makes audio recordings of oral arguments available on the Web. The Ohio Supreme Court began a similar program in 2004, and tries to limit commercial and political use of the broadcasts. Ohio also makes archived video of oral arguments and other programs held at the Court since the spring of 2004 available via links from its homepage.

C. THE MECHANICS: PRODUCING A BROADCAST OR A WEBCAST

The way in which the broadcasting and webcasting is accomplished varies from state to state. Several supreme courts, like those in Michigan, Washington, Florida, Ohio, and California, broadcast through state public television channels or government telecommunication agencies. Some supreme courts, like those in New Jersey, Massachusetts, and Florida, broadcast in partnership with a university. New Hampshire has installed a camera at its own expense—the cost of doing so starting as low as $5,000.00—and feed[s] the video directly to its website.

The configuration of the cameras in the courtroom also runs the gamut. New Hampshire has installed one camera facing the court, while New Jersey has seven (one for each justice). Other courts, like Florida's and Indiana's, have four cameras. Those courts with multiple cameras typically provide for a close-up of the justice or the attorney speaking. Court staff, or hired personnel, operate the joysticks for the camera work.

The manner of the video feed varies considerably. It may fall to the government channel or university to execute the feed for purposes of streaming the video to the internet or to other stations. Mississippi, for example, allows outside media to observe and tape arguments for broadcast only after giving the court notice and receiving its consent, and allows only one broadcast camera in the courtroom at a time. Similarly, Ohio has required the media to form pooling agreements in order to limit the disruption likely to be caused by additional equipment in the courtroom should the Court's own video feed be unavailable or inadequate. Other states, like Alaska and Iowa, delay their webcasts.

Some state supreme courts, like Michigan's, provide that the Chief Justice may exclude coverage relating to sensitive subjects, such as the identities of sex-crime victims, police informants, and relocated witnesses. Reaction shots of audience members designed to sensationalize the issues before the court are universally prohibited. And any movement of equipment or personnel that might cause a distraction during oral argument is verboten.

D. THE RISKS

Although most state courts that broadcast or webcast their arguments have had positive experiences, several concerns remain. First and foremost is the impact of cameras in the courtroom and the threat that justices or attorneys might have a tendency to play to the cameras, or, at the very least, to be unsettled by their presence. Despite this concern, no state that currently provides video of its oral arguments cites grandstanding as a problem, and some court administrators, like the New Jersey communications director, have specifically concluded that televising has had no negative effect. But there are exceptions. An attorney appearing before the Ohio Supreme Court made reference, for example, to an argument "for your viewers at home." He was promptly admonished by the chief justice.

Unfavorable film clips that can be taken out of context by the media or (in those states in which appellate judges are elected) by political opponents is a second oft-stated worry about videotaping. The fear that a justice's political opponents might make use of unflattering clips, however, does not appear to be borne out in reality. Nevertheless, legislation is pending in Texas at the time of this writing to make political use of audio or video tapes of oral arguments a misdemeanor.

Examples of adverse political use occurring as a direct result of videotaping oral arguments have not surfaced in my research. In New Jersey, media reports about the Supreme Court may on occasion be unfavorable because of disagreement with an opinion, but this could happen "with or without recording." And in Florida, archived oral arguments on videotape are regarded as providing a check against the possibility that a justice will be misquoted, while attorneys appearing before the Florida Supreme Court tend now to be "far more professional because they know they are being watched by their bosses and clients."

Another potential problem that has surfaced recently is the open microphone. According to Judge Raker of Maryland's highest court, comments by judges between oral arguments, though largely inaudible, were on one occasion picked up by the court's sound system. Trial judges watching the broadcast wrote to the court, urging its members to be more careful.

Notes and Questions

1. Three arguments often raised in favor of televised Court coverage include: (1) the educational value of televised Court proceedings; (2) notions of transparency and open government; and (3) the success of cameras in courts at the state level. Which of these arguments do you find the most persuasive? The least persuasive? Why?

2. Of the arguments against televised Court coverage, some frequently voiced concerns include: the potential for adverse effects on judicial proceedings; separation of powers concerns; the potential for misinterpretation; security and privacy concerns; and costs and implementation issues. Which of these arguments do you find the most persuasive? The least persuasive? Why?

3. If Congress passed a bill mandating cameras in the United States Supreme Court, would this be a separation-of-powers violation? Why or why not? For debate on the issue, see Bruce G. Peabody & Scott E. Gant, *Congress's Power to Compel the Televising of Supreme Court Proceedings*, 156 U. Pa. L. Rev. Pennumbra 46 (2007); Bruce G. Peabody, *"Supreme Court TV": Televising the Least Accountable Branch?*,

33 J. Legis. 144 (2007); Brandon Smith, *The Least Televised Branch: A Separation of Powers Analysis of Legislation to Televise the Supreme Court*, 97 Geo. L.J. 1409 (2009).

4. Why do you think the states have surpassed the federal judiciary in terms of their embrace of new technology that enables televised access to judicial proceedings?

5. Beginning in 1968, the Court began transcribing the proceedings in all oral arguments. Currently, written transcripts are publicly released the same day the oral arguments occur, and they indicate the names of the Justices who posed questions to the advocates. This, however, has not always been the case. The Court did not begin issuing same-day transcripts until 2006. Moreover, prior to 2004, questions were simply noted as being from "the Court" on transcripts rather than listing the name of specific Justices. This allowed only lawyers witnessing the arguments, not the general public, to identify individual Justices' comments and questions.

Given that today's Court issues same-day written transcripts of oral arguments, should the release of written transcripts be viewed as a substitute for videotaped proceedings? Why might advocates for cameras in the courtroom not see written transcripts as an adequate substitute for televised proceedings?

6. In March 2012, as the Supreme Court prepared to hear landmark oral arguments about the constitutionality of the Affordable Care Act, C-SPAN petitioned the Court to televise the arguments. Specifically, C-SPAN argued that the case would affect every American's life, and it argued that the unusual amount of time—five-and-a-half hours—that the Court chose to allocate for oral argument cried out for camera coverage. The Court ultimately did not allow cameras to film the arguments; however, it did release audio recordings of the arguments on the same day that the arguments took place. Normally, the Court releases audio recordings at the end of the week when the arguments took place.

7. For a thorough discussion of the issue of cameras in courtrooms, see Ronald L. Goldfarb, *TV or Not TV: Television, Justice, and the Courts* (1998). Publishing his book in 1998, Goldfarb stated: "I expect that all courtrooms of the future—state and federal, trial and appellate—will be equipped with cameras." *Id.* at 188. Some 15 years later, however, his expectation of cameras in all courtrooms has not proven true. Do you think his expectation will be met in 10 more years? 20 years? 30 years? Or never?

2. Releasing Retired Justices' Papers

Besides access to the Court's oral arguments via written transcripts, audio tapes, and—perhaps someday—televised Court proceedings, another prime source of information about the Court lies in the Justices' own papers and records kept while sitting as a Justice on the Court. This material includes draft opinions, notes from private conferences, and correspondence with fellow Justices or law clerks. For example, when Justice Thurgood Marshall's papers were publicly released in 1993, researchers and members of the press immediately dug through the papers and reported the history behind seminal cases. *See, e.g.*, *O'Connor Shift Saved* Roe *Ruling*, Chi. Trib., May 24, 1993, at 3 (reporting how Marshall's newly released papers revealed that the Court came so close to overturning *Roe v. Wade* in 1989 that three Justices had drafted an angry dissent). The release of Justice Harry Blackmun's papers led to similar archeological digs through history. *See, e.g.*, Joan Biskupic, *Peer Back to Turbulent Times in Justice's Papers*, USA Today, Feb. 27, 2004, at 5A.

Currently, there is no judicial rule or standard uniformly resolving questions about how Justices' papers should be handled upon their retirement or death.

Rather, the Federal Judicial Center has made it clear that disposition of a judge's papers is up to each judge, stating:

> The chambers papers of a federal judge remain the private property of that judge or the judge's heirs, and it is prerogative of the judge or the judge's heirs to determine the disposition of those papers. Neither federal statute nor the policies of the Judicial Conference of the United States make any provision for the preservation of federal judges' papers. Judges' staffs or the clerks of court cannot determine where the papers go, and the National Archives cannot accept the collections as part of the records of the courts. Nor are court funds available for the preservation of judges' papers, and the federal records centers do not provide temporary storage of judges' chambers papers.

Fed. Judicial Ctr., *A Guide to the Preservation of Federal Judges' Papers* 1 (2d ed. 2009), available at http://www.fjc.gov/public/pdf.nsf/lookup/judgpa2d.pdf/$file/judgpa 2d.pdf.

In light of this wide discretion given to individual Justices and their heirs, it is not surprising that significant differences have emerged in how Justices handle their papers. Many recent Justices have chosen to donate their papers to a particular repository, such as the Hoover Institution Archives at Stanford University (where Chief Justice William H. Rehnquist left his papers) or the Library of Congress (where Justice Thurgood Marshall left his papers), subject to certain negotiated restrictions. For example, when Justice David Souter left the Court in 2009, he agreed to leave his papers in his home state by assigning his papers to the New Hampshire Historical Society. However, he also sealed his papers for 50 years—meaning until 2059.

In contrast, Justice Thurgood Marshall's papers were immediately released upon his death in 1993 by the Library of Congress—just two years after Justice Marshall retired from the Court. This led to a dispute between the Library of Congress, which claimed it was carrying out the Justice's exact intentions in immediately releasing the collection upon his death, and his family and the Supreme Court, which questioned the Library of Congress's decision to release papers containing documents from cases decided as recently as 1991. *See* Benjamin Weiser, *Marshall Lawyer Tries to Close Access to Papers,* Wash. Post, May 25, 1993, at A1; Benjamin Weiser & Joan Biskupic, *Librarian Rejects Restrictions; Marshall Files to Stay Open Despite Pressure from Court, Family,* Wash. Post, May 27, 1993, at A1. Congress noted the dispute, and the U.S. Senate Committee on Governmental Affairs held a hearing called "Public Papers of Supreme Court Justices: Assuring Preservation and Access." A statement made by Senator Joseph Lieberman at the hearing is excerpted below. It highlights some of the many (still unresolved) questions surrounding Justices' working papers.

Public Papers of Supreme Court Justices: Assuring Preservation and Access: Hearing before the Subcomm. on Regulation and Gov't Info. of the Comm. on Gov't Affairs

103d Cong., S. Hrg. 103-847, at 1-3 (1993) (opening statement of Sen. Joseph I. Lieberman)

The recent release of the papers of Justice Thurgood Marshall has brought into full public view a host of questions that has been left unattended for a number of years. I must say that I read with great fascination the series of articles in The Washington

Post based on Justice Marshall's papers that examined the Supreme Court's decision-making process in some very controversial areas such as abortion rights and civil rights.

As fascinating as it was to read about the discussions and negotiations in chambers . . . I must say that I read with a certain discomfort, two kinds of discomfort. The first was that as fascinated as I was and as much as I learned, I felt, in some senses, as if I had been—as if the curtain separating me and the public from the inner world of the Supreme Court had been pulled back and I had been let in, much to my surprise, to the inner workings of the Court. In some senses, I will own up to having felt, if I may use this term, something like a judicial peeping tom.

Perhaps that is because I approach these papers as a lawyer, as an occasional litigator, as an admirer—one might almost say a devoted fan—of the Supreme Court. On the other hand, I felt a very different kind of discomfort as I thought about the dispute that followed the release of Justice Marshall's papers, and that was that they may not have ever been released at all. Indeed, they may not have ever been preserved to be published and available for scholars, researchers and journalists. . . .

. . . [T]he Marshall papers episode, in addition to raising questions such as those that I myself felt as I watched it unfold, I think shows the need for some set of ground rules to govern preservation of, and access to, a Supreme Court Justice's working papers. . . .

Now, the hearing this morning is designed to consider a number of questions that are related to the preservation and publication of judicial records. First, how, through rules of the Court or otherwise, perhaps through legislation, can we be assured that the drafts and work products related to the business of the Court are preserved for posterity? Second, is it prudent to continue to rely on individual Justices, their estates and institutions to which Justices may have donated papers to weigh adequately the competing interests surrounding record preservation and disclosure and to set the terms and conditions of such preservation and disclosure?

At present, for instance, the archivist receiving the donation is bound by the wishes of the donor. There are no fixed rules. Who, then, should write the rules if there should be rules? If Congress does, is this too invasive an act, given separation of powers considerations? If the Court sets the rules, will they be adequately enforceable against third parties or against successors?

And third, if ground rules are needed, what is the right balance between the interest of the public in access and the interest of sitting Justices and the Court as an institution in safeguarding the deliberative process? In fact, if I may just explain a little bit for a moment the unease I felt about the Marshall papers. It was that not only was Justice Marshall, in his papers, revealing to us the thought process that he was going through. But he was also revealing his own interpretation or recording of the thought processes of some of his colleagues, some of whom are still sitting on the bench, and considering areas of case law that he comments on and that are still developing.

What other interests, such as the interest of the parties to the litigation, are implicated by disclosure of predecisional work of sitting Justices and how should these interests be accommodated? If restrictions on access are set, how long should they run, given the long lifespan of issues before the Supreme Court?

Notes and Questions

1. Should Congress pass legislation dictating how retired Justices' papers are to be handled for the sake of uniform release? For one voice, see Kathryn A. Watts, *Judges and Their Papers*, 88 N.Y.U. L. Rev. _____ (forthcoming 2013) (arguing that Congress should declare judicial papers to be public property but should leave the details concerning preservation and release of the papers up to the judiciary). Would such legislative action raise separation-of-powers concerns? Alternatively, should the Court itself adopt a rule governing public release of the Justices' papers? What might such a rule look like in terms of time and access restrictions?

2. Currently, presidential and judicial papers are not treated similarly because of a federal statute—the Presidential Records Act of 1978 (PRA), 44 U.S.C. §2201-2207 (2006)—that requires former presidents to release their records. Under the PRA, as amended, the U.S. government asserts complete ownership of all presidential and vice-presidential records. *See* 44 U.S.C. §2202 (2006) ("The United States shall reserve and retain complete ownership, possession, and control of Presidential records; and such records shall be administered in accordance with the provisions of this chapter."). Upon conclusion of the president's term in office, the National Archivist is required to take custody of the records. These records are then made available to the public under the terms of the PRA, subject to certain exceptions. The president has the authority to specify time durations, not to exceed 12 years, for which access to certain records shall be restricted, such as records including "confidential communications requesting or submitting advice, between the president and his advisers, or between such advisers." 44 U.S.C. §2204(a)(1)(A)(5)(2006). Should judicial papers be subjected to a similar rule? Or are presidential and judicial papers sufficiently different, such that a rule would be ill-advised in the judicial context? Notably, in 1977, the National Study Commission on Records and Documents of Federal Officials, a commission established by Congress to study problems concerning control and disposition of federal records in the wake of the Nixon Watergate scandal, recommended that a Justice's working papers be treated as public, rather than private, property publicly accessible beginning 15 years after the Justice left the Court. *See* Natl. Study Commn. on Records and Documents of Fed. Officials, Final Report of the National Study Commission on Records and Documents of Federal Officials 22-27 (1977). Although Congress responded to portions of the Commission's report that dealt with presidential records by enacting the Presidential Records Act of 1978, Congress ultimately punted on the issue of judicial records. Some 35 years later, neither the judiciary nor Congress has adopted a uniform rule on the subject, leaving the ultimate disposition of judicial papers to the whims of individual Justices or judges. Professor Kathryn Watts has argued that judicial papers—like presidential papers—should be treated as governmental property. See Kathryn A. Watts, Judges and Their Papers, 88 N.Y.U. L. Rev. _____ (forthcoming 2013).

3. Modern technology has enabled wide dissemination of some retired Justices' papers. For example, Lee Epstein, Jeffrey Segal, and Harold Spaeth created a digital archive of many papers from Justice Blackmun's files. Their digital archive is freely available to the public over the Internet; it includes cert pool memos from the 1986 to 1993 Terms as well as accompanying docket sheets. *See* Lee Epstein, Jeffrey A. Segal & Harold J. Spaeth, The Digital Archive of the Papers of Justice Harry A. Blackmun (2007), *available at* http://epstein.usc.edu/research/BlackmunArchive. html. The pool memo from the *Perreault* case included in Chapter 4 on certiorari (see p. 250) was acquired from this digital archive.

3. Confidentiality and Leaks

Those who work at the Court, including law clerks, aides and even the Justices themselves, serve as another major source of information about the Court's business and inner workings. Although those who work at the Court generally remain very tight-lipped about what goes on behind the scenes, leaks sometimes occur.

This section will explore three prominent leaks. First, this section explores revelations about the Court made by Edward Lazarus, a former law clerk to Justice Harry Blackmun, in *Closed Chambers: The First Eyewitness Account of the Epic Struggles Inside the Supreme Court,* a book which was published in 1998. Second, this section considers an article published by *Vanity Fair* in which various anonymous former law clerks divulged behind-the-scenes details about *Bush v. Gore,* 531 U.S. 98 (2000), the highly political case that put the Court front and center in deciding the 2000 presidential election. Finally, this section considers various leaks that occurred in the wake of the Supreme Court's blockbuster June 2012 ruling on the constitutionality of the Affordable Care Act.

a. Controversy Surrounding *Closed Chambers*

In 1989, Chief Justice Rehnquist helped implement a "Code of Conduct for Law Clerks of the Supreme Court of the United States," which imposes a duty of confidentiality on Supreme Court clerks. *Closed Chambers,* a book published in 1998 by Edward Lazarus, provides great fodder for discussion about what this duty of confidentiality should entail, as well as the purposes it serves.

In *Closed Chambers,* Lazarus describes a highly polarized Court full of partisanship and factions, and he includes many behind-the-scenes details about the Court and its inner workings. For example, Lazarus describes a shouting match between a liberal and conservative law clerk that erupted over a Court opinion involving abortion. The altercation resulted "in shoves and swings that drove them into the courtyard fountain." Edward Lazarus, *Closed Chambers* 419 (1998). Lazarus describes the goal of his book as "both an indictment—a revelation of how a Court can come to lose its essential character—and a hopeful plea that, as a new generation at the Court searches for balance, such character may be restored." *Id.* at 14.

In thinking about Lazarus's book and the propriety of Lazarus writing *Closed Chambers* after serving as a law clerk, consider a rather scathing review written by Judge Alex Kozinski, a judge on the United States Court of Appeals for the Ninth Circuit who, earlier in his career, clerked for then-Judge (now Justice) Anthony Kennedy and for Chief Justice Warren Burger.

Alex Kozinski, Conduct Unbecoming

108 Yale L.J. 835, 834-38, 840-42 (1999)

Until the publication of *Closed Chambers* last year, it was well understood that whatever a clerk learned about case deliberations during his term of service would never be disclosed outside the Court. This was made clear to the new clerks during conversations with the Justices, and it was part of the institutional ethos—the bedrock of assumptions shared by those working within the Court. During the 1988 Term, it was embodied in a written Code of Conduct for Supreme Court Law Clerks which provides: "A law clerk should never disclose to any person any confidential information received in the course of the law clerk's duties, nor should the law clerk employ such information for personal gain."

Edward Lazarus, who clerked for Justice Blackmun during the 1988 Term, pokes a sharp stick in the eye of this tradition when he declares on the front cover of his book that he has written "The First Eyewitness Account of the Epic Struggles Inside the Supreme Court." The point is driven home by the dust jacket blurb, which declaims in breathless prose:

> Never before has one of these clerks stepped forward to reveal how the Court really works—and why it often fails the country and the cause of justice. In this groundbreaking book, award-winning historian Edward Lazarus, a former clerk to Justice Harry A. Blackmun, guides the reader through the Court's inner sanctum, explaining as only an eyewitness can the collision of law, politics, and personality as the Justices wrestle with the most fiercely disputed issues of our time. . . . Unprecedented in its revelations and unparalleled in the brilliance of its analysis, *Closed Chambers* is the most important book on the Supreme Court in a generation.

While much of the book consists of sober, sometimes turgid, analysis of the Court's case law concerning the death penalty, the right to privacy, and affirmative action, the book is also a memoir of Lazarus's life and times at the Court. He thus fulfills his publicist's promise by disclosing many communications—oral and written—that supposedly took place within the Court during his tenure there. This raises a number of questions: Has Lazarus violated any ethical norms? Are the disclosures justified because they serve an important public purpose? Does the book contribute to our understanding of the Court and its processes? . . .

I. No One Here but Us Chickens

Contrary to the claims of his publicist, Lazarus has denied he did anything out of the ordinary: " 'This idea of absolute silence is really a myth,' " he told the *Washington Post.* " 'Clerks speak to reporters all the time. The difference is they don't put their names to it,' " he told the Associated Press. Lazarus has likened himself to former clerks who have written about cases decided during their clerkships, about the clerking process, or about their Justices. Lazarus also points to the fact that Supreme Court Justices have released their working papers, sometimes very soon after their death or retirement.

On this point—whether Lazarus did something unprecedented—the book jacket has it exactly right. The claim that "former clerks . . . routinely talk to the press" is simply not true; clerks may have spoken anonymously on occasion, but the overwhelming majority do not because they consider it ethically improper. In any group there are those who break the rules; they remain anonymous because they are doing wrong. Such surreptitious disclosures no more legitimize Lazarus's wholesale (and highly profitable) release of confidential information than petty shoplifting legitimizes armed robbery.

Nor can Lazarus find cover in the work of academic scholars who have written about the Supreme Court. Using one's understanding of cases as a basis for scholarly discourse is very different from quoting internal Court memoranda, describing the Justices' conduct, and telling stories about how law clerks supposedly interacted with their Justices and each other. Finally, Lazarus cannot sanitize his actions by pointing to the fact that the Justices themselves have released their papers. Justices enjoy a different status from Court employees, and it is misleading and presumptuous for Lazarus to try to shoehorn himself into the same category.

Just how far Lazarus has departed from accepted norms of law clerk conduct is illustrated by the fact that not a single former Supreme Court clerk has come to his defense—none of the three dozen who clerked with Lazarus during the 1988 Term; none of the ninety or so former Blackmun clerks; not even one of the thousand other living former clerks now serving in law practice, academia, and the judiciary. At the same time, a number of former clerks have responded to press queries or written articles expressing outrage. If Lazarus's conduct were benign and ordinary, as he claims, some of the hundreds of others who have served at the Court—among them Lazarus's friends and colleagues—should have rallied to his defense. That none have, despite repeated public statements impugning his honor, is a fair indication that Lazarus went where no clerk has gone before.

II. It's OK Because I Heard Myself Say It

Lazarus states unequivocally that he " 'violated absolutely no legal or ethical obligations.' " He elaborates upon this in his author's note:

> [I]n describing the private decision-making of the Justices, I have been careful to avoid disclosing information I am privy to *solely* because I was privileged to work for Justice Blackmun. In other words, I have reconstructed what I knew and supplemented that knowledge through primary sources (either publicly available or provided by others) and dozens of interviews conducted over the last five years.

The word "solely" is emphasized because it is crucial to Lazarus's ethical hairsplitting. Lazarus takes the position that he did not breach any confidences because all the inside information he discloses, he learned—or relearned—after he left the Court. In that respect, he argues, he is just like an investigative journalist who develops sources, conducts interviews and examines documents provided by others.

There are a number of difficulties with this position, the most basic of which is that we must believe Lazarus about where he got his information. But why should we? Lazarus provides no proof for the implausible proposition that when he tells us things he saw and heard while at the Court, he is not relying on his own perceptions and recollections, but on accounts of the same events he gathered from others. In fact, the book contains several passages where Lazarus reveals information he could not have obtained from other sources. . . .

But even if Lazarus did reconstruct everything by talking to others, it seems absurd to argue that a former clerk honors his own duty of confidentiality by inducing other clerks to betray theirs. Moreover, Lazarus admits he made full use of his insider status in piecing together his "reconstruction." In his author's note, he tells us that his "experience as a law clerk for Justice Harry A. Blackmun was indispensable" in writing the book. He continues:

> The clerkship gave me unusual access to sources knowledgeable about the Court and armed me with questions others might not think to ask. It also gave me a significant advantage in evaluating and interpreting publicly available primary source material about the Court, in particular the unpublished draft opinions and memorandum contained in the paper of various former Justices. Finally, the clerkship left me with specific memories and a general view of life at the Court against which to evaluate the information I subsequently gathered.

A little later on, he explains that he did his best "to sift out information that was not independently corroborated or inherently credible in light of [his] own experience."

This kind of "reconstruction" is very different from what an ordinary journalist would do. A journalist who set out to write an insider account of what transpired during the 1988 Supreme Court Term would call people who worked at the Court—primarily former law clerks—and try to get them to talk about their experiences. Since publication of *The Brethren* in 1979, former clerks have been especially skittish about discussing Court confidences with the press, so the journalist would have to spend much time and effort cultivating sources and persuading them to part with documents illicitly taken from the Court. Lazarus, by contrast, only had to call his former colleagues and chat. . . .

Lazarus's reconstruction also has a far greater air of authenticity than that of an ordinary journalist. This is no trivial point. An investigative reporter starting from scratch cannot be certain that any story he picks up is accurate or complete. Reputable journalists therefore require multiple sources or tangible corroboration. Lazarus by contrast provided his own corroboration; he himself functioned as an automatic second source. Readers, moreover, would find disclosures from one who was there inherently more credible than those pieced together by an outsider. Lazarus and his publicist play up this fact when explaining why *Closed Chambers* is superior to other books that have plowed this terrain.

Notes and Questions

1. Not everyone agreed with Judge Kozinski's scathing attack of Lazarus's book. Erwin Chemerinsky, a prominent constitutional scholar who is currently Dean of the University of California's Irvine School of Law, wrote a defense of Lazarus in which Chemerinsky argued:

> Kozinski's accusations are completely unfounded. There is little indication that Lazarus used confidential information that he gained as a result of being a clerk. Much of the new information in the book comes from papers that Justice Thurgood Marshall made publicly available, and much of the rest comes from interviews that Lazarus conducted over several years of working on the book.

Erwin Chemerinsky, *Opening* Closed Chambers, 108 Yale L.J. 1087, 1088 (1999). Chemerinsky went on to state that "if the claim of a breach of trust is based on disclosure of confidential information, that disclosure did not occur; if it is based on Lazarus's saying unflattering things about the Court, there is no duty imposed on former clerks only to praise the institution." *Id.* at 1104.

2. Lazarus himself tried to defend his actions, writing an op-ed for the *Washington Post* that was published in July 1998. In the op-ed, Lazarus asserted that "the Law Clerk Code of Conduct, including its confidentiality provision, applies only to clerks during their time at the court (to protect deliberation on pending and impending cases) and has no bearing on the propriety of a former clerk writing a book." Edward Lazarus, *The Supreme Court Must Bear Scrutiny,* Wash. Post., July 6, 1998, at A19. In addition, Lazarus asserted that the book was "a work of research and reportage, undoubtedly benefitting from the perspectives I gained as a clerk, but not employing any confidential material that I was privy to solely because of that experience." *Id.* Specifically, he noted that the source for most of his book was Justice Thurgood Marshall's papers, which were available in the Library of Congress. *Id.*

3. What is the main reason for imposing confidentiality duties on law clerks? Consider the answer that three former law clerks gave in the wake of *Closed Chambers:*

> There are, in fact, a number of very good reasons why Courts (including the Supreme Court) keep their internal discussions confidential. The first, of course, is that reasoned decisionmaking requires a free exchange of ideas, including ideas that in the end can be kind of embarrassing. In deciding whether material is pornographic, the Court had to watch some pretty gamey stuff and then talk about it. It is natural that judges would be less likely to analyze untested ideas, or to exchange ideas about experimental, theoretical or disfavored concepts, if they feared that these preliminary musings would be recorded and published. These fears are compounded by the fact that the people most likely to disclose unformed thoughts are one's detractors.
>
> Second, as a practical matter, clerks and Court staff receive information with significant insider trading value. It is not too difficult to imagine how knowing in advance how the Court will decide its upcoming local phone deregulation case could give insiders a significant financial advantage. In addition, even after a decision has been issued, information about a Justice's private thoughts about its effect on other cases would give some parties a significant advantage over others in framing cases or predicting outcomes.
>
> Third, and perhaps most significantly, the Court as an institution derives most of its authority from public respect. While certain formalities may seem arcane, the marble palace, the red velvet drapes, the black robes, the ritualistic intoning of "God save this honorable Court," and the secrecy of the Court's proceedings all add an air of mystery and formality to Court proceedings that helps assure respect and legitimacy for the Court's pronouncements. Because the Court lacks the cruder forms of persuasion (such as an army) available to the coordinate branches, the Court must depend upon the persuasive force of its decisions and general respect for the institution to maintain authority. The Court could not maintain the respect it needs if all its secrets were exposed, because no human institution (or human being) can ever consistently live up to our highest ideals. As Winston Churchill aptly put it, "no man is a hero to his valet." Confidentiality does not just protect the Justices, it protects the Court.
>
> Finally, even if one considers the reliance of Justices on clerks to be an "evil," it is a necessary evil. It is not reasonable to expect all nine individuals to examine carefully 7,000 legal petitions, review hundreds of stay applications and requests for reconsideration, digest several hundred more briefs in highly charged and complex cases, hear and prepare for 80 to 90 oral arguments, write dozens of opinions, and be thoughtful, meticulous arbiters in all of these matters without getting a little help. Justices need clerks to assist them in all of this delicate work and are entitled to expect the clerks they choose to function according to the rules each Justice sets for himself or herself. And of course Justices should be able to count on their clerks to maintain the confidentiality of these necessary disclosures.
>
> Interestingly, *Closed Chambers* does not directly quarrel with the notion that the Court is entitled to some confidentiality, or that the Court is fairly open about its decision-making compared to other branches. What other governmental institution actually goes to the trouble of explaining in writing its decision, including all of the points of disagreement? Instead, the book implies only that certain "corrosive" or "corrupt[ing]" elements need to be exposed and corrected: namely partisan politics and out-of-control clerks. . . .

Jeff Bleich, Kelly Klaus & Lise Earle Beske, Closed Chambers: *Has the Integrity of the Supreme Court Been Breached?*, Or. St. B. Bull., July 1998, at 15, 17-18.

For additional thoughts on this question that were written prior to the *Closed Chambers* controversy, see Comment, *The Law Clerk's Duty of Confidentiality,* 129 U. Pa. L. Rev. 1230, 1236 (1981) ("The necessity for frank and open communication in an atmosphere of trust is the reason most frequently given by commentators and judges for preserving the confidentiality of the inner workings of the judiciary.").

b. Controversy Surrounding *Bush v. Gore*

Another prominent debate involving law clerk confidentiality centers around *Vanity Fair*'s October 2004 issue, in which various former Supreme Court clerks from the Court's 2000 Term spoke, under the condition of anonymity, about what happened behind the scenes in *Bush v. Gore*, 531 U.S. 98 (2000). The article paints a picture of highly political maneuvering at the Court. Notably, the *Vanity Fair* article specifically highlighted how unusual it was for law clerks to talk, stating:

> The Court's proceedings are shrouded in secrecy, and the law clerks, who research precedents, review petitions, and draft opinions, are normally notoriously, maddeningly discreet. In addition, Rehnquist makes them all sign confidentiality agreements, then reiterates the point to them in person. A surprising number of clerks talked to Vanity Fair for this article, however. . . . To the inevitable charges that they broke their vows of confidentiality, the clerks have a ready response: by taking on *Bush v. Gore* and deciding the case as it did, the Court broke its promise to them. "We feel that something illegitimate was done with the Court's power, and such an extraordinary situation justifies breaking an obligation we'd otherwise honor," one clerk says. "Our secrecy was helping to shield some of those actions."

David Margolick, from David Margolick, Evgenia Peretz & Michael Shnyerson, *The Path to Florida: What Really Happened in the 2000 Election and What's Going Down Right Now!*, Vanity Fair, Oct. 2004, at 310.

The article received significant attention and was the subject of much debate; however, as one news article noted, the buzz focused less on the article's content than on the fact that some of the Justices' law clerks broke their vows of silence. *See* Charles Lane, *In Court Clerks' Breach, a Provocative Precedent*, Wash. Post, Oct. 17, 2004, at D01.

On the one hand, the *Vanity Fair* article prompted nearly 100 former law clerks and Court practitioners to write a letter, which was published in the *Legal Times*, asserting that the disclosures to *Vanity Fair* were improper and inexcusable and that they represented conduct that was "unbecoming" of any legal advisor who holds a position of trust. *See High Court Clerks and Appellate Lawyers Decry Vanity Fair Article*, Legal Times, Sept. 27, 2004. On the other hand, Edward Lazarus, the author of *Closed Chambers*, defended the actions of those former clerks who chose to divulge information about *Bush v. Gore* to *Vanity Fair*. Excerpts from Lazarus's defense are included below.

Edward Lazarus, The Supreme Court's Excessive Secrecy: Why It Isn't Merited

Findlaw.Com, Sept. 30, 2004,
http://writ.news.findlaw.com/lazarus/20040930.html

In the October issue of *Vanity Fair* magazine, David Margolick offers a deeply troubling expose of how the Supreme Court actually decided *Bush v. Gore*. (In that notorious 2000 decision, as readers will doubtless recall, five conservative justices stopped the vote recount in Florida and thereby handed the presidency to George W. Bush.)

The article is the first to penetrate the Justices' aggressive efforts to maintain the secrecy of their internal deliberations in this case. Margolick succeeded in getting several former Supreme Court clerks from 2000 to describe precisely what happened. Based on their reports, Margolick tells the disturbing story of how a highly polarized and politicized Court stumbled inexorably towards an intellectually indefensible decision—in arguably the most important case of our time.

The article shows that Justices Antonin Scalia and Sandra Day O'Connor essentially pre-judged the election case. It explains how, with a vital assist from Justice Anthony Kennedy, they drove the Court towards a decision handing victory to the candidate with whom they were politically aligned. And it reveals that critics' worst fears were <u>factually true</u>: Five unelected justices, by a single vote, hijacked a presidential election at least in part out of fear that, left unchecked, the Florida recount would put Al Gore in the White House. The Justices weren't applying the law; they were choosing a President.

Margolick's article has generated a firestorm in the community of Supreme Court watchers. Unfortunately, this firestorm has little or nothing to do with the article's extremely important substantive allegations.

Instead, the firestorm has focused on what should be a minor side issue: Were Margolick's law clerk sources, on whom the Justices had imposed an oath of permanent confidentiality, justified in breaking that oath to speak out about *Bush v. Gore?*

Former Attorney General Richard Thornburgh, former Deputy Attorney General William Barr, former Solicitor General Theodore Olson, and close to 90 former law clerks—mostly right-wingers—have written a letter excoriating the clerks who spoke to Margolick as traitors to the Court and to their profession. Several U.S. Senators have now gone so far as to call upon the Senate Judiciary Committee to look into these breaches of judicial confidence.

These critics of Margolick's clerk sources are asking the wrong question. Reasonable people may reasonably disagree over when a former clerk is justified in breaching his duties of confidentiality to the Court. Surely, a strong case can be made that Margolick's sources were justified in enlightening the American people about how five unelected justices, by a single vote, hijacked a presidential election at least in part out of fear that, left unchecked, the Florida recount would put Al Gore in the White House.

After all, *Bush v. Gore* was no ordinary case. And the facts the law clerks decided to reveal were no ordinary facts. To the contrary, the clerks chose to expose a Court that was teetering on—arguably even falling over—the brink of constitutional illegitimacy. And the clerks weren't the only ones who interpreted the facts this way: Several Justices shared their view.

But the real issue in all this has nothing to do with this particular story or these particular clerks. The real issue here is whether the Supreme Court is justified in its aggressive attempts to suppress investigation of its internal decision-making process. And the real scandal here is the way most of the Supreme Court press corps abets this enterprise by all but abandoning the concept of investigative reporting. . . .

Even in everyday cases—and this was no everyday case—Supreme Court secrecy is far more complete than necessary. Indeed, the Supreme Court demands far greater secrecy than that enjoyed by the elected branches of our government—when, given its unelected, life-tenured personnel, it ought to demand far less. . . .

Some claim that public revelation of the Court's internal deliberations—even years after decisions are rendered—will "chill" the free flow of ideas between clerks and their justices and among the justices themselves. This may be true to some extent: Some people may be less willing to share their candid views about sensitive issues if they know that these views will become public down the road. But this concern is easily exaggerated:

Just look at the executive branch. It has become commonplace for presidential aides and other high ranking officials to write memoirs including detailed revelations about internal executive branch decision-making. Yet open and frank advice-giving within the Executive Branch has hardly come to a grinding halt.

To the contrary, such firsthand internal accounts are generally considered an important tool for maintaining government accountability and for assessing, in hindsight, the substance and process of contemporary policymaking. Whatever minor chilling effect these publications may engender (if any) is overwhelmed by these affirmative public benefits.

Is advice giving or the exchange of ideas within the judicial branch somehow more fragile or more in need of protection than advice-giving in the executive branch? I can't think why.

If anything, executive branch deliberations would seem to be <u>more</u> sensitive than the judicial deliberations. Exchanges of views inside the court ordinarily don't touch on issues of national security. Nor do they involve the sensitive, strategic trade-offs that executive branch officials have to make with legislators, or between competing agencies.

Generally, deliberations within the Supreme Court focus on issues of high abstraction: How should certain precedents be read? What is the best reading of a particular statute? How should the concept of due process of law be applied to a given set of facts?

In discussing such things, will clerks or justices really start looking over their shoulders if they think their candidly expressed views may someday become public? I'm highly skeptical.

And perhaps if clerks do need to look over their shoulders, they should think about <u>why that is</u>: Is it because they know their views will be looked upon with horror and scorn by future generations? If clerks and Justices don't have the courage of their convictions—and the courage to make these convictions public—it may be because even they know, at some level, that their convictions are wrong, illegal or unethical. If they know their children—and their children's children—will judge them ill, shouldn't they take that into account? . . .

Besides the "chilling effect," defenders of Court secrecy tend to cite the fact that the Court supposedly is open in that it issues opinions giving the reasons for its decisions to the public—whereas other branches supposedly often do not.

The brilliant Justice John Paul Stevens recently made this very argument. Unfortunately, even Justice Stevens makes mistakes. And upon closer examination, this argument doesn't pass the laugh test.

To start with, it simply is not true that the other branches of government do not give public explanations for their actions. Congress, for example, routinely accompanies new laws with elaborate legislative histories explaining the purposes and reasons behind their enactment. . . .

Bush v. Gore presents an excellent example of why the "just read our opinions" approach to judicial accountability is so problematic. The majority "per curiam" opinion in *Bush v. Gore* is based on a theory of the Constitution's Equal Protection Clause that is—as commentators have pointed out ad nauseam—transparently unworkable. In light of Margolick's reporting, we now can be pretty sure that almost all the Justices shared this dim view of the Equal Protection reasoning. Indeed, it may be that only Justice Kennedy, who minted the Equal Protection argument, actually was sincere in deciding the case on this basis.

Granted, the Court's published opinions may be an accurate guide to the justices' decisionmaking in many cases. But in other cases—and these, not coincidentally, tend to be the hard cases, and the controversial cases, the cases that really matter—the opinions, instead, sometimes mask a hidden set of justifications and strategies.

For this reason, the mere publication of opinions in no way qualifies the Supreme Court as the most public of our governmental institutions. Nor should the issuance of those opinions immunize the Court from internal scrutiny. The question of whether the Supreme Court is properly performing the function assigned it in our democracy cannot be answered solely by reference to the Court's public statements.

The reason is this: We grant extraordinary authority to this unelected arm of government precisely because we think that its process of decision—deliberative and significantly removed from political and partisan concerns—elevates its ultimate judgments above those of the elected branches. Unless we achieve some window into the Court's internal decisionmaking, we have no way of evaluating whether the Court is, in fact, living up to this constitutional trust.

If we think that the Court should be accountable in any way—even accountable for only the very worst breaches one can imagine—then we cannot live with a cloak of total secrecy over its decisionmaking.

Notes and Questions

1. Is Lazarus right or wrong to suggest that we should "not be vilifying those brave enough" to provide "crucial facts" about the Court? Why?

2. From a Justice's standpoint, why might loyalty and confidentiality be crucial? Do you think the need for confidentiality is greater in the judicial branch than the executive branch, where Lazarus says it is common for presidential aides to write memoirs revealing internal executive branch decisions?

3. For an analysis of law clerks' duty of confidentiality following the *Vanity Fair* article, see David Lane, Bush v. Gore, Vanity Fair, *and a Supreme Court Law Clerk's Duty of Confidentiality*, 18 Geo. J. Legal Ethics 863 (2005).

c. The Affordable Care Act Case

Yet another prominent example of a secrecy breach at the Court came on the heels of the blockbuster ruling in *National Federation of Independent Business v. Sebelius*, 132 S. Ct. 2566 (2012). In the case, Chief Justice Roberts joined the four more liberal members of the Court to largely uphold the constitutionality of the Affordable Care Act, leaving Justices Scalia, Kennedy, Thomas, and Alito in dissent. Just days after the Court's ruling, a *CBS News* report—relying upon two anonymous sources with specific knowledge of the deliberations that took place among the Justices during the case— reported that Chief Justice John Roberts initially sided with the Court's four conservative Justices to strike down the Affordable Care Act but later changed his position to uphold the bulk of the law. *See* Jan Crawford, *Roberts Switched Views to Uphold*

Health Care Law, CBS News (July 1, 2012, 1:29 PM), http://www.cbsnews.com/8301-3460_162-57464549/roberts-switched-views-to-uphold-health-care-law. According to CBS's inside sources, Chief Justice Roberts's position change stirred the ire of the four conservatives and pushed them to independently craft a highly unusual unsigned joint dissent. *See id.*

In the wake of these revelations, rumors and speculation about the source and veracity of the leaks infectiously spread—especially across the blogosphere. Some speculated that law clerks were not to blame for the leaks and, perhaps, one or more of the Justices may have been to blame. Justice Antonin Scalia personally challenged the veracity of the leaks, telling NPR that information about the Court's deliberations was either made up or came from an unreliable source.

Notes and Questions

1. For hypothetical purposes, imagine that a Justice leaked details to CBS about Chief Justice Roberts's position switch. Would this be more or less problematic than if a law clerk was the source of the leak? Why?

2. Law clerks face an affirmative duty of confidentiality as a result of the Law Clerk Code of Conduct, but do the Justices? What keeps a Justice from leaking behind-the-scenes details about a case right after the Court hands down the decision?

3. What harms might result from post-decisional leaks like those surrounding the Affordable Care Act? Do such contemporaneous leaks tarnish the Court's reputation as an institution above the fray of politics? Do they damage the Court's collegial decision-making process? Are the potential harms that contemporaneous leaks raise different, in either kind or severity, from the potential harm raised by public access to a Justice's working papers years or decades after the Court decides a case? Are there any countervailing benefits to such leaks?

Appendix A

Selected Constitutional and Statutory Provisions

U.S. Constitution, Article III

Section 1. The judicial Power of the United States, shall be vested in one supreme Court, and in such inferior Courts as the Congress may from time to time ordain and establish. The Judges, both of the supreme and inferior Courts, shall hold their Offices during good Behaviour, and shall, at stated Times, receive for their Services, a Compensation, which shall not be diminished during their Continuance in Office.

Section 2. [1] The judicial Power shall extend to all Cases, in Law and Equity, arising under this Constitution, the Laws of the United States, and Treaties made, or which shall be made, under their Authority;—to all Cases affecting Ambassadors, other public Ministers and Consuls;—to all Cases of admiralty and maritime Jurisdiction;—to Controversies to which the United States shall be a Party;—to Controversies between two or more States;—between a State and Citizens of another State;—between Citizens of different States;—between Citizens of the same State claiming Lands under Grants of different States, and between a State, or the Citizens thereof, and foreign States, Citizens or Subjects.

[2] In all Cases affecting Ambassadors, other public Ministers and Consuls, and those in which a State shall be Party, the supreme Court shall have original Jurisdiction. In all the other Cases before mentioned, the supreme Court shall have appellate Jurisdiction, both as to Law and Fact, with such Exceptions, and under such Regulations as the Congress shall make.

[3] The Trial of all Crimes, except in Cases of Impeachment, shall be by Jury; and such Trial shall be held in the State where the said Crimes shall have been committed; but when not committed within any State, the Trial shall be at such Place or Places as the Congress may by Law have directed.

Section 3. [1] Treason against the United States, shall consist only in levying War against them, or in adhering to their Enemies, giving them Aid and Comfort. No Person shall be convicted of Treason unless on the Testimony of two Witnesses to the same overt Act, or on Confession in open Court.

[2] The Congress shall have Power to declare the Punishment of Treason, but no Attainder of Treason shall work Corruption of Blood, or Forfeiture except during the Life of the Person attainted.

627

U.S. Constitution, Amendment 11

The Judicial power of the United States shall not be construed to extend to any suit in law or equity, commenced or prosecuted against one of the United States by Citizens of another State, or by Citizens or Subjects of any Foreign State.

STATUTORY PROVISIONS
(FROM TITLE 28 U.S. CODE—JUDICIARY AND JUDICIAL PROCEDURE)

§1.   Number of justices; quorum
§2.   Terms of court
§3.   Vacancy in office of Chief Justice; disability
§4.   Precedence of associate justices
§5.   Salaries of justices
§455.   Disqualification of justice, judge, or magistrate judge
§1251. Original jurisdiction
§1253. Direct appeals from decisions of three-judge courts
§1254. Courts of appeals; certiorari; certified questions
§1257. State courts; certiorari
§1258. Supreme Court of Puerto Rico; certiorari
§1259. Court of Appeals for the Armed Forces; certiorari
§1291. Final decisions of district courts
§1292. Interlocutory decisions
§1294. Circuits in which decisions reviewable
§1651. Writs
§2101. Supreme Court; time for appeal or certiorari; docketing; stay
§2284. Three-judge court; when required; composition; procedure

PART I—ORGANIZATION OF COURTS
CHAPTER 1—SUPREME COURT

§1. Number of justices; quorum

The Supreme Court of the United States shall consist of a Chief Justice of the United States and eight associate justices, any six of whom shall constitute a quorum.

§2. Terms of court

The Supreme Court shall hold at the seat of government a term of court commencing on the first Monday in October of each year and may hold such adjourned or special terms as may be necessary.

§3. Vacancy in office of Chief Justice; disability

Whenever the Chief Justice is unable to perform the duties of his office or the office is vacant, his powers and duties shall devolve upon the associate justice next in precedence who is able to act, until such disability is removed or another Chief Justice is appointed and duly qualified.

§4. Precedence of associate justices

Associate justices shall have precedence according to the seniority of their commissions. Justices whose commissions bear the same date shall have precedence according to seniority in age.

§5. Salaries of justices

The Chief Justice and each associate justice shall each receive a salary at annual rates determined under section 225 of the Federal Salary Act of 1967 (2 U.S.C. 351-361), as adjusted by section 461 of this title.

Part I, Chapter 21—General Provisions
Applicable to Courts and Judges

§455. Disqualification of justice, judge, or magistrate judge

(a) Any justice, judge, or magistrate judge of the United States shall disqualify himself in any proceeding in which his impartiality might reasonably be questioned.

(b) He shall also disqualify himself in the following circumstances:

(1) Where he has a personal bias or prejudice concerning a party, or personal knowledge of disputed evidentiary facts concerning the proceeding;

(2) Where in private practice he served as lawyer in the matter in controversy, or a lawyer with whom he previously practiced law served during such association as a lawyer concerning the matter, or the judge or such lawyer has been a material witness concerning it;

(3) Where he has served in governmental employment and in such capacity participated as counsel, adviser or material witness concerning the proceeding or expressed an opinion concerning the merits of the particular case in controversy;

(4) He knows that he, individually or as a fiduciary, or his spouse or minor child residing in his household, has a financial interest in the subject matter in controversy or in a party to the proceeding, or any other interest that could be substantially affected by the outcome of the proceeding;

(5) He or his spouse, or a person within the third degree of relationship to either of them, or the spouse of such a person:

(i) Is a party to the proceeding, or an officer, director, or trustee of a party;

(ii) Is acting as a lawyer in the proceeding;

(iii) Is known by the judge to have an interest that could be substantially affected by the outcome of the proceeding;

(iv) Is to the judge's knowledge likely to be a material witness in the proceeding.

(c) A judge should inform himself about his personal and fiduciary financial interests, and make a reasonable effort to inform himself about the personal financial interests of his spouse and minor children residing in his household.

(d) For the purposes of this section the following words or phrases shall have the meaning indicated:

(1) "proceeding" includes pretrial, trial, appellate review, or other stages of litigation;

(2) the degree of relationship is calculated according to the civil law system;

(3) "fiduciary" includes such relationships as executor, administrator, trustee, and guardian;

(4) "financial interest" means ownership of a legal or equitable interest, however small, or a relationship as director, adviser, or other active participant in the affairs of a party, except that:

(i) Ownership in a mutual or common investment fund that holds securities is not a "financial interest" in such securities unless the judge participates in the management of the fund;

(ii) An office in an educational, religious, charitable, fraternal, or civic organization is not a "financial interest" in securities held by the organization;

(iii) The proprietary interest of a policyholder in a mutual insurance company, of a depositor in a mutual savings association, or a similar proprietary interest, is a "financial interest" in the organization only if the outcome of the proceeding could substantially affect the value of the interest;

(iv) Ownership of government securities is a "financial interest" in the issuer only if the outcome of the proceeding could substantially affect the value of the securities.

(e) No justice, judge, or magistrate judge shall accept from the parties to the proceeding a waiver of any ground for disqualification enumerated in subsection (b). Where the ground for disqualification arises only under subsection (a), waiver may be accepted provided it is preceded by a full disclosure on the record of the basis for disqualification.

(f) Notwithstanding the preceding provisions of this section, if any justice, judge, magistrate judge, or bankruptcy judge to whom a matter has been assigned would be disqualified, after substantial judicial time has been devoted to the matter, because of the appearance or discovery, after the matter was assigned to him or her, that he or she individually or as a fiduciary, or his or her spouse or minor child residing in his or her household, has a financial interest in a party (other than an interest that could be substantially affected by the outcome), disqualification is not required if the justice, judge, magistrate judge, bankruptcy judge, spouse or minor child, as the case may be, divests himself or herself of the interest that provides the grounds for the disqualification.

Part IV—Jurisdiction and Venue
Chapter 81—Supreme Court

§1251. Original jurisdiction

(a) The Supreme Court shall have original and exclusive jurisdiction of all controversies between two or more States.

(b) The Supreme Court shall have original but not exclusive jurisdiction of:

(1) All actions or proceedings to which ambassadors, other public ministers, consuls, or vice consuls of foreign states are parties;

(2) All controversies between the United States and a State;

(3) All actions or proceedings by a State against the citizens of another State or against aliens.

§1253. Direct appeals from decisions of three-judge courts

Except as otherwise provided by law, any party may appeal to the Supreme Court from an order granting or denying, after notice and hearing, an interlocutory or permanent injunction in any civil action, suit or proceeding required by any Act of Congress to be heard and determined by a district court of three judges.

§1254. Courts of appeals; certiorari; certified questions

Cases in the courts of appeals may be reviewed by the Supreme Court by the following methods:

(1) By writ of certiorari granted upon the petition of any party to any civil or criminal case, before or after rendition of judgment or decree;

(2) By certification at any time by a court of appeals of any question of law in any civil or criminal case as to which instructions are desired, and upon such certification the Supreme Court may give binding instructions or require the entire record to be sent up for decision of the entire matter in controversy.

§1257. State courts; certiorari

(a) Final judgments or decrees rendered by the highest court of a State in which a decision could be had, may be reviewed by the Supreme Court by writ of certiorari where the validity of a treaty or statute of the United States is drawn in question or where the validity of a statute of any State is drawn in question on the ground of its being repugnant to the Constitution, treaties, or laws of the United States, or where any title, right, privilege, or immunity is specially set up or claimed under the Constitution or the treaties or statutes of, or any commission held or authority exercised under, the United States.

(b) For the purposes of this section, the term "highest court of a State" includes the District of Columbia Court of Appeals.

§1258. Supreme Court of Puerto Rico; certiorari

Final judgments or decrees rendered by the Supreme Court of the Commonwealth of Puerto Rico may be reviewed by the Supreme Court by writ of certiorari where the validity of a treaty or statute of the United States is drawn in question or where the validity of a statute of the Commonwealth of Puerto Rico is drawn in question on the ground of its being repugnant to the Constitution, treaties, or laws of the United States, or where any title, right, privilege, or immunity is specially set up or claimed under the Constitution or the treaties or statutes of, or any commission held or authority exercised under, the United States.

§1259. Court of Appeals for the Armed Forces; certiorari

Decisions of the United States Court of Appeals for the Armed Forces may be reviewed by the Supreme Court by writ of certiorari in the following cases:

(1) Cases reviewed by the Court of Appeals for the Armed Forces under section 867(a)(1) of title 10.

(2) Cases certified to the Court of Appeals for the Armed Forces by the Judge Advocate General under section 867(a)(2) of title 10.

(3) Cases in which the Court of Appeals for the Armed Forces granted a petition for review under section 867(a)(3) of title 10.

(4) Cases, other than those described in paragraphs (1), (2), and (3) of this subsection, in which the Court of Appeals for the Armed Forces granted relief.

PART IV—JURISDICTION AND VENUE
CHAPTER 83—COURTS OF APPEALS

§1291. Final decisions of district courts

The courts of appeals (other than the United States Court of Appeals for the Federal Circuit) shall have jurisdiction of appeals from all final decisions of the district courts of the United States, the United States District Court for the District of the Canal Zone, the District Court of Guam, and the District Court of the Virgin Islands, except where a direct review may be had in the Supreme Court. The jurisdiction of the United States Court of Appeals for the Federal Circuit shall be limited to the jurisdiction described in sections 1292(c) and (d) and 1295 of this title.

§1292. Interlocutory decisions

(a) Except as provided in subsections (c) and (d) of this section, the courts of appeals shall have jurisdiction of appeals from:

(1) Interlocutory orders of the district courts of the United States, the United States District Court for the District of the Canal Zone, the District Court of Guam, and the District Court of the Virgin Islands, or of the judges thereof, granting, continuing, modifying, refusing or dissolving injunctions, or refusing to dissolve or modify injunctions, except where a direct review may be had in the Supreme Court;

(2) Interlocutory orders appointing receivers, or refusing orders to wind up receiverships or to take steps to accomplish the purposes thereof, such as directing sales or other disposals of property;

(3) Interlocutory decrees of such district courts or the judges thereof determining the rights and liabilities of the parties to admiralty cases in which appeals from final decrees are allowed.

(b) When a district judge, in making in a civil action an order not otherwise appealable under this section, shall be of the opinion that such order involves a controlling question of law as to which there is substantial ground for difference of opinion and that an immediate appeal from the order may materially advance the ultimate termination of the litigation, he shall so state in writing in such order. The Court of Appeals which would have jurisdiction of an appeal of such action may thereupon, in its discretion, permit an appeal to be taken from such order, if application is made to it within ten days after the entry of the order: Provided, however, That application for an appeal hereunder shall not stay proceedings in the district court unless the district judge or the Court of Appeals or a judge thereof shall so order.

(c) The United States Court of Appeals for the Federal Circuit shall have exclusive jurisdiction—

(1) of an appeal from an interlocutory order or decree described in subsection (a) or (b) of this section in any case over which the court would have jurisdiction of an appeal under section 1295 of this title; and

(2) of an appeal from a judgment in a civil action for patent infringement which would otherwise be appealable to the United States Court of Appeals for the Federal Circuit and is final except for an accounting.

(d)(1) When the chief judge of the Court of International Trade issues an order under the provisions of section 256(b) of this title, or when any judge of the Court of International Trade, in issuing any other interlocutory order, includes in the order a statement that a controlling question of law is involved with respect to which there is a substantial ground for difference of opinion and that an immediate appeal from that order may materially advance the ultimate termination of the litigation, the United States Court of Appeals for the Federal Circuit may, in its discretion, permit an appeal to be taken from such order, if application is made to that Court within ten days after the entry of such order.

(2) When the chief judge of the United States Court of Federal Claims issues an order under section 798(b) of this title, or when any judge of the United States Court of Federal Claims, in issuing an interlocutory order, includes in the order a statement that a controlling question of law is involved with respect to which there is a substantial ground for difference of opinion and that an immediate appeal from that order may materially advance the ultimate termination of the litigation, the United States Court of Appeals for the Federal Circuit may, in its discretion, permit an appeal to be taken from such order, if application is made to that Court within ten days after the entry of such order.

(3) Neither the application for nor the granting of an appeal under this subsection shall stay proceedings in the Court of International Trade or in the Court of Federal Claims, as the case may be, unless a stay is ordered by a judge of the Court of International Trade or of the Court of Federal Claims or by the United States Court of Appeals for the Federal Circuit or a judge of that court.

(4)(A) The United States Court of Appeals for the Federal Circuit shall have exclusive jurisdiction of an appeal from an interlocutory order of a district court of the United States, the District Court of Guam, the District Court of the Virgin Islands, or the District Court for the Northern Mariana Islands, granting or denying, in whole or in part, a motion to transfer an action to the United States Court of Federal Claims under section 1631 of this title.

(B) When a motion to transfer an action to the Court of Federal Claims is filed in a district court, no further proceedings shall be taken in the district court until 60 days after the court has ruled upon the motion. If an appeal is taken from the district court's grant or denial of the motion, proceedings shall be further stayed until the appeal has been decided by the Court of Appeals for the Federal Circuit. The stay of proceedings in the district court shall not bar the granting of preliminary or injunctive relief, where appropriate and where expedition is reasonably necessary. However, during the period in which proceedings are stayed as provided in this subparagraph, no transfer to the Court of Federal Claims pursuant to the motion shall be carried out.

(e) The Supreme Court may prescribe rules, in accordance with section 2072 of this title, to provide for an appeal of an interlocutory decision to the courts of appeals that is not otherwise provided for under subsection (a), (b), (c), or (d).

§1294. Circuits in which decisions reviewable

Except as provided in sections 1292(c), 1292(d), and 1295 of this title, appeals from reviewable decisions of the district and territorial courts shall be taken to the courts of appeals as follows:

(1) From a district court of the United States to the court of appeals for the circuit embracing the district;

(2) From the United States District Court for the District of the Canal Zone, to the Court of Appeals for the Fifth Circuit;

(3) From the District Court of the Virgin Islands, to the Court of Appeals for the Third Circuit;

(4) From the District Court of Guam, to the Court of Appeals for the Ninth Circuit.

PART V—PROCEDURE
CHAPTER 111—GENERAL PROVISIONS

§1651. Writs

(a) The Supreme Court and all courts established by Act of Congress may issue all writs necessary or appropriate in aid of their respective jurisdictions and agreeable to the usages and principles of law.

(b) An alternative writ or rule nisi may be issued by a justice or judge of a court which has jurisdiction.

PART V, CHAPTER 133—REVIEW—MISCELLANEOUS PROVISIONS

§2101. Supreme Court; time for appeal or certiorari; docketing; stay

(a) A direct appeal to the Supreme Court from any decision under section 1253 of this title, holding unconstitutional in whole or in part, any Act of Congress, shall be taken within thirty days after the entry of the interlocutory or final order, judgment or decree. The record shall be made up and the case docketed within sixty days from the time such appeal is taken under rules prescribed by the Supreme Court.

(b) Any other direct appeal to the Supreme Court which is authorized by law, from a decision of a district court in any civil action, suit or proceeding, shall be taken within thirty days from the judgment, order or decree, appealed from, if interlocutory, and within sixty days if final.

(c) Any other appeal or any writ of certiorari intended to bring any judgment or decree in a civil action, suit or proceeding before the Supreme Court for review shall be taken or applied for within ninety days after the entry of such judgment or decree. A justice of the Supreme Court, for good cause shown, may extend the time for applying for a writ of certiorari for a period not exceeding sixty days.

(d) The time for appeal or application for a writ of certiorari to review the judgment of a State court in a criminal case shall be as prescribed by rules of the Supreme Court.

(e) An application to the Supreme Court for a writ of certiorari to review a case before judgment has been rendered in the court of appeals may be made at any time before judgment.

(f) In any case in which the final judgment or decree of any court is subject to review by the Supreme Court on writ of certiorari, the execution and enforcement of such judgment or decree may be stayed for a reasonable time to enable the party aggrieved to obtain a writ of certiorari from the Supreme Court. The stay may be granted by a judge of the court rendering the judgment or decree or by a justice of the Supreme Court, and may be conditioned on the giving of security, approved by such judge or justice, that if the aggrieved party fails to make application for such writ within the period allotted therefor, or fails to obtain an order granting his application, or fails to make his plea good in the Supreme Court, he shall answer for all damages and costs which the other party may sustain by reason of the stay.

(g) The time for application for a writ of certiorari to review a decision of the United States Court of Appeals for the Armed Forces shall be as prescribed by rules of the Supreme Court.

PART VI—PARTICULAR PROCEEDINGS
CHAPTER 155— . . . THREE-JUDGE COURTS

§2284. Three-judge court; when required; composition; procedure

(a) A district court of three judges shall be convened when otherwise required by Act of Congress, or when an action is filed challenging the constitutionality of the apportionment of congressional districts or the apportionment of any statewide legislative body.

(b) In any action required to be heard and determined by a district court of three judges under subsection (a) of this section, the composition and procedure of the court shall be as follows:

(1) Upon the filing of a request for three judges, the judge to whom the request is presented shall, unless he determines that three judges are not required, immediately notify the chief judge of the circuit, who shall designate two other judges, at least one of whom shall be a circuit judge. The judges so designated, and the judge to whom the request was presented, shall serve as members of the court to hear and determine the action or proceeding.

(2) If the action is against a State, or officer or agency thereof, at least five days' notice of hearing of the action shall be given by registered or certified mail to the Governor and attorney general of the State.

(3) A single judge may conduct all proceedings except the trial, and enter all orders permitted by the rules of civil procedure except as provided in this subsection. He may grant a temporary restraining order on a specific finding,

based on evidence submitted, that specified irreparable damage will result if the order is not granted, which order, unless previously revoked by the district judge, shall remain in force only until the hearing and determination by the district court of three judges of an application for a preliminary injunction. A single judge shall not appoint a master, or order a reference, or hear and determine any application for a preliminary or permanent injunction or motion to vacate such an injunction, or enter judgment on the merits. Any action of a single judge may be reviewed by the full court at any time before final judgment.

Appendix B

Rules of the Supreme Court of the United States
adopted January 12, 2010
effective February 16, 2010

PART I. THE COURT

Rule 1. Clerk

1. The Clerk receives documents for filing with the Court and has authority to reject any submitted filing that does not comply with these Rules.

2. The Clerk maintains the Court's records and will not permit any of them to be removed from the Court building except as authorized by the Court. Any document filed with the Clerk and made a part of the Court's records may not thereafter be withdrawn from the official Court files. After the conclusion of proceedings in this Court, original records and documents transmitted to this Court by any other court will be returned to the court from which they were received.

3. Unless the Court or the Chief Justice orders otherwise, the Clerk's office is open from 9 a.m. to 5 p.m., Monday through Friday, except on federal legal holidays listed in 5 U.S.C. §6103.

Rule 2. Library

1. The Court's library is available for use by appropriate personnel of this Court, members of the Bar of this Court, Members of Congress and their legal staffs, and attorneys for the United States and for federal departments and agencies.

2. The library's hours are governed by regulations made by the Librarian with the approval of the Chief Justice or the Court.

3. Library books may not be removed from the Court building, except by a Justice or a member of a Justice's staff.

Rule 3. Term

The Court holds a continuous annual Term commencing on the first Monday in October and ending on the day before the first Monday in October of the following year. See 28 U.S.C. §2. At the end of each Term, all cases pending on the docket are continued to the next Term.

Rule 4. Sessions and Quorum

1. Open sessions of the Court are held beginning at 10 a.m. on the first Monday in October of each year, and thereafter as announced by the Court. Unless it orders otherwise, the Court sits to hear arguments from 10 a.m. until noon and from 1 p.m. until 3 p.m.

2. Six Members of the Court constitute a quorum. See 28 U.S.C. §1. In the absence of a quorum on any day appointed for holding a session of the Court, the Justices attending—or if no Justice is present, the Clerk or a Deputy Clerk—may announce that the Court will not meet until there is a quorum.

3. When appropriate, the Court will direct the Clerk or the Marshal to announce recesses.

PART II. ATTORNEYS AND COUNSELORS

Rule 5. Admission to the Bar

1. To qualify for admission to the Bar of this Court, an applicant must have been admitted to practice in the highest court of a State, Commonwealth, Territory or Possession, or the District of Columbia for a period of at least three years immediately before the date of application; must not have been the subject of any adverse disciplinary action pronounced or in effect during that 3-year period; and must appear to the Court to be of good moral and professional character.

2. Each applicant shall file with the Clerk (1) a certificate from the presiding judge, clerk, or other authorized official of that court evidencing the applicant's admission to practice there and the applicant's current good standing, and (2) a completely executed copy of the form approved by this Court and furnished by the Clerk containing (a) the applicant's personal statement, and (b) the statement of two sponsors endorsing the correctness of the applicant's statement, stating that the applicant possesses all the qualifications required for admission, and affirming that the applicant is of good moral and professional character. Both sponsors must be members of the Bar of this Court who personally know, but are not related to, the applicant.

3. If the documents submitted demonstrate that the applicant possesses the necessary qualifications, and if the applicant has signed the oath or affirmation and paid the required fee, the Clerk will notify the applicant of acceptance by the Court as a member of the Bar and issue a certificate of admission. An applicant who so wishes may be admitted in open court on oral motion by a member of the Bar of this Court, provided that all other requirements for admission have been satisfied.

4. Each applicant shall sign the following oath or affirmation: I, _____, do solemnly swear (or affirm) that as an attorney and as a counselor of this Court, I will conduct myself uprightly and according to law, and that I will support the Constitution of the United States.

5. The fee for admission to the Bar and a certificate bearing the seal of the Court is $200, payable to the United States Supreme Court. The Marshal will deposit such fees in a separate fund to be disbursed by the Marshal at the direction of the Chief Justice for the costs of admissions, for the benefit of the Court and its Bar, and for related purposes.

6. The fee for a duplicate certificate of admission to the Bar bearing the seal of the Court is $15, and the fee for a certificate of good standing is $10, payable to the United States Supreme Court. The proceeds will be maintained by the Marshal as provided in paragraph 5 of this Rule.

Rule 6. Argument *Pro Hac Vice*

1. An attorney not admitted to practice in the highest court of a State, Commonwealth, Territory or Possession, or the District of Columbia for the requisite three years, but otherwise eligible for admission to practice in this Court under Rule 5.1, may be permitted to argue *pro hac vice.*

2. An attorney qualified to practice in the courts of a foreign state may be permitted to argue *pro hac vice.*

3. Oral argument *pro hac vice* is allowed only on motion of the counsel of record for the party on whose behalf leave is requested. The motion shall state concisely the qualifications of the attorney who is to argue *pro hac vice*. It shall be filed with the Clerk, in the form required by Rule 21, no later than the date on which the respondent's or appellee's brief on the merits is due to be filed, and it shall be accompanied by proof of service as required by Rule 29.

Rule 7. Prohibition Against Practice

No employee of this Court shall practice as an attorney or counselor in any court or before any agency of government while employed by the Court; nor shall any person after leaving such employment participate in any professional capacity in any case pending before this Court or in any case being considered for filing in this Court, until two years have elapsed after separation; nor shall a former employee ever participate in any professional capacity in any case that was pending in this Court during the employee's tenure.

Rule 8. Disbarment and Disciplinary Action

1. Whenever a member of the Bar of this Court has been disbarred or suspended from practice in any court of record, or has engaged in conduct unbecoming a member of the Bar of this Court, the Court will enter an order suspending that member from practice before this Court and affording the member an opportunity to show cause, within 40 days, why a disbarment order should not be entered. Upon response, or if no response is timely filed, the Court will enter an appropriate order.

2. After reasonable notice and an opportunity to show cause why disciplinary action should not be taken, and after a hearing if material facts are in dispute, the Court may take any appropriate disciplinary action against any attorney who is admitted to practice before it for conduct unbecoming a member of the Bar or for failure to comply with these Rules or any Rule or order of the Court.

Rule 9. Appearance of Counsel

1. An attorney seeking to file a document in this Court in a representative capacity must first be admitted to practice before this Court as provided in Rule 5, except that admission to the Bar of this Court is not required for an attorney appointed under the Criminal Justice Act of 1964, see 18 U.S.C. §3006A(d)(6), or under any other applicable federal statute. The attorney whose name, address, and telephone number appear on the cover of a document presented for filing is considered counsel of record, and a separate notice of appearance need not be filed. If the name of more than one attorney is shown on the cover of the document, the attorney who is counsel of record shall be clearly identified. See Rule 34.1(f).

2. An attorney representing a party who will not be filing a document shall enter a separate notice of appearance as counsel of record indicating the name of the party represented. A separate notice of appearance shall also be entered whenever an attorney is substituted as counsel of record in a particular case.

PART III.   JURISDICTION ON WRIT OF CERTIORARI

Rule 10.   Considerations Governing Review on Certiorari

Review on a writ of certiorari is not a matter of right, but of judicial discretion. A petition for a writ of certiorari will be granted only for compelling reasons. The following, although neither controlling nor fully measuring the Court's discretion, indicate the character of the reasons the Court considers:

(a) a United States court of appeals has entered a decision in conflict with the decision of another United States court of appeals on the same important matter; has decided an important federal question in a way that conflicts with a decision by a state court of last resort; or has so far departed from the accepted and usual course of judicial proceedings, or sanctioned such a departure by a lower court, as to call for an exercise of this Court's supervisory power;

(b) a state court of last resort has decided an important federal question in a way that conflicts with the decision of another state court of last resort or of a United States court of appeals;

(c) a state court or a United States court of appeals has decided an important question of federal law that has not been, but should be, settled by this Court, or has decided an important federal question in a way that conflicts with relevant decisions of this Court.

A petition for a writ of certiorari is rarely granted when the asserted error consists of erroneous factual findings or the misapplication of a properly stated rule of law.

Rule 11.   Certiorari to a United States Court of Appeals Before Judgment

A petition for a writ of certiorari to review a case pending in a United States court of appeals, before judgment is entered in that court, will be granted only upon a showing that the case is of such imperative public importance as to justify deviation from normal appellate practice and to require immediate determination in this Court. See 28 U.S.C. §2101(e).

Rule 12.   Review on Certiorari: How Sought; Parties

1. Except as provided in paragraph 2 of this Rule, the petitioner shall file 40 copies of a petition for a writ of certiorari, prepared as required by Rule 33.1, and shall pay the Rule 38(a) docket fee.

2. A petitioner proceeding *in forma pauperis* under Rule 39 shall file an original and 10 copies of a petition for a writ of certiorari prepared as required by Rule 33.2, together with an original and 10 copies of the motion for leave to proceed *in forma pauperis*. A copy of the motion shall precede and be attached to each copy of the petition. An inmate confined in an institution, if proceeding *in forma pauperis* and not represented by counsel, need file only an original petition and motion.

3. Whether prepared under Rule 33.1 or Rule 33.2, the petition shall comply in all respects with Rule 14 and shall be submitted with proof of service as required by Rule 29. The case then will be placed on the docket. It is the petitioner's duty to notify all respondents promptly, on a form supplied by the Clerk, of the date of filing, the date the case was placed on the docket, and the docket number of the case. The notice shall be served as required by Rule 29.

4. Parties interested jointly, severally, or otherwise in a judgment may petition separately for a writ of certiorari; or any two or more may join in a petition. A party not shown on the petition as joined therein at the time the petition is filed may not later join in that petition. When two or more judgments are sought to be reviewed on a writ of certiorari to the same court and involve identical or closely related questions, a single petition for a writ of certiorari covering all the judgments suffices. A petition for a writ of certiorari may not be joined with any other pleading, except that any motion for leave to proceed *in forma pauperis* shall be attached.

5. No more than 30 days after a case has been placed on the docket, a respondent seeking to file a conditional cross-petition (*i.e.,* a cross-petition that otherwise would be untimely) shall file, with proof of service as required by Rule 29, 40 copies of the cross-petition prepared as required by Rule 33.1, except that a cross-petitioner proceeding *in forma pauperis* under Rule 39 shall comply with Rule 12.2. The cross-petition shall comply in all respects with this Rule and Rule 14, except that material already reproduced in the appendix to the opening petition need not be reproduced again. A cross-petitioning respondent shall pay the Rule 38(a) docket fee or submit a motion for leave to proceed *in forma pauperis*. The cover of the cross-petition shall indicate clearly that it is a conditional cross-petition. The cross-petition then will be placed on the docket, subject to the provisions of Rule 13.4. It is the cross-petitioner's duty to notify all cross-respondents promptly, on a form supplied by the Clerk, of the date of filing, the date the cross-petition was placed on the docket, and the docket number of the cross-petition. The notice shall be served as required by Rule 29. A cross-petition for a writ of certiorari may not be joined with any other pleading, except that any motion for leave to proceed *in forma pauperis* shall be attached. The time to file a conditional cross-petition will not be extended.

6. All parties to the proceeding in the court whose judgment is sought to be reviewed are deemed parties entitled to file documents in this Court, unless the petitioner notifies the Clerk of this Court in writing of the petitioner's belief that one or more of the parties below have no interest in the outcome of the petition. A copy of such notice shall be served as required by Rule 29 on all parties to the proceeding below. A party noted as no longer interested may remain a party by notifying the Clerk promptly, with service on the other parties, of an intention to remain a party. All parties other than the petitioner are considered respondents, but any respondent who supports the position of a petitioner shall meet the petitioner's time schedule for filing documents, except that a response supporting the petition shall be filed within 20 days after the case is placed on the docket, and that time will not be extended. Parties who file no document will not qualify for any relief from this Court.

7. The clerk of the court having possession of the record shall keep it until notified by the Clerk of this Court to certify and transmit it. In any document filed with this Court, a party may cite or quote from the record, even if it has not been transmitted to this Court. When requested by the Clerk of this Court to certify and transmit the record, or any part of it, the clerk of the court having possession of the record shall number the documents to be certified and shall transmit therewith a numbered list specifically identifying each document transmitted. If the record, or stipulated portions, have been printed for the use of the court below, that printed record, plus the proceedings in the court below, may be certified as the record unless one of the parties or the Clerk of this Court requests otherwise. The record may consist of certified copies, but if the lower court is of the view that original documents of any kind should be seen by this Court, that court may provide by order for the transport, safekeeping, and return of such originals.

Rule 13.   Review on Certiorari: Time for Petitioning

1. Unless otherwise provided by law, a petition for a writ of certiorari to review a judgment in any case, civil or criminal, entered by a state court of last resort or a United States court of appeals (including the United States Court of Appeals for the Armed Forces) is timely when it is filed with the Clerk of this Court within 90 days after entry of the judgment. A petition for a writ of certiorari seeking review of a judgment of a lower state court that is subject to discretionary review by the state court of last resort is timely when it is filed with the Clerk within 90 days after entry of the order denying discretionary review.

2. The Clerk will not file any petition for a writ of certiorari that is jurisdictionally out of time. See, *e.g.*, 28 U.S.C. §2101(c).

3. The time to file a petition for a writ of certiorari runs from the date of entry of the judgment or order sought to be reviewed, and not from the issuance date of the mandate (or its equivalent under local practice). But if a petition for rehearing is timely filed in the lower court by any party, or if the lower court appropriately entertains an untimely petition for rehearing or *sua sponte* considers rehearing, the time to file the petition for a writ of certiorari for all parties (whether or not they requested rehearing or joined in the petition for rehearing) runs from the date of the denial of rehearing or, if rehearing is granted, the subsequent entry of judgment.

4. A cross-petition for a writ of certiorari is timely when it is filed with the Clerk as provided in paragraphs 1, 3, and 5 of this Rule, or in Rule 12.5. However, a conditional cross petition (which except for Rule 12.5 would be untimely) will not be granted unless another party's timely petition for a writ of certiorari is granted.

5. For good cause, a Justice may extend the time to file a petition for a writ of certiorari for a period not exceeding 60 days. An application to extend the time to file shall set out the basis for jurisdiction in this Court, identify the judgment sought to be reviewed, include a copy of the opinion and any order respecting rehearing, and set out specific reasons why an extension of time is justified. The application must be filed with the Clerk at least 10 days before the date the petition is due, except in extraordinary circumstances. For the time and manner of presenting the application, see Rules 21, 22, 30, and 33.2. An application to extend the time to file a petition for a writ of certiorari is not favored.

Rule 14.   Content of a Petition for a Writ of Certiorari

1. A petition for a writ of certiorari shall contain, in the order indicated:

(a) The questions presented for review, expressed concisely in relation to the circumstances of the case, without unnecessary detail. The questions should be short and should not be argumentative or repetitive. If the petitioner or respondent is under a death sentence that may be affected by the disposition of the petition, the notation "capital case" shall precede the questions presented. The questions shall be set out on the first page following the cover, and no other information may appear on that page. The statement of any question presented is deemed to comprise every subsidiary question fairly included therein. Only the questions set out in the petition, or fairly included therein, will be considered by the Court.

(**b**) A list of all parties to the proceeding in the court whose judgment is sought to be reviewed (unless the caption of the case contains the names of all the parties), and a corporate disclosure statement as required by Rule 29.6.

(**c**) If the petition exceeds five pages or 1,500 words, a table of contents and a table of cited authorities. The table of contents shall include the items contained in the appendix.

(**d**) Citations of the official and unofficial reports of the opinions and orders entered in the case by courts or administrative agencies.

(**e**) A concise statement of the basis for jurisdiction in this Court, showing:

(**i**) the date the judgment or order sought to be reviewed was entered (and, if applicable, a statement that the petition is filed under this Court's Rule 11);

(**ii**) the date of any order respecting rehearing, and the date and terms of any order granting an extension of time to file the petition for a writ of certiorari;

(**iii**) express reliance on Rule 12.5, when a cross-petition for a writ of certiorari is filed under that Rule, and the date of docketing of the petition for a writ of certiorari in connection with which the cross-petition is filed;

(**iv**) the statutory provision believed to confer on this Court jurisdiction to review on a writ of certiorari the judgment or order in question; and

(**v**) if applicable, a statement that the notifications required by Rule 29.4(b) or (c) have been made.

(**f**) The constitutional provisions, treaties, statutes, ordinances, and regulations involved in the case, set out verbatim with appropriate citation. If the provisions involved are lengthy, their citation alone suffices at this point, and their pertinent text shall be set out in the appendix referred to in subparagraph 1(i).

(**g**) A concise statement of the case setting out the facts material to consideration of the questions presented, and also containing the following:

(**i**) If review of a state-court judgment is sought, specification of the stage in the proceedings, both in the court of first instance and in the appellate courts, when the federal questions sought to be reviewed were raised; the method or manner of raising them and the way in which they were passed on by those courts; and pertinent quotations of specific portions of the record or summary thereof, with specific reference to the places in the record where the matter appears (*e.g.*, court opinion, ruling on exception, portion of court's charge and exception thereto, assignment of error), so as to show that the federal question was timely and properly raised and that this Court has jurisdiction to review the judgment on a writ of certiorari. When the portions of the record relied on under this subparagraph are voluminous, they shall be included in the appendix referred to in subparagraph 1(i).

(ii) If review of a judgment of a United States court of appeals is sought, the basis for federal jurisdiction in the court of first instance.

(h) A direct and concise argument amplifying the reasons relied on for allowance of the writ. See Rule 10.

(i) An appendix containing, in the order indicated:

(i) the opinions, orders, findings of fact, and conclusions of law, whether written or orally given and transcribed, entered in conjunction with the judgment sought to be reviewed;

(ii) any other relevant opinions, orders, findings of fact, and conclusions of law entered in the case by courts or administrative agencies, and, if reference thereto is necessary to ascertain the grounds of the judgment, of those in companion cases (each document shall include the caption showing the name of the issuing court or agency, the title and number of the case, and the date of entry);

(iii) any order on rehearing, including the caption showing the name of the issuing court, the title and number of the case, and the date of entry;

(iv) the judgment sought to be reviewed if the date of its entry is different from the date of the opinion or order required in sub-subparagraph (i) of this subparagraph;

(v) material required by subparagraphs 1(f) or 1(g)(i); and

(vi) any other material the petitioner believes essential to understand the petition.

If the material required by this subparagraph is voluminous, it may be presented in a separate volume or volumes with appropriate covers.

2. All contentions in support of a petition for a writ of certiorari shall be set out in the body of the petition, as provided in subparagraph 1(h) of this Rule. No separate brief in support of a petition for a writ of certiorari may be filed, and the Clerk will not file any petition for a writ of certiorari to which any supporting brief is annexed or appended.

3. A petition for a writ of certiorari should be stated briefly and in plain terms and may not exceed the word or page limitations specified in Rule 33.

4. The failure of a petitioner to present with accuracy, brevity, and clarity whatever is essential to ready and adequate understanding of the points requiring consideration is sufficient reason for the Court to deny a petition.

5. If the Clerk determines that a petition submitted timely and in good faith is in a form that does not comply with this Rule or with Rule 33 or Rule 34, the Clerk will return it with a letter indicating the deficiency. A corrected petition submitted in accordance with Rule 29.2 no more than 60 days after the date of the Clerk's letter will be deemed timely.

Rule 15.   Briefs in Opposition; Reply Briefs; Supplemental Briefs

1. A brief in opposition to a petition for a writ of certiorari may be filed by the respondent in any case, but is not mandatory except in a capital case, see Rule 14.1(a), or when ordered by the Court.

2. A brief in opposition should be stated briefly and in plain terms and may not exceed the word or page limitations specified in Rule 33. In addition to presenting other arguments for denying the petition, the brief in opposition should address any perceived misstatement of fact or law in the petition that bears on what issues properly would be before the Court if certiorari were granted. Counsel are admonished that they have an obligation to the Court to point out in the brief in opposition, and not later, any perceived misstatement made in the petition. Any objection to consideration of a question presented based on what occurred in the proceedings below, if the objection does not go to jurisdiction, may be deemed waived unless called to the Court's attention in the brief in opposition.

3. Any brief in opposition shall be filed within 30 days after the case is placed on the docket, unless the time is extended by the Court or a Justice, or by the Clerk under Rule 30.4. Forty copies shall be filed, except that a respondent proceeding *in forma pauperis* under Rule 39, including an inmate of an institution, shall file the number of copies required for a petition by such a person under Rule 12.2, together with a motion for leave to proceed *in forma pauperis*, a copy of which shall precede and be attached to each copy of the brief in opposition. If the petitioner is proceeding *in forma pauperis*, the respondent shall prepare its brief in opposition, if any, as required by Rule 33.2, and shall file an original and 10 copies of that brief. Whether prepared under Rule 33.1 or Rule 33.2, the brief in opposition shall comply with the requirements of Rule 24 governing a respondent's brief, except that no summary of the argument is required. A brief in opposition may not be joined with any other pleading, except that any motion for leave to proceed *in forma pauperis* shall be attached. The brief in opposition shall be served as required by Rule 29.

4. No motion by a respondent to dismiss a petition for a writ of certiorari may be filed. Any objections to the jurisdiction of the Court to grant a petition for a writ of certiorari shall be included in the brief in opposition.

5. The Clerk will distribute the petition to the Court for its consideration upon receiving an express waiver of the right to file a brief in opposition, or, if no waiver or brief in opposition is filed, upon the expiration of the time allowed for filing. If a brief in opposition is timely filed, the Clerk will distribute the petition, brief in opposition, and any reply brief to the Court for its consideration no less than 10 days after the brief in opposition is filed.

6. Any petitioner may file a reply brief addressed to new points raised in the brief in opposition, but distribution and consideration by the Court under paragraph 5 of this Rule will not be deferred pending its receipt. Forty copies shall be filed, except that a petitioner proceeding *in forma pauperis* under Rule 39, including an inmate of an institution, shall file the number of copies required for a petition by such a person under Rule 12.2. The reply brief shall be served as required by Rule 29.

7. If a cross-petition for a writ of certiorari has been docketed, distribution of both petitions will be deferred until the cross-petition is due for distribution under this Rule.

8. Any party may file a supplemental brief at any time while a petition for a writ of certiorari is pending, calling attention to new cases, new legislation, or other intervening matter not available at the time of the party's last filing. A supplemental brief shall be restricted to new matter and shall follow, insofar as applicable, the form for a brief in opposition prescribed by this Rule. Forty copies shall be filed, except that a party proceeding *in forma pauperis* under Rule 39, including an inmate of an institution, shall file the number of copies required for a petition by such a person under Rule 12.2. The supplemental brief shall be served as required by Rule 29.

Rule 16.   Disposition of a Petition for a Writ of Certiorari

1. After considering the documents distributed under Rule 15, the Court will enter an appropriate order. The order may be a summary disposition on the merits.

2. Whenever the Court grants a petition for a writ of certiorari, the Clerk will prepare, sign, and enter an order to that effect and will notify forthwith counsel of record and the court whose judgment is to be reviewed. The case then will be scheduled for briefing and oral argument. If the record has not previously been filed in this Court, the Clerk will request the clerk of the court having possession of the record to certify and transmit it. A formal writ will not issue unless specially directed.

3. Whenever the Court denies a petition for a writ of certiorari, the Clerk will prepare, sign, and enter an order to that effect and will notify forthwith counsel of record and the court whose judgment was sought to be reviewed. The order of denial will not be suspended pending disposition of a petition for rehearing except by order of the Court or a Justice.

Part IV.   Other Jurisdiction

Rule 17.   Procedure in an Original Action

1. This Rule applies only to an action invoking the Court's original jurisdiction under Article III of the Constitution of the United States. See also 28 U.S.C. §1251 and U. S. Const., Amdt. 11. A petition for an extraordinary writ in aid of the Court's appellate jurisdiction shall be filed as provided in Rule 20.

2. The form of pleadings and motions prescribed by the Federal Rules of Civil Procedure is followed. In other respects, those Rules and the Federal Rules of Evidence may be taken as guides.

3. The initial pleading shall be preceded by a motion for leave to file, and may be accompanied by a brief in support of the motion. Forty copies of each document shall be filed, with proof of service. Service shall be as required by Rule 29, except that when an adverse party is a State, service shall be made on both the Governor and the Attorney General of that State.

4. The case will be placed on the docket when the motion for leave to file and the initial pleading are filed with the Clerk. The Rule 38(a) docket fee shall be paid at that time.

5. No more than 60 days after receiving the motion for leave to file and the initial pleading, an adverse party shall file 40 copies of any brief in opposition to the motion, with proof of service as required by Rule 29. The Clerk will distribute the filed documents to the Court for its consideration upon receiving an express waiver of the right to file a brief in opposition, or, if no waiver or brief is filed, upon the expiration of the time allowed for filing. If a brief in opposition is timely filed, the Clerk will distribute the filed documents to the Court for its consideration no less than 10 days after the brief in opposition is filed. A reply brief may be filed, but consideration of the case will not be deferred pending its receipt. The Court thereafter may grant or deny the motion, set it for oral argument, direct that additional documents be filed, or require that other proceedings be conducted.

6. A summons issued out of this Court shall be served on the defendant 60 days before the return day specified therein. If the defendant does not respond by the return day, the plaintiff may proceed *ex parte.*

7. Process against a State issued out of this Court shall be served on both the Governor and the Attorney General of that State.

Rule 18. Appeal from a United States District Court

1. When a direct appeal from a decision of a United States district court is authorized by law, the appeal is commenced by filing a notice of appeal with the clerk of the district court within the time provided by law after entry of the judgment sought to be reviewed. The time to file may not be extended. The notice of appeal shall specify the parties taking the appeal, designate the judgment, or part thereof, appealed from and the date of its entry, and specify the statute or statutes under which the appeal is taken. A copy of the notice of appeal shall be served on all parties to the proceeding as required by Rule 29, and proof of service shall be filed in the district court together with the notice of appeal.

2. All parties to the proceeding in the district court are deemed parties entitled to file documents in this Court, but a party having no interest in the outcome of the appeal may so notify the Clerk of this Court and shall serve a copy of the notice on all other parties. Parties interested jointly, severally, or otherwise in the judgment may appeal separately, or any two or more may join in an appeal. When two or more judgments involving identical or closely related questions are sought to be reviewed on appeal from the same court, a notice of appeal for each judgment shall be filed with the clerk of the district court, but a single jurisdictional statement covering all the judgments suffices. Parties who file no document will not qualify for any relief from this Court.

3. No more than 60 days after filing the notice of appeal in the district court, the appellant shall file 40 copies of a jurisdictional statement and shall pay the Rule 38 docket fee, except that an appellant proceeding *in forma pauperis* under Rule 39, including an inmate of an institution, shall file the number of copies required for a petition by such a person under Rule 12.2, together with a motion for leave to proceed *in forma pauperis,* a copy of which shall precede and be attached to each copy of the jurisdictional statement. The jurisdictional statement shall follow, insofar as applicable, the form for a petition for a writ of certiorari prescribed by Rule 14, and shall be served as required by Rule 29. The case will then be placed on the docket. It is the appellant's duty to notify all appellees promptly, on a form supplied by the Clerk, of the date of filing, the date the case was placed on the docket, and the docket number of the case. The notice shall be served as required by Rule 29. The appendix shall include a copy of the notice of appeal showing the date it was filed in the district court. For good cause, a Justice may extend the time to file a jurisdictional statement for a period not exceeding 60 days. An application to extend the time to file a jurisdictional statement shall set out the basis for jurisdiction in this Court; identify the judgment sought to be reviewed; include a copy of the opinion, any order respecting rehearing, and the notice of appeal; and set out specific reasons why an extension of time is justified. For the time and manner of presenting the application, see Rules 21, 22, and 30. An application to extend the time to file a jurisdictional statement is not favored.

4. No more than 30 days after a case has been placed on the docket, an appellee seeking to file a conditional cross-appeal (*i.e.,* a cross-appeal that otherwise would be untimely) shall file, with proof of service as required by Rule 29, a jurisdictional statement that complies in all respects (including number of copies filed) with paragraph 3 of this Rule, except that material already reproduced in the appendix to the opening jurisdictional statement need not be reproduced again. A cross-appealing appellee shall pay the Rule 38 docket fee or submit a motion for leave to proceed *in forma pauperis.* The cover of the cross-appeal shall indicate clearly that it is a conditional cross-appeal. The cross-appeal then will be placed on the docket. It is the cross-appellant's duty to notify all cross-appellees promptly, on a form supplied by the Clerk, of the date of filing, the date the cross-appeal was placed on the docket, and the docket number of the cross-appeal. The notice shall be served as required by Rule 29. A cross-appeal may not be joined with any other pleading, except that any motion for leave to proceed *in forma pauperis* shall be attached. The time to file a cross-appeal will not be extended.

    5. After a notice of appeal has been filed in the district court, but before the case is placed on this Court's docket, the parties may dismiss the appeal by stipulation filed in the district court, or the district court may dismiss the appeal on the appellant's motion, with notice to all parties. If a notice of appeal has been filed, but the case has not been placed on this Court's docket within the time prescribed for docketing, the district court may dismiss the appeal on the appellee's motion, with notice to all parties, and may make any just order with respect to costs. If the district court has denied the appellee's motion to dismiss the appeal, the appellee may move this Court to docket and dismiss the appeal by filing an original and 10 copies of a motion presented in conformity with Rules 21 and 33.2. The motion shall be accompanied by proof of service as required by Rule 29, and by a certificate from the clerk of the district court, certifying that a notice of appeal was filed and that the appellee's motion to dismiss was denied. The appellant may not thereafter file a jurisdictional statement without special leave of the Court, and the Court may allow costs against the appellant.

    6. Within 30 days after the case is placed on this Court's docket, the appellee may file a motion to dismiss, to affirm, or in the alternative to affirm or dismiss. Forty copies of the motion shall be filed, except that an appellee proceeding *in forma pauperis* under Rule 39, including an inmate of an institution, shall file the number of copies required for a petition by such a person under Rule 12.2, together with a motion for leave to proceed *in forma pauperis,* a copy of which shall precede and be attached to each copy of the motion to dismiss, to affirm, or in the alternative to affirm or dismiss. The motion shall follow, insofar as applicable, the form for a brief in opposition prescribed by Rule 15, and shall comply in all respects with Rule 21.

    7. The Clerk will distribute the jurisdictional statement to the Court for its consideration upon receiving an express waiver of the right to file a motion to dismiss or to affirm or, if no waiver or motion is filed, upon the expiration of the time allowed for filing. If a motion to dismiss or to affirm is timely filed, the Clerk will distribute the jurisdictional statement, motion, and any brief opposing the motion to the Court for its consideration no less than 10 days after the motion is filed.

    8. Any appellant may file a brief opposing a motion to dismiss or to affirm, but distribution and consideration by the Court under paragraph 7 of this Rule will not be deferred pending its receipt. Forty copies shall be filed, except that an appellant proceeding *in forma pauperis* under Rule 39, including an inmate of an institution, shall file the number of copies required for a petition by such a person under Rule 12.2. The brief shall be served as required by Rule 29. If a cross-appeal has been docketed, distribution of both jurisdictional statements will be deferred until the cross-appeal is due for distribution under this Rule. Any party may file a supplemental brief at any time while a jurisdictional statement is pending, calling attention to new cases, new legislation, or other intervening matter not available at the time of the party's last filing. A supplemental brief shall be restricted to new matter and shall follow, insofar as applicable, the form for a brief in opposition prescribed by Rule 15. Forty copies shall be filed, except that a party proceeding *in forma pauperis* under Rule 39, including an inmate of an institution, shall file the number of copies required for a petition by such a person under Rule 12.2. The supplemental brief shall be served as required by Rule 29.

9. If a cross-appeal has been docketed, distribution of both jurisdictional statements will be deferred until the cross-appeal is due for distribution under this Rule.

10. Any party may file a supplemental brief at any time while a jurisdictional statement is pending, calling attention to new cases, new legislation, or other intervening matter not available at the time of the party's last filing. A supplemental brief shall be restricted to new matter and shall follow, insofar as applicable, the form for a brief in opposition prescribed by Rule 15. Forty copies shall be filed, except that a party proceeding *in forma pauperis* under Rule 39, including an inmate of an institution, shall file the number of copies required for a petition by such a person under Rule 12.2. The supplemental brief shall be served as required by Rule 29.

11. The clerk of the district court shall retain possession of the record until notified by the Clerk of this Court to certify and transmit it. See Rule 12.7.

12. After considering the documents distributed under this Rule, the Court may dispose summarily of the appeal on the merits, note probable jurisdiction, or postpone consideration of jurisdiction until a hearing of the case on the merits. If not disposed of summarily, the case stands for briefing and oral argument on the merits. If consideration of jurisdiction is postponed, counsel, at the outset of their briefs and at oral argument, shall address the question of jurisdiction. If the record has not previously been filed in this Court, the Clerk of this Court will request the clerk of the court in possession of the record to certify and transmit it.

13. If the Clerk determines that a jurisdictional statement submitted timely and in good faith is in a form that does not comply with this Rule or with Rule 33 or Rule 34, the Clerk will return it with a letter indicating the deficiency. If a corrected jurisdictional statement is submitted in accordance with Rule 29.2 no more than 60 days after the date of the Clerk's letter it will be deemed timely.

Rule 19.   Procedure on a Certified Question

1. A United States court of appeals may certify to this Court a question or proposition of law on which it seeks instruction for the proper decision of a case. The certificate shall contain a statement of the nature of the case and the facts on which the question or proposition of law arises. Only questions or propositions of law may be certified, and they shall be stated separately and with precision. The certificate shall be prepared as required by Rule 33.2 and shall be signed by the clerk of the court of appeals.

2. When a question is certified by a United States court of appeals, this Court, on its own motion or that of a party, may consider and decide the entire matter in controversy. See 28 U.S.C. §1254(2).

3. When a question is certified, the Clerk will notify the parties and docket the case. Counsel shall then enter their appearances. After docketing, the Clerk will submit the certificate to the Court for a preliminary examination to determine whether the case should be briefed, set for argument, or dismissed. No brief may be filed until the preliminary examination of the certificate is completed.

4. If the Court orders the case briefed or set for argument, the parties will be notified and permitted to file briefs. The Clerk of this Court then will request the clerk of the court in possession of the record to certify and transmit it. Any portion of the record to which the parties wish to direct the Court's particular attention should be printed in a joint appendix, prepared in conformity with Rule 26 by the appellant or petitioner in the court of appeals, but the fact that any part of the record has not been printed does not prevent the parties or the Court from relying on it.

5. A brief on the merits in a case involving a certified question shall comply with Rules 24, 25, and 33.1, except that the brief for the party who is the appellant or petitioner below shall be filed within 45 days of the order requiring briefs or setting the case for argument.

Rule 20.   Procedure on a Petition for an Extraordinary Writ

1. Issuance by the Court of an extraordinary writ authorized by 28 U.S.C. §1651(a) is not a matter of right, but of discretion sparingly exercised. To justify the granting of any such writ, the petition must show that the writ will be in aid of the Court's appellate jurisdiction, that exceptional circumstances warrant the exercise of the Court's discretionary powers, and that adequate relief cannot be obtained in any other form or from any other court.

2. A petition seeking a writ authorized by 28 U.S.C. §1651(a), §2241, or §2254(a) shall be prepared in all respects as required by Rules 33 and 34. The petition shall be captioned "*In re* [name of petitioner]" and shall follow, insofar as applicable, the form of a petition for a writ of certiorari prescribed by Rule 14. All contentions in support of the petition shall be included in the petition. The case will be placed on the docket when 40 copies of the petition are filed with the Clerk and the docket fee is paid, except that a petitioner proceeding *in forma pauperis* under Rule 39, including an inmate of an institution, shall file the number of copies required for a petition by such a person under Rule 12.2, together with a motion for leave to proceed *in forma pauperis,* a copy of which shall precede and be attached to each copy of the petition. The petition shall be served as required by Rule 29 (subject to subparagraph 4(b) of this Rule).

3. **(a)** A petition seeking a writ of prohibition, a writ of mandamus, or both in the alternative shall state the name and office or function of every person against whom relief is sought and shall set out with particularity why the relief sought is not available in any other court. A copy of the judgment with respect to which the writ is sought, including any related opinion, shall be appended to the petition together with any other document essential to understanding the petition.

(b) The petition shall be served on every party to the proceeding with respect to which relief is sought. Within 30 days after the petition is placed on the docket, a party shall file 40 copies of any brief or briefs in opposition thereto, which shall comply fully with Rule 15. If a party named as a respondent does not wish to respond to the petition, that party may so advise the Clerk and all other parties by letter. All persons served are deemed respondents for all purposes in the proceedings in this Court.

4. (a) A petition seeking a writ of habeas corpus shall comply with the requirements of 28 U.S.C. §2241 and 2242, and in particular with the provision in the last paragraph of §2242, which requires a statement of the "reasons for not making application to the district court of the district in which the applicant is held." If the relief sought is from the judgment of a state court, the petition shall set out specifically how and where the petitioner has exhausted available remedies in the state courts or otherwise comes within the provisions of 28 U.S.C. §2254(b). To justify the granting of a writ of habeas corpus, the petitioner must show that exceptional circumstances warrant the exercise of the Court's discretionary powers, and that adequate relief cannot be obtained in any other form or from any other court. This writ is rarely granted.

    (b) Habeas corpus proceedings, except in capital cases, are *ex parte,* unless the Court requires the respondent to show cause why the petition for a writ of habeas corpus should not be granted. A response, if ordered, or in a capital case, shall comply fully with Rule 15. Neither the denial of the petition, without more, nor an order of transfer to a district court under the authority of 28 U.S.C. §2241(b), is an adjudication on the merits, and therefore does not preclude further application to another court for the relief sought.

5. The Clerk will distribute the documents to the Court for its consideration when a brief in opposition under subparagraph 3(b) of this Rule has been filed, when a response under subparagraph 4(b) has been ordered and filed, when the time to file has expired, or when the right to file has been expressly waived.

6. If the Court orders the case set for argument, the Clerk will notify the parties whether additional briefs are required, when they shall be filed, and, if the case involves a petition for a common-law writ of certiorari, that the parties shall prepare a joint appendix in accordance with Rule 26.

PART V.   MOTIONS AND APPLICATIONS

Rule 21. Motions to the Court

1. Every motion to the Court shall clearly state its purpose and the facts on which it is based and may present legal argument in support thereof. No separate brief may be filed. A motion should be concise and shall comply with any applicable page limits. Rule 22 governs an application addressed to a single Justice.

2. (a) A motion in any action within the Court's original jurisdiction shall comply with Rule 17.3.

    (b) A motion to dismiss as moot (or a suggestion of mootness), a motion for leave to file a brief as *amicus curiae,* and any motion the granting of which would dispose of the entire case or would affect the final judgment to be entered (other than a motion to docket and dismiss under Rule 18.5 or a motion for voluntary dismissal under Rule 46) shall be prepared as required by Rule 33.1, and 40 copies shall be filed, except that a movant proceeding *in forma pauperis* under Rule 39, including an inmate of an institution, shall file a motion prepared as required by Rule 33.2, and shall file the number of copies required for a petition by such a person under Rule 12.2. The motion shall be served as required by Rule 29.

    (c) Any other motion to the Court shall be prepared as required by Rule 33.2; the moving party shall file an original and 10 copies. The Court subsequently may order the moving party to prepare the motion as required by Rule 33.1; in that event, the party shall file 40 copies.

3. A motion to the Court shall be filed with the Clerk and shall be accompanied by proof of service as required by Rule 29. No motion may be presented in open Court, other than a motion for admission to the Bar, except when the proceeding to which it refers is being argued. Oral argument on a motion will not be permitted unless the Court so directs.

4. Any response to a motion shall be filed as promptly as possible considering the nature of the relief sought and any asserted need for emergency action, and, in any event, within 10 days of receipt, unless the Court or a Justice, or the Clerk under Rule 30.4, orders otherwise. A response to a motion prepared as required by Rule 33.1, except a response to a motion for leave to file an *amicus curiae* brief (see Rule 37.5), shall be prepared in the same manner if time permits. In an appropriate case, the Court may act on a motion without waiting for a response.

Rule 22. Applications to Individual Justices

1. An application addressed to an individual Justice shall be filed with the Clerk, who will transmit it promptly to the Justice concerned if an individual Justice has authority to grant the sought relief.

2. The original and two copies of any application addressed to an individual Justice shall be prepared as required by Rule 33.2, and shall be accompanied by proof of service as required by Rule 29.

3. An application shall be addressed to the Justice allotted to the Circuit from which the case arises. An application arising from the United States Court of Appeals for the Armed Forces shall be addressed to the Chief Justice. When the Circuit Justice is unavailable for any reason, the application addressed to that Justice will be distributed to the Justice then available who is next junior to the Circuit Justice; the turn of the Chief Justice follows that of the most junior Justice.

4. A Justice denying an application will note the denial thereon. Thereafter, unless action thereon is restricted by law to the Circuit Justice or is untimely under Rule 30.2, the party making an application, except in the case of an application for an extension of time, may renew it to any other Justice, subject to the provisions of this Rule. Except when the denial is without prejudice, a renewed application is not favored. Renewed application is made by a letter to the Clerk, designating the Justice to whom the application is to be directed, and accompanied by 10 copies of the original application and proof of service as required by Rule 29.

5. A Justice to whom an application for a stay or for bail is submitted may refer it to the Court for determination.

6. The Clerk will advise all parties concerned, by appropriately speedy means, of the disposition made of an application.

Rule 23. Stays

1. A stay may be granted by a Justice as permitted by law.

2. A party to a judgment sought to be reviewed may present to a Justice an application to stay the enforcement of that judgment. See 28 U.S.C. §2101(f).

3. An application for a stay shall set out with particularity why the relief sought is not available from any other court or judge. Except in the most extraordinary circumstances, an application for a stay will not be entertained unless the relief requested was first sought in the appropriate court or courts below or from a judge or judges thereof. An application for a stay shall identify the judgment sought to be reviewed and have appended thereto a copy of the order and opinion, if any, and a copy of the order, if any, of the court or judge below denying the relief sought, and shall set out specific reasons why a stay is justified. The form and content of an application for a stay are governed by Rules 22 and 33.2.

4. A judge, court, or Justice granting an application for a stay pending review by this Court may condition the stay on the filing of a supersedeas bond having an approved surety or sureties. The bond will be conditioned on the satisfaction of the judgment in full, together with any costs, interest, and damages for delay that may be awarded. If a part of the judgment sought to be reviewed has already been satisfied, or is otherwise secured, the bond may be conditioned on the satisfaction of the part of the judgment not otherwise secured or satisfied, together with costs, interest, and damages.

PART VI. BRIEFS ON THE MERITS AND ORAL ARGUMENT

Rule 24. Briefs on the Merits: In General

1. A brief on the merits for a petitioner or an appellant shall comply in all respects with Rules 33.1 and 34 and shall contain in the order here indicated:

(a) The questions presented for review under Rule 14.1(a). The questions shall be set out on the first page following the cover, and no other information may appear on that page. The phrasing of the questions presented need not be identical with that in the petition for a writ of certiorari or the jurisdictional statement, but the brief may not raise additional questions or change the substance of the questions already presented in those documents. At its option, however, the Court may consider a plain error not among the questions presented but evident from the record and otherwise within its jurisdiction to decide.

(b) A list of all parties to the proceeding in the court whose judgment is under review (unless the caption of the case in this Court contains the names of all parties). Any amended corporate disclosure statement as required by Rule 29.6 shall be placed here.

(c) If the brief exceeds five pages, a table of contents and a table of cited authorities.

(d) Citations of the official and unofficial reports of the opinions and orders entered in the case by courts and administrative agencies.

(e) A concise statement of the basis for jurisdiction in this Court, including the statutory provisions and time factors on which jurisdiction rests.

(f) The constitutional provisions, treaties, statutes, ordinances, and regulations involved in the case, set out verbatim with appropriate citation. If the provisions involved are lengthy, their citation alone suffices at this point, and their pertinent text, if not already set out in the petition for a writ of certiorari, jurisdictional statement, or an appendix to either document, shall be set out in an appendix to the brief.

(g) A concise statement of the case, setting out the facts material to the consideration of the questions presented, with appropriate references to the joint appendix, *e.g.*, App. 12, or to the record, *e.g.*, Record 12.

(h) A summary of the argument, suitably paragraphed. The summary should be a clear and concise condensation of the argument made in the body of the brief; mere repetition of the headings under which the argument is arranged is not sufficient.

(i) The argument, exhibiting clearly the points of fact and of law presented and citing the authorities and statutes relied on.

(j) A conclusion specifying with particularity the relief the party seeks.

2. A brief on the merits for a respondent or an appellee shall conform to the foregoing requirements, except that items required by subparagraphs 1(a), (b), (d), (e), (f), and (g) of this Rule need not be included unless the respondent or appellee is dissatisfied with their presentation by the opposing party.

3. A brief on the merits may not exceed the word limitations specified in Rule 33.1(g). An appendix to a brief may include only relevant material, and counsel are cautioned not to include in an appendix arguments or citations that properly belong in the body of the brief.

4. A reply brief shall conform to those portions of this Rule applicable to the brief for a respondent or an appellee, but, if appropriately divided by topical headings, need not contain a summary of the argument.

5. A reference to the joint appendix or to the record set out in any brief shall indicate the appropriate page number. If the reference is to an exhibit, the page numbers at which the exhibit appears, at which it was offered in evidence, and at which it was ruled on by the judge shall be indicated, *e. g.*, Pl. Exh. 14, Record 199, 2134.

6. A brief shall be concise, logically arranged with proper headings, and free of irrelevant, immaterial, or scandalous matter. The Court may disregard or strike a brief that does not comply with this paragraph.

Rule 25. Briefs on the Merits: Number of Copies and Time to File

1. The petitioner or appellant shall file 40 copies of the brief on the merits within 45 days of the order granting the writ of certiorari, noting probable jurisdiction, or postponing consideration of jurisdiction. Any respondent or appellee who supports the petitioner or appellant shall meet the petitioner's or appellant's time schedule for filing documents.

2. The respondent or appellee shall file 40 copies of the brief on the merits within 30 days after the brief for the petitioner or appellant is filed.

3. The petitioner or appellant shall file 40 copies of the reply brief, if any, within 30 days after the brief for the respondent or appellee is filed, but any reply brief must actually be received by the Clerk not later than 2 p.m. one week before the date of oral argument. Any respondent or appellee supporting the petitioner or appellant may file a reply brief.

4. If cross-petitions or cross-appeals have been consolidated for argument, the Clerk, upon request of the parties, may designate one of the parties to file an initial brief and reply brief as provided in paragraphs 1 and 3 of this Rule (as if the party were petitioner or appellant), and may designate the other party to file an initial brief as provided in paragraph 2 of this Rule and, to the extent appropriate, a supplemental brief following the submission of the reply brief. In such a case, the Clerk may establish the time for the submission of the briefs and alter the otherwise applicable word limits. Except as approved by the Court or a Justice, the total number of words permitted for the briefs of the parties cumulatively shall not exceed the maximum that would have been allowed in the absence of an order under this paragraph.

5. The time periods stated in paragraphs 1, 2, and 3 of this Rule may be extended as provided in Rule 30. An application to extend the time to file a brief on the merits is not favored. If a case is advanced for hearing, the time to file briefs on the merits may be abridged as circumstances require pursuant to an order of the Court on its own motion or that of a party.

6. A party wishing to present late authorities, newly enacted legislation, or other intervening matter that was not available in time to be included in a brief may file 40 copies of a supplemental brief, restricted to such new matter and otherwise presented in conformity with these Rules, up to the time the case is called for oral argument or by leave of the Court thereafter.

7. After a case has been argued or submitted, the Clerk will not file any brief, except that of a party filed by leave of the Court.

8. The Clerk will not file any brief that is not accompanied by proof of service as required by Rule 29.

9. An electronic version of every brief on the merits shall be transmitted to the Clerk of Court and to opposing counsel of record at the time the brief is filed in accordance with guidelines established by the Clerk. The electronic transmission requirement is in addition to the requirement that booklet-format briefs be timely filed.

Rule 26. Joint Appendix

1. Unless the Clerk has allowed the parties to use the deferred method described in paragraph 4 of this Rule, the petitioner or appellant, within 45 days after entry of the order granting the writ of certiorari, noting probable jurisdiction, or postponing consideration of jurisdiction, shall file 40 copies of a joint appendix, prepared as required by Rule 33.1. The joint appendix shall contain: (1) the relevant docket entries in all the courts below; (2) any relevant pleadings, jury instructions, findings, conclusions, or opinions; (3) the judgment, order, or decision under review; and (4) any other parts of the record that the parties particularly wish to bring to the Court's attention. Any of the foregoing items already reproduced in a petition for a writ of certiorari, jurisdictional statement, brief in opposition to a petition for a writ of certiorari, motion to dismiss or affirm, or any appendix to the foregoing, that was prepared as required by Rule 33.1, need not be reproduced again in the joint appendix. The petitioner or appellant shall serve three copies of the joint appendix on each of the other parties to the proceeding as required by Rule 29.

2. The parties are encouraged to agree on the contents of the joint appendix. In the absence of agreement, the petitioner or appellant, within 10 days after entry of the order granting the writ of certiorari, noting probable jurisdiction, or postponing consideration of jurisdiction, shall serve on the respondent or appellee a designation of parts of the record to be included in the joint appendix. Within 10 days after receiving the designation, a respondent or appellee who considers the parts of the record so designated insufficient shall serve on the petitioner or appellant a designation of additional parts to be included in the joint appendix, and the petitioner or appellant shall include the parts so designated. If the Court has permitted the respondent or appellee to proceed *in forma pauperis,* the petitioner or appellant may seek by motion to be excused from printing portions of the record the petitioner or appellant considers unnecessary. In making these designations, counsel should include only those materials the Court should examine; unnecessary designations should be avoided. The record is on file with the Clerk and available to the Justices, and counsel may refer in briefs and in oral argument to relevant portions of the record not included in the joint appendix.

3. When the joint appendix is filed, the petitioner or appellant immediately shall file with the Clerk a statement of the cost of printing 50 copies and shall serve a copy of the statement on each of the other parties as required by Rule 29. Unless the parties agree otherwise, the cost of producing the joint appendix shall be paid initially by the petitioner or appellant; but a petitioner or appellant who considers that parts of the record designated by the respondent or appellee are unnecessary for the determination of the issues presented may so advise the respondent or appellee, who then shall advance the cost of printing the additional parts, unless the Court or a Justice otherwise fixes the initial allocation of the costs. The cost of printing the joint appendix is taxed as a cost in the case, but if a party unnecessarily causes matter to be included in the joint appendix or prints excessive copies, the Court may impose these costs on that party.

4. (a) On the parties' request, the Clerk may allow preparation of the joint appendix to be deferred until after the briefs have been filed. In that event, the petitioner or appellant shall file the joint appendix no more than 14 days after receiving the brief for the respondent or appellee. The provisions of paragraphs 1, 2, and 3 of this Rule shall be followed, except that the designations referred to therein shall be made by each party when that party's brief is served. Deferral of the joint appendix is not favored.

(b) If the deferred method is used, the briefs on the merits may refer to the pages of the record. In that event, the joint appendix shall include in brackets on each page thereof the page number of the record where that material may be found. A party wishing to refer directly to the pages of the joint appendix may serve and file copies of its brief prepared as required by Rule 33.2 within the time provided by Rule 25, with appropriate references to the pages of the record. In that event, within 10 days after the joint appendix is filed, copies of the brief prepared as required by Rule 33.1 containing references to the pages of the joint appendix in place of, or in addition to, the initial references to the pages of the record, shall be served and filed. No other change may be made in the brief as initially served and filed, except that typographical errors may be corrected.

5. The joint appendix shall be prefaced by a table of contents showing the parts of the record that it contains, in the order in which the parts are set out, with references to the pages of the joint appendix at which each part begins. The relevant docket entries shall be set out after the table of contents, followed by the other parts of the record in chronological order. When testimony contained in the reporter's transcript of proceedings is set out in the joint appendix, the page of the transcript at which the testimony appears shall be indicated in brackets immediately before the statement that is set out. Omissions in the transcript or in any other document printed in the joint appendix shall be indicated by asterisks. Immaterial formal matters (*e.g.,* captions, subscriptions, acknowledgments) shall be omitted. A question and its answer may be contained in a single paragraph.

6. Two lines must appear at the bottom of the cover of the joint appendix: (1) The first line must indicate the date the petition for the writ of certiorari was filed or the date the appeal was docketed; (2) the second line must indicate the date certiorari was granted or the date jurisdiction of the appeal was noted or postponed.

7. Exhibits designated for inclusion in the joint appendix may be contained in a separate volume or volumes suitably indexed. The transcript of a proceeding before an administrative agency, board, commission, or officer used in an action in a district court or court of appeals is regarded as an exhibit for the purposes of this paragraph.

8. The Court, on its own motion or that of a party, may dispense with the requirement of a joint appendix and may permit a case to be heard on the original record (with such copies of the record, or relevant parts thereof, as the Court may require) or on the appendix used in the court below, if it conforms to the requirements of this Rule.

9. For good cause, the time limits specified in this Rule may be shortened or extended by the Court or a Justice, or by the Clerk under Rule 30.4.

Rule 27. Calendar

1. From time to time, the Clerk will prepare a calendar of cases ready for argument. A case ordinarily will not be called for argument less than two weeks after the brief on the merits for the respondent or appellee is due.

2. The Clerk will advise counsel when they are required to appear for oral argument and will publish a hearing list in advance of each argument session for the convenience of counsel and the information of the public.

3. The Court, on its own motion or that of a party, may order that two or more cases involving the same or related questions be argued together as one case or on such other terms as the Court may prescribe.

Rule 28. Oral Argument

1. Oral argument should emphasize and clarify the written arguments in the briefs on the merits. Counsel should assume that all Justices have read the briefs before oral argument. Oral argument read from a prepared text is not favored.

2. The petitioner or appellant shall open and may conclude the argument. A cross-writ of certiorari or cross-appeal will be argued with the initial writ of certiorari or appeal as one case in the time allowed for that one case, and the Court will advise the parties who shall open and close.

3. Unless the Court directs otherwise, each side is allowed one-half hour for argument. Counsel is not required to use all the allotted time. Any request for additional time to argue shall be presented by motion under Rule 21 in time to be considered at a scheduled Conference prior to the date of oral argument and no later than 7 days after the respondent's or appellee's brief on the merits is filed, and shall set out specifically and concisely why the case cannot be presented within the half-hour limitation. Additional time is rarely accorded.

4. Only one attorney will be heard for each side, except by leave of the Court on motion filed in time to be considered at a scheduled Conference prior to the date of oral argument and no later than 7 days after the respondent's or appellee's brief on the merits is filed. Any request for divided argument shall be presented by motion under Rule 21 and shall set out specifically and concisely why more than one attorney should be allowed to argue. Divided argument is not favored.

5. Regardless of the number of counsel participating in oral argument, counsel making the opening argument shall present the case fairly and completely and not reserve points of substance for rebuttal.

6. Oral argument will not be allowed on behalf of any party for whom a brief has not been filed.

7. By leave of the Court, and subject to paragraph 4 of this Rule, counsel for an *amicus curiae* whose brief has been filed as provided in Rule 37 may argue orally on the side of a party, with the consent of that party. In the absence of consent, counsel for an *amicus curiae* may seek leave of the Court to argue orally by a motion setting out specifically and concisely why oral argument would provide assistance to the Court not otherwise available. Such a motion will be granted only in the most extraordinary circumstances.

PART VII.   PRACTICE AND PROCEDURE

Rule 29.   Filing and Service of Documents; Special Notifications; Corporate Listing

1. Any document required or permitted to be presented to the Court or to a Justice shall be filed with the Clerk.

2. A document is timely filed if it is received by the Clerk within the time specified for filing; or if it is sent to the Clerk through the United States Postal Service by first-class mail (including express or priority mail), postage prepaid, and bears a postmark, other than a commercial postage meter label, showing that the document was mailed on or before the last day for filing; or if it is delivered on or before the last day for filing to a third-party commercial carrier for delivery to the Clerk within 3 calendar days. If submitted by an inmate confined in an institution, a document is timely filed if it is deposited in the institution's internal mail system on or before the last day for filing and is accompanied by a notarized statement or declaration in compliance with 28 U.S.C. §1746 setting out the date of deposit and stating thatfirst-class postage has been prepaid. If the postmark is missing or not legible, or if the third-party commercial carrier does not provide the date the document was received by the carrier, the Clerk will require the person who sent the document to submit a notarized statement or declaration in compliance with 28 U.S.C. §1746 setting out the details of the filing and stating that the filing took place on a particular date within the permitted time.

3. Any document required by these Rules to be served may be served personally, by mail, or by third-party commercial carrier for delivery within 3 calendar days on each party to the proceeding at or before the time of filing. If the document has been prepared as required by Rule 33.1, three copies shall be served on each other party separately represented in the proceeding. If the document has been prepared as required by Rule 33.2, service of a single copy on each other separately represented party suffices. If personal service is made, it shall consist of delivery at the office of the counsel of record, either to counsel or to an employee therein. If service is by mail or third-party commercial carrier, it shall consist of depositing the document with the United States Postal Service, with no less than first-class postage prepaid, or delivery to the carrier for delivery within 3 calendar days, addressed to counsel of record at the proper address. When a party is not represented by counsel, service shall be made on the party, personally, by mail, or by commercial carrier. Ordinarily, service on a party must be by a manner at least as expeditious as the manner used to file the document with the Court.

4. (a) If the United States or any federal department, office, agency, officer, or employee is a party to be served, service shall be made on the Solicitor General of the United States, Room 5614, Department of Justice, 950 Pennsylvania Ave., N.W., Washington, DC 20530-0001. When an agency of the United States that is a party is authorized by law to appear before this Court on its own behalf, or when an officer or employee of the United States is a party, the agency, officer, or employee shall be served in addition to the Solicitor General.

(b) In any proceeding in this Court in which the constitutionality of an Act of Congress is drawn into question, and neither the United States nor any federal department, office, agency, officer, or employee is a party, the initial document filed in this Court shall recite that 28 U.S.C. §2403(a) may apply and shall be served on the Solicitor General of the United States, Room 5614, Department of Justice, 950 Pennsylvania Ave., N.W., Washington, DC 20530-0001. In such a proceeding from any court of the United States, as defined by 28 U.S.C. §451, the initial document also shall state whether that court, pursuant to 28 U.S.C. §2403(a), certified to the Attorney General the fact that the constitutionality of an Act of Congress was drawn into question. See Rule 14.1(e)(v).

(c) In any proceeding in this Court in which the constitutionality of any statute of a State is drawn into question, and neither the State nor any agency, officer, or employee thereof is a party, the initial document filed in this Court shall recite that 28 U.S.C. §2403(b) may apply and shall be served on the Attorney General of that State. In such a proceeding from any court of the United States, as defined by 28 U.S.C. §451, the initial document also shall state whether that court, pursuant to 28 U.S.C. §2403(b), certified to the State Attorney General the fact that the constitutionality of a statute of that State was drawn into question. See Rule 14.1(e)(v).

5. Proof of service, when required by these Rules, shall accompany the document when it is presented to the Clerk for filing and shall be separate from it. Proof of service shall contain, or be accompanied by, a statement that all parties required to be served have been served, together with a list of the names, addresses, and telephone numbers of counsel indicating the name of the party or parties each counsel represents. It is not necessary that service on each party required to be served be made in the same manner or evidenced by the same proof. Proof of service may consist of any one of the following:

(a) an acknowledgment of service, signed by counsel of record for the party served, and bearing the address and telephone number of such counsel;

(b) a certificate of service, reciting the facts and circumstances of service in compliance with the appropriate paragraph or paragraphs of this Rule, and signed by a member of the Bar of this Court representing the party on whose behalf service is made or by an attorney appointed to represent that party under the Criminal Justice Act of 1964, see 18 U.S.C. §3006A(d)(6), or under any other applicable federal statute; or

(c) a notarized affidavit or declaration in compliance with 28 U.S.C. §1746, reciting the facts and circumstances of service in accordance with the appropriate paragraph or paragraphs of this Rule, whenever service is made by any person not a member of the Bar of this Court and not an attorney appointed to represent a party under the Criminal Justice Act of 1964, see 18 U.S.C. §3006A(d)(6), or under any other applicable federal statute.

6. Every document, except a joint appendix or *amicus curiae* brief, filed by or on behalf of a nongovernmental corporation shall contain a corporate disclosure statement identifying the parent corporations and listing any publicly held company that owns 10% or more of the corporation's stock. If there is no parent or publicly held company owning 10% or more of the corporation's stock, a notation to this effect shall be included in the document. If a statement has been included in a document filed earlier in the case, reference may be made to the earlier document (except when the earlier statement appeared in a document prepared under Rule 33.2), and only amendments to the statement to make it current need be included in the document being filed.

Rule 30. Computation and Extension of Time

1. In the computation of any period of time prescribed or allowed by these Rules, by order of the Court, or by an applicable statute, the day of the act, event, or default from which the designated period begins to run is not included. The last day of the period shall be included, unless it is a Saturday, Sunday, federal legal holiday listed in 5 U.S.C. §6103, or day on which the Court building is closed by order of the Court or the Chief Justice, in which event the period shall extend until the end of the next day that is not a Saturday, Sunday, federal legal holiday, or day on which the Court building is closed.

2. Whenever a Justice or the Clerk is empowered by law or these Rules to extend the time to file any document, an application seeking an extension shall be filed within the period sought to be extended. An application to extend the time to file a petition for a writ of certiorari or to file a jurisdictional statement must be filed at least 10 days before the specified final filing date as computed under these Rules; if filed less than 10 days before the final filing date, such application will not be granted except in the most extraordinary circumstances.

3. An application to extend the time to file a petition for a writ of certiorari, to file a jurisdictional statement, to file a reply brief on the merits, or to file a petition for rehearing shall be made to an individual Justice and presented and served on all other parties as provided by Rule 22. Once denied, such an application may not be renewed.

4. An application to extend the time to file any document or paper other than those specified in paragraph 3 of this Rule may be presented in the form of a letter to the Clerk setting out specific reasons why an extension of time is justified. The letter shall be served on all other parties as required by Rule 29. The application may be acted on by the Clerk in the first instance, and any party aggrieved by the Clerk's action may request that the application be submitted to a Justice or to the Court. The Clerk will report action under this paragraph to the Court as instructed.

Rule 31. Translations

Whenever any record to be transmitted to this Court contains material written in a foreign language without a translation made under the authority of the lower court, or admitted to be correct, the clerk of the court transmitting the record shall advise the Clerk of this Court immediately so that this Court may order that a translation be supplied and, if necessary, printed as part of the joint appendix.

Rule 32. Models, Diagrams, Exhibits, and Lodgings

1. Models, diagrams, and exhibits of material forming part of the evidence taken in a case and brought to this Court for its inspection shall be placed in the custody of the Clerk at least two weeks before the case is to be heard or submitted.

2. All models, diagrams, exhibits, and other items placed in the custody of the Clerk shall be removed by the parties no more than 40 days after the case is decided. If this is not done, the Clerk will notify counsel to remove the articles forthwith. If they are not removed within a reasonable time thereafter, the Clerk will destroy them or dispose of them in any other appropriate way.

3. Any party or *amicus curiae* desiring to lodge non-record material with the Clerk must set out in a letter, served on all parties, a description of the material proposed for lodging and the reasons why the non-record material may properly be considered by the Court. The material proposed for lodging may not be submitted until and unless requested by the Clerk.

Rule 33. Document Preparation: Booklet Format; 8½- by 11-Inch Paper Format

1. *Booklet Format:* **(a)** Except for a document expressly permitted by these Rules to be submitted on 8½- by 11-inch paper, see, *e.g.,* Rules 21, 22, and 39, every document filed with the Court shall be prepared in a 6⅛- by 9¼-inch booklet format using a standard typesetting process (*e.g.,* hot metal, photocomposition, or computer typesetting) to produce text printed in typographic (as opposed to typewriter) characters. The process used must produce a clear, black image on white paper. The text must be reproduced with a clarity that equals or exceeds the output of a laser printer.

(b) The text of every booklet-format document, including any appendix thereto, shall be typeset in a Century family (*e.g.,* Century Expanded, New Century Schoolbook, or Century Schoolbook) 12-point type with 2-point or more leading between lines. Quotations in excess of 50 words shall be indented. The typeface of footnotes shall be 10-point type with 2-point or more leading between lines. The text of the document must appear on both sides of the page.

(c) Every booklet-format document shall be produced on paper that is opaque, unglazed, and not less than 60 pounds in weight, and shall have margins of at least three-fourths of an inch on all sides. The text field, including footnotes, may not exceed 4⅛ by 7⅛ inches. The document shall be bound firmly in at least two places along the left margin (saddle stitch or perfect binding preferred) so as to permit easy opening, and no part of the text should be obscured by the binding. Spiral, plastic, metal, or string bindings may not be used. Copies of patent documents, except opinions, may be duplicated in such size as is necessary in a separate appendix.

(d) Every booklet-format document shall comply with the word limits shown on the chart in subparagraph 1(g) of this Rule. The word limits do not include the questions presented, the list of parties and the corporate disclosure statement, the table of contents, the table of cited authorities, the listing of counsel at the end of the document, or any appendix. The word limits include footnotes. Verbatim quotations required under Rule 14.1(f), if set out in the text of a brief rather than in the appendix, are also excluded. For good cause, the Court or a Justice may grant leave to file a document in excess of the word limits, but application for such leave is not favored. An application to exceed word limits shall comply with Rule 22 and must be received by the Clerk at least 15 days before the filing date of the document in question, except in the most extraordinary circumstances.

(e) Every booklet-format document shall have a suitable cover consisting of 65-pound weight paper in the color indicated on the chart in subparagraph 1(g) of this Rule. If a separate appendix to any document is filed, the color of its cover shall be the same as that of the cover of the document it supports. The Clerk will furnish a color chart upon request. Counsel shall ensure that there is adequate contrast between the printing and the color of the cover. A document filed by the United States, or by any other federal party represented by the Solicitor General, shall have a gray cover. A joint appendix, answer to a bill of complaint, motion for leave to intervene, and any other document not listed in subparagraph 1(g) of this Rule shall have a tan cover.

(f) Forty copies of a booklet-format document shall be filed.

(g) Word limits and cover colors for booklet-format documents are as follows:

Type of Document	Word Limits	Color of Cover
(i) Petition for a Writ of Certiorari (Rule 14); Motion for Leave to File a Bill of Complaint and Brief in Support (Rule 17.3); Jurisdictional Statement (Rule 18.3); Petition for an Extraordinary Writ (Rule 20.2)	9,000	white
(ii) Brief in Opposition (Rule 15.3); Brief in Opposition to Motion for Leave to File an Original Action (Rule 17.5); Motion to Dismiss or Affirm (Rule 18.6); Brief in Opposition to Mandamus or Prohibition (Rule 20.3(b)); Response to a Petition for Habeas Corpus (Rule 20.4)	9,000	orange
(iii) Reply to Brief in Opposition (Rules 15.6 and 17.5); Brief Opposing a Motion to Dismiss or Affirm (Rule 18.8)	3,000	tan
(iv) Supplemental Brief (Rules 15.8, 17, 18.10, and 25.5)	3,000	tan
(v) Brief on the Merits for Petitioner or Appellant (Rule 24); Exceptions by Plaintiff to Report of Special Master (Rule 17)	15,000	light blue
(vi) Brief on the Merits for Respondent or Appellee (Rule 24.2); Brief on the Merits for Respondent or Appellee Supporting Petitioner or Appellant (Rule 12.6); Exceptions by Party Other Than Plaintiff to Report of Special Master (Rule 17)	15,000	light red
(vii) Reply Brief on the Merits (Rule 24.4)	6,000	yellow
(viii) Reply to Plaintiff's Exceptions to Report of Special Master (Rule 17)	15,000	orange
(ix) Reply to Exceptions by Party Other Than Plaintiff to Report of Special Master (Rule 17)	15,000	yellow
(x) Brief for an *Amicus Curiae* at the Petition Stage or pertaining to a Motion for Leave to file a Bill of Complaint (Rule 37.2)	6,000	cream
(xi) Brief for an *Amicus Curiae* in Support of the Plaintiff, Petitioner, or Appellant, or in Support of Neither Party, on the Merits or in an Original Action at the Exceptions Stage (Rule 37.3)	9,000	light green
(xii) Brief for an *Amicus Curiae* in Support of the Defendant, Respondent, or Appellee, on the Merits or in an Original Action at the Exceptions Stage (Rule 37.3)	9,000	dark green
(xiii) Petition for Rehearing (Rule 44)	3,000	tan

(**h**) A document prepared under Rule 33.1 must be accompanied by a certificate signed by the attorney, the unrepresented party, or the preparer of the document stating that the brief complies with the word limitations. The person preparing the certificate may rely on the word count of the word-processing system used to prepare the document. The word-processing system must be set to include footnotes in the word count. The certificate must state the number of words in the document. The certificate shall accompany the document when it is presented to the Clerk for filing and shall be separate from it. If the certificate is signed by a person other than a member of the Bar of this Court, the counsel of record, or the unrepresented party, it must contain a notarized affidavit or declaration in compliance with 28 U.S.C. §1746.

2. *8½- by 11-Inch Paper Format:* (**a**) The text of every document, including any appendix thereto, expressly permitted by these Rules to be presented to the Court on 8½- by 11-inch paper shall appear double spaced, except for indented quotations, which shall be single spaced, on opaque, unglazed, white paper. The document shall be stapled or bound at the upper left-hand corner. Copies, if required, shall be produced on the same type of paper and shall be legible. The original of any such document (except a motion to dismiss or affirm under Rule 18.6) shall be signed by the party proceeding *pro se* or by counsel of record who must be a member of the Bar of this Court or an attorney appointed under the Criminal Justice Act of 1964, see 18 U.S.C. §3006A(d)(6), or under any other applicable federal statute. Subparagraph 1(g) of this Rule does not apply to documents prepared under this paragraph.

(**b**) Page limits for documents presented on 8½- by 11-inch paper are: 40 pages for a petition for a writ of certiorari, jurisdictional statement, petition for an extraordinary writ, brief in opposition, or motion to dismiss or affirm; and 15 pages for a reply to a brief in opposition, brief opposing a motion to dismiss or affirm, supplemental brief, or petition for rehearing. The exclusions specified in subparagraph 1(d) of this Rule apply.

Rule 34. Document Preparation: General Requirements

Every document, whether prepared under Rule 33.1 or Rule 33.2, shall comply with the following provisions:

1. Each document shall bear on its cover, in the order indicated, from the top of the page:

(**a**) the docket number of the case or, if there is none, a space for one;

(**b**) the name of this Court;

(**c**) the caption of the case as appropriate in this Court;

(**d**) the nature of the proceeding and the name of the court from which the action is brought (e.g., "On Petition for Writ of Certiorari to the United States Court of Appeals for the Fifth Circuit"; or, for a merits brief, "On Writ of Certiorari to the United States Court of Appeals for the Fifth Circuit");

(**e**) the title of the document (e.g., "Petition for Writ of Certiorari," "Brief for Respondent," "Joint Appendix");

(**f**) the name of the attorney who is counsel of record for the party concerned (who must be a member of the Bar of this Court except as provided in Rule 9.1) and on whom service is to be made, with a notation directly thereunder identifying the attorney as counsel of record and setting out counsel's office address, e-mail address, and telephone number. Only one counsel of record may be noted on a single document, except that counsel of record for each party must be listed on the cover of a joint appendix. The names of other members of the Bar of this Court or of the bar of the highest court of State acting as counsel, and, if desired, their addresses, may be added, but counsel of record shall be clearly identified. Names of persons other than attorneys admitted to a state bar may not be listed, unless the party is appearing *pro se*, in which case the party's name, address, and telephone number shall appear.

(g) The foregoing shall be displayed in an appropriate typographical manner and, except for identification of counsel, may not be set in type smaller than standard 11-point, if the document is prepared as required by Rule 33.1.

2. Every document exceeding five pages (other than a joint appendix), whether prepared under Rule 33.1 or Rule 33.2, shall contain a table of contents and a table of cited authorities (i.e., cases alphabetically arranged, constitutional provisions, statutes, treatises, and other materials) with references to the pages in the document where such authorities are cited.

3. The body of every document shall bear at its close the name of counsel of record and such other counsel, identified on the cover of the document in conformity with subparagraph 1(f) of this Rule, as may be desired.

4. Every appendix to a document must be preceded by a table of contents that provides a description of each document in the appendix.

5. All references to a provision of federal statutory law should ordinarily be cited to the United States Code, if the provision has been codified therein. In the event the provision has not been classified to the United States Code, citation should be to the Statutes at Large. Additional or alternative citations should be provided only if there is a particular reason why those citations are relevant or necessary to the argument.

Rule 35. Death, Substitution, and Revivor; Public Officers

1. If a party dies after the filing of a petition for a writ of certiorari to this Court, or after the filing of a notice of appeal, the authorized representative of the deceased party may appear and, on motion, be substituted as a party. If the representative does not voluntarily become a party, any other party may suggest the death on the record and, on motion, seek an order requiring the representative to become a party within a designated time. If the representative then fails to become a party, the party so moving, if a respondent or appellee, is entitled to have the petition for a writ of certiorari or the appeal dismissed, and if a petitioner or appellant, is entitled to proceed as in any other case of nonappearance by a respondent or appellee. If the substitution of a representative of the deceased is not made within six months after the death of the party, the case shall abate.

2. Whenever a case cannot be revived in the court whose judgment is sought to be reviewed, because the deceased party's authorized representative is not subject to that court's jurisdiction, proceedings will be conducted as this Court may direct.

3. When a public officer who is a party to a proceeding in this Court in an official capacity dies, resigns, or otherwise ceases to hold office, the action does not abate and any successor in office is automatically substituted as a party. The parties shall notify the Clerk in writing of any such successions. Proceedings following the substitution shall be in the name of the substituted party, but any misnomer not affecting substantial rights of the parties will be disregarded.

4. A public officer who is a party to a proceeding in this Court in an official capacity may be described as a party by the officer's official title rather than by name, but the Court may require the name to be added.

Rule 36. Custody of Prisoners in Habeas Corpus Proceedings

1. Pending review in this Court of a decision in a habeas corpus proceeding commenced before a court, Justice, or judge of the United States, the person having custody of the prisoner may not transfer custody to another person unless the transfer is authorized under this Rule.

2. Upon application by a custodian, the court, Justice, or judge who entered the decision under review may authorize transfer and the substitution of a successor custodian as a party.

3. (a) Pending review of a decision failing or refusing to release a prisoner, the prisoner may be detained in the custody from which release is sought or in other appropriate custody or may be enlarged on personal recognizance or bail, as may appear appropriate to the court, Justice, or judge who entered the decision, or to the court of appeals, this Court, or a judge or Justice of either court.

(b) Pending review of a decision ordering release, the prisoner shall be enlarged on personal recognizance or bail, unless the court, Justice, or judge who entered the decision, or the court of appeals, this Court, or a judge or Justice of either court, orders otherwise.

4. An initial order respecting the custody or enlargement of the prisoner, and any recognizance or surety taken, shall continue in effect pending review in the court of appeals and in this Court unless for reasons shown to the court of appeals, this Court, or a judge or Justice of either court, the order is modified or an independent order respecting custody, enlargement, or surety is entered.

Rule 37. Brief for an *Amicus Curiae*

1. An *amicus curiae* brief that brings to the attention of the Court relevant matter not already brought to its attention by the parties may be of considerable help to the Court. An *amicus curiae* brief that does not serve this purpose burdens the Court, and its filing is not favored. An *amicus curiae* brief may be filed only by an attorney admitted to practice before this Court as provided in Rule 5.

2. (a) An *amicus curiae* brief submitted before the Court's consideration of a petition for a writ of certiorari, motion for leave to file a bill of complaint, jurisdictional statement, or petition for an extraordinary writ may be filed if accompanied by the written consent of all parties, or if the Court grants leave to file under subparagraph 2(b) of this Rule. An *amicus curiae* brief in support of a petitioner or appellant shall be filed within 30 days after the case is placed on the docket or a response is called for by the Court, whichever is later, and that time will not be extended. An *amicus curiae* brief in support of a motion of a plaintiff for leave to file a bill of complaint in an original action shall be filed within 60 days after the case is placed on the docket, and that time will not be extended. An *amicus curiae* brief in support of a respondent, an appellee, or a defendant shall be submitted within the time allowed for filing a brief in opposition or a motion to dismiss or affirm. An *amicus curiae* shall ensure that the counsel of record for all parties receive notice of its intention to file an *amicus curiae* brief at least 10 days prior to the due date for the *amicus curiae* brief, unless the *amicus curiae* brief is filed earlier than 10 days before the due date. Only one signatory to any *amicus curiae* brief filed jointly by more than one *amicus curiae* must timely notify the parties of its intent to file that brief. The *amicus curiae* brief shall indicate that counsel of record received timely notice of the intent to file the brief under this Rule and shall specify whether consent was granted, and its cover shall identify the party supported.

(b) When a party to the case has withheld consent, a motion for leave to file an *amicus curiae* brief before the Court's consideration of a petition for a writ of certiorari, motion for leave to file a bill of complaint, jurisdictional statement, or petition for an extraordinary writ may be presented to the Court. The motion, prepared as required by Rule 33.1 and as one document with the brief sought to be filed, shall be submitted within the time allowed for filing an *amicus curiae* brief, and shall indicate the party or parties who have withheld consent and state the nature of the movant's interest. Such a motion is not favored.

3. (a) An *amicus curiae* brief in a case before the Court for oral argument may be filed if accompanied by the written consent of all parties, or if the Court grants leave to file under subparagraph 3(b) of this Rule. The brief shall be submitted within 7 days after the brief for the party supported is filed, or if in support of neither party, within 7 days after the time allowed for filing the petitioner's or appellant's brief. Motions to extend the time for filing an *amicus curiae* brief will not be entertained. The 10-day notice requirement of subparagraph 2(a) of this Rule does not apply to an *amicus curiae* brief in a case before the Court for oral argument. An electronic version of every *amicus curiae* brief in a case before the Court for oral argument shall be transmitted to the Clerk of Court and to counsel for the parties at the time the brief is filed in accordance with guidelines established by the Clerk. The electronic transmission requirement is in addition to the requirement that booklet-format briefs be timely filed. The *amicus curiae* brief shall specify whether consent was granted, and its cover shall identify the party supported or indicate whether it suggests affirmance or reversal. The Clerk will not file a reply brief for an *amicus curiae*, or a brief for an *amicus curiae* in support of, or in opposition to, a petition for rehearing.

(b) When a party to a case before the Court for oral argument has withheld consent, a motion for leave to file an *amicus curiae* brief may be presented to the Court. The motion, prepared as required by Rule 33.1 and as one document with the brief sought to be filed, shall be submitted within the time allowed for filing an *amicus curiae* brief, and shall indicate the party or parties who have withheld consent and state the nature of the movant's interest.

4. No motion for leave to file an *amicus curiae* brief is necessary if the brief is presented on behalf of the United States by the Solicitor General; on behalf of any agency of the United States allowed by law to appear before this Court when submitted by the agency's authorized legal representative; on behalf of a State, Commonwealth, Territory, or Possession when submitted by its Attorney General; or on behalf of a city, county, town, or similar entity when submitted by its authorized law officer.

5. A brief or motion filed under this Rule shall be accompanied by proof of service as required by Rule 29, and shall comply with the applicable provisions of Rules 21, 24, and 33.1 (except that it suffices to set out in the brief the interest of the *amicus curiae*, the summary of the argument, the argument, and the conclusion). A motion for leave to file may not exceed 1,500 words. A party served with the motion

may file an objection thereto, stating concisely the reasons for withholding consent; the objection shall be prepared as required by Rule 33.2.

6. Except for briefs presented on behalf of *amicus curiae* listed in Rule 37.4, a brief filed under this Rule shall indicate whether counsel for a party authored the brief in whole or in part and whether such counsel or a party made a monetary contribution intended to fund the preparation or submission of the brief, and shall identify every person other than the *amicus curiae*, its members, or its counsel, who made such a monetary contribution. The disclosure shall be made in the first footnote on the first page of text.

Rule 38. Fees

Under 28 U.S.C. §1911, the fees charged by the Clerk are:

(a) for docketing a case on a petition for a writ of certiorari or on appeal or for docketing any other proceeding, except a certified question or a motion to docket and dismiss an appeal under Rule 18.5, $300;

(b) for filing a petition for rehearing or a motion for leave to file a petition for rehearing, $200;

(c) for reproducing and certifying any record or paper, $1 per page; and for comparing with the original thereof any photographic reproduction of any record or paper, when furnished by the person requesting its certification, $.50 per page;

(d) for a certificate bearing the seal of the Court, $10; and

(e) for a check paid to the Court, Clerk, or Marshal that is returned for lack of funds, $35.

Rule 39. Proceedings *in Forma Pauperis*

1. A party seeking to proceed *in forma pauperis* shall file a motion for leave to do so, together with the party's notarized affidavit or declaration (in compliance with 28 U.S.C. §1746) in the form prescribed by the Federal Rules of Appellate Procedure, Form 4. The motion shall state whether leave to proceed *in forma pauperis* was sought in any other court and, if so, whether leave was granted. If the United States district court or the United States court of appeals has appointed counsel under the Criminal Justice Act of 1964, 18 U.S.C. §3006A, or under any other applicable federal statute, no affidavit or declaration is required, but the motion shall cite the statute under which counsel was appointed.

2. If leave to proceed *in forma pauperis* is sought for the purpose of filing a document, the motion, and an affidavit or declaration if required, shall be filed together with that document and shall comply in every respect with Rule 21. As provided in that Rule, it suffices to file an original and 10 copies, unless the party is an inmate confined in an institution and is not represented by counsel, in which case the original, alone, suffices. A copy of the motion, and affidavit or declaration if required, shall precede and be attached to each copy of the accompanying document.

3. Except when these Rules expressly provide that a document shall be prepared as required by Rule 33.1, every document presented by a party proceeding under this Rule shall be prepared as required by Rule 33.2 (unless such preparation is impossible). Every document shall be legible. While making due allowance for any case presented under this Rule by a person appearing *pro se*, the Clerk will not file any document if it does not comply with the substance of these Rules or is jurisdictionally out of time.

4. When the documents required by paragraphs 1 and 2 of this Rule are presented to the Clerk, accompanied by proof of service as required by Rule 29, they will be placed on the docket without the payment of a docket fee or any other fee.

5. The respondent or appellee in a case filed *in forma pauperis* shall respond in the same manner and within the same time as in any other case of the same nature, except that the filing of an original and 10 copies of a response prepared as required by Rule 33.2, with proof of service as required by Rule 29, suffices. The respondent or appellee may challenge the grounds for the motion for leave to proceed *in forma pauperis* in a separate document or in the response itself.

6. Whenever the Court appoints counsel for an indigent party in a case set for oral argument, the briefs on the merits submitted by that counsel, unless otherwise requested, shall be prepared under the Clerk's supervision. The Clerk also will reimburse appointed counsel for any necessary travel expenses to Washington, D.C., and return in connection with the argument.

7. In a case in which certiorari has been granted, probable jurisdiction noted, or consideration of jurisdiction postponed, this Court may appoint counsel to represent a party financially unable to afford an attorney to the extent authorized by the Criminal Justice Act of 1964, 18 U.S.C. §3006A, or by any other applicable federal statute.

8. If satisfied that a petition for a writ of certiorari, jurisdictional statement, or petition for an extraordinary writ is frivolous or malicious, the Court may deny leave to proceed *in forma pauperis.*

Rule 40.   Veterans, Seamen, and Military Cases

1. A veteran suing under any provision of law exempting veterans from the payment of fees or court costs, may proceed without prepayment of fees or costs or furnishing security therefor and may file a motion for leave to proceed on papers prepared as required by Rule 33.2. The motion shall ask leave to proceed as a veteran and be accompanied by an affidavit or declaration setting out the moving party's veteran status. A copy of the motion shall precede and be attached to each copy of the petition for a writ of certiorari or other substantive document filed by the veteran.

2. A seaman suing under 28 U.S.C. §1916 may proceed without prepayment of fees or costs or furnishing security therefor and may file a motion for leave to proceed on papers prepared as required by Rule 33.2. The motion shall ask leave to proceed as a seaman and be accompanied by an affidavit or declaration setting out the moving party's seaman status. A copy of the motion shall precede and be attached to each copy of the petition for a writ of certiorari or other substantive document filed by the seaman.

3. An accused person petitioning for a writ of certiorari to review a decision of the United States Court of Appeals for the Armed Forces under 28 U.S.C. §1259 may proceed without prepayment of fees or costs or furnishing security therefor and without filing an affidavit of indigency, but is not entitled to proceed on papers prepared as required by Rule 33.2, except as authorized by the Court on separate motion under Rule 39.

PART VIII.   DISPOSITION OF CASES

Rule 41.   Opinions of the Court

Opinions of the Court will be released by the Clerk immediately upon their announcement from the bench, or as the Court otherwise directs. Thereafter, the Clerk will cause the opinions to be issued in slip form, and the Reporter of Decisions will prepare them for publication in the preliminary prints and bound volumes of the United States Reports.

Rule 42.   Interest and Damages

1. If a judgment for money in a civil case is affirmed, any interest allowed by law is payable from the date the judgment under review was entered. If a judgment is modified or reversed with a direction that a judgment for money be entered below, the courts below may award interest to the extent permitted by law. Interest in cases arising in a state court is allowed at the same rate that similar judgments bear interest in the courts of the State in which judgment is directed to be entered. Interest in cases arising in a court of the United States is allowed at the interest rate authorized by law.

2. When a petition for a writ of certiorari, an appeal, or an application for other relief is frivolous, the Court may award the respondent or appellee just damages, and single or double costs under Rule 43. Damages or costs may be awarded against the petitioner, appellant, or applicant, against the party's counsel, or against both party and counsel.

Rule 43.   Costs

1. If the Court affirms a judgment, the petitioner or appellant shall pay costs unless the Court otherwise orders.

2. If the Court reverses or vacates a judgment, the respondent or appellee shall pay costs unless the Court otherwise orders.

3. The Clerk's fees and the cost of printing the joint appendix are the only taxable items in this Court. The cost of the transcript of the record from the court below is also a taxable item, but shall be taxable in that court as costs in the case. The expenses of printing briefs, motions, petitions, or jurisdictional statements are not taxable.

4. In a case involving a certified question, costs are equally divided unless the Court otherwise orders, except that if the Court decides the whole matter in controversy, as permitted by Rule 19.2, costs are allowed as provided in paragraphs 1 and 2 of this Rule.

5. To the extent permitted by 28 U.S.C. §2412, costs under this Rule are allowed for or against the United States or an officer or agent thereof, unless expressly waived or unless the Court otherwise orders.

6. When costs are allowed in this Court, the Clerk will insert an itemization of the costs in the body of the mandate or judgment sent to the court below. The prevailing side may not submit a bill of costs.

7. In extraordinary circumstances the Court may adjudge double costs.

Rule 44.   Rehearing

1. Any petition for the rehearing of any judgment or decision of the Court on the merits shall be filed within 25 days after entry of the judgment or decision, unless the Court or a Justice shortens or extends the time. The petitioner shall file 40 copies of the rehearing petition and shall pay the filing fee prescribed by Rule 38(b), except that a petitioner proceeding *in forma pauperis* under Rule 39, including an inmate of an institution, shall file the number of copies required for a petition by such a person under Rule 12.2. The petition shall state its grounds briefly and distinctly and shall be served as required by Rule 29. The petition shall be presented together with certification of counsel (or of a party unrepresented by counsel) that it is presented in good faith and not for delay; one copy of the certificate shall bear the signature of counsel (or of a party unrepresented by counsel). A copy of the certificate shall follow and be attached to each copy of the petition. A petition for rehearing is not subject to oral argument and will not be granted except by a majority of the Court, at the instance of a Justice who concurred in the judgment or decision.

2. Any petition for the rehearing of an order denying a petition for a writ of certiorari or extraordinary writ shall be filed within 25 days after the date of the order of denial and shall comply with all the form and filing requirements of paragraph 1 of this Rule, including the payment of the filing fee if required, but its grounds shall be limited to intervening circumstances of a substantial or controlling effect or to other substantial grounds not previously presented. The petition shall be presented together with certification of counsel (or of a party unrepresented by counsel) that it is restricted to the grounds specified in this paragraph and that it is presented in good faith and not for delay; one copy of the certificate shall bear the signature of counsel (or of a party unrepresented by counsel). The certificate shall be bound with each copy of the petition. The Clerk will not file a petition without a certificate. The petition is not subject to oral argument.

3. The Clerk will not file any response to a petition for rehearing unless the Court requests a response. In the absence of extraordinary circumstances, the Court will not grant a petition for rehearing without first requesting a response.

4. The Clerk will not file consecutive petitions and petitions that are out of time under this Rule.

5. The Clerk will not file any brief for an *amicus curiae* in support of, or in opposition to, a petition for rehearing.

6. If the Clerk determines that a petition for rehearing submitted timely and in good faith is in a form that does not comply with this Rule or with Rule 33 or Rule 34, the Clerk will return it with a letter indicating the deficiency. A corrected petition for rehearing submitted in accordance with Rule 29.2 no more than 15 days after the date of the Clerk's letter will be deemed timely.

Rule 45.   Process; Mandates

1. All process of this Court issues in the name of the President of the United States.

2. In a case on review from a state court, the mandate issues 25 days after entry of the judgment, unless the Court or a Justice shortens or extends the time, or unless the parties stipulate that it issue sooner. The filing of a petition for rehearing stays the mandate until disposition of the petition, unless the Court orders otherwise. If the petition is denied, the mandate issues forthwith.

3. In a case on review from any court of the United States, as defined by 28 U.S.C. §451, a formal mandate does not issue unless specially directed; instead, the Clerk of this Court will send the clerk of the lower court a copy of the opinion or order of this Court and a certified copy of the judgment. The certified copy of the judgment, prepared and signed by this Court's Clerk, will provide for costs if any are awarded. In all other respects, the provisions of paragraph 2 of this Rule apply.

Rule 46.   Dismissing Cases

1. At any stage of the proceedings, whenever all parties file with the Clerk an agreement in writing that a case be dismissed, specifying the terms for payment of costs, and pay to the Clerk any fees then due, the Clerk, without further reference to the Court, will enter an order of dismissal.

2. (a) A petitioner or appellant may file a motion to dismiss the case, with proof of service as required by Rule 29, tendering to the Clerk any fees due and costs payable. No more than 15 days after service thereof, an adverse party may file an objection, limited to the amount of damages and costs in this Court alleged to be payable or to showing that the moving party does not represent all petitioners or appellants. The Clerk will not file any objection not so limited.

(b) When the objection asserts that the moving party does not represent all the petitioners or appellants, the party moving for dismissal may file a reply within 10 days, after which time the matter will be submitted to the Court for its determination.

(c) If no objection is filed—or if upon objection going only to the amount of damages and costs in this Court, the party moving for dismissal tenders the additional damages and costs in full within 10 days of the demand therefor— the Clerk, without further reference to the Court, will enter an order of dismissal. If, after objection as to the amount of damages and costs in this Court, the moving party does not respond by a tender within 10 days, the Clerk will report the matter to the Court for its determination.

3. No mandate or other process will issue on a dismissal under this Rule without an order of the Court.

PART IX.   DEFINITIONS AND EFFECTIVE DATE

Rule 47.   Reference to "State Court" and "State Law"

The term "state court," when used in these Rules, includes the District of Columbia Court of Appeals, the Supreme Court of the Commonwealth of Puerto Rico, the courts of the Northern Mariana Islands, and the local courts of Guam. References in these Rules to the statutes of a State include the statutes of the District of Columbia, the Commonwealth of Puerto Rico, the Commonwealth of the Northern Mariana Islands, and the Territory of Guam.

Rule 48.   Effective Date of Rules

1. These Rules, adopted January 12, 2010, will be effective February 16, 2010.

2. The Rules govern all proceedings after their effective date except to the extent that, in the opinion of the Court, their application to a pending matter would not be feasible or would work an injustice, in which event the former procedure applies.

3. In any case in which a petitioner or appellant has filed its brief on the merits prior to the effective date of these revised Rules, all remaining briefs in that case may comply with the October 1, 2007, version of the Rules of the Supreme Court of the United States rather than with these revised Rules.

Index